MW00991572

NATIONALIZING
EMPIRES

NATIONALIZING
EMPIRES

Edited by
STEFAN BERGER

and

ALEXEI MILLER

Central European University Press
Budapest–New York

Published in 2015 by

Central European University Press
An imprint of the
Central European University Limited Liability Company
Nádor utca 11, H-1051 Budapest, Hungary
Tel: +36-1-327-3138 or 327-3000
Fax: +36-1-327-3183
E-mail: ceupress@ceu.hu
Website: www.ceupress.com

400 West 59th Street, New York NY 10019, USA
E-mail: meszarosa@ceu.hu

ISBN 978-963-386-016-8

Library of Congress Cataloging-in-Publication Data

Nationalizing empires / edited by Alexei Miller and Stefan Berger.
    pages cm. — (Historical studies in Eastern Europe and Eurasia ; volume III)
    Includes bibliographical references and index.
    ISBN 978-9633860168 (hardbound)
1. Europe—Territorial expansion—History—19th century. 2. Europe—Foreign relations—1815–1871. 3. Europe—Foreign relations—1871–1915. 4. Europe—Politics and
government—19th century. 5. Imperialism—History—19th century. 6. Nation-building—History—19th century. 7. Nationalism—History—19th century. 8. Nation-state—
History—19th century. 9. Military history, Modern—19th century. I. Miller, A. I. (Aleksei
I.) II. Berger, Stefan.

    D359.7.N39 2014
    325'.3209409034—dc23

                        2013048034

Printed in Hungary by
Prime Rate Kft., Budapest

Table of Contents

COMMENTS

Preface

The interrelationship between nation-formation and empire-building in Europe's long nineteenth century is an eminently complex and novel theme. Its proper treatment requires concerted efforts and ample time. Luckily, circumstances allowed for bringing together the best specialists in the comparative history of empires. This book was first conceived during the academic year 2003–04, when Alexei Miller was visiting professor at the Center for Border Studies at the University of Glamorgan, which was directed by Stefan Berger at the time. Our conversations naturally focused on the complex interrelationship between empire and nation-building, due to Miller's expertise in the Romanov Empire, his long-standing interest in the relationship between nationalism and empire-building, and Berger's interest in the comparative history of nationalism and national identity formation in Europe. In subsequent years, we organized several conferences on this theme, in Budapest and in Manchester. Here we recruited the authors, who are now represented in this volume, and we discussed drafts of the subsequent chapters. We refined our theoretical ideas as well as our specific guidelines for those authors who had written chapters on specific empires and we also thought about comparative themes that emerged from the empire chapters. Subsequently we asked specialists in the comparative history of empires to write shorter articles on those thematic concerns. During another stint as visiting professor at the School of Languages, Linguistics and Cultures at the University of Manchester in 2010–11, Miller and Berger—the latter of whom directed the Jean-Monnet-Center of Excellence at the University of Manchester between 2005 and 2011—had the opportunity to finalize all the contributions and write the biggest part of the introduction to this volume. After another two years of further revisions and changes to individual chapters, the introduction to this volume could be completed in the spring of 2014. So, in sum, this volume has been in gestation for about 10 years and we hope that our prolonged work on it will help to bring our understanding of the interrelationship between nation-formation and empire building in Europe's long nineteenth century one step forward.

Over the course of a decade, we have amassed a range of debts to a range of individuals and institutions, which we would like to thank. First and foremost, we would like to thank the authors of this volume, some of whom have accompanied our ten-year journey on the road to this book and have been incredibly patient with our repeated demands for revisions and changes as well as our plans to involve more and different authors on specific themes and empires. And we would also like to thank some of our colleagues who have been involved in some of the workshops and conferences but who ultimately, for one reason or another, are not among the authors. They include, in particular, Feroze Yasamee, Vincent Viaenne, and Miguel Jeronimo. Furthermore, Miller would like to thank Central European University in Budapest and the Institute for Scientific Information in Social Sciences in Moscow, where he held positions during these years, as well as the Universities of Glamorgan and Manchester, where he was visiting Professor in 2004 and 2010–11. Berger would like to thank the Universities of Glamorgan, Manchester, and Bochum, where he held professorships during the years of the production of this volume. All of these institutions and the many colleagues in these institutions provided an extremely stimulating atmosphere for research. Furthermore, Berger is grateful to the Freiburg Institute of Advanced Studies, which provided him with a Senior Fellowship during the academic year 2009–10. Here in particular his many discussions with Jörn Leonhard and Ulrike von Hirschhausen on the topic of the comparative histories of empire furthered his own thinking about the topic. While many institutions and individuals contributed a great deal to making this volume possible, as always, the remaining shortcomings and mistakes contained here are solely the responsibility of the editors.

STEFAN BERGER and ALEXEI MILLER
Bochum and Budapest

INTRODUCTION:

Building Nations In and With Empires—A Reassessment

STEFAN BERGER AND ALEXEI MILLER

"It is hardly likely that anyone in the future will achieve what Charles V, Louis XIV and Napoleon I failed to do. The founding of a new Roman Empire or of a new Carolingian empire would now be impossible ... France, England, Germany and Russia will, for centuries to come, no matter what may befall them, continue to be individual historical units, the crucial pieces on a checkerboard whose squares will forever vary in importance and size but will never be wholly confused with each other. Nations, in this sense of the term, are something fairly new in history." Isn't it striking that Renan in his famous lecture *Qu'est-ce qu'une Nation* names four of the strongest European Empires (or rather their imperial core areas) as examples of nations? And isn't it also striking how little attention has been paid to that curious fact by historians? This famous passage from Ernest Renan's lecture is one of the most often quoted definitions of the national principle:

> A nation is a soul, a spiritual principle. Only two things, actually, constitute this soul, this spiritual principle. One is in the past, the other is in the present. One is the possession in common of a rich legacy of remembrances; the other is the actual consent, the desire to live together, the will to continue to value the heritage which all hold in common ... A heroic past, of great men, of glory ... that is the social principle on which the national idea rests. To have common glories in the past, a common will in the present; to have accomplished great things together, to wish to do so again, that is the essential condition for being a nation.[1]

---

[1] Ernest Renan, "Qu'est qu'une nation?" [1882] in *Nationalism*, eds. John Hutchinson and Anthony D. Smith (Oxford: Oxford University Press, 1994), 17–29.

The passage is formulated in and for an age of nation-state formation, for which the nation-state seemed almost the natural spatial reference point. Renan goes on to say a lot about the imagined nature of that reference point, but his article ultimately also helped to make the nation-state the dominant form of thinking about nation, thereby pushing to the sideline what was, still at the point where Renan wrote these lines, the dominant state form in Europe—the imperial state. Whether we think of sea-based empires in the west or contiguous empires in Central and Eastern Europe, imperial imaginations had been vital for state formation and continued to be the dominant imaginations during the nineteenth century. National imaginations, as we shall argue in this volume, were taking place within such imperial frameworks.

If we jump from Renan's famous nineteenth-century definition of nation to one of the most impressive contemporary attempts to portray the history of a nation-state in Europe—the German Historical Museum in Berlin—we observe an interesting shift, backwards and forwards, in representations of nation and empire. When the visitors enter the main hall of the museum, they are confronted with maps of Germany from the Middle Ages to the present day, which project very different imperial and national shapes and constantly elide the national and the imperial. When entering the exhibition proper, almost the first thing that the visitors are confronted with is a sign reading "Wir sind ein Volk"—a phrase made famous in the revolution of 1989, but it can also be read here as being projected to all German history. However, ethnic Germanness historically stood uneasily between very different imperial, national, and regional state-building efforts: the histories of the Bavarian, Saxon, Swiss states, states of the Holy Roman Empire, Imperial Germany, or National Socialist Germany are not congruent with the notion of "one people." Hence we would argue that the German Historical Museum in Berlin is a fine example of how today, the categories of the national and the imperial are still often deeply entangled and intertwined.[2] It therefore appears to us as extremely timely to re-assess the relationship between nation-states, nationalism, and empires in European history.

The strict opposition between empire and nation-state as two profoundly different types of political organization of society and space has dominated historiography for decades. Recently, several authors began to question this dichotomy.[3] Here, we

---

[2] For an early and thought-provoking call to take seriously the entangled nature of the diverse spatial and non-spatial histories of Europe see Philipp Ther, "Beyond the Nation: the Relational Basis of a Comparative History of Germany and Europe," *Central European History* 36, no. 1 (2003): 45–73.

[3] Jürgen Osterhammel, *Die Verwandlung der Welt. Eine Geschichte des 19. Jahrhunderts* (Munich: Beck, 2009); Henry Kamen, *Empire: How Spain Became a World Power, 1492–1763* (New York: Perennial, 2004); Ronald G. Suny, "The Empire Strikes Out: Imperial Russia, 'National' Identity, and Theories of Empire," in *A State of Nations: Empire and Nation-Making in the Age of Lenin and Stalin*, eds. Ronald G. Suny and Terry Martin (Oxford: Oxford University Press, 2001), 23–66, esp. 27; Stefan Berger and Alexei Miller, "Nation-Building and Regional Integration, c. 1800–1914: the Role of Empires," *European Review of History* 15, no. 3 (2008): 317–30; Alexei Miller, *Imperia Romanovykh i natsionalizm. Esse po metodologii istoricheskogo issledovaniia* (Moscow:

want to build on such re-assessments and develop them further. In order to do so, we shall focus on nation-building in the imperial core, which, until now, largely escapes theoretical reflection. So, for example, Ernest Gellner's famous definition of nationalism as a political principle, which holds that the political and the national unit should be congruent, does not fit the case of nationalism in the imperial core.[4] Projects of building nations in the imperial metropolis aim at the preservation and extension of empires rather than at the dissolution of empires or the transformations of entire empires into nation-states. In some cases nation-building projects in imperial core areas had to be adjusted to the circumstances of imperial collapse, but causality here again puts imperial dynamics first. In many European societies, memories of empire came to shape the nation-state in the nineteenth and twentieth centuries.[5]

Jürgen Osterhammel was one of the first to challenge the dominance of the traditional framework among historians. As he pointed out, the nineteenth century was not the age of nation-states; rather it has to be described as the age of empires and nationalism. He described four different types of formation of nation-states in the nineteenth century. The first type was "revolutionary autonomization." European cases included Greece, Belgium, Serbia, Montenegro, Romania, and Bulgaria. Greece achieved its own state and independence from the Ottoman Empire in 1827 because of a combination of an indigenous independence movement, cross-European Philhellenism, and a military naval intervention by Britain, Russia, and France. What was internationally recognized as a Greek state in 1830, was, Osterhammel argued, not yet a Greek nation, which was still in the making. Over the course of the nineteenth and early twentieth centuries, Serbia, Montenegro, Romania and Bulgaria all made use of the weakness of the Ottoman Empire and followed the Greek example. The Belgian case was entirely different, as it was not a struggle against imperial domination but rather resistance to autocratic rule in the form of a revolutionary movement demanding secession from the Netherlands. But, like in the Greek case, the European great

---

NLO, 2006) [English language edition—*The Romanov Empire and Nationalism: Essays in Methodology of Historical Research* (Budapest: Central European University Press, 2008)]. Political scientists and sociologists addressed this issue much earlier, but without clear conclusions. See S. N. Eisenstadt and Stein Rokkan, eds., *Building States and Nations*, 2 vols. (Beverly Hills: Sage, 1973); Stein Rokkan, "Nation-Building: A Review of Models and Approaches," in *Nation-Building*, eds. Stein Rokkan, Kirsti Saelen, and Joan Warmbrunn (The Hague–Paris: Mouton, 1971), 7–38; Joseph W. Esherick, Hasan Kayali, and Eric van Young, eds. *Empire to Nation: Historical Perspectives on the Making of the Modern World* (Lanham, Md.: Rowman and Littlefield, 2006).

[4] Ernest Gellner, *Nations and Nationalism* (Ithaca: Cornell University Press, 1983), 1: "Nationalism is primarily a political principle, which holds that the political and the national unit should be congruent (...) Nationalist *sentiment* is the feeling of anger aroused by the violation of the principle, or the feeling of satisfaction aroused by its fulfillment. A national *movement* is one actuated by a sentiment of this kind."

[5] For Britain, see the impressive "Memories of Empire" trilogy by Bill Schwarz, in particular: *The White Man's World*, vol. 1 of *Memories of Empire* (Oxford: Oxford University Press, 2011).

powers, all of them empires, once again played a crucial role in facilitating the Belgian dream. The second type of nation-state, Osterhammel argued, came about through "hegemonic unification." Classic cases were Germany and Italy, where one part— Prussia in Germany and Piedmont-Sardinia in Italy—took the initiative to unify the nation. We should note that in both cases the emerging states immediately embraced imperial legacies and pursued imperial policy in order to consolidate the nation and join the club of European great powers.[6] Osterhammel also subsumes cases like the Netherlands and Switzerland under "hegemonic unification," although he has to admit that there was considerable polycentrism in the federal unification processes in these countries. The third type of nation-state that emerges in the course of the nineteenth century, according to Osterhammel, comes about through "evolutionary autonomization." The only European example he cites here is Norway, which, after a long process of gaining more and more autonomy, finally ended its dynastic union with Sweden in a peaceful way in 1905.[7] Osterhammel's fourth type includes former centers of empires abandoned by their imperial possessions. His prime examples are Spain and Portugal. Especially in Spain he sees the first post-imperial nation-state in Europe. However, in this typology, the older conceptual underpinnings of nationalism, as represented by Gellner, strangely survive, as this typology barely mentions one of the most paradigmatic cases of nation-building in the nineteenth century, namely the nationalism that aimed at building imperial nations at the heart of empires, including Britain, France, Spain, Germany, and Russia. Osterhammel does mention that "diverse nationalisms could be found in empires and in nation-states" and that pride in the empire became an important facet of nationalism in the imperial metropoles.[8] But overall, he tends to underestimate the close entanglement of nation and empire in the major imperial nations of nineteenth-century Europe. In fact, in his contrasting comparison of "nation-states" on the one hand and "empires" on the other, Osterhammel re-enforces the identification of nation with nation-state.

Nation-Building in Imperial Nations

Where the term "imperial nation" appears in the literature on empire, it usually denotes an unrealistic project of total assimilation of all the subjects/citizens into a single nation, thus in fact transforming empire into a nation-state. By contrast, we would like to use the term "imperial nation" to refer to the nation-building project which was conceived and implemented in the imperial core. These projects never aimed at including all the subjects/citizens of an empire into a nation. They equally never aimed at including all the territorial possessions of an empire into the concept of national

[6] On Italy see also Giuseppe Maria Finaldi, *Italian National Identity in the Scramble for Africa: Italy's African Wars in the Era of Nation-Building 1870–1900* (Bern: Peter Lang, 2009).
[7] Osterhammel, *Verwandlung*, 586–96; 601–03, 607–16.
[8] Osterhammel, *Verwandlung*, 671.

territory, but they unlike separatist peripheral projects, saw empire as a political and economic asset of its own. Instead of being anti-imperial, the proponents of these projects were pro-imperial in terms of their support for the preservation and further extension of the existing empire or its reorganization in order to make it more effective. A closer look at European history of the nineteenth century shows that the biggest and often most advanced nation-building projects were implemented with different degrees of success in the imperial core areas, but they were invariably very closely linked to empire in a variety of ways. States created nations,[9] and empires provided those states with various resources. Frederick Cooper suggested a term "empire-state" to challenge the historiographical tradition which is focused on the nation-state.[10] The territorial, institutional, and cultural designs of these imperial nations were very much linked to the development of empires. In this sense, the imperial dimension and the nation-building dimension cannot be treated separately in the case of imperial nations. In the existing literature, this link was acknowledged in its negative aspects only, that is, how empires hindered nation-building projects.[11] However, we would like to restore the balance and draw attention to both the obstacles that empires posed to nation-building projects and the incentives and (broadly understood) resources empires provided for building nations at the core of empires.

There is, in fact, a whole host of areas where the imperial is closely entangled with the national in the process of building imperial nations. Without trying to provide here an exhaustive list, we should mention, first, various aspects of managing space, including the imagined geography of national territory, migrations, the development of communication systems, urban development, particularly in the capital cities, which combined the roles of national and imperial capitals. For Spain it has recently been pointed out that the geographical societies played the most important role in promoting Spanish Africanism from the last third of the nineteenth century onwards. These associations, such as the Sociedad Africanista y Colonial (Africanist and Colonialist Society) promoted a racially-based affinity between Morocco and Spain and presented Morocco both as a case of backwardness in need of development and as a landscape of desire. National and imperial imagination, as Ferrán Archilés has pointed out, were closely interwoven in the Spanish ambitions in Africa.[12] Secondly, we would like to highlight the cultural and linguistic consolidation on both the elite and mass levels, as well as the importance of concepts of "the Other" and concepts of civilizing missions, which worked both in imperial and national contexts. Thirdly, we underline the importance of the development of economic ties between various

---

[9] See also John Breuilly, *Nationalism and the State*, 2nd edn. (Manchester: Manchester University Press, 1993).

[10] See: Frederick Cooper, *Colonialism in Question: Theory, Knowledge, History* (Berkeley: University of California Press, 2005), 174.

[11] E.g., Geoffrey Hosking, *Russia: People and Empire 1552–1917* (London: HarperCollins, 1997).

[12] Ferrán Archilés, "Maurische Exotik, imperialer Traum. Imperialismus, Nation und Geschlecht im Spanien der Restaurationsmonarchie," *Mittelweg 36*, no. 6 (2013): 36 – 54.

regions, which were vital both in imperial and national contexts. Fourthly, we think it necessary to discuss mechanisms of political involvement on the elite and mass levels, which included concepts of citizenship, as well as gradually emerging social rights linked to citizenship. Foreign policy in general, and interimperial competition in particular, were extremely important factors. Finally, we should also like to draw attention to institutions, which were central both for empires and imperial nations, ranging from the army to scientific societies.

The subsequent articles in this volume will take account of all of these factors from the perspective of their respective case studies or their thematic concerns. However, as we did not want to make these factors into a straitjacket for individual cases—they will be dealt with and emphasized to a very different degree in the different chapters. Chapter authors had to take account of the existing research for their particular empires and recognize that in some areas there was not yet sufficient work being done. As is particularly evident in the chapters by Broers and Komlosy, the very concept of nation and imperial core could acquire a dramatically new meaning under different circumstances of place and time. Thus, Broers shows that Napoleon never saw the whole of France but rather some northern parts of France, Belgium, and some parts of western Germany as the core of his future pan-European empire. Komlosy demonstrates how the consolidation of the Habsburg Empire—or, rather, of her Austrian parts after 1867—was based on economic integration and legal equality and not on processes of cultural and linguistic unification. In this area the Habsburg Empire achieved far higher levels of integration than many so-called nation-states.[13] To a large extent that became possible due to Ausgleich, which as a matter of fact gave Hungarians their own sub-empire in Transleithania, where they could pursue an aggressive strategy of imperial nation-building. It should be noted in this context that the model of Habsburg dualism was perceived as attractive by Catalanism in the early twentieth century.[14]

During the high point of the age of historiographical nationalism, roughly between 1850 and 1950, historians atomized the spatial entities that dominated the nineteenth century, that is, empires, into smaller, national units and, at the same time, they downplayed the imperial components of nation-states. In this perspective, the "normal" historical development went from empire to nation-state. This legacy lived on in nationalism studies during the second half of the twentieth century. With the rise of

[13] For a detailed comparison of the Habsburg, Ottoman, and British Empires and their different strategies of integrating core and periphery and for a convincing argument that, of those three, only the British Empire attempted to nationalize its British core, see Andrea Komlosy, "Habsburgermonarchie, Osmanisches Reich und Britisches Empire—Erweiterung, Zusammenhalt und Zerfall im Vergleich," *Zeitschrift für Weltgeschichte* 9, no. 2 (2008): 9–62.

[14] In addition to the article of Xosé M. Núñez Seixas in this volume, see Josep M. Colomer, "Empire-, State- and Nation-Building and Deconstructing in Spain" (2007) in http://works.bepress.com/cgi/viewcontent.cgi?article=1020&context=josep_colomer&sei-redir=1#-search=%22Alfred%20Stepan%2C%20Linz%20Yogendra%20Yadav%20State-nation%22 [Accessed on Jan. 27, 2014].

imperial studies in the 1990s—which has many diverse origins, among them the collapse of the Soviet Union and the globalization of historical studies figure prominently—much new research was produced on empires and imperialism, but it remained, at least as far as it was about Europe, almost entirely separate from the research on nationalism and nation-states.[15] Overall, by bringing together these two distinct bodies of scholarship, one on empires and one on nationalism and nation-states, we are confident that we can provide intriguing new perspectives on both phenomena—empires and nations—and highlight the much neglected sphere of their entanglement.

A Word on Chronology

Our project does not have firm chronological borders. In some respects we can talk about the long nineteenth century being the focus of our investigation. The First World War marks a convenient end point, as it had a profound transformative impact on European empires. In the initial stages it triggered powerful processes of nationalist mobilization rallying around notions of the imperial fatherland. In the later stages, for various reasons, it contributed to the rise of secessionist sentiments and the strengthening of organizational structures of peripheral nationalisms.[16] Some empires collapsed entirely, e.g. the Ottoman and Habsburg Empires. Some were re-integrated into the framework of a profoundly different imperial project, e.g. the USSR. Even those empires in Western Europe who survived the First World War faced new challenges with Wilson's and Lenin's championing of the principle of national self-determination. Of course, the First World War was much less of a decisive event in Spain and Denmark then it was for the rest of the empires dealt with here. Nevertheless, the

---

[15] These issues were perceived as very much entangled within post-colonial and subaltern studies, but they generally focused on colonial peripheries, not European metropolitan areas. For an introduction, see Rochona Majumdar, *Writing Postcolonial History* (London: Bloomsbury Academic, 2010).

[16] One important reason was the support for secessionist nationalisms in enemy empires by opposing rival empires. Political and financial support of secessionist politicians in enemy countries was supplemented by the use of POW camps for nationalist mobilization. István Deák believes that the "the dissolution of the (Habsburg) monarchy into hostile national entities had begun in the POW camps" during the First World War. See István Deák, *Beyond Nationalism: a Social and Political History of the Habsburg Officer Corps, 1848–1918* (Oxford: Oxford University Press, 1990), 198. On analogous processes in the POW camps for the soldiers of the Russian army in Germany and Austria, see Chapter 7 of Miller, *The Romanov Empire*. The occupational politics of the Central powers and Russia were also designed to support the secessionist political forces in rival empires. See F. Grelka, *Die ukrainische Nationalbewegung unter deutscher Besatzungsherrschaft 1918 und 1941/42* (Wiesbaden: Harrassowitz, 2005); M. von Hagen, *War in a European Borderland: Occupations and Occupation Plans in Galicia and Ukraine, 1914–1918* (Seattle: University of Washington Press, 2007); V. G. Liulevicius, *War Land on the Eastern Front: Culture, National Identity, and German Occupation in World War I* (Cambridge: Cambridge University Press, 2000).

years immediately after the First World War marked the rise of the nation-state as a normative spatial unit. However it does not bring to an abrupt end the age of empires, which is why all chapters, in a kind of coda or outlook, consider the continued interrelationship between empires and nations after the First World War.

The age of empire is, of course, not strictly speaking, a modern age only. As the article of Jean-Frédéric Schaub in this book demonstrates, early modern empires were already an extremely powerful force in nation-building processes and their legacies reach deep into the nineteenth century. This makes it difficult to find a clear watershed which could mark the beginning of the period under investigation here. Conventionally, the beginning of the long nineteenth-century and the age of nationalism is linked to the French revolution and the Napoleonic conquest of Europe. However, for our purposes it will be vital to take into account the seventeenth and eighteenth centuries. The traditional dichotomy of empire and nation-state, which we are aiming to overcome, neglects important developments which precede the nineteenth century and manifest themselves prior to the rise of nationalism. If we assume that a state is necessarily a nation-state and an empire is always pre-modern,[17] we cannot reconcile this understanding with the experience of the eighteenth and early nineteenth centuries, because the processes of state-building, inspired by the ideas of the Enlightenment and the well-ordered police-state, were prerequisites of nationalism and not its product. State-building in the eighteenth century in fact very much happened in an imperial framework—something which remains valid to a large extent for the nineteenth century.[18] Industrialization, urbanization, universal conscription, alphabetization, mass schooling—all of these phenomena, which we associate with the rise of the modern state, can in fact be linked to empires and inter-imperial competition as well as nations and nationalism and indeed, regionalism. The variety of experiences of state-building in the nineteenth-century included the German states within the post-1815 German Confederation, especially Bavaria, which was well on its way toward a nation-state in the 1860s. There was no teleology of nation-state building. The phenomena, mentioned above, helped to modernize regions as well as empires, enhanced their competitiveness (which was usually the main rationale) and also created the conditions for nation-building at various spatial levels. This is precisely why all the chapters consider the period before 1789 in a kind of preface or introductory section. How far back in time they go depends on how far back these modernizing impulses can be

---

[17] There is a long tradition of juxtaposing empires as traditional polities with modern states, which are supposed to be nation-states. In 1962, Rupert Emerson wrote "empires have fallen on evil days and nations have risen to take their place." This statement can be seen as paradigmatic of the clear juxtaposition of nation and empire which once held supreme. See Rupert Emerson, *From Empire to Nation* (Cambridge, Mass.: Harvard University Press, 1962), 3; see also, for example, Shmuel N. Eisenstadt, *The Political Systems of Empires* (New York: Free Press of Glencoe, 1963); Charles Tilly, *Coercion, Capital and European States, AD 990–1992* (Oxford: Blackwell, 1990), 91.

[18] Ronald Suny once remarked that "many, if not most, of the oldest nation-states of our own time began their historic evolution as heterogeneous dynastic conglomerates with the characteristics of imperial relationships between metropole and periphery." Suny, *The Empire Strikes Out*, 27.

traced. Although they were important foundations of the subsequent process of consolidation of imperial nations, they are not analyzed in any detail, as we would like to maintain our focus on the long nineteenth century.

A Word on Geography

In terms of the spatial boundaries of the current volume, the analysis in particular chapters goes beyond the limits of Europe to include imperial peripheries on all five continents. Those peripheries are vital for our analysis insofar as they impacted on the development of the core. They were involved in the transfer of human and material resources and carried issues of prestige. Migrations were absolutely vital in imperial/national contexts, as a recent British survey has impressively underlined.[19] Core–periphery relations involved various versions of the idea of a "civilizing mission" and racialism. Both were important elements of the development of nationalism at the core of imperial nations. This is also true for cases, such as Italy and Germany, which did not have empires at the time they commenced the building of their nation-states in 1861 and 1871 respectively. However, the legacies of past empires (the Roman and the Venetian Empires as well as the Holy Roman Empire) and the imagining of future empires (in Africa, elsewhere overseas, and Eastern Europe) played an extremely important role for nation-state building even here.

In attempts to relate notions of imperial space to nation, the category of race was of crucial importance.[20] The population of the imperial core was often constructed as racially complementary and racial differences were downplayed in contrast to the function of race in the colonies, where the idea served the purpose of segregating and isolating the colonizers from the colonized. Thus, the Scots, the Irish, and the Welsh were regarded as of similar "racial standing" as the English, even if Anglo-Saxonism often drew important racial distinctions between an allegedly superior English race and its inferior Celtic counterparts.[21] The Celts were, however, rarely depicted in the same racial terms as the people on the Indian sub-continent.[22] And, of course, to use Paul Gilroy's famous title, there was no "black in the Union Jack" well into the

---

[19] Marjory Harper and Stephen Constantine, *Migration and Empire* (Oxford: Oxford University Press, 2010).

[20] See many of the brilliant essays in Catherine Hall and Keith McClelland, eds., *Race, Nation and Empire: Making Histories, 1750 to the Present* (Manchester: Manchester University Press, 2010).

[21] Hugh MacDougall, *Racial Myth in English History. Trojans, Teutons and Anglo-Saxons* (Montreal: Harvest House, 1982); L. P. Curtis, *Anglo-Saxons and Celts: a Study of anti-Irish Prejudice in Victorian England* (New York: New York University Press, 1968).

[22] Mrinilina Sinha, "Gender and Imperialism: Colonial Policy and the Ideology of Moral Imperialism in Late Nineteenth Century Bengal," in *Changing Men: New Directions in Research on Men and Masculinity*, ed. Michael S. Kimmel (London: Sage, 1987), 217–31.

twentieth century.[23] In the Russian project, the Eastern Slavs played the key role, but the Finno-Ugric population was also described as complementary, and sometimes as inseparable part of Russia.[24]

The relations between the imperial authorities (particularly their more traditionalist wing) and emerging dominant nationalisms (both as public sentiment and organized movement) were usually complicated. But, from the late eighteenth century onwards, both aimed at transforming the core areas of empires, previously defined mostly in dynastic terms, into "national territories." These nation-building projects usually were expansionist, in other words they claimed certain peripheral regions as parts of these newly conceived national territories. Nationalism thus brought with it new ways of imagining and structuring imperial space. In some cases, the idea of "national territory" even incorporated regions that were located beyond the current borders of the empire. Thus, for example, Eastern Galicia for decades was claimed by Russian nationalism as "Russian land," and it was indeed occupied in 1914 under irredentist slogans, and the German claims on Alsace precisely as "German land" led directly to the annexation of the territory after the Franco-Prussian war in 1871.[25] It is often intriguing to look at such bordering and also border transgressions between empires.[26]

Success or failure of particular empires in their imperialist endeavors overseas could have a profound impact on competition between dominant and secessionist nationalist projects in their European core or metropolitan areas. They also provided the means to integrate imperial elites by involving peripheral elites in Europe into the business of running the empire. At times, even patterns of nationalism were imported from the periphery into the core area—as is very evident in the chapter on the Spanish empire in this volume, which shows how political developments in her American colonies influenced diverse regionalisms in Spain and their relationship with the Castilian core. However, overall we concentrate on the imperial nations that are located in Europe. We recognize that Japan and the United States can be approached from the same perspective, but they will not form part of our analysis here.

---

[23] Paul Gilroy, *"There Ain't No Black in the Union Jack." The Cultural Politics of Race and Nation* (Chicago: University of Chicago Press, 1987).

[24] See Miller, *Imperiia Romanovykh I natsionalizm*, 147–71.

[25] For Galicia see Alexei Miller, "A Testament of the All-Russian Idea: Foreign Ministry Memoranda to the Imperial, Provisional and Bolshevik Governments," in *Extending the Borders of Russian History. Essays in Honor of Alfred Rieber*, ed. Marsha Siefert (Budapest: Central European University Press, 2003), 233–44; for Alsace compare Christopher J. Fischer, *Alsace to the Alsatians: Visions and Divisions of Alsatian Regionalism, 1870–1939* (Oxford: Berghahn Books, 2010).

[26] For the Habsburg-Russian context, see, for example, Malte Rolf and Jörn Happel, eds., *Grenzgänger in Vielvölkerreichen: Grenzziehungen und -überschreitungen in Russland und Österreich-Ungarn (1840–1918)*, special issue of *Zeitschrift für Geschichtswissenschaft* 59, no. 5 (2011): 397–462.

Imperial Modernities

This volume seeks to provide new material for understanding the mechanisms of social and political transformations that were at work in Europe and which are often
grouped together under the concept of modernity.[27] We look at these transformations
through the experience of building imperial nations. Two ways to classify empires generally prevail in historiography. Empires are divided into maritime and land based, or
contiguous. If Britain and Spain can be seen as exemplary cases for a maritime empire, the Russian, Habsburg and Ottoman Empires fit well the definition of the contiguous empire. Of course, there are certain cases that fit this classification less comfortably. France had substantial overseas possessions; however, she also engaged in a
breathtaking Napoleonic project of building a pan-European contiguous empire, and
Napoleonic France was more willing to sacrifice some of her overseas possessions for
the sake of her European expansionist project. Germany was initially a land-based empire, but soon after its unification it embarked on the race for overseas colonies. Even
England and Spain had an important element of contiguous empire in their structure.
Britain—with Scotland, Wales, and Ireland—was a composite contiguous structure in
the eighteenth and nineteenth centuries. Spain was also a composite imperial structure, as far as Catalonia, the Basque country, and other peripheral kingdoms were concerned, plus Spain had quite a tricky relationship with Portugal, including a period
where the latter had become part of Spain. Edward Ross Dickinson suggested an elegant solution to this problem, by imagining empires lying at various points on a continuum. Some were rather close to the ideal type of relatively homogenous European
core and considerable overseas periphery, like Portugal or the Netherlands after the
loss of Belgium in 1830. Others were more heterogeneous in their European core, like
France or Britain. Yet others had major extra-European continental components contiguous with their core territories, like the Ottoman and Russian Empires. The respective proportions of European, contiguous extra-European, and overseas possessions
could change considerably over time, like in the case of Germany.[28]

The sea could play a very different role for different empires, both function-
ally and in the imperial imagined geography.[29] Thus, it could act as a dividing space,
but also as a comfortable means of communication. Whether Ireland was part of the

---

[27] The concept of modernity in the singular has recently been problematized and for good reasons. See
Shmuel N. Eisenstadt, *Multiple Modernities* (New York: American Academy of Arts and Sciences,
2000); also Dominic Sachsenmaier, Jens Riedel, and Shmuel N. Eisenstadt, eds., *Reflections on
Multiple Modernities: European, Chinese and Other Interpretations* (Leiden: Brill, 2002); while we
do not centrally engage with this debate, we are providing information relevant to it.

[28] Edward Ross Dickinson, "The German Empire: an Empire?" *History Workshop Journal* 66
(2008): 129–62.

[29] Robin A. Butlin, *Geographies of Empire. European Empires and Colonies, c. 1880–1960* (Cambridge: Cambridge University Press, 2009).

British core was hotly debated throughout much of the nineteenth-century, whereas there was rather less debate on Algeria belonging to the French core—areas therefore separated by stretches of water could be perceived as part of the core. Even in the Spanish Empire overseas peripheries were not always clearly identified as different from the nation.

There are several other criteria which one can use to build such continuums. Take, for example, the proportion of modern and traditional elements in various aspects of empire. The Russian, Ottoman and Habsburg Empires are usually seen as examples of traditional empires, while France and Britain are depicted as modern versions, thus creating a false impression that the category of modern coincides with maritime empires, while traditional empires were land-based. There are several caveats to this scheme. First, there are maritime empires which in many ways failed to modernize, e.g. Spain and Portugal. Secondly, some of the land-based empires in certain respects modernized rather effectively—Prussia/Germany in economic and military terms, Austro-Hungary in economic terms, and even Russia and the Ottoman Empires were partially successful in modernizing themselves.[30] Finally, those empires usually referred to as modern very often contained many traditional elements, and, even more to the point, they used the imperial periphery to preserve these traditional elements in their own structure.[31] In general, the European aristocracy proved to be very resilient and adoptive to new realities during the nineteenth century—losing influence, but still clinging on to power. Only the twentieth century brought about the more-or-less complete destruction of Europe's aristocracy.[32]

One of the important elements of political modernization was the gradual introduction of democratic representation in European core areas of empires, creating inevitable tensions. Jürgen Osterhammel's definition of empire pinpoints exactly this conflict: "An empire is a large, hierarchical structure of domination of polyethnic and multireligious character, the coherence of which is secured by threats of violence, administration, indigenous collaboration, and the universalist programs and symbols of an imperial elite ... but not by social and political homogenization and the idea of universal citizenship rights."[33] But was the idea of citizenship rights from the very beginning tailored to be universal? It excluded various groups of the metropolitan population, in fact the overwhelming majority, along criteria of gender, social status, and wealth. Was the concept of citizenship exclusively based on membership in a nation? Citizenship rights are most clearly represented by the right to participate in elections. From this perspective, Austria after 1867 and Russia after 1905 followed a different

---

[30] Once again, the concept of multiple modernities is very helpful for conceptualizing these phenomena. See Shmuel Eisenstadt, "Multiple Modernities," *Daedalus* 129 (2000): 1–29.
[31] See David Cannadine, *Ornamentalism. How the British Saw Their Empire* (Oxford: Oxford University Press, 2001).
[32] See Dominic Lieven, *The Aristocracy in Europe. 1815–1914* (London: MacMillan Press, 1992).
[33] Jürgen Osterhammel, "Europamodelle und imperiale Kontexte," *Journal of Modern European History* 2 (2004): 157–81, esp. 172.

logic—participation in elections was granted to the population in the imperial peripheries, even if it was through the curia system, based on estates, and containing various other limitations. The Russian Empire after 1905 also extended access to State Duma elections far beyond ethnic Russians, no matter how broad was the interpretation of Russianness at that time.

These limitations and exclusions of various groups in the metropolis and in the periphery were debated in direct connection to each other and to the imperial issues.[34] On balance, two different logics of exclusion operated within imperial cores and peripheries—in the former those tended to be exclusions of social status, wealth, gender and citizenship, while in the peripheries exclusions operated along lines of race, ethnicity, and civilization. However, in the French Empire at various times we also witness attempts to codify citizenship without recognizing the race barrier,[35] and in the British Empire, a strong notion of imperial citizenship developed in the nineteenth century, which directly tied citizenship to belonging to a white-man's empire. Although it ultimately failed in the twentieth-century, it is an intriguing example of the intricacies of the relationship between citizenship and empire.[36]

Inter-Imperial Rivalries

Another possibility to locate empires at various points on a continuum would be their role in world politics. Dominic Lieven defines empire as "a very great power that has left its mark on the international [or, as we would prefer, inter-imperial] relations of the era." Inter-imperial competition was directly linked to nation-building in more than one way. One of these connections is rather obvious—since warfare after Napoleon became more and more based on universal conscription and national armies, the empires faced the tricky task of controlling vast and heterogeneous territories and populations and mobilizing their resources in order to maintain the great power status while at the same time nationalizing the imperial core, which was also a requirement for inter-imperial competitiveness.

But the status and prospects of empires in the world system, as well as their perception, were also linked to scenarios of nation-building. We might want to distinguish between empires in decline and empires on the rise in nineteenth century Europe. Some empires were constantly shrinking, while some felt too vulnerable to think of further expansion, and others were still willing (or just beginning) to expand.

---

[34] See Jennifer Pitts, *A Turn to Empire: The Rise of Imperial Liberalism in Britain and France* (Princeton: Princeton University Press, 2005).

[35] On Blaise Diagne, the first black in the French parliament before World War I, see, G. Wesley Johnson, *The Emergence of Black Politics in Senegal: The Struggle for Power in the Four Communes, 1900–1920* (Palo Alto: Stanford University Press, 1971).

[36] Daniel Gorman, *Imperial Citizenship: Empire and the Question of Belonging* (Manchester: Manchester University Press, 2006).

That would mean that nation-building in the core area in Spain, Denmark, Sweden, the Ottoman Empire, and, to some extent, the Habsburg Empire would be guided by the logic of cutting one's losses. Turning imperial space(s) into national core space was made more difficult by imperial decline, particularly in cases where the core remained heterogeneous. Spain, for example, lost 85% of its overseas possessions in the early nineteenth century. But it was only defeat in the war against the USA in 1898 and the ensuing loss of Cuba and the Philippines which led to a crisis of national consciousness threatening the integration of continental peripheries such as Catalonia or the Basque country.[37] The Ottoman Empire faced a whole range of challenges on the Balkans, starting from the Greek war of independence. Ultimately the Young Turks had to use the collateral effect of imperial decline, namely the massive influx of the Muslim population into Anatolia, in their successful attempt to salvage the previously neglected core area of the empire, transforming it into the Turkish state.

In the Habsburg Empire, which again was widely perceived to be in decline, German nationalism could not launch an expansionist nationalizing project as the German-speaking parts of the empire widely clung to the idea of a German nation, incorporating the German Empire to the north. But even here the program, adopted by German nationalists in Linz in 1882, called for autonomy for those lands which they claimed as German, and for the defense of their German character. The program suggested to transfer Bosnia and Hercegovina, Dalmacia, and possibly, Galicia and Bukovina to Transleitania, while the "German character" of Bohemia, Moravia, and Slovenia, the transalpine regions of today's Italy and the Silesian lands, which still remained under Habsburg rule, had to be strengthened.[38]

In contrast to this "defensive" nation-building in the Habsburg Empire, imperial elites in Britain, Germany, France, and Russia were thinking in terms of expanding empire, and, at least in German and Russian cases, in terms of expanding the national core of their respective empires, perceiving imperial expansion, among other things, as a means of consolidating that core. A similar logic was to be adopted by a much newer and weaker Italian empire in the making. The construction of imperial heroes often aimed at establishing national legends and demonstrates the close interconnection between the imperial and the national.[39] The recent historiographical boom in imperial biographies also underlines, by and large, to what extent imperial actors reflected both the national and the imperial as space for opportunities, experiences, and imaginings. Extremely mobile, imperial elites across diverse nineteenth-century empires were the

---

[37] Angel Smith and Emma Aurora Davila Cox, eds., *The Crisis of 1898: Colonial Redistribution and Nationalist Mobilization* (Basingstoke: Palgrave MacMillan, 1999).

[38] Michael John, "National Movements and Imperial Ethnic Hegemonies in Austria, 1867–1918," in *The Historical Practice of Diversity: Transcultural Interactions from Early Modern Mediterranean to the Postcolonial World*, ed. Dirk Hoerder (Oxford: Berghahn Books, 2003), 87–105.

[39] Berny Sèbe, *Heroic Imperialists in Africa: The Promotion of British and French Colonial Heroes, 1870–1939* (Manchester: Manchester University Press, 2013).

key hub for circulating specific forms of knowledge and practice that connected the national and the imperial. These elites frequently performed empire in a way that connected empire to nationalism and notions of *Heimat*.[40]

When trying to construct a continuum based on inter-imperial competition and to locate empires on it we should also keep in mind the role of empires in producing international (or, rather, inter-imperial) order. Some empires belonged to the first league of great powers, as it was formally established at the congress of Vienna, where five empires (Britain, Russia, Prussia, Austria, and France) were represented in all the committees. Others belonged to the second-class powers, represented on some of the committees only. The Ottomans were not part of the European concert at all. This difference imposed certain very important imperatives on the ruling elites—maintaining their great-power status, or striving to win recognition in the system. Part of such a strategy in peripheral empires was the promotion (and sometimes imitation) of nation-building at the core, as well as of some patterns of imperial domination ("borrowed colonialism" or "borrowed Orientalism"), characteristic for those European powers who were among the most prestigious.[41]

The impact of inter-imperial competition on nation-building within particular empires is extremely important. Inter-imperial competition was the incentive for a general politics of consolidation of the core as a means to increase the military potential and resilience of the empire. Nationalism in turn provided a new justification for imperialist contests over colonial possessions, as imperial space was now perceived as the space for implementing *national* missions. Nationalist slogans and various irredentist ideologies were also employed in inter-imperial rivalry over certain contested borderlands in Europe. Since the middle of the nineteenth century, Russian nationalism claimed Eastern Galicia and some trans-Carpathian regions of Hungary (so-called Red Russia) as Russian lands inhabited by Russian people. In 1914, Petr Struve, formulating the tasks of the empire in the Great War, included the "liberation of Galicia" among the three most important aims, together with the unification of Poland under Russian control and the capture of the Bosporus. The Habsburg reaction was to promote a Ukrainian identity among local Ruthenians and, during the war, to implement the mass imprisonment of the Russofile population in the first concentration camps on European soil in Talerhof and Terezin. To give another example, after the unification of Germany, the Romanov Empire, acknowledging the danger of German claims over the Baltic littoral as national territory, had to change its nationality policy in these territories, promoting weak Latvian and Estonian nationalisms in order to undermine the domination of Baltic Germans, even in spite of their invariable loyalty to the dynasty. Alsace was annexed by the German Reich after the Franco-Prussian War of 1870–71, on the grounds that it had belonged for centuries to the Holy Roman Empire of the

---

[40] See, for example, the special issue on imperial biographies in *Geschichte und Gesellschaft* 40, no. 1 (2014), edited by Malte Rolf.

[41] Ussama Makdisi, "Ottoman Orientalism," *The American Historical Review* 107, no. 3 (2002): 768–96.

German Nation before it became French in the seventeenth century. Its indigenous population spoke a German dialect and were allegedly ethnically German. Hence national arguments were pursued in the conflict between rival empires about a region of some geopolitical importance. Tens of thousands of French speakers, among them a good part of the administrative and political elite of the region, left for France, and the loss of Alsace (and Lorraine) remained a major sore on the national consciousness in France, keeping alive calls for revenge and the redrawing of boundaries into the First World War. The French also argued in national terms that the region was culturally French and that, in line with civic notions of Frenchness, the population felt an allegiance to France. When Alsace returned to France after the First World War, the French were careful to accommodate Alsatian regionalism. The strong interrelationship between regional and national belonging and the rival imperial aspirations of France and Germany were to continue with two more swaps (in 1940 it was re-incorporated into the German Reich before it returned to France in 1945) in the twentieth century.[42]

Locating Empires—Space, Economics, and Culture

It would also be possible to group empires according to their geographical location. Thus, we can describe Britain and Russia as "flank" empires in the geostrategic meaning of the word,[43] while France and Germany can be seen as central powers with the potential to claim pan-European hegemony. While geographical location was important, economic correlations were also vital. Hence it mattered hugely whether the core area of empires lay in the area of traditional urban centers (parts of France and Austria, most of Germany, Britain, Belgium and the Low Countries), which became the powerhouse of capitalist development, or whether, like in the cases of the Russian, Spanish and Ottoman Empires, it came to lie in the periphery of the European economic space or semi-periphery of the world economic system, if we are to follow Wallerstein's concept.[44] Certainly, empires were increasingly networking the globe through people, goods, and capital that in turn allowed the differentiation of a core from diverse peripheries.[45]

---

[42] Fischer, *Alsace to the Alsatians.*

[43] Dominic Lieven, "Empire on Europe's Periphery: Russian and Western Comparisons," in *Imperial Rule*, eds. Alexei Miller and Alfred Rieber (Budapest: Central European University Press, 2004), 135–52.

[44] Immanuel Wallerstein, *The Modern World-System IV: Centrist Liberalism Triumphant, 1789–1914* (Berkeley: University of California Press, 2011). See also special issue "Models on the Margins: Russia and the Ottoman Empire," *Kritika* 12, no. 2 (2011). Initially the project included also Spain.

[45] Gary B. Mageem and Andrew S. Thompson, *Empire and Globalization. Networks of People, Goods and Capital in the British World, c. 1850–1914* (Cambridge: Cambridge University Press, 2010).

And, quite apart from geography and economics, another important factor for the grouping of empires was the degree of cultural and linguistic homogeneity in their core areas, which empires inherited from the premodern period. Ethnic and linguistic divisions here would be very important for the trajectories of the nation-building process during the period of mass mobilization. As an understanding of the importance of linguistic unity for nation-building processes was growing throughout the nineteenth century, empires did not necessarily insist on mono-lingualism but rather on bilingualism,[46] where the dominant language of the imperial core would supplement local languages and vernaculars rather than fully suppress them. France, with her aggressive politics of the suppression of vernaculars in the nineteenth century, is often taken for the norm, but it should be rather considered as one end of the extreme. Overall, there was a huge variety of politics aiming not at the total suppression of vernaculars in empires, but rather at achieving a situation of bilingualism in which local tongues would be supplemented with imperial language. This was typical for the Russian and Spanish empires as well as the Habsburg Empire. Such an approach gradually became a legal norm in the second half of the twentieth century for the majority of nation-states and in those states some political scientists now suggest to call "state-nations."[47]

Apart from language, ethnicity and race were seen as points of departure for the foundation of nations in nineteenth-century empires. However, as with language, ethnicity/race was not necessarily perceived as exclusive. Thus, the Habsburg idea of a federative multiethnic nation found some parallels in other empires. The fact that, in the end, it did not work, should not lead us to conclude that it could not have worked. In fact, a recent comparison of the way in which the Habsburg and British Empires dealt with ethnic heterogeneity comes to the conclusion that the principle of ethnic neutrality was far more developed in the Habsburg Empire, whereas ethnic differentiation and hierarchization characterized ethnic politics in the British Empire. Hence, in this perspective, the Habsburg Empire suddenly appears to be more "modern" than its British equivalent.[48] Certain versions of understanding nationality in empires gained

---

[46] Karen Barkey and Mark von Hagen, *After Empire—Multiethnic Empires and Nation-Building. The Soviet Union and the Russian, Ottoman and Habsburg Empires* (Boulder: Westview Press, 1997); Tomasz Kamusella, *The Politics of Language and Nationalism in Modern Central Europe* (Basingstoke: Palgrave MacMillan, 2009); Rosita Rindler Schjerve, ed., *Diglossia and Power: Language Policies and Practice in the 19th Century Habsburg Empire (Language, Power & Social Process)* (Berlin: Mouton de Gruyter, 2003).

[47] See Alfred Stepan, Juan J. Linz, and Yogendra Yadav, *Crafting State-Nations: India and Other Multinational Democracies* (Baltimore: Johns Hopkins University Press, 2011); idem. "The Rise of 'State-Nations,'" *Journal of Democracy* 21, no. 3 (2010): 50–68.

[48] Benno Gammerl, *Untertanen, Staatsbürger und andere. Der Umgang mit ethnischer Heterogenität im britischen Weltreich und im Habsburgerreich 1867–1918* (Göttingen: Vandenhoeck & Ruprecht, 2010); on the intricacies of the relationship between empire and ethnicity, with special reference to the British Empire and the emergence of "imperial ethnicities" within that empire, see also John Darwin, "Empire and Ethnicity," *Nations and Nationalism* 16, no. 3 (2010): 383–401. For recent interesting perspectives on the comparative and transnational history of empire,

prominence or lost appeal depending, to a very large extent, on the outcome of the competition between empires.

There are many possible continuums where we could locate empires based on various factors which are more or less directly linked to building imperial nations. Overall, we would suggest that it might be possible to group empires according to the combination of factors of imperial nation-building discussed above. We hope that our volume provides reliable foundations for such a classification, which should, among other things, help us avoid the traditional binary oppositions so typical for the existing classifications.

Linking Nation and Empire

As should be clear by now, it is our conviction that concepts of nation and empire were linked in a variety of ways during the long nineteenth century. These links reflected attempts of elites to make nation fit imperial plans and vice versa. As a matter of fact, the understanding of nation and empire was changing together, as these concepts were strongly entangled.

In Russia the concepts of nation and empire entered political discourse almost simultaneously during the second decade of the eighteenth century.[49] During the whole eighteenth century there was no tension between these concepts—they were rather seen as supplementary. Nation referred to a sovereign polity, and was often used in diplomatic practice to refer to Russia. Paragraph 11 of the treaty of Kuchuk-Kainardzha (1774) with the Ottoman Empire spoke about the English, French, and other nations, using the term synonymously with empire.[50] By the end of the eighteenth century the term nation (*natsiia*) became closely associated with the concept of popular political sovereignty and constitution. The draft of *La charte constitutionelle*

---

see Jörn Leonhard and Ulrike von Hirschhausen, *Empires und Nationalstaaten im 19. Jahrhundert* (Göttingen: Vandenhoeck & Ruprecht, 2009); Jörn Leonhard and Ulrike von Hirschhausen, eds., *Comparing Empires: Encounters and Transfers in the Long Nineteenth Century* (Göttingen: Vandenhoeck & Ruprecht, 2010); Jane Burbank and Frederick Cooper, *Empires in World History: Power and the Politics of Difference* (Princeton: Princeton University Press, 2010).

[49] Alexei Miller, "Istoria poniatiia Natsiia v Rossii," in *Poniatia o Rossii*, eds. Alexei Miller, D. Sdvizhkov and I. Schierle (Moscow: NLO, 2012), vol. 2, 7–49. But protonational discourse can be traced to the 17th century, when the concept of *narod* was adopted from the Hetmanate. See Serhii Plokhy, *The Origins of the Slavic Nations/ Premodern Identities in Russia, Ukraine, and Belarus* (Cambridge: Cambridge University Press, 2006), 250–99; Zenon E. Kohut, "A Dynastic or Ethno-Dynastic Tsardom? Two Early Modern Concepts of Russia," in *Extending the Borders*, ed. Siefert, 17–30.

[50] See *Pod stiagom Rossii* (Moscow: Russkaia Kniga, 1992), 80, 81, 83, 84. The treaty was written in three languages. The French version speaks of "toutes les nations Tartar" where the Russian version speaks of "Tatar peoples." The latter uses the term "natsiia" where the French speaks of "état politique et civil." See Karl Strupp, ed., *Ausgewählte diplomatische Aktenstücke zur orientalischen Frage* (Gotha: F.A. Perthes, 1916).

de l'Empire de Russie, prepared in 1818 by the order of Alexander I, stated in article 91: "*La nation russe aura à perpétuité une représentation nationale.*"[51] The relationship between nation and empire became more complicated in the second third of the nineteenth century, when autocracy had abandoned the idea of introducing a constitution for the empire. Furthermore, the ethnic heterogeneity of empire had increased dramatically with multiple annexations, such as the ones of Poland, Finland, and Bessarabia around the turn of the nineteenth century. The Polish uprising of 1830–31 put into question the mechanisms by which peripheral elites were incorporated into managing empire. Between the 1830s and the 1850s the concept of nation was consciously replaced with a vague concept of nationality (*narodnost*). But from the 1860s onwards the concept of nation made a comeback, first as part of a liberal vocabulary, but from the 1880s on as a key concept of general political discourse. The last two tsars consequently used nationalism as a source of legitimacy for the monarchy.[52]

In the British Isles the national discourse is much older than the discourse on empires. Some historians have traced a prominent discourse about nation to the middle ages.[53] Certainly, by the early modern period, there was an established idea of an English nation.[54] The discursive construction of Britishness and the British nation, however, is also, by and large, only a product of the eighteenth century. As Linda Colley has shown, it was forged in the struggles of a Protestant England, Scotland, and Wales against a Catholic France.[55] In the course of the nineteenth and twentieth centuries, the discourse on Britishness came to eclipse the discourse on Englishness, and while the notion of a Scottish nation survived throughout and the discourse about a Welsh nation was revived towards the end of the nineteenth century,[56] the English

---

[51] Cited in: Theodor Schiemann, *Kaiser Alexander I und die Ergebnisse seiner Lebensarbeit* (Berlin: Verlag Georg Reimer, 1904), 365.

[52] Richard Wortman, *Scenarios of Power: Myth and Ceremony in Russian Monarchy from Peter the Great to the Abdication of Nicholas II* (Princeton: Princeton University Press, 2006), vol. 2; Alexey Miller, "*Natsiia, Narod, Narodnost'* in Russia in the 19th Century: Some Introductory Remarks to the History of Concepts," *Jahrbücher für Geschichte Osteuropas* 56, no. 3 (2008): 379–90; Maureen Perrie, "Narodnost': Notions of National Identity," in *Constructing Russian Culture in the Age of Revolution: 1881–1940*, eds. C. Kelly and D. Shepherd (Oxford: Oxford University Press, 1998), 28–37; N. Knight, "Ethnicity, Nationality and the Masses: Narodnost' and Modernity in Imperial Russia," in *Russian Modernity: Politics, Knowledge, Practices*, eds. D. L. Hoffmann and Y. Kotsonis (New York: Palgrave MacMillan, 2000), 41–65.

[53] Most prominently Adrian Hastings, *The Construction of Nationhood: Ethnicity, Religion and Nationalism* (Cambridge: Cambridge University Press, 1997).

[54] Herbert Grabes, ed., *Writing the Early Modern English Nation: the Transformation of National Identity in Sixteenth and Seventeenth-Century England* (Amsterdam: Rodopi, 2001).

[55] Linda Colley, *Britons: Forging the Nation, 1707–1837* (New Haven: Yale University Press, 1992).

[56] On the Scottish national discourse see Graeme Morton, *Unionist Nationalism: Governing Urban Scotland, 1830–1860* (Edinburgh: Tuckwell Press, 1999); also Murray Pittock, *Celtic Identity and the British Image* (Manchester: Manchester University Press, 1999); on Wales, compare Kenneth O. Morgan, *Rebirth of a Nation: Wales, 1880–1980*, Part I (Oxford: Oxford University Press, 1981).

nation seemed happy to dissolve into a wider Britishness, in which it was undoubtedly dominant.[57] Protestant Ulster was desperate to belong to Britain and developed a sectarian and overly orthodox discourse on Britishness which ultimately only highlighted its difference from the English, Scottish, and Welsh core areas of Britishness. Catholic Ireland, before the establishment of the Free State in 1922, was only on occasion imagined as part of Britishness.[58] And while there were attempts by J. R. Seeley and Froude, amongst others, to extend Britishness to the white settler societies of the empire and produce a discourse on a "Greater Britain,"[59] such wider Britishness comprising large parts of the overseas empire remained the concern of a minority elite discourse. There is, in fact, some evidence that among the core British population, sentiments of empire were at times eclipsed by little England, Scottish, and Welsh sentiments which were not only bereft of but even skeptical of notions of empire. While describing the British as "absent-minded imperialists" might be overstating the case, it reflects the frustration of those, like Seeley, who wanted to move to a "Greater Britain."[60]

In Germany the national discourse can also be traced to the late Medieval and early modern periods. During the centuries of German humanism and the Reformation, the idea of Germany was closely intertwined with the notion of empire, and it is not by chance that the suffix "of the German nation" began to be added to the term "Holy Roman Empire" from the late fifteenth century onwards.[61] The national imagination became deeply intertwined with notions of empire and led to an "imperial patriotism" (Reichspatriotismus) that flowered in the late eighteenth century.[62] Recent arguments, directed against the Prussian view of the Holy Roman Empire as a monstrosity that prevented an earlier nation-state formation, have put forward the alternative view of

[57] Krishan Kumar, *The Making of English National Identity* (Cambridge: Cambridge University Press, 2003), explains this tendency of the English to dissolve into Britishness with the peculiar missionary nationalism of the English.

[58] On Protestant Ulster see James Loughlin, *Ulster Unionism and British National Identity since 1885* (London: Pinter, 1995); on the othering of Catholic Ireland and its ambiguous position within an Anglicized United Kingdom, see James H. Murphy, *Abject Loyalty: Nationalism and Monarchy in Ireland During the Reign of Queen Victoria* (Washington: Catholic University of America Press, 2001).

[59] Duncan Bell, *The Idea of Greater Britain: Empire and the Future of World Order, 1860–1900* (Princeton: Princeton University Press, 2007); Anthony Robert Froude, *Oceania, or England and Her Colonies* (Cambridge: Cambridge University Press, 2010) [Reprint, originally published 1886].

[60] Bernard Porter, *The Absent-Minded Imperialists: Empire, Society and Culture in Britain* (Oxford: Oxford University Press, 2004); see also generally on the topic of Britishness: Paul Ward, *Britishness since 1870* (London: Routledge, 2004).

[61] On the middle ages, see Joachim Ehlers, *Die Entstehung des Deutschen Reiches* (Munich: Oldenbourg, 2010); on the early modern period see Thomas Lau, *Teutschland: eine Spurensuche 1500–1650* (Stuttgart: Konrad Theiss, 2010); Jason Philip Coy, Benjamin Marschke, and David Sabean, eds., *The Holy Roman Empire Reconsidered* (Oxford: Berghahn Books, 2010).

[62] Jörg Echternkamp, *Der Aufstieg des deutschen Nationalismus, 1770–1840* (Frankfurt: Campus, 1998), 77 ff., 203 ff.

the Holy Roman Empire as first German nation-state.[63] Several authors have severely criticized this point of view,[64] and we share the prevailing view that the Holy Roman Empire cannot be described as a nation-state. However, both views seem to us to be beside the point, because it is precisely the interaction between the national and the imperial discourse which characterized the German situation. Even when the small-German Prussian camp won in 1871, the German nation-state that came into being was called an "empire" (Deutsches Reich), and over the next seven decades of its existence it demonstrated very clear imperial ambitions, not just overseas but also at its European, and especially East European, borders.[65] It was arguably only after the Second World War that the close discursive link between nation and empire in Germany came to an end. The examples of Russia, Britain, and Germany demonstrate that in all three cases the pattern was different but that nation and empire were closely entangled.

Pan-ethnic ideologies could become important mediators between the imperial and the national, but one should keep in mind that nationalizing projects in imperial cores had very complex relations to such pan-ethnic ideologies, as Pan-Slavism, Pan-Germanism, or Pan-Turkism. Pan-Germanism fitted well the program of German nation building.[66] Pan-Slavism, dear to the heart of proponents of the romantic-conservative Slavophile version of Russian nationalism, was perceived by the more modernist and liberal nationalists as damaging, as it undermined their focus on unity of the Eastern Slavs as the core of the Russian nation. Pan-Turkism for a long time remained an export product, mostly for the Turkic groups in the Romanov Empire, but later was adopted by the Young Turks as a resource for their nation-building project in Anatolia.[67]

Some less famous pan-ideologies also combined imperial and national motives. Iberianism could be utilized by Spanish nationalists to understand Portugal as an essential part of Spain. After all, not only did the two nations share mythical figures,

---

[63] Georg Schmidt, *Geschichte des alten Reiches. Staat und Nation in der frühen Neuzeit* (Munich: C.H. Beck, 1999).

[64] Powerful critiques of Schmidt's thesis have been presented by Heinz Schilling, "Reichs-Staat und frühneuzeitliche Nation der Deutschen oder teilmodernisiertes Reichssystem: Überlegungen zu Charakter und Aktualität des Alten Reichs," *Historische Zeitschrift* 272, no. 2 (2001): 377–95; and Wolfgang Reinhard. "Frühmoderner Staat und deutsches Monstrum: die Entstehung des modernen Staates und das alte Reich," *Zeitschrift für historische Forschung* 29, no. 3 (2002): 339–57. For a good introduction to the debate in English, see Coy, Marschke, and Sabean, eds., *The Holy Roman Empire.*

[65] See the chapter on the German empire nation below with many additional references.

[66] Roger Chickering, *We Men Who Feel Most German: a Cultural Study of the Pan-German League, 1886–1914* (London: Allen and Unwin, 1984).

[67] Fikret Adanir and Hilmar Kaiser, "Migration, Deportation and Nation-Building: The Case of the Ottoman Empire," in *Migrations and Migrants in Historical Perspective: Permanencies and Innovations*, ed. René Leboutte (Brussels: Peter Lang, 2000), 273–92, esp. 279–81; Kemal H. Karpat, *The Politicization of Islam: Reconstructing Identity, State, Faith, and Community in the Late Ottoman State* (Oxford: Oxford University Press, 2001).

such as Viriato, the Hispanic shepherd who resisted the might of the Roman empire in the second century BC, but the annexation of Portugal by Spain in 1580 was portrayed as the end point of a century-old struggle for the reunification of the peninsula. However, Iberianism also had some followers in Portugal, who attributed a common spirit to all Iberian peoples. It originated in the Roman conquest and the joint efforts of the Reconquista against the Muslims. Iberianists were quick to argue that the relative isolation of the Iberian peoples from the rest of Europe made for a more homogeneous Iberian civilization and culture, which found expression in a peculiar mixture of individualist thinking and mystic belief. But Iberianists remained divided over whether or not such commonalities should result in common statehood. It was characteristic for the stronger all-inclusive Iberianism in Spain that cartographical representations of Spain tended to incorporate the whole of the peninsula whereas Portuguese maps showed only Portugal and not the entire Iberian peninsula.[68]

Scandinavianism was based on the assumption of a Nordic family of peoples, whose histories had been interrelated for centuries. These histories had a strong imperial dimension—Danes had ruled over Iceland and Norway, Swedes over Finland and Norway. Swedes and Danes had been major competitors in the North for power and influence. There has been a great deal of linguistic compatibility and proximity in Scandinavia, which allowed for the conceptualization of the differences between various peoples as more regional than national. This in turn opened the possibility of imagining Scandinavian space within the perspective of imperial nations.[69]

The re-imagination of a part of imperial as national space necessitated the re-assessment of regionalisms. In empires, regional peculiarities were tolerated under the dynastic principle. The nationalist transformation was less tolerant of regionalisms which challenged the unity of the imagined nation, but it was willing to consider "unity in diversity," that is, regionalisms within the imagined national territory were acceptable and sometimes even encouraged as long as those regionalisms were willing to endorse the greater good of the nation. In the German case much scholarly attention has been focused on showing conclusively how the nation was made from regional building blocks.[70] Over recent years, it has increasingly been recognized that

---

[68] Xosé-Manoel Núñez, "The Iberian Peninsula: Real and Imagined Overlaps," in *Disputed Territories and Shared Pasts: Overlapping National Histories in Modern Europe*, eds. Tibor Frank and Frank Hadler (Basingstoke: Palgrave MacMillan, 2011), 329–48; Xosé-Manoel Núñez, "History of Civilization: Transnational or Postimperial? Some Iberian Perspectives (1860–1930)," in *Nationalizing the Past: Historians as Nation Builders in Modern Europe*, eds. Stefan Berger and Chris Lorenz (Basingstoke: Palgrave MacMillan, 2011), 384–403.

[69] Peter Aronsson, "National Cultural Heritage—Nordic Cultural Memory: Negotiating Politics, Identity and Knowledge," in *Transnationale Erinnerungsorte: nord- und südeuropäische Perspektiven*, eds. Bernd Henningsen, Hendriette Kliemann-Geisinger and Stefan Troebst (Berlin: Berliner Wissenschafts-Verlag, 2009), 71–90.

[70] The strong interrelationship between regionalism and the making of the nation is discussed in Maiken Umbach, ed., *German Federalism: Past, Present, Future* (Houndmills: Palgrave MacMillan, 2002); Abigail Green, *Fatherlands. State-Building and Nationhood in Nineteenth*

this strong interrelationship between nationalism and regionalism was not a German peculiarity.[71] As the chapters on Spain, France, Russia, and Italy, among others, show, the relationship between nationalism and regionalism within nations-in-the-making was always closely linked with the imperial contexts.

Thinking in terms of imperial nations had also changed the perception of regionalisms in the imperial peripheries, which were not seen as part of the national territory. Here empires could tolerate and even promote certain peripheral regionalisms with an explicit nationalist agenda, under the condition that they stopped short of separatist tendencies. Imperial elites, e.g. in the Habsburg Empire, often supported what they thought to be weaker local nationalisms in order to neutralize claims to contested territories from alternative powerful expansionist projects. In the Western borderland of the Romanov Empire the authorities supported Lithuanian nationalism (and sometimes even Little Russian and White Russian regionalisms) in the hope of undermining challenges from Polish nationalism, who claimed the territory of the Grand Duchy of Lithuania. Since 1870 a similar tactic was pursued vis-à-vis Latvian and Estonian nationalisms in order to counterbalance German nationalist claims over the Baltic provinces. In Finland the empire supported the Finnish movement at the expense of Swedish elites. In Western Europe this phenomenon of the promotion of regionalist nationalisms was far less prominent, partly because borders in nineteenth-century Western Europe were far more stable than in Central and Eastern Europe.

Even loyal regional elites within empires came under pressure when their status within the empire changed. The Baltic Germans in Russia, the Poles in Prussia, and the Armenians and Greeks-Fanariots in the Ottoman Empire suddenly found themselves in much more hostile environments when the traditional logic of imperial rule was replaced or supplemented by nationalist perspectives.[72] The transition from traditional to modern anti-Semitism, which happened all over Europe in the 1870s and 1880s, also reflected this trend. Jewish capital was now perceived not only as a rival of "national capital" both in the imperial core areas and peripheries, but also as an agent of rival nationalist projects. Nationalists in the peripheries saw Jews as agents of the

---

Century Germany (Cambridge: Cambridge University Press, 2001); Michael B. Klein, *Zwischen Reich und Region. Identitätsstrukturen im Deutschen Kaiserreich (1871–1918)* (Stuttgart: Steiner, 2005); Daniel Ziblatt, *Structuring the State. The Formation of Italy and Germany and the Puzzle of Federalism* (Princeton: Princeton University Press, 2006).

[71] Compare the contribution by Xosé Manoel Nuñez and Maiken Umbach, "Hijacked Heimats: National Appropriations of Local and Regional Identities in Germany and Spain, 1930–1945," *European Review of History* 15, no. 3 (2008): 295–316; Celia Applegate, "A Europe of Regions: Reflections on the Historiography of Sub-National Places in Modern Times," *American Historical Review* 104 (1999): 1157–82.

[72] John A. Armstrong, "Mobilized and Proletarian Diasporas," *The American Political Science Review* 70 (1976): 393–408. For a good example of the increasing ethnic tensions between different ethnic groups under conditions of a nationalizing empire see Ulrike von Hirschhausen, *Die Grenzen der Gemeinsamkeit. Deutsche, Letten, Russen und Juden in Riga, 1860–1914* (Göttingen: Vandenhoeck & Ruprecht, 2006).

imperial nationalism, while nationalists in the center often saw Jews as an obstacle for imperial nationalizing projects at the core.[73]

Traditional elites of birth as well as new elites of capital and education were crucial for the remapping of imperial space into nationalized spaces that we discussed above.[74] In some empires, the elites were extremely homogeneous and shared the same social and educational background. France would perhaps be the most prominent example. In others, notably Russia, the elites came from a great variety of ethnic and educational backgrounds. Having launched nationalizing projects, empires had to choose between different strategies towards peripheral elites. Traditional loyalty to the center was not sufficient any more. In peripheral areas, which were not claimed as national territory, empires were usually satisfied with a certain level of acculturation, which was necessary for the functioning of the modernizing state machine. But in peripheral regions which were supposed to belong to the nationalizing core, much effort was put into the integration or, in case of strong opposition, the replacement of local elites.[75]

Thus, the traditional imperial indirect rule was transformed into a new imperial politics, which was now informed by a nationalist agenda: in some cases it resulted in a new type of toleration or even promotion of regionalism, while in other cases it led to the more aggressive imposition of direct rule and a politics of assimilation. The concept of national space, later supplemented by Darwinist visions of nation, brought with it new expectations for the level of regional integration in linguistic and cultural terms compared with traditional empires that existed before the advent of modern nationalist thinking. This created additional tensions and problems for imperial politics. However, much of the existing literature on empires is focused exclusively on the

---

[73] Christhart Hoffmann, "Geschichte und Ideologie: Der Berliner Antisemitismusstreit 1879/81," in *Vorurteil und Völkermord: Entwicklungslinien des Antisemitismus*, eds. Wolfgang Benz and Werner Bergmann (Freiburg: Herder, 1997), 219–51; David Feldman, "Was Modernity Good for the Jews?" in *Modernity, Culture and "the Jew,"* eds. Bryan Cheyette and Laura Marcus (Cambridge: Polity Press, 1998), 171–87; Zygmunt Bauman, "Allosemitism: Premodern, Modern, Postmodern," in *Modernity*, eds. Cheyette and Marcus, 143–56. An important exception was the Hungarian policy of incorporation of Magyarized Jews as a necessary component of the emerging Hungarian bourgeoisie.

[74] On the formation of national elites see Andreas Kappeler, Fikret Adanir, and Alan O'Day, eds., *The Formation of National Elites* (Dartmouth: New York University Press, 1992). For comparison of elites in contiguous empires see Hans Peter Hye, "Elity i imperskie elity v Gabsburgskoj imperii, 1815–1914" (150–76); Aksin Somel, "Osmanskaja Imperija: Mestnye elity i mekhanizmy ikh integratsii" (177–205); Alexander Kamenskij, "Elity Rossijskoj Imperii i mekhanizmy administrativnogo upravlenija" (115–39) in *Rossiiskaia Imperiia v sravnitel'noi perspektive. Sbornik statei*, ed. Alexey Miller (Moscow: Novoe izdatelstvo, 2004); Andreas Kappeler, "Imperiales Zentrum und Eliten der Peripherie" (conference paper, delivered at: "Rulers and ruled in contiguous empires," Vienna, Austrian Academy of Sciences, 2003).

[75] The move away from the ideal typical distinction between ethno-cultural and civic-political nationalisms is confirmed by the more recent literature on nationalism. See, for example, the contributions in Timothy Baycroft and Mark Hewittson, eds., *What is a Nation? Europe 1789–1914* (Oxford: Oxford University Press, 2006).

centrifugal impact of these new developments in the imperial peripheries and is underestimating the success of empires in fostering such integration processes before the First World War.

Mapping the Imperial Nation

Imagining national territories of imperial nations was inevitably linked to the concept of the functional core of empires. However, these two concepts of mental mapping were significantly different. National territory could reach far beyond the territories of the functional core into the peripheries and sometimes even beyond the imperial borders.[76] The functional core of empires, defined by such factors as economic development, communications, elite integration, and homogeneity of legal space, was usually smaller than the imagined national territory of imperial nations. However, the functional core of empires sometimes would include territories that were not regarded as part of national space, as exemplified by the Napoleonic and Habsburg Empires.[77]

Nationalist perspectives would gradually supplement the purely functional rationale of military and economic factors. So, for example, the nationalist perspective was gaining in importance in the essentially imperial programs seeking to develop systems of communications. In turn the results of these developments provided new means for nationalist appropriations of imperial space.[78]

The overlapping of national and imperial symbolism in the representation of institutions and the appropriation of space can be exemplified in many empires. Of course, each empire had its peculiarities also in this respect. In Britain it was rather national symbolism which was supplemented with vestiges of empire.[79] In Russia the

---

[76] Eastern Galicia, which belonged to the Habsburg Empire, was claimed as a part of national territory by Russian nationalists. Many parts of the Habsburg and Romanov empires were seen as part of national territory by greater German and pan-German nationalists. Alsace and Lorraine, part of the German Empire after 1871, were perceived as part of national territory by French nationalists. Schleswig and Holstein, part of the German Confederation after 1864 and the German Empire after 1871, were still reclaimed as national territory by Danish nationalists. The examples could be multiplied here.

[77] See the chapters by Michael Broers and Andrea Komlosy in this book.

[78] On telecommunication and its global networks see Roland Wenzlhuemer, ed., *Telecommunication and Global Flows of Information in the Late Nineteenth and Early Twentieth Century*, special issue of *Historical Social Research* 35, no. 1 (2010).

[79] Queen Victoria in Britain was celebrated not only as head of the British state, but she was also Empress of India. Oxford University did not only regard itself as the first university in Britain, but also as an "imperial university." See Richard Symonds, *Oxford and Empire* (Basingstoke: Palgrave MacMillan, 1986). The river Thames "is consistently seen both as the embodiment of British liberty, and as the umbilical link between the territorial island and commercial globalism" and, one might add, empire. See Geoff Quilley, "'All Ocean is Her Own': the Image of the Sea and the Identity of the Maritime Nation in Eighteenth-Century British Art," in *Imagining Nations*, ed. Geoff Cubitt (Manchester: Manchester University Press, 1998), 135–52, esp.140.

opposite is true—the imperial symbolism of the dynasty was gradually nationalized in the second half of the nineteenth century.[80]

Geographers were, of course, vital for the provision of images, above all, maps, which demonstrated spatial unity and defined national and imperial space. In Britain, Halford Mackinder was arguably the most important geographer to situate Britain centrally in global representations, moving it from Europe's edge to the world's center. In his geographical imagination, the British were an island race ideally qualified both to defend its rural English heartlands and to bring its values to all corners of the world.[81] When the German Empire lost its colonies at the end of the First World War, it led to a re-mapping of the world which had repercussions not only on the tourist industry but also on the way that Germans came to visualize their own nation.[82] In Russia, the geographer V.P. Semenov-Tianshanskii singled out a special "cultural-economic entity"—a "Russian Eurasia" (spanning the space between the Volga and the Enisei and from the Arctic Ocean to the empire's southern borders on the Caspian sea) that must not be regarded as a borderland, but should be spoken of as a "native and fully equal Russian land."[83]

Nationalist historical narratives were constructed in order to "prove" conclusively the belonging of certain imperial spaces to "national territory." The German concept of "Kulturboden" (cultural territory), for example, gained wider currency as an attempt to move territorial claims of German nationalism as far to the east as possible. Even where the population was overwhelmingly non-German, it was argued that the superior cultural ambitions of German settlers, past or present, made that territory German. The German Empire thus developed imperialist concepts in order to further the extension of national space.[84] Similar tactics were used when Siberia was appropriated as a Russian national territory in the late nineteenth and early twentieth centuries. In the western borderlands of the Romanov Empire, the Russian national historical narrative was used to claim the eastern borderlands of the partitioned Polish Commonwealth as Russian national territory on the grounds that both the Medieval Kievan Rus' and the Grand Duchy of Lithuania were Russian states. In Britain, to take another example, Irish history became a battlefield between Tory and Whig Anglo-Irish conceptions of how the Irish story was to be related to a wider British one. Between Froude and Lecky, the conception of how to achieve such integration was

---

[80] Richard S. Wortman, *Scenarios of Power: Myth and Ceremony in the Russian Monarchy*, 2 vols. (Princeton: Princeton University Press, 1999).

[81] Halford J. Mackinder, *Britain and the British Seas* (London: Heinemann, 1902); Mackinder's historical equivalent was, of course, J. R. Seeley, *The Expansion of England* (London: MacMillan, 1883).

[82] Rudy Koshar, *German Travel Cultures* (Oxford: Berg, 2000), 80.

[83] V.P. Semenov-Tian-Shanskii, "O mogushchestvennom territorial'nom vladenii primenitel'no k Rossii," *Arabeski istorii* 7 (*Rozhdenie natsii*) (Moscow, 1996), 603–04, 608–09.

[84] Jan M. Piskorski, Jörg Hackmann, and Rudolf Jaworski, eds., *Deutsche Ostforschung und polnische Westforschung im Spannungsfeld von Wissenschaft und Politik. Disziplinen im Vergleich* (Osnabrück: fibre, 2002).

different and contested, but the historical narratives on both sides had a direct political purpose: to provide stability through historical discourse for an Ireland which was to remain closely allied to England, Scotland, and Wales.[85]

The merging of national and imperial motifs was also evident in such domains as managing space in urban development. Metropolitan cities, such as London, Paris, Berlin, and St. Petersburg, now became national capitals with architectural designs that combined imperial and national languages.[86] In nineteenth century Britain, most architects saw architecture as an expression of national personality,[87] and while much of English architecture reflected visions of Englishness, many of the public buildings, such as town halls and civic centers, also reflected the wider imperial ambitions of the island nation. Victorian cities were not only built in Britain, but also in the empire, the prime example perhaps being Melbourne.[88] In other cases, urban spaces, constructed as imperial centers, were acquiring national meaning, e.g. St. Petersburg, where the classicist empire style in architecture was replaced with an often awkward mixture of Byzantine and pre-imperial Russian motives. One can easily see what we mean when looking at the peculiar mixture of neo-Moscovite and neo-Byzantine styles in the Church of the Resurrection of Christ (of the Savior on the Spilled Blood), erected in St. Petersburg in 1883–1907 on the place where Alexander II had been assassinated.[89] The image of a capital was shaped by both imperial and national agendas. This was also true for Budapest as the capital of the sub-empire of Hungary, which was developed as an imperial and national city after the Constitutional Compromise of 1867. It was consciously borrowing from other imperial-national capitals, such as Budapest (Andrássy út), Vienna (the Ringstrasse; various public buildings, e.g. the Opera), and London (Parliament building). The whole Buda hill was reshaped in view of the coronation of the Austrian emperor as the Hungarian king and the construction of the new *Königlich und Kaiserlich* residence.

---

[85] On Froude see the forthcoming biography: Ciaran Brady, *James Anthony Froude: an Intellectual Biography of a Victorian Prophet* (Oxford: Oxford University Press, 2013); on Lecky see Benedikt Stuchtey, *W.E.H. Lecky (1838–1903)* (Göttingen: Vandenhoeck & Ruprecht, 1997); generally on the importance of history for constructions of the Irish story see the excellent book: Roy Foster, *The Irish Story. Telling Tales and Making It Up in Ireland* (Oxford: Oxford University Press, 2002).

[86] See David Cannadine, "The Context, Performance and Meaning of Ritual: The British Monarchy and the 'Invention of Tradition,' c. 1820–1977," in *The Invention of Tradition*, eds. E. J. Hobsbawm and T. O. Ranger (Cambridge: Cambridge University Press, 1992), 101–64. Takashi Fujitani's admirable analysis of the Japanese experience provides many examples of how elites in Japan were consciously melting together the cult of the emperor, nation and empire building, largely following their understanding of the policies of European empires. See Takashi Fujitani, *Splendid Monarchy : Power and Pageantry in Modern Japan* (Berkeley: University of California Press, 1998), 1–28, 197–229, esp. 24.

[87] Robert Colls, *Identity of England* (Oxford: Oxford University Press, 2002), 235.

[88] Asa Briggs, *Victorian Cities* (London: Odhams, 1963), chapter 7.

[89] More than ten other churches in "new Russian style" in the capital were destroyed after 1917.

Opera gained central importance through all Europe precisely because it had both an imperial and at the same time national role.[90] Churches were both imperial and national spaces. The rope ornaments that we find in much of neo-Manueline Portuguese as well as in Spanish architecture linked national space to maritime, that is, imperial adventures. Important second cities in imperial nations such as Liverpool, Hamburg, Barcelona, Marseille, or Porto (all ports) were very much tied into the imperial enterprise and into narratives of empire.[91]

A new nationalizing agenda crept into imperial institutions such as schools, universities, learned societies, bureaucracies, armies, and churches. School curricula were rewritten in order to facilitate the nationalization of imperial space. In Russia, the author of an important national narrative, N. Ustrialov, was awarded the prize for the best textbook in history already in the 1830s. Books on geography for children in all empires followed the pattern of the French *Le Tour de la France par deux enfants* by Augustine Fouillée, telling the story of friends who traveled all over "our land" and admired its richness, beauty, and variety, but recognized its national unity.[92] Diverse "geographies of empire" underpinned different practices of imperial rule and also helped to negotiate the relationship between the imperial and the national within empires.[93]

Key institutions of the nationalizing empires (army, law courts, bureaucracies, and universities) were staffed by peripheral elites keen to take material and status advantage of the promised integration of peripheries. The prominence of Scots, Welsh- and Irishmen in the imperial administration and the colonial services of Britain has long been the focus of considerable attention.[94] The officer corps (and military schools) worked as a unifying mechanism in many empires.[95] In the Romanov Empire the officer corps proved to be the most efficient tool not only for the acculturation and consolidation of the imperial elite, but later for the Russification of numerous representatives of the Baltic German, Georgian, and even Polish nobility as well. The Prussian army and navy had a long-term influence on the German unification process in the 1860s and early 1870s, as its officer corps set many of the core values and

---

[90] Peter Stachel and Philipp Ther, *Wie europäisch ist die Oper? Die Geschichte des Musiktheaters als Zugang zu einer kulturellen Topographie Europas* (Munich: Oldenbourg, 2009).

[91] Maiken Umbach, "A Tale of Second Cities," *American Historical Review* 110, no. 3 (2005): 659–92; Sheryllynne Haggerty, Anthony Webster, and Nicholas J. White, *The Empire in One City? Liverpool's Inconvenient Imperial Past* (Manchester: Manchester University Press, 2008); See also, more generally, Felix Driver and David Gilbert, eds., *Imperial Cities: Landscape, Display and Identity* (Manchester: Manchester University Press, 1999).

[92] First published in 1877 it had sold 6 million copies by 1900.

[93] Robin A. Butlin, *Geographies of Empire: European Empires and Colonies, c. 1880–1960* (Cambridge: Cambridge University Press, 2009).

[94] See, for example, Kevin Kenny, ed., *Ireland and the British Empire* (Oxford: Oxford University Press, 2006); Nigel Leask, "Imperial Scots," *History Workshop Journal* 59, no. 1 (2005): 262–70.

[95] On the Habsburg army see Deák, *Beyond nationalism*.

ambitions which were prominent in Imperial Germany after 1871.[96] Imperial armies, particularly after the introduction of universal conscription, also played a crucial role for the acculturation and sometimes the assimilation of the peasant populations of the empires.[97] But, as the First World War shows clearly, anxieties to upset global racial hierarchies informed the warring nations' attitudes towards colonial troops on all sides, indicating to what extent the army was a marker of cores and peripheries in all European empires.[98]

State-centered elites, in particular state bureaucracies, had a vital impact on the interrelationship between nationalizing empires and their peripheries. The growth of bureaucracy provided, among other things, new positions (and incentives for loyalty) for the representatives of regional elites. The relatively small Cossack elite and the Baltic nobility could find enough attractive career opportunities in the Romanov Empire even in the eighteenth century, while later it proved impossible to accommodate a much more numerous Polish nobility, partly due to the comparative numerical weakness of the bureaucracy in the Romanov Empire.[99] It was the imperial elites that produced the "cultures of empire" that also informed nation-building within empires.[100]

The role of representatives of organized religion in the implementation of nationalizing projects varied significantly. Positioned both at the core of power in empires (at courts and close to government) and in the localities (through parish priests), they were vital interlocutors for nationalizing empires, as in Spain and France.[101] Missionary activities of the Orthodox church were of crucial importance in the effort to Russify the population of the Volga-Kama region, which was gradually included into the nationalized core. At the same time, representatives of religion were also the backbone of the secessionist national movements defining their nation in religious terms against another religion or confession of the imperial oppressors. Polish Catholic priests, Muslim clergy in the Caucasus and Asian periphery of the Romanov Empire, and Orthodox priests in Bulgaria and Serbia were vital to the national resistance against Tsarism and Ottomanism alike.

---

[96] Ute Frevert, *Die kasernierte Nation. Militärdienst und Zivilgesellschaft in Deutschland* (Munich: C.H. Beck, 2001), chapter IV.

[97] Jörn Leonhard and Ulrike von Hirschhausen, eds., *Multi-Ethnic Empires and the Military: Conscription in Europe between Integration and Disintegration, 1860–1918*, special issue of *Journal of Modern History* 5, no. 2 (2007), 194–307.

[98] Santanu Das, ed., *Race, Empire and First World War Writing* (Cambridge: Cambridge University Press, 2011).

[99] Steven Velychenko, "The Size of the Imperial Russian Bureaucracy and Army in Comparative Perspective," *Jahrbücher für Geschichte Osteuropas* 3 (2001): 346–62; Theodore R. Weeks, *Nation and State in Late Imperial Russia. Nationalism and Russification on the Western Frontier, 1863–1914* (DeKalb: Northern Illinois University Press, 1996).

[100] For the British example, see Catherine Hall, ed., *Cultures of Empire: A Reader* (Manchester: Manchester University Press, 2000).

[101] For France see, for example, Owen White and James Patrick Daughton, eds., *In God's Empire: French Missionaries and the Modern World* (Oxford: Oxford University Press, 2012).

The Imperial Nation in a Nutshell

The examples we have given above are tilted toward the Russian, British, and German Empires—the histories of which are most familiar to the authors of this introduction. However, the reader of this book will find many more examples in the diverse empire chapters in this book. The lengthy imperial case studies provided here will inevitably provoke comparative reflections in the minds of the readers. However, we also asked a number of renowned historians to write shorter comparative reflections on a number of those themes that feature prominently in almost every chapter on specific empires. What emerges from the empire chapters and the comparative commentaries on those chapters are three interrelated arguments, which also adequately summarize the editors' intentions with this volume: First, nations did not build empires—instead, nations emerged within empires and in the context of inter-imperial competition; secondly, nation-building cannot be understood without its imperial context—this is true for secessionist nation-building projects in imperial peripheries, but also for the nation-building processes in imperial cores; and thirdly, nation building and empire were very much entangled processes—nation-building in the core of empires was in fact one of the key instruments of empires to enhance and improve their competitiveness.

"A World Empire, Sea-Girt"[1]: The British Empire, State and Nations, 1780–1914

NEIL EVANS

Introduction: The Nature of the British Empire

The imperial historian Hugh Egerton was a rare example of a commentator who managed to sum up the British Empire of the Victorian era in a neat phrase. Cartoonists could portray it as a lion but this was a symbol which did very little to reveal its nature.[2] Many found it defied easy description. *Encyclopaedia Britannica,* in its classic edition of 1911, had difficulty and saw it as: "the name now loosely given to the whole aggregate of territory, the inhabitants of which, under various forms of government ultimately look to the British crown as the supreme head. The term 'empire' is in this connection used rather for convenience than in any sense equivalent to that of the older or despotic empires of history."[3] There was a valiant search for statistics to fill the conceptual gap. It comprised a quarter of the land surface of the globe, mainly in temperate zones seen as suitable for European settlement, but with enough diversity to be half in light and half in dark at any one time. The summer produce of some parts could supply the winter needs of others and vice-versa. It was easy to characterize it in superlatives: It contained some of the highest mountains and biggest lakes in the world and of a total population of 400 million, of whom around one eighth were of European ancestry. It has vast land frontiers as well as extended sea routes. Lord Curzon counted them at some 21,000 miles and observed that: "We commonly speak of Great Britain as the greatest sea-power, forgetting that she is also the greatest land-power in the universe."[4]

---

[1] Hugh Edward Egerton, *A Short History of British Colonial Policy* (London: Methuen Press, 1920), 5.

[2] Mark Bryant, *Wars of Empire in Cartoons* (London: Grub Street Books, 2008).

[3] *Encyclopaedia Britiannica,* 1911 edition, sub BRITISH EMPIRE, retrieved from http://en.wikisource.org/wiki/1911_Encyclop%C3%A6dia_Britannia/British_Empire. The following details come from this source unless credited otherwise.

[4] Lord Curzon, Frontiers Romanes Lecture (Oxford, 1907). Text available at: https://www.dur.ac.uk/resources/ibru/resources/links/curzon.pdf (accessed on April 30, 2014).

This meant it did not fit easily into the conceptions of seaborne empires and land based empires which were being elaborated by Halford Mackinder and Alfred T. Mahan at that time, though it was clearly not a contiguous land empire Mackinder saw as the form of the future.[5] Its extent and diversity made it difficult even to count its population accurately. From 1840, there had been efforts to produce a single, coordinated imperial census. They were regularly frustrated by difficulties of distance, communication, and wildly differing social structures (including non-sedentary populations in some colonies), which made statistical measures difficult to agree and were not aided by the reluctance of colonial administrations to spend scarce resources on such projects. Only in 1901 was this achieved, though with a few remaining gaps. In 1911, there was a more complete effort but a comprehensive general report was never published because of the intervention of the First World War. The difficulties tell us much about the nature of this sprawling mass.[6]

Maps were a means of representing the empire as a more coherent entity than it in fact was. The Mercator projection distorted the edges of the map in a way which emphasized the size of the empire while basing it on the Greenwich Meridian, established as the international standard in 1884, making the British Isles the focal point of the world. The empire could be shown in pink or red while the rest of the world was blank or lacking in detail. This gave a spurious impression of unity.[7]

One of the problems with trying to create a census was the fact that the empire was a rapidly moving target. It never seemed to stay still for long enough to measure, a problem familiar from quantum physics. Growth was a constant process throughout our period. The so-called first British Empire was based in the Atlantic and dominated by trade which was suffused with the enslavement of Africans and colonies of white settlement. The core was the thirteen colonies in North America where settlers of British origin predominated while the outlier in Quebec was primarily French and Catholic in ethnicity. The West Indian possessions were overwhelmingly slave societies with a tiny white elite but their sugar, along with the tobacco of the Chesapeake and the naval supplies of New England, were the backbone of this imperial economy. On a lesser scale in the eighteenth century were the possessions—managed by the East India Company—in the Indian sub-continent. After the American colonies won their independence, expansion in India seemed to be the new trend, though in fact the two were parallel in many ways. The Atlantic remained the focus of British trade into the nineteenth and twentieth centuries, though with a

---

[5] Paul Kennedy, "Mahan versus Mackinder: Two Interpretations of British Sea Power," in *Strategy and Diplomacy 1870–1945* (Glasgow: Fontana Press, 1983).

[6] A. J. Christopher, "The Quest for a Census of the British Empire, 1840–1940," *Journal of Historical Geography* 34 (2008): 268–85.

[7] Linda Colley, "'This Small Island': Britain, Size and Empire," *Proceedings of the British Academy*, 121 Lectures, 2002, 170–90, at 170–74; Felix Driver, "In Search of the Imperial Map: Walter Crane and the Image of Empire," *History Workshop Journal* 69 (Spring 2010): 147–57, points out the specificity of the map which Colley employs and advocates a wider search for cartographic images.

lesser presence of formal possessions, and much greater reliance on informal control and influence. The subsequent freeing of the Spanish and Portuguese colonies tended to place them under British tutelage. They shifted from a formal empire to an informal zone of influence.[8] The colonies in Canada and South Africa maintained an Atlantic presence as did the West Indies, though the last area declined in significance with the abolition of the slave trade and then of slavery. So while there was something of a "swing to the east" after 1783 it was not a direction which was unknown to the British before that date.[9] Part of the push was to replace America as a convict destination, the need to find somewhere else to empty their domestic "jakes" (chamber pots) as Benjamin Franklin had charmingly described the North American penal colonies.

Even the loss of the American colonies in 1776 did little to halt the inexorable growth of colonial possessions. In 1792 Britain had 26 colonies; in 1815 it emerged from the Napoleonic Wars with 42. The dynamism continued to the mid century. Cape Town and Sri Lanka were retained as strategic bases especially important given the dynamism of the East India Company to produce a territorial empire in the sub-continent. Fears of Russian and French expansion led to involvement in Central Asia and the beginnings of the "Great Game." Besides Cape Colony there were other footholds in Africa, such as Sierra Leone. Tasmania was added to the colony in New South Wales and Trinidad and Tobago to possessions in the West Indies.[10] While the early nineteenth century was sometimes seen as a period of relative lack of interest in empire and of commitment to "the imperialism of free trade" possibly more territory was annexed between 1815 and 1875 than in the so-called new imperialism of the next quarter century. Gains in the Victorian period before 1875 included Western Australia, New Zealand, Western Canada, Burma, more of India, Natal, the Gold Coast, and Lagos.[11]

India became a new sub-center of the empire. Gradually it shifted from an informal zone of influence to empire in the opposite direction from Atlantic colonies.[12] While economically it never eclipsed the Atlantic, it became a vital market, source of raw materials, and foreign exchange with which to balance Britain's highly skewed trade in Asia. Expansion in India was based on acquiring tax and land revenues so the process was self-financing. The process was one of strategic leapfrog—territorial acquisition to protect existing territory and to pre-empt (real or imagined) French ambitions. The process became regional (in that American sense of the word in the era of globalization) extending into Burma and along the shores of the Indian Ocean. Indian

---

[8] David B. Abernethy, *The Dynamics of Global Dominance: European Overseas Empires, 1415–1980* (New Haven: Yale University Press, 2000), 20–24, 175.

[9] P. J. Marshall, *The Making and Unmaking of Empires: Britain, India, and America, c. 1750–1783* (Oxford: Oxford University Press, 2007).

[10] Douglas M. Peers, "Britain and Empire," in *A Companion to Nineteenth-Century Britain*, ed. Chris Williams (Oxford: Oxford University Press, 2004), 53–78, at 57–60.

[11] John Darwin, "Imperialism and the Victorians: The Dynamics of Territorial Expansion," *English Historical Review* CXII, no. 442 (June 1997): 614–42, at 630–32.

[12] Abernethy, *Dynamics of Global Dominance*, 175.

trade and revenues financed British consumption and the defense of the empire. Little wonder that once India won its independence in 1947 the bulk of the empire had crashed down within twenty years.[13]

Between 1870 and 1900 the empire grew four times in size, penetrating the African interior, the Pacific, and South East Asia. Africa, with less developed states, lower population densities, and less unified cultures than in Asia, was amenable to the occupation and partition of creeping colonialism. Some of this expansion was the result of a complex game of chess between the European powers: territories were acquired to check the ambitions of others and to prevent checkmate in India. Extractive industries, like diamonds, gold, rubber, and ivory, established in many of these new possessions required more territory than did a mercantile empire. Unlike in India, Britain did not run up against the formidable Russian Empire but the collective, divided forces of the other European powers which were easier to manage and contain, without the general imperial crisis which a clash with Russia would entail.[14] Throughout the long nineteenth century the white settler colonies of the temperate zones expanded along moving frontiers in previously thinly settled areas, with varying levels of opposition from the native peoples displaced, marginalized, and murdered in the brutal process.[15]

The outcome of this process—much more dynamic than those of other European empires—was an extreme disproportion between the territorial size of the core state and the peripheral empire. In the early twentieth century the British Empire was 125 times the size of the British Isles while the Dutch Empire was 50 times the size of the Netherlands and the French Empire merely 18 times the size of France. It required some shift in perceptions to see such a colossus as being viable. According to eighteenth-century perceptions it would not have been, but shifting perspectives in the nineteenth century made it seem more tenable. It was an outlet for surplus population, sustainable by an industrial nation which by the mid-nineteenth century seemed to be the center of the world economy. Its use of some groups of colonists to conquer others economized on the resources devoted to empire. From within the British Isles, Highlanders and the Irish were at the forefront while Indian troops became available for ventures in Egypt, Malaya, Burma, Afghanistan, and China.[16]

---

[13] Anil Seal, *The Emergence of Indian Nationalism Competition and Collaboration in the Later Nineteenth Century* (Cambridge: Cambridge University Press, 1968), ch. 1; Anil Seal, "Imperialism and Nationalism in India," *Modern Asian Studies* 7, no. 3 (May 1973): 321–47 and in John Gallagher, Gordon Johnson, and Anil Seal, eds., *Locality, Province and Nation: Essays on Indian Politics, 1870 to 1940* (Cambridge: Cambridge University Press, 1973): 1–28.

[14] Peers, "Britain and Empire," 61–65; Darwin, "Imperialism and the Victorians," 634.

[15] James Belich, *Replenishing the Earth: The Settler Revolution and the Rise of the Angloworld, 1783–1939* (Oxford: Oxford University Press, 2009).

[16] Colley, "This Small Island," 171–74 and 181–86.

Historians, Britain, and the Empire

Given these realties it is perhaps unsurprising that historians have found it difficult to tell the story of Britain and its empire as a single entity. The existing historiography is of limited use in confronting the question raised in this volume, for it has rarely addressed the issue—at least directly—of the impact the empire had upon state making at the center. However the richness of writing about both British domestic development and the empire make it possible to pose the question by reading critically the existing writing. Briefly reviewing the trends in historical writing provides both an overview of the questions which have been asked in the past and of the material available for interrogation from the point-of-view of state formation at the center.

After World War Two there was a massive divergence between the manner of writing British domestic history and imperial historiography. The latter shifted its focus from Whitehall and became (rightly) more concerned with conditions on the periphery and increasingly linked with histories written in the newly liberated colonies. John Gallagher and Ronald Robinson, the most influential imperial historians of the 1950s and 60s, rejected economic interpretations of empire (which might have linked core and periphery) in favor of an anti-Leninist, strategic interpretation of the partition of Africa, mainly motivated by the defense of India. Such an approach linked empire to diplomacy and foreign policy but made little connection with Britain's domestic history.[17] There was some room for a connection with the domestic economy through the notion of the "imperialism of free trade," the informal empire alleged to be the preferred British method, with formal empire being something of a last resort.

Historians of Britain itself developed concerns focused on social and economic history and often adopted the viewpoint of "history from below" rather than "the official mind" which dominated imperial historiography when it did engage with the center. As David Cannadine has observed, "there has never been an authoritative social history of the empire," but in British domestic history by the 1970s social history seemed to sweep all before it.[18] The separation was emphasized in the trajectory of a popular textbook, *Empire to Welfare State*. In this view empire had no future

---

[17] Henk Wesserling, "Overseas History," in *New Perspectives on Historical Writing*, ed. Peter Burke (Oxford: Blackwell Publishers, 1991), 67–92, esp. 70–72; C. C. Eldridge, ed., *British Imperialism in the Nineteenth Century* (London: Macmillan, 1984), 3–19, 168–89. John Gallagher and Ronald Robinson, "The Imperialism of Free Trade," *The Economic History Review*, Second Series, VI, no. 1 (1953): 1–15; John Gallagher, Ronald Robinson, and Alice Denny, *Africa and the Victorians: the Official Mind of Imperialism* (London: Macmillan, 1961).

[18] David Cannadine, *Ornamentalism: How the British Saw their Empire* (London: Allen Lane, 2001), xviii, 202, fn 12. The only real exception he notes is: Asa Briggs, *Victorian Cities* (Harmondsworth: Penguin, 1968) ch. 7, a study of the development of Melbourne.

and welfare became the culmination of a re-jigged and more popular Whig history.[19] Linda Colley has given a vivid account of her student perspective on imperial history in the early 1970s. It was more than usually about chaps, studied by them in a fusty way which emphasized diplomacy and administration, and (most damningly) the University of Bristol's lecturer in the subject habitually wore a safari jacket![20]

Not only did British history fail to engage with the empire, it failed to engage with large portions of the land mass of Britain and their populations. Despite a growing tendency to speak of British history rather than English history, it was still largely an English story with Scotland and Wales having a tangential contact. The change in nomenclature has little effect on the content, at least in a geographical sense. Scottish and Welsh history both enjoyed post-war renaissances, largely inspired by the predominance of social and economic history, and clawed their way into the modern period. The previous emphasis on the state meant that Scottish and Welsh historians tended to see their national stories as melding into the English one at some point after the middle ages, but a social and economic approach allowed them to have a distinct story or at least to claim an important part of the general story. It would be a highly partial social and economic history of modern Britain which found no place for Merthyr Tydfil, the Rhondda, the Clyde, and Dundee. As indications of the post-war discovery of modern history in Scotland and Wales, the *Welsh History Review* started publication in 1960, joining the *Scottish Historical Review* which had resumed publication in 1947 after a hiatus of some twenty years. Each country in turn developed its own structures of labor history and women's history and Scotland had a separate journal of social and economic history, as well.[21]

So Scotland and Wales tended to be apart from an essentially English story. Ireland was a little different for, despite the separation of the twenty-six counties from the UK in the twentieth century, Ireland impinged more obviously on UK politics and had to be accorded a place. The renewal of the Irish "troubles" from the late 1960s gave Irish history a new urgency and relevance. This inspired what came to be known as "revisionism," seen by its detractors as anti-nationalist in inspiration and driven by the need to find a less confrontational past in the hope of producing a less deadly present and future. The production and scholarly achievements were massive but it generated a counter-current, often in interdisciplinary Irish Studies (largely literature, in fact) which was founder of colonial and imperial models of Irish

[19] T. O. Lloyd, *Empire to Welfare State: English History, 1906–1967* (Oxford: Oxford University Press, 1970); David Cannadine, "British History: Past, Present—and Future?" *Past and Present* 116 (August 1987): 169–91.
[20] Linda Colley, "What is Imperial History Now?" in *What is History Now?*, ed. David Cannadine (London: Palgrave Macmillan, 2002), 132.
[21] Ernst Bruckmüller, Neil Evans, and Lluís Roura y Aulinas, "Striving for Visibility: Nationalists in Multinational Empires and States," in *Setting the Standards: Institutions, Networks and Communities of National Historiography*, eds. Ilaria Porciani and Jo Tollebeek (London: Palgrave Macmillan, 2012) 378–84.

developments. The imperial connections—and the disavowal of them—are central to Irish historiography.[22]

Anglo-centric history was challenged by "the new British history" from the late 1980s, one which would give due weight to the experience of the whole of the British Isles and not simply focus on England. Some of the inspiration for this came from Ireland, though Irish scholars were prone to conceive of their situation as being simply one end of Anglo-Irish relations and many British historians confined their attentions to the larger of the Britannic islands. But the most wide-ranging work came to be concerned with the British Isles as a whole and to raise the question of whether the empire could be included.[23] At least one historian rejected the framework of the nation and argued for an imperial one as the only necessity.[24] Indeed the inspiration for this work was often the suggestive essays of the New Zealand-born J. G. A. Pocock who had written programmatic essays from the 1970s, inspired by the severing of many of Britain's ties with the Dominions on its entry to the European Economic Community in 1973.[25] But generally both an effective new British history for the British Isles has been elusive as far as the modern period is concerned and the integration of the overseas empire remains an aspiration rather than a reality.[26]

Perhaps, in some ways, the project was made even more difficult by the turn taken in imperial history in the period. In 1993, Peter Cain and Tony Hopkins published a provocative and justly influential account of *British Imperialism* from 1688 to 1990. But their thesis, consciously placing economic development and the British core back in the center of things, in opposition to Gallagher and Robinson, saw the dynamic as being "gentlemanly capitalism," an amalgam of landed and financial wealth centered in the City of London: "Africa and the Victorians have become the Victorians and Africa."[27] Their core was a particularly restricted British one which was hard to reconcile with the so-called new British history.[28] More generally a "new imperial history" which began to emerge around this time focused on the impact of the center on

---

[22] Stephen Howe, *Ireland and Empire: Colonial Legacies in Irish History and Culture* (Oxford: Oxford University Press, 2002).

[23] Hugh Kearney, *The British Isles: A History of Four Nations* (Cambridge: Cambridge University Press, 2006).

[24] Antionette Burton, "Who Needs the Nation? Interrogating 'British' History," *Journal of Historical Sociology* 10, no. 3 (1997): 227–48.

[25] Many of Pocock's essays are collected in: *The Discovery of Islands: Essays in British History* (Cambridge: Cambridge University Press, 2005).

[26] Colley, "This Small Island," 188–90; A. G. Hopkins, "Back to the Future: From National History to Imperial History," *Past and Present* 164 (August 1999): 198–243.

[27] Andrew Porter, "The South African War (1899–1902): Context and Motive Reconsidered," *Journal of African History* 31, no. 1 (1990): 50.

[28] P. J. Cain and A. G. Hopkins, *British Imperialism, Vol. I: Innovation and Expansion, 1688–1914; Vol. II: Crisis and Deconstruction, 1914–1990* (London: Longman, 1993).

the periphery—of the state on the empire rather than upon the impact of the empire on the state which is the concern of this essay.[29]

But an indication of what had changed historiographically came with the publication of Linda Colley's landmark book, *Britons*, in 1992.[30] This deservedly took center stage in the new approaches and has gone through several paperback editions and almost a reincarnation in 2009. It is a permanent classic of British historiography. Colley argued that Britain was created as a new nation, comparable with the United States, in 1707 by the Union of England and Wales with Scotland and that in the crucible of frequent wars a British identity was forged which, while it did not expunge existing English, Welsh, and Scottish identities, did overlay them with a new nationhood. Britishness, characterized by Protestant unity, was defined against Catholic "Others" in France and Ireland, and against the conquered civilizations of the expanding British Empire. The mobilization of women and their incipient assertion was central to the process. She devoted little attention to working class mobilization, once seen as the key to the period,[31] or to the union with Ireland in 1800, a Catholic and civilizational "Other" not capable of integration into this sense of Britishness. Her story ended with the accession of Queen Victoria to the throne in 1837 but was seen as having implications for the present, though the intervening period was one not with which she directly engaged.

As far as British writing is concerned Colley's book might be seen as the point at which the concerns of the present volume begin; that is the way in which the core state was shaped by its imperial context. One of the key things which produced this new state was its imperial nature. It is convenient to take such a fine, provocative, and seminal book as a foil. I want to suggest that we need to make some modifications to her thesis in order to engage with the questions posed in this volume. In the process I offer a sketch of a history which attempts to integrate domestic (meaning the whole of the British Isles) and imperial history.

First of all, while the idea of a new nation is provocative and illuminating, more weight needs to be given to the English state which formed the core of the new British polity. Secondly, more emphasis can be given to the divisions within Britishness, the continuing and developing separateness of the Welsh and Scots within the new polity. Thirdly, the coming of Ireland into the union had a profound impact which needs to be confronted. Fourthly, the empire needs to be much more present and not simply hover on the fringes as a defining "Other." Fifthly, the story needs to continue beyond 1837 and to engage with the major issues of the late nineteenth century, particularly the conflicts generated by Irish home rule which posed serious

---

[29] Andrew Thompson, "Empire and the British State," in *The British Empire: Themes and Perspectives*, ed. Sarah Stockwell (Oxford: Blackwell Publishing, 2008), 39–61 at 42.

[30] Linda Colley, *Britons. Forging the Nation 1707–1837* (New Haven: Yale University Press, 1992).

[31] Edward Countyman, *Americans: Collisions of History* (New York: Hill and Wang, 1996). This is in some ways a similar study but gave much more attention to class and had graphic descriptions of the changes to the American landscape effected by industrialization.

questions for the whole of the empire. Sixthly, economic issues are engaged with more directly. These perspectives are addressed in the remainder of the essay.

From English Empire to British Empire

If Britain was a new state created in 1707 its core English state was ancient. When Germanic tribes conquered Gaul they adopted the name of Franks. A similar process in the Roman province of Britannia had a very different outcome. The invaders conquered around half the island and eventually adopted a new identity as English while ideas of being British survived and were developed in the western fringes and a Scottish polity emerged in the north.[32] Generally the English rulers claimed overlordship of the whole of the British Isles, though before the Norman Conquest of the eleventh century they could do little to enforce these claims. Their efforts to impose rule over the whole island—and later Ireland—were intermittent for the next few centuries but led to what has been called "The First English Empire" with the twelfth century being seen as "the first century of English imperialism." So within the British Isles multiple identities were created and not simply an English much less a British state.[33]

The English state which was created was more ambitious in its administrative functions than the Carolingian equivalents and it has been seen as fostering a very early form of nationalism.[34] There is certainly evidence that some people thought of an English nation but it is unlikely that this was widely enough shared to constitute nationalism in any meaningful sense.[35] But conflicts with the internal opponents in Britain as well as in France did create a more widespread sense of Englishness by the end of the middle ages. The commitments of English rulers to France obstructed the process of conquest in the periphery. Only after the Angevin possessions in France were lost in the early thirteenth century were the resources and energy to conquer Wales (1277–83) found and serious attempts made to control Scotland. New

---

[32] Bryan Ward-Perkins, "Why did the Anglo-Saxons not become More British?" *English Historical Review* 115, no. 462 (June 2000): 513–33.

[33] Rees Davies, *The First English Empire* (Oxford: Oxford University Press, 2000), ch. 1; John Gillingham, "The Beginnings of English Imperialism," *Journal of Historical Sociology* 5, no. 4 (December 1992): 392–409; R. R. Davies, "Buchedd a Moes y Cymru" [The Manners and Morals of the Welsh], *Welsh History Review* 12 (1984/85): 155–80.

[34] James Campbell, *Essays in Anglo-Saxon History* (Gloucester: Hambledon Press, 1986), chs. 10 and 11; Gerald E. Alymer, "The Peculiarities of the English State," *Journal of Historical Sociology* 3, no. 2 (June 1990): 91–108; Derek Sayer, "A Notable Administration: English State Formation and the Rise of Capitalism," *American Sociological Review* 97, no. 5 (March 1992): 1382–1415.

[35] H. R. Loyn, *The Making of the English Nation: From the Anglo-Saxons to Edward I* (London: Thames and Hudson, 1991), ch. 1; Patrick Wormold, "Engla Lond: The Making of an Allegiance," *Journal of Historical Sociology* 7, no. 4 (March 1994): 1–24; Adrian Hastings, *The Construction of Nationhood: Ethnicity, Religion and Nationalism* (Cambridge: Cambridge University Press, 1997), ch. 2.

commitments in France obstructed the efforts in Scotland and it found an alliance with France to be a valuable strategy.

Nor did the Reformation bring increased uniformity. The Anglican settlement was imposed upon Wales with little resistance—far less than in the English periphery—and the grip of the central state on Wales and the English periphery was tightened by measures to incorporate Wales into the English polity and to end the jurisdictions of the English palatinates in the 1530s. Ireland was proclaimed a kingdom ruled from England in 1541 but not finally conquered until 1601. The reformation was not easily imposed upon Ireland, where the coincidence of religious change and colonization/expropriation of land helped build into the British Isles a deep religious divide. Scotland had its separate and distinctive, more radical and Calvinist Reformation to add to the diversity. When there were efforts to impose religious uniformity in the early seventeenth century relations between the polities collapsed into civil war and revolution.[36] So the past did not provide a picture of a single culture and polity and the focus of identity for the core of the state was England rather than Britain; the latter identity was associated with Wales and Scotland.

The English state was distinctive in its social basis. Charles Tilly describes the general pattern of European state building in this period by reference to two polar ideal types. On the one hand there were vast territorial empires which historically had mustered the power to crush rival polities like cities. Authoritarian rule and a certain pragmatic devolution on cultural matters were their central political features. They tended to be economically backward lacking in integration both territorially and governmentally. On the other hand, there were regions of city-states and small polities like principalities and dukedoms where the density and power of the towns and their trade had defeated centralized efforts at state-building. England was something of a hybrid: the early growth of its state had allowed for a good deal of centralization and state power. But London had erupted powerfully into this structure and provided much of the basis for a challenge to absolutism. It, too, was the fulcrum of an overseas empire, mired in slavery, which did much to power the social and economic transformation of the state. London was the only really large city but the power of the towns was increased by virtue of the fact that the gentry came to be their parliamentary representatives and the House of Commons was a hybrid of urban and landed representatives.[37]

Between the sixteenth century and the early eighteenth, the society and economy of Britain were also transformed and it moved from being a marginal force on the periphery of Europe to one of its dynamic centers. Its rapid population growth also provided the people for colonial settlements across the Irish Sea, across the Atlantic, and beyond. The new empire was emphatically one of settlement, drawing on these domestic

[36] Neil Evans, "Internal Colonialism? Colonization, Economic Development and Political Mobilization in Wales, Scotland and Ireland," in *Regions, Nations and European Integration: Remaking the Celtic Periphery*, eds. Graham Day and Gareth Rees (Cardiff: University of Wales Press, 1991), 235–64.

[37] Charles Tilly, *Coercion, Capital and European States, 990–1990* (Oxford: Blackwell, 1990).

resources, and not one of conquest like those of Spain and Portugal. Staple crops and new luxury goods were produced: sugar, tobacco, rice, and much else, much of it realized through slave labor which the British became the major suppliers of in the Atlantic trade as well as major exploiters of in the West Indies and the North American colonies. Slavery, the underpinning of the eighteenth-century empire, ran through the whole trading and manufacturing complex, animating it with its cruelties and with the fruits of its production. An earlier generation of historians erred in trying to establish direct connections, slave-generated money being used nakedly for factory finance. In fact there were few economic activities which were not touched by slavery at some point; in a sense it was more important than Eric Williams claimed, the life breath of the whole enterprise.[38]

By the late seventeenth century these developments had created a distinctive form of the state. The Stuart monarchy had tried to create an empire on the French, Catholic model. Divine right at home would be supported by landed colonies providing goods from across the seas. But a different conception of empire cut across this model, inspired by the Dutch example of a trading empire and drawing strength from the long tradition of representative government, including the struggles over the constitution in the mid-seventeenth century. This would provide a state which was the foundation for effective rivalry with other European powers, including waging war against France, the major imperial competitor.[39]

In the process, an internal balance of forces had been produced. In the mid-seventeenth century, touched off by attempts to impose some religious unity on England, Scotland, and Wales, there was a decade of civil wars which in turn created a revolution in 1649 in which the king lost his head, the monarchy was abolished and replaced by a republic, and the House of Lords and the Bishops followed a similar course. The restoration of the monarchy in 1660 was, however, far from being a simple triumph of the court party. The center's power was tempered by an effective devolution of some functions of government to local level, with "low politics" being the province of justices of the peace recruited from local landowners. Parliament became the fulcrum of the system, a means by which conflicts between the center and the periphery could be resolved peacefully. High politics, the constitution, religion, and diplomacy were functions of the center. The lynchpin was the idea of parliamentary sovereignty.

By the middle of the eighteenth century Britain had a distinctive state, derived from peculiar circumstances in the early Medieval era, which had been reproduced in many of its essentials in the succeeding centuries. Imperial ambitions within the island and beyond it had clearly affected its nature, while the trading empire which lay behind its urban growth was the foundation for its representative form. At its core was an English identity which had been formed early and nourished by frequent wars and the "Others" which they provided. This issue was how this kind of formation could adapt to the new state of Great Britain that was created in the early eighteenth century.

---

[38] Eric Williams, *Capitalism and Slavery* (Chapel Hilll: University of North Carolina Press, 1944).

[39] Steven Pincus, "A Fight for the Future," *History Today* 59, no. 10 (October 2009): 10–16; Aylmer, "Peculiarities of the English State."

Britain and its Empire, 1780–1860

In the mid-eighteenth century Britain was one of five European empires which were vying for power in the world. By 1830 it had achieved dominance over them all.[40] The Spanish and Portuguese empires had shriveled in the face of colonial rebellions and revolutions in the Americas and the Dutch and French Empires had shrunk in competition with the British. The long nineteenth century would in many ways be the British century in the way that the twentieth was the American century.

This period of the development of world hegemony coincided with Britain's industrialization, which seemed equally spectacular to contemporaries, even if the current generation of econometric historians are harder to impress.[41] Of course, the term means more than simply the growth of industry. It encompassed massive shifts in the size and distribution of the population which had profound consequences for the social and cultural relationships within Britain, major developments in communications and media, as well as reinforcing Britain's hegemonic grip on the world economy.

At the outset we might ask to what extent this process which transformed nineteenth-century Britain was itself related to Britain's imperial trade and economy. At one time economic historians were virtually unanimous in finding domestic consumption to be the motor of Britain's industrial growth, relegating international trade to the margins. In a famous phrase, Patrick O'Brien argued that; "the periphery was peripheral." A fairly recent survey of the period by Pat Hudson—and one rightly admired—barely mentions foreign trade and has no index entries for empire and colony. The one real dissenting voice was that of Eric Hobsbawm, who built his whole interpretation of economic and social history after 1750 around the relationship of *Industry and Empire*.[42] Recent analysis has swung closer to his view, and the change in interpretation is analogous with that on the role of Atlantic slavery in the earlier British Empire, noted previously.[43]

The major generators of domestic demand in the eighteenth century were urban areas, many of which were ports involved in global trade. Over the course of the century the major markets for British goods shifted from Europe to North America

---

[40] J. R. Ward, "The Industrial Revolution and British Imperialism," *Economic History Review* 2nd Series 47, no. 1 (February 1994): 44.

[41] N. F. R. Crafts, *British Economic Growth during the Industrial Revolution* (Oxford: Oxford University Press, 1985).

[42] D. E. C. Eversley, "The Home Market and Economic Growth in Britain, 1750–1780," in *Land, Labor and Population in the Industrial Revolution: Essays presented to J. D. Chambers*, eds. E. L. Jones and G. E. Mingay (London: Arnold, 1967), 206–59; Patrick O'Brien, "European Economic Development: The Contribution of the Periphery," *Economic History Review* 35, no. 1 (February 1982): 1–18, quotation 16; Pat Hudson, *The Industrial Revolution* (London: Arnold, 1992); Eric Hobsbawm, *Industry and Empire: An Economic History of Britain since 1750* (London: Weidenfeld and Nicholson, 1968).

[43] See above.

and the West Indies and later to India. Imports contributed 10% of national income in the period from 1700–70 but 15% in the early nineteenth century. Exports accounted for 50% of cotton production in 1760 and 65% of a much larger production in 1831. As early as 1801, ¼ of iron production was exported. Exports were concentrated in narrow areas of the economy but vital to those sectors. They were especially vital in the new transformative industries of cotton and iron manufacture. And in comparative terms they made a huge difference. In 1840, 13% of British GNP derived from exports, which shows that the home market was dominant, but it is necessary to show that only 6% of French GNP derived from exports in the same year to show the significance of the British pattern of growth.[44]

Not all imports and exports were imperial, of course, but in many ways empire had shaped consumer demand in Britain. Key consumer goods—sugar, tobacco, tea, and coffee—all came from warmer climates and had an imperial connection. Porcelain from China had created a taste for the product which was increasingly satisfied by Wedgewood and other potters in Staffordshire. The new lighter cotton cloths produced by Lancashire and Glasgow mills in the early nineteenth century were essentially cheaper and machine made copies of goods which had formerly been imported from India. Imports of tropical goods also stimulated exports in order to pay for them. Colonial economies were not simply "traditional" or feudal remnants but based on the revolutionary organization of the plantation and its attendant slave labor which were the means of supplying burgeoning European demand. The modern word for this is "agribusiness." Other colonies—South-East Africa, the Cape, Mozambique, the Seychelles, Mauritius, and Réunion—became necessary to protect and supply the trade routes along which tropical commodities traveled.[45]

Trade enhanced Britain's industrial revolution, a position to which even the formerly skeptical O'Brien is now converted. While it was not been found to be larger in volume than previously thought, it is seen as having a major influence on the rate and pattern of growth. The luxury market, as we have seen, reshaped consumption and stimulated innovation, imitation, and adaptation. Industry returned the compliment by forging empire. The new demand for tea was largely from the urbanized working class. The East India Company had numerous influences upon the British economy: it employed perhaps 30,000 people in supplying its demand for trade goods and spent some £70M on such commodities in the period 1756–1834. Beyond this it employed merchant sailors. The full force of Asian demand was felt in Britain only after 1833, especially with the export of cheap cotton back to the countries which had given Britain the inspiration to develop its industry. There is little doubt that many of the patterns of economic and social transformation which will be discussed later had their origins

[44] M. J. Daunton, *Progress and Poverty: An Economic History of Britain, 1700–1850* (Oxford: Oxford University Press, 1995), 370–82.
[45] Carole Shammas, "The Revolutionary Impact of European Demand for Tropical Goods," in *The Early Modern Atlantic Economy*, eds. John McCusker and Kenneth Morgan (Cambridge: Cambridge University Press, 2000), 163–85.

in Britain's imperial polity.[46] The reverse impact is less clear. Britain's late eighteenth century creation of a "Bengal bridgehead" was done before there was much serious influence from exports from Lancashire but later expansion, the breakout from this foothold, may well have been influenced by industrial needs. And in less direct ways earlier expansion was influenced by Britain's economic needs. As J. R. Ward writes, "[d]uring the later eighteenth century broadly based industrial progress gave the British a new cutting edge."[47]

The eighteenth-century British polity has been described as a "military-fiscal state."[48] It was efficiently organized for war and was the engine of the imperial growth achieved in the eighteenth and early nineteenth centuries. It managed to extract a large revenue in taxation from its subjects. States always rely on military force at some level and the nature of the British Empire posed particular problems. It had the advantage of not requiring a large standing army. While it did not enjoy the advantage which the United States gained from the Atlantic in having virtually free defense, the English Channel was a surrogate which meant that for normal purposes a small army was sufficient. A powerful navy was essential. The empire, however, acquired long exposed land frontiers and sea lanes which required garrisons and patrols: being a world power made huge demands. This was recognized by an acute observer in 1874:

> The nature of our Empire, made up of possessions all over the world, entails upon our army duties unknown to the same extent by all other nations, but ... the insular position of the Mother Country, and our superiority at sea—good protecting elements against invasion—are good reasons why it is not necessary to keep on foot an immense armed force.
>
> As a nation, we are led to content ourselves with a military force at home just barely large enough ... [and] To supply the small contingent of troops required for wars with the savage nations that our commerce and the scattered nature of our empire occasionally brings us into collision with.[49]

But if such a state was instrumental in generating imperial power, and the product of a quest for imperial power, from the late eighteenth century onwards it became the subject of increasing radical attacks. It came to be seen as "Old Corruption" or "the Thing," an engine for a regressive redistribution of wealth. On radical platforms orators would explain the robbing of the poor through the excise to provide sinecures for

[46] H. V. Bowen, *The Business of Empire: The East India Company and Imperial Britain, 1756–1833* (Cambridge: Cambridge University Press, 2006).
[47] Ward, "The Industrial Revolution," 62.
[48] John Brewer, *The Sinews of Power: War, Money and the English Economy, 1688–1783* (London: Hyman, 1989); Lawrence Stone, ed., *An Imperial State at War: Britain from 1689 to 1815* (London: Routledge, 1994).
[49] TNA, War Office 33/26 Major General G. J. Wolseley "Our Army Reserve" [1874], 2.

members of the political elite.[50] Such attacks reached their crescendo with the Chartist movement of the 1830s and 40s but they were not confined to plebeian radicals.[51] Equally, the Manchester School assaulted this elite which was imbricated in the British Empire; Richard Cobden memorably described the empire as a "gigantic system of out relief for the aristocracy." Efforts to clean up this system started with the Younger Pitt but were diverted by the Napoleonic Wars. They consumed much of the time and energy of parliament from the end of the wars until the mid century. Along with the removal on restrictions on civil liberty based on religious exclusions and the reform of parliament, they constituted a central part of the changing nature of the British state in the early nineteenth century.

Excise was the corner stone of this regressive system and free trade was therefore part and parcel of the reform. Income tax plugged some of the gap in revenue but generally the absolute and relative take of the state in taxation fell after 1815 and in the process a state endowed with a much higher level of popular legitimacy was created. The Crimean War was the swan song of old corruption and the occasion for Cobden's withering comment. Its heroes were the ordinary soldiers not their lamentable officers and generals. Army reform followed in a decade and a half, too. The British State had not shifted its boundaries since 1800 but it had been the subject of massive internal transformation.

Famously, Britain avoided revolution in 1848 but this was to some extent because some of its tensions had been displaced to the empire. Much of the burden of the fiscal military state was shifted to the overseas possessions. There was a bad precedent for this, as the attempt to shift the costs of empire to the periphery after the Seven Years' War had precipitated the American Revolution. Yet this is just what British governments did after 1825—the fear of unrest at home was much greater than the concern for imperial revolt. In the spring of 1848 this was intensified as military expenditure was cut in the colonies and the burden of defense shifted to colonial troops supported by local taxes. The periphery's share of taxation increased, which allowed the center's share to fall. The colonial assemblies of the West Indies and of the settler colonies had less power than their eighteenth century predecessors, and Indian peasants who came to bear much of the burden had no representation at all. This did produce some colonial unrest but the tensions were handled. Domestic radicals were transported to penal settlements, though the role of the empire as a safety valve was existing on borrowed time. Reform there would see the end of transportation. But there is little doubt that

---

[50] Iorwerth Prothero, "William Benbow and the Concept of the 'General Strike,'" *Past and Present* 63 (May 1974): 132–71; Gareth Stedman Jones, *Languages of Labour: Studies in English Working Class History 1832–1982* (Cambridge: Cambridge University Press, 1983), ch. 3.

[51] Philip Harling and Peter Mandler, "From 'Fiscal-Military' State to Laissez Faire State, 1760–1850," *Journal of British Studies* 32, no. 1 (January 1993): 44–70; Martin Daunton, *Trusting Leviathan: The Politics of Taxation in Britain, 1799–1914* (Cambridge: Cambridge University Press, 2001); Peter Mandler, ed., *State and Society in Victorian Britain* (Oxford: Oxford University Press, 2006).

the empire was one of the reasons why Britain was able to negotiate the social crisis of the early nineteenth century.[52]

Old corruption was one form of state adjusted to imperial competition; it was replaced by a state form better adapted to a situation where Britain was the dominant military and industrial force in the world. The repeal of the Corn Laws and the Navigation Acts opened Britain and its empire to the trade of the world but its political and economic power was such that it had nothing to fear from the new situation—"[f]ree trade was ... a form of imperialism that did not, perhaps dare not, speak its name."[53] Territorial expansion did not diminish, nor was there serious opposition to providing infrastructure in India to allow free trade to function or to forcibly opening markets. The sinews of the old state had been cut but the new one still supported the empire and perhaps all the more efficiently because it increasingly recruited according to ability and professional expertise rather than through nepotism.[54] Equally, the state adjusted to the new realities of economic and political power in its imperial world.

But these changes were not the only ones to affect the nature of the British state in the early nineteenth century. The Act of Union of 1800 made Ireland an integral part of the state rather than a colonial possession. This was the result of considerable pressure on its political elite. Its Protestant parliament had won some independence of Westminster in the 1780s and raised issues of self government analogous to those of the American colonies. But the rising of the United Irishmen and the French landings of 1798, in the context of the global war against the Napoleonic Empire, seemed to call for different measures in London. This was clearly a restructuring of the state called forth by an imperial crisis; as we will see it was to have profound but unanticipated consequences for the nature of Britain and its relationship with its empire. The union of Ireland and Great Britain came into effect on January 1, 1801 but it never had any real prospect of being as popular as the union with Scotland—or indeed with Welsh acceptance of their incorporation on 1536–43.

This was not a minor change: Ireland in 1801 provided a third of the population of the United Kingdom and posed serious issues about the nature of the entity. If the eighteenth-century UK had been a "confessional state" in which either Anglicans—or Protestants in general—played the central and privileged role, Ireland was immediately a challenge to this.[55] The bulk of its population was Catholic in allegiance and many of its Protestants were not Anglicans. Such a structure of belief was

---

[52] Miles Taylor, "The 1848 Revolutions and the British Empire," *Past and Present* 166 (February 2000): 146–80. Daunton, *Trusting Leviathan*, ch. 5.

[53] Thompson, "Empire and the British State" 44.

[54] Thompson, "Empire and the British State" 43–48.

[55] J. C. D. Clark, *English Society, 1688–1832: Ideology, Social Structure, and Political Practice During the Ancien Regime* (Cambridge: Cambridge University Press, 1985). Clark stresses the role of the Anglican establishment. Colley's alternative view, developed in opposition to this, found Protestant unity to be a more significant factor.

not easily digestible in the nation-state created in 1707 as was recognized in a number of ways. Catholics had to be given the vote in the state of 1800 but the franchise qualification in Ireland was immediately raised to reduce their impact on the polity. The act of union was passed with a commitment to full Catholic rights but the king demurred and the promise was reneged upon. Yet, as was recognized in the negotiations for the union, the old confessionalist state was inappropriate. It took a major mobilization of Catholics in Ireland to secure this, something which under the leadership of Daniel O'Connell, made it a European pioneer of mass political activism.[56] Along with the admission of Dissenters to more-or-less full civil liberties, at the same time it induced a severe political crisis in the late 1820s. English, Welsh, and Scots Catholics could not have forced this change: it was Ireland that made the difference.

But Ireland was only brought partially into the polity. Its parliament was ended and MPs sent to Westminster, but there were still penal laws in operation and Ireland was governed by a lord lieutenant appointed in London and a permanent secretary. It had a distinct civil service. The analogy with colonial forms of government has not been ignored by Irish historians.[57] Ireland was distinct in its forms of policing which had a paramilitary style and became the model for many colonial police forces. It was frequently governed by "coercion"—the suspension of habeas corpus—something which was not done in Britain after the expiry of the "six acts" in the 1820s. Social legislation was also distinct. Its poor law was even less generous than those which operated in England and Wales, as well as Scotland, and they contributed to the disaster of the famine of 1845–50, when something like a million people died and a million and a half emigrated. Relief policy was wavering and infused with a kind of sado-Malthusianism rooted in obedience to the "laws" of political economy and evangelical conceptions of providence. It was a deadly combination.[58] While older accusations of genocide are not sustainable, it is difficult to believe that a similar lack of sympathy would have been evinced anywhere else in the UK. Indeed, the contemporary famine

---

[56] Oliver MacDonagh, *The Hereditary Bondsman: Daniel O'Connell, 1775–1829* (London: Weidenfeld and Nicholson, 1988); and Oliver MacDonagh, *The Emancipist: Daniel O'Connell, 1830–1847* (London: Weidenfeld and Nicholson, 1989); Gearoid O' Tuathaigh, *Ireland Before the Famine 1798–1848* (Dublin: Gill and Macmillan, 1972); Joseph Lee, *The Modernization of Irish Society, 1848–1918* (Dublin: Gill and Macmillan, 1973).

[57] Christine Kinealy, "At Home with the Empire: The Example of Ireland," in *At Home With The Empire*, ed. Catherine Hall and Sonya O. Rose (Cambridge: Cambridge University Press, 2006), 77–100.

[58] Christine Kinealy, "Was Ireland a Colony? The Evidence of the Great Famine," in *Was Ireland a Colony? Economics. Politics and Culture in Nineteenth-Century Ireland*, ed. Terence McDonough (Dublin: Irish Academic Press, 2005); Kevin Whelan, "The Revisionist Debate in Ireland," *Boundary* 2-31, no. 1 (Spring 2004): 179–205; Peter Gray, "Famine Relief Policy in Comparative Perspective: Ireland, Scotland, and Northwestern Europe, 1845–1849," *Éire–Ireland* 32, no. 1 (1997): 86–108. I adapt the term "sado-Malthusianism" from Denis Healey's key phrase of the 1983 election, "sado-monetarism."

in parts of the Scottish Highlands got priority in relief operations. Famine policy in Ireland may be compared, without serious strain, with that in India.[59]

And yet the Irish gentry, at least, supplied many colonial administrators while lower down the scale the army was an outlet for the surging population of the sister island and the response was disproportionately high. Catholics found opportunities to spread the word by missionary activities in the nominally Protestant British Empire, while a fair proportion of the Irish Diaspora found its way to the settlement colonies—Canada and Australia in particular.[60] Some Irish people were reconciled to the new state by the opportunities it provided in the empire.

The state created in 1707, of course, had not been uniform. Wales had been incorporated in 1536–43 with a distinct system of courts administering English law, a slightly different distribution of county seats in parliament and a supervisory agency, the Council in the Marches of Wales, to oversee its defense and justice. This last had been abolished in 1689 while the distinctive Courts of Great Session were abolished in 1830. Legislation applied to England and Wales which became the legal unit. The Anglican Church was established but conducted its services in Welsh rather than English.

Scotland entered the British state with far more distinctiveness; a separate legal code as well as a distinct system of courts, even if legislation was passed in Westminster it was specific legislation geared to Scottish law. Even more importantly, perhaps, it had an established church which was Presbyterian rather than Anglican and Episcopalians became dissenters north of the border. Scottish universities had a different (and far superior) curriculum from Oxford and Cambridge while its system of parochial schools was unparalleled in England and Wales, even if its virtues are frequently exaggerated.

Scots and Welsh people generally regarded their unions in favorable, even enthusiastic terms. But there was never widespread enthusiasm for the union in Ireland. While many Victorian Scots were proud to use the term "North Briton," in Ireland "West Briton" was a term of abuse and suggested treason to the (Irish) nation. In Ireland the union was open to renegotiation right from the beginning and mainstream politicians pushed for this. Daniel O'Connell, after the success of his campaign for Catholic Emancipation, pushed for a repeal of the union, though in practice, he and most of his successors would have been content with a radical renegotiation of it.[61] There was also a republican fringe which repudiated the whole monarchical and unit-

[59] Simon Schama, *A History of Britain, Vol. 3: The Fate of Empire, 1776–2000* (London: BBC, 2002): 295–312; Peter Gray, "Famine and Land in Ireland and India, 1845–1880: James Caird and the Political Economy of Hunger," *Historical Journal* 59, no. 1 (March 2006): 193–215.

[60] Jeffrey Keith, ed., *An Irish Empire? Aspects of Ireland and the British Empire* (Manchester: Manchester University Press, 1996); Kevin Kenny, ed., *Ireland and the British Empire* (Oxford: Oxford University Press, 2004).

[61] Oliver MacDonagh, *Ireland; the Union and its Aftermath* (London: Allen and Unwin, 1977); Oliver MacDonagh, *States of Mind: A Study of Anglo-Irish Conflict, 1780–1980* (London: Allen and Unwin, 1983).

ed enterprise though the two would not come together as a powerful, united and convincing case for a separate state until the era of the First World War. It was symptomatic of the potential economic effects of union that free trade was not established until the 1820s and a whole literature bemoaning the effects of the British markets grew up in the period. Ireland, however, sat uneasily in the United Kingdom and its discomfort raised fears for the integrity of the empire itself. It was on the cusp of the relationship between state-making and the empire and must occupy a central role in any analysis of their relationship.

Imagined Territories

We have so far considered the way in which the British polity may be delineated by contemporary historians. But how was it imagined by contemporaries? Did the peoples of Britain and the empire see themselves as a single united people? If not, how did the empire shape their perceptions? The Act of Union of 1707 had enjoined the use of the term "Great Britain" and some even remembered to use it. But the problem remained the power of older associations. Many Scots had been keen to promote the idea of Britain and subsume themselves within it as North Britons, and the Welsh had historically identified themselves as Britons. But it has been argued that Britishness pertained more to the state than to ethnicity and identity.[62] To paraphrase the problem posed by an Anglo-Saxon historian, the key issue was the extent to which the English would become more British.

As we have seen, some sense of Englishness has been traced back as far as the Venerable Bede, while Medieval historians have outlined the development of both an English polity and an identity. The early emergence of this and its tight institutional structure made the rest of the British Isles hard to absorb into it and may have helped form the separate identities of Wales, Scotland, and Ireland.[63] English identity was rooted in a sense of "deep England," a rural idyll which has been traced back at least as far as Shakespeare's Forest of Arden, and English identity was carried forward into the present by a sense of the rights of an ancient constitution and the rights of "freeborn" Englishmen.[64] The Gothic style of architecture became something of an English style and, it has been argued, was hardly in need of a revival in the Victorian age—it had not really been eclipsed. It reflected a country with bishops—cathedrals and parish churches were predominantly in the Gothic style. The elite was educated in colleges

---

[62] Robert J. C. Young, *The Idea of English Ethnicity* (Oxford: Blackwell, 2008).

[63] Davies, *First English Empire.*

[64] Adam Nicholson, *Earls of Paradise: England and the Dream of Perfection* (London: Harper Collins, 2008); Miranda Seymour, "House and Home," *Guardian* 12 (January 2008); Robert McCrum "A Perfect Wilton Weave," *Observer* 6 (January 2008); Patrick Parrinder, *Nation and Novel: The English Novel from its Origins to the Present Day* (Oxford: Oxford University Press, 2006), 15, 16, 19.

built in the same style and ruled through a crown, parliament, and courts which also had Medieval origins. The architectural tradition faded in the late seventeenth and eighteenth centuries but was still a living tradition and by the mid-eighteenth century it experienced a revival. The French Revolution enhanced the symbolism of ancient origins and deprived the besieged English of the classical models of the Grand Tour as well as their neo-classical declensions.[65]

Such influences fed into the ideas of Whig history which were so central to nineteenth-century Englishness. When the competition opened for a design for the new House of Commons, after the disastrous fire of 1834, it was decreed that the only permissible entries were gothic of Elizabethan: "Medievalism had become a signifier of national identity."[66] Colley's period of the emergence of Britishness has been seen by another scholar as crucial for the rise of English nationalism.[67] This is no contradiction, as the English most usually envisaged Britain as England and tended to apply their old identity to the new. It was assumed that Anglicization would take place within the new polity, aided by rampant great national chauvinism. John Stuart Mill, for instance, for all his advocacy of the right to be different and abhorrence of the herd instinct, was content to see such cultural divisions erased in the interest of the advance of civilization.[68]

Empire was usually excluded from the view of the British past and Whig notions of English liberty occupied center stage. But when Sir John Seeley drew attention to this historiographical neglect, he wrote of the expansion of *England* rather than of Britain—his view of empire had much in common with Mill's and not least in its assimilation of the Celtic countries into England.[69] Even Matthew Arnold, who thought the Celts could inject some imaginative insights into the cold and calculating English, was happy to see the demise of the Welsh language. The metamorphosis was seen as racial rather than cultural and Celts were to revivify an English-speaking Empire.[70]

In the early nineteenth century Englishness was enhanced by rooting it in a conception of the Teutonic race. The key proponent of the idea was Thomas Arnold and his approach resonated with many. William Stubbs was a later exponent of the idea of a racially based approach to English history—and sales from his publications

---

[65] Simon Bradley, *St. Pancras, Station* (London: Profile Books, 2007), 23–29.

[66] Ibid., 28.

[67] Gerald Newman, *The Rise of English Nationalism: A Cultural History, 1740–1830* (London: Palgrave Macmillan 1997).

[68] John Stuart Mill, *On Liberty* [1859] (Cambridge: Cambridge University Press, 1989).

[69] J. R. Seeley, *The Expansion of England: Two Courses of Lectures* [1883] (Chicago: University of Chicago Press, 1973).

[70] Matthew Arnold, *The Study of Celtic Literature* (London, 1867); Rachel Bromwich, *Matthew Arnold and the Study of Celtic Literature* (O'Donnell Lecture, Oxford: Oxford University Press, 1965); Patrick Sims-Williams, "The Visionary Celt: The Construction of an 'Ethnic Preconception,'" *Cambridge Medieval Celtic Studies* 11 (Summer 1986): 71–96; Daniel Williams, *Ethnicity and Cultural Authority: From Matthew Arnold to W. E. B. Du Bois* (Edinburgh: Edinburgh University Press, 2006).

were sufficient to make him rich. He could accommodate a very limited Celtic admixture but he argued that the post-Saxon invaders were of the same racial stock: "The English nation is of distinctly Teutonic or German origin ... the main stock of our forefathers: sharing the primeval German pride of purity of extraction ... Every infusion of new blood since the first migration has been Teutonic; the Dane, the Norseman, and even the French-speaking Norman of the Conquest, serve to add intensity to the distinctiveness of the national identity."[71]

The thrust of this view was to imagine a tightly defined English identity. But this rather flew in the face of a great deal of knowledge of the remoter regions of Britain that had been collected and placed in the public sphere. A succession of travelers had toured the polity and each seemed to have produced a book about it. This process, which had begun in England in the Tudor age and later reached out into the Celtic periphery, accelerated during the Napoleonic Wars when the grand tour was denied to the English upper classes. To some extent this produced an upland and romantic "Other" for the English but there was also an internal English highland zone in the shape of the Lake District. Wordsworth and the other Lake Poets produced a rugged and romantic rural idyll rather different from the arbors of the Forest of Arden or Sherwood Forest.[72]

Jane Austen provides an exchange which gets to the heart of Englishness and its "Others." In *Northanger Abbey*, her heroine, Catherine Morland, entertains gothic fantasies of murder and mischief in the eponymous country house. Her mentor and soon to be husband, Frederick Tilney, instructs her in the nature of her country: "Remember that we are English ... Consult your own understanding your sense of the probable, your own observation of what is passing around you. Does our education prepare us for such atrocities? Do our laws connive at them?"[73] Mrs Radcliffe's Gothic works were charming but "it was not in them perhaps that human nature, at least in the midland counties of England, was to be looked for. Of the Alps and Pyrenees, with their pine forests and their vices, they might give a faithful delineation; and Italy, Switzerland, and the South of France, might be as fruitful in horrors as they were there represented." Catherine comes to see the wisdom of this view: "... in the central part of England there was surely some security for the existence even of a wife not beloved, in the laws of the land, and the manners of the age. Murder was not tolerated, servants were not slaves, and neither poison nor sleeping potions to be procured, like rhubarb, from every druggist."[74]

---

[71] William Stubbs, *Select Charters and Other Illustrations of English Constitutional History from the Earliest Times to the Reign of Edward the First* (Oxford: Oxford University Press, 1895), sixth edition, 1–2.

[72] W. G. Hoskins, "The Discovery of England," in *Provincial England* (London: Macmillan, 1963); Esther Moir, *The Discovery of Britain: The English Tourists, 1540–1840* (London: Routledge, 1964).

[73] Jane Austen, *Northanger Abbey* (ed. Anne Ehrenpreis, London: Penguin Books, 1972), 199–200. The novel was published in 1818 but essentially written c. 1798–99 and accepted for publication in 1803.

[74] Ibid., 202.

Austen's characters argue for the civilizing process as expressed in a highly cultivated English garden. The landscape is a compound of broadleaf forest with scarce stone, intensively farmed and then framed by ideal vistas, formed by landscape gardeners which took inspiration from classical and native models. Widespread enclosure of the land over a long period in the south of England and the Midlands added to the sense of a manicured, managed landscape.[75]

The capital was difficult to reconcile with such an image. It was regularly excoriated by radicals as "the Great Wen," a consuming cancer on the face of rural England.[76] It has been argued that London came to be seem as a capital of the empire rather than as one for England or Britain, the natural focus of a growing expatriate community which spread around the world.[77] In 1800, London was imperial only in size but lacked the architectural vista and ceremonial display of its European equivalents. But victory in the Napoleonic Wars was marked by a vast remodeling of central London, largely in the classical style of John Nash. St. Paul's Cathedral acquired a national pantheon of heroes, the National Gallery, and the remodeled British Museum displayed art and archaeological treasures appropriate to a superpower: to the victor the spoils.[78] Even London's status was equivocal—there was the ancient City of London but this was a closed and unreformed corporation with a highly restricted geographical remit. Westminster was also a city but the rest of the sprawling metropolis was simply London "town" a chaos of vestry government and inspiring little in the way of civic pride.

But if the conventional idea of England rested on the rural south and midlands, it was increasingly challenged by the impact of economic and social change in the midlands and north. The English North had long been the poor relation, an alien territory within, but now industrialization gave it much more weight within the polity and some envisaged it as eclipsing the south in importance. The six major industrial cities of the north formed both an east–west and a north–south axis: Liverpool, Manchester, Sheffield, and Leeds—none more than forty miles apart—while from north to south, Sheffield to Nottingham and Birmingham were no more than fifty miles from each other. Such concentration increased their impact, physically and mentally.[79] By the time the Manchester Ship Canal was built, there were even visions of Liverpool and Manchester growing until they formed a single conurbation and as a

---

[75] John Keegan, "England is a Garden," *Prospect* 24 (November 1997). Jane Austen shows familiarity with the cultivated naturalness of the landscapes of Repton in *Mansfield Park* (1814), ch. 6, where there is much talk of the "improvement of the landscape." The title of the novel is itself telling.

[76] William Cobbett, *Rural Rides* [1830] (London: Penguin Books, 2005).

[77] Young, *Idea of English Ethnicity*.

[78] Holger Hoock, *Empires of the Imagination: Politics, War and the Arts in the British World, 1750–1850* (London: Profile Books, 2010).

[79] Helen M. Jewell, *The North-South Divide: The Origins of Northern Consciousness in England* (Manchester: Manchester University Press, 1994); J. A. Banks, "A Contagion of Numbers," in *The Victorian City: Images and Realities, vol. 1*, eds. H. J. Dyos and Michael Wolff (London: Routledge, 1973), 105–06.

new commercial capital. Imaginations would not stretch far enough to see it as the political capital but had they done so it would have been one which was geographically more appropriate for the United Kingdom than was London.[80] Industrial strength was associated with the production of dialect literature and a refusal to be absorbed into the center. The two strands coalesced as "the industrial muse," the dialect forms in which popular culture was celebrated.[81] In the northeast of England the newspaper magnate Joseph Cowen promoted such a viewpoint right to the end of his life in 1900 and made a point of speaking in the dialect in Parliament.[82] Some in the northeast defined it as British rather than English, stressing its affinity to Scotland, but it was more usual to define it as English and to use the bishops of Durham as analogs of the kings and queens of England in writing the history of the region. More generally northern England adhered to a sense of Englishness in which the local distinctiveness was expressed at the level of the county rather than of the industrial region—something which the more orthodox historiography of Durham expressed perfectly.[83] But if the northeast possibly had the most distinctive regional culture in England, it was far from unique in displaying a regional cultural difference.[84]

Such regional consciousness was paralleled—and even more strongly—in the national identity of Scotland and Wales. Neither country had a large population which resisted the British project but they sought to maintain their distinctiveness within it and to define it as not simply England extended or writ large. Scotland both benefited from and helped shape European romanticism. The second-century Gaelic poet Ossian, via the forgeries of James McPherson, reached a wide audience, while the Highlands attracted tourists in ever-increasing numbers. Tartan, once a symbol of rebellion, became associated with the monarchy and Scottish regiments. Walter Scott, who did most to popularize its image, did so in folklore, ballad, and folk tale collections as well as in verse and novels which sold well enough to restore his shattered

---

[80]   Victor Kiernan, "Victorian London: Unending Purgatory," *New Left Review* 76 (November–December 1972): 76.

[81]   Donald Read, *The English Provinces, c. 1760–1960: A Study in Influence* (London: Edward Arnold, 1964); John Langton, "The Industrial Revolution and the Regional Geography of England," *Transactions of the Institute of British Geographers*, New Series, 9, no. 2 (1984): 145–67; Pat Hudson, ed., *Regions and Industries: A Perspective on the Industrial Revolution in Britain* (Cambridge: Cambridge University Press, 1989); Martha Vicinus, *The Industrial Muse: A Study of Nineteenth-Century British Working Class Literature* (London: Barnes & Noble Books, 1974); Mike Higgins and Keith Gregson, "Northern Songs, Sporting Heroes and Regional Consciousness, c. 1800–80," *Northern History* 44, no. 2 (September 2007): 141–58.

[82]   Nigel Todd, *The Militant Democracy: Joseph Cowen and Victorian Radicalism* (Whitley Bay: The Bewick Press, 1991); Joan Allen, *Joseph Cowen and Popular Radicalism on Tyneside, 1829–1900* (London: Merlin Press, 2007).

[83]   C. Delheim, "Imagining England: Victorian Views of the North," *Northern History* 23 (1987): 216–30.

[84]   Edward Royle, ed., *Issues of Regional Identity: In Honor of John Marshall* (Manchester: Manchester University Press, 1998).

fortunes. Robert Burns became a cult figure and a lowlander to complement the Highland images that were widely adopted throughout Scotland. What had been a highly divided society—Jacobite rebellions were Scottish civil wars—now united around an image compounded from its diverse elements.[85]

Wales had less spectacular mountains, though Snowdonia passed muster as the center piece of a renewed Welsh identity, forged (often literally) in the crucible of Romanticism. Manuscripts of early Welsh literature were collected and published, a largely mythical history proclaimed and patriotic societies created. The most important of these, the Honourable Society of Cymmrodorion, was created in London in 1751, in response to metropolitan English jibes that the Welsh had no literature and culture. The United Kingdom state had brought many Welsh people to the capital but they did not meekly accept a state of cultural inferiority and absorption. "Cymmrodorion" means the "first inhabitants" of the island. They were thus the first of the British, and the whole British enterprise made little sense without them and their distinctive contribution. The Eisteddfod, a Medieval cultural institution to maintain standards in the bardic class, was revived from its moribund state and transformed into a popular competitive cultural festival featuring music, poetry, and essay prizes.[86] A national network of local and county eisteddfodau was crowned by a peripatetic National Eisteddfod in 1858.

Iolo Morganwg (Edward Williams, 1747–1826) grafted onto the eisteddfod the Gorsedd of Bards, the product of his opium-fed imagination and the pinnacle of his forgery which included poems he claimed had been written by Dafydd ap Gwilym in the fourteenth century. Some thought them the finest poems of that acknowledged Welsh master. By the mid-nineteenth century a nonconformist definition of the Welsh nation had been grafted onto this. The 1851 religious census showed that Wales had the highest levels of attendance in the UK and more than that three quarters of Wales's attenders were nonconformists. Those sects along with Liberalism and the Welsh language came to define Welshness in the Victorian era. While railways were a powerful link across the border and the main lines were west–east, there was a more ramshackle north–south link and a network. Religion, language, transport, and migration linked Wales as a unit more than at any time in its past and perhaps more than anything would unite the country in the twentieth century. It was the railway which made the national eisteddfod possible.[87]

Ultimately Wales and Scotland were comfortable with the United Kingdom, and simply required recognition of their distinctive culture, religion, and history.

---

[85] Richard Finlay, *A Union for Good: Scotland and the Union since 1880* (Edinburgh: John Donald, 1997).

[86] R. T. Jenkins and Helen Rammage, *A History of the Honourable Society of Cymmrodorion, 1751–1951* (London: Honourable Society of Cymmrodorion, 1951); Prys Morgan, *The Eighteenth Century Renaissance* (Llandybie: Christopher Davies, 1981); Emrys Jones, ed., *The London Welsh, 1500–2000* (Cardiff: University of Wales Press, 2001).

[87] Prys Morgan, *Iolo Morganwg* (Cardiff: University of Wales Press, 1975); Neil Evans, "Gogs, Cardis and Hwntws: Region, Nation and State in Wales, 1840–1940," in *National Identity in the British Isles*, ed. Neil Evans (Harlech: Coleg Harlech Occasional Papers in Welsh Studies, no. 3, 1989).

Ireland was much harder to envision as part of the Union or to ignore by placing some blanket of English cultural imperialism over it. It was in George Bernard Shaw's phrase, "John Bull's other island" and the third word in the phrase could quite happily take a post-colonialist capital letter to indicate its place in the English imaginary. The "wild Irish" were rebellious and truculent while the English were peaceful and constitutional. Welsh and Scots spokespeople hastened to claim these characteristics for their own populations and were happy to use the Irish as a negative measuring stick. Protestant Britain had to accommodate largely Catholic Ireland. The British were industrious and progressive; the Irish lazy and backward and in the eyes of many British caricaturists they were little if anything above the ape. The awareness of Irish difference was amplified by the presence of so many Irish migrants in mainland Britain, particularly after the potato famine of the late 1840s. This coincided with the efforts to restore the Catholic hierarchy in Britain and the Anglo-Catholic movement in the Church of England, which led to numerous pilgrimages to Rome. This made religious concerns quite central to British politics between the 1830s and the 1870s.[88] Seemingly constant rebellions and governing the island through coercive policies deemed inappropriate for Britain increased the sense of difference. The English might nourish the illusion that they could digest the Welsh and the Scots, but Ireland meant chronic dyspepsia.

So the space was imagined in rather conflicting ways. The dominant notions of Englishness did not carry into the north country and were countered in Wales and Scotland. Ireland was its antithesis. Industry also produced a world that was difficult to fit into such images, apart from negatively as some kind of blot on the English landscape. But all could respond to the empire.[89]

Empire might not appear to enter into many of the visions but in fact it framed them all. Englishness, Scottishness, and Welshness had to be defined against something which was not these things and empire often filled the role: "The culture of Britain ... was permeated with empire."[90] The eponymous Mansfield Park of Jane Austin's novel was the property of Sir Thomas Bertram, who owned slave plantations. His absence in Antigua is central to the plot. The slave trade is referred to as something which could not be talked about in the household. Austen's own family was implicated in the slave trade; her father was a trustee of slave-owning estates in Antigua.[91]

---

[88] Jim Maclaughlin, *Reimagining the Nation-State: Contested Terrains of Nation-Building* (London: Pluto Press, 2001).

[89] Robert Colls and Philip Dodd, eds., *Englishness: Politics and Culture, 1880–1920* (London: Routledge, 1986).

[90] Catherine Hall, "Culture and Identity in Imperial Britain," in *The British Empire: Themes and Perspectives*, ed. Sarah Stockwell (Oxford: Blackwell, 2008), 202.

[91] Edward W. Said, *Culture and Imperialism* (London: Chatto and Windus, 1993), 95–116; Cora Kaplan, "Imagining Empire: History, Fantasy and Literature," in *At Home with the Empire: Metropolitan Culture and the Imperial World*, ed. Catherine Hall and Sonya O. Rose (Cambridge: Cambridge University Press, 2006), 193–98; Paula Byrne, *The Real Jane Austen: A Life in Small Things* (London: HarperCollins, 2013), chs. 2 and 12.

Imperial issues were not to the fore in English novels in the early nineteenth century. They provided context, reasons for absence, and places to which central characters might emigrate. But they nonetheless intruded into what are superficially only domestic fictions. The writings of the Brontë sisters respond to a society in which the anti-slavery consensus of the 1830s had fragmented. Edward Rochester, one of Jane Eyre's suitors, had lived in Jamaica and brought back with him an insane, mulatto wife—a fearsome and dangerous racial "other." She inherits a fortune which had been made in the triangular trade. Her other suitor, St. John Rivers becomes a missionary and dies in India. Jane described her childhood of that of a "rebel slave" and the basic narrative of the novel has been compared with a slave narrative. Heathcliff, the central presence in *Wuthering Heights*, was described in the book as a heathen, gypsy, a lascar and an Indian or Chinese prince. He may have been suggested by a visit of Bramwell Bronte to Liverpool during the Irish Famine. He seems to be a kind of universal "other," capable of being interpreted in a whole variety of ways but always suggesting danger and violence.[92] Thackeray provided a kind of imperial panorama in *Vanity Fair* (1847) or at least "some of the wallpaper and colour." These are commodities, black servants (portrayed in inferior and stereotypical ways), white characters with imperial connections with the imperial armies, and mocking portrayals of humanitarians concerned with slaves and indigenous peoples which would later be echoed by Dickens in *Bleak House* (1852–53).[93] This was not an imperialist novel as places in England and Europe were in its foreground but in the late nineteenth century novels set in the empire became more frequent, from adventure stories like H. Rider Haggard's *King Solomon's Mines* (1886), and Rudyard Kipling's *The Light that Failed* (1890) and *Kim* (1901), to dissections of evil as in Joseph Conrad's *Heart of Darkness*, (1902).[94]

The changing nature of the empire increased the sense of "otherness." Even the settler colonies which became the United States had experienced a problem of identity with the core state. In the eighteenth century the American colonists were increasingly seen from the center as Americans and depicted as Red Indians, rather than as the British subjects, claiming English rights, as they saw themselves.[95] Henry Longfellow popularized the idea that Paul Revere warned on his famous ride in 1776 that "The British are coming." He actually said "The regulars are coming out." For him it was unthinkable that he was not British and a similar consciousness in the metropolis might have helped avert the conflict.[96]

[92] Parrinder, *Novel and Nation*, 202–08, 320; Kaplan, "Imagining Empire," 205–08; Elsie Michie, "From Simianized Irish to Oriental Despots: Heathcliffe, Rochester and Racial Difference," *Novel* 25, no. 2 (Winter 1992): 125–40.
[93] Parrinder, *Novel and Nation*, 322–26; Hall, "Culture and Identity," 208.
[94] Hall, "Culture and Identity," 206–07; Parrinder, *Novel and Nation*, 322–23.
[95] David Waldstreicher, "Rites of Rebellion, Rites of Assent: Celebrations, Print Culture, and the Origins of American Nationalism," *Journal of American History* 82, no. 1 (June 1995): 37–61.
[96] David Hackett Fischer, *Paul Revere's Ride* (Oxford: Oxford University Press, 1994), 109–10.

Once the American colonies had broken away the problem was exacerbated. By the late eighteenth century the majority of its subjects were black people and it took a considerable effort of imagination to envisage them as fellow citizens, while India, with its diverse climates, came to be defined increasingly as a "tropical" territory very different from temperate Britain and Europe. Macaulay referred to it as a "thick darkness" and it was frequently seen as being peopled with of effete Bengalis in contrast to the "manly" British. When Britain acquired increasing areas of Africa in the late nineteenth century the issue was further exacerbated.[97] Henry Morton Stanley proclaimed that he had come back from "In Darkest Africa" and the image was quickly adopted for the urban areas which Victorians found most repulsive. William Booth took his readers *Into Darkest England* while shortly afterwards the *South Wales Daily News* offered a series of exposés of "Darker Cardiff."[98] The empire was essentially an "Other" against which Englishness and Britishness could be defined, so it clearly formed a part of the way in which the core state was imagined. Part of it could be seen as integral—the settler colonies which had grown in the course of the nineteenth century were often seen as children and as part of the expansion of the Anglo-Saxon race. The imaginings of England and Britain were deeply rooted and drew upon European contrasts but clearly they were increasingly framed by imperial borders.[99]

The sense of difference was also influenced by political theory. This pivoted on the sense of the immense distances which separate the United Kingdom from its empire. Edmund Burke stressed the limitations placed by nature on the unity of the empire and this became the conventional wisdom of the age. It made representation in parliament impossible, he argued. Jeremy Bentham agreed with him on this, if on little else. Spain was said to face problems akin the governing of the moon. Burke respected local traditions and sovereignty, which he thought Warren Hastings had ridden roughshod over. Humanity was diverse and "strangers" at such a distance could not be understood.[100]

But nineteenth century views of the empire—mainly expressed in political theory—were complex, not least because of the complexity of the empire. Burke had to deal with an empire which was essentially just the colonies in the Atlantic and India. His

---

[97] David Killingray, "'A Good West Indian, a Good African, and, in Short, a Good Britisher': Black and British in a Colour-Conscious Empire, 1760–1950," *Journal of Imperial and Commonwealth History* 36, no. 3 (September 2008): 363–81; David Arnold, "India's Place in the Tropical World, 1770–1930," *Journal of Imperial and Commonwealth History* 26, no. 1 (January 1998): 1–21, 199–217; Hall, "Culture and Empire," 212–14; Michael Howard, "Empire, Race and War in Pre-1914 Britain," in *Empires, Nations and Wars*, ed. Michael Howard (Stroud: Spellmount Books, 2007), 64.

[98] Henry Morton Stanley, *In Darkest Africa* (C. Scribner's Sons, 1891); William Booth, *In Darkest England and the Way Out* (London: International Headquarters of the Salvation Army, 1891); *South Wales Daily News,* 1892–93.

[99] Thompson, "The State and the British Empire"; Charles Wentworth Dilke, *Greater Britain* (New York, 1869).

[100] A. S. Duncan, "Dissolving Distance: Technology, Space and Empire in British Political Thought, 1770–1900," *Historical Journal* 77, no. 3 (September 2005): 523–62, 526–27, and 532–40.

solution was to respect local sovereignties in each case. Adam Smith thought the only future for colonies was freedom or federation with the mother country. Distance and slow
travel was generally held to make the latter impossible, so for people of a similar persuasion, the end of empire was inevitable and desirable. This was not least because the habits of rule developed in India might be extended to home and threaten English liberties.
Charles James Fox was a frontrunner in a line of radicals who feared this outcome.[101]

The thinkers of the enlightenment form a brief interlude of anti-imperialism in a liberal tradition which has generally been much more comfortable with such
an idea.[102] In the early nineteenth century, normal service was resumed. James Mill's
History of British India was judgemental and broke with the positive Orientalist views
which had animated Burke and earlier critics of Empire. His son would justify despotism on the basis of differences in civilization which did not allow for Indian self-government soon.[103] The settler colonies developing in the early nineteenth century eased
Malthusian fears of over-population and could be interpreted as being akin to Greek
colonies founded on freedom and not presenting problems of tyranny to be confronted at home.[104] India was hard to shift out of the Roman mould but with a difference
in civilizations seen as being central, it was harder to envisage the Indian model being
applied in Britain. The danger was reduced by the separation of civilizations—and
races—practiced in India. The Romans were seen as having erred in allowing the melding of peoples and the ready granting of citizenship to conquered peoples. The British
in India did not make such overtures to the conquered.[105]

---

[101] Miles Taylor, "Imperium et Libertas? Rethinking the Radical Critique of Imperialism during the
Nineteenth Century," *Journal of Imperial and Commonwealth History* 19, no. 1 (January 1991):
1–23.

[102] Sankar Muthu, *Enlightenment against Empire* (Princeton: Princeton University Press,
2003); Bhiku Parekh "Liberalism and Colonialism: A Critique of Locke and Mill," in *The
Decolonization of the Imagination*, ed. Jan Nederveen Pieterse and Bhiku Parekh (London:
Zed Books, 1995), 81–99; and Bhiku Parekh, "Decolonizing Liberalism," in *The End of Isms?
Reflections on the Fate of Ideological Politics after Communism's Collapse*, ed. Alexander Stromas
(Oxford: Blackwell, 1994), 85–103.

[103] Kanura Mantena, "The Crisis of Liberal Imperialism," in *Victorian Visions of Global Order:
Empire and International Relations in Nineteenth Century Political Thought*, ed. Duncan Bell
(Cambridge: Cambridge University Press, 2007), 113–35; Eileen P. Sullivan, "Liberalism and
Imperialism: J. S. Mill's Defense of the British Empire," *Journal of the History of Ideas* 44, no. 4
(October–December 1983), 599–617.

[104] Sullivan, "Liberalism and Imperialism"; Duncan Bell, "Ancient and Modern in Victorian
Imperial Thought," *Historical Journal* 49, no. 3 (September 2006): 735–59; Taylor, "Imperium
et Libertas?"

[105] Raymond F. Betts, "The Allusion to Rome in British Imperialist Thought of the Late Nineteenth
and Early Twentieth Centuries," *Victorian Studies* 15, no. 2 (December 1971): 149–59; Javeed
Majeed, "Comparativism and References to Rome in British Imperial Attitudes to India," in *Roman
Presences: Receptions of Rome in European Culture, 1789–1945*, ed. Catherine Edwards (Cambridge:
Cambridge University Press, 1999), 88–109; Phiroze Vansunia, "Greater Rome and Greater Britain,"
in *Classics and Colonialism*, ed. Barbara Goff (London: Duckworth, 2005), 38–64.

THE BRITISH EMPIRE

This map shows all the territories ever to be part of the British Empire, including post WW1 Mandates. This has the disadvantage of exaggerating its
size at any one time but it serves to stress its overall size and dynamism.
The 13 colonies in North America became independent in 1783 but after
that the process of growth in the long nineteenth century was constant.
Mandates under the League of Nations were awarded after WW1 for the administration of former Central Powers colonies. The map also stresses the
diversity of the empire by distinguishing Dominions from other forms of
colonial relationships.

■ United Kingdom of
Great Britain & Ireland

▨ Dominions

▨ British India, Princely States

▨ Protectorates

■ Mandates, Trust Territories

☐ Other dependencies

Empire formed the way in which the British polity was envisaged. It provided "others" and a framework of common enterprise in which the distinct but overlapping conceptions of the four nations of the British Isles could coexist. It also offered the British state an exalted place in world history, as not simply ranked with Rome but superior to it because of its allegedly safer handling of the issues of racial difference. There was some suspicion of empire as a threat to political liberty and an obstacle to free trade and universal peace but in practice it was difficult to envisage Britain without its empire.

Britain and its Empire, 1860–1914

After 1860 Britain's position in the world changed fundamentally. Louis Bonaparte was already presenting a more aggressive French face in Europe in the 1850s and in the next decade the map of Europe was redrawn. Unified states emerged in west central Europe where once there had been small kingdoms, principalities, duchies, and city states of little account in international relations. The Union victory in the American Civil War made it even more aggressively expansionist in the west. In 1803 Thomas Jefferson had made the Louisiana Purchase from Napoleon, predicting that he had acquired enough land for a thousand years of expansion. In 1890, famously, the Bureau of the Census proclaimed the frontier to be closed: in less than a century it had overrun even more land than the second president had bought. The US became a more conventional imperial power when its interventions in Cuba and the Philippines in 1898 gave the *coup de grace* to the Spanish Empire. Britain had little choice but to accept that the programmatic Monroe Doctrine of 1823, proclaiming the western hemisphere as the zone of influence of the US, was now a geopolitical reality. Russia's expansion in Central Asia and Siberia was similarly relentless and for most of the period Britain's politicians saw it, along with France, as its main rival.

Industrial transformation made the United States and Germany into serious rivals, while Italy, France, and even Russia gained in economic power. Britain was still, of course, the fulcrum if the world economy and "Pax Britannica" was the handy term for the international system. But appeasement began to be a central part of British foreign policy in the period as there were now too many challenges to confront.[106] By the end of the century many politicians articulated a sense of imperial overstretch, none more poignantly than Joseph Chamberlain who referred to the condition of the state he hoped to transform through tying it more closely to its empire, as a "weary titan."[107] Germany's naval program and turn to *Weltpolitik* in the 1890s—as well as its potent economic competition—finally fixed it as the major rival by 1900. Britain's view of the

---

[106] Paul Kennedy, "The Tradition of Appeasement in British Foreign Policy, 1865–1939," in *Strategy and Diplomacy*, 13–39.

[107] Cited in Peter T. Marsh, *Joseph Chamberlain: The Entrepreneur in Politics* (New Haven: Yale University Press, 1994), 532.

world in the mid nineteenth century had been transformed in ways which made the previous vista hard to recognize.

The problems were also revealed in the fears which inspired bestselling writers of (highly) imaginative fiction. The Channel could be circumvented by a surprise attack whether by the French through a secretly built channel tunnel, erupting in the Battle of Dorking or (when the enemy changed) by Germans launching a surprise attack on East Anglia with barges hidden on the Friesian Islands.[108] The Empire could be defended if the eruptions were localized but a generalized revolt of a Pan-African scale or an outbreak of Islamic fundamentalism gave nightmares to novelists and their readers.[109]

Creating an Imperial Economy, 1850–1914

The British economy became increasingly well integrated into its empire in the second half of the nineteenth century. It was rooted in the diaspora of British people in the sixty years before the First World War. Fifty million Europeans moved to the New World in the period—and a quarter of them were British. This represented over thirteen million free laborers. The bulk of them went to the United States, especially those from Ireland. But about half the total flow went to the dominions and after 1900 there was an especially rapid switch of destination as unskilled labor flowed into the US from eastern and southern Europe and the domestic market supplied its skilled labor. Australia and New Zealand had suffered from the "tyranny of distance" and Australia from its image as a penal settlement, though this was mostly dispelled by the gold discoveries of the 1850s.[110] These migrants created dense networks of connections back to the home country, aided by surprising levels of return migration and postal and telegraph networks. Networks of this kind created trust and came to influence the directions of markets, trade, and investment. The "psychic distance" was far less than the physical distance. The place of origin of these migrants conditioned their tastes and helped provide markets for British products. Scotch whisky and milk chocolate were distinctive products for which recent migrants hankered; Cadbury's targeted such migrants who provided its only non-UK market. Between 1873 and 1913, the empire's take of British exports rose from 26.8% to 35%. Most of this increase was accounted for by the dominions and India. In this period most of the growth of exports to the dominions was accounted for by their growth in GDP. The migrants simply had increasing amounts of money to spend. But cultural links ensured that a large proportion of

---

[108] I. F. Clarke, *Voices Prophesying War, 1763–1984* (Oxford: Oxford University Press, 1966); Erskine Childers, *The Riddle of the Sands* [1903] (London: Vintage, 2013).

[109] John Buchan, *Prester John* (New York: George H. Doran Co., 1910) and *Greenmantle* (New York: George H. Doran Co., 1916).

[110] Geoffrey Blainey, *The Tyranny of Distance: How Distance Shaped Australia's History* (Melbourne: Sun Books, 1983).

their spending ended up in British pockets. At the same time the share of British exports to the developed world fell from 47.25 to 35.9%.

The export of capital became a central part of the British economy with a massive £4.1B invested abroad between 1865 and 1914. This represented almost 4% of earnings and rose to over 5% in some of the Edwardian years. The trend was away from Europe and towards the US, the dominions, and Argentina. Especially important were investments in the infrastructure required in settlement colonies—ports, telegraphs, railways, etc. London supplied 70% of funds for settlement colonies for such investments in infrastructure in the period. Such areas were seen as relatively safe by investors—almost as well known as home. The fact that the UK provided defense, law and order, justice, and institutions (including the monetary system) aided the flow of funds along the paths cut out by settlers who kept close contact with the home country.

Particular regions and industries could be very closely integrated into the empire. It has recently been demonstrated that the development of Glasgow and Bombay was closely entwined. This "interconnected synchronicity" was driven by commodity movements between the two ports. Industry was a vital part of this, for shipping required engineering and shipbuilding—it cannot be seen simply as a service industry. The complex of economic interests in Glasgow, involving banks, shipping, and industry, were linked with Scottish merchants and bankers in Bombay through kinship and cultural ties. Their close links with the colonial government smoothed the way for acquiring land for port development in Bombay. The deepening of the Clyde to make it more navigable had ramifications for its trading partners in Bombay, which could draw on the expertise acquired in Scotland. A large wet dock was something needed for imperial trade, rather than for local needs and the interests of those who used the shores for such trades were trampled by the power of the global trading and manufacturing interests centered in Glasgow and with a substation in Bombay.[111] More than that, substantial amounts of money flowed back in the form of remittances—a net gain of £120–200 million in the period 1873–1914. Cornwall, suffering from the decline of its metal mining industries, became much dependent on the flow of money from Cousin Jacks abroad.[112]

Empire and free trade were generally held to be important to Britain's economic health in the period. There was some questioning of free trade as tariffs began to rise in Europe from the 1870s. Some in the Conservative Party campaigned for "fair trade" but their efforts to end free trade had no political outcome. The conflicts

---

[111] Sandip Hazareesingh, "Interconnected Synchronicities: The Production of Bombay and Glasgow as Modern Global Ports, c. 1850–80," *Journal of Global History* 4 (2009): 7–31.

[112] For the previous four paragraphs I have drawn freely on Gary B. Magee and Andrew S. Thompson, *Empire and Globalization: Networks of People, Goods and Capital in the British World, c. 1850–1914* (Cambridge: Cambridge University Press, 2010) and Gary B. Magee, "The Importance of Being British? Imperial Factors and the Growth of British Imports, 1870–1960," *Journal of Interdisciplinary History* 37, no. 3 (Winter 2007): 341–69.

over tariffs were to raise important issues about empire and they also connect with recent debates on the nature of the British economy and society in the period. It was once the conventional wisdom that the nineteenth-century economy was dominated by industry and the manufacturers of the midlands and north. But more recent work has suggested an uninterrupted dominance of the city and "gentlemanly capitalism," the service sector, and the south in general.[113] Some of this analysis is based on now much disputed probate evidence which shows a preponderance of landed and finance fortunes amongst the very wealthy. But this is likely to be a bias built into the sources which do not ensnare industrial wealth passed on in the lifetime to heirs, as was often the case. It is generally unwise, anyway, to seek an overweening dominance for any one sector in the nineteenth-century British economy. Undoubtedly finance was vital throughout but industrial production was also a central pillar of the economy. The leading economic historian of the period offers the sage opinion that no one interest dominated the British economy in the period. Free trade, it had been suggested, was favored by the City while manufacturers favored tariffs. Certainly some industries questioned free trade and looked for retaliation and reciprocity in trade agreements. But free trade was always more than a simple matter of economic interest. Attachment to it was influenced by religion and cultural factors. Nor was it as simple as export industries favoring free trade and domestic manufacturers wanting protection, for the same reasons. In addition, individuals might have multiple interests and find it difficult to make a rational economic choice between them; but there was always more involved than rational choice, anyway.[114] Internal reform of firms might be seen as a counter to tariff reform—another way of meeting competition, rather than stressing the unfairness of the conditions of trade, while alternately some industrialists could be attracted to tariff reform as an alternative to the high income tax that the Liberals offered in its place.[115]

But whatever the balance of interests in the British economy overall in the nineteenth century, there is little doubt that there was a shift back to London and away from the provinces in the late nineteenth century.[116] The city even began to look like the imperial capital it was. A foundation for this had been laid by Nash and the

---

[113] For the basic argument and evidence, expanded in many subsequent publications, see: W. D. Rubinstein "Wealth, Elites and the Class Structure of Modern Britain," *Past and Present* 76 (August 1977): 99–126; Cain and Hopkins, *British Imperialism*; C. H. Lee, "Regional Growth and Structural Change in Victorian Britain," *Economic History Review* 34, no. 3 (August 1981): 438–52.

[114] Frank Trentmann, *Free Trade Nation: Commerce, Consumption and Civil Society in Modern Britain* (Oxford: Oxford University Press, 2008).

[115] M. J. Daunton, "'Gentlemanly Capitalism' and British Industry 1820–1914," *Past and Present* 122 (February 1989): 119–58; Martin Daunton, *Wealth and Welfare: An Economic and Social History of Britain, 1851–1951* (Oxford: Oxford University Press, 2007), ch. 6.

[116] Brian Robson, "Coming Full Circle: London against the Rest, 1890–1960," in *Regional Cities in the U.K., 1890–1980*, ed. George Gordon (London: Harper and Row, 1986), 217–32.

Prince Regent, as we have seen, but it was really in the late nineteenth century that the city began to look like the hub of a world empire.[117]

Imperial Expansion

The empire was not tightly controlled from the center; it was too vast and diverse for this to be the case and communications were too slow. Imperial power was in a sense devolved but ultimately it forced a response from the center. The extent of the imperial state was in large part shaped by the periphery. Perhaps the central dynamic was the way in which the diversity of the empire was matched by a diversity of interests at home. There were diverse interests in the British economy and all of these might have their reasons for promoting particular expansions in particular places and added to this were humanitarian groups. Pressure groups called many of the tunes: "The rough conditions of a decentralized imperial state were hardly favorable to the authority, or even the coherence, of an official mind."[118] At the imperial bridgeheads were a variety of forces, variously commercial, proconsular, missionary, or settler, or even all four. Exploiting the local environment required the assistance of the power of the metropolis. But if the local forces could develop a source of revenue and a military force, they had the possibility of expanding without reference to the metropolis. In the mid-Victorian period a variety of currents of public opinion supported imperial expansion and could be aggressive in their demands. Evangelicals, Utilitarians, free traders and opponents of slavery could between them mobilize powerful lobbies. But their impact was limited by constraints abroad. Britain was a superior power but did not have total dominance, especially in the Near East and in the Americas. China was contested by other powers. But where a suitable bridgehead could be established the possibilities of conquest were considerable. British people might have endorsed ideas associated with the "imperialism of free trade," much as Americans do today, but they operated in a very different world. In 1816 only 24% of the world was occupied by sovereign territories, 11% by colonies, with the remainder "unrecognized." In 1946, as the US became a global hegemon, the respective figures were 71%, 20%, and 9%.[119]

---

[117] M. H. Port, *Imperial London, Civil Government Building in London, 1851–1915* (New Haven: Yale University Press, 1995); M. H. Port, "Government and the Metropolitan Image: Ministers, Parliament and the Concept of a Capital; City, 1840–1915," in *The Metropolis and its Image: Constructing Identities for London, c. 1750–1950*, ed. Dana Arnold (Oxford: Blackwell, 1999), 101–26; Alex G. Brenner, "Nation and Empire in the Government Architecture of Mid-Victorian London: the Foreign Office and India Office Reconsidered," *Historical Journal* 48, no. 3 (September 2005): 703–42; Jonathan Schneer, *London, 1900: The Imperial Metropolis* (New Haven: Yale University Press, 1999).

[118] John Darwin, "Imperialism and the Victorians: the Dynamics of Territorial Expansion," 614–42, quotation 624.

[119] Julina Go, "Global Fields and Imperial Forms: Field Theory and the British and American Empires," *Sociological Theory* 26, no. 3 (September 2008): 201–29, at 212.

The key strategic locations in this world complex had their proconsular regimes. India had one with its own dynamic. Ireland, nearest to home, could have been
used by a hostile power to control the English Channel. Napoleon and the Kaiser
both attempted to do this, in alliance with disaffected Irish people at the chronological limits of our period. Canada and South Africa occupied the transatlantic diago-
nal, though the latter was mainly concerned with the protection of the Indian Ocean
and the route to the subcontinent. Gibraltar and Egypt occupied opposite ends of the
Mediterranean and again held the route to India open, especially after the opening of
the Suez Canal in 1869. Finally the Straits of Malacca and Singapore controlled access
to the Far East, including Australia and New Zealand. Each of these areas had a proconsul (titles varied) with a large measure of independent control, including direction
of substantial military forces. They mediated between local interests of British merchants, traders, and missionaries, and the government in Whitehall. In practice they
exercised great power because they were the men "on the spot," an especially advantageous position if communications were less than perfect. They had initiative which
they often used. Central government was often presented with a *fait accompli*.[120]

Such men were key points on the vast "turbulent frontier" of the empire.[121]
Some of these spots were also areas of large-scale white settlement. These had especially dynamic frontiers as Britons abroad sought their place in the sun. Canada and
South Africa were complicated by the presence of substantial non-British white settlers of French and Dutch origin respectively. French Canadians headed south for the
US rather than to the frontier but the Boers trekked into the interior to evade British
control. British proconsuls tried to tether them especially after gold and diamonds
were discovered, adding to the value of the arid interior. In each case (apart from New
Zealand) the sprawling settlement pattern and multiple colonization was drawn into
the net of a federal constitution in efforts to increase the coherence of the scatter, making each more unified and integrated with the metropolitan core. Each had stirrings
(and more) of a distinct nationality but it was generally expressed within an imperial
framework. James Belich detects a late nineteenth-century process of "re-colonization"
in New Zealand and finds the idea applicable elsewhere.[122]

In the late nineteenth century influence from the center became tighter because
of improved communications but it could never exert total control.[123] This feature of
Britain's expansion was not paralleled in other European countries. France had an over-

---

[120] John Benyon, "Overlords of Empire? British 'Proconsular Imperialism' in Comparative Perspective," *Journal of Imperial and Commonwealth History* 19, no. 2 (May 1991): 164–202.

[121] John S. Galbraith, "The 'Turbulent Frontier' as a Factor in British Imperial Expansion,"
Comparative Studies in Society and History 2, no. 2 (January 1960): 150–68.

[122] James Belich, *Making Peoples; A History of the New Zealanders from the Polynesian Settlement to
the End of the Nineteenth Century* (London: Allen Lane, 1996); James Belich, *Paradise Reforged:
A History of New Zealanders from the 1880s to the Year 2000* (Honolulu: University of Hawaii
Press, 2002).

[123] David Powell, *Nationhood and Identity: The British State since 1800* (London: I.B. Tauris, 2002), 98.

seas empire but none of the population growth to fuel such a creation. Germany had the population growth but not the naval power at the right time to open up the lands for settlement. The Dutch Empire lost its main potential area of settlement to Britain in the Napoleonic Wars. The industrial and demographic regime therefore shaped the British Empire in a unique way and with consequences to which we will return.

Mixing the British Peoples

Population Growth in the United Kingdom, 1801–1911

	Population (000s)					% of UK Total			
	Eng	Wales	Scot	Ire	UK	Eng	Wales	Scot	Ire
1801	8.32	0.58	1.6	5.2	15.7	53	3.7	10.2	33.1
1811	9.53	0.67	1.8	6.0	18.0	53	3.7	10.0	33.3
1821	11.21	0.79	2.1	6.8	21.9	51	3.6	9.6	31.0
1831	13.00	0.90	2.4	7.8	24.1	54	3.7	10.0	32.3
1841	14.86	1.04	2.6	8.2	26.7	56	3.9	9.7	30.7
1851	16.74	1.16	2.9	6.5	27.3	61	4.2	10.6	23.8
1861	18.82	1.28	3.1	5.8	29.0	65	4.1	10.7	20.0
1871	21.29	1.41	3.4	5.4	31.3	68	4.5	10.9	17.3
1881	24.43	1.57	3.7	5.2	34.9	70	4.5	10.6	14.9
1891	27.23	1.77	4.0	4.7	37.7	72	4.7	10.6	12.5
1901	30.49	2.01	4.5	4.5	41.5	74	4.8	10.8	10.8
1911	33.68	2.42	4.8	4.4	45.3	74	5.3	10.6	9.7

Source: *Calculated from data in Chris Cook and John Stevenson, The Longman Handbook of Modern British History, 1714–1980 (London: Routledge, 1983), 97; and Digest of Welsh Historical Statistics, Vol. 1, ed. John Williams (Cardiff: Welsh Office, 1985), 7.*

To what extent did the transformation of British society in this imperial context produce a melded British society? Industrialization and migration produced major shifts in the balance of population between the nations of Britain. England always had half the population, at least, but came to hold three quarters of it. The major loser was Ireland after the catastrophe of the famine and its related out-migration. Its share of the UK population fell from a 33% high to under 10%. Scotland's share remained fairly static at 10% but it came to eclipse Ireland by the end of the period. Wales steadily increased its share as the result of the massive industrialization of the south. Its share of the UK population rose by some 70% in the course of the nineteenth century, but it remained only half that of Scotland and Ireland. Twenty years ago it was fashionable to call the UK a multi-national state. Certainly, it was, in many ways but it is not sufficient to leave the analysis there. The imbalance between England and the rest is a notable feature. It was numerically much more dominated by its core population than was the Habsburg Empire, for instance.[124]

But, of course such crude population figures have limited usefulness. Place of residence is not the same as ethnicity. Many of the migrating Irish moved to England, Scotland, and Wales. English migrants moved into south Wales in large numbers while Scots spread themselves more widely, but with some concentrations in the north of England. Indeed it has been argued that the northeast of England might be seen as a region of Britain rather than of England such was the composition of its population at the turn of the twentieth century, with so many migrants from Scotland and Ireland.[125] So the population of England is far from being the same as the ethnic English population—and this distinction is even more apposite in the case of Ireland where religious identity was more significant than birth.[126] In reality we are dealing with multiple regional and religiously based cultures rather than four nations. Urbanization and the flight from the land had the effect of mixing the populations of the UK more than ever before. But it did not blend them. Hibernian societies were to be found everywhere in the UK and in big cities there would be Caledonian Societies and Cymmrodorion Societies, as well as county-based fraternal organizations. All of this was also true of the Empire where such groupings were also found.

The political impact of this varied enormously. The Irish were rarely a force for integration, given the reaction of much of the population of Britain to their arrival. Merseyside, particularly Liverpool, organized its politics around an ethnic and religious divide and the proletarian city did not have a Labour majority on its council until 1955. Many English and Scottish-born workers allied with the Protestant/Conservative cause rather than create a class alliance with the Irish incomers.[127] Clydeside was similar, though it channeled much of the violence through sport and the "old firm" clashes of Celtic and Rangers with their symbolic (though often real) violence. But the home rule

---

[124] Neal Ascherson, *Games with Shadows* (London: Radius Books, 1988); Evans, *National Identity*.

[125] David Byrne, "Immigrants and the Formation of the North Eastern Industrial Working Class," *North East Labour History* 30 (1996): 29–36.

[126] F. S. L. Lyons, *Culture and Anarchy in Ireland, 1890–1939* (Oxford: Oxford University Press, 1979).

[127] Tony Lane, *Liverpool: Gateway of Empire* (London: Laurence and Wishart, 1987); Frank Neal, *Sectarian Violence: The Liverpool Experience, 1819–1914, An Aspect of Anglo-Irish History* (Manchester: Manchester University Press, 1988); P. J. Waller, *Democracy and Sectarianism: A Political and Social History of Liverpool, 1868–1939* (Liverpool: Liverpool University Press, 1981); John Belchem, *Merseypride: Essays in Liverpool Exceptionalism* (Liverpool: Liverpool University Press, 2000); John Belchem, *Irish, Catholic and Scouse: The History of the Liverpool-Irish 1800–1939* (Liverpool: Liverpool University Press, 2007) John Belchem, ed., *Popular Politics, Riot and Labour: Essays in Liverpool History 1790–1940* (Liverpool: Liverpool University Press, 2000).

split in the Liberal Party created a bastion of Liberal Unionism in Western Scotland based on the rejection of home rule in much of the native population. Wales was different again with initial hostility to the Irish giving way to a political and trade union alliance from the 1880s. Public demonstrations of religious belief often produced violence in Lancashire and southwest Scotland. In Wales, by contrast, the Corpus Christi parades inaugurated in Cardiff in 1872 (with the patronage of the Third Marquess of Bute, a Catholic convert) were held for over a century with no serious conflict at all.[128] But in general, by 1914 the bitter conflicts between the Irish and British had subsided. People of Irish descent generally settled into an alliance with a Liberal Party offering home rule for Ireland, though in Liverpool, the inappropriately named Scotland Division returned an Irish Nationalist M.P. from 1885 to 1922.

The South Wales Coalfield also had large numbers of English incomers, largely from the border counties, and mainly towards the end of the period. They tended to settle in distinct areas of the crowded valley communities. Anecdotal evidence suggests that the Welsh predominated in the better paid coalface jobs while the English clustered in underground haulage, but there has been no systematic study of this. It is much clearer that the Irish were removed from the Rhondda valleys by violence in the 1850s and that few of them found jobs as miners. They remained clustered in the ports—Cardiff, Newport, and Swansea—and the older iron-working centers at the heads of the Valleys, and Merthyr Tydfil in particular. Before 1880 English migrants had predominantly headed for the ports rather than the coalfield and something of a split labor market can be detected by close analysis of the structure of opportunities in Cardiff.[129] Yet a certain amount of sorting by ethnicity did not lead to entrenched hostility: after a brief flurry of separate ethnically-based unions for English and Welsh in the 1870s, and the occasional hint of ethnic tensions into the 1890s, they came to see themselves as an English-speaking but Welsh identifying working class, very much integrated into the British labor movement.[130]

The movements of population within the British Isles were, of course, lopsided. The Irish moved in vast numbers and even more of them went abroad, to the

---

[128] Paul O' Leary, "Processions, Power and Public Space: Corpus Christi at Cardiff, 1872–1914," *Welsh History Review* 24, no. 1 (June 2008): 77–101.

[129] Neil Evans, "Immigrants and Minorities in Wales, 1840–1990: A Comparative Perspective," *Llafur* 5, no. 4 (1991): 5–26; Philip N. Jones, "Some Aspects of Immigration into the Glamorgan Coalfiled, 1881–1911," *Transactions of the Honourable Society of Cymmrodorion*, 1969; Philip N. Jones, "The Welsh Language in the Valleys of Glamorgan, c. 1800–1914," in *A Social History of the Welsh Language, Vol. 3 Language and Community in the Nineteenth Century*, ed. Geraint H. Jenkins (Cardiff: University of Wales Press, 1998), 147–80; Philip Davies, "Migration and Women's Work in Late Victorian Cardiff" (unpublished University of Glamorgan M.A. thesis, 2008).

[130] Paul O'Leary, *Immigration and Integration: The Irish in Wales, 1798–1922* (Cardiff: University of Wales Press, 2000); Neil Evans, "Comparing Immigrant Histories: The Irish and Others in Modern Wales," in *Irish Migrants in Modern Wales,* ed. Paul O'Leary (Liverpool: Liverpool University Press, 2004), 156–77.

United States in particular and less frequently to the British settler colonies. Their lesser inclination to move to imperial locations might be seen as a political comment.[131] Some moved within Ireland to change the ethnic composition of Belfast from a mainly Protestant small city to a very mixed Protestant and Catholic large one. It became the most divided and bitterly fought over city in the UK. "We have no Ulster in Wales" observed a smug Welsh commentator in 1894 analyzing the linguistic divide in Wales but measuring it against what he saw as the archetype of ethnic division.[132] Highland Scots were vigorous migrants, too, with many going to the US and the dominions but others fetching up in Glasgow and the industrialized central belt of Scotland. The Welsh were less serious long-range movers and many were kept within the bounds of Wales by the forces of industrialization. But it is no longer tenable to view them as not migrating out of Wales in large numbers after 1851. In reality, something like three crossed the border for each one who shifted within it.[133] So the Welsh colonized not only south Wales but also Merseyside, London, and Teesside, as well as the United States and the dominions.[134] They seem to have been only a small presence in the empire and as John Mackenzie perceptively points out, the attention given to a small settlement in Chubut suggests there may have been no bigger battalions to investigate.[135]

Nations within the Empire

If there was a considerable degree of ethnic mixing in Britain there was also, in many ways, a clarification and redrawing of national boundaries. We should not see the formation of Britain as being one of melding into uniformity but of the creation of distinct identities within the framework offered by the United Kingdom and the British Empire.

---

[131] Magee and Thompson, *Globalization and Empire.*

[132] Sybil Baker, "Orange and Green: Belfast, 1832–1912," in *The Victorian City,* ed. Dyos and Wolff, Vol. 2, 789–814; T. Darlington, "The English-Speaking Population of Wales," *Wales* 1, no. 1 (May 1894): 16.

[133] Brinley Thomas, "Wales and the Atlantic Economy," in *The Welsh Economy: Studies in Expansion,* ed. B. Thomas (Cardiff: University of Wales Press, 1962). Thomas argues for massive internal migration within Wales and relatively small emigration, which is seriously challenged by Dudley Baines, *Migration in a Mature Economy: Emigration and Internal Migration in England and Wales, 1861–1900* (Cambridge: Cambridge University Press, 1985), ch. 10.

[134] Colin G. Pooley, "Welsh Migration to England in the Nineteenth Century," *Journal of Historical Geography* 9, no. 3 (1983): 287–306; R. Merfyn Jones and D. Ben Rees, *The Liverpool Welsh and their Religion* (Liverpool: New Welsh Publications, 1984); Richard Lewis and David Ward, "Culture, Politics and Assimilation: The Welsh on Teesside, c. 1850–1940," *Welsh History Review* 17, no. 4 (Dec. 1995): 550–70; W. D. Jones, *Wales in America: Scranton and the Welsh, 1860-1920* (Cardiff: University of Wales Press, 1993); Bill Jones, "Welsh Identities in Ballarat, Australia, during the late nineteenth century," *Welsh History Review* 20, no. 2 (Dec. 2000): 283–307.

[135] John M. Mackenzie, "Empire and National Identities: The Case of Scotland," *Transactions of the Royal Historical Society* 8 (1998): 215–31, at 219–20.

Perhaps the clearest case is that of Scotland. The Union of 1707 had a fairly direct and quick impact on the economy, making Glasgow the center of the tobacco trade in Britain. The Union was interpreted as marking the beginnings of the empire as a joint venture between England and Scotland and as being at the root of the intellectual glories of the Scottish enlightenment.[136] Younger sons of the gentry flocked to jobs in the Empire under the patronage of political fixers who sought to control its politics. Once Jacobitism was defeated, the Highlands became one of the richest recruiting grounds for the army and Scots could be found in disproportionate numbers in imperial outposts, usually sporting the kilt, after it had been shorn of its subversive, Stuart, associations. Glasgow proclaimed itself to be the "second city of the empire" and one English historian has wondered whether there was more enthusiasm for empire in Scotland than there was in England.[137] Scots were the most likely of all the peoples of the islands to embrace Britishness and even the particular name North British, a term which was emblazoned on an Edinburgh Hotel until within living memory.

So a Scottish nation could be built very comfortably within the framework of the Empire and even be enhanced by it. Scotland had always had a distinct civil society from England and the separation of its law, education, and religion continued into the nineteenth century and was enhanced by distinctive legislation. In 1853 it secured Sunday Closing and in 1885 it gained substantial administrative devolution with the creation of the Scottish Office, run by a secretary of state. Scots could both celebrate their role in the empire and enjoy what has been variously described as "unionist nationalism" and effective autonomy from the center. Many Scottish intellectuals plied their trades in London and became influential figures. The British Empire worked for most Scots.[138]

We know far less about Welsh attitudes towards the empire but this in itself suggests a less enthusiastic embrace of it. That is not to say that there was hostility towards it, nor a rejection of the Union, simply that it was far less central to Welsh consciousness.[139] The "Union"[140] was celebrated as bringing peace, order and parlia-

---

[136] John M. Mackenzie, "On Scotland and the Empire," *International History Review* 15, no. 1 (November 1991): 714–39; Mackenzie, "Empire and National Identities."

[137] John M. Mackenzie, "'The Second City of the Empire': Glasgow—Imperial Municipality," in *Imperial Cities: Landscape, Display and Identity*, eds. Felix Driver and David Gilbert (Manchester: Manchester University Press, 1999), 215–37; Bernard Porter, *Absent-Minded Imperialists* (Oxford: Oxford University Press, 2003).

[138] Lindsay Patterson, *The Autonomy of Modern Scotland* (Edinburgh: Edinburgh University Press, 1994); Graeme Morton, *Unionist Nationalism: Governing Urban Scotland, 1830–60* (East Linton: Tuckwell Press, 1999); Christopher Harvie, *Scotland and Nationalism* (London: Allen and Unwin, 1977).

[139] Neil Evans, "Writing Wales into the Empire: Rhetoric, Fragments and—Beyond?" in *Wales and the British Overseas Empire: Interactions and Influences, 1650–1830*, ed. H. V. Bowen (Manchester: Manchester University Press, 2012): 15–39.

[140] Technically the Acts of 1536 and 1543 incorporated Wales into the English realm and were only referred to retrospectively as the Acts of Union by comparison with the Scottish and Irish unions.

mentary representation to Wales but not really as the foundation of modern Wales. It was often seen as almost ending the separate existence of Wales, at least in a legal and administrative sense; "oddiar hyny [Acts of Union] hyd yn awr, mae cynnrychiolaeth Cymru yn rhan o gynnrychiolaeth Lloegr, megys ag y mae Cymru ei hun wedi ymsuddo i fod yn rhan o Loegr" [from then until now, Welsh [political] representation has been part of English representation, so that Wales itself has merged into a part of England].[141] Welsh historians confirmed these views and often added that the real business of creating modern Wales had been done *after* the Union and by the people themselves. This involved the growth of nonconformity—the root of Welsh identity by the mid-nineteenth century—the Welsh language press, and its educational system.[142] After 1868, Wales became a bastion of the Liberal Party, which won the vast majority of its parliamentary seats for the rest of our period. Welsh Liberalism had a few distinctive features, notably the promotion of a series of specific measures for Wales. In 1881 a Sunday Closing Act was passed; in 1889, intermediate schools supported by the rates were instituted over a decade before England had an equivalent system; and the three university colleges established between 1872 and 1884 were crowned by a degree awarding University of Wales in 1893. Disestablishment, a long-running demand of Welsh nonconformity, was placed on the statute book in 1914, and implemented in 1920 after having been suspended for the duration of the war. Campaigns for land reform and home rule were less intensive and unsuccessful but overall Welsh Liberals could feel that the British state was responsive to their needs, especially to the argument that a nation with a Nonconformist majority had to be treated differently from England. At the same time English institutions could be preserved by a kind of devolution of power. Minor administrative devolution created the Welsh Board of Education and a Welsh Board of Health.[143]

Empire was generally endorsed in Wales, though sometimes with the reservation that it was the preserve of the Anglican and Tory gentry, a group increasingly defined as being outside the nation. The nation was seen as dwelling in the cottage and not in the mansion. George Cornewall Lewis was a notable Wakefieldite advocate of empire, commemorated in a massive monument in New Radnor (almost big enough to be a space probe!) but his family's cross-border estates seem to have produced no

---

[141] J. Jones, *Llawlyfr Etholiadaeth Cymru* [Handbook of Welsh Elections] (Llangollen, 1867), 16. My thanks to Paul O'Leary for this reference.

[142] These remarks are based on the following: John Rhŷs and David Brynmor Jones, *The Welsh People: Chapters on their Origin, History, Laws, Language, Literature and Characteristics* (London: T. Fisher Unwin, 1900); Owen M. Edwards, *Wales* (1901); Owen M. Edwards, *A Short History of Wales* (London, 1906); Howell T. Evans, *The Making of Modern Wales* (Cardiff: Educational Publishing Company, 1917); Gilbert Stone, *Wales: Her Origins, Struggles and Later History, Institutions and Manners* (London: Ulan Press, 1911); Llewelyn W. Williams, *The Making of Modern Wales* (London: Macmillan, 1919).

[143] Kenneth O. Morgan, *Wales in British Politics, 1868–1922* (Cardiff: University of Wales Press, 1963); Kenneth O. Morgan, *Rebirth of a Nation: Wales, 1880–1980* (Oxford: Oxford University Press, 1981).

awareness of the distinctiveness of Wales and it is notably absent from his writings on colonialism.[144] What limited evidence there is suggests that Wales did not produce large numbers of imperial administrators. Was this because its MPs needed no management under "Old Corruption"? But this is an area in which research is lacking and we have only more-or-less informed speculation to go on.[145]

If Scotland was over-represented in the ranks of the British army, Wales was notably under-represented and remained so until the First World War.[146] The Welsh electorate was not, as was once thought, notably pro-Boer in the khaki election of 1900 but the country did harbor eleven pro-Boer MPs out of a total of 32.[147] This did not mean root and branch hostility to the empire, however. Lloyd George was the most famous of these dissidents but he was a consistent supporter of the empire, and only a missed train had prevented him from lining up with Joseph Chamberlain in 1886. As prime minister in the First World War, he was hospitable to the arch imperialists of Lord Milner's "kindergarten."[148] But it was mainly the Conservative Party who raised issues of empire in Welsh politics and they were always content to refer to England as their place of origin. Such attitudes gave them some 25% of the popular vote but rarely more than four MPs, and none at all in the Liberal landslide of 1906.[149] Empire did appear in statements and celebrations of Welsh identity but it was not one of the first things to be thought of and often it seemed like an afterthought.[150]

England's identity was always muddied by the British problem. That is, that people who spoke about England rarely bothered to distinguish it from Britain, and often did not understand the distinction and simply employed the words as synonyms. James Bryce pointed out that: "An Englishman has but one patriotism, because England and the United Kingdom are to him practically the same thing. A Scotchman

---

[144] George Cornewall Lewis, *An Essay on the Government of Dependencies* (Oxford: Clarendon Press, 1841); R. W. D. Fenn and Sir Andrew Duff Gordon, *The Life and Times of Sir George Cornewall Lewis, Bart* (Herefordshire: Logaston Press, 2005).

[145] These issues will be addressed in H. V. Bowen and Paul O'Leary, eds., *Wales and the British Empire, 1830–1914*, forthcoming.

[146] Neil Evans, "Loyalties: State, Nation, Community and Military Recruitment in Wales, 1840–1918," in *Wales at War*, eds. Matthew Cragoe and Chris Williams (Cardiff: University of Wales Press, 2007), 38–61.

[147] Henry Pelling, "Wales and the Boer War," and Kenneth O. Morgan, "Wales and the Boer War: A Reply," *Welsh History Review* 4, no. 4 (1969); Paul Readman, "The Conservative Party, Patriotism, and British Politics: The Case of the General Election of 1900," *Journal of British Studies* 40, no. 1 (January 2001): 107–45.

[148] John Grigg, *Lloyd George: The Last Best Hope of the British Empire* (Caernarfon: Lloyd George Memorial Lecture, 1999).

[149] Neil Evans and Kate Sullivan, "'Yn Llawn o Dân Cymreig' [Full of Welsh Fire]: The Language of Politics in Wales, 1880–1914," in *A Social History of the Welsh Language, Vol. 4: Social Domains of the Welsh Language 1801–1911*, ed. Geraint H. Jenkins (Cardiff: University of Wales Press, 2000), 561–85. Morgan, *Wales in British Politics*.

[150] This comment is based on a brief survey of Welsh periodicals at the turn of the twentieth century, especially *Young Wales* and *Wales* which will be reported elsewhere.

has two."[151] But empire was one of the few areas of discussion where generally the term British was fairly consistently used: the phrase "The English empire" has a peculiar ring to it, though it was not absent from discussion. Popular enthusiasm for empire has generally been seen as confined to the later part of the nineteenth century, though the rapidity of its decline has been questioned. This popular enthusiasm has been particularly associated with London and its music hall culture but there has been little exploration of the theme on a regional basis.[152] Bernard Porter's iconoclastic study doubts the depth and intensity of this feeling and suggests there was much indifference to it. Certainly we know little of the reception of imperial propaganda. Mackenzie's work on the topic is very much top-down in approach with an emphasis on the purveyors of propaganda. Public opinion is seen as being manipulated. At the very least we may suggest that this is overly simple. Extensive research on Nazi propaganda has uncovered sources on its reception and found a much more complex pattern than simple absorption. Reception depended upon prior beliefs and age amongst other factors, including whether the message agreed with alternative sources of information.[153] Research on Britain will certainly benefit from thinking in these terms, but evidence about reception may be difficult to obtain.

Politics and the Empire

Politics was one of the spheres of the British state most affected by the empire. It was an imperial issue—slavery—which prompted the first mass campaign, the first modern social movement.[154] The extent of mobilization was remarkable and involved meetings, lectures, tract distribution, and petitions to parliament. Eventually it was held together by a newspaper, the *Anti-Slavery Reporter*, which flourished from 1825 to 1836. The abolition of the slave trade in 1807 and the abolition of slavery in the empire in 1833 were very much the product of the popular movement and not simply of the maneuverings of its parliamentary leaders. Parliament came to be impressed with not simply the number of signatories of petitions but their weight. The first petition of 1787 attracted 10,700 signatures in Manchester, which had a population of 50,000. The petitioning campaign in France in 1846–47 got just over that number of signatories in a popu-

---

[151] Cited in: David Lowenthal, "British National Identity and the Rural Landscape," *Rural History* 2, no. 2 (1991): 209.

[152] John M. MacKenzie, *Propaganda and Empire: The Manipulation of British Public Opinion, 1880–1960* (Manchester: Manchester University Press, 1984); Gareth Stedman Jones, *Languages of Class: Studies in English Working Class History* (Cambridge: Cambridge University Press, 1985); Porter, *Absent Minded Imperialists*; Andrew Thompson, *The Empire Strikes Back? The Impact of Imperialism on Britain from the Mid-Nineteenth Century* (London: Pearson Educational, 2005).

[153] Ian Kershaw, "How Effective was Nazi Propaganda?," in *Nazi Propaganda: The Power and Limitations,* ed. David Welch (London: Croom Helm, 1983), 180–205.

[154] Charles Tilly, *Social Movements, 1768–2004* (Boulder: Paradigm Publishers, 2004), 31–34.

lation of 35 million. In the 1830s, there were 4,000 who gave value to the idea of free labor; they probably exceeded the number of signatories of Chartist petitions as well as those of the Anti-Corn Law League. It was soon placed high on the political agenda and the signatories forced the issue. Women's mobilization was a key feature, not paralleled in other popular mobilizations of the period, and the "Ladies of England" petition of 1833 took four men to carry it.[155] Empire forced a reconsideration of the nature of humanity and in the process created the conditions in which a mass mobilization could occur; such campaigns were central to transforming the nature of the British state in the nineteenth century and anti-slavery itself kicked away one of the props of "old corruption."[156]

"Old corruption" included large East Indian and West Indian interests but in the early nineteenth century they faded out of the picture. The end of the slave trade and then of slavery, as well as the increasing absorption of the East India Company into the state, marked their decline. But empire was so central to the British polity that this did not mean the end of the imperial impact on British politics. It is now clear that anti-imperialism was largely a rhetorical position and that very few politicians or intellectuals seriously contemplated the immediate demise of the empire, even if many thought it had a limited long term life and railed against its costs. Empire was common ground on which most politicians stood: "no responsible statesman during the 'Little England' era embraced the view that separation of the colonies from Britain was a desirable prospect."[157] Goldwin Smith is often seen as the notable separatist of the period but even he thought this applied to the settlement colonies and not to India. Richard Cobden did advocate dissolution and thought free trade was the mechanism which would achieve it but he was an isolated voice on this. The common ground was clearly for holding on to existing colonies though generally not for expansion of them, particularly as this involved costly land forces and compromised the idea of a maritime empire. The ideas of a separation between "little Englanders" and "Jingos" comes from the political debates of the period, particularly from the insults flung at political opponents, but they do not reflect the realities of divisions in the political classes. Empire

---

[155] Seymour Drescher, "Public Opinion and the Destruction of British Colonial Slavery," in *Slavery and British Society, 1776–1846*, ed. James Walvin (London: Macmillan, 1982), 22–48 and 216–21; James Walvin, "The Public Campaign in England against Slavery, 1787–1834," in *The Abolition of the Atlantic Slave Trade*, ed. David Eltis and James Walvin (Madison: University of Wisconsin Press, 1981), 63–79; James Walvin, "The Rise of British Popular Sentiment for Abolition, 1787–1832," in *Anti-Slavery, Religion and Reform: Essays in Memory of Roger Anstey*, eds. Christine Bolt and Seymour Drescher (London: Dawson, 1980), 149–62; James Walvin "The Propaganda of Anti-Slavery," in *Slavery and British Society*, ed. Walvin (Baton Rouge: Louisiana State University Press, 1982), 49–68 and 221–24; Clare Midgley, *Women against Slavery: The British Campaigns, 1780–1870* (London: Routledge, 1992).

[156] Thomas C. Holt, "Explaining Abolition," *Journal of Social History* 24, no. 2 (Winter 1990): 371–79.

[157] John S. Galbraith "Myths of the 'Little England' Era," *American Historical Review* 67, no. 1 (October 1961): 35.

was therefore seen as the very way in which the state was constituted, germane to its whole nature.[158]

When the franchise was extended in 1867 the debates occurred in a clear imperial context, including the rebellion in Jamaica, emancipation and enfranchisement of African Americans in the United States, claims for women's suffrage, and the experience of male suffrage in Australia. The sense of British supremacy in the world was palpable.[159] English men were deemed suitable for self-government unlike other races and women. At the same time as the franchise was extended at home, Jamaica had its representative government removed. This was a creature of the planters but extending its reach would raise the issue of the participation of non-whites: "Citizens it was decreed were men with homes, men with property, men with families, men with jobs ... Property was no longer the basis of the suffrage, but 'race', gender, labor and the level of civilization now determined who was included in and excluded from the political nation."[160]

Benjamin Disraeli sought to give empire a new prominence in British politics in the mid-nineteenth century in an effort to preserve what he saw as the old traditions of England.[161] Just when he introduced such ideas into policy has been the subject of much debate but it is possible to find considerable continuity in his thinking with empire as a means of ensuring the flourishing of the ideas which had animated "Young England" in the 1840s. His thinking became apparent as a kind of social imperialism reacting to the changed situation in Europe, aiming to unite the classes at home in the late 1860s and culminating in the unveiling of the Queen as the "Empress of India" in 1876.[162] Doing so was a central part of the late Victorian conception of monarchy that was related firmly with the empire: it became an imperial institution.[163]

---

[158] R. E. Robinson, "Imperial Problems in British Politics, 1880–1895," in *The Cambridge History of the British Empire, Vol III: The Empire-Commonwealth, 1870–1939*, ed. E. A. Berhens, James Butler, and C. E. Carrington (Cambridge: Cambridge University Press, 1959), 127–80; John S. Galbraith, "Myths"; Ged Martin, "Anti-Imperialism in the Mid-Nineteenth Century and the Nature of the British Empire, 1820–1870," in *Reappraisals in British Colonial History*, eds. R. Hyam and G. Martin (London: Macmillan, 1975), 88–120; G. K. Pentling, "Victorian Imperial Theorist? Goldwin Smith and Ireland," in *Victoria's Ireland: Irishness and Britishness, 1837–1901*, ed. Peter Gray (Dublin: Four Courts Press, 2004), 27–36; Anthony Howe, "Free Trade and Global Order: the Rise and Fall of a Victorian Vision," in *Victorian Visions of Global Order: Empire and International Relations in Nineteenth-Century Political Thought*, ed. Duncan Bell (Cambridge: Cambridge University Press, 2007), 26–46.

[159] Catherine Hall, "Rethinking Imperial Histories: The Reform Act of 1867," *New Left Review* 208 (November–December 1994): 3–29. This analysis is extended in Catherine Hall, Keith McClelland, and Jane Rendall, *Defining the Victorian Nation. Class, Race, Gender and the Reform Act of 1867* (Cambridge: Cambridge University Press, 2000).

[160] Hall, "Rethinking Imperial Histories," 19–29.

[161] J. P. Parry, "Disraeli and England," *Historical Journal* 43, no. 4 (September 2000): 699–728.

[162] C. C. Eldridge, *Disraeli and the Rise of a New Imperialism* (Cardiff: University of Wales Press, 1996); Freda Harcourt, "Disraeli's Imperialism, 1866–68: A Question of Timing," *Historical Journal* 23, no. 1 (March 1980): 87–109.

[163] Paul Ward, *Britishness since 1870* (London: Routledge, 2004), ch 1 and 14.

The Queen lived long enough to celebrate two jubilees, the golden in 1887 and the diamond in 1897. Both, but particularly the latter, were occasions when leaders of the empire came to London for the festivities: "the whole empire in microcosm parade through the streets of London."[164] In 1897 the opportunity was taken to hold an imperial conference on the occasion. The same kinds of scenes were re-enacted when Victoria died in 1901 and for the coronations of her successors, Edward VII and George V. Not only did the empire come to London but members of the royal family increasingly visited the empire, including the massive Durbars in India. In 1912, Elgar's masque "Crown of India" was staged to celebrate the Durbar. When William Walton composed "Crown Imperial" for the Coronation of George VI in 1937 it was a succinct recognition of the way in which the monarchy had become linked with the empire. This was central to its modernization in the late nineteenth century as an archaic but reassuring survival in a world of dramatic change. It was of course, an "invented tradition" in many respects playing a role seemingly above politics and with a newly perfected ceremonial, a kind of Disneyland on wheels.[165]

After 1860, politics were deeply affected by imperial issues. One indicator was the controversy over Governor Eyre's behavior in Jamaica in 1865. A protest movement, possibly an insurrection, was harshly repressed and summary executions conducted under martial law. 439 black people were killed, 600 whipped, and a thousand homes destroyed. Many liberals were outraged and demanded the governor's punishment. John Stuart Mill was their figurehead. But intellectuals divided on the issue and many rallied behind Thomas Carlyle who had effectively sided with the plantation owners and condoned slavery in an article of 1849: "On Occasional Disquisition on The Negro Question." This was later reissued as a pamphlet with the word "Negro" changed to "Nigger" a succinct indication of its intellectual roots. Eyre was recalled but not prosecuted, and conflicts between the Jamaica Committee and the Eyre Defence Committee raged for some time.[166] A fault line was established which would later open much wider.

---

[164] David Powell, *Nationhood and Identity: The British State since 1800* (London: I.B. Tauris, 2002), 100.

[165] David Cannadine, "The Context, Performance and Meaning of Ritual: The British Monarchy and the 'Invention of Tradition' c. 1820–1977," in *The Invention of Tradition*, eds. Eric Hobsbawm and Terence Ranger (Cambridge: Cambridge University Press 1983), 120–33; Elizabeth Hammerton and David Cannadine "Conflict and Consensus on a Ceremonial Occasion: the Diamond Jubilee in Cambridge in 1897," *Historical Journal* 24, no. 1 (March 1981): 111–46.

[166] Bernard Semmel, *Democracy versus Empire: The Jamaica Riots of 1865 and the Governor Eyre Controversy* (New York: Anchor Books, 1969); Thomas C. Holt, *The Problem of Freedom: Race, Labor and Politics in Jamaica and Britain, 1832–1938* (Baltimore: Johns Hopkins University Press, 1992); Catherine Hall, *White, Male and Middle Class: Explorations in Feminism and History* (Cambridge: Polity Press, 1992); Catherine Hall, *Civilizing Subjects: Metropole and Colony in the English Imagination, 1830–1867* (Cambridge: Polity, 2002), 243–64, 406–24; Gad Heuman, *'The Killing Time': The Morant Bay Rebellion in Jamaica* (London: Macmillan, 1994).

Just eleven years later popular agitations protested against Turkish atrocities in Bulgaria, where irregular troops massacred some 15,000 Christians. A massive campaign of public meetings demanded that the Turks withdraw their forces from the area. It was essentially a campaign of nonconformists in England and Wales (Scotland was much less involved) and orchestrated by newspapers such as the *Northern Echo* and the *South Wales Daily News*. Traditionally, Britain had backed the Ottoman Empire, seen as capable of modernization, but the behavior revealed turned much public opinion. Gladstone, who had nominally retired from the leadership of the Liberal Party, assumed the leadership of the campaign and fulminated against the Disraeli government's failure to intervene. Gladstone and British Nonconformity adopted what might be seen as an ethical foreign policy which meant condemnation of the Muslim empire and alliance with the Orthodox Christianity of Russia.[167] Disraeli's stance was the opposite of this; the Ottoman Empire was a bulwark against Russian expansion which was seen particularly as pressing into Afghanistan and by extension into India. He stood for what political scientists would now call realism, not to mention preserving the policy of Lord Palmerstone of the mid-Victorian period.

Gladstone led a moral crusade against this and created a convenient hate figure which he dubbed "Beaconsfieldism." In the process he propagated the idea that his opponent was creating a sinister system and a conspiracy and was profligate with government expenditure as well, which exacerbated the economic crisis of the period.[168] This sustained the Liberal Party through the election campaign of 1880 in which it won a resounding victory. Prominent in it was Gladstone's own campaign in a formerly Tory seat of Midlothian, when he was greeted by vast crowds and enthusiasm, redolent of the American elections which Lord Rosebery, his campaign manager, had observed in the United States. But it also allowed the Conservatives to castigate Liberals as being anti-imperial and this became central to their rhetoric from Disraeli's Crystal Place speech of 1872 onwards.[169]

In some ways Gladstone's victory was less impressive than it seemed. He won by a hundred seats but many were marginal and the surplus of votes was very small. He quickly became embroiled in imperial adventures of his own with the bombardment of Alexandria and the occupation of Egypt in 1882, which took some of the luster from

---

[167] Richard Shannon, *Gladstone and the Bulgarian Agitation of 1876* (Hassocks: Harvester Press, 1975); Ann Pottinger Saab, *Reluctant Icon: Gladstone, Bulgaria and the Working Classes, 1856–1878* (Cambridge, Mass.: Harvard University Press, 1991).

[168] Disraeli had been elevated to the House of Lords in 1876 as Lord Beaconsfield. P. J. Durrans, "A Two-Edged Sword: The Liberal Attack on Disraelian Imperialism," *Journal of Imperial and Commonwealth History* 10, no. 3 1982, 262–84; P. J. Durrans, "Beaconsfieldism," in "Empire, Politics and Popular Culture," ed. C. C. Eldridge, Special Issue of *Trivium* 24 (1989): 58–75; Peter Cain, "Radicalism, Gladstone and the Imperial Critique of Disraelian 'Imperialism'," in *Victorian Visions of Global Order: International Politics in Nineteenth-Century Political Thought*, ed. Duncan Bell (Cambridge: Cambridge University Press, 2007), 215–38.

[169] H. C. G. Matthew, "Rhetoric and Politics in Great Britain, 1860–1950," in *Politics and Social Change in Modern Britain*, ed. P. J. Waller (Brighton: Harvester Wheatsheaf, 1987), 34–58.

his moral stance, while the perception that he had failed to rescue General Gordon from the insurgents of Khartoum in 1885 produced a counter-image of weakness and failure. The Liberal Party began to lose the support of the propertied over Bulgaria and of influential sections of public opinion. The *Daily Telegraph*, in its inception a Liberal newspaper, switched its allegiance to the Tories over the issue. Gladstone had used the rhetoric of "the classes against the masses" in the campaigns, and like Disraeli was apart from majority opinion in his own party. He frightened much Liberal support particularly in the intelligentsia.

This split was made deeper and irreconcilable by his announcement of his conversion to Irish home rule shortly before Christmas in 1885. Ireland was clearly one of the central problems for British governments in the nineteenth century. The Union clearly lacked legitimacy and Ireland was never fully integrated into the polity. Beyond this it had bitter conflicts over land. Home rule was raised as a slogan by the Protestant Isaac Butt in the 1870s as part of a federal approach to British government, but in the 1880s it became the cause of Charles Stuart Parnell who yoked behind it the fervor and organization of the land campaigns.[170] As in 1876, Gladstone saw a divinely given opportunity to lead the masses in a campaign.[171] It may have been a means of heading off issues of social reform which were repugnant to him as well. He had found his earlier Irish measures—disestablishment of the Anglican Church in Ireland and two measures of land reform—inadequate, a failure symbolized by the murder of the chief secretary and permanent under secretary in Phoenix Park in 1882. He bent his voracious reading to Irish history and convinced himself that home rule was the only just solution.

Much of his party failed to agree and subsequently split, leaving its majority in the political wilderness for the next two decades. Ireland was clearly contentious for many reasons but chief among them was the imperial context in which it was set. Very early in the debate, *The Spectator* proclaimed a domino theory by which it would be the first tile to fall but would inevitably lead to the collapse of the whole empire. It had been beaten to the point by Lord Salisbury in 1883, a theory by which if Ireland went there would be a chain reaction and a step-by-step disintegration of the empire. The philosopher and economist Henry Sidgwick saw it as a social and imperial danger and similarly James Fitzjames Stephen feared both social revolution and the loss of India.[172] Such issues ran through the whole presence of the question in British pol-

---

[170] Alan O'Day, "The Irish Problem," in *Later Victorian Britain*, eds. T. R. Gourvish and Alan O'Day (London: Macmillan, 1988), 229–49; Charles Townshend, "The Home Rule Campaign in Ireland," in *The Challenge to Westminster Sovereignty: Devolution and Independence*, eds. H. T. Dickinson and Michael Lynch (West Linton: Tuckwell Press, 2000), 102–12.

[171] Richard Shannon, "Gladstone and Home Rule, 1886" in *Ireland after the Union*, Proceedings of the Second Joint Meeting of the Royal Irish Academy and the British Academy (Oxford University Press, 1989), 45–59.

[172] Cited in H. V. Brasted, "Irish Nationalism and the British Empire in the Late Nineteenth Century," in *Irish Culture and Nationalism, 1750–1950*, eds. Oliver MacDonagh, W. F Mandle, and Pauric Travers (London: Macmillan, 1983), 84; Tom Dunne, "*La Traison des Clercs*: British Intellectuals and the First Home Rule Crisis," *Irish Historical Studies* 23, no. 90 (November 1982): 134–73, at 136.

itics. Bonar Law articulated the fears in Londonderry, 1912: "Once more you hold the pass for the Empire, you are a besieged city."[173] Gladstone had to evolve an answer to this which involved arguing that on the contrary resolving the Irish question meant strengthening the empire and conceiving of it as a free association of peoples. He argued that there were in reality four nations in the UK. This became a signal for Welsh Liberals to argue for disestablishment in Wales, while some Scots called for home rule there. Eventually it was summed up in the slogan "home rule all round."[174] Gladstone went on a pilgrimage to Swansea in June 1887 to commend the moral example of the firmly Protestant Welsh who had strongly endorsed home rule for the overwhelmingly Catholic Irish in the elections of 1886.[175] Along the way he offered telegraphic statements of his argument as counters to Tory accusations of imperial dissolution: at Llanymynech he asserted that whatever system of government emerged out of his ideas would "really conduce both the happiness of Wales and the union and strength of the empire," while at Llanidloes he claimed that "the people of Wales do not for one moment believe the preposterous and absurd statement that we are persons engaged in dissolving and breaking up the British Empire. On the contrary we are engaged in tightening the bonds and confirming the foundations of that great union [Which was built not on pieces of paper and statutes] ... but in the hearts and affections of the people."[176] Four nations was a view of the British state analogous to that of empire, one which derived from a view of England as the new Greece.[177]

Home rule was defeated in the House of Commons in 1886, passed there in 1894 only to be struck down my the House of Lords. It looked set to become law in 1914 once the Parliament Act of 1911 had reduced the upper house's veto to a suspensory one of three years. Passions ran high with threats of rebellion in Ulster, an actual mutiny of officers at the Curragh and the prospect of civil war in 1914. Much, though not all, of it was discussed in essentially colonialist terms—the fitness of the Irish to govern themselves and the shackling of Protestant and enterprising Ulster to Catholic and peasant reaction.[178] Often something more than the details of particular pieces of Irish legislation were involved.

---

[173] Cited in Christine Kinealy, "At Home with the Empire: The Example of Ireland," in *At Home with the Empire: Metropolitan Culture and the Imperial World,* eds. Catherine Hall and Sonya O. Rose (Cambridge: Cambridge University Press, 2006), 96.

[174] Elfie Rembold, "'Home Rule All Round': Experiments in Regionalizing Great Britain, 1886–1914," in *Reforming the Constitution: Debates in Twentieth-Century Britain,* eds. Peter Caterall, Wolfram Kaiser, and Ulrike Walton-Jordan (London: Cass, 2000), 201–24.

[175] Mike Benbough-Jackson and Neil Evans, "Ritual, Symbol and Politics: Gladstone, Swansea and Wales in 1887," *Welsh History Review* 26, no. 3 (June 2013): 454–81.

[176] *Mr Gladstone in South Wales* pamphlet in West Glamorgan Record Office D141/1, unpaginated; *Western Mail,* June 3, 1887.

[177] Dunne, *"La Traison,"* 164.

[178] Dunne, *"La Traison,"* passim; Paul Bew, *Ideology and the Irish Question: Ulster Unionism and Irish Nationalism, 1912–1916* (Oxford: Oxford University Press, 1994).

The Liberal Party was shattered by the issue but its fortunes revived from 1903 when Joseph Chamberlain announced his ideas for tariff reform. This was a means of trying to draw together the empire but it was countered by a Liberal reaffirmation of the free trade principles of the 1840s with the slogan of the big loaf versus the little loaf. Free trade connected Britain with the world in a very different way, particularly a looser connection with the empire.[179] The Edwardian era in British politics in some respects moved forward from the issues of the 1880s. If Gladstone had sought to frustrate social reform his policy was not effective in the long run.[180] Both major parties as well as the growing labor movement made the case for social measures. While there were many indigenous pressures for reform as well as the European model of the Bismarckian measures in Germany and close connections with American reformers, some of the impetus and example came from parts of the empire where the social and political balances were different and progressive legislation was enacted before it was in Britain. Australia and New Zealand's enacting of Old Age Pensions, trade boards, and compulsory arbitration influenced British campaigners and legislation.[181] The rejection of many potential recruits into the army in the Boer War also highlighted social conditions and linked them with empire in a graphic way: this was the major imperial war of the century but British cities seemed incapable of producing a population fit to be soldiers.

Women's suffrage was also enhanced by imperial examples, though the empire could also be used as an argument against it. Conservatives and Liberal imperialists often argued that women could vote in local government in Britain or in dominion elections because such bodies never declared war on other countries. It was argued that the imperial parliament was a different matter simply because it could wage war and it would be inappropriate for women who did not fight to be a part of a process by which men were sent to fight. Only men should make such decisions, it was argued. Neither of these arguments was decisive—there was a parliamentary majority for the cause from 1906 but conflicting party considerations blocked legislation before the First World War. Part of the case for women's suffrage was that women should shoulder an imperial burden and make the case for their helpless (though inferior) Indian sisters.[182] But imperial examples, considerations, and arguments shaped the debate as with much of British politics in the period.

---

[179] E. H. H. Green, *The Crisis of Conservatism: The Politics, Economics and Ideology of the British Conservative Party, 1880–1914* (London: Routledge, 1995); Peter Clarke, *Hope and Glory: Britain 1900–1990* (London: Allen Lane, 1996), ch 1.

[180] E. H. H. Green, "The Conservative Party, the State and Social Reform, 1880–1914," in *The Conservatives and British Society, 1880–1990*, eds. Martin Francis and Ina Zweiniger-Bargielowska (Cardiff: University of Wales Press, 1997), 226–39.

[181] Thompson, "British State," 48–50; Antionette Burton, "New Narratives of Imperial Politics in the Nineteenth Century," in *At Home with the Empire*, eds. Hall and Rose, 212–29.

[182] Antoinette Burton, *Burdens of History: British Feminists, Indian Women, and Imperial Culture, 1865–1915* (Chapel Hill: University of North Carolina Press, 1994); Clare Midgley, "New Imperial Histories," *Journal of British Studies* 35, no. 4 (October 1996): 547–53; Kay Cook and

COUNTRIES OF THE BRITISH EMPIRE

DRAW ON A UNIFORM SCALE ACCORDING TO THEIR WHITE POPULATION

BRITISH ISLES, 45 millions

CANADA
7 millions

AUSTRALIA
$4\frac{1}{2}$ millions

SOUTH AFRICA
1 million

NEW ZEALAND
1 million

NOTE.—In this diagram South Africa is drawn about $\frac{1}{45}$ the size of the British Isles, because the White Population of South Africa is about $\frac{1}{45}$ of the Population of the British Isles

Ideas of Imperial Federation stressed the links between Britain and the Dominions. This map illustrates the very different ratios between population and land in the UK and in the Empire. The census of the Empire in 1911 confirmed that the non-white populations were vastly bigger. In 1909 a Welsh missionary claimed there were 360M non-white people in the British Empire.

Imperial issues therefore ran through nineteenth-century politics and they shaped some of the most contentious issues. Parliamentary reform was contentious in 1832 but became more a matter of negotiation and agreement subsequently, and religious issues remained alive and sometimes bitter. But politics very much related to Britain's place in the world—even when overtly imperial issues were not to the fore.

Neil Evans, "'The Petty Antics of the Bell-Ringing Boisterous Band?' The Women's Suffrage Movement in Wales, 1890–1918," in *Our Mother's Land: Chapters in Welsh Women's History, 1830–1939,* ed. Angela John (Cardiff: University of Wales Press, 2011), 157–85.

A Federal Empire and Britain?

Improved communications drew the empire into a tighter and tighter net. In 1873, Jules Verne sent his factional Phileas Fogg *Around the World in Eighty Days*. In 1890 the real life journalist Nellie Bly managed it in seventy three.[183] One of the victims was the conventional wisdom that distance made close political relations in the empire impossible.[184] This offered a solution to the emergence of rival powers to challenge British hegemony. The empire could be integrated into a single state—federal in nature—by drawing the bonds ever tighter. An essentially maritime empire could then compete with the land-based empires which were coming to be seen as the preferred form of the future. As the historian J. A. Froude put it in 1870: "Other nations once less powerful or not more powerful than ours are growing in strength and numbers, and we too must grow if we are to remain on a level with them."[185] Such schemes developed from the 1860s in the minds of travelers and thinkers but they found it hard to make the transition to practical politics.

They could offer potential benefits like sharing the tax and defense burdens of the empire and relieving the logjam of legislation in Westminster and they were a way of addressing the problem of the disparity in size between the imperial core and the expanding periphery. The empire had grown but its political system had not reflected this. The Imperial Federation League was created in 1884 in the wake of the publication of Seeley's lectures on imperial history, and it helped create much public discussion about the issue. But it proved fruitless and the league was dissolved in 1893. There were too many competing schemes and an imperfect understanding of just what imperial federation—and federal government—meant. The cracks were papered over with rhetoric and sentiment, with a particular stress on the bonds of race. This of course confined it to the dominions but inevitably questions of the place of India in any such federation were raised. Race also conjured up the prospect of re-union with the United States of America, perhaps the clearest indication of the realms of fantasy that could be explored.[186]

A wholesale reconfiguration of the British state was at least conceivable. Why didn't it happen? Most political discussion found it hard to think of anything other than the "flexible" British unwritten constitution and the traditions of this were impossible to displace. A written constitution would have been necessary. As in other

---

[183] Stefan Lorent, ed., *Pittsburgh: The Story of an American City* (New York: Doubleday, 1964), 331.
[184] Duncan Bell, *The Idea of Greater Britain: Empire and the Future of World Order, 1860–1900* (Princeton: Princeton University Press, 2007).
[185] Cited in John Kendle, *Federal Britain: A History* (London: Routledge, 1997), 41.
[186] Kendle, *Federal Britain*, 45, 49, and ch. 3 *passim*. See also John Kendle, *Ireland and the Federal Solution: The Debate over the United Kingdom Constitution, 1870–1921* (Kingston: McGill-Queen's University Press, 1989) and Michael Burgess, *The British Tradition of Federalism* (Madison, NJ: Fairleigh Dickinson University Press, 1995).

spheres of constitutional discussion, as Linda Colley has observed, the good became the enemy of the best. A polity which had limited the powers of its rulers at a remarkably early time found it hard to adjust to changing times and new problems.[187] Sovereignty was seen as being as single and indivisible as any good Jacobin would have liked and the idea of divided sovereignty was widely understood as being a source of conflict and weakness. Divided sovereignty was seen as a reduction of sovereignty, whereas it should not have had any such impact within the defined spheres of a federal constitution. The very size of England within the UK posed a huge problem for any federal solution and in a speech in Dundee in 1912, Winston Churchill recognized that England would have to be divided into ten or twelve self governing regions in order for a federal United Kingdom to work. There was no political basis for regionalism in England and proponents had to look back to the (semi-mythical) Anglo-Saxon Heptarchy to find a precedent. Regionalism in England was economic and cultural but not political.[188] Schemes were developed but, as in the whole discussion of federalism, they never became the program of any significant politician much less of any political party.[189]

Ireland linked the United Kingdom and imperial dimensions of this discussion through "home rule all round" or as part of a federal solution for the British Isles. But in the end Chamberlain was not the only politician who preferred to see Ireland separate than to grant it home rule. Solutions outside the ambit of a centralized English state were hard to envisage. Devolution of power, such as to the Scottish Office or varying territorial arrangements, were compatible with this, but not any genuine federalism or major realignments of the state. It has recently been argued that federalism is successful where the infrastructural power of the central state is sufficient to exert pressure on its periphery but not sufficient to overwhelm it.[190] In the case of the empire, the power of Westminster was sufficient to suggest the idea of imperial federation but distances were still too great and communications too slow to allow this to be practicable. In the case of the United Kingdom, Westminster had quite sufficient power to overwhelm or integrate the periphery—apart from in Ireland—though it had learned not to impose uniformity upon it. The status quo could be preserved, but at the cost of spewing up the indigestible part of Ireland which had always lain heavily on the English stomach.

---

[187] Linda Colley, *Taking Stock of Taking Liberties: A Personal View* (London: British Library, 2008).

[188] John K. Walton, "Britishness," in Chris Wrigley, ed., *A Companion to Early Twentieth-Century Britain* (Oxford: Blackwell, 2003), 517–31.

[189] Kendle, *Federal Britain*, 71. Christopher Harvie, "English Regionalism: the Dog that Never Barked," in *National Identities: The Constitution of the United Kingdom*, ed. Bernard Crick (Oxford: Blackwell, 1991), 105–18; C. B. Fawcett, "Natural Divisions of England," *Geographical Journal* 49, no. 2 (February 1917): 124–35; C. B. Fawcett *Provincial England* (London: Williams and Norgate, 1919).

[190] Daniel Ziblatt, "Rethinking the Origins of Federalism: Puzzle, Theory, and Evidence from Nineteenth-Century Europe," *World Politics* 57, no. 1 (October 2004): 70–98.

Kendle provides a key argument:

Federalism was simply unacceptable to a political community so deeply wedded to the concept of parliamentary sovereignty. It was natural
that the English should view the division of sovereignty with some trep-
idation; it could mean a weakening of English dominance within the
British Isles. ... The furthest the Welsh or Scots would go was home rule
all round, a strictly devolutionary device. National consciousness, such
as it was, did not demand "national" legislatures with clear sovereignty;
all that was required were enhanced but delegated administrative and
legislative powers within the comforting embrace of a unitary system of
government. ... [to] Irish Nationalists, ..., federation was simply a devious means of denying them greater autonomy on the colonial model. It
might work as a means of resolving internal Irish tensions but it was not
acceptable as a means of satisfying self-governing aspirations.[191]

But something had to be done. Increasing, military needs made stringent financial demands on the state and created a "warfare state" in parallel with the incipient welfare
state. The response to international competition was to create something analogous to
the military-fiscal state of the eighteenth century, in the sense that it relied on naval
supremacy and employed advanced technology produced by its industrial strength to
counter its deficiencies in manpower. In 1914, Britain had not only the largest navy in
the world but contained the largest submarine force and the largest naval air service.
Britain needed an army—but a small and professional army that the Edwardian army
reforms were aimed at producing.[192]

The military was increasingly brought under civilian control and defense coordinated through the Committee of Imperial Defense, usually chaired by the prime
minister, created in 1902. Some of the largest and most advanced firms in Britain were
concerned with armaments and they tended to displace the government's own production of arms through naval dockyards.[193] The army became more popular because of its
association with colonial wars in the nineteenth century and the development of the
idea of the Christian soldier; it had always used regional and national identities as part
of its ethos, recruiting in Ireland, the Highlands, and Wales, as well as having county
regiments in England. The army reforms enhanced such identities. Much of the old
hostility to the army as a threat to liberty evaporated, aided by the fact that there was
no real argument in favor of mobilizing the whole nation in arms through conscription, and the idea that an island location meant volunteer defense forces were adequate

---

[191] Kendle, *Federal Britain*, 61.
[192] David Edgerton, "Liberal Militarism and the British State," *New Left Review* 185 (January–February 1991): 138–69, quotation 142.
[193] Edgerton "Liberal Militarism"; and David Edgerton, *Warfare State: Britain, 1920–1970* (Cambridge: Cambridge University Press, 2005), 35–41.

to repel invasion. The navy also embraced the separate identities of the UK and the empire through frequent and widespread naval displays in Britain and the colonies. Technology, popular support, and strengthened links with the dominions created a military system adjusted to the new needs of the late Victorian and Edwardian eras. The dominions increasingly bore some of the cost of the navy, even if the Admiralty's priorities were always home defense with colonial defense something that could be dealt with when Britain itself was safe. The empire helped strengthen the British state rather than led to imperial overstretch.[194]

The key to resolving these issues and re-jigging the British state was who would pay for the new needs. Ultimately Chamberlain thought it would be the foreigner and the consumer through imperial preferences and tariffs. This had implications for empire—federalism, a customs union, and a greater centralization. Liberals came up with ways of raising revenue which had less impact on the overall structure of the imperial state. Campbell-Bannerman and Lloyd George thought it should be landowners and plutocrats who should provide the funds through progressive taxation and death duties. There was a fiscal crisis of the state to pay for social welfare and for the new military needs but it was resolved by taxing the rich rather than by a radical reconfiguring of the state.[195]

So how was the empire integrated in 1914? In essence the answer is by allowing difference and diversity to be expressed in non-political areas of life, by sentiment and by patterns of migration. Keith Robbins has asked the question of what integrated the United Kingdom at the outbreak of the First World War. Tolerance of diversity is his essential answer—there was unity in difference.[196] It was a complex web but it helped hold the whole enterprise together because it allowed people to follow their inclinations in many areas. There were many volunteers for the fight, even in Ireland. It was only when conscription was mooted that the bonds with Irish volunteers broke asunder. The war needed a centralized state and equal sacrifice. It proved too much for many Irish Catholics and enough rebelled to induce a revolutionary crisis there. Such a crisis is defined by troops who refuse to obey and breach the state's monopoly of violence. Clearly this had occurred in Ireland by 1919–20.

Much the same applied in the empire. By the end of our period, the dominions had formed states and had clear elements of national consciousness. Self

---

[194] Jörn Leonhard, "Nations in Arms and Imperial Defence: Continental Models, the British Empire and its Military before 1914," *Journal of Modern European History* 5 (2007): 287–308; Jan Rüger, "Nation, Empire and Navy: Identity Politics in the United Kingdom, 1887–1914," *Past and Present* 185 (November 2004): 157–87; Phillips Payson O'Brien, "The Titan Refreshed: Imperial Overstretch and the British Navy before the First World War," *Past and Present* 172 (August 2001): 146–69.

[195] Jose Harris, "The Transition to High Politics in English Social Policy, 1880–1914," in *High and Low Politics in Modern Britain*, eds. Michael Bentley and John Stevenson (Oxford: Oxford University Press, 1983), 58–79.

[196] Keith Robbins, *Nineteenth-Century Britain: Integration and Diversity* (Oxford: Oxford University Press, 1988), ch. 7.

government had been achieved in domestic affairs though diplomacy. Defense and foreign policy remained matters for Westminster. In most cases these new nations were comfortable with a dual British/dominion identity and they gained a political theorist in the shape of Richard Jebb who visited all of them in the early twentieth century and pressed the cases for their nationality. Australia and New Zealand sought protection from Russian, German, and especially, Japanese expansion in the Far East while Canada needed protection from an aggressive American cultural imperialism. If nationalism has been likened to a warm and comforting blanket in which to hide from the modern world this applies very well to colonial nations which could seem to be adrift in dangerous waters.[197] Cricket and rugby teams provided some common elements in popular culture and national teams from the dominions toured from the later nineteenth century, sometimes having the effrontery to beat the mother country. Troops from the dominions had rallied to the imperial cause from Gordon's death in Khartoum onwards. (Only New Zealand failed to respond then, but did so in later crises). Support correlated with areas with high proportions of British birth and descent. Sentiment proved strong, as theorists of empire like Richard Jebb had argued, but there was no realistic basis for a federal state. Despite this, representatives of the dominions joined the war cabinet and to some extent the empire functioned as a coherent unit in the conflict. Indian and West Indian troops found their way to Europe while Africans were conscripted to fight in battles in their own continent.

The late nineteenth century offered the vision of a radical re-forging of the British state, one which would bind it securely to the empire. But the bonds of rail, boiler, and wire proved insufficient. The substance, as opposed to the vision, of the new means of communication was inadequate to overcome the global reach which was necessary. At root there were vested interests in the existing state of governmental affairs, not least in the dominions themselves, and the fact that no one economic interest dominated the British state in the period suggests that decisive action and remodeling was unlikely. Compromise or the status quo was always more likely.[198] Free trade, a central component of the remodelled mid-Victorian state, also militated against change in the wider imperial system, which would have required tariffs. The Liberals won those particular arguments by introducing graduated income tax in 1894, securing the survival of free trade against Tory tariff reformers in the landslide election victory of 1906 and taxes on the rich to pay for social reform in the "people's budget" of 1909. The last two were based on substantial popular support, and free trade was rooted in a kind of "moral economy" providing cheap bread for the poor. The state had been transformed in the mid-Victorian era but in many ways the developments of the Edwardian era only confirmed this. Financing social reform through taxing the rich kept the structure of government intact.

[197] John Eddy and Deryk Shreuder, eds., *The Rise of Colonial Nationalism: Australia, New Zealand, Canada and South Africa first assert their nationalities, 1880–1914* (Sydney: Allen and Unwin, 1988); J. D. B. Miller, *Richard Jebb and the Problem of Empire* (London: Athlone Press, 1956).
[198] M. J. Daunton, "'Gentlemanly Capitalism' and British Industry 1820–1914," *Past & Present* 122 (February 1989): 119–58.

Tariff reform and imperial federation were the enemies of this but rallying their scattered, muddled, and disparate forces was too great a task for any realistic politics.

Imagining the Past

We might seek some illumination about the nature and integration of the empire from its historiography. History is an important way of self-understanding in any society, but in the long nineteenth century, it became an increasingly academic subject, with much of the research and teaching of it undertaken in universities. Clearly one of the conditions for being a modern nation was to have a closely documented and professional corpus of historical work. This was a strong growth as far as English history was concerned but the United Kingdom and the empire posed much knottier problems if their pasts were to be confronted and analyzed.

Nineteenth-century Britain was a superpower but its historians had some difficulty in engaging with that fact. The dominant narrative of its historians was that of a struggle for freedom and that was something which was the property of the English people rather than their empire. There were variants of the story: William Stubbs traced the English constitution—cautiously—back to Tacitus's account of German society and stressed its continuity through local institutions like shire courts in order to obviate the problem of the discontinuity of the Norman conquest. Others like E. A. Freeman saw continuity between the Saxon Witan and parliament and developed this in opposition to the Whigs influenced by Thomas Babbington Macaulay who put parliament in the center of the frame and could find little to place in it before the epic struggles with the king which had been inaugurated in the thirteenth century.[199] Of these only Macaulay could really engage with the empire in any meaningful way, linking empire with progress. He was arrogant about the cultural ascendancy of the British over the Indians and stressed the benevolence of British rule, of which he had direct experience.[200]

A school textbook which went through many editions and was advertised as being suitable for the main military and civil service examinations claimed to be a *History of the British Empire* but was mainly the standard account of England, reign by royal reign, with the addition of some consideration of Scottish kings and passing comments on imperial matters at appropriate points in the narrative.[201] The occasional sweeping claim did not alter the fact that it did not offer a very coherent account

---

[199] John W. Burrow, *A Liberal Descent: Victorian Historians and the English Past* (Cambridge: Cambridge University Press, 1981).

[200] William Roger Louis, "Introduction," in *The Oxford History of the British Empire, Vol V: Historiography,* eds. Robin W Winks and Aline Low (Oxford: Oxford University Press, 1999), 5–7.

[201] William Francis Collier, *History of the British Empire* (London: Nelson School Series, Senior Class Book, 1870). The National Library of Wales has seven different editions dated between 1859 and 1881.

of the empire and its growth. After the discovery of the mainland of North America by "English enterprise" in the reign of Henry VII: "...ever since, while rich and useful products of distant lands have been borne into our harbors, from the British Islands as a center there have been flowing towards the rising and the setting of the sun, our sciences, our literature and our language, and best of all, the faith in Jesus, which we prize as the chief blessing of our nation."[202] The fact that it ended with a gazetteer of "British Colonies and Dependencies" only emphasized the disjunction between the main narrative and the empire.[203]

Empires were the antithesis of freedom and they had a distressing tendency to decline. Edward Gibbon had published his *Decline and Fall of the Roman Empire* at just the time at which Britain was losing its American colonies to reinforce the point.[204] At a rhetorical level there was an expectation that the existing British Empire would decline or secure its freedom. Few contemporaries in the early nineteenth century contemplated its rapid expansion. If empire had no future it was hard to find a pattern in is past—easier than to see it as the result of random and unplanned events and not to yoke it with the destiny of the English nation which powered all the variants of Whig history.

Sir John Seeley's *The Expansion of England*, published with much acclaim in 1883, sought to challenge these trends; within two years it had sold 80,000 copies and did not go out of print until the year of the Suez crisis. Seeley was a devotee of the German school of history and rejected the popular histories of Thomas Carlyle and Macaulay as well as the picturesque invocations of the past which used conjecture, poetic narrative, and omitted dull detail, such as the historical novels of Sir Walter Scott. Facts had to be accumulated, analyzed, correlated, and explained. He thought there was too much stress on the Whiggish idea of constitutional liberty and domestic affairs; Macaulay was a "charlatan" whose romanticism was to be despised.[205] The most celebrated aphorism in the book is almost always misquoted as indicating Seeley's view that the British Empire had been acquired in a "fit of absence of mind." In fact he was commenting on the emphasis historians had given to the past in England and "[r]estored to its original context, Seeley's celebrated remark about the empire seemingly having been acquired in a 'fit of absence of mind' is less a comment on English history than on English historiography."[206] Seeley wanted to prove the opposite of the common misapprehension of his views: that foreign policy had primacy and that by portraying the eighteenth century as a sort of second hundred years war, the growth of the empire was amenable to rational explanation. Nor was it the work of Carlyle's

---

[202] Collier, *History of the British Empire*, 153.
[203] By the 13th edition in 1888 this feature had been dropped.
[204] Colley, *Britons*, 102; Louis, "Introduction," 3–5.
[205] Peter Burroughs, "John Robert Seeley and British Imperial History," *Journal of Imperial and Commonwealth History* 1, no. 2 (January 1973): 193–94; Louis, "Introduction," 7–10.
[206] John Gross, "Editor's Introduction," in J. R. Seeley, *The Expansion of England* (Chicago: University of Chicago Press, 1971), xv.

heroes. India had been conquered by ordinary men because of the decay of the Mughal emperors, the use of Indian troops, and the divisions in Indian society which lacked a sense of nationhood.[207]

Seeley was far from being a cold rationalist, however. He thought the problem with the Whig approach was that it suggested that English history had ended because liberty had been achieved and that it placed too much emphasis upon freedom of the individual and too little on the security of the state. His work was a sudden inspiration and clearly informed by the growing international rivalry of the 1880s. He, in turn, inspired ideas of imperial federation and clearly saw both destiny and strength in the growth of the dominions. India was much more problematic for him. History had to end with a moral. Empire provided this. Since the seventeenth century, the key theme was the growth of empire. England had become "Greater Britain," in the title of Charles Dilke's political travelogue which had clearly been one of his inspirations.[208]

Seeley ultimately inspired the development of imperial history as a university subject. By the First World War there were three chairs of the subject in the "golden triangle" of London, Oxford, and Cambridge and aspirations to create them in every university.[209] Yet such an aim remained unfulfilled and imperial history still struggled for legitimacy and attention. Seeley's work was warmly received but his biographer surmises that he would have been disappointed with the quality of the response to it. His approach to the study of history—and what concerns us here, his attempt to change the object of study—was generally disregarded for the political implications of his work.[210] The standard work on the development of history as a university discipline in the late nineteenth and early twentieth centuries has no index entry for empire or imperial history and a mere four pages on imperialism.[211] Seeley's work was a kind of manifesto and his own more substantive research to develop it was incomplete at his death in 1895, though a version was published posthumously. He published some articles but the process was hindered by the onset of health problems from 1890.[212]

It was left to others to develop Seeley's legacy. In 1897 Hugh Edward Egerton published his *A Short History of British Colonial Policy*, and still felt that he had to justify his subject in the preface. He imagined an objector saying there was no such thing as imperial policy and that "Great Britain has merely blundered into the best places

---

[207] Gross, "Editor's Introduction," xi–xv.

[208] Burroughs, "John Robert Seeley," 191–96; Gross, "Editor's Introduction," xiv–xvii.

[209] The Beit Chair of Colonial History was established at Oxford in 1905. The Rhodes Chair of Imperial History in London in 1919 and the Vere Harmsworth Chair of Naval History at Cambridge (also 1919) became a chair of Imperial and Naval History in 1933. David Fieldhouse, "Can Humpty Dumpty be Put Back Together Again? Imperial History in the 1980s," *Journal of Imperial and Commonwealth History* 12, no. 2 (January 1984): 9.

[210] Deborah Wormell, *Sir John Seeley and the Political Uses of History* (Cambridge: Cambridge University Press, 1980), 98–99.

[211] Reba N. Soffer, *Discipline and Power: The University, History and the Making of the English Elite, 1870–1930* (Stanford: Stanford University Press, 1994).

[212] Wormell, *Sir John Seeley*, 99–107.

of the earth and means to keep them." However, he argued that there were "forces at work fitting events, apparently fortuitous, into the scheme of a mighty system."[213] Elsewhere he gave a thumbnail sketch of his views: "It seems to be a law of life that, when a nation has reached a certain stage of internal development, it finds in overseas expansion a natural and healthy outlet for its superabundant energies."[214] Egerton offered an overview of the process which, as this cameo suggested, was developmental. The origins of the subject in the seventeenth century were dominated by the search for an appropriate constitutional form for English overseas colonies developed by trading companies. A new phase began with the passing of the Navigation Act of 1651, which ensured that colonies were run for the benefit of the mother country, but with this tempered by kind treatment. Free trade undercut this policy of monopoly from the late eighteenth century and raised the issue of whether colonies were of any use. But this was quickly countered by the systematic colonization schemes of Edward Gibbon Wakefield, though the lack of any possibility of close control from London meant that the end result of this was likely to be self government. But the advent of "democracy" from the 1860s meant there was a constituency for the empire which was receptive to their democratic constitutions. This coincided with the resurgence of militarism and protectionism in Europe, which raised the possibility of an imperial economic union in which the one side supplied raw materials and the other manufactured goods. There was therefore an explicable pattern of British colonial policy, not random responses to events, which fitted into a wider international history and ended with "Greater Britain."[215] This was Egerton's answer to those who saw only formlessness. He could not only trace a pattern but assert an answer to the doubters: "behind the mistakes and failures of individuals and generations, there grows upon us as we study the history, the sense of an unseen superintending Providence controlling the development of the Anglo-Saxon race. Through the vistas of the ages the voice is heard, 'Be fruitful and multiply, and replenish the earth.'"[216]

Egerton provided what has been described as a whole-hearted and quasi-religious commitment to the imperial credo which was alien to Seeley.[217] Egerton became the first Beit professor at Oxford in 1905 and thereafter devoted much of his attention to teaching and promotion of the subject. But, despite this and his providential views, his approach failed to carry the conviction and popular resonance of English history. In the run up to the First World War promoters of imperial history had to counter the view that the real story was domestic history and the empire was merely a sub-field of

---

[213] Egerton, *Short History*, viii.

[214] H. E. Egerton, *Is the British Empire the Result of Wholesale Robbery?* (Oxford Pamphlets, 1914), 3–4.

[215] Egerton, *Short History*, 1–7.

[216] Egerton, *Short History*, 525.

[217] J. G. Greenlee, "'A Succession of Seeleys' The 'Old School' re-Examined," *Journal of Imperial and Commonwelath History* 4, no. 3 (May 1976): 267–68.

the "real" story.[218] As late as 1937 Eric Walker felt the need to defend the subject, in a way no historian would have been compelled to defend English history, in his inaugural lecture at Cambridge. Its detractors felt it was dull and lacking in human interest. He argued that as a *Volkswanderung* the story did not lack human interest and also had coherence and continuity. But he looked forward to a time when imperial and national history could be effectively integrated. Clearly the development of imperial history had not achieved this goal—it remained an aspiration: "Some day perhaps, a history will be written which will show the interaction of the different parts of this world empire, an interaction which has long been more significant than the history of any one part, even, I would respectfully submit, than that of the United Kingdom standing by itself alone."[219]

Part of the problem was in the sheer variety of the British Empire. The author of a history published in 1921 saw the need to divide the volume into separate sections on the dominions and the dependent empire for the nineteenth century. Clearly it was difficult to tell a story of the inevitable development of responsible government in the one while keeping a narrative of autocratic government in the other going even if the object was to "tell the story as a whole."[220] The rather nebulous concept of growth could be used to square the circle. The empire was "a growth with all the diversity that comes from growth, and the more it grows, the more it differs from the thing from which it grew ... We are concerned with the slow addition and replacement of particles, with sometimes here a lopping of a branch and there the pruning of a twig."[221]

Despite these advances the whole subject of colonial history remained rather undeveloped in Britain. Apart from English history the most developed areas were modern Germany and France and the ancient world: when Reginald Coupland was asked by the Clarendon Press in 1916 to suggest authors for histories of colonies and colonial development, he replied that "[t]he whole subject of Colonial History has been so much neglected that very few people in this country would be qualified to write."[222] He suggested that colonial universities might provide the best recruiting areas for the press. What was lacking, especially, was the new "scientific" and rigorous history which Seeley advocated. Many well-known English historians were interested in empire and imperial federation but this was usually a matter of politics and almost travel writing rather than of academic analysis.[223] Froude's *Oceana* looked back to Macaulay and Carlyle, rather than to the modern academic writers. Civil servants and journalists often published much of the colonial history which existed. The Historical

---

[218] Greenlee, "Succession of Seeleys," 269–76.

[219] Eric A. Walker, *The Study of British Imperial History: An Inaugural Lecture* (Cambridge: Cambridge University Press, 1937), 22.

[220] C. S. S. Higham, *History of the British Empire* (London: Longman, 1921), 127–28.

[221] J. Fairgrieve and Ernest Young, *The Growth of Greater Britain* (London: George Philip, 1924), 1.

[222] Leslie Howsam, "Imperial Publishers and the Idea of Colonial History," *History of Intellectual Culture* 5, no. 1 (2005): 1–15.

[223] Robert J. C. Young, *The Idea of English Ethnicity* (Oxford: Blackwell, 2008), ch. 7.

Geography of the Colonies which Charles Prestwood Lucas offered to edit was seen as a commentary on contemporary history rather than as serious history. Many publishers and their readers were hostile to colonial history—colonies were seen as having no history before the process of colonization and subsequent events were seen as being too few and brief to interest metropolitan audiences.[224] Assuming they knew their readers, this surely tells us something about the depth and width of interest in the empire in general.

Geographers could sometimes offer a more coherent approach. Indeed, the geologist Sir Roderick Murchison (1792–1871) could make the story messianic: "He was convinced that Britain's greatness as an industrial power had been predestined because her rocks contained abundant supplies of coal and iron ore. Here geology and geography combined to promote the image of Britain's imperial greatness."[225] Two geographers found the logic of the empire not in historical development but in the pattern of trade: "The British Empire ... is scattered all over the world, and the separate pieces are united mainly by sea routes, the safety of which depends upon the British Navy ... it has been necessary to control, for various purposes, a certain number of quite small areas, most of which are peninsulas, and therefore quite easily accessible to ships."[226]

But most historians seemed to despair of any simple story. For Basil Williams it was "an abnormal and incongruous entity ... difficult to describe ... It has never been the same from century to century ... either in extent or constitutional character."[227] Again there was some sense of growth or at least of vitality. A full description (dissection?) would only be possible if the subject were dead. The Indian Empire was founded "almost by chance." But fortunately for Williams the British nation woke up before it was too late to its responsibility for this romantic heritage, and therefore became as truly master of India's destiny as of its own. Like Egerton, he concluded that there were stages in the process of development of empire.[228] Ultimately he drew the full conclusion which the geographers had hinted only upon. The empire was "distributed round the world along the world's main trade routes," he wrote, "in a way that could hardly have been improved upon had some great schemer originally plotted out the whole design."[229]

A providential view might provide the great schemer. Williams merely suggested an inner logic. Imperial history received the imprimatur of a Cambridge history in due course. It is doubtful if this helped unify the subject or integrate it with the domestic story. For one thing it was an extremely protracted process of publication. The first volume appeared in 1929 and it was completed with the eighth volume in 1959, a

---

[224] Howsam, "Imperial Publishers," *passim*.

[225] Peter J. Bowler, *The Fontana History of the Environmental Sciences* (London: Fontana, 1992), 220.

[226] Fairgrieve and Young, *Greater Britain*, 180.

[227] Basil Williams, *The British Empire* (London: Thornton Butterworth, 1928), 175.

[228] Williams, *British Empire*, 7, 84, 123.

[229] Williams, *British Empire*, 181.

total of thirty years which spanned one of the decisive events of the twentieth century, though most of the volumes appeared within a decade of the first volumes. Only the first volume had a chapter which was redolent of social history and this presumably reflected a period when the empire lacked the diversity of its later incarnations. The volumes often had distinct geographical foci with India getting two volumes and Canada, South Africa, and Australia and New Zealand one each.[230]

Imperial history suffered because it was crowded out by the compelling public place of English history. The same fate awaited the histories of the rest of the United Kingdom. English history was like the Upas Tree of Java which, according to legend poisons and blights all other growth within fifteen miles.[231] Scottish historians struggled to break free of its influence. Ironically the prowess of Scottish writers in creating more general historical approaches had left little space for the story of the Scottish nation.[232] Only in the later nineteenth century did history become a serious concern of the universities with chairs being established in the 1870s—though here they emphasized Stubbsian English history.[233] Pressure from many directions, stressing equality for Scotland, led to the establishment of chairs of Scottish history at Edinburgh in 1901 and Glasgow in 1913. University scholarship rejected and challenged the popular and romantic myths of the past but remained solid rather than inspirational. The subject remained marginalized within the universities with only small student numbers and often obstructed by the general history departments.[234] Much the same was true of the history of Wales. In a state-centered historiography it was hard to engage with the history of Wales after the defeat of the native princes. History became established as a university subject in the late nineteenth century, usually on Oxbridge models but with some reference to the early history of Wales which had been put on secure foundations

---

[230] J. Holland Rose, A. P. Newton, and E. A. Benians, eds., *The Cambridge History of the British Empire*, 8 Vols. (1929–59). By the final (published not chronological) volume in 1959 Benians (by then deceased), Sir James Butler and C. E. Carrington were series editors. Each volume had individual editors as well. Volumes I and VI appeared in 1929; Volume VI in 1930; Volume V in 1932; Volume VII (2 parts) in 1933; Volume VIII in 1936; Volume II in 1940, and Vol. III in 1959. The Australian and New Zealand volumes were separately published parts of Vol. VII; hence there were effectively nine volumes.

[231] S. G. Checkland, *The Upas Tree: Glasgow, 1875–1975—and after, 1975–80* (Glasgow: Glasgow University Press, 1981).

[232] W. Ferguson, *Scotland, 1689 to the Present* (Edinburgh: Oliver & Boyd, 1968), 210–14; Marinell Ash, *The Strange Death of Scottish History* (Edinburgh: Ramsey Head Press, 1980); Murray G. Pittock, "Enlightenment Historiography and its Legacy: Plurality, Authority and Power," in *History, Nationhood and the Question of Britain*, eds. Helen Brocklehurst and Robert Phillips (London: Palgrave Macmillan, 2004), 33–44; Colin Kidd, "*The Strange Death of Scottish History* Revisited: Constructions of the Past in Scotland, c.1790–1914," *Scottish Historical Review* 76, no. 2001 (April 1997): 86–102.

[233] Lenman, "Teaching of Scottish History," 173–76; J. H. Burns "Stands Scotland Where it Did?," *History* 70 (1985): 46.

[234] Donaldson, *Scottish History*, 4; Burns, "Stands Scotland Where it Did?"

by the work of John Edward Lloyd. He emphasized that it was early history which really formed a nation.[235]

Ireland was somewhat different. J. A. Froude produced work on Irish history which contrasted the fecklessness of the Irish with the polished performance of their conquerors. It was explicitly unionist in intent and his work appeared against a background of Gladstone's land bill, Fenianism, and Disestablishment. Froude was an imperialist who claimed to love the Irish but not their faults which he enumerated as priests, superstition, demagoguery, cowardice, idleness, and unruliness. It might be wondered if there was, in fact, anything left to love! Froude referred to the English as "the nobler and wiser set of men" and had a clear sense of racial superiority. A modern scholar has found it to be a foretaste of English imperialism "in its more extreme and repulsive forms" and that "the Irish were simply the whiteman's burden nearer home." This clearly integrated Irish historiography with the empire but in ways most Irish people would reject.[236]

Froude was answered by the work of William E. H. Lecky, (1838–1903) also based in the archives and also unionist in intent but less concerned to libel the Irish. Donal McCarthy describes his response as cool, and he exposed the one-sidedness of Froude's sources. Nationalists seized upon this as they had upon Froude and ransacked them for evidence of harsh treatment of the Irish to use in the cause of home rule. For Froude *all* the Irish shared the qualities he abhorred; for Lecky the Irish gentry were exempt and showed admirable qualities.[237]

Scholars of a nationalist persuasion began to write histories of Ireland, sometimes using Gaelic sources, which offered an alternative reading of the past. But the widely read writers of the late nineteenth century were nationalists like Alice Stopford. Her title—*The Making of Ireland and its Undoing* (1908)—made her point succinctly.[238]

Historiography provided a patchwork account of the empire. Separate national histories characterized the United Kingdom and there was no clear connection between imperial history and the multiple domestic histories. The empire was more easily imagined in space than in time.

---

[235] Huw Pryce, "From the Neolithic to Nonconformity: J. E. Lloyd and the *History of Caernarfonshire*," *Transactions of the Caernarvonshire Historical Society* 66 (2005): 14–37.

[236] A. F. Pollard and William Thomas, "Froude, James, Anthony, (1818–1894)," *Oxford Dictionary of National Biography* http://www.oxforddnb.com/view/article/10202 (accessed on December 3, 2008); Donal McCartney, "James Anthony Froude and Ireland: A Historiographical Controversy of the Nineteenth Century," in *Historical Studies* 8, ed. T. Desmond Williams (Dublin 1971): 171–90, quotations 187; Anne Wyatt, "Froude, Lecky and the Humblest Irishman," *Irish Historical Studies* 19, no. 75 (March 1975): 261–85.

[237] McCartney, "James Anthony Froude," 179–82; Donal McCartney, "Lecky's *Leaders of Public Opinion in Ireland*," *Irish Historical Studies* 14, no. 54 (September 1964): 119–14. Joseph Spence, "Lecky, (William) Edward Hartpole, (1838–1903), Historian," *Oxford Dictionary of National Biography* http://www.oxforddnb.com/view/article/34461 (accessed on December 3, 2008).

[238] "Alice Stoppford Green," (1847–1929)' in *The Oxford Companion to Irish History*, ed. Sean Connolly (Oxford: Oxford University Press, 1998), 240.

Conclusion

How might Britain and its empire have been better integrated and transformed in the late nineteenth century? Any scheme to do so faced at least two major and perhaps insuperable obstacles: the diversity of the empire and the deeply rooted, constantly reproduced, sense of English identity, institutions, and history. As the empire became more diverse over the course of the long nineteenth century and the numerical dominance of the English over the United Kingdom increased, the problems confronting any project for an integrated empire intensified.

To integrate the whole empire would have required a color blindness which it would be quite unhistorical to seek in the period. Racial hierarchy was a mainstay of empire, even if it was bolstered and sometimes challenged by class.[239] The survival of the empire required at least a softening of racial edges. The slave trade and then slavery itself were abolished in the early nineteenth century. Humanitarians concerned with these issues also turned to the protection of native rights, while some of the conquest of India could be justified as the protection of the human rights of the indigenous peoples through the suppression of customs like *suttee*. All of these concerns rested on some fundamental sense of human equality and uniformity. But could an empire be run on such lines? It required at least the fiction that this was the case. One by-product of the imperial census were statistics of the balance of races in British territories across the globe. Roughly this was 400 million black people to 50 million white, figures which were printed in *Encyclopaedia Britannica* in 1911, and quickly used as ammunition by black politicians claiming their rights as British subjects. So justice and fairness had to be claimed for the empire.

However the most plausible ideas of imperial integration operated on the opposite principle of some kind of racial unity founded on the expansion of the Anglo-Saxons across the globe. Its danger—if it had succeeded—was that it would create a kind of *Kleindeutsch* empire. Settler colonies were often the sites of the deepest fault lines of racial cleavage, with genocidal histories and an obsession with racial segregation and hierarchy. This often meant the exclusion of the other great nineteenth century diaspora, that of Asians across the globe, from their territories. The tighter political bonds envisaged between white people in schemes of imperial federation would be difficult (to say the least) to reconcile with the fictions of equality required to rule over black peoples. More than that, imperial federation would have required a challenge to the tradition of undivided parliamentary sovereignty which were so important in Westminster and Whitehall. Ultimately it posed problems for the core which could not be met. The problems were exacerbated by the changing nature of the British core state in the long nineteenth century. The distinct identities and to a lesser extent polities of Scotland and Wales posed no real challenge to Britain, but this was not true of

---

[239] Cannadine, *Ornamentalism*, passim.

Ireland. It was throughout the period subject to a quasi-colonial administration which was unacceptable to many. If its landlords, soldiers, and missionaries were enthusiasts for empire many of its nationalists (certainly the republican fringe) were not. There were significant numbers of committed anti-imperialists as they showed in anti-monarchist demonstrations and even in raising forces to fight with the Boers. A line of division over empire ran through Ireland. This was entirely appropriate given the entanglement of the Irish Question in empire. The most ferocious opposition came from those who saw it as the first domino to fall in an effect which would spread through the whole of the empire.

Federalism might have been a solution to this but as with imperial federation it ran up against the brick wall of parliamentary sovereignty and the numerical dominance of England at the core of the UK. This made federalism virtually impossible unless it were combined with regionalism in England, a polity which had been more-or-less united and centralized since the tenth century.

None of these issues were resolved by 1914. As the First World War broke out, Ireland seemed to be on the verge of civil war over home rule. As we have seen the empire rallied to the cause but at the end of hostilities much of it was riven by crisis and conflict, particularly nationalist revolt. Ireland's revolution led to dominion status for the 26 counties and home rule for Northern Ireland, a truncated six county version of the historic nine counties of Ulster.

Britain presented a vision of racial equality in some aspects of its empire—a mother country to which subjects were free to travel and would remain so until 1962. There could be no official and pan-empire version of the segregation and racial hierarchy of the dominions or of individual colonies. As a small example, the British state appeased the racist demands of merchant seamen for privileged or exclusive access to jobs in the shipping industry by winking at the fiction that most of the black sailors were not British subjects. The latter could not be subject to discrimination. *Alien* colored seamen were a different matter.[240]

There was no imperial federation but a continuing reliance on fraternal bonds which were compatible with dominion nationalism. Richard Jebb, the Du Bois of the master class, had seen settlers as having roots in two soils and tight and formal integration which have involved uprooting from one of them.[241] Imperial federation had its practical impact on the world not in the empire but as a model and inspiration for

---

[240] Neil Evans, "Across the Universe: Racial Conflict and the Post-War Crisis in Imperial Britain, 1919–1925," *Immigrants and Minorities* 13, no. 2 & 3 (July–October 1994): 59–88; and Neil Evans, "Regulating the Reserve Army: Arabs, Blacks and the Local State in Cardiff, 1919–1945," *Immigrants and Minorities* 4, no. 2 (July 1985): 68–115.

[241] Cf. W. E. B. Du Bois, *The Souls of Black Folks* (1903) available at: http://etext.lib.virginia.edu/toc/modeng/public/DubSoul.html. Du Bois stresses the dual African and American heritage of American blacks. See also Richard Hofstadter, *The American Political Tradition and the Men who Made It* (London: Jonathan Cape, 1962), ch. 4: "John C. Calhoun: The Marx of the Master Class."

the League of Nations.[242] Tariff reform, proclaimed by the Tories in the 1923 election, proved to be a means of returning a minority Labour government committed to free trade. Only in the 1930s did some of these ideas bear fruit. The Ottawa Conference of 1932 produced a limited kind of imperial preference while Bebb is now often seen as the person who most closely envisaged the form of Commonwealth which emerged.

The British state—or at least its representative system and administration—was not transformed by empire. It proved extremely resilient, partly reflecting its ancient English origins. But empire had a profound effects on civil society in the long nineteenth century. The British economy was deeply and ever more closely imbricated with imperial markets in the period. Less directly this influenced the distribution of population and provided something of a safety valve for the social tensions on an industrial society. Empire provided a clear reason for the non-English peoples of the British Isles to remain in the United Kingdom. Diversity and multiple tensions made the flexibility of an unwritten constitution attractive to most politicians. The bonds of empire were resistant to strenuous tightening, but they still did much to shape the British state and polity.

---

[242] Mark Mazower, *No Enchanted Palace: The End of Empire and the Ideological Origins of the United Nations* (Princeton: Princeton University Press, 2009).

The First Napoleonic Empire, 1799–1815

Michael Broers

Napoleonic history was once seen only in terms of the "great man" and his deeds, and those deeds were, almost entirely, military and diplomatic. His shadow, whether for good or ill, sweep across Europe—"the trail of the comet" was a recurring metaphor for the Napoleonic period—and that was that. The legacy of the years 1799–1814 was centered on the man and his legend. When historians ventured into this period on any other errand than the military, biographical, or diplomatic, it was either in the spirit of French nationalism writ large, or with something close to a sense of shame. The former attitude is encapsulated in the very title of Jacques Godechot's classic study of expansion under the Directory, *La Grande Nation*, which almost says it all.[1] Historians of the non-French parts of the Empire too often equated the period of Napoleonic hegemony with collaboration and national defeat. Most of these scholars were too professional to identify their interpretations directly with the Nazi occupations of the 1940s, but their sensitivities were obviously influenced by the climate of their times. Something of this tradition survives in more sophisticated form. For those who interpreted the empire in a purely nationalist context, the former assessment is still a powerful current in military and diplomatic history, as in Paul W. Schroeder's *The Transformation of European Politics*, and has, perhaps, found a postmodernist exponent in David Bell's *The First Total War*. Both are powerful works, rooted in diplomatic and military concerns, which see the essence of the Napoleonic experience as a negative dynamic.[2] Nevertheless, the winds of change have blown through Napoleonic history, with considerable force.

---

[1] J. Godechot, *La Grande Nation*, 2 vols. (Paris: Aubier Montaigne, 1956).
[2] P. W. Schroeder, *The Transformation of European Politics, 1763–1848* (Oxford: Oxford University Press, 1994); D. Bell, *The First Total War: Napoleon's Europe and the Birth of Warfare as We*

The study of the First Napoleonic Empire has undergone a renaissance in the last quarter of a century. It was galvanized by the appearance of Stuart Woolf's *Napoleon's Integration of Europe* in 1991.[3] The very title indicates that a major part of the revival of Napoleonic period history centered on the imperial character of Napoleon's empire, in that its nature could no longer simply be described as an extension of France: For Woolf and the majority of scholars who have followed his lead, Napoleon's domination of Europe marks a seminal period in the development of the modern history of the continent precisely because it bore signs of being an imperialist project. There is a growing sense that there was more than crude military expansion and material exploitation to Napoleonic rule beyond France, nor was such rule a mere extension of France. Although the new Napoleonic historiography launched by Woolf, and driven forward by so many others, is now central to Napoleonic studies, it does not stand alone or remain without its detractors, just as it is not without its internal divisions.

Woolf's decisive break with the dominant historiography was driven by the need he perceived to redirect the emphasis from "the man" to his system and the support it received from the bureaucrats and local elites needed to run the imperial edifice, together with a determination to locate the importance of Napoleonic expansion in a truly European context beyond France. It is significant that most of the literature influenced by Woolf's emphasis on European integration as the essence of the Napoleonic Empire has come from outside France, and concerns itself with the non-French parts of the empire. Studies of the German, Italian, Dutch, and Spanish elements of the empire now abound,[4] where once the histories of these regions under foreign domination were regarded as too problematic to explore in depth largely through potential analogies with the Third Reich. Increasingly, it is the history of

Know It (Boston: Houghton Miffin, 2007). This is also evident in the work of Charles Esdaile, put most emphatically in Charles Esdaile, "Popular Resistance in Napoleonic Europe: Issues and Perspectives," in *Popular Resistance in the French Wars*, ed. Charles Esdaile (Basingstoke: Palgrave, 2005), 201–21.

3 S. J. Woolf, *Napoleon's Integration of Europe* (London: Routledge, 1991).

4 The literature is vast. An important collection of specialist articles is: P. Dwyer, ed., *Napoleon and Europe* (London: Longman, 2001). Among the major regional studies: M. Rowe, *Reich to State: the Rhineland in the Revolutionary Age, 1780–1830* (Cambridge: Cambridge University Press, 2003); J. Davis, *Napoleon and Naples, Southern Italy and the European Revolutions, 1780–1860* (Oxford: Oxford University Press, 2006); M. Broers, *Napoleonic Imperialism and the Savoyard Monarchy, 1773–1821* (Lampeter: Edwin Mellen Press, 1997); U. Planert, *Der Mythos vom Befreiungskriege: Frankreichs Kriege und der deutsche Süden: Altag, Wahrehmung, Deutung, 1792–1841* (Paderborn: Schöningh, 2007); J. M. Lafon, *L'Adalouise et Napoléon. Contre-insurrection, collaboration et resistances dans le midi de l'Espagne (1808–1812)* (Paris: Nouveau monde, 2007); J. Joor, *De adelaar en het lam: onrust, opruiing en onwilligheid in Nederland ten tijde van het Koninkrijk Holland en de inlijving bij het Franse keizerrijk (1806–1813)* (Amsterdam: Bataafsche, 2000).

Napoleonic France in this period that now suffers from comparative neglect.[5] Whereas general studies written just before or soon after Woolf—in English, notably Martin Lyons' *Napoleon Bonaparte and the Legacy of the French Revolution*[6]—could content themselves with a solitary chapter on non-French lands, almost all subsequent English-language surveys, to say nothing of the seminal work of the Dutch-based French scholar, Annie Jourdan, actually center themselves on the empire, rather than France.[7] The shift from the "supra-national" to the genuinely European and imperial has been emphatic at every level of historiography, and seems set to continue.[8]

Nevertheless, with change comes complexity. Woolf's original thrust was to underpin and explore the origins of the states that succeeded the Napoleonic Empire, to examine the roots of the institutional ethos of the European nation-state that came to dominate the post-Napoleonic world. This is reflected in the important collection of essays edited by Lucy Riall and David Laven in 1997 and by the general tenor of Alex Grab's recent survey of the period.[9] The initial impact of Woolf's thesis was, essentially, Eurocentric and he quickly retreated from his own attempt to broaden it, after the criticisms of Geoffrey Ellis, since re-enforced by Alex Grab.[10] This has not prevented a "second wave" of the development of the new Napoleonic historiography, however, and it has two cardinal aspects: The first is to set the First Napoleonic

---

[5] Much of the recent work on Napoleonic France concentrates on the earliest period: I. Woloch, *Napoleon and his Collaborators: The Making of a Dictatorship* (New York: Norton, 2001); M. Crook, *Napoleon Comes to Power: Dictatorship and Democracy in Revolutionary France, 1795–1804* (London: Longman, 1998); H. Brown, *Ending the French Revolution: Violence, Justice and Repression from the Terror to Napoleon* (Charlottesville: University of Virginia Press, 2006). Almost unique are I. Woloch, *The New Regime. Transformations of the French Civic Order, 1789–1820s* (New York: Norton, 1994) and T. Lentz, *Nouvelle Histoire du Premier Empire*, vol. III, and *La France et l'Europe de Napoléon 1804–1814* (Paris: Fayard, 2007), the former for taking the history of institutions, widely defined, through the whole period, the latter for concentrating on the later years of the period.

[6] M. Lyons, *Napoleon Bonaparte and the Legacy of the French Revolution* (London: Macmillan, 1994).

[7] A. Jourdan, *L'Empire de Napoléon* (Paris: Aubier, 2000); A. Grab, *Napoleon's Transformation of Europe* (Basingstoke: Palgrave, 2003); C. J. Esdaile, *The Wars of Napoleon* (London: Longman, 1995); M. Broers, *Europe Under Napoleon* (London: Arnold, 1996). T. Lentz, *Nouvelle Histoire*.

[8] For example: M. Broers, A. Guimera, and Peter Hicks, eds., *El imperio napoleónico y la nueva cultura politica europea* (Madrid: Centro de Estudios Politicos y Constitucionales, 2010).

[9] D. Laven and L. Riall, eds., *Napoleon's Legacy: Problems of Government in Restoration Europe* (Oxford: Berg, 2000).

[10] For Woolf's original position: S. J. Woolf, "French civilization and ethnicity in the Napoleonic Empire," *Past & Present* 124 (January 1989): 96–120. For the clearest expression of Ellis' critique: G. Ellis, "The nature of Napoleonic Imperialism," in Dwyer, *Napoleon and Europe*, 97–117. For Woolf's reassessment of his initial position: S. J. Woolf, "Napoleon and Europe Revisited," *Modern and Contemporary France* 8 (April 2000): 69–478. Grab's direct refutation of the importance of the "civilizing mission" is: A. Grab, "Napoleon: A Civilizing Missionary or a Pragmatic Imperialist?" in *Consortium on Revolutionary Europe, 1750–1850: Selected papers 2007*, eds. F. Schneid, and J. Censer (High Point NC: High Point University, 2008), 238–49.

Empire in the wider context of European imperialism, and particularly in that of the colonial empires of the later nineteenth century, to examine it as something of a nursery—a testing ground—for extra-European experiences. This potential was indicated by Victor Kiernan as early as 1969, when he wrote with almost nonchalance that "French imperialism even in its earlier career inside Europe had two aspects, the arrogance as well as the enlightenment of the Great Nation."[11] Woolf's hasty retreat from Ellis' critique has shown just how controversial this course is, but the increasing acceptance of the importance of Napoleonic rule for the wider course of European history has led to its reassessment in the equally revivified context of "Atlantic history," led by Annie Jourdan. Jourdan argues that the emergence of a new wealth of local studies now enables scholarship to accomplish what R. R. Palmer and Jacques Godechot attempted—probably prematurely—in the late 1960s, to produce a truly "western" history of the revolutionary epoch.[12] Jourdan, interestingly, centers the argument for this as much on the Napoleonic period as on the 1790s. That is, as much on the influence of overtly imperial expansion and reform, as on the spread and attempted adaptation of revolutionary ideology.

All this leads, almost inexorably, towards the second, and probably seminal, element of the second wave of post-Woolf Napoleonic studies: For the Napoleonic Empire to have influenced either the character of later European imperialism or the subsequent history of Europe, that empire had to have a "project," a determined program of reform—ideological intent, if not necessarily a dogmatic ideology—to drive it. Ideology is intrinsic to imperialism, if not to empire, as such. Even to sustain Woolf's original, purely European, proto-national thesis, the very character—not just the later ramifications—of Napoleonic rule had to have a purpose from its outset in a given region, which reached beyond pragmatic control or naked exploitation. Ellis and Grab pose qualifications to this, insisting on the opportunist nature of Napoleonic expansion and the pragmatic approach to the occupied territories they see as the Napoleonic norm. In this optic, the Napoleonic Empire was simply "empire" bereft of imperialism. "Pragmatic traditionalism"—or the tradition of pragmatism—retains its power in the manner in which the empire was created and defended; the "imperialist" ideological approach finds its power in the manner in which the French and their sympathizers attempted to govern that empire.

[11] V. Kiernan, *The Lords of Human Kind: European Attitudes to Other Cultures in the Imperial Age* (London: Serif, 1969), 96. The term "the great nation" refers to Jacques Godechot's *La Grande Nation*.
[12] R. R. Palmer, *The Age of the Democratic Revolutions*, 2 vols. (Princeton: Princeton University Press, 1959). J. Godechot, *France and the Atlantic Revolution of the Eighteenth Century, 1770–1799* trans. Herbert H. Rown (London: Collier-Macmillan, 1971).

The Origins and Growth of Napoleonic Europe

The French revolutionaries did, indeed, do something truly revolutionary—they invented a new form of international relations. They declared that France was possessed of "natural frontiers"—the Atlantic Ocean, the Mediterranean Sea, the Alps, the Pyrenees, and the Rhine—but this was a minor matter. *Ancien régime* diplomats had long thought in such terms, but this had been a matter for negotiation with other powers.[13] Under the new regime, however, it became a matter for assertion and aggressive action. In February, 1793, Danton only told the National Convention what its predecessor, the Legislative Assembly had already proclaimed as grounds for war almost two years earlier, when at the height of the war he thundered: "The boundaries of France are marked by Nature. We shall reach them..."[14] Following the peaceful absorption of Savoy, Nice and Avignon in 1790, the Rhine was the only one yet to be achieved. It was enough, however, for to do so entailed war with the Holy Roman Empire. When the revolutionary—not yet even republican—France set its own frontiers, clearly defined, it also fixed the point when, by its own definition, it would change from a nation-state into an empire. Conversely, when it fixed those frontiers as lying along natural boundaries which were not, in 1791, within its traditional borders, it became an aggressive, aspiring imperial power in the eyes of the rest of Europe. Either way, the declaration of France's rights to its "natural frontiers" drew emphatic lines of definition, as well of international conflict, long before Napoleon came to power. On November 19, 1792, now as a republic at war, the revolutionaries issued the famous "Edict of Fraternity" by which the French nation "grants fraternity and assistance to all peoples desiring the recovery of their liberty." They had invented the "war of liberation," and with it, a proto-Trotskyite form of hegemonic expansion. This ideologically-driven expansionism came and went before 1814. It would soon sour into disillusion under the Directory (1795–99), a period when the French could tell Irish revolutionaries that their liberation would depend on their own ability to generate a revolution,[15] while they forced all extra-French regions they did succeed in "liberating"—the Low Countries, Germany west of the Rhine, most of northern and central Italy—to pay for their liberation by quartering and supplying the French armies. When, by 1797, the French had marched to the Rhine and secured this last "natural frontier"—at least until 1814—they had become an empire to the rest of Europe. When they first stepped beyond it, with the annexation of Piedmont in 1802, they became an empire by their own rights, even if Napoleon still called himself First Consul and his regime the Republic. From the outset, the French liberators were met with

---

[13] See for example, P. Sahlins, *Boundaries: The Making of France and Spain in the Pyrenees* (Berkeley: University of California Press, 1989).

[14] Cited in Sahlins, *Boundaries*, 186–87.

[15] M. Elliott, *Partners in Revolution: The United Irishmen and France* (New Haven: Yale University Press, 1982).

more resistance than collaboration, culminating in the massive peasant revolts of 1798 in Belgium and 1799 in Italy, in tandem with a successful Allied counter-offensive that threw the French back beyond the Rhine and the Alps for the first time since 1793. Thus, Napoleon seized power in 1799 when even expansion to the "natural frontiers" seemed in danger of reversal and when the concept of hegemony through liberation was at its lowest ebb. Ideologically colored or not, territorial expansionism was reborn with a vengeance as soon as Napoleon resumed the war late in 1799.

However much subsequent phases of Napoleonic expansion were driven by war, the period from 1800–05 that followed the successful military campaigns in Italy, Switzerland, the Low Countries, and Germany saw only one case of direct annexation—that of Piedmont—beyond the "natural frontiers." Napoleon's chief objectives at the Peace of Amiens in 1801 were the recovery of those frontiers and recognition of this by the other powers. Nevertheless, these years were seminal for both the character of the regime—they mark the point in time when the "Napoleonic model" of the modern state was forged within the natural frontiers—and for the geographic direction subsequent imperial expansion would take.

Napoleon's first exercises in imperialism actually ended in failure and retreat, and led to a complete reorienting of French expansionist aims. He quickly abandoned most of the residues of the *ancien régime's* North American territories, one willingly—the Louisiana territory sold to the United States for a derisory sum in 1803—and the other, Saint Domingue, now Haiti, after a brutal, costly, and futile struggle to retake it from a successful slave revolt led by Toussaint l'Ouverture, which ended with the repulsion of a French army in 1804. In the meantime, Napoleon turned French ambitions firmly towards expansion within Europe.

The expansion of French power into Europe in this period was characterized by indirect if powerful influence over a power vacuum of small, weak states in western and southern Germany, as well as Italy. Such expansion culminated in the dissolution of the Holy Roman Empire in 1804 not by Napoleon, but by its own sovereign, Francis II of the House of Habsburg, so fearful had he become of French influence among the German princes in the intervening years. This relative "soft power" Napoleon achieved over the middle states of Germany—the *Mittelstaaten*—proved far more lasting and important, if less resounding, than his post-1805 conquests, which were won by purely military successes. This represents a period of expansion by hegemony rather than expansion by annexation or the creation of satellite kingdoms—the successors of the "sister republics"—that marked his later period. In Germany, Napoleon chose to work with and through the established rulers, turning them away from, and ultimately against, the House of Habsburg. It was a complex diplomatic process, but by offering to guarantee the German princes his support should Francis oppose them, Napoleon not only changed the balance of power in Germany, but did so to allow the princes of the middle-sized states—chiefly Bavaria, Baden, Württemberg, Nassau, and Darmstadt—to absorb most of the very small territories of the Imperial Knights and the Prince-Bishops, a process euphemistically called "meditization." Once achieved, Francis effectively lost all influence with them, becoming instead Napoleon's allies, grouped together in the new Confederation of the Rhine, of which Napoleon was the head. Their territorial aggrandizement was paid for by supplying France with troops and money in time of war, a promise honored without real opposition until 1813. In Italy, Napoleon was able to re-establish the satellite state of the Republic (later Kingdom) of Italy in 1800, centered on Lombardy and Bologna, together with the satellite republic of Liguria, around Genoa. The French military presence south of the Alps effectively ended Habsburg influence in the peninsula, but expanded its own territories no further at this stage. Beyond the "natural frontier" of the Belgian departments, now definitively annexed to France, Napoleon was able to restore another satellite republic, the Batavian, the revolutionary successor of the old Dutch Republic, and was also to gain indirect control of Switzerland—the Helvetic Republic. By 1805, France was the dominant regional power in western and southern Europe.

Most of this power was indirect—hegemonic—in nature, but it was very real, nonetheless. These areas became Napoleon's power base, even if almost all of the extra-French parts of his hegemony were not under his direct rule. They became his surest sources of conscripts and revenue when the wars recommenced after 1805. More than this, this entire zone now underwent a period of intense internal institutional reform in the Napoleonic period, whether it came directly from Paris, in the case of the annexed territories, or in adapted form, from their traditional rulers, as in the Confederation of the Rhine. Importantly, the Napoleonic reforms took place in France and the rest of its hegemony simultaneously, in the period 1800–05. In the context of its subsequent expansion, this macro-region might be seen as an "inner empire," in contrast to less well assimilated later conquests.[16] This initial zone of expansion and, indeed, this period of Napoleonic history, arguably represent the most important aspect of the First Empire, for it was in these regions that the institutional legacy of Napoleonic rule was longest lived and most deeply felt after 1814. Moreover, if there was a "Napoleonic model" of both the state and the civil society it was meant to govern, it took clear shape in these places and in these years. Napoleon used the almost five year "peace dividend" from 1800–05 to create the prefectoral system, which tightened the control of central government over the departments. He standardized conscription, assigning quotas to each department based on its population, and reformed and strengthened the gendarmerie—the rural, para-military police force composed of army veterans—to ensure its vigorous enforcement. Perhaps most importantly, he oversaw the completion of a new code of civil law, completed in 1804 and named the *Code Napoléon*, which guaranteed equality before the law, the equal division of property among all children, open public trials, and confirmed in statute the abolition of all forms of feudalism, first proclaimed in general terms by the revolutionaries in August, 1789. The Code also decreed freedom of conscience and religious belief. The general lines of these reforms were adopted—and adapted—in all the states within the Napoleonic sphere of influence in these years. As the empire expanded after 1805,

---

[16] M. Broers, "Napoleon, Charlemagne and Lotharingia: Acculturation and the Borders of Napoleonic Europe," *Historical Journal* 44 (April 2001): 135–54.

attempts were made—usually with less success than in the earlier period—to implant these reforms in the newly acquired territories of the empire proper and in the allied and satellite states under its indirect control. The concept of the Napoleonic Empire as more than a vehicle for Napoleon's personal power, or for the enrichment of France, itself, largely rests on the commitment of the regime to export and establish these reforms throughout its territories.

The resumption of war in 1805 brought a series of resounding victories over first the Austrians and Russians, and then against the Prussians in 1806, and the Russians again in 1807. These campaigns carried the French armies beyond the borders of modern Poland into Lithuania, and culminated in the Treaties of Tilist in 1807, caricatured—not without some truth—by the British satirist Gillray, as Napoleon and Tsar Alexander I of Russia carving up the world. In terms of power politics, it transformed the Napoleonic Empire from the hegemonic power in western Europe into a pan-European super-power. The empire now expanded into far flung places for two different reasons, both of which are marked by political and military expediency: The first was the perceived need to punish, coerce, and militarily emasculate Austria, Prussia, and their minor allies. The second was to reduce the one, seemingly unassailable hostile power, Britain. Napoleon chose to achieve the first objective through the creation and redistribution of territory in central and eastern Europe, not merely by imposing heavy restrictions on the military establishments of Prussia and Austria. In 1805, he stripped the petty Austrian princes of their Italian possessions in Parma and Tuscany, eventually annexing these regions to France. As punishment for deserting him for Austria in 1805, he deposed the Neapolitan Bourbons, who fled to Sicily, placing his elder brother, Joseph, on their throne. In Germany, he seized Hanover from Prussia and merged most of it with the former Electorate of Hesse-Kassel, Prussia's ally in 1806, to form the new Kingdom of Westphalia, under his youngest brother, Jerome. The Batavian Republic was now the Kingdom of Holland, under his brother, Louis, but its status within the wider hegemony changed little as a result. Napoleon seized all of Prussian Poland and was awarded some of Russian Poland, to create the Grand Duchy of Warsaw, in 1807, under his ally, the King of Saxony. When Austria confronted him again, without success, in 1809, Napoleon continued this policy, stripping it of Polish Galicia and uniting it with the Grand Duchy of Warsaw.

The other motor of expansion was driven by the creation of the Continental System and the Continental Blockade in 1807. These were the twin prongs of Napoleon's attempt to reduce Britain by economic warfare, and they drove the French into the direct annexation of most of the coastal areas of western Europe, from 1807 until 1811. The blockade was meant to keep British goods out of Europe, and so starve the enemy of markets and, consequently, of the capital Britain used to finance her continental allies. Its effectiveness depended on control of the coasts—events proved that Napoleon could seize them, but not police them, and the only tangible results were, first, the acquisition of more territory, and then the ruination of the economies of these same areas, as the blockade destroyed maritime trade, but put nothing in its place. Conquest was possible, nonetheless. This process had already begun in 1805, with the annexation of Liguria to France, but accelerated after Tilsit. The need to enforce the Blockade led Napoleon to depose his own brother in Holland in 1810, and to annex his kingdom, together with the whole of German North Sea Coast as far as Denmark, in the same year. The same imperatives led him to invade Spain in 1808, and place Joseph on the throne, with his sister Caroline and brother-in-law and cavalry commander, Murat, going to Naples. In 1809, he arrested and deposed Pope Pius VII and annexed Rome to France. It was the need to enforce the blockade in the Adriatic, as much as to punish Austria, that he seized its Balkan possessions and grouped them into the "Illyrian Provinces" in 1809, governed from Paris. By the end of this process, in 1812, the empire proper numbered 130 departments, with a population of 44 million inhabitants. Together with the allied and conquered states, it straddled Europe and was known even at the time as the Grand Empire. It lasted barely two more years, however. It was the need to hound Alexander into the blockade that drove Napoleon to invade Russia, and so to his own ruin. By 1814, Napoleon had been deposed and France reduced to the borders of 1791, stripped even of its self-proclaimed "natural frontiers," at least along the Rhine and the Alps.

The Continental System was a more complex construct. Through it, Napoleon hoped to reorient European markets, agriculture, and industry away from reliance on Britain, with the intention of creating a new market design centered on the continent. It had more nuanced, regionally diverse results than the blockade; in general, agriculture benefitted, but industry beyond the tariff boundaries drawn by the Trianon Treaty of 1810 were deliberately undermined. The Trianon Treaty drew a tariff wall around the natural frontiers of 1791, effectively treating most of the imperial departments as "foreign" in terms of trade: Even regions annexed as early as Piedmont (1802) were kept outside this preferential zone, as were all the satellite kingdoms and the states of the Confederation of the Rhine. The silk industry of northern Italy was destroyed to make Lyon the "silk city" of Europe; the light metallurgical industries of the Grand Duchy of Berg, centered on Düsseldorf—and ruled over by Napoleon, himself after 1808—were decimated to the profit of the departments on the west bank of the Rhine.[17] Napoleon even blocked a proposed free trade treaty between his own Kingdom of Italy and Bavaria, probably his most loyal ally.[18] The general aim was to direct raw materials toward French industry on low tariffs and re-export manufactured goods at higher rates. Some sectors of non-French economies benefitted, but the over all impact was what Napoleon intended when he declared "France first." Louis Bergeron has called the system "a one-way Common Market." Geoffrey Ellis put it

---

[17] On Berg: C. Schmidt, *Le grand-duché de Berg (1806–1813): Étude sur la domination française en Allemagne sous Napoléon Ier* (Paris: Felix Alcan, 1905). On Milan: A. Pillepich, *Milan, capitale napoléomienne 1800–1814* (Paris, 2001). E. V. Tarlé, *La Vita Economica dell'Italia nell'età napoleonica* (Turin: Einaudi, 1950).

[18] M. Dunan, *Napoléon et l'Allemagne, le système continental et les débuts du Royaume de Bavière, 1806–1810* (Paris: Plon, 1942).

even better, as a formula for an "uncommon market."[19] This was economic imperialism that bordered on colonialism.

Even from this outline, the central arguments of the traditionalist, anti-Woolf historiography become as powerful as they are clear: The latter phase of expansion was rapid, driven wholly by desperation, of short duration, marked by ruthless material exploitation for the war effort and, above all, brutal and makeshift in its methods of control. French troops and gendarmes were quartered along the new coastal departments to fight smugglers—often the better part of the local population—and extract conscripts and taxes from increasingly destitute communities. French administrators arrived in ever greater numbers to assume posts at ever lower levels, as it became clear how few locals could be relied upon, and how little even willing collaborators grasped the workings of an alien state, conceived of and forged far away. Although harder to sustain when applied to the earlier annexations and alliances, the vision of empire as little more than a transient, traumatic system of exploitation becomes obvious in the areas affected after 1807. Nevertheless, the conduct of the French in all the regions they attempted to absorb was not one-dimensional, and this is where the debate over the nature of the First Napoleonic Empire, and the very existence—or not—of the concept of Napoleonic imperialism, takes shape.

Manifest Destiny: French Nationalism and European Empire

The French elites, particularly those associated with the Napoleonic regime, emerged from the 1790s—and even more from the series of breath-taking military victories between 1805 and 1807, with a belief that France was, indeed *la Grande Nation*, to be imitated and obeyed by the rest of Europe. What might be termed their "cultural confidence"—to put it mildly—separated the French in their own minds from the other Europeans they came to rule over during the Napoleonic period. Their self-belief was based on three things: They had freed themselves from the decrepitude of the *ancien régime* by their own efforts—the revolution. They had then—again by their own efforts—curbed the worst excesses of that revolution, and salvaged the best of their pre-revolutionary past from the wreckage: that is, they had reconciled *le grand siècle* and the enlightenment to the revolution. The practical benefits of this were the civil code, the administrative system, and finally, the state which produced the *Grande Armée*. The lightning victories of 1805–07 were the fruits of this. Well before, during the 1790s, the French had proved arrogant and inflexible in their dealings with those who, unlike them, had failed to liberate themselves. Their dealings with the foreign patriots became increasingly high-handed, as the failure of the latter to produce spontaneous, indigenous revolutions beyond France only served to convince the French

---

[19] L. Bergeron, *France under Napoleon*, trans. R. R. Palmer (Princeton: Princeton University Press, 1981), 173. Ellis, *Napoleonic Empire*: 112.

not only of their own innate superiority to other Europeans, but of their uniqueness. From this came a concept of imperialism predicated on French "otherness," and on the intrinsic need for the imperial power to be "other" from its *administrés*. This was the essence of imperialism, as expressed clearly in a report to Napoleon by the minister of justice in 1811:

> Almost all the institutions of Europe were created by the conquerors ... Men would never have escaped barbarism, had they continued to live in small, isolated settlements: They would have remained sunk in anarchy and brutishness. Such has always been the fate of peoples who were not held in check by a superior force: such was the fate of the Gauls, when they were conquered by the Romans, such was the state of the peoples of Italy until only recently, until they were reunited to France. Only great empires provide the encouragement and rewards for talent, that make for progress. Empire fosters the spread of law and, of necessity, perfects it through so many diverse states ... The first rays of gentility shone on Europe through the exploits of Charlemagne.[20]

This raw exposition of the imperialist rationale is all the more forceful, perhaps, because it reveals how a powerful sense of national identity among the French elites was now intrinsically bound up with the concept of empire.

Nowhere is this cultural confidence recounted more emphatically than in the memoirs of Jacques-Claude Beugnot, one of Napoleon's leading imperial civil servants. Recalling his first trip to Germany in 1807, to take over the administration of the Grand Duchy of Berg, his recollections are those of a French elite at the zenith of its imperial power:

> It was something in Europe, to be a Frenchman...I was, in Germany, what the Roman pro-consuls had been, once upon a time. There was the same respect, the same obedience on the part of the nobles, the same wish to please and to win my favor ... I lived in an age of ambition, and the road opened before me, wide and strewn with flowers; I could no more doubt my good fortune than that of the Empire ... and I can still recall that sort of drunkenness which I felt crossing that eternally famous river (the Rhine), now bent under our yoke, after our victories. It was not easy, be it as a soldier or a civil servant of Napoleon, to be modest; the best one could hope for, was not to be insolent.[21]

---

[20] Archives Nationales de Paris (ANP) BB18 700 (Affaires criminelles, Rome) Min. of Justice, Report to Napoleon, Oct. 29, 1811.
[21] J. C. Beugnot, *Le Grand-Duché de Berg (Extrait des Mémoires inédits du Comte Beugnot)* (Paris: E. Dentu, 1852), 18, 26.

There is a term for this, and it is bound inextricably to imperialism: Manifest Destiny. It translated into the view of history laid down by the minister of justice, and into the emotions of Beugnot as he went forth to govern. Soon, as the French came into their destiny, for however brief a time, it would test itself against the other societies of Europe and, in so doing, harden their perceptions of themselves as a nation apart, made so by its grandeur.

The historical relationship between France and her empire cannot be described as alien, but the French did not conceive of it in any way as equal. In his *Memoire pour servir à l'histoire de la société polie en France*, written in the 1820s[22] after his own experiences as an imperial administrator in Naples and Germany, and those of his son as a prefect in Umbria, Pierre-Louis Roederer—one of the leading proto-anthropologists of the period and a member of the *Institut*—portrays the intelligent, civilized character of native conversation: "... that social instinct which seems to belong to the French, more than to any other nation ... that French pleasure which is the envy of all other civilized nations," as the hallmark of a uniquely French identity. He forges this as a direct result of his close interaction with other Europeans. When French imperial administrators in Germany or Italy denounced the lack of salons among the local elites, it was a very profound condemnation, indeed. In Rome, Tournon, the French Prefect remarked that "[i]t hardly exists in this country, where the taste for reading is not widespread."[23] Norvins, the police commissioner for the Roman departments, condemned the locals as "these people who prefer processions to dancing, and sermons to the theatre."[24] Even the Dutch, whom the French generally regarded as highly cultivated, were not entirely immune from the process of "salonization." In the newly annexed Dutch departments, in 1810, François-Joseph Beyts, the Franco-Belgian magistrate sent to organize the judiciary there, turned to it almost instinctively. Beyts sought to bring together everyone involved in the law, in every town, into a *societe letteraire de jurisprudence*. Beyts had already created something similar in the Hague, with its own library, but these were meant to be more than reading rooms:

> Quite apart from the support of these immense collections of printed literature, and the facility to consult and study them, the lawyers can have the opportunity gradually to initiate themselves into the mysteries of our higher jurisprudence; their instruction will take place through sociability, through amicable discussion ... In a word, they will learn by forms of amusement.[25]

---

[22] P. L. Roederer, *Mémoire pour servir à l'histoire de la société polie en France* (Paris: Institut Royal de France, 1835).

[23] J. Moulard, ed., *Lettres inédites du comte Camille de Tournon, préfet de Rome 1809–1814 : 1ère partie : La politique et l'esprit public* (Paris, 1914), Tournon to his mother, Nov. 3, 1810.

[24] ANP F7 7018 (Bulletins, Rome) Norvins to Min. Police-Générale, May 21, 1812.

[25] ANP BB5 288 (Organisation Judiciaire, Holland) Beyts to Min of Justice, May 1, 1811.

Among so many other prejudices embedded in the remarks of Norvin and Degerando is the belief prevalent among the French in the superiority of the text over the image in an Italian context. Their colleague, the prefect Tournon, considered Italy "a country where all men judge and respect themselves, according to how much they spend, and by external show."[26] The French believed the way to deal with this was straightforward "culture war." This led to a direct challenge to the opera, by the French theatre. The French prefect of Parma, Nardon, welcomed its disappearance in Parma. He thought the *opera buffa* might provide a "half way house" to wean Italians from the grosser aspects of their native opera, towards "proper" theatre. It would be "a great aid for education and shaping public opinion." However, his loathing went much deeper than aesthetic taste. Nardon saw the opera as an active agent of moral depravity that had to be eradicated: "The theatres in Italy today are horrible, and serve only to propagate indecency, corrupt morality, encourage bad taste, and harbor notions of violent thoughts and crude passions."[27]

> No other issue underlines the French sense of superiority better than religion. When confronted by Italian Catholicism, the French set themselves directly against the cultural of the visual, in its most potent sphere of expression. There are times, when reading their correspondence, that it is hard to believe the French and Italians both came from Catholic backgrounds. Indeed, the French found it hard to credit it themselves. Wrote Degerando, a member of the French administration in Rome, ethnographer and member of the *Institut*, on Roman piety:
>
>> Religion, as it is understood by enlightened men and felt by virtuous men, as it generally exists in France, that is—as the product of a reasoned and reasonable conviction, the main aim of which is to improve morals—is scarcely even perceived to exist by the Romans ... Relics, indulgences, the 40 Hours, the Rosary, the little medals are what interest them...Many thousands of men who come to kiss the feet of the statue of Jupiter—now transformed into that of the Prince of the Apostles—scarcely even suspect that there might even be such a thing as the Gospel.[28]

Religion—or, more correctly, the tolerance of religion and the equality of opportunity demanded by the civil code—drew the French into a different confrontation in their Dutch provinces. When the Empire faced north and east, the barriers to Napoleonic progress were often different in kind, if perhaps not quite in essence, even if the goals of the empire-builders were the same. Few parts of the empire could have been more different from Rome than the flat, highly urbanized commercial and multi-confessional world of the Dutch maritime provinces. They were first a sister republic—the

---

26　Cited in Moulard, *Camille*, ii, 130.
27　ANP F^{1c} 85 (Parme, Plaisance et Guastelle) Nardon to Min. Int., Sept. 10, 1806.
28　ANP F20 102 (Statistique, Rome) "Rapport sur Rome et les états romains," 1810.

Batavian—in 1795, then a satellite kingdom ten years later under Napoleon's brother
Louis, and finally, imperial departments ruled directly from Paris in 1810. In this final
stage of assimilation, they received—like Novi—the full French judicial and administrative model unaltered in its essentials. The Franco-Belgian jurist, Beyts, was sent to
these new departments to organize the judiciary, and he felt none of the fundamental
prejudices about his new *administés* that Roederer or Tournon held for the Italians.
The Dutch were highly educated; Beyts even considered many of their magistrates to
be more so than the French.[29] The problem here was that, however highly educated,
the French now acquired a society where religious discrimination was deeply rooted, at
least in the public sphere. Almost all the candidates are Reform Church—it was the established religion, and almost all public offices demanded adherence to it. It is still the
religion of the vast majority of the people. However, Beyts grouped all candidates for
judicial posts together, regardless of their religion, "because we have proposed them
on their ability, without regard for their confessional attachements,"[30] perhaps a revealing window on what a specifically French Empire stood for in such matters. Beyts
and Lebrun, the senior French official in charge of the annexation of the Netherlands,
were very anxious to push this still further, however. They were determined to include
both Catholics and Jews in the magistracy—they wanted all faiths represented, if possible, and took great care over this: "all now under a law equal to the justness of our
great monarch."[31] On the practical level of appointments, the French were doing their
best to operate something like a quota system here—and towards a religion they were
generally at odds with over much of their empire. Even more, perhaps, and the fact
that the Protestant culture has done much to make the Dutch quite "like us" not with-
standing, the principle of toleration etc. is being brought home in the context of this
multi-confessional society. This is a crucial difference between even the most advanced
ancien régime, the Dutch Republic, and the new regime of the code and 1789. The
French were different everywhere.

    In a long passage in his *Histoire*, Louis Roederer points specifically to the
unique role played by women at the center of French polite society and their importance for preventing the descent of French discourse to the barren metaphysics of the
German university or the boorish "techno-jargon" of the English club. It ran in the
family. Perhaps the most damning comment on Italian womanhood comes from his
daughter-in-law, the wife of Antoine Roederer, the prefect of Umbria, who spoke
Italian well and spent almost five years in Spoleto, at her husband's side. In a letter to
her father-in-law, she lambasted her Italian gardener for refusing to take orders from a
woman, but turned her real venom on the women of the Umbrian elite:

> I got up and took over running the house ... five days after giving birth.
> They regard that as some sort of miracle in this part of the world, where

---

[29] ANP BB5 288 (Organisation Judiciaire, Holland) Beyts to Min of Justice, Feb. 25, 1811.
[30] Ibid.
[31] Ibid.

the accepted wisdom is that, without exception, you have to spend forty days in bed after a birth. I, however, am a good little French peasant girl, healthy and of good heart.[32]

Here, too, stands the shared myth of France, a homeland filled with a brave, sturdy yeomanry, and a peasant heritage the young professionals on the periphery shared in the face of a decadent "other." Far removed from the realities of the French metropole, Madame Roederer took upon the role of the rational, energetic enlightened woman of business. She had to set an example to the weak, trivialized, and decadent women of Italy. It is too often forgotten that Napoleonic imperialists regarded the high status they accorded women in social affairs as among the most important attributes defining their uniqueness.

Couples could set the example, too. After his marriage, Tournon adapted his patterns of *sociabilité* to suit his new status, but made even fewer concessions to Italian social habits. He and his wife, Adèle née de Pancemont—the daughter of a family of *parlementaires* from Nîmes[33]—opened their house to the Roman elites in a style wholly in keeping with the imperial mission. The character of their *salon* was stamped by cultural imperialism. In his unpublished memoirs Tournon is reported to have said:

> In the home of the prefect, there was less din, and certainly less unseemliness and debauchery that made up for its scandalous past history. *Un bon ton* prevailed there, good manners, an honest cordiality... The excellence of the food, the amiable nature of the welcome, the grace and perfect tact of the mistress of the house, the clever conversation combined with songs, concerts, dances, alongside courteous discussions about politics and public affairs, all gave these gatherings variety, and a charm that endured right to the end.[34]

Restraint, directness, and genuine friendliness replaced Roman lasciviousness, falsity, and extravagance. Above all, the Tournons' salon was a place of culture and intelligence. It was not about the visual, but the life of the mind, and a place where people knew how to behave. Even at table, they set a culinary example of superiority. Tournon asked his father to send 100 bottles of Cornas, the daily drink of their native northern Rhone, and also to throw in one or two cases of Côte-Rotie and Hermitage, the truly great wines of the region, "in order to tell them of the wines of my country, and to set an example of what is truly the best."[35] Even as a bachelor, Tournon revealed a very French, neo-classical approach to "space," in which he threw down a cultural gauntlet to Italian baroque. He told his mother, on taking up residence in the city:

---

[32] ANP 29-AP -16, Madame A. Roederer to P. L. Roederer, Sept. 23, 1812.
[33] Moulard, *Lettres*, Tournon to his mother, Dec. 3, 1810.
[34] Moulard, *Camille*, ii, 126, 129.
[35] Moulard, *Lettres*, Tournon to his father, Oct. 8, 1810.

> (E)very Monday, I open my apartment to all comers ... My apartment ...
> is very airy and tasteful, but also very simple. This is the only way to com-
> bat the magnificence of the Roman palaces, which are gilded, but lacking
> in all grace.[36]

These first steps in his tenure of the prefecture reveal a great deal about the nature of the French civilizing mission in the Italian departments and even more about those aspects of the French self-image that drove a wedge between rulers and ruled. Tournon's immediate concern was to replace darkness with light, to open up cramped, confined spaces and create freshness from the stale, obscurantist debris of the old order. Although a noble, his almost automatic response to what he found in his Roman *palazzo* bears the essential hallmarks of the cleansing of public spaces through light and air so prevalent among the early revolutionaries studied in Ozouf's work on official festivals.[37] A shared culture, based on enlightened sensibilities—in the pristine sense of the term—drove Tournon's initial steps in an alien Rome. The neoclassicism of the *Grand Siècle* was now allied to the air and light of the whole enlightenment, not only a discernible French aesthetic. Tournon, the prefect of Rome, set out the stall of French national superiority in typical style, and he did so not in some remote, primitive outpost, but in the place Napoleon, himself, had styled "the second city of the Empire." French identity was not forged only in isolated postings, but at the traditional heart of European civilization. The rest of Europe had lost its way; only the French could show the way to a civilized future.

The key to French superiority was their ability to achieve "balance" in all things; for contemporary imperialists, "balance" was the essence of French genius and, so, of French "otherness." Their "balance," when set in the imperial context of ruling other peoples, made the French unique, as well as superior in Europe, in their own eyes. It is ruthlessly expressed in this passage from the memoirs of General Rocca, who had served in the *Grande Armée* all over Europe under Napoleon. He knew the countries and peoples of which he spoke at first hand. Familiarity bred contempt. This is his parallel assessment of the Spaniards and the Germans:

> As regards learning and the improvement of social customs, Spain was
> a century behind the rest of Europe...(T)he Spaniards were much given
> to indolence and their government was corrupt and disorderly, the inev-
> itable results of a long-lived despotism: their government, although ar-
> bitrary, had none of the militaristic, absolutist power which existed in
> Germany, where the constant submission of one and all to the orders of
> one man incessantly compromised individuality.[38]

[36] Moulard, *Lettres*, Tournon to his mother, April 1, 1810.
[37] M. Ozouf, *Festivals of the French Revolution*, trans. Alan Sheridan (Cambridge, Mass.: Harvard University Press, 1989), passim.
[38] A. J. M. de Rocca, *Mémoires sur la guerre des français en Espagne* (Paris, 1814), 272–73.

Here, then, is the clearest expression of the "French balance," the self-image of the French genius: more civilized and disciplined than the Spaniard; more intelligent and enterprising than the German.

The French read, rather than watched; they talked intelligently, rather than sang or played parlour games; they knew how to behave in mixed company, and preferred it to isolating the sexes. They were disciplined, but self-disciplined, and the distinction was important to them. Their religion was reasoned, based on its ability to impart earthly, civilized values, rather than divine favor. Their style was a balance between gaiety and restraint; their taste was elegant minimalism. They had no doubt all this set them apart, but even more interesting is how the experience of empire brought opposites—indeed, former enemies—together not just in imperial service, but in their mutual realization that they were united in culture. The Roederers were a staunchly revolutionary family of Alsatian Lutherans, and their cultural reactions to life abroad are quite predictable. Hugues Nardon, in Parma, was a former Jacobin and school friend of Napoleon, and his loathing of Italian culture is even more pre-ordained. Tournon, however, shows how the practice of imperial rule forged a cultural unity unimaginable in the France of the 1790s or, at least, made Frenchmen aware of its existence and its centrality to their identity. Tournon was the embodiment of this. He was the scion of an aristocratic family who had fled Collot d'Herbois' Jacobin assault on Lyon in 1794 holding his mother's hand for dear life;[39] his father was an *émigré*, but Tournon had trained wholly in the Napoleonic system, and learned through imperial service that he had far more in common with Roederer, his colleague in Umbria—or even with Nardon—than with the Roman nobility.

The French looked for people and societies they felt most resembled their own. It was, in one way, as simple as that, from their own perspective, and was made all the more so, through the clear vision they had of themselves. They seldom, if ever, looked at the novel characteristics of another society with admiration; it seldom occurred to them to "borrow" from the institutions or practices of even their close neighbors, unless they already possessed something very close to their own ideas. They never adapted or compromised their own legal or administrative systems, still less their cultural habits, with anyone, anywhere.

Napoleon intended Paris to be the center of the new imperial universe. He told Las Cases on St. Helena:

> It came into my perpetual dreams, to make of Paris the veritable capital of Europe: In time, I wanted it to become (a city) of two, three, even four million inhabitants...in a word, something fabulous, colossal, something unknown before our own times.[40]

---

[39] J. Moulard, *Le Comte Camille de Tournon*, 3 vols. (Paris, 1927), vol I. *La Jeunnesse, Paris, Bayreuth*: 87–95.

[40] Quoted in M.-B. d'Arneville, *Parcs et Jardins sous le Premier Empire. Reflets d'une société* (Paris: Fayard, 1981), 31.

He was neither lying nor exaggerating his original thoughts, and there is a wealth of material evidence to bear witness to these particular "words from the Rock." More to the point, he gave Paris the coveted privilege of very low conscription quotas, and was capable of resorting to tactics worthy of both the *Parlement* of Paris and the Commune in times of subsistence crisis, notably just before the onset of the Russian campaign in 1812, when he used nothing less than the Imperial Guard to forage ruthlessly in the Norman departments for provisions for the city, in the manner of the *Armée Révolutionaire*.[41] In short, he became the city's protector, in the manner of both the *Parlement* and Hébert. However, Paris was meant to protect him, in return. It was to be both a magnet for those who rallied and wished to amalgamate or, failing that, a cage for those who refused to integrate, and had to be forcibly assimilated. Napoleon sought to draw to Paris the very best minds and talents of the lands under his sway; Goethe and Canova were the most prominent of those he courted. He had little success with foreigners, but it was quite the reverse for the French "abroad."

The France of the imperial servants was the France of the northern cities, and of Paris, above all. Their vision of home, and of the cradle of "the Great Nation," did not embrace the "wild west" of the rural, Catholic, royalist Vendée any more than it did the hot, violent, valley of the Rhone or Provence. If it was not couched in quite these terms at the time, it came to be, with the formulation of the concept of the Maggiolo Line, at the end of the nineteenth century. This hypothetical division of France by a line running northwest to southeast, between St. Malo and Geneva, was based on levels of literacy, and first devised by Louis Maggiolo in 1879. It corresponded very much to the France of Napoleon's Frenchmen—and women—abroad. At its heart—and in theirs—stood Paris, above all, however. The administrative centralization that defined the imperial public sphere drew them there to begin their careers, in the great educational institutions created in the very first moments of the consulate.

Around them, grew a renewed cultural and intellectual private sphere, from which the servants of empire went out, and to which—far more than their own provincial homes—they usually longed to return. No one embodied the spirit of the young imperial professional more than Antoine Roederer. In his determination to make the regime's writ run in Umbria and, perhaps even more, he wrote these words to his father in late 1811:

> Today, I have been two years and four days in Spoleto. It seems more like
> a month. In six months, I hope to come to see you...for I desire nothing
> more than to go to Paris, to see Paris.[42]

When his counterpart in Rome, Camille de Tournon, returned on leave, he was suitably impressed by the new splendor of the imperial capital, noting in his memoirs, "[a]

---

[41] J. Vidalenc, "L'industrie dans les départements notmands à la fin du Ier Empire," *Annales de Normandie* 7 (April 1957), 281–307.

[42] ANP 29 AP- 15, A. Roederer to P-L Roederer, Dec. 14, 1811.

Frenchman abroad, like the Roman of an earlier time, bowed his head before the *sum civis romanum.*[43] Thus, the center kept its emotional hold on its loyal servants in the furthest flung corners of the periphery. It was Napoleon's hope and the regime's determined policy that others from all over Europe would feel the same. The prospects for advancement were here more than anywhere else, and the routes were informal as well as institutional, even in so professionalized a state.

Imperial Paris was also the heart of that talismanic emblem of French imperial identity, the *salon*. The Duchesse de Chastenay remarked of the *salon* of Champagny, a holder of a succession powerful ministries throughout the period, that he "received, generally, the hopefuls, the *auditeurs*, the prospective protégés, in truth, and those who had more ephemeral relations with him, who rather passed through."[44] Even the young Comte de Montesquiou, from a background ill-disposed to the new order, still believed his father did him a favor by introducing him to the *salon* of the Duchesse de Luynes, for "it was generally regarded as a most honorable recommendation."[45] The old order carried on in this ambience, and the new evolved its own variants on the great tradition. Such were the routes open to newcomers, and if they regarded Paris more as a cage than a city of golden threaded networks, it was certainly as well gilded a cage as Napoleon's means could fashion. Of the charms of the *salon*, Montesquiou could recall "the grace, elegance and glowing youth" brought to his milieu *préféré* by Mlle de Narbonne, while the German composer Reichardt spoke of Juliette Récamier in almost ravening terms.[46]

The physical urban ambience surrounding these private spaces was intended to seduce and impress, simultaneously. The Napoleonic period saw more than the well-known grandiose public building projects, as attention was turned to the parks and gardens of the city for the first time since the 1780s. They, coupled to its *salon* society, set an agreeable stage for the processes of acculturation and professional advancement, in stark, deliberate contrast to the horrors of the battlefields on the imperial frontier, or the rudeness and perceived backwardness of its peripheries. The Napoleonic regime put special emphasis on the parks, gardens, and other public green spaces of the capital. In the hands of the imperial regime, the park became a tool of enlightenment, the public equivalent of Tournon's opening up of his baroque palace in Rome. To Napoleon, private parks were "Gothic" relics of a drab old order. As Marie-Blanche d'Arneville has said, "The Empire wanted to put an end to the era of closed gardens."[47] Napoleon opened the restored gardens of the Tuileries to the public, in direct contrast to their layout under the monarchy, yet he kept them in the neo-classical style of the seventeenth century, as he also did with

---

43 Cited in Moulard, *Camille*, II, 123.
44 Cited in A. Fierro, ed., *Le Consulat et l'Empire: anthologie des memorialistes du Consulat et de l'Empire* (Paris: Fayard, 1998), 795.
45 Fierro, *Consulat*, 797–98.
46 Ibid., 798, 800–03.
47 d'Arneville, *Parcs et Jardins*, 31.

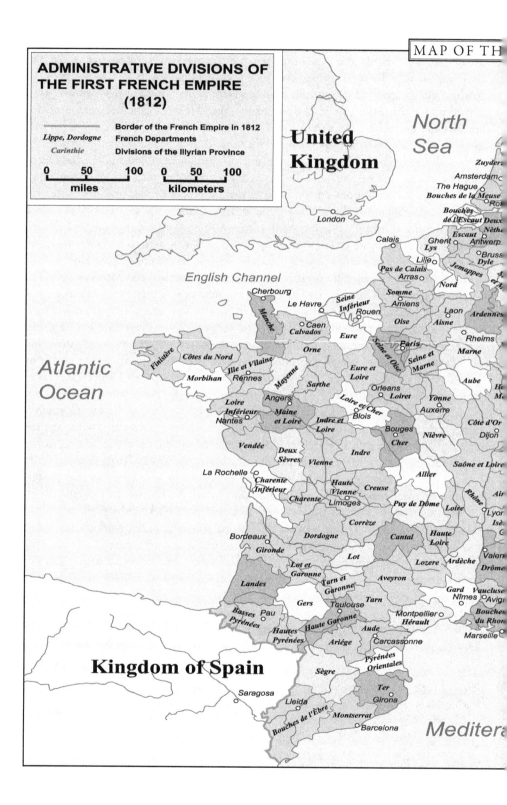

ADMINISTRATIVE DIVISIONS OF THE FIRST FRENCH EMPIRE (1812)

Border of the French Empire in 1812
Lippe, Dordogne   **French Departments**
Carinthie   **Divisions of the Illyrian Province**

0   50   100   0   50   100
miles   **kilometers**

North
Sea

United
Kingdom

Zuyder

Amsterdam
The Hague
Bouches de la Meuse
Ro

Bouches
de l'Escaut Deux
Escaut Nèthe
Ghent Antwerp
Lys
London Brussels
Lille Jemappes
Calais Pas de Calais Dyle
Arras
Nord

English Channel

Cherbourg
Le Havre   Seine   Somme
Inférieur   Amiens
Rouen   Laon   Ardennes
Caen   Oise   Aisne
Calvados   Eure   Rheims

Orne   Paris   Marne
Côtes du Nord   Eure et   Seine et
Ille et Vilaine   Loire   Marne
Finistère   Morbihan   Rennes   Mayenne   Sarthe   Aube

Atlantic
Ocean

Orleans   Loiret   Yonne   He
Loire   Angers   Loire et Cher   Auxerre   M
Inférieur   Maine   Blois   Côte d'Or
Nantes   et Loire   Indre et   Bouges   Nièvre   Dijon
Loire   Cher

Vendée   Deux   Indre   Saône et Loire
Sèvres   Vienne
La Rochelle   Allier   Air
Charente   Haute   Creuse
Inférieur   Vienne   Puy de Dôme   Rhône   Lyon
Charente   Limoges   Loire   Ise

Corrèze   Haute   Valen
Bordeaux   Dordogne   Cantal   Loire   Drôme
Gironde   Lot   Lozere   Ardèche
Lot et   Gard   Vaucluse
Garonne   Aveyron   Nîmes   Avig
Landes   Tarn et   Bouches
Garonne   Tarn   Montpellier   du Rhon
Gers   Toulouse   Hérault   Marseille
Basses   Pau
Pyrénées   Haute Garonne   Aude
Hautes   Ariége   Carcassonne
Pyrénées   Pyrénées
Orientales

Kingdom of Spain

Sègre

Saragosa   Ter
Lleida   Girona
Bouches de l'Èbre   Montserrat
Barcelona

Mediterra

NIC EMPIRE

1-Lucca   2-Neuchâtel

Denmark

Swedish Pomerania

Kingdom of Prussia

Grand Duchy of Warsaw

Lübeck
Hamburg
Bouches de l'Elbe
Bouches du Wesser
érieur
nabrück
Hannover
Berlin
Breslau

Kassel
Leipzig
Dresden

Confederation of the Rhine
blenz
Mainz
Prague

Bayreuth
nt
nnerre

Stuttgart

ssbourg
Ulm
Munich
Salzburg

Vienna
Buda Pest

Austrian Empire

sel
Zurich

Confederation
n

Carinthie

Trient
Ljubljana
Carniole

Milan
Padua
Venice
Istrie
Croatie Civitas
Fiume

Sesia
Vercelli
Croatie Militaire

Marengo
Taro
Parma
Génes
Apennins

Kingdom of Italy

Illyrian Province

Ottoman Empire

Montenotte
Savona
Génes
La Spezia
1
San Marino
Zara
Dalmatie

Livorno
Florence
Arno
Méditerranée
Siena

Adriatic Sea

Piombino
Ombrone
Trasiméne
Spoleto

Ragusa
Ragusa

Corse
Ajaccio

Rome
Rome

Kingdom of Naples

Pontecorvino

Benevento

ea

Naples

the Luxembourg gardens. This could almost serve as a metaphor for the regime: It embraced the powerful legacy of "the great century" of Louis XIV. It did not turn its back on the glorious past, yet equally, Napoleon sought to maintain a bond to the new, revolutionary attitudes of "nation" and "people." The public parks of Napoleonic Paris were physical plebiscites, and an opening of a culture previously the preserve of the privileged, to the nation. Nevertheless, Parisian space was also used to affirm emphatically the authoritarian character of the regime. Many of the other great spaces recreated by Napoleon doubled as public parks and parade grounds. Paris was the permanent headquarters of the Imperial Guard, the cream of the army, which was under Napoleon's exclusive command, and the open spaces of the capital were used to showcase it. Thus, "[i]f the Tuileries affirmed the Empire as the master of France over its capital, and if it was used to proclaim its power as that of the army, the park also represented ... the point of permanent contact between the people of Paris and its government."[48] The public spaces of Paris, its parks especially, encapsulate the contradictions just as much as the aspirations of the imperial regime.

This was to be the very French heart of a very French Empire, but the reality was far more complex, not only within France, but even more so, beyond it. From beginning to end, the intense sense of French cultural superiority, and the shared high culture that went with it, was the preserve of an administrative and judicial elite and, to a certain extent, of the army. Just as this elite had an imagined geographical homeland—that of Paris and the urban northeast—it had an opposition. Rural France—still largely traditionally Catholic in the south and west, groaning under the yoke of conscription after war was renewed in 1805 everywhere—shared very little in the elation, confidence, or arrogance of those who willingly assumed the role of empire-builders. The experience of the French masses had more in common with their fellows in the annexed and subjugated lands beyond the borders of 1790. There were no popular risings to save Napoleon as the Allies advanced into France in 1814, perhaps the clearest sign that his cult would have to wait a generation—until the experience of war and conscription had faded into a nostalgic haze. Ironically, if the empire-builders found support beyond their narrow ranks, it was among sections of the elites of the non-French parts of their empire.

A Historical Geography of Napoleonic Europe

The character of the Napoleonic empire is marked not only by its brevity and rapaciousness, but also by the heterogeneous nature of the many areas it ruled over, the great variation in the lengths of time it occupied different parts of the territory under its sway, and the relentlessly uniform, uncompromising manner in which it sought to rule the extent of its empire. Even given the shortness of Napoleonic rule everywhere,

---

[48] Ibid.

the regions annexed directly to France or brought into the wider net of French hegemony—the satellite states and the members of the Confederation of the Rhine—
had lived as long as France under the Napoleonic state, as reformed and consolidated
under the Consulate, 1800–05. Thus, it seems reasonable to speak in terms of an inner
and an outer empire, distinguished principally on grounds of the length of Napoleonic
rule, especially when the durability of the Napoleonic reforms of the public sphere
after 1814 is born in mind.

The lands of the inner empire clustered around the eastern borders of France,
but they were not synonymous with those of *l'ancienne France*, for as time progressed,
it became clear that the interior of the empire was really the Rhine-Saône-Rhone axis.
The writ of Paris ran more surely, and was accepted with better comprehension in
Belgium, the left bank of the Rhine, and Piedmont than it was in the *Vendée militaire*,
Roussillon, or the Cevennes.[49] This was not only because the roads were safer in these
eastern regions than in the west and south, or because these departments came—after
periods of ferocious, if successful, pacification—to yield up their sons to conscription
more easily than many parts of pre-imperial France. The administrative norms of the
centralized, professional state born in the 1790s and honed in the first half decade of
Napoleonic rule took root more readily in these places, as did the code. This is seen
not just in its workings, but through the alacrity and facility with which the legal
classes of these new provinces adapted to the norms of the new order. Rhinelanders
may have looked down on the new Napoleonic jurisprudence in comparison to their
own, but they knew how to absorb and work within it, to the point they demanded
and received from their new Prussian rulers, in 1814, the right to retain the French
code and court system.[50] Several Piedmontese magistrates rose high in the Napoleonic
service. Some—the most distinguished being Peyretti di Condove and Botton di
Castellamonte—chose to remain in Paris in 1814,[51] while another, Dal Pozzo, became
a highly influential theoretical interpreter and intermediary for the code among the
legal classes of Restoration Italy.[52] It was a Belgian jurisconsulte, Beyts, who brought

49 On Roussillon: M. Brunet, *Le Roussillon. Une société contre l'État, 1780–1820* (Toulouse:
    Editions Eché, 1986); on the Midi: Brown, *Ending the French Revolution.* There is a huge liter-
    ature on the Vendée; for a good general survey see: J.-C. Martin, *La Vendée et la France* (Paris:
    Seuil, 1987); D. Sutherland, *The Chouans. The Social Origins of Popular Counter-Revolution in
    Upper Britanny, 1770–1796* (Oxford: Oxford University Press, 1982); Roger Dupuy, *De la
    Révolution à la Chouannerie* (Paris: Flammarion, 1988). All three are classic studies of a phenom-
    enon of collective resistance that endured well into the Napoleonic period.

50 Rowe, *Reich,* 137; J. Engelbrecht, "The French Model and German Society: the Impact of the *Code
    Pénal* on the Rhineland," in *Révolutions et justice pénale en Europe. Modèles français et traditions na-
    tionales, 1780–1830,* eds. X. Rousseau, M.-S. Dupont, and C. Vael (Paris, 1999), 101–08.

51 Broers, *Napoleonic Imperialism,* 449–50.

52 F. Dal Pozzo, *Opuscli di un avvoccato Milanese,* 8 vols. (Milan, 1817); M. Broers, *The Napoleonic
    Empire in Italy, 1796–1814: Cultural Imperialism in a European context?* (Basingstoke: Palgrave,
    2005), 289–90.

the code to the Dutch and Hanseatic departments.[53] Neither the Vendean nor the Provençale departments could boast such service to the new regime, at least not in the sphere most fundamental to its ethos.

There is a marked irony about the inner empire. Its template was forged in France, by a generation of Frenchmen who felt their national experience to be simultaneously unique and universal. They alone had liberated themselves from the old order. They, alone in Europe, had first unleashed and then tamed their own peculiar revolution to the point they felt confident enough by 1800 to draw on their pre-revolutionary past where it suited them. They stood above and apart from other Europeans. Almost perversely, however, they felt they had created a model of the state and, above all, a legal code, that could serve as universal model. Napoleon and his collaborators felt that, in the Civil Code, they had finally brought to fruition the bold declaration of the moderate revolutionary, Condorcet, in 1790: "A good law is a good law for all men." Indeed, the code was imposed, virtually unaltered, not only in all those parts of Europe from Hamburg to Rome that became French departments, but in the satellite kingdoms and, in buffered form, in the states of the Confederation of the Rhine. The Napoleonic new regime, like the revolution it sprang from, was a unique French creation, but made-to-measure for export, not just in the eyes of its creators, but in those of a significant element of the ruling elites of western Europe.

The proof of this seeming contradiction is found in the composition of the inner empire. It was made up of far more than regions annexed directly to France. Indeed, its bulk was not made up of imperial departments—there were far more annexed territories in the outer empire—nor even of satellite kingdoms under Bonapartes: there were two satellite kingdoms within it, those of Italy and Holland, and even the latter was only briefly one. There were four Rhenish, five Piedmontese, nine Belgian and, eventually, four Dutch departments. The core of the inner empire may have been eastern and northern France and the annexed regions immediately to its east, but its bulk comprised the states of the Confederation of the Rhine, and the Helvetic Republic. With the partial exception of Republic/Kingdom of Italy—which was ruled by a French viceroy, Eugène de Beauharnais, but staffed almost entirely by Italians—there is a lesson of sorts to be taken from this: Napoleonic institutions did not need direct French rule to take root, whatever the French, themselves, may or may not have come to think.

Ralliement and *amalgame* were, initially, how Napoleon expressed the Consulate's determination to end the political divisions of the 1790s. The former signified a general, usually passive, acceptance of the regime, more or less synonymous with an attitude of "live-and-let-live" among former adversaries, under the broad umbrella provided by the new regime. The latter involved direct participation in the Napoleonic state. The Consular regime pursued a deliberate policy of harnessing former antagonists to its service—former royalists in the diplomatic corps, ex-Jacobins in the police,

---

[53] On Beyts: A.N.P., Série BB 5 (Organisation Judiciaire) 268–70, (départements hanséatiques) 288–94, (départements hollandaises).

moderate revolutionaries in the magistracy—thereby submitting them to its control and making them work according to its own rules. The state was both arbiter and the guarantor of toleration, if not of political liberty as experienced at the height of the revolution.[54]

The willingness of the princes of the Confederation of the Rhine to embrace the Napoleonic template is probably the most striking example of the extension of Napoleon's dual policies *ralliement* and *amalgame* from the internal politics of France to an imperial construct, just as his relationship to them corresponds more closely to the vision he set out in his memoirs on St. Helena of a federal Europe, centered on an Emperor with kings allied to and ultimately subject to him. These rulers remained more loyal to him than any of his family—Louis in Holland, and Joseph in Spain— since he did not depose them, and they had to be carefully, and with difficulty, won over by the Allies in 1813. They were bound to Napoleon because he had enabled them to expand their states at the expense of the smallest German polities, and he had shown in subsequent wars against Austria and Prussia that, if they aided his war effort, he would defend their gains, just as his reforms and his unwillingness to restore Louis XVIII in 1800 showed Frenchmen that he would defend the practical gains of the revolution. In their changed circumstances, with ex-feudal nobles and new, often hostile communities to absorb, the German princes soon found the essence of the Napoleonic reforms essential to their own survival. Above all, the new regime worked best where indigenous cultural mediators introduced key institutions and laws of the new order, the cardinal example being the Helvetic Republic, the last "sister republic" still in existence.[55] Here, the centralized administrative system could be mutated almost out of being to accommodate the traditional cantons, yet this vital compromise, followed by others often disliked by the French at the time, also allowed the essence of the code to embed itself in the republic. It is arguable that the code, certainly, and the centralized administrative system, up to a point, flourished best when introduced by indigenous rulers more ready to adapt French norms to their own needs, although such rulers were also usually as insensitive as Napoleon to local conditions of which they disapproved. This emerged in the Tyrolese revolt against Bavarian rule in 1809 and the longstanding, if peaceful, legal wrangles between the Imperial Knights of the ex-*kriese* and the mediatized princes.[56] Such struggles sharpened the minds of the indigenous princes and taught them the need for the code in particular and the vital role of the centralized ethos of the new regime in general.

In an empire bent on institutional uniformity, identity of interest was crucial. This may reveal a deeper, underlying element of unity, however. The legacy of

---

[54] F. Bluche, *Le Bonapartisme: Aux origines de la droite autoritaire (1800–1850)* (Paris: Presses Universitaires de France, 1981), 13–94.

[55] G. Clemens, "El caso de la Suiza" in Broers, Guimera, Hicks, *El imperio napoleónico*, 123–37.

[56] On the Tyrol: F. G. Eyck, *Loyal Rebels. Andreas Hofer and the Tyrolean Uprising of 1809* (New York: University Press of America, 1986). On the Imperial Knights: K. Epstein, *The Genesis of German Conservatism* (Princeton: Princeton University Press, 1966), 607.

Cameralism in the *longue durée*, and of Josephism in contemporary terms, played a crucial role in Germany and Lombardy, for both were signs that these were, in essence, public spheres similar to that of post-revolutionary France. Montegelas, the chief minister of Bavaria, and his counterparts in Baden—von Reitzenstein and von Bieberstein in Nassau—were all protégés of Joseph II, as was Melzi d'Eril, the Vice President of the Italian Republic from 1800–04. There were similar if not identical reforming aspirations to draw upon. It could seem to run deeper, however. Direct contact with the elites of southern Germany in particular proved very easy and even agreeable for the French. There was a sense of natural partnership. The French often sensed this, themselves. Montbreton de Norvins recalled of his time as the French *chargé d'affaires* in Baden, that "The Grand Duchy became a second Alsace united, rather than separated, by the Rhine, to the point it was impossible to be more in France than in that German state."[57] Baden was, emphatically for this imperial civil servant, within the "French" circle. Here, then, was the ideal "imperial model" of the First Empire: a confederation of well established rulers whose attitude to institutional reform matched that of the French exactly because it stemmed from similar intellectual roots and comparable internal conditions. If French rule was meant to turn on the twin pillars of *ralliement* and *amalgame*, harnessed together, it did so far more in those states free from direct French control, where indigenous rulers and bureaucracies did the reforming, not men from Paris.

Napoleon understood the power of dynastic legitimacy precisely because he did not, himself, possess it. Hence his reticence to deposing the House of Savoy and annexing Piedmont directly to France: he was driven to this only by the Savoyards' own double-dealing with Austria.[58] Nor did he depose either the Spanish or Neapolitan Bourbons until utterly exasperated by them. He hesitated far more in these circumstances than he did with members of his own family. Thus, the ideal imperial relationship was that which he established with the Wittelsbachs of Bavaria. Substituting indigenous rulers with his siblings was the penultimate resort, and annexation to France was the last: the blockade transformed the fate of the Batavian Republic, first into a satellite kingdom in 1806 and finally into French departments in 1810. Similarly, in Catalonia, stripped from Joseph's Spain in an effort better to protect the Pyrenean "natural frontier" by ruling both sides of it, demonstrated less imperial ambitions than the failure to extend the model of the Confederation of the Rhine beyond the "natural frontiers" of the inner empire. Those frontiers were not defined by physical geography, however, but by societal, cultural, and political mores.

The inner empire was an elitist construct, for all its relative success. The European masses, from the core of *l'ancienne France* to the furthest flung outposts of the empire, including all of its satellite states save Spain, were subject to conscription, to a newer, more efficient system of taxation, and to all the oppression of an active bureaucracy in time of war. The inner empire was successful and it laid the foundations

---

[57] J. Norvins de Montbretonne, *Souvenirs d'un historien de Napoléon*, 3 vols. (Paris, 1896–97), iii, 62.

[58] P. Gaffarel, "L'annexation du Piémont à la France," *Révolution Française* 19 (June 1890): 281–314.

for the pattern of government in most of western Europe for the rest of the nineteenth century, but this in no way made it a popular, still less a populist regime, anywhere. Indeed, its support was often limited only to those sections of the elite who served it. Nevertheless, rulers and their bureaucracies became powerful enough to maintain themselves, and the number of rulers who adhered to the Napoleonic vision of the law and the state actually swelled in 1814 rather than diminished. For example, William I, the new king of the Netherlands, did not dismantle what he found, even if he denied its origins.[59] Gradually, the House of Savoy returned to the Napoleonic template, until by 1831, the state resembled a Napoleonic clone, more than the eighteenth century absolutism it still claimed to be.[60] Across this band of territory, a vital nerve had been touched by the experience and, above all, the example of Napoleonic rule, however elitist and confined that nerve might have been.

Ironically, the heavy hand of direct rule from Paris excluded local elites from real power in most of the outer empire. The civil administration and the courts of the imperial departments were everywhere, from Rome to the Baltic, dominated by Frenchmen, as were the higher echelons of the governments of the new satellite kingdoms of Naples and Westphalia. Effectively, this made the implementation of *ralliement* and *amalgame* in the outer empire difficult and often impossible. The indigenous elites were excluded from real power, even on the lowest rung on the judicial hierarchy. A poignant example is the post of public prosecutor. All the public prosecutors in the new departments were French, as defined by the "natural frontiers." This office was not only responsible for bringing cases for the state, but oversaw the internal discipline of the courts, a sign the local judiciary could not really be trusted, whether politically or in terms of pure professional competence. More emphatically, all the six-man gendarmerie brigades beyond the "natural frontiers" were composed of four Frenchmen. Only Spain remained largely in Spanish hands, although its position as a war zone meant that the Josephist government remained largely fictitious outside Madrid and Catalonia. Where French rule was real—as in Valencia and Andalucia between 1810 and 1812—it was usually due to the efforts of interested military commanders, Suchet and Soult, respectively.

A direct French presence, whether in the annexed departments or the satellite kingdoms, did not guarantee the triumph of French policies. It was in Westphalia that the Napoleonic regime came closest to reverting to feudalism itself. The new kingdom lost land to *majorats* and *dotations*, lands whose revenues were earmarked for the support of families who had distinguished themselves in imperial service and carried Napoleonic titles of nobility. There were *majorats* and *dotations* in the territories of the Grand Duchy of Warsaw and the former Venetian territories of the Kingdom of Italy as well. In Westphalia, especially, their scale subtracted revenues from the new state on

---

[59] M. van der Burg and M. Lok, "El caso holandés," in Broers, Guimera, and Hicks, *El imperio napoleónico*, 72–97.

[60] M. Broers, "The Restoration in Piedmont-Sardinia, 1814–1848. Variations on Reaction," in Laven and Riall, *Napoleon's Legacy*, 151–64.

an appreciable scale.[61] Westphalia and the Grand Duchy of Warsaw also proved ready sources of conscripts after 1807. Conscription weighed heavily on both the inner and outer empires, if by different means: in the former, it was achieved through intensive administrative reforms and the diffusion of gendarmeries throughout its rural peripheries; its success signified the triumph of the new state. In the latter, however, conscription succeeded where it did because the new state halted at the gates of the great feudal estates of central Germany and Poland, compromised with the manorial system, and received fresh levies as a result. In the Kingdoms of Naples and Spain, Napoleonic rule did not even achieve this. This much appears indisputable: the continued, seemingly perpetual extraction of conscripts from rural Europe on an unprecedented scale provoked fierce and intransigent popular resistance right across all the states under Napoleonic hegemony. If it was usually too atomized to pose any real threat to authority, the "blood tax"—so-called all over Europe by peasant communities who could not understand dialects only a few miles from their own villages—ensured that all the Napoleonic regimes were never popular beyond a narrow elite. Where conscription worked, it was either because resistance was not feasible, as in Nassau, where two per cent of the total population was always under arms between 1806 and 1813, or in the Auvergne region of central France, whose mountain communities were simply worn down by 1810, after a decade of determined "policing" by the gendarmerie and the army.[62] Seen from the perspective of the common people of Europe, there was little tangible, immediate evidence that the new, imperial order was anything other than, quite literally, a blood sucker. Its novelty for them lay in its efficiency, an efficiency based on the omnipresence of its police.[63] Indeed, the recent work of Johan Joor on the great cities of the Netherlands has shown that determined resistance need not be confined to rural peripheries where the terrain lent itself to the ruthless game of "hide-and-seek" so common across Napoleonic Europe. Joor's work is also a salutary lesson that the success of policing—the quashing of overt, collective, violent resistance to the state—should not be equated with acquiesce or acceptance of its norms, as has been argued by Isser Woloch for France.[64]

---

[61] H. Berding, *Napoleonische Herrschafts- und Gesellschaftspolitik in Königreich Westfalen 1807–1813* (Frankfurt: Vandenhoeck and Ruprecht, 1973), 51.

[62] On Nassau: C. Anderson, "State-building in Early Nineteenth Century Nassau," *Central European History* 24 (October 1991): 222–47. On the Auvergne: I. Woloch, "Napoleonic Conscription: State Power and Civil Society," *Past & Present* 111 (June 1986): 101–29.

[63] For France: A. Forrest, *Conscripts and Deserters: The Army and French Society during the Revolution and Empire* (Oxford: Oxford University Press, 1989). For the Kingdom of Italy: A. Grab, "Army, State, and Society: Conscription and Desertion in Napoleonic Italy (1802–1814)," *Journal of Modern History* 67 (January 1995). Most of the regional studies cited here have chapters devoted to conscription.

[64] J. Joor, *De Adelaar en het Lam. Onrust, opruiing en onwilligheid in Nederland ten tijde van het Koninkrijk Holland en de Inlijving bij het Franse Keizerrijk (1806–1813)* (Amsterdam: Uitgeverij De Bataafsche Leeuw B.V., 2000). Woloch, *New Regime*, 418–20.

One way to reconcile the concept of the empire set out by Woolf—that of a determinedly reforming regime whose policies were underpinned by a discernable ideology—with a more traditional analysis which sees the Napoleonic Empire as, at best, purely pragmatic or, at worst, simply rapacious, is to regard both views as valid within the inner and outer empires, respectively. To follow this line of thought, the inner empire was not only under Napoleonic control for a more appreciable amount of time, it often adapted Napoleonic reforms at the behest of indigenous rulers—most of its territories were already moving toward similar patterns or reform before the French Revolution. Conversely, the outer empire was occupied only briefly, it had been acquired for different reasons, and in a different manner. It was the result of either the need to enforce the blockade, or the spiteful desire to punish perceived treason. Its origins were purely negative; its only practical purpose became the extraction of human and material resources as the blockade faltered and it became increasingly obvious that neither Prussia nor Austria had been cowed into reliable submission by the loss of territory.

Nevertheless, however great the gap between what the French sought to achieve and their failure to do so in the face of the "pragmatic" exigencies of war, they insisted on trying to introduce reforms which they knew from experience made the tasks of conscription, routine administration—and even the restoration of order—very difficult and often impossible. Why they did so brings the debate to the heart of the matter: whether there was such a thing as "Napoleonic imperialism," as quite distinct from the First Napoleonic Empire, rests on how French behavior throughout Europe is perceived, and not just within the confines of the inner empire. Indeed, it is arguable that the makeshift, often ephemeral nature of the later annexations and the later satellite kingdoms stemmed, in part, from French attempts to integrate them too rapidly, that their rule was weaker because they rejected pragmatism in favor of confrontation.

"Napoleonic Civilization": a Contradiction in Terms or the Essence of a Regime?

No one can doubt the truth of Christof Dipper's verdict on the reforming impulses of Napoleonic imperialism as marked by "the gulf between the program and the reality,"[65] an assessment that at least allows the existence of a reforming program, an assumption that, itself, is far from universally accepted. Jerome's Westphalia was to be a "model state" run through sane, rational, and enlightened legislation. Napoleon told him famously that good French government would prove a better protection from Prussian bayonets than the *Grande Armée*. Yet, this same kingdom was full of *dotations* and *majorats* within months. This does not exempt the historian from trying to understand the nature of that program. Nor does it automatically annul the possibility

---

[65] C. Dipper, W. Schieder, R. Schultze, eds., *Napoleonische Herrschaft in Deutschland und Italien—Verwaltung und Justiz* (Trier: Duncker & Humblot, 1995), 13; Ellis, *Napoleonic Empire*, 101.

of that program acquiring a lasting influence beyond its own times. Neither should any analysis of that program allow itself to be hidebound or discredited by Napoleon's own assertions in his memoirs.

Many of the reforms inherent in Napoleonic rule were driven by expediency. The dogmatic insistence on the imposition of the French system of departments headed by centrally appointed prefects, like the introduction of the *État civil* created in France as early as 1790, were both essential to the process of conscription. The departments were rational units of administration, and the prefect, in whom all managerial responsibility was concentrated, was the perfect tool for an operation which involved all the main branches of local administration—civil, military, judicial, and police—in concert, at least three and often four times a year. The *État civil* placed all birth, death, and marriage records in the hands of the civil authorities, thereby making the statistics vital for conscription—age, marital status, and the overall number of conscription-aged men per department—readily available to the state. Thus, however much rage the introduction of such reforms provoked, they were unavoidable if the Napoleonic war machine was to be supplied and more generally were deemed fundamental to the extension of state power. This centralized system of administration was adopted for exactly these reasons almost *in toto* in the allied states of the Confederation of the Rhine, and retained by many restored rulers who otherwise detested Napoleon—notably William I of the Netherlands—for just these reasons. It is more than possible to divorce much of the process of Napoleonic reform from any deep ideological basis. Put another way, even in its rigid, uncompromising uniformity—and all the local resistance it could provoke—the essence of the system can be interpreted as an exercise in pragmatism, because the war was the regime's *raison d'être*.

Nevertheless, there were other reforms which were not essential to the war, but were axiomatic to the French. The French, from Napoleon down, insisted on implementing "awkward" reforms, as well as necessary evils, wherever they went, be it by direct annexation or the creation of a satellite kingdom: in Naples, Napoleon ordered Joseph to publish the code in full despite his brother's openly expressed misgivings regarding the consternation legalized divorce would cause among all social classes. Indeed, the introduction of the code, and even more of the French system of court administration, had the potential to make the indigenous legal classes redundant throughout Napoleonic Europe. The increasing presence of French magistrates at even the lowest rungs of the judicial ladder—and always in the key positions of first presidents and public prosecutors—made this a reality in the annexed departments of the outer empire. This greatly compromised the potential for *ralliement* in these places, and made *amalgame* virtually a dead-letter. In this context, however, the point is that a less rigid insistence on the wholesale introduction of both the code and the court system may have left the door open to wider collaboration. This was seldom the case, however.

The Concordat was as axiomatic as the code for the French, in their satellite states just as within the imperial departments, and it lost them more friends and made them more enemies than almost anything else, arguably even than conscription, for the "blood tax" fell largely on the lower classes—those with money could buy replacements—but the religious reforms antagonized people of all social classes and, with the insistence of both code and Concordat on freedom of conscience, those most angered were the majority religion. The abolition of the regular clergy brought the new regimes properties of the contemplative orders, but this was the only tangible gain that accrued from the Concordat. Its capacity to unsettle and disrupt religious life did not always lead to overt, collective violence, but it bred alienation and could, as in the departments of the former Papal states, produce widespread campaigns of passive, civil resistance capable of paralyzing local administration.[66] Reform of the Catholic church struck at, and was evident in, daily life like few other aspects of Napoleonic reform. The Josephist kingdom of Spain is a revealing case in point. In seeming contrast to the other Napoleonic states, Joseph's constitution recognized Catholicism as the only official religion, but the introduction of the code, with its guarantee of freedom of conscience, virtually negated its importance. Moreover, in the midst of the war and the *guerrilla*, Joseph pressed ahead with the suppression of the regular orders and the seizure of their property. One of his first acts was to abolish the Inquisition.[67] Napoleon continually put pressure on Bavaria to emancipate the Jews, with no success it is true, but it is, perhaps, revealing that he risked antagonizing his loyalist ally over such an issue.

The proto-colonialist mind set of the imperial bureaucracy emerged most emphatically in their handling of the administration of the meridional regions of the empire, as can be sensed in Joseph's insistence on ecclesiastical reform in the teeth of the Spanish *guerrilla*. In the imperial departments of Italy, it also pervaded that most necessary and pragmatic of all evils, "the blood tax." Conscription was regarded not only as a means to tame the "wild" communities of the mountain peripheries, but, literally, to reinvigorate the decadent, priest-ridden youth of the urban upper classes. It assumed the magnitude of a campaign of moral regeneration that was itself the culmination of an arduous process of fostering a martial spirit in the hearts and minds of Italian males. One unfortunate young noble was Connestabile Stoffa, who Antoine Roederer, the French prefect of the department of Trasimeno, was determined to hound into the *garde d'honneur*. He was worth more than 100,000 francs in rents and carried "le plus beau nom d'Italie," but this was not Roederer's reason for "targeting" him for active service:

> His father is dead and his mother treats him like a little girl. She is a respectable woman who imagines she could not do better than to have three priests bring up her boy. This young man is eighteen. Judge for yourself what a blow this will [be] for the poor mother! It creates a great

---

[66] M. Broers, *The Politics of Religion in Napoleonic Italy: The War against God, 1801–1814* (London: Routledge, 2002).

[67] J. Mercader Riba, *José Bonaparte: Rey de España*, 2 vols. (Madrid: Instituto Jerónimo Zurita, 1971), i; J. Mercader Riba, *Estructura del Estado Español Bonapartista* (Madrid: Instituto Jerónimo Zurita, 1983), 453–81. On the Inquisition: E. de la Lama Cereceda, *J. A. Llorente, un ideal Burgesia* (Pamplona: Ediciones Universidad de Navarra, 1991).

good chance for this young man. There have been attempts to exempt him under thousands of pretexts.[68]

Roederer had a duty to Connestabile Stoffa to free him from a baroque Catholicism which had robbed him of his ancestral glory. For the director-general of police in Florence:

> Nothing proves better, the faults of former institutions and running of these various small states, than the estrangement of the inhabitants of this part of the Empire, from the profession of arms; they have inherited none of the inclinations of their earliest ancestors or the warlike peoples who have successively invaded this beautiful part of the Empire.[69]

The severity of their judgements marks a clear perception of "the other," of incompatibilty as well as of hostility, between opposing cultures. The European view of Latin America, as drawn by Kiernan, may even have part of its origins here: "From the distance of Europe all Latin America was much the same, and much oftener decadent than virile."[70]

In the nobility, weak government allowed cases such as the young Stoffa to abound, while on the periphery of these states—usually synonymous with the Apennine uplands—it fostered unchannelled aggression where, according to Rome's director-general of police, "their youth turns to brigandage, whereas long ago in France, it had turned to soldiering."[71] Embedded in these remarks are the enlightenment concepts that made possible the seemingly incongruous association between militarism and civilized life so central to the ideology of Napoleonic imperialism. For enlightenment thinkers such as De Pauw and Buffon, a *société polie* could exist only within a *société policée*.[72] Military service, far from brutalizing youth, would curb the latent effeminacy of its privileged members and the barbarism of its peasantry. Absorbing *ancien régime* power vacuums meant something more than international security, at least south of the Alps and Pyrenees.[73]

Perhaps it is in the character of these "awkward reforms" and their insistence on implementing them, as well as in their attitudes to the "morality" of conscription, that a French national identity emerges, and it was based on the tenets of the revolution of 1789. In the public sphere, it rested on the abolition of feudalism, the

---

[68] Archives Nationales de Paris, Archives Privées, Fondes Roederer 29-AP-15, A. Roederer to P-L Roederer, April 28, 1813.
[69] ANP F⁷ (Police Générale) 6523A (Toscane, Rapports du Directeur Général), D. Gen. to Min. 3 arrondissement de police, Aug. 1810.
[70] Kiernan, *The Lords*, 302.
[71] ANP F⁷ (Police Générale) 8889 (dépt. Rome) D. Gen. to Min. Police Générale, Sept. 20 1812.
[72] See Michelle Duchet, *Anthropologie et histoire au siècle des Lumières* (Paris: Albin Michel, 1971).
[73] Broers, *Napoleonic Empire in Italy*, passim.

sacredness of the separation of powers in the administration. Nor was it confined to southern, Catholic Europe, although it emerged in different ways further north. The commercial, maritime world, with its emphasis on money, its aversion to public service in terms of a formal career, and its perceived amateurish ethos in the public sphere—to say nothing of the general absence of codified law or centralized, uniform administration—was no more in harmony with the Napoleonic state than baroque Catholicism or seigneurial tenure. Joseph Faure, a former president of the Tribunate and a Bonapartist of the first hours, had the task of organizing the judiciary of the new Hanseatic departments. His reports emphasize the gulf between the people of the Hansa ports and France and, interestingly, Faure did not see their commercial economy as an agent of civilization. Quite the reverse:

> The character of these cities is such that they are dominated by commercial interests, and so they have little liking for Roman law, which they should learn to respect. There are some civil and criminal regulations that, even if they have largely fallen into disuse, are not compatible with the mores of civilized nations.[74]

The ideal of empire was a world of commerce in rivers and canals, not of the open sea, of well trodden routes, not new horizons. It was an urban world, but in a very traditional sense—secular and literate, the world of the *salon* but not the *caffè*, of the theatre but not the opera, of enlightenment yet not of restless innovation. These were not stereotypes or merely the contents of after-dinner conversational prejudice, but the bases which the French formed judgments and relationships with those around them, and these benchmarks excluded vast swathes of their fellow citizens, just as they did many beyond the old frontiers. They allowed a considerable number of "new Frenchmen" in, as well. It all crystallized around the receptiveness of a given society to the fundamentals of the Napoleonic Code, for this determined family structures, concepts of property, the ethos of civic pride and the regard in which society held public service, and the innate respectability of a given polity, confirmed by a willingness to accept the world of the open, published trial, in place of inquisitorial justice. If the new subjects were seen as malleable to the mores embodied in the code, they were civilized men who recognized the universal truth of a good law; if not, they had to learn such truths through the good government Napoleonic hegemony would bring them. Above all, the empire was a society governed by reason rather than tradition, and tradition was not there to be respected. This was as necessary to impress upon the advanced, urbanized commercial worlds of the Hansa and Holland, as on the hinterlands of the Apennines. It was as big a challenge in the Vendée as in Croatia. Napoleonic "civilization" had a regional core, and beyond that core it had a civilizing mission. From all this emerges a final irony, however. There was a marked discrepancy between the "nation of

---

[74] ANP BB5 268 (Organisation Judiciaire, dépts. hanséatiques) Faure to Minister of Justice, January 26, 1811.

mind," which was France, and the real core of the empire, which was anchored in the Rhineland and northern Italy more than in large swathes of France itself.

Empire, State and Nation: the Legacy of the First Napoleonic Empire

Napoleon trumpeted his credentials as the godfather of European nationalism on St. Helena, but his own empire was its antithesis, in all but one case—that of France, itself. Only his furthest flung creations—the Grand Duchy of Warsaw and, more obliquely, the Illyrian Provinces—corresponded with nationalist aspirations. Annie Jourdan has astutely observed that Napoleon's own political creations—his reordering of western Germany through the Confederation, like his division of Italy—were not true nation-states in size, but small or middle-sized states.[75] They could not defend themselves from the great eastern powers without his support, a hard fact that bound the diverse elements of the inner empire—the allied states and the annexed departments—together and to France. Above all, he ruthlessly sought to make every element of his hegemony conform to the French template of the public sphere. There was no room for diversity; the First Napoleonic Empire was not a composite state, even as regards its allied and satellite kingdoms.

Napoleon turned to nationalism in his last exile because he was looking forward even as he appeared to be reminiscing. He was also aware that, in France at least, his demise had made "empire" unfashionable. In 1813, Benjamin Constant, a longstanding opponent of Napoleon, published a damning critique not only of the Emperor but of the imperialist ideal itself.[76] Interestingly, Constant actually did an about face and supported Napoleon during the Hundred Days, which perhaps—it is impossible to know—awakened the possibilities of nationalism in him, on St. Helena. In any case, Napoleon and his collaborators lived in the world of the possible, and it was states rather than nation-states that they forged successfully and left as their greatest legacy to post-1814 Europe. The state system in Germany, with a few alternations, endured for half a century to come; the most potent and popular forms of Italian unification proposed in the early nineteenth century tended to revolve around confederations of states not unlike Napoleon's own partition. The pattern Annie Jourdan has discerned so clearly—middle-sized states which could be controlled by the Great Powers—were well suited to their times. From below, they corresponded better, if hardly perfectly, to a world built on local and dynastic loyalties. From above, they posed no threats to the great Chancelleries of Europe. From the perspective of rulers for whom modern communications were still in the future, they were manageable

---

[75] A. Jourdan, *L'Empire de Napoléon* (Paris: Flammarion, 2000), 124.

[76] B. Constant, "The Spirit of Conquest and Usurpation and Their Relation to European Civilization," in F. Biancamaria, ed. and trans., *Constant: Political Writings* (Cambridge: Cambridge University Press, 1993), 51–169.

in the same way as the French model of the department on a lower scale. The manner in which the states of post-Napoleonic Europe were governed proved more enduring still. The model of the Napoleonic state proved powerful, so much so that, by mid-century, even his enemies had adopted its major hallmarks where they had never been abandoned. As Marta Lorente has declared, Napoleon did conquer Spain, but he did so in 1843, when the monarchy adopted the Council of State, the lynchpin of the Napoleonic executive.[77] To assert this in the case of Spain is, perhaps, the most poignant testimony of all to the durability of the Napoleonic legacy in Europe.

The example of Napoleonic imperialism as an imperialist model is more debatable, but its uncompromising centralism, its clear sense of cultural superiority, and above all, the increasing emergence of a civilizing mission among its servants, stamped this aspect of its character on the future, more than the false claims of proto-nationalism Napoleon tried to clothe it in after its demise.

---

[77] M. Lorente, "De los Consejos de la Monarquía Católica al Consejo de Estado Español. (Análysis Crítico de un transplante institucional, España, 1808–1845)," in Broers, Guimera, and Hicks, *El imperio napoleónico*, 232–57.

Colonialism and Nation-Building in Modern France

ROBERT ALDRICH

France occupies a tidy place on maps of Europe, a hexagonal shape, with Paris at its center, a country whose borders seem to have varied little over the past several centuries, and whose culture—despite great diversity in landscapes, architecture, and culinary specialities—remains immediately identifiable both to outsiders and to residents. Recurrent references in political rhetoric to the indivisibility of the nation and to the constancy of republican values reinforce the appearance of unity. However, the impression is something of a mirage; France is a nation and state constructed over a very long period, and with deep fractures of regional, religious, political, and social strife.

Over the *longue durée*, the contours of the French state and nation, as is the case with most others, have changed dramatically. Empire has occupied an important place in the making of France, both nation and state, though not without paradoxes, contradictions, and challenges that proved impossible to resolve. Forging a nation meant not only molding together a disparate set of regions, cultures, and people inside that roughly hexagonal stretch of land inside Europe, but it also meant working out the relationship between continental France and its overseas possessions scattered from the Caribbean to Oceania. The very existence of these far-flung corners of France around the world inevitably posed questions about France as nation, as state, and as empire, and indeed, in our day, as a post-imperial country. If empire only exceptionally occupied center-stage in French concerns—perhaps during the imperial scramble of the late 1800s, certainly during the Algerian war of the 1950s and early 1960s—it always hovered somewhere in the background. One politician remarked just after the Second World War, as France's empire was starting to come undone, that with empire France was a great country, but without it, France was only a parcel of Europe, a comment that underscored the role that the empire had played in the French self-image of their nation and its role in the world. In history and in maps, both global and mental, the colonies and the metropole have overlapped.[1]

The principal argument of this chapter begins with the supposition that modern France, in particular from 1830 to 1962 but with antecedents in the old regime, revolutionary, and Napoleonic periods, is an imperial nation-state—French nationalism was an *imperial* nationalism.[2] However, nation-building involved the construction of that imperial nation-state, with carefully circumscribed integration of the colonies into the French polity, economy, and cultural universe, making them in a sense overseas provinces. Accompanying this task came an effort to instil support for colonialism in the cities and regions of France. Moreover, particular regional interests could be galvanized in the colonial endeavor, but those interests could also persuasively agitate, at the national center, for overseas expansion. The ideal for colonialists—though ending in ultimate and perhaps inevitable failure—was a unified nation indefectibly linked to its colonies, a *plus grande France* stretching seamlessly from the towns and villages of the metropole to the furthest frontiers of the empire.

The Old and New Empires of New Regime France

A new sort of nation-building became a necessity for the revolutionaries of 1789, reconstructing a nation on the ruins of the old regime that they had dismantled. Constitutional monarchists, republicans, Jacobin radicals, and proto-socialists disagreed on both the processes and the goals, but several significant developments occurred in the first years of the revolution that remained in place despite the turbulent regime changes that followed. One was a new sense of the nation as a collective of citizens rather than as subjects of a monarch who ruled by divine right. Not all citizens were equal; for a time, "active" citizens enjoyed the right to vote while "passive" citizens did not, and women (and indigenous and enslaved people in the colonies) remained disenfranchised. The Declaration of the Rights of Man and Citizen nevertheless declared liberty for citizens and equality before the law, with the added promise of fraternity for members of the body politic: a dramatic departure from the institutionalized estates of the Bourbon era. Furthermore, the revolution mandated representation for the citizens, with the implication of mass politicization, elections, and the primacy of the parliament. The new nation thus constituted a compact of men (and that word conveys the gendered sense of entitlement) whose Frenchness both endowed them with the privileges of the declaration of rights and whose status as citizens gave them control over the state. In return, they accepted certain responsibilities: to obey the law, pay taxes, and defend the *patrie* from

---

[1] The most comprehensive discussion can be found in Martin Thomas, ed., *The French Colonial Mind* (Lincoln: University of Nebraska Press, 2011).

[2] Jane Burbank and Frederick Cooper, *Empires in World History: Power and the Politics of Difference* (Princeton: Princeton University Press, 2010), provides the most incisive discussion of the inter-linked role of nations and empires in the modern world.

enemies at home and abroad—the *levée en masse*, a particularly important expression of the new nationalism. Indeed, nationalism as it emerged throughout Europe in the nineteenth century, as many theorists of nationalism have argued, owed much to the ideology of the French Revolution, the contract between citizens bound together by their belonging to a state and their adherence to its ideals. Such allegiance to the ideals and the institutions of the new regime, in the French case, formed the bedrock of inclusive nationalism, whereas in other conceptions (sometimes in opposition to French revolutionary imperialism) nation-building philosophers and politicians stressed ancestral lineage, the sharing of language and culture, and a more spiritual sense of the nation to which outsiders of whatever sort could have but limited access.

Another nation-building aspect of the revolution was the attempt to wield the congeries of different regions and cultures into a unit. Several policies symbolized this effort. The revolutionary assemblies adopted the metric system to replace the various weights and measures current in old France. They abolished the provinces, dividing France into a set of *départements* (and, below them, *cantons*), administrative districts mapped out by the distance of the furthest village from the local center (*chef-lieu*). Paris appointed a prefect (*préfet*) for each *département*, an official duty-bound to execute and enforce political policy made by the parliament and administration in Paris, and to safeguard the nation against illegitimate departures from norms decreed by the center. The legislators adopted uniform codes of civil and criminal law, codifications that replaced the baffling array of statutes of the old regime. In each of these measures, the leaders of the revolutionary regimes, and then Napoleon—who in fact reinforced such provisions—sought to standardize governance, from an agreed system of measurements to a canon of law and an artifice of administration, and thereby they strove to homogenize a nation.[3]

Such attempts obviously faced resistance from opponents of the revolution. They also came up against the question of the place of the French colonies in this system, and of the place of those European territories that came under French rule after conquest by the revolutionary and Napoleonic armies. The revolutionaries pronounced their creed universalistic and evangelical, and their armies' campaigns to defend the new republic and *la patrie en danger* led to invasions of neighboring countries and the sponsoring of new sister republics in the Low Countries, Switzerland, and Italy. The revolutionaries also maintained control over the remnants of New France (essentially the vast territory of the Mississippi valley and the tiny islands of Saint-Pierre and Miquelon), the colonies of the Caribbean (Saint-Dominigue, Martinique, and Guadeloupe key among them) and French outposts along the coast of western Africa and in the Indian Ocean. The sponsored new regimes on the European borders of France were not incorporated into the French Republic, their relationship one of

---

[3] On nationalism in the old regime and revolutionary period, see David A. Bell, *The Cult of the Nation in France: Inventing Nationalism, 1680–1800* (Cambridge, Mass.: Harvard University Press, 2003). On the later period, a good starting point for further reading is Rogers Brubaker, *Citizenship and Nationhood in France and Germany* (Cambridge, Mass.: Harvard University Press, 1992).

alliance with the French state not integration into the French nation, though the establishment of republican (or, in Napoleon's iteration, hereditary) governments often provoked opposition to France and its revolutionary principles. The colonies, however, came under direct French rule, though their exact relationship to European France was unclear. Local (white) elites initially had grave suspicions about the post-1789 regime in Paris, especially with talk of the abolition of the slavery that formed the basis for economic life and political power in the plantation colonies. Attacks on the planters in such islands as Guadeloupe (where many were massacred) and the Convention's abolition of slavery in 1794 not surprisingly roused even greater opposition. Political leaders in the metropole no doubt thought of their distant kin in the colonies as members of the nation and the state, covered by the declaration of rights and fit to elect representatives to the legislature. Few considered the indigenous peoples and the slaves as part of the nation, only as wards of the state. Only the most radical argued that equality extended to the colonized, even if the occasional black delegate, duly vested with a tricolor sash of office, appeared in the assemblies in Paris.[4]

The question of the boundaries of the French nation and state became more acute in the Napoleonic regime. In the West Indies, Napoleon reinstituted slavery but proved incapable of defeating the secessionist rebels in Saint-Dominigue (Haiti).[5] He sold the Louisiana Purchase to the United States, putting paid to any discussion of the place of the North American French in the *patrie*. Despite de-accessioning this vast territory, Napoleon not only made himself emperor but became an ardent imperialist: the double meaning of "empire" during Napoleon's reign—a particular form of state organization and rule over conquered countries—itself pointed to the quandary of where France, Frenchness, and French rule began and ended.[6] Napoleon's short-lived conquest of Egypt, and even briefer incursions into Palestine, are legendary, and Napoleon and supporters harbored visions of forcing the British out of India or at least of conquering part of the subcontinent for the French. These distant dreams evaporated, and British military victories removed most of the French colonies, either temporarily or permanently, from Paris's overlordship. Any hopes for a great overseas empire vanished when Napoleon was forced to evacuate Egypt, even if he tried to spin his defeat into a success for the audience back at home, and his sights then turned to a European continental empire.[7]

France the nation thus was France the empire (as it had been, in a somewhat different configuration, in the old regime) under Napoleon. Setting his relatives and commanders on European thrones, Napoleon exported his legal codes and political

---

[4] Yves Benot, *La Révolution française et la fin des colonies* (Paris: La Découverte, 1997).

[5] Laurent Dubois, *A Colony of Citizens: Revolution and Slave Emancipation in the French Caribbean, 1787–1804* (Chapel Hill: University of North Carolina Press, 2004).

[6] Partly because of the double meaning (and the revival of "empire" in France under Napoleon III), "empire" was generally not used in French to refer to the colonies until the early twentieth century, and even so rarely appeared in official nomenclature.

[7] Maya Jasanoff, *Edge of Empire: Lives, Culture and Conquest in the East, 1750–1850* (New York: Vintage Books, 2005); Paul Strathern, *Napoleon in Egypt* (New York: Vintage Books, 2006).

institutions to conquered territories and extracted their resources for the use of France, transforming much of western and central Europe essentially into a set of French protectorates (if not outright colonies).[8] It would be interesting, in fact, to think about the "colonial" aspects of Napoleon's continental empire, even with the profound differences that separated his domains in Europe from the overseas possessions denoted in the more generally accepted notion of colonialism. Not only satisfaction of Napoleon's megalomania, but also the survival of his regime, and the power and prestige of France, depended on the success of his military expansion. Empire-building, at great expense of men and blood, became part of the program of Bonapartist nation-building, as his armies marched across the Iberian, Germanic, and Italian lands and on into eastern Europe and towards the gates of Moscow. Meanwhile, the French and British navies battled for supremacy in the Caribbean Sea and the Indian Ocean. Looking further afield, Napoleon chartered an expedition to Australia, led by Captain Baudin, to reconnoiter interests in the South Seas. The French nation and state in Europe thereby lay at the heart of a global and imperialist system.

The life span of Napoleon's European empire proved too brief to fully ascertain the place that the countries and people he conquered would have played in the French nation and state. Would the new territories have been reduced to permanent appendages to the French state? How far might a Napoleonic *mission civilisatrice* have extended in an effort to Gallicize subject European peoples? Would Napoleon have designed some enduring supranational institutional system—a prequel to the French Union of the 1940s or a European Union of the present day—to exercise European hegemony? How would Bonaparte's administrators have ruled the colonies that France conquered, or others that might have been acquired if his armies had not been pushed back? The answers to such questions can only involve speculation.

Despite the defeat of his imperial system, Napoleon left many legacies to later imperialists and nation-builders. French ideologists and power brokers never lost the idea that acquisition of foreign territory, whether in Europe or, increasingly more likely, overseas, could be a benefit and even an imperative in building and preserving the French nation, especially in the continuing competition with a now triumphant Britain. The strategy of military conquest and the imposition of French-style centralized law and administration provided a template for later colonial rule. The emperor's successors reaffirmed France's cultural mission as universalistic and always envisaged its geopolitical rights extending beyond the hexagonal boundaries. With Waterloo, the French Empire overseas severely contracted and the French Empire in Europe disintegrated, but only fifteen years passed before a new effort at nation-building through empire-building occurred. The heritage of Napoleonic rule would be marshalled to that new campaign: the sense of national greatness, the advancement of the frontiers of French rule, the takeover of points around the globe providing geopolitical and commercial advantage.

---

[8] For a good overview, see: Philip G. Dwyer, ed., *Napoleon and Europe* (London: Bloomsbury, 2001).

Even during that hiatus in empire-building before 1815 and 1830, imperial questions in fact never disappeared from the national agenda. The French reimposed rule in their remaining possessions, from Martinique and Guadeloupe to the *comptoirs* of India and the island of La Réunion. They undertook initiatives to settle and develop the colonies, some dramatically ill fated, such as the expedition of the *Méduse* to re-establish control over coastal enclaves in Senegal. Trading ships still sailed between such ports as Bordeaux and the Antilles, and judges sent convoys of prisoners to the "green hell" of Guyane. Debates continued about slavery and slave-trading, emancipationists seeking to reverse Napoleon's restoration of slavery and to combat the now illicit slave trade. In the *"guerre des deux sucres,"* competition intensified between producers of cane sugar in the tropical plantation colonies and the refiners of beet-sugar in northern France (whose efforts dated back to the Continental Blockade). Penologists considered the possibility of replicating (though, they thought, by perfecting) the British system of transportation of criminals, and scouted for an overseas site where convicts might be punished and rehabilitated as settlers. The Navy campaigned for acquisition of supply stations and ports at vital nodes on the globe. Newly set up missionary orders, hoping to rebound from the onslaught of revolution and de-Christianization, sent out priests to evangelize the heathen of Africa and Oceania. Even in what might be thought the most un-colonial period in the nineteenth century, from the loss of most French colonies by 1815 to the conquest of Algiers in 1830, the French nation and state did not live in isolation from its overseas empire and imperial concerns. But it is to the subsequent "new imperialism" and its role in nation-building that we now turn.

France: Nation and Empire after Napoleon

The historical links between post-Napoleonic imperialism, on the one hand, and nation- and state-building, on the other, have traditionally attracted less attention in French historiography than other themes. Indeed, from the period following decolonization until fifteen or twenty years ago, colonial history as a strand of national history had become a rather neglected subject except for a small, if dedicated and accomplished, cohort of scholars. By contrast, subjects such as the revolution, socio-political movements, Marxist-oriented economic history, *Annales*-style social history, and Foucault-inspired cultural history galvanized historians' workshops, and provided the grids for understanding the "making" of modern France. Historians considered domestic issues the prime movers in the country's history, the empire a literally and metamorphically distant part of the engine of nation-building. The French public, for its part, showed little interest in an empire that seemed a relic of the past, a quaint enterprise that occasionally inspired nostalgia for the tropical life of jungles and pith-helmets, but that also evoked painful memories of wars in Indochina and Algeria (and the French defeat in those theatres), the difficult "repatriation" and assimilation of *pieds-noirs* from North Africa, and France's reduced role in international affairs in a post-imperial world.

The old neglect, avoidance, occlusion or "amnesia" about colonialism has now disappeared, with colonialism a hot topic over recent years in the public sphere, in parliament and in academia.[9] Political issues over the two decades or more have animated discussion of the heritage of colonialism: questions about large-scale migration from the former Maghrebin and black African colonies, and issues surrounding multiculturalism, secularism, and communitarianism revealed by debates on the wearing of Muslim headscarves and burqas, riots in suburbs with large ethnic populations, arguments on social mobility, discrimination (and potential measures of positive discrimination) and a debate on "national identity." Conflict has raged about the imperial record, from the slave trade of the first empire to the violence and torture of the Algerian war of 1954–62. Political figures, sometimes maladroitly, have made public pronouncements about the balance sheet of colonialism. Parliament passed a law in 2001 declaring the slave trade a "crime against humanity," and more controversially in 2005 adopted legislation recognizing the "positive" side of colonialism with a clause—subsequently voided by the President—requiring that positive aspects of French expansion be taught in schools. Officials have unveiled new monuments commemorating colonialism, and museums of *arts premiers* and migration have opened in the French capital and other cities.[10] Meanwhile, a formidable array of theses and books on colonialism, both ones written in France and others authored by foreign scholars, fill the bookshelves.[11] In short, the empire is once again seen as an important part of what made (and makes) France what it is.

One outcome of the rediscovery of empire is a wholesale re-evaluation of the role that colonialism occupies in the narrative of French history and in the construction of French identity. Opinions differ about how deeply imperialism planted its roots

---

[9] The notion of post-colonial "amnesia" is generally associated with the work of Benjamin Stora (e.g. *La gangrène et l'oubli: la mémoire de la guerre d'Algérie* (Paris: La Découverte, 1991)), but has been widely adopted by other writers.

[10] The Musée du Quai Branly combines the non-European collections of the Musée de l'Homme (founded in 1937 as successor to the Musée d'Ethographie, set up in 1878) and the Musée des Arts d'Afrique et d'Océanie, opened for the Exposition coloniale internationale of 1931—clear links in the museum's genealogy to the colonial past. The Palais de la Porte Dorée, which housed the ex-Musée colonial (and whose decorative murals and bas-reliefs still celebrate colonialism), now somewhat ironically houses the Cité Nationale de l'Histoire de l'Immigration.

[11] Among a proliferating number of books on the memory of colonialism, and the debates it has engendered in contemporary French society, the following are particularly insightful: Romain Bertrand, *Mémoires d'empire: la controverse autour du "fait colonial"* (Bellecombes-en-Bauges: Editions du Croquant, 2006); Catherine Coquery-Vidrovitch, *Enjeux politiques de l'histoire coloniale* (Marseille: Agone, 2009); Sébastien Jahan and Alain Ruscio, eds., *Histoire de la colonisation: réhabilitations, falsifications et instrumentalisations* (Paris: Les Indes savantes, 2007); and Daniel Lefeuvre, *Pour en finir avec la repentence coloniale* (Paris: Flammarion, 2006). On specific themes and regions, see: Patricia M. E. Lorcin, ed., *Algeria and France, 1800–2000: Identity, Memory, Nostalgia* (Syracuse: Syracuse University Press, 2006); Alain Ruscio and Serge Tignères, *Dien Bien Phu: mythes et réalités, 1954–2004—cinquante ans de passions françaises* (Paris: Les Indes savantes, 2005); and Françoise Vergès, *La mémoire enchaînée: questions sur l'esclavage* (Paris: Albin Michel, 2006).

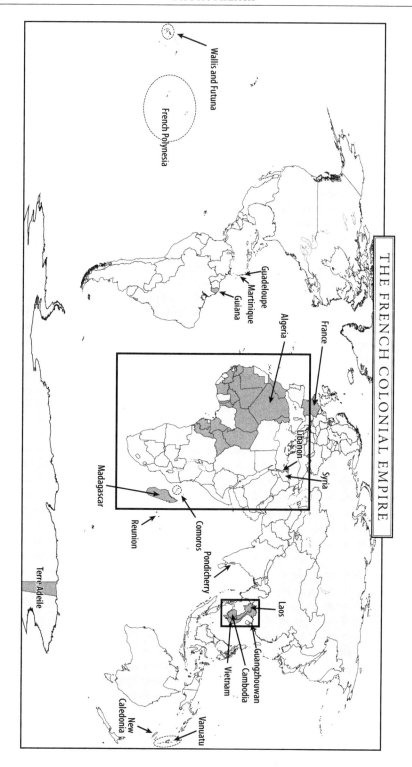

THE FRENCH COLONIAL EMPIRE

Wallis and Futuna

French Polynesia

Guadeloupe
Martinique
Guiana

Algeria

France

Libanon

Syria

Madagascar

Reunion

Comoros

Pondicherry

Laos

Guangzhouwan
Cambodia
Vietnam

New
Caledonia

Vanuatu

Terre Adelie

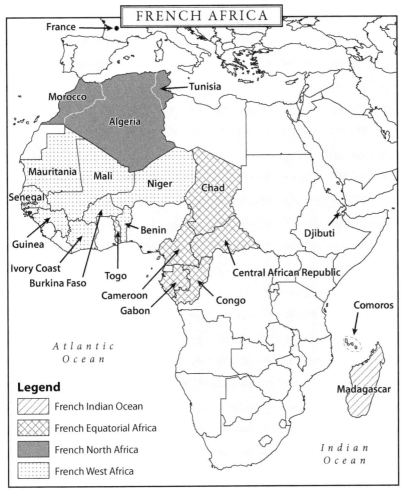

FRENCH AFRICA

France

Morocco

Tunisia

Algeria

Mauritania   Mali   Niger   Chad

Senegal   Djibouti

Guinea   Benin

Ivory Coast

Burkina Faso   Togo   Central African Republic

Cameroon   Congo

Gabon   Comoros

Atlantic Ocean

Legend

French Indian Ocean

French Equatorial Africa

French North Africa

French West Africa

Madagascar

Indian Ocean

FRENCH INDO–CHINA

Guangzhouwan

Vietnam

Laos

Cambodia

South China Sea

into French society. As in Britain and elsewhere, opposing perspectives suggest that colonialism was either of concern to a restricted if committed and vocal number of promoters and interest groups, or rather that it was powerfully omnipresent throughout
society, directly or indirectly suffusing all of public life and touching countless private
lives.[12] Certain it is that colonialism spread like a rhizome across the Hexagon, sending
its shoots into academic and cultural life, industry and trade, military actions and geopolitics, the to and fro of migration, the gospel of Christian evangelization, as well as
the dissemination of revolutionary and republican ideals. The tendrils may have been
more superficial than profound, but they indubitably crept over and covered much of
the Hexagon, raising questions about national unity, race and ethnicity, the universalism or exceptionalism of French culture, and the capacity of France to integrate different countries and cultures into a single polity and commonwealth.

Focusing on nation-building and empire-building in France in the late 1800s
and first half of the 1900s, that is, during the period when the new overseas empire—
the world's second largest—was conquered, and when the ideology of imperialism reached its zenith, this chapter will now trace some of the parameters of France,
Hexagon and empire, specifically the traits of regionalism, nationalism and imperialism during the Third Republic. It will subsequently discuss the strategies that French
authorities used to make the colonies French, the ways in which the overseas outposts
were incorporated into the republic through legal mechanisms, *mise en valeur*, and the
creation of social and cultural French outposts (little "Frances") in distant continents.
The viewpoint afterwards shifts to the role of colonialism in the French provinces, the
different fashions in which colonialism functioned at the local level, and the tactics by
which regional elites instrumentalized expansionism to advance their own objectives.
Trying to draw together these strands, the conclusion will suggest that parallel dyna-
misms worked in nation-building in the colonial age, "colonializing" the provinces and
"provincializing" the empire.

Nation and Empire from the New Imperialism to the "Confetti of Empire"

Any historian would be foolhardy to argue that colonialism provides *the* key to French
history, nation-building or identity, and even "maximalists" who underline the po-
tency of imperialism allow that the French public demonstrated only intermittent

---

[12] This "maximalist" position is represented, for instance, in Pascal Blanchard, Nicolas Bancel and
Sandrine Lemaire, *La fracture coloniale: la société française au prisme de l'héritage colonial* (Paris:
La Découverte, 2005), and other works by these authors and their associates in the "Groupe de
recherches ACHAC" (For a list of the publications, see www.achac.com). The different essays
in a volume that they have co-edited, *Culture coloniale en France: de la Révolution française à nos
jours* (Paris: Autrement, 2008)—including an essay by the present author on colonial museums—
represent a variety of perspectives.

and less than unanimous enthusiasm for *la plus grande France*. Many other causes and affairs—1789 and all that, the *enracinement* of the French psyche in rural life, the conflict between left and right, between Paris and provinces, between the church and anti-clericals—no doubt provided more essential ingredients to the composition of the French identity, past and present, than Timbuktu or Tahiti, even though some of those conflicts played out overseas as well as at home. "*Plutôt la Corrèze que la Zambèze*," as one slogan put it: better to concentrate on domestic problems than worry about distant domains. Nevertheless, one might remark, in a Galileo-style protestation, that empire did count.[13]

Even in the more obvious issues that dominated French life in the late 1800s the distinct traces of colonialism are evident. The emancipation of slaves, proclaimed by the Convention and revoked by Napoleon, reappeared as an issue in the 1848 revolution (when emancipation was definitively adopted). Some of the rebels of 1848 were exiled to Algeria, and defeated Communards in 1871 were sent to New Caledonia. The rights and obligations of Frenchmen overseas, and their representation in the parliament in Paris, reappeared as a question for each new regime and constitution. Each new regime indeed restructured colonial administration, with Napoleon III, for instance, imagining the creation of an "Arab kingdom" under his rule, and the Third Republic replacing military (often naval) officers with civilian administrators and centralizing the direction of much of the empire under a new Ministry of Colonies in Paris. The rise and fall of political leaders—notably, the fall of *Ferry le Tonkinois* with reaction against Jules Ferry's expansionism in Indochina in the 1880s—occasionally had colonial precipitants. Priests and anti-clericalists bickered in foreign parts as well as on the mainland, though with a more symbiotic *modus vivendi* between church and state abroad than at home. Emergent ideologies encompassed plans for the colonies—Saint-Simonians perhaps expressed the greatest interest in colonial prospects (and a mania for canal-building in places such as Suez), Fourierists hoped to build colonial phalansteries, and Marxist socialists vested hope in the revolutionary potential of colonial proletarians. The military defeat of France in 1870 and the economic crisis of the following years directed the spotlight on colonies as sources of raw materials, markets, and soldiery. Discussions of economic development and the theories underpinning it almost inevitably encompassed some consideration of colonial resources and potential. Debates about free trade versus tariffs and protectionism stumbled on the questions of whether colonial imports comprised domestic or foreign commodities, and on whether traders or manufacturers stood to gain greater advantages from imperial preference. For some reformers, the "social question" might have colonial answers, with continued concern, as a case in point, about whether the transport of convicts to New Caledonia (from the 1860s until the 1890s) or Guyane (until the 1930s) provided

---

[13] There are a number of general works on the history of French colonialism. See, for example: Robert Aldrich, *Greater France: A History of French Overseas Expansion* (London: Macmillan, 1996); and Gilles Manceron, *Marianne et les colonies: une introduction à l'histoire coloniale de la France* (Paris: La Découverte, 2005).

a good solution to the punishment of criminals, and whether the *misérables* of city or countryside might be usefully and happily settled in Algeria or other colonies. Domestic crises produced colonial repercussions, for example, in the anti-Semitic vitriol and violence in Algeria at the time of the Dreyfus affair. Colonial scandals, such as the Voulet-Chanoine affair, provoked outrage in the metropole.[14] Although historians have not yet investigated the colonial aspects of all domestic issues and conflicts, the inter-linking of national and colonial in the background (or perhaps middle ground) of French life provides evidence enough for the importance of the empire in the project and process of nation-building.

However, there are also some more specific ways in which the empire loomed, and its heritage continues to appear in the public arena. To begin with a statement that, though banal, sometimes escaped the attention of scholars of the history of French nation-building: for more than four hundred years, France has ruled over places outside its European boundaries. With the invasion of Algiers in 1830, France began rebuilding an overseas empire reduced to a small constellation of islands and enclaves, even if it took two decades to occupy fully and "pacify" Algeria, the jewel of that new empire. In the 1840s and 1850s, policy-makers were less interested in taking over continental expanses, however, than in *points d'appui* for the naval and commercial fleets, ports where ships could obtain or stockpile supplies, maintain and repair ships, trans-ship cargoes, keep a watchful eye on rivals, and station garrisons. Islands provided perfect sites to meet these objectives. In 1841, France purchased Mayotte, situated between the east African coast and Madagascar, affording, it was hoped, good port facilities in the Indian Ocean. The following year, the navy established a protectorate over Tahiti and the Society Islands, a riposte to British expansion in Australia and New Zealand; colonialists promised they would become key staging posts in the growing trans-Pacific trade. New Caledonia was added in 1853, site for a penal colony and a launching pad for trade in the southwest Pacific and onwards to Asia and Australasia. After several unsuccessful efforts to gain a toehold in eastern Asia (with the British firmly ensconced in Penang, Singapore, and more recently Hong Kong), the French finally blasted their way into Saigon, and took Cochinchina, at the end of the 1850s—a transitional moment between the acquisition of *points d'appui* and larger continental territories. Further expansion in North Africa, sub-Saharan Africa, Madagascar and Indochina followed, completed by League of Nations mandates in the Middle East after the First World War. By the 1930s, Greater France encompassed a portfolio of some 11 million square kilometers of territory and 100 million citizens and subjects. In a century, France had tectonically transformed itself from a "parcel of Europe" with only a few, scattered overseas shards into a global empire spreading across the continents.

French nation-building in the long nineteenth century was not a process of the unification of different political entities under one flag, as was the case in Germany

---

[14] Betrand Taithe, *The Killer Trail: A Colonial Scandal in the Heart of Africa* (Oxford: Oxford University Press, 2009).

and Italy. Nor did it involve secession and the creation of a separate state, as occurred in Belgium and Greece, or in a different way in the creation of the Habsburg Dual Monarchy. The French state already existed, but as in the case of other great powers of Europe, empire-building formed part of the nineteenth-century nation-building project. Big powers such as Britain and France (and the Russians in central and eastern Asia) sought to extend, maintain and exploit their empires. Other veteran imperial powers—Spain, Portugal and the Netherlands—consolidated control over their old possessions (though Spain's empire was aging in much reduced circumstances). Colonial promoters in newly unified countries such as Italy and Germany argued that obtaining colonies would confirm their status in the concert of powers, and the ruler of a small and newish country like Belgium saw the conquest of an empire as a once-in-a-lifetime opportunity to join the club of the world powers. A nation without an empire, in short, was not a state of consequence, and empire-building proved a vital component in nation-building across Europe (as well as in the United States and Japan).[15]

The overseas empire constituted an organic part of the nation in various ways. Although this is not the place in which to detail the multifarious links between the French nation and the empire, it is worth emphasizing at this point one aspect of that linkage. *Algérie française*, ultimately divided into three *départements* (and a military territory), constitutionally formed as much a part of France as any of the regions of the metropole. Europeans in Algeria were fully-fledged French citizens from the late 1880s, as were the inhabitants (of all races) of the *quatre communes* of Senegal (Saint-Louis, Dakar, Gorée, and Rufisque), and some of the residents of the French *comptoirs* in India and the Society Islands in Polynesia, joined in 1946 by those in the *vieilles colonies* (Martinique, Guadeloupe, Guyane, and La Réunion).[16] Those who were not citizens could technically became so (on which more presently). France, so it seemed at least to colonialists, was a nation inseparable from its empire; indeed, for the most ardent defenders of empire, as they continued to imagine even at the time of the Algerian crisis, France was inconceivable without its empire.

The heyday of empire, however, was short-lived. In the *Exposition coloniale internationale* held in Paris in 1931, France and the other countries it invited—including Italy, Spain, Portugal, the Netherlands, Belgium, Denmark and the USA, though Britain declined to take part—consecrated and celebrated imperialism. Yet already anti-colonial nationalism contested the ideology and fact of imperialism, and French troops had been deployed to quell the Rif rebellion in Morocco and the Druze revolt

---

[15] See Robert Aldrich, ed., *The Age of Empires* (London: Thames and Hudson, 2007). The chapter on the Habsburg Empire, by Walter Sauer, suggests that Bosnia in some ways was an Austrian colony (and reveals the imperial ambitions of other Austrian figures), while Knud J.V. Jespersen discusses the little known history of Scandinavian imperialism—even countries not thought of as imperialist were not immune to the colonial movement.

[16] There is an American imperial parallel in the granting of statehood to non-contiguous Alaska and Hawaii in 1959 and 1960, and the extension of citizenship to residents of several other off-shore territories.

in Lebanon. Less than a decade after the Paris colonial fair (and even earlier in eastern Asia), war would throw all of the empires into chaos, soon to begin the painful and protracted loss of empire, with the necessary task for European countries of redefining themselves, *sans* empire, for a post-colonial age. If nation-building for 130 years since 1830 had involved empire-building for France, the nation-building of the post-1945 period involved deconstructing that very empire.

France, as is well known, decolonized reluctantly. It unhappily relinquished Syria and Lebanon at the end of the Second World War. It fought an eight-year war trying to retain Indochina, finally withdrawing from Vietnam, Cambodia, and Laos in 1953 and 1954. Rising nationalism and preoccupation with *Algérie française* forced the French hand in the protectorates of Morocco and Tunisia, which regained independence in 1956. After vain efforts to turn the sub-Saharan African colonies into member territories of the French Union (in 1946) and the Community (1958), recasting the old colonial ties in new constitutional forms—and after quitting Guinea, which declared independence in 1958—President de Gaulle accepted what seemed the inevitable and granted independence to the sub-Saharan African colonies as fast as ministers could fly around the continent for the lowering and raising of flags in 1960. The Algerian war, which had begun in 1954, dragged on in all its bloody fury, until 1962, when the French had to give up their major overseas outpost, only major settler colony and, according to law, an integral piece of French territory.[17] Empire had come to an end, or almost so, with several remaining possessions subsequently going free.

Yet France has held on to a dozen outposts around the world, generally diminutive territories referred to by some rather disobligingly as the "confetti of empire."[18] Advocates, however, lauded these remaining territories as sites for nuclear testing (French Polynesia), space exploration (Guyane), settlement (New Caledonia), and the diffusion (*rayonnement*) of French culture, *as well the resources* that could be derived from exclusive maritime zones of economic exploitation. There survives a discourse of promotion that vaunts these *pays d'outre-mer* (the current appellation) as an opportunity and good fortune (*chance*) for France and indeed for Europe. Various campaigns for independence, notably in New Caledonia in the 1980s, proved unsuccessful, though regular bouts of social upheaval occur. The "mini-empire" lives on, the scattered remnants still part of the French nation and the republican state.

---

[17] Independence subsequently came to French Somaliland (Djibouti), the Comoros Islands (minus Mayotte), and the Anglo-French condominium of the New Hebrides (Vanuatu).

[18] The French *outre-mer* now comprises Saint-Pierre et Miquelon (off the coast of Newfoundland), Martinique, Guadeloupe, Saint-Barthélémy and Saint-Martin in the West Indies, Guyane in South America, La Réunion and Mayotte in the Indian Ocean, New Caledonia, Wallis and Futuna, and French Polynesia in the South Pacific, and the "French Austral and Antarctic Lands" (including Terre Adélie in Antarctica and several uninhabited sub-Antarctic islands). See Robert Aldrich and John Connell, *France's Overseas Frontier: Départements et Territoires d'Outre-Mer* (Cambridge: Cambridge University Press, 1992).

A minor but recurrent theme in contemporary French politics—to digress for a moment to an issue that reveals the fraught nature of the national-colonial relationships over the long run—is the exact administrative positions of these dozen overseas territories in the republic. Paris continually experiments with arcane modifications of the constitutional statutes of the "ultra-peripheral regions" or "overseas countries and territories" (as they are labeled in the European Union nomenclature). In some instances, they have moved towards greater autonomy, as has been the case with French Polynesia: since the 1980s, it enjoys such signifiers of national status as its own flag. New Caledonia, whose ultimate status is meant to be decided in the 2010s, is probably also moving in that direction with, in the meantime, an esoteric distinction between those who possess French *nationalité,* which includes all in New Caledonia who do not hold foreign citizenship, and those who have New Caledonian *citoyenneté* based on indigenous ancestry or a prescribed period of residence. Another direction is shown by Mayotte, an island of less than 400 square kilometers populated with 186,000 mostly Muslim inhabitants, which gained quasi-*département* status in 2011. Constitutional questions about statutory arrangements are not just debates on the finer points of law and administration, as the particular type of statute has great implications for ordinary people—the level of family allocations and other social security payments, for example. Most legal experts accept that a *département* has no constitutional right of secession or independence, while the territories and, probably, a *pays d'outre-mer* do so. Attempts to work out appropriate arrangements also reflect on how the French conceive of their polity and society, what are the limits of parity and equality, and what it means to be French even when one lives on the other side of the world from Paris.

Problems of unemployment (at times reaching as high as a quarter of the workforce), economic dependency on metropolitan subsidies, social friction, and cultural soul-searching remain ever-present in these overseas regions, yet the likelihood of immediate or complete separation between France and the remnants of its vestigial colonial empire appears small. Around 2.5 million people live in the *outre-mer* (as well as another one million in the metropole whose parents or ancestors hail from the current overseas territories) and benefit from full rights of citizenship including the right of abode in France. Moreover, they elect representatives to the French parliament and vote in elections for the European parliament, though the abstention rate is always high. Advocates of the *outre-mer* staunchly reject claims that the existence of these territories provides proof of continued colonialism, but their attachment to the republic does point to the long life of formal French engagement with extra-European countries, and the vagaries of colonial administration over the years. For better or worse, the boundaries of the French state still extend to Saint-Pierre et Miquelon off the Canadian coast, to the Antilles and South America, and to the Indian and Pacific Oceans. The French nation encompasses a diversity of West Indian, Indian Ocean, and Pacific peoples who live under the tricolor. The subject of the present-day French overseas outposts may be a postscript to a longer history of imperialism and nation-building, but discussions about their statutory place in the republic, debates on the benefits France derives from them, and questions about the ways their particularistic cultures fit into or together with the culture of the French nation in general mirror the larger place that the old, "real" empire played in the nation in former times.

Nation-Building and the Uses of Empire

Imperialism was historically significant to French life not just because of the existence of extra-European territories *per se*, but also for the tangible and dense network of links woven between France and its outposts. Much has been written about the cultural history of colonialism, the colonial gaze, the vision of the other, and the import into France of images and stereotypes of the exotic world via the conduits of colonialism.[19] That impact is undeniable, and cultural exchange moved in both directions. The export of French notions of constitutionalism, egalitarianism and socialism ironically fuelled the ideologies of anti-colonial militants in resistance to colonialism; the ideologies of French nation-building and regime change could be applied in the colonies as well as in the metropole. The universalistic image of French culture depended partly on the capacity of the French to export it to the colonial world, with French culture itself enriched and changed with engagement with the wider world: *chinoiserie* and perspectives on the *bons sauvages* in the Enlightenment, Orientalism in the nineteenth century, modernism and the encounter with "primitive" arts at the beginning of the twentieth century.[20] From Egyptology at the time of Napoleon through the new anthropological theories developed by researchers working overseas, imperial scholarship (the *sciences coloniales*) pushed back the frontiers whose development and outreach formed part of the French nation-building project.[21]

Empire also presented economic benefits, though it is pointless to try to tally up monetary gains and losses in any comprehensive calculation. The colonies accounted for only about 10% of France's exports and imports at the time of the First World War, but that proportion rose dramatically during the depression, by necessity, with a French-style imperial preference that relied increasingly on the empire as a fall-back preserve in a tough economic environment. Certain French companies with primarily

---

[19] E.g., Pascal Blanchard and Armelle Chatelier, *Images et colonies* (Paris: Syros, 1993); Pascal Blanchard et al., *L'Autre et nous: "Scènes et types"* (Paris: Syros, 1995); Nicolas Bancel, Pascal Blanchard, and Francis Delabarre, *Images d'Empire, 1930–1960* (Paris: Editions de la Martinière, 1997).

[20] See, among many other works, Dawn Jacobson, *Chinoiserie* (London: Phaidon Press, 1993); Jean-Marcel Humbert, *L'Egypte à Paris* (Paris: Action artistique de la Ville de Paris, 1993); Lynn Thornton, *Les Orientalistes: peintres voyageurs* (Paris: ACR Editions, 1994); Roger Benjamin, *Orientalist Aesthetics: Art, Colonialism and French North Africa, 1880–1930* (Berkeley: University of California Press, 2003); and Petrine Archer-Straw, *Negrophilia: Avant-garde Paris and Black Culture in the 1920s* (London: Thames and Hudson, 2000).

[21] The links between anthropology and colonialism are discussed in Alice L. Conklin, *In the Museum of Man: Race, Anthropology, and Empire in France, 1850–1950* (Ithaca, NY: Cornell University Press, 2013).

colonial implantations—the Messageries maritimes shipping line, the Banque de l'Indochine, the Compagnie française de l'Afrique noire—represented major players in French commercial life, and many niche industries relied on colonial supplies or markets even if the dynamic titans of modern capitalism generally found their outlets in Europe or in the non-colonial world. From its colonies, France nevertheless acquired much of its nickel, phosphate, exotic hardwoods, tropical foodstuffs ranging from bananas to coffee and chocolate, and a host of other commodities.[22] In the 1950s, the last full decade of imperialism, France invested more in the colonies than ever before, the new technocratic and *dirigiste* doctrines of economic development finding terrain in the colonies just as in the metropole.

Soldiers also provided a benefit of empire. Soldiers from the colonies, especially the *tirailleurs sénégalais* (recruited from throughout western Africa and not just Senegal), provided much of the manpower for further French expansion, used by French generals from the mid-1800s down to the Indochinese War. During the First World War, France drew on what one general called the *force noire* (the reserve of indigenous servicemen) and the French settlers. The French mobilized 134,000 overseas citizens and 545,000 indigenous men. A total of 87,000 soldiers from the colonies died in the Great War. France also brought 221,000 "natives" to France, from as far away as Indochina (and China), to work in war industries during the 1914–18 period.[23] Colonial soldiers played their part in the Second World War, as well, particularly in the liberation of the Mediterranean coast. Despite the heroization of soldiers from the world wars in French nation-building mythology, only belatedly did the Arabic, African, and Asian soldiers enter the pantheon in the popular imagination. The 2006 film *Indigènes*, which highlighted the service of North African soldiers in the Liberation, revealed to many the hitherto unrecognized contributions of the colonial troops.

If colonial soldiers came to the rescue of France in the world wars, French intervention overseas had also brought about wars of empire. French international relations and geopolitics have been inextricably linked with the colonies. France and Britain almost went to war because of Fashoda in the 1890s, and France and Germany similarly almost came to blows a few years later over Morocco.[24] Nationalist ideology and military strategy targeted the British until the signing of the Entente Cordiale, the Germans from the 1870s onwards, and the Italians when Mussolini made noises about Italian rights over Tunisia, Djibouti, and even Corsica. Nation-building meant defense

---

[22] Jacques Marseille, *Empire colonial et capitalisme français: histoire d'un divorce* (Paris: Albin Michel, 1984); Hubert Bonin et al., eds., *L'esprit économique impérial (1830–1970): groupes de pression et réseaux du patronat colonial en France et dans l'empire* (Paris: Publications de la Société française d'histoire d'Outre-mer, 2008). These two volumes offer a number of case studies. There are various volumes on particular régions, e.g., Pierre Brocheux, *Histoire économique du Viet Nam: la palanche et le camion, 1850–2007* (Paris: Les Indes savantes, 2009).

[23] Jacques Frémeaux, *Les colonies dans la Grande Guerre: combats et épreuves des peuples d'outre-mer* (Paris: 14–18 Editions, 2006).

[24] See Jacques Frémeaux, *De quoi fut fait l'empire: les guerres coloniales au XIXe siècle* (Paris: CNRS, 2010).

of French interests and territory in the empire as well as the Hexagon, even though it proved impossible to forestall Japanese occupation of Indochina in the 1940s. Yet the *ralliement* of the colonies to General de Gaulle formed a vital part of France's position during the Second World War.[25] The French role in the invasion of Egypt during the Suez crisis of 1956 was motivated partly by opposition to President Nasser's support for the Algerian nationalists. Over a million Frenchmen served in the war against Algerian independence, a formative experience for many young Frenchmen (including such future politicians as Jacques Chirac and Jean-Marie Le Pen). Since decolonization, the French military has on a number of occasions intervened in former colonies in Africa, with a barely disguised assumption that its old colonial realm remains a sphere of legitimate French influence and action. National defense justifies, in the French view, the maintenance of military bases in several former colonies and, when deemed necessary, military action in *Françafrique*. Geostrategic objectives have continued to be apparent even in the reduced "post-colonial" French *outre-mer*. Through the 1980s, and again in the early 1990s, French nuclear testing at Mururoa (and the sinking of Greenpeace's *Rainbow Warrior* ship in the harbor of Auckland, New Zealand, in 1985) were said to be necessary for defense, even if they poisoned relations between Paris and the nations of Australasia and the South Pacific, and left Polynesians with long-term health problems that the French for long denied. Nation-building always includes securing national frontiers, even when they lie in the colonial world, and the colonies have afforded France sites for garrisoning, manoeuvers, offensive attacks, and testing of weaponry.

Cultural imports, trade goods and military advantage total only three of the provisions that the empire supplied France. Nation-building in nineteenth- and early twentieth-century France meant the *mise en valeur* of the resources and people of the empire. The nation, colonialists argued, *required* essential goods from the empire and the markets that the colonies offered to French investment and trade. France might require soldiers from the colonies, too, especially with the decline in French birth rates and France's reduced European position after 1870, then again in 1914 and at the end of the 1930s. The colonies gave France a big-power status and garrisons around the world. Nation-building meant defending French territory to the furthest borders of the empire against outside attack and domestic rebellion, and marshalling the men and matériel that the colonies promised. The colonies, once joined to the imperial nation-state, provided their own mandate for geopolitical manoeuvers, economic stimulation, and political calculations.

For some conservatives, the empire even represented "true" France. Colonialist literature, implicitly or explicitly, often juxtaposed the strong, heroic colonial with the increasingly effete metropolitan: the life of action versus the life of impotent contemplation, work in the spartan and disciplined rigor of the *brousse* rather than idle luxury in the pleasure quarters of the cities, "traditional" values versus the

---

[25] Martin Thomas, *The French Empire at War, 1940–1945* (Manchester: Manchester University Press, 2007). See also Eric Jennings, *La France libre fut africaine* (Paris: Perrin, 2014).

lure of cultural and moral dilettantism. Marshal Hubert Lyautey—hero of a colonial war in Indochina, administrator in Madagascar, French proconsul in Morocco, organizer of the 1931 colonial exhibition, and colonial elder statesman—preached to his troops that the empire was the true home for the man of action, a place where the French with the "right stuff" could succeed as pioneers, builders, and civilizers. For Lyautey and others critical of a France in the inter-war years of the twentieth century that they feared was prey to socialism, moral decadence, questioning of religious belief, weak allegiance to the nation, and a loss of will, the empire offered a way to regenerate the French themselves. Laying roads and raising cities, developing agriculture and trade, imposing law and order, and creating dynamic settler societies provided proof of virility and fertility, of national effort and patriotic initiative.[26] For writers of the *École d'Alger* (with Albert Camus taking up a variation on the theme), the *pieds-noirs* of North Africa represented new Frenchmen and Frenchwomen, burnished by the sun, hardened by honest labor, hard-talking and full of *bonhomie*, re-creating Europe on the southern shore of the Mediterranean. It is no surprise, therefore, that the some of the principles of the "national revolution" proclaimed by Marshal Pétain meshed well with the doctrines of colonialism: *travail, famille, patrie* seemed an apt set of principles for colonials and colonized, the sense of duty, obedience, and defense championed in the metropole in the early 1940s, a recapitulation of the very virtues preached in the colonies. The sense of racial distinctions enforced in the colonies with renewed energy meanwhile paralleled the racist policies of the Vichy regime.[27] Not all colonials, nor all colonialists, were right-wing at the time of Lyautey, or collaborationist under Pétain, but many of the ideals propagated by promoters of empire coincided nicely with conservative rhetoric aiming at national regeneration.

Yet, somewhat contradictorily, the empire increasingly had to incarnate the modern as well as the traditional. The pith-helmeted colonial already appeared quaint by the 1920s, part of the reason for the push to project an image of the colonies as modernizing, and to use new methods—films, the Croisière noire and Croisière jaune automobile expeditions in Africa and Central Asia in the 1930s, photographs of new aerodromes, and the celebration of aviators such as Antoine de Saint-Exupéry—to challenge anachronistic stereotypes. Such a version of colonial and metropolitan modernization persisted right through the 1950s, as colonial magazines filled their pages with pictures of engineers and business managers, the empire now harnessed to the

---

[26] The most recent biography, written by a former French minister, is Hervé de Charette, *Lyautey* (Paris: Lattès, 1997); see also Robert Aldrich, "Marshal Lyautey's Funerals: The Death and Afterlife of a French Colonial Hero," in Vesna Drapac and André Lambelet, eds., *French History and Civilization: Papers from the George Rudé Seminar*, H-France, Volume 2 (2009), 137–52.

[27] Eric Jennings, *Vichy in the Tropics: Pétain's National Revolution in Madagascar, Guadeloupe, and Indochina, 1940–1944* (Stanford: Stanford University Press, 2001); Jacques Cantier and Eric Jennings, eds., *L'empire colonial sous Vichy* (Paris: Odile Jacob, 2004); Anne Raffin, *Youth Mobilization in Vichy Indochina and Its Legacy, 1940–1970* (Lanham, Mass.: Lexington Books, 2005); Ruth Ginio, *French Colonialism Unmasked: The Vichy Years in French West Africa* (Lincoln: University of Nebraska Press, 2006).

nation-building project of postwar reconstruction and the economic growth and development of the *trente glorieuses*.

In nineteenth- and early twentieth-century nation-building, therefore, the colonies had many roles to play. They extended national territory and resources, they provided a geostrategic bulwark against enemies, they offered a domain for spread of French culture and justification of its civilizing mission, they were a forcing-ground where the French could prove their mettle, and they evidenced French engineering advancement and business acumen. It would not be a real exaggeration to say that the empire—at least in the eyes of advocates—was France at its best, a model for the homeland: technologically innovative with rail networks and bridges, commercially entrepreneurial with vineyards, rubber plantations and nickel mines, intellectually curious with the work of the archaeologists and natural scientists, the enforcer of law and order, the conveyor of civilization. Contrary images often presented themselves—the brutal soldier or planter, the corrupt official, the dissolute settler "gone native" and addicted to drink, opium, and sex, the mad adventurer—and opponents of colonialism missed few chances to shine light on these darker sides of colonialism (as in the anti-colonial exhibition organized by surrealists, Communists and other opponents of empire in 1931). But for the spokesmen who adroitly dominated parliament, media, military, and the education system and other official sectors of public life, the colonies, at their idealized best, were no less than the paragons of what France could be and achieve.

This, it should be added, was rhetoric rather than reality; the best and brightest graduates, colonialists lamented, did not enter the colonial civil service but applied for jobs in other branches of the administration. The military brass sometimes depreciated the capabilities of colonial officers and soldiers, the *tirailleurs sénégalais* the object of amused affection, the Foreign Legion an always dubious, if mythologized, force. It was, in general, smaller, old-fashioned businesses rather than the most dynamic, modernizing firms that focused on colonial trade. For many of the French, the bright lights of Paris far outshone the attractions of the Sahara, the Congo or the Mekong. Only gradually did recalcitrant political groups come round to the idea of colonialism. After 1870, apostles of *revanchisme* argued that France's efforts should target the recovery of the "lost provinces," with one parliamentarian remarking that colonial "domestics" were no replacements for the sons and daughters of Alsace and Lorraine forced to live under the German flag. Radicals and socialists continued to express reservations about colonialism on ideological grounds, and shared with others the fear that imperial expansion took attention and funding away from more urgent problems at home. Only gradually did they rally to the colonial cause. Anti-colonialism—and simple lack of interest in the empire—remained persistent in the Third Republic, with opposition gaining new strength under the Communist Party after 1920.

Important as the empire was to the nation, in the colonialist view, the French nevertheless had to be convinced of that fact. If the nation were fully to encompass and embrace the empire, colonial promoters faced the challenge of making the French colonialists and of making the colonies French. That issue points to the particular traits inherent in the building of the French Empire, and of the French nation and state.

Building an Imperial Nation

Many similarities characterized the connections between empire-building and nation-building in those states that carried out overseas expansion. All believed that enlarged territories made their states greater ("Greater Britain," *la plus grande France*) in both real and metaphorical terms, and that great-power status necessitated imperial extension. It was taken for granted that empire should produce rewards, economic profits, land, geopolitical advantage, prestige, and leverage against rivals. All states had to articulate the relationships between centers and peripheries on the bases of race or ethnicity, political enfranchisement, defense and national cultures. All preserved a notion of the superiority of core populations over those in the marches of empire (both overseas and in Europe—as in the case of the "Celtic fringe" in the United Kingdom), and of the beneficence of a carefully modulated civilizing mission to those brought under national flags with the backing of strong-armed and militarily safeguarded authority. Central elites also believed in the permanency of empire, conceding that bonds could be loosened only when the colonized might merit some autonomy, but seldom foreseeing the relatively complete decolonization that eventually took place, in many cases only a few decades after colonies were acquired.

Nevertheless, significant differences also appeared among the imperial powers, each a *sui generis* case of expansion mirroring not only the general international context at the moment of the imperialist impulse, but also domestic considerations. In the case of France, it is worthwhile to underline some of these particularities. France's empire was, from 1871 onwards (with the exception of the Vichy period), that of a republican state with roots in the revolution, not a monarchy, as were all the other European and non-European empires, save the United States. While the residents of Britain were "subjects" of Queen Victoria, the French were "citizens" of the republic. A monarch held supra-political powers by birth, descent, and the role that the sovereign played in national life, prerogatives that could not entirely be shared by an elected president or government. A king or queen claimed many domains—even today, Elizabeth II remains the Queen of the United Kingdom of Great Britain and Northern Ireland, but she also carries the titles of Queen of Australia, Queen of New Zealand, Queen of Canada and queen of other realms; the crown in some senses (though with legalistic debate on the issue) is divisible. Queen Victoria reigned as Empress of India, the Italian king ambitiously usurped the title of Emperor of Ethiopia, and the Russian ruler was traditionally tsar of "all the Russias" and emperor.

France ruled the colonies with monarchical imperialism until 1871 (other than during a brief period after the 1848 revolution), but the republican regime was configured differently. Awkwardly, it was a republic with an empire (that, ironically, included protectorates over countries with monarchical regimes: from the emperor of Annam and the sultan of Morocco to the kings of Wallis and Futuna). The sort of "ornamentalism" that David Cannadine posited for the British Empire—a parallelism in status between inherited elites, and the indirect rule that followed from it—could be accommodated less easily in the French republican empire which placed premiums on equality of representation, centralized administration and, in principle, an unmediated relationship between citizen and republic.[28]

The republican ideology of nationalism suggested that all who accepted the compact enshrined in that republican order enjoyed the sacrosanct "liberty, equality, and fraternity" that the revolutionary slogan promised. Yet, as has been pointed out, those blessings did not exist for women in France and the vast majority in its empire: the republic was a racialized and gendered construction. The question facing colonial authorities, never effectively resolved, was how to reconcile the idealistic principles of republicanism with colonialism, a subject that has been examined in detail, in the case of West Africa, by Alice L. Conklin.[29] Who should be citizens and what rights would they enjoy? "*Périssent les colonies plutôt qu'un principe*," Robespierre famously said in promoting the decree in the Convention emancipating slaves, but in fact legislators never intended the principle of republican egalitarianism to apply to the "non-civilized," and, in any case, principles generally gave way to colonial imperatives. In imperialistic countries of an authoritarian sort (such as Russia or Germany), questions of liberty and equality did not really arise, and in monarchies, where the existence of legally-recognized aristocracies and unelected assemblies were commonplace, philosophers and policy-makers felt less of a need to square the circle than in France.

In the nineteenth century, a policy of "assimilation" had suggested that, in theory, the colonies (and the colonized) could potentially be treated just as the metropole; black, brown or yellow natives, with suitable acculturation, could become fully-fledged Frenchmen and Frenchwomen, and the French political system could simply be transported overseas. Such a rigidly Cartesian and mimetic approach proved unworkable, and around the turn of the century, "association" replaced "assimilation" in the policy handbooks: some local leaders should be left in place, colonies might need to be ruled differently from the metropole and from each other, accession to French rights (and Frenchness) was unlikely for many and would require a long initiation: the colonies did not just form a geographical extension of the metropole. Neither catchword, however, articulated a detailed program of governance, nor did either policy resolve the issue of what republican colonialism meant in theory and in practice.[30] This problem bedevilled French ideologues and legislators right to the end of empire. Ironically, in the last decades of empire, with the *départementalisation* of the *vieilles colonies* in 1946, the policy, for at least some of the French outposts, was finally defined. Imperial nation-building remained a legal quandary, and the very effort to systematize it, in a way not considered so urgent in Britain, a country free both of the

---

[28] David Cannadine, *Ornamentalism: How the British Saw Their Empire* (London: Penguin, 2002).
[29] Alice L. Conklin, *A Mission to Civilize: The Republic Idea of Empire in France and West Africa, 1895–1930* (Stanford: Stanford University Press, 1997).
[30] Raymond Betts, *Assimilation and Association in French Colonial Theory, 1840–1914* (Lincoln: University of Nebraska Press, 2005), originally published in 1960, remains the standard work on this issue.

written constitutions that imposed codification demanded of French law-makers and of the dramatic regime changes that occurred in 1871, 1940, 1946, and 1958.

France was (and is) a highly centralized state, despite the persistence of significant regional differences and an ideological counter-current of regionalism that will be discussed later in this chapter. This is an inheritance of the age of Louis XIV, the revolution and the Napoleonic order, never contested by the republicans. The structure differed from the one obtained in a German Reich, which remained a federal state, for example, or from Britain, which tolerated different legal codes and established churches between Scotland and England. The British reconciled themselves with the continued power of local rulers, as in the princely states of India, integrating maharajahs and sultans into colonial power structures. And they saw little difficulty in designing varying laws and regulations for different colonies. For the French, this proved more difficult, even in the protectorates where the pre-colonial rulers retained certain prerogatives. Administration, in the French view, was the business of a civil service formed in the French universities, responsible to Paris, and enforcing rules and regulations decreed by the national parliament. While the British accepted devolution of political, administrative and budgetary powers to colonial elites, at least in the white settler colonies, the French adamantly did not. Almost a hundred years after the British granted self-government to the Australian colonies, Canada, and New Zealand, the French, at the Brazzaville conference held in the 1940s, explicitly ruled out the possibilities of "self-government" (the word used in the English, so foreign was the concept) for the French colonies. By contrast, the French possessions had gained representation in the Senate and the National Assembly (just as the colonies of Spain and Portugal also enjoyed representation in their parliaments), something that never occurred at Westminster. Representatives from the far corners of the French Empire, even if men (and generally white men at that) elected under very restricted suffrages, dutifully made their way to the Palais-Bourbon and the Palais du Luxembourg for the sittings of parliament. Indeed, by the 1950s, several men from the *outre-mer* served as ministers in the Fourth Republic. Nation-building in imperialist France thus brought representatives of the colonies into parliament and sent plenipotentiary administrators to the colonial outposts.

Another primary trait of the French *outre-mer* was that it was not an empire of migration, nor did the colonialists primarily promote expansion as the quest of land for migrants or a solution to overpopulation (as was the case, *mutatis mutandis*, in Britain, Germany, and Italy). France did not set its eyes on *Kulturboden* in Europe or elsewhere—even Napoleon I did not think of his conquests in terms of irredentist campaigns to win territory to which the French claimed ancestral rights. There were no designs by colonialists on incorporation of Wallonia, the Francophone cantons of Switzerland or the Vallée d'Aoste. Similarly, colonialists did not argue a need for *Lebensraum* for the French population. France itself was a fertile country that, in most parts, was not too densely populated. Land redistribution at the time of the revolution and over the course of the nineteenth century meant that a larger proportion of French people had some access to land, through ownership or long-term lease, than elsewhere in Europe. The slower path to industrialization followed by France, by comparison notably with Britain, also meant fewer landless peasants and a smaller deracinated proletariat (though France did experience large-scale rural-to-urban migrations in the 1800s). The French did not have a migratory population comparable to the Irish or the Scottish in terms of ethnicity, peripheral geographical position, or disparities of wealth. The French birth rate remained notoriously low, the natality crisis exercising commentators who worried about the rising population and higher birth-rate of Germany (especially after 1870). The challenge was not to find lands for settlement, but to find settlers to populate the colonies.

France sent relatively few migrants to its colonies—Indochina, at the time of the Second World War, counted only around 35,000 ethnically French residents. Algeria and New Caledonia comprised the only real French settler colonies. Transported convicts provided the majority of New Caledonia's initial European population, with prisoners transported to the South Pacific territory from the mid-1860s to the mid-1890s in the hope of reforming the malefactors and turning them into honest yeoman farmers and pastoralists for the new France of Oceania. In Algeria, from the 1830s until the 1880s, the bulk of the European population came from outside France—from Spain, Italy, and Malta. France gained instant "French" populations when, in 1870, the Crémieux degree granted citizenship to the substantial population of indigenous Jews in Algeria and, in 1889, when the foreign Europeans also gained citizenship. Migration, enfranchisement, and a high birth rate among settlers, with a growing but never massive stream of French migrants, ultimately produced a population of a million *pieds-noirs*. Colonialist promoters tried to persuade compatriots to move to Algeria and elsewhere in the empire, but without dramatic success. The French did prove adept at moving some of the colonized around, recruiting Indian laborers for the West Indies and La Réunion after the abolition of slavery, appointing Vietnamese to the administration in Cambodia, bringing Chinese laborers to Tahiti, and dispatching Antillean bureaucrats to equatorial Africa.

The French Empire was thus the most geographically and culturally diverse of overseas empires other than the British Empire, but not one of widespread European settlement. The ties of kinship that linked Britain to its dominions existed only for a small number of French possessions, with a smaller population compared to the British domains. In no colony did the French and other Europeans outnumber the indigenous population, as was the case in Australia, New Zealand and Canada, and only in Algeria and New Caledonia did the Europeans represent a large minority of the total, even if they did control political and economic power. Imperialist nation-building thus necessitated co-opting, assimilating or associating populations in the colonies that remained overwhelmingly "native." This was coupled with the necessity of aligning colonial administration to the principles of republican ideology, constitutional legislation, and centralized statecraft: a heady challenge.

The colonies, as this chapter has argued, helped make France France, especially from the mid-nineteenth century to the beginning of the 1960s. But to what extent was the empire really French? How did the French try to make their colonies French, to bring those multiple territories into the framework of a universalistic culture (as the French saw it) and under a centralized administration? Several decades ago, in *Making Peasants French*, Eugen Weber argued that the Third Republic had to turn multitudes of peasants, stubbornly clinging to particularistic local cultures, into true Frenchmen and Frenchwomen. He noted, in passing, that this domestic *mission civilisatrice* was not unlike the parallel exercise carried out in the colonies, as the French tried to instil patriotism, a common standardized language, the national French culture, productive economic habits, and the institutions of governance into sometimes recalcitrant and even "savage" populations at home and abroad. Electoral campaigns, the press, military service and, especially, the education system—the pride of the early Third Republic—provided the agencies for this "Frenchification" of the population inside the metropole. Other historians have advanced critiques of Weber's thesis, emphasizing the persistence of regionalism. Indeed, national authorities harnessed regionalism to nationalism, so long as it did not threaten the integrity of the nation. Teachers might well dissuade students from speaking Breton or some dialectical variation of school-book French, but public authorities adopted folklore and local customs as part of the rich French patrimony. Nevertheless, a key part of nation-building in the Third Republic's policy was to inculcate a sense of the republican nation that superseded regional, ethnic, religious and other identities, and to develop those regions—the Massif Central, Brittany, Corsica, remote Alpine hillsides, parts of the Midi—that seemed to lag behind Paris and the more dynamic and industrialized areas of northern France.[31]

Certain parallel tracks are evident in nation-building at home and abroad in late nineteenth- and early twentieth-century France. The French had to be made colonialist, and the colonies had (to a certain degree) to be made French in order to bring the *petites patries* of the provinces together with the colonies of *la plus grande France* into a single, united, more perfect *patrie*. That project was doomed to failure, the rapid rise of anti-colonialism and the violence of decolonization were dramatic proofs of a lack of long-term success. However, for several generations, those efforts, futile though they seem in retrospect, constituted aspects of the continuing process of nation-building for imperial France.

Making the Colonies French

Authorities tried to recast the empire in a French crucible in a variety of sometimes contradictory strategies—a process of nation-building overseas in order to impose authority, develop resources, safeguard settlement, and promote French culture. However, and the point is worth emphasizing, both in intention and in achievement, the effort remained intentionally limited. Colonialist rhetoric might well advertise

---

[31] Eugen Weber, *Peasants into Frenchmen: The Modernization of Rural France, 1870–1914* (Stanford: Stanford University Press, 1976); cf. James R. Lehning, *Cultural Contact in Rural France during the Nineteenth Century* (Cambridge: Cambridge University Press, 1995).

the availability of French citizenship, the existence of elective institutions and the
benefits of a capitalist economy. Yet no one expected that the colonies would become
fully French, or should do so. One politician pertinently quipped that the principle
of "one person, one vote" extended to the colonies, for example, would mean that the
colonized, who greatly outnumbered residents of the metropole, would rule France.
Complete Gallicization would destroy the very bases of racial and civilizational inequality on which the foundations of colonialism rested.

Race, of course, created an almost unbreachable gap between the French
and the "natives," especially with the emergence of "scientific" ideas of racialism in
the nineteenth century that saw race as genetic and biological, endowing individuals
with inalterable capacities (or incapacities), physically, mentally and even morally. Few
questioned the "primitive" character of some colonized peoples—Melanesians, in particular, appeared survivors of the Stone Age. Africans might lack brain-power equal to
that of Europeans, said racial theorists, but nature endowed them with strength, virility, and courage. They thus made, military strategists added, excellent soldiers. Asians
were hard workers, able to support the heat of the tropics. Such stereotypes filled
the European imaginary, and policy implications followed. During the First World
War, the French used Africans as auxiliary troops; despite the bravery of a cohort of
Indochinese soldiers, authorities consigned most of the Vietnamese brought to France
to work in factories, considering them less fit for the battlefront. If the French found
Africans "primitive," Asians carried the stigma of decadence typified by opium-smok-
ing, and burden of the decline of their ancestral societies, represented by the ruins of
Angkor Wat.

Colonial scientists created spuriously scientific racial typologies, and the *politique des races* favored those (such as Berbers) considered to be closer to Europeans in
biological and cultural make-up.[32] In the racial hierarchy codified in scientific thought,
the Europeans triumphed at the apex, and in many ways, the French defined themselves *against* the peoples of the empire: white versus colored, advanced versus primitive or decadent, intellectual versus physical, modern versus backward. Stories of can-
nibalism, harem-keeping, foot-binding and opium-smoking comforted the French in
their sense of a racially defined moral superiority. For many scholars working in the
sciences coloniales, as well as ordinary citizens, the natives were different, and never
could they be equals. When the twain did meet, the mixed-race populations that were
engendered fit uneasily in the hierarchies of race and culture. Unwillingness to jettison
ideas of race helped to doom any real possibility of a greater France in which *métropol-
itains* and *ultramarins* would be equal.

Nevertheless, even with the racialized and racist theories and practices that
separated European from native, imperial nation-building mandated strategies of

[32] Patricia M. E. Lorcin, *Imperial Identities: Stereotyping, Prejudice and Race in Colonial Algeria*
(New York: I.B. Tauris, 1995), is the most comprehensive case study. See also: Sue Peabody and
Tyler Stovall, eds., *The Color of Liberty: Histories of Race in France* (Durham: Duke University
Press, 2003).

incorporation of the colonies, and the colonized, into the French polity, society, and culture—especially under a republican regime based, however tenuously, on a notion of inclusiveness. One constitutional action, to which allusions have already been made, transformed parts of the empire into regions of France. In 1848, Paris divided the Algerian littoral into three French *départements*; almost a hundred years later, the *vieilles colonies* of Martinique, Guadeloupe, Guyane, and La Réunion became *départements d'outre-mer*. In the first instance, conservative authorities intended to solder a new society of settlement and geopolitical influence to the Hexagon. In the second, the instigation came from left-wing members of parliament, representatives from the *vieilles colonies* (led by the poet-politician Aimé Césaire) who hoped that wholesale integration would diminish the overbearing power of the small white (*Béké*) elite to the advantage of the black and *métis* majority. In principle, Algeria and the later overseas *départements* were fully integrated into the territory of the Republic (and inseparable from it), yet the limits to such inclusion were manifest by great economic and social disparities between the metropole and these outposts.

Another strategy of imperial nation-building was the granting of citizenship to individuals or particular groups in the empire, pioneered in the cases of the Jews and Europeans of Algeria. In 1848, the French had already given citizenship, and (for men) voting rights, to the emancipated slaves and other residents of the *vieilles colonies*, with citizenship subsequently extended, *en masse*, to residents of the *quatre communes* of Senegal where France claimed a particularly long-established imperial presence. Some Polynesians joined the club of citizens when the French protectorate over the Society Islands turned into annexation in the 1880s. Most everywhere else, acquisition of citizenship during the Third Republic became a matter of the acceptance of a personal application rather than the extension of group rights. The process for naturalization remained arduous, with grants of nationality parsimoniously given. In general, procedures obliged a "native" to prove that he or she was Gallicized. Evidence demanded included that the postulant demonstrate knowledge of the French language and live in a French manner (though what that meant was not specified). Employment in the French colonial civil service was of help, and soldiers who served faithfully in French forces, especially if recipients of the Médaille militaire or the Légion d'Honneur, stood a reasonable chance of becoming citizens. The application process was intentionally onerous, and before becoming a citizen, a "native" had to renounce his or her traditional civil status (*statut personnel*). For many, this step was unacceptable. Muslim leaders regarded such renunciation as heresy, and those who nevertheless renounced their *statut personnel* occasionally became victims of violence on the part of anti-colonial nationalists. Renunciation meant that an individual abandoned rights inherent in traditional legal codes, such as the right, in polygamous societies, for a man to take several wives, the right to have various legal matters decided by chiefly or religious courts and law-codes, and rights to property adjudication through pre-colonial mechanisms. Relatively few of the colonized made the effort to secure citizenship, or had applications accepted by the authorities—from 1865 to 1962, fewer than 7,000 Algerian Muslims became French citizens through this route. The benefits, in any case,

were limited, though they included exemption from the hated system of arbitrary punishments meted out by administrators (under the *code de l'indigénat*), enjoyment of
the right to vote and stand for election, and the privilege of being considered an *évolué*,
an assimilated Frenchman or Frenchwoman.

The post-Second World War regime effected significant changes in the relationship between metropole and *outre-mer*, such as the abolition of the *code de l'indigénat* and the *départementalisation* of four veteran colonies. The Lamine Guèye law
of April 25, 1946 extended citizenship to all residents of the colonies, though the law
was not definitively confirmed by France's highest judicial organ for administrative affairs (the Conseil d'État) until nine years later. According to Article 82 of the 1946
constitution, the colonized were declared citizens, but there was much subsequent debate among jurists about whether this was citizenship of the Republic or the French
Union; the French Union having no autonomous existence apart from the republic,
its elected assemblies could exercise only purely consultative rights, and French Union
citizenship meant almost nothing. For elections to the French parliament, where true
power lay, separate electoral colleges remained, with whites massively overrepresent-
ed, and some colonized populations, such as the Melanesians of New Caledonia, did
not vote until 1956. In that year, Minister of the Interior Gaston Defferre set up local
assemblies in the *outre-mer*, but powers remained very strictly circumscribed, and the
Paris-appointed (and always non-indigenous) High Commissioners served as their
presidents.

Such measures demonstrated a very hesitant striving to incorporate the colonized into citizenship, representation, and administration, but French authorities expressed pride that *députés* and senators from around the *outre-mer* sat in parliament
and occasionally, as was the case with Léopold Sedar Senghor and Félix Houphouët-
Boigny, held ministerial portfolios. However, even as these changes took place, the
empire was falling apart—the Indochinese countries and the protectorates gained independence before the new assemblies of 1956 convened—while anti-colonial nationalism gained ground in sub-Saharan Africa, and the Algerian War became increasingly
violent and fratricidal. That war brought down the Fourth Republic, and led to the
return to power of Charles de Gaulle, whose prerequisite for taking office was a new
constitution. The 1958 constitution for the Fifth Republic recast the French Union as
Communauté (without the "French" adjective), with overseas *départements* and *territoires*. Paris invited each colony to hold a referendum to choose one of those statuses,
or to choose independence. Only Guinea, under the leadership of Sékou Touré, opted
for immediate independence. The constitution reaffirmed the citizenship rights of residents of the overseas *départements* and territories, though it removed the limited powers given to the local assemblies in favor of heightened central control, and it maintained separate, and unequal, electoral colleges in some of the overseas regions, such as
Algeria.

In the final years of empire, constitutional lawyers and policy-makers continued arcane discussions about who was a citizen and what entitlements various sorts of
status provided, their eyes now focused on avoiding a situation in which the residents

of former colonies that became independent might claim rights of residence, voting or other benefits in France. Indeed, as Todd Shepard has shown, when French withdrawal from Algeria became more and more certain, the bureaucrats frantically tried to redraw legislation to make certain that the (white) *pieds-noirs* who desired to move to France would be able to do so, and benefit from all the rights of citizenship, but that Muslims would not have equal rights of migration or automatic citizenship in the post-colonial republic. At the end of empire, therefore, race trumped other criteria in determining the actual exercise of the rights of a citizen.[33] Extension of full citizenship as a mode of creating a great imperial republic, except for the relatively few inhabitants of a handful of exceptional colonies, had been a remote possibility.

Another strategy that marked imperial nation-building, though one less explicitly elucidated than the various constitutional provisions for citizenship, was the "Frenchification" of the empire. This was inevitably an incomplete process; colonialists never intended to make the colonies into replicas of France, and in any case, they lacked the wherewithal to do so. Some colonialists of both conservative and liberal persuasions wanted to keep the "natives" cushioned against Frenchification, either because they were considered unassimilable or because, in a more progressive formulation, they should be allowed to preserve their cultures, languages, and habits. Those who retained their own ways earned grudging admiration even from the most diehard racists, while *évolués* and *métis* sometimes provoked scorn or ridicule for mimicking French ways. The problems were impossible to solve. Should the French, for instance, protect the nomadic lifestyles of Tuaregs in North Africa, or should they be "sedentarized" with European-style properties and land title, and Gallicized with French education, law, and even religion? To what extent could or should colonial authorities promote the Gallicization of the "hill tribes" (*Montagnards*) of the Indochinese highlands, whose cultures already differentiated them markedly from the lowland Vietnamese and Laotians? They might be distant inhabitants of the French state—Republic, Union, Community—but might they ever become true members of the French nation?

Similar questions faced all imperial powers, with changing views and varying policies. Nevertheless, for purposes of administration, *mise en valeur*, and the much heralded *mission civilisatrice*, a do-nothing policy was unacceptable. A highly policed and violently enforced order—with the underpinnings of law codes and administrative regulations—had to be instituted to guarantee colonial control. Economic development according to Western norms, with creation of suitable infrastructures, investment, taxation and export-oriented economies, was required to extract the profits that, after all, provided a key rationale for imperialism. Humanitarianism meant the building of schools and hospitals. Settlers, traders and *fonctionnaires* demanded the facilities that all colonials except those hoping for a rustic life in the outback would expect.

---

[33] Todd Shepard, *The Invention of Decolonization: The Algerian War and the Remaking of France* (Ithaca: Cornell University Press, 2006) discusses the question of citizenship in late colonial Algeria.

The French tried to create "little Frances" overseas and to join these colonial outposts to the motherland in many ways. Transport and urbanism offer two introductory examples. The "transport revolution," at home and in the colonies, provided new means of nation-building in the nineteenth century. Railways proved particularly important, mobilizing capital and technology in a nationwide enterprise. The rail connected Paris and the provinces, city and countryside, inland areas and ports, raw materials, factories and markets; it accelerated the movement of goods and people. Grandiose railway stations rose in regional centers and smaller junctions as symbols of modernity, mobility, and national cohesion, the neat timetables and carefully calibrated schedules of the railways proof of the coordination of national interests and ambitions. So too the train in the colonies. Throughout the empire rail lines linked colonial centers with one another—the Saigon to Hanoi express, for instance. Engineers sketched out vast rail systems (many never completed) between the French colonies in Africa, with designs for trains that would speed from Algiers to Dakar and Brazzaville, even to Djibouti, and that would join Casablanca with Tunis along the coast of North Africa. Shipping-lines continued the rail tracks, connecting colonial ports with each other and with the metropole: Saigon to Nouméa, Dakar to Bordeaux, Algiers to Marseille. The rail and shipping lines (and, later, air routes) functioned as the arteries and capillaries of the great imperial body. Already at the end of the nineteenth century, advertisements for the newly developing tourist industries informed travelers that within a few hours on the PLM railway they could journey from Paris to Marseille, and then with just a few more hours by steamer arrive in Algiers. The Michelin company—famous for guidebooks and the tires which it produced from tropical rubber, some sourced from plantations in Indochina—touted imperial tourism as a way for the French to experience exoticism and explore their empire. New transport networks represented in real and metaphorical terms one of the prime achievements of nineteenth-century nation-building, and the extension of those networks to the colonies projected similar hopes of combining foreign parts into an imperial whole.[34]

Urbanism stands as another example of imperial nation-building via technology, capital, and state action, motivated by the objective of transforming distant colonies into sites fit for settlers and profitable commercial activities, showcases for French culture, and environments for the advancement of those colonized people who could be nurtured into European society. In the first stages of conquest, the French (as did other imperialists) often demolished reminders of the pre-colonial world, from the citadel walls of Hanoi to grand mosques in central Algiers, both to attack the bases of the old order, and—with the proclaimed justification of hygiene and modernization—to allow construction of new cities and the imprinting of French rule on the landscape.

---

[34] A comparison with the British Empire brings out the role of transport in nation- and empire-building: the role of shipping companies such as P&O, the rail system of India, the joining of the extremities of continental colonies with the Canadian-Pacific railway in North America and the Indian-Pacific in Australia.

Next to casbahs and "native towns," there arose *villes nouvelles* or *villes européennes*, ornamented with Haussmann-style broad boulevards and monumental buildings. Pictures of new schools, hospitals, wharves and warehouses filled the pages of colonialist propaganda, testifying to the French prowess at city-building.[35]

If the French proudly labeled Hanoi the "Paris of the East," or happily compared Algiers to Marseille, such claims did not solely bespeak the rhetoric of colonialism, but revealed an attempt to remake the environments so that they would both look and function like metropolitan centers. Giving the names of colonial heroes, national statesmen or other *grands hommes* or cultural luminaries to streets and squares— with many a Place de la République or an Avenue Foch or a Square Victor-Hugo or some variant in the colonies—offered further proof of integration. That some of the constructions were objectionable to local people—a statue of Empress Joséphine on the Savane of Fort-de-France in Martinique, a monument to the colonial "genius" of France in Algiers—could hardly provoke concern as the urban builders erected symbols of the new French order. They aimed to mark the colonies visibly with signs and symbols of the French *imperium*.

Hanoi, with its French precinct now beautifully restored, serves as a prime example of such city-building as part of the imperial and national project. The French cleared a huge tract of land between the old citadel (which, ironically, had been constructed for the emperors of Annam in the pre-colonial period with the assistance of French engineers) and the Red River for the *ville française*. A grand Parisian-type avenue linked the Hoan Kiem lake with the Municipal Theatre, generally known as the Opera, a splendid building with cornices and columns, mirrors and velvet curtains modelled on the opera houses that graced the French capital and provincial cities. Not far away loomed the massive palace of the Governor-General of Indochina, a vaguely Gothic-style cathedral that would not look out of place in a French province, and the swank Hôtel Métropole, imposing buildings for banks, trading companies and branches of the administration, and the grim Maison Centrale prison. The Pont Doumer Bridge (still in service, but renamed the Long Bien Bridge) was perhaps the single best-known engineering feat of the French Empire. Until the early twentieth century, French constructions in Vietnam displayed impeccable European style, complete with neo-classical or Beaux-Arts ornamentation: the Paris of the east indeed. Only with the work of Ernest Hébrard, a colonial architect active in the 1920s, did East Asian motifs (sometimes a motley of Vietnamese, Cambodian, and Chinese features) appear on buildings such as a new art museum and the University of Hanoi. The change in design perhaps indicated that Frenchmen such as Hébrard envisioned a hybridization of cultures in the French imperial nation. Soon Art Deco made its appearance in Hanoi, as the colony followed the metropole in cultural innovation; Hanoi

---

[35] Two pioneering works on French colonial urbanism are Gwendolyn Wright, *The Politics of Design in French Colonial Urbanism* (Chicago: University of Chicago Press, 1991), and Zeynep Çelik, *Urban Forms and Colonial Confrontations: Algiers under French Rule* (Berkeley: University of California Press, 1997).

could boast buildings that recalled the Paris of Haussmann, but also buildings that paralleled the new Art Deco structures of the capital, such as the Palais de Chaillot and the Musée colonial erected in the 1930s.[36]

Similar urban change occurred elsewhere (the program of urbanism in Rabat, Morocco, a source of particular pride for colonialists). Smaller towns, as well as larger cities, had their church and *mairie*, embodiments of the religious and secular nodes of colonial power in African towns just as in the French provinces, alongside a market-place, a rail station, a school and other typical French edifices. A few buildings were even transported lock, stock, and barrel from France to the colonies—one exhibition pavilion from Paris became the Bibliothèque Schoelcher in Martinique, another was re-erected at the palace of the Khmer king in Phnom Penh. Such undertakings were not just decorative, but embodied the ideological foundation of colonial urbanism: to make certain neighborhoods of colonial cities look European (or to create a hybrid-ized style that blended European and indigenous influences), and thus to transform the built environment into a suitable setting for the imperial nation-state. Though some of these structures (especially the colonial statuary) have disappeared, pulled down by post-colonial regimes, and others have been neatly recycled to post-colonial uses (the old Palace of the Governor-General of Indochina now serves as the official residence of the president of the Socialist Republic of Vietnam), the boulevards, many buildings, and a few monuments remain as reminders of the colonial period and the Gallicization of even the physical space of the imperial world: imperial nation-building carved in marble, moulded in concrete, and cast in iron.

In many other ways, the centripetal forces of imperial nation-building pulled remote regions into the French cultural orbit. For the colonialists, each dam and road-way, every school and hospital and hotel, each school lesson and theatre performance represented a further building block in the construction of an overseas France that was, they hoped, increasingly and indefectibly French. Not unsurprisingly, colonialists referred to the French overseas possessions as "provinces," while travelers thrilled at the exoticism but also found satisfaction and reassurance in French-style buildings, French food and drink, and the clubs and churches that made even distant outposts seem like home. The colonies were different provinces, to be sure, the gentle rivers and valleys of the Loire replaced by the jungles along the Mekong or the endless Saharan desert, but provinces they were, part of the imperial republic and, at least to a degree, part of the French nation. Not surprisingly at international exhibitions, such as the one held in Paris in 1937, neighboring pavilions displayed the specialities of various regions of metropolitan France *and* of various colonies.

Local indigenous and even settler elites did not always welcome this Galliciz-ing effort in the colonies, however, a negative response that offers another reminder of the difficulties of building a nation that encompassed an empire. Settlers often rankled

---

[36] France Mangin, *Le patrimoine indochinois: Hanoi et autres sites* (Paris: Éditions Recherches, 2006), William Logan, *Hanoi: Biography of a City* (Kensington: University of New South Wales Press, 2000); Pierre Papin, *Histoire d'Hanoi* (Paris: Fayard, 2001).

at the imposition of control from the center, especially when such regulations limited their profit-making or constrained their freedom in "native affairs." They objected in particular to reformist administrators, missionaries, and others who seemed to hold the interests of natives more to heart than, they complained, the interests of the empire or the settlers themselves. Regular disputes on taxation, development subsidies, duties on colonial products entering the metropole, relations with other powers and most other issues pitted settlers against central authorities, their discontent frequently aggravated when governors arrived with little knowledge of local conditions and moved on to their next postings after brief terms of office. The *Français d'Algérie* developed a convinced sense of their special position—a European elite (yet one formed, as Robert Randau and Albert Camus pointed out, from a melding of European backgrounds) of French citizens, resident in fully-fledged *départements*. The *Algériens* (as the white settlers often called themselves) were French, but French with a proud local identity and loyalty. The *métis* populations of the Antilles and La Réunion, cadres for the local administration and liberal professions, also prickled at any slights, taking seriously the equality that the revolutionary credo heralded. Yet *métis*, in general, exemplified some of the paradoxes and inevitable failures of imperial nation-building. When recognized by a French father (as most were products of liaisons between a French man and an indigenous woman), a *métis* enjoyed citizenship, but since parental unions often lacked the sanction of legal marriage, and the soldier or administrator fathers returned home leaving their families, the mixed-race children were usually raised in an indigenous milieu. In some parts of the empire, as in western Africa, the French established special schools and orphanages for the *métis* children, with the intention of "protecting" them from native influences and turning them into auxiliary workers for the state. *Métis* thus were intended to serve the colonial order, but they came up against relatively low ceilings in their professional advancement and faced discrimination in daily lives, hostility from both the French colonials and their indigenous kith and kin. Europeans and "full-blood" natives had doubts about the real loyalties of this in-between population.[37] The situation of enracinated settler elites and *métis* showed that not all who claimed French citizenship, and proclaimed their Frenchness, thought of themselves, or were regarded by others, in the same way.

Meanwhile, for the old (pre-colonial) and new (*évolué*) indigenous elites, the very forums and conduits designed for the inculcation of Frenchness and empire loyalty, such as schools, administrative employment, and the press, also incubated anti-colonialist nationalism. Most of the leaders of anti-colonial movements issued from the system meant to instil national pride and allegiance. Soldiers in the colonial army, students at French schools, indigenous priests and pastors, employees in the civil service,

---

[37] On *métissage*, see Owen White, *Children of the French Empire: Miscegenation and Colonial Society in West Africa, 1895–1960* (Oxford: Oxford University Press, 1999); Emmanuelle Saada, *Les enfants de la colonie: les métis de l'empire français entre sujétion et citoyenneté* (Paris: La Découverte, 2007); and Adrian Carton, *Mixed-Race and Modernity in Colonial India: Changing Concepts of Hybridity Across Empires* (London: Routledge, 2012).

migrants to the metropole: all became familiar with the precepts of constitutionalism, nationalism and sometimes Marxism that became the philosophical weapons in their fights for independence.[38] At some point, every colonized person became painfully conscious of his or her difference from compatriots in the *mère-patrie*; most famously, perhaps, Aimé Césaire recorded his sentiments when he realized that no matter the fact of his being a citizen and a university student, when he arrived in France he was most aware of being a black man, a person whom other Frenchmen did not think of as equal. Frantz Fanon, the Martinique-born psychiatrist, famously analyzed the phenomenon of "black skin, white masks": the forced interiorization of European culture, but the vain hope of the colonized trying to pass as Europeans.[39] Ironically, but perhaps not unpredictably, the building of an empire-nation in the long run helped to undermine imperialism, educating anti-colonial nationalists, providing the ideologies of rebellion, creating the situations of land spoliation, economic exploitation, and cultural alienation in which demands for autonomy or independence could take hold.

The French, it is useful to repeat, never intended the colonies to become *fully* French. Yet the French did have to bring the far-flung countries over which they ruled into the French orbit, and to Frenchify the empire sufficiently so that it would be (they hoped) eternally tied to France, to "pacify" the empire to maintain control, to develop it enough so that it would return profits, and to Gallicize it enough to secure support at home. Imperial nation-building, in the French case, meant provincializing the colonies, endowing them—within strict limits—with political representation, economic modernization, French culture, and even a built environment that was identifiably French. That undertaking these massive efforts would finally produce contrary effects to what was intended, a rising movement that aimed at nation-building *outside* the bounds of the imperial nation-state, escaped most of the colonialists.

Colonialism on the Home Front

Imperialist nation-building required not only an effort overseas but also at home: promoting the empire in the metropole. Colonialism initially attracted limited enthusiasm in France, with much doubt about the value of expending men and money (the *or et sang de la France*), the diversion of national energies away from domestic or other international priorities, the adventurism that often marked colonial efforts, and the occasional scandals that erupted. Colonialists waged an on-going battle, never entirely won, to convince fellow citizens of the merits of empire, a campaign that necessitated

---

[38] The Senegalese leader Léopole Sedar Senghor was an *agrégé*, holder of France's highest teaching qualification; the Congolese nationalist leader, Fulbert Youlou, a Roman Catholic priest; the Polynesian nationalist Pouvana'a a Oopa, a decorated First World War veteran; Ho Chi Minh joined the Communist Party while living in France.

[39] On these two seminal thinkers, see, most recently, Pierre Bouvier, *Aimé Césaire, Frantz Fanon: portraits de décolonisés* (Paris: Les Belles Lettres, 2010).

both inculcating a colonialist spirit in the population and capitalizing on the particular benefits seen to accrue to different sectors from colonial expansion: land for settlers, profits for businessmen, soldiers for the military, souls for missionaries. Spreading
awareness of (and, they hoped, support for) the colonies, and tapping into specific
colonial interests throughout the nation thus became two sets of dynamics for the incorporation of colonialism into the nation-building project at home, the one a general
mission of proselytizing for the colonial cause, the other activation of particular colonial vocations of individuals or groups in French society.

It should be remembered that, despite the centralizing tendencies of the state,
France remained a country of culturally distinct regions. Provincials maintained a
steadfast loyalty to the *petites patries* of village, town, and province. As travelers often
noticed, and Graham Robb has illustrated in his popular account of the "discovery"
of France, the Hexagon at the end of the nineteenth century and well beyond formed
a mosaic of different languages, traditions, architectures, styles of clothing, and most
everything else.[40] A substantial number of people still spoke Breton or Alsatian or
Corsican, though the teachers in Jules Ferry's universal, free, and secular educational
system worked hard to teach standard French. Even with the new rail system, parts of
the Massif Central and the Alps remained very remote indeed. In some areas, such as
Brittany, Catholic observance was regular and pious,[41] while other regions were notorious for the small number of *pratiquants.* "Making" modern France in the late nineteenth century was, in part, a program of bringing these diverse regions and cultures,
and the loyalties that they embodied, together into a unified republican nation—a
program complicated by the need to do more or less the same thing for the colonies.

Regionalism thus remained strong in France. Anne-Marie Thiesse, Jean-
François Chanet, Caroline Ford, and Stéphane Gerson, among others, have emphasized the ways in which regionalists revived, preserved, and vaunted local cultures even
in the midst of the Third Republic's centralization.[42] Indeed, the last decades of the
nineteenth century witnessed a recrudescence of proud provincialism. Regionalist intelligentsia, especially in the Occitan country, promoted the particularity of local folklore and essayed to preserve and institutionalize it in museums, *sociétés savantes,* and
compendia of local oral literature and modern vernacular writing. School-teachers,
though the *hussards* of Paris-directed nationalism, nevertheless vaunted local tradi-

---

[40] Graham Robb, *The Discovery of France* (London: Picador, 2007).

[41] Britanny also provided many missionaries; see Joseph Michel, *Missionnaires bretons d'outre-mer:
XIX–XXe siècles* (Rennes: Presses Universitaires de Rennes, 1997) [1946]. On earlier Bretons
overseas, see Jean-Yves Mérian, *Les aventures des Bretons au Brésil à l'époque coloniale* (Rennes: Les
Portes du large, 2007).

[42] Jean-François Chanet, *L'École républicaine et les petites patries* (Paris: Aubier, 1996); Caroline
Ford, *Creating the Nation in Provincial France: Religion and Political Identity in Brittany*
(Princeton: Princeton University Press, 1993); Anne-Marie Thiesse, *La création des identités
nationales: Europe XVIIIe–XXe siècles* (Paris: Editions du Seuil, 2001); Stéphane Gerson, *The
Pride of Place: Local Memories and Political Culture in Nineteenth-Century France* (Ithaca:
Cornell University Press, 2003).

tions, valorized artistic and architectural patrimonies, and often became amateur anthropologists. Just as industrialization and urbanization diminished differences between zones of France, ethnographers and folklorists busily collected and studied rural
traditions that varied from place to place. Authors such as Frédéric Mistal (1830–1914)
and his colleagues in the Félibrige worked to safeguard the Provençal language and
culture, and similar groups emerged in Alsace, Brittany, and the Basque country.

In a more avowedly political sense, Maurice Barrès (1862–1923) mourned the
German takeover of his native Lorraine, and he bemoaned the uprooting of those who
no longer had an attachment to the "soil and the dead" of the regional homeland that
gave them heritage, character, and a sense of place. Barrès developed an organicist theory of nationalism combining a cult of the soil, nostalgia for the rural world and its
values, and a belief that true France emanated from provinces contesting the individ-
ualism, *étatisme*, and modernity rampant in Paris.[43] Somewhat paradoxically, this provincialism in the metropole could prove conducive to French colonial provincialism
(especially in *Algérie française*), and it is not surprising that Barrès' ideas won support
from such a person as Marshal Lyautey, a fellow son of Lorraine. As Resident-General
of Morocco, Lyautey professed his respect for Islamic and Arabic culture and heritage.
Morocco, like Lorraine, was a province with its own traditions to be defended even
with the imposition of French colonial authority. Lyautey—whose chateau boasted a
"Lorraine room" and a "Moroccan salon," and whose funeral bier was backed by the
banners of Lorraine and Morocco, as well as the tricolor—saw no contradiction between his regionalism, nationalism and colonialism.

The nation was the interface between the provinces and the colonies, uniting
a people and an empire from the smallest village to the most far-away overseas outpost. The ideology of nationalism and the agencies of the central state aimed to bring
together these different components and draw on their complementary resources.
French-style nationalism allowed for the preservation of provincial traits so long as
they did not endanger national unity, and mobilized regionalist sentiments and energies for the glory of the *patrie*, but it also was an imperialist nationalism. The title
of a memoir by Robert Delavignette, colonial administrator, historian and teacher at
France's École Coloniale, encapsulated a tripartite denomination of his personal origins in the French provinces, his work in Paris and allegiance to the nation, and his
colonial service in French West Africa: *Soudan-Paris-Bourgogne*. For Delavignette,
who shared some of Barrès' views on the spiritual value of the French *terroir*, the nexus
between the *petite patrie*, the *patrie*, and what might be called the *plus grande patrie* of
the empire was both obvious and important.[44]

How then were the provinces connected with the colonies? Bilateral links between regional France and the empire were multiple, but colonialists articulated strategies for spreading the mission of colonialism around the country, to propagandize for
the empire and its advantages, to create support at the grass-roots level. As the colonial

[43] Maurice Barrès' novel *Les Déracinés* (1897) provides a *mise en scène* of his ideas.
[44] Robert Delavignette, *Soudan-Paris-Bourgogne* (Paris: B. Grasset, 1935).

lobby tried to "colonialize" provincial France, many local *notables* saw in colonialism a way to advance their own regions (sometimes at the expense of other regions), particularly with the development of commercial activities, and they simultaneously found in colonialism a tool for buttressing local identities often counterpoised to the centralizing, standardizing tendencies of Paris and the state.

An examination of some of those provincial-colonial networks and ambitions reveals a dynamic that constituted an important feature of the imperial adventure and of nation-building. A comparative case from another empire offers an introduction and suggests that the phenomenon occurred in many imperialist contexts. This non-French example of links between regionalism, nationalism and imperialism comes from Japan, a case of what Jeremy Phillips usefully refers to as "Imperialist Regionalism." Kanazawa, located on the Sea of Japan, had enjoyed a period of prosperity as a major trading city under the Tokugawa regime, but its fortunes declined in the Meiji era. Isolated from trans-Pacific trade routes, failing to industrialize, suffering a population decline, Kanazawa seemed to have little hope for revival until a conjunction of Japanese imperialist ambitions with the designs of city fathers offered a chance for renewal. Local promoters argued that industrialization (including mechanization of the city's silk industry) pointed the way forwards, and in the 1930s, Japanese expansion on the Asian continent added an extra target for municipal boosterism. Tokyo transferred an army division stationed in Kanazawa to China after the Shanghai incident of 1931—violent clashes between Japanese and Chinese that precipitated further Japanese incursions into the Celestial Empire. The following year, the Japanese established the puppet-state of Manchukuo, trumpeting its new possession as a veritable treasure-trove of vital resources. Kanazawa's elite, evoking the possibility of creating a port only a few kilometers away (Kanazawa itself was landlocked) and stimulating a profitable trade route directly across the Sea of Japan, championed their city as the gateway to Manchuria. Fortuitously, plans were already underway for an ambitious Great Kanazawa Industry and Tourism Exposition, to be held in 1932, and the organizers immediately spun the themes to emphasize defense and the sacrifices of local soldiers in China; pavilions dedicated to Taiwan, Korea and Manchuria displayed Japan's burgeoning overseas dominion. The show highlighted the potential for Kanazawa to play a key role in this new enterprise, both revitalizing the Hokuriku region and recasting its vocation away from an old daimyo-centered identity towards a new national one, and at the same time contributing to the Japanese effort at imperialism. As Phillipps concludes, "Local goals ... were cleverly packaged as a national good: local development was promoted as an integral part of national development." In the event, local ambitions were not realized. Other cities along the coast successfully competed for Manchurian trade, and the port meant to be a great Asian metropolis (as some propagandists wishfully intimated) was not completed until after the Second World War. The delay in building it preserved Kanazawa from destruction through bombing in the Pacific war.[45]

---

[45] Jeremy Phillipps, "City and Empire: Local Identity and Regional Imperialism in 1930s Japan," *Urban Studies* 35, no. 1 (2008): 116–33, quotation from 124.

Though circumstances and geography differ between the Japanese and the European overseas empires, Kanazawa illustrates well the regionalist and state-building concerns current in the West. Colonialism provided an opportunity for initiatives argued to be beneficial for local areas *and* the nation, cities branded themselves gateways to the empire; expositions and similar propagandistic and educational undertakings attempted to rouse imperialist sentiment. In an ideal outcome, all would come out ahead. Cities and their hinterlands would gain new sources of revenue and civic pride, the nation would be strengthened by a *désenclavement* of peripheral, isolated or declined zones, and the empire would be firmly connected to the grassroots of the metropole.

The exact configuration of those connections varied from empire to empire, but the lateral connections were everywhere present. In Britain, the old port cities such as Bristol, whose connection with the overseas world dated back to the days of the slave trade, remained centers of imperialism. Liverpool is a case of the "empire in one city." Catherine Hall has shown how Birmingham thrust itself into a prime position in imperial life thanks to traders, emancipationists, and civic boosters. John Mackenzie portrays Glasgow as the second city of empire in the British Isles, and T. M. Devine has evaluated the many-stranded connections between Scotland and the empire.[46] In the Netherlands, The Hague established a reputation as a "colonial" city for administrators and retirees, joining the ports of the East India Company, such as Amsterdam, in their centuries-old colonial vocation pioneered by the VOC. The German Reich's second city, Hamburg, played a role as spearhead of German expansion and trade in Africa and the Pacific. In Italy, if traders, explorers and scientists from Turin stood in the forefront of expansion, colonialists touted the Mezzogiorno as a major future beneficiary, with colonies providing land and labor for impoverished peasants from the south.[47] And back in Asia, Japan's colonies, especially Manchuria, gained favor as sites of settlement for migrants from the densely populated Ryukyu Islands. In cases of "sub-imperialism" as well, regionalist overtures proved significant. In the South Seas, traders from Queensland and missionaries from Victoria, far more than settlers in New South Wales, provided a vanguard for British, and later Australian, interests in New Guinea and the New Hebrides; the elite in La Réunion proved instrumental in French expansion in Madagascar and Djibouti. In each case, regional interests provided the building blocks for imperial nation-building.

---

[46] Catherine Hall, *Civilizing Subjects: Metropole and Colony in the English Imagination, 1830–1867* (London: Polity, 2002); Sheryllynne Haggerty, Anthony Webster, and Nicholas J. White, eds., *The Empire in One City? Liverpool's Inconvenient Imperial Past* (Manchester: Manchester University Press, 2009); John Mackenzie, "The Second City of the Empire: Glasgow—imperial municipality," in Felix Driver and David Gilbert, eds., *Imperial Cities* (Manchester: Manchester University Press, 1999), which also contains essays on several other cities and their imperial links; T.M. Devine, *Scotland's Empire, 1600–1815* (London: Penguin, 2004).

[47] Aliza S. Wong, *Race and the Nation in Liberal Italy, 1861–1911: Meridionalism, Empire, and Diaspora* (London: Palgrave Macmillan, 2006). For a German example, see Markus Seemann, *Kolonialismus in der Heimat: Kolonialbewegung, Kolonialpolitik und Kolonialkultur in Bayern, 1882–1943* (Berlin: Christophe Links, 2011).

"Regionalist imperialism" in France, in part, was the implanting or growing of pro-colonialist sentiments around provincial France. The nineteenth-century cults of association and sociability facilitated this effort. So did vogues for exhibitions, the opening of new museums, the increased circulation of newspapers and illustrated periodicals, and the conduit provided by schooling and textbooks.

Voluntary associations have played an important role in modern France, providing sites of sociability and entertainment, forums for debate, and centers for like-minded people to pursue their intellectual and political agendas. Such groups proliferated in the late nineteenth century, from lodges of Freemasons to *sociétés savantes,* from sports clubs to professional associations. Colonialism was not absent in French associative life. Geographical societies that sprang up around France, in the wake of the establishment of the Société de Géographie de Paris in 1821, promoted the sort of exploration that segued into conquest, and these societies stood in the front lines in lobbying for the expansion and exploitation of the French Empire with the expeditions they sponsored and funded, their journals, lectures, library collections, and receptions and prizes for the hardy adventurers who charted the unknown world. (Several prizes established at the Paris society rewarded "geographical work on France or on regions subjected to French influence.") Provincial geographical societies followed the Paris lead, although only from the 1870s, perhaps not coincidentally the period of revived interest in imperialism, with the foundation of sister societies in Lyon (1873), Bordeaux (1874), Bourges (1875), Marseille (1876), Montpellier, Valenciennes, Rochefort and the Algerian city of Oran (all in 1878), with three dozen eventually set up around France.[48]

Colonialism was not the sole brief of the geographical societies, but in the last years of the nineteenth century and first decades of the twentieth, new *instituts coloniaux,* as their names implied, specifically focused on the empire. Most important cities counted an *institut colonial* among their civic organizations: Marseille (from 1893), Bordeaux (1901), Nancy (1902), Nice (1927), Le Havre (1929), Montpellier (1931), etc. Businessmen were often prime movers in setting up the institutes, sometimes under the aegis of local chambers of commerce and industry, but membership included academics, military officers, explorers, *fonctionnaires,* and old colonials. They mounted a variety of activities, similar to those of the geographical societies, including lectures and publications, and sometimes also founded colonial training academies or colonial museums. In general, they served as provincial clearing-houses for colonial interests. In Nice, for example, the colonial institute, with key participation from former colonials who had retired to the Côte d'Azur, held public lectures on the politics of imperialism or the exotic marvels of France's possessions, published a regular newsletter (complete

---

[48] Dominique Lejeune, *Les Sociétés de géographie en France et l'expansion coloniale au XIXe siècle* (Paris: Albin Michel, 1993); Pierre Singaravélou, ed., *L'Empire des géographes: géographie, exploration et colonisation (XIXe–XXe siècles)* (Paris: Belin, 2008), and, more generally, Pierre Singaravélou, *Professer l'Empire: Les 'sciences coloniales' en France sous la IIIe République* (Paris: Publications de la Sorbonne, 2011).

with advertisements from companies hoping for patronage from colonials and colonialists, such as the *pharmacie centrale et coloniale* in central Nice) and otherwise tried
to rouse support for France's empire.[49] The institutes formed a useful link between the
ground-roots of the provinces and the colonies, their importance significant enough
that by the 1920s, Paris tried to inventory the organizations and prompt the setting up
of *instituts coloniaux* in cities that did not already have them.

   Complementing colonial institutes were the *expositions coloniales* and *musées
coloniaux* that appeared throughout France. Displays of exotic objects had been a fad
since the *cabinets de curiosités* of the old regime, but the 1800s experienced a growing
mania for museum-building. Museums incarnated the civic spirit in nineteenth-century
municipalities—every city worth its mettle needed a fine-arts museum, a natural history
museum, a concert hall or theatre, and a library. Exotica remained a treasured part of
collections. In Paris, the Louvre had already created a gallery of Egyptian artifacts after
Napoleon's campaign in the 1790s, then put on display objects from explorations of the
South Pacific. The Muséum d'histoire naturelle in the Jardin des Plantes collected and
cataloged specimens of flora and fauna from overseas, and the Musée d'Ethnographie,
set up in 1878 in the Palais de Trocadéro (the ancestor of the Musée de l'Homme and
the present-day Musée du Quai Branly) exhibited the arts and crafts, and occasionally
human remains, of "primitive" peoples. Similar museums multiplied in the provinces,
almost always combining displays of ethnography and natural history in the one building, enriched by donations from explorers, military officers and colonial public servants. Private individuals also set up museums for their lovingly gathered collections,
including Emile Guimet's museum of Asian religions in Lyon (subsequently transferred
to Paris), the Musée africain established by a missionary order, also in Lyon, the museum of Georges Labit, a gentleman explorer in Toulouse, and one set up by a big-game
hunter on the Ile d'Aix. These museums, quite literally, brought the empire home to
the provinces. All of the important cities in France had natural history museums, often
with collections of impressive amplitude—Strasbourg's boasts 18,000 preserved birds,
30,000 mollusks and 80,000 species of insects, as well as 30,000 mineralogical samples.
Given the vogue for exoticism, animals preserved by the taxidermists' craft, pressed and
dried plants, displays of weaponry, clothing and utensils from around the world attracted many museum-goers. On the walls of fine-art museums, meanwhile, hung paintings
of Arab souks, African jungles, or colorful ports in Asia, part of the Orientalist wave in
nineteenth-century painting that reflected an interest in the wider world, and that for
some artists was intentionally colonialist. Displays of natural history and fine-art collections were not just intended as entertainment for the masses, but as edification for
the citizens, a way of educating them about science, art and, in the case of the exotica, of
informing them about France's empire and the peoples over whom it ruled.[50]

---

[49] Laurent Morando, *Les Instituts coloniaux et l'Afrique, 1893–1940: ambitions nationales, réussites
      locales* (Paris: Karthala, 2007).
[50] Robert Aldrich, *Vestiges of the Colonial Empire in France: Museums, Monuments and Colonial
      Memories* (London: Palgrave Macmillan, 2005).

More forthrightly propagandist were *musées coloniaux*, often the work of chambers of commerce or operated in conjunction with *instituts coloniaux*. In most of the colonial museums in the provinces—in Marseille, Lyon, Nancy, and elsewhere— exhibitions hitched themselves to commerce, with displays of items produced in the colonies that could be useful to metropolitan businesses, and products that could be exported to the colonies. Indeed, some of the museums combined "colonial" and "commercial" in their names, demarcating themselves from the museums of natural history and fine arts (which their developers thought complementary), though most exhibited enough artifacts to capture the interest of school students taken on guided tours to whet their vocation as future colonials. What would now be called "documentation centers" provided information about colonial trade and migration. Many of the colonial museums remained small-scale, and they never rivalled the museums of fine arts and natural history in scope or visitor numbers—surviving pictures show some fairly unexciting places on the tourist trail. However, they too served to sensitize the public to the benefits of the colonies to the *mère-patrie*.

Periodically, colonial expositions were held throughout France, either as part of general fairs or as dedicated colonial jamborees. Bordeaux led the way with a colonial exhibition at the city fair organized by the Société philomathique in 1850, and over the next eighty years, most cities hosted similar exhibitions, such as ones in Nantes in 1861, Le Havre in 1868, and Cherbourg in 1869. Cities rivalled each other for the grandeur of their expositions just as they competed for colonial business and for the title of colonial capitals in France. When Lyon's authorities announced that they would hold a colonial exposition in 1894, Bordeaux's colonialists immediately laid plans for one in 1895, saying that they would do as well as if not better than the Lyonnais. Marseille held the biggest colonial fairs yet seen in 1906 and 1922, and Bordeaux responded by including a large colonial section at its yearly trade fair *(foire)*. (Marseille's success, or perhaps, hubris, indeed helped stimulate national and Parisian authorities to organize the greatest colonial exhibition of all, held in 1931, in the capital.) Many smaller cities held similar expositions, a combination of the work of civic elites, colonialists, and private promoters, including the ones that set up *villages noirs* that became a stock feature of the events. Mock African (or sometimes Arabic, Asian, or Pacific Island) villages were constructed for the duration of the fairs, peopled by "natives" brought from the colonies and instructed to go about their daily routines in full view of spectators. Scholars disagree about the degree of exploitation of the "natives" in the *villages noirs*, and whether their presence simply reinforced notions of primitivism and barbarity, or might indeed have helped soften some of the old racialist ideas.[51] Whatever the case, the *villages noirs*, expositions, and trade fairs that punctuated the last decades of the nineteenth century and the early decades of the twentieth

---

[51] Nicolas Bancel, et al., *Zoos humains: au temps des exhibitions humaines* (Paris: La Découverte, 2002); J. M. Bergougnou, R. Clignet, and P. David, *"Villages noirs" et visiteurs africains et malgaches en France et en Europe, 1870–1940* (Paris: Karthala, 2001).

represented some of the most visible and dramatic ways in which colonialism came to the provinces.

Yet another forum for the nurturing of colonial sentiment in provincial France was the parish. The champions of *laïcité* combated the intervention of the Catholic church in education and public life (leading to the separation of church and state in 1905), and de-Christianization gradually reduced the number who actively practiced their religion. The Catholic church, however, remained strong, especially in Brittany and in cities like Lyon, and evangelical activities, and the work of such religious orders as the Sacred Heart missionaries and the Marists, had provided a way to revitalize religion by taking it overseas. Memoirs and magazines published by the missionary orders (enhanced with photographs of new converts) circulated around parishes, visiting missionaries gave talks on their apostolic work and the wonders of the colonies, mother-houses of missionary orders opened little museums contrasting paganism and Christian religion, the missionaries themselves engaged in ethnographical work (dictionaries of indigenous languages counted as a particular achievement), church leaders collected donations for the priests and religious working overseas, worshippers offered prayers for the conversion of the heathen, and priests exhorted young people with a religious vocation to take up missionary work. Seminaries around France, notably the one in Lille, made particular provisions for training indigenous men from the colonies preparing for the priesthood. Catholic parishes formed a dense network in regional and rural France for the promotion of colonial missionary activities, and French Protestants, though fewer in number, engaged in missionary activities with equal zeal and a parallel network of support groups, publications, and training of ministers, both French and indigenous. Parishioners in even small towns and villages could thereby find a linkage both with the colonies—letters from missionaries to their families and orders, often widely read and published, provided one way of keeping in touch—and the national colonial vocation, as well as with the biblical injunction to spread the faith.[52]

Monuments, too, played a part in the provincial theatre of colonialism. One of the other great vogues in late nineteenth-century France, in addition to museum-building, was *statuomanie* (as Maurice Agulhon has called it), the erection of statues to the great and good and, a bit later, the raising of *monuments aux morts* to the glorious war dead. Consecration of heroes with statues in Paris was replicated in the provinces, where statues, monuments, or plaques honored native sons who distinguished themselves on the national, international, or colonial stage. The Alpine city of Chambéry, for instance, boasts a fountain featuring four elephants holding up a column symbolizing a palm tree; on top is a statue of Benoît de Boigne. A soldier

---

[52] J. P. Daughton, *An Empire Divided: Religion, Republicanism, and the Making of French Colonialism, 1880–1914* (Oxford: Oxford University Press, 2006), is the best study of the colonialism and the church (and the tensions between church and state). See also: Sarah A. Curtis, *Civilizing Habits: Women Missionaries and the Revival of the French Empire* (Oxford: Oxford University Press, 2010).

in the armies of Louis XV, de Boigne also served Catherine the Great in Russia, was taken prisoner by the Turks, and ended up working for the British in India. He then fought against the British with Maharajah Mahadji Scindia, before returning to his hometown of Chambéry, where Napoleon unsuccessfully beseeched him to organize an expeditionary force against the British in India—a missed colonial intervention, perhaps, but nevertheless, a career "statuified" in Chambéry. On the other side of France, a monument decorated with two other elephants, in La Rochelle, honors three local men hailed as the "pioneers" of French colonization in the Ivory Coast. In Saint-Vincent de Mercuze, in the Dauphiné, a mock Angkorian tower commemorates Ernest Doudart de Lagrée, a native son who led the first French expedition up the Mekong from 1866 to 1868. The town of Dinan, in Brittany, put up a statue to its favorite son, Auguste Pavie, credited with bringing Laos under French control. In the cathedral of Nantes, a monumental sarcophagus entombs the remains of General Lamoricière, a plaque recording that "In Africa, with authority and wisdom, he pushed back and strengthened the borders of the *patrie*."[53]

Along the sea-front in Marseille stands a grandiose monument to the *Armée d'Orient*, French forces in the eastern theatres of the First World War. One of the figures carved on the monument is a colonial soldier, and the inscriptions pay tribute to those from the colonies who fought for France. The argument that colonial soldiers would buttress French troops in wartime became evident in the Great War when tens of thousands of "native" soldiers died for France. The sojourns of these colonial troops (and imported colonial workers) provided a very visible and new example of the place of the empire in the imperial nation, and in the defense of the *patrie*. Their presence sometimes created problems, with official concerns about intimate links that might develop between the colonial soldiers and French women, and about the effects that war service, stays in France and fraternization with the French might have on the their views of the world and their submission to French authority. Violence between colonials and indigenous Frenchmen sometimes erupted, including some racially motivated attacks, but there were also examples of great care and solicitude for the colonial soldiers, as revealed in Lucie Cousturier's memoir about African soldiers in her village. The Mediterranean port of Fréjus, headquarters of the *troupes coloniales*, provided the garrison and transit area for the colonial soldiers, and offered a warmer climate to which troopers were sent from the front during the winter months, when the death rate for the Africans rose especially high. During the Great War, a committee of support for the Indochinese soldiers built a pagoda for the Buddhist troops (and it remains a functioning Buddhist temple). Colonial troops continued to be stationed in Fréjus after the war, and a mosque for Muslims was constructed in the 1920s in the style of the great mosque of Djenné in the French Soudan (now Mali). The drawing of a black man used to advertise the breakfast drink Banania was transformed during the war into a smiling *tirailleur sénégalais*, an African soldier in France, one of the most

---

[53] Aldrich, *Vestiges of the Colonial Empire.*

enduring colonial images. Though later commentators branded the advertising image a paternalist stereotype, the service of the soldiers in the Great War helped transform the reputation of the Africans from primitive rebels that France must pacify to warrior auxiliaries in the defense of the French nation. Except for a group of colonial war memorials on the grounds of the Jardin botanique colonial in Paris, the colonial soldiers were nevertheless only belatedly recognized in monuments—Fréjus unveiled a monument to the *armée noire* in the 1990s—but the memorials that do exist, as well as the statues of explorers and other colonialists, provided a clear reminder in *la France profonde* of the connections between provinces and colonies, the nation and its empire.

Schools and textbooks drove home lessons about the merits of empire. Although French children were taught about *Nos ancêtres les Gaulois* (even, infamously, in some colonial schools), the curriculum also included material on the empire. Textbooks reinforced the notion of a French *grandeur* manifested in its imperial domains, maps mounted in classrooms showed the extent of the empire, and stories of swashbuckling explorers no doubt provided "boy's own" entertainment for juvenile audiences. Teachers took children on excursions to visit colonial fairs and museums. One especially active colonial support group in Bordeaux had as its particular mission to promote empire to children, prizes (often of books about the colonies) rewarded school students in Nice who wrote essays on imperial topics. The Jardin botanique colonial in Paris dispatched specially constructed display panels of tropical hardwoods, and similar collections of colonial specimens, around public schools. Board games with colonial themes marketed for youngsters reinforced the indoctrination provided by teachers and texts. For more advanced students, *écoles coloniales* offered specialized tertiary diplomas in a number of French cities as well as Paris, and universities established chairs of colonial geography, history, and medicine.

Geographical societies, colonial institutes, expositions, museums, schools, monuments, and parishes promoted colonialism at the grass roots, welcomed by national authorities as a means of stimulating colonialist sentiment and providing commercial initiatives, secular and religious vocations, and electoral support for the colonial venture. In other ways as well—through cinema and music, for example—colonialism was projected to the French public, a form of propaganda mixed with popular entertainment. Those who saw films such as *Pépé le Moko*, one of the most famous features set in Algeria, or who sang along to *Ma Petite Tonkinoise* might or might not have had a deep interest in French colonialism, but they could hardly have been unaware that imperial France extended to northern Africa and eastern Asia.[54] These man-

---

[54] On these media, see David Henry Slavin, *Colonial Cinema and Imperial France, 1919–1939: White Blind Spots, Male Fantasies, Settler Myths* (Baltimore: Johns Hopkins University Press, 2001); and Alain Ruscio, *Que la France était belle au temps des colonies...: anthologie de chansons coloniales et exotiques françaises* (Paris: Maisonneuve et Larose, 2001). For further discussions of different aspects of colonial culture see Bancel et al., *Culture coloniale en France*; and Martin Evans, ed., *Empire and Culture: The French Example, 1830–1940* (London: Palgrave Macmillan, 2004).

ifestations formed part of imperial nation-building, ways in which provincials could be made aware of France's colonies and its proclaimed benefits, and opportunities where the colonies and the achievements of colonialists could be showed off to citizens, voters, and those who might be persuaded to join the colonial army, apply for admission to the École Coloniale, take the vows of a missionary order, or seek employment with a firm doing business in the colonies. It is not coincidental that the future Nobel Prize-winner Albert Schweitzer, whose medical and humanitarian career took him from Alsace to Gabon in French West Africa, recalled how his interest in the wider world and colonies had been stimulated when he stopped regularly as a child to admire a fountain in Colmar. Decorated with allegorical figures of the four continents, the work was designed by Auguste Bartholdi to honor Admiral Bruat, a Colmar native who sailed to the Atlantic and Pacific, established a French protectorate over Tahiti, and served as a governor in the Antilles.

The roots of colonial culture in the provinces, manifested in these various ways, did not perhaps reach deep into the soil of France—for some, unlike Schweitzer, colonial interests were but a hobby, and colonial fairs just an agreeable entertainment—but the shoots of colonialism did spread across the country. Reine-Claude Grondin's research on a region with improbable colonial ties gives insight into how the colonialist phenomenon developed even in areas seemingly far removed from the internationalist currents of imperialism. The landlocked Limousin remained one of the most rural provinces in France, separated from busy ports and growing industrial centers, yet even there, dedicated colonialists stirred up interest in empire. Geographical societies, there as elsewhere, served as popular conduits for colonialism, interest in the wider world combining with *sociabilité savante* (as Grondin puts it). In 1900, a man billing himself as an explorer instigated the setting up of a Société de Géographie in Brive, and the club successfully sought affiliation with the Paris geographical society. In nearby Tulle, an engineer who had worked on the construction of the port in Dakar organized a committee promoting local economic development. Both men saw in the empire a way, as did spokesmen for colonialism in far-away Kanazawa, to revive a region with a shrinking population and a declining economy. Stay-at-homes in the Limousin maintained contacts with associations of local migrants to Algiers and Tunis, the settlers forming a personal connection between the colonies and the province. Along with former colonials in the Limousin, local lobbyists held meetings, backed activities to raise consciousness about colonialism, and proposed the establishment of a colonial museum to house artifacts collected by Louis Parfait Monteil, another local explorer, who had traveled through Africa, Asia, and Oceania. However, their efforts did not always meet with great support, as some local *notables* feared that if the empire did become popular, migration would further drain people away. In the *dénouement* of one regionalist novel, a sun-burnished colonial soldier returns home to his farm and lady-love in a Limousin village, the author explicitly contrasting rural France and colonial France, the true France versus the France of adventure and danger. Grondin concludes that what existed was a "reticulated" colonial culture in the Limousin, with hardy boosters but without coordinated, tightly-knit support for

France overseas.[55] The limits of colonialism as a pivot for regional development, whether in Kanazawa or the Limousin, were obvious, though that fact hardly constrained the ambitious producers of novels and exhibitions, or the founders of colonial institutes and museums.

Promotion of colonialism could come from top down or the bottom up, from the convinced colonialists or those simply receptive to colonial culture, from the authorities in Paris or from provincial centers, from powerful lobby organizations to activist individuals. Perhaps the major argument to be made in this regard is that colonialism, and the promotion of empire, served a *functionalist* purpose. Individuals and organizations, public and private, could take up imperialism to advance their own causes, and in such a fashion colonialism became the instrument *both* of nationalism and nation-building, on the one hand, *and* the maintenance or recrudescence of regionalism (or municipalism) on the other: "regionalist imperialism," in the words of Jeremy Phillips, or "municipal imperialism," in the concept developed by John Laffey for the case of Lyon (on which more presently). The colonialist movement, after all, constituted a broad church in which lobbyists, adventurers, entrepreneurs, and other converts could seek and often find inspiration for their undertakings and benediction for their efforts, an assembly bound together by the creed of imperialism and the vocation of those who advanced it. Empire-building thus served for both nation-building and region-building.

Regions and Colonies

Colonialism functioned in varying ways in particular regions, with "regionalist imperialism" contributing in different fashions to nineteenth-century nation-building. Not all regions were equally touched by colonialism, though as the example of the Limousin has indicated, few provinces and towns stayed completely isolated from the empire, or unaffected by the colonialists' efforts to shape public opinion. In several cities and provinces, however, empire held a special role, offering the possibility of stimulating regional revivification as part of the project of national modernization, of providing a home for settlers under the French flag, and of welding peripheral regions to the *patrie*.

The first of those functions is illustrated by the cities of the Atlantic seaboard and, in a somewhat different way, by Lyon and Marseille.[56] The western littoral of France, by its very geography, enjoyed prime position in France's expansion from the 1500s through the 1700s. The regions of Atlantic France, nevertheless, did not champion later colonialism with an equal degree of enthusiasm. Brittany was particularly important in the French move into the Americas in the 1600s. Many of the explorers

---

[55] Reine-Claude Grondin, *L'Empire en province: Culture et experience coloniales en Limousin (1830–1939)* (Toulouse: Presses universitaires du Mirail, 2010).

[56] The following paragraphs do not claim to convey a comprehensive discussion of the regions covered, nor to suggest that there were no colonial interests in other areas of provincial France.

of the new world hailed from cities near the Breton coast, and Bretons were numerous among the seamen who manned ships of exploration and trade. Bretons also dominated fishing in the Atlantic, and provided numerous settlers for colonies in New France.[57] Yet Emmanuel Godin argues that the renewed colonialism of the nineteenth century proved slow to win support in the region. Local newspapers reported on colonial expansion with interest but without fervor. In rhetoric that revealed the conservative, and sometimes anti-Semitic turn, of some journalists, newspapers even expressed suspicion about the empire, especially Algeria, which writers characterized as a colony created by the French *Midi* in throes to rapacious settlers, Freemasons and anti-clericals, and Jews. Colonialism did win favor in the Catholic milieu in Brittany, with a considerable cohort of missionaries and donations sent from the region to the empire; the caveat needs to be made that Catholics, in Brittany and elsewhere, always thought of their mission as universal rather than exclusively colonial, reaching around the globe not just to the boundaries of the empire. In contrast to the church, the chamber of commerce in Rennes, the Breton capital, at least down to the end of the nineteenth century, seemed little interested in international or colonial affairs. It declined to participate in colonial exhibitions, promote the colonies as possible markets, or engage in the sort of colonial entrepreneurship and propaganda that marked such organizations of local *patronats* in other cities. The explanation is that French and European markets seemed more promising to exporters of the agricultural products that comprised the bulk of Breton trade than did colonial ones. Efforts to set up fishing villages of Bretons in Algeria and Tunisia, in an attempt to redress a crisis in Atlantic fishing in the late 1800s, met with little success. Few fishermen were tempted to try their fortunes in North Africa, and many other settlers there judged Bretons less adaptable to local conditions than migrants from the *Midi*. Newfoundland and Canada seemed more propitious destinations, and a Canadian lobby agitated for migration of Bretons to Canada, where they could settle in a Francophone, conservative, Catholic and traditional society, and find ample land and fertile fisheries. The sights of most of the expatriates and migrants from Rennes, Saint-Malo and other parts of Brittany thus set more on North America than on North Africa.[58] Nevertheless, Bretons did find in their international connections confirmation of a centuries-old maritime orientation and a continuation of their privileged ties with America, where the colonial legacy of language and religion persisted in Québec even if the French flag no longer flew over the Canadian province. Furthermore, the sending out of missionaries signalled a way in which the Bretons could still claim to make their contribution to the new national vocation of colonialism, all the while promoting a certain idea of France increasingly at odds with the secularism, de-Christianization and *laïcité* gaining ground; imperialism presented a chance for Bretons to reaffirm the faith of a Christian France.

---

[57] Damien Aupias, *Les immigrés bretons à l'île Bourbon de 1665 à 1810* (Saint-Paul, La Réunion: Grand Océan, 2006).
[58] Emmanuel Godin, "Greater France and the Provinces: Representations of the Empire and Colonial Interests in the Rennes Region 1880–1905," *French History* 13, no. 1 (2007): 45–66.

Other cities in Atlantic France invested more heavily in the new empire. Indeed, nineteenth-century expansion offered an opportunity for reinventing themselves, modernizing their commercial infrastructures, finding new sources of profits, and affirming their commercial positions in national life.[59] In the 1600s and 1700s, cities such as Nantes, La Rochelle, and Bordeaux had provided the major ports for exchanges with western Africa, the Caribbean, and New France, the triangular trade that crossed the Atlantic with French-manufactured commodities, African slaves, and products from the new world, in particular, the sugar of the Antilles, but also the furs and skins of Acadia and Québec.[60] The ship-builders and merchants of these cities amassed fortunes from the Atlantic commerce, including the trade in human cargo of slaves that continued from the mid-1600s until the early 1800s. The construction of ships in Nantes, Le Havre, and elsewhere also provided major economic activity. Meanwhile, the Compagnie des Indes Orientales, set up in the late 1660s, established its headquarters at Lorient, and the city becoming a virtual company town with arsenal, docks, and warehouses: the major port for trade between France and Asia.[61]

By the early 1800s, the glory days of this early trade with Africa and the "Indies," west and east, lay in the past. France had lost most of its American empire, Britain had outdistanced France in the acquisition of territory in India and ports in eastern Asia, the French East India Company had folded, competition from European products (such as beet sugar) attacked traditional commodities of the Caribbean, the slave trade was banned (with slaves emancipated in 1848), and the *notables* of the Atlantic ports tried to hide and forget their participation in a slave trade now considered ignominious. Yet trade with Africa and the Americas continued from the Atlantic and Channel ports, and the heritage of the earlier days served local promoters agitating for a new imperialist direction for the now somewhat somnolent cities. Terminal economic decline, in contrast with the dynamism of cities gearing up for industrialization, indeed threatened by the mid-1800s. Ship-builders, importers and exporters, and civic promoters thus tried to revive urban life through links with the newer colonies.

Nantes and Bordeaux serve as examples from western France. Already in the 1600s, Nantes' commercial elites built fortunes from the triangular trade in the Atlantic and trade with Asia. In the 1700s, 42% of French slave-trading expeditions involved *Nantais* ships, and the Nantes hinterland provided supplies for the voyages, labor, and the textiles traded in Africa and America. The "loss" of Saint-Domingue

---

[59] For an extended study of one example, see: Claude Malon, *Le Havre colonial de 1880 à 1960* (Mont-Saint-Aignan: Publications des Universités de Rouen et du Havre / Presses universitaires de Caen, 2006).

[60] Olivier Pétré-Grenouilleau, *Nantes au temps de la traite des Noirs* (Paris: Aubier, 1998); A. Roman, *Saint-Malo au temps des négriers* (Paris: Karthala, 2001); Jean-Michel Deveau, *La traite rochelaise* (Paris: Karthala, 2009); *Lorient, la Bretagne et la traite* (Cahiers du Musée de la Compagnie des Indes, Nos 9/10, 2006); Eric Saugéra, *Bordeaux, port négrier. XVIIe–XIXe siècles* (Paris: Karthala, 1995).

[61] Philippe Haudrère and Gérard Le Bouëdec, *Les Compagnies des Indes* (Rennes: Ouest-France, 2001).

and then the end of legal slave trading threatened ruin for the *Nantais* traders, who clawed back some of their profits by reorienting commerce from the Atlantic to the Indian Ocean. Trade with Mauritius (a French colony until Napoleon's defeat) and La Réunion helped maintain Nantes' commercial position, and the city remained the fourth largest port in France in 1860, though a plant disease was soon to wreak havoc on sugar plantations in the Indian Ocean islands on which it had laid its bets. Traders found other products to import and sell, including palm oil from France's African outposts and nickel from New Caledonia. New industries grew up to process these products—soap factories and sugar refineries, for example. Nantes also developed a prosperous export industry with a specialization in foodstuffs, and nearby Saint-Nazaire became one of the largest sites of ship-building in France. Though colonial trade never regained the primacy it had once enjoyed in Nantes, this international commerce, including the import-export business with France's colonies, provided a motor for local industrialization and modernization that formed part of the broader project of economic nation-building in the nineteenth century and afterwards. Advertisements for a trade-fair held in Nantes in 1932 enumerated the diverse activities of the city with the signal inclusion of a colonial vocation: "Industry, Commerce, Agriculture, Colonies," and another poster championed "Nantes, a great industrial and colonial port"—metropolitan industrialism and imperialism there neatly joined. The heritage of slave-trading nevertheless weighed heavily in Nantes, becoming a subject of embarrassment and a taboo in public life from the mid-nineteenth century until the 1980s, its newly appropriated "industrial and colonial" mandate one that hid a less glorious, if vital and prosperous, aspect of the municipal past.

Bordeaux, at the end of the eighteenth century, was France's most important *entrepôt* for colonial imports, the key port for trade with the Antilles. Connections with Africa through the triangular trade help explain the early role played by *Bordelais* in extending French business and conquest in western Africa, where *Bordelais* merchants established trading outposts in the 1820s. Within several decades, Senegal would be the major center for Bordeaux's colonial business activities; one booster in 1900 went so far as to say that "Senegal is essentially a *Bordelais* colony." Increasingly important in the difficult economic times of the mid-1800s, colonial trade became even more significant for Bordeaux after the mid-1880s, when phylloxera badly affected the Gironde's vineyards. The city owed much of its prosperity at the end of the century and the years before the Great War to trade with Senegal and other parts of that region of western Africa, as well as Morocco. A group of Bordeaux merchants and traders (the most famous the Maurel and Prom families, both firmly established in Senegal over several generations) imported diversified shipments of goods from western Africa, ground-nuts the most important of them; refineries in Bordeaux extracted oil and made animal food from the nuts. Tropical woods, phosphates, rice, and other products were unloaded on Bordeaux's docks. The city monopolized the indigo and salt-cod trade. In the *fin-de-siècle*, over half of all ships in Bordeaux arrived from colonial ports, and a third of those that departed headed for the empire. Merchants doing business with the colonies, such as the Maurel dynasty, dominated civic institutions.

A host of colonial groups and activities in Bordeaux—a colonial institute, colonial museum, geographical society, publications, colonial courses at the university, one of the Navy's colonial medical schools, etc.—worked hard to promote both the city and the empire, whose fortunes so closely intertwined. Moreover, *Bordelais* showed particular enthusiasm in holding colonial expositions and trade fairs. Competition with other colonialist cities, notably Lyon and Marseille, provided continued instigation for the city to make the most of its self-appointed vocation as "colonial capital of France." Colonialism thus proved something of a salvation for Bordeaux, but there was a price to be paid, according to Souad Boukarta. Having a proudly mercantile and colonialist outlook, the city's reliance on colonial markets and trade which was based on imports and was dominated by family firms, worked against a more go-getter industrialization and modernization.[62]

Lyon, like the Atlantic ports, prided itself on an extroverted international reputation. Famously the city of the "two hills"—the hill that prays and the hill that works—Lyon's role in the *outre-mer* came from commerce and Christianity. The manufacture of silk textiles traditionally represented Lyon's most important economic activity, with some raw silk produced locally, but much imported from the Levant or the Orient; in the mid-1800s disease that affected local silkworms made it necessary to augment supplies from Asia. Several *Lyonnais* entrepreneurs hoped for development of French relations with China and Southeast Asia as a way of assuring supplies, but also as conduits for greater regional benefits from trade and investment.

John Laffey developed the concept of "municipal imperialism" in the 1970s to explain this *Lyonnais* push into Asia.[63] The argument does not enjoy unanimous support from specialists in Lyon's history, who dispute the implied breadth of support for France's colonial ventures in the city, yet the concept retains convincing merits for its focus on the local impetus in expansionist ventures and also its emphasis on the lead part played by the regional business elite. The businessmen who dominated the powerful chamber of commerce and the city government, such as the industrialist Ulysse Pila (nicknamed the "viceroy of Indochina"), developed their own interests—and, they argued, those of their hometown—by advancing French positions in the South China Sea. *Lyonnais* encouraged French intervention, alongside the British, in the Chinese empire. They argued strongly for the acquisition of a French domain in Southeast Asia; indeed, *Lyonnais* took considerable credit for instigating the French takeover of

---

[62] Christelle Lozère, *Bordeaux colonial* (1850–1940) (Bordeaux: Éditions Sud-Ouest, 2007); Souad Boukarta, *Bordeaux, une économie et une société coloniales au début du XXe siècle* (Bordeaux: Institut aquitain d'études sociales, 2004); and Danielle Pétrissans-Cavaillès, *Sur les traces de la traite des noirs à Bordeaux* (Paris: L'Harmattan, 2004).

[63] John Laffey, "Municipal imperialism in France: the Lyon Chamber of Commerce, 1900–1914," *Proceedings of the American Philosophical Society* 119 (1976): 8–23. On Lyon's involvement in the empire, see Jean-François Klein, *Un Lyonnais en Extrême-Orient: Ulysse Pila, vice-roi de l'Indochine* (Lyon: Editions lyonnaises d'art et d'histoire, 1994); and Bruno Benoît and Gilbert Gardes, *Être Lyonnais. Identité et régionalité* (Lyon: J. André, 2005).

Vietnam and the neighboring countries of Indochina from the late 1850s to the 1890s. They suggested, too, that France might establish a dominant trade position in southern China, in Yunnan, from its base in Tonkin.

Evangelization complemented trade, even though Lyon's business and religious communities did not always collaborate easily. Lyon became the center for the church's revivalism with the establishment of the Propagation de la Foi in 1822. For the next century, until the pope transferred the society's headquarters to Rome, it was from Lyon that the association coordinated the Catholic Church's missionary efforts (alongside the Société des Missions Étrangères, whose mother-house in Paris dated to the 1600s). Several new missionary orders also emerged in Lyon. The Society of Mary (Marists), founded in 1816, grew into an important order for missionary work and education in Oceania and Australasia, while the Société des Missions Africaines from 1856 directed its efforts towards sub-Saharan Africa. The SME maintained branches in France for recruiting missionaries as well as its mission stations overseas, alongside an energetic publications program and a wide support network. In addition to the interest in spreading Catholicism witnessed by such congregations, particular *Lyonnais* were attracted to Asian religions. Émile Guimet, a wealthy entrepreneur who had traveled in Turkey, India, and Japan, opened a museum of Asian art and religions in 1879; faced with a lukewarm reception among his fellow townsmen, Guimet moved his museum to Paris in 1885 (where it is now the national museum of Asian arts).[64]

Lyonnais invested in both trade goods and souls in the colonies, with a particular focus on southeastern Asia, which some boosters liked to see as almost a *Lyonnais* reserve in the colonial world, similar to the *Bordelais* hegemony in Senegal and the neighboring region of Africa. A *Lyonnais* colonial culture, complete with colonial institute, geographical society, colonial training academy, and *musée colonial*, provided the infrastructure for municipal colonialism. Lyon thereby affirmed its role in the commercial and civilizational tasks of imperial nation-building overseas, and used the empire to advance its own economic well-being, assert its municipal identity, and compete with other cities in France. The colonial connection was important in Lyon's efforts to promote itself as a regional metropolis, and aspire to the rank of France's second city—an ambition contested by Marseille.

Lyon's and, in particular, Bordeaux's great competitor was Marseille, "portal to the Levant" (*porte de l'Orient*), the real "colonial capital of France," as its city fathers and promoters branded the city. Marseille benefitted from its location, and a history of trade in North Africa stretching back to the 1500s. However, the fortunes of Marseille's port declined precipitously in the early 1800s because of competition from northern European shipping, and the empire provided a perfect opportunity to restore

---

[64] Yannick Essertel, *L'aventure missionnaire lyonnaise 1815–1962* (Paris: Les Editions du Cerf, 2001); Françoise Chappuis and Francis Macouin, eds., *D'Outremer et d'Orient mystique... les itinéraires d'Émile Guimet* (Suilly-la-Tour: Editions Findakly, 2001); and various chapters of Claude Prudhomme, *Une appropriation du monde: missions et missionnaires XIXème–XXème siècles* (Paris: Publisud, 2004).

the city's status, just as it did for the Atlantic ports and the capital of the Rhône region. The conquest of Algeria, expansion of French interests in western Africa, and the opening of the Suez Canal in 1869 increased opportunities, and the city's energetic chamber of commerce—more important than the city council as the heart of municipal power—avidly sought to capitalize on these conditions. Not only would shipping benefit, so too would Marseille's industries, including the processing of tropical products: *savon de Marseille* made from colonial palm and coconut oils became one of the city's specialities. Marseille firms, such as the Compagnie du Sénégal et de la Côte occidentale de l'Afrique, the Compagnie française d'Afrique occidentale, the Messageries maritimes, and Freissinet shipping lines counted among the very largest business operations in the French Empire, transforming the city into the busiest port in France and the major *entrepôt* for colonial trade by the late 1800s.[65]

The colonial interests of *Marseillais* entrepreneurs earned them fortunes, and also leveraged them into positions of regional, national, and international importance. Jules Charles-Roux stands head and shoulders above fellow townsmen as an exemplar for the mixing of local, national, and colonial initiatives.[66] Born in 1841, Charles-Roux cut his political teeth when sent by the family soap-making company to Paris in 1873 to campaign against a new tax that disadvantaged oil importers and soap manufacturers. Like many in his milieu, Charles-Roux would remain an ardent supporter of free trade, and a defender of liberal capitalism and republicanism. His personal empire was diversified. In addition to owning a large share of the soap industry, he administered a sugar refinery, and presided over the Freissinet shipping company and its affiliated shipbuilding and repair company. He also served as president of the Compagnie Générale Transatlantique, an even bigger shipping line, and chaired the organization of French ship-builders. He sat on the board of several banks, the Paris–Lyon–Méditerranée railway company and the Suez Canal Company. Charles-Roux won election to Marseille's city council in 1881 and to the French parliament in 1889, offices he held for a decade, making him perhaps the most powerful figure in Marseille and the most influential *Marseillais* in Paris.

Colonialism went hand in hand with regional and national development for Charles-Roux. He was a founding member of the Marseille geographical society, and played a role in the establishment of a colonial institute, a colonial museum and a colonial medical school in Marseille.[67] He organized the colonial section at the world's fair in Paris in 1900, and the Marseille *exposition coloniale* of 1906, the latter a partic-

---

[65] See Marcel Courdurie and Guy Durand, eds., *Entrepreneurs d'empires* (Marseille: Chambre de commerce et d'industrie Marseille-Provence, 1998); and Hubert Bonin, *L'esprit économique imperial,* for detailed studies on local businesses. The Chambre de Commerce et d'Industrie de Marseille has also published a series of volumes on Marseillais commercial activities in the empire.

[66] The following biographical account comes from Isabelle Aillaud, et al., *Jules Charles-Roux, le grand Marseillais de Paris* (Rennes: Marines Editions, 2004).

[67] See Eric Deroo, ed., *L'École du Pharo: cent ans de médecine outre-mer, 1905–2005* (Panazoli: Lavauzelle, 2005).

ular triumph for his vision of Marseille as the commercial headquarters of the French Empire.[68] Charles-Roux was instrumental in setting up two lobby groups, the Comité de l'Afrique française and the Comité de Madagascar, and he was elected president of the Union Coloniale Française, the peak body of colonial businesses. Charles-Roux saw acquisition of colonies as a means to compensate for the defeat of 1870. He argued that colonialism represented a "peaceful solution" to France's economic problems and a wise economic investment: "Our colonies are in a way a reserve for the future, the supreme home for our industry and trade." A civilizing impulse imbued colonialism in the eyes of the Marseillais entrepreneur as well: "We claim to be the representatives of a superior civilization, and it is on this superiority that we found our rights to colonial power."

Amidst his other activities, Charles-Roux made time for his local cultural interests. He was an early supporter of the Félibrige movement of his friend Frédéric Mistral and its promotion of Provençal language and literature. He helped set up museums of Provençal folklore in Arles and Avignon, and he authored a small stack of monographs on the history of various towns in southern France. Charles-Roux, in short, was a regionalist, a nationalist, and a colonialist—and indeed it is possible to say that for him colonialism provided a link between the province and the nation. Empire advanced the fortunes of Marseille and of France (as well, of course, Charles-Roux himself), a way in which a city such as Marseille could contribute to a national cause and underline its status as a regional, political, and commercial center. Colonialism was vital to the French nation, Charles-Roux argued, and Marseille's key position served to bring the fruits of empire to France and to channel France's material and moral investments and exports to the colonies. The evidence of colonialism was everywhere present in Marseille, as visitors and writers noted: in the procession of ships unloading in the port, in the plethora of colonial organizations, in the stately buildings housing the colonial companies and the chamber of commerce (its walls decorated with motifs inspired by the colonies), and in the variegated population of Europeans, Arabs, black Africans, West Indians and others who passed through the boulevards and alleys, the cafés and brothels of the Mediterranean metropolis.[69] Marseille earned a reputation as the most cosmopolitan city in France—an image that sometimes tarnished it in the eyes of other Frenchmen, somewhat disoriented by the rough, ebullient and multi-cultural ambiance of the port that for the colonial boosters provided proof positive of the city's dynamism.

Was Marseille a colonialist city? Some historians dispute the label, arguing that Marseille was first and foremost a trading city, able to adapt and take advantage of colonialism, but later also able to adapt to decolonization. They point out that

---

[68] Laurent Morando, "Les expositions coloniales nationales de Marseille de 1906 et 1922: manifestations locales ou nationales?," *Provence historique* 54, no. 216 (2004): 229–52.

[69] See, for instance, Albert Londres, *Marseille, porte du Sud* (Paris: Le Serpent à plumes, 1995 [1927]); Joseph Roth, *The White Cities: Reports from France, 1925–39* (London: Granta, 2004); and Claude McKay, *Banjo* (London: X Press, 2000 [first published in 1932]).

many Marseille businesses did not depend fully on colonial markets, and that by no means all *Marseillais* manifested great support for colonialism (except perhaps when they trooped out to exhibitions). They argue that colonialism was more a question of opportunism than vocation for Marseille. Though municipal imperialism might have projected Marseille into the forefront of French expansion in the late 1800s and at the time of the 1906 and 1922 expositions, the real center of colonial power lay in Paris—exemplified by the holding of the 1931 colonial fair in the capital, not the provinces—and other cities, such as Bordeaux and Lyon, had their place among the "imperial cities" of the metropole.[70] Such arguments have much merit, but it is hard to deny that Marseille's elite engaged in colonial activities in a particularly ambitious fashion, pocketing the profits and trumpeting Marseille's colonial engagement; they certainly wished to portray Marseille as the colonial center of France. The image and reality of Marseille's primacy among colonial outposts, and its position as France's second city during the Third Republic, owed much to its colonial orientation.[71] There existed, in sum, no more manifest site in the metropole for imperialist nation-building than Marseille.

In the cases of such cities as Nantes, Bordeaux, Lyon, and Marseille, colonialism became a constituent part of regional identities and helped define their place in the nation—trading points that served as conduits between the empire and the metropole, sites of the ship-building, industrialization, entrepreneurship, and urban renewal considered necessary for the construction of a modern nation. Their activities underlined France's position as an international and colonial power in a way that other regional centers could not: a nation open to exchange with foreign countries, taking its products and its culture around the globe. The imperial nation-state needed the commitment of men, money, and support to the empire, and these cities provided the places, local colonialists argued, where they were to be found. Moreover, colonialism provided the pivot for the revival of the ports, their path to prosperity, the means by which they could restyle themselves and gain leverage against the often overweening power of Paris.

In several other regions, colonialism served different functions in the nation-building project. Alsace, in eastern France, was not an obviously "colonialist" territory of the Hexagon, though promoters convinced a small stream of settlers from Alsace to settle in Algeria in the mid-1800s. However, the French defeat in the war against Prussia in 1870–71, and the forced cession of Alsace and Lorraine to the new German Reich, pointed to a potentially new relationship between the "lost provinces" and the newly founded empire. Alsatians who did not wish to live under German

---

[70] See Xavier Daumalin, *Marseille et l'ouest africain: l'outre-mer des industriels (1841–1956)* (Marseille: Chambre de commerce et d'industrie Marseille-Provence, 1992), and the chapter by Guy Durand in Bonin, *L'esprit économique impérial.*

[71] On "second cities," and their need to find a particular vocation, see Maiken Umbach, "A Tale of Second Cities: Autonomy, Culture, and the Law in Hamburg and Barcelona in the Late Nineteenth Century," *American Historical Review* 110, no. 3 (2005): 659–92.

rule (including many Catholic Alsatians who looked with suspicion on the Protestant Prussians) seemed to have little choice but exile in France. The French colonialists suggested another option: migration to Algeria. To the colonial lobby, this represented an ideal solution to the Alsatian problem. The Alsatian refugees could live under the French flag, re-creating their communities and enjoying the benefits of land and liberty in North Africa, while Algeria would gain a populace of willing settlers eager to develop the land and defend French interests. Several thousand migrants heeded the siren call, and journalists waxed lyrical about tidy new hamlets bearing Alsatian names, where settlers decorated their gardens with geraniums, brewed beer, chatted in the Alsatian *patois*, and kept alive the traditions of their homelands, all the while waving the tricolor. The men and women of the diaspora, it was hoped, though never ceasing to work for the return of Alsace and Lorraine to France, would do their part in making Algeria veritably French: a triangulated relationship in which the "lost provinces" (soon, it was hoped, to be reclaimed) and the new province of Algeria would contribute to the good of the *patrie* that offered the common point of allegiance for both provincials and colonials. The results never lived up to such expectations, as the Alsatian communities in North Africa disaggregated with the move of migrants to the growing cities of the Maghreb. However, the idea of Alsatians as colonial pioneers melded well into the pro-colonial ideology of the late 1800s in which acquisition of an overseas empire was seen as some compensation, at least temporarily, for the loss of the two French provinces, and an invigorated empire could eventually provide resources for a successful reversal of the defeat of 1870.[72]

Of all the French regions, Corsica was, arguably, the one where colonialism held the greatest sway. As I have discussed elsewhere, Corsica was, in many ways, France's colonial island. Acquired from Genoa in the 1760s, staunchly retaining its own language and customs even against the tide of Gallicization, Corsica's peripheral position in France was not only geographical. Corsicans' age-old involvement in military activity, confirmed by Napoleon's imperialist actions, provided a rare avenue of social mobility in an island that remained impoverished, and the expanded French public service offered yet another route of social ascension to a population composed largely of shepherds and farmers. Colonialism swelled the army and the administration, and Corsicans readily volunteered. Although they accounted for less than one percent of France's total population, Corsicans totalled a fifth of colonial administrators, and a similar proportion of the European soldiers in France's colonial army. Corsicans seemed omnipresent in the empire as soldiers, customs-inspectors, tax officers, postal clerks, and bureaucrats working in other administrative offices. "Without the Corsicans, there would be no colonies," one general congratulated the islanders-turned-colonial pioneers.

---

[72] Fabienne Fischer, *Alsaciens et Lorrains en Algérie: histoire d'une migration 1830–1914* (Nice: Editions Jacques Gandini, 1999); Odile Goerg, "Exotisme tricolore et imaginaire alsacien—L'Exposition coloniale, agricole et industrielle, Strasbourg, 1924," *Revue d'Alsace*, no. 20 (1994): 239–268.

The Corsicans indeed became a key expatriate group in the colonies, though their somewhat ambivalent reputation—"continentals" considered Corsicans clannish, sometimes corrupt and occasionally criminal—followed them around the empire. Corsicans organized friendly associations (*amicales*) that provided mutual aid to members and venues for solidarity and sociability. *L'Echo de la Corse et de l'Algérie*, published in Algiers, counted among the Corsican periodicals that brought settlers news from home, while, *Saïgon-Cyrnos* was the organ of the Corsican community in Indochina. Colonial Corsicans held fêtes and banquets to share their food, wine, and songs and to celebrate the accomplishments of their compatriots, brave soldiers and meritorious administrators held up as role-models for Corsicans and proof that continental stereotypes were wrong. Corsicans abroad sent earnings home to their often needy families, a valued injection of capital into the island. At the end of military or administrative tours of duty, many returned to their native land enriched enough to buy land, gain status as *notables*, and win political office. Government service in the colonies, therefore, became a mainstay in the economic and social welfare of the Mediterranean island, promoters even arguing that Corsicans' heritage and character endowed them with a particular talent for colonialism.

Empire supplied an outlet for Corsicans who nevertheless remained painfully aware of the limited opportunities at home. Indeed, Corsican newspapers in the colonies regularly bemoaned the problems of Corsica and the inattention of the government in Paris to the poor transport systems on the island, the high cost of shipping between the mainland and island ports, continued prevalence of malaria, and lack of support for economic diversification and development. Some contrasted the interest shown in Paris for distant colonies with the relative disinterest for Corsica, ironically depicting the great growth of modern Algiers against the stagnation of Ajaccio or Bastia. If the tone occasionally showed bitterness at the neglect of Corsica, and at the necessity for Corsicans to choose "exile" to the mainland or the colonies, the papers also lauded the benefits of colonialism and constantly reminded fellow Frenchmen of the vital role played by the Corsicans in the extension and maintenance of the empire. Corsicans, the spokesmen declared, through their contributions to colonialism demonstrated that they were productive citizens and eternally loyal Frenchmen, their commitment to the nation evidenced by the work and the sacrifices made in the empire.[73]

Colonialism provided a platform for new (or renewed) regionalist vocations, including the profit-making associated with trade, shipping, and investment, the more or less successful revival of age-old colonial interests in Brittany and the Atlantic ports,

---

[73] Robert Aldrich, "France's Colonial Island: Corsica and the Empire," in *French History and Civilization: Papers from the George Rude Seminar*, ed. Gemma M. Betros (Brisbane, 2009), 112–25. See, in particular, Marien Martini, *Les Corses dans l'expansion française* (Ajaccio: Les Myrtes, 1953); two books, one the catalog of an exhibition, the other the proceedings of a conference, both published under the title *Corse-Colonies* (Corte: Musée de la Corse, 2004); Charlie Galibert, *La Corse, une île et le monde* (Paris: Presses universitaires de France, 2004); and Francis Arzalier, *Les Corses et la question coloniale* (Ajaccio: Albiana, 2009).

the development of a new focus on Asian expansion in Lyon, the specialization in links between Bordeaux and Senegal and between Marseille and North Africa, and the adoption of colonialism as a means of economic and social salvation in Corsica. The empire offered career opportunities—at sea, in trade, missionary endeavors, the civil service, the army—for the sons (and, at least in the religious congregations, for the daughters) of families with horizons and fortunes otherwise circumscribed by the limitations of provincial life. It helped solder peripheral regions to the nation, provided a means for the rebranding of port cities, and gave an opportunity for local elites to underline the contributions of their cities to great national undertakings. It also was a chance to reinforce local particularities, to differentiate regions from each other and from Paris. It offered a platform for competition between cities and regions, and sometimes for the expression of grievances against the central government. Colonialism helped bring Corsica closer into the ambit of the nation-state, and to keep Alsace, temporarily out of the French system, demographically and ideologically within its orbital field of gravity; Breton missionaries could help preserve Francophone culture and the Catholic religion in the former colonies of North America. Colonialism provided a new vocation, as least as represented in the propaganda that tried to shape public opinion, which extended France overseas, creating a domain for the energies of its population: part of a triangulated scheme, from the *petite patrie* to the national *patrie* to the *grande patrie* of empire. Economically, politically, socially and culturally, therefore, colonialism stood as an essential component in the mechanism of nation-building in the Third Republic.

The Dynamics of Empire and Nation-Building

Through the nineteenth century and into the twentieth, nationalists sought to weld together culturally and politically diverse regions, particularistic local cultures, and different economies into a whole. This they did through law, extension of the franchise, electoral and party politics, standardization of weights and measures and language, the creation of national economies and transport systems, the inculcation of patriotism through universal education, the defense of the fatherland by a (generally) conscripted army, and diplomatic strategies designed to increase national power and prestige. The aims were unity and a sense of national purpose, but the program of nation-building also encompassed the strengthening of military might, economic modernization and industrialization, the creation of international networks to provide geopolitical and commercial advantage. Overseas expansion, for all of the major European countries (and others, such as Japan and the United States), formed part of this comprehensive project of nation-building, whether for states that already possessed an empire but which were eager to expand and safeguard their holdings, or for new states that saw acquisition of colonies as confirmation and guarantee of great-power status.

Like the other great powers, France was proudly an imperialist nation-state. For much of the nineteenth century and the first six decades of the twentieth, the nation-building project encompassed empire-building: the relics of the empire of the old regime, Napoleon's short-lived continental empire and his overseas schemes, the construction of a formal global empire and its maintenance over more than three generations. Colonialists boasted that the *Marseillaise* could echo from Brittany to Vietnam, and that the tricolor flew over Toulouse and Timbuktu as the *coq gaulois* strutted the globe. The colonial lobby sought to convince the citizenry and the political elite that the colonial periphery constituted a vital adjunct to the metropolitan center. Nation and empire could never be completely fused, not only because of the manifest differences between the Corrèze and the Congo but because affirmation of differences between Europe and the *outre-mer*, civilized and primitive (or decadent), was the bedrock on which imperial rule rested. Rail lines and shipping lanes might well connect the provinces and the colonies, but issues of race and political entitlement always separated them. The white settlers of the empire might be fully-fledged French, but only rarely was it possible for the black, brown, or yellow inhabitants of the colonies to accede to the status of citizenship or recognized "Frenchness" (even if they aspired to such goals, which many decidedly did not). Only in a very unequal fashion did the colonies gain representation in parliamentary institutions and the other centers of power. Not until the Fourth Republic—with the end of the *code de l'indigénat*, the establishment of the *départements d'outre-mer*, the short-lived functioning of (largely consultative) local assemblies—did there emerge a policy that aimed at real integration of the colonies and the colonized into the nation, or at least the French Union, with anything even remotely resembling parity. Only the constitution of the Fifth Republic in 1958 made it clear that all those in the *outre-mer* were indeed citizens with the right to vote, and even so, different electoral colleges preserved inequalities of representation while bureaucrats wrestled with esoteric questions about what citizenship actually meant for the citizens of the nation recharted as part of a vague *Communauté* doomed to disappear.[74]

Following decolonization, France had to recast itself as a nation without an empire, a post-colonial state. Ironically, authorities would nevertheless have to confront independence movements in remaining outposts (notably, in the 1980s, in New Caledonia), as well as secessionist tendencies (in Corsica) that drew on rhetoric and militant strategies borrowed from the anti-colonialist movements in the now deceased empire. Demands for devolution of budgetary and administrative powers to local government authorities revived the regionalist tendencies that had never disappeared.

In the long run, the building of an imperial nation-state—a vast continuum from the villages of *douce France* to the exotic outposts at the far corners of the world—had failed. Many of the colonized did not want citizenship, despite the

---

[74] Frederick Cooper, *Citizenship between Empire and Nation: Remaking France and French Africa, 1945–1960* (Princeton: Princeton University Press, 2014), discusses the issue of citizenship and suffrage in sub-Saharan Africa, convincingly arguing that many French African leaders, at least initially, campaigned for recognition of their full rights as citizens and for administrative autonomy within the French Union and Community rather than for independence.

decades of indoctrination about the *mère-patrie*, the promises of advancement and de-velopment, the recruitment of soldiers and sending out of teachers and missionaries, the building of government houses and opera houses, the laying of railways, and the catchphrases about *la France des cinq continents, la France de 100 millions d'habitants, la plus grande France*. The French at home, despite decades of similar propaganda and lobbying, found that they could do without the colonies. Post-war reconstruction, *rapprochement* with Germany and the construction of a more cooperative Europe, the consumer revolution, the *trente glorieuses* of economic growth could all be effected without the colonies. Already in the 1950s, during the Indochinese war, some said that France should withdraw gracefully from Asia, falling back on its positions on the Afri-can continent. Few protested the accession to independence of the sub-Saharan colo-nies, and most were relieved when the Algerian war came to an end. No one much no-ticed when the colonial museums closed, the colonial institutes turned off the lights, and the colonial associations disbanded.[75]

France found new strategies for a post-colonial nation-building, for na-tion-building is always a work in progress. A nuclear arsenal (with a testing site in French Polynesia) buttressed the military clout previously said to be assured only by colonial bases and troops; the defense establishment successfully negotiated to main-tain French garrisons in former colonies such as Chad, Djibouti, and the Ivory Coast. The *Français d'Algérie* and other colonial French were repatriated, though in some for-mer colonies of west Africa, there would be more French residents thirty years after independence than in the days of empire. Many colonial companies changed their names, but continued business as usual, and entrepreneurs and investors found new opportunities and markets in the now independent countries that had once belonged to the empire: "neo-colonialism" in the eyes of critics, overseas profit-making with-out the burdens of imperial administration or the exigencies of the *mission civilisa-trice*. France continued to treat most of its former colonies in sub-Saharan Africa as a *pré-carré*, an exclusive domain, directing its interventions through a special office at the Elysée Palace in charge of African relations (and with a generous budget to secure the amity of post-independence states and their dictatorial rulers), the French African franc serving as a common currency, and the French language spoken as a lingua fran-ca: a continuing dream of "Françafrique," according to those who castigated the new order.[76] Cultural connections between France and its colonies found a new structure

[75] On the period of decolonization, see, most recently, Martin Thomas, *Fight or Flight: Britain, France, and their Roads from Empire* (Oxford: Oxford University Press, 2014).

[76] See Robert Aldrich, "When Did Decolonization End? France and the Ending of Empire," in Alfred W. McCoy, Josep M. Fradera, and Stephen Jacobson, eds., *Endless Empire: Spain's Retreat, Europe's Eclipse, America's Decline* (Madison: University of Wisconsin Press, 2012), 216–29. The notion of *Françafrique* is associated with the works of François-Xavier Verschave, such as *La Françafrique: le plus long scandale de la République* (Paris: Stock, 1999); the Élysée's African of-fice was for long the domain of Jacques Foccart, on whom see: Pierre Péan, *L'Homme de l'ombre* (Paris: Fayard, 1990).

in *Francophonie*, a cultural movement born in the early 1960s that has evolved into an institutionalized set of international activities under the effective auspices of Paris. Migrants from the old colonies flowed into France in far greater numbers in the last years of empire and afterwards than ever before, providing a cheap source of labor for agriculture, industry, and public works. France, however, proved increasingly unwelcoming to these migrants, who now had no colonial lien on citizenship, right of abode, or other entitlements.

Though nation-building in France after the early 1960s was a project that no longer included an extensive formal empire, the heritage of colonialism has resurfaced in debates about migration, multi-culturalism and national identity. Around the turn of the twentieth to the twenty-first century, France rediscovered its empire and its colonial heritage, from revelations about torture in Algeria to demonstrations by the *Indigènes de la République*, from a successful move by parliament to declare slavery and slave-trading crimes against humanity to a disastrous legislative move to require the teaching of the "positive" aspects of colonialism in schools, from the erection of a national monument to the dead of the Algerian war to the unveiling of private monuments to diehard defenders of *Algérie française*, from a vogue for *nostalgérie* to the cultural movements of world music and Francophone literature, from debates on the wearing of Islamic head-scarves to riots in ethnically populous suburbs. Not all of these developments should be interpreted as the pure product of France's colonial history, but it has become increasingly evident that the legacy of a defunct empire—a colonial past once considered buried—has an afterlife in contemporary France. Contemporary nation-building in France must now address the heritage of the country's long-lasting efforts to construct an imperial nation-state.

Nation-Building and Regional Integration: The Case of the Spanish Empire, 1700–1914

Xosé-Manoel Núñez

This article will provide an overview on the political-territorial dynamics that the imperial dimension of the Spanish political community has provoked in its peninsular territory since the eighteenth century. It focuses particularly on the inter-territorial dynamics and cleavages, as well as on the consequences that the imperial dimension, an aspect often neglected by Iberian historiography, has played in the evolution of the national question in modern Spain. This has particularly to do with one factor: unlike the Ottoman, the Russian, or the Austro-Hungarian cases, Spain has been a transatlantic empire, whose main core was placed in Europe, and particularly in the Iberian Peninsula. In the case of the Spanish Empire, it is possible to refer to a Castilian core and a first layer of peripheries of other Iberian territories, in particular those belonging to the former Crown of Aragon, and then a second layer, to which Portugal, during its short-lived incorporation, belonged (between 1580 and 1640). A third layer of Spanish colonies followed in America and (to a lesser extent) Asia, where at least in late nineteenth century, the idea of territorial integration was harbored, which collapsed in the course of the first quarter of the nineteenth century. The three remaining major possessions in this third layer, where integration was not achieved, were lost by the empire in 1898. A fourth layer of possessions in Africa consisted of a largely indigenous population and very few settlers. Until the 1950s, these colonies were never perceived as being in any way assimilable into the core.

The tendency to deal with the overseas territories as integrated bodies of the Spanish monarchy was parallel to the increasing integration of the different Iberian lands—the Aragonese kingdom, Castile, Navarre, and Portugal (between 1580 and 1640), which joined the Spanish political community since the end of the fifteenth century—as well as to the development of a Spanish proto-nationalism or dynastic patriotism, particularly since the coming of the Bourbon dynasty and the reforms carried out by enlightened absolutism from the middle of the eighteenth century. This tended to identify the Iberian territories as "Spain," the core of an empire whose overseas and European lands were seen as separate bodies from each other, in spite of the fact that many efforts were made by writers and political theorists to assess the continuity of the same Catholic and dynastic community along several continents.[1] However, both dynamics were deeply intertwined: the increasing integration of the Iberian core-lands of Spain was also dependent on the influences and transfers received from the overseas territories. This oscillated between their aim at becoming fully-fledged members of the Spanish political community and their parallel claim, which became dominant after 1810 under North American influence, to set up separate sovereign bodies.

The "late Spanish Empire," which lasted from 1826 to 1898, as well as the "new empire," which replaced the American one and was composed of some territories in Africa, also had an important influence on the process of territorial integration (or disintegration) of Spain as a nation-state. However, the progressive losses of territory that the Spanish Empire suffered from the beginning of the nineteenth century was a process that underwent several phases. For example, independence of the largest part of the American colonies between 1810 and 1824; loss of the last overseas colonies— Puerto Rico, Cuba and the Philippines, as well as some archipelagos in Micronesia— as a result of the Spanish–American war of 1898; wars in the Spanish Protectorate of Northern Morocco from 1907–25, and later independence of Morocco in 1956; independence of Equatorial Guinea in 1968; and the loss of Western Sahara in favor of Morocco (and Mauritania) in 1975. The continuous losses of overseas territories deeply affected the inner dynamics of regional integration within the Spanish nation-state in an opposite way. This also leads one to question whether the colonies, and the multi-continental dimension of the empire, have ever been incorporated into the cultural repertory of images and nationalist discourses of what Spain was and is today. Therefore, it also questions whether the fact of having been an overseas empire (or a nation-state which ruled over territories outside Europe until as late as 1975) also exerted an influence on the dynamics of both nation-building and "nation-destroying," as Walker Connor has affirmed.[2] With a few exceptions, the most up-to-date existing models on the relationship between the "center" and the "periphery" in Spain during the modern period frequently tend to ignore or at least to undermine the colonial/imperial dimension of the state, and this has had a double consequence for historical research.

Firstly, it has been ignored to an extent where political tensions between metropolitan Spain and the colonies were translated into the political cleavages arising

---

[1] H. Kamen, *Spain's Road to Empire: The Making of a World Power, 1492–1763* (London: Allen Lane, 2002); J. H. Elliott, *Empires of the Atlantic World: Britain and Spain in America, 1492–1830* (New Haven: Yale University Press, 2006); and his classic work: J. H. Elliott, *Imperial Spain, 1469–1716* (London: Penguin Books, 1990 [1963]). A useful and relatively well updated synthesis in English is W. S. Maltby, *The Rise and Fall of the Spanish Empire* (London: Palgrave Macmillan, 2009).

[2] W. Connor, *Ethnonationalism. The Quest for Understanding* (Princeton: Princeton University Press, 1994), 28–66.

between the capital (Madrid, or more precisely the Central Government) and the regions where territorial claims for home rule, and later on ethnonationalism, emerged and developed. The central elites did not see separatism emerge in the last years of the nineteenth century, through both the creation of the Basque Nationalist Party in the Basque Country (1895) and the first electoral success of the Catalan Regionalist League in Barcelona in 1901. Actually, such a perception arose earlier, as the first Cuban demands for home-rule were voiced in the 1830s and radicalized after 1868. These claims coming from the "distant" periphery merged with the tensions caused by the persistence of Basque *Fueros*, a premodern form of territorial privileges which survived during the process of liberal state-building since 1833. To put it simply, the first Iberian separatists were seen as something like European "Cubans." Furthermore, until the coming of the Spanish Civil War (1936–39), the inner discussion on the structure of the state was also linked to the problem of how to rule the new colony (Protectorate) of Northern Morocco.

Secondly, the disregard of the imperial dimension of Spanish politics and culture during the nineteenth and twentieth century has also led most historians to overemphasize the supposed "euro-centrism" of Spanish nationalism since the beginning of the liberal revolution. This belief has deeply impregnated the prevailing approach to the process of nation-building and regional integration in nineteenth-century Spain. Accordingly, in 1826 Spanish liberals and traditionalists alike did not complain very much about the loss of the greatest part of the American empire. It was interpreted that the king had lost his overseas possessions, as most individuals who were integrated in the practice of political representation did not see America as a part of the nation. Thereafter, the Spanish project was defined in purely European terms: Spain had to aim at becoming a modern nation-state, following in particular the French model, although—and unlike its beloved mirror—the state-led process of nation-building was partially unable to attain a final success in culturally homogenizing the whole peninsular territory of Spain. However, the different Spanish historiographies on modern nationalism have not yet achieved a consensus regarding the set of historical problems that should be addressed using a long-term view of national construction in Spain.[3]

The historiographic thesis of the prevailing "eurocentrism" of Spanish nationalism and identity politics in the long nineteenth century fails to explain the relevance

---

[3] See, for example: J. Álvarez Junco, *Spanish Identity in the Age of Nations* (Manchester: Manchester University Press, 2011). Nevertheless, it has to be noted that the question whether the nation-building process in nineteenth-century Spain can be characterized as a "failure" or simply as a "relative success" constitutes a matter of discussion for recent Spanish historiography. See: J. Moreno Luzón, ed., *Construir España. Nacionalismo español y procesos de nacionalización* (Madrid: CEPC, 2007); and X. M. Núñez, "La questione nazionale in Spagna: Note sul recente dibattito storiografico," *Mondo Contemporaneo* 2 (2007): 105–27. See also S. J. Jacobson, "Spain: The Iberian Mosaic," in *What is a Nation? Europe 1789–1914*, eds. T. Baycroft, and M. Hewitson (Oxford: Oxford University Press, 2006), 211–27.

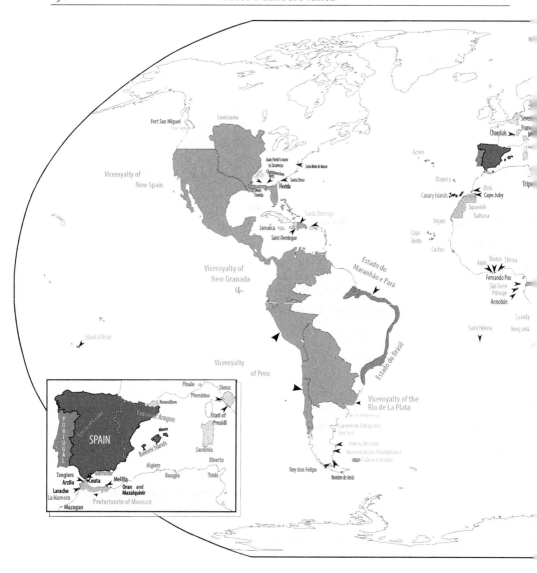

of the imperial (and late imperial) experience. This interpretation has often neglected how the beginning of the process of modern state- and nation-building in Spain, which can be dated back to the first decades of the eighteenth century,[4] coincided with the forging of the empire, or at least with the process of consolidation of the old empire. Many questions were left unanswered with such a historical approach: What of the

---

[4] Some authors date this process further back: see A. M. Bernal, *España, proyecto inacabado. Los costes/beneficios del imperio* (Madrid: Marcial Pons, 2005); and A. M. Bernal, *Monarquía e Imperio* (Barcelona: Crítica/Marcial Pons, 2007).

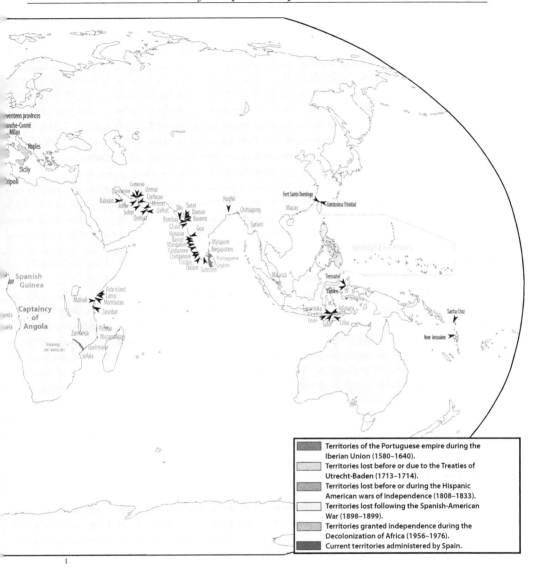

Territories of the Portuguese empire during the Iberian Union (1580–1640).

Territories lost before or due to the Treaties of Utrecht-Baden (1713–1714).

Territories lost before or during the Hispanic American wars of Independence (1808–1833).

Territories lost following the Spanish-American War (1898–1899).

Territories granted independence during the Decolonization of Africa (1956–1976).

Current territories administered by Spain.

remaining colonies such as Cuba, Puerto Rico, and the Philippines, whose economic importance for the development of peninsular Spain is undeniable? What of the new, though meager, territories in Africa, including the Protectorate of Northern Morocco since 1904? What happens to the influence of "Orientalist" and "Africanist" culture on the definition of the Spanish national narrative?[5] To what extent were the relics of the

---

[5] See a first approach in: A. Rivière Gómez, *Orientalismo y nacionalismo español: estudios árabes y hebre-os en la Universidad de Madrid: (1843–1868)* (Madrid: Instituto Antonio de Nebrija/ Universidad Carlos III/ Dykinson, 2000); as well as in V. Morales Lezcano, *Africanismo y orientalismo en el siglo*

"classic" empire of the sixteenth century integrated within a national worldview? In other words: Why did the social and intellectual reaction in Spain to the defeat of 1898 (the "Disaster" that marks a decisive turning-point in Spanish history) provoke in the (former) colonial power a new wave of cultural pessimism, to the point of considering that the lost territories had been "amputated" from the national body?[6] This brief outline of the problem suggests that to deal with the liaison between regional integration and the role of empire in the Spanish case confronts the historian with a number of unanswered questions by existing historiography, and forces us to advance an interpretative synthesis largely based on a selective reassessment of up-to-date historical research.

The Spanish Empire in the Eighteenth Century: Reform and Reaction

Under the Treaties of Utrecht (April 1713), the European great imperial powers decided what the fate of Spain would be in terms of the continental balance of power. The new Bourbon King Philip V, who was the winner of the War of Spanish Succession (1701–14), retained the overseas empire, partly because France and the maritime powers were aware that Philip's cause was very popular in America and did not risk waging another war on the new continent. However, the Spanish monarchy ceded the rest of its European sixteenth-century Empire—such as the Spanish Netherlands, Naples, Milan, and Sardinia—to the Austrian Empire. Sicily and some parts of Milan were handed over to the Duchy of Savoy. And, finally, some parts of the peninsular territory were transferred to the British Empire. The British retained Gibraltar and Menorca, captured during the War of Spanish Succession. Menorca could not be regained by the Spanish monarchy until the Treaty of Amiens (1802). The disastrous performance of the Spanish army in the War of the Quadruple Alliance (1718–20), which put a definitive end to any attempt by Spain to recover its past possessions in Italy and Northern Africa, also exposed the level of weakness the Spanish empire had fallen to.

Moreover, the new Spanish king granted the British the exclusive right to slave trading in the Spanish colonies of America for thirty years, as well as licensed voyages to ports in Spanish colonial dominions. Philip had already granted the French the right to trade in the Caribbean area. Spain's economic and demographic recovery had only begun slowly in the last decades of the Habsburg dynasty. This was evident from the growth of its trading convoys and much more rapid growth of illicit trade during the period. But this recovery did not translate into institutional improvement due to deficiencies in command of the last Habsburg kings.

XIX (Madrid: UNED, 1988); M. Marín, "Orientalismo en España: Estudios árabes y acción colonial en Marruecos (1894–1943)," *Hispania*, no. 231 (2009): 117–46; and B. López García, *Orientalismo e ideología colonial en el arabismo español (1840–1917)* (Granada: Universidad de Granada, 2011).

[6] See C. Serrano, *Final del Imperio: 1895–1898* (Mexico: Siglo XXI, 1984), and S. Balfour, *The End of the Spanish Empire, 1898–1923* (Oxford: Clarendon, 1997).

After 1720, the new Bourbon monarchy took a much more cautious approach to international relations, built upon a family alliance with Bourbon France, and continuing to follow a program of institutional renewal that was directly inspired from French enlightened reformism. A repertory of Bourbon mercantilist ideas based on a centralized state, that reflected the thinking of Richelieu and Jean-Baptiste Colbert, was put into effect in America slowly at first but with increasing momentum during the century. They designed their administrative reforms to enhance the rule of the crown. The Spanish Bourbons' broadest intention was to break the power of the entrenched aristocracy of the creoles (*criollos*) in America, elites which were composed of locally born colonials of European descent. The monarchs also aimed to loosen the territorial control of the Jesuits over the reductions, virtually independent theocracies (*missions*) inhabited by Guarani natives in the territories of today's Paraguay. The armed resistance of the Guarani, fostered by the Jesuits, could only be defeated by a joint Spanish–Portuguese army during the War of the Seven Reductions or Guarani War (1756). This was part of the regalist policies of the Bourbon Kings, which aimed to enforce royal control over universities, the Inquisition, and ecclesiastical appointments. This policy also maintained that vast lands held by the Catholic Church were an obstacle for economic development. In fact, the Jesuits were expelled from the metropolis and from all Spanish America in April 1767. However, by removing the Jesuits from all territories of the empire, the new King Charles III destroyed the most vital part of the Spanish empire's educational system, and may actually have harmed the broader interests of the crown in the long term. The Spanish monarch may have neutralized what might have been an intellectual ally in the near future, which could have challenged, thanks to its defense of economic reform and scientific learning, the progress of revolutionary political theories among Creoles.[7]

The Spanish economy's emerging sectors exploited the overseas territories either as consumers or as producers of food or industrial raw materials. The basis of all this was still the highly regulated labor of the Native Americans, supplemented with the abundant use of slave labor, particularly of African origin.[8] The Iberian peninsula's most prosperous economic sectors that developed over the course of the eighteenth century, which had traditionally channeled part of their production to the Americas, considered the American markets as an important reserve.[9]

---

[7] See Maltby, *The Rise and Fall*, 159–60, as well as C. M. MacLachlan, *Spain's Empire in the New World. The Role of Ideas in Institutional and Social Change* (Berkeley: University of California Press, 1988), 67–98.

[8] See H. Thomas, *The Slave Trade; The History of the Atlantic Slave Trade 1440–1870* (London: Papermac, 1997).

[9] See S. J. Stein and B. H. Stein, *Apogee of Empire. Spain and New Spain in the Age of Charles III, 1759–1789* (Baltimore: Johns Hopkins University Press, 2003), as well as S. J. Stein and B. H. Stein, *Edge of Crisis. War and Trade in the Spanish Atlantic, 1789–1808* (Baltimore: Johns Hopkins University Press, 2009).

Mercantilist ideas were also enacted in the economic field. First, Bourbon reformists set up new chartered "companies" based on the British model for the exploitation of the American colonies, which also opened the overseas territories' trade to other territories of Spain rather than just Castile. Thus, the Caracas Guipuzcoana Company offered Basque traders a monopoly over commerce with Venezuela, in particular the rapidly growing business in cacao. The Catalonia Company was also licensed to trade with the island of Saint Domingue. By 1746, thanks to his reforms, the administration had been rationalized and the country's finances had been restored. The opening of the American trade to the Kingdom of Aragon and other ports in the Crown of Castile had acted as a powerful means to integrate the Iberian territory and to make Catalan claims for recovering the self-government (lost in 1714) gradually disappear from the public sphere. By 1789, every port within the Empire had the right to trade with any of the others. This did not mean that nostalgia for the lost regional liberties in 1714, when the Catalan territorial privileges had been abolished by the new monarchs, had completely vanished from the public sphere. In fact, several intellectuals and opinion-makers in Catalonia and Aragon continued to raise the banner of the restoration of the regional privileges.[10]

Under Charles III, a protectionist economic policy aimed at strengthening Catalan textile and Basque metalworking and shipbuilding industry had developed. The import of cloth from India was already banned in 1718. This led to an increasing dependency on cotton imported from the West Indian colonies and woven in Catalonia. Much of the finished cloth was then exported to the American colonies.[11] This also meant that textile manufacturers in Latin America were forced to close. A ban on imported iron and copperware was also issued in 1775. All these reforms achieved a fundamental realignment of the Spanish imperial economy. While in 1700 merely 10–12% of all manufactured goods imported by the American colonies came from metropolitan Spain, by the end of the 1780s that percentage had risen to 55%.

The eighteenth century was also a period of prosperity for the overseas Spanish Empire as trade within grew steadily, particularly in the second half of the century. A number of Spanish victories against the British fleet helped it secure the Bourbons' dominance of the Americas until the early nineteenth century. Rapid shipping growth from the mid-1740s until the Seven Years' War (1756–63) reflected, in part, the success of the Bourbons in bringing previous forms of illicit trade under control. After the end of that war, shipping trade within the Empire once again began to expand, reaching an extraordinary rate of growth in the 1780s.[12] Spanish control

---

[10] See E. Lluch, *Las Españas vencidas del siglo XVIII: Claroscuros de la Ilustración* (Barcelona: Crítica, 1999).

[11] See C. Martínez Shaw, *Cataluña en la carrera de Indias, 1680–1756* (Barcelona: Crítica, 1981) and H. A. Silva, *El comercio entre España y el Río de la Plata (1778–1810)* (Madrid: Banco de España, 1993).

[12] See Stein and Stein, *Apogee of Empire*; J. M. Delgado Ribas, *Dinámicas imperiales (1650–1796): España, América y Europa en el cambio institucional del sistema colonial español* (Barcelona,

over the Indies trade was improved by reforming the navy and by licensing private vessels to seize foreign interlopers. Moreover, the Spanish Bourbon kings set up the renewed structures for governing the colonies. This obeyed the priorities settled by the Bourbon government since Utrecht: to reclaim initiative for the state in matters of war finance, and to recover control of external trade. This would enable the control of sources of revenue, which were crucial for reconstructing Spain's military capacity.[13] First, the monarchy reformed the tariff system, and in 1717 transferred the administrative powers of the variegated councils that had flourished in the Habsburg imperial administration, and which had served as sources of information and guarantors of consensus, to the new secretaries of state. For example, the previously influential Council of the Indies (*Consejo de Indias*) merely retained its influence on patronage, as well as its role as an appellate court. The *Casa de Contratación* was moved to the emergent port of Cádiz, which became the one port for all Indies trading. Individual sailings at regular intervals were slow to displace the old habit of armed convoys, but by the 1760s there were regular packet ships crossing the Atlantic between Cádiz and Havana and Puerto Rico, and at longer intervals to the emerging region of the River Plate, where a further viceroyalty was created in 1776 that joined the existing ones of New Spain, Peru, and New Granada. The contraband trade that had been the lifeblood of the Habsburg Empire declined in proportion to registered shipping. Between 1764 and 1786, Charles III extended his governmental and administrative reforms to the overseas territories. In general, and like his predecessors, Charles III's reforms aimed at expanding royal power, as well as increasing the crown revenues. However, they also aroused serious misgivings among the Creole elites and colonists.

The eighteenth century has traditionally been regarded as a relatively peaceful period in Hispanic America. However, several upheavals since the Tzetal revolt in Mexico (1712–13) registered unease within the American colonies, while demonstrating the renewed resiliency of the reformed imperial system. The most important was the uprising led by Tupac Amaru that broke out in Peru in 1780 and lasted until 1783, when a series of Indian revolts that had taken place since 1740 in Upper Peru peaked. Local resentment for abusive practices and the demand for reform of the vice regal system mixed with indigenous claims for better treatment and abolition of compulsory work services. There was also, in 1781, the less relevant revolt of the *comuneros* in the viceroyalty of New Granada (today's Colombia and parts of Venezuela), where indigenous claims mixed with protests against taxation and the abundance of metropolitans in administrative offices. Although their causes were related to different reasons, and cannot be considered as forerunners of the late independence movements, they also meant in part, reactions to tighter control from imperial power.[14]

Edicions Bellaterra, 2007); J. R. Fisher, *The Economic Aspects of Spanish Imperialism in America, 1492–1810* (Liverpool: Liverpool University Press, 1997).

[13] Kamen, *Spain's Road*, 449–50 and ff.

[14] See S. Rinke, *Revolutionen in Lateinamerika. Wege in die Unabhängigkeit 1760–1830* (Munich: Beck, 2010).

The uprisings were severely repressed. However, and partly as a response to the revolts, the imperial power introduced some reforms in the colonial administrations. In 1784, the former systems of *repartimientos* (forced labor draft allocated to Indians) had been abolished, and a new intendant system was introduced to Peru. Sub-delegates dependent on the intendants replaced the corrupt previous network of *corregidores* (chief responsible for a provincial jurisdiction) and majors. The intendant system was also introduced in 1786 in the northern part of Spanish America (New Spain). Although the sub-delegates did not achieve the level of administrative efficiency that was expected from them, the new system experienced some success in urbanized areas, where reinforced supervision produced some improvements in public services and infrastructures. However, the Bourbon reforms favored the interests of the crown at the cost of the Creole elites, and restrained the "de facto home-rule" that the latter had enjoyed so far. After 1750, the Spanish crown gave priority to the appointment of Europeans to new vacancies in *Audiencias* (appellate courts with advisory functions to the chief executive power) and other colonial offices, instead of selling them to prominent Creoles, as had been the policy of the late Habsburgs. Administrative efficiency and greater control from the metropolis was supposed to be achieved through this measure. Intendants, who in their majority were born in the metropolis, also appointed metropolitans for *cabildos* and other offices, and commissions in the colonial army were also reserved for them.[15]

Therefore, the Creole elite, which had governed its own affairs for almost a century and a half, saw itself now excluded from political influence and from the ability to negotiate spheres of power, as they had traditionally enjoyed during the Habsburg period, characterized by an often inefficient and corrupt exercise of power from the metropolis. Moreover, few American subjects of the Spanish empire accepted the Enlightenment concept of reason that supposedly laid at the core of the metropolitan policy of administrative reform. In many Creoles' eyes, the Bourbons set in motion a second conquest of America.

The Bourbon institutional reforms were to bear some fruit militarily when Spanish forces easily retook Naples and Sicily from the hands of the Austrians in 1734 during the War of Polish Succession, and they also rejected successfully British attacks during the War of Jenkins' Ear (1739–42). Although the Spanish monarchy lost territories to the British Empire during the Seven Years' War (1756–63), Spain recovered these losses and seized the British Bahamas during the ensuing American War of Independence (1775–83). Despite all these partial victories, the Spanish Empire had not returned to first class power status. Certainly, it had recovered considerably from the difficult days at the beginning of the eighteenth century. The relatively peaceful century under the Bourbon monarchy had allowed Spain to rebuild and start the long process of modernizing its institutions and economy, with the important contribution of a renewed empire. The demographic decline had been reversed, as it also became

[15] See J. Lynch, "The Institutional Framework of Colonial Spanish America," *Journal of Latin American Studies* 24, no. 15 (1992): 69–81; MacLachlan, *Spain's Empire*, 99–111.

evident in the overseas colonies—revenues from America had increased dramatically from the 1740s.

On the other hand, most of rural metropolitan Spain and its empire lived in relatively backward conditions, at least compared to eighteenth-century West European standards. Although there were some substantial improvements by the late eighteenth century, Spain was still an economic backwater. Under the mercantile trading arrangements, the Spanish monarchy had difficulty providing the goods demanded by the strongly growing markets of its empire, and providing adequate outlets for return trade. The economic integration of the metropolitan lands of the empire was far from being achieved. In Henry Kamen's words, Spain's return to an imperial role under the new Bourbon dynasty was "deceptive, fragile and in the long run disastrous," and this would not substantially change during the rest of the century.[16]

The growth of trade and wealth in the colonies also contributed to an increase of political tensions as frustration grew with the improving but still restrictive trade with Spain, whose colonial administrative reforms did not follow the accelerated path opened by commerce. Some observers remarked on this contradiction. On his return from a scientific expedition in 1795, Alessandro Malaspina wrote a memorandum dealing with the situation of Spanish colonial institutions. He recommended transforming the empire into a more or less looser confederation of states, which would maintain strong commercial ties, as a means to improve governance and trade so as to undermine the growing political tensions between the elites of the empire's periphery and the center.[17]

Late imperial Spain of the eighteenth century was also a new opportunity for regional integration. First, the term "colonies" was hardly used in the Spanish metropolis since the sixteenth century. The Spanish-American dominions were not colonies, but "discrete parts of the crown of Castile," which had come to be regarded by their inhabitants as quasi-autonomous kingdoms. A part of them even came to be called *Magna Hispaniae*, Greater Spain. And this would make them no different, independently on their real status from the legal point of view, from other European dominions of the monarch, such as Aragón, Naples, or the Low Countries.[18] Secondly, the Catalano-Aragonese part of the kingdom, and in particular the Catalan emerging trade bourgeoisie, gained free access to the "race of the Indies." This contributed to shape economic interests of a wider spectrum that linked more territories of the Iberian "periphery" to empire, which until that moment had been almost exclusively exploited by the Castilian part of the Spanish Crown. Now its benefits extended to practically all regions of metropolitan Spain, and the crown gained enthusiastic support from new social sectors of the Iberian "periphery" to the defense of the empire, abandoning or postponing their past sentiments of grievance towards the Castilian core.

---

[16] Kamen, *Spain's Road*, 453, 489.

[17] See J. C. Kendrik, *Alejandro Malaspina: Portrait of a Visionary* (Montreal: McGill-Queen's University Press, 1999).

[18] A. Pagden, *Spanish Imperialism and the Political Imagination* (New Haven: Yale University Press, 1990), 91–92.

However, the traditional concept of the Hispanic political community as a composite monarchy, which had been advocated by the Habsburg dynasty (an addition of territories united by a common Catholic faith and a common dynasty, which was evident in the official name of the Spanish empire, *La Monarquía Católica*, the Catholic Monarchy), was progressively replaced with a more nuanced one. The sum of the inhabitants of the territories ruled by the Spanish Crown had to become homogenized in order to transform itself into a "coherent" political and legislative body, placed under the direct authority of the king. The concept "patria" (fatherland) steadily emerged as a common denominator to all Iberian territories of the Spanish Crown, although this concept was deprived of sovereignty.[19] However, it was quite uncertain whether the "patria" also embraced those subjects who were living in the overseas colonies. And, if it did include them, what kind of inhabitants were they? Were American Spaniards just the "neighbors" of white color and European descent, the creoles? In theory, the concepts of inclusion and exclusion that were applied to the inhabitants of the colonies in their respective local communities and territorial bodies were not particularly different from those existing in the European core of the empire. And the development of notions of political community in Spain and Hispanic America can only be understood in relation to each other.[20] However, there was in this respect a subtle difference between theory and practice.

The Habsburg concept of a composite monarchy began to be replaced, both in the metropolitan core of the empire and to some extent in its periphery, with a proto-national one, which tended to administratively deal with the overseas territories as mere colonies. This actually constituted an accurate reflection of what was taking place at the economic level. The higher economic integration of the empire was flanked by the increasing self-perception of the Iberian core being something more than a conglomerate of different kingdoms united by a common Catholic faith and a shared monarch. But this perception was not entirely shared by Creole elites. On the contrary, at the end of the eighteenth century, a new sense of belonging had emerged among many inhabitants of the American dominions. In spite of sharing a common religion, a common language and many cultural values with metropolitan Spain, they no longer saw themselves as Spanish. A number of intellectuals and prominent Creoles had begun to think of their territories in terms of a separate political community and no longer as parts of the Spanish "Catholic Monarchy." This was partly rooted in the previously existing and autonomously evolving idea of being part of a "New World" that deserved another historical narrative to be explained.[21]

---

[19] See J. Fernández Sebastián, "España, monarquía y nación. Cuatro concepciones de la comunidad política española entre el Antiguo Régimen y la Revolución liberal," *Studia Historia. Historia Contemporánea* 12 (1994): 45–74.

[20] See T. Herzog, *Defining Nations: Immigrants and Citizens in Early Modern Spain and Spanish America* (New Haven: Yale University Press, 2003).

[21] A. Pagden, "Identity Formation in Spanish America," in *Colonial Identity in the Atlantic World, 1500–1800*, eds. N. Canny and A. Pagden (Princeton: Princeton University Press, 1987), 51–94;

Independence Movements in the Americas and the Spanish Political Community Redefined

The turmoil of the French revolutionary wars, which affected Spain directly, and the oscillations in the foreign alliances pursued by the decadent Bourbon monarchy under the reign of Charles IV, which finally brought him under the patronage of the French emperor Napoleon, led the Spanish Empire to a series of disastrous maritime wars against Britain. The peak moment was the defeat of a joint Spanish–French fleet at the battle of Trafalgar in October 1805. The success of Britain's war against Spanish trade made things worse. Most of the economic damage came from the British maritime blockade. To prevent economic collapse in America, the Spanish crown sanctioned neutral trade throughout the empire in November 1797. Then, the United States, Britain and the Netherlands became the Creoles' economic lifeline, along with the emerging commercial bourgeoisie of Buenos Aires, Veracruz, Havana or Caracas benefited from this new possibility of free trade with ports other than Spain.[22] Therefore, the claim of freedom of trade became a crucial point of their political claims, particularly when things suddenly changed some years later. Moreover, no more Spanish ships loaded with treasures arrived to the port of Cádiz. Spain's commercial links with its overseas colonies weakened at a crucial moment when political resentment against the metropolis grew among Creoles. The revolutionary ideas from France and the United States also reached Creole private libraries in such distant places as Peru and the River Plate.

As Napoleon ordered his army to enter Spain and war broke out on metropolitan soil after the popular rising of Madrid on May 2, 1808, a complex conflict developed in the Iberian peninsula. This led to a politically unstable coalition of Ancient Regime supporters and liberals who shared little but an emerging sentiment of patriotism and hatred against Napoleon and the French, as well as some Spanish liberals, the *afrancesados*, who collaborated with the invaders. The struggle in the metropolis left the Spanish Empire without a functioning central government for six years, replaced with a number of regional *juntas* and supreme command in Seville, which was supposed to coordinate the resistance. The later renamed War of Independence concluded with the withdrawal of Napoleonic troops in 1814 and the American colonies were left to their own devices.

In 1808, there was no widespread desire in America to "get rid" of Spain. Most Creoles resented Bourbon "despotic" reforms and a monarchy hostile to colonial interests. Some of them were inspired by the North American example and were imbued with French enlightened ideas. However, the process of "emancipation" of the colonies

---

D. A. Brading, *The First America. The Spanish Monarchy, Creole Patriots and the Liberal State, 1492–1867* (Cambridge: Cambridge University Press, 1991).

[22] J. R. Fisher, "Commerce and Imperial Decline: Spanish Trade with Spanish America, 17978–1820," *Journal of Latin American Studies* 30, no. 3 (1998): 419–79.

had more to do with the Spanish monarchy's "desertion" from America than with extended popular support for national independence in the new continent. The dissolution of imperial power in America was not caused by the emergence of Creole national projects. Instead, the emergence of Hispanic American nationalist projects may be regarded as a somewhat unexpected consequence of the breakdown of the imperial order. The Hispanic American wars of independence were, above all, civil wars among Creoles themselves, confronting those who supported the legitimacy of the Catholic monarchy with those who opted for getting free from that power. Both shared a kind of "Creole patriotism," which could be labeled as a vaguely defined kind of proto-nationalism. But for most inhabitants of the Spanish American race, class and skin color were far more relevant than the sentiment of belonging to a political community.[23] At the outset of the process of independence, just a minority of Creoles and a handful of charismatic leaders, such as Simón Bolívar, Francisco Miranda or José de San Martín, were firm supporters of republicanism and enlightened ideas. Where no such leaders emerged, the attachment to the Spanish monarchy survived longer. The social conditions of each territory, and its recent history, also mattered. In several areas, like Peru and New Spain (Mexico), Creole fear of social revolts that would reverse the existing racial hierarchies contributed to the long endurance of the loyalist option.[24] The example of the Haitian revolt that had led to the establishment of a Black Republic in 1804, and the remembrance of the Indian uprisings in the previous century, conditioned the attitudes of Creole elites. In other areas, such as the River Plate, the process of independence followed a more straightforward dynamic.

The first wave of American independence that started in 1808 and ended in 1810 ran parallel to the formulation of the first modern national project by the Spanish liberals, in particular since the Junta of Seville convened a meeting of the *Cortes* with the purpose of writing Spain's first constitution, which was approved in 1812. This meant a turning point in the way in which American creoles considered themselves part of the newly-found Spanish political community. The liberals wanted Spain to continue to be a multi-continental polity, and proclaimed that the American territories were also, in theory, a part of the nation, whose inhabitants were as Spanish as

---

[23] Apart from J. Lynch, *The Spanish American Revolutions, 1808–1826* (New York: Norton, 1973), see the most recent interpretations of Rinke, *Revolutionen*; J. K. Adelman, *Sovereignty and Revolution in the Iberian Atlantic* (Princeton: Princeton University Press, 2006); A. Ávila and P. Pérez Herrero, eds., *Las experiencias de 1808 en Iberoamérica* (Mexico DF: El Colegio de Mexico/Universidad de Alcalá, 2008); F. Colom González, ed., *Relatos de nación: La construcción de las identidades nacionales en el mundo hispánico* (Madrid: Iberoamericana/Vervuert, 2008); J. E. Rodríguez, *The Independence of Spanish America* (Cambridge: Cambridge University Press, 1998 [Mexico DF 1996]); T. Pérez Vejo, *Elegía criolla. Una reinterpretación de las guerras de independencia hispanoamericanas* (Mexico DF: Tusquets, 2010), and P. Cagiao Vila and J. M. Portillo Valdés, eds., *Entre imperio y naciones. Iberoamérica y el Caribe en torno a 1810* (Santiago de Compostela: USC, 2012).

[24] See J. Ch. Chasteen, *Americanos: Latin America's Struggle for Independence* (Oxford: Oxford University Press, 2008), 66–94.

metropolitans. From the theoretical point of view, the first Spanish liberal constitutional draft was highly inclusive. Thus, the national project that emerged with the Napoleonic Wars and which continued until the years of the liberal revolution in the 1830s was also a genuinely imperial project of multi-continental compass. Its objective could be summarized as the creation of a liberal community that included both "European Spaniards" and "American Spaniards" as the foundation of a renewed empire. Furthermore, the burdens of colonial servitude would be abolished or deeply reformed, in a way acceptable to the ideology of political equality that was overwhelmingly dominant in the political rhetoric of this period.[25]

The American representatives at the first liberal Assembly of Modern Spain (the "Cádiz Parliament" of 1810–12) also played an unexpected role in the formulation of the first concept of Spain as a modern nation. Spain had to become a nation of citizens, though permeated by history and religion as allegedly necessary preconditions for the emergence of the Spanish political body as a new demos. The Cádiz constitution envisioned a limited constitutional monarchy based on civil equality, personal liberty, and the rights of property. Creoles were to be granted citizenship and parliamentary representation. However, the number of American representatives was carefully limited. It also made no concessions on the subject of free trade, so as not to harm the commercial interests of the local merchant communities of the metropolis. This was the outcome of a relevant contradiction that soon emerged within the liberal project: American representatives could attain majority in the future legislative chamber, thus undermining the ability of metropolitan Spanish liberals to set up a new institutional order. While the American representatives claimed their territories were equal parts of the new [Spanish] nation, and therefore that the American citizens were equal in rights to those living in Europe, including equal representation, Spanish liberals were not able to go this far. Spanish Americans amounted to 16 million in 1810, while metropolitan Spaniards were just 10 million. Equal representation meant the electoral hegemony of the former colonies over the European core of the empire. A first limitation approved by the Cádiz *Cortes* was the exclusion of a part of the American population—the free descendants of African slaves, the so-called *castas pardas* ("brown castes"), regardless of how relevant the portion of "African blood" in a given person was—from full citizenship. This discussion overlapped with the political dilemma between centralism and federalism. Most metropolitan liberals were afraid of leaving too much room for self-government in the hands of the Creoles, while also opposing Iberian "regional liberties," regarded as a relic of the territorial organization of the Habsburg monarchy of the sixteenth and seventeenth centuries.[26]

---

[25] J. M. Fradera, "The Empire, the Nation, and the Homelands: 19th Century Spain's National Idea," in *Nation and Region: Nation-Building, Regional Identities and Separatism in Nineteenth-Century Europe*, eds. J. Augusteijn and E. Storm (Basingstoke: Palgrave, 2012), 131–48; J. M. Fradera, *Colonias para despuěs de un Imperio* (Barcelona: Bellaterra, 2005), 80–103.

[26] See J. S. Pérez Garzón, *Las Cortes de Cádiz: El nacimiento de la nación liberal* (Madrid: Síntesis, 2007).

A basic problem that underpinned the discussion was that for many metropolitan liberals, but in particular for the American representatives, the nation was not only defined as a community of free-born individuals, but also as an aggregation of territories and bodies whose existence was legitimized in history. This would have enabled the advantageous integration of the overseas territories. Nevertheless, the perception of what a Spanish citizen is was different on each side of the ocean. While the Creole patriots believed their territories to be equal in rights and historical legitimization (as "bodies" that reached an agreement with the Spanish Monarchy, like the self-perception of the Basque territories), they came to be increasingly seen by the Bourbon reformers, and later on by the metropolitan liberals, as territories which were not constitutional parts of the Spanish nation but possessions of the nation. This contradicted with the Creole dream of achieving unity with the Spanish liberal nation in terms of *primi inter pares*. The American Creoles were keen to be subjects of the king, but not to become subjects of the new Spanish nation—they wanted to be both citizens and national subjects of an emergent political community.[27] However, this point of view was not accepted by Iberian liberals, who wanted to reconcile the full recognition of equality of rights among European and American citizens on the one hand, and the exclusion in practice from citizenship of a relevant part of the American Spaniards on the other. The metropolitan liberals were obsessed with maintaining political control over the colonies. This became evident in the 1810–12 debate and then again, in the 1820–23 parliamentary discussion on the structure of provincial administrative institutions (*Diputaciones*), for which a different system was envisaged in the overseas provinces that would guarantee the political control by metropolitans and, in particular, by military governors. Metropolitans would also continue to be preferably appointed for public offices in the colonies.[28]

All this meant that Spain was to become a nation extended in the empire, but molded in its Iberian model. From the outset of the liberal revolution, Spain was conceived as a political community composed of "Spaniards living in both hemispheres," as stated by the Cádiz Constitution of 1812. The necessity of coping with an immense territory caused the first Spanish liberals some additional problems to define the restructuring of the state. Some of them preferred centralism as a model of organization of the territories which were located at the core of the empire. This concept was not accepted by "peripheral" liberals of the peninsula—not to speak of traditionalists and supporters of the return to the Ancient Regime, and particularly by the Basque representatives. The final agreement was reached when a new form of the ancient territorial privileges of the

[27] J. M. Portillo Valdés, "'Americanos españoles': Historiografía, identidad y patriotismo en el Atlántico hispano," in *Fénix de España. Modernidad y cultura propia en la España del siglo XVIII (1737–1766)*, ed. P. Fernández Albadalejo (Madrid: Marcial Pons, 2006), 327–44; see also J. M. Portillo Valdés, *Crisis atlántica: Autonomía e independencia en la crisis de la Monarquía hispana* (Madrid: Marcial Pons, 2006).

[28] A. Martínez-Riaza, "Las diputaciones provinciales americanas en el sistema liberal español," *Revista de Indias* 52 (1992): 647–91; J. M. Fradera, *Gobernar colonias* (Barcelona: Península, 1999), 82–85.

Basque provinces (the *Fueros*) was granted, partly a consequence of the first concessions made by metropolitan liberals to the Creole liberals, whose aim was to preserve a certain degree of home-rule for their territories within a Spanish nation regarded as being composed of different "bodies." The preservation of the Basque *Fueros*, and the long-term tolerance displayed by a great part of the Spanish liberals toward the survival of an idealized relic of "pre-Liberal constitutionalism," equated by enlightened intellectuals to the Republic of San Marino or the Swiss Grisons, was also linked to the liberal state's necessity of integrating the rest of a multicontinental empire.[29]

The Cádiz Constitution and its legacy held little attraction for those Creoles who admired the American and French revolutions. A majority of them came to the conclusion that, if they wanted to enjoy the taste of revolutionary liberalism, they had to choose independence. Even the most conservative Creoles were left with no option other than to rule themselves due to the Spanish monarchy's enduring failure to govern the empire since the Napoleonic invasion. The restoration of King Ferdinand VII (1814) and the General Rafael del Riego's revolt (January 1820) forced the king to restore the constitution of 1812 by means of a military coup. This coup was triggered by the refusal of several army units (up to 20,000 men) to fight the rebels in the Americas. The result of this uprising was the short-lived restoration of liberal rule in Spain until the French invasion, supported by the Holy Alliance of the European absolutist powers, in October 1823. No further army units were sent from the metropolis to America. This sealed the destiny of the remaining lands of the Spanish Empire in the new continent and paved the way for the definitive success of the alternative solution among supporters of liberalism in the American colonies.[30] At first came the openly federalist proposals, which were expressed by some deputies from New Spain (Mexico) in 1822–23 and rejected by metropolitans, something that left no other solution for the Mexicans than open independence, although Mexico had been a stronghold of the loyalists.[31] The late proposals of establishing a sort of confederation of independent American republics and the Spanish liberal monarchy, which were advanced by the Creole liberal Francisco Antonio de Zea, were damned to oblivion.[32]

The ultimate effort made by Spanish liberals to preserve the empire under a new form became a new argument for the opponents of a Jacobin state-structure within Iberian Spain, who gained some audience and preserved their spheres of influence.[33]

---

[29] See J. M. Portillo Valdés, *El sueño criollo: La formación del doble constitucionalismo en el País Vasco y Navarra* (San Sebastián: Nerea, 2006).

[30] See J. M. Delgado Ribas, "La desintegración del Imperio español. Un caso de descolonización frustrada (1797–1837)," *Illes i Imperis* 8 (2006): 5–44. See also M. Chust and J. A. Serrano, eds., *Debates sobre las independencias americanas* (Münster–Madrid– Frankfurt a. M.: AHILA/Iberoamericana/Vervuert, 2007).

[31] See an exhaustive analysis of the process in Rodríguez, *The Independence*, 192–205.

[32] See L. Ovalles, *Francisco Antonio de Zea y sus proyectos de integración ibero-americana* (Caracas: Academia Nacional de la Historia, 1994).

[33] M. P. Costeloe, *Response to Revolution: Imperial Spain and the Spanish American Revolutions, 1810–1840* (Cambridge: Cambridge University Press, 1986).

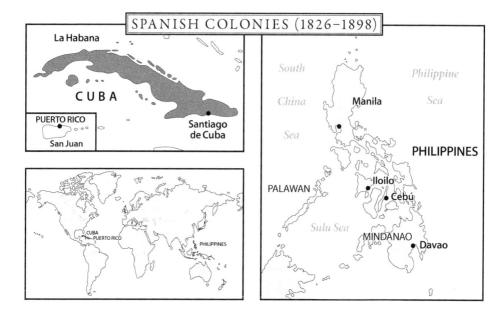

SPANISH COLONIES (1826–1898)

This heritage of the empire persisted within the European territory of Spain after the final defeat of the most important contingent of royalist troops still remaining in South America at the battle of Ayacucho (December 1824), which forced the Spanish Crown to recognize the independence of Peru and to withdraw, in practice, from continental South and Central America the following year. The last campaigns of the insurgent Creoles were also aided by political divisions among the royalists themselves, split between supporters of King Ferdinand VII and those who were in favor of the restoration of the liberal constitution. By 1826, Spain had lost all its territories in the Americas with some noteworthy exceptions: Cuba, Puerto Rico, and, in Asia, the Philippines.

Two or One? The "Overseas Spain" and Metropolitan Spain (1826–1898)

After the definitive loss of most of the American territories in 1824–26, the notion of imperial rule apparently vanished from the Spanish public sphere. Even the proper term "empire" was replaced, with the more ambiguous term "overseas territories" or simply "overseas" (*Ultramar*); a process that had already begun during the Cádiz parliament in 1812.[34]

---

[34] See J. M. Fradera, "Las fronteras de la nación y el ocaso de la expansión hispánica," in *Más se perdió en Cuba. España, 1898 y la crisis de fin de siglo*, ed. J. Pan-Montojo (Madrid: Alianza, 2006), 483–557 (here, 494).

The fiction of maintaining a small part of the pre-modern empire may have been, for Spanish ruling elites, very important to maintain the delusion of still being a great world power, despite the evidence of the increasing decadence of Spain in the face of expanding colonial empires of Britain and France. However, there is some historiographic discussion regarding the effective social impact on the metropolis of the first wave of American independence. Most historians have argued that the majority of "ordinary Spaniards" were highly indifferent towards the colonial losses of the 1820s. The main concern of Spanish liberals was making the nation in Europe. Therefore, liberal imperialism was weak because Spanish liberals did not care about the colonies. According to Martin Blinkhorn, the crisis of the 1820s did not produce any feeling of national agony in the metropolis, as most Spaniards had "little consciousness of empire or attachment to it."[35]

Nevertheless, it has to be noted that what has been called the "Ayacucho syndrome" continued to be present among the moderate liberal governments through the 1840s and 1850s. The Spanish government maintained the aim of restoring its sovereignty over the new republics by denying them diplomatic recognition and supporting the hispanophile elites in the political turmoil of the first decades of independence. Until 1836, Spain did not recognize the independence of Mexico. In several cases, it took more than thirty years for the Spanish government to extend that recognition to all American "successor states" of the past empire.[36] The prevailing public discourse of Spanish moderate liberalism insisted too on imperial restitution, gradually replaced with a rhetorical emphasis on cultural and "racial" brotherhood between Spain and its former colonies. The Minister of Foreign Affairs, Joaquín F. Pacheco, affirmed in June 1864 that "We [Spaniards] can never be foreigners in America as long as Americans speak our language, as long as they share our blood and are from our race, and this will be so until the end of the centuries."[37]

Those sectors of Spanish society that had economic interests in Hispanic America, particularly merchant elites of harbors such as Barcelona and Cádiz, were increasingly concerned by the loss of the colonies and even took some initiatives to raise funds to send troops to America. After 1826 they had to reorient their production and

[35] See M. Blinkhorn, "Spain, the 'Spanish Problem' and the Imperial Myth," *Journal of Contemporary History* 15, no. 1 (1980): 5–25. A similar point of view in J. Álvarez Junco, "La nación en duda," in *Más se perdió en Cuba*, especially 411–12.

[36] See J. Castel, *El restablecimiento de las relaciones entre España y las repúblicas hispanoamericanas* (Madrid: Cuadernos de Historia de las Relaciones Internacionales y Política Exterior de España, 1955); as well as J. C. Pereira and A. Cervantes, *Las relaciones diplomáticas entre España y América* (Madrid: Mapfre, 1992), 28–32.

[37] Parliamentary speech, June 21, 1864, quoted by J. A. Inarejos Muñoz, *Intervenciones coloniales y nacionalismo español. La política exterior de la Unión Liberal y sus vínculos con la Francia de Napoleón III, 1856–1868* (Madrid: Sílex, 2007), 101–02. On the nostalgic discourse towards Hispanic America in the decades after American independence of mid-nineteenth century Spanish liberalism, see L. López-Ocón Cabrera, *Biografía de "La América": Una crónica hispano-americana del liberalismo democrático español (1857–1886)* (Madrid: CSIC, 1987).

look for new markets that replaced the lost ones. European markets then became particularly important and absorbed around 30% of Spanish exports. The rest of the territories that were a relic of what had been the broad pre-modern empire (Cuba, Puerto Rico, and the Philippines) constituted a handful of islands which were quite distant from each other. However, between 1833 and 1868, Spanish public policy began to pay greater attention to all these territories. The military and administrative presence of the Spanish state on the islands increased. Administration of the empire depended on the Ministry of Overseas (*Ministerio de Ultramar*)—which was not founded until 1863—and the Ministry of State (Foreign Affairs). The communications network within each of these territories also improved. This process was particularly noticeable in Cuba, where new settlements spread to the interior of the island throughout the nineteenth century, new lands were also cultivated, and an increasing economic integration was fostered among its different parts. Havana had 300,000 inhabitants by 1895, and was the third largest city of the Spanish polity; nearly 20 percent of all Spanish railroads were located in Cuba.[38]

Puerto Rico, the Philippines, and particularly Cuba also experienced an increasing process of economic integration with the Iberian territories of the Spanish Crown during the second and third quarters of the nineteenth century. This made them in practice three more provinces of the new liberal state, which since 1833 adopted a centralized structure based on the implementation of the provinces. This new structure respected (unlike the French *départements*) the limits of the pre-modern historical regions, but was designed as the real intermediary between the central state and the population. Once liberalism's triumph was ensured in the metropolis with the defeat of Carlist legitimism after the end of the first Carlist War (1833–39), the liberal moderate faction began rapidly restructuring the political system. Even earlier there was both a change in mood toward concentrated state power, to the detriment of local and provincial democratic forms of governance, as well as the creation of an electoral franchise with very restrictive criteria. In 1837, the liberal government approved the expulsion of the inhabitants of Cuba, Puerto Rico, and the Philippines from the institutional and representative framework of the state, denying them rights of political participation—yet another example of the steady closure of the political system. Using as a pretext a local uprising in Cuba, which proclaimed the Constitution of 1812, and the fear of a possible contagion to the metropolis, Spanish moderate liberals approved what would be a typical feature of colonial rule: centralization and militarization of the political command in the Caribbean islands and the Philippines. This measure intended to leave apart the colonies from the political changes that were taking place in the Iberian peninsula, such as the difficult transition from the *ancien régime* to a new liberal order after the death of King Ferdinand VII in 1833. This left in practice no space for any attempt at institutionalizing some form of local government, and meant a radicalized version of some of the tendencies that were also observed in

---

[38] C. Naranjo Orovio, "Evolución de la población desde 1760 hasta la actualidad," in *Historia de Cuba*, ed. C. Naranjo Orovio (Madrid: CSIC / Doce Calles, 2009), 29–58.

the governance of the metropolis. The fear of social unrest in the colonies due to the steady increase in the slave population, in particular in Cuba, also played a significant role in the decision.

The Spanish government intended to replace the former "Laws of the Indes" (*Leyes de Indias*) with special laws in their overseas provinces, but these new laws, initially promised by the 1837 constitution, were never passed and therefore never enacted. Several projects of colonial reform and special administration were sporadically contemplated by the Spanish parliament, thanks to the initiative of some Cuban reformists like José Antonio Saco and Domingo Delmonte. Likewise, committees were set up in Spain to visit the Caribbean islands in 1838–39 and to analyze the *Leyes de Indias* (1840). But none of these initiatives, like the establishment of an Information Committee in 1865 by the young Minister of Overseas Antonio Cánovas del Castillo, brought any practical results.[39] Many Cubans began to contemplate a separatist solution, and in the 1840s many reform leaders and their disciples agitated for Cuba's annexation to the United States.

In practice, the Spanish liberal state subjected Cuba, Puerto Rico, and the Philippines to exceptional rule. Political control in the colonies was concentrated in the office of the military governors, the captain-generals, which had been awarded arbitrary powers since 1835. Although the "special laws" were successively debated throughout the nineteenth century every time a new constitution was drafted in metropolitan Spain (1845, 1869, and 1876), the Spanish government did not display any special interest in entering the discussion in detail. The fundamental reason was economic—the metropolitan government wanted above all to exploit the economic resources of its overseas possessions, vital for the difficult balance of public finances. Control of tax policy was in this respect crucial. Moreover, the racial argument was thoroughly discussed by Spanish liberals in 1837. The basic principles of liberalism— equality, justice, and fraternity—could not be applied to societies where the racial structure was completely different from Europe, and where the seeds of liberty would stir up unrest among African slaves. The same argument was used for excluding the Philippines from parliamentary representation, as well as for maintaining the characteristics of the pre-modern colonial empire in the Asian colonies—such as monopolies, compulsory labor services for natives, and different taxations according to racial groups—that had been abolished, in theory, by the *Cortes* in Cádiz in 1812.[40]

---

[39] Fradera, *Gobernar colonias*, 93–94, 102–03; M. P. Alonso Romero, *Cuba en la España liberal (1837–1898): Génesis y desarrollo del sistema autonómico* (Madrid: CEPC, 2002), 25–35; J. Alvarado Planas, *Constitucionalismo y codificación en las provincias de Ultramar. La supervivencia del Antiguo Régimen en la España del siglo XIX* (Madrid: CEPC, 2001), 197–227.

[40] J. M. Fradera, "Why were Spain's special overseas laws never enacted," in *Spain, Europe and the Atlantic world*, eds. R. L. Kagan, and G. Parker (Cambridge: Cambridge University Press, 1995), 334–49; J. M. Fradera, "Ciudadanía, ciudadanía congelada y súbditos residuales: Tres situaciones bajo un mismo estado," *Illes i Imperis* 7 (2004): 113–34. On the Philippines, see also L. A. Sánchez Gómez, "Los debates sobre la prestación personal en Filipinas durante el siglo XIX," *Anuario de Estudios Americanos* 57, no. 2 (2000): 577–99.

The "federalist" option of setting up a system of autonomous assemblies and governments in the overseas territories, which could control the activity of military governors and was largely inspired by the system implemented by the British in the West Indies and, afterwards, in the white dominions like Canada, was also definitively set aside by metropolitan liberals in 1837.[41] Thereafter, the political role of military governors in the Caribbean, which had been exceptionally reinforced as a provisory measure in May 1825, was not abolished but reconfirmed in 1834–35, under Captain-General Miguel Tacón in Cuba. This link was not, however, strongly separated from the administration of the metropolis. In the case of the military governors of Cuba, their instability and short permanence in office—with there being sixteen captain-generals between 1834 and 1868—was related to the fact that Havana was one possible destination among many others in the metropolis. Being sent to the Balearic Islands was considered by many generals a worse place than being dispatched to Havana or Puerto Rico, from where some influential members of the military later became presidents of the Spanish government.[42] Cuba was the most important military base of Spain and likewise an important platform for prominent members of the military endorsing their prospects for a successful political career. Yet, the Spanish army in the Caribbean was not a typically colonial army in the proper sense. There were neither creoles nor black soldiers enrolled on a regular basis, contrary to the British and French cases.[43]

The empire—as a market for the weak industrial production of some Spanish regions, above all, textile goods from Catalonia, and as a producer of sugar, tobacco and other minor products—undoubtedly contributed toward the reinforcement of economic integration in the new Spanish nation-state, since the latter was given a protected market, restricted to the colonies. This did not prevent economic inequalities from growing among the different metropolitan regions, although the role of the state in promoting the economic integration of the peninsula territory by improving communications and extending the networks of railroads has been recently emphasized.[44] Moreover, since the mid-nineteenth century, thousands of Iberian Spaniards, as well as Canary islanders, had left for the island, attracted by the better prospects of life in the flourishing colony. They added to the thousands of Metropolitan civil servants, military officers, and American Creoles who were loyal to the Spanish Crown but that had moved from former areas of the Spanish Empire to Cuba after 1820–26.

---

[41] See J. C. M. Ogelsby, "Una alternativa a la revolución: Los autonomistas cubanos y el modelo canadiense, 1837–1898," *Boletín de la Academia Nacional de la Historia*, Caracas 288 (1989): 5–46. See also the contemporary interpretation by J. A. Saco, *Paralelo entre la isla de Cuba y algunas colonias inglesas* (Madrid: Imp. Tomás Jordán, 1837).

[42] This was the case with Captain-Generals Leopoldo O'Donnell (1844–48), Francisco Serrano (1859–62) and Juan Prim (1847–48).

[43] See J. G. Cayuela Fernández, *Bahía de Ultramar. España y Cuba en el siglo XIX. El control de las relaciones comerciales* (Madrid: Siglo XXI, 1993), 178–205.

[44] See S. Calatayud, J. Millán, and M. C. Romeo, eds., *Estado y periferias en el siglo XIX: Nuevos enfoques* (Valencia: PUV, 2009).

Metropolitan Spaniards in Cuba and Puerto Rico temporarily lost their political rights, but cultivated a self-awareness of being the most "Spanish" of all Spaniards. They also founded mutual-aid associations and developed a very intense regional and local sociability. Metropolitan migrants to Cuba and Puerto Rico became merchants and landowners, particularly major planters, and those who came back to the metropolis as successful return migrants or *indianos* invested a part of their savings into nascent modern sectors of the Spanish economy.[45] Some of the most influential merchant families of Spain during the nineteenth century, whose fortunes last until the present day, came from Cuba and had their main economic interests based in the Caribbean. Their regional origin was also variegated. While on the eastern part of the island, Catalans shaped the overwhelming majority—over 75%—of all Spanish merchants, their percentage decreased in Western Cuba, where Galicians, Cantabrians, Asturians and Castilians were also abundant. The Spanish merchant elite of Cuba acted as a powerful means of regional integration, and the percentage of Catalans was noteworthy—over 40% of the total amount. In Puerto Rico, merchants from the Balearic Islands, as well as from Catalonia, were particularly abundant.[46]

High tariffs directed against foreign goods and carriers protected Spanish manufactures, foodstuffs, and shipping. More than 25% of Spanish exports were concentrated in Cuba, Puerto Rico, and the Philippines. Cuba alone accounted for almost 20% of Spanish goods in the 1850s, and for 14.7% during the 1890s.[47] Furthermore, these territories also contributed decisively to the Spanish public budget. Moreover, the goods produced by the colonies, in particular Cuban sugar, tobacco, and coffee, were distributed in America and Europe by Spanish companies. Nevertheless, this was just one side of the coin. The Cuban merchant and planters' elite also succeeded in using the Iberian peninsula as a useful platform to place its products, in particular sugar, on the world market, and displayed a strong ability to influence Spanish politics, often using metropolitan political leaders as efficient representatives of its interests. With the exception of Puerto Rican coffee in the 1880s and 1890s, Caribbean exports received no protection in the Spanish market. A big proportion of the Cuban sugar production was sent to the United States and Great Britain. Therefore, the financial investments of the Cuban elite also followed multiple directions, and just a

---

[45] On the social and economic role of Spanish settlers in Cuba during the second half of the nineteenth century, see J. Maluquer de Motes, *Nación e inmigración: Los españoles en Cuba (siglos XIX y XX)* (Colombres: Archivo de Indianos, 1992); as well as P. Cagiao and S. Guerra, eds., *De raíz profunda. Galicia y lo gallego en Cuba* (Santiago de Compostela: Xunta de Galicia, 2007). On the economic role of the *indianos*, see A. Bahamonde and J. G. Cayuela, *Hacer las Américas: Las elites coloniales en el siglo XIX* (Madrid: Alianza, 1992).

[46] See Ch. Schmidt-Nowara, "National Economy and Atlantic Slavery: Protectionism and Resistance to Abolitionism in Spain and the Antilles, 1854–1874," *Hispanic American Historical Review* 78, no. 4 (1998): 603–29 (here, 609).

[47] See figures in L. Prados de la Escosura, *De imperio a nación: Crecimiento y atraso económico en España (1780–1930)* (Madrid: Alianza, 1988), 202.

minority of them were placed in the emerging modern sectors of Spanish economy.[48] Slavery was the crucial factor in the internal economic restructuring of the Caribbean colonies. Cuba alone imported more than 750,000 slaves from 1780 to 1867, when the Cuban slave trade was finally abolished. This accounted for more than the total amount of slaves that were imported by the Spanish Empire during the three previous centuries.[49]

Despite their relevance for Spanish economy, the overseas territories were not considered provinces of the liberal state—after its restructuring in 1833, following the French model of *departments*—and their inhabitants were not viewed as equal citizens to Spaniards. Slavery was not abolished in the Caribbean Islands until 1886.[50] This constituted a major theme in the articulation of interests of the Spanish settlers, and particularly of the Spanish planters and merchant elites in the Caribbean, the majority of whom were interested in keeping the empire free from the wave of abolitionism that extended throughout the Americas since the American Civil War. A high population of slaves in Cuba (350,000 in 1868), as well as the pro-abolitionist stance adopted by Cuban supporters of independence, prevented the Spanish authorities from taking up abolition, considered too dangerous for the stability of colonial rule over the island. Even the new democratically-oriented Spanish regime emerging out of the September 1868 revolution, which lasted until the failure of the First Spanish Republic in 1873, did not dare to abolish slavery. Only in Puerto Rico, where the amount of slaves was much smaller than in Cuba (40,000 in 1868), did the metropolitan Republican government suppress slavery, in March 1873. Republicans extended to the island the Spanish constitution, and installed an abolitionist captain-general who sided with ex-slaves and creoles against metropolitan conservatives and planters. However, the threat of broadening this regime to the neighboring island of Cuba hastened the counter-revolution that finally put an end to the Spanish First Republic in January 1874.[51]

Abolitionists were organized in the metropolis since 1865, and were supported by the suppression of slavery in the United States (1865) and the progressive abolition of slave trade in the Spanish Caribbean (1867–70). However, the Cuban planters and their allies among the business elites, landowners, and manufacturers in metropolitan Spain, who also regarded the maintenance of slavery as a last barrier of defense of the Catholic civilization and social hierarchies on the island, delayed abolition for

---

[48] See J. G. Cayuela, "Reacción colonial y elite hispano-cubana en la España del XIX," *Studia Historica. Edad Contemporánea* 15 (1997): 21–34.

[49] See M. Moreno Fraginals, *El ingenio: Complejo económico-social cubano del azúcar* (Havana: Editorial de Ciencias Sociales, 1978), 3 vols. See also R. J. Scott, *Slave Emancipation in Cuba: The Transition to Free Labor, 1865–1899* (Princeton: Princeton University Press, 1985). An interesting view from a comparative perspective in M. Moreno Fraginals, F. Moya Pons, and S. L. Engerman, eds., *Between Slavery and Free Labor: The Spanish-Speaking Caribbean in the Nineteenth Century* (Baltimore: Johns Hopkins University Press, 1985).

[50] The British Empire had abolished slavery in its Caribbean possessions in 1834–38.

[51] See Ch. Schmidt-Nowara, *Empire and Antislavery: Spain, Cuba, and Puerto Rico, 1833–1874* (Pittsburgh: University of Pittsburgh Press, 1999), 339–86.

as long as possible.[52] This racial element present in Cuba—and, to a lesser extent, in Puerto Rico—was constantly invoked as a legitimizing argument by the metropolitan government to maintain a militarized administrative apparatus in the Caribbean that differed from the liberal order in Spain. "If Cuba ceases to be Spanish, it will be black" remarked metropolitan deputy Vicente Sancho in 1837.[53]

Military governors in Cuba held political power, and they tended to exert it in a very authoritarian manner. However, this was not particularly different from the metropolis, where civil governors of the peninsula provinces were often subject to the dominance of military governors on the occasion of social unrest and political crises.[54] Colonial administrations were not professionalized enough, and therefore often fell under the exclusive authority of military governors imbued with special powers whose everyday practices were corrupt.

Militarization of the colonial rule ran parallel to economic liberalization. This was a necessary response in the case of the Asian territories of Spain due to the loss of most of the Americas, which until the beginning of the nineteenth century, had functioned as the link between the Philippines and the European core of the empire through the naval route between Manila and Mexico.[55] The Philippines had been an anomaly among Spanish overseas possessions in many respects. Very little territory of the immense archipelago had been conquered by Spain, and the monarchy hardly endorsed any attempts to introduce the use of the Spanish language among natives. The city of Manila was similar to the Portuguese colonies scattered over Asia, such as Macau or Goa: a trading station where some military units and bureaucrats were permanently stationed. No more than 5,000 Spanish-speaking Filipinos could be numbered by 1800, and the majority of the population, divided ethnically and linguistically, was unable to generate a strong sentiment of community. The age of independence in the Americas passed with only minor incidents for the colonial rule. And the Filipino elites felt comfortably integrated within the nascent liberal Spain, thanks to the symbolic presence of two representatives of the islands in the Spanish parliament. Spain was only interested in maintaining a close access point to China in order to import Chinese laborers to Cuban sugar plantations—metropolitan commerce with the Philippines was of little relevance. The full-fledged Spanish citizens who resided on the islands were a tiny minority (around 6,000 by the mid-nineteenth century, out of a total 30,000 metropolitan Spaniards residing on the archipelago), and their views were barely represented by anyone in the Spanish parliament. During the pe-

[52] D. R. Murria, *Odious Commerce: Britain, Spain, and the Abolition of the Cuban Slave Trade* (Cambridge: Cambridge University Press, 1980).

[53] Quoted by Fradera, *Gobernar colonias*, 122–23.

[54] J. A. Piqueras, "La vida política entre 1780 y 1878," in Naranjo Orovio, ed., *Historia de Cuba*, 273–302. For a comparison with the role of military and civil governors in the metropolis, see M. Risques, *El govern civil de Barcelona al segle XIX* (Barcelona: PAM, 1995).

[55] See X. Huetz de Lemps, *L'archipel des "épices": La corruption de l'administration espagnole aux Philipinnes (fin XVIIIe–fin XIXe siècle)* (Madrid: Casa de Velázquez, 2006).

riod 1868–74 and beyond, the extension of provincial status to the Philippines was never considered by the Spanish parliament, not even the devolution of the right of political representation to the islands. While the Caribbean islands came to be regarded as an extension of Spain, the Philippines were always considered a typical colony. All affairs related to the Philippines were exclusively discussed in the administrative sphere and dealt with by the Overseas Ministry, as well as by the consultative bodies called "Overseas Councils" (*Consejos de Ultramar*), which since 1870 also dealt with the emerging Spanish possessions in Africa. Social control over the territory was exerted by Catholic clergymen, who in some cities enjoyed, in practice, the monopoly of power.

From the beginning of the 1880s, Spain began to reinforce its economic links with the Philippines by opening the tobacco trade to private enterprises and increasing its exports to the islands. However, tensions arose between the Spanish administration and the local elites. This contributed to the emergence of a Filipino nationalist movement in the 1880s, first inspired by the writings of the reformist intellectual José Rizal, and later controlled by the insurgent faction represented by the secret organization *Katipunan* (1892), which unleashed a separatist uprising in August 1896.[56]

The inhabitants of the Philippines were divided in the Spanish population censuses into four categories, depending on their skin color and their origin. Also, Spain was considered a civilizing mission to the archipelago, settled by people which were seen as "Spaniards," but not as Spanish citizens, as conservative premier Cánovas del Castillo clearly stated in 1890. Not surprisingly, modern Spanish anthropology and ethnography were born out of the interest for the native populations of the Philippines. They became a beloved object of study by Spanish anthropologists, and were portrayed as primitive people who had not yet reached their coming of age. In the face of black Cubans and Philippine's diverse ethnic groups, Iberian Spaniards emphasized their self-perception as being civilized and modern.[57] This notion of otherness served indirectly to emphasize the continuity of the civilizing role of Spain, now presented as an updated version of what had been the ideological legitimization of the

---

[56] See A. Sánchez Andrés, "Los organismos consultivos del Ministerio de Ultramar y el gobierno de las colonias del Pacífico," *Revista Española del Pacífico* IV, no. 4 (1994): 65–74; J. S. Arcillas, *Rizal and the emergence of the Philippine Nation* (Quezon City: Ateneo de Manila University Press, 1991); J. N. Schumacher, *The Propaganda Movement, 1880–1895: The Creation of a Filipino Consciousness, the Making of a Revolution* (Manila: Ateneo de Manila University Press, 1997); H. Goujat, *Réforme ou Révolution? Le projet national de José Rizal (1861–1896) pour les Philippines* (Paris: Connaissances et Savoirs, 2010).

[57] See L. A. Sánchez Gómez, *Un imperio en la vitrina. El colonialismo español en el Pacífico y la Exposición de Filipinas de 1887* (Madrid: CSIC, 2003), as well as L. A. Sánchez Gómez, "Las exhibiciones etnológicas y coloniales decimonónicas y la Exposición de Filipinas de 1887," *Revista de Dialectología y Tradiciones Populares* LVII, no. 2 (2007): 79–104, and F. Archilés, "Maurische Exotik, imperialer Traum. Imperialismus, Nation und Geschkecht in Spanien der Restaurationsmonarchie" *Mittelweg 36*, no. 6 (2013): 36–54.

conquest and colonization of the Americas in the early modern period: to civilize and to expand the Catholic faith.

From 1885, Spain carried out isolated efforts to acquire Micronesian islands in the aftermath of the Berlin Conference, with limited success. Spain had to face German ambitions over the same territory, and lacked the resources to occupy some of the distant islands that the country was given.[58] However little relevance, in economic terms, the Pacific islands may have had, feelings of popular nationalism were aroused by the government throughout the 1880s. Anti-German demonstrations accompanied a diplomatic dispute with the German Empire over the Spanish-held Caroline Islands in August 1885, a quarrel that was finally solved with the mediation of the pope—the archipelago was finally sold to Germany in 1899.[59]

The Spanish case in the nineteenth century was not exceptional. As in the majority of European overseas empires, the combination of complex situations where liberal rights in the core coexisted with special regimes in the colonial periphery was not the exception, but the norm.[60] However, in the Caribbean region it faced U.S. expansionism toward the south, which made Cuban and Puerto Rican elite discontent with imperial rule particularly explosive. The fact that they were Spanish provinces excluded from the benefits granted by the successive liberal constitutions made nationalization of the colonial crisis into something inevitable, partly because there was a very intertwined relationship between metropolitan and colonial societies, particularly in Cuba. This also affected the way in which the Spanish national project was regarded, both as a nation with colonies and as an integrated political community of all national territories. Both dimensions maintained a steady ambivalence.[61]

This nationalist dimension of the colonial empire in the self-understanding of the metropolitan core had deep roots, and could be traced back to the late eighteenth century. For some authors, the model of nation-state that linked Spain to its colonies after 1824 through 1898 was a reelaboration of the old concept born during the Enlightenment, which established the existence of an organic, cultural link between the metropolis and its colonies and gave rise to the idea of Cuba, Puerto Rico, and the Philippines being an integral part of the Spanish nation. Thus, the place of the colonies in the Spanish "imagined community" of mid-nineteenth-century nation-builders was a crucial one, as in their view the colonies were bound to the peninsula "not only by the 'national economy' but also by centuries of Spanish rule that had implanted language, religion, and political institutions in the Caribbean and Pacific, effectively

---

[58] F. Rodao, "Asia: Filipinas, percepciones y los empujes tardíos," in *La política exterior de España. De 1800 hasta hoy*, ed. J. C. Pereira (Barcelona: Ariel, 2010), 487–96.

[59] A. R. Rodríguez González, "La crisis de las Carolinas," *Cuadernos de Historia Contemporánea* 13 (1991): 25–46.

[60] See J. M. Fradera, "Reading Imperial Transitions: Spanish Contraction, British Expansion, and American Irruption," in *Colonial Crucible: Empire in the Making of the Modern American State*, eds. A. McCoy and F. Scarano (Madison: The University of Wisconsin Press, 2009), 34–62.

[61] M. Moreno Fraginals, *Cuba/España, España/Cuba. Historia común* (Barcelona: Crítica, 2002).

assimilating, culturally and biologically, the conquered people into the march of Spanish history." When the Spanish historians of the nineteenth century attempted to craft a new collective identity based on the emerging concept of the modern nation, they strongly relied upon the narrative that had been fabricated one century earlier to endorse the legitimacy of the empire. Hence, there was a broad consensus among Spanish liberal and traditionalist elites alike that the colonies were not separate territories with a history of their own but "integral parts of the Spanish nation-state" that accounted for specific chapters in the march of Spanish history.[62] Some recent reassessments have further reflected on this concept, but have instead underlined the existence of a dual relationship expressed in the formula of "peninsular Spain" vs. "overseas Spain." This binomial concept expressed itself in the coexistence of two administrative apparatuses and two societies that did not merely maintain a typically colonial link, but a kind of juxtaposition, characterized by a scarcely hierarchical relationship marked by intersection rather than by dominance.[63]

Spanish liberal historians considered Spain as being a national community which had recreated itself in the colonies, thus integrating them into their own metropolitan narrative. They also took over many of the arguments harbored by eighteenth century historians to counteract the attacks of British and French historians on the Spanish Empire, blaming it for its purported backwardness and lack of rationality, science, and progress. Spanish national historians of the nineteenth century also re-utilized the rhetorical strategies crafted by their forerunners in order to reassert the benign and positive character of Spanish early modern imperialism, and transferred them to the present. In doing so, Spanish national historians stated that the colonies did not have any history before 1492. Their history began with the Spanish conquest, through several wars that, continuing the argument of the previous Habsburg Empire to legitimize the Spanish conquest, had been just wars, fought on behalf of civilization and the Catholic faith.[64] They also maintained that the racial mixing of people had characterized Spanish colonialism, which—in contrast to perverse British imperialism—had favored the blending of conquistadors and indigenous people, and of settlers and natives. This gave rise to new racial communities that could only be considered as a further continuity with the "racial alloy" that had taken place earlier in the Iberian peninsula. The shaping of the Cuban, Philippine, or Puerto Rican people had been similar to the variegated origins of the Spanish race in the Middle Ages, as a result

[62] Ch. Schmidt-Nowara, "'La España ultramarina': Colonialism and Nation-building in Nineteenth-Century Spain," *European History Quarterly* 34, no. 2 (2004): 191–214.

[63] F. J. Martínez Antonio, "Von Spanien im Übersee zum Spanien in Afrika: Über die Eigentumlichkeit des spanischen Imperiums im 19. Jahrhundert," *Mittelweg 36*, no. 6 (2013): 18–35.

[64] This was already present in Juan Bautista Muñoz's *Historia del Nuevo mundo* (1793). See J. Cañizares-Esguerra, *How to Write the History of the New World: Histories, Epistemologies, and Identities in the Eighteenth-Century Atlantic World* (Stanford: Stanford University Press, 2001). For the precedent arguments on the conquest as a "just war," see Pagden, *Lords of all the World*, 92–94.

of the mixing of different substrata, from Celts to Basques to Romans. Spanish anthropologists actually applied to the overseas Spain the same explanatory model they had used for interpreting racial diversity in the metropolis. Spaniards had never been a pure race, but were a result of the mixing of people which had inhabited and traversed the Iberian peninsula over the centuries. And this process of long-scale racial fusion had simply been continued and reproduced in the Americas.

According to this interpretation, the Spanish colonial behavior in the past had been a sheer continuation of the process of nation-building from an anthropological point of view. And it was hence logical that Spaniards conducted a benevolent conquest that embraced a catholicizing mission, according to Spanish traditionalist historians, and a civilizing mission according to liberal historians, bringing barbarian people like the Aztec or Mayas from practicing human sacrifices to a superior civilized stage. Even the most brutal aspects of Spanish colonization, such as the system of forced labor or *encomiendas*, were dealt with in a positive way, as their main critic in the past, the Dominican friar Bartolomé de las Casas, was simply refashioned as an author of moral guidelines for conquest and colonization.[65]

Therefore, it is not surprising that the process of American independence that took place between 1808–10 and 1826 was also explained within this framework. According to Spanish liberal and later Republican historians, the Creole supporters of independence did not rise against the Spanish nation but against a form of despotic government—that of the late years of absolutist monarchy. The lack of tolerance of the monarchs had led those liberal Spaniards to move away from the political community and establish new republics, which in essence had to be seen as re-creations of a better Spain. The Creole "liberators" of America, like Simón Bolívar and José de San Martín, were not supposed to have conducted a war against the other, a foreign enemy. They were sons rebelling against their fathers.

The resilience of the concept of the Caribbean islands as a continuation of Spain prevented most metropolitan governments from granting self-government to Cuba and Puerto Rico. When General Juan Prim, who became provisory head of the government after September 1868, planned to grant greater autonomy and even independence to Cuba under the condition that the island pay economic compensation to Spain under the guarantee of the United States, the Cuban lobby in the metropolis exerted severe pressure and ensured the failure of the project. According to Prim, the "noble Spanish pride, the interests of commerce in general, those of important provinces, and the sympathy towards the numerous co-nationals settled on the island" had

---

[65] See in detail Ch. Schmidt-Nowara, *The Conquest of History: Spanish Colonialism and National Histories in the Nineteenth Century* (Pittsburgh: University of Pittsburgh Press, 2006), as well as some insights in J. Goode, *Impurity of Blood: Defining Race in Spain, 1870–1930* (Baton Rouge: Louisiana State University Press, 2009). For the specific case of Puerto Rico, see also A. Cubano-Iguina, "Visions of Empire and Historical Imagination in Puerto Rico under Spanish Rule, 1870–1898," in *Interpreting Spanish Colonialism: Empires, Nations, and Legends*, eds. Ch. Schmidt-Nowara and J. Nieto Phillips (Albuquerque: University of New Mexico Press, 2005), 87–107.

to be confronted with "an exhausted treasure, lost credibility, the lack of soldiers and weapons."[66]

However, the enlarged representation given to the "overseas territories" in the new constitution passed in June 1869 was not enough for Cuban patriots, who attempted to exploit the conjuncture of political instability that opened itself in the metropolis following the "democratic revolution" of September 1868 and launched a new war in the following month. However, during the Cuban Ten Years War (1868–78), the island of Puerto Rico, which was far less conflictive, became the laboratory for reform. First, slavery was abolished in 1873; then, the political regime of the island was made relatively equal to that of the metropolis.[67] While the inhabitants of the Philippines were systematically excluded from the benefits granted by the 1876 Constitution, and a significant part of the Cuban population rebelled, the Puerto Rican elites advanced down the road to an agreement with the Spanish liberal regime. They organized autonomous political parties and elected representatives to the Madrid parliament. The Cubans would only follow this path ten years later, after the Treaty of Zanjón (February 1878) was signed as a consequence of the fact that neither the insurgents nor the imperial army were able to defeat the enemy.[68]

The armed conflict in the Antilles transformed Spanish politics in the years of the first restoration monarchy, ensuring the failure of the First Spanish Republic in 1874.[69] A consequence was that the model of Spanish nation-building that had characterized the nineteenth century liberal project was subject to discussion. The beginning of the home-rule agitation in the Caribbean islands set in motion a debate about the structure of the Spanish state as the renewed home-rule projects for Cuba and Puerto Rico were debated in the metropolitan public sphere. In particular, during the brief Republican period of 1873, both islands were mentioned in the constitutional draft for a Federal Spanish Republic as "states" able to join the federation, unlike the rest of the colonies. Cuban politics oscillated among three positions. First, those who aimed at full-fledged secession: the followers of Máximo Gómez and Antonio Maceo, military leaders of the Ten Years war, but also the later supporters of José Martí's Cuban Revolutionary Party—*Partido Revolucionario Cubano*, PRC—and Cuban exiles in the United States.[70] Second, the majority of the Iberian settlers supported the continuity of the colonial status quo and regarded any form of decentralization as a gateway to separatism. A third group of "autonomist" and reformist liberals, supported by

---

[66] Letter from Juan Prim to Captain General Antonio Caballero de Rodas, Madrid, September 10, 1869, quoted by C. Lida, "Cuba: Un desastre anunciado, 1868–1898," *Illes i Imperis* 8 (2006): 69–82.

[67] See Schmidt-Nowara, *Empire and Antislavery*, as well as Scott, *Slave Emancipation*.

[68] T. Gallego y García, *La insurrección cubana. Crónicas de la campaña. I. La preparación de la guerra* (Madrid: Imprenta Central de los Ferrocarriles, 1897), 59.

[69] I. Roldán de Montaud, *La Restauración en Cuba. El fracaso del proceso reformista* (Madrid: CSIC, 2000).

[70] See A. Ferrer, *Insurgent Cuba: Race, Nation, and Revolution, 1868–1898* (Chapel Hill: The University of North Carolina Press, 1999).

middleclass Creoles, considered Canadian self-government as a possible model to be imitated.

A steady broadening of the electoral rights for Cuban citizens was constantly postponed—Spain viewed Cuban enfranchisement as a threat to control over the island. After the treaty of Zanjón, Cuba and Puerto Rico steadily regained, between 1878 and 1881, the condition of Spanish territories "assimilated" to the same juridical condition of metropolitan ones. This concession was not made to the Philippines. However, the metropolitan government never fully applied the 1876 constitution in the Caribbean, and maintained a much more restrictive census suffrage than in European Spain.

The "autonomists" sustained the view that it was necessary to have its own legislative chamber and government to defend the interests of Cuba within the wider framework of the Spanish Empire, and to definitively separate the military government from the sphere of civilian politics on the island. This should be carried out by an autonomous parliament and a general-governor elected by the Cuban citizens. Its more ambitious model continued to be the model of home-rule that Canada enjoyed within the British Empire, as it was embraced by the Liberal Autonomist Party (*Partido Liberal Autonomista*), founded in 1881 as opposition to the fiercely Spanish nationalist party of Constitutional Union (*Unión Constitucional*). A more flexible and pragmatic objective consisted of attaining a model of "insular autonomy" or "colonial autonomy" more restrictive as far as the political competencies of the Cuban legislative bodies were concerned.[71] Although Cuba ("the Island") was defined by them as the Fatherland of the Cubans, Spain remained the "greater Nation" to which it belonged, but generous political and financial compensation was demanded from the metropolis.[72] Quite similar projects, which oscillated between the "Canadian model" and the more moderate designs of "colonial home-rule" were also proposed by the Puerto Rican reformists.[73] Caribbean autonomists often referred to the "provincial liberties" invoked by Basque *fueristas* or Catalan and Galician regionalists in Europe to endorse their demands. However, the diverse projects of "colonial home-rule," like that presented by Cuban and Puerto Rican representatives of the Spanish parliament in 1886, were systematically rejected by metropolitan governments.[74] A similar failure was the

---

[71] See the different outlook of two Cuban autonomist leaders: A. Govín, *Las Leyes especiales. Colección de artículos publicados en "El Triunfo," órgano oficial del Partido Liberal de la Isla de Cuba* (Havana, n. ed., 1880), and R. M. De Labra, *La autonomía colonial en España* (Madrid: Imp. Sucesores de Cuesta, 1892).

[72] See A. Sánchez Andrés, "La crisis colonial y la reforma del Estado liberal: La construcción de un modelo alternativo de política colonial durante la Restauración (1879–1897)," *Cuadernos de Historia Contemporánea* 19 (1997): 183–201. See also F. Lambert, *Cuba and the Autonomists in the Politics of the First Spanish Restoration* (Glasgow: University of Glasgow Papers on Latin America, 1996), and M. Bizcarrondo and A. Elorza, *Cuba/España. El dilema autonomista, 1878–1898* (Madrid: Colibrí, 2000), 84–107.

[73] See L. R. Rivera, "El autonomismo puertorriqueño en el siglo XIX," *Revista Jurídica. Facultad de Derecho de la Universidad Interamericana de Puerto Rico* 43, no. 1 (2008/09): 1–16.

[74] Alonso Romero, *Cuba en la España liberal*, 60–74; Bizcarrondo and Elorza, *Cuba/España*, 199–227.

reform of administrative decentralization in the Caribbean islands sustained by the liberal ministers Antonio Maura in 1893 and Buenaventura Abárzuza in 1895, which came too late to satisfy any of the political factions of the islands.[75]

Partly as a consequence of this, the new generations of Cubans grew up bearing a sentiment of exclusive national identity. Schoolmasters taught the history of the island as a separate entity from the Spanish political community. Pro-independence manifestos and propaganda circulated throughout the entire insular territory with the increasing help of the Cuban nationalist groups based abroad, particularly in the United States. The University of Havana, after its secularization in 1842, increasingly educated new Cuban students in nationalist belief and popular resentment against the colonial rule.[76]

The metropolis reacted with indifference, and sometimes hostility, to these demands for Caribbean home-rule principally because they required a fundamental reshaping of the concept of the Spanish nation that characterized the restoration regime. This was based on the notion of an organic unity, which was seldom politically inclusive of regional differences and cultural diversity. Recognition of diversity in the distant periphery would have unleashed dangerous similar demands and "demonstration effects" on the metropolitan territory, particularly on the non-Castilian periphery. Between 1878 and 1895, Spanish Republicans had attempted to build a political alliance with Cuban autonomists and abolitionists to incorporate an autonomous Cuba, including freed slaves, into a new, democratic and multi-racial imperial project, which challenged both Cuban separatism and the colonial status quo, aiming to reconstruct a transatlantic Spanish nation.[77] However, most Spanish Republicans experienced increasing difficulties in incorporating the autonomist claims from overseas and extending to the Caribbean the same rights that they defended in the metropolis. Since 1895, racial fear moved them to embrace a view of the Cuban insurgents as black slaves who threatened white civilization. This also included many federalists who advocated full decentralization of the Spanish polity, and even refounding the nation from the bottom up on a federal principle, and who therefore were in favor of devolution to the "historical regions" or "nationalities" of metropolitan Spain.

There were some exceptions, like the Federal Party led by the chief ideologue of Spanish federal republicanism, Francesc Pi i Margall. He maintained in 1882 that colonial home-rule was the best way to preserve the overseas provinces' attachment to Spain. Thanks to the implementation of federalism, and much in the same way as Austria had come to an arrangement with the Hungarians and Britain had maintained the ties to its colonies, "we [federal republicans] will unite Spain and Portugal,

[75] See A. Marimon i Riutort, *La política colonial d'Antoni Maura. Les colònies espanyoles de Cuba, Puerto Rico i les Filipines a finals del segle XIX* (Palma de Mallorca: Documenta Balear, 1994).

[76] See Ferrer, *Insurgent Cuba*; E. Ramírez Cañedo and C. J. Rosario Grasso, *El autonomismo en las horas cruciales de la nación cubana* (Havana: Ed. de Ciencias Sociales, 2008); L. A. Pérez, *Cuba between empires, 1878–1902* (Pittsburgh: University of Pittsburgh Press, 1983).

[77] See Ch. Schmidt-Nowara, "From Slaves to Spaniards: The failure of Revolutionary Emancipationism in Spain and Cuba, 1868–1895," *Illes i Imperis* 2 (1999): 177–90.

something that three centuries of monarchy have not yet achieved, and will retain the colonies of Cuba and Puerto Rico."[78]

Cuban politics was not a distant matter of empire rule. The involvement of Spanish settlers in the Cuban war and the intricate net of human relationships that linked Cuban society to Spain affected the whole destiny of the Spanish nation. The defense of the colonial order acted as a powerful unifying factor across different regions of Spain. They all framed their interests in terms of national integrity. The Caribbean islands were a deeply interrelated part of the Spanish national imagination, although the social relations that dominated there were supposed to be peculiar and restricted to the overseas space. Most Spanish intellectuals and opinion-makers saw no contradiction in endorsing this attitude.

The maintenance of the colonial status quo in the Antilles, together with the defense of protectionism and the opposition to free trade, was also a shared claim by Catalan, Basque, and Castilian merchants in the metropolis alike. In spite of the increasing demands for political decentralization that particularly came from significant sectors of the Catalan middle class since the 1860s, which were not yet framed in eth-nonationalist terms, most Catalan political representatives and even many supporters of cultural Catalanism were fierce centralists when they were confronted with the issue of colonial reform and abolition of slave trade. Most of them gave priority to the defense of a protected national market in the Caribbean, vehemently opposed Cuban demands for home-rule after 1878, and raised their voice against trade liberalization. An example of this was the republican and federalist-oriented Catalanist Víctor Balaguer, who claimed in his historical works the glorious past of Catalonia and the role played by the Aragonese Crown in forging the Spanish empire. Balaguer occupied the office of Minister of Overseas and then Finances in 1871–72, and became a devoted supporter of Spanish colonialism in the Philippines, as well as a fierce defender of Spanish and particularly Catalan commercial interests in the Pacific. According to him, Spain recreated itself, implicitly including its Iberian linguistic variety, in the colonies thanks to the implantation of metropolitan institutions, as well as through miscegenation.[79] Steamship companies of Catalan and Basque origin became main protagonists of Spanish commerce with the Philippines.[80]

---

[78] Parliamentary speech, July 8, 1886, quoted by Sánchez Andrés, "La crisis colonial," 195. See also J. Conangla i Fontanilles, ed., *Cuba y Pi y Margall* (Havana: Ed. Lex, 1947), and J. Pich i Mitjana, "Francisco Pi I Margall y el problema cubano," *Cuba de colonia a República*, ed. M. Rodrigo (Madrid: Biblioteca Nueva, 2006), 299–319. Other Republican authors also expressed the view that a Spanish Republic was the sole way to tempt the Cubans to remain Spanish: see F. Calcagno, *La República: Unica salvación de la familia cubana* (Barcelona: Maucci, 1898).

[79] Schmidt-Nowara, "La España ultramarina," 208–09; M. Comas i Güell, *Victor Balaguer i la identitat collectiva* (Catarroja: Afers, 2008).

[80] See J. M. Valdaliso, "Bandera y colonias españolas, navieros y marinos vizcaínos, y capital y comercio británicos. Las navieras anglo-bilbaínas en el último tercio del siglo XIX," *Itsas Memoria. Revista de Estudios Marítimos del País Vasco* 4 (2003): 455–71.

Also among Iberian settlers in Cuba were to be found strong supporters of regional decentralization in the Iberian core of the empire, who held opposite views when faced with the home-rule demands from the colonies. The main argument was the superior *civilization* that reigned in peninsula regions. Some of the fiercest opponents of Cuban home-rule, like the Galician journalist Enrique Novo, saw no contradiction between this tenet and the upholding of regionalism and decentralization for the future restructuring of Iberian Spain.[81] But the look inside of metropolitan identity politics by returned migrants became different after 1898. For example, the last Spanish major of Manila was the Basque businessman José Manuel de Etxeita, a man very well connected to the establishment of Spanish business and politics of the turn of the century, who after his return from the Philippines became known for his passionate defense of the Basque language and leaned towards pro-Basque nationalist attitudes.[82]

In November 1897, Cuba and Puerto Rico were given a new status of "colonial home-rule," which recognized the politico-juridical existence of the islands as separate entities within the Spanish state, and foresaw the constitution of a bicameral parliament, as well as a council of administration. The insular parliament would have competency in all matters not reserved to the national parliament, that is, justice, treasury, education, agriculture, insular administration, monetary and financial affairs. The local executive power would be designated by a general-governor, who would act as a representative of the metropolitan government and would command the colonial army on each island. The project was much more far-reaching than the drafts that had been systematically rejected by Spanish conservative liberals and their counterparts in Cuba, the followers of the *Constitutional Union*, who fiercely opposed the new autonomy and were therefore excluded from its governance.

A provisory regional government was set up in December 1897, presided over by the autonomist leader José-María Gálvez, and the first elections for Cuban deputies in the Spanish parliament were held in conditions of universal male suffrage in March 1898. A month later the first regional elections for the Cuban chamber of representatives were held. Both electoral contests were won by the reformist autonomists. However, the United States intervention in the Cuban conflict, decided by the American Congress and Senate in April 1898, prevented autonomy from being wholly implemented. The home-rule solution came too late, as Spain would soon lose its

---

[81] See E. Novo García, *Cuba y España: Réplica a juicios de Curros Enríquez sobre un libro de Montoro* (Havana: n. ed., 1894), who blamed the Galician regionalist and Republican Manoel Curros Enríquez, also a journalist in Havana, for having written that the home-rule claimed by Cuban autonomists was similar in nature to that desired by the rest of the Spanish regions. Enrique Novo differentiated metropolitan "regionalism," based on politico-administrative decentralization, from insular "autonomism," whose objective was creating separate spheres of government that only aimed at secession.

[82] J. Kortazar, "Analysis of the personality of Jose Manuel Etxeita (1842–1915) through a study of his letters," *Revista Internacional de Estudios Vascos* 53, no. 2 (2008): 476–506.

SPANISH POSSESSIONS IN AFRICA

overseas colonies. After a short war, the Spanish government demanded the end of the armed hostilities on August 4, and eight days later signed the armistice in Washington, ratified by the Peace Treaty of Paris in December. On January 1st, 1899 Spanish sovereignty ceased to exist in Cuba and Puerto Rico.[83]

A New Empire of Substitution?
Spanish Imperialism in Africa

The new empire Spain saw as compensation for the loss of the "old" American one was found in Africa. This related to the idea of "regeneration" of the Spanish nation, which crossed the whole political spectrum from traditionalists to republicans throughout the second half of the nineteenth century. If the Spanish polity had to be redeemed from its present state of "decadence," it was not only necessary to reform the state and educate the citizens, but also to recover the past status of colonial power. Inner

---

[83] See C. Aguado Renedo, "El primer precedente directo de los actuales Estatutos de Autonomía: las 'Constituciones Autonómicas' de Cuba y Puerto Rico," *Historia Constitucional* 3 (2002), available at: http://www.historiaconstitucional.com/index.php/historiaconstitucional/article/view/180/160; Alonso Romero, *Cuba en la España liberal*, 110–98, and Roldán de Montaud, *La Restauración*, 617–27.

territorial disputes emerging in Spain since the first civil war—the Carlist War of 1833–39—were regarded as a consequence of the lack of imperial ambition.[84]

To restore the Spaniards' national pride meant rebuilding an empire. First of all, it meant they had to achieve new minor colonies, which Spain obtained in Africa. The attention paid by the Spanish governments to the Moroccan territories that surrounded the cities of Ceuta and Melilla had been scarce, and Spanish action oriented itself towards the maintenance of the Spanish rule in the two cities, which were sporadically subject to border incidents and threatened by the Northern Moroccan tribes. After the so-called ultimatum crisis (1844), the situation in Northern Africa had become fairly stable for Spanish interests. However, a minor incident in the Ceuta's border in 1859 was exploited by the liberal government in Spain to launch a short and successful war against the Moroccan tribes, known as the Hispano-Moroccan War. An army of 45,000 soldiers was dispatched to Northern Africa under the direct command of General Leopoldo O'Donnell, who was the president of the government, as we will see below.

Apart from these enclaves in Morocco, there were basically two territories claimed by Spain throughout the last quarter of the nineteenth century and beyond: Equatorial Guinea and Western Sahara. What came to be known as Equatorial Guinea, comprising the island of Fernando Po and the continental enclave of Río Muni, was first acquired by Spain in 1778. The territory was merely an object of some exploration travels undertaken by naval officers and missionaries of English Protestant and Spanish Catholic religious orders,[85] and the colony was not really incorporated into the Spanish administration until 1843. Thereafter European presence continued to be minimal.[86]

The successive Spanish governments displayed little interest in a distant colony, where the number of Spanish and European settlers was very low due to the tropical climate, and whose economic profits were seen as minimal. French diplomatic interests also pushed Spanish ruling elites towards abandoning the area. However, Spain did not give up its formal sovereignty over the territory, partly because of the propaganda campaign made by the Africanist sectors of the Spanish middle class, which spread the idea that remaining in Guinea was a matter of national pride. It was not

[84] M. C. Romeo, "Nación e Imperio en el siglo XIX. Comentario," in *Viejos y nuevos Imperios. España y Gran Bretaña, s. XVII–XX*, eds. I. Burdiel and R. Church (Valencia: Episteme, 1998), 173–96.

[85] See J. Creus, "Sexe i missió. Desfici i desfetes en l'evantgelització claretiana de Guinea, 1883–1910," *Illes I Imperis* 2 (2000): 87–104; M. Vilaró i Güell, "Missioners o viatgers? Els claretians a la Guinea espanyola," in *Una Mirada catalana a l'Àfrica: viatgers i viatgeres dels segles XIX i XX (1859–1936)*, eds. M. D. Garcia Ramon, J. Nogué, and P. Zusman (Barcelona: Institut d'Estudis Catalans, 2008), 113–35; M. Vilaró i Güell, "Los avatares de la primera expedición misionera a las posesiones españolas del Golfo de Guinea a cargo de los eclesiásticos ilustrados Jerónimo Mariano Usera y Alarcón y Juan del Cerro," *Hispania Nova* 9 (2009), available in: http://hispanianova.rediris.es.

[86] See J. B. Vilar, "La proyección española en África," in Pereira, ed., *La política exterior*, 459–85.

until the period between 1900—when the Treaty of Paris clearly established the territorial lines of demarcation between French and Spanish colonization in that area—and 1926, when the continental lands of Guinea were more systematically explored and the Spanish administrative apparatus expanded there from the island of Fernando Po (today known as Bioko). However, real interest in the exploitation of the colony's raw materials began after 1940.[87] The same could be said about the government's concern with "hispanicizing" the indigenous inhabitants, which did not begin until the Francoist period (1939–75). In 1904 a so-called *Patronato de Indígenas* was established, with the task of "tutoring" the natives, who were legally considered minors, a legal strategy also used by other colonial powers in Africa.[88]

Western Sahara was claimed by Spain in 1884 as the Protectorate of Western Sahara. The Crown of Castile had already unsuccessfully attempted to extend its presence from the Canary Islands to the Western African coast as early as 1478. However, the later focus of all Spanish energies on America's colonization left this territory unattended. Spain only expressed interest in the area to avoid the establishment of other European settlers in front of the Canary Islands' coast. The pressure exerted by the vociferous but relatively reduced Africanist elites of Madrid, as well as the interest displayed by some fishing entrepreneurs from the Canary islands, and the necessity to counteract British attempts at taking over the Western African territory, pushed the Spanish government to affirm its right to occupy Western Sahara. Some expeditions were sent between 1877 and 1883 to explore the territory. They declared Spanish sovereignty on its soil and founded some settlements. However, the relevance of Western Sahara for the Spanish colonial imagination continued to be weak. The territory was not really occupied until 1934, when a complete colonial administration was deployed.[89]

---

[87] M. L. De Castro and M. L. Calle, *Origen de la colonización española en Guinea Ecuatorial (1777–1860)* (Valladolid: Universidad de Valladolid, 1992); A. R. Rodríguez González, "Prólogo a una colonia: La estación naval de Guinea (1858–1900)," *Cuadernos de Historia Contemporánea* 25, no. 2 (2003): 337–46; M. L. De Castro Antolín, D. Ndongo-Bidyogo, and J. U. Martínez Carreras, *España en Guinea. La construcción del desencuentro: 1778–1968,* (Madrid: Sequitur, 1998); G. Álvarez Chillida and E. Martín Corrales, "Haciendo Patria en África: España en Marruecos y en el Golfo de Guinea," in *Ser españoles. Imaginarios nacionalistas en el siglo XX*, eds. J. Moreno Luzón and X. M. Núñez (Barcelona: RBA, 2013), 399–432.

[88] R. Sánchez Molina, "*Homo infantilis*: asimilación y segregación en la política colonial española en Guinea Ecuatorial," *Revista de Dialectología y Tradiciones Populares* LVII, no. 2 (2002): 105–20; G. Nerín, *La última selva de España. Antropófagos, misioneros y guardias civiles* (Madrid: Libros de la Catarata, 2010).

[89] See J. Salom, "Los orígenes coloniales del Sahara occidental en el marco de la política española," *Cuadernos de Historia Contemporánea*, extraordinary issue (2003): 247–72; J. Martínez Milán, *España en el Sahara Occidental y en la zona Sur del Protectorado en Marruecos, 1885–1945* (Madrid: UNED, 2003); A. García, *Historia del Sahara y su conflicto* (Madrid: La Catarata, 2010); A. Rumeu de Armas, *España en el África atlántica* (Madrid: CSIC, 1956–57), 2 vols.; A. R. Díez Torre, ed., *Ciencia y memoria de África* (Madrid: Ateneo de Madrid / Universidad de Alcalá de Henares, 2002).

The Sahara's case illustrates how, in accordance with the apparently scarce interest of the Spanish public sphere in African colonies in economic and political terms, "Africanism" played a comparatively minor role in the national imagination of Spaniards until the beginning of the 1920s. There were some relevant public figures, like the conservative politician Cánovas del Castillo, who before 1874 had devoted some attention to the proclaimed necessity for Spain to find a substitute empire in Africa.[90] However, the mainstream of Spanish Africanist thinking emerged relatively late, as a pale reflection of the first International Conference of Geography held in Brussels in 1876. This event led immediately to the foundation in Madrid of the Spanish Association for the Exploration of Africa and the *Sociedad Geográfica* (Geographical Society), as well as the *Sociedad de Africanistas y Colonistas*—which later became the *Sociedad de Geografía Comercial*.[91] This process peaked with the celebration of the First Spanish Conference of Mercantile and Colonial Geography in November 1883, and the subsequent foundation of a Spanish Association of Africanists. Its leaders, the geographer Francisco Coello and the influential reformist intellectual Joaquín Costa, attempted to awaken middle class interest in African expansion. The Africanist associations gathered important figures of Spanish public sphere, and were able to influence politics as well as achieve prominent visibility.[92]

The scientific attention to Africa continued during the first decades of the twentieth century, as became evident with the attention paid to Spain's African territories on the occasion of the Ibero-American Exhibition held in Seville in 1929. However, this exhibition also displayed the existing differences in the Spanish colonial imagination between the "old" and the "new" models of empire. The American "traditional" pattern aimed at a religious conversion and a cultural assimilation of the native populations, as well as their "assimilation" into Spanish civilization through the creation of a new colonial society. The African model of imperialism was imagined by some Spanish colonialist elites as a recreation of the old Empire through the constitution of a so-called Hispano-American-African community. However, it merely consisted of superficial economic exploitation, which did not envision any intense cultural

[90] A. Pedraz Marcos, "El pensamiento africanista hasta 1883: Cánovas, Donoso y Costa," *Anales de la Fundación Joaquín Costa* 11 (1994): 31–48.

[91] See J. A. Rodríguez Esteban, *Geografía y colonialismo. La Sociedad Geográfica de Madrid (1875–1936)* (Madrid: UAM, 1996); J. A. Rodríguez Esteban, ed., *Conmemoración de la expedición científica de Cervera-Quiroga-Rizzo al Sáhara occidental en 1886* (Madrid: CSIC, 2008); A. Pedraz Marcos, *Quimeras de África. La Sociedad Española de Africanistas y Colonistas: El colonialismo español a finales del siglo XIX* (Madrid: Polifemo, 2000); A. Martínez Salazar, *Manuel Iradier. Las azarosas empresas de un explorador de quimeras* (Madrid: Miraguano Eds., 2004).

[92] See M.-C. Lécuyer and C. Serrano, *La Guerre d'Afrique et ses répercussions en Espagne. Idéologie et colonialisme en Espagne, 1859–1904* (Paris: PUF, 1976), 227–81; G. De Reparaz, *Política de España en África* (Barcelona: Imprenta Barcelonesa, 1907); J. García Figueras, *África en la acción española* (Madrid: Instituto de Estudios Africanos-CSIC, 1949); J. García Figueras, *La acción Africana de España en torno al 98 (1860–1912)* (Madrid: CSIC, 1966), 2 vols.

assimilation of natives. Moreover, in the Moroccan case, the Spanish rule refused to aim at a religious conversion of the natives, while in Guinea it simply regarded the indigenous population as mostly being unassimilable savages.[93]

Dreaming of a new empire also meant looking back at the lost one by attempting to recover some of the former territories of the monarchy. Under the guidance of the new government of the *Unión Liberal* (moderate liberals) that rose to power in Madrid between 1858 and 1863, presided by General Leopoldo O'Donnell, an aggressive foreign policy was supposed to overcome what had been so far regarded as a decadent and inefficient diplomacy. This strategy aimed at reinforcing the national cohesion of Spaniards, as well as undermining the influence of the political opposition—conservatives and republicans—and "restoring" the lost prestige of Spain in world affairs.[94] As the novelist Benito Pérez Galdós, one of the main crafters of the national narrative in Spanish literature of the second half of the nineteenth century, wrote, O'Donnell set in motion a "cleaning-up of Spanish collective psychology" by imitating French Emperor Napoleon III, "looking for a means of integrating the nation thanks to military glory, to discipline the souls and make them more docile for political action."[95]

Such was the rationale behind the Spanish intervention in Mexico, together with Great Britain and France, in 1861–62, when the Mexican government refused to pay foreign debts, which affected Spanish financial interests. Following a short military campaign, the British and Spanish troops withdrew after being guaranteed by the Mexican president Benito Juárez the payment of the remaining debts, leaving alone the French, who launched a war with Mexico to make it a satellite kingdom. A similar rationale held in the Spanish intervention in South Vietnam—in the Kingdom of Annam—in 1857–63. In collaboration with British and French troops, the intervention was presented to the Spanish public opinion as a civilizing crusade. However, this endeavor did not obtain any territorial compensation.

There were also some initiatives to reaffirm Spain's imperial role in the American sphere. These were, firstly, the so-called Pacific War from 1864 to 1866 against Peru, Ecuador, Bolivia, and Chile. Spain sent a navy to the Pacific to display its new naval power, with the objective of forcing the South American republics to make some economic concessions. They also wanted to endorse a scientific expedition organized by the Scientific Committee on the Pacific founded in 1862, which had declared Spanish sovereignty on the Chincha Islands and their rich guano deposits. The army, commanded by Admiral Casto Méndez-Núñez, limited itself to bombing some harbor

---

[93] See L. A. Sánchez Gómez, "África en Sevilla. La exhibición colonial de la Exposición Iberoamericana de 1929," *Hispania*, no. 224 (2006): 1045–82.

[94] See A. Arnalte, *Delirios de grandeza. Las quimeras coloniales del siglo XIX español* (Madrid: Síntesis, 2009), as well as Inarejos Muñoz, *Intervenciones coloniales*.

[95] B. Pérez Galdós, *Aita Tettauen* (Madrid: Obras de Pérez Galdós, 1905), 45.

cities. This campaign was greeted with enthusiasm by Spanish public opinion, which elevated Méndez-Núñez to the category of a new national hero.[96]

A second campaign was the re-annexation by Spain of the Republic of Santo Domingo (1861–65), which responded to the interest of some Dominican elites to enjoy the ancient metropolis' protection against the neighboring Republic of Haiti. Spanish presence was not welcomed by the majority of the local population, and moreover Spanish soldiers and bureaucrats experienced some trouble in dealing with people of color who, unlike in Cuba, were free men, and whose cultural habits and concepts of community strongly differed from Catholic beliefs. Since August 1863, the Dominican guerrillas created permanent difficulties for the Spanish government, forcing them to send soldiers to an island of little economic interest. When the moderate liberals took office again in 1864, Santo Domingo was abandoned by the Spaniards. Apart from some sectors of metropolitan public opinion that lamented the impact of such a withdrawal on Spain's prestige, protests in the metropolis were much reduced. It was difficult to reconcile the maintenance of slavery in some parts of the empire, while in other parts it was abolished.[97]

The final results of these new campaigns of imperial prestige were highly ambivalent for the Iberian hardcore. On the one hand, Spanish nationalist mobilization peaked and created a popular atmosphere of support towards the liberal governments, particularly to the liberal-progressive generals, O'Donnell and Prim, who a few years later conspired against the monarchy and were protagonists of the "Glorious Revolution" of 1868. On the other hand, the financial and human costs of the wars in distant lands were not compensated by the long-term incorporation of new territories which could bring imperial gains in economic terms for Spain. During the following decades, the Spanish army became unpopular among the lower classes, due to its adoption of socially discriminating models of conscription that allowed the rich to escape enlisting.[98]

However, all these splendid little wars contributed toward enriching and renewing alike the repertory of Spanish national myths, which incorporated some new heroes and heroic deeds to the nationalist *lieux de mémoire*, from Admiral Méndez

---

[96] See Inarejos Muñoz, *Intervenciones coloniales*, 99–108 and ff; L. López-Ocón and M. A. Puig-Samper, "Los condicionantes políticos de la Comisión Científica del Pacífico: Hispanoamericanismo y nacionalismo en la España bajoisabelina," in *Estudios sobre Historia de la Ciencia y de la Técnica*, eds. M. Esteban de Vega, et al. (Valladolid: Junta de Castilla y León, 1988), vol. II, 615–19.

[97] See R. González Tablas, *Historia de la dominación y última guerra de España en Santo Doimngo* [1870] (Santo Domingo: Editora de Santo Domingo, 1974); E. González Calleja and A. Fontecha Pedraza, *Una cuestión de honor. La polémica sobre la anexión de Santo Domingo vista desde España (1861–1865)* (Santo Domingo: Fundación García Arévalo, 2005); C. Robles Muñoz, *Paz en Santo Domingo (1861–1765). El fracaso de la anexión a España* (Madrid: CSIC, 1987).

[98] See F. Luengo, *Servir a la patria. El servicio militar en las provincias vascas (1877–1931)* (Madrid: Maia Eds., 2009); R. Núñez Florencio, *Militarismo y antimilitarismo en España (1888–1906)* (Madrid: CSIC, 1996).

Núñez to the battles of Wad-Ras (1860) and Tetuán (1860), which found reflection in contemporary literature and in the renaming of streets in Madrid and other cities.[99] The colonial wars also reinforced existing stereotypes of the nation's "other," which were now given additional meanings. The role of the nation's other was played during some phases by the Cuban rebels (the *mambises*), but particularly by the Northern African Muslims or Moors. Furthermore, this confrontation, mostly symbolic but sometimes violent, was regarded as a continuation of the so-called reconquest of the Middle Ages, which according to the master narrative of Spanish historiography had been the first common cause to unite all Iberians under a community of destiny, whose final result could not be other than Spain. The Moors were then resuscitated at several moments as a kind of counter icon for nation-building and regional integration, as it was first expressed in Orientalist paintings.[100]

This was particularly noticeable on the occasion of the victorious campaign against Morocco in 1859–60, regarded as a civilizing crusade aimed at uniting Spaniards on behalf of civilization and the Catholic faith.[101] Moreover, a significant number of volunteers came from Catalonia. They were subsequently represented wearing typically Catalan peasant hats (*barretines*), and were commanded by General Juan Prim, who was himself a self-conscious Catalan.[102] Even Catalan federalist-oriented republicans and some representatives of the Barcelona's workers movement saw in the Moroccan campaign a progressive fight, directed toward an uncivilized neighbor who did not yet deserve democracy.[103] The short Spanish–Moroccan war of 1893–94, provoked by an incident in the Spanish border around the town of Melilla, was regarded from a similar angle. The regions of Spain were now supposed to help their brethren living on the enclave towns of Ceuta and Melilla. And even federal republicans like Francesc Pi i Margall held the view that no step backward should be taken in face of an

---

[99] See abundant examples in Lécuyer and Serrano, *La Guerre d'Afrique*, 121–219.

[100] See E. Arias Anglés, "La visión de Marruecos a través de la pintura," *Mélanges de la Casa de Velázquez. Nouvelle Série* 37, no. 1 (2007): 13–37; M. A. Moreta Lara, *La imagen del moro y otros ensayos marruecos* (Málaga: Aljaima, 2005). See also P. Hertel, *Der erinnerte Halbmond. Islam und Nationalismus auf der Iberischen Halbinsel im 19. und 20. Jahrhundert* (Munich: Oldenbourg, 2012).

[101] E. Martín Corrales, ed., *Marruecos y el colonialismo español (1859–1912): De la Guerra de África a la "penetración pacífica"* (Barcelona: Bellaterra, 2002); S. Acaso Deltell, *Una guerra olvidada: Marruecos, 1859–1860* (Barcelona: Inédita, 2007); A. Bachoud, *Los españoles ante las campañas de Marruecos* (Madrid: Espasa-Calpe, 1988); J. Álvarez Junco, "El nacionalismo español como mito movilizador: Cuatro guerras," in *Cultura y movilización en la España contemporánea*, eds. R. Cruz, and M. Pérez Ledesma (Madrid: Alianza, 1997), 35–67.

[102] P. Anguera, *El general Prim: Biografía de un conspirador* (Barcelona: Edhasa, 2003).

[103] See V. Balaguer, *Jornadas de gloria o los españoles en África* (Madrid/Havana: Librería Española, 1860); Lécuyer and Serrano, *La Guerre d'Afrique*, 35–92; A. García Balañá, "Patria, plebe y política en la España isabelina: La Guerra de África en Cataluña (1859–1860)," in Martín Corrales, ed., *Marruecos*, 13–77; Inarejos Muñoz, J. A. "La campaña de África de la Unión Liberal: Una Crimea española?," *L'Atelier du Centre de Recherches Historiques* 3, no. 1 (2009): available at: http://acrh.revues.org/index1805.html#text.

uncivilized kingdom like Morocco.[104] Last but not least, similar icons were diffused—though their social impact still remains to be researched—during the long "African war" of 1907–25.[105]

Morocco became the main object of Spanish African imagination, and the area where Spanish neo-imperial dreaming really achieved some concrete realization. This was partly due to the fact that the African Northern coast had been traditionally regarded as an area of natural expansion of the Iberian Peninsula. Moroccans were sometimes regarded backward Spaniards: people who needed to be directed to civilization by Spain, which precisely by virtue of its intermediary position between Europe and Africa was in a better situation to rule over Moroccan territory.[106] This aim eclipsed the other African territories that were being colonized by Spain to a secondary position. According to Joaquín Costa, Morocco required to be formally independent under the guidance and tutelage of Spain, much in the same way that Britain had sustained Greece's independence, giving it an intermediate status between a colonial relationship and another one based on mutual respect of independence. Spain should bring civilization to Morocco, trying to "reproduce down there the characters of our homeland, making it an African Spain."[107] Engineers, doctors, military advisers, civil servants and qualified personnel in general would be sent to Morocco in order to modernize its administration under the patronage of Spain. There were several lines of continuity between this concept of an "African Spain," which flourished during the period 1885–1905, and the previous project of "overseas Spain."[108]

As was the case with the 1895–98 Cuban War, the African War that began shortly after the Algeciras International Conference in 1907 stirred up contradictory reactions that affected the degree of regional integration in the core territory of the

---

[104] J. Pich i Mitjana, *Francesc Pi i Margall y la crisis de Melilla de 1893–94* (Barcelona: Bellaterra, 2008).

[105] See S. Balfour, "War, nationalism and the Masses in Spain, 1898–1936," in *La transición a la política de masas. V Seminario Histórico Hispano-británico*, eds. E. Acton and I. Saz (Valencia: Universitat de València, 2001), 75–91; S. Balfour, *Deadly Embrace: Morocco and the Road to the Spanish Civil War* (Oxford: Oxford University Press, 2002), particularly 184–202; V. Morales Lezcano, *España y el mundo árabe: Imágenes cruzadas* (Madrid: Instituto de Cooperación con el Mundo Árabe, 1993), and Mª D. Fígares Romero de la Cruz, *La colonización del imaginario: Imágenes de África* (Granada: Universidad de Granada, 2003).

[106] See A. Martin-Márquez, *Disorientations. Spanish Colonialism in Africa and the Performance of Identity* (Yale: Yale University Press, 2008).

[107] Joaquín Costa's speech at the *Ateneo* of Madrid, 1884 (quoted in Martínez Antonio, "Vom Spanien im Übersee," 31). See also an useful compilation of texts in *Intereses de España en Marruecos* (Madrid: n. ed., 1947), as well as F. J. Martínez Antonio, *Intimidades de Marruecos. Miradas y reflexiones de medicos españoles sobre la realidad marroquí a finales del siglo XIX* (Madrid: Miraguano Eds., 2009).

[108] See for example: M. Olivié, *Aspiraciones nacionales de España. Marruecos* (Barcelona: Heinrich and Co., 1893); G. De Reparaz, *Política de España en África* (Barcelona: Imprenta Barcelonesa, 1907); Y. Akmir, *De Algeciras a Tetuán. Orígenes del proyecto colonialista español en Marruecos (1875–1906)* (Rabat: Instituto de Estudios Hispano-Lusófonos, 2010).

Spanish Crown. On the one hand, the war was simply hated by the lower classes, due to the fact that the Spanish Army was far from being a really "national army" based on compulsory male conscription. This hatred was particularly intense among the Catalan working class. The Moroccan "rebels," on the other hand, came to be considered later by some Basque and Catalan nationalists as a potential ally against a common enemy, the Spanish state. In spite of this, the solidarity with the Northern Africans never went beyond the level of rhetorical provocation, as a contradiction persisted between advocating solidarity with Spain's enemies and embracing a common cause with colonial people, which were denied the category of equal nations.[109]

Therefore, the new imperial wars of Spain provoked very divergent reactions in the Iberian periphery, which were already expressed in the social protests that took place in Barcelona in 1909, known as the "Tragic Week," once the substate nationalist agitation had been successfully launched. Reaction against recruitment of conscripted soldiers to Northern Africa unleashed the common rejection of the workers' movement, republicans, and the emerging substate nationalists, who for different reasons— such as pacifism, the rejection of a socially discriminating military conscription system, and refusal to participate in a Spanish national project—joined in the protest. Unlike Cuba or Puerto Rico, Northern Africa was never considered by most Spaniards, not even by Spanish army officers, as a part of Spain. It was regarded as a "backward" land where some of the primitive qualities of the ancient Spaniards had been preserved. And it played little role in the regional integration of the Spanish core territory.

However, the Moroccan wars reinforced the centralist worldview of Spanish civil servants and particularly of army officers. Neither were the Moroccans integrated in *Hispanity*, nor was there a belief that Spain was ready to integrate the Moroccans. The discourse of otherness was much stronger than it had been regarding the American colonies in the past. Not even in economic terms was the Northern African Protectorate a push factor for economic regional integration, since the exploitation of its mines and resources hardly produced benefits.

Spanish Colonial "Integralist" Nationalism—and Regional Disintegration

A parallel phenomenon of the spreading of autonomist and separatist mobilization in the overseas territories was that a significant sector of the Iberian settlers, particularly in Cuba and Puerto Rico, increasingly radicalized their Spanish nationalist tenets and started to embrace a kind of paramilitary and radical "unionism" that manifested itself

---

[109] See R. M. de Madariaga, "Le nationalisme basque et le nationalisme catalan face au problème colonial au Maroc," *Pluriel* 13 (1978): 31–54; E. Ucelay-Da Cal, "Els enemics dels meus enemics. Les simpaties del nacionalisme català pels 'moros': 1900–1936," *L'Avenç*, no. 28 (1980): 29–40; and A. Ugalde Zubiri, *La Acción Exterior del Nacionalismo Vasco (1890–1939): Historia, Pensamiento y Relaciones Internacionales* (Oñati: IVAP, 1996), 229–35, 285–89.

into a new form of integral and militaristic nationalism. Unlike Spanish nationalism in the Iberian core, its overseas counterpart adopted a form of a structured social movement, counting on volunteers, newspapers, war symbols and even militias of their own, particularly since the first Cuban War of Independence. This led to a reinvention of Spanish nationalism on a new model in the Caribbean: the *Incondicionales* in Puerto Rico and the radical supporters of coercive assimilation in Cuba, who endorsed the radical hispanicization of the island and hoped to increase the figures of metropolitan settlers to favor that process, turning Cuba into another province of Spain. The Spanish volunteers' militias (*Cuerpo de Voluntarios*) in Cuba, founded in 1855, which numbered around 80,000 men in 1872, became the best expression of this tendency. Although two thirds of the volunteers were assimilationist Cuban-born creoles, the militias constituted a real expression of lower middle-class nationalism, as many of its metropolitan members typically were shop assistants and clerks. The volunteers were the armed expression of what first came to be labeled as the Spanish Party (*Partido Español*), whose main focus was located at the *Casino Español* of Havana founded in March 1869, and then extended to other Cuban towns.[110]

The political mobilization of the Spanish settlers and their organs of expression often were intertwined with the mutual-aid associations founded by metropolitan immigrants. The Spanish Party had an inter-class character, but its leadership was clearly in the hands of sugar and tobacco planters, as well as of merchants. It became a key factor in Cuban politics, which played an increasing role in the decisions taken by captain-generals and, in practice, governed the island during the whole period of political instability that reigned in the metropolis until the breakdown of the First Spanish Republic in 1873. They also developed a simplified image of the other—the uncivilized black people who rejected Catholicism and civilization—as well as a preference for a strong authority and a permanently mobilized society. Certainly a current of sympathy and solidarity between Cuban patriots and metropolitan republicans and anarchists also emerged after 1874. Political prisoners from Cuba and Spain often met at the prisons located in Northern Africa or Guinea, and Spanish supporters of the workers' movement in Cuba became strategic allies in the fight for independence. But they did not shape the mainstream of the Spanish settlers' public opinion.[111]

The Spanish metropolitan-born civil servants and military officers stationed in Cuba were also imbued with the idea of fighting a different war, whose objective was to annihilate a barbarian enemy that had more in common with African slaves than with Americans. However, and despite the later accusations by Cuban nationalist historiography of an extermination policy on the island, the Spanish colonial military's concept of the war in the Caribbean did not correspond to the twentieth century wars of extermination. The policy of setting up "re-concentration" areas for

---

[110] See Roldán de Montaud, *La Restauración*, 25–41.

[111] See J. Casanovas Codina, *Bread or Bullets! Urban Labor and Spanish Colonialism in Cuba, 1850–1898* (Pittsburgh: University of Pittsburgh Press, 1998).

the civil population from the eastern rural areas of the isle, which was followed by General Valeriano Weyler, military governor of the island, was understood as a means to prevent the guerrilla fighters from being supported by local peasants. Although these measures were not aimed at physically exterminating the local population, lack of means and prevention on the part of the Spanish authorities led to starvation and death by disease of several thousands of Cubans. The rebels were certainly considered to be aliens and bandits, not citizens at all, while most Cubans regardless of their skin color were simply regarded as second-class Spaniards who still had to be elevated to the category of full civilization.[112]

Some of these representations of the colonial war were later applied on European soil against new opponents—the "Anti-Spaniards" who were fighting for the republic or for communism in 1936–39—although without the final consequences that were experienced in the Nazi case. But it must be noted that shared representations of the enemy followed two complementary directions across the ocean. The visual representations of the Cuban rebels as the enemy during the first Cuban War (1868–78) were to a certain extent also imported from the last civil war between supporters of the Ancien Regime (the Carlists) and the liberal state that took place almost simultaneously on Spanish peninsula territory. In fact, the Third Carlist War (1872–76), during which the Carlist rebels, a great part of them coming from Navarre and the Basque provinces, were often depicted in the liberal and republican public sphere as uncivilized reactionaries—"primitive Basques"—which did not deserve the honor to become fully-fledged Spanish citizens. Some liberal military officers even proposed measures to subjugate the Carlist-supporting Basque population, treating them as colonial subjects without any rights of citizenship. However, these suggestions were simply rejected. There was still a gap between the cultural perception of the Basque supporters of the Ancien Regime as uncivilized Spaniards, but in spite of this, Europeans, and the more extreme image of the Cuban insurgents, associated with race stereotypes that converted them into rebel slaves from African origin.[113]

In effect, a new variant of "integral nationalism" came to be very strong among the military who were stationed in the Philippines and in the Caribbean islands. This variant "returned" to the Iberian peninsula in the 1880s, and more intensively after the final defeat of 1898, instilling some of the new thoughts which became very present among Spanish military officers, but also counted on many supporters among returned civilians who preferred to go back to the Iberian peninsula after the independence (or the American take over) of the former colonies.[114] To express their views roughly, Spain had to be intransigent towards regional "separatism" from the peninsula periph-

[112] See A. Stucki, *Aufstand und Zwangsumsiedlung. Die kubanischen Unabhängigkeitskriege 1868–1898* (Hamburg: Hamburger Edition, 2012).

[113] See F. Molina Aparicio, *La tierra del martirio español. El País Vasco y España en el siglo del nacionalismo* (Madrid: CEPC, 2005).

[114] See A. Elorza, and E. Hernández Sandoica, *La Guerra de Cuba (1895–1898): Historia política de una derrota colonial* (Madrid: Alianza, 1998).

ery. Otherwise, the Catalans would follow the path which had been opened up by the Cubans and would be the next to leave.[115]

The intense patriotic mobilization that spread throughout Spain in 1898 faded away after the disastrous defeat of the Spanish navy in the Philippines and Cuba by the U.S. navy. However, the remains of that mobilization were visible in the impact left by "Cuban nostalgia" on the Spanish national culture of the twentieth century. In a way, Cuba had been the "jewel of the Spanish Crown," due to its economic relevance for Spain during the second half of the nineteenth century, but also because of the important number of European settlers on the island. This military mobilization was a driving force behind the emergence in peninsula Spain of a new form of "integral" nationalism, undoubtedly fuelled and partially brought about by the former colonies, whose dimensions and social spread—through the return of former settlers, army officers and conscripted soldiers, etc.—have not yet been accurately researched. In fact, the memory of Spanish patriotic mobilization among Spanish settlers in Cuba, whose flow continued and even increased after 1902, endured until the 1930s and eventually created a permanent atmosphere of nostalgia for empire. The "young Spaniards" of Cuban background who then returned as army officers to the metropolis turned their eyes toward the core of the empire in order to make it a stronger and unified nation-state where authority had to be reinforced regardless of democracy and individual rights.[116] It was stated that Spain had to become more "Spanish" in the near future, while any attempt to integrate the colonies in the national repertory of images of what Spain was had to be marginalized.

The sociological influence in Spain of "returned nationalism" from the colonies is a topic to be researched in depth. However, it seems to have had a compensating effect to the contrary phenomenon: the fact that the Spanish army had never adopted an "imperial" bias—as the Austro-Hungarian model displayed—and therefore had not played an integrating role. Only metropolitan Spaniards were accepted—indigenous auxiliary forces were used particularly in the police forces—and compulsory male conscription was not adopted until the second decade of the twentieth century. Moroccan mercenaries were accepted into the Spanish army of northern Africa in the second decade of the twentieth century, but only as members of separate auxiliary corps. However, they were forged on the model of French and British colonial troops, rather than on the model of the Austro-Hungarian army. And they were simply regarded by ordinary Spaniards as foreign troops, particularly during the Spanish Civil War, as

---

[115] See E. Ucelay-Da Cal, "Cuba y el despertar de los nacionalismos en la España peninsular," *Studia Historica/Historia Contemporánea* 15 (1997): 151–92; E. Ucelay-Da Cal, "Self-fulfilling prophecies: Propaganda and Political Models between Cuba, Spain and the United States," *Illes i Imperis* 2 (1999): 191–220; and J. Romero Maura, *The Spanish Army and Catalonia: The "Cu-Cut!" Incident and the Law of Jurisdictions* (London: Sage, 1976).

[116] See G. Jensen, *Irrational Triumph: Cultural Despair, Military Nationalism, and the Ideological Origins of Franco's Spain* (Reno: University of Nevada Press, 2002).

their presence in the insurgent army made it appear as an "invading horde" in the eyes of the Republicans.[117]

Patriotic mobilization among the Spanish settlers who remained in the former colonies contributed towards reinforcing the sense of belonging among them. The memory of the fallen from the colonial wars, for instance, remained alive among Spanish migrants in Cuba and Puerto Rico, while there were almost no monuments or commemorations to the remembrance of the dead soldiers for the empire in the Iberian Peninsula.[118] Perhaps the most striking phenomenon is that in some of the former colonies, particularly in Puerto Rico but also in the Philippines, a new Spanish Creole identity emerged, which was incorporated into the native narratives of anti-colonial identity and turned toward the new rulers: the United States and—as in the case of the Philippines after 1941—Imperial Japan. This was particularly striking in the case of some urban areas of the Philippines, particularly in Manila, where the Spanish language was maintained as a sign of distinction not only by the upper middle classes, but also by some creolized sectors of the lower middle class.[119]

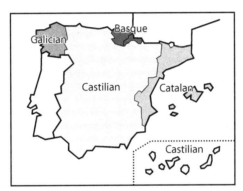

The transfer of ideas from the colonies to Spain also influenced the development of substate nationalisms within the metropolitan territory. The colonial defeat of 1898

[117] See G. Nerín, *La Guerra que vino de África* (Barcelona: Crítica, 2005), and X. M. Núñez, *¡Fuera el invasor! Nacionalismos y movilización bélica durante la guerra civil española, 1936–1939* (Madrid: Marcial Pons, 2006), 124–44; V. Moga Romero, "Los tejedores de ensueños: Tras la 'pared de tela de araña' del Protectorado (1912–1956)," *Mélanges de la Casa de Velázquez* 37, no. 1 (2007): 109–29.

[118] See J. M. Klein, "Spaniards and the Politics of Memory in Cuba, 1898–1934," PhD Dissertation, University of Texas at Austin, 2002 (available at: http://www.lib.utexas.edu/etd/d/2002/kleinj029/kleinj029.pdf). For a contrasting view of the relatively scarce attention paid by the metropolitan public opinion to the warrior myths of the Caribbean wars, see C. Serrano, *El nacimiento de Carmen. Símbolos, mitos, nación* (Madrid: Taurus, 1999).

[119] F. Rodao, "Departure from Asia: Spain in the Philippines and East Asia in the Nineteenth and Twentieth Centuries," in *Nation and Conflict in Modern Spain: Essays in Honor of Stanley G. Payne*, eds. B. D. Bunk, S. Pack, and C. G. Scott (Madison: Parallel Press/The University of Wisconsin, 2007), 104–22.

constituted a potential source for regional disintegration, since the Cuban and Puerto Rican autonomists became models to be imitated by metropolitan regionalists—and, later on, full-fledged ethnonationalists. Some Catalans, Basques, Galicians, and even Filipino students in the metropolis were to a certain extent influenced by this transfer of ideas and examples from the Caribbean. Their precise impact beyond some symbolic attitudes must not be overestimated. But certainly it was not by chance that some of the symbols hung up by the supporters of Catalan independence since the first decade of the twentieth century found clear inspiration in the Cuban fight, such as the new separatist Catalan flag, which consists of an open remake of the Cuban flag, introduced for the first time in 1904–08 after the return of some radical Catalanists from the Caribbean.[120] However, this imitation of symbols was not consistent with any general refusal of all imperialisms. The founder of Basque nationalism, Sabino Arana, openly admired Britain and, though embracing the cause of the Cuban and Filipino independence, also took into consideration the possibility of the Basque Country becoming a protectorate of the benign British Empire.[121]

The imperial imagination also impregnated the first political models of autonomist regionalisms and emergent ethnonationalisms in the Iberian periphery. The sudden dissolution of the empire, and the example of Cuban, Puerto Rican, or Philippine nationalists and their charismatic leaders—from Carlos Manuel de Céspedes and Antonio Maceo to José Rizal—led Basque, Catalan, and later on Galician regionalists (who later became fully-fledged ethno-nationalists) to think of Spain in terms of a historical failure. The economic interests of a great part of the Catalan bourgeoisie—particularly those behind the rising cotton and textile industry of the region—were also seriously damaged by the loss of the Cuban market. If the nation-state could not fully survive as an empire, then Spain as such was considered to be a decadent entity; an ill body that was damned to die in the age of imperialism. Classic interpretations of the emergence of Catalan nationalism at the end of the nineteenth century as a mass movement have pointed out the fact that the loss of confidence of Catalan middle-classes in the Spanish project, after it had failed in preserving the rest of the empire, made them turn their patriotic loyalties to the subnational entity they were attached to. Imperial decline is certainly not the only factor that explains this turn of loyalties vis-à-vis the nation-state, but it undoubtedly played an important catalyzing role. Regional patriotism was then increasingly replaced by a new form of exclusive feeling of identity, and became a fully-fledged national identity. Once Spain had ceased to be a successful empire in the age of empires, it did not deserve to survive as a nation-state anymore, but had to be re-founded from a multinational perspective.[122]

---

[120] See J. Crexell, *Origen de la bandera independentista* (Barcelona: El Llamp, 1988).

[121] See A. Ugalde, ed., *Patria y Libertad. Los vascos y las guerras de independencia de Cuba (1868–1898)* (Tafalla: Txalaparta, 2012).

[122] See B. de Riquer, *Lliga Catalana: La burgesia catalana i el nacionalisme, 1898–1904* (Barcelona: Eds. 62, 1977); A. Marimon, *La crisis de 1898* (Barcelona: Ariel, 1998), and A. Smith, *The Origins of Catalan Nationalism, 1770–1898* (Basingstoke: Palgrave, 2014).

However, the main political objective of mainstream Catalan nationalism was not to set up a separate and independent nation-state, but instead to set up a new Iberian empire, based on a new relationship among the territories which integrated the European core of Spain. Particularly among some sectors of Catalan conservative nationalism, the loss of the American empire was also regarded as a consequence of the implementation of centralism in the Spanish State. Not unsurprisingly, they flattered the "liberal" and "tolerant" British Empire, and declared that a Catalan hegemony in Spanish politics, and therefore a federal or confederal restructuring of the Spanish state by closely following the Austro-Hungarian model of compromise or *Ausgleich*— as it was explicitly demanded by some Catalanist organizations since the 1880s[123]— would facilitate a reinvigorated imperial presence of Spain in the world, particularly in Latin America. Since the essence of empires was diversity, the key for recovering Spain's past greatness was first to undertake a territorial reform within its European borders, and to incorporate the regenerating impulse from the Catalan periphery. The Empire was seen as a consequence of the autonomy of its parts, not as a function of the center's authority and its strength. The "imperial model" of the state was also considered to be an alternative to the consolidation of a Spanish nation-state exclusively based on a homogenized Castilian-centered identity. However, this imperial imagination was full of uncertainties which made it a metaphor rather than a politically influential model. How was it possible to reconcile a "bi-national monarchy" at the European core of the empire with an imperial treatment of Cuba, Puerto Rico, or the Philippines as dominions or protectorates, particularly in the later case of Morocco? Despite its contradictory character, this idea, expressed by the most important and foundational thinker of Catalan conservative nationalism, Enric Prat de la Riba, in 1906 (*La nacionalitat catalana* [Catalan nationhood]), impregnated most political projects of Catalan nationalism until the 1930s.[124]

Even more complicated was to formulate a kind of Austro-Hungarian solution for Spain, based on a dual Monarchy (Castilian/Catalan), where the Catalan part would take over the economic but not administrative control of the empire. At the same time, Catalonia would be entitled to launch a political offensive to regain the lost territories of Hispanic America in economic and cultural terms, which would be flanked by a parallel offensive in the Mediterranean basin for "recovering" Catalonia's past sphere of cultural and political influence. This also included the cultural and economic expansion towards

---

[123] E. Ucelay-Da Cal, "'El Mirall de Catalunya': Models internacionals en el desenvolupament del nacionalisme i del separatisme català, 1875–1923," *Estudios de Historia Social* 28–29 (1984): 213–19; J. Llorens i Vila, *Catalanisme i Moviments Nacionalistes Contemporanis (1885–1901): Missatges a Irlanda, Creta i Finlàndia* (Barcelona: Dalmau, 1994); and J. Burgaya Riera, "La formació del catalanisme conservador i els models 'nacionals' coetanis. Premsa catalanista i moviments nacionalistes contemporanis, 1868–1901" (PhD Thesis, Universitat Autònoma de Barcelona, 1999).

[124] Extensively on this aspect, see E. Ucelay-Da Cal, *El imperialismo catalón. Prat de la Riba, Camby, D'Ors y la conquista moral de Espaca* (Barcelona: Edhasa, 2003).

Southern France—the Occitanian lands and the Catalan-speaking Roussillon—as well as the former territories of the Catalan Empire of the late Middle Ages.[125]

Nevertheless, this *peripheral* appeal to the recovery of an empire as compensation for the restructuring of the centralist model of nation-state was simply not understood by the Spanish public opinion, which increasingly identified the necessity of an empire not as a substitute for a central state, but instead as a kind of "mission," a project which, like in the past, should unite all Spaniards from all social backgrounds and regional origins in a "common destiny," once again around the aegis of Castile. This idea was coined by the so-called 1898 intellectual generation, and particularly expressed by the influential philosopher José Ortega y Gasset in 1921.[126] The lust for empire would act again as an efficient factor of regional integration. The Spanish fascists picked up this idea and cloaked it with a dense coat of aggressive rhetoric. Nevertheless, they distinguished between imperial aims toward Latin America, defined as the search for recovery of cultural hegemony in the world, and the territorial claims regarding Portugal and northern Africa, where a more ambitious tone was expressed until 1943–44.[127] In fact, one of the most influential theoreticians of the idea of Spanish Empire during the 1940s was the philosopher Eugeni D'Ors, who until 1919 had been closely linked to the Catalan nationalist elites and first coined the concept of "Catalan Empire," according to which Catalonia should aim at regenerating the whole Spanish state, turning it into a plural federation of nations. This new Spain would then be able to incorporate new territories, beginning with Portugal, to a more flexible political community whose ultimate destiny was to rebuild, in economic and cultural terms, the old Spanish Empire, now filled with a new economic and commercial spirit.

Conclusion

The functions of empire in Spanish history varied according to time and place and very much depended on chronology. There were at least four imperial stages: the pre-modern one, 1500–1826; the modern one, based on the relics of the classic overseas empire, 1826–98; the new empire of substitution in Africa, 1907–56; and the final imperial stage of Francoism, 1956–75. Each of them had different effects on the making of proto-national and national identity in the Iberian lands. They were not parallel processes running independently of each other, but rather closely intertwined and hence complementary phenomena.

---

[125] See A. Rafanell, *La il.lusió occitana. La llengua dels catalans, entre Espanya i França* (Barcelona: Quaderns Crema, 2006), 2 vols.

[126] J. Ortega y Gasset, *España invertebrada* (Madrid: Espasa-Calpe, 1921).

[127] See I. Saz, *España contra España. Los nacionalismos franquistas* (Madrid: Marcial Pons, 2002); E. González Calleja and F. Limón Nevado, *La Hispanidad como instrumento de combate. Raza e Imperio en la prensa franquista durante la guerra civil espacola* (Madrid: CSIC, 1988); M.-A. Barrachina, *Propagande et culture dans l'Espagne franquiste 1936–1945* (Grenoble: ELLUG, 1998), 139–78.

The function of Empire in the process of Spanish nation-building may be regarded as ambiguous, something that could be probably applied to other European cases. The empire played an integrating role in some phases and a disintegrating function in other periods. The mechanisms of regional integration facilitated by the Spanish Empire were rather informal, contrary to the British case. No established practices granted Catalans, Basques or Galicians access to the benefits of the empire, with much depending on their own initiative. Moreover, the metropolitan regions did not exist as such until 1833. Regions were split up into provinces, and even in the Basque case there were no "Basque" institutions but provincial ones—that is, assemblies of Biscay, Alava, and Guipúzcoa—with very limited powers. Participation in imperial affairs was as open to the "periphery" as to the "center." And the benefits of the empire were not perceived as collective achievements by metropolitan territories. Since the loss of Cuba, Puerto Rico, and the Philippines in 1898, the political representatives of the emergent nationalist movements of the peninsular periphery, particularly Catalan speakers of the home-rule movement, framed some of their demands in neo-imperial terms. Thus, on the one hand, the empire played an integrating role and became a complementary tool in the strategies of nation-building implemented by Spanish elites.

On the other hand, the empire also constituted a potential source for nation-destroying, as armed conflicts in distant lands and the demonstration effect caused by the successes of anti-colonial nationalists also provoked reactions of divergent nature in the Iberian core of the empire. While war in the overseas periphery fostered the emergence of radical Spanish nationalism and fuelled the appeal to achieve national unity in the core in order to better defend the imperial grandeur, it also exerted a potentially multiplying influence on the regionalist and nationalist movements that also emerged in the Iberian territories of the empire since the last decades of the nineteenth century. Imperial decay demonstrated the historical failure of Spain as a political community, as well as the weakness of its central power. And further inability to put a definitive end to the Moroccan revolts since 1911, which peaked in 1919–22, also uncovered the structural deficiencies of a state that lacked modernizing appeal for some sectors of the peripheral middle classes. However, this did not give rise to a mass-scale rejection of Spanish identity in each of these territories. Returned soldiers from the African wars, widespread images of the enemy, and the persistent appeal to Spain's civilizing mission in Africa counteracted in many respects the decadent images of Spanish military defeats in some critical conjunctures.[128] The extent to which the imperial nation-building process was able to overcome, counteract, or at least resist its parallel nation-destroying effect still remains a process to be satisfactorily researched from the bottom up.

---

[128] See X. M. Núñez and F. Sevillano, "Introducción: Las Españas y sus enemigos," in *Los enemigos de España: Imagen del otro, conflictos bélicos y disputas nacionales siglos XVI–XX*, eds. X. M. Núñez, and F. Sevillano (Madrid: CEPC, 2010), 13–27.

Building the Nation Among Visions of German Empire

Stefan Berger

Introduction

When Theodor Schieder published his influential book on Imperial Germany in 1961, he pondered about the complexity of its constitutional, cultural, and ethnic setup. He was well aware of the symbolic strength of Medievalism and of the Holy Roman Empire of the German Nation for the new-found nation-state of 1871. Not for nothing was it called a *Reich*, an empire; it had an emperor as head of state and it was to develop imperial ambitions, both in Central and Eastern Europe and overseas. And yet Schieder was to define Imperial Germany as a "nation-state." He thus followed in the footsteps of the nineteenth-century Prussian historians who had been so successful in anchoring in the historical consciousness the idea of the Germans' alleged centuries-long search for a unified nation-state. The national struggle and the national movement dominated so much of what had been written on nineteenth-century German history that it was hard to think of the German state that came into being after the Franco-Prussian War of 1870–71 as anything else than a nation-state.[1]

---

[1] Theodor Schieder, *Das Deutsche Kaiserreich von 1871 als Nationalstaat* (Düsseldorf: Westdeutscher Verlag, 1961); the extremely influential book by Hans-Ulrich Wehler, *Das Deutsche Kaiserreich* (Göttingen: Vandenhoeck&Ruprecht, 1973) followed in the footsteps of Schieder, who was much admired by Wehler, so much in fact, that Wehler re-issued Schieder's history in 1992. The most influential recent syntheses of nineteenth-century German history all emphasize the character of Imperial Germany as a nation-state. See especially Thomas Nipperdey, *Deutsche Geschichte 1866–1918*, 2 vols. (Munich: Beck, 1990 and 1992); Wolfgang Mommsen, *Der autoritäre Nationalstaat: Verfassung, Gesellschaft und Kultur im deutschen Kaiserreich* (Frankfurt: Fischer, 1992); Hans-Ulrich Wehler, *Deutsche Gesellschaftsgeschichte*, 5 vols., in particular vol. 2: *Von der Reformära bis zur industriellen und politischen "Deutschen Doppelrevolution" 1815–1845/49*, and vol. 3: *Von der "deutschen Doppelrevolution" bis zum Beginn des Ersten Weltkrieges 1849–1914* (Munich: Beck, 1987 and 1995).

THE GERMAN REICH
1871–1918

Kingdom
of
Denmark

Kingdom
of Sweden

Copenhagen

Malmö

Noth Sea

Province

Flensburg

Schleswig

Heligoland
(until 1890 part of the UK)

Schleswig Kiel

Rostock   Stralsund

Kolberg

Holstein

Hanseatic City
of Lübeck

Grand Duchy
of Mecklenburg-
Schwerin

Province

of Pomerania

Wilhelmshaven

Bremer-
haven

Hanseatic City
of Hamburg

SCHWERIN

Grand Duchy of
Mecklenburg-Strelitz

Stettin [Szczecin]

Groningen

OLDENBURG

Hanseatic
City of
Bremen

Province of
Hanover

NEUSTRELITZ

Province of
Brandeburg

Kingdom of the
Netherlands

Grand Duchy
of Oldenburg

Ems

Aller

Weser

Province of
Saxony

BERLIN

Potsdam

Küstrin
[Kostrzyń
nad Odrą]

Warta

Amsterdam

The Hague   Arnhem

Osnabrück

Hanover

BRUNSWICK

Magdeburg

Frankfurt
(Oder)

Oder

Münster

Dortmund

Province of
Westphalia

Göttingen

Duchy of Brunswick

DESSAU

Duchy of Anhalt

Essen   Ruhr

Düsseldorf

Halle   Leipzig

Principality of
Schwarzburg-Sondershausen

Kingdom of Saxony

Liegnitz
[Legnica]

Pro

Liège

Cologne

Bonn

Principality
of Waldeck-
Pyrmont

Kassel

GOTHA

SWE

WEIMAR

GERA

SA

DRESDEN

Kingdom of
Belgium

Rhine Province

Marburg

Giessen

Province of Hesse-Nassau

SCG

SSR

SWE

RJL

Chemnitz

Koblenz

Wetzlar

Grand Duchy
of Hesse

MEININGEN

SMG

SCG

Wiesbaden

Frankfurt (Main)

COBURG

Elbe

Prague

Grand Duchy
of Luxembourg

Trier

Mainz

DARMSTADT

Main

Vltava

Luxembourg

Grand Duchy
of Hesse

Würzburg

Nuremberg

Meuse

Verdun

Metz

Moselle

KARLSRUHE

Grand Duchy of Baden

Kingdom of Bavaria

Regensburg/
Ratisbon

Isar

Danube

Austrian

Nancy

Imperial Territory
of Alsace-
Lorraine

STRASBOURG

Kingdom

STUTTGART

of Württemberg

Ulm

Augsburg

Lech

Linz

VIE

France

Colmar

Freiburg

MUNICH

Salzburg

Empire

Basle

Zurich

Princ. of
Liechtenstein

Inn

Innsbruck

Mur

Graz

BERNE

Geneva

Switzerland

Rhône

Balzano

Adige

Piave

Klagenfurt

Drave

Marbur
[Maribo

Kingdom

of Italy

FHZ = Principality of Hohenzollern (part of Prussia)
GH = Grand Duchy of Hesse
LD = Principality of Lippe
OLD = Part of the Grand Duchy of Oldenburg
RÄL = Principality of Reuss-Greiz
RJL = Principality of Reuss-Gera
SA = Duchy of Saxe-Altenburg
SCG = Duchy of Saxe-Coburg and Gotha
SL = Principality of Schaumburg-Lippe
SMG = Duchy of Saxe-Meiningen
SR = Principality of Schwarzburg-Rudolstadt
SWE = Grand Duchy of Saxe-Weimar-Eisenach
W = Principality of Waldeck-Pyrmont (Region Pyrmont)

Only recently, the global and imperial dimensions of the German nation-state have been emphasized more prominently. In line with the move to transnationalism in historical writing, the German Empire has been scrutinized and re-evaluated.[2] Sebastian Conrad has argued that the dynamism of Wilhelminian nationalism cannot be explained satisfactorily without taking into account its global contexts.[3] The Wilhelminian discourse on nation was, to a significant extent, shaped by the discourse on globalization. Global exchanges and interactions determined the construction of the German nation. Many of these global factors were in fact imperial factors. In other words, the German nation was shaped significantly through empire. Imperial Germany cannot be adequately understood by looking at it merely through the lens of an imperializing nation-state. One also needs to take seriously the impact of a nationalizing empire on the constructions of German nationhood.

Since the second half of the 1990s, a growing literature on German imperial fantasies,[4] on real-life colonialism and imperialism in Africa, the Near East,

---

[2] Sebastian Conrad and Jürgen Osterhammel, eds., *Das Kaiserreich transnational. Deutschland in der Welt 1871–1914* (Göttingen: Vandenhoeck & Ruprecht, 2004).

[3] Sebastian Conrad, "Globalisierungseffekte: Mobilität und Nation im Kaiserreich" in *Das deutsche Kaiserreich in der Kontroverse*, eds. Sven Müller and Cornelius Torp (Göttingen: Vandenhoeck&Ruprecht, 2009), 406–21; see also Sebastian Conrad, *Globalisierung und Nation im deutschen Kaiserreich* (Munich: Beck, 2006).

[4] See the pioneering study of Susanne Zantop, *Colonial Fantasies. Conquest, Family, and Nation in Precolonial Germany, 1770–1870* (Durham: Duke University Press, 1997); also: Sara Friedrichsmeyer, Sara Lennox, and Susanne Zantop, eds., *The Imperialist Imagination: German Colonialism and its Legacy* (Ann Arbor: University of Michigan Press, 1998); Birthe Kundrus, ed., *Phantasiereiche; zur Kulturgeschichte des deutschen Kolonialismus* (Frankfurt a.M.: Campus-Verlag, 2003); Ulrich van der Heyden and Joachim Zeller, eds., *Kolonialismus hierzulande. Eine Spurensuche in Deutschland* (Erfurt: Sutton, 2007).

and Oceania,[5] and on German designs for a German Empire in Central and Eastern Europe[6] has given rise to views that take the name of empire of the first German nation-state more seriously. Philip Ther, for example, has argued that empire is crucial to any understanding of the character of Imperial Germany.[7] And Edward Ross Dickinson has reminded us of a possible German peculiarity in the entanglement of empire and nation before 1914: those who referred to themselves as culturally German could be found in three different empires, namely the Hohenzollern, Habsburg and Romanov Empires and in one republic, namely Switzerland. This kind of transnationalism produced a range of productive tensions and synergies between the imperial and the national.[8] This article will build on this more recent literature in seeking to understand Imperial Germany as an imperial nation, in line with other imperial nations in late nineteenth-century Europe, which are discussed in this volume. It will explore the diverse ways in which nation-building took place at the heart of the German Empire.

The National Core of the Empire and Four Peripheries

In his comparative study on the collapse of empires, Alexander J. Motyl argued that Germany belonged to those empires which made a hard distinction between core and periphery, the core being the nation-state and the periphery being possessions overseas.[9] Such a view, however, does not capture the complexity of the relationship

---

[5] See in particular J. Noyes, *Colonial Space: Spatiality in the Discourse of German South West Africa, 1884–1915* (Philadelphia: Harwood Academic Publishers, 1992); M. Seligmann, *Rivalry in Southern Africa: the Transformation of German Colonial Policy* (Basingstoke: Palgrave MacMillan, 1998); D. Walther, *Creating Germans Abroad. Cultural Policies and National Identity in Namibia* (Athens: Ohio University Press, 2002); E. Wareham, *Race and Realpolitik: The Politics of Colonization in German Samoa* (Frankfurt: Peter Lang, 2002); Birthe Kundrus, *Moderne Imperialisten. Das Kaiserreich im Spiegel seiner Kolonien* (Cologne: Böhlau, 2003); Dirk van Laak, *Imperiale Infrastruktur. Deutsche Planungen für eine Erschliessung Afrikas 1880–1960* (Paderborn: Schöningh, 2004); Michael Pesek, *Koloniale Herrschaft in Deutsch-Ostafrika. Expeditionen, Militär und Verwaltung seit 1880* (Frankfurt: Campus-Verlag, 2005); M. Fuhrmann, *Der Traum vom deutschen Orient. Zwei deutsche Kolonien im Osmanischen Reich 1851–1918* (Frankfurt: Campus-Verlag, 2006); George Steinmetz, *The Devil's Handwriting: Precoloniality and the German Colonial State in Qingdao, Samoa and Southwest Africa* (Chicago: The University of Chicago Press, 2007).
[6] See Robert L. Nelson, ed., *Germans, Poland, and Colonial Expansion to the East. 1850 Through the Present* (Basingstoke: Palgrave MacMillan, 2009); Vejas Gabriel Liulevicius, *The German Myth of the East, 1800 to the Present* (Oxford: Oxford University Press, 2009).
[7] Philip Ther, "Imperial instead of National History: Positioning Modern German History on the Map of European Empires," in *Imperial Rule*, eds. Alexei Miller and Alfred J. Rieber (Budapest: Central European University Press, 2004), 47–68.
[8] Edward Ross Dickinson, "The German Empire: an Empire?" *History Workshop Journal* 66 (2008): 129–62.
[9] Alexander J. Motyl, *Imperial Ends. The Decay, Collapse and Revival of Empires* (New York: Columbia University Press, 2001), 14.

between nation-state and empire in Germany. For a start, the nation-state itself had a very marked core and periphery. Arguably, Prussia was the nation's core, the driving force behind German unification, with the other German states and statelets forming a first-line periphery to be incorporated into the nation-state. Especially in the southern German states, memories of Prussian occupation after the German "civil war" of 1866 remained both painful and prevalent, and anti-Prussian sentiment lingered on for a very long time thereafter.[10] However, it should be noted that Prussia itself was very much a former periphery of the Holy Roman Empire of the German Nation. Its eastern parts had never formed part of the empire, and during much of the late Medieval and early modern period, Prussia can hardly be described as an entity that was in any way, shape or form an important factor on the map of Europe. This was only to change in the eighteenth century, and it was only in the nineteenth century that Prussia was replacing the Habsburg Empire as the most important and powerful state in the German Confederation.[11]

1871 was in many respects not the end point of a long process of nation formation but the beginning of a remarkably successful and rapid process of nation building under the umbrella of empire.[12] After all, during the first half of the nineteenth century, most Germans living in the German lands connected the terms patriotism and even nation to their particular territorial states, such as Bavaria, Württemberg, Hanover, Hamburg, or Saxony. The "small fatherlands" of the German Confederation embarked on their own state-building measures after 1815, in order to ensure the integrity of their territories and the loyalty of their subjects.[13] The process of regionalizing those identities and making them part of a German nation was a process which came fully into its own only after 1871. The liberal-national politician August Ludwig von Rochau spoke for many when he lamented the lack of cohesion among Germans on the eve of unification in 1869: "The German love for the fatherland is made up of much fiction and little truth … there is no national spirit in the political sense of the word … We carry German unity on our lips but not in our hearts."[14] Historians, such as John Breuilly, have argued against the grain of Prussian historiography that the German national movement was essentially quite weak before the 1860s and that therefore the real task

---

[10] For a convincing interpretation of the war between Prussia and the Habsburg Empire of 1866 as a German "civil war," see James J. Sheehan, *German History, 1770–1866* (Oxford: Oxford University Press, 1989).

[11] Christopher Clark, *Iron Kingdom. The Rise and Downfall of Prussia, 1600–1947* (London: Allen Lane, 2006). See also Alexei Miller's chapter, who equally notes how former peripheries (Moscow) became national/imperial centers (in the 16th century, in Moscow's case) and how former centers declined to become peripheries.

[12] John Breuilly, *The Formation of the First German Nation-State, 1800–1871* (Basingstoke: Palgrave MacMillan, 1996).

[13] Abigail Green, *Fatherlands. State-Building and Nationhood in Nineteenth-Century Germany* (Cambridge: Cambridge University Press, 2001).

[14] Quoted in Wehler, *Deutsche Gesellschaftsgeschichte*, vol. 3, 940.

of nation building only began after the foundation of the German Reich.[15] After all, the first elections in the newly founded Imperial Germany demonstrated the urgent need for regional integration—only half of those eligible bothered to turn up and of those who did, half voted for parties who were either opposed to or were at best luke-warm about German unification. In subsequent decades empire, as we shall see below, had a major role to play in the successful stabilization of a national core. Prussia essen-tially faced the task of integrating the other territorial states in the German Empire and forging the nation-state through empire.

In promoting national unity under the umbrella of empire, Prussia also had to contend with ethnic minorities which did not regard themselves as German and were not regarded by "the core" as German. They formed the second layer of a colonial periphery. Polish speakers in Prussia's eastern provinces, Danish speakers in Schleswig and Alsatians and Lorrainers in the annexed Reichsland of Elsass-Lothringen were wary of the claims of the new nation-state to their allegiance and the nation-state ul-timately failed to integrate them fully before 1914.[16] 4 million citizens of the German Reich out of a total of 65 million belonged to those linguistic/ethnic minorities. One of every ten inhabitants of Prussia did not speak German as their mother tongue.

The Poles formed the most numerous and arguably the most important na-tional minority. In East and West Prussia as well as in Upper Silesia Polish speakers formed a clear majority in many districts. Often predominantly Polish settlements could be found next to predominantly German settlements—with a sizable Jewish population identifying almost entirely with the German nationality against the Polish one—despite their own exclusion from a Protestant Prussian fatherland, in which di-verse forms of anti-Semitism were widespread.[17]

After the Polish uprising of 1863 the Prussian/German political elites saw grave dangers for the Prussian/German state in every form of Polish national senti-ment which they therefore sought to counter with deliberate Germanization policies in the "German east." Poles should not be able to use their language in schools and

---

[15] John Breuilly, "Nationalism and the First Unification," in *Germany's Two Unifications: Anticipa-tions, Experiences, Responses*, eds. Ronald Speirs and John Breuilly (Basingstoke: Palgrave Mac-Millan, 2005), 101–21.

[16] Hans Henning Hahn and Peter Kunze, eds., *Nationale Minderheiten und staatliche Minderhei-tenpolitik in Deutschland im 19. Jahrhundert* (Berlin: Akademie-Verlag, 1999); Kai Struve and Philipp Ther, eds., *Die Grenzen der Nationen. Identitätenwandel in Oberschlesien in der Neuzeit* (Marburg: Verlag Herder-Institut, 2002).

[17] Mathias Seiter, *Jewish Identities Between Region and Nation: Jews in the Borderlands of Posen and Alsace-Lorraine, 1871–1914* (University of Southampton, PhD, 2010); Elizabeth A. Drummond, "On the Borders of the Nation: Jews and the German-Polish National Conflict in Poznania, 1886–1914," *Nationalities Papers* 29, no. 3 (2001): 459–75; Chris Clark, "The 'Christian' State and the 'Jewish Citizen' in Nineteenth-Century Prussia," in *Protestants, Catholics and Jews in Germany 1800–1914*, ed. Helmut Walser Smith (Oxford: Berg, 2001), 67–96; also Till van Rahden, *Jews and Other Germans: Civil Society, Religious Diversity and Urban Politics in Breslau 1860–1925* (Madison: The University of Wisconsin Press, 2008).

public life; they should not own land and the migration of more Poles (from Russia and Austria-Hungary) into the Prussian/German East had to be prevented. 48,000 Poles, allegedly not Prussian citizens, were deported from Prussia between March and June 1885. The Prussian migration law of 1886 tightly limited the movement of non-Prussian Poles into Prussia. The German Ostmarkenverein, founded in 1894, hysterically attacked Poles and promoted the Germanization of the Prussian east. By 1914 it organized around 54,000 members in 400 local associations. An expropriation law was passed in 1908 and used against Polish landowners for the first time in 1912. Civil servants in Wilhelmine Germany received a special allowance (Ostmarkenzulage) for serving in the ethnically and nationally highly contested "German east" and to encourage them to pursue Germanization policies with greater fervor. After German had also been introduced as compulsory language of instruction in religious education in schools in 1906–07, a school strike of 50,000 Polish children was met with an uncompromising response by the German authorities who imprisoned many parents and withdrew parental rights from others. Children were taken into state care and separated from their families. The Prusso-German authorities in the east also routinely manipulated statistics in favor of Germany, and the 1908 Association Law only allowed German to be used in assemblies of associations, including associations of national minorities. Prussia had clearly left its multi-ethnic past and its tolerance for ethnic minorities behind and set about nationalizing its minorities. The empire nation was to destroy the worlds of plurality and cosmopolitanism which had, to a certain extent, characterized Prussian statism in the eighteenth century. In some respects the German empire nation was at its most vociferous at the margins and the peripheries, for it was here that it came in direct conflict with other national movements. This would be true for the Prussian provinces of Posen, East and West Prussia and Upper Silesia, but also for the Bohemian lands.[18]

Schleswig and Holstein had, of course, been bones of contention of the German national movement almost throughout the first half of the nineteenth century. When both duchies returned to the German Association following the Prussian–Danish war of 1864, national jubilation was great. But Germany had now acquired an ethnic minority which spoke Danish and saw themselves as Danes. Like in the east and in the west, the Imperial German authorities stressed the need for their assimilation, underlining their desire to create a homogeneous national core of the empire nation. German anti-Danish propaganda in the nineteenth century had portrayed Denmark as an autocratic and backward peasant state. Hence the Danes which had come under German sovereignty were portrayed as being in need of progressive and superior German culture. In Northern Schleswig (a region the Danes referred to as

---

[18] Rolf Petri and Michael G. Müller, *Die Nationalisierung von Grenzen: zur Konstruktion nationaler Identität in sprachlich gemischten Grenzregionen* (Marburg: Herder-Institut, 2002); Gary Cohen, *The Politics of Ethnic Survival: Germans in Prague 1861–1914* (Princeton: Princeton University Press, 1981); William Hagen, *Germans, Poles and Jews. The Nationality Conflict in the Prussian East 1772–1914* (Chicago: University of Chicago Press, 1980).

Southern Jutland), Danes formed a majority in the countryside. From the late 1870s Germanization was adopted as a strategy here. In 1888 German became the sole language of instruction in schools. Danish-speaking families whose sons refused to become recruits in the German army were threatened with expulsion. A German Association for German Schleswig was founded in order to promote the thorough Germanization of Northern Schleswig.[19]

The annexation of Alsace and Lorraine after the Franco-Prussian war was celebrated in Germany as the return of arch-German territories with a German-speaking population. The Francophone elites of Alsace, however, identified wholeheartedly with France. After the annexation, more than 130,000 people left the region and resettled in France. The reluctance of the German Reich to give the Reichsland the same federal autonomies and freedoms that other federal states of the Reich enjoyed remained a sign of the empire nation's distrust in its newly acquired territories. Germanization policies were far less rigorous here than elsewhere on the borders of the German Reich, but German was also introduced as the sole language of instruction in schools in 1873. Overall, many Alsatians and Lorrainers felt like second-class citizens and retained a marked regionalism, which was often formulated in opposition or at least with the aim of distancing themselves from the German nation and German nationalism.[20]

Although Alsatians and Lorrainers had been welcomed to the Reich in 1871 as long-lost sons, they were often treated by German administrators, officials, military officers, and others coming into daily contact with the Reichsland as a quasi-colonial people who could not be fully trusted and who certainly could not be regarded as being fully German. The abrasive, if not outright abusive treatment of Alsatians by German officials, who came overwhelmingly from the right bank of the Rhine, was legendary. The foundation of a first-class German university in Strasbourg by the German authorities was meant as an important means of demonstrating to Alsatians the superiority of German culture and to contribute to the acculturation of the colonial periphery into the German core.[21] Inversely, large parts of the regionalist movement in Alsace before 1918 were precisely about overcoming the quasi-colonial status of the Reichsland and becoming more fully integrated into the core of the German nation. The Zabern affair of 1913[22] as well as the mistrust against Alsatian soldiers in

---

[19] Uffe Østergård, "Danish-German Historiographical Overlap Concerning Schleswig and Holstein," in *Borders and Nations: Confrontations and (Re-)Conciliations*, eds. Tibor Frank and Frank Hadler (Basingstoke: Palgrave MacMillan, 2011), 200–23.

[20] Christopher Fischer, *Alsace to the Alsatians? Visions and Divisions of Alsatian Regionalism, 1870–1939* (Oxford: Berghahn, 2010).

[21] John E. Craig, *Scholarship and Nation-Building. The Universities of Strasbourg and Alsatian Society, 1870–1939* (Chicago: University of Chicago Press, 1984).

[22] A young officer had slighted the local people in the small Alsatian town of Zabern and called on recruits to use weapons against locals if challenged. He even put out a reward of 10 Goldmark for each stabbed Alsatian. When this became public, a storm of protest arose both in Alsace and the entire Reich. But locally, the commanding officer mobilized the army and arrested 30 civilians

the German army during the First World War demonstrated to what extent the core of the empire nation remained unwilling to accept Alsace and Lorraine as equal part of the core. Reich officials repeatedly emphasized that German officers in Alsace were "almost in enemy territory," thus drawing a clear line between Germany and Alsace.

Beyond this second periphery inside the nation-state there was a third periphery outside the nation-state. Central and Eastern Europe contained numerous settlements of ethnic Germans. About 24 million German speakers found themselves outside the borders of the German Reich after 1871.[23] Specific associations were founded in Imperial Germany to represent their interests, such as the Allgemeine Deutsche Schulverein, later renamed Verein für das Deutschtum im Ausland (VDA). They promoted the idea that all German speakers belonged to the German nation. Eastern Europe was widely regarded by the German empire nation as German "cultural soil" (*Kulturboden*),[24] that is, territories to which Germany had a civilizational claim.[25] Germans had an imperial duty to bring culture to these areas, which, if left to the Slav population, would sink into barbarism. Language and culture took on a determinedly imperial dimension. German colonization in Europe's east (*Ostsiedlung*) can be traced back to the middle ages and produced German linguistic islands throughout Central and Eastern Europe. The very name of Prussia was a reminder of that early colonization, as it derived from a Slav tribe, the Pruzzen, which had been vanquished by German-speaking settlers. From the middle of the nineteenth century onwards the idea of Germans as the main carriers of culture in Eastern Europe became an ideology underpinning vast plans for the Germanization of Eastern Europe.

Notions of an imperial cultural nation (Kulturnation), which was already at times infused with völkisch ideas (that were to come to the fore in and after the First World War), stood side by side with state nationalist sentiments in Imperial Germany which were focused on the Imperial German state. Undoubtedly, many citizens of Imperial Germany felt strong loyalties first and foremost to Imperial Germany (and, of course, to their territorial states which preceded unity). Many knew and cared little about the Germans in Austria-Hungary and different parts of Eastern Europe. The historian Hermann Oncken complained in 1911 that Reich Germans knew next to nothing about their Austrian fellow nationals.[26] Nevertheless, there existed a hori-

---

which were imprisoned and maltreated. The legal challenge to this action, which followed, produced no reprimand of the officers by the army hierarchy. In Alsace this left many people feeling that it was a telling sign of Germany's unwillingness fully to accept Alsatians as Germans.

[23] Wehler, *Deutsche Gesellschaftsgeschichte*, vol. 3, 951.

[24] Guntram Herb, *Under the Map of Germany: Nationalism and Propaganda, 1918–1945* (London: Routledge, 1997); also Jan Piskorski, Jörg Hackmann, and Rudolf Jaworski, eds., *Deutsche Ostforschung und polnische Westforschung im Spannungsfeld von Wissenschaft und Politik. Disziplinen im Vergleich* (Osnabrück: fibre-Verlag, 2002).

[25] On civilizational missions of empires see Jürgen Osterhammel et al., eds., *Zivilisierungsmissionen* (Konstanz: UVK-Verlagsgesellschaft, 2005).

[26] Hermann Oncken, "Deutschland und Österreich seit der Gründung des Neuen Reiches (1871–1911)," in *Historisch-politische Aufsätze*, vol. 1, ed. Hermann Oncken (Munich: Oldenbourg,

zon of vague emotional solidarity with Germandom outside of the borders of Imperial Germany. The Russification policies towards the Baltic Germans created widespread outrage in Imperial Germany. The VDA campaigned vigorously to maintain German schools in Hungary, and the writings of Paul de Lagarde can be seen as an early example of a völkisch nationalism which was to blossom after 1918.[27]

And yet the German diaspora in Eastern Europe was not an irridenta, that is, it was not oriented towards incorporation into the existing Imperial German state. German settlements in Eastern Europe perceived themselves as ethnically and culturally German, but they often were loyal citizens of the states they lived under. The Baltic Germans were a good case in point. They widely ignored the political nature of national questions in the Baltic before 1914 and let both Baltic and Russian nationalisms develop without putting a firm German nationalism that was clearly oriented towards the German nation against it.[28] In the interwar period the historian Reinhold Wittram chastised the Baltic German leadership for not developing a more state-centered völkisch consciousness oriented towards the radical Germanization of the Baltic. These strategies became popular in the Third Reich, but they were not pursued, by and large, during the long-nineteenth century. Germans in Southeastern Europe remained oriented towards Vienna and the Habsburg Empire rather than Imperial Germany in any case. By the time of the First World War the national core of the German Empire had been so strictly defined within the borders of the Kaiserreich that Austrian-German interests, let alone the interests of Germans in Eastern Europe, were by and large regarded as secondary to the interests of the Reich. While Imperial Germany celebrated the ethnic community with Austrian Germans and glorified it as eternal comradeship-in-arms (Nibelungentreue), the Habsburg Empire was allocated the tasks of keeping its Slav peripheries in the war alongside the Mittelmächte. As the treatment of the German minority in Hungary and the attitude towards the Polish question during the First World War demonstrated, the state interests of Imperial Germany clearly came before any völkisch or ethnic ideas of nation. While notions of a newborn Holy Roman Empire and Mitteleuropa contributed to a more focused concern with völkisch ambitions in the war, the geopolitical and economic interests of the Reich continued to be by far more important to Imperial German policymakers and opinion leaders between 1914 and 1918. Most Mitteleuropa enthusiasts, even before 1914, were not so much driven by pan-Germanism than by a desire to

---

1914), 122–44. For a spirited argument about the preeminence of state nationalism in Imperial Germany over völkisch nationalism throughout the period of the First World War see Jan Vermeiren, *Brothers in Arms: The Dual Alliance in World War One and German National Identity* (University College London PhD, 2009).

[27] Fritz Stern, *The Politics of Cultural Despair: a Study in the Rise of the Germanic Ideology* (Berkeley: University of California Press, 1961), 3–96 on Lagarde.

[28] Anders Henriksson, *Vassals and Citizens. The Baltic Germans in Constitutional Russia, 1905–1914* (Marburg: Herder-Institut, 2009).

formulate a strategy for the Imperial German pursuit of power politics and economic imperialism.[29]

Beyond that third periphery of Imperial Germany, there was a fourth periphery consisting of the overseas colonies. A racial discourse of insurmountable biological difference increasingly prevented the German colonialists from perceiving their colonial subjects as potential Germans. Their essential otherness meant that German Kultur would be wasted on them; there was no point in bringing them its blessings. The dehumanization of the indigenous population to a level where they could be compared with animals helps to explain the extraordinary brutality of German colonial wars in Africa, which have been described as laboratories for the National Socialist holocaust.[30] The colonies, whether in Eastern Europe or overseas, became, in Dirk van Laak's words, "laboratories of modernity" more generally, in which a range of things, from gun boats to steam ships, from the telegraph to electrical technology, and from transport networks to drainage systems, were tried out before they were adopted for and in the national core. Medical, botanical, military, and geographical experimentation joined forces with cultural proselytization and an education towards German culture, which together spanned the field of the German colonial administration in the years before the First World War. The envisioned Pax Germanica often followed an explicit British model and took its cue from the way in which colonial space and metropolitan space were bound together in a discourse of all-encompassing modernity.[31]

However, at the same time we also find a colonial discourse which seeks to make the German colonial territories outside of Germany into an integral part of the German nation. Diverse visualizations of the overseas empire in Germany around 1900 sought to appropriate the colonies through the idiom of Heimat.[32] Heavily focusing on landscape photography, these images carried a message that the colonies were some kind of *terra nulla* awaiting the German settlers who could appropriate the land for Germandom. Newspaper and journal reports, information materials from Christian missions, live exhibits of indigenous people in Imperial Germany, advertising, school textbooks, postcards, or the popular dioramas all spread this message at the core of the German nation and sought to make the colonies part and parcel of

---

[29] Vermeiren, *Brothers in Arms*.

[30] Jürgen Zimmerer and Joachim Zeller, eds., *Genocide in German South-West Africa: the Colonial War of 1904–1908 and its Aftermath* (London: Merlin Press, 2007); for a critical riposte see Stephan Malinowski and Robert Gerwarth, "Der Holocaust als 'kolonialer Genozid': europäische Kolonialgewalt und nationalsozialistischer Vernichtungskrieg," *Geschichte und Gesellschaft* 33 (2007): 439–66.

[31] Laak, *Imperiale Infrastruktur*. On visions of colonial space outside of Europe as "greater Germany," see also Horst Gründer, ed. "...*da und dort ein junges Deutschland gründen." Rassismus, Kolonien und kolonialer Gedanke vom 16. bis zum 20. Jahrhundert* (Munich: Deutscher Taschenbuch-Verlag, 1999).

[32] Jens Jäger, "Colony as Heimat? The Formation of Colonial Identity in Germany around 1900," *German History* 27, no. 4 (2009): 467–89; see also: Jens Jäger, "'Heimat' in Afrika, oder: die mediale Aneignung der Kolonien um 1900," *Zeitenblicke* 7 (January 10, 2008): URL: http://www.zeitenblicke.de/2008/2/jaeger/index_html.

everyday reality of German national life. Stollwerck chocolate, for example, explicitly used imperial images in order to increase its appeal to German but also to global consumers.[33] Expensive coffee table books about the German colonial possessions were produced as well as cheap popular editions, which sold tens of thousands of copies.[34] *Avant garde* expressionist artists, such as Emil Nolde and Ernst-Ludwig Kirchner were inspired by the "primitive" art of Africa. Walter von Ruckteschell famously painted Mount Kilimanjaro as "Germany's highest mountain." The incredibly popular novels of Karl May portrayed German heroes in colonial settings, where they could prove the superiority of Germandom. May's celebration of German virtues was also a form of nation building through empire.[35] German orientalists were not single-minded racists intent on demonstrating the inferiority of the Orient, but rather developed complex relationships to the object of their studies which could meander between admiration, adaptation and rejection.[36] Colonial imagery was extremely widespread in popular culture,[37] and by no means restricted to advertising for colonial products (Kolonialwaren) but also for everyday products such as toothpaste or washing powder.[38]

A national claim over the colonies was already visible in the very naming of them: German South-West Africa; German East-Africa, but also others were often referred to with the prefix "German," such as German-Samoa, German-New Guinea or German-Cameroon. This claim of the nation over territorial colonial space was also at times extended to include "our black compatriots" (*unsere schwarzen Landsleute*)— something that was particularly prominent in missionary discourse on the colonies.[39] Jim Retallack has argued that the language of civilizing mission and improvement was all-pervasive in German colonies such as Togo.[40] It brought German colonialism closer to its British and French counterparts, where the idea of "the white man's burden" (Rudyard Kipling) of civilizing colonial subjects and transforming them into English gentlemen and French republicans respectively played an influential role in

[33] Angelika Epple, "Das Auge schmeckt Stollwerck. Die Bildsprache einer 'Weltmarke' zwischen Imperialismus und Globalisierung," *Werkstatt Geschichte* 45 (2007): 13–32.

[34] See, for example, Kurd Schwabe, *Die deutschen Kolonien*, 2 vols. (Berlin: Carl Weller, 1910); the cheap edition of the same volume followed suit in 1912.

[35] N. Berman, "Orientalism, Imperialism and Nationalism: Karl May's Orientzyklus," in *The Imperialist Imagination: German Colonialism and its Legacy*, eds. S. Friedrichsmeyer, S. Lennox, and S. Zantop (Ann Arbor: University of Michigan Press, 1998), 51–68.

[36] Suzanne L. Marchand, *German Orientalism in the Age of Empire: Religion, Race, and Scholarship* (Cambridge: Cambridge University Press, 2009).

[37] D. Ciarlo, "Rasse konsumieren: von der exotischen zur kolonialen Imagination in der Bildreklame des wilhelminischen Kaiserreichs," in *Phantasiereiche*, ed. Kundrus, 135–79.

[38] R. A. Berman, *Enlightenment or Empire: Colonial Discourse in German Culture* (Lincoln: University of Nebraska Press, 1998); A. Honold and K. P. Scherpe, eds., *Mit Deutschland um die Welt. Eine Kulturgeschichte des Fremden in der Kolonialzeit* (Stuttgart: Metzler, 2004).

[39] Michael Schubert, *Der schwarze Fremde. Das Bild des Schwarzafrikaners in der parlamentarischen und publizistischen Kolonialdiskussion in Deutschland von den 1870er bis in die 1930er Jahre* (Stuttgart: Steiner, 2003).

[40] James Retallack, *Imperial Germany 1871–1918* (Oxford: Oxford University Press, 2008), 220.

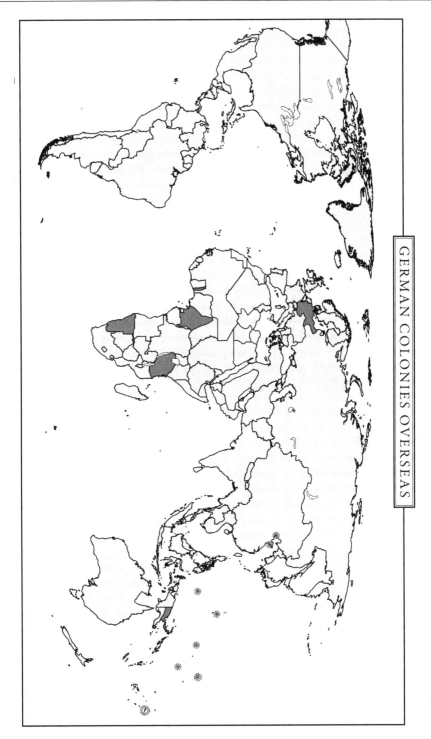

GERMAN COLONIES OVERSEAS

the colonial projects. Colonialism, whether in Eastern Europe or overseas, thus was a means of constructing the nation in and through empire.

Visions of Overseas and Contiguous Empire and the Imperial Nation

Colonial expansion brought in its wake considerable domestic conflict. Bismarck and his conservative allies had partially embarked on colonialism in order to placate the working classes and create a more unified and homogeneous nation-state.[41] They argued that the colonies would bring economic benefit to all social classes in Imperial Germany, and the idea that the Imperial German nation-state needed colonies in order to become a world power that could see eye to eye with empire nations such as Britain and France, proved remarkably popular among the liberal middle classes. Max Weber famously argued that the creation of the German nation-state would have been a folly had it not taken the inevitable second step of becoming a world power. And the Leipzig-based historian Karl Lamprecht also argued very similarly that the German people had only climbed a hill in 1871 and that the real towering tops of the mountains still lay ahead of them.[42] The only problem with this was that Germany was a latecomer to the race for colonies. A reluctant Bismarck only embarked on the acquisition of colonies in 1884. Hence colonialism produced, above all, international rivalries and tensions. It played a role in forging the pre-war alliance system, in which Imperial Germany and Austria-Hungary found themselves "encircled" by hostile powers. And domestically, their social imperialism was not too successful either, because left liberals, Catholics and socialists were highly critical of Imperial Germany's colonialism. The erosion of Bismarck's political prestige could not be halted through imperial adventures in the 1880s and the utopian horizon of a German Empire might have given many Germans a new aim and telos after the fulfillment of their national ambition, but it was as divisive and contentious as the one leading to 1871. However, if colonialism did not produce greater unity among Germans, it gave Germans a common framework for discussion and helped to define Germanness in invariably plural and contested ways. Perhaps in this more modest sense, colonialism was successful in contributing towards the making of Germans in Wilhelmine Germany.

Apologists for German colonialism in the late nineteenth century liked to postulate a continuity of a German colonial mission since 1680, when Brandenburg acquired a colony in Western Africa (today's Ghana) and founded Gross-Friedrichsburg. However, the "Brandenburg-Africanische Compagnie" was economically unsuccessful and was sold to the Dutch West Indies Company in 1717, making Brandenburg's colonialism a rather short-lived episode. This did not prevent

---

[41] Hartmut Pogge von Strandmann, "Domestic Origins of Germany's Colonial Expansion under Bismarck" *Past and Present* 42 (1969): 140–59.

[42] Wehler, *Deutsche Gesellschaftsgeschichte*, vol. 3, 1140 f.

the Imperial German state under Wilhelm II to promote the Brandenburg example as a model in its own pursuit of the acquisition of colonies. It was vigorously assisted by a variety of non-governmental civic associations, such as the German Colonial Society (founded in 1882), the Centralverein für Handelsgeographie und Förderung deutscher Interessen im Ausland (founded in 1878), and the Westdeutscher Verein für Kolonisation und Export (founded in 1881). Many of these associations focused the export interests of the German economy, promoted social imperialism, and sought to regulate migration from Germany. In many of these groups a strong völkisch thinking prevailed which also meant that they were positively inclined towards pan-Germanism. There was considerable overlap between the membership of the Colonial Association and the Pan-German League, founded in 1894. Prominent members included leading national liberal politicians such as Rudolf von Benningsen and Johannes von Miquel, as well as leading industrialists, such as Karl Ferdinand von Stumm, and intellectuals such as Gustav Schmoller and Gustav Freytag. The associations tended to be overwhelmingly middle class with a preponderance of bankers, conservative politicians, industrialists, and professors amongst its members. Colonial associations also collaborated closely with other nationalist pressure groups such as the Naval League, the Ostmarkenverein, the Allgemeiner Deutscher Sprachverein and the VDA. Imperialism proved to be very popular among students as well.

Apart from the assumed economic benefits to the nation and the desire to promote social imperialism, colonies also allowed Imperial Germany to put forward a solution to the demographic problems of the nation-state. Colonies, whether in Eastern Europe or overseas, would allow Germans to stay German rather than become Americans or be absorbed by other nationalities. The idea of a Germanic world catering for a Germanic race was used to construct greater cohesion also at the core of empire. Taking their cue from models, very largely provided by the British Empire (settlement schemes, women as saviors of national identity), they promoted the building of a "New Germany"—settler colonies for emigrating Germans, where they could retain their Germandom and would not be lost to the "national community," as was the case with the mass migration of Germans, mainly to the United States of America, during the nineteenth century.[43] The governor of German East-Africa, Eduard von Liebert, argued that the Germandom abroad was Germany's most important colony.[44] Like many other colonialists, he envisioned the colonial German as the one who would ultimately overcome the many divisions between regional and social hierarchies that threated national unity at the core of empire. Colonial settlements were frequently connected with imaginings of an ideal German nation, a laboratory of a German nation which can be seen as part and parcel of a colonial "laboratory of

---

[43] Klaus J. Friedrich Bade, *Friedrich Fabri und der Imperialismus in der Bismarckzeit: Revolution, Depression, Expansion* (Freiburg: Atlantis, 1975).
[44] Cited from Conrad, *Globalisierunseffekte*, 412.

modernity."[45] However, these ideas proved to be dreamlands. The largest German settler colony, German South-West Africa, had no more than 14,000 Europeans on the
eve of the First World War. If one compares this to the nine million German migrants
to the United States alone before 1914, it is painfully obvious that constructions of
a Germanic world were part and parcel of a never-never land of the promoters of
German colonialism.

Already in the 1880s it became clear that the idea of agricultural colonies in
South America was a chimera and that most of the colonies in Africa were unsuitable
for mass white settler communities. Such disillusionment fueled more concerted efforts at creating a German Empire in Central and Eastern Europe. Many groups in
the German Empire of 1871 were unhappy with the borders of that empire and concerned with Germans, defined by culture and ethnicity, who found themselves outside of those borders and in need of national integration. Essential parts of the core
nation, they argued, still lay outside the empire and had to be brought in. The gym-
nasts' movement, for example, remained very *grossdeutsch* in orientation throughout
the 1870s.[46] Associations, such as the General German Linguistic Association and the
Pan-German League expressed the desire of important sections of German civil society to bring Germans into the Reich.[47] Empire therefore was crucial for legitimating an
aggressive colonialism and its claims over East Central Europe.

A good example is the journal Archive for Inner Colonization, founded by
Paul Sering in 1908 and the Society for Advancement of Inner Colonization, founded
in 1912. Sering's models were the Canadian prairies and the American midwest, which
he experienced first hand. Eastern Europe was to be Germany's "frontier." Eastern
Europe could be constructed as "empty land" via the concept of culture in the same
way as some of Germany's overseas territories were constructed as terra nulla. If only
cultured people counted as inhabitants, Poles/Slavs disappeared and a highly populated area suddenly turned into "empty wilderness." Historians, scientists, officers, teachers, journalists, and civil servants supported such endeavors. The British and Russian
Empires were widely represented as models, and in particular Russia was seen as "most
comparable continental colonial power" with similar interests in Eastern Europe.
Eastern Europe and not Africa was the real vocation of German imperialism, as settlement schemes in Eastern Europe promised not only a greater Germany but also the
solution to the social question through vast projects of social engineering.[48]

---

[45] Dirk van Laak, *Ueber alles in der Welt. Deutscher Imperialismus im 19. und 20. Jahrhundert*
(Munich: Beck, 2005).

[46] Svenja Goltermann, *Körper der Nation. Habitusformierung und die Politik des Turnens 1860–*
1890 (Göttingen: Vandenhoeck & Ruprecht, 1998); Stefan Illig, *Zwischen Körperertüchtigung*
und nationaler Bewegung. Turnvereine in Bayern, 1860–1890 (Cologne: SH-Verlag, 1998).

[47] Roger Chickering, *We Men Who Feel Most German: a Cultural Study of the Pan-German League*
1886–1914 (London: Allen & Unwin, 1984).

[48] Robert L. Nelson, "The *Archive for Inner Colonization*, the German East, and World War I," in
Germans, ed. Nelson, 65–94.

The topic of Eastern Europe as Germany's frontier also emerged in innumerable colonial novels, the most famous of which was Gustay Freytag's *Soll und Haben*.[49] Its middle-class German hero Anton was the archetypal pioneer at the frontier: "I stand here now as one of the conquerors who, in the name of ... human culture, have taken control of this land from a weaker race. We and the Slavs: it is an old struggle; and with pride, we find that cultural development (Bildung), industriousness, and financial credit are on our side."

Such emphasis on the spread and protection of Germandom went hand in hand with attempts to raise the race consciousness of Germans both in the colonies and "at home." In particular the women's association of the Colonial Society tirelessly campaigned against the mixing of races in the colonies and promoted the settler women as the savior of Germandom overseas, which, without her, would be overwhelmed by indigenous colonial cultures and the male German colonialists' tendency to "go native." Women's organizations thus promoted women's issues and thereby helped to feminize the nation within the discourse of racism and imperialism. If women were indeed crucial in allowing Germandom to survive and prosper in the colonies, imperialism became a strong argument in favor of women's rights. As Lora Wildenthal has shown, the values of racial purity and domesticity were closely intertwined, as the gendering of both the colonized and the colonizer developed.[50] The indigenous population was routinely described as the negative other of Germandom, that is, unmanly (for men), undomestic (for women), and generally, lazy, dirty, untrustworthy, brutal, and stupid.[51] This othering and the simultaneous discursive construction of Germandom was an important act of self-assurance of a nation still in search of regional integration and unsure of itself and its inner unity. The great fear that the German colonialist could go native and abandon his Germandom was exacerbated by such comparative insecurity about national identity. It reflected the growing importance of ethnic nationalism in the Kaiserreich, where the discourse of colonialism was invariably bound up with an organicist concern about preserving and developing the "people's body" (*Volkskörper*).

---

[49] Kristin Kopp, "Reinventing Poland as German Colonial Territory in the Nineteenth Century: Gustav Freytag's *Soll und Haben* as Colonial Novel," in *Germans*, ed. Nelson, 11–38, quote on 11.

[50] Lora Wildenthal, *German Women for Empire, 1884–1945* (Durham: Duke University Press, 2001); see also Birthe Kundrus, "Weiblicher Kulturimperialismus. Die imperialistischen Frauenverbände des Kaiserreichs," in *Kaiserreich transnational*, eds. Conrad and Osterhammel, 213–35, and Katharina Walgenbach, *"Die weiße Frau als Trägerin deutscher Kultur." Koloniale Diskurse über Geschlecht, "Rasse" und Klasse im Kaiserreich* (Frankfurt: Campus-Verlag, 2005), as well as Marianne Bechhaus-Gerst, Mechthild Leutner, and Hauke Neddermann, eds., *Frauen in den deutschen Kolonien* (Berlin: Links, 2009).

[51] Reimer Gronemeyer, ed., *Der faule Neger. Vom weissen Kreuzzug gegen den schwarzen Müssiggang* (Reinbek: Rowohlt, 1991); on the gendering of the racial discourse in Germany, see also Sandra Maß, *Weisse Helden, schwarze Krieger: zur Geschichte kolonialer Männlichkeit in Deutschland, 1918–1964* (Cologne: Böhlau, 2006).

At the same time as the colonialist discourse spread, colonial exoticism surrounded Germans in the Reich: in literature, film, the arts and sciences, advertisements, city planning, law and associationalism, images of the colonies and the colonial subjects abounded.[52] Arguably these images contributed to the self-perception of people from very different parts of the Reich as Germans—in contrast to the colonial subjects. Intriguingly, the only German settler colony of any significance, German South-West Africa, made great efforts to use German names for areas, towns, and regions in order to lay claim to territory in the name of Germandom. It self-consciously replicated the federal structure of the Reich underlining to what extent the territorial states in Germany were in the process of becoming building blocks of the nation-state. Hence there were suggestions to rename whole regions in German South-West Africa as "New Bavaria," "New Baden," "New Saxony," etc., in order to signal to Germans from the different regions that they could rebuild in the colonies not only "New Germany" but also their specific Heimats within Germany. The regionalist discourse within the Reich was thus replicated in the colonies.[53]

Some prominent colonialists, however, deplored the strong regionalism in the German Empire and sought to overcome it through colonialism. Take, for example, Carl Peters, the notorious German colonialist adventurer, a kind of German Cecil Rhodes, whose admiration for the British Empire was only kept in check by his ardent nationalism. In his most successful publication entitled "England and the English" (*England und die Engländer*, published in 1904, it ran through six editions and sold more than 20,000 copies), Peters depicted England as the model empire nation and at the same time advocated a continental European power block, led by Germany, which would be strong enough to compete with and stand up to the British Empire and the Anglo-Saxon power block. The future, he argued, belonged to large-scale empires, and Germany only had the choice to become one or sink into mediocrity.[54] Peters advocated colonialism as the key to future German greatness, but he also saw its importance for regional integration and inner nation building: "We have tribal characteristics, Swabian, lower German, upper Bavarian folk cultures, but we do not yet possess a German national character." Peters advocated militarism and Prussianism as the basis for the German national character of the future, which, he insisted, had to be forged and developed through colonialism.[55]

[52] Alexander Honold and Oliver Simons, eds., *Kolonialismus als Kultur. Literatur, Medien, Wissenschaft in der deutschen Gründerzeit des Fremden* (Tübingen: Francke, 2002).
[53] Krista O'Donnell, Renate Bridenthal, and Nancy Reagin, eds., *The Heimat Abroad: The Boundaries of Germanness* (Ann Arbor: University of Michigan Press, 2005); Kundrus, *Moderne Imperialisten*, especially 176–88, 281–94.
[54] Arne Perras, *Carl Peters and German Imperialism 1856–1918. A Political Biography* (Oxford: Clarendon Press, 2004), 234–36.
[55] Carl Peters, "Das Deutschtum als Rasse" [1905] in *Gesammelte Schriften*, vol. 3, ed. Walter Frank (Munich: Beck, 1943), 355–65, quote on 356.

Both the ambitions and the limitations of the uses of empire for regional integration and inner nation building among the first periphery were visible in the national
elections of January 25, 1907, quickly dubbed the Hottentotten elections.[56] The national liberal and conservative parties, with support from industry and nationalist pressure
groups, heavily campaigned on a nationalist ticket defending the German war against
the Herero in German South-West Africa and alleging that the Catholic Center Party
and, even more so, the Social Democratic Party were unreliable when it came to national issues. While the result (the number of SPD deputies went down from 81 to 43)
was a confirmation that imperial nationalism was a vote winner in Imperial Germany, it
also demonstrated just how far away the imperial nation still was from achieving inner
unity—the Catholic and even more so, the socialist milieu remained far removed from
identifying wholeheartedly with Imperial Germany and its colonialist projects. In addition many left liberals argued that imperialism was threatening free trade and harming
rather than benefiting the German economy. The Social Democrats also belonged to
the most consistent opponents of Germanization policies in Eastern Prussia. Taking up
the mantle of the left in 1848, they argued that Germanization policies were incompatible with the rule of law and the rights of national/ethnic minorities. And yet, despite
this domestic opposition, the struggle against the ethnic minorities inside the Reich,
the idea of German "cultural soil" stretching deep into Central and Eastern Europe,
the construction of ethnic others, in particular Slavs, and the colonialist imagination
were all remarkably capable of bringing the different regions of the German Reich together as Germans. There can be little doubt that issues of colonialism, empire and na-
tion-buidling were strongly interrelated.[57]

Continuities of Empire before the Nineteenth Century

At this stage of the argument, it is vitally important to say a few words about the
German imperial nation before the long nineteenth century, as there exist some long-
term continuities in the construction of the "mental maps" of the German imperial
nation. During the later middle ages and throughout much of the early modern period, the idea of Germany and of German national consciousness was rooted in ideas of
a German language, a wider German culture, a specific German legal tradition, and the
notion of an empire, the *Reich*. Of course, the proto-nationalist discourse of Medieval
and early modern Europe was in some respects fundamentally different from the modern nationalist discourse in terms of its definition of the nation (bounded territories,
citizenship within bounded territories etc.), and yet many of the tropes of modern

[56] Ulrich van der Heyden, "Kolonialkrieg und deutsche Innenpolitik—die Reichstagswahlen von
1907," in http://www.freiburg-postkolonial.de/Seiten/Heyden-Reichstagswahlen1907.htm.
[September 19, 2014]

[57] Michael Perraudin and Jürgen Zimmerer, eds., *German Colonialism and National Identity*
(London: Routledge, 2010) provides many intriguing examples of this strong interconnection.

national identity construction are rooted deeply in the past. Historians have traced explications of the idea of the German Reich to the fifteenth century. The earliest mention of the Holy Roman Empire *of the German Nation* [my emphasis] can be found around 1409. Humanist scholars, such as Jakob Wimpfeling, Konrad Celtis, Heinrich Bebel, and Johannes Cochlaeus, were crucial in linking ideas of German nationhood with pride in empire. In fact, Wimpfeling in particular, was to combine regionalist, sub-national, and empire transnational discourses in order to frame powerful arguments relating to the character of the German nation. Hence he stressed his commitment to the city of Schlettstadt, the region of Alsace and the Holy Roman Empire of the German Nation as three interlocking parts of his patriotism.

The "laudes Germanica" were a specific genre of historical writing in German humanism that was meant to fill contemporary Germans with pride and make them want to emulate the ancient German tribes. Praise for Germanic virtues invariably took place within the framework of empire. The most clear-cut example of such nationalist-imperialist-humanist history was Wimpfeling's *Epitome Germanorum* of 1505. In fact the whole idea of the Four Empires, which we find with Wimpfeling, but also with Schedel, Nauclerus, and a whole host of other humanist writers, was instrumentalized for national purposes, as the Holy Roman Empire of the German Nation was portrayed as the last successor of the Roman Empire charged with fulfilling its mission. Thus the theory of the Four Empires, initially part of a Christian-providentialist historical thinking, was secularized into an imperialist-nationalist-providential concept.[58]

The humanists emphasized that the emperor had to be German for meritocratic and historical reasons. Charlemagne, they argued, had been German and as he was the worthy successor of the Roman emperors, he also transposed the mission of those emperors to the Germans. Because the Germans were portrayed by the humanists as a warrior people *par excellence*, they were also seen as predestined for empire building and for becoming a world power. The Germans had to be at the core of empire, not just because they were superior warriors, but also because they were superior Christians. It was ultimately only to strengthen and promote the Christian religion that Germans undertook the mission to reforge the empire. Unsurprisingly therefore, the Germans were also portrayed as the nation with the greatest number of saints. And finally, Germans were also of superior nobility to all other nobles in Europe which marked them out additionally as rightful empire builders. The German soil contained resources richer than anywhere else, the German air was so healthy that it made Germans grow older than any other people. The humanist discourse on empire and nation therefore already constructed national cores and imperial peripheries, which in turn helped to put the national core into sharper relief.

---

[58] Caspar David Hirschi, *Wettkampf der Nationen. Konstruktionen einer deutschen Ehrgemeinschaft an der Wende vom Mittelalter zur Neuzeit* (Göttingen: Wallstein-Verlag, 2005); see also Ulrich Muhlack, *Geschichtswissenschaft im Humanismus und in der Aufklärung. Die Vorgeschichte des Humanismus* (Munich: Beck, 1991).

According to Georg Schmidt, the first German proto-state was an imperial nation. It went back to the reforms of Maximilian I between 1495 and 1500.[59] Maximilian, of course, was a Habsburg, and throughout much of the late Medieval and early modern period, ideas of the German nation were associated with the Habsburgs much more than with Prussia. From the fifteenth to the eighteenth centuries, it was the Habsburgs rather than the Hohenzollerns who sought to nationalize the core of the empire. The Emperor Maximilian I used this humanist national discourse to bring the different parts of his empire closer together during the last decades of the fifteenth century. Humanist national histories helped him to portray himself as *pater patriae* and defender of German liberties against foreign threats.

It was the Prussian annexation of Silesia in the 1740s that formed the basis for its rise to great power status in the eighteenth century. But within the old empire, the territorial powers retained their wide-reaching sovereignty, as guaranteed by the Golden Bull of 1356, even if central Reich institutions, such as the Law Court (Reichskammergericht) in Wetzlar, the parliament (Reichstag) in Regensburg and the emperor himself, defined the core of the empire to which very different regions and territories could and did subscribe. After all, the unprecedented legal culture and the imperial system of law guaranteed relative peace for the regions belonging to the empire over the centuries, although the system did occasionally break down, e.g. during the Thirty Years' War (1618–48) and the Seven Years' War (1756–63).

The confessional division of the empire at the time of the Reformation brought calls for the emperor to serve as a mediating institution, but this was not successful. In fact, the popularization of the humanist discourse of the imperial nation by Martin Luther and Ulrich von Hutten ensured the close links between ideas of the German nation and Protestantism. The national discourse became a weapon against the universalism of the Catholic Church and a Catholic emperor (e.g. the explicitly universal conception of empire developed by the imperial chancellor Gattinara under Charles V). The nation, in Protestant national discourse, found itself in the Reformation. Protestant humanist proto-nationalists were quick to distance themselves from notions of *sacerdotium* and *imperium*. Martin Luther was to become the nation's foremost national hero. The Reformation was thus of crucial importance in weakening the link between nation and empire. In the early modern *Reich*, the idea of the expansion of the state in the name of an empire nation was not entirely absent, but it was never prominent and had no material consequences.[60]

---

[59] Georg Schmidt, *Geschichte des alten Reiches. Staat und Nation in der Frühen Neuzeit, 1495–1806* (Munich: Beck, 1999).

[60] For the Protestant bias of national tropes and patriotic rhetoric see also Alexander Schmidt, *Vaterlandsliebe und Religionskonflikt. Politische Diskurse im Alten Reich (1555–1648)* (Leiden: Brill, 2007). More generally see Heinz Schilling. "Nationale Identität und Konfession in der europäischen Neuzeit," in *Nationale und kulturelle Identität: Studien zur Entwicklung des kollektiven Bewusstseins in der Neuzeit*, ed. Bernhard Giesen (Frankfurt: Suhrkamp, 1991), 192–252.

By the time of the Seven Years' War, we encounter two competing ideas of nation within the empire: on the one hand, the idea of a Prussian nation, which found its "other" in the Catholic Habsburg Empire, and, on the other hand, the idea of a reformed empire, where federalism merged with German patriotism. One of the most prominent propagators of this Reich patriotism (Reichspatriotismus), Friedrich Carl von Poser, argued that only the empire nation could guarantee the rule of law, security, and liberty. The diversity of the empire nation's regions and territories was one of its greatest strengths. Poser and other Reich patriots denounced the centralization of the French and English nation-states which was allegedly out of line with "German freedoms." However, Reich patriotism remained a diffuse movement full of internal contradictions. It undoubtedly had its moments during humanism in the fifteenth century, between 1683 and 1740, and again towards the end of the eighteenth century. Especially in the context of the revolutionary wars with France, Reich patriots, such as the legal scholars at the universities in Halle and Göttingen, held high the idea of the unique legal culture of the Reich and its constitution.[61]

And yet the German variant of a Whig national master narrative that focused on ideas of German liberty and constitutional development did not become powerful in the late eighteenth century or thereafter. Nevertheless, the Reich could mobilize positive sentiment, which also explains why there was, across the German lands (and in particular in the non-Prussian areas), a genuine sense of loss and sadness when Napoleon dissolved the Holy Roman Empire of the German Nation in 1806. The memory of the Reich managed to live on, which was also the reason why the language of empire could be mobilized with such ease after 1871.

Multiple State-Building Projects and the Idea of a German Nation Before 1866

Before the emergence of the imperial nation-state in 1871, the larger territorial states inside the German Confederation (Deutscher Bund) sought to develop their own state-building measures between 1815 and 1866. The German Confederation continued the tradition of a strong federalism in the German lands. It had few central institutions, such as the Confederal Diet in Frankfurt, and its presidency was taken on by Austria. In most areas real power lay with the federal territorial states. Many of them had acquired new territories in the territorial settlement of the Vienna Congress and therefore they were keen to ensure the rapid integration of these territories into their states. They strengthened their state administrations in order to increase the reach of the state into the most distant corners of their territories. They developed communication systems, in particular the railway network, in order to ensure the shrinking of space inside their territories. Some of them even sought to combine state building with

---

[61] Jörg Echternkamp, *Der Aufstieg des deutschen Nationalismus (1770–1840)* (Frankfurt: Campus-Verlag, 1998), 83–89.

nation building. It has often been observed that the 1848 revolution was too many revolutions in one: a liberal, a social, and a national revolution. But it was the national aspect, the desire to create one united German fatherland, which threatened the territorial states and in turn prompted them to reinforce their own attempts to construct "small fatherlands."[62]

The Bavarian king Maximilian II and his successors went furthest in pursuing the project of a Bavarian monarchical nation-state.[63] They sought systematically to construct Bavarian national consciousness through political celebrations, customs, heritage, dress, language, monuments, science, educational policy, history, and popular festivals such as the Oktoberfest, which became the Bavarian national festival *par excellence*. The 700 year anniversary of Munich in 1858 and the wedding anniversaries and birthdays of the royal couple were events in which the Bavarian nation celebrated the unity between the dynasty and the people. A Bavarian national theatre was founded, in which patriotic Bavarian theatre plays were staged. In particular civil servants and priests were educated to become muliplicators of the Bavarian national consciousness.

Several of the larger territorial states had the potential of developing into fully fledged nation-states. In the 1850s and 1860s many of the territorial states consciously generated a good deal of patriotic sentiment using the language of "patriotism," "fatherland," "tribe" (Stamm) and even "nation." At the heart of the attempt to construct "small fatherlands" lay the popular marketing of the ruling dynasty, an emphasis on the cultural achievements, the constitutional liberties and the material well-being of the subjects of the territorial state. Yet it was one of the peculiar characteristics of the nation-state building at federal level that it could go hand in hand with the discursive construction of Germandom. While the monarchs of the big territorial states were busy building up small nations, there was a gray zone where the territorial states were willing to sponsor and foster a sense of wider German national consciousness, which was cultural and not directed toward state-building. Hence, for example, the willingness of King Maximilian II to sponsor, in 1858, a historical commission at the Bavarian Academy of Sciences that pursued not just Bavarian but explicitly German national aims. The commission became a major stalwart in publishing sources, documents, and monographs on German national history. And in his inaugural speech at the official opening of the commission, the Prussian historian Wilhelm von Giesebrecht made it clear that it was to foster knowledge about the whole of German history.[64] While this

---

[62] Green, *Fatherlands*.

[63] Manfred Hanisch, *"Für Fürst und Vaterland." Legitimitätsstiftung in Bayern zwischen Revolution 1848 und Deutscher Einheit* (Munich: Oldenbourg, 1991); Regina Bendix, "Moral Integrity in Costumed Identity: Negotiating 'National Costume' in Nineteenth-Century Bavaria," *The Journal of American Folklore* 111, no. 440 (1998): 133–45.

[64] Christoph Freiherr von Maltzahn, "Außeruniversitäre Organisationsformen in der deutschen Geschichtswissenschaft im 19. und 20. Jahrhundert," in *Formen außerstaatlicher Wissenschaftsförderung im 19. und 20. Jahrhundert: Deutschland im europäischen Vergleich*, ed. Rüdiger vom Bruch (Stuttgart: Steiner, 1990), 185–210, here 189 ff.

directly clashed with Maximilian's attempts to foster a Bavarian national consciousness, it was typical of the volatile and ambiguous relationship between the different
national discourses in the German lands: an all-German cultural national discourse
(which came in a grossdeutsch and kleindeutsch variant) often stood side by side with
a state-centered national discourse focused on the individual territorial states within
the German Confederation.

However, the tensions between a Prussianized concept of the nation and
the German territorial states, especially in southern Germany, led to the widespread
rejection of Prussianism in Germany's south, which was only gradually overcome in
Imperial Germany. In the 1860s, in the southwest of Germany, Heimat celebrations
adopted a strong anti-Prussian and anti-centralist tone and remained skeptical of the
Prussianized nation-state after 1871. The erections of monuments to Bismarck and
Wilhelm I, for example, were far less popular in southern Germany than in Prussia.
Similarly, "the Germans remained interested in local not national history."[65] Most
German territorial states sponsored historical associations, which promoted the study
of patriotic history of the territorial states, the collection of patriotic antiquities,
and the publication of historical source material. The Württemberg Association for
Fatherland Studies gave out guidelines for patriotic history in 1822, which explicitly promoted the historic symbiosis of dynasty and people.[66] Senior state officials and
establishment figures heavily dominated the membership in the historical societies and many of them enjoyed monarchical patronage. When, in 1852, the General
Association of German Historical and Antiquarian Societies, was founded as an
umbrella organization of the many historical associations, it only "paid lip-service to
German nationalism, but in essence it was very much in keeping with the particularist
bias of existing historical societies."[67] Furthermore, the Heimat discourse of the first
two thirds of the nineteenth century emphatically included the German-speaking
parts of the Habsburg Empire. Hence the commitment of the Germans to ideas of
Heimat in the nineteenth century did not necessarily foreshadow the formation of
the German Empire in 1871.

As the kleindeutsch national movement gathered strength in the 1860s, the
"small fatherlands" doubled their efforts to focus patriotic sentiments on the territorial state and leave commitment to a German nation rather vague. In 1860, the Württemberger Staats-Anzeiger, for example, argued that the division of Germany into territorial states might well have been responsible for preventing the rise of a powerful
Germany, but it most certainly was the source of an unparalleled cultural richness and
superiority of the German lands over all other nations of Europe.[68] It was the fusion
of the language of empire with the language of the "small fatherlands" through the
Heimat discourse which allowed the successful regional integration of diverse parts

---

[65] Green, *Fatherlands*, 103.
[66] Ibid., 278 f.
[67] Ibid., 109.
[68] Ibid., 281.

of Germany, as Heimat increasingly became a spectacle to be consumed by increasing number of national tourists. Tourist guides in Imperial Germany became important places for the reflection and self-reflection of national identity.[69]

Heimat Discourses, Monument Politics, and Germanization Policies in the Imperial Nation

Several scholars, above all Celia Applegate and Alon Confino, have established beyond reasonable doubt, how closely linked German national consciousness was with the construction of a sense of Heimat.[70] The Heimat idea successfully mediated between the everyday experience of the local and the more abstract notion of national belonging. 400 Heimat museums were founded between 1871 and 1918. Innumerable Heimat books were being published. Heimat associations were legion and Heimat studies became part of the primary school curriculum. But Heimat cannot be equated with regionalism. In the context of patriotism promoted by the "small fatherlands," Heimat also mediated between these "small fatherlands" and the larger Germany that emerged in 1871. Thus Heimat, together with empire, ultimately allowed the fusion of the "small fatherlands" into the larger Germany as it decentralized German national discourse and avoided the need to define a firm and fixed core of the nation. It was thus able to overcome, or rather sideline, anti-Prussian sentiments outside of Prussia and thereby facilitate a Prussian-dominated empire in which its peripheries did not necessarily feel marginalized. At the same time, empire also appropriated the language of cultural superiority (in Heimat discourse a direct result of the diversity of the many fatherlands) in order to justify further expansion in Eastern Europe and overseas.

The hagiographers of the Prussian state and the Hohenzollern dynasty were adamant that it was Prussia which, through its military prowess, had created Germany. As the popular biographer of several Hohenzollern monarchs, Bernhard von Kugler, put it in 1893: "Before the glorious war of 1870–71 there existed Prussians, Saxons, Bavarians, Mecklenburgers etc. There were dozens of tribes [Landsmannschaften], who spoke German, but Germans as such did not exist."[71] The "iron chancellor" of German unity, Otto von Bismarck, understood the territorial states as nations: "The special nationalities, which have formed in our midst on the basis of dynastic family property, understand themselves mostly as heterogeneous. Their togetherness is not linked to their belonging to the same tribe or their sharing of a common historical development,

---

[69] Rudy Koshar, *German Travel Cultures* (Oxford: Berg, 2000).

[70] Celia Applegate, *A Nation of Provincials: the German Idea of Heimat* (Berkeley: University of California Press, 1990); Alon Confino, *The Nation as Local Metaphor. Württemberg, Imperial Germany and National Memory 1871–1918* (Chapel Hill: University of North Carolina Press, 1997).

[71] Bernhard von Kugler, *Deuschlands grösster Held!* (Dresden: Vaterländischer Buchverlag, 1893), from the unpaginated preface.

but exclusively to the territories having been acquired by particular dynasties in circumstances, which, in many cases, are rather questionable."[72] Reducing the "small fatherlands" to artificial dynastic constructions was one way of nudging them toward a common perception as Germans who assembled under a single and shared roof of empire. The cult around empire and the emperor served the purpose of finding commonalities between and above the "small fatherlands." This was in large measure directed also against Bismarck's previous allies, the Prussian conservatives, who retained a strong sense of a national-dynastic identity as Prussians and were skeptical of the new German Empire. They shared their skepticism with those who remained loyal to their small fatherlands in the non-Prussian territorial states. The story of the German Empire after 1871 is to a large extent the story of eroding such skepticism and forging an imperial nation.

One way of doing this was through a politics of national monuments.[73] Take the example of the Walhalla, erected on the orders of King Ludwig I of Bavaria just outside Regensburg between 1830 and 1842. His chief architect, Leo von Klenze, built a classicist Greek temple that was decorated by figures representing the German states on its southside eaves, while it displayed on its northern side scenes from the battle of the Teutoburg Forest. The historian Johannes Müller advised the king on the selection of fitting heroes who would find a place inside this hall of national fame. The ultimate principle of selection was language, which meant that Swiss and Dutch heroes found themselves alongside Germans. Thus the Walhalla was effectively designed along imperial lines.

Apart from the Walhalla, the Kyffhäuser memorial, built between 1892 and 1896, linked the new German Empire, represented by its Emperor Wilhelm I, nicknamed Barbablanca, directly to the idea of the Medieval Reich, by depicting, just below Wilhelm, the Medieval emperor Frederick I, nicknamed Barbarossa, who had expanded the borders of the Reich far to the south and who was, according to national myth, awaiting the return of Germany to national greatness inside the Kyffhäuser mountain. The symbolism of the monument carefully merged ancient, Medieval, and contemporary German history to demonstrate the inner continuity of the German empire nation.[74]

Hamburg, one of the gateways of Imperial Germany to the world, was marked by a distinctive imperial iconography in its late nineteenth and early twentieth century monument politics that carefully mediated between region, nation, and empire.[75]

---

[72] Otto Fürst von Bismarck, *Gedanken und Erinnerungen* (Berlin: Cotta, 1920), vol. 1, 321.

[73] George Mosse, *The Nationalization of the Masses: Political Symbolism and Mass Movements in Germany from the Napoleonic Wars through the Third Reich* (New York: Howard Fertig, 1975), 53 ff.

[74] Monika Arndt, "Das Kyffhäuser Denkmal—ein Beitrag zur politischen Ikonographie des Zweiten Kaiserreiches," *Wallraff-Richartz Jahrbuch* 40 (1978) 75–122.

[75] Mark A. Russell, "The Building of Hamburg's Bismarck Memorial, 1898–1906," *Historical Journal* 43 (2000): 133–56. On the importance of monuments to nation-building in Imperial Germany compare also Reinhard Alings, *Monument und Nation. Das Bild vom Nationalstaat im Medium Denkmal—zum Verhältnis von Nation und Staat im deutschen Kaiserreich* (Berlin: de Gruyter, 1996).

The 15 meter high, giant Bismarck statue, complete with armor and sword, overlooking the harbor in Hamburg, is a good example. Facing the global mission of empire, having forged the nation, the heraldic figures at the bottom of the monument represent the agreement of the diverse German tribes to Bismarck's work. Völkisch monuments, above all the Monument to the Battle of Nations (*Völkerschlachtdenkmal*) in Leipzig, inaugurated in 1913, represented Germany's military mission in the creation of empire and at the same time underlined the message that the empire nation could only be forged through war. The *völkisch* propagandist Julius Langbehn spoke of the "fine barbarism" of a Germanic artistic style revealed in the monument. It was a 91 meter high pyramidical structure—the biggest memorial in Europe at the time. Its symbolical language emphasized the sacrifice, courage, manliness and strength of a German warrior people. The nation had become one, the monument alleged, through sacrifice in war. The people (*Volk*) had been consecrated through war. Not only architecture and monuments, but also songs and poems illustrated the close association between empire and nation in the nineteenth century. Hoffmann von Fallersleben's "Deutschlandlied" and Arndt's poetry are good examples, as they illustrate the imperial dimensions of the national movement.

Nowhere were such imperial dimensions more visceral than in those regions of the German Association which were ethnically mixed. In Bohemia, for example, or the Prussian areas of divided Poland, national movements arose which challenged the dominance of the German discourse of empire nation and in turn heightened German imperial-national consciousness. In these regions we see an increasingly vociferous contestation between opposed national discourses over nationally defined territory. When dynasty had still been the anchor point of Prussian national consciousness, ethnic and linguistic differences did not matter so much, but when language and ethnicity became the anchor points of national identity, the existence of linguistic/ethnic minorities was seen as major stumbling block on the road to nationalizing the empire. However, one should be careful not to idealize the dynastic attitude to ethnic difference. After all, following the division of Poland, Frederick the Great had already been in favor of Prussianizing the Polish gentry. If he did little to Prussianize ordinary Poles, it was because he was convinced that gradual mixing would ultimately make Poles Prussians. He was less sanguine about the Jewish population, much of which he wanted to expel (with the notable exception of rich Jews). While Prussian dynasticism under Frederick can therefore hardly be described as tolerant, it remains true that in so far as these ethnically mixed areas became part of the German Empire after 1871, the empire nation strove for national homogeneity inside the core of the nation and embarked on ever more radical nationalization policies.

In the Polish-speaking parts of Eastern Prussia, for example, the circles of Prussian civil servants, of Protestant clergy, and of the German-speaking bourgeoisie engaged in commerce and trade served in effect as an imperial elite engaged on an imperial mission to Germanize these territories, i.e to spread the German language, Protestantism, and German *Kultur*. The land wars in Eastern Prussia were the clearest sign of the increasingly desperate attempts of the German Empire to prevent what it perceived as the "Slav flood" to enfold Germany. The 1908 Expropriation Law which planned to expropriate 70,000 hectares of land in Polish hands and turn it into land for German settlers, provoked a storm of international protests. The land wars were not the only facet of nationalization policies in Eastern Prussia. Wilhelmine Germany also sought to Germanize the Polish church and get rid of the Polish language altogether. Ultimately, the Imperial German government (unlike the National Socialist government) shied away from policies of ethnic cleansing or genocide, and it also did not commit enough resources to break the strong resistance from the Polish-speaking population who boycotted the German agency attempting to buy up land for German settlers. By 1914, Imperial Germany had spent one billion marks to transfer Polish lands into German hands, but Poles, through various counter-schemes, had in fact increased their landholding in Prussia. In addition there was no sign of the deterioration of the Polish language either. Nor did Poles slacken in their enthusiasm for their church. However, the Imperial German state succeeded in raising the nationality conflict in Eastern Prussia to fever-pitch.[76]

The Germanization policies vis-à-vis the Slavs did not only affect the Poles but also small minorities such as Kashubians, Masurians, and Sorbs. They were not fully developed nationalities and they did not possess a strong national consciousness. They found themselves crushed between the major nationality conflict of Poles and Germans in the last half of the nineteenth and the first half of the twentieth century. Take the example of the Masurians, located between Ermland in the west and northwest and Masowia/Podlachia in the south and southeast. In this southern part of eastern Prussia, most famous for its lakes, people tended to think of themselves mainly as belonging to a particular locality rather than to a specific nation. The Polish language and the Protestant religion were important reference points for their identity as was loyalty to the ruling Prussian dynasty of the Hohenzollern. Within the multi-ethnic Prussian state, these self-declared "Polish Prussians" often were seen as mediators between German and Slav culture across the Prussian border with Russian Poland. Yet within the framework of the German empire nation, any expression of sympathy for Poland became "national treason." Hence Masurians' Polishness needed to be extinguished and they had to become fully German. Masurian place names and family names were changed in order to make them sound more German. German-speaking Protestant pastors often saw themselves as ramparts of German culture amongst the hybrid Masurians. There were some attempts amongst Masurians to maintain their hybrid identity and resist encroachments on the use of the Polish language, yet these attempts were quickly assimilated into the Polish national response against Germanization. Without a self-confident urban elite, universities, or other civic associations that could have developed strategies of resistance, pre-national non-dominant

---

[76] Hagen, *Germans, Poles and Jews*; Scott M. Eddie, *Landownership in Eastern Europe Before the Great War* (Oxford: Oxford University Press, 2008).

ethnic groups, such as the Masurians, vanished from the European map in the first half of the twentieth century, crushed between the rival claims on their loyalty by the German empire nation and its Polish rival.[77]

The national minorities were not the only groups treated as colonial subjects and national Others. Jews were also prominently constructed as a powerful force undermining Germandom in Imperial Germany. The tragedy of German Jewry was that most German Jews wanted to be part and parcel of the nationalizing core of empire. However, the eminent historian Heinrich von Treitschke reminded them in 1879 that they, in his view, were Germany's "misfortune." Culturally and ethnically, they could not be integrated into the German nation. Treitschke's comments started a major public debate, which saw mainly Jewish authors (with some prominent exceptions, such as Theodor Mommsen, who was immediately ridiculed by the anti-Semites as Mommsohn) defend the Jews against the charge that they lacked national sentiment.[78] The fears of many Germans that their country might be swamped with "Eastern Jews" (Ostjuden)—religiously Orthodox, uneducated and "un-German"—made many susceptible to Treitschke's arguments. In the German press, anti-Semitism was often combined with anti-Chinese rhetoric and images, thus showing the importance of a global colonial imagination for the construction of the nation's Others. It has frequently been pointed out that the political parties promoting anti-Semitism in the Kaiserreich remained a marginal phenomenon, winning only about 2 per cent of the popular vote in national elections. This also made the Jewish defense organizations, such as the Central Union of German Citizens of Jewish Faith (Centralverein deutscher Staatsbürger jüdischen Glaubens), confident that German anti-Semitism was on the wane. They were, however, all-too painfully aware that anti-Semitism remained socially acceptable in wide circles of Imperial German society. Conservative newspapers, such as the *Kreuzzeitung* regularly deplored the alleged economic dominance of Jews in Germany. The powerful agrarian pressure group Bund der Landwirte (BdL) was very anti-Semitic and the Catholic milieu was still dominated by traditional anti-Judaism. In the Prussian legal profession, Jews were hardly ever appointed judges and there were no Jewish officers in the regular Prussian army and only a handful reserve officers, despite the fact that there would have been no shortage of candidates.[79]

---

[77] On the Masurians see, in particular, Richard Blanke, *Polish-Speaking Germans? Language and National Identity among the Masurians since 1871* (Cologne: Böhlau, 2001); Andreas Kossert, *Preussen, Deutsche oder Polen? Die Masuren im Spannungsfeld des ethnischen Nationalismus, 1870–1956* (Wiesbaden: Harrassowitz, 2001).

[78] Christhard Hoffmann, "Geschichte und Ideologie: Der Berliner Antisemitismusstreit 1879/81," in *Vorurteil und Völkermord. Entwicklungslinien des Antisemitismus*, eds. Wolfgang Benz and Werner Bergmann (Freiburg: Herder, 1997), 219–51.

[79] Amos Elon, *The Pity of it All: a History of Jews in Germany 1743–1933* (Harmondsworth: Penguin, 2002).

Racializing the Imperial Nation

As we have seen above, Africans and Asians could not be turned into Germans easily, as the racial prejudices were far higher than with other Europeans. The imperial nation restricted the movement of its colonial subjects to the metropole for fear of any racial mixing, and it did not allow any naturalization of colonial subjects. The racialization of the citizenship law in Imperial Germany found expression in a clear-cut segregation of whites and non-whites that was even prepared to overrule paternalist principles in law. So, for example, children of mixed marriages were not German, even if their father was German, and mixed marriages could easily be annulled. Despite protests of German family fathers, who wanted their black children to receive German citizenship and despite a rather uneasy practice of the law vis-à-vis the naturalization of children from mixed marriages, the principle was established that "blood" beats paternity.[80] The construction and definition of a German citizenship in 1913 owed a great deal to the experience and concept of empire, as it sought to codify an ethnic principle of descent expressing a *völkisch* imperialist ideology which wanted to do both, preserve the purity of Germandom inside the Reich and preserve Germandom outside the borders of the German Reich, especially in Eastern Europe and the overseas colonies. The concern with keeping the "German blood pure" was fuelled by fears of a "flood" of migrants from Russia, many of them Jewish and Polish, who went westwards, many of them staying in Imperial Germany only for a short while, en route to North America. It should also be noted that, until the reform of the citizenship law in 1913, there was no national German citizenship. Germans were citizens of their respective territorial states and only through that did they become citizens of the Reich. Even after 1913 they stayed citizens of their respective territorial states. A unitary German citizenship was only introduced by the Nazis in 1934.[81] Overall, the development of the citizenship law in Imperial Germany once again demonstrated that the making of nation was taking place inbetween the reforging of region and the construction of empire.

Many of the colonial fantasies even before the onset of colonialism were obsessed with the issue of race.[82] One of the earliest ideologues of race, Christoph Meiners, a Göttingen-based professor of philosophy, spread the idea about a link between physical properties—such as dense beards, white skin, or tall size—and intellectual abilities as early as the second half of the eighteenth century. The obsession with the purity and homogeneity of the national core vis-à-vis the periphery of the empire also extended to the Slav population in Eastern Europe. Despite the fact that

[80] Dieter Gosewinkel, *Einbürgern und Ausschliessen. Die Nationalisierung der Staatsangehörigkeit vom Deutschen Bund bis zur Bundesrepublik Deutschland* (Göttingen: Vandenhoeck & Ruprecht, 2001), 278 ff.
[81] Klaus J. Bade, *Migration in European History* (Oxford: Blackwell, 2003), 151–53.
[82] Susanne Zantop, *Colonial Fantasies,* 87–90.

the economy in Eastern Prussia urgently needed cheap seasonal agricultural laborers to work the estates during the harvesting season, the Imperial German state restricted even such seasonal work migration, as it became increasingly obsessed with a racial threat to the national core emanating not only from the overseas colonies but also from Slav Eastern Europe.

In many respects Germany's "white man's burden" lay eastwards, but still in Europe.[83] The rebuilding and restoration of the Marienburg in the nineteenth century became one of the most potent symbols for this German mission. In the fourteenth and fifteenth century it had been the governmental and administrative center of the German Order, who, according to nationalist mythology, served as colonizers in the East, already attempting to bring German culture to the area. Rebuilding of the monument began after the Napoleonic Wars and lasted until the early twentieth century. When Marienburg came to Prussia in 1772 with the first division of Poland, Frederick II showed no great interest in it. It was decided to destroy parts of it altogether, while others were to be used as corn magazine. Enlightened Protestant Prussia certainly had no sense of being in any way a successor state to the one created by the Catholic German Order of the Middle Ages. German historians such as Heinrich Luden and Johannes Voigt came up with very negative judgements on the Order during the first half of the nineteenth century. It was only with the arrival of German neo-Gothicism after 1800 that a campaign got under way to rebuild the Marienburg.[84] Theodor Schön, the influential president (Oberpräsident) of Prussia, oversaw the first phase of rebuilding between 1815 and 1850, and he made the castle into a "national monument" of Prussia, a "pantheon of the provinces of Prussia" and a Prussian Walhalla or a Prussian Westminster. Schön very much influenced a change in the historical understanding of the German order. It was only now that the state created by the knights became the base from which Prussia could rise to one of Europe's great powers. The eagle of the Order's Hochmeister became a direct relation to the Hohenzollern eagle, and the Cross of the Order was turned into a precursor to the Iron Cross of the Wars of Liberation against France. The fighters for German liberty and unity of the early nineteenth century were standing in a direct line of tradition to the Medieval knights. The newly commissioned color windows of the Marienburg amounted to a pictorial program of German imperialism in Eastern Europe; the decline of the castle between

---

[83] Gregor Thum, "Mythische Landschaften. Das Bild vom 'deutschen Osten' und die Zäsuren des 20. Jahrhunderts," in *Traumland Osten: deutsche Bilder vom östlichen Europa im 20. Jahrhundert*, ed. Gregor Thum (Göttingen: Vandenhoeck & Ruprecht, 2006), 181–211; see also Hartmut Boockmann, "Das ehemalige Deutschordensschloss Marienburg 1772–1945. Zur Geschichte eines politischen Denkmals," in *Geschichtswissenschaft und Vereinswesen im 19. Jahrhundert. Beiträge zur Geschichte historischer Forschung in Deutschland*, eds. Hartmut Boockmann, et al. (Göttingen: Vandenhoeck & Ruprecht, 1972), 99–162.

[84] In some respect it can be seen as a parallel project to the equally successful campaign to finish building the Gothic cathedral in Cologne.

1457 and 1772 was depicted as part and parcel of the inability of Slavs and Poles in particular to maintain and care for cultural traditions.

After 1871, the German imperial nation used the image of the German Order to construct a century-old continuity of German claims on a "German East." In fact it became one of the official residences of Emperor Wilhelm II, who resided in the castle 50 times until 1918. On June 5, 1902 he staged a knights' procession in the castle—a kind of historical costume drama, so beloved by Wilhelm II. In his speech for the occasion, he reminded everyone of the "German mission" east of the Weichsel as part and parcel of maintaining the German heritage in Eastern Europe. In Wilhelmine Germany the castle also became a model for modern buildings. Thus, the building of the Naval Cadet School in Flensburg-Mürwik, opened by the Kaiser in 1910, was very much inspired by the Marienburg. The historical imperialism of the Order was thus connected directly to the naval ambitions of the German Empire. The Ordensburg was now widely seen as "bulwark of Germandom in the East." Associations, promoting Germandom in the East, such as the Ostmarkenverein, identified themselves completely with the German Order, and it is no coincidence that the idea of the Order was still strong with leading National Socialists, such as Alfred Rosenberg.

The Imperial German government supported attempts to strengthen Germandom both inside the borders of the Reich and outside, that is, among those groups of ethnic Germans who settled outside the borders of the Reich and were perceived as bridgeheads of German culture in Eastern Europe. The Association for the Encouragement of Germandom in the Eastern Marches, founded in Posen (today Poznań) in 1894 is a good example of a pressure group created to further the imperial aims of Germany in Eastern Europe. On the eve of the First World War it had 55,000 members, among them many priests and teachers. It propagated the Germanization of Eastern Europe, if necessary, by means of violence and sought to foster the use of the German language and the colonization of the land. Its propaganda was shrill at time and it was allied to a variety of other imperialist pressure groups in the Reich.

If Germany's key imperial project lay in Central and Eastern Europe, it is a telling sign of the imperial nation's desire to construct its national core around various peripheries that it developed mini-imperialist projects also on its western and northern borders, as discussed above with Alsace, Lorraine, Schleswig, and Holstein. Overall then, we can see that the German Empire was engaged upon imperial, colonizing projects on many of the borders of its national core, where it sought to use those projects to eliminate ethnic difference as far as possible and consolidate that national core. At the same time it was held back by a parallel process of othering, which ensured that these territories were depicted as (not yet) fully nationalized and therefore not part of the national core. Both processes of inclusion and exclusion led to a significant racialization of the national discourse, which was intimately connected to imperialist designs in Eastern Europe and overseas. These, in turn, proved helpful in achieving the regional integration of non-Prussian parts of the German Empire into the national core.

Continuities of the Imperial Nation in the Twentieth Century

It was this German commitment to an increasingly racialized imperial project in Eastern and Central Europe that made the loss of territories in the east, as a result of the 1919 Versailles Treaty, particularly difficult to accept, ensuring that National Socialist imperialism would pick up the cause of civilizing the east with a vengeance. Whereas the loss of Alsace and Lorraine in the west was easier to stomach, at least for the more conciliatory of Weimar politicians seeking some kind of rapprochment with France in the 1920s, the loss of the "German east" was opposed by virtually everyone in the Weimar Republic. It underlined the strength of the belief in an imperial mission of Germany in Eastern Europe and the complete inability of Germans to come to terms with the loss of what was very widely perceived as core national territory to Slav nations, above all to newly reconstituted Poland.[85]

Under the National Socialist occupation of Poland, the land was Germanized with utmost brutality, and National Socialist plans for the Polish population included extermination of the Polish elites and the transformation of Polish peasants and workers into slave laborers. True, German civil servants had already developed ideas of ethnic cleansing and of a "cleared racial space" in Eastern Europe during the First World War. But regardless of the many continuities that can be observed in the planning of a German Empire in Eastern Europe during the First and Second World War, important differences remained. The cultural chauvinism which dominated attitudes towards Eastern Europe in Imperial Germany was qualitatively different from the biological racism which characterized National Socialist policies in Eastern Europe. Although "race thinking" can be traced back to the nineteenth century and the idea of the colonial laboratory was also not an invention of National Socialism, the genocidal re-ordering of space in Europe undertaken by the National Socialists was not a part of mainstream thinking in Imperial Germany.[86]

While it is important to point out that not all of the images of "the east" were negative in Germany,[87] there is undoubtedly a strong line leading from ideas of a race-based empire in Imperial Germany to National Socialism, which marked the most radical version of the German colonial project in Eastern Europe. And it went further than this. As Andreas Hillgruber has shown, National Socialist foreign policy was based on the idea of creating, first, German hegemony over Europe, then, in a second step, to take over British colonial space and ultimately, achieve world hegemony

---

[85] Jonathan Wright, *Gustav Stresemann: Weimar's Greatest Statesman* (Oxford: Oxford University Press, 2002).

[86] Vejas Gabriel Liulevicius, "The Languages of Occupation: Vocabularies of German Rule in Eastern Europe in the World Wars," in *Germans*, ed. Nelson, 121–40.

[87] The ambivalences of German images of the east are clearly brought out in Gerd Koenen, *Der Russland Komplex. Die Deutschen und der Osten 1900–1945* (Munich: Beck, 2005).

against its final potential rival, the United States.[88] For a long time there has been controversy between those historians who attribute greater importance to the National Socialists' conquest of *Lebensraum* in Eastern Europe and those who underline the more global aspirations of German foreign policy under Nazism. However, for our purposes, we can simply state that the National Socialist attempts to build a German nation at the heart of layers of empire was entirely in line with earlier attempts to forge the nation within a framework of empire, which had a distinct Eastern European and a wider global dimension.

Under Nazism, Germans living in states other than Germany were emphatically regarded as an integral part of the *Volksgemeinschaft*. Roughly fifteen million Germans lived in what the National Socialists described as *geschlossener Volkssiedlungsboden*, that is, areas of dense German settlement in Poland, Czechoslovakia, Austria, Switzerland, Belgium, and Luxembourg. Another four million lived in other parts of Europe and 16 million were living overseas, the overwhelming majority in the United States. Already in the 1930s the National Socialists had argued vigorously for uniting the German territories outside the borders of the Reich with the core Germany as far as possible. The *Anschluss* of Austria in 1938 and the occupation of the Sudetenland in 1939 were the most spectacular incidences of such policies. Where there was no immediate prospect of making German settlements part of the German core, the National Socialists devised plans to bring Germans "home into the Reich." The resettlement scheme for Baltic Germans in 1939–40 was perhaps the most prominent example of this policy. However, in the context of the war against the Soviet Union, the idea of a vast German Empire over Eastern Europe, stretching deep into Asia, became a vision with increasing attraction to German policy makers. Germans overseas were supposed to work for and identify with their ethnic brethren in the core lands of the German empire nation. The German *Volksgemeinschaft* was imagined time and again against the background and within the framework of empire, even if those ideas of empire were forever shifting during the 1930s and 1940s. Only Germany's ultimate and utter defeat in the Second World War left Europe in ruins and put an end to dreams of a German imperial nation. However, the negative stereotypes regarding East Europeans and the feelings of superiority towards Eastern Europe survive in Germany to the present day.[89]

---

[88] Andreas Hillgruber, *Deutsche Großmacht- und Weltpolitik im 19. und 20. Jahrhundert* (Düsseldorf: Droste, 1977); Klaus Hildebrand, *Vom Reich zum Weltreich. Hitler, NSDAP und koloniale Frage 1919–1945* (Munich: Wilhelm Fink, 1969); see also in English: Klaus Hildebrand, *The Foreign Policy of the Third Reich* (London: B.T. Batsford, 1973).

[89] Oliver Schmidtke, "The Threatening Other in the East: Continuities and Discontinuities in Modern German-Polish Relations," in *Germans*, ed. Nelson, 171–98; Hubert Orlowski, *"Polnische Wirtschaft." Zum deutschen Polendiskurse der Neuzeit* (Wiesbaden: Harrassowitz, 1996).

Prussianizing the Idea of Empire

Returning to the nineteenth century, it is in many respects surprising that the Prusso-German state after 1871 adopted the language of empire. After all, the Seven Years' War had witnessed the emergence of a Prussian national discourse which was opposed to the idea of empire. And in the debates surrounding either a small-German or great-er-German solution to the German question, the imperial idea was very much associated with greater-German propagandists such as Julius Ficker and Edmund Jörg. They glorified the Medieval legitimacy of the empire, whereas the small Germans, such as Johann Gustav Droysen, Gustav Freytag, and Treitschke saw in the empire nothing but misery for the development of the German nation. In the famous controversy between the historians Heinrich Sybel and Ficker about the attempt of Frederick Barbarossa to build an empire, which included Italy, Ficker defended the emperor with reference to the greater glory of the empire, whereas Sybel saw in Barbarossa's Italian adventure nothing but adverse effects for the development of the German nation. Although a debate on Medieval history, the contemporary context was very clear: history served both historians as legitimation for greater-German or small-German concepts of the nation-state in the present.[90]

The idea of Reich had been mobilized in particular in Austrian efforts to harness the power of the national discourse to its power politics in the early nineteenth century. Friedrich Wilhelm Schlegel's *Lectures on Universal History* of 1805–06 and his *Lectures on Modern History* of 1810–11, both held at the University of Vienna, glorified the Medieval emperors and the Holy Roman Empire more generally as a golden age of Catholic Christianity. Medieval knights were transformed into "German heroes," who expressed what was best and most virtuous in the German national character.[91]

After the victory of the small-German idea in 1871, we therefore witness the attempt to Prussianize the idea of empire. Celebrations of the emperor and the dynasty of the Hohenzollern carried a strong Prussian element. In particular the construction of a popular Emperor was vital for regional integration. Wilhelm I was still too much a traditional Prussian king for this to work, but his grandson Wilhelm II was a different matter. He sought to fuse Hohenzollern ceremonials with all the trappings of empire.[92] Wilhelm united in his person the old pre-modern dynastic ideas, including the idea of the dynastic nation, with the dynamic processes of industrial society,

---

[90] Thomas Brechenmacher, "Wieviel Gegenwart verträgt historisches Urteilen? Die Kontroverse zwischen Heinrich von Sybel und Julius Ficker über die Bewertung der Kaiserpolitik des Mittelalters (1859–1862)," in *Historisierung und gesellschaftlicher Wandel in Deutschland im 19. Jahrhundert*, ed. Ulrich Muhlack (Berlin: Akademie-Verlag, 2003), 87–112.

[91] Echternkamp, *Aufstieg des deutschen Nationalismus*, 203–15.

[92] Isabel V. Hull, "Prussian Dynastic Ritual and the End of Monarchy," in *German Nationalism and the European Response 1890–1945,* eds. Carole Fink, Isabel V. Hull, and MacGregor Knox (Norman: University of Oklahoma Press, 1985), 13–42.

technological progress, and modernity, epitomized by the German middle classes. In addition, the much-publicized travels of the emperor to the colonies were also a means of bringing together people from different parts of the Reich. However, there remained clear limits to these attempts. Thus Wilhelm II, in most non-Prussian parts of the German Empire, was still closely associated with Prussia. Sedan Day, the celebrations of the victory over France in 1871, remained unpopular in many non-Prussian parts of Germany. The same is true for the celebrations surrounding the proclamation of empire on January 18. The Kaiser cult, which was started by Wilhelm II with reference to his grandfather, Wilhelm I, remained artificial.[93] More popular was "Kaiser's birthday" (*Kaisergeburtstag*), which became a widely celebrated national day in Imperial Germany associated with the Hohenzollern. The emperor also made a point of visiting the different regions of Germany regularly, in order to bring into line sentiments of regional Heimat with the nationalizing schemes of the Wilhelmine governments.

Overall, the emperor and empire were symbolically important for the desired regional integration in the German Empire. A good example is provided by the Wilhelm monument in Heilbronn, where Germania was portrayed as reconciling two young boys representing North and South Germany. Wilhelm was shown in a medaillon, but on the very top of the monument stood Victoria with the imperial crown. The monument was thus giving expression to the desired integration of the small fatherlands into the new Germany via conceptions of empire. The small-German Nationalverein, the most important association to promote German unity under Prussia's leadership in the 1860s, had already been remarkably successful in mobilizing members from various parts of the German lands. Among its leadership were 16 Prussians, 10 Bavarians, 9 Badenese, 7 Württemberger, 6 Coburg-Gothaer, 4 Hanoverians, 4 Bremeners, and three each from Hamburg, Saxony, Nassau, Kurhessen, Schleswig-Holstein, and Frankfurt, as well as one each from Hessen-Darmstadt and Mecklenburg. If the Nationalverein was successful in integrating the different regions of small Germany, it partly did so already with reference to a strong German navy, which was widely perceived as precondition for winning back Schleswig and Holstein from the Danish Empire.[94]

Although the new German Empire was still a multi-confessional state, Protestantism was now clearly the dominant religion. Among the Nationalverein's leadership one could find only 9 Catholics and three Jews; the rest were staunchly Protestant. The Habsburg Empire as bulwark of Catholicism was excluded from the Prussian-led imperial nation, and the remaining Catholic regions, such as Bavaria, struggled to combine their confessional orientation with the dominant Protestant Prussianism. At the same time, however, as the idea of empire was Prussianized, the idea of Prussia was effectively regionalized (alongside the regionalization of the "small fatherlands") and hencewith the idea of empire was also nationalized, producing the

---

[93] Nipperdey, *Deutsche Geschichte 1866–1918*, vol. 2 *Machtstaat vor der Demokratie*, 259.

[94] Andreas Biefang, *Politisches Bürgertum in Deutschland 1857–1868. Nationale Organisationen und Eliten* (Düsseldorf: Droste, 1994), 185–91, 300; on the Schleswig-Holstein Krise see 310–56.

imperial nation of Imperial Germany. Stalwarts of the old Prussia and stalwarts of the old Holy Roman Empire of the German Nation were both opposed to this new imperial nation, but the latter's appropriation of the idea of empire was successful. It gave historical depth and justification to the new-found nation-state, which was important in an age of historism.

Empire became a key ideology of integration. Imperial mythologies were prominent. Treitschke chaired the advisory committee for the erection of a national monument to Kaiser Wilhelm I, while Houston Stewart Chamberlain celebrated Wilhelm II as new Caesar. The Medieval idea of empire was also foregrounded in Sybel's recreation of the Goslarer Kaiserpfalz. Overall, imperial visions were extremely widespread among historians who inserted them into German historical consciousness. Karl Lamprecht hailed the institution of the emperor and Wilhelm II in particular, as it allegedly fulfilled the need for an integrating institution capable of uniting all Germans. National unity was routinely depicted as the achievement of the Hohenzollern dynasty. Thus it is not surprising that monarchist ideology (or better: ideology of the emperor) became the centerpiece of imperial nationalism. It proclaimed the unity of emperor and people. In the writings of Friedrich Rohmer, Julius Fröbel, Lorenz von Stein, and Friedrich Naumann, the emperor was the protector of the fourth estate. The idea of a social emperorship was strongly influenced by ideas from France, where forms of plebeian Caesarism flourished under both Napoleon I and Napoleon III. English ideas, such as Bolingbroke's "patritotic king" or Walter Bagehot's notion of a democratic monarchy also were widely adapted in Imperial Germany.[95]

The Prussianization of the idea of empire was also helped by the framing of Berlin as imperial city and national capital.[96] Berlin became an international center for the study of African and Asian languages and cultures. As German science (*Wissenschaft*) rose to world-fame before 1914, many of the areas that Germans excelled in and that were internationally regarded as a German strength were located in Berlin and had to do with empire: anthropology, ethnology, eugenics, oceanography, tropical medicine, and zoology to name only the most obvious areas.[97]

In archaeology, for example, the renowned Gustaf Kossinna put his discipline in the service of empire, demonstrating that Germanic tribes had colonized much of Eastern Europe. Kossinna's work was clearly not only informed by the desire to learn about the past, but instead he was keen to justify contemporary imperial ambitions

---

[95] Peter Burg, "Monarchism as a National Ideology," in *German and American Nationalism: a Comparative Perspective*, eds. Hartmut Lehmann and Hermann Wellenreuther (Oxford: Berg, 1999), 71–96.

[96] Ulrich van der Heyden and Joachim Zeller, eds., *Kolonialmetropole Berlin. Eine Spurensuche* (Berlin: Berlin-Ed., 2002).

[97] Paul Weindling, *Health, Race and German Politics between National Unification and Nazism, 1870–1945* (Cambridge: Cambridge University Press, 1989); P. Grosse, *Kolonialismus, Eugenik und bürgerliche Gesellschaft in Deutschland, 1850–1918* (Frankfurt: Campus-Verlag, 2000).

of Germany in Eastern Europe.[98] And in literature, the most famous historical epic of nineteenth-century Germany was the *Nibelungenlied*, whose Germanic hero, Siegfried, is defeated by Hagen not in open battle but through devious backstabbing. The myth served as warning in Wilhelmine Germany of the deviousness of Germany's enemies and as a model for the heroism of Germanic heroes. German truthfulness and loyalty could be juxtaposed with either French or Slav deviousness. In the nineteenth century the myth had been immortalized by Richard Wagner's opera cycle and Wagner himself, of course, was soon to become a nationalist icon. Outside of Berlin, many German cities associated with the *Nibelungen*, from Passau to Worms, erected monuments dedicated to the *Nibelungen* or commissioned paintings and murals (often for public buildings, such as the town hall in Passau) with *Nibelungen* motifs.

It is true to say that Berlin had far fewer memorials associated with colonialism than imperial cities such as London or Paris. Two memorial stones and one obelisk were erected to the memory of those soldiers who died in the colonial wars in China and German South-West Africa. Although Imperial Germany saw a major debate about a larger memorial for all Germans who died for the fatherland in the colonies, no specific plans were realized before the outbreak of war in 1914. A central memorial to the memory of the German colonies was only erected in 1932, and then it was built in Bremen and not in Berlin. However, the capital of the imperial nation saw the creation of an "African quarter" in Berlin Wedding. In 1899 the first two streets were named Kameruner Strasse and Togostrasse. 21 other names followed, names of colonies, of particular places in colonies, of famous colonizers and colonial generals. The renaming of streets with a colonial theme continued into the 1920s, demonstrating the strength and the appeal of colonial revisionism in the Weimar Republic.[99]

Before 1900 Berlin held several colonial exhibitions, the biggest of which took place in 1896–97, when a Kongo village, exhibiting "50 wild Kongo women" was one of the attractions of the Berlin Trade Exhibition in Treptower Park, which attracted 3,780 exhibitors from around the world. The exhibition included a German Colonial Exhibition comprising of several halls of exhibition space. Visitors could witness a war dance of the Massai or they could watch how a house was built by the indigenous people of Cameroon. When the Kaiser visited the trade exhibition (by boat, of course), he made a point of spending most of his time at the colonial exhibition. The import of live exhibits of indigenous people from the colonies was a frequent occurrence in Wilhelmine Germany. Live exhibits of Africans were mostly held

---

[98] Gustaf Kossinna, "Ueber die vorgeschichtliche Ausbreitung der Germanen in Deutschland," *Correspondenzblatt der deutschen Gesellschaft für Anthropologie, Ethnologie und Urgeschichte* 26 (1895): 109–12; Gustaf Kossinna, "Die indogermanische Frage archäologisch beantwortet," *Zeitschrift für Ethnologie* 34 (1902): 161–221.

[99] On the memory of empire from the Weimar Republic to today see: Britta Schilling, *Postcolonial Germany: Memories of Empire in a Decolonized Nation* (Oxford: Oxford University Press, 2014). On the memorial landscape of colonialism in Germany, see Jürgen Zimmerer, ed., *Kein Platz an der Sonne. Erinnerungsorte der deutschen Kolonialgeschichte* (Frankfurt: Campus, 2013).

at zoological gardens, where their display was combined with both racist and sexist messages.[100] While blacks were thus dehumanized, German colonialists were turned into German heroes. Hermann von Wissmann, who had led many brutal and bloody colonial wars in Africa, had a room of honor all to himself at the 1896 Berlin trade exhibition. Berlin school classes were shipped to the exhibition *en masse*—they did not even have to pay an entrance fee. The colonial ambitions of the empire were underlined by the simulation of a naval battle against a painted background complete with cliffs, forts, and islands. Six times daily the visitors could watch ships sink amidst the thunder of heavy artillery, and the catalog of the exhibition commented on this elaborate simulation that it was meant to bring home to visitors the message that battleships are "the key to national power and freedom." It was hardly a coincidence that German heavy industry and German electrical industry displayed major items for battleships in the trade halls of the exhibition. Certainly German industrialists were ready to fulfill the nation's naval destiny as future colonial and world power. Added to all this, the trade exhibition also featured a special exhibition on Cairo, complete with Arab horse displays, the reconstruction of pyramids which could be visited from the inside (where one would find real mummies, delivered to Treptow by the Berlin museums), and the chamber orchestra of the Egyptian *Khedive*, which played Janissary music. The architect of the main building of the exhibition constructed a façade which seemed to come straight out of Ali Baba. All of this was, of course, a homage to the Orient politics of the Kaiserreich.[101]

Berlin was also home to a German Colonial Museum. It was located near the Lehrter Bahnhof in a building which had previously housed a panorama. It opened its gates in 1899, and it was not by coincidence that a statue of the Emperor Wilhelm II greeted the visitor in the entrance hall. The museum stressed the economic attractiveness of empire, and it documented German missionary work in the colonies. Real landscapes were to give an impression of the physicality of empire, as were the cultural artifacts from the colonized. The exotic was "the other" against which definitions of Germandom could appear more clearly. The museum was not a state museum, but a private shareholding company, in which the Colonial Association was heavily involved. It had to close its gates because of financial difficulties in 1915. In addition to the colonial museum, Berlin had a colonial panorama, which opened on the Wilhelmstrasse in December 1885 and for two years was a runaway success with

---

[100] Anne Dreesbach, *Gezähmte Wilde. Die Zurschaustellung "exotischer" Menschen in Deutschland 1870–1940* (Frankfurt: Campus-Verlag, 2005); Werner Michael Schwarz, *Anthropologische Spektakel. Zur Schaustellung "exotischer" Menschen, Wien 1870–1910* (Vienna: Turia und Kant, 2001).

[101] Paul Thiel, "Berlin präsentiert sich der Welt. Die Treptower Gewerbeausstellung 1896," in *Die Metropole: Industriekultur in Berlin im 20. Jahrhundert*, eds. J. Boberg, T. Fichter, and E. Gillen (Munich: Beck, 1986), 16–27; see also Paul Greenhalgh, *Ephemeral Vistas: The Expositions Universelles, Great Exhibitions and World's Fairs 1851–1939* (Manchester: Manchester University Press, 1988).

the Berlin public. In addition to the colonial panaroma, the *Kaiserpanorama*, which opened its doors in Berlin in 1883, featured many picture cycles with colonial themes (on colonial wars, expeditions, world exhibitions, and travel itineraries).[102]

If Berlin was struggling to become a symbol of German colonialism in the way that London, for example, was a symbol of British colonialism, it had much to do with the federal setup of Germany. The multiplicity of second cities offering federal national identities, which were themselves often infused with the discourse of colonialism (especially in major cities associated with shipping, such as Hamburg), made it difficult for Berlin to develop an iconography of empire aimed at national integration. As museums sprang up in every capital city of the German lands after 1815, its collections were often used to engender patriotic sentiment for the "small fatherlands" with the help of colonial displays.[103]

Education and the Empire Nation

Empire also defined the nation in education—both at school and in higher education. In the German Confederation after 1815 school curricula were redesigned and history, geography, and nature studies were given pride of place, as those were regarded as being particularly useful subjects when it came to fostering patriotism focused on the territorial state. The territorial states attempted to win over school teachers through a mixture of disciplinary threats and pay raises, and school teaching was supposed to strengthen dynastic loyalty.[104] Even in Imperial Germany school teaching, especially history teaching, "encouraged pupils to identify with the particular state, rather than the nation as a whole."[105] However, the schools and their curricula were also nationalized to a significant extent after 1871. In history and geography, in particular, an earlier particularist and dynastic orientation was replaced with an orientation towards Kaiser and Reich. The imperial ambition of the Reich was taken very seriously in songs sung in schools, and in reading books, such as Wünsche's mentioned below. Naval and colonial themes were particularly popular in seminars for teachers. The inculcation of patriotism was, without a doubt, one of the main aims of Imperial German schools. Take, for example, this extract from a reading book for higher classes in Franconia: "Why do you love your fatherland? You love it, because your mother is German; because the blood, which flows through your veins, is German; because the soil is German in

---

[102] Erhard Senf, "Das kostümierte Imperium. Bildsequenz aus dem Kaiserpanorama," in *Die Metropole*, eds. Boberg, Fichter, and Gillen, 28–32.

[103] H. G. Penny, *Objects of Culture: Ethnology and Ethnographic Museums in Imperial Germany* (Chapel Hill: University of North Carolina Press, 2002); H. Thode-Arora, *Für fünfzig Pfennig um die Welt. Die Hagenbeckschen Völkerschauen* (Frankfurt: Campus-Verlag, 1989).

[104] Green, *Fatherlands*, 201, 226.

[105] D. Kennedy, "Regionalism and Nationalism in South German history lessons 1871–1914," *German Studies Review* 12 (1989): 11–33.

which the dead are buried who are mourned by your mother and honored by your father; because the location, where you were born, the language that you speak, because your brother, your sister, the people, in whose midst you live, the beautiful nature, which surrounds you, and everything that you see, that you love, that you learn, is German."[106]

Geography teachers in Wilhelmine Germany routinely referred to the *Kilimanjaro* as the highest German mountain and German school children learned that the highest point of the volcanic crater on top of the *Kilimanjaro* was called *Kaiser-Wilhelm-Spitze*. A. Wünsche's *The German Colonies—Portrayed for the Use in Schools* [*Die deutschen Kolonien—für die Schuled argestellt*] of 1912 was used widely in the classroom as were a number of other readers and primers produced largely after 1900. From around 1900 there were constant debates about the introduction of a separate school subject entitled "colonial studies," and educationalists such as Bruno Clemenz, argued vigorously that "colonial studies" would be a vital contribution to nation building. In Prussian schools, the teaching of colonialism was compulsory for all types of schools after 1908. Heimat studies, which were taught in Prussian primary schools, were increasingly not only informing pupils about their immediate locality and region, but also about German colonies, indicating how tightly intertwined ideas of Heimat and ideas of colonialism were in the forging of the German nation around 1900.[107]

Wissenschaft was also very much in the vanguard of constructing and underpinning notions of core and periphery in the empire nation. The above mentioned Gustaf Kossinna, who occupied a chair of pre-history at the University of Berlin after 1902, formulated the idea of "cultural circles" or "cultural provinces" which the archaeologist could isolate and which he identified with specific ethnic and national formations. He thus related archaeology directly to ethnic national discourses and national-ethnic continuity.[108] A convinced racist and Social Darwinist, Kossinna paved the way for a racist archaeology attempting to demonstrate that all innovation in European history derived from the expansion of a superior Aryan race. Its heirs, the modern-day Germans, had the historical duty to bring culture and civilization to the east. In the 1930s this was exploited by Nazi archaeologists, who sought to justify the territorial expansion of Germany with reference to archaeological finds, which allegedly demonstrated that Germanic tribes once occupied a vast territory—not just in the east, but also in the west. In fact, one could argue that both *Ost-* and *Westforschung*

---

[106] Cited in Nipperdey, *Deutsche Geschichte 1866–1918*, vol. 1 *Arbeitswelt und Bürgergeist*, 539.

[107] Katherine Kennedy, "African Heimat: German Colonies in Wilhelmine and Weimar Reading Books," *Internationale Schulbuchforschung* 24 (2002): 7–26; Hans-Dietrich Schulz, "Das 'größere Deutschland' muss es sein!—Der koloniale Gedanke im Geographieunterricht des Kaiserreichs und darüber hinaus," in *Schule und Unterricht im Kaiserreich*, eds. Reinhard Dithmar and Hans-Dietrich Schulz (Ludwigsfelde: Ludwigsfelder Verlags-Haus, 2006), 183–234; also Horst Gies, "Nationale Identitätsbildung als Aufgabe des Geschichtsunterrichts in der Volksschule," in *Schule und Unterricht im Kaiserreich*, eds. Dithmar and Schulz, 109–35.

[108] S. Jones, *The Archaeology of Ethnicity* (London: Routledge, 1997), 16.

only fully came into its own after the Versailles Treaty, when *Wissenschaft* had a major role to play in fostering revisionism and demanding the restitution of Germany to its former borders.[109]

Historians in Wilhelmine Germany were moving from the promotion of Prussia's vocation in Germany (i.e., the vocation to unify the German lands) to advocating Germany's world mission. Once again, region, nation, and empire were tightly interrelated in the construction of a usable past.[110] German history was proof of the superiority of German culture over those European nations which were at best "merely" civilized (i.e., the French and the British) and at worst barbaric (much of the Slav nations of Eastern Europe). The role of German historians in promoting the German empire nation in Wilhelmine Germany was a prominent one, not the least because history was widely regarded as the "lead science" in late nineteenth and early twentieth century Germany. The intellectual elite of the country was in the grip of a historism, which rallied the nation around notions of Heimat and empire.

Next to history, which provided a cultural identity to Germans, anthropology was particularly important in anchoring a biological identity in German historical consciousness. Even the liberal politician and scientist Rudolf von Virchow pursued with great passion a project which provided comprehensive statistics on school children's eye, skin, and hair color, something, which would, so Virchow's hope, help classify German racial characteristics.[111] The intellectual appeal of diverse forms of Social Darwinism were vital for the construction of nation at the heart of and through empire. Notions of the Aryan race not only provided a justification for colonization, the ideas of "natural selection" and the "survival of the fittest" also lent scientific legitimation to racial theories. From anthropologists, such as Otto Ammon, to industrialists such as Alexander Tiller and zoologists such as Ernst Haeckel, Social Darwinism provided a blueprint for constructions of nationality within the framework of empire. A third group of scientists, who were absolutely crucial in constructing the imperial nation, were geographers. A range of geographical societies in Germany produced maps and circulated information, which played a vital role in promoting a national understanding of space that differentiated between core and various peripheries outlined above. Overall, German scientists played an important role in what could be termed imperial information gathering that served the purpose of nationalizing the empire.

---

[109] On Ostforschung and the völkisch "sciences" more generally see Ingo Haar and Michael Fahlbusch, eds., *Handbuch der völkischen Wissenschaften. Personen, Institutionen, Forschungsprogramme, Stiftungen* (Munich: Saur, 2008); on one of the key proponents of Westforschung, see Karl Ditt, "Die Kulturraumforschung zwischen Wissenschaft und Politik: das Beispiel Franz Petri (1903–1993)," *Westfälische Forschungen* 46 (1996): 73–176.

[110] Wolfgang Hardtwig, *Geschichtskultur und Wissenschaft* (Munich: Deutscher Taschenbuch-Verlag, 1990), 103–60.

[111] Andrew Zimmerman, *Anthropology and Antihumanism in Imperial Germany* (Chicago: University of Chicago Press, 2001).

Historians, anthropologists, geographers, academics from a variety of other disciplines and the professions more generally were very transnational in their orientations, which ironically helped them to nationalize the imperial core: world exhibitions and the debates among German architects, medics, musicians, and professors focused on what made their endeavors "national" in what they perceived to be a rapidly globalizing world.

Geographers, following in the footsteps of Friedrich Ratzel (1844–1904), played a hugely influential role in forging ideas of the nation against the background of globalization and empire. Ratzel, a zoologist by training, turned to geography and introduced Social Darwinism to the study of cultural geography, most famously in his *Political Geography* of 1897. A staunch nationalist, he also developed the concept of *Lebensraum* in an attempt to justify imperial expansion. Peoples with great culture, and invariably none were greater than the Germans, naturally tended towards expansion, in order to bring less cultured peoples the benefits of their superior culture. It was no coincidence that Ratzel was a founding member of the Colonial Society in 1882 and later helped to set up the Pan-German League. His pupils Paul Langhans and Felix Hänsch played prominent roles within the Pan-German League. Other prominent geopolitics scholars such as Karl Haushofer and the Swede Rudolf Kjellén, drew heavily on Ratzel and made the idea of space and the extension of space a central ingredient of German imperialist-national discourse.[112]

The concept of *Mitteleuropa* was another example of the importance of science to underpinning German colonialist projects within Europe. Various, mutually incompatible versions of *Mitteleuropa* existed in historical-geographical-political discourse from around 1800 onwards, but the definition of a German core and a non-German periphery, which was constructed as a de facto colonial empire, were particularly prominent in the German imperialist imagination. The specific geographical sphere of *Mitteleuropa* remained unclear, and yet East-Central Europe in particular figured prominently in concepts of a German colonial space in Europe. The German core was to be surrounded by border areas, including the Netherlands, Belgium, Switzerland, the Bohemian lands and Poland, which were all imagined in terms of quasi-colonies, dependent on the German core. It gave all those who were unhappy with the borders of the German Reich after 1871 a concept with which to demand the expansion of those borders in line with Social Darwinist ideas that larger orders of space would determine the future of Europe. One of the most prominent proponents of the idea of *Mitteleuropa*, Friedrich Naumann, explicitly referred to the old Reich in setting out his ambitions for the new one. According to him it was this old Reich, which "was now emerging from underneath the earth and preparing itself for its return

---

[112] Marc Bassin, "Imperialism and the Nation-State in Friedrich Ratzel's Political Geography," *Progress in Human Geography* 11, no. 4 (1987): 473–95.

after a long slumber."[113] The idea of a German-dominated *Mitteleuropa* was to be revived in the revisionist literature of the inter-war period and the war-time designs of
the National Socialists during the Second World War.

The Pan-German movement actively sought to harness the power of *völkisch
Wissenschaft* to its overall aim of spreading the culture of Germandom in Europe.
Leading national historiens such as Dietrich Schäfer and Karl Lamprecht willingly lent
their services. Lamprecht routinely presented Flanders and Holland as well as Austria
and Switzerland as Germanic provinces and tirelessly promoted common spiritual interests among the Germanic peoples. At the same time he warned against the encroachments of Slav peoples, such as Poles and Czechs on cultural territory belonging to the
Germanic "races." Germanic colonization of Eastern Europe was portrayed as the only
hope for civilization and progress. German expansionism was part and parcel of an inevitable historical development leading to the consolidation of German settlements across
the European continent and beyond. Clear affinities between his variant of cultural history and *völkisch* nationalism in the Kaiserreich also translated into strong sympathies of
some of his students, such as Otto Hoetzsch, for the cause of Pan-Germanism.[114]

Militarism and the Imperial Nation

The Pan-German League and the Colonial Association were arguably the most prominent among a variety of civil society organizations which sought to spread the idea
of the imperial nation. They were supported by state institutions, including the universities (already mentioned under *Wissenschaft* above), civil service, law courts, and
the military. The role of the military in uniting Imperial Germany has long been recognized. After all, unity came about after three successful military campaigns against
Denmark (1864), the Habsburg Empire (1866) and France (1870–71). The Emperor's
Kaiserparaden effectively functioned as a means of national integration of the army.
They took place outside Prussia up to four times a year in different parts of Germany
under the new national flag.[115] In Protestant Germany, annual national celebrations

---

[113] Friedrich Naumann, *Mitteleuropa* (Berlin: G. Reimer, 1915), 42. See generally on the career of the concept of Mitteleuropa Hans-Dietrich Schultz and Wolfgang Natter, "Imagining
Mitteleuropa: Conceptualisations of 'its' Space in and outside German Geography," *European
Review of History* 10, no. 2 (2003): 273–92. On recent publications describing the dense
entanglements of Mitteleuropa see also Wolfram Siemann, "Habsburg, Deutschland und
Mitteleuropa im 'langen neunzehnten Jahrhundert'," *Sehepunkte* 11, no. 5 (2011), [May 15,
2011], URL: http://www.sehepunkte.de/2011/05/11838.html.

[114] Roger Chickering, *Karl Lamprecht: a German Academic Life (1856–1914)* (Atlantic Highlands:
Humanities Press, 1993), 399–403.

[115] Jakob Vogel, "Militärfeiern in Deutschland und Frankreich als Rituale der Nation (1871–
1914)," in *Nation und Emotion: Deutschland und Frankreich im Vergleich, 19. und 20.
Jahrhundert*, eds. Etienne François, Hannes Siegrist, and Jakob Vogel (Göttingen: Vandenhoeck
& Ruprecht, 1995), 199–214.

(*Sedanfeiern*) took place to celebrate the victory of the Prusso-German troops against the "hereditary enemy" France. In September of each year the Imperial fall manoeuvers were hosted by a different province of the empire to bring the different parts of the core closer together through several days of celebrations, parades, dinners, inspections, fireworks, and speeches, all of which was generously covered by the national media. All German recruits had to swear an oath of allegiance, which was another important means of integrating different regions of Germany. For some, such as the chief of staff of the Imperial Army, Helmuth von Moltke, the different oaths that were sworn in different parts of the empire demonstrated not integration but disunity: "One gets an intimation of our divided political circumstances from the reading of the different forms of oaths. First, it is the Prussian subjects, the Protestants, the Catholics. Then, those from Brunswick, then Württemberg, then the subjects of all the other small federal states and finally those from Alsace-Lorraine, all their special oaths!"[116] However, the intimate relationship between Heimat, nation, and empire, referred to above, arguably ensured only the greater effectiveness of national integration. The importance of militarism to German nationalism in the Kaiserreich is also underlined by the budgetary prominence of military expenditure. In 1913, the military devoured 75 to 80% of the entire Reich budget and the individual states within the Reich all had their own military budgets in addition to the national one. A massive 250% increase in military expenditure between 1880 and 1913 was due, above all, to the naval race with Great Britain.[117]

Celebrations of the army were indeed massively augmented by celebrations of the navy in Wilhelmine Germany. Especially the German Navy League (Deutscher Flottenverein), founded in 1898, promoted the building of a strong German battlefleet with considerable official governmental support. Leading industrialists, politicians and intellectuals joined hands to propagate the idea of Germany's naval mission as precondition for its rise as an imperial and world power. So-called naval professors, such as the historian Karl Lamprecht or the economists Gustav Schmoller and Adolf Wagner, traveled up and down the country to propagate navalism in innumerable public meetings. In 1913 the Navy League had 1.1 million members; even if we take into account that 790,000 of those were corporate members, the association was an important part of an increasingly radical nationalist milieu in Germany, which sought to anchor the nation within an overall framework of imperialism and Weltpolitik.[118] The strong connection between navalism and imperial nationalism in Wilhelmine Germany impacted on a variety of different areas, which in turn demonstrates how deeply this imperial nationalism penetrated everyday life and work in Wilhelmine Germany. The navy became a theatre of identity, in which a variety of symbols and ceremonies clearly

---

[116] Helmuth von Moltke, *Erinnerungen: Briefe und Dokumente 1877–1916*, ed. by Eliza von Moltke (Stuttgart: Der Kommende Tag A.G. Verlag, 1922) 153 f. (Nov. 18, 1889).

[117] Ute Frevert, *A Nation in Barracks: Modern Germany, Military Conscription and Civil Society* (Oxford: Berg, 2004), chapter 4.

[118] Geoff Eley, *Reshaping the German Right: Radical Nationalism and the Political Right after Bismarck* (Ann Arbor: University of Michigan Press, 1991).

demonstrated the entanglements of the imperial and the national.[119] Take for example historical research on the *Hanse*, the Medieval trading association that dominated trade in the Baltic between the fourteenth and sixteenth centuries. *Hanse* historians such as Dietrich Schäfer began to nationalize the *Hanse* thoroughly, making it a kind of Germanic precursor to Wilhelmine navalism. Schäfer, another "naval professor," completely ignored the social and economic dimensions of the topic and tied *Hanse* research to diplomatic and high politics history. Or take the popularity of dressing little boys in naval uniform in Wilhelmine Germany, and the general enthusiasm generated by ocean liners and dreadnoughts. Research institutes, such as the Royal Institute for Maritime Transport and World Economics, were specifically set up to provide a scientific basis for navalism.

In this respect it is also important to recognize the role of colonial wars for the regional integration of Imperial Germany. The military campaigns in German East-Africa and German South-West Africa were not only incredibly numerous, they also were fought with genocidal force and generated much colonial enthusiasm in the German Empire. The extremely brutal treatment of the indigenous population also created much criticism, especially from Social Democrats, Catholics, and the missionary movement, but the colonial wars were undoubtedly a means of constructing Germanhood in the face of its "barbarian" Other. Military setbacks and defeats in the colonies were met with outcries of revenge in the mainstream liberal and conservative German newspapers, which sought to rally the nation around the colonial wars. Black soldiers were widely seen as key Other to the German soldier and images of black soldiers as "wild children" or "bestial niggers" circulated widely in Germany.[120] However, the German colonial army, like other colonial armies, recruited black soldiers as auxiliary troops, identifying particular races, such as the Askari or Zulu who allegedly were particularly warrior-like. Yet it was a sign of the prevalent racism among German officers and troops that there were hardly any attempts to "civilize" the auxiliary troops, teach them the German language or even treat them half-decently.[121] In addition, the Empire actively promoted the maintenance of military vigilance against the "Slavic east." The Prussian Eastern Railway for example was built for military purposes, that is, imperial designs in Eastern Europe which would safeguard "the German East."[122]

The First World War was fought by Germany at least partly as an imperial war. The peace treaty of Brest-Litovsk made it very clear that nothing short of the complete re-ordering of the landscape of Eastern Europe was on the cards. Eastern Europe was

---

[119] These theatres of identity are examined in exemplary comparative fashion by Jan Rüger, *The Great Naval Game: Britain and Germany in the Age of Empire*. (Cambridge: Cambridge University Press, 2007).

[120] Eberhardt Kettlitz, *Afrikanische Soldaten aus deutscher Sicht seit 1871: Stereotype, Vorurteile, Feindbilder und Rassismus* (Frankfurt: Lang, 2007).

[121] Thomas Morlang, *Askari und Fitafita. "Farbige" Söldner in den deutschen Kolonien* (Berlin: Links, 2008).

[122] Green, *Fatherlands*, 241.

to become the imperial periphery of the German imperial nation. Erich Ludendorff and other leading German officers in the First World War vigorously pursued the idea of a German settler colony *Ober-Ost* in Eastern Europe, which could have become potentially part of the core.[123] And some researchers have recently pointed to continuities between the colonial wars and the *Generalplan Ost* during the Second World War, which made the war in the East in effect a racial war against Jews and Slavs.[124] Like the Nazis sought to exterminate and ethnically cleanse territories in the east for German settlement, the war against the Hehe in German East-Africa was fought in the name of allowing more German settlers into the colony.[125] The dehumanization of Jews and Slavs was prefigured by the dehumanization of the indigenous population in Germany's African colonies. The leading German general in the war against the Herero in German South-West Africa, von Trotha, explicitly perceived the war as an "existential race war," in other words, a war of annihilation. His opinion was shared by the head of the Imperial army in Berlin, von Schlieffen. After the successful completion of the campaign against the Herero, von Trotha was celebrated as a German hero by the public and received the order *Pour le Merite* from the emperor. German colonial associations organized popular charity collections for German soldiers fighting in Africa, and a whole host of colonial memoirs, diaries, popular histories, novels, and children's books with a colonial theme were published in Wilhelmine Germany, all of them carrying a strong racial-national discourse. One of the most popular was *Peter Moors Fahrt nach Südwest. Ein Feldzugsbericht* (1906) by Gustav Frenssen. Even in the inter-war period, colonial novels underpinned not just colonial revisionism, but also the radical-nationalist discourse of the right more generally,[126] and as late as 1961, H. O. Meissner produced a bestseller with his nostalgic travel book on South-West Africa, which emphasized the German legacies without any criticism of German colonialism.[127]

In China, the Boxer War was fought in 1900 as war for German (and European) civilization. The aim was to teach respect to "savages." As Wilhelm II formulated

---

[123] Vejas Gabriel Liulevicius, *War Land on the Eastern Front. Culture, National Identity, and German Occupation in World War I* (Cambridge: Cambridge University Press, 2000).

[124] Jürgen Zimmerer, "Die Geburt des 'Ostlandes' aus dem Geist des Kolonialismus. Die nationalsozialistische Eroberungs- und Beherrschungspolitik in (post-)kolonialer Perspektive," *Sozial. Geschichte* 19 (2004): 10–43; Jürgen Zimmerer, "Colonialism and the Holocaust. Towards an Archaeology of Genocide," in *Genocide and Settler Society: Frontier Violence and Child Removal in Australia*, ed. Dirk A. Moses (New York: Berghahn, 2004), 49–76.

[125] Thomas Morlang, "'Die Wahehe haben ihre Vernichtung gewollt.' Der Krieg der 'Kaiserlichen Schutztruppe' gegen die Hehe in Deutsch-Ostafrika (1890–1898)," in *Kolonialkriege. Militärische Gewalt im Zeichen des Imperialismus*, eds. Thoralf Klein and Frank Schumacher (Hamburg: Hamburger Edition, 2006), 80–108.

[126] See for example: Konrad Seiffert, *Farm Nasslowhöhe. Bericht aus unserer alten Kolonie Deutsch-Südwestafrika* (Cologne: Volker-Verlag, 1928); Herbert Patera, *Der weiße Herr Ohnefurcht. Das Leben des Schutztruppenhauptmanns Tom von Prince* (Berlin: Deutscher Verlag, 1939).

[127] H. O. Meissner, *Traumland Südwest. Südwestafrika: Tiere, Farmen, Diamanten* (Stuttgart: Cotta, 1961).

it in his famous "Hun's speech," German troops were sent to China "so that never again a Chinese would dare even to look strangely at a German."[128] On the occasion of the Boxer expedition, the painter Hermann Knackfuß exhibited a painting entitled "Peoples of Europe, protect what is holiest to you." The arc-angel Michael occupied the center of the painting defending German and European civilization. Participants of the East Asian Expedition Corps received a German China memorial coin, which depicted the Prussian eagle with the Chinese dragon in its claws.[129] Colonial wars were invariably defended in terms of the protection of national honor and German settlers.[130] This went hand in hand with a more general discourse on the dangers of "niggerization" (*Verkafferung*), which warned (at time hysterically) against Germans going native in Africa as a major threat to nationdom and civilization. Any criticism of either the inhumanity of the warfare or colonialism more generally was attacked as an unpatriotic gesture, and the Hottentot elections of 1907 demonstrated clearly how public opinion could be mobilized against Socialist or Catholic "fellows without a fatherland."[131]

The military elites in Wilhelmine Germany came to see the German Empire increasingly as an arena in which they could prove themselves and win important experience. When German colonialism got fully into its own in the 1890s, almost a whole generation had lived under conditions of peace. The Franco-Prussian war was for many aspiring young officers at best a distant memory, and for many it was a boyhood memory. Hence the colonial wars attracted no shortage of volunteers among the officer corps. Their experiences in the colonies often reinforced a strong commitment to forms of ethnic and *völkisch* nationalism. Whether the officers came from Baden, Mecklenburg, or Saxony, it was in the colonies that they became fully aware of their

---

[128] Bernd Sösemann, "Die sog. Hunnenrede Wilhelms II. Textkritische und interpretatorische Bemerkungen zur Ansprache des Kaisers vom 27. Juli 1900 in Bremerhaven," *Historische Zeitschrift* 222 (1976): 342–58; S. Kuss and B. Martin, eds., *Das deutsche Reich und der Boxeraufstand* (Munich: Iudicium-Verlag, 2002).

[129] Thoralf Klein, "Straffeldzug im Namen der Zivilisation: der Boxerkrieg in China (1900–1901)," in *Kolonialkriege*, eds. Klein and Schumacher, 145–81.

[130] Susanne Kuss, "Kriegführung ohne hemmende Kulturschranke: die deutschen Kolonialkriege in Südwestafrika (1904–1907) und Ostafrika (1905–1908)," in *Kolonialkriege*, eds. Klein and Schumacher, 208–47; on the popularization of colonial wars in Germany see also Medardus Brehl, "'Das Drama spielte sich auf der dunklen Bühne des Sandfeldes ab.' Die Vernichtung der Herero und Nama in der deutschen (Populär-)Literatur," in *Völkermord in Deutsch-Südwestafrika: der Kolonialkrieg (1904–1908) in Namibia und seine Folgen*, eds. Jürgen Zimmerer and Joachim Zeller (Berlin: Links, 2003), 86–96; Peter Heine and Ulrich van der Heyden, eds., *Studien zur Geschichte des deutschen Kolonialismus in Afrika. Festschrift zum 60. Geburtstag von Peter Sebald* (Pfaffenweiler: Centaurus-Verlags-Gesellschaft, 1995).

[131] Wolfgang Reinhard, "'Sozialimperialismus' oder 'Entkolonisierung der Historie'? Kolonialkrise und 'Hottentottenwahlen' 1904–1907," *Historisches Jahrbuch* 97/98 (1978): 384–417; Ulrich van der Heyden, "Die 'Hottentottenwahlen' von 1907," in *Völkermord in Deutsch-Südwestafrika*, eds. Zimmerer and Zeller, 97–102.

Germandom and it was here that they saw themselves as defending German national honor and winning national glory for the fatherland.[132]

Elites and the Empire Nation

But it was not just the intellectual and military elites discussed above for which notions of nation became intertwined with ideas of Heimat and empire. Both served as important ideologies of integration for other elites in Wilhelmine Germany as well. Within the strongly federal constitutional setup of Imperial Germany, elites remained strongly regionalized, in other words, Saxons, Bavarians, Hamburgers etc. continued to play an important role in their respective territorial states. Initially, after 1871, the administrative and governmental elites of Imperial Germany were heavily dominated by the Prussian elites, but over time, the national arena became a viable career option for political and administrative elites from other parts of Germany. The increasing participation of elected representatives of the people in public life, at the municipal, regional (state parliaments), and national (Reichstag) levels produced a parliamentary, party-political elite. Liberal politicians had been the main carriers of the national idea throughout nineteenth-century Germany. Their compromise with Bismarck and their firm belief that the national future belonged to them and to their liberal political ideas integrated them firmly into Imperial Germany. Here, with the exception of a few left Liberals, they became the most vociferous supporters of colonialism and *Weltpolitik*, tying the fortunes of the nation to the fortunes of empire.

The economic and financial elites of Imperial Germany were, qua their profession, transnational in their orientation, and yet they carried their own nationalism into their transnational business affairs and arrangements.[133] For the Krupps and Stumms of Germany, the building of the German navy and the idea of a German Empire was both a business opportunity and a national concern. In an age in which transnational corporations, such as Siemens, perceived international success as benchmark for national excellence, transnationalism, empire, and nationalism were closely intertwined. The existing economic data underline the relative economic importance of Eastern Europe in comparison with Germany's overseas empire as prime markets for German exports. In 1913, for example, exports of Germany industry to Romania alone were three times as high as all exports to the German colonies taken together.[134] The promotion of global

---

[132] Heiger Ostertag, *Bildung, Ausbildung und Erziehung des Offizierskorps im deutschen Kaiserreich, 1871–1918: Eliteideal, Anspruch und Wirklichkeit* (Frankfurt: Lang, 1990).

[133] Cornelius Torp, *Die Herausforderung der Globalisierung. Wirtschaft und Politik in Deutschland 1860–1914* (Göttingen: Vandenhoeck & Ruprecht, 2005); Morten Reitmayer, *Bankiers im Kaiserreich. Sozialprofil und Habitus der deutschen Hochfinanz* (Göttingen: Vandenhoeck & Ruprecht, 1999).

[134] David Blackbourn, "Das Kaiserreich transnational. Eine Skizze," in *Kaiserreich transnational*, eds. Conrad and Osterhammel, 302–24, see 322.

economic concerns went hand in hand with a belief in German *Weltpolitik*. The close proximity of German business and finance to the state meant that economic interests and imperial-national concerns of the state were often difficult to separate.

This was particularly visible in the economic expansion of Wilhelmine Germany into the Ottoman Empire after 1896. It was a German conglomerate under the leadership of Deutsche Bank that was building the Anatolian railway beginning in 1888. The Ottoman market was an attractive one for the German export industry, which worked closely with the Imperial German political and administrative elites to develop that market. The German ambassador to the High Porte, Marshall von Bieberstein, perceived his own role as one of actively fostering German economic interest. The Anatolian railway project was widely seen as the entry ticket to securing an informal economic empire in the Near East. Economic and imperial/national interests were closely intertwined. Wilhelm II traveled to Damascus in 1898, portraying himself as protector of all Muslims and supporting Sultanism in the form of the ailing regime of Sultan Abdülhamit.[135] When Georg von Siemens, the head of Deutsche Bank, proposed to internationalize the Anatolian railway project, he was severely reprimanded by German government officials, who emphasized the importance of economics for the promotion of imperial interests. They expected the German economic and financial elite to play ball, which, to be fair to them, they largely did.[136]

The concentration of economic power in the hands of fewer and fewer big companies and big banks and the formation of cartels made the close cooperation between economic elites, interests groups, and state administration much easier. In 1887, Gustav von Caro compared the state with an architect who was at the service of industry: "Industry is the client for whom a house is being built ... [the state] is the architect; we come to him and show him that the roof is leaking and demand that he repairs it. How he does it, that's his concern."[137] In line with such thinking the Imperial German state was not shy in actively intervening in economic processes in order to prevent recession and protect companies against mighty (especially foreign) rivals. The state also helped industry accommodate to new situations on the world market, and it developed and fostered new branches of industry so as to make them internationally competitive. Just to give one example, export-oriented shipping lines in Imperial Germany were generously subsidized by the state in order to help the German export economy. Economics was always also understood as a means of foreign policy and vice versa—foreign policy became a means of fostering German economic interests. Even with regard to Imperial German labor policies, the idea of the state having a duty to

---

[135] Mehmet Cebeci, *Die deutsch-türkischen Beziehungen in der Epoche Abdulhamids II (1876–1908). Die Rolle Deutschlands in der türkischen Außenpolitik unter besonderer Berücksichtigung der bulgarischen, ägyptischen und armenischen Frage* (Marburg: Tectum-Verlag, 2010).

[136] Jonathan S. McMurray, *Distant Ties: Germany, the Ottoman Empire, and the Construction of the Baghdad Railway* (Westport: Praeger, 2001).

[137] Cited in Wehler, *Deutsche Gesellschaftsgeschichte*, vol. 3, 667.

protect "national labor" confirmed the important role which administrative elites sought the state to play in the imperial nation's economic life.[138]

And, of course, there were the colonial administrators and civil servants work-ing both in the colonies and the Colonial Department in the Foreign Office, estab-lished in April 1890.[139] For them colonialism was not just career advancement, but also service to the imperial nation. The colonial resources had to be mobilized for the ben-efit of the German nation. German settlers had to be protected. German values and culture had to be spread.[140] The Hamburg-based Colonial Institute was responsible for the training of colonial civil servants. It emphasized that the civil servants could only hope to succeed in the colonies if they remained true to their national character. Yet the colonial pioneer at the frontier of German colonialism also had freedom from many social and cultural conventions in the fatherlands which were perceived as sti-fling initiative and personality. Hence the colonies were a space where Germandom could not only be reproduced, but in fact remade. Everywhere the German colonizers were the masters qua their Germandom and everywhere the colonized were the sub-jects who simply followed orders.[141] Colonial governors often aped the social conven-tions of the aristocracy thereby reproducing what they saw as elite culture of Germany in the colonies.

Next to the colonial civil servants and the colonial military personnel, an-other important group of Germans in the colonies were the missionaries. As Philippe David's study on Togo demonstrates, missionaries were vital for producing visual ma-terial about the colonies which shaped the image of the colonies in the metropole.[142] The missionaries came in order to Christianize and civilize "the negroe," and invari-ably they did so in a nationalizing way. The indigenous population was to adopt a German ethos alongside a Christian one. Just like the Inner Mission inside of Imperial Germany sought to civilize the worker and turn him into a good German, the mis-sionaries in Africa and elsewhere in the German colonies sought to civilize the "bar-barians" and inculcate them with German culture. Catholic missionaries promot-ed German values not only for the benefit of the indigenous population, but also to

---

138 Wehler, *Deutsche Gesellschaftsgeschichte*, vol. 3, 622 ff., 632 ff., 666–77, 949.

139 The latter became a fully fledged Colonial Office only in 1907. It was perhaps not coincidence that a former banker, Bernhard Dernburg, became its first head.

140 L. H. Gann and Peter Duignan, *The Rulers of German Africa: 1884–1914* (Palo Alto: Stanford University Press, 1977); Jutta Bückendorf, *"Schwarz-Weiss-Rot über Ostafrika!" Deutsche Kolo-nialpläne und afrikanische Realität* (Münster: Lit-Verlag, 1997); Karin Hausen, *Deutsche Kolo-nialherrschaft in Afrika. Wirtschaftsinteressen und Kolonialverwaltung in Kamerun vor 1914* (Zurich: Atlantis-Verlag, 1970).

141 Andreas Eckert and Michael Pesek, "Bürokratische Ordnung und koloniale Praxis. Herrschaft und Verwaltung in Preussen und Afrika," in *Kaiserreich transnational*, eds. Conrad and Osterhammel, 87–106.

142 Philipp David, "Les cartes postales sur l'Afrique noire (1890–1960)," in *Kolonialausstellungen— Begegnungen mit Afrika?*, eds. Robert Debusmann and János Riesz (Frankfurt: Verlag für Interkulturelle Kommunikation, 1995), 103–08, see 106.

consequences, as it encouraged Russia to move closer to France because it felt snubbed by Imperial Germany.[151] Overall, the East Elbian elites are a good example of how important elements of the imperial core worked only for their regional/social interests and against any idea of nationalizing the core in the pursuit of imperial strategies.

Apart from the railways, roads, and canals, the German Empire also took pride in a well-developed telegraph system. The first electromagnetic telegraph lines were installed between Bremen and Vegesack and between Berlin and Frankfurt/ Aachen from 1847–49. They replaced optical telegraph lines, which were cumbersome to build and very dependent on the weather. From the 1880s, Imperial Germany witnessed the rapid spread of the telephone, yet for the second half of the nineteenth century it was, above all, the telegraph that revolutionized communication systems and ensured the integration of region, nation and empire.

The nineteenth century also saw a massive proliferation of newspapers in the German lands, which was unparalleled in Europe. The number of journals in the German lands increased from 1,102 in 1850 to 1971 in 1,875. Literacy rates in the German lands were high in European comparison: in 1850 over 80% of the population could read and write. Public communication became more and more dense already in the first half of the nineteenth century. About half the male population read newspapers and journals. The daily newspapers had a total circulation of 300,000 with which they reached roughly 3 million readers. Commercial libraries became more and more popular, as did reading circles.[152]

The territorial states sponsored official newspapers in the hope of managing the news and guiding their subjects/citizens towards supporting the governments/ dynasties of the territorial states. Unsurprisingly they tended to be anti-Prussian in southern Germany, but few could withstand creeping nationalization tendencies. While many carried news from the territorial states before they carried news from other "German" states or international news, the order was reversed in most papers during the 1860s: now "national" news came first, followed by international news and then news from the territorial state came last. Even after 1871, there were few genuinely national newspapers, but the major regional newspapers all carried extensive national news. Newspapers that aspired to being national in their distribution, such as the socialist *Vorwärts*, the conservative *Kreuzzeitung*, or the liberal *Frankfurter Zeitung* still had a regional flair to them, even if they were soon read widely across the empire.

In terms of circulation figures the daily newspapers were easily outperformed by weekly illustrated journals, the most successful of which was *Die Gartenlaube*, which reached a circulation of 382,000 in 1875, the highest of any journal anywhere in the world at the time. It had an estimated three to four million readers every week and

[151] Wehler, *Deutsche Gesellschaftsgeschichte*, vol. 3, 678 f., 975–77.

[152] Sybille Obenaus, "Buchmarkt, Verlagswesen und Zeitschriften," in *Deutsche Literatur: eine Sozialgeschichte*, vol. 6, ed. Horst-Albert Glaser (Reinbek: Rowohlt, 1982), 44–62; Dieter Barth, "Zeitschriften, Buchmarkt und Verlagswesen," in *Deutsche Literatur: eine Sozialgeschichte*, vol. 7, ed. Horst-Albert Glaser (Reinbek: Rowohlt, 1982), 70–88.

sought to provide entertainment and education across all classes and ages. Avoiding any overt party-political stance, it pursued a consistently strong national line and contributed to defining the national core within the German Empire. There was a whole host of similar weekly journals, such as *Illustrierte Welt* (founded in 1853), *Über Land und Meer* (1858) and *Illustriertes Familien-Journal* (1854). They all pursued similar nationalizing aims, even if none of them was as successful as *Die Gartenlaube*. From the 1880s onwards they all covered both the overseas German Empire and the issue of the "German east" extensively, using both themes to forge constructions of a German national core and diverse layers of peripheries.

Berlin had been the most important center of a German-language press since the early nineteenth century. The transport revolution discussed above was a vital precondition for the more efficient and quicker distribution of newspapers and journals across the German lands. Even the remotest areas could now be reached easily. In 1868 the postal system in the German lands brought approximately 150 million newspapers and journals to subscribers. The effective privatization of the media market between 1869 and 1871 and the relative lack of censorship further contributed to a booming newspaper market that was increasingly focused on the Berlin metropolis. After 1871, the news was made in this imperial/national center and from this center ideas and opinions spread to the imperial peripheries.[153]

Economic Growth, Migration, and the Making of the Imperial Nation

Not only was the communication infrastructure second to none in early twentieth century Germany, its economy had overtaken that of Great Britain to become the most important economy in Europe, second only in its modernity and dynamism to that of the United States of America. Between 1908 and 1913 Imperial Germany saw a 25% increase in its gross national product. Throughout much of the nineteenth century, economic growth alone could not sustain a massive population explosion in the nineteenth century. The population in the borders of the post-1871 German Reich rose from 20 million in 1800, to 33.7 million in 1850, to 56 million in 1900. Population growth had been particularly marked in Prussia. It grew from 10.5 million in 1816, to 19.5 million in 1866, 24.6 million in 1870, and 40.1 million in 1913. Berlin grew from approximately 145,000 people in 1784 to 412,000 in 1848. By the mid-1870s it had passed the one million mark. In 1871 Imperial Germany had a mere eight cities (Grossstädte) with 4.8% of the population living there. In 1910 that figure had risen to 48 with 21.3% of total population living in cities. In 1871, 63.9% of the total population

---

[153] Kurt Koszyk, *Geschichte der deutschen Presse. Teil 2. Deutsche Presse im 19. Jahrhundert* (Berlin: Colloquium-Verlag, 1966).

lived in communities with less than 10,000 inhabitants. By 1910 that figure had been reduced to 40%.[154]

The only German state that managed to keep up with Prussian population growth and even to outperform, in relative terms, Prussia, was Saxony, which also saw considerable levels of migration to its industrial centers. The second half of the nineteenth century saw the biggest population movement in German history. By 1907 450,000 Polish and Masurian speaking Prussians had moved to the Ruhr. In the industrial regions of Rhineland and Westphalia the population increased sevenfold between 1850 and 1900.

Almost throughout the nineteenth century, millions of Germans emigrated from the German lands, the overwhelming majority to North America. The emigration saw its high point during the years 1880 to 1893. Between 1816 and 1847, almost 600,000 Germans emigrated. In the late 1860s and early 1870s more than 100,000 people left the North German Confederation/German Reich every year. Between 1880 and 1893, 1.8 million people left. Overall, between 1820 and 1914 a total of 5.1 million Germans turned their backs on Germany. Added to emigration was domestic migration, which, during high industrialization between the 1880s and the 1910s, according to the economic historian W. Köllmann, was the "greatest mass movement in German history [...] almost every second German participated in it."[155] By 1907, 48% of the population of the Reich lived outside the parish where they were born. Every second German was a migrant. Nine million Germans had moved outside of their province/territorial state to another province/territorial state. Massive urbanization followed, as migrants were moving from the surrounding countryside into the big cities. Hundreds of thousands went from rural East and West Prussia and Posen to the industrial conurbations of Berlin, the Ruhr, Silesia, and Saxony. Whereas emigration from Germany caused the debates surrounding the loss of national potential, referred to above, domestic migration levelled regional differences and contributed in a major way to the regional integration of the core within the imperial nation. In the 1870s and 1880s, most domestic migrants who left the borders of their territorial federal states behind thought of themselves as emigrants. On the eve of the First World War this was markedly less the case for Germans who moved outside of their federal territorial states but stayed inside of Imperial Germany.[156]

[154] Jürgen Reulecke, *Geschichte der Urbanisierung in Deutschland* (Frankfurt: Suhrkamp, 1985); Klaus J. Bade, ed., *Population, Labor and Migration in Nineteenth and Twentieth-Century Germany* (Oxford: Berg, 1987).
[155] W. Köllmann, "Bevölkerungsgeschichte 1800–1970," in *Handbuch der deutschen Wirtschafts- und Sozialgeschichte*, vol. 2, eds. H. Aubin and W. Zorn (Stuttgart: Klett-Cotta, 1971), 9–50, quote on 20.
[156] Peter Marschalck, "Die Bevölkerungsentwicklung in Deutschland, 1850–1980: Entwicklungslinien und Forschungsprobleme," in *Auswanderer, Wanderarbeiter, Gastarbeiter. Bevölkerung, Arbeitsmarkt und Wanderung in Deutschland seit der Mitte des 19. Jahrhunderts*, 2 vols, ed. Klaus J. Bade (Ostfildern: Scripta-Mercaturae-Verlag, 1984), 78–109.

Regional integration through labor migration was only the case where this domestic labor migration was by ethnic Germans. The example of the Ruhr Poles demonstrates that labor migration by other ethnic groups, even if they were German citizens, did not lead to greater integration of those groups into the German imperial nation. To the contrary, they formed their own separate milieus and policies of isolation and self-isolation went hand-in-hand in order to produce "Polish ghettoes" in the Ruhr.[157] The population explosion in nineteenth-century Germany meant that it was not necessary to import labor from beyond the national borders to any significant extent. During the early phases of industrialization, some skilled labor was imported mainly from England and later on, agricultural seasonal labor was imported into the Prussian northeastern provinces.

Despite the limitations of labor migrations from outside the borders of the German Reich, we can observe with Klaus Bade a major change. During the long nineteenth century, the German lands changed from being a major country of emigration to being a country of immigration. According to the official statistics, only 207,000 foreigners were living in the German Reich in 1871. By 1910 that figure had grown to 1,259,880, but the real figure was probably much higher, as many foreign workers were living illegally in Germany and the counting was done in winter, when hundreds of thousands of foreign seasonal laborers working in East Prussian agriculture had returned to their homes outside of the Reich. Poles and Ruthenes were the biggest groups of seasonal migrant laborers in Imperial Germany, and Italians were also numerous. 70 to 80% of all foreign laborers migrated to Prussia, providing another indication that the economic dynamo of Imperial Germany was located in Prussia. Prussia had no labor restrictions except for Poles. In 1885 mass expulsions of foreign Poles from the Prussian border provinces led to catastrophic labor shortages. From the early 1890s the Prussian authorities regulated labor migration and introduced "mandatory registration" and a system of "compulsory return." The latter was imposed either on the basis of citizenship (Russian) or on the basis of nationality (Polish). Indeed, some areas of industry and especially agriculture had become dependent on foreign labor before the First World War, and the necessary import of foreign labor made it even more necessary to distinguish between a national core and a wider imperial area, which could serve as a recruiting ground for much-needed labor.[158]

As a matter of fact, foreign laborers were never recognized as immigrants. Instead they were widely referred to as *Wanderarbeiter* (migrant laborers), signaling

---

[157] John J. Kulczycki, *The Foreign Worker and the German Labor Movement: Xenophobia and Solidarity in the Coalfields of the Ruhr, 1789–1914* (Oxford: Berg, 1994); Christoph Klessmann, *Polnische Bergarbeiter im Ruhrgebiet 1870–1945: soziale Integration und nationale Integration einer Minderheit in der deutschen Industriegesellschaft* (Göttingen: Vandenhoeck & Ruprecht, 1978).

[158] Bade, *Migration*, 157–60; also: Klaus J. Bade, "Vom Auswanderungsland zum 'Arbeitseinfuhrland': kontinentale Zuwanderung und Ausländerbeschäftigung in Deutschland im späten 19. und frühen 20. Jahrhundert," in *Auswanderer, Wanderarbeiter, Gastarbeiter.* vol. 2, ed. Klaus J. Blade, 433–85.

the intention of the state to send them back to their countries of origin after their labor was no longer needed. Labor migration policies thus indicated clearly how concerned the Imperial German state was with differentiating a national core from an imperial periphery. Not until the 1990s did Germany become a country which saw itself as a country of immigration.[159]

Migration from the overseas colonies into Germany also became tightly restricted and did not amount to more than a few hundred people, mainly men, who were never awarded the status of German citizens. In fact, the German state expressly forbade the "export" of indigenous people from the colonies in 1901. Pressure groups, such as the Colonial Association and the Pan-German League campaigned heavily against any form of sexual relations between Germans and foreigners, especially when the latter came from the colonies or Eastern Europe. *Rassenschande* (dishonoring one's race) was not a word invented by the National Socialists in the 1930s; it was already a well-established propaganda trope in Imperial Germany.[160] Hence, there were considerable tensions between the desire to use imperial space as recruiting ground for much-needed labor and the intention to keep non-Germanic elements before the gates of the inner core of the imperial nation.

Economically, the German Empire was well on its way to leading the world markets in coal, iron, and electricity production by the turn of the century, when its chemical and motor industries were already setting the standards globally. German industrialization entered its take-off phase only around 1850 which made the progress all the more rapid and impressive. The primary agricultural sector declined from 51.2% in 1867 to 34.5% in 1913, while the secondary industrial sector increased from 27.1% in 1867 to 37.8% in 1913, and the tertiary administrative sector also increased from 21.4% in 1867 to 27.6% in 1913. The scale of Germany's industrial growth was staggering: iron production grew from 214,560 tons in 1850, to 988,200 tons in 1865, to 1,390,490 tons in 1870. Steel and coal had similarly fantastic growth rates. Prussia was by far the most important coal producing region in the German Confederation and the German Reich. Coal production in Prussia increased from 4.5 million tons in 1850 to 32.4 million tons in 1873. Regions showing high levels of industrialization in Prussia included the Ruhr, the Rhineland between Krefeld, Cologne and Aachen, the Bergisches Land, the Eifel, the Saar region, and Upper Silesia. They were rivalled only by the industrializing regions of Saxony, especially Chemnitz, Leipzig, and the Lausitz. Industrial growth in Prussia and elsewhere in the German lands was based on the rapid expansion of share-holding companies, which were capable of raising major investment capital—they were the preconditions for the phenomenal rise of big companies and big banks in Imperial Germany. Much of the industrial growth in the nineteenth century was driven by railway construction, but, more importantly, Germany was leading all of its European competitors in the second industrial revolution, based on electrical

[159] Klaus J. Bade, ed., *Auswanderer, Wanderarbeiter, Gastarbeiter.*
[160] Pascal Grosse, "Zwischen Privatheit und Öffentlichkeit: Kolonialmigration in Deutschland, 1900–1940," in *Phantasiereiche*, ed. Kundrus, 91–109.

and chemical industries. Imperial Germany's economic success was arguably the most important factor for the successful regional integration and imperial expansion of Germany after 1871.[161]

Prussia consolidated its prominent economic role among the German lands by founding the customs union of 1834, which facilitated the exchange of goods and led to a massive increase in trade inside the customs union. Prussia's economic influence thus expanded far beyond its borders, consolidating its role as core of the North German lands. The customs union was directed against the Habsburg Empire and it was a major tool of Prussia to contest the leading role of the Habsburgs inside the German Confederation. There were many financial and governmental advantages for those small and medium-sized states that were to join the customs union. Their administrative costs decreased and they benefitted from a much simplified and more efficient customs system. The chancellor of the Habsburg Empire, Metternich, had already instituted a customs union of his own in 1828, the *Mitteldeutsche Handelsverein*, but it was to wither away in the face of Prussian economic might. By excluding the German-speaking lands of the Habsburg Empire from the customs union, Prussia in effect treated them as a foreign country economically, thereby taking a first important step on the road of distinguishing between a national core, which excluded the Habsburg Empire, and a German-speaking periphery in southeastern Europe, for which Vienna was to become the core reference point.[162]

German colonies were to add to the economic luster of the empire nation by providing important commodities, such as cotton, for German industry and serving as markets for finished German goods.[163] Hamburg, in its own self-perception, was the second city of the Reich with a proud independent tradition as a city-state. The city benefitted enormously from overseas transcontinental trade. The very strength, virility, and power of the German Empire left Hamburgers far more comfortable with the federal idiom of the imperial nation and integrated it firmly into the national core of the empire. This was in marked contrast to second cities, such as Barcelona, in failing empires such as Spain.[164]

However, German industry, the most dynamic export economy in the world before 1914, overall was far more interested in the markets of Central and Eastern Europe than in overseas markets—it was remarkably successful in penetrating the

---

[161] A good overview in English of the development of the economy in the German lands during the nineteenth century is provided by Toni Pierenkemper and Richard Tilly, *The German Economy during the Nineteenth Century* (Oxford: Berghahn, 2004).

[162] H. W. Hahn and Marco Kreutzmann, *Der deutsche Zollverein. Ökonomie und Nation im 19. Jahrhundert* (Cologne: Böhlau, 2012); H. W. Hahn, *Geschichte des deutschen Zollvereins* (Göttingen: Vandenhoeck & Ruprecht, 1984); W. O. Henderson, *The Zollverein*, 2nd ed. (London: Frank Cass & Co, 1968).

[163] For cotton production in German East-Africa, see Sven Beckert, *The Empire of Cotton* (New York: Knopf, 2014), chapter nine.

[164] Maiken Umbach, "A Tale of Second Cities: Autonomy, Culture and the Law in Hamburg and Barcelona in the Late Nineteenth-Century," *American Historical Review* 110, no. 3 (2005): 659–92,

economies of these regions. Much of the Central and East European banking system was under German control and German capital owned major shares in Central and Eastern European companies. Eastern Europe was widely perceived as German bread basket and provider of vital commodities, such as oil and ore. Hence the third circle of the imperial periphery was not just about spreading German *Kultur*, but it was also about very material economic interests of German capital.

By the outbreak of the First World War, Wilhelmine Germany had become a globalization leader. Terms such as "German quality craftsmanship" (*deutsche Wertarbeit*) and "Made in Germany" became expressions of an economic imperialism which was global in its aspirations and was closely intertwined with imperial ambitions. The Institute of World Economy, founded in Kiel in 1911, was the scientific expression of such aspirations.[165]

The strong export orientation of German industry was born out of the long economic crisis between 1873 and 1879. As domestic markets seemed incapable of solving the crisis, a strong export orientation was widely seen as remedy and subsequently became the dominant ideology of German industry. Between 1873 and 1894, industrial exports increased twice as much as industrial production. Around 1900, Imperial Germany was the second most successful export country behind the US. Justifications for colonialism in the 1880s routinely referred to the help it would provide for the German export economy. Colonies were seen as security valve for an export-oriented German industry. In the golden years of German industrialization, between 1895 and 1913, when the German economy showed year on year growth rates of 3.3%, German exports increased by 180%. As Germany had taken the lead in the second industrial revolution, it was particularly successful in exporting products associated with the chemical, electrical, and machine-building industries.[166]

Conclusion

The first German Empire had ended before the rise of modern mass nationalism in the nineteenth century. The second German Empire rose in the context of mass nationalism, which is precisely why we find an extremely uneasy, interlocking, and confusing conceptualization of empire and nation. The third German Empire, through its destructive dynamism, buried the imperial nation once and for all. Germany's overseas colonial empire only lasted for 30 years, even if colonial revisionism persisted in the two decades after the end of the First World War. Nevertheless it was no coincidence that National Socialist imperialism concentrated, above all, on Eastern Europe. As we noted above, the idea of a German civilizing mission in Eastern Europe was very old

---

[165] Niels Petersson, "Das Kaiserreich in Prozessen ökonomischer Globalisierung," in *Kaiserreich transnational. Deutschland*, ed. Conrad Osterhammel, 49–67.

[166] Wehler, *Deutsche Gesellschaftsgeschichte*, vol. 3, 564 f., 585, 595 ff., 613 ff., 983.

and was used most effectively in defining Germanness. It served the purpose of integrating a national core within the empire after 1871.

Overall, this chapter has shown how the concept of nation in Germany developed alongside the concept of empire and how both were entangled in a complex web of meanings and imaginations. The idea of a national core within the empire evolved alongside the differentiation between four layers of periphery: non-Prussian ethnic Germans from regions outside of Prussia; ethnic "others" inside Germany, above all Jews and Poles; ethnic "others" outside Germany, above all Slavs in Eastern Europe; and ethnic "others" in Germany's overseas colonial possessions. Empire was thus of crucial importance for framing answers to the age-old question: who was German and where did Germany's borders end. Christian Geulen has stressed how concepts of race brought ideas of Heimat and region in connection with ideas of empire. In his view, the bonding between those sub-national and transnational ideas left the idea of the nation significantly weakened.[167] However, the analysis here points toward an entirely different direction. Nation-building took place at the heart of reconfigurations of both Heimat and empire and ideas of race were crucial to the whole process.[168]

Imperial Germany undertook strenuous efforts to nationalize non-ethnic Germans inside its borders and to prevent the move of further non-ethnic Germans into the Reich. Vast areas of Eastern Europe were German "cultural soil" (*Kulturboden*) on the mental map of German imperialists, who imagined German settler communities bringing culture and civilization and replacing "Slav barbarism" in the East. The Nazis attempted to turn these mental maps into actually-existing maps with terrifying consequences. The fourth layer of the periphery, the overseas colonial empire of Imperial Germany, was also partly imagined as German *Kulturboden*, where German settlers were to create the "New Germany." If there was some debate about the question of whether it was possible to assimilate ethnic Slavs in Germany and its borderlands, the assimilation of the indigenous populations of Africa and Oceania was largely beyond the German national imagination.

The article has traced how the imperial imagination defined a national core via diverse peripheries within variants of German Empire, concentrating on the long nineteenth century (but taking side glances at the Holy Roman Empire of the German Nation and National Socialist Germany). The rise of Prussia since the eighteenth century reconfigured the idea of a German national core. Although state-building in the German Confederation was a characteristic of most German states after 1815, some of which even embarked on forms of nation-state building (e.g. Bavaria), it was Prussia which ultimately had the political and economic clout to bring about a unified

---

[167] Christian Geulen, *Wahlverwandte. Rassendiskurs und Nationalismus im späten 19. Jahrhundert* (Hamburg: Hamburger Edition, 2004).

[168] For National Socialism, this intertwining of Heimat and Empire has recently been emphasized by many of the essays in Claus-Christian W. Szejnmann and Maiken Umbach, eds., *Heimat, Region, and Empire: Spatial Identities under National Socialism* (Basingstoke: Palgrave MacMillan, 2012).

Germany. This new nation on the map of Europe was at the same time an empire, in which ideas of Heimat were of paramount importance in defining a core which went beyond Prussia and incorporated most of the other regions of Imperial Germany. The overseas empire and the idea of a "German frontier" in Eastern Europe were both vital for further integrating the national core by defining distinct peripheries.

The role of NGOs and pressure groups such as the Colonial Association, the Pan-German League and the Naval League in promoting empire as a means of achieving regional integration of the core nation has been emphasized. Monument politics and the Germanization policies adopted by Imperial Germany were important aspects of nationalizing the core of empire. While the idea of empire was Prussianized in the nineteenth century and Berlin became both a national as well as an imperial city, the idea of the imperial nation was racialized to a significant extent under the influence of Social Darwinist ideas and the need to differentiate a national core (increasingly understood as an ethnic core) from a non-national (non-ethnic) periphery. The treatment of Jews, ethnic minorities, and black colonial subjects in the Kaiserreich all indicated the growing significance of this ethnic-imperial-national understanding, which was also the underlying rationale behind the reformulation of the German citizenship laws in 1913.

Militarism was important for building the imperial nation and hence became a major ideology of legitimation and part and parcel of the core identity of the imperial nation after 1871. Other aspects of consolidating the national core of empire included transport and communication revolutions as well as migration and economic development. The imperial nation's elites, from colonial civil servants to directors of major transnational companies and banks, from missionaries to leading politicians, from scientists to school teachers, all played their part in building the nation within the framework of empire.

Given the predominance of understanding Germany as a successful or failed nation-state in historiography, much still needs to be done in order to arrive at a fuller understanding of Germany as an imperial nation. Nineteenth-century Germany has long been perceived as a nation-state in the making, which decided, belatedly, to acquire an empire. However, as this articles underlines, there was no stark dichotomy between imperializing nations and nationalizing empires. Germany in the nineteenth century was both: it sought to form a nation via an empire and it built the nation at the heart of empire. I hope that this article can make a small contribution to re-orienting research towards an understanding of Germany between the sixteenth century and 1945 as an imperial nation, for which ideas of empire were crucial for constructing notions of a national core and an imperial periphery.

The Romanov Empire and the Russian Nation

ALEXEI MILLER

For decades, the relationship between empire and Russian nationalism has been a blind spot of historiography for both political and methodological reasons. Russian nationalism was almost a taboo topic under the Soviet rule inside the USSR, and foreign scholars also didn't have much to offer.[1] The dissolution of the USSR produced a captivating impact on many historians, particularly those working in the post-Soviet space, who started to look at the Romanov Empire through the prism of the political map at the end of the twentieth century. That is also rather typical for Russian historians, who write about "Russia in the Romanov Empire," usually having in mind the contemporary Russian Federation.[2]

---

[1] Even Andreas Kappeler (in his book which deservingly became a classic) mostly covers peripheral nationalisms, and does not deal much with the Russian one. See Andreas Kappeler, *The Russian Empire: A Multiethnic History* (Harlow: Pearson Education, 2001). The German edition appeared much earlier—*Russland als Vielvolkerreich: Enstehung, Geschichte, Zerfall* (Munich: C.H. Beck, 1992).

[2] A perfect example is provided by Boris Mironov's recent study of Russian social history. See Boris Mironov, *Sotsial'naia istoriia Rossii perioda imperii (XVIII–nachalo XX v.)*, vols. 1 and 2 (St. Petersburg: Dmitrii Bulanin, 1999). The title of the book, *A Social History of Russia During the Imperial Period*, already presupposes that Russia can be separated from the empire. Mironov suggests that one can write the social history of the Russians in the empire in isolation. Mironov believes that the social history of the empire as a whole can be presented as the mechanical sum of the histories of the various ethnic groups. See Boris N. Mironov, "Response to Willard Sunderland's 'Empire in Boris Mironov's Sotsial'naia istoriia Rossii,'" *Slavic Review* 60, no. 3 (2001): 579.

When Rogers Brubaker wrote that "nowhere is theoretical primitivism in the study of nationalism more striking than in the literature (and quasi-literature) on this subject," what he had in mind was Eastern Europe and political science.[3] However, the perspectives on the range of problems of Russian nationalism, and on the relationship between this nationalism and the empire that, to a large extent, continue to dominate today's historiography, show convincingly that this criticism partly concerns historians as well. I will cite examples from several recent publications. David Rowley in his article comes to the conclusion that there is no basis for discussing Russian nationalism "in [the] generally accepted meaning" during the age of the Romanovs. The "generally accepted meaning," for Rowley, is the definition of Ernest Gellner, who stated that "nationalism is primarily a political principle, which holds that the political and the national unit should be congruent ... Nationalist *sentiment* is the feeling of anger aroused by the violation of the principle, or the feeling of satisfaction aroused by its fulfillment. A national *movement* is one actuated by a sentiment of this kind." Consequently, Rowley concludes, "Russian nationalist resentment ... could be manifested in two forms: either the Russian nation could draw a boundary around the territory in which Russians lived, and separate itself from all non-Russian territories, or it could seek to turn all the residents of the Russian state into members of the Russian nation. The first alternative would mean to disband the empire and to create a Russia of, by, and for its people. The second would mean the thorough enculturation with Russian ethnicity (Russification) of all peoples of the state."[4] In this passage, Rowley clearly expresses and takes to their logical conclusion the theoretical theses that form the basis of many works on Russian nationalism.

The thesis that the Russians did not differentiate between the empire, the nation-state, and the nation is repeatedly cited in various publications, and leads many historians to conclude that the Russian nationalist program was nothing else but the clearly unrealistic project of transforming the whole empire into a nation-state. It is this thesis that Robert Kaiser, for one, employs, when he writes that the "distinction between Russia, the ancestral homeland—and Rossiya—the geographic extent of the Russian Empire—lost its clear meaning over the course of time," and defines "the Russian nationalist vision" as "re-creating the Russian Empire as a Russian nation-state."[5] Kaiser continues: "The great question for Russian leaders during the nineteenth and twentieth century might be formulated as to whether they could instill something analogous to British compound national identity in their empire's more diverse ethnic elements." This is also the spirit in which Geoffrey Hosking writes his book about, "how the building of an empire impeded the formation of a

---

[3] Rogers Brubaker. "Myths and Misconceptions in the Study of Nationalism," in *The State of the Nation: Ernest Gellner and the Theory of Nationalism*, ed. John A. Hall (Cambridge: Cambridge University Press, 1998), 272–306, here 302.

[4] David Rowley, "Imperial versus National Discourse: The Case of Russia," *Nations and Nationalism* 6, no. 1 (2000): 23–42, quotations from 24, 25.

[5] Robert J. Kaiser, *The Geography of Nationalism in Russia and the USSR* (Princeton: Princeton University Press, 1994), 85.

nation."[6] "Imaginative geography: Russian Empire as a Russian nation-state" is both the title of a chapter and the subject of the entire recent book by Vera Tolz.[7]

But to what extent is Gellner's definition of nationalism, on which all the quoted and many similar discussions are based, applicable in the Russian case? Nationalists inevitably come to ask what space their nation should occupy in terms of political control and as a "national territory." In the case of non-imperial nations, it can be said that a national territory encompasses what the nationalists believe to be "their" state ideally or "rightfully." That is, a "national territory" and the space of political control are congruent. With imperial nations, these two categories of space may differ significantly. The point is that an effort to consolidate the nation, including a definition of a certain part of the territory of the empire as the "national territory," does not necessarily signal an intention to "disband" the empire.

For Russian nationalism, just as for French, British, or Spanish nationalisms, an attempt to consolidate the nation was far from irreconcilable with an attempt to preserve and, given the opportunity, expand the empire. Gellner's formula of nationalism fits the experiences of the movements that tried to "cut" new states out of the existing ones, but it does not work in cases when a particular nationalism could adopt as its "own" an already existing state, including an empire.[8]

What follows is an attempt to tell the story of Russian nation-building before 1917 as the story in which imperial context was far from being just an obstacle in this process, while imperial actors were important players in this story. The chronologically organized narrative, which I see as more comfortable for the readers without special expertise in Russian history, is supplemented by thematic sub-chapters on the nationalist discourse of territoriality, migrations, urbanization, industrialization, and infrastructure.

From a Periphery of the Golden Horde to the Russian Empire

During the fourteenth and fifteenth centuries, the Grand Duchy of Muscovy gradually incorporated, often by force, those principalities and city republics that had appeared in the north and east of the Kievan Rus' after its dissolution in the twelfth and thirteenth century. Muscovy's success was determined mainly by its princes' skillful exploitation of their role as privileged peripheral agents of the huge Chengisid Empire and later of the Golden Horde. Moscow imposed a single political system on the annexed territories and

---

[6] Geoffrey Hosking, *Russia. People and Empire. 1552–1917* (Cambridge, Mass.: Harvard University Press, 1997), XIX, XXI. See also our recent exchange of opinions on this matter in "Forum, Empire, Nation, and Society in the Work of Geoffrey Hosking," *Kritika: Explorations in Russian and Eurasian History* 13, no. 2 (2012): 419–28, 459–65.

[7] Vera Tolz, *Inventing the Nation: Russia* (London: Bloomsbury Academic, 2001), 155.

[8] On the inapplicability of Gellner's model to the British case, see Ben Wellings, "National and Imperial Discourses in England," *Nations and Nationalism* no. 1 (2002): 95–109.

successfully overcame, sometimes by rather brutal measures, the separatism of the regional elites. Thus, already during this period, the themes of empire and regional integration were an important component of the historical development in this part of Eastern Europe.

In the mid-sixteenth century, the armies of Ivan IV conquered the khanates of Kazan' (1554) and Astrakhan' (1556). As a result, the imperial center was relocated into a former periphery, to Moscow, while the former imperial center in the Volga region became, in its turn, a periphery of a newly emergent empire. Soon Moscow made the first, and largely unsuccessful, attempts at territorial expansion in the Baltic region. Moscow's earlier experience of cooptation of Tatar servicemen into its elite helped it to integrate the privileged groups in the Volga region relatively quickly, a substantial part of which converted to Orthodoxy and gradually fused with the Russian gentry.[9]

At the beginning of the seventeenth century, the Muscovite state survived a grave crisis, during which it could easily have lost the status of a center of power and turned into a periphery of the Jagiellonian Polish Commonwealth that sought to expand its possessions in the east. The fortress of Smolensk that lay so close to Moscow in the West remained under Polish rule until the middle of the seventeenth century. Muscovy came out of this crisis having consolidated the elites around the Romanov dynasty in 1613. In the mid-seventeenth century, the Cossack uprising against the Polish Commonwealth led by Bogdan Khmelnitskii offered Muscovy an opportunity to change dramatically the balance of power on her western borders. Having supported Khmelnitskii after some hesitation, Moscow managed to push the border of her control to the left bank of the Dnieper. An autonomous Cossack polity (the Hetmanate) appeared here, whereas the part of the Hetmanate territory on the right bank of the Dnieper returned to Poland in accordance with the treaty of 1667.

The annexation of the Khanate of Kazan' in 1554 opened the possibility of Russian settlement beyond the Ural Mountains. Here, after the defeat of the Tatar Khan Kuchum by a small group of Russian adventurers and criminals under the command of Ermak, the expansion did not encounter an organized resistance and therefore was taking place largely without the participation of the state. The state was rather following the lead of the colonists and to the best of its ability trying to establish control over the new territories.

The reign of Peter I at the end of seventeenth and the first quarter of the eighteenth centuries constitutes a major landmark in the development of the Russian Empire and in the process of nation-building. This was the time of a successful war

---

[9] By the 19th century many of the noble Tatar families were firmly assimilated and incorporated into the Russian elite. A very incomplete list of the prominent Russian cultural figures who had Tatar ancestors would include poets Gavriil Derzhavin, Denis Davydov, and Anna Akhmatova, writers Nikolai Karamzin (also famous as historian), Ivan Turgeniev, Ivan Bunin, and Mikhail Bulgakov, composers Mikhail Balakirev, Sergei Rahmaninov, Nikolai Rimskii-Korsakov, and Alexander Skriabin, publicists and philosophers Piotr Chaadaev, Mikhail Leontjev, Ivan and Konstantin Aksakovs, Nikolai Berdiaev. Among statesmen, generals and politicians with Tatar roots we find Sergei Uvarov, Alexander Ermolov, Alexander Maklakov, Mikhail Tukhachevskii, Dondukov-Korsakovs, Jusupovs, Kochubeis, etc.

with the Swedish Empire, giving Russia a stable control over a large part of the Baltic littoral. The Russian army and navy underwent radical modernization in the course of this war. The administrative system, many elements of culture, and the education of the elites were also substantially transformed within the general framework of Peter's program of the country's westernization. Radical changes took place in elites way of life and elements of the public space appeared for the first time. Peter introduced in 1718 the Table of Ranks, which stressed even more the state character of nobility.[10] The Table also created the formal mechanism of ennoblement through state service.

The control of the tsar and of the laic bureaucracy over the Orthodox Church was strengthened after the refusal of Peter to appoint a new Patriarch in 1700. In 1721, the Patriarchate was formally abolished, to be reestablished only after the fall of the monarchy. Peter I used brutal measures to overcome the split between those who accepted the reforms of his father, Alexei Mikhailovich, and Patriarch Nikon and those who persisted in the "old faith." However, the Old Believers never reunited with the official Orthodox Church, always remaining a more or less acutely perceived challenge to the official image of the unity of all Orthodox subjects of the tsar. The number of "schismatics" was usually estimated between 10 and 15% of the Orthodox population throughout the eighteenth and nineteenth centuries.

The term "nation" (*natsiia*) as a way of the elites' self-description, came into use in Russian even somewhat earlier than the term "empire." The exact time of composition of the "Lexicon of the New Vocables Arranged in the Alphabetical Order," i. e. a dictionary of notions newly incorporated into the Russian language, is unknown, but it is certain that it was prepared on the order of Peter I, who personally edited the entries of the first four letters.[11] The word "nation" is explained in it as "Russian, German, Polish or other people (*narod*)." It is highly likely that a "*narod*" in this case was understood in the sense of early modern nation, i. e. as a designation of the nobility.[12] However, the word *narod* in the meaning of Orthodox Christian folk, united by some common cultural features, had also been introduced into Muscovy through Kiev clerical circles in the middle of the seventeenth century.[13]

---

[10] Mostly following the Danish concept of Dienstadel.

[11] 1st edition. See, appendix to N. A. Smirnov, *Zapadnoie vlianie*, 362–82.

[12] See, for example, *naród szlachecki, natio Hungarica*, which meant, respectively, Polish and Hungarian nobility. In this meaning the word had been used in Russia until the end of the 18th century. See Aleksei Miller, "Priobretenie neobhodimoe, no ne vpolne udobnoe: transfer poniatiia Natsiia v Rossiiu, nachalo 18—pervaia polovina 19 v.," in *Imperium inter pares*, eds. M. Aust, R. Vulpius, A. Miller (Moscow: NLO, 2010).

[13] See: Serhii Plokhy, *The Origins of the Slavic Nations: Premodern Identities in Russia, Ukraine, and Belarus* (Cambridge: Cambridge University Press, 2006), 250–99; Zenon E. Kohut, "A Dynastic or Ethno-Dynastic Tsardom? Two Early Modern Concepts of Russia," in *Extending the Borders of Russian History: Essays in Honor of Alfred J. Rieber*, ed. Marsha Siefert (Budapest: Central European University Press, 2003), 17–30. An important role in this process belonged to "Synopsis," a collection of short extracts from chronicles about "the beginning of Slavic-Russian people (*slavenorossiiskii narod*), first published in 1674.

The "Regulation for Skippers" (1714) uses the word "nation" in the sense of state belonging: "When a foreign [skipper] finds in water something lost by the people of our nation, let him declare it."[14] In 1721, Peter assumed the title of the emperor and the Tsardom of Muscovy turned into the Russian (*Rossiiskaia*) Empire. Through the course of the entire eighteenth century, one did not feel the contradiction between *empire* and *nation*; rather, they were seen as synonymous. The article 11 of the Russian version of Kuchuk-Kajnardja Treaty of 1774 speaks about French, English, and other "nations," using this word as a synonym of "empire" and "great power."[15]

During the reign of Catherine II (1762–96) the empire accorded increasing attention to the incorporation of the German elites of the Baltic provinces as well as of the Cossack *starshina* of the Hetmanate. The difference of the goals and measures of policy towards these two groups is striking. Although Catherine spoke of the necessity to "russify" both, she clearly meant two different things. As far as the Baltic German nobility was concerned, she made cautious steps toward weakening their corporate exclusiveness and partly "domesticating them at court" in the spirit of absolutist policy.

An entirely different policy was pursued in the Hetmanate, where the local elite did not have a consolidated noble status, belonged to the same Orthodox Church as the Russian nobility and was largely fluent in Russian. The ennoblement of the representatives of the *starshina* by the tsars took place as early as the seventeenth century, but its character was highly limited and selective. Since the reign of Peter, the incorporation of the clergy of the Hetmanate into the all-Russian church hierarchy and the attraction of some representatives of the secular elites to the Russian state service was paralleled by the limitation of the Hetmanate's autonomy.

However, a crucial change occurred in the second half of the eighteenth century. Already at the beginning of her reign, Catherine took measures toward the final abolition of the autonomy of the Hetmanate and the dissolution of the Cossack regiments. At the same time, the elites of the Hetmanate were offered significant personal benefits. During the formal ennoblement of the Cossack *starshina*, Catherine consciously permitted a mass falsification of the documents that was exploited by more than 20,000 individuals. Simultaneously, new members of the imperial nobility were widely attracted to military and civil administrative posts outside the Hetmanate. This allowed for the abolition of the autonomy without any mass outbreaks of protest. The nobility of the Hetmanate "had gradually come to accept the fact that they represent a part of empire and not a separate country. In order to secure their interests as well as the interests of their region they sought to acquire a decent role in the imperial

---

[14] Cited after N. A. Smirnov, *Zapadnoie vlianie na russkii iazyk v Petrovskuiu epokhu* (Saint Petersburg, 1910), 203.

[15] See: *Pod stiagom Rossii: Sbornik arkhivnykh dokumentov* (Moscow: Russkaia kniga, 1992), 80–84. The text of the treaty was composed in three languages. The French version uses the expression "état politique et civil" whereas the Russian version uses the term "natsia." (See Karl Strupp, ed., *Ausgewählte Aktenstücke zur orientalischen Frage*. Gotha, 1916.)

system."[16] With time, the identity based on the Hetmanate took the form of a "Little Russian" regional identity. Another, perhaps even more numerous, part of the nobility sought to fuse with the Great Russian nobility and make a career in the service of empire, first of all, in St. Petersburg.

This success in regional integration was largely caused by imperial achievements in expansion. Russian victory in the war against the Ottoman Empire of 1768–74 and the first partition of Poland (1772) played an important role in the predominance of the loyalist attitudes among the *starshina*. Subsequent partitions of Poland have pushed the imperial borders even farther away from the borders of the former Hetmanate, which therefore turned from a borderland into an internal province of empire.

Seeking to forestall the toughening of the imperial policy in the region, immediately after the suppression of Polish uprising of 1830–31, the governor-general of Little Russia, Repnin, wrote to Nicholas I: "The Little Russians are really quite Russians and they have confirmed it by the events of the last summer. The dialect, the customs and the dress are somewhat different, but the faith, the tsar and Russia are a single untouchable sacred object for them, whereas a hereditary enmity towards the neighboring Catholic Poles makes them ... the best guardians against Polish thoughtlessness. Of course it is desirable that any difference within a kindred people disappear ... but, according to the words of Catherine II, bad is the policy that prescribes by law what has to be changed by customs."

In 1835, the already russified Sloboda-Ukrainian *gubernia* was renamed the Kharkov *gubernia* and placed under the authority of the governor-general of Little Russia. In this way, the authorities diluted the attachment of the Little Russian governor-generalship to the tradition of the Hetmanate. Both in geopolitical and internal political aspects, Little Russian governor-generalship was turning from a borderland contested by the Polish Commonwealth, the Ottoman Empire, and Russia into an internal province of the Russian Empire, and in many respects, even into an integral part of the imperial core that provided human and material resources for the assimilation of new territories and the administration of the whole empire. The abolition of Little Russian governor-generalship in 1856 only symbolized this new status.[17]

The assimilation of the privileged groups of the Hetmanate was the last successful incorporation of a whole regional elite, not only into the imperial elite, but also into the Russian nobility. As in the case of the Tatar elites, acquiring the status of Russian nobles was one of the key factors which facilitated the process. In the

---

[16] Zenon E. Kohut, *Russian Centralism and Ukrainian Autonomy: Imperial Absorption of the Hetmanate, 1760s–1830s* (Cambridge, Mass.: Harvard University Press, 1988), 248. See also Zenon E. Kohut, "The Ukrainian Elite in the Eighteenth Century and Its Integration into the Russian Nobility," in *Nobility in Russia and Eastern Europe*, eds. I. Banac and P. Bushkovich (New Haven: Slavica Publishers, 1983).

[17] Kimitaka Matsuzato, "Iadro ili periferia imperii? General-gubernatorstvo i malorossiiskaia identichnost," *Ab Imperio*, no. 2 (2002): 605–15.

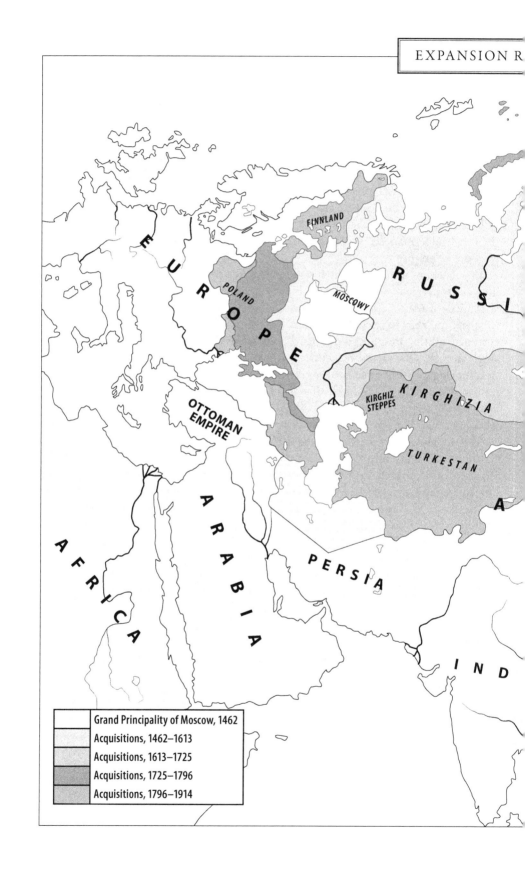

EUROPE

FINNLAND

POLAND

MOSCOWY

RUSSI

OTTOMAN
EMPIRE

KIRGHIZ
STEPPES

KIRGHIZIA

TURKESTAN

A

AFRICA

ARABIA

PERSIA

IND

	Grand Principality of Moscow, 1462
	Acquisitions, 1462–1613
	Acquisitions, 1613–1725
	Acquisitions, 1725–1796
	Acquisitions, 1796–1914

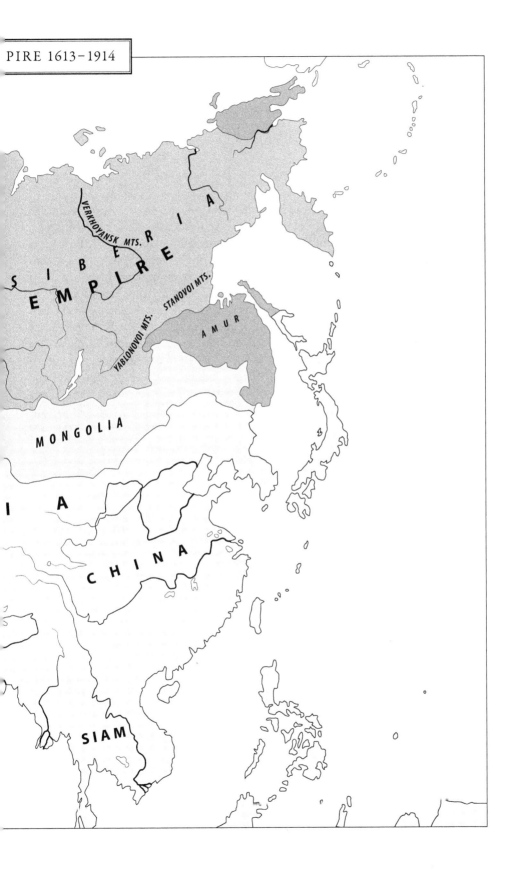

PIRE 1613–1914

VERKHOYANSK MTS.

S I B E R I A

E M P I R E

STANOVOI MTS.

YABLONOVOI MTS.

AMUR

MONGOLIA

I A

CHINA

SIAM

nineteenth century, these mechanisms didn't work any more for whole groups and the assimilation into Russianness rather became an element of individual strategies of integration.

Nation and Empire in the Early Nineteenth Century

As the result of the partitions of the Polish Commonwealth of 1772, 1793, and 1795, the empire annexed the territory of the former Grand Duchy of Lithuania (463 sq. km. with a population of 5.5 million people), it annexed Finland in 1809, Bessarabia in 1812, and the Kingdom of Poland (with a population of more than 3 million people) in 1815. At the end of the eighteenth century, East Slavs constituted about 84% of the empire's population. As a result of subsequent annexations, the share of East Slavs decreased to 68%, and that of Great Russians to 46%. The heterogeneity of the empire increased drastically, including its European part. Policies towards the periphery gained a new importance because of the structural changes in the empire's architecture as a whole. All the newly acquired territories were granted significant territorial autonomy. They were clearly perceived as principally different from the imperial core. The Kingdom of Poland, created after the Vienna Congress, in fact received a status closer to dynastic unity with the empire than autonomy, with a separate crown, diet, constitution, army, budget, and currency. Poland had immediately turned into an alternative center of gravitation for the nobility in the wide belt of the former lands of the Polish-Lithuanian Commonwealth annexed by Russia.

Russian elites and imperial bureaucracy's emerging consciousness of the changing character of the empire was only one of the major new factors. Turning France from the main source of cultural borrowings into a major military threat, the Napoleonic Wars and their victory in them gave a powerful impetus to the cultural emancipation of the Russian nobility. Even earlier, the French revolution immediately made problematic the political meaning of nation in the consciousness of the Russian elite, by linking it inextricably to the theme of political representation and constitution. The French "Declaration of the Rights of Man and Citizen" of 1789 wrote that "nation is the source of the sovereign power. No institutions, not a single individual can have the power that does not explicitly originate from the nation."

On September 27, 1797, the apparent heir and future tsar, Alexander I, sent a letter to his former tutor Frederick Cesar LaHarpe in Geneva. Alexander reported that the person bringing the letter, his close friend Nikolai Novosiltsev, was coming to ask for "council and guidance in a matter of highest importance—securing the well-being of Russia under the condition of introducing a liberal constitution in it." Alexander formulated the essence of his plan to grant freedom "from above" in order to avoid the horrors of revolution in the following way: "I will do an incomparably better thing by devoting myself to the task of granting freedom to the country and thereby preventing it from becoming a toy in the hands of some madmen ... I think this would have been the best of all revolutions, since it would have been carried out by the supreme authority, which would have ceased to exist the moment the constitution is finished and the nation has elected its representatives."[18]

Constitutional reformism did not evaporated entirely after Alexander became a tsar. In 1815, he granted a constitution to the Kingdom of Poland and in 1816 ordered a draft constitution for Russia.[19] The "Fundamental State Charter" or rather *La charte constitutionelle de l'Empire de Russie*, was written on his order in 1818–19—a French-language document completed in Warsaw at the Chancery of the Imperial Commissioner in the Kingdom of Poland Nikolai Novosiltsev. Article 91 of the project read: "*La nation russe aura à perpétuté une representation nationale.*"[20] One of the collaborators on the project was the poet Petr Viazemskii. Since 1816, he was assigned the task of translating some of the Emperor's speeches, originally written in French, into Russian, and now he was supposed to create a Russian version of the constitutional charter. It is at this juncture that the word *narodnost'* appeared in 1819 in his correspondence as the translation of the word nation.[21]

In 1823–25, not only the high imperial officials, but also noble conspirators seeking to dethrone the emperor (the Decembrists) worked over the project of a future constitution. During its meeting in 1825, the secret Southern Society adopted "Russian Justice" written by Colonel Pavel Pestel, which represented a mixture of a constitution and a political program of the future revolutionary dictatorship. Article 16 of the document eloquently titled "All tribes should be fused into a single people" wrote:

> One people and all different shades are to be fused into a single mass so that the inhabitants of the entire space of the Russian state be all Russians … The general measures consist mainly in, first, making Russian the only dominant language in the space of the Russian state: all intercourse will thereby be greatly facilitated; the notions and the way of thinking will become homogenous; people speaking the same language will acquire the closest possible connection, and, being uniform, will compose one and the same people … all these different names [of the tribes] be annihilated and everywhere fused in

---

[18] Cited after N. Schilder, "'Alexander I,' Russkii biograficheskii slovar." Vol. 1. (St. Petersburg, 1896,) 141–384. Quotation on 159–60.

[19] On reformist plans of the early 19th century see: S. V. Mironenko, *Samoderzhavie i reformy. Politicheskaia borba v Rossii v nachale 19 veka* (Moscow: Nauka, 1989).

[20] Cited after: Theodor Schiemann, *Kaiser Alexander I und die Ergebnisse seiner Lebensarbeit* (Berlin: Verlag von Georg Reimer, 1904), 365. For a complete French text, see *La charte constitutionelle de l'Empire de Russie*. Préface de M. Théodore Schiemann. (Berlin, 1903). Also interesting is article 94 about "nationalized foreigners" [*étrangers nationalizes*] who can occupy official positions after five years of irreproachable living and on condition of mastery of the Russian language (Ibid.). The criteria of admission are thus acceptance of citizenship (civic understanding of the nation) and successful acculturation.

[21] Alexey Miller, "*Natsiia, Narod, Narodnost'* in Russia in the 19th Century: Some Introductory Remarks to the History of Concepts," *Jahrbücher für Geschichte Osteuropas* 56, no. 3 (2008): 379–90.

a single Title of the Russians. Third: that the same laws and the same mode of government exist in all parts of Russia and thereby, in the political and civic respect, the whole of Russia, in its entire space, have the appearance of single origin, uniformity and the same way of thinking. The experience of all centuries and all states proved that the people are everywhere what the government and the laws under which they live make of them.[22]

By dividing peoples into great and small, Pestel does not consider a people or a tribe as an immanent essence and views the small peoples to be the objects of assimilation. He opposes the "Right of Nationality," important for the epoch of Romanticism, to the "Right of Well-being" and subordinates the former to the latter (Chapter I, art. 1), considering that the "the right of Nationality truly exists only for those peoples, which, benefiting from it, have the possibility to preserve it," i. e. are capable of defending it by force. The small peoples, according to Pestel, are deprived of this possibility which is why "it will be better and more useful for them to join spiritually and socially with a big State and completely fuse their Nationality with the nationality of the Dominant People, composing a single People with it and ceasing to dream uselessly about something that is impossible and cannot be fulfilled."[23]

For Pestel, the criteria of belonging to "different nations" are 1) citizenship and 2) political loyalty and cultural identification. It is clear from Pestel's following considerations that he considers nation to be an ethnically open community, bound by the political ties of citizenship as well as cultural and linguistic uniformity. Confessional belonging appears to be secondary in Pestel's discussion, although he clearly hopes with time to turn all Russian citizens into Orthodox Christians. "Russian Justice" must have been inspired by the French model of nation-building, based on the leading role of a centralized secular state as well as cultural and linguistic homogenization.

Other official and oppositionist constitutional projects of that time, being less aggressive in their assimilation fervor, also stressed literacy in Russian as a necessary prerequisite for access to any official positions and to citizenship rights. In fact, this view was quite revolutionary in its nature, as the number of imperial subjects that were literate in Russian was by that time smaller in comparison to those literate in French or Polish.[24]

A Conservative Turn: Narodnost' against Nation

By 1820, Alexander I had lost his enthusiasm for constitutional projects, partly because of his personal experience during the visit to the Warsaw Diet, where he felt offended by the speeches of the opposition, and partly because of the events in Spain, where

---

[22] *Vosstanie dekabristov*. Dokumenty, Vol. VII, 149.

[23] *Vosstanie dekabristov*. Dokumenty. Vol. VII, 121–22.

[24] See D. Altoen, *That Noble Quest: From True Nobility to Enlightened Society in the Polish-Lithuanian Commonwealth, 1550–1830*. PhD dissertation, University of Michigan, 2000.

Rafael de Riego was a reminder that a constitution could become a revolutionary slogan. Soon, the Decembrist uprising of 1825, the revolutions in Europe of 1830 and the Polish uprising of 1830–31 reinforced a conservative turn in the politics of the Tsar Nicholas I (1825–55). The uprising of 1830–31 put an end to the illusion that the Polish *szlachta* could become a loyal regional elite of the empire similar to the German nobles of the Baltic area. The Polish constitution was abolished in 1831, and the very idea of constitutionalism was proclaimed unsuitable for Russia. Also, the Bessarabian experiment with autonomy was brought to an end by 1829. The autocracy never came back to plans of arranging imperial borderlands as a chain of autonomous units, controlled through the system of indirect rule, based on loyal local elites. Only the Grand Duchy of Finland survived as an exception which underlines the rule.

The new ideology was expressed with a triad formula, coined in 1832 by the minister of popular education, Count Sergei Uvarov: *"Pravoslavie-Samoderzhavie-Narodnost'"* (usually translated as "Orthodoxy-Autocracy-Nationality"). The word *Narodnost'* (Nationality), invented by Viazemskii to be an adequate Russian translation of the term Nation, was now used to create a cognitive gap with the concept of Nation—which was inseparably linked to the idea of political representation—and constitution. In Uvarov's formula, *Narodnost'* was free of constitutional connotations; instead it presumed loyalty to the autocrat and evoked such issues as Russian cultural individuality and "coming of age," in other words claim for equal standing (in terms of development and civilization) with the Western European empire nations. Nikolai Nadezhdin, one of the leading journalists of the period, expressed this new mood in his article, "Europeanism and Nationality, with Regard to Russian Literature": "If we really want to be European, to resemble Europeans in more than dress and external manners, we should begin by learning from them how to respect ourselves, how to cherish our national personality, though without the ridiculous boastfulness of the French, the superior snobbery of the English or the dumb self-content of the Germans."[25]

While rejecting the political contents of the concept Nation, the activities of Uvarov were strongly influenced by the ideas of nationalist politics. Among his first moves as minister was the introduction of Russian as the only language of instruction at the universities[26] and establishing new chairs for Russian history and literature in all the universities of the empire. Uvarov also promoted a new official version of the Russian historical narrative, shaped mostly by Nikolai Ustryalov, which was much more nationalized than the statist and dynastic narrative of the multivolume bestseller *The History of the Russian State*, by Nikolai Karamzin.[27] One of the important measures was the pressure on noble families throughout empire to abandon home

---

[25] See: N. I. Nadezhdin, *Literaturnaia kritika. Estetika* (Moscow: Khudozhestvennaia literatura, 1972), 441.

[26] All Polish educational institutions in the Western borderland were abolished, instead of the Vilna university a new Russian university was created in Kiev, where Polish influence was much weaker.

[27] See Aleksei Miller, *The Romanov Empire and Nationalism: Essays in the Methodology of Historical Research* (Budapest: Central European University Press, 2008), ch. 5.

education for their sons and to send them instead to the universities where they would study together with the young people of other social strata. Uvarov also strove to harmonize university programs, so as to make it easier for students to move to another university during their course of study, hoping in to mix students from the central regions with students from the borderlands.[28]

Nicholas I always had a pretty suspicious attitude to the universities, and rather put his hopes in a newly created system of cadet corps for the young sons of the poor, mostly provincial Russian nobility, in order to shape a loyal officer corps based on corporate solidarity, which would be more Russian in its nature. But each in its own way, the universities and cadet corps were aimed at shaping a more nationalized Russian elite, which had to become a new solid base for the empire after the system of indirect imperial rule of the provinces turned out to be unreliable.

Uvarov's "nationalism" was ultimately just as pragmatic as his interpretation of "religion" and "autocracy" in the triad. His task, as he saw it, was to protect the integrity and stability of the empire, which were the most important elements of Uvarov's formula even if they were not the declared ones. Perhaps it would be most accurate to define Uvarov as an imperial bureaucrat who realized the importance of Russian nationalism for the future of the empire.

Modernizing the empire meant, among other things, transition from a policy of indirect rule based on the recognition of broad autonomy for traditional elites in the imperial peripheries to a more centralized policy which relied on a modern bureaucracy.[29] Such a policy meant that a fairly high degree of national consolidation would be needed at the core of the empire. This was the general trend of all modernizing empires. Uvarov was one of the first among the upper echelons of the Russian imperial bureaucracy to understand this trend and to demonstrate an ability to take account of it in his policy.

In the reign of Nicholas I, the autocracy was trying to use elements of nationalist politics without changing the political nature of the regime. These politics mostly targeted educated or privileged groups and the aim was mostly acculturation rather than assimilation as far as the peripheral elites were concerned. Nicholas and

---

[28] Increasing numbers of Poles began to enroll in institutions of higher education in St. Petersburg, Moscow, Kazan, and such an influx of the Polish youth in the educational centers of the empire was in part consistent with the intentions of the authorities who hoped to create a loyal generation of Poles until the uprising of 1863. Nicholas also hoped to "re-educate" Polish nobles through the state service inside Russia. In 1837, Poles were banned from the service in the central ministries and offices of the capital unless they had served 5 years in a Great Russian province and had a good command of the Russian language. By the 1850s, the share of Poles among the central bureaucracy had reached 6 percent. See, e.g.: A. Kappeler, *Russland als Vielvolkerreich: Enstehung, Geschichte, Zerfall* (Munich: C.H. Beck, 1992); A. Chwalba, *Polacy w służbie Moskali* (Warsaw–Cracow: PWN, 1999).

[29] Uvarov's program to develop university education was, among other things, also a reaction to the conflict of the "elites of education" and the hereditary elites, which had already begun in the 18th century.

his minister, Uvarov, were clearly thinking of the empire, which would later make increasing use of Russian nationalism as the source of its legitimacy and as an instrument of mobilization. In order for these new mechanisms to function in the future, the regional elites had to be acculturated and their loyalty to the Empire now had to include respect for Russia and Russian culture as "having reached maturity." On this point, the aims of domestic policy for the outlying regions were linked both with the aims of shaping the ideology of Russian nationalism and also the ideological solution to the question of Russia's relationship with Europe.

In such perspective, not only the mutinous Polish gentry, but also the Baltic German nobility loyal to the dynasty, became a problem. Acknowledging the steadfast "feeling of devotion to the legal sovereign" manifested by the nobility of the Baltic region, Uvarov also saw a problem since the "idea that their supposed nationality is *German* has firmly taken root amongst them," and since they were "hardly likely to recognize Russians as intellectually equal."[30] The top bureaucracy now wanted "confirmation of respect for Russian accomplishments" even from loyal regional elites who were used to looking at themselves, and were previously recognized by the imperial center, as being more developed than the Russian nobility. These ideas strongly resonated with the views of those Russian nobles who were more and more loudly expressing dissatisfaction with the privileged position of the Baltic Germans in the *Ostsee* provinces and at the court.

Russian scientists soon started to challenge, often successfully, the leading role of German experts in the newly created imperial academic institutions.[31] A telling example, is the story of the founding of the Imperial Russian Geographical Society. Some German scholars in Russian service saw the main task of the ethnographic division of the society in studying small non-Russian ethnic groups, while their Russian colleagues insisted on focusing the research on the Russian people. The first ethnographic map of Russia, prepared by Peter Köppen in 1848, didn't reflect the Russian population, but focused on minorities.[32] Soon, however, even German scientists began to adopt the Russian nationalist agenda. Already, the maps of the western provinces of the empire, published in 1863 by Roderich von Erckert, were focused on "the fight" of Polish and Russian ethnic groups in the contested region, manipulating the data in order to diminish Polish presence in the French edition to show lack of basis for Polish claims, and increasing the Polish presence in the Russian version in order to mobilize

---

[30] *Desyatiletie Ministerstva narodnogo prosvescheniia, 1833–1843* (Zapiska predstavlennaia G[osudariu] I[mperatoru] Nikolaiu Pavlovichu Ministrom N[arodnogo] P[rosveschenia] grafom Uvarovym v 1843 godu i vozvraschennaia s sobstvennoruchnoi nadpisiu E[go] V[elichestva]: "Chital s udovolstviem") (St. Peterburg: Tipografiia Imperatorskoi AN, 1864, 49–51).

[31] N. Knight, "Science, Empire and Nationality: Ethnography in the Russian Geographical Society, 1845–1855," in *Imperial Russia: New Histories for the Empire*, eds. J. Burbank and D. L. Ransel (Bloomington: Indiana University Press, 1998), 108–42.

[32] Petr Keppen, *Etnograficheskii Atlas Evropeiskoi Rossii, sostavitel' Petr Keppen, chlen Russkogo geograficheskogo obschestva* (St. Petersburg, 1848).

public opinion against the danger.[33] In 1875, Alexander Rittich (Rittikh) prepared an ethnographic map of European Russia with focus on assimilation processes.[34] The same year, the map was presented at the International Geographical Congress in Paris and awarded a first-class medal. The map produced the desired impression: "It [Rittikh's map] exhibited in a most striking manner, the gradual absorption of the minor nationalities by the great Russian race; and showed clearly that the time is not far distant when the whole of that vast empire will be inhabited by *one* people speaking the same language," remarked one of the reviewers.[35] Later in his lectures, Rittikh wrote: "if our literacy becomes obligatory and all-embracing, if the Russian school becomes strong among 25% of our non-Russian population, within just 100 years, within three generations, there will be no other language in all Russian territory but Russian, which is only desirable from the state and ethnographic perspectives."[36]

Coming back to Uvarov: his strategy in acculturation of elites was rather cautious. He knew where to make exclusions[37] and he was always looking for allies in the targeted groups.[38] Uvarov was prepared to wait for the results of his policy. The minister described the strategy of his program as being intended to last for decades. "This is not a new idea" he wrote, "it was that of all brilliant rulers, from the Romans to Napoleon—those who intended to unite the tribes they conquered with the victorious tribe, invested all their hopes and all the fruits of all their labors in future generations instead of the present generation."[39] However, on the individual level we see a growing number of people who had chosen the strategy of assimilation into Russianness already in the 1830s and 1840s.

By introducing nationality into the formula of official ideology and encouraging public debates on the concept, Uvarov aimed not only at marginalizing the constitutional aspect of the concept Nation. By including nationality in his triad, and leaving a large amount of room for different interpretations, Uvarov, as far as was possible in the Russia of Tsar Nicholas I, created an opportunity for a public debate to be held on

---

[33] R. d'Erkert, *Atlas ethnographique des provinces habitées, en totalité ou en partie, par des Polonais, par R. d'Erkert, capitaine aux gardes, membre effectif de la Société Géographique Impériale de la Russie* (St. Petersburg, 1863); and R. F. Erkert, *Etnograficheskii atlas Zapadno-Russkikh gubernii i sosednikh oblastei. Sostavlen R.F.Erkertom, gvardii polkovnikom, deistvitelnym chlenom Imperatorskogo Russkogo Geograficheskogo Obschestva* (St. Peterburg, 1863).

[34] *Etnograficheskaia karta Evropeiskoi Rossii. (sost. A. Rittikh)* (St. Peterburg, 1875).

[35] Ernest George Ravenstein, "Statistics at the Paris Geographical Congress," *Journal of the Statistical Society of London* 38, no. 4 (December, 1875): 428.

[36] Alexander F. Rittikh, *Chetyre lekcii po russkoi etnografii* (St. Petersburg, 1895), 14.

[37] Dorpat University (Tartu) functioned in German until the 1860's.

[38] Most telling example: the introduction of Russian language schools for the Jews, which was successful exactly because Uvarov managed to find support among the maskils. The origins of Russian-Jewish intelligentsia are rooted exactly in this period. Michael Stanislawski, *Tsar Nicholas and the Jews. The Transformation of Jewish Society in Russia, 1825–1855* (Philadelphia: The Jewish Publication Society, 1983).

[39] *Desyatiletie Ministerstva narodnogo prosvescheniia, 1833–1843*, 142.

this concept.[40] However, the more the public debated nationality, the more two un-solved burning issues were coming to the surface—serfdom and constitution. Growing impatience with the lack of any concessions was translated into the mood of despair and apathy during the late 1840s, when the regime tightened its control over the pub-lic sphere in the context of European revolutions. The famous "parting of ways" be-tween the regime and the intelligentsia intensified exactly at that time. Uvarov, who would rather put stress on dialog with the educated part of the society, had to retire.

Great Reforms and Nationalist Politics

The legitimacy of the old regime was dramatically undermined in the Crimean War (1853–56) when Russia was defeated and her backwardness painfully exposed.

The defeat in the war coincided with the new reign of Alexander II, who soon launched the so-called Great Reforms of 1860–70s.[41] The new mood was symbolized by the pompous opening of the Monument of Russian Millennium in Novgorod in 1862. The project of the monument, which featured over 150 historical figures, led to tense negotiations between the imperial bureaucracy and the public about who exactly should be presented. All the reforms had direct impact on nation-building, and were perceived by many contemporaries exactly in this perspective.[42]

The abolition of serfdom in 1861 opened the opportunity for nationalization of a huge mass of peasant population. It made the development of popular education of largely illiterate peasantry a practical issue. Questions of the language(s) of instruc-tion and of organizing and financing primary schools were placed high on the agenda. Issues of acculturation and assimilation ceased to be just the matter of elite politics.

Starting with 1859, the authorities used language politics as an instrument of shaping identity and loyalty of the imperial subjects, regulating the usage of various languages and alphabets. In some cases (forbidding the use of the Latin alphabet for Lithuanian and Latvian language in areas with a Polish gentry presence in 1865) the primary goal was to promote de-Polonization.[43]

In the case of Ukrainians and Belorussians, the restrictions were designed to prevent emancipation of these vernaculars and to establish Russian as the sole

---

[40] All the projects of the previous period were secret—be it those of clandestine organizations or official.

[41] Ben Elkof, John Bushnell, and Larissa Zakharova, eds., *Russia's Great Reforms, 1855–1881* (Bloomington: Indiana University Press, 1994).

[42] M. Dolbilov, "The Emancipation Reform of 1861 in Russia and the Nationalism of the Imperial Bureaucracy," in *The Construction and Deconstruction of National Histories in Slavic Eurasia*, ed. T. Hayashi (Sapporo: Slavic Research Center, Hokkaido University, 2003), 205–30.

[43] D. Staliunas, "Assimilation or Acculturation? Russian Imperial Policy Toward Lithuanians in the 1860s," *Central & Eastern European Review* 2 (2008): 1–20; D. Staliunas, *Making Russians. Meaning and Practice of Russification in Lithuania and Belarus after 1863* (Amsterdam: Rodopi, 2007).

language of education. In 1859, the use of Latin script for Ukrainian and Belorussian language was forbidden in order to minimize Polish influence. In 1863, during the Polish uprising, the authorities banned Ukrainian publications of primaries and other cheap books for peasants. This decision blocked attempts by the emerging Ukrainian nationalist movement to promote Ukrainian language in primary schools.[44] In 1857, the official translation of the Holy Scriptures from Church-Slavonic into Russian was finally allowed (which sold more than 1 million copies within two years), providing the state with a powerful instrument of promoting Russian among the Orthodox peasants. The Russian translation of the bible appeared much later than translations in languages of other nationalizing empires.[45] The publication of the Ukrainian translation of the Bible was forbidden together with primers in 1863.[46]

After serfdom was abolished, peasants, particularly those who did not have communal property of land, could move either to the cities, which fueled a dramatic rise in population, or to other, mostly peripheral parts of the empire where they could get more land.

The reform of the court system provided peasants with the opportunity to participate actively in judicial processes, and they were happy to use it.[47] Court reforms also introduced competitive processes, barristers, and a jury—creating new important areas of civil participation. Military reform replaced recruits with conscription, finally, although belatedly in comparison with other European Empires, opening the way to use the army as an instrument of mass socialization (nationalization). Most of the Asian subjects of the Empire, who were not included into the nationalist image of the Russian nation, were not conscripted. Ethnic principle was not taken into consideration when forming the military units, which makes the nationalizing role of the army even more obvious. *Zemstvo* (1864) and town (1870) reforms created a system of local self-government, which was perceived by many as the first step to the formation of a system of national representation. *Zemstvo* reforms were introduced only in those areas where Russian nobility could play a leading role—borderland regions with weak or absent Russian nobility were not included. When *zemstvo* structures had been gradually introduced into some of the borderlands, it reinforced Russian presence and the

---

[44] Miller, *Romanov Empire and Nationalism*, Ch. 3.

[45] The previous attempts to publish the Russian translation, including that of the Biblical Society in 1821, were blocked by the Orthodox hierarchy, who were not prepared to see this issue in nationalist terms. See: S. K. Batalden, "Printing the Bible in the Reign of Alexander I: Toward a Reinterpretation of the Imperial Russian Bible Society," in *Church, Nation and State in Russia and Ukraine*, ed. Geoffrey A. Hosking (Edmonton: Canadian Institute of Ukrainian Studies Press, 1993); I. Smolitsch, "Geschichte der russischen Kirche. Teil 2," *Forschungen zur osteuropaischen Geschichte*, 45 (1991).

[46] Alexei Miller, *The Ukrainian Question: The Russian Empire and Nationalism in the 19th Century* (Budapest: Central European University Press, 2003); R. Vulpius, "Iazykovaia politika v Rossiiskoi imperii i ukrainskii perevod Biblii (1860–1906)," *Ab Imperio*, no. 2 (2005): 191–224.

[47] Jane Burbank, *Russian Peasants Go to Court: Legal Culture in the Countryside, 1905–1917* (Bloomington: Indiana University Press, 2004).

Russian public sphere in the contested areas.[48] The nationalist aspect of the new structure was thus obvious.

A significant part of imperial bureaucracy, mostly grouped around the Miliutin brothers,[49] openly admitted that they followed a nationalist logic in their policy towards the Russian population of the Empire, as well as to the non-Russian population of the borderlands. An exemplary case is the policy of Russian administration headed by Nikolai Miliutin in Poland after the suppression of the uprising of 1863–64. The administration did not pursue an assimilation strategy, but tried to influence the formation of the Polish nation by deepening the split between the nobility and the peasants and attempting to create a Polish nation in which the *szlachta* would be marginalized, while Polish peasants, getting land from the tsar, would be loyal to the empire.[50] This strategy was probably informed by the tactics of the Habsburg administration in Galicia in the late 1840s, when the Austrian Governor Count F. Stadion didn't hesitate to provoke peasant revolt against the *szlachta* in 1846 and to issue the decree about the abolition of peasants' personal obligations to the landlords in Spring 1848, before the nobles could do it themselves.

Since the 1860s, Russian officials in the borderlands were often undertaking initiatives in Russification which had no approval from the central bureaucracy, and sometimes acted even against explicit instructions from St. Petersburg.[51] Their nation-

---

[48] See, e.g., Charles Steinwedel, "How Bashkiria Became Part of European Russia, 1762–1881," in *Russian Empire: Space, People, Power, 1700–1930*, eds. Jane Burbank, Mark von Hagen, and Anatolyi Remnev (Bloomington: Indiana University Press, 2007), 94–124.

[49] Dimitrii was the war minister and Nikolai the head of the civil administration in Warsaw in 1864–65.

[50] Alexei Miller and M. Dolbilov, "'The Damned Polish Question'—The Romanov Empire and the Polish Uprisings of 1830–31 and 1863–64" in *Comparing Empires: Encounters and Transfers in the Long Nineteenth Century*, eds. Joern Leonhardt and Ulrike von Hirschhausen (Goettingen: Vandenhoek and Ruprecht, 2010), 425–453.

[51] Such was the case of alphabet politics for the Lithuanian language. While the authorities in Saint Petersburg didn't see their task in Russification, and explicitly supported the development of the Lithuanian language in Cyrillic alphabet as an anti-Polish measure (and that could count on a positive response from the emerging Lithuanian educated strata), some local Russian officials in Vilna wanted to transform alphabet change into straight forward Russification policy, and, as a result, mobilized the Lithuanians against the Cyrillic alphabet. See: D. Staliunas, "Assimilation or Acculturation? Russian Imperial Policy Toward Lithuanians in the 1860s," *Central & Eastern European Review* 2 (2008): 1–20; D. Staliunas, *Making Russians. Meaning and Practice of Russification in Lithuania and Belarus after 1863* (Amsterdam: Rodopi, 2007). G. Subačius, "Development of the Cyrillic Orthography for Lithuanian in 1864–1904," *Lituanus* 51, no. 2 (2005): 29–55. For more general observations on the contradictions of nationality politics, see: M. Dolbilov, "Russification and the Bureaucratic Mind in the Russian Empire' North-Western Region in the 1860s," *Kritika* 5, no. 2 (2004): 245–72; D. Staliunas, "Did the Government Seek to Russify Lithuanians and Poles in the Northwest Territory after the Uprising of 1863–64?" *Kritika* 5, no. 2 (2004): 273–90; and A. Kappeler, "The Ambiguities of Russification," *Kritika* 5, no. 2 (2004): 291–98.

alist drive was often going much further than official instructions. That was partly the consequence of yet another crucially important reform of 1863—the abolition of the preventive censorship. Newspapers had sharply increased their circulation; the distribution of the papers and the networks of correspondents dramatically broadened in geographical as well as social terms.[52] The leading figure of Russian nationalist journalism, Mikhail Katkov, had "reloaded" the word *narodnost'* with the meaning synonymous to nation. He had immense influence not only among the reading public, but also in the top echelons of bureaucracy. Minister of Interior Petr Valuev maintained systematic correspondence with Katkov, recognizing the importance of his newspaper for government policy. It was already a situation of reciprocal influence—in the 1860s Katkov was often able to shape the agenda of the bureaucracy. The new phenomenon of a nationalist public was gradually becoming an important political factor, showing its force in the 1870s during the build up of the Russo-Turkish war when Slavic Benevolent Committees managed to organize massive financial support for the numerous volunteers who were going to Serbia in spite of clear disapproval from the government.

Nationalism, represented by Katkov in the 1860s, had many elements typical of the nationalism of imperial nations. It was assimilation-oriented, inclusive, ethnically open, and religion did not play a decisive role. In 1866, Katkov wrote:

> Neither Christianity nor Orthodoxy coincides with any one nationality ... Just as non-Russian people can be, and in fact some are, Orthodox Christians, Russians, in exactly the same manner, can be non-Orthodox ... It would be highly incompatible both with the universal character of Orthodoxy and with Russia's national interests to sweep away from the Russian people all Russian subjects of Catholic or Evangelical faith as well as of the Jewish law, and turn them, contrary to reason, into Poles or Germans. Peoples differ from each other not by religious faith but primarily by language, and as soon as Russian Catholics and Evangelicals, as well as Jews, adopted the Russian language not only for their everyday use but also for their spiritual life, they would cease to be an ethnically alien, hostile and dangerous element for Russian society.[53]

Based on these principles, Katkov openly argued for the emancipation of the Jews, who constituted around 5% of the population of the empire, and were mostly concentrated in the western borderlands, where Russian nationalism expected to fight its main battles. Katkov insisted that emancipation would open the way to Jewish

---

[52] A. Renner, *Russischer Nationalismus und Öffentlichkeit im Zarenreich* (Cologne: Böhlau, 2000).

[53] *Moskovskie vedomosti*, no. 53, March 10, 1866. Quoted from: M. N. Katkov, *Sobranie peredovykh statei "Moskovskikh Vedomostei." 1866* (Moscow, 1897), 154. See more in Miller, *The Romanov Empire*, ch. 2.

assimilation into Russianness, instead of pushing them towards Poles and Germans.[54] "The Jews," emphasized Katkov, "are acting in the interests of the political unity of the state everywhere their rights are recognized.[55]

The borrowed, "western" nature of this ideology was clear to Katkov's critics. "Congratulations with the triumph of Latin classicism on Russian Orthodox soil! Now there is no doubt about Russian nation joining the European family. Down with *narodnost'* and faith, long live nation, religion and civilization"—thus was the sarcastic comment of Alexander Rachinskii, one of the most outspoken critics of western influences at the time.[56]

The reunification of Germany became a permanent reference point in Russian nationalist thought of the time. The story, as Russian observers saw it, was that of overcoming regional cultural and linguistic differences and building a strong German nation. Such a nation was capable of establishing the national character of the territories, contested by the peripheral nationalists,[57] to claim "the national" territories under foreign rule,[58] become competitive in the great power game, and pursue successful imperialist policy far beyond the imperial borders. The motif of insufficient national unity, and insufficient national energy emerged invariably in Russian discourses on nation when compared to the British, French, and German models.

This new nationalism was particularly hostile to those elite groups in the borderlands who were perceived as potential rivals in the efforts to expand the territorial and the ethnic limits of the Russian nation. In the western borderlands, the usual suspects—the Poles were joined by Ukrainian nationalists in the 1860s, although the latter were still pretty weak and limited in numbers—were able to present their views

---

[54] Pointing at the dissemination among the Jews of the German, not Russian, language, Katkov wrote in 1866: "Can the Russian government wish for a German outpost in our one-million-and-a-half Jewish population, wedged almost into the very heart of Russia?" See *Moskovskie Vedomosti*, no. 143, July 8, 1866. Quoted from Katkov, *Sobranie peredovykh statei*, 294.

[55] See: *Moskovskie vedomosti*, no. 53, March 10, 1866. Quoted from Katkov, *Sobranie peredovykh statei*, 155. Katkov's position was not an isolated voice, and found reflection in government policy. A total of 69 statutes and directives concerning Jews were issued in the period between 1859 and 1869. Only three of them (in 1859, 1861, and 1868) were making the situation of the Jews worse, 19 had an explanatory or clarifying purpose, and the remaining 47 expanded Jewish rights. The period during which the "liberal invitation to acculturation and assimilation" remained in force was the same in Russia as in Germany—from the late 1850s to the late 1870s, though the factors that contributed to this coincidence were not identical. Full emancipation couldn't happen as there was no period when liberals would safely control the Russian government.

[56] Letter of A. V. Rachinskii to the Head of Vilna Educational District I. P. Kornilov from June 11, 1871. Manuscript division of Russian National Library, F. 377, ed.kh. 1034, l. 34.

[57] Germanization policy in Mazuria and Silezia were resonating with Russian nationalist agenda in the western borderlands, where they had to face the same Polish rival.

[58] For Russian nationalism Eastern Galicia under Habsburg rule was a "tormented Russian land" similar to German nationalist view of Alsace.

in public for the first time. Partly due to tactical reasons, they would speak about two Russian nationalities—Southern or Little Russian, and Northern, Great Russian. "It is a scandalous and absurd sophism that there can be two Russian nationalities and two Russian languages, as if there could ever exist two French nationalities and languages!" reacted Katkov, clearly defining the reasons for his enmity towards Ukrainophilism. He portrayed the Ukrainian movement as a division within the national body, and commented that attempts to collect money for Ukrainian publications was "even more dangerous than voluntary donations in Rus' for the Polish mutiny."[59] Ukrainian nationalism was soon identified as the most important challenge to the Russian nation-building project as it was undermining its key element, the concept of unity among Great, Little, and White Russians as the branches of one single nation. The idea of a triune Russian nation, which had to embrace Great Russians, Little Russians, and White Russians, so dear to Katkov, was shared also by the Slavophiles. In 1861, the Slavophile Vladimir Lamanskii wrote: "Little Russians and Great Russians, for all their differences and mutual ridiculing, form one Russian people, one Russian land that is closely, inseparably connected by one banner of faith and civil institutions ... The alienation of Kiev and its region would lead to disintegration of the Russian nation, to the collapse and division of the Russian land."[60]

But for early 1860, the main danger came from the Poles. The uprising of 1863–64, as previously the uprising of 1830–31, greatly influenced all the aspects of life across the empire, including the development of nation-building processes. The issue of nation-building played an important role in the uprising of 1863 and its aftermath, both in the rebels' tactics and in the activities of the imperial authorities. The rebels were aiming toward the creation of a nation as a vertically integrated community that would unite the nobility and the unprivileged classes of society in the fight for a national idea. The Russian government was looking for ways to re-formulate the Polish identity so that it would include ideas of loyalty to the dynasty and to a "Slavic unity." It aimed to create a "new" Polish nation based on the peasantry, excluding the nobility which was now seen not just as a difficult object of educational efforts but as an incurably hostile group. In the 1830s and 40s, imperial authorities used a nationalist policy with much reservation, blocking discussion of the subject and of the very notion of "nation" in the press.[61] In 1863, however, authorities actively used nationalist rhetoric and policies and at the same time experienced pressure from an even more radical Russian public opinion.

After 1863, the Western borderland was imagined on mental maps of the imperial bureaucracy as a site of the fiercest struggle between Russianness and Polishness. Just as characteristic was the organicist metaphor of a sacral part of the national body, subjected to a painful disease, a crippling sickness. The effort to proclaim the

---

[59] M. N. Katkov, *1863 god. Sobranie statei po pol'skomu voprosu, pomeshchavshikhsia v Moskovskikh vedomostiakh, Russkom vestnike i Sovremennoi letopisi* Vol. 1 (1887), 276, 282.
[60] *Den'*, 1861, no. 2, October 21, 15.
[61] See Miller, "*Natsiia, Narod, Narodnost'*."

unequivocally Russian character of the Western borderland made governmental policy in this region different from the russification policy in the kingdom. While none of the administrators in the Kingdom of Poland declared as their aim (and very few pursued in practice) the destruction of the Polish language and culture, in the Western *guberni-as* such a goal determined an entire series of governmental actions. "The Poles must surrender their place to the Russian people on this side of the Neman and the Bug," governor-general Konstantin Kaufman wrote to Nikolai Miliutin from Vilna in 1865. In less official circumstances, Kaufman's predecessor in the position of Vilna governor-general, Mikhail Muraviev, formulated his final goal thus: "Discontent will die here when the [Polish] landlords, like Kazan Tatars, will begin selling dressing-gowns and soap."[62]

Before the uprising of 1830, the western province was under full economic, social, and cultural control of the Polish nobility. After 1831, the nobility's economic power and social control were largely preserved, but cultural control was contested and partially undermined by the empire. As a result, in the period between the two uprisings, the Polish movement already began a gradual transition from the concept of the "eastern *kresy*" as a Polish region to the search for local allies represented by the Ukrainian movement, from the concept of the "Commonwealth of two nations" (Poland and Lithuania) to the concept of the Commonwealth of three nations (Poland, Lithuania and Rus'-Ukraine). The Western Province, after the uprising of 1863, became an object of noticeably more intensive depolonization and russification efforts on the part of the empire, which included a total ban on Polish language in public sphere and presupposed the full elimination of the Polish regional elite. However, in the course of this struggle, both the Polish movement and the empire awakened local nationalisms—Ukrainian, Lithuanian, Belorussian—and supplied them with resources. This complicated the implementation of the program of consolidation of eastern Slavs into a single all-Russian nation precisely at the moment after the abolition of serfdom when assimilating efforts had to target not only the elites but the peasant masses as well.

Another challenge to Russian nation-building efforts emerged in the Volga region, where Tatar Muslim elites, instead of concentrating on trade in "dressing-gowns and soap," promoted a Turkic-Islamic project,[63] which challenged the slow process of Christianization and russification of the animist populations and even caused the re-conversion into Islam of previously baptized Tatar peasants. Russian press described the situation in apocalyptic terms: "We did not pay attention that from Kasimov to Samarkand and from Samara to the borders of China Muslim spirit is being spread, and Muslim propaganda is secretly moving and spiritual kingdom of Mohammed is being built. It is known that small non-Russian pagan groups baptized and non-baptized from those regions of Russia where they live close to Muslims, are absorbed by Muslim communities and replenish the number of followers of Islam. Now even

---

[62] OR RGB, f. 169, k. 65, ed. khr. 22, l. 5ob; RO RNB, f. 628, ed. khr. 6, l. 1.

[63] On the origins of Pan-Islamic and Pan-Turkic ideas in the Russian Empire see Kemal H. Karpat, *The Politicization of Islam: Reconstructing Identity, State, Faith and Community in the Late Ottoman State* (Oxford: Oxford University Press, 2001), particularly 276, 286.

Orthodox Russians are accepting Islam."[64] Up to the middle of the nineteenth century, Tatar interpreters and merchants were perceived by the imperial authorities as perfect mediators in the Volga region and in the Steppe, but since nation-building issues came into the picture things changed significantly.[65]

As a reaction to this challenge, a Russian Orthodox missionary, Nikolai Il'minskii, developed local written languages in order to promote Christianization, hoping that linguistic russification will follow later.[66] A special anti-Muslim department was established in Kazan Ecclesiastic Academy, together with the practical missionary society.[67]

The Russian nationalist public was ready to support the imperial authorities in their confrontation with the Polish insurgency and with the western powers, but it also demanded voice and participation in imperial enterprise. A prominent Slavophile Jurii Samarin claimed in 1863 that "We, the Russians, must now become what the French are in the French Empire, and the English in the British Empire."[68] In 1864, historian Nikolai Pogodin expressed his genuine indignation at an argument that a tsar had to be a monarch who was equally close to all the people living in his empire:

> The Russian sovereign was born and grew up on Russian soil and acquired all the provinces with Russian people, with the help of Russian labor and Russian blood! [...] to see in the sovereign not a Russian but a man made up of all the ethnic groups living in Russia is an absurdity which no true Russian can hear of without feeling indignant.[69]

One element was missing on the list of the reforms, and this element was crucial—the expectations of a constitution and some representative body were not met. The

[64] *Missioner* [Missionary] no. 24, June 15, 1875, 194.
[65] *Pis'ma N.I. Il'minskogo k ober-prokuroru Sviateishego sinoda K.P. Pobedonostsevu.* Kazan, 1895; R. P. Geraci, *Window to the East: National and Imperial Identities in Late Tsarist Russia* (Ithaca: Cornell University Press, 2001); P. W. Werth, *At the Margins of Orthodoxy: Mission, Governance, and Confessional Politics in Russia's Volga-Kama Region, 1827–1905* (Ithaca: Cornell University Press, 2001); N. Knight, "Grigor'ev in Orenburg, 1851–1862: Russian Orientalism in the Service of Empire?" *Slavic Review* 59, no. 1 (2000): 74–100; N. Knight, "On Russian Orientalism: A Response to Adeeb Khalid," *Kritika* 1, no. 4 (2000): 701–15.
[66] "I believe that such small, separate nationalities [*narodnosti*] cannot exist permanently, and that in the end, they will join the Russian people by the historical course of life itself." N. N. Il'minskii to Pobedonostsev on April 21, 1891, about the peoples of the Volga area, see: *Pis'ma N. N. Il'minskogo k ober-prokuroru Sviateishego Sinoda Pobedonostsevu* (Kazan, 1895), 399.
[67] M. Mashanov, *Obzor deyatel'nosti bratstva Svyatitelya Guriya za 25 let ego suschestvovaniya (1867–1892)* (Kazan, 1892).
[68] *Perepiska Ju.F.Samarina s baronessoiu E.A.Raden, 1861–1876* (Moscow, 1893), 28. (Letter dated 5/17 of October 1864).
[69] M. P. Pogodin, *Pol'skii vopros. Sobranie rassuzhdenii, zapisok i zamechanii, 1831–1867* (Moscow, 1867), 189.

disappointment was deep, and the authorities had lost, probably, the last opportunity to bridge the growing split between the autocracy and the educated public. Unable to sacrifice the autocratic power, the regime soon had to limit the prerogatives of *zemstvos*, prohibiting their interaction beyond *gubernia* borders in order to prevent a danger that the representative body would be shaped from below. The government didn't know how to manage the growing strength of Russian nationalism. Symbolically, in 1874 Katkov was instructed by the minister of interior to avoid any topics related to nationalism.[70]

Many other reforms failed to use the nation-building potential they initially contained. Having paid compensation to the landowners after the abolition of serfdom, the state put all the created debt on the peasants. The government didn't bother to use the experience of the Habsburg Empire; where all the social groups had to participate in paying "indemnization" after the abolition of peasant obligations to the landlords in 1848. In the Russian context, such a solution could have a powerful impact on shaping national solidarity beyond the social borders. By keeping the peasant community and even reinforcing it during the reform, the government, for several decades, created a strong obstacle for social and geographic mobility of the Russian peasants. Elementary education, considered a crucial issue after the abolition of serfdom did not receive until the mid-1890s any serious attention from the government, which covered only 11% of the costs of primary schools.[71] The last three decades of the nineteenth century, when the peripheral nationalist movements were still rather weak, were not fully used by the government for assimilation pressure through the school system.

The government failed to provide student stipends and career opportunities for university graduates, contributing to the growing radicalization of elites of education, potentially the main driving force of nationalist and socialist movements.[72] In the 1870s, radical groups of intelligentsia (*narodniki*) started their efforts to mobilize the peasants against authorities. The idea that decent people should not collaborate with the government gradually acquired the status of a dogma in the ethos of the intelligentsia. The authorities, on their side, started to see the intelligentsia more and more as the spoiler in the relationship between the state and the people.

The notion of *narod* (i.e., folk, common people, and primarily peasantry) as a community that the intelligentsia should enlighten and unite with against the authority became established in the 1860s and especially the 1870s. The *narodnik* version of these views presupposed that the people (*narod*) were the keeper of true values and morals, and that the intelligentsia, while bringing enlightenment to the people,

---

[70] V. G. Chernukha, *Vnutrenniaia politika tsarizma s serediny 50-h do nachala 80-h godov XIX v* (Leningrad: Nauka, 1978).

[71] B. Eklof, *Russian Peasant Schools: Officialdom, Village Culture and Popular Pedagogy, 1861–1914* (Berkeley: University of California Press, 1986).

[72] Daniel R. Brower, *Training the Nihilists: Education and Radicalism in Tsarist Russia* (Ithaca: Cornell University Press, 1975).

should simultaneously absorb the people's spirit. In this, the *narodniks* were preceded by Slavophiles. The liberal version emphasized the idea of the intelligentsia's duty to the people. The monarchy, especially during the last two reigns, also claimed a unity with the people "above" the obstacles created by bureaucracy and the educated classes. For example, in both cases the notion of national unity was structured as a triangle in which one element was conceptualized as superfluous—for the authority it was the intelligentsia, for the intelligentsia, the autocracy, bureaucracy or sometimes the state as such.

The Russian state was severely under-governed compared to other European powers. The ratio of officials to the population rather resembled that of Algeria and French Indo-China, than that in the metropolitan European empire-states.[73] Partly because of the limited resources, partly because of its autocratic nature, partly due to the mistrust between the ruling elite and the intelligentsia, the state in the last decades of the nineteenth century failed to offer a sufficient number of decently paid administrative positions and career opportunities to the growing number of educated Russians. This situation had the most damaging impact on the process of Russian nation-building and was one of the main causes of the crisis of the state in the last decades of the empire.

All the weaknesses of the empire became particularly visible and acute by the 1860s. The traditional patterns of imperial rule—when politics, including the politics of acculturation and assimilation, were mostly the business of the elite groups both in the center and in the borderlands—were now giving way to much broader involvement of the imperial subjects, largely due to the competing efforts of the state and various elite groups in nation-building.

"Nationalist Turn" of the Monarchy under Alexander III

The assassination of Alexander II crowned a series of terrorist acts by political radicals who hoped to provoke mass movement with this first systematic campaign of terror in European history. Many liberals were so irritated with the autocratic regime that they were not prepared to side unequivocally with the monarchy. In fact, their hopes that the terrorist campaign would force the autocracy to allow some sort of political representation were close to realization, but all the reforms planned by the tsar and his reform-oriented minister Mikhail Loris-Melikov in 1880 were cut short with the assassination on March 1, 1881.

Alexander III decided to promote nationalization of the dynasty without sacrificing autocratic principle.[74] The most visible element of the new scenario

---

[73] S. Velychenko, "The Size of the Imperial Russian Bureaucracy and Army in Comparative Perspective," *Jahrbücher für Geschichte Osteuropas* 49, vol. 3 (2001): 346–62.

[74] R. Wortman, *The Scenarios of Power: Myth and Ceremony in Russian Monarchy* (Princeton: Princeton University Press, 2000).

of power was the adoption of neo-Russian style in the architecture of churches and public buildings. The new tsar refused to revise the most irritating and counterproductive russifying measures adopted in the 1860s and 1870s, and stressed the direct link between the tsar and "the people," simple folk loyal to autocracy.[75] The tsar openly privileged "true Russians" with access to administrative positions and education. The former teacher of the new tsar, and now the influential chief procurator of the Holy Synod, Konstantin Pobedonostsev, saw conversion to Orthodoxy as the most effective means of Russification.[76] A long list of discriminatory measures were introduced against the Jews, Poles, and other *inorodtsy* (aliens). Instead of the ethnically inclusive liberal nationalism of 1860–70, an exclusive nationalism with clear racial motives, accentuated by Orthodox faith and a conservative political agenda, moved to the forefront of Russian politics. Referring to the neo-Russian style in architecture and art as an awkward attempt to come back to the pre-Petrine Rus' of the seventeenth century, State Council Petr Valuev wrote sarcastically in his diary that "[t]he *mot d'ordre* now is Russian roots, Russian forces, Russian people—in a word, Russicism of all kinds."[77]

The 1880s brought a new example of Russian–German entanglement into nation-building. From 1883–85, when Germany forcibly expelled 32,000 Russian subjects from Prussia to the Russian Empire, the Russian authorities proved to be rather good pupils. They learned fast how to use citizenship as a tool for restricting the ability of foreign subjects to acquire landed property in the western borderlands, and imposed a system, which closely resembled one used in Germany, upon Chinese and Korean laborers in railroad construction and gold mining industries, preventing them from settling permanently in the empire.[78] Imposing these restrictions, the authorities, however, still welcomed immigration into big cities, where they hoped for relatively quick assimilation of the newcomers.

The concept of Nation, which had remained almost exclusive to liberal property in the previous decades, was now successfully claimed by anti-liberal forces. Russian liberals, feeling more and more alienated from the state and dynasty, at the same time began to distance themselves from the nationalist rhetoric and agenda. During the last decades of the nineteenth century, the assimilating drive of liberal Russian nationalism was gradually replaced by the new, exclusivist approach. Racial thinking and social Darwinism went hand in hand with the wish to exploit the empire and her borderlands as the property of the Russian nation. The non-Russian

---

[75] The painting of Ilia Repin which presents the Tsar surrounded by venerating peasants was reproduced in numerous prints. Alexander III was the first Romanov after Peter I's father Alexey Mikhailovich to wear a beard, and its shape was similar to that of Russian peasants.

[76] A good analysis of Pobedonostsev's Russification program can be found in Edward C. Thaden, *Conservative Nationalism in Nineteenth Century Russia* (Seattle: University of Washington Press, 1966), 183–203.

[77] P. A. Valuev, *Dnevnik 1877–1884 gg.*, 181

[78] Eric Lohr, *Russian Citizenship: From Empire to Soviet Union* (Cambridge: Harvard University Press, 2012).

population in the borderlands, particularly Asiatic borderlands, were seen more and more as the object of exploitation and suppression, rather than assimilation and elevation to the level common with Russians. Russian nationalism soon became dissociated with the agenda of political liberation and closely linked to the image of the repressive autocracy not only in the minds (and in propagandistic efforts) of peripheral elites but also among Russian counter-elites who were growing in numbers and influence.

Constitutional Period: 1905–1914

The revolution of 1905, triggered by defeat in the war with Japan, finally forced the monarchy to make concessions on the constitutional issue.[79] The Manifesto of October 17, 1905 introduced an empire-wide political representation—the State Duma. All parts of the empire and all groups of the population, including the Jews, could vote, although the electoral system clearly privileged the internal *gubernias* and Russian population.

However, even after the revolution, the monarchy and the liberals from the Constitutional Party (*Kadets*) failed to forge an alliance or at least establish some basic mutual trust. Locked in the opposition to the monarchy and government, Russian liberals found themselves in a situation where they had to look for allies in elections among non-Russian nationalist elites in the borderlands, because their main rivals on the right had captured the agenda of Russian nationalism for themselves. This tactic worked in some cases when local nationalists gave *Kadets* enough votes to beat their rightwing opponents. But the alliance was based on shaky tactical ground, not on ideological proximity. Being decisively opposed to any demands for federalization of the empire made by their partners in the borderlands, *Kadets* still had to introduce the slogans of autonomy into their program and electoral campaigns. They were trying to dissociate the idea of autonomy from nationalism, suggesting the introduction of autonomous units, which would not coincide with the national territories of the peripheral national groups.[80] Their partners in the borderlands were never satisfied with what *Kadets* could offer without alienating their Russian sympathizers. In their negotiations, *Kadets* and the borderland nationalists were both trying to avoid thorough debate of the nationality issues, of autonomy and federation, because both sides knew that at the end of the day their positions were irreconcilable.

---

[79] Abraham Ascher, *The Revolution of 1905: A Short History* (Palo Alto: Stanford University Press, 1988).

[80] See Kadet constitutional projects in: "Konstitucionnoe gosudarstvo. Sbornik statei. SPb.," *Obschestvennaia pol'za*, 1905 C. 527–73. For the party program on autonomy see: "Programma konstitucionno-demokraticheskoi partii, vyrabotannaia s'ezdom partii 12–18 oktiabria 1905 g.," in *S'ezdy i konferencii konstitucionno-demokraticheskoi partii* (Moscow: ROSSPEN, 1997), vol. 1, 1905–1907, 37.

Despite this, Russian liberals invariably sided with the nationalist representatives of the borderlands in the Duma. The attempts of Prime Minister Petr Stolypin to invite liberals into the government failed, while his reformist policy in agrarian and colonization issues were making him also a target for the political attacks by the conservative right, as well as terrorist attacks by the revolutionaries. Throughout the constitutional period, Russian nationalism failed to provide the ground for a broader political coalition.

The structure of the political field after 1905 created a situation in which Russian nationalism became clearly divorced from the agenda of political liberalism, and was rather associated with the revanchist autocratic monarchy and xenophobic quarters of Russian society. Nicholas II developed close ties with the extreme nationalist right, including the Black Hundred. The authorities were intensively using various anniversary celebrations, including 300 years of the Romanov dynasty in 1913, to mobilize nationalist public support for the monarchy. The appeal of such a policy was, however, limited. The failure of Nicholas II to accept the role of a constitutional monarch caused deepening alienation between the dynasty and liberals in spite of the growing strength of radical socialist groups. Peripheral nationalists did their best to link their demands to the all-imperial agenda of political liberation, while trying to present their enemies, Russian nationalists in the borderlands, as a purely reactionary and undemocratic force. Russian nationalists in the borderlands were not always as reactionary and undemocratic as their opponents tried to present them, but they felt that their alarming voices about the danger of peripheral separatism were ignored by the majority of the Russian liberal public in the center and had to rely mostly on cooperation with the monarchy and the ministers.

On the other hand, Nicholas II was the first monarch who paid really serious attention to the development of elementary education. Between 1896 and 1900, state funding for primary schools duplicated, and the next double increase was achieved by 1907; from 1907 to 1914 spending in this area had quadrupled. In 1881, spending on education constituted 2.69% of the state budget and primary schools were getting a fraction of this money, while in 1914 education received 7.21% of the state budget, and the portion assigned to primary schools also increased.[81] Systematic increase in state funding of primary education brought Russia very close to the introduction of obligatory primary schooling on the eve of WWI.[82] Together with intensification of urbanization and migration flows, this measure could have potentially had a long lasting impact on the nation-building processes across the empire.

---

[81] Eklof, *Russian Peasant Schools*, 89–90.
[82] Only 32.6 percent of recruits in 1912 were illiterate, which was not much worse than 24.9 percent of illiterate Americans drafted in 1917. See Joshua Sanborn, "The Mobilization of 1914 and the Question of the Russian Nation: A Reexamination," *Slavic Review* 59, no. 2 (Summer 2000): 267–89, figures on 285.

The Nationalist Discourse of Territoriality in the Western Part of the Empire

Territoriality invariably plays an important role in imagining and building a nation. Imagining national territory within Russian nationalism was inextricably related to the imperial context. First, in a continental empire like Russia, carving out a national territory within the imperial space was difficult and fraught with contradictions. Secondly, in Russia, more than in any other empire, the idea of national territory was not fixed and the latter tended to expand with time, which was conditioned by the migration processes (to be considered in the next section) and the on-going territorial expansion in the nineteenth century. Finally, the structure of imperial space not only opened perspectives for national territorial expansion, but also produced spaces of struggle between Russian nationalism and alternative projects of national consolidation on the imperial peripheries.

In the eighteenth century, nation and empire largely coincided.[83] The very notions of empire and nation were used in the Russian language of the epoch as synonyms that could be used to refer to Russia.[84] Eastern Slavs, most of whom were Greek Orthodox, constituted over 80% of the population. Already at that time, the differences between Great, Little, and White Russians were often perceived as differences between the branches of a single "Slaveno-Russian" people, rather than between three different nations. This is testified by "Synopsis," written in the Kiev Cave Monastery in 1674, soon after the Hetmanate on the left bank of the Dnieper came under the authority of Moscow. During the eighteenth century, "Synopsis" remained the main historical text that by the beginning of the nineteenth century went through more than 30 editions.[85] However, this view still had to be translated into the language of modern nationalism and become dominant. Before the partitions of Poland, the image of common nationhood of the Great and Little Russians included only the territory of the Hetmanate that is, up to the left bank of the Dnieper, and did not spread beyond the imperial borders of the time.

According to the eighteenth-century notions, only the Baltic provinces in the West and Siberia in the East were non-Russian territories. The Asiatic part of the empire was seen as a colony and the new border of Europe was drawn along the Ural Mountains (and not the Don River), which made the empire look more like a

---

[83] Willard Sunderland, "Imperial Space: Territorial Thought and Practice in the Eighteenth Century," in *Russian Empire*, eds. Burbank, von Hagen, and Remnev, 33–66; Yuri Slezkine, "Naturalists Versus Nations: Eighteenth-Century Russian Scholars Confront Ethnic Diversity," *Representations* 2 (1994): 170–95, 174.

[84] Aleksei Miller, "Narodnost' i natsiia v russkom iazyke XIX veka: podgotovitelnye nabroski k istorii poniatii," *Rossiiskaia istoria*, no. 1, 46–60.

[85] A. Ju. Samarin, *Rasprostranenie i chitatel' pervykh pechatnykh knig po istorii Rossii (konets XVII–XVIII v.)* (Moscow: MGUP, 1998).

European power and corresponded to its new European identity.[86] This ideological conceptualization of space took place against the background of great efforts at mapping the empire. Willard Sunderland describes the eighteenth century as the period of "high territoriality" and notes that "the eighteenth-century elite's preoccupation with defining the Russian nation produced a related impulse to define both the national territory and the territory of the empire. Eighteenth-century scholars did indeed draw some distinction between national and imperial space ... but at the same time, these very scholars also had a variety of reasons for conflating the two spaces."[87]

For the Russian Empire, the late eighteenth and early nineteenth century was a time of considerable territorial acquisitions in the west, resulting from the partitions of Poland and the victory over Napoleon. This greatly increased the ethnic heterogeneity of the population. Suffice it to say that numerous Polish *szlachta* and almost half of European Jewry became imperial subjects. Initially, all new territories were perceived as imperial borderlands and were granted various forms of autonomy.[88] Among the noble radicals and future Decembrists, already during the 1820s there were projects of transforming the empire into a national state-republic by strong assimilatory pressures. However, these ideas did not gain much currency in the first half of the nineteenth century. Projects of radical assimilation were not popular among the imperial elite, which undoubtedly preferred indirect rule and various forms of compromise with the regional elites. Until the end of the 1820s, most newly-acquired territories were still considered non-Russian imperial borderlands. In 1818–19, Alexander I even considered transferring to the Kingdom of Poland some territories of the former Grand Duchy of Lithuania, which were incorporated into the Russian Empire as a result of Polish partitions.

A drastic change in the dominant discourse about the limits of Russian national territory in the west occurred as part of the reaction to the Polish uprising of 1830–31. Among the most important elements of the ideological response to the uprising was the official promotion of a new, much more nationalized historical narrative. It was most consistently presented by Nikolai Ustryalov, who, in 1837, was awarded the prize for the best Russian history textbook. Ustryalov was patronized by the imperial Minister of Education Count Serguey Uvarov. Ustryalov gave the clearest definition of the aims of history as being national history, in direct opposition to Karamzin who

---

[86] Mark Bassin, "Russia between Europe and Asia: The Ideological Construction of Geographical Space," *Slavic Review* 50, no. 1 (1991): 1–17; Willard Sunderland, "Imperial Space," 43. Vasilii Tatischev, who suggested the Urals as the new border of Europe, wrote of Russia proper (*Rossija sama soboju*) and its peripheries.

[87] Willard Sunderland, *Taming the Wild Field: Colonization and Empire on Russian Steppe* (Ithaca: Cornell University Press, 2004), 77.

[88] Victor Taki, "Istoricheskaia pamiat' i konstruirovanie regiona posle prisoedinenia k imperii: Osobaia forma upravlenia Bessarabii, 1812–1828," *Ab Imperio: History and Theory of Nationalism in the Post-Soviet Realm*, no. 3 (2004): 223–58.

wrote the history of the state and ruling dynasty.[89] According to Ustryalov, the history of the state was less extensive than the history of the nation, since for a long time the state did not include Western Russia, that is, the lands of the Great Principality of Lithuania.[90] This assertion, in turn, allowed Ustryalov to provide a new historical basis for claims to the lands annexed during the partitions of the Polish-Lithuanian Commonwealth and their inclusion in Russian national territory—a basis which fitted in neatly with Uvarov's policy on this issue.[91] The claim that Little Russia and White Russia belonged not only to the empire but also to Russian national territory became a doctrine of Russian nationalism ever since, and remained unchanged until the twentieth century. According to Ustryalov, the Russian notions of the Great Lithuanian Principality were corrupted and its "Russian nature" obfuscated by the Poles, "who, having subsequently enslaved the best part of the Russian land, also tried to deform its history."[92] The anti-Polish sentiment in Ustryalov's arguments was attractive to the Little Russian elites of the Western Province who entertained anti-Polish feelings.[93] Quoting Ustryalov at length demonstrates how dominate his nationalist perspective became in Russia's historic narrative of the nation:

> The history of the Lithuanian Principality which emerged in the Russian lands, preserved the main conditions of the Russian nationality, served as a cause for almost all the conflicts between the sovereigns of Muscovy and the Polish kings, and which finally returned to the bosom of the ancient father state—the history of this Principality deserved the same attention of the writer as the fate of Muscovy, especially if one takes into consideration that: 1) the Lithuanian Principality before the final union with Poland, in the first half of the 16th century, and before the Church Union, had been Russian in the full sense ... 3) the union of the Lithuanian Principality and Poland was a matter of chance 4) its inhabitants, despite all the efforts of the Polish government, have never abandoned the idea of kinship with Russia ... 6) that, finally, the striving, on the one hand, for domination over all of the Russian land and the effort

[89] N. Ustryalov, *O sisteme pragmaticheskoy russkoy istorii* (St. Petersburg, 1836), 21.
[90] Ustryalov meant the Great Principality of Lithuania before its unification with Poland, i.e., with the lands along the river Dnieper. See N. G. Ustryalov, *Issledovanie voprosa, kakoe mesto v russkoy istorii dolzhno zanimat' Velikoe knyazhestvo Litovskoe?* (St. Petersburg: MNP, 1839).
[91] Meanwhile, as early as 1819, N. M. Karamzin had used every argument imaginable in his so-called "Letter from a Russian Citizen," in which he objected to Alexander I's plan to unite part of this territory with the Kingdom of Poland—apart from this one. See more in Alexei Miller, *The Romanov Empire*, Ch. 6.
[92] Ustryalov, *O sisteme pragmaticheskoi russkoi istorii*, 72.
[93] "Here we stand and take up arms against the Polish spirit for holy, ancient, first-called Kievan Rus,'" wrote M. A. Maksimovich to Vyazemsky in 1840. See "Pis'ma M. P. Pogodina, S. P. Shevyreva i M. A. Maksimovicha kniaziu P. A. Vyazemskomu," *Starina i novizna* (St. Petersburg, 1901), book 4, 199.

not to allow its unification, on the other, was the sole source of all the wars between Russia and Poland ... To show the fate of the Russian people beyond the Dnieper, all the sufferings it experienced under the Polish yoke, all the policies of the Roman Court and the Warsaw Sejm, is one of the most important tasks of History ... The intrigues of the Polish magnates and Jesuits were the only obstacle to the reunification of the two peoples of one tribe, one faith, separated by accidental circumstances.[94]

Comparing the views of Ustryalov and Karamzin, one can see that this system of argumentation is radically different from the discourses of "the last chronicler." In 1819, Karamzin was ready to admit that the policy of Catherine II in regard to the Polish-Lithuanian Commonwealth was an aggressive and worthy of regret, while Ustryalov wrote of "the unification of almost all the Russian lands in one whole by Catherine II."[95] We must also note that Ustryalov fully repeats the interpretation of the Russian-Polish conflict by Alexander Pushkin in his poems of 1831. Minister Uvarov himself translated Pushkin's poem "Klevetnikam Rossii" ("To the Slanderers of Russia") into French, and, on October 8, 1831, sent his translation to the author, "in admiration for the beautiful, truly *national* verses." It is indicative that one of the staunchest opponents of autocracy, Petr Chaadaev, called Pushkin a "national poet" for the same poem.[96] Nationalism had immediately demonstrated its effectiveness as a basis for the union of the oppositional elite and the authorities in times of crises and external threats.

Before 1830, the peasantry and other unprivileged groups of the western region were considered to be Polish nobility's cultural property of a kind. After the uprising, the better part of these lands were proclaimed as being "eternally Russian" (or "Russian since the time immemorial") and the empire started an intense struggle against Polish cultural influence. Measures aimed at "restoring" the Russian character of the lands that had suffered from a prolonged Polish dominance, included "bringing back the Uniates into the Orthodox fold" in 1839, an active study of early texts in order to substantiate a new conceptualization of this territory,[97] as well as closure of the Polish educational establishments and transfer of the education system to the Russian language.

The theme of national property rights on the territories of the western region was discussed with a renewed intensity in the wake of the Polish uprising of 1863–64. More specifically, close attention to property rights constituted a new element of the politics of territoriality in the western borderlands. Whereas, after the uprising of 1830–31, the *szlachta*'s economic dominance in the region remained unquestioned,

---

[94] Ustryalov, *O sisteme pragmaticheskoi russkoi istorii*, 36–37, 44.

[95] Ibid., 47.

[96] Letter of Chaadaev to Pushkin of September 18, 1831. See: *Perepiska Pushkina v dvukh tomakh*, vol. 2 (Moscow: Khudozhestvennaia literatura, 1982), 281.

[97] Imperial Commission for the Study of Early Texts (Archeographical Commission) was created in 1834.

now, the empire took a number of measures in order to undermine Polish and strengthen Russian landownership here. Land owned by participants in the uprising was confiscated. While Poles were prohibited from buying land in the region, a special tax was imposed on all Polish landowners in order to prompt them to sell their possessions. A large number of landless *szlachta* and those of its members who owned little land were deprived of noble status.[98] A system of special measures facilitated the acquisition of lands by Russian nobles. The right to buy land in the western region accorded to the Jews on the eve of the uprising was abolished in 1864, as they were not corresponding to the new policy of russification of the landed property. Later, the government introduced restrictions on the acquisition of land by any foreign subjects, while in the last decades of the nineteenth century, as Russian relations with the united Germany deteriorated, similar limitations were imposed on the Russian subjects of German origin.

Special attention paid to the composition of large landowners is partly explained by the role they played in the *zemstvo* organizations. Only on the left bank of the Dnieper were the latter created simultaneously with their counterparts in the Great Russian *gubernias*. This was yet another testimony to the fact that the territory of the Hetmanate was successfully incorporated into national territory already in the first half of the nineteenth century. Immediately after the uprising, there were plans to include some of the districts of the *gubernias* of the Western region into the left-bank *gubernias*. "Firmer social foundations of Russian way of life" in the left-bank *gubernias* served as an argument for such a transfer.[99]

An active campaign for the restoration of Orthodox churches in the region took place, which in practice often meant confiscating and rendering the Orthodox churches that had been built as Orthodox, but were then turned into Catholic churches at the time of the Polish-Lithuanian Commonwealth. New Orthodox churches were built in places of the earlier existing ones that had been destroyed. At the end of the nineteenth century and beginning of the twentieth century, a number of new Orthodox churches were built in the particularly sensitive locations in order to emphasize the Russian character of this territory. A pertinent illustration is offered by the Trinity Cathedral of the Orthodox Pochaev monastery (near Ternopol', close to the western border of the empire) that belonged to the Greek-Catholic Church between 1720 and 1831. It was built under personal patronage of Nicholas II from 1906–12, in

---

[98] Daniel Beauvois, *Gordiev uzel Rossijskoi Imperii: vlast,' shlikhta i narod na Pravobereznoi Ukraine (1793–1914)* (Moscow: NLO, 2011).

[99] That was the way Ivan Aksakov saw the Left-Bank Ukraine and Novorossia in the 1860s; he suggested that particular districts of the Southwestern province be included, for their "sanation," into these territories. See I. Aksakov, "Ob izmenenii granits Zapadnogo kraia," in I. S. Aksakov, *Sochineniia. Vol. 3. Pol'skii vopros i zapadno-russkoe delo. Evreiskii vopros. 1860–1886* (St. Petersburg, 1900), 265–66. He suggested similar measures for the Northwest province as well. It should be noted that his arguments are always presented within the framework of the Russian nationalist discourse; his main criterion is "more of the Russian public element" (267). (First published in *Den'*, October 26, 1863).

the Novgorod version of Russian architectural modernism amidst the ensemble of buildings in the style of Austrian baroque.

New elements in the discourse of the Russian national character in the western region appeared, in the second half of the nineteenth century, as a challenge to the emerging Ukrainian nationalism, complementing the threat of Polish nationalism in these territories. All-Russian national unity was emphasized often through comparison with Western European nations. Nikolai Kostomarov, who wrote the article, "Two Russian Nations" [*narodnosti*], treating Great Russians and Little Russians as separate nations, received a scathing rebuke from the most prominent Russian nationalist journalist of the time, Katkov, who wrote: "An outrageous and absurd sophistry ... that two Russian nations and two Russian languages are possible—it's as if two French nations and two French languages were possible!"[100] References to the German example of national unification, despite the existence of different historical traditions and dialects of the German lands, became frequent after 1866 and especially after 1871. A monument to Bogdan Khmelnitskii was built in Kiev in 1888, the inscriptions on the pedestal of which read: "We want to go under the Eastern, Orthodox tsar" and "United and indivisible Russia to Bogdan Khmelnitskii." Suggested by an enemy of the Ukrainian nationalists, a Little Russian nobleman Mikhail Iuzefovich, the second inscription referred specifically to the indivisibility of the Russian nation comprising the Great and the Little Russians.

At the same time, the logic of this discourse was pushing the boundaries of the "Russian national territory" beyond the empire's borders, into the provinces of the Habsburg Empire populated by East Slavs. The discourse of *Cherwonaja* (Red) Rus' (Eastern Galicia) and *Ugorskaja* (Ugric) or *Karpatskaja* (Carpathian) Rus' (Bukovina and present-day Transcarpathian Ukraine) was different in principle from the general Russian panslavist discourse on the Slavs of the Habsburg and Ottoman Empires. It was, in essence, a discourse of nationalist irredenta. Already in the nineteenth century, the Russian nationalists repeatedly criticized "Catherine's mistake"—in the course of partitions, the Empress left the "Russian" population of East Galicia to the Austrian empire where it remained "under the Polish rule."

Thus, according to this vision, the "truly Russian lands" were divided into "well-accommodated," that is those where their Russian character was well established; "ailing," that is those that required an eradication of hostile influences in the western borderland; and, finally, the ones that remained "torn away," that is, not included in the empire, and, as a result, into the national body.

This discourse remained in force up until the collapse of the empire. When in 1911, the creation of the Kholm (Chelm) *gubernia* was discussed in the Duma (that is, transferring Kholmshchina (Chelm region) from the Kingdom of Poland to South-Western Province), Vladimir Bobrinskii II argued that this territory should be "in an uncontested national possession not of Russia—everything here is Russia—but of

---

[100] M. N. Katkov, *1863 god. Sobranie statei, po pol'skomu voprosu, pomeshchavshikhsia v Moskovskikh Vedomostiakh, Russkom Vestnike i Sovremennoi Letopisi. Vypusk 1* (Moscow, 1887), S. 276

Rus', so that this land would be not only a part of the Russian state, but be universally recognized as an ancient Russian land, that is Rus.'"[101] This did not prevent Bobrinskii from admitting that the population of *Kholmshchina* was deeply polonized, but this fact served as an argument in favor of urgent steps to "save" "its original Russian nature," which was not altogether lost. "This is an exceptionally sickly, tormented Russian land," wrote Bobrinskii, "and so it is singled out to treat it with a particular attention and care."[102] The symbolism of Russian nationalism transpires with particular clarity in the image of the national body distinct from the empire, and an ailing part of the national body distinct from an imperial province.

It is in connection with the western peripheries that it becomes possible to trace how the discourse of the national territory was reflected in the concepts of such prominent Russian nationalist liberals and imperialists as Petr Struve prior to and during the First World War. He begins his article "Great Russia and Holy Rus'" with the statements that "Russia is a nation-state" and so, as it is "expanding its nucleus geographically, the Russian state has turned into a state that, while multiethnic, possesses, at the same time, a national unity."[103] It is exactly these quotations that are often presented in the argument that nation-state and empire have been conflated in the Russian perception. Meanwhile, in that same article, Struve speaks of a "national nucleus state," in which "Russian tribes melted into a single nation." He notes the ability of this national nucleus to expand, and differentiates it from imperial expansion. The connection of various peripheries to the "state-national nucleus" could be, according to Struve, "purely or predominantly a state matter," or, possibly, that of "state and culture, leading in its final development to the complete assimilation, russification of the 'aliens.'" Struve's ideal is, of course, a gradual expansion of the nation-state to fill the boundaries of the imperial state, based on "the law and a representative political system," but he, first of all, clearly sees the differences between them, and secondly, he understands his ideal as a distant perspective. Some time earlier, in his polemic with Ukrainian nationalism, Struve repeatedly used the formula "a Russian Russia," meaning exactly the "all-Russian nation."[104]

When Struve goes on to formulate the goals of Russia in the war, it turns out that the most important task, in his opinion, is to "reunite and blend together with the empire all parts of the Russian people," which means the annexation of the "Russian Galicia." Here, he resorts again, as is generally typical of the nationalist discourse of organic unity, to the metaphor of sanitation of the national body, proving that the annexation of Eastern Galicia is necessary for the "internal sanitation of Russia, since the life of a Little Russian tribe under Austrian rule here has generated and given support

---

[101] *Gosudarstvennaia Duma, 3-ii sozyv. Stenograficheskie otchety 1911 g., Sessia* V, *Chast'* 1. *Zasedanie* 30, December 25, 1911. (St. Petersburg, 1911), 2745.

[102] Ibid., 2746.

[103] *Russkaia mysl'* no. 12 (1914): 176–80.

[104] P. B. Struve, "Obshcherusskaia kul'tura i ukrainskii partikuliarizm," *Russkaia mysl'* no. 1 (1912): 68, 82.

to the ugly so-called Ukrainian question." The second task, from Struve's standpoint, is to "regenerate Poland as a single national organism." This exclusion from the empire of the ethnically Polish lands becomes a dear idea of the Russian nationalists since Katkov. After the uprising of 1863, Katkov argued in his letters to Alexander II that ethnic Poland should be "expelled" from the empire because of her detrimental influence on the Russian nation-building in the western borderlands. The control over the straits comes only third in Struve's argument about the aims of Russia in the Great War. Thus, in this hierarchy, Struve places first and second tasks that come directly from nationalist discourse, and does not bother to substantiate them as being obvious, concentrating instead on a lengthy explanation as to why Russia still needs Constantinople.

Already, the observations made in this section allow a better understanding of the discourse about the "core of Russia" emerging in the nineteenth century. It may be instructive to analyze the terms that were used for the spatial organization of the empire. The core of the empire was often described as an almost perfect circle with a diameter of 450 km centered on Moscow.[105] These lands were called "interior" (*vnutrenniaja*), "native" (*korennaja*), or "central" (*tsentral'naiia*) Russia. The lands of the Russian principalities annexed by Muscovy at the end of the fifteenth century were called "native Russia." In the historical narrative, the process of territorial expansion of the Grand Duchy of Muscovy was described as "gathering of the Russian lands." (Ustryalov also uses this trope to refer to the annexation of the territories of the Grand Duchy of Lithuania in the late eighteenth century.) Native Russia was thought to be characterized by ethno-cultural and religious homogeneity and an unquestioned loyalty to the dynasty and the state.

Moscow as the contemporary "heart," the embodiment of Russianness, and as the center of "gathering" the Russian lands was undoubtedly present in Russian nationalist discourse. In the traditionalist version of Russian nationalism, it was Muscovy that was contrasted to St. Petersburg's Imperial Russia. But the historical boundaries of Muscovy did not "work" in this discourse, or were perceived as a tool in the adversary discourses, as those clearly unacceptable boundaries to which her enemies want to reduce Russia.[106] It is noteworthy that "native Russia" could be imagined by means of "nodes" or "points of control," which, alongside Moscow, invariably included Novgorod and Kiev. The last two cities made part of this list in their capacity as major political and cultural centers of pre-Mongol Rus', which for a nineteenth century observer was embodied not only in the increasingly *national* historical narrative, but also in the majestic Orthodox churches of pre-Mongol epoch, especially in the Novgorod and Kiev cathedrals of Saint Sophia. The aesthetics of Novgorod churches inspired

---

[105] Leonid Gorizontov, "The Great Circle of 'Interior Russia': the Representations of Imperial Center in the Nineteenth and early Twentieth Century," in *Russian Empire*, eds. Burbank, von Hagen, and Remnev, 67–93.

[106] Shrinking Russia to the borders of Muscovy remains a nightmare scenario in Russian discourse even in the 21st century.

one of the variants of Russian modernist religious architecture of the late nineteenth century and the early twentieth century. For its part, Kiev acquired in this discourse the title of the "mother of Russian cities" and, in this capacity, partly took over Moscow. South Russia was gradually assimilated in the Russian nationalist discourse as different from Great Russia, but nevertheless, just as "native" as Muscovy. The growing currency of this view in the Russian society of the 1830s formed the basis of the fantastic popularity of Nikolai Gogol's early works on the Little Russian and South Russian way of life. In the nineteenth century, Kiev became the site of active archaeological excavations, initiated by nationally motivated enthusiasts from St. Petersburg and Moscow who were looking for the roots of Russia.[107]

The terms "central" and "interior" denoted the position of territories in the empire and referred to its functional core rather than to a national homeland. Interior *gubernias* had a standard civil administration, whereas the borderlands were ruled by viceroys and governor-generals, whose personal military and administrative authority compensated for the bureaucratic weakness of the empire and Russian society in the peripheries. The notions of interior and central Russia tended to expand with time, among other things, due to the replacement of governor-generals by a civil administration. This, in turn, created a new critical mass of educated Russians, often of noble origin, in the new *gubernia* centers and later, with the spread of *zemstvo* institutions, in the districts. For example, as the empire expanded beyond the Ural Mountains and into the Steppe region, the territories between the Volga and the Urals gradually turned from a periphery into a part of the core area.[108] Such an expansion of the center was reflected in bureaucratic practice. The Kokovtsev commission "on the impoverishment of the Center" (*ob oskudenii tsentra*), created in 1901, covered with its study not only the nine Great Russian *gubernias*, traditionally considered "central," but also Poltava, Kharkov, Chernigov, Orenburg, Kazan, Ufa and Don Cossack Host territory, altogether 18 *gubernias*.

Thus, one can see a gradual expansion of the notions of Russian national territory and functional center of the empire. These territorial entities often did not coincide and the processes of their expansion, while interrelated, had different logic. The mechanisms of extending "Russian national territory" likewise varied depending upon the region. In the south and the east of the empire, the nature of the process was described as *osvoenie zemel'*, a civilizing mission. "Making it Russian" primarily meant here "making a land Russian." In the western borderlands the task was formulated as recovering the Russian character of the land and of the people, while in the south and the east that meant giving the land a Russian character for the first time. The nature of the processes was indeed very different, as well as the nature of the claimed spaces. In

---

[107] Soon their finding will be claimed also by Ukrainian nationalists as Ukrainian heritage.
[108] Robert Geraci suggested calling this region an "internal borderland," but its borderland characteristics were steadily diminishing. For a close analysis of the mechanisms of introducing civil administration and zemstvo institutions in Bashkiria as well as their russifying effect, see Steinwedel, "How Bashkiria Became."

the south and in the east the space was perceived as mostly empty or sparsely populated by various sorts of "barbarians" or *inorodtsy*. Western borderlands were the "original Rus'" (that is what was expressed with the term *Malaia Rus'*), the population there was very numerous, and generally was not perceived by Russians as inferior in terms of civilization. These territories never constituted an object of any significant Great Russian peasant migration.

Migrations and Discourse of Territoriality in the South and East

"The history of Russia is the history of a land which is undergoing colonization" (*Istoriia Rossii est' istoriia strany, kotoraia kolonizuetsia*), stated one of the most influential Russian historians of the imperial period.[109] Migrations and colonization did indeed play a crucial role in various areas of life in the Russian Empire. They were particularly important for nation-building, since in the Russian Empire, more than in any other, the formation of an imperial nation until the First World War was tied to the spatial extension of the "national territory."[110]

Agricultural migration was predominant throughout most of Russian imperial history. Its development can be divided into two stages. Before the abolition of serfdom in 1861, most of the migrations were either illegal, that is, flights from serfdom and from state control, or forced, when serfs were resettled by decision of their proprietors, as described, for example, in Gogol's "Dead Souls" or in Leskov's stories. Migrations also took place when Cossaks were ordered by the central authorities to settle in a new borderland. The state provided some support for voluntary agricultural settlers, but most of them were immigrants (Germans, Serbs, Bulgarians, etc.).

After 1861, migrations became mostly voluntary—the driving forces behind them were the rural overpopulation of the central regions and the migrants' hope to acquire land and to create new, more prosperous homesteads in the empire's borderlands. The migrations of this period were partly contained by the peasant community (*obschina*) which presupposed a collective responsibility for taxation and a communal property of land. Within the post-reform era, one can single out the transitional period from the 1860s to the mid-1890s, when the state did not generally facilitate migrations, but, however reluctantly, had to meet the peasants' demand for resettling

---

[109] V. O. Kliuchevskii, *Russkaia istoriia. Polnyi kurs lektsii v trekh knigach*, vol. 1 (Moscow 1995), 20. Although the ethnic composition of the migratory and colonizing movements was extremely diverse, Kliuchevskii speaks mostly of the colonizing mission of the Russian peasant.

[110] It's possible to argue that migrations played no lesser role in the nation-building in the British Empire than in the Romanov Empire, but it was not linked, as in Russia, with the territorial expansion of the nationalized core.

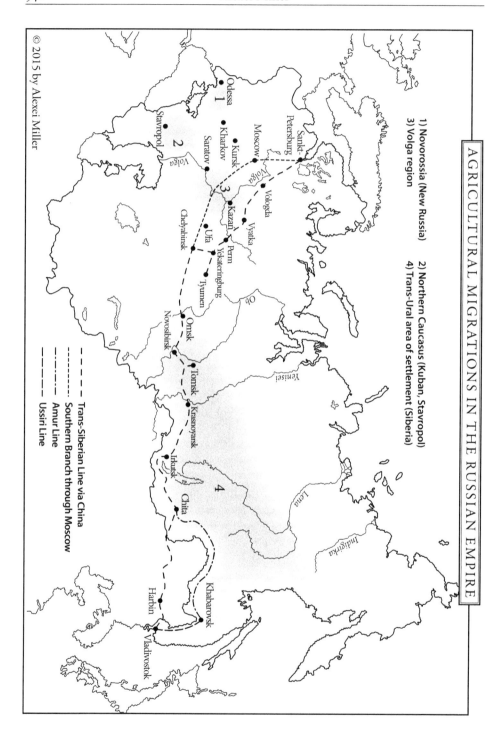

AGRICULTURAL MIGRATIONS IN THE RUSSIAN EMPIRE

1) Novorossia (New Russia)   2) Northern Caucasus (Kuban, Stavropol)
3) Volga region   4) Trans-Ural area of settlement (Siberia)

– – – – Trans-Siberian Line via China
········· Southern Branch through Moscow
– · – · – Amur Line
– – – – Ussiri Line

by passing laws that regulated the spontaneous movement.[111] Since the late nineteenth century, the state became a very active organizer in agricultural migration, especially as part of Prime Minister Petr Stolypin's program (1906–11). After 1861, and particularly in the late nineteenth and early twentieth centuries, migrations were "associated with the idea of a heroic national cause."[112]

During the different stages of migrations, migrants settled in different places. From 1782 to 1858, the main destinations were New Russia (1,510,000) and the Volga and Ural regions (968,000). During this period, the number of migrants to the North Caucasus reached 565,000 and to Siberia and the Steppe Province, 517,000. The transitional period from 1870 to 1896 is clearly marked by changes in the direction of migrations. The number of migrants to the already saturated Volga and Ural regions decreased by almost two-thirds (358,000), and to New Russia by one-third (1,045,000). The North Caucasus, where the long war with the indigenous mountain peoples had finally come to an end in the 1860s, experienced the inward migration of 1,687,000 in the last thirty years of the nineteenth century. The flow of migrants to Siberia and the Steppe Province sharply increased in this period, up to 926,000. The period between 1897 and 1915, particularly after 1906, when the state started to pursue active migration policies by means of supporting agricultural resettlement,[113] saw a real revolution in the directions of migratory flows. The number of migrants in all the traditional directions plummeted sharply—to New Russia it was down to 333,000, to the Volga and Ural regions down to 80,000, and to the North Caucasus to 296,000. The main destination was now the Trans-Ural part of the empire, where 3.5 million people resettled in this period.[114]

These migrations were radically changing the ethnic balance in the target regions, as well as the perception of the character of these lands. Thus, in the latter half of the nineteenth century, the Russians already constituted over 50 percent of the entire population of the Volga-Ural region, and were numerically predominant in all the

[111] During this period, particularly after 1881, the authorities demonstrated similar dubious attitude to the Jewish migration outside the Empire—not preventing it, but, for a long time, not providing legal ground for such movement.

[112] Alberto Masoero, "Territorial Colonization in Late Imperial Russia: Stages in the Development of a Concept," *Kritika: Explorations in Russian and Eurasian History* 14, no. 1 (Winter 2013): 59–91, quotation on 63. See also Lutz Hafner, "Russland und die Welt: Das Zarenreich in der Migrationsgeschichte des langen 19. Jahrhunderts," in *Globalisierung imperial und sozialistisch. Russland und die Sowjetunion in der Globalgeschichte 1851–1991*, ed. Martin Aust (Frankfurt: Campus Verlag, 2013), 64–83.

[113] Created in 1905, the Main Administration for Land Management and Agriculture (*Glavnoe upravlenie zemleustroistva i zemledeliia*) in 1906 had a 5 million rouble budget for colonization, in 1914 it was more than 30 million. See: Willard Sunderland, "The Ministry of Asiatic Russia: The Colonial Office that Never Was but Might Have Been," *Slavic Review* 69, no. 1 (2010): 120–50; Donald W. Treadgold, *The Great Siberian Migration: Government and Peasant in Resettlement from Emancipation to the First World War* (Princeton: Princeton University Press, 1957); George Yaney, *The Urge to Mobilize: Agrarian Reform in Russia, 1861–1930* (Urbana: University of Illinois Press, 1982).

[114] See B. N. Mironov, *Sotsial'naia istoriia Rossii*, vol. 1 (St. Petersburg, 1999), 22–25.

cities of the area, annexed to the empire in the sixteenth and seventeenth centuries after the conquest of the Kazan and Astrakhan khanates. This provided a basis for a rather active assimilation policy in regard to the Volga region's native minorities— through conversion to the Orthodox faith and the dissemination of the Russian language and of Russian agricultural practices.

The Muslim Tatar elite, which in the eighteenth century had been regarded by authorities as a convenient intermediary in communication with the indigenous population of the Volga and Steppe areas, was by the nineteenth century recognized to be the main danger to the russification policy, a carrier of the pan-Turkic ideology and, primarily, an Islamization agency. When Islamic proselytism was identified as a challenge, the missionary and educator N. I. Ilminskii proposed the idea of Christianization through translations of prayers and religious books into indigenous languages, believing that the most urgent task was to prevent the spread of Islam among heathens and the return to Islam of previously baptized Tatars, while linguistic assimilation was to follow later.[115] In the 1860s, further anti-Islamic and anti-Tatar measures included founding the missionary organization of the Brotherhood of St. Gurii, the abolition of Tatar self-government in Kazan, and the closing of Tatar language instruction in the Kazan gymnasium in order to limit the formation of laic educated strata among Kazan Tatars.

However, it would be incorrect to describe the Russians' relations with the Muslims of the Volga exclusively through the prism of confrontation. It was in that region that the authorities were gradually developing a model for peaceful coexistence between Christians and Muslims.[116] By having created a formal hierarchy of Muslim clergy loyal to the state, authorities also opened opportunities for ordinary Muslims to complain about clerical abuses to the state bodies, thus creating additional loyalty mechanisms.[117]

---

[115] N. I. Ilminskii, *Iz perepiski po povodu del o primenenii russkogo alfavita k inorodcheskim iazykam* (Kazan, 1883). See also: Alexei Miller, "Rossiiskaia imperiia, natsionalism i protsessy formirovaniia natsii v Povolzh'e," *Ab Imperio*, no. 3 (2003): 393–406; W. Dowler, *Classroom and Empire: The Politics of Schooling Russia's Eastern Nationalities, 1860–1917* (Montreal: McGill-Queen's University Press, 2001); P. W. Werth, *At the Margins of Orthodoxy: Mission, Governance and Confessional Politics in Russia's Volga-Kama Region, 1827–1905* (Ithaca: Cornell University Press, 2001).

[116] Robert Crews, *For Prophet and Tsar: Islam and Empire in Russia and Central Asia* (Cambridge, Mass.: Harvard University Press, 2006); L. A. Taimasov, "From 'Kazan's Newly Converted' to 'Orthodox Inorodtsy': The Historical Stages of the Affirmation of Christianity in the Middle Volga Region," in *Imperiology: From Empirical Knowledge to Discussing the Russian Empire*, ed. K. Matsuzato, *Slavic Eurasian Studies* no. 13 (Sapporo: Slavic Research Center, Hokkaido University, 2007), 111–38. See also: Daniel R. Brower and E. J. Lazzerini, eds., *Russia's Orient: Imperial Borderlands and Peoples, 1700–1917* (Bloomington: Indiana University Press, 1997).

[117] Crews, *For Prophet and Tsar*; Robert Crews, "Empire and the Confessional State: Islam and Religious Politics in Nineteenth-Century Russia," *American Historical Review* 108, no. 1 (2003): 50–83; Elena Campbell, "The Autocracy and the Muslim Clergy in the Russian Empire (1850s–1917)," *Russian Studies in History* 44 (2005): 8–29.

For the Finno-Ugric and Turkic peoples (Chuvash, Mari, Mordva) of the Volga region, a discourse was formulated that emphasized the complementary qualities of the Russian and indigenous populations. In this area, Russian nationalism spoke unashamedly of an age-old process of miscegenation between the Finno-Ugric groups and the Great Russians.[118] Marriages between Russian peasants and indigenous people were officially welcomed. "It seems to me that a russification or assimilation of the Chuvash with the Russian people can only be reached in three ways: the first, and most important, is through their adoption of Orthodoxy—anyone knows what importance our ordinary folk ascribe to a difference of faith; secondly, through conjugal unions; and thirdly, through the learning of Russian by the Chuvash," wrote Ivan Iakovlev, a student of Kazan University and a Chuvash, in his 1870 report to the trustee of the Kazan School District Petr Shestakov. It is perfectly clear that Iakovlev does not have the slightest doubt that not only adoption of faith and language, but also intermarriage of the Chuvash and Russians would not raise any objections from his addressee.[119] Although the results of the Christianization and russification of the indigenous population were time and time again questioned by Russian observers,[120] the perception of this region as a Russian national territory was already well established by the 1870s, and the river Volga acquired the status of a key national symbol.[121]

The fertile land of New Russia, adjacent to the Black Sea coast, was annexed by the Russian Empire in the eighteenth century as a result of the successful wars with the Ottoman Empire. The annexation of the Crimean Khanate in 1783 made the area secure for agricultural colonization. It was the main object of agricultural colonization

---

[118] It was different in the western borderlands, where Russian nationalism and the authorities emphasized the unquestionable Slavic-ness of the Russians in response to the Polish theories of the "Turkic" origins of the Great Russians, which were used by the empire's enemies in their fight over the influence on the Little and White Russians. See I. Rudnytsky, *Essays in Modern Ukrainian History* (Edmonton: Canadian Institute of Ukrainian Studies, 1987); and Miller, *The Ukrainian Question.*

[119] *Agrarnyi vopros i krest'ianskoe dvizhenie 50–70-kh godov XIX v. Materialy po istorii narodov SSSR.* Vypusk 6. (Moscow–Leningrad, 1936), 333. "The circumstances have made me into a Russian, and I am proud of this name, without, however, feeling ashamed for being a Chuvash and without forgetting my origins. As a Christian, who loves Russia and believes in her great future, I would wish with all my soul that the Chuvash, my compatriots, were enlightened by the light of the Gospel and would become one with the great Russian people," wrote Iakovlev of himself. (331–32).

[120] R. P. Geraci, "Ethnic Minorities, Anthropology, and Russian National Identity on Trial: The Multan Case, 1892–96," *The Russian Review* 59 (October 2000): 530–54; R. P. Geraci, *Window to the East: National and Imperial Identities in Late Tsarist Russia* (Ithaca: Cornell University Press, 2001); P. W. Werth, *At the Margins of Orthodoxy: Mission, Governance, and Confessional Politics in Russia's Volga-Kama Region, 1827–1905* (Ithaca: Cornell University Press, 2001); P. W. Werth, "'Inorodtsy' ob obrusenii: religioznoe obrashchenie, dukhovenstvo iz korennogo naseleniia i politika assimiliatsii v Rossii kontsa imperskogo perioda," *Ab Imperio,* no. 2 (2002): 105–34.

[121] See, e.g., A. N. Pypin, "Volga i Kiev," *Vestnik Evropy* (July 1885): 188–215

throughout the nineteenth century. The settlers included large numbers of Germans, Balkan Slavs, Greeks, and Jews from the Pale of Settlement,[122] but most of them were Little Russian and Great Russian peasants. Great Russians constituted more than 20 percent of the population of New Russia by the end of the nineteenth century, and Great and Little Russians combined, over 50 percent. The cultural russification of the region had greatly advanced by the end of the nineteenth century, and the Ukrainian movement that had sprung up into the empire in the mid-nineteenth century was weak there.

The peculiarity of the North Caucasus migrations was in the preliminary mass removal from these territories of the indigenous Muslim population. It had not always been a direct expulsion, but the authorities had invariably welcomed Muslim migration to the Ottoman Empire, the so-called *Muhajir* movement.[123]

In the Caucasus, like in other troubled areas, the settlers were headed by the Cossacks.[124] There were repeated conflicts between the peasants and the Cossacks, including land feuds. The Cossacks were prone to regard themselves as a separate group, which led them to attempt to formulate a particular Cossack nationalism in the early twentieth century.[125] However, the Cossacks were predominantly loyal to the state and understood themselves as a special part of the Russian nation.

More than two million migrants who settled in the North Caucasus in the nineteenth century, in combination with the Muslim migration out of the region, had significantly changed the demographical balance.[126] As a result, the Stavropol Province was separated in 1899 from the Caucasus general-governorship and became an ordinary *gubernia*, gradually acquiring, like Kuban, the status of Russian national territory. In other regions of the Caucasus, like subsequently in Turkestan, the Russian settlements were essentially enclaves, outposts of imperial influence. Being imperial possessions, but avoiding a total demographic occupation, Turkestan and the South Caucasus were not marked by Russian nationalism as *national* property.

By the end of the nineteenth century, the migration beyond the Urals, especially to Siberia and the Far East, becomes particularly important. The number of Trans-Ural migrants ran into millions even before the Stolypin reform, and reached

[122] That was the only at least partially successful program of Jewish agricultural settlement in the 19th century in the world, which created several dozens of stable settlements.

[123] I. Babich, V. Bobrovnikov, eds., *Severnyi Kavkaz, v sostave Rossiiskoi imperii* (Moscow: NLO, 2007), Chapter 7; Justin McCarthy, *Death and Exile: The Ethnic Cleansing of Ottoman Muslims, 1821–1922* (Princeton: Darwin Press, 1995).

[124] N. B. Breyfogle, *Heretics and colonizers: forging Russia's Empire in the South Caucasus* (Ithaca: Cornell University Press, 2005); N. B. Breyfogle, A. Schrader, and W. Sunderland, eds., *Peopling the Russian Periphery: Borderland Colonization in Eurasian History* (London: Routledge, 2007).

[125] Shane O'Rourke, "From Region to Nation: The Don Cossacks 1870–1920," in *Russian Empire*, Burbank et al., eds., 218–38.

[126] A. Tsutsiev, *Atlas etnopoliticheskoi istorii Kavkaza (1774–2004)* (Moscow: Europa, 2006).

about 3.5 million under Stolypin's resettlement program that was enacted in 1906.[127] The number of Little Russian peasant migrants suffering from the lack of land—as Great Russian peasants did—was very high.[128] The mechanism that worked both in New Russia and in the Caucasus for Little and Great Russian peasant settlers—namely, the acceleration of their coming together and assimilation under the conditions of migration—manifested itself with a particular clarity here. It was partly caused by the fact that in new places, especially when surrounded by a very different and sometimes hostile local population, the features of cultural similarity and religious commonality prevailed over the differences. Another reason was the separation of Little Russian peasants in new places from contacts with the Ukrainian movement activists and their propagandistic efforts. According to the 1926 census, half of the Ukrainians who had resettled in the Far East in the early twentieth century indicated Russian as their native language, despite the fact that the census was conducted in the midst of the *korenizatsiia* campaign, when Ukrainian-ness was highly welcomed by Soviet power.[129]

---

[127] Steven G. Marks, "Conquering the Great East: Kulomzin, Peasant Resettlement, and the Creation of Modern Siberia," in *Rediscovering Russia in Asia. Siberia and the Russian Far East*, eds. Stephen Kotkin and David Wolff (London: M. E. Sharpe, 1995), 23–39.

[128] E.g., there were no Ukrainians (Little Russians) in the Steppe Province (North Kazakhstan) in 1858. By the end of the century there were already about 100,000 Ukrainians, and by 1917, when Stolypin's program was fully underway, the number of Ukrainians in Kazakhstan exceeded 789,000. A similar tendency was observed in other Trans-Ural regions. With practically no Ukrainians there in 1858, the censuses of 1897–1900 show 137,000 Ukrainians in West Siberia, 25,000 in East Siberia, and 61,000 in the Far East. By 1917, the number of Ukrainians in West Siberia jumped to 375,000, in East Siberia to 96,000, and in the Far East to 427,000. In the Lower Volga region (Samara, Saratov, and Astrakhan gubernias) the number of Ukrainians in 1917 exceeded 545,000. Thus, in 1917, the number of Ukrainians living in the regions not adjacent to their ethnic territory amounted to almost 2.5 million. See S. I. Bruk and V. M. Kabuzan, "Chislennost' i rasselenie ukrainskogo etnosa v XVIII–nachale XX v.," *Sovetskaia etnografiia*, no. 5 (1981): table 3, 20–221.

[129] Andreas Kappeler, "Chochly und Kleinrussen: Die ukrainische ländische und städtische Diaspora in Russland vor 1917," *Jahrbücher fur Geschichte Osteuropas* 45 (1997), H. 1, 48–63, esp. 58; A. A. Novoselova, "Sibirskie khokhly: k voprosu ob etnicheskoi prinadlezhnosti," in *Etnografiia Altaia i sopredel'nykh territorii*, Issue 5 (Barnaul, 2003), 27–28; A. A. Novoselova, "Ukraintsy v Srednem Priirtysh'e: identifikatsiia i samoidentifikatsiia v kontse 19–nachale 20 v.," in *Ukraina-Zapadnaia Sibir': dialog kul'tur i narodov* (Tiumen, 2004), 51–62; A. A. Novoselova, "Potomki belorusskikh pereselentsev v derevniakh Srednego i Nizhnego techeniia reki Tary," in *Etnokul'turnye vzaimodeistviia v Sibiri (17–20 vv.)* (Novosibirsk, 2003). It is fairly difficult to assess the progress of assimilation among the Little Russian peasants in the early twentieth century, since many of the results of these process were annulled by the Soviet policy of ukrainization. However, in all the regions with massive Little Russian populations left outside of Soviet Ukraine (Siberia, the Far East, Kuban, Stavropol) and thus less susceptible to the ukrainization policy of the 1920s, the descendants of the early-twentieth century migrants are still calling themselves *Russian khokhly*.

Calculations show that in the second half of the nineteenth century, 1.5 million Little Russians/Ukrainians were "russified."[130]

The imperial authorities had always been extremely cautious about manifestations of Siberian separatism; whether it was real or imaginary. As early as the 1860s, a group of young men came up with a demand to grant Siberia the status of a colony, after the British model. They argued that Russians in Siberia had acquired such different qualities as to have become a nation in its own right, and proclaimed a possible separation of Siberia from Russia in the future. Their leaders, Grigorii Potanin and Nikolai Iadrintsev, were arrested and given long prison sentences.[131] The authorities used the celebration of the 300th anniversary of the incorporation of Siberia in 1882 for the propaganda of Siberian-Russian unity. It should be noted that in this official imperial discourse, the words "inseparable part" of Russia became a keynote. One of the sixteenth-century conquerors of Siberia, Ermak, was mythologized, included in history textbooks, and even in the pantheon of the most important historical figures represented in the Russia Millennium Monument, erected in Novgorod in 1862. Even though the Ermak expedition was not commissioned by the state, the new narrative emphasized this unbreakable bond between the state and the "people moving east" and received an academic confirmation in the complete geographical description of Russia undertaken by the H. M. Russian Geographical Society (IRGO).[132]

The Siberian jubilee coincided with the abolishing of the West-Siberian general-governorship, which marked the extension to Siberia of the administrative system characteristic of the inner *gubernias*. The strategic goal of these reforms was to establish a view that "Siberia does not and must not constitute a separate entity."[133] The late nineteenth century and early twentieth century marked a turning point in the Russian discourse of Siberia—from the Asian colonial possessions, an "alien land," Siberia was

---

[130] Bruk and Kabuzan, "Chislennost' i rasselenie," 26, 30.

[131] The Senate sentenced the society's leader G. N. Potanin to fifteen years of forced labor and N. M. Iadrintsev to ten years of imprisonment in a fortress. See: Dimitri Von Mohrenschildt, *Toward a United States of Russia: Plans and Projects of Federal Reconstruction of Russia in the Nineteenth Century* (Madison, NJ: Fairleigh Dickinson University Press, 1981), 104–05; I. Popov, "Iz vospominanii o G.N. Potanine," *Golos minuvshego*, no. 1 (1922): 141. Their sentences were later reduced, but Potanin still served five years in Sveaborg. Such a harsh punishment during the reformist era of Alexander II presented a sharp contrast to how the generally more repressive regime of his father Nicholas I had treated a similar group of Ukrainian separatists from the Cyril and Methodius Society—none of them were imprisoned. See: Miller, *The Ukrainian Question*. On Siberian regionalism, see also: W. Faust, *Russlands goldener Boden. Der sibirische Regionalismus in der zweiten Hälfte des 19. Jahrhunderts* (Cologne: Böhlau, 1980); Anatolii V. Remnev, "Rossiia i Sibir' v meniaiushchemsia prostranstve imperii (XIX–načalo XX v.)" in *Rossiiskaia imperiia v sravnitel'noi perspektive. Sbornik statei*, ed. Aleksei Miller (Moscow: NLO, 2004), 286–319.

[132] *Rossiia. Polnoe geograficheskoe opisanie nashego otechestva* (St. Petersburg, 1907), vol. 16 (*Zapadnaia Sibir'*), 174.

[133] S. G. Svatikov, *Rossiia i Sibir' (K istorii sibirskogo oblastnichestva v XIX v.)* (Prague, 1930), 77.

gradually turning into a "Russian land," an inalienable part of Russia as a nation.[134] Against the background of the speculations that the Russians would number 350–400 million by the end of the twentieth century, the image of Siberia as a living space for future generations and the image of a Eurasian Russian nation were becoming increasingly well established. The geographer Veniamin Semenov-Tianshanskii, for example, singled out a special "cultural-economic entity"—a "Russian Eurasia" (spanning the space between the Volga and the Enisei and from the Arctic Ocean to the empire's southern borders on the Caspian Sea) that must not be regarded as a borderland, but should be spoken of as a "native and fully equal Russian land."[135]

One of the aspects of the national appropriation of the colonized territories was toponymic russification. Initially, the formation of a toponymic system in the zone of Russian influence was arbitrary, a part of folk culture. It was a process of "landscape immersion" and of adoption (appropriation) of the native toponyms as being Russian; with the change of generations; they became a part of a national "world-view" and collective memory. Except for towns, the names of other geographical objects, such as rivers, lakes, marshes, mountains, and, most importantly, villages, were given and established by the Russians in convention with the indigenous population.[136] Equally important were the "transferred" toponymics—the place names brought by settlers from their places of origin to Asiatic Russia. The migrants transferred familiar geographical names to a new territory believing that those names belonged to the Russian toponymic system regardless of their past origin. The prefix "Novo-" ("New") reflected both a nostalgia for the native land left behind, and a hope for a new life in a new place, which would in time also become their own.[137]

The situation began to change in the mid-nineteenth century, when, along with the increasing state control over peasant migrations, the state's role in place naming also increased. A number of big city names in the borderlands had a typically imperial ring to them, such as Vladikavkaz, Vladivostok [Rule(r) of the Caucasus, Rule(r) of the East]. The authorities often prescribed for new towns names associated with the names of the imperial family.[138] The manager of the Siberian Railroad Committee,

[134] A. V. Remnev, "300-letie prisoedineniia Sibiri k Rossii: v ozhidanii 'novogo istoricheskogo perioda'," in *Kul'turologicheskie issledovaniia v Sibiri* (Omsk, 2007), no. 1 (21), 34; Claudia Weiß, *Wie Sibirien "unser" wurde. Die Russische Geographische Gesellschaft und ihr Einfluss auf die Bilder und Vorstellungen von Sibirienim 19. Jahrhundert* (Göttingen: V&R unipress GmbH, 2007).

[135] V. P. Semenov-Tian-Shanskii, "O mogushchestvennom territorial'nom vladenii primenitel'no k Rossii," in *Arabeski istorii* (Moscow: Tanais, 1996), Issue 7 (*Rozhdenie natsii*), 603–04, 608–09.

[136] For detail, see: V. N. Kurilov, *Russkii subetnos Zapadnoi Sibiri v seredine XIX v.: rasselenie i toponimiia*. Dissertatsia na soiskanie uchenoi stepeni kandidata istoricheskikh nauk (Novosibirsk: Novosibirsk State University, 2002).

[137] V. P. Nepoznak, "Perenesennaia toponimiia Zapadnoi Sibiri," in *Vostochnoslavianskaia onomastika* (Moscow: Nauka, 1979), 175–83.

[138] A. D. Kolesnikov, "Pereseleniia krest'ian v Zapadnuiu Sibir' v kontse XIX v.," *Voprosy istorii Sibiri*, issue 9 (Tomsk, 1976), 71.

Anatolii Kulomzin, gave the following recommendation to local officials during his trip to Siberia in 1896: "It is necessary, whenever possible, to lead the settlers to the idea to name their settlements in honor of the members of the imperial family, so as to contribute by all means necessary to the consolidation of this periphery with the native crucible."[139] This remark shows that the authorities did not always attempt to dictate their toponymic policy to the migrants, but engaged them in a kind of negotiating process on the subject. At the same time, migration to the uncultivated lands or lands inhabited by nomadic people created a new situation for the settlers, which fostered group solidarity and a connectedness with the authority, and also with the empire that played the role of a protector here.

"Russification" of the landscape of the newly settled territories became a widespread idea, which presupposed, primarily, large stretches of plough land, Russian Orthodox churches in villages, and, with time, monasteries.[140] In the "russifying" scenarios (imperial, Orthodox, and popular—which were close but not congruent), the mechanisms of turning an "unknown" land into a Russian Christian space included, along with the ploughing of the land, the awareness of it as being God-given and consecrated by Russian Orthodox symbolism.[141]

In all cases of mass migration, both the authorities and public opinion expressed fears that the peasants were losing certain features that were considered key elements of Russianness in the traditionalist discourse. It primarily concerned Russian Orthodox piety, which was weakened as the living standard rose, or else was threatened by unorthodox beliefs.[142] It was often noted that, as his standard of living went up, the peasant demonstrated not only less religious fervor, but less obedience to authority and less communal collectivism. Any information on cases of Russian settlers who had gone native received wide exposure.[143] However, the importance of these

---

[139] A. N. Kulomzin, *Perezhitoe*. RGIA. F. 1642., op. 1, d. 202, l. 19.

[140] See: S. V. Maksimov, "Sibirskaia sviatynia," in *Sobranie sochinenii S.V. Maksimova* (St. Petersburg, 1910), vol. 16, 115–275.

[141] P. P. Liubimov, "Religii i veroispovednyi sostav naseleniia Aziatskoi Rossii," in *Aziatskaia Rossiia* (St. Petersburg, 1914), vol. 1, 214.

[142] In New Russia, it was the protestant "shtundisty" (from German *Stunde*), and in the Caucasus and Siberia sect members and Old Believers who played the role of religious "seducers." See, e.g., Sergei Zhuk, "'A Separate Nation' of 'Those Who Imitate Germans': Ukrainian Evangelical Peasants and Problems of Cultural Identification in the Ukrainian Provinces of Late Imperial Russia," *Ab Imperio* 3 (2006); Nicholas Breyfogle, *Heretics and Colonizers: Forging Russia's Empire in the South Caucasus* (Ithaca: Cornell University Press, 2005).

[143] Anatolyi Remnev and Nataliia Suvorova, "'Russkoe delo' na aziatskikh okrainakh: 'russkost'' pod ugrozoi ili 'somnitel'nye kulturtregery,'" *Ab Imperio*, no. 2 (2008): 157–222; Remnev and Suvorova, "'Obrusenie' aziatskikh okrain Rossiiskoi imperii: optimism i pessimism russkoi kolonizatsii," *Istoricheskie zapiski* 11 (129) (Moscow: Nauka, 2008), 132–79; Willard Sunderland, "Russians Into Iakuts? 'Going Native' and the Problem of Russian National Identity in the Siberian North, 1870s–1914," *Slavic Review* 55, no. 4 (1996): 806–26; Robert Geraci, "Ethnic Minorities, Anthropology, and Russian National Identity on Trial: The Multan Case, 1892–96," *Russian Review* 59, no. 3 (2000): 530–54.

cases was usually marginal, and was highly exaggerated in the alarmist discourse. An alternative discourse was gradually formed, which described the said changes as positive, attesting to the fact that the settlers were turning from traditional peasants into individual farmers.[144] In this view, the "effective" Russian colonizer transformed the "alien" (indigenous, pagan/Muslim, savage, nomadic) space into "his own" (Russian, Orthodox, peasant/land-cultivating).[145]

All the borderlands, to which mass flows of agricultural migrants were headed, had two common features. First, the level of their economic development and, as a whole, their civilization development was perceived to be lower compared to the empire's core. That is why colonization was ideologically supported not only by the idea of a national appropriation of the territory but by the slogan of the civilizing mission. Not only did the civilizing mission justify imperial expansion. It allowed the educated Russians, on the one hand, to confirm their European-ness constantly questioned by the West, and on the other, to claim the role of a more "humane" patron of the indigenous population, as compared with the West European colonizers.[146]

Secondly, all these borderlands throughout the nineteenth century remained outside the sphere of direct influence of other major powers, which created beneficial conditions not only for the institution of the Russian imperial authority but also for the demographic occupation and nationalist appropriation of huge territories.

Compared to other empires, Russia was unique in the scale of her success in nationalizing enormous territories in the imperial borderlands. This success was mostly achieved by the Great Russian and Little Russian peasant and Cossack colonization in the east and south of the empire. In the western borderlands, inward migration of the Great Russians was limited, mostly urban, and consisted mainly of state servants and industrial workers. In the lands of contemporary Ukraine and Belorussia, these migrations together with the process of cultural russification of the local urban population created significant areas which strongly gravitated towards Russian national core.

Industrialization, Urbanization, and Development of Communications

After the abolition of serfdom in 1861, industrial development and urbanization were gradually picking up speed. In most of the cases, the city played the role of an assimilating mechanism. This concerns not only the largest imperial centers—Moscow and

---

[144] I. N. Smirnov, "Obrusenie inorodtsev i zadachi obrusitel'noi politiki," *Istoricheskii vestnik*, no. 3 (1892): 725–65; N. N. Kharuzin, "K voprosu ob assimiliatsionnoi sposobnosti russkogo naroda," *Etnograficheskoe obozenie* 23, no. 4 (1894): 43–78.

[145] Remnev and Suvorova, "'Obrusenie' aziatskikh okrain."

[146] Alexander Morrison, "Russian Rule in Turkestan and the Example of British India, c. 1860–1917," *Slavonic and East European Review* 84, no. 4 (October 2006): 666–707

St. Petersburg—which attracted their labor force from various parts of the empire.[147] In the Ukraine, Poltava was the only city where the majority of the population indicated the Ukrainian language (or, more exactly, Little Russian) as their primary language of communication, according to the 1897 census. In the meantime, more than 80 percent of the urban population in the Ukraine came from surrounding rural locations.[148] In 1860, Kiev had a population of 55,000 (an increase of just 10,000 compared with 1840), Kharkov 50,000, and Odessa 112,000. By 1874, the population of Kiev rose to 127,000; Kharkov in 1881 had 128,000, and Odessa 220,000 inhabitants. To better assess the urban population growth in the Russian part of the Ukraine, suffice it to say that Lemberg, belonging to the Habsburg Empire, had 70,000 inhabitants in 1860 and was only second, to Odessa, among the cities on the lands of the contemporary Ukraine, but by the early 1880s, having a population of 100,000 people, was already noticeably behind not only Odessa, but also Kiev and Kharkov.[149]

Russia however continued to lag behind leading European countries in terms of urbanization throughout the latter half of the nineteenth century: even in 1890, its urban population constituted just 12.5%, compared to 47% in Germany, 37.4% in France, 32.5% in Austro-Hungary, to say nothing of Great Britain (72%).[150] Such a low figure is reason why mass agrarian migrations in Russia continued up to the First World War, while such processes in other European empires had ended in the second half of the nineteenth century or earlier.

Industrial migration began to develop actively only from the late nineteenth century onwards. One of its main directions was the Donetsk coal basin (Donbass) where coal mining began in the late 1890s. The flow of workers—Little and Great Russian peasants—meant that Donbass also acquired the functions of a melting pot. According to the all-Russian census of 1897, the Donbass population in the earliest stages of industrial development constituted 1,136,000, 62.5% (710,000) of which were Little Russians/Ukrainians and 24.2% Great Russians. It was to some extent similar to the development of South Wales, which underwent a gradual Anglicization, in contrast to North Wales, where absence of industrial development preserved traditional culture.[151]

---

[147] J. Bradley, *Muzhik and Muscovite: Urbanization in Late Imperial Russia* (Berkeley: University of California Press, 1985); Evel Economakis, *From Peasant to Petersburger* (London: Macmillan Press, 1998); Shevyrev Alexander, "The Axis Petersburg–Moscow: Outward and Inward Russian Capitals," *Journal of Urban History* 30 (Nov. 2003): 70–84; James Bater, *St. Petersburg: Industrialization and Change.* (Montreal: McGill-Queen's University Press, 1976).

[148] Peter Woroby, "The Role of the City in Ukrainian History," in *Rethinking Ukrainian History*, ed. Ivan L. Rudnytsky (Edmonton: Canadian Institute for Ukrainian Studies, 1981), 208.

[149] Patricia Herlihy, "Ukrainian Cities in the Nineteenth Century," in *Rethinking Ukrainian History*, ed. Ivan L. Rudnytsky (Edmonton: Canadian Institute for Ukrainian Studies, 1981), 136–37.

[150] B. N. Mironov, *Sotsial'naia istoriia Rossii perioda imperii (XVII–nachalo XIX v.)*, vol. 2 (St. Petersburg: Dmitri Bulanin, 1999), table 4, 381.

[151] One of the founders of the coal mining industry in Donbass was the Welsh engineer John Hughes, whose name was soon given to one of the main urban centers of the region, Iuzovka (now Donetsk).

Migration, especially beyond the Urals, was closely tied to the development of infrastructural projects on the imperial scale, primarily railroad construction. The Trans-Siberian Railway was built between 1891 and 1916. While being an important geopolitical imperial project, it also became the main channel for the migratory flow of peasants during the Stolypin reform. The Siberian Railroad administration was an important colonization organizer and russification agent. The Siberian Railroad Committee made it one of its priorities to build schools and churches beyond the Urals.[152]

The first railroad in Russia was constructed only two years after the first continental railways in 1837. However, Russia was too late for the railroad boom of the 1840s, and only began attempting to catch up in the 1860s. By the last two decades of the nineteenth century, it was second only to the United States in the number of newly completed railway branches. This development was mostly motivated by military strategy. The Crimean War had demonstrated the importance of railways extremely painfully and thus convincingly. However, the nation-building aspect of the issue also acquired great importance as early as the 1860s.[153]

Baron Korf who was sent to the Ukraine immediately following the Polish uprising of 1863–64 to assess the threat of Ukrainian nationalism and the methods of countering it, reported to the tsar: "At the present moment, the Little Russian people sees its connection with Russia in monarchy, its affiliation in religion, but the connection and affiliation will become even stronger, even more unbreakable ... The way to it is through the railroad. ... It is not only the goods that move along this road, but also books, ideas, customs, views ... The Great Russian and Little Russian capitals, ideas, views will mix, and these two peoples, already standing close, will first become related

---

[152] Marks, "Conquering the Great East"; Steven G. Marks, *Road to Power. The Trans-Siberian Railway and the Colonization of Asian Russia, 1850–1917* (Ithaca, Cornell University press, 1991); Anatolyi V. Remnev, "Rossiia i Sibir' v meniaiushchemsia prostranstve imperii (XIX–nachalo XX v.)" in *Rossiiskaia imperiia v sravnitel'noi perspektive. Sbornik statei*, ed. Alexei Miller (Moscow: NLO, 2004), 286–319. See also: Sergei Iu. Vitte, "Vsepoddanneishii doklad upravliaiushchego ministerstvom finansov o sposobakh sooruzheniia Velikogo Sibirskogo Zheleznodorozhnogo puti i o naznachenii soveshchaniia dlia obsuzhdeniia sego dela. 6 noiabria 1892 g.," in *Sobranie sochinenij i dokumental'nykh materialov v piati tomakh*, vol. 1: *Puti soobshcheniia i ėkonomicheskoe razvitie Rossii*, book 2, part 1, ed. Alexei Miller (Moscow: Nauka, 2006), 159–83.

[153] On railroad construction and its impact on the visions of the empire and the nation see: Walter Sperling, *Der Aufbruch in die Provinz. Die Eisenbahn und die Neuordnung der Räume im Zarenreich* (Frankfurt: Campus Verlag, 2011); F. Benjamin Schenk, "Die Neuvermessung des Russländischen Reiches im Eisenbahnzeitalter," in *Osteuropa kartiert—Mapping Eastern Europe*, eds. Jörn Happel and Christophe von Werdt (Berlin: LIT Verlag, 2010), 13–35; F. Benjamin Schenk, "Das Zarenreich als Transitraum zwischen Europa und Asien. Russische Visionen und westliche Perzeptionen um die Jahrhundertwende," in *Globalisierung imperial und sozialistisch. Russland und die Sowjetunion in der Globalgeschichte 1851–1991*, ed. Martin Aust (Frankfurt: Campus Verlag, 2013), 41–63; F. Benjamin Schenk, "Travel, Railroads, and Identity Formation in the Russian Empire," in *Shatterzone of Empires. Coexistence and Violence in the German, Habsburg, Russian, and Ottoman Borderlands*, eds. Eric Weitz and Omer Bartov (Bloomington: Indiana University Press, 2013), 136–51.

and then become one."[154] The proposition that loyalty to the dynasty is a less stable foundation for unity than a railroad, presented to the monarch by a colonel in his entourage, speaks volumes. Katkov, expressing his opinion in 1865 on the most pressing measures that should be taken to russify the South-West Province, also suggested as the first priority the task of connecting the basins of the Volga and Dnieper through railway communication.[155] From 1865 to 1875 the railroad network in the Ukraine more than tripled.[156]

For the Great Russian provinces, too, railroad-building became an important stimulus to nationalist thinking. To discuss the routes of new roads, local initiative committees were set up. It was their task to prove that building the road through the town they represented was most fully compatible not only with local interests but with Russian national interests. Soon, interest in local history and culture, expressed in the rise of *kraevedenie*, became a typical feature of Russian provincial intellectual landscape and started to influence also the educational programs.[157] The discourse of the local Motherland usually comfortably coexisted with the nationalist discourse of the imperial Fatherland.

The thesis that railways have a special importance for national unity of such a huge country as Russia became commonplace in late nineteenth century discourse. It should be noted that these arguments were accompanied by references that for the contemporaries signified the national, rather than imperial, type of state. The engineer Pavel Mel'nikov who became, in 1865, the first Russian minister of ways of communication traveled the US for one year in 1839–40, in order to collect information on the

---

[154] RGIA, f. 733, op. 193 (1863), ed. Khr. 86, l. 20. Korf also paid attention to the migration of labor force as an instrument of assimilation, referring to the example of the factories of merchant N. Tereshchenko in the Chernigov gubernia, where two-thirds of the 5,000 workers were Great Russians. Ibid., l. 20ob.

[155] See M. N. Katkov, *Sobranie peredovykh statei "Moskovskikh vedomostei." 1865 g.* (Moscow, 1897), 757.

[156] It should be noted that not only the Russian, but also the Ukrainian nationalists expected much from the railroads as an instrument of nation-building. Mikhail Dragomanov characteristically wrote in 1861: "We have to admit that the things which at first glance do not have anything in common with nationality and even are not born from the nation's own desire, as railways, for instance, which Austria and Russia are building now from pure strategic reasons, are very important for they give the people of our nation a chance to know each other better. And before it, for example, Bantysh, the author of "The History of Little Russia," was not sure whether the same Little Russians live in Hungary; I met lots of educated people, who were surprised to know that in Volhynia live the same people as in Poltava; Stets'kyi, the author of Polish books on Volhynia, was very serious in persuading my sister that the Volhynian embroidery pattern can't be the same as in Poltava and so on. Now the roads from the Left Bank to the Right, and then to Galicia and Hungary made much more than books to get Ukrainians together." See: Mykhailo Dragomanov, *Lysty na Naddniprians'ku Ukraiinu* (Kolomyia, 1894), 27.

[157] M. V. Loskoutova, "A Motherland with a Radius of 300 Miles: Regional Identity in Russian Secondary and Post-Elementary Education from the Early Nineteenth Century to the War and Revolution," *European Review of History* 9, no. 1 (2002): 7–22.

new means of transportation. After his return to St. Petersburg, he claimed that "railroads are essential for Russia ... it can be said that they were invented for Russia and for America more than for any European country."[158]

Also important, particularly for the Volga-Urals region, was the development of steamship communication. Steamship lines appeared in the Volga basin in the 1850s and developed into a regular means of transporting goods and people by the 1870s. This development was extremely important in transforming the former borderland of Volga-Kama basin and the Bashkir lands (Ufa *gubernia*) into a part of internal Russia (*vnutrenniaia Rossiia*), and, gradually, into a part of Russian national territory.[159]

During the second half of the nineteenth century, Russian entrepreneurs gradually became vocal in expressing their nationalist agenda. Russian merchants, united in the Moscow Entrepreneurial group, became active at the very beginning of the reform era, organizing their first journal *Vestnik promyshlennosti* [The Industrial Messenger] from 1858–61. Later, they controlled many other periodicals, including such titles, as *Rus', Russkii trud* [Russian Labor], *Golos Moskvy* [The Voice of Moscow], *Russkoe delo* [Russian cause], and *Russkoe obozrenie* [Russian review]. They also financially supported several important nationalist intellectuals and journalists. The group consisted predominantly of ethnic Russians—often they were Old Believers—dominated by rich merchants and factory owners (Timofei Morozov, the Mamontovs, Alexei Khludov, Ivan Liamin, Kozma Soldatenkov, to name a few).[160] They argued for reliance on domestic capital and investment in key spheres, first of all railroad construction and banking. They wanted to make Moscow the central hub of a railroad network controlled by Russians, and tried to organize a Russian railroad company. Lacking experience and bureaucratic connections, they were initially not successful in attempts to enter the railroad construction business. But their lobbying brought some results, in the sense that the government opted to construct certain key lines, including the southern line from Odessa to Moscow, at state expense instead of giving concessions to foreigners.[161] In the 1870s, the Moscow group managed to win support of several key ministers and to take under their direct control an important railroad line from Kursk to Vologda. The Moscow group also became involved in the organization of the Arkhangelsk-Murmansk Steamship Company. They were also active in banking, organizing the Moscow Merchants' Bank, later the Moscow Merchants' Society of Mutual Credit and a whole set of small banking institutions. In the 1870s, Moscow banks financed the first domestic production of rails by N. I. Putilov's plant, and later, when

---

[158] Pavel Mel'nikov, "Svedeniia o russkikh zheleznykh dorogakh," in *P.P. Mel'nikov. Inzhener. Uchenyi. Gosudarstvennyi deiatel'*, eds. Mikhail I. Voronin and M. M. Voronina (St. Petersburg: Gumanistika, 2003), 223–398, 276.

[159] Steinwedel, "How Bashkiria Became," 107, 122.

[160] What follows on the Moscow Entrepreneurial group is based on Alfred J Rieber, *Merchants and Entrepreneurs in Imperial Russia* (Chapel Hill: University of North Carolina Press, 1976).

[161] Alfred Rieber, "The formation of La Grande Société de Fer Russes," *Jahrbücher für Geschichte Osteuropas* 21 (1973): 375–91.

Putilov ran into serious financial difficulties they managed to force the government for the first time to subsidize the Russian industrial enterprise.

In the 1870s, Russian merchants had organized the Society for Encouragement of Russian Industry and Trade, the purpose of which was defined as to "stand guard permanently over Russian industrial interests and profits in our trade with Europe, preventing foreigners from exploiting us exclusively for their own gain."[162] Already in the first year of its existence, the society was joined by over five hundred men from 65 towns and cities.

By the 1880s, Russian entrepreneurs became rather active also in city councils and gained experience in city politics through town Duma elections. According to Alfred Rieber, "by its vigorous lobbying and propaganda, the Moscow group demonstrated conclusively that native Russian capitalists could organize to defend their interests and thus, influence the course of economic development. By the end of the nineteenth century, the government had blessed the blend of economic and political nationalism that the Moscow group had fostered from its beginning."[163]

It can be generally concluded that by the outbreak of the First World War Russia was still in the midst of the industrialization and urbanization and was a long way from the completion of the period of agrarian migrations. In the countries where these processes had already happened or were developing more quickly, more advanced stages of industrialization and urbanization was bringing intensification of the assimilation processes. That would inevitably be the case also in Russia. However, lagging behind in economic development also meant that the final stages of industrialization and urbanization would not precede, but rather coincide, with the rise in activity of nationalist movements in the imperial periphery.

The First World War, the collapse of the empire, the victory of the Bolsheviks, and the Soviet policy of *korenizatsia* (indigenization) in the 1920s deprived historians of the possibility to check which tendency would prevail in various regions and ethnic groups.

WWI: the Destruction of the Romanov Empire and Mobilization of Ethnicity

The economic and military potential of the empire, her political integration, and achievements in Russian nation-building at its expanding core were put to a severe test during WWI, and ultimately the empire failed to survive it. For the Romanov Empire, WWI was the first war in which it participated as nation-in-arms, with mass conscription and mobilization of the reservists. The patriotic excitement was quite high at the early stages of this long war, and nationalist motifs were playing the first fiddle instead

---

[162] Quoted in Rieber, *Merchants and Entrepreneurs*, 199.
[163] Rieber, *Merchants and Entrepreneurs*, 217–18.

of traditional peasant monarchism.[164] However, from 1916, what initially had looked as nation-in-arms was gradually turning into increasingly revolutionized armed peasants and workers, as nationalist mobilization was giving way to class tensions and hatreds. The Russian imperial elites failed to cope with this challenge; in fact liberals were often trying to use growing social unrest against the monarchy, which was becoming more and more isolated before it collapsed in 1917.

The Great War triggered a whole set of processes which resulted in the mobilization of ethnic nationalism in the peripheries of the Russian Empire, particularly in the western provinces which became one huge war theatre.[165] The very beginning of a pan-European war mobilized the political imagination of the nationalist elites. Their first step was to escalate demands for national autonomy in exchange for their loyalty to the imperial center. Soon, however, particularly after the summer of 1915, when the Russian army suffered painful defeats from the German troops and the frontline moved several hundred kilometers east, some among the peripheral elites started thinking about potential advantages to be gained from shifting loyalty to the German side. In general, unlike the German–French front in the west, in the east the front-line moved quite dramatically many times in both directions, which created serious challenges for imperial integration in the most important and most vulnerable western borderlands. Still, we cannot see a decisive reorientation of loyalty of peripheral nationalist elites until the Bolshevik coup in the autumn of 1917, when the legitimate center of the Russian Empire ceased to exist. By that time, even those Russians in Petrograd who didn't support the Bolsheviks started to invest their hopes in the German occupation of the city.

In the course of the war, the neighboring empires—Russia, Austria-Hungary, and Germany—that had previously been extremely reserved about playing up the ethnic card in their interrelations, and were even compelled to a sort of solidarity because of their joint involvement in the partitions of the Polish Commonwealth, were now fully involved in promoting ethnic separatism in the enemy camp. In the occupied territories, the German occupational administration (*Ober Ost*) supported local languages, making them the official languages of administration and forbidding Russian in this capacity. *Ober Ost* civil servants put together an *Atlas of the Division of Peoples of Western Russia*, claiming it demonstrated that "the state -structure, which before the war was considered a uniform Great Russian Empire, is to a large extent formed out of territories of independent ethnicities, who do not stand closer to Muscovite nature than to us."[166]

---

[164] Joshua A. Sanborn, *Drafting the Russian Nation: Military Conscription, Total War, and Mass Politics, 1905–1925* (DeKalb: Northern Illinois University Press, 2003); and Sanborn, "The Mobilization of 1914."

[165] Mark von Hagen, "The Great War and the Mobilization of Ethnicity," in *Post Soviet Political Order: Conflict and State-Building*, eds. B. R. Rubin and J. Snyder (London: Routledge, 1998), 34–57.

[166] Vejas Liulevicius, *War Land on the Eastern Front: Culture, National Identity, and German Occupation in World War I* (Cambridge: Cambridge University Press, 2000), 117.

Both the German and Habsburg Empires made many other important moves to support anti-Russian nationalism in the borderlands, including separate POW camps for the Ukrainian soldiers, where they were exposed to the propagandistic efforts of Ukrainian nationalists.[167] Significant funding was provided to support various nationalist activists with desirable orientation.[168] The Russian side was doing similar things by creating separate camps for the POW Habsburg Slavs, and assigning the Special Political Department of the Foreign Ministry the task of organizing propaganda among these people.[169]

The ethnic and religious affiliation was turning into an important factor in the evaluation of population's loyalty. Many of the German and Jewish subjects of the tsar, so numerous in the western provinces, were targeted by military authorities as potential traitors and subjected to deportations from the front zone and expropriations of real estate on a mass scale.[170]

The German advance caused a massive refugee movement, which involved over six million people. Most of them had left towns and cities that were Russian strongholds in the region. Many territories were occupied and re-occupied more than once with all the niceties of retaliation of the advancing side against those who had (in fact or allegedly) expressed their sympathy to the enemy. "Nationalization" processes were taking place in the refugee communities. It was partially caused by the natural desire to keep the company of one's natives in an alien environment and in difficult circumstances, and partially encouraged by the authorities themselves who kept track of the refugees' numbers and distributed aid according to the ethnic principle. The activists of the refugee movement would often attempt to use this situation for national mobilization. Many of the leaders of refugee organizations would later play prominent roles in postwar nationalist movements and in the new states.[171]

---

[167] Frank Grelka, *Die Ukrainische Nationalbewegung unter deutscher Besatzungsherrschaft 1918 und 1941/42*, Studien der Forschungsstelle Ostmitteleuropa an der Universität Dortmund, band 38 (Wiesbaden: Harrassowitz Verlag, 2005); Mark von Hagen, *War in a European Borderland: Occupations and Occupation Plans in Galicia and Ukraine, 1914–1918* (Seattle: Herbert J. Ellison Center for Russian, East European, and Central Asian Studies, 2008).

[168] O. Kuraev, *Der Verband "Freie Ukraine" im Kontext der deutschen Ukraine-Politik des Ersten Weltkriegs* (Munich: Osteuropa-Institut), *Mitteilungen*, no. 35 (August 2000).

[169] Alexei Miller, "A Testament of the All-Russian Idea: Foreign Ministry Memoranda to the Imperial, Provisional and Bolshevik Governments," in *Extending the Borders of Russian History: Essays in Honor of Alfred Rieber*, ed. Marsha Siefert (Budapest: Central European University Press, 2003).

[170] E. Lohr, *Nationalizing the Russian Empire: The Campaign against Enemy Aliens during the World War I* (Cambridge, Mass.: Harvard University Press, 2003). On the other side of the front Ruthenian ethnicity was sufficient factor for repressions of the Habsburg authorities in Galicia. Detention camps for alleged Galician Russophiles in Tallerhof and Terezin became the first concentration camps on the European continent, modeled after the British camps in the Boer war.

[171] On the refugee phenomenon, see P. Gattrell, *A Whole Empire Walking: Refugees in Russia During World War I* (Bloomington: Indiana University Press, 1999).

The collapse of the dynasty in February 1917 brought to power the liberal provisional government. It encouraged the local politicians in the borderland regions to form separate administrations, at the same time having no clear plans about how to address the issue of autonomy and federation. All these questions were supposed to be solved by the Constitutional Assembly, which met in October 1917. The provisional government was desperately trying to keep the country in the war. In the summer of 1917 the top military command ordered the nationalization of army units in an attempt to limit the impact of Bolshevik propaganda among the troops. It didn't help much in this respect but it did have a profound impact after the Bolshevik coup. That is how these events were remembered in 1919 by Pavel Skoropadskii—in 1917 the loyal imperial general trusted by Supreme Commander General Lavr Kornilov with the Ukrainization of the corps under his command: "I answered Kornilov saying that I had just been to Kiev where I observed Ukrainian activists, and that they had produced rather a negative impression on me, that the corps may consequently become a serious basis for the development of Ukrainophilia in the sense undesirable for Russia, etc. The frivolous attitude of Kornilov to this question showed me his incompetence and lack of understanding. I tried to turn his attention to the seriousness of the question, realizing that the kind of national feeling that the Ukrainians possessed should be treated with tact and without exploiting it for its sincerity."[172] Unexpected popularity amongst Ukrainians, gained by the general while implementing the order he so strongly objected, soon propelled him, together with German support, to the role of the Hetman of the Ukraine. In this capacity he attempted to fight Bolsheviks in the east and social unrest inside the ephemeral Ukrainian state.[173]

By 1918 the space of the ruined empire was sinking into the chaos of civil war, or rather multiple civil wars. Bolshevik Reds, in control of the central *gubernias*, were fighting all sorts of Russian Whites, from monarchists and liberals to moderate socialists, based in the peripheries. The majority of the peasants fought their own wars, trying to protect their regions both from the Reds and the Whites. In the borderlands, local forces were desperately trying to drift as far as possible from the Bolshevik center, sometimes building coalitions with the Whites, more often fighting them, as well as the neighbors, with whom they had to measure force while trying to establish control over the territories, contested in mutually conflicting images of national territory. Several peripheral regions in the south and the north were occupied in 1918–19 by

---

[172] P. Skoropadskii, *Spogadi. Kinets' 1917—gruden' 1918* (Kiev–Philadelphia: Instytut istorii, 1995), 64. Skoropadskii reminisced about his childhood and his family thus: "Ukraine was understood as the glorious past of my homeland, but it was not at all related to the present; in other words, there were no political considerations connected to the restoration of Ukraine. My entire family was deeply devoted to the Russian tsars, but it was always somehow stressed that we were not Great Russians, but Malorussians of, as they used to say, noble origin" (quoted on 387).

[173] By that time the Habsburgs had their own, separate from German, scenario for Ukraine, which had to become a Kingdom under Wilhelm von Habsburg, who learned Ukrainian and became known in Ukraine as Vasyl Vyshyvany. See Timothy Snyder, *The Red Prince: The Secret Lives of a Habsburg Archduke* (New York: Basic Books, 2008)

British, French, and American forces. As the Red Army (and *Cheka*) was marching into the peripheral regions of the former empire in the final stages of the civil war, it was first of all hunting the Whites and, more generally, the "class enemies"—in other words, the bearers of the pre-revolutionary Russian nationalism.[174]

Conclusion: the Formation of the USSR and the Deconstruction of Russian Nationalism

Summing up the years of WWI and revolution, this cataclysmic era resulted in power-ful mobilization of peripheral nationalisms and the destruction of many achievements of Russian nation-building, particularly in the western borderlands. It can be said that the explosive growth of nationalism in the western borderlands was to a great extent the consequence of the burdens of a total war in general and of the new competitive imperial policies in particular. Prior to the war, secessionist nationalism—with the ex-ception of the Poles—was not strong in the Romanov Empire, and it was rather the product of the imperial collapse than its cause. As a result of the Bolshevik victory, the Russian center of the post-imperial space lost its legitimacy not only in the eyes of many peripheral actors, who were initially loyal to the empire, but also for the majority of the old elites who felt themselves part of the Russian nation. These elites suffered complete destruction of their social and economic status, and huge numerical losses as a result of the war, Red terror, and emigration.

A good way to understand the significance of the Bolshevik coup is to imag-ine counterfactually that after the collapse of the monarchy Russia, even losing the war, could have avoided the Bolshevik victory in 1917. One can also imagine that the Whites could have managed to reestablish some anti-Bolshevik regime (liberal, or, much more probably, right wing authoritarian) in the capitals in 1918–19. In both cases it would be quite probable that in some peripheries, local nationalists would try to implement secessionist projects. While it is unlikely, for example, that Belorussian nationalists would be strong enough to succeed, Ukrainian nationalists could form an independent Ukrainian state. In case the Ukrainian state survived the inevitable confrontation with the reemerging Poland and a nationalist Russia, the situation would, to some extent, resemble that of the Polish-German borderland after WWI, where many regions were contested and became parts of postwar Germany or Poland after referenda and/or military clashes. Significant parts of the areas—which became the southern and eastern parts of the Soviet Ukraine, including Kharkov, Donetsk coal basin, and New Russia—would have been claimed by Russia and almost certainly

---

[174] In Kiev, for example, the Reds in 1918 shot dead all 78 members of the Kiev Club of Russian Nationalists, whom they managed to find. What was one of the most influential nationalist organization in the western borderlands by 1913, with over 700 members, simply disappeared without a trace by 1918.

become part of the Russian state.[175] That is what happened on the Ukrainian-Polish border, where the Poles successfully claimed Galicia. Such a clash of competing nationalist projects, Russian and peripheral, would, to some extent, serve as a test for achievements and failures of the prewar russification policy. In any case, it is clear that the geography of nationalism in Eastern Europe would be quite different from what we know today.

In reality, Bolsheviks came to power in autumn 1917 and survived in the civil war of 1918–19. They decisively rejected the Russian nationalism, which was supported mostly by the social groups hostile to the new regime. From the very early days of the Soviet power those groups were subjected to terror and expulsion.

The creation of the Ukrainian and Belorussian Soviet Socialist Republics and official recognition in the USSR of the Ukrainian and Belorussian nations as separate entities, along with the vigorous Soviet policy of Ukrainization and Belarussization within the framework of the general drive toward *korenizatsia* (nativization, or indigenization) in the 1920s, all were policies deconstructing the very backbone of the Russian nation-building project of the imperial time—the concept of the unity of Great, Little, and White Russians as the branches of a single nation. All the eastern territories of contemporary Ukraine and Belorussia, which were deeply russified before WWI, were transferred to those Soviet republics, often in spite of the protests of the local population, like in the case of the Vitebsk or Donetsk regions. That move was motivated by the wish of the Bolsheviks to create Belorussian and Ukrainian Soviet republics which would be attractive for those Ukrainians and Belorissians who found themselves under Polish rule after the Soviet-Polish war of 1920.

By rejecting and suppressing Russian nationalism as a hostile force and ideology,[176] Bolsheviks followed an entirely different project of political consolidation in the space of the former Romanov Empire. Many achievements of the russification policy in the borderlands were deconstructed within the logic of the Soviet project of territorialization of ethnicity[177] and *korenizatsia*.[178] Russian agricultural settlements in many borderland regions of the Caucasus, Steppe, and Central Asia were declared mistakes, and many settlers moved back to central Russia. Cossacks, who performed the role of the armed vanguard of the settlement movement, were targeted with brutal repressions as the foes of the Soviet power, which the majority of them truly were. The Orthodox Church and the clergy, who were also important elements of Russian presence in the peripheral regions, remained targets of systematic repression throughout the interwar period all over the USSR.

---

[175] See Vladimir Kornilov, *Donetsko-Krivorozhskaia respublika: rassstereliannaia mechta* (Donetsk: Folio, 2011).

[176] Veljko Vujacic, "Stalinism and Russian nationalism: A reconceptualization," *Post-Soviet Affairs* 23 (2007): 156–83.

[177] R. Kaiser, *The Geography of Nationalism in Russia and the USSR* (Princeton: Princeton University Press, 1994).

[178] Terry Martin, *The Affirmative Action Empire* (Ithaca: Cornell University Press, 2001).

Korenizatsia institutionalized ethnicity as a key factor of individual identification. "Correct" ethnicity became a great career asset in the new national republics.[179] Liquidation of illiteracy was implemented in the 1920s in the local languages. Several dozens of languages which used to have a Cyrillic alphabet were transferred to Latin script.[180] In sum, during the 1920s the Bolsheviks had eliminated or suppressed by force the social strata which were associated with Russian nationalism, dismantling many of those results of russification in the borderlands that still survived after the civil war, and introducing a new model of political organization of the imperial space, based on territorialization of ethnicity and promotion of ethnic particularism. All this makes it extremely difficult to assess the advancement and trends of Russian nation-building in the late Romanov Empire.

---

[179] J. Slezkine, "The USSR as a Communal Appartment, or How a Socialist State Promoted Ethnic Particularism," *Slavic Review* 53, no. 2 (Summer 1994).

[180] Alexei Miller, "Identité et allégeance dans la politique linguistique de l'Empire russe dans les territoires peripheriques occidentaux au cours de la seconde moitié du XIXe siècle," in *Cacophonies d'empire. Le gouvernement des langues dans l'Empire russe et l'Union sovietique*, ed. Juliette Cadiot, Dominique Arel, and Larissa Zakharova (Paris: CNRS Editions, 2010), 37–60.

Imperial Cohesion, Nation-Building, and Regional Integration in the Habsburg Monarchy

ANDREA KOMLOSY

It was a widely acknowledged wisdom in the twentieth century that multi-national empires had suffered from challenging national aspirations inside and outside their territories, subsequently ceding power to the nation-state. Recent research questioned this idea by pointing at the active participation of imperial elites in nation-building processes in the core areas of their empires, exercising pressure on national minorities to more or less assimilate to the dominant imperial nation.[1] Great Britain, France, or Spain have been used to illustrate the consolidation of a core nation, a transformation from imperial to national core throughout the nineteenth and the early twentieth centuries.[2] Nation building is no longer seen as a challenge, and possible danger for these empires, but as a part of their strategy for survival against the challenges of national movements within the empires as well as of inter-(imperial) state rivalry. Additionally, the Russian and the Ottoman Empire showed tendencies to replace the multi-ethnic and pluri-religious character of their empires by Russian or Turkish identity.[3] The Habsburg Monarchy has been exempted from this tendency, maintaining an imperial, multi-ethnic self-understanding of its state, which was characterized by a graduated regional self-government

---

[1] Stefan Berger and Alexei Miller, "Nation-Building and Regional Integration, c. 1800–1914: the Role of Empires," *European Review of History* 15, no. 3 (2008): 317–30.

[2] L. Colley, *Britons: Forging a Nation* (London: Pimlico, 1992); H. Kamen, *Spain's Road to Empire. The Making of a World Power* (Harmondsworth: Penguin 2002); E. Weber, *Peasants to Frenchmen: The Modernization of Rural France, 1870–1914* (Palo Alto: Stanford University Press, 1976).

[3] Alexei Miller, *The Ukrainian Question: The Russian Empire and Nationalism in the 19th Century* (Budapest: Central European University Press, 2003); K. Barkey and Mark von Hagen, eds., *After Empire: Multiethnic Societies and Nation-Building. The Soviet Union and the Russian, Ottoman and Habsburg Empires* (Boulder: Westview Press, 1997); M. S. Hanioglu, *Preparation for a Revolution: The Young Turks, 1902–1908* (Oxford: Oxford University Press, 2001).

and by constitutional rights of the various ethnic and religious groups.[4] This ethnic diversity is said to have turned into national opposition movements, which finally rejected the imperial framework and formed new nation-states. Hungary is understood as an exception from the exception, setting up in the lands of the Hungarian Crown a nationalizing transformation of the imperial state similar to the West European empires.[5]

This contribution aims at examining if and in which respect the above assumption is correct and what were the reasons for the preponderance of a multi-ethnic dynastic understanding of nationhood in Austria (Cisleithania) and of the nationally homogenizing ideology in Hungary (Transleithania). It collects empirical evidence for the two models of state-building—ethnic pluralism in Austria and national homogenization in Hungary—which mutually reinforced each other and were embedded into the great power relations in Europe.

Cisleithania and Transleithania only exist since the Dual Settlement or Compromise of 1867, which established the separate rule of the Austrian and the Hungarian part of the Monarchy as distinct political entities, held together by a common sovereign and only submitting military, foreign policy and some finances to a common government.[6] This paper will focus on the period from 1806–1918. It was the only period when the "Austrian" (1804–67 *Österreichisches Kaiserreich*) then "Austro-Hungarian" Empire (1867–1918 *Österreich-Ungarn*) existed as a distinctive imperial unity, which was not part of and did not overlap with the Holy Roman Empire, enabling its Habsburg rulers to bear the title emperor until its dissolution in 1806.

Despite a focus on this time period, the relationship between the imperial, the national, and the regional dimension of the Habsburg lands is shaped by older developments. They are characterized by the fact that the imperial dimension existed in two forms. The official one is resulting from the fact that Habsburg rulers were Holy Roman emperors first in 1273 and from 1438 onwards (with an interruption 1740–45). This title went far beyond the Habsburg possessions and binds Austrian history inseparably with the Holy Roman Empire, and as a consequence with the German question. Unofficially the title of emperor was also applied to the Habsburg lands, which represented the largest territorial political entity within the Holy Roman Empire and transcended its boundaries with the inheritance of Hungary (1526) and its later conquest, as well as with the newly acquired provinces in eastern and southeastern Europe since the 1770s. When contemporaries called Habsburg rulers emperor or empress (Maria Theresia), they did not only refer to the Holy Roman Empire, but to the sum of the Habsburg lands—the legal declaration and international assertion of their unity was a central issue of Habsburg diplomatic efforts. In spite of

---

[4] R. Kann, *The Multinational Empire. Nationalism and National Reform in the Habsburg Monarchy 1848–1918*, 2 vol. (New York: Columbia University Press, 1950); E. Bruckmüller, *The Austrian Nation: Cultural Consciousness and Socio-Political Processes* (Riverside, Cal.: Ariadne Press, 2004).

[5] Berger and Miller, "Nation-Building," 1.

[6] The border between Austria and Hungary is partly following the river Leitha, giving the name Transleithania to the lands belonging to the Kingdom of Hungary, while the Habsburg possessions west of the Leitha were called Cisleithania.

their entanglement with the Holy Roman Empire, the Habsburg lands, as a distinctive state unity with a sovereign imperial ruler, experienced efforts of centralization and unification, bringing along a highly developed process of state formation in the fields of administration, legal affairs, conscription and recruitment, transport and communication infrastructure, education, church administration, finance, market formation, and control of mobility.[7] These reforms strengthened the central government at the expense of self-governing institutions on the local (towns and manors) and the regional (estates and church) level.

Dualism between Austria and Hungary in 1867 was to a large extent the consequence of German unification under Prussian dominance on the one hand, and a fear of pan-slavic tendencies within and beyond the Habsburg Monarchy on the other.[8] Austrian Prime Minister Friedrich Ferdinand von Beust in 1871 argued in favor of a leading role of German-speaking Austrians in Cisleithania—if Slavs were also granted a compromise, German Austrians would be reduced to a minority, endangering the power balance with the Prussian-dominated German Empire.[9] This is why the Compromise only included Austria and Hungary, and Bohemian demands for similar constitutional autonomy were rejected, allowing Austria to establish the doctrine of multi-ethnicity under German leadership and conceding the Hungarian government the right to pursue a policy of national assimilation.

The balance between the two sub-empires, based on the complementarity of Austrianness and Magyarism, required adjustments in each entity in order to maintain stability. Poles and Croats were able to achieve smaller agreements, similar to the one between Austria and Hungary: Poles with the Austrian government in Galicia, Croats with the Hungarian government in Croatia-Slavonia, allowing exceptions from the respective dominant model. Privileging the noble nationalities of Poles and Croats fuelled dissatisfaction among nationalities who were not dominated by nobles, but by peasants, workers, or urban middle classes—first of all the Czechs, who represented a possible republican challenge toward dynastic reign. So, practically, multi-ethnic pluralism in Austria and Magyarization in Hungary, although following different principles of national integration, supported each other.

In Austria, German never stopped being the leading language, opening careers in higher administration, academia, and political life. At the same time, the

---

[7] H. Matis, ed., *Von der Glückseligkeit des Staates. Staat, Wirtschaft und Gesellschaft in Österreich im Zeitalter des aufgeklärten Absolutismus* (Berlin: Dunker & Humblot Verlag, 1981).

[8] Compare: H. Lutz, *Österreich-Ungarn und die Gründung des Deutschen Reiches. Europäische Entscheidungen 1867–1871* (Frankfurt–Berlin–Vienna: Propyläen Verlag, 1979), 416–37; J. Redlich, *Das österreichische Staats- und Reichsproblem. Geschichtliche Darstellung der inneren Politik der habsburgischen Monarchie von 1848 bis zum Untergang des Reiches* (Leipzig: Der Neue-Geist Verlag, 1920), vol. II, 557, 561.

[9] H. Lutz, "Zur Wende der österreichisch-ungarischen Außenpolitik 1871. Die Denkschrift des Grafen Beust für Kaiser Franz Joseph vom 18. Mai," *Mitteilungen des Österreichischen Staatsarchivs* 25 (1972):169–84; J. Koralka, *Tschechen im Habsburgerreich und in Europa 1815–1914. Sozialgeschichtliche Zusammenhänge der neuzeitlichen Nationsbildung und der Nationalitätenfrage in den böhmischen Ländern* (Vienna: Verlag für Geschichte und Politik, 1991), 152.

non-German nationalities were able to establish their languages on a local and region-al level, opening possibilities of national self-representation and nation-building, but equally blocking their compatriots' access to high state positions that required German language skills. In the climate of inter-ethnic rivalry, a supra-national Austrianness could hardly develop: if at all, it manifested in a common identification with the em-peror or the dynasty, identification that lost momentum with the development of par-liamentarism and the military defeats against Sardinia-Piedmont and France (1859) and Prussia (1866).

In Hungary, Magyarization was a common theme, involving Hungarians of all nationalities. After all, Magyarization was less effective than agents and opponents would have suggested, and Hungary's ethnic landscape remained as pluralistic as the Austrian one. These developments, which were impeding the official doctrines of Dualism, are presented and analyzed in a final section in a counter-factual way, look-ing at empirical evidence of German-led nation-building in Austria and the survival of multi-ethnicity in Hungary.

Hungary, in spite of all resistance and difficulties of integration, will be looked at as a constitutive part of the Habsburg Empire, as part of a territorial unit with a common sovereign. Hungary equally can and must be looked at as a distinct entity—a separate political and territorial unit—that requires comparison with Austria. The per-spective on Hungary in this article will change between the two perspectives.

In Search of an Imperial Core

In order to decide if an imperial core was transformed into an imperial nation in the course of the nineteenth century, the term requires genesis and interpretation. Like in all composite monarchies, the state territory of the Habsburgs resulted from a pro-cess of enlargement, which added new provinces to the territories initially assigned to represent Austria.[10] A province is labeled as "core" if it represented a key role for state unity and state identity. Provinces which did not represent a core are regarded as sup-plementary, or marginal, for state unity and identity. Hence an imperial core reflects the rank that is attributed to a province in the hierarchy of possessions. Definitions vary between the moment of acquisition itself and later interpretations of the signifi-cance of a province. Here the term core is used regardless of the economic function of a province. The following chronological overview of the territorial formation of what used to be Austria in different periods[11] cannot be isolated from various layers of his-torical interpretations that heavily resist deconstruction. It elaborates which of the ac-quisitions were core territories and which were considered more peripheral.

---

[10] F. W. Putzger and E. Bruckmüller, *Historischer Weltatlas zur allgemeinen und österreichischen Geschichte* (Vienna: Verlag Hölder-Pichler-Tempsky, 1998).

[11] A. Komlosy, "Habsburgermonarchie, Osmanisches Reich und Britisches Empire-Erweiterung, Zusammenhalt und Zerfall im Vergleich," *Zeitschrift für Weltgeschichte* 9, no. 2 (2008): 9–62.

The political unit called Austria (*marchia orientalis, Ostarrichi*) came into being as a small strip of land established as a border region of the Frank and the Ottonian Empires against the rival Avar and Hungarian Empires in the ninth and tenth century. When this region achieved political sovereignty and grew by military conquest and diplomatic expansion, a nuclear Austrian state came into existence. The process of initial enlargement consolidated a small territorial complex in the eastern Alps and the adjacent river basins of the Danube, Mur and Sava, which in the fifteenth century reached more or less the size of the later Republic of Austria (including South Tyrol and parts of Slovenia and Friulia but not including Salzburg and the Burgenland). Shall we consider this state the imperial core? This would satisfy expectations of twentieth century history books that establish continuity between initial and contemporary Austria. It would, however, not be in line with the changes in size, political constitution, and territorial integration that Austria experienced from the fifteenth to the beginning of the twentieth century. The shape of the Austrian territory changed significantly, when the Habsburg family included the Bohemian and the Hungarian lands into their hereditary possessions in 1526. While Habsburg rule in Bohemia was immediately put into practice, the bigger part of the Hungarian Kingdom was conquered by the Ottoman army and came under direct (Hungary) or indirect (Transylvania) Ottoman rule, until the Habsburg army re-conquered Hungary from the Ottomans and established Habsburg rule from 1687–1718. From a retrospective angle all these territories were regarded as core and key countries for Habsburg imperial unity. Conversely, other expansions realized in these years, like the inclusion of Burgundy (1477) and Spain (1516) with its overseas colonies, were not considered core, because they were lost by conquest, by exchange, or by the partition of the Spanish and the Austrian possessions of the Habsburg dynasty. This secondary significance was also linked with those former Spanish possessions that came under Austrian rule after the War of Spanish Succession in 1714 (Southern Netherlands, Lombardy, Naples, and Sicily), even if some remained part of the Austrian possessions for as long as 1859 (Lombardy). Although the Austrian Netherlands and Austrian Lombardy were economically central, their significance for empire building was small. They were located at the fringes of the Habsburg Empire, with different local traditions, and often without direct territorial connections. Their relations to the Austrian core provinces were loose. Attempts to include these provinces into the system of central administration which the imperial core imposed on all hereditary lands against strong estate opposition were less ambitious in these cases. The empire did not integrate these provinces into modern state institutions and its political economy that were instituted during the seventeenth and eighteenth centuries.[12] The southern

---

[12] H. Van der Wee, ed., *The Rise and Decline of Urban Industries in Italy and in the Low Countries* (Leuven: Leuven University Press, 1988); G. Galasso, ed., *Storia d'Italia, vol. 11: Il Ducato di Milano 1535–1796, vol 18/1: L'Italia di Napoleone dalla Cisalpina al Regno, vol. 18/2: Il Regno Lombardo-Veneto* (Torino: UTET 1984–1987); R. Zedinger, *Die Verwaltung der Österreichischen Niederlande in Wien (1714–1795)* (Vienna–Cologne–Weimar: Böhlau Verlag, 2000).

Netherlands were welcome because of the high standard of textile and other industries from which Austrian crafts would be able to benefit, but expectations that the
southern Netherlands would help establish Austrian East Indian trade did not come
to fruition.[13] The lands of the Hungarian Crown were not included into modern state
formation either. In the sixteenth and seventeenth century this was due to Ottoman
rule which did not touch upon feudal rights if taxes were delivered. Attempts to establish central administrative measurements after the Habsburg conquest of 1687
were rejected by the aristocracy, hence limiting the integration of the Hungarian
lands into the imperial, absolutist state.[14]

The expansions of the eighteenth and the nineteenth centuries (Galicia,
Bukovina, Venetia and former Venetian coastal provinces, as well as Bosnia and
Hercegovina) had a different character. As the setup of Austrian overseas trade relations and colonial activities from the southern Netherlands were not successful, efforts
of imperial territorial consolidation turned eastwards. The new acquisitions, achieved
by military and diplomatic means, brought territorial gains in regions claimed by
neighboring empires. Galicia, Bukovina, Venetia, and Dalmatia were not considered
core provinces, while the acquisition of west Istria fulfilled a long lasting Habsburg
territorial claim on the Istrian peninsula. The Berlin Congress (1878) entitled the
Habsburgs to the occupation of Bosnia and Hercegovina. Bosnia and Hercegovina
formally remained part of the Ottoman Empire until their annexation by Austro-
Hungary in 1908. Bosnia and Hercegovina stayed outside the dual partition of the empire, representing a common Austrian–Hungarian colony. Even if some of the newly
acquired territories exceeded older provinces in size, they were seen as strategic borderlands, fulfilling military, economic, or colonial missions, refraining rivals from exercising influence and delivering manoeuvring space vis-à-vis enemy or rival neighbors.
The new acquisitions, even if they were uncontested economic centers like Venetia or
strategic territories like Galicia, were considered marginal in imperial significance and
not part of the imperial core. This initial perception underwent change, like in the case
of Galicia, which turned from an object of inter-imperial exchange to a province with
much closer ties to the imperial center, without ever being considered part of the imperial core, however.[15]

Did the ranking of imperial significance depend on the belonging of a
province to the Holy Roman Empire or not? The case of Hungary shows that the
Habsburg mainland extended beyond the Holy Roman Empire's boundaries. All further expansions rather confirm the idea that the Holy Roman Empire's provinces were

[13] J. Dullinger, "Die Handelskompagnien Oesterreichs nach dem Oriente und nach Ostindien in
der ersten Hälfte des 18. Jahrhunderts," *Zeitschrift für Social- und Wirthschaftsgeschichte* 7 (1900):
43–83.
[14] L. Kontler, *Millennium in Central Europe: A History of Hungary* (Budapest: Atlantisz Publishing
House, 1999).
[15] H.-C. Maner, *Galizien. Eine Grenzregion im Kalkül der Donaumonarchie im 18. und 19.
Jahrhundert* (Munich: IKGS Verlag, 2007).

superior to others. However, the collapse of the empire under Napoleon's imperial expansions rendered this question a secondary one, strengthening the imperial cohesion of the Austrian Empire.

The territorial formation of the Habsburg Monarchy gave way to a composite empire, consisting of initial and early constitutive provinces, of hereditary land expansions of the sixteenth century, the conquest of Ottoman provinces at the turn from the seventeenth to the eighteenth century, and the new acquisitions of the eighteenth and nineteenth centuries. While the first three were retrospectively considered the imperial core, the latter were marginal from the perspective of imperial state unity.

Overlapping of Imperial, Economic, and National Core

Until the nineteenth century, the imperial core did not have a national or ethnic connotation. Over the course of the nineteenth century, however, language and ethnicity became key indicators for belonging to a nation or not. Empires faced the challenge of being transformed into nation-states. One possible answer was ranking their provinces along the principle of a leading nation, which represented the national core, while other nations or nationalities were regarded minorities, squeezed between subordination or assimilation. The multiethnic composition of the Habsburg lands prevented the imperial cores from being easily translated into a national core. A third understanding of a core region or province is economic—core being defined as an agglomeration with a complexity of economic and financial functions, attracting capital, investment, and migration. Conversely, an economic periphery is characterized by a dependent relationship vis-à-vis one (or several) cores, supplying an unequal division of labor with products based on agriculture, natural resources, or (wo)manpower.[16]

How does imperial core status relate to the economic significance of a province, its core role in the inter-regional division of labor? Many examples show that economic cores and economic peripheries were located both in provinces considered the imperial core as well as in regions that were more marginal for the unity of the empire. From the perspective of state unity, core and marginal provinces showed a broad economic heterogeneity ranging from metropolitan, financial, and industrial centers to agricultural, raw material, industrial outsourcing, or labor recruitment provinces.[17] Economic and political weight (centrality), or weakness (peripherality), did not always coincide. In the case of the lands of the Hungarian Crown, an economically rather peripheral region enjoyed a high degree of political autonomy, achieving almost

---

[16] A. Komlosy, *Grenze und ungleiche regionale Entwicklung. Binnenmarkt und Migration in der Habsburgermonarchie* (Vienna: Promedia Verlag, 2003), 41.

[17] A. Komlosy, "Innere Peripherien als Ersatz für Kolonien? Zentrenbildung und Peripherisierung in der Habsburgermonarchie," in *Zentren, Peripherien und kollektive Identitäten in Österreich-Ungarn*, eds. E. Hárs, W. Müller-Funk, U. Reber, and C. Ruthner (Tübingen–Basel: A. Francke Verlag, 2006), 55–78.

complete political independence. In the case of the lands of the Bohemian Crown, the provinces of Bohemia and Moravia were not able to translate their strong economic centrality into a political autonomy for the Bohemian state.[18]

If the economic significance of a province did not necessarily indicate its status as political core or periphery, the same can be said for the ethnic or national composition of the population. The German (Swiss) origin of the Habsburg dynasty and their leading role as kings and emperors of the Holy Roman Empire did not privilege German-speaking regions or the German language within the Habsburg Monarchy. Rulers, governors, and state officials administered the territories in many different languages, and the language of the imperial court and the dynastic suite varied along with administrative necessities (use of Latin) as well as with noble fashions (use of Italian or French). Nonetheless it goes without saying, that there was no equality of languages. Languages that were not represented in urban surroundings, especially if they had no written codification, were for oral use only. Their speakers had to assimilate to German, Italian, Magyar, or Polish, if they left their rural environment and approached the world of trade, arts, education, or state administration.[19]

When nation building entered the arena of the multi-national empire, centrality and peripherality of regions both in a political and an economic understanding were translated into national terms. From the national movements' perspective, which represented the majority in a province, their respective national language and ethnicity were considered national core. Provincial borders did not coincide with national territories, however. Were the Habsburg dynasty and central state institutions successful in establishing a supra-ethnic imperial nationhood against the national endeavors of single ethnic groups to form their own ethnic nation? Were they able to promote state integration on a supra-ethnic level?

Only German had the potential to represent the core nation of the empire. German preponderance was not due to a numerical majority, but due to the fact that German speakers were not limited to specific regions, settling across the empire. The German language dominated trade, administration, and education, hence rendering German an instrument of social advancement. Along with the enlightened state reforms under Joseph II in the 1780s, Germanizing tendencies received state support, but they faced equal resistance from the side of the "awakening" nationalities. The following sections will investigate attempts, successes, and failures of Germanizing the empire against the background of national resistance from non-German nationalities on the one hand, and a supra-national definition of imperial identity on the other.

Magyar was limited to the Hungarian part of the monarchy, where it was admitted as an official language only on the county level (*comitatus*). In most Hungarian

---

[18] L. Klusáková, "The Czech Lands in the Habsburg Empire (Economic Center but Political Periphery)," in *Internal Peripheries in European History*, ed. H.-H. Nolte (Göttingen–Zurich: Muster Schmidt Verlag, 1991), 169–94, 183; Koralka, *Tschechen im Habsburgerreich*, 146–74.

[19] E. Niederhauser, *1848 Sturm im Habsburgerreich* (Budapest: Corvina; Vienna: Kremayr & Scheriau, 1990). 22–33.

towns urban administration, economic, and political life was dominated by the German language—Magyar was mainly spoken in the country-side. The official language of the Hungarian Diet was Latin and jurisdiction was equally carried out in Latin. Joseph II's advances to Germanize county and district administration failed. Attempts of establishing and developing Magyar as a urban language started in the late eighteenth century as part of the national "awakening." In 1843–44, the Diet adopted the official status of the Magyar language in the Kingdom of Hungary.[20] The Magyarization of the country could only be carried out after the Dual Settlement of 1867 had opened legal possibilities of a Hungarian language policy and did not gain momentum before the 1880s.[21]

While the Cisleithanian Constitution (Austria) declared the right of every "ethnic people to preserve and to cultivate one's nationality and language" and the "equal right of all native languages in schools, offices and public life,"[22] the Transleithanian (Hungary) attitude towards non-Magyar citizens aimed at assimilation. The integration of the ethnic and linguistic diversity of the citizens was based on two different principles: negotiated co-existence in Cisleithania and assimilation in Transleithania. Czech, Slovene, Polish, Ruthenian (Ukrainian), Italian etc. were admitted as official languages in Cisleithania within the limits of those administrative entities, where their speakers were majority or relevant minority, while they could not achieve full equality in central institutions and in higher education, where German was dominant. Other languages only slowly and against strong resistance were able to gain ground on a provincial level. Slovak, Serbian, Romanian etc. did not enjoy similar rights in Transleithania. Hungary after 1867 set up for a process of transforming the royal Hungarian lands into a national core, aimed at ethnic assimilation in the course of state building. Magyar became the only official language in the Hungarian sub-empire, with the exception of the Kingdom of Croatia-Slavonia, which achieved administrative autonomy in 1868.

The different handling of ethnicity and languages in the Austrian and the Hungarian realm met with imbalances in the political and economic position of the single provinces within the Habsburg Empire. The following sections concentrate on specific circumstances of the state-building process in different parts of the monarchy, throwing light on the different developments and strategies in the fields of nation-building, political administration, and economic integration, and in conclusion discussing the non-synchronicity of an economic and a political understanding of core and periphery.

---

[20] Kontler, *Millennium in Central Europe*, 155, 224, 244.

[21] The author uses the term Magyar for ethnic and linguistic issues of nationality, while the term Hungarian is reserved for the political nation, in the case of Hungary including the different ethnic groups, or nationalities, which lived in the Lands of the Hungarian Crown.

[22] "Staatsgrundgesetz über die allgemeinen Rechte der Staatsbürger für die im Reichsrate vertretenen Königreiche und Länder," December 21, 1868, article 19; compare Kann, *The Multinational Empire*.

Nation-Building

DIFFICULTIES OF FORMING A GERMAN NATION

The imperial rather than national foundation of Habsburg state-formation is a result of the specific structure of the Holy Roman Empire, which only partially corresponded with the Habsburg territories. In spite of carrying the appendix "of German Nation" since the fifteenth century, nation was not defined on ethnic and linguistic grounds—a majority of Czech speakers in the Bohemian Lands and Polish speakers in parts of Silesia did not hinder these provinces from being integral parts of the Holy Roman Empire.

The Habsburg possessions extended beyond the Holy Roman Empire's borders, a situation that was prolonged after the abolition of the empire in 1806, when the Austrian Empire was member of the German Confederation (*Deutscher Bund*). Inspired by national ideas, which went along with the claim for democratization of the old regimes, former imperial unity faced transformation into national unity, causing tensions between the great powers aspiring for hegemony in the confederation. Austria represented supra-national imperial continuity, while Prussia stood for unification of the German states on national grounds. After a period of competition, when Habsburg Austria formed coalitions with those German states that opposed Prussian hegemony, the leadership was clarified by Prussia's military victory in 1866. The leading role in the process of German state-formation was taken over by Prussia, and the way opened to a new German imperial project based on the national principle and aimed at the Germanization of the empire. The Habsburg Monarchy was not included in the process of German unification, which was realized in the form of a "Small German" solution.[23] By transforming imperial into national unity, Prussia was able to establish and exercise control over the German Empire, defining the imperial by national unity.

German-speaking Austrians in the Habsburg Monarchy were deprived of an imperial frame that suited national endeavors. They could adopt a loyal position vis-à-vis the throne, either accepting the multi-ethnic character of the monarchy or pushing for as much Germanization of the empire as possible. They could also adopt a critical position vis-à-vis the separation of the Habsburg Monarchy and fight for a revision of the German question, that is, an all-German or "Great German" solution including

---

[23] Compare W. Schmidt, "The Nation in German History," in *The National Question in Europe in Historical Context*, eds. M. Teich, and R. Porter (Cambridge: Cambridge University Press, 1994), 148–80; H. A. Winkler, "Nationalism and Nation-state in Germany," in *The National Question in Europe in Historical Context*, eds. M. Teich and R. Porter (Cambridge: Cambridge University Press, 1994), 181–95; for the German Customs Union see K. Koch, "Österreich und der Deutsche Zollverein (1848–1871)," in *Die Habsburgermonarchie 1848–1918, Bd. 6/1: Die Habsburgermonarchie im System der internationalen Beziehungen,* ed. A. Wandruszka (Vienna: Verlag der Österreichischen Akademie der Wissenschaften, 1989), 537–60.

the German-speaking parts of the Habsburg Monarchy instead of the "Small German" project, from which the Austrian Germans were excluded. German-speaking Austrians were split in this regard.

The separate development of the German and the Habsburg Empires did not offer chances to realize all-German aspirations within the given state borders, hence convincing major wings of German nationals to accept the Habsburg state as a framework for their national endeavors. Radical wings fought for an all-German project. Both German-liberal and German-radical circles argued for a leading role for the German language and the German nation, which they considered an imperial nation, meriting priority over other ethnic communities. The percentage of German-speaking Austrians had risen, when Lombardy (1859) and Venetia (1866) disassociated from the Habsburg Empire and the lands of the Hungarian Crown had formed an autonomous Hungarian sub-empire with a separate parliament and government. The majority of the German-speaking population did not oppose these developments, and somehow agreed with the trans-national, multi-ethnic self-understanding of the Habsburg Empire—all the more so, as German was the language of the court, the army, the central bureaucracy, and the universities, clearly privileged vis-à-vis other national languages. So Austrian Germans were ready to identify with Austrianness as the official doctrine of statehood as long as their privileges as German speakers were not put in question. Only a small minority advocated the unification of the German (speaking) provinces with the German Empire.

In 1918, after the dissolution of the empire and the split of the non-German nationalities into independent nation-states, an all-German identity was quickly adopted in the German-speaking regions. Deprived of the imperial framework, the majority of the population, parliamentary deputies, and major political parties claimed that the Republic of "*Deutschösterreich*" would unite with the German state, which was transformed into a republic in 1918. It was widely acknowledged that "'Austria' was a state that nobody wanted."[24] Continuity was preserved on the level of provincial instead of national identity (*Landesbewusstsein*). Positive associations with being "Austrian" only developed after the defeat of the Third German Reich and the emergence of a neutral state and mediator in international politics.

AUSTRIANNESS: POTENTIALS AND LIMITS OF A MULTI-ETHNIC NATION

If Germanness was not an option on which an Austrian state identity could be built, we have to investigate the possibilities of developing a multi-ethnic understanding of the state and its citizens, Austrianness (*Österreichertum*). For this reason the various notions of Austria have to be kept in mind. They came up at successive moments in history, each of them persisting when new manifestations were developed, hence forming an overlapping structure of identities in which some were compatible and

---

[24] H. Andics, *Der Staat, den keiner wollte* (Vienna: Herder 1962)

others contradictory.[25] First of all, Austria had a geographical meaning, designating the Duchies (1156), later Archduchies (1358–59) of Lower and Upper Austria (*Österreich unter und ober der Enns*). This designation never ended, transforming the regional identity of their inhabitants into a national one. It took a while, until later acquisitions of the Austrian Archdukes were considered "Austria" as well. "Austria" in a broader sense was mainly confined to the German hereditary lands, including the Bohemian lands, but usually not the lands of the Hungarian hereditary Crown. There was no common denomination for the Austrian territories, therefore the plural was used to address them, summing them up in a long list. No allusion to a national definition was made, as the following quotation from 1739 shows, in which all terms are used in a strictly regional, not a national sense: "... *kein Unterschied der Nation gemachet wird und ... nicht allein Oesterreicher, sondern auch Steyermärker, Kärntner, Crainer, Tyroler, Croaten, Böhmen, Mähren und Schlesier, Hungarn, Siebenbürger, Spanier, Welsche und Niederländer sich befinden.*"[26]

"Austria" had a second, strictly dynastic meaning, denominating the lands under a common sovereign, identifying Austria with the ruling family whose possessions were the "house" of Austria. The Hungarian Lands were theoretically included, just like later acquisitions, but in practice the term Austria was more often applied for the German hereditary lands. The more the ruling dynasty wanted to underline the unity of their possessions as a great power within the Holy Roman Empire, the more "Austria" denoted a unified state rather than a plurality of territories. The unifying term "Austrian Monarchy" was first used in 1673 with the succession of the Spanish Habsburgs, and was confirmed in 1713 in a document called "Pragmatic Sanction," which declared the indivisibility of the Austrian Lands, hence transforming the dynastic unity into territorial terms without limiting expansion. Still there was no common name for the composite conglomeration of "hereditary kingdoms and provinces," which only became "empire" (*Österreichischer Kaiserstaat*) in 1804, when Emperor Franz I (II) claimed equality with Emperor Napoleon.[27] In the meanwhile, the penetration of the Austrian lands by public administration, common legislation, and the integration of the provinces into a common market during the eighteenth century had contributed to a widening identification with the "House of Austria": the first

---

[25] Bruckmüller, *The Austrian Nation*; G. Klingenstein, "Was bedeuten 'Österreich' und 'österreichisch' im 18. Jahrhundert? Eine begriffsgeschichtliche Studie," in *Was heißt Österreich. Inhalt und Umfang des Österreichbegriffs vom 10. Jahrhundert bis heute*, eds. R. Plaschka, G. Stourzh, and J. P. Niederkorn (Vienna: Verlag der Österreichischen Akademie der Wissenschaften, 1995), 149–220; E. Zöllner, "Der Österreichbegriff. Aspekte seiner historischen Formen und Wandlungen," in ibid., 19–33.

[26] F. Gatti, *Geschichte der k. k. Ingenieurs- und k. k. Genie-Akademie 1717–1869*, vol. 1 (Vienna, 1901), 20: "No difference of nation is made ... there were not only Austrians, but Styrians, Carinthians, Crainers, Tyrolians, Croats, Bohemians, Moravians and Silesians, Hungarians, Transylvanians, Spaniards, Italians and Netherlandians." Compare G. Klingenstein, "Was bedeuten Österreich," 165.

[27] Klingenstein, "Was bedeuten Österreich," 187, 191, 204.

advances of an Austrian nation-building from above were made by central state civil servants, giving rise to the idea of a "*Hofratsnation*," a "nation of counselors to the emperor."[28] When legal reforms under Joseph II and his successors introduced the idea of citizenship and citizens' rights, replacing the status of legal dependence from a feudal lord, "Austria" could potentially acquire a broader meaning, rendering identity to the state citizens instead of being restricted to the dynasty.

The idea of being Austrian was equally rooted in the estates, which arose on the provincial (lands) level from the fourteenth century onwards, giving rise to the representation of the nobility, the clergy, urban burghers, and in rare cases also the landed peasantry in the diet. As institutions of self-representation and self-government land estates (*Landstände*) and diets (*Landtage*) developed provincial identity, Archduchies identified themselves with "Austria," and in other lands emerged a Styrian, a Carinthian, or a Tyrolian identity. On the grounds of provincial consciousness, the estates identified with the ruling dynasty, and they equally opposed it in the name of "Austria," "Styria," or "Bohemia" if the sovereign increased imperial domination and central state control. Provincial identity on the level of the lands was restricted to those represented in the estates, with the potential of being extended from the privileged to broader circles of the provincial population. It could easily have turned into a national identification from below, if the estates were not besieged by the absolutist ruler and their self-governing competence subordinated to central state authorities. Another source of extending Austrian nationhood beyond the ruling classes was represented by the Austrian Freemasons and Jacobins, who for a short period were backed and instrumentalized by Archduke Franz von Lothringen, Josef II, and Leopold II in support of their state reforms, before they were suppressed by their successors.[29] The fight against Napoleon, which required general armament in Vienna in 1797,[30] gave way to a broad patriotic, national feeling, and was also suppressed after the defeat of 1809.

So the broadening of identification with the "House of Austria" was enacted from above, based on the separation of the Austrian Empire from the Holy Roman Empire, and the codification of citizenship in the Civil Code of 1811 (*Allgemeines Bürgerliches Gesetzbuch*), liberating Austrianness from its exclusive imperial connotation.[31]

On the contrary, the movements of national awakening and the Revolutions of 1848 were supporting the ethno-linguistic understanding of nation-building. Democracy was identified with national liberation, the neo-absolutist reaction with the dynasty, and its multi-ethnic interpretation of nationhood ("prison of nations").

---

[28] Bruckmüller, *The Austrian Nation*, 224.

[29] Bruckmüller, *The Austrian Nation*, 334.

[30] At this occasion the national anthem, praising "our good Emperor Franz," was performed for the first time: Bruckmüller, *The Austrian Nation*, 225f.

[31] H. Burger, "Paßwesen und Staatsbürgerschaft," in *Grenze und Staat. Paßwesen, Staatsbürgerschaft, Heimatrecht und Fremdengesetzgebung in der österreichischen Monarchie (1750–1867)*, eds. W. Heindl and E. Saurer (Vienna–Cologne–Weimar: Böhlau Verlag, 2000), 108.

Contrarily to Germany, where an exclusive ethno-linguistic definition of the German nation gained ground, the Habsburg Monarchy foresaw multiple identities. Austrianness allowed German speaking Austrians to belong to the German culture as well as to the Austrian political nation at the same time.

In theory, the idea of Austrianness (*Österreichertum*) was a supra-national category, relying on the common sovereign, and common Central European culture and history beyond ethnic and linguistic differences. As pointed out, the Constitution of 1867 declared the "equal right of all native languages." So Austrianness offered a potential identity for all peoples; and indeed, we may observe Czechs, Poles, Ruthenians, Slovenes and other nationalities adopting a feeling of being part of the Austrian nation.[32] Very often, the common army and navy is taken as an example to underline the multi-ethnic character of the Habsburg state. Recruitment was carried out on a territorial basis, not making any social, ethnic or religious differences. Recruits served in provincial military corps, where everyday communication was carried out in the recruits' language(s) (*Regimentssprachen*). Officers were obliged to learn the regiments' languages within three years. Conversely, recruits were relocated to other provinces during several years of their military service, confronting the young men with other regional, social and cultural environments. As German was the language of command (*Kommandosprache*), recruits had to learn some elementary German, making German the *lingua franca* for all nationalities.[33]

In practice, it was much easier for German speakers to identify with Austria than for non-Germans. Austrianness was closely linked with the German language, serving as an instrument of communication, rule, and dominance, superposing regional languages in the domains of politics, trade, law, and science, providing Austrianness with German traits in the self-understanding of both German speaking and non-German speaking Austrians.

Nevertheless Austrianness was present as a popular feeling under the reigns of Franz II, Ferdinand I, and Franz Joseph I. It only ceased being a cohesive force with the defeat in World War I. It would not be appropriate to apply the anti-Austrian sentiments after 1917, which gave rise to new nation-states, to the period between 1848 and 1914.

What was the nature of loyalty to the Austrian state? First, identification with Austria was identification with the sovereign and the dynasty, the House of Austria. Despite strong objections vis-à-vis specific measures and single representatives, the

---

[32] For Czechs see Koralka, *Tschechen im Habsburgerreich*, 37; for Ruthenians (Ukrainians) see S. Cholij, "The Modernization of the Armed Forces—a Chance for the Galician Population? The personal development of the recruits, 1868–1914," paper presented on the conference *Galizien. Peripherie der Moderne—Moderne der Peripherie*, Vienna, Nov. 9–11, 2011 (Marburg: Verlag Herder-Institut, 2013).

[33] Cholij, "The Modernization of the Armed Forces"; E. A. Schmidl, "Die k. u. k. Armee: Integrierendes Element eines zerfallenden Staates?" in *Das Militär und der Aufbruch in die Moderne, 1860–1890. Armeen, Marinen und der Wandel von Politik, Gesellschaft und Wirtschaft in Europa, den USA sowie Japan*, ed. M. Epkenhans (Munich: Oldenbourg Verlag, 2003), 143–50.

dynasty was regarded as a force that balanced antagonistic social, ethnic, and religious interests based on the idea of a just ruler and giving rise to a high popularity of the Habsburg family. Second, identification was the result of empire-wide economic, cultural, and political integration, allowing many groups and individuals to experience the extended empire as beneficial for their purposes. Productive forces, sales markets, job and labor markets, transport facilities, educational standards, cultural interactions and transfers, all these cohesive factors contributed to make the monarchy a reality for the inhabitants, much easier to perceive than the polarizing forces, which were inscribed in social inequality and regional disparity of the empire. Even from a critical point of view, which many opponents shared because of class and ethnic exclusion, belonging to the monarchy led to an ambiguous feeling, combining rejection and attraction. Even the opposition was loyal to the emperor, illustrated by a legend reported about Viktor Adler, the leader of the Social Democrat Party. When Adler was supposed to welcome his son Friedrich home from prison, who had assassinated the wartime prime minister in 1916, he had a problem. In the same hour Adler was invited by the emperor who was in his last days in power. In order to be able to meet his son, a state enemy, at the station and reach the emperor's reception, he was offered an imperial coach with a driver, allowing him to fulfill both duties.

A third source of Austrianness, shared across social boundaries, was based on distancing itself from other nations, first of all from Prussia and the German Empire, which was perceived as an enemy and a competing national project after the defeat of 1866, but also from France for being a centralist state and from Russia for being a militarist one. In contrast, the Habsburg Monarchy was perceived as a milder, Central European alternative, based on multi-ethnicity and plural identities, even if it was hard to realize equality in practice.

In the end, the limits were overwhelming the potentials of Austrianness. Austrian Germans' parties and associations blocked the "right of every ethnic people" to become realized, fueling the vision of national self-determination first within— then beyond—the Habsburg Monarchy's boundaries. Paradoxically, concessions the imperial government made to single ethnic groups in order to guarantee their parliamentary cooperation strengthened ethno-national imperial identity. So Austrianness was put under increasing pressure and competition from German and non-German nationalisms, the first being able to operate in harmony with the official trans-national doctrine, and the latter—although claiming ethno-linguistic equality—in opposition to it. A major source of conflict was inherent in the compromise with Hungary. It was not possible to include the lands of the Hungarian Crown into the framework of power on the same grounds as other nationalities: guaranteeing the compromise of dualism proved the multi-ethnic commitment of the constitution. On the other hand, offering the Hungarian government autonomy in regulating inner-Hungarian ethnic affairs on the grounds of assimilation to the dominant nation was regarded as a betrayal of the state guiding principles, inevitably causing imbalances and tensions with Bohemia and its Czech majority. Such imbalances prevented Bohemian Czechs and Germans from developing a positive identification with "Austria."

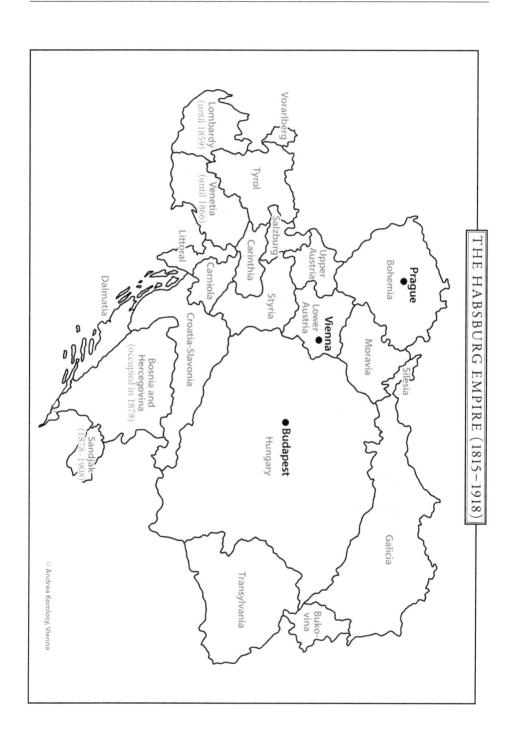

THE HABSBURG EMPIRE (1815–1918)

Vorarlberg

Lombardy
(until 1859)

Venetia
(until 1866)

Tyrol

Salzburg

Carinthia

Littoral

Carniola

Dalmatia

Croatia-Slavonia

Bosnia and
Hercegovina
(occupied in 1878)

Sandjak
(1878–1908)

Upper
Austria

Lower
Austria

Styria

Vienna

Bohemia

Prague

Moravia

Silesia

Budapest

Hungary

Galicia

Transylvania

Buko-
vina

© Andrea Komlosy, Vienna

DEPARTURE TOWARDS A HUNGARIAN NATION

Being a language of the countryside, the Magyar language for a long time did not enter the world of higher administration, law, science, and literature. Magyar co-existed in a close relationship with German and Latin, which were serving as trans-regional languages of communication in Hungary, and other vernacular languages, spoken in specific Hungarian regions. The idea of the Hungarian nation, represented by the estates, was carried by the Hungarian nobility—including its high, medium, and low ranking members, which comprised around 6% of the population. Adherence relied on noble status, land-ownership, and the availability of peasants and serfs to cultivate one's land, supplying the Hungarian nation with a strong material foundation, including noble land owners and excluding all other subjects. Language neither played a role for inclusion nor for exclusion: Any noble land owner, regardless of language and ethnicity, was part of it, while landless Magyar speakers did not belong to the Hungarian nation. Hence the symbiotic relationship with German, Latin, and other languages did not contradict the idea of the Hungarian nation.[34]

The reforms of Joseph II met resistance first of all because of their centralizing ambitions, reducing the autonomy of the county as a self-governing body and imposing taxation on the lords' revenues. Going hand in hand with the introduction of German as language of administration on the county-level, language became politicized. Attempts from above to Germanize the local administration kicked off the transformation of the Hungarian nation from a noble to an ethno-linguistic nation, corresponding with the idea of a "national awakening," which brought social change all over Europe at the beginning of the nineteenth century. The new concept of a Hungarian nation no longer was restricted to the landed nobility, but also included—and mobilized—other subjects and citizens, if they were Magyar speakers or ready to adopt the Magyar language and culture.[35]

In the first half of the nineteenth century a broad movement of language reform was set up to bring Magyar up to the standards of modern literature, science, and administration. Grammar books, dictionaries, and literature prospered, supporting the idea that belonging to the Hungarian nation required command of the Magyar language.[36] The Revolution of 1848 was rooted in the new concept of the Hungarian nation, pushing for democratization and self-administration on national grounds. Seizing power and drafting a Hungarian constitution in April 1848 opened up possibilities for the revolutionary government to Magyarize the society. Magyarization was carried out on a primarily symbolic level: changing names of streets and places, adopting Magyar instead of non-Magyar family names, introducing the Magyar language in as

---

[34] E. Niederhauser, "The National Question in Hungary," in *The National Question in Europe in Historical Context*, eds. M. Teich and R. Porter (Cambridge: Cambridge University Press, 1994), 251.

[35] Kontler, *Millennium in Central Europe*, 215.

[36] Ibid., 220f.

many domains as possible, including city councils, theatres, clubs, religious services, and schools. German was identified with the language of the political oppressor, Viennese absolutism and centralism, which had to be overcome through Magyarization. This attitude put German-speaking revolutionaries into a difficult situation. But Slovak, Serbian, or Romanian-speaking revolutionaries were hardly accepted as partners—they saw the revolution as a chance for their own national claims to be realized instead of accepting Magyarization as the appropriate revolutionary expression.

When the central imperial government regained power during and after the revolutionary period, it abolished all democratic achievements, and with them the advance of the Magyar language. The Austrian authorities, until 1854 under a state of siege, re-established old street names, exchanged revolutionary with reactionary monuments, stopped the use of Magyar for debates and notes in the Buda and Pest city-councils, and forced persons who had adopted Magyar family names back into their old names.[37] The anti-Magyar backlash strengthened the Magyar cause—it re-affirmed the idea of Magyarization as part of the struggle for national self-determination, linking national liberalization with democratization. More and more people rallied behind the idea of establishing identity between state, people, and language—despite the fact, that Magyar speakers in 1850 did not make up more than 44.5% of the Kingdom's population, and 22.9% in Budapest respectively.

When the Compromise re-introduced a Hungarian government, Magyarization could be pursued on an official level, using language and language policy as a major means of nation-building: public events, media and inscriptions, toponyms, and family names were the areas where Magyarization could symbolicly be pursued. Monuments were erected to remember the past according to national principles, history books and curricula were rewritten, and collective memory produced. Education and school became major fields of state intervention, aimed at founding the Hungarian identity both from above and from below.

Robert Nemes has pointed out how Budapest during this process lost its German character. He confronts the mobilizing aspect of the national awakening with its repressive character vis-à-vis non-Magyar languages and their speakers: German, especially in Budapest, which lost its hegemonic role in media, literature, and public life to Magyar; and the languages of the national minorities, which were not supposed to be developed in their own rights and purposes, remaining secondary languages and facing discrimination in administration and education.

Magyar was imposed on the Hungarian society by a complex set of attractive and legal measurements. Magyarization was attractive because it allowed its speakers social advancement. Thousands of non-Magyar Hungarians assimilated with the Magyar culture, contributing to a merger between nation and language. This was attractive for Slovaks and Croats, many of whom became Magyarized; it was less attractive for Serbs and Romanians, whose nationality was inseparably linked with their

---

[37] Robert Nemes, *The Once and Future Budapest* (Illinois: DeKalb, 2005), 150, 155.

Christian-Orthodox confession. Many prominent Hungarians who dedicated their life and work to the Magyar cause had Slavic origins, such as the revolutionary poet Sándor Petőfi, who was born as Alexander Petrovics. Jews from all nationalities, including Zionists, responded to the offer Magyar represented for social assimilation and voluntarily adopted Magyar for religious service and social life. Only the Jewish Orthodox did not follow the Neolog majority in the question of language and religious reform.[38]

In Budapest, Jews were prominent fighters of the Hungarian Revolution, and they became pillars for and representatives of the inclusive concept of Magyarization. Magyarization was a means of overcoming anti-Judaist sentiments. The Dual Settlement of 1867 was accompanied by a law that guaranteed Jews equal civic and political rights.[39] The equality of the nationalities was codified in 1868: The Nationality Law declared the unity and the indivisibility of the Hungarian nation.[40] The same law was regulating the use of different languages, hence defining the national question of non-Magyar nationalities in terms of language, subordinated under the Hungarian nation, including every citizen and hence laying the grounds for a Hungarian citizenship. Elementary schooling, which was subject to a law in 1868, was supposed to teach children in their mother tongue, hence acknowledging linguistic diversity in the kingdom.[41] In reality, however, the overall trend towards Magyarization put pressure on the existence of non-Magyar schools and moved many children into Magyar schooling. In Budapest, while 34.4 % declared German their mother tongue in 1880, there was not a single German language school in Budapest, and only six out of more than 100 schools were bilingual.[42] Public voices attacked linguistic pluralism, achieving a reform bill in 1879, which rendered Hungarian the compulsory language of education in public elementary schools.[43] Every citizen should be able to speak the national language, it argued, and non-Magyar speaking teachers were given three years time to learn Magyar. A fundamental advance in Magyarization came along in 1907 in the form of administrative measures, regulating the salary of school teachers. Community and confessional schools were put under state control, hence eliminating last resorts of teaching in non-Magyar languages.[44] These laws, named after the Minister of Public Instruction Albert Apponyi, marked a major shift towards Magyarization, stressing the restrictive character of language policy vis-à-vis its integrative obligation.

---

[38] Nemes, *The Once and Future Budapest*, 164, 174.
[39] Hungarian State Law, Art. 1867: 17. See complete collection of Hungarian laws (in Magyar language) http://www.1000ev.hu. I am grateful to Susan Zimmermann for the translation.
[40] Art. 1868: 44; L. Gogolák, "Ungarns Nationalitätengesetze und das Problem des Magyarischen National- und Zentralstaates," in *Die Habsburger Monarchie 1848–1918, vol. 3, Die Völker des Reiches,* eds. A. Wandruszka and P. Urbanitsch (Vienna: Verlag der österreichischen Akademie der Wissenschaften, 1980), 1207–1303; Nemes, *The Once and Future Budapest*, 177.
[41] Art. 1868: 38; Kontler, *Millennium in Central Europe*, 285.
[42] Nemes, *The Once and Future Budapest*, 176.
[43] Hungarian State Law, Art. 1879: 18.
[44] Art. 1907: 36, 37; Kontler, *Millennium in Central Europe*, 298.

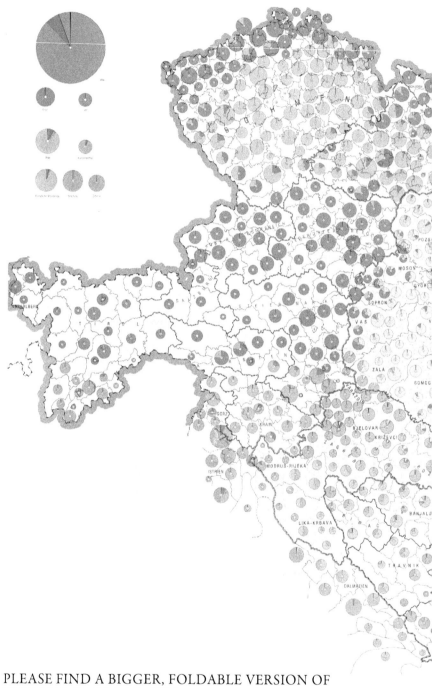

PLEASE FIND A BIGGER, FOLDABLE VERSION OF
THIS MAP IN COLOR AT THE END OF THE BOOK

LANGUAGES AND NATIONALITIES IN THE AUSTRIAN-HUNGARIAN MONARCHY (1910)

The map shows the distribution of nationalities by regions, with Vienna, Graz, Linz (top left) and Budapest (bottom right).
Nationalities/religious confession according to the census of 1910.

Germans — Dt	Slovaks — Slo	Italians l, Ladins	Gipsies — Z	Jews grey raster on nationality
Chechs — T	Slovenes — Sle	Romanians — Run	Bulgarians — B	Others 0–1%
Poles — P	Serbes — Se	Magyars — M	Muslim Bosniaks	Others 1–2%
Ruthenians — Rur	Croats — K	Dalmatinians, Illyrians a.o.	Spaniols in Bosnia-Her-cegowina — Sp	

Marriage policies were also instrumental for the process of nation building. In 1894, marriage registers were transferred from the church to the state.[45] This facilitated inter-confessional marriages and because of the strong link between ethnicity and religion, encouraged inter-ethnic marriages.[46] Mixed couples more easily adopted a Hungarian identity, opting voluntarily for the Maygar language, while eventually maintaining other languages for local or private purposes.

Political Administration: Conflict between Central Administration and Regional Self-Government—Between and Beyond Ethnic Lines

Central state institutions strengthened vis-à-vis regional elites in the process of state-formation in the seventeenth and eighteenth centuries. The process of modern state-building took place regardless of the ethnic composition of the regions and localities, which were deprived of their self-governing bodies or reduced in their self-governing competences. If local and regional elites, who had to cede power to central state institutions, were non-German nationals, regional opposition against centralizing state reforms obtained a national character. The conflict between local/regional and central interests intermingled with ethnic diversity, which always had a regional, very often a social, and sometimes also confessional, foundation.

The tension between regional and central power requires differentiation between the major provinces of the empire—each case shows a different socio-ethnic and socio-religious composition of the provincial population, with different issues for the conflict between central and regional elites, depending on the specific geopolitical conditions and the historical timing. The following case studies refer to the lands of the Bohemian and the Hungarian Crown.[47]

In the lands of the Bohemian Crown,[48] where Germans and Czechs lived side-by-side since the German settlement in the Middle Ages, regional self-govern-

---

[45] Art. 1894: 33.

[46] Z. Tóth, "Was wird im Schmelztiegel geschmolzen? Assimilationsweisen in Pest in der zweiten Hälfte des 19. Jahrhunderts," in *Wien–Prag–Budapest. Urbanisierung, Kommunalpolitik, gesellschaftliche Konflikte (1867–1918)*, eds. G. Melinz and S. Zimmermann (Vienna: Promedia Verlag, 1996), 210–18.

[47] Komlosy, "Innere Peripherien," 62–67.

[48] K. Bosl, ed., *Handbuch der Geschichte der böhmischen Länder, vol. 3: Die böhmischen Länder im Habsburger Reich, 1848–1919* (Stuttgart: Anton Hiersemann Verlag, 1968); J. K. Hoensch, *Geschichte Böhmens von der slavischen Landnahme bis ins 20. Jahrhundert* (Munich: C.H. Beck Verlag, 1992); A. Klíma, "The Czechs," in *The National Question in Europe in Historical Context*, eds. M. Teich and R. Porter (Cambridge: Cambridge University Press, 1994), 228–47; Kořalka, *Tschechen im Habsburgerreich*; M. Teich and R. Porter, eds., *The National Question in Europe in Historical Context* (Cambridge: Cambridge University Press, 1994); O. Urban. *Die tschechische*

ment suffered a backlash after the Bohemian estates' defeat in the Battle of the White Mountain (1620). The conflict between the court and the estates was embedded in and raised to a confessional conflict, in which the estates identified with the Protestant religion, while centralizing state ambitions were linked with Roman Catholic universalism. Catholic aristocratic families of various ethnic or national backgrounds, which had proven their loyalty to the emperor, replaced Protestant families who were expelled from the Bohemian Lands. After the expulsion of both German and Czech protestant nobles and the re-Catholization of the country, German was declared the language of administration and education. The confessional conflict, underlying the competition between the central state and regions, was transformed into a national conflict, thus referring to the Hussite revolutionary movement of the fourteenth century, which was fuelled by religious and national dissent. As a consequence of the Germanization of the central governing, administrative, and educational institutions, Czech was pushed off to local, rural, and agricultural spheres of life, where it suffered official neglect and was only revived by the national movement arising in the nineteenth century, gradually promoting the acceptance of the Czech language in public life. In the nineteenth century, Bohemian regionalist aspirations—in spite of inter-ethnic rivalry—were supported by German and Czech elites, who were united by their demand to obtain "Bohemian Constitutional Rights" (*Böhmisches Staatsrecht*) that is, a common parliament and government for the lands of the Bohemian Crown, hence extending the Dual Austrian-Hungarian Settlement into a trilateral compromise. When this Bohemian project failed, the nationalist voices among Bohemian Germans and Czechs gained the upper hand in a severe fight for national positions. In Moravia, the conflict was less intense and practical solutions for bi-national co-existence were found more easily.[49]

Several factors contributed to the deterioration of the relations between Germans and Czechs, reinforcing each other mutually.[50] In the first half of the nineteenth century the Czech national movement aspired biliguality and equality of the Czech and German language, in Bohemia called "utraquism." After the failure of a

---

Gesellschaft 1848–1918, 2 vol. (Cologne–Weimar–Vienna: Böhlau Verlag: 1994). The author prefers the term Bohemian to Czech because it included all ethnic groups; and the Lands of the Bohemian Crown to Bohemia, because it refers to all parts—Bohemia, Moravia and Silesia—as well as to the unity of the Kingdom.

[49] Koralka, *Tschechen im Habsburgerreich*, 159.

[50] Bosl, *Die böhmischen Länder*, 154–70; P. M. Judson, *Guardians of the Nation: Activists on the Language Frontiers of Imperial Austria* (Cambridge, Mass.: Harvard University Press, 2006); F. Svátek, "Tschechischer und deutscher Nationalismus. Der "Sprachkampf" der Minderheiten an der Südgrenze Böhmens im 19. Jahrhundert," in *Kulturen an der Grenze. Waldviertel-Weinviertel-Südböhmen-Südmähren,* eds. A. Komlosy, V. Bužek, and F. Svátek (Vienna: Promedia Verlag, 1995), 238–45; N. Wingfield, *Flag Wars and Stone Saints: How the Bohemian Lands Became Czech* (Cambridge, Mass.: Harvard University Press, 2007); T. Zahra, *Kidnapped Souls: National Indifference and the Battle for Children in the Bohemian Lands, 1900–1948* (Ithaca: Cornell University Press, 2008).

Bohemian compromise Czech, nationalist positions gained ground at the expense of utraquism. At the same time, social and demographic changes occurred, leading to a rise of Czechs among the urban, industrial, and educated population. The inclusion of broader layers of the population into franchise led to an increased political representation of Czechs in municipal and provincial parliaments. Hand in hand with the rise of eligibility went the rise of the more radical, nationally oriented party of the "Young Czechs" (*Jungtschechen*), marginalizing the conservative "Old Czechs," who had a closer relationship with the court and the central government and had been the advocates of an utraquist compromise. Rising political representation of Czechs and their endeavors to establish Czech as the leading language wherever they had the demographic majority reinforced nationalist positions among the German population. Germans lost their majorities not only in municipal governments, but in 1883–84 also in the Bohemian diet and important chambers of commerce. As a reaction they asked for an administrative division of the crown-land into a German and a Czech Bohemia, or—another option which was partly realized—into German and Czech districts, which were not obliged to practice bilinguality in public administration, introduced by language laws in 1880. Czech parties heavily opposed a division, criticizing it for "tearing the land in pieces" ("*Landeszerreissung*"), hence endangering the unity of the Bohemian Lands. The "Young Czechs adapted the ideas, represented by the old claim for "Bohemian Constitutional Rights" to the battle for maintaining a homogeneous provincial administration, obliging all districts, and not only those with a Czech majority, to respect the equality of languages. Provincial unity was also aspired, because the economically more prosperous Germans paid a higher tax share, and an administrative division would have deprived Czechs from participation. Attempts at achieving a compromise were regularly blocked, and as a consequence both sides mobilized to win those people who were nationally indifferent or ethnically mixed to a single national cause. Language frontiers were created where there had been none before, challenging and obstructing the consolidation of Austrianness in the Bohemian lands.

In the lands of the Hungarian Crown after Ottoman rule, the centralizing aspirations of the Viennese court opened a long lasting dispute between estates and regional nobility on the one side and the central government on the other, which now and again took military form.[51] In Hungary the Habsburgs' centralizing aspirations had to take account of the Ottoman occupation of large parts of the country. When the House of Habsburg extended its rule over the whole Kingdom of Hungary after 1687, the court was not able to establish the administrative and political control in the same way as in the Bohemian Lands. In Hungary the tradition of aristocratic self-government had suffered under Ottoman rule, but the landed nobility also experienced a high degree of autonomy with regard to feudal relations, culture, and religion, as long

---

[51] P. Hanák, *Ungarn in der Donaumonarchie. Probleme der bürgerlichen Umgestaltung eines Vielvölkerstaates* (Munich: Verlag für Geschichte und Politik, 1984); Kontler, *Millennium in Central Europe*, 181–215; Niederhauser, "The National Question"; I. G. Tóth, ed., *Geschichte Ungarns* (Budapest: Corvina Kiadó, 2005).

as they delivered taxes to central Ottoman authorities. Immediately after the takeover of former Ottoman Hungary and the acceptance of Habsburg rule by the estates, the War of Independence broke out (1703–11). Military defeat obliged the Hungarian nobility to accept central government and institutions; but they were also successful in restoring the estates' rights of 1670, that is, the abolition of central state interference in regional affairs, including political, economic, cultural, and religious issues. Hungary did not join the census and conscription system established in the Austrian and Bohemian Lands, and it did not join the fiscal system, thereby preventing Viennese central authorities from direct taxation of landlords' and subjects' incomes. And it did not accept re-Catholization of the various protestant groups who had been able to survive and enjoyed a high degree of religious freedom under Ottoman rule. In the 1690s, when the Habsburgs took over Hungarian rule, counter-reformation could not be achieved against a population that had long ago adopted Lutheran or Calvinist beliefs. As a consequence of the compromise between the estates and the court, Hungary did not participate in the economic and administrative integration of the Habsburg state; the major political reforms of Enlightened Absolutism ended at the Leitha border, which maintained its function as a customs frontier until 1851. High customs on the export of Hungarian goods compensated the central state for the lacking access to internal taxation of the Hungarian noble economy. Hungarian resistance could not prevent Habsburg authorities under Joseph II to impose an ambitious program of centralization on Hungarian institutions, which aimed at the Germanization of the district administration. This program met with strong resistance in Hungary and elsewhere and was stopped in 1790. Previous estates' rights were re-confirmed.

Another militarization of the conflict took place in 1848, when the Hungarian estates' declaration of independence was put down militarily with Russian assistance. Hungary, deprived of all its regional self-governance, was submitted to direct Viennese administration—a status which was not accepted by Hungarian elites and was overcome as soon as the central government was weakened by internal conflicts and military defeats abroad, leading to the loss of Lombardy (1859) and Venetia (1866) and surrender to Prussia in the German question (1866). The readiness of the court to give Hungary political autonomy went hand in hand with the increasing political demands of German Austrians in the Austrian sub-empire, who were granted a constitution in 1867.

In Hungary, the conditions of the Dual Settlement of 1867 led to a conflict between the Deák Party, which supported a close cooperation with Vienna, and the Left Center Party, which advocated more autonomy. The Compromise was fundamentally rejected by the Independence Party, which followed the ideas of Lajos Kossuth.[52] Hungary's first Prime Minister, Gyula Andrássy, belonged to the Deák Party. While the radical Independists wanted to push forward democratization and broader political participation within a Hungarian nation-state, the moderates and conservatives stressed that geopolitical realities as well as economic viability necessitated union with

---

[52] Kontler, *Millennium in Central Europe*, 284; also see Hanák, *Ungarn in der Donaumonarchie*, 70–77.

Austria. The Compromise did not question the strong economic power of the landed nobility. By establishing a customs regime in favor of the big agricultural estates, it enabled the landlords to maintain high food prices, perpetuating the endemic poverty of the rural population, who maintained their deep dependence on the landlords. Political participation was limited by franchise restrictions, which depended on status and income. The number of Hungarian citizens entitled to vote for the national parliament never exceeded six to seven percent of the population.[53] The Compromise helped stabilize the empire by integrating the Hungarian aristocracy into the ruling political class. It supported national self-determination and tolerated the Magyarization of the country—at the expense of the revolutionary demands for independence and more democratization.

When the centralizing ambitions of the Viennese government could not be fully applied in former Ottoman Hungary after the Habsburg conquest, they were more successful in Transylvania, the Banat, and the Military Border, provinces of the Hungarian Crown where Vienna could establish central control. The unity of the lands of the Hungarian Crown, as demanded by the Hungarian estates, was not realized.[54] Transylvania had enjoyed a high degree of regional autonomy under Ottoman suzerainty. When Transylvania came under Habsburg rule in 1699, the establishment of a Transylvanian Chancellery (*Siebenbürgische Hofkanzlei*) in Vienna acknowledged this special status, but also opened the door for Viennese influence over the Transylvanian estates at the expense of Hungarian ambitions. Leopold I (*Leopoldinisches Diplom 1691*) confirmed the Transylvanian Constitution, based on the *Unio trium nationum* (1437) of Magyar nobles, Saxon peasants and burghers, and Székely soldiers.[55] It also confirmed religious freedom for Protestant believers. Romanian serfs, who worked on the Magyar manors, were subjected to religious conversion, however. As they were Greek Orthodox Christians, the program consisted of pushing their bishops to abdicate their previous religious authority, the Greek Orthodox Patriarch and accept the Roman Catholic Pope instead, while keeping their religious rites. The ecclesiastic union with Rome, creating so-called United Greek Catholics, was only successful with a part of the Romanian bishopry (1701), while others kept the Orthodox belief.[56] It shows that the centralizing ambitions of Habsburg rule were present and adapted to specific regional situations. Unifying Romanian Orthodoxy with the Catholic Church at the same time weakened the power of the Magyar nobility vis-à-vis their Romanian serfs.

---

[53] A. Gerö, *The Hungarian Parliament (1867–1918): A Mirage of Power* (New York: Columbia University Press, 1997), 49.

[54] Kontler, *Millennium in Central Europe*, 197.

[55] Name for a group of Magyar speaking inhabitants and their Carpathian region, who in medieval times obtained privileges for fulfilling military functions for the Kingdom of Hungary.

[56] V. Roman and H. Hofbauer, *Transsilvanien—Siebenbürgen. Begegnung der Völker am Kreuzweg der Reiche* (Vienna: Promedia Verlag, 1996), 74.

The Banat of Temes, a province in the south of Hungary which was annexed to the Habsburg Empire in 1719, was exempted from Hungarian control and directly subjected to the Imperial Military Council and the Imperial Treasury in Vienna for strategic reasons. This status was maintained until 1778, when Hungarian rule was established over those parts of the province that did not belong to the Military Border Region (*Militärgrenze*).[57]

The Kingdom of Croatia-Slavonia was granted regional self-government leading to the Hungarian-Croat constitutional agreement (Nagodba) in 1868.[58] This compromise within the Compromise reflects the conflict between central administration and regional self-government in Transleithia itself. However, large parts of Croatia-Slavonia were included into the Military Border, hence submitting regional Croat aristocracy to central Viennese authorities.

The Habsburg regions bordering the Ottoman Empire had become a distinctive administrative unit under direct control of the central administration (*Militärgrenze, Confin, Vojna Krajna*).[59] Established in 1535 in Croatia, they changed their territorial extension along with the Habsburg-Ottoman front-line and were extended along with Habsburg territorial conquests to Slavonia (1702), to the Banat (1742), and Transylvania (1764).[60] The Military Border followed a specific military logic mobilizing military peasants for self-subsistent agrarian settlement. Most soldier-peasants belonged to ethnic or religious minorities, many of them fleeing from Ottoman advance into Habsburg territories, where they enjoyed property rights, political freedoms, and religious privileges in exchange for their military service, hence representing an important pillar of court and central government. In the Croatian, the Slavonian and the Banat sections of the Military Border they were overwhelmingly Orthodox Serbians, who were the first non-Catholic Christians to experience religious tolerance in the Habsburg Monarchy.[61] In the Transylvanian section of the Military Border, Christian-Orthodox Romanians prevailed, who underwent union with the Catholic Church. The Military Border was located on Hungarian territories. Apart from its military significance, it represented a means of diminishing Magyar and Croat noble influence on peasants, who were directly subjected to the Imperial Military Council (*Hofkriegsrat*), hence undermining control by central Hungarian authorities as well as regional and local self-government by provinces, counties, and manorial estates. Hence it was an

---

[57] Kontler, *Millennium in Central Europe*, 197; A. Paulinyi, "Ungarn 1700–1850," in *Handbuch der europäischen Wirtschafts- und Sozialgeschichte vol 4*, ed. W. Fischer and I. Mieck (Stuttgart: Klett Kotta Verlag 1993), 916–47, 924; I. Karaman, "Die südslawischen Länder der Habsburger Monarchie," in ibid., 1027–47, 1036.

[58] Kontler, *Millennium in Central Europe*, 197, 283.

[59] J. Amstadt, *Die k. k. Militärgrenze 1522–1881* (Würzburg, 1969); Heeresgeschichtliches Museum, *Die k. k. Militärgrenze* (Vienna: Österreichischer Bundesverlag, 1973).

[60] C. Göllner, *Die Siebenbürgische Militärgrenze. Ein Beitrag zur Sozial- und Wirtschaftsgeschichte 1762–1851* (Munich: Oldenbourg Verlag, 1974).

[61] I. Silbernagel, *Verfassung und gegenwärtiger Bestand sämtlicher Kirchen des Orients*, ed. Jos. Schnitzer (Regensburg: Manz, 1904), 208–10.

efficient instrument that strengthened the central state in the conflict with regional aristocratic ambitions for autonomous rule. The Military Border stayed outside the Compromise regulations of 1867. It was gradually abolished between 1851 and 1881 and finally became an integral part of the Hungarian sub-empire.

Economic Integration

While in the sixteenth and seventeenth centuries Habsburg state building aimed at the loyalty and the political control of the estates—the provincial self-governing bodies—the eighteenth-century administrative reforms aimed at the economic integration of the Habsburg lands. Rather than a sum of lands under common rule, hereditary lands as well as old and new acquisitions were conceived as a territorial unity which required economic policies in order to realize integration. In a plea for market integration, Emperor Joseph II argued for thinking of the monarchy in its totality.[62] Internal customs on the local, regional, and provincial level were gradually abolished during the eighteenth and nineteenth centuries, integrating more and more provinces into a free-trade area protected by high customs. Capital was raised by merchants and aristocratic landowners. Lack of capital was overcome by state subsidies and official attempts to attract foreign investors, while banks were only established in the nineteenth century.[63] Industrial investment was encouraged by state privileges and monopolist rights granted to certain enterprises and industry was gradually liberated from guild's regulations. After new trades were introduced, monopolies were transformed into general factory laws.[64] The labor market was encouraged by the reduction if not abolition of seigniorial rights over their subjects. Migration control was transferred from the manorial and municipal into the competence of newly created district authorities on behalf of the central state, which developed new criteria for empowering or refraining local population from migration. The Habsburg free-trade area initiated in 1775 comprised of the hereditary Austrian and Bohemian provinces, with the exception of the Tyrol. The abolition of internal customs, combined with subsidies and privileges (temporary

---

[62] "Einige Gebirgsgegenden in Böhmen, hundert Fabrikanten in Wien werden zu Grunde gehen, dies sei jedoch einer Betrachtung nicht würdig, denn jetzo sehen diese Fabrikanten, diese Leinwandhändler nur auf sich, jeder Herr nur auf seine Herrschaft, jeder Kreishauptmann auf seinen Kreis, jedes Land nur auf sein Wohl und kein Mensch auf das Ganze der Monarchie" –Joseph II in a memorandum for the abolition of internal customs borders, in: A. Beer, "Die Zollpolitik und die Schaffung eines einheitlichen Zollgebietes unter Maria Theresia," *Mittheilungen des Instituts für oesterreichische Geschichtsforschung* XIV (Innsbruck, 1893): 274.

[63] The first bank for industrial financing, organized as a stock company, was founded in 1793. H. Matis, *Die Schwarzenberg-Bank. Kapitalbildung und Industriefinanzierung in den habsburgischen Erblanden 1787–1830* (Vienna: Verlag der Österreichischen Akademie der Wissenschaften, 2005).

[64] H. Freudenberger, *Lost Momentum. Austrian Economic Development 1750s–1830s* (Vienna–Cologne–Weimar: Böhlau Verlag, 2003); Matis, *Von der Glückseligkeit*.

monopoly rights) for investors, technical development as well as highly protectionist customs barriers, were considered to be an efficient industrial policy, which supported big, government-backed, export-oriented industries against smaller competitors, who produced for local markets. There were only a few Tyrolean export industries that could have profited from market liberalization, while transit trade would have suffered from protectionist customs. Tyrol therefore stayed outside the customs union, only joining in 1825, together with Lombardo-Venetia, when the process of state territorialization of the Habsburg Monarchy no longer allowed single provinces to stay outside.[65] The Tyrol and Lombardo-Venetia stayed at the margin of the common market, however, and maintained strong legal and illegal ties with neighboring states.[66] The province of Galicia, which came under Habsburg rule only in 1772, joined the customs union in 1784, although it also was a transit trade area without domestic industrial capacities, and merchant circles opposed integration. Joining the union opened the Galician market for Bohemian and Austrian industries in exchange for agricultural goods, and these interests prevailed.

Hungary stood apart.[67] In their case, the reason for not entering the Habsburg customs union was a reciprocal one: customs on Hungarian imports into the common trade area made up for the refusal of Hungarian nobles to be subjected to taxation by Vienna. The government in Vienna was strong enough to impose much higher taxes on imports from the common trade area to Hungary than on exports. The division of labor between the agrarian east and the industrializing west of the monarchy, which also reflected different agricultural constitutions, was deepened by the active discrimination of Hungarian industrial development at that time.[68] The Hungarian agrarian oligarchy did not object to the industrial neglect, as long as their feudal privileges were not put into question. The division of labor between the Austrian and the Bohemian lands on the one side and the Hungarian lands on the other represented a balanced antagonism, from which the elites of both sides benefited, exempting Hungary from modern industrial development and socio-political reforms that were achieved in the western parts of the Habsburg lands.

When in the first half of the nineteenth century some Hungarian nobles engaged in industrial projects and advocated a re-negotiation of the customs-barrier, there was no support from the Austrian side, which benefited from the unequal

---

[65] Beer, "Die Zollpolitik"; Komlosy, *Grenze und ungleiche*, 134.

[66] E. Saurer, *Straße, Schmuggel, Lottospiel. Materielle Kultur und Staat in Niederösterreich, Böhmen und Lombardo-Venetien im frühen 19. Jahrhundert* (Göttingen: Vandenhoeck & Ruprecht, 1989).

[67] Komlosy, *Grenze und ungleiche*, 137–40; J. Komlos, *Die Habsburgermonarchie als Zollunion. Die wirtschaftliche Entwicklung Österreich-Ungarns im 19. Jahrhundert* (Vienna: Österreichischer Bundesverlag, 1986), 27–31.

[68] Compare K. M. Fink, *Die österreichisch-ungarische Monarchie als Wirtschaftsgemeinschaft* (Munich: Trofenik Verlag, 1968); O. Jaszi, *The Dissolution of the Habsburg Monarchy* (Chicago: University of Chicago Press, 1967). Jaszi supports the discrimination thesis, which is rejected by Kontler, *Millennium in Central Europe*, 203–25.

division of labor.[69] After the defeat of the 1848 revolution and the establishment of direct Viennese rule, the customs border was finally lifted (1851). Its abolition marked the end of the compromise and the subordination of the Hungarian provinces under Viennese rule. The lack of administrative control and the strong resistance of the Hungarian nobility against central government interference hindered the effective integration of the Hungarian provinces into the Viennese Empire.

The Dual Settlement of 1867 separated the k. u. k. monarchy into two k. sub-empires.[70] It enabled the Hungarian government to pursue state investment in infrastructure and economic policies promoting rapid industrialization. Traffic policies clearly show the central role of railroad and road networks, establishing Budapest as the main transport hub between all Hungarian provinces. The industrial advance of Austrian and Bohemian firms prevented Hungarian investors from competing in the same industrial branches. As a consequence, Hungarian industry initially turned toward building up processing capacities for agricultural goods, which gave way to a machine building industry expanding beyond agricultural processing.[71] The disinterest of aristocratic land owners and the lack of capital and industrial labor limited the success of Hungarian industrial development. It was concentrated in Budapest and western Hungary and therefore increased regional disparities and created social and political tensions between the industrial and agricultural parts of the Hungarian sub-empire. Nevertheless it gave rise to industrial agglomeration and upgraded the Hungarian agricultural exports from raw materials to processed food. New industrial branches were introduced. The build up of highly industrialized flour milling plants impacted the Austrian and Bohemian provinces, where milling had been a widespread local industry often carried out in combination with peasant farming. Peasants and small millers at the end of the nineteenth century could no longer compete against Hungarian cereal and flour companies which benefited from the large internal market. So Austrian and Bohemian industrialists and Hungarian big landowners, backed by an emerging agro-industrial complex, shared a common interest in maintaining the division of labor and the common market.[72]

The western, Austrian part of the Empire was characterized by imbalances in regional development as well. On the one hand they existed between industrial regions that in the second half of the eighteenth century attracted investment and state support (especially in Lower and Upper Austria, Styria, Bohemia and Moravia-Silesia)

---

[69] Kontler, *Millennium in Central Europe*, 224.

[70] One k. represented the "kaiserlich" imperial Austrian crown, the other the "königlich" royal Hungarian crown.

[71] D. F. Good, *The Economic Rise of the Habsburg Empire 1750–1914* (Berkeley: University of California Press, 1984).

[72] J. Becker and A. Odman, "Von den inneren zu äußeren Grenzen. Die Auflösung von Habsburgermonarchie und Osmanischem Reich im Vergleich," in *Grenzen weltweit. Zonen, Linien, Mauern im historischen Vergleich*, eds. J. Becker and A. Komlosy (Vienna: Promedia Verlag, 2004), 75–100.

and agrarian regions, some of which specialized in supplying the growing urban markets, while others maintained self-sufficient agricultural production. In Lower and Upper Austria, Styria and the Bohemian Lands, industrial and agrarian specialization co-existed close to each other, forming a division of labor based on a core-periphery relationship on a small scale. Galicia and Bukovina were large agrarian provinces, Dalmatia and the Littoral were so on a smaller scale, and the urban centers of these regions were hardly interrelated with the countryside, as their main commercial centers (Trieste/Littoral and Brody/Galicia) were privileged free trade areas exempted from the single market. Conversely to the old hereditary provinces, where internal cores and peripheries were involved in an intense interrelationship, the Carpathian and Littoral-Dalmatian acquisitions represented overall internal peripheries, which showed a colonial-type of dependency on the economic core regions, even if their inhabitants enjoyed the same legal status. Some of the most important economic and commercial centers were not located in the core provinces, but in regions at the very fringes of the empire, e.g. Ostende, Milano, Venice, or Trieste, the majority of which used to be under Habsburg rule only temporarily. The southern Netherlands, Lombardy, and Venetia had important functions in linking the Habsburg economy with leading technical, financial, and commercial developments in Europe and the world, thus representing economic centers without fully participating in the political or economic integration of the monarchy. The only permanent Habsburg port cities were Trieste/Triest/Trst, forming part of the Austrian hereditary lands, and nearby Rijeka/Fiume/St. Veit an der Pflaum, which belonged to the Kingdom of Croatia-Slavonia. Both were declared privileged free ports in 1719, the latter annexed to Hungary in 1778.

The single market formation brought about the integration of the Habsburg political economy. Along with the integration of regions into a trans-regional division of labor, existing differences between the regions gave way to growing imbalances, hence contributing to the polarization of the economic structure, deepening but also transforming existing differences. Much as the critics had predicted, the smaller-sized, locally oriented, lower productivity industries fell victim to concentration and faced difficulties competing with bigger, often state-subsidized companies. In this process Bohemian industries fell behind those of Lower Austria, Upper Austria, and Styria, which became the leading industrial centers between 1780 and 1870.[73] It was only after the economic crisis of 1873 that Bohemia and Moravia-Silesia properly recovered. They became major centers of economic growth attracting investment by the availability of raw materials, energy supply, or cheap labor. Industrial outsourcing went hand in hand with new technological developments, which allowed the better exploitation of Bohemian and Moravian iron and coal and gave rise to a complex of heavy industries. This development was reinforced by a shift in the Austrian use of North Sea harbors for exports, rather than the Mediterranean ones, which clearly favored the Bohemian Lands over the Alpine provinces, contributing to the relative decline of Trieste.

---

[73] A. Komlosy, "State, Regions, and Borders: Single Market Formation and Labor Migration in the Habsburg Monarchy, 1750–1918," *Review Fernand Braudel Center* 27, no. 2 (2004): 150.

The Non-Synchronicity of an Economic and Political Understanding of Core and Periphery

The picture of center-periphery relations in the Habsburg Monarchy is complicated by the non-synchronicity of core and periphery on an economic and a political level. While in some regions both economic and political features of the core or periphery applied, in other cases an economic core position went hand in hand with political peripheralization and vice versa. Let us investigate the relationship in the last third of the nineteenth century, region by region.

The Bohemian lands, which belonged to the economic core, were denied constitutional self-determination (*Staatsrecht*), initially claimed by German and Czech elites.[74] They were kept in a provincial status. As the aspirations for self-government were not met, German as well as Czech elites in Bohemia shifted towards national aspirations for their respective ethnic collectives, ending in a clash of Czech and German nationalism. At the same time Bohemian and Moravian business elites, both German and Czech, enjoyed economic success: they profited from the unequal interregional division of labor, offering Bohemian and Moravian industrial goods vast markets in the agrarian parts of the empire. This is why Czech national aspirations did not question the imperial frame as long as economic integration was intact. Pan-Slavism was a political challenge, but it did not offer a viable economic alternative to the Habsburg common market. German trades in the Bohemian lands were split, depending on whether they were integrated within the Habsburg Monarchy like in the east and south or if they were, like in the northwestern part of the country, oriented towards German markets. After the disintegration of the empire following World War I, Czech and German nationals adopted the idea of a nation-state. The Czech–Slovak alliance can be regarded as a regional variety of pan-Slavism, aimed at strengthening the Slavic element in the Czechoslovak Republic. The union included another big national minority, Slovak Magyars, into the new state, which became politically viable because of Allied support against German, Austrian, and Hungarian dominance in Central Europe.

The Alpine lands from the Tyrol to Styria, although they contained vast economic peripheries in their mountainous regions, were considered a political core, not least because they belonged to the old hereditary lands. The Archduchies of Lower and Upper Austria were definitely the heartlands of the monarchy, where political and economic core were congruent. Together with Vienna, the imperial capital, financial and cultural center, they represented the imperial core.

The southeastern and Carpathian lands, acquisitions of Habsburg eastward expansions between the seventeenth and nineteenth centuries, were typical internal peripheries, fulfilling initially strategic and—as a result of market integration—economic functions for the imperial core. Economic and political peripherality went

---

[74] Hoensch, *Geschichte Böhmens*; Klusáková, "The Czech Lands"; Komlosy, "Innere Peripherien"; Koralka, *Tschechen im Habsburgerreich*.

hand in hand. From an economic point of view, the delivery of raw materials, agricultural goods, and migrant labor to the core blocked a balanced and sustainable economic and social development of these provinces and made them dependent on foreign investment based on an extractive economy and subsidies from the central state. The national elites of the newly acquired territories did not belong to the old imperial elites, and thus their political influence on Austrian politics was not very strong. Nevertheless their national elites forged alliances with the imperial core, despite the presence of a "national awakening" that sought self-determination. These tactical alliances aimed at maintaining regional hegemony over ethnic rivals (e.g. Galician Poles versus Ruthenian claims, Littoral and Dalmatian Italians versus Croat and Slovene claims) or they aimed at mobilizing imperial support against neighboring empires, Ottoman or Romanov, which had claims over their national territories.[75] In Galicia, Poles were able to improve their political position because their representatives in the *Reichsrat* were considered a partner to the Viennese government against national claims of both Germans and Czechs. In order to prevent a Slavic coalition with the Czechs in the boycott of the Reichsrat, the Poles were granted a regional compromise in 1868 that increased Galician self-governing and encouraged Polonization of the province.[76] Economically, the increase in regional autonomy did not change the peripheral role of the province.

Dalmatia and the Littoral—a province comprising of Görz-Gradisca, Triest, and Istria, with a population of less than a tenth of Galicia and ethnically heterogeneous—were neglected regions with the lowest per capita product of Cisleithania. The port city of Triest represented a regional economic and cultural center with a long tradition of urban self-government, which was reflected in the provincial status of the town and its role as the administrative center of the Littoral.

Hungarian aspirations to form a nation-state in the framework of the monarchy suffered the defeat of the Revolution of 1848, but were realized in 1867. Political autonomy, guaranteed by the Dual Settlement of 1867, did not imply an economic core position, however. Industrial policies of the Hungarian government encouraged some important trades and industries, but they could not overcome their dependency on foreign capital, which came from Austria and Bohemia-Moravia initially but was gradually replaced by West European capital at the end of the nineteenth century.[77] Industrial development specialized in refining agricultural products and machinery. Apart from the mining industry in central Slovakia (Upper Hungary),[78] the indus-

---

[75] Maner, *Galizien*; A. Moritsch and A. Krahwinkler, eds., *Alpen Adria. Zur Geschichte einer Region* (Klagenfurt–Vienna: Hermagoras Verlag, 2001).

[76] Maner, *Galizien*.

[77] I. Berend and G. Ránki, *Underdevelopment in Europe in the Context of East-West Relations in the 19th Century* (Budapest: Akadémia Kiadó, 1980), 77; I. Berend and G. Ránki, *The European Periphery and Industrialization 1780–1914* (Cambridge: Cambridge University Press, 1982), 87.

[78] D. Kovács, M. Teich, and M. Brown, eds., *Slovakia in History* (Cambridge: Cambridge University Press, 2011).

trial sector was concentrated in a few industrial islands in and around Budapest and the western part of the country, while the majority of the country was agricultural. While political autonomy was not able to overcome the peripheral economic status and strong regional imbalances, it allowed the implementation of language and education policies, aiming at linguistic and cultural homogenization, equating Hungarian to Magyar identity. After an initial period in which the Nationality Law and the law on elementary schooling of 1868 guaranteed minorities the right for culture and education in their language if they amounted to more than 20 percent of the regional population, Magyarization attempts were enforced from the 1880s.[79] In 1907 it culminated in a law on non-state elementary schools and the salaries of elementary school teachers, the so-called Lex Apponyi, which imposed Magyar schooling on every child and teacher.[80] This corresponded with Magyar as the language of administration all over the Hungarian provinces. Persons, towns, and villages were forcibly pushed to Magyarize their names. Ethnic minorities in the Kingdom of Hungary (Slovaks, Romanians, Serbs, Germans and other ethnic minorities) relied on vernacular skills and private organizations to preserve language and culture, as well as cooperation in cultural affairs with their co-nationals abroad as well as within diaspora communities in the Cisleithanian core.

The Dual Settlement succeeded in overcoming the secessionist ambitions of Hungarian independentist nationalists by offering the Hungarian elites political autonomy, which came near to independence and could be interpreted as such by Hungarian politicians. The Hungarian government was able to pursue sovereign politics, while Hungary at the same time benefited from a huge market where Hungarian agricultural products enjoyed a quasi monopoly. The inclusion of Hungary into the common market favored the existing unequal division of labor between agrarian and industrial provinces. So the common Austrian-Hungarian market served Austrian and Bohemian industrial interests on the one side and Hungarian landlords on the other side, both advocating the protection of the common market from foreign competition. The abolition of the customs barrier improved Hungarian agricultural products' access to Cisleithanian markets. Peasant agriculture in the Cisleithanian provinces now faced much stronger competition from Hungarian cash crops, which forced many Austrian and Bohemian peasants to give up agriculture and become workers. In Hungary the division of labor reinforced by the specialization on agriculture. Export revenues were raised by increasing the industrial processing of agricultural goods, however.

The political appeasement of Hungary by compromising on the Dual Settlement was fueling tensions with the Bohemian Lands. Representing an economic core without the political autonomy comparable to Hungary, Bohemian elites—both German and Czech—felt excluded from the balance of power. While German speaking Bohemians could benefit from being part of the leading nation, Czechs lacked institutionalized representation: not astonishingly they demanded the

---

[79] Hanák, *Ungarn in der Donaumonarchie*, 311; Kontler, *Millennium in Central Europe*, 283.
[80] Hungarian State Law, Art. 1907: 37.

acknowledgement of the Czech nationality and language and pursued a policy of establishing Czech institutions in the Bohemian Lands. Migration from the largely Czech populated countryside into towns, traditionally a domain of German speaking burghers, led to better representation of Czechs in city councils. The advent of a Czech middle class, which was inspired by the idea of the "national awakening," was interpreted as competition by the German bourgeois class, which for a long time had controlled industries and urban politics. The Czech language was implemented into secondary education. The Prague Carolo-Ferdinandea-University was divided into a Czech and a German speaking section in 1882. In 1889, a second Czech Technical University was opened in Brno near the German one. Theatres, media, and cultural institutions promoted the Czechization of public life. In contrast to Hungary, the Bohemian Germans, although they had to make concessions, were able to keep their hegemonic position. The Czech language was accepted in more and more sectors of public life, though it never achieved equality with German—a constant and growing factor of dissatisfaction for a rising Czech bourgeois class.

Belonging to the economic core of the empire did not prevent people from rural and peripheral Bohemian and Moravian regions from migrating to urban and industrial centers. The main attracting regions for Czech as well as for German Bohemians and Moravians, especially those from the southern parts of the country, were the core regions in Lower and Upper Austria. Migrants from northern Bohemia also headed toward Prague, though later than migration to Vienna. At the end of the nineteenth century there was a migration watershed between the Prague and the Vienna region, crossing Bohemia south of Prague.[81] The same pattern of migration applied to other German speaking peripheries, like the Waldviertel, the Mühlviertel, or the Alpine regions, which maintained migrant relations with regional or imperial cores. Like Czechs, they formed distinct migrant networks, supporting each other in their new home communities and maintaining narrow relations with the home region.

Although in a peripheral economic position, Hungarians were less attracted by the Austrian core region. On the one hand, Hungary was a distinctive universe for internal migrants from rural areas, including ethnic minorities, heading seasonally or permanently into harvesting areas, rural towns, or the Budapest service or industrial sector. On the other hand, overseas migration by all ethnic groups across Hungary was much greater than German and Czech overseas migration.[82] Hungary showed a specific national pattern of migration—migrants concentrating on the Hungarian lands and in the case of long-distance migration replacing the Austrian labor-attracting core regions by overseas destinations. The Hungarian migration pattern reflects the unevenness of economic development within Hungary, attracting laborers into agricultural

---

[81] Compare Komlosy, *Grenze und ungleiche*, 182.

[82] J. Puskás, *From Hungary to the United States, 1880–1914* (Budapest: Akadémia Kiadó, 1982); J. Puskás, "Hungarian Migration Patterns, 1880–1930: From Macroanalysis to Microanalysis," in *Migration Across Time and Distance: Population Mobility in Historical Contexts*, eds. I. Glazier, and L. DeRosa (New York: Holmes & Meier, 1986), 231–54.

regions and workers to Budapest and surroundings. It also reflects migrant competition: Czech and German migrants' networks were well established in Lower and Upper Austria, the main regions demanding migrant labor, preventing Hungarians from obtaining access to good positions.

Galician Poles, as well as Ruthenians (Ukrainians) and Jews, immigrated to the United States.[83] The Austrian core only played a minor role for Galician immigrants, who were underrepresented in Lower and Upper Austria compared to Czech and German migrants—only in Moravia Galician migrants held a considerable portion of internal migration.[84] The attraction of the Vienna metropolis was the biggest for Galician Jews.[85] Educated Jewish elites easily assimilated into the dominant national culture. Orthodox Jews, especially from Galicia and Bukovina, only arrived at the end of the nineteenth century, when other European and overseas destinations had erected barriers against poor Jewish immigrants. When they migrated to Vienna in bigger numbers, they faced competition from settled migrant communities, including Jewish ones, and had difficulty adapting to the new situation.[86] They formed a separate community and became object of strong anti-Jewish sentiments, though anti-Semitism was not restricted to this group.

Between 1900 and 1910, when overseas emigration significantly increased, migrants from the Austrian-Hungarian Monarchy accounted for 25% of the total number of immigrants to the United States, the majority of them Magyars, Poles, Serbs, Croats, and Slovaks, originating from the Monarchy's eastern and southern provinces. German and Czech speaking migrants comprised only a minor share of overseas migrants.[87] Despite nationalist rivalries, Czechs and Germans developed a symbiotic relationship that strengthened their migration to the Austrian core and thereby weakened migration to the same area by other ethnic groups. Hungarian Slovaks were in a somewhat intermediary position, migrating within Hungary, to overseas as well as to Austrian destinations, above all to neighboring Lower Austria and Vienna.[88]

Migrant competition reflects a region's position within the inter-regional division of labor. It takes place between countries and regions exercising demand on the one hand, and between groups of migrants looking for promising destinations on the other hand. The German east and the United States were the main competitors for

---

[83] L. Caro, "Auswanderung und Auswanderungspolitik in Österreich," *Schriften des Vereins für Socialpolitik* 131 (Leipzig, 1909).

[84] Komlosy, *Grenze und ungleiche*, 177.

[85] G. Kohlbauer-Fritz, *Zwischen Ost und West. Galizische Juden und Wien* (Vienna: Mandelbaum, Buch zur Ausstellung, Jüdisches Museum Wien, 2000).

[86] Kohlbauer-Fritz, *Zwischen Ost und West.*

[87] Komlosy, "State, Regions, and Borders," 154.

[88] M. Glettler, "Ethnizität als gesellschaftliches Konfliktfeld in Preßburg und Budapest," in *Wien–Prag–Budapest. Urbanisierung, Kommunalpolitik, gesellschaftliche Konflikte (1867–1918)*, eds. G. Melinz and S. Zimmermann (Vienna: Promedia Verlag 1996), 219–29; M. John and A. Lichtblau, *Schmelztiegel Wien einst und jetzt. Zur Geschichte und Gegenwart von Zuwanderung und Minderheiten* (Vienna: Böhlau Verlag, 1990).

migrants from the Habsburg Monarchy. There was a dividing line, depending on ethnicity, religion, and timing. Bohemian and Moravian Czechs and Germans, as well as
Alpine Austrians, were the first to depart to the Austrian core regions and to distribute
attractive jobs among their followers, thus establishing migration chains or migration
networks which promoted their co-nationals' local acquaintance. Czechs were used to
coresiding and interacting with Germans for a long time, which facilitated integration.
In spite of nationalist rivalries, the Czech–German relationship was a narrow, almost
symbiotic one. All other ethnic groups migrating to the Austrian core lagged behind.
They were handicapped by language and religion (in the case of Christian Orthodoxs,
Greek Catholics, and Jews) in a mainly catholic, German speaking surrounding, but
first of all it was the networking of German and Czech speaking migrants which monopolized the Austrian and particularly the Viennese labor market. Whether preserving the Czech language or assimilating, Czechs became socially integrated in their
new place of residence, at the same time maintaining contacts and exchange with their
homelands. Hence migration strengthened the axis between the economic cores of
the Bohemian Lands and the Austrian Archduchies, omitting Hungary as a separate
sphere of migration. At the same time it reflects imbalances within the core regions,
encouraging feelings of German superiority and ranging Czech migrants on the lower
end of public estimation in Vienna.

Imperial Cohesion

It has become a common place to attribute backwardness to the Habsburg Monarchy
due to a lack of state integration.[89] The final collapse of the monarchy in 1918 and its
break-up into national successor states seems to confirm this view. The discussion
about backwardness lacks precise definitions about criteria and indicators of success
and failure, however, and needs useful and suitable units of comparison. For example,
can we compare the dissolution of the Habsburg Monarchy, with all its internal peripheries, with the dissolution of overseas colonies in sea-based empires and states like
Great Britain, France, or Belgium?[90]

A close examination shows that the Habsburg Monarchy displays a dynamic
and sophisticated type of state-building process, in particular with regard to market
integration, administrative reform, and legal homogenization. Although the growth
of a central administration favored the use of the German language, state building in
the Habsburg Monarchy did not aim for national homogenization in the sense of assimilating different ethnic groups to the language and culture of a leading nation. In

---

[89] A prominent representative of the thesis of backwardness: A. Gerschenkron, *Economic
Backwardness in Historical Perspective* (Cambridge, Mass.: The Belknap Press, 1966); A.
Gerschenkron, *An Economic Spurt that Failed: 4 Lectures in Austrian History* (Princeton:
Princeton University Press, 1977).

[90] Compare Komlosy, "Habsburgermonarchie,"

the context of the Habsburg Monarchy, this leading nation would undoubtedly have been the German one, not because Germans held the majority of the population (their share depended on the actual geographical extension of the monarchy and the interpretation of ethnicity in a multi-ethnic context at a given time), but because the origin and the mission of the Austrian state, the historical core of the monarchy, has been linked to its role as a frontier province in the Holy Roman Empire from the ninth to the twelfth century (803–907 *Marchia orientalis*, 960–1156 Ottonian frontier system) by the historiography of the nineteenth century. The Babenbergs ruling from 976 until 1246 and the Habsburgs ruling from 1273 until 1918 were German-speaking dynasties, the latter holding the crown of the Holy Roman Empire, which also was defined as "of the German nation."

Conversely, the ruling dynasties did not found their legitimacy on a national principle but on power. The pending character of nationality in the Holy Roman Empire as well as the Habsburg extensions into provinces, which definitely were non-German and which did not belong to the Holy Roman Empire, supported the ethnic diversity of the state. Habsburg sovereigns were fluent in Italian or French, the *lingua franca* of the European high aristocracy, and open to integrate and to speak the languages of non-German nationalities along with the expansion of the empire. The multi-ethnic understanding did not change when in the nineteenth century it came under pressure from nationalist movements within and outside its borders.

Habsburg state integration began long before, without relying on nationalism as a cohesive force. The cohesive pillars of the Habsburg state integration between 1750 and 1870 were anchored in the territorialization of the state, declared an empire in 1804, by forming territorial unity with marked and controlled borders. Other factors of state integration included a multi-layered system of state administration on the local, regional, provincial and central levels; a single army and a system of public conscription based on the cohabitation of nationalities; a single market area; state control of migration, both internal and external, allowing migrants to move independently; general laws for compulsory schooling and higher education; program of traffic and communication infrastructure planned and supported by the state; and a process of legal unification, eliminating differences between provinces in each legal domain. The main steps toward legal unification of state subjects were the Civil Code (*Allgemeines Bürgerliches Gesetzbuch*, 1811) and the State Constitution (1867), defining the civil rights of citizens.

The results of market integration, administrative reform, and legal homogenization were ambiguous, however. On the one hand, adjustment and assimilation of the different provinces of the empire were achieved, showing empirical evidence in many respects. The architectural development of the empire, which culminated in a k. u. k. style used for railway stations, schools, office buildings, courts, theatres, or barracks, continues to unite the successor states today.[91] Interregional division of labor, trade,

---

[91] A. Moravánszky, *Die Architektur in der Habsburgermonarchie 1867–1918* (Budapest: Corvina Kiadó, 1988).

and commodification contributed to adjustments in life-style and consumer culture, superposing regional traditions. All these factors supported a process of integration, which was characterized by convergence and a reduction of regional and cultural differences, contributing to a degree of homogenization in the empire.

At the same time, one could observe opposed tendencies, preserving existing differences and creating new imbalances. A polarizing effect of integration could be observed in regional imbalances of wages and incomes, in spite of an adjustment in prices. Migration itself mirrors the divergence between regions of out-migration and regions of in-migration.[92] Regional gaps, often in combination with social polarizations, can be regarded as an immediate outcome of the process of integration. If factors aiming at homogenization meet very different preconditions and capacities to participate in the common game, that is, the single market, polarization cannot be avoided and homogenizing measurements propel the rise of imbalances. In this process, economic cores and peripheries gain new meaning, transforming the regional structure and influencing trans-regional or international divisions of labor. Polarization may impede imperial cohesion, but it also may represent a form of integration not based on convergence but on the cohesions of holding together and integrating very heterogeneous parts, which fulfill different functions in an interregional division of labor. In this latter sense, imbalances can be seen as an integrative factor, which do not necessarily break up a state, but forge differences together.[93]

What applies to the hereditary lands in Central Europe, as well to the northeastern and southeastern acquisitions of the eighteenth and nineteenth centuries, does not hold true for the lands of the Hungarian Crown. From a Habsburg, or court perspective, the acquisition of Hungary as the result of a Habsburg–Jagiello marriage treaty (1506), which became effective in 1526, was one among many other enlargements aimed at integrating the new territories into the framework of the Habsburg state-building process. Ottoman occupation, or suzerainty, of the largest parts of Hungary delayed the establishment of Habsburg rule for more than 150 years. From an Austrian perspective, seizing power after victory over the Ottomans, beginning in 1683, was interpreted as a reunification with Hungary. This view has dominated Austrian historiography up to today. Conversely, Hungarian historiography focuses on noble resistance against Habsburg ambitions, particularly the enthronement of Jan Zápolya/Szapolyai as King of Hungary by the estates in 1526, contesting the Habsburg claim. Zapolya sought the help of the Ottomans against Ferdinand, the Habsburg pretender. In the Treaty of Constantinople (1528) he was recognized as the only lawful ruler of the land conquered by the sultan.[94] This perspective in many respects corresponds with Ottoman, or Turkish historiography, which underlines the importance of the Ottoman role in the dispute about a legitimate king.

---

[92] Komlosy, *Grenze und ungleiche*.
[93] Ibid.
[94] Kontler, *Millennium in Central Europe*, 139f.

If the legal claim on the Hungarian throne is questioned, the label "unification" cannot hold true for the military advance of Habsburg troops into Hungarian provinces after the victory of Vienna in 1683. It rather corresponds to a conquest and occupation, legitimized by historical claims, although approved by the Hungarian Diet in 1687. Since the acquisition of the Hungarian Crown by a Habsburg king, Hungarian elites opposed central state reforms aimed at the legal homogenization of the Habsburg possessions and the integration of Hungary into central institutions. Strong Hungarian resistance led to relative exclusion from the integration process.

The ability to resist centralization was based on the economic and political power of the Hungarian aristocracy. Their strong independence was shaped by the pragmatic handling of Ottoman domination. Hungary had no interest in replacing Ottoman dominance with a Habsburg hegemon, despite loyalty to a Habsburg sovereign on Saint Stephen's throne. Economically it was grounded in their landed property and labor resources of serfs and dependent peasants. The opposition against central state dominance was carried by the nobility, which formed the nation. This nation must not be confounded with the political nation, which only emerges in the course of the nineteenth century, extending nationhood to all social classes, regardless of whether they were noble or not. In the eighteenth century Hungarian resistance against the Habsburg centralizing state was still rooted in the concept of an aristocratic nation.

Imperial cohesion was also unrealized at the margins of the empire, which—both in core and peripheral functions—never experienced full integration into the Habsburg political core, like the southern Netherlands, the southern Italian provinces (Naples, Sicily), or the scattered territories in southern Germany (*Vorlande*). The loss of these provinces did not put the empire's legitimacy into question. Additionally, Lombardy and Venetia, although they had become part of the single market area in 1825–26, maintained separate legal and administrative structures without being regarded key provinces. Conversely, Hungary was regarded as a key province for historical reasons, primarily to preserve great power status in the inter-imperial competition with the Ottoman Empire. This explains why compromising with Hungary was a priority for the empire. The success of the Dual Settlement was based on its exclusive character, thereby increasing tensions with other provinces and nationalities.

In provinces which fulfilled peripheral economic roles for the core, political hegemony by the imperial core was not questioned—tactical alliances were forged in order to achieve certain improvements. Most successful in forming a political alliance with Vienna were Galician Poles, who were rewarded for their loyalty with a Galician Compromise.

In economic core regions of the monarchy, the denial of political autonomy supported political tensions between the province and the core. Such regional identities existed among the provincial elites of Styria, Carinthia, or the Tyrol, and they also existed in sub-regions below the provincial level. These crown lands or regions were considered and considered themselves an integral part of the imperial core, however. Secession was unthinkable, and as their citizens were overwhelmingly German speaking Austrians, nationalism could not serve as a means to express dissent. It was possible to maintain regional identities, while at the same time national—or imperial state—consciousness was developed, which integrated regional forms of identification.

Not so in the Italian provinces: after the suppression of the national uprising of 1848, secessionist ambitions in Lombardy and Venetia, fuelled by Italian aspirations of unification and nationhood, could not be stopped. The loss of Lombardy and Venetia weakened the Habsburg state internally and externally: in combination with the defeat in Königgrätz/Hradec Králové against the Prussian army it initiated the shift from a neo-absolutist to a constitutional system, and from single to dual centralism in 1867.

From that moment onwards, imperial cohesion was effective on three distinct levels: the Cisleithanian entity (Austria), the Transleithanian entity (Hungary) and the common imperial space (Austria-Hungary). The common empire was represented by the sovereign who acted as Emperor of Austria and King of Hungary, bound together in the spirit of the pragmatic sanction by the centralized command of the armed forces, the customs union, the joint ministries of common imperial affairs (defense, foreign affairs, common finances), and the economic compromise, which had to be re-negotiated every ten years. The common institutions always risked conflict with the ambitions of the two sub-states, their parliaments, and specific sub-imperial interests. Re-balancing diverging interests within and between the two entities was a complicated and delicate task, uniting the ruling classes of both sub-empires.

As a consequence of the Dual Settlement, state integration from 1867 onwards also had a Hungarian side. Hungarian state building in many respects differed from the one in the Austrian old and new provinces. First of all, Hungarian state-building started one century later than in the hereditary lands. The Ottoman legacy, as well as the noble reluctance to comply with Viennese centralism, meant a late start for modern state-building. Structures, institutions, and a legal corpus for taxation, census, and policies in various fields had to be built up. A common capital was created, uniting Buda, Pest, and Obuda, which were separate communities until 1872.

The Austrian provinces served as a model for integration: they set the standards against which pace and success of Hungarian state building was to be measured. Hungary faced the problem of being treated as a younger brother who was not up to par with the standards of the older one. As a result, institutional catching-up by copying Austrian structures and institutions co-existed with ambitions and attempts to develop a genuine Hungarian form of state building and modernization, different from the Austrian one.

When the concept of the noble nation was transformed into the Hungarian political nation, Hungary adopted a principle of linguistic and cultural assimilation dominant in Western European nation-states, particularly in France. By defining the political nationhood by Magyar nationality, or by the obligation to adapt the Magyar language and culture, Hungary followed France, where Briton, Occitan, German, or Basque speaking citizens were transformed into Frenchmen and women. While in France the forcible assimilation led to an almost complete Frenchization of the society, Hungarian ethnic minorities survived. Nevertheless, and in contrast to Cisleithania with its commitment to multi-ethnicity, assimilation to the political nation was the guiding principle of nation building.

From the perspective of a Hungarian national economy, the preponderance of export agriculture to the western provinces of the empire—in exchange for manufactured goods—required up-grading. Economic plans aimed at setting up infrastructure, modernizing agriculture, developing industrial enterprises, and substituting imports from Austria, the Bohemian Lands, and Western Europe. At the same time the government represented and was to meet the interests of the landed aristocracy, who wanted to pursue their agricultural export economy, based on cheap, low-skill and dependent laborers, and therefore rejected the development of industry, industrial labor-markets, and educational training of the labor force. They did not object the build up of industries, as long as the common Austrian-Hungarian single market met their interests. That meant protection of agricultural production against world market competition from colonial agriculture, which since the 1870s had led to a sharp decline in prices for grain, meat, and wood. With the help of high customs barriers, agreed upon in the Compromise, Hungarian landlords could maintain their way of production and sell their products in the Habsburg lands, pushing out smaller peasants and producers in less fertile regions. Hungarian labor was reserved for big agriculture. Industry was restricted to Budapest and its surroundings, specializing in agricultural processing, though it suffered a lack of capital, qualified labor, and a weak Hungarian banking sector. Contrary to the national ambitions of modernizing the economy according to the ideal of a broad variety of economic sectors with strong linkage effects, Hungary's role as agricultural export economy hardened. It did not catch up with the developed industrial regions in Cisleithania. This situation contradicted the aim of a self-reliant national economy and led to an even stronger drive toward nationalism to compensate for economic and social deficiencies.

In spite of the differences, measurements of state-building in Hungary in many respects resembled the ones achieved in the period of enlightened absolutism in the hereditary lands, although showing specific Hungarian characteristics. They included the territorialization of the Hungarian state, integrating Transylvania, the Banat, and the Kingdom of Croatia-Slavonia under common Hungarian rule, extended to the Military Border between 1851 and 1881. A multi-layered system of state administration developed, containing local, regional (county), and the central levels. Provincial self-governing institutions were restricted to Croatia-Slavonia.

The armed forces and military conscription belonged to the common k. u. k. affairs, though additional armed forces were established for internal purposes in Austria (*k. k. Landwehr*)[95] and Hungary (*k. u. Honvéd*),[96] administered by separate ministries of defense. In Hungary the internal armed forces for territorial defense

---

[95] Kaiserlich österreichische, königlich böhmische Landwehr (imperial Austrian, royal Bohemian Landwehr).
[96] Königlich ungarische Landwehr (Honvéd) (royal Hungarian Honvéd).

derived from the Hungarian army, which had been formed under the short-lived independent Hungarian revolutionary government in 1848–49.[97]

When Hungary established state instruments for controlling migration, serfdom no longer existed. Moreover, empowerment of migrants vis-à-vis their landlords, which had guided Austrian migration laws of the eighteenth century in order to establish mobility on a trans-regional labor-market, was no longer on the agenda. Internal migration, both in Austria and in Hungary, were controlled by laws of domicile, which regulated the conditions under which a migrant achieved permanent rights of domicile, including social welfare, in their new place of residence. Due to the lower legal obligations, standards, and costs of public social welfare, Hungarian conditions to become domiciled at a new place were less restrictive than the Austrian ones.[98] In 1867, the Austrian State Constitution abolished restrictions for emigration abroad, and Hungary adopted similar laws. Census data collections recorded the present population according to place of birth, place of residence and place of legal domicile—they also distinguished between citizens and foreigners. In contrast to the common single market for goods and capital, Hungarian migrants in Austria were listed as foreigners, and vice versa, without restricting access, however. Labor migration between Austria and Hungary was of minor importance for other reasons, as mentioned above.

Elementary schooling and higher education was of crucial importance in the multi-ethnic settings of Austria and Hungary. In Hungary, school and education laws were major instruments of state building via national homogenization. Unlike in Austria, assimilation through state education standards was arguably the most important tool for Hungarian state building. The Civil Code of 1811 was established when the Hungarian lands were provinces of the Austrian Empire (*Österreichisches Kaiserreich* 1804–67), laying common legal grounds, which were influencing separate legal developments after 1867. There was no common citizenship—people were either Austrian or Hungarian citizens. Except for common affairs, which were administered in common ministries, parliaments and governments acted independently.

In the lands of the Bohemian Crown—an integral part of the hereditary lands and at the same time an economic core region strongly integrated into the Habsburg single market with its distinctive inter-regional division of labor—a nation-state was not on the agenda. Bohemia, Moravia, and remaining Silesia were bi-national provinces; all-German, all-Czech, and pan-Slavic ideas lacked economic perspectives. When the Bohemian demands for compromise were rejected, the cohesion of the Habsburg lands was at risk.

---

[97] Hungarian State Law, Art. 1868: 41.
[98] G. Melinz and S. Zimmermann, "Die aktive Stadt. Kommunale Politik zur Gestaltung städtischer Lebensbedingungen in Budapest, Prag und Wien," in *Wien–Prag–Budapest*, eds. Melinz and Zimmermann, 161f; S. Zimmermann, *Prächtige Armut. Fürsorge, Kinderschutz und Sozialreform in Budapest. Das "sozialpolitische Laboratorium" der Doppelmonarchie im Vergleich mit Wien. 1873–1914* (Sigmaringen: Jan Thorbecke Verlag, 1997).

Counterfactual Approach:
Germanizing for the Sake of Imperial Unity?

Arguing that the idea of Habsburg Austria was based on the dynastic cohesion of the multi-ethnic empire does not deny that nationalizing tendencies were going on in the imperial core. As to the national movements of the non-German nationalities, this finding is uncontested if not seen as the main reason for the collapse of the monarchy. But what about the nationalizing aspirations of the Austrian Germans—or German speaking Austrians—and their efforts to define Austrian identity as a German one? Which counterfactual evidence for Germanizing tendencies can be found in Austrian history and what was their importance? Did they fail and if so why? The following chapter will investigate the successes of transforming the imperial core into a (German) national core by collecting empirical evidence. The same counterfactual approach will be applied to the Hungarian case, which apparently functioned along the Magyarizing principle: Were Hungarian nationality policies successful in transforming Transleithania into a political, Magyar speaking nation? Which counterfactual evidence for surviving multi-ethnicity can be found in the Hungarian sub-empire?

NATIONALIZING ELEMENTS IN THE AUSTRIAN CORE

The Germanization of Austria can be the result of active intervention into the use of languages by state institutions on the local, regional, or central state level. It can be advanced by single actors—individuals, lobby-groups, parties, and associations—who push for and contribute to the Germanization of public life. Thirdly, Germanization can be the unintended (though perhaps not unwanted) result of centralization and modernization.[99] As a privileged language and language of the privileged, German had different means of achieving or maintaining dominance over non-German languages. This structural difference could only be perceived from the side of the underprivileged. It inspired the director of the Hungarian Capital Office of Statistics, József Körösi, to state: "In the history of nationhood in our capital, we have repeatedly been witness to forcible Germanization. There could never be discussion of forcible Magyarization."[100] When Körösi compared Germanizing to Magyarizing tendencies in 1881, a time when Magyar was on the way to dominate all fields of public life in Budapest, his observation hardly complied with reality. At the same time it expressed perfectly the feeling of subordination that the Magyar language had faced for a long time and which was to be overcome by privileging it vis-à-vis German.

Examples of active implementation of German as the single language of administration in Austria are rare. Even the constitution imposed on Bohemia and

---

[99] Benedict Anderson, *Die Erfindung der Nation. Zur Karriere eines folgenreichen Konzepts* (Frankfurt: Campus Verlag, 2005).

[100] Joseph Körösi, 1881, quoted in: Nemes, *The Once and Only Budapest*, 152.

Moravia after the estates' defeat in 1620 (*Verneuerte Landesordnung*) did not ban Czech from public life, although it promoted German as the language of administration and education.[101] Joseph II's attempts to establish German as the common language of administration on all levels of parliaments and administrations[102] are well known, less for their success than for their failure and for the resistance they inspired against linguistic homogenziation, especially in Hungary. They aimed for administrative standardization by introducing German as a *lingua franca* of political administration in all provinces. The idea was based on the existing functional hegemony of German in political and commercial life as well as the advanced level of linguistic standardization of the German language. Such a project failed to appreciate the importance of language as a means of identity and emancipation for non-German nationalities. Joseph's decrees achieved the opposite from what was intended: They contributed to the desire of establishing the legal equality of languages among the non-German nationalities, which was achieved by the Austrian Constitution of 1867.

A hundred years after Joseph II, the Viennese mayor and founding member of the Christian-Social Party, Karl Lueger, set out to redefine the imperial capital, which had become multi-ethnic by migration. Vienna had developed into a melting pot of nations coming from all corners of the empire, raising the question of ethnic separation, multi-cultural integration, or assimilation of migrants with the German culture. With some of his sayings, Lueger declared his preference for the assimilating option, underscoring the German and at the same time Catholic character of the city.[103] His exclusionism was directed against Jews, whom he blamed for dominating economic life, and against Czechs, the biggest group of migrants to Vienna. Lueger's interpretation of the national character aimed at an Austrian national identity as defined by the German language, Roman Catholicism, and Habsburg imperial rule. Lueger's opinions were shared by several groups of Cisleithanian German speakers.

Austrian Germans, who supported an all-German unification of the German speaking provinces of Cisleithania with the German Empire, had their own parties, associations, lobby-groups and media, most of them linked with Georg von Schönerer, who became more and more radical over the years.[104] His followers represented a minority position, not least because the legal separation of the two empires did not offer the chance to realize unification, the ultimate national agenda. On the one hand they were a national liberation movement, which resembled Polish, Romanian, or Italian

---

[101] Hoensch, *Geschichte Böhmens*, 228, 296.

[102] *Handbuch aller unter der Regierung des Kaisers Joseph II. für die k. k. Erbländer ergangenen Verordnungen und Gesetze*, vol. 7 (Vienna, 1786), e.g. Imperial Decree from 18.V.1784.

[103] J. W. Boyer, *Political Radicalism in Late Imperial Vienna: Origins of the Christian Social Movement, 1848–1897* (Chicago: University of Chicago Press, 1981), xii; A. Fuchs, *Geistige Strömungen in Österreich 1867–1918* (Vienna: Löcker Verlag, 1984), 58–62; M. Seliger, and K. Ucakar, *Wien–Politische Geschicht vol. 1* (Vienna–Munich: Jugend und Volk Verlag, 1985), 590f.

[104] K. Berchtold, ed., *Österreichische Parteiprogramme 1868–1966* (Vienna: Verlag für Geschichte und Politik, 1967), 69–83.

movements, who sought to join their co-nationals in neighboring nation-states. All-Germans who fought for a Great German solution opposed the dynastic understanding of Austrian imperial statehood.

Another group of German Austrians (so defined because they identified with the Austrian state) pleaded for a German understanding of the Austrian Monarchy while accepting the imperial Habsburg frame. They differed from the irredentist all-German national movements insofar as their aspired core, German Austria, was located in Austria, not abroad. In practice all-German and German Austrian demands often overlapped, especially with regard to German language and culture, which was to be granted a privileged role in the state. Activities aimed at the acknowledgement of the German character of the Austrian Empire were as manifold as the actors who pursued them.[105] They were supported by groups with an explicit German nationalist self-understanding, aimed at unification with Germany, who became organized in various German National or All-German Parties, but they could also be found in movements and parties with a social focus, like the Christian-Social Party or the Social-Democratic Party. Moreover, all three political camps, which succeeded the liberal clubs of early parliamentarism, had a common political origin: the German-National Association (*Deutscher Nationalverein*), founded in 1882. This association based on the "*Linzer Programm*," which opposed political liberalism and proclaimed German national and social issues together with a broadening of democratic participation.[106] On these common grounds, later mass parties elaborated distinct political profiles according to class and professional interests.

The Austrian "German-Nationals," who had founded several political projects over the years that split and re-united over the degree of loyalty with the Habsburg state, interpreted the monarchy to be a German Empire. This is why they advocated loosening the relationship with those parts of the Empire where non-German citizens prevailed: Hungary was to be transformed into a separate, sovereign sub-empire, and the political union to be reduced to the common sovereign. Galicia, Bukovina, Dalmatia, and Bosnia and Hercegovina were to be ceded to Hungary or should be given special status.[107] Schönerer in "My Program" of 1879 demanded to give sovereignty to Bosnia and Hercegovina, eventually under a Habsburg prince.[108] The Bohemian lands, which had been an integral part of the Holy Roman Empire as well as the German Confederation, were regarded as a German core, and German was proclaimed the common language all over the former Holy Roman Empire—Czech was not seen as a language deserving equality with German in public and political life, but

---

[105] Berchtold, *Österreichische Parteiprogramme*, 69–83.

[106] Berchtold, *Österreichische Parteiprogramme*, 95, 198–203.

[107] "Linzer Programm" [Linz Programme] 1882, § 1, in: Berchtold, *Österreichische Parteiprogramme*, 199.

[108] "Mein Programm" [My Program] 1879, in: Berchtold, *Österreichische Parteiprogramme*, 187.

reserved for everyday communication,[109] traditional culture, and folklore. German national parties on the one hand were part of the political establishment, participating in all kind of parliaments and state institutions, and they represented influential parts of the economic elite, both from industry and the free professions. On the other hand they were opposed to the imperial philosophy of multi-cultural equality, which was the state-building ideology of the ruling dynasty. Thy dynasty had to cooperate with them and reluctantly accept their German national commitment. At the same time, German national parties accepted the entire monarchy as an attractive economic market.

The Germanizing tendencies among the Christian-social movement, which arose from older aristocratic Christian-conservative circles as a modern, democratic mass movement with social concerns in the 1880s, were even more ambiguous. On the one hand Christian-socials identified themselves with the Habsburg Monarchy and the multi-ethnic conception of dynastic rule. On the other hand they declared themselves both a Christian and German project. Originating from Lower Austria—the *Ostarrichi* nucleus of the later Austrian state defined by nineteenth century historiography as a bulwark of German civilization—they started their activities in a German speaking surrounding. The combination of Germanness and Roman Catholicism was maintained when they received empire-wide support at the beginning of the twentieth century. The conviction to defend the German character of Austria[110] strongly contradicted their state and nationality program,[111] which demanded the abolition of the Dual Settlement and the re-construction of the "United States of Austria" by replacing the traditional crown lands with a confederation of autonomous regions along ethnic principles.[112] Nonetheless this new union was to be founded on the leading role of German language and culture, anti-Semitism serving as a unifying ideology. While German-nationals in their visions for a German Austria rather aimed at separating the German from non-German provinces and reducing common state institutions,

---

[109] Everyday communication included the communication between German speaking masters and Czech speaking servants, resulting in a hybrization of languages, typical for bilingual regions, e.g.: "Naša Anna pucovala našemy hausherovi vintrok." Compare linguistic inter-actions in bilingual surroundings: M. Janečková, and A. Jaklová "'Das Lébn ist lajdr kaine Wurst nicht, es hat núr ajn Ende.' Sprachcharakteristika der südböhmischen Region," in *Kulturen an der Grenze. Waldviertel-Weinviertel-Südböhmen-Südmähren*, eds. A. Komlosy, V. Bužek, and F. Svátek (Vienna: Promedia Verlag, 1995), 232; J. King, *Budweisers into Czechs and Germans: A Local History of Bohemian Politics, 1848–1948* (Princeton: Princeton University Press, 2002).

[110] "Pfingstprogramm" [Pentecostal Program] 1899, in: Berchtold, *Österreichische Parteiprogramme*, 210–25; Wahlmanifest der christlichsozialen Reichspartei 1907, in: Berchtold, *Österreichische Parteiprogramme*, 174–78.

[111] "Eggenburger Entschließung" [Eggenburg Resolution] 1905, in: Berchtold, *Österreichische Parteiprogramme*, 172f.

[112] Following a proposal from the Transylvanian Romanian Aurel Popovici to establish "United States of Great Austria." Compare Berchtold, *Österreichische Parteiprogramme*, 54; A. C. Popovici, *"Die Vereinigten Staaten von Groß-Österreich. Politische Studien zur Lösung der nationalen Fragen und staatsrechtlichen Krisen in Österreich-Ungarn* (Leipzig: Elischer Nachfolger, 1906).

the Christian-Socials' understanding of Austria's Germanness was based on German hegemony within a fairly multi-cultural surrounding. In other words: German-Nationals pleaded for a separation of the German core from non-German peripheries, while Christian-socials conceived a German core that embraced and subordinated non-German provinces as well as non-German citizens to the German-Austrian heartlands (*Stammländer*). This explains the erratic attitudes vis-à-vis Czechs and Slovaks, who were blamed for undermining the German character of Vienna by mayor Karl Lueger, while at the same time his party supported Czech and Slovak critics of Magyar dominance at the imperial level as well as within Hungary. In the programmatic Christian-social documents, Magyars were treated in a pejorative manner, more or less denounced as Judeo-Magyars.[113]

The Social Democratic Party, which was closely linked with the trade unions, believed that being a class party with a clear internationalist orientation would put social-democrats beyond national conflicts. Indeed in the first years after 1867, when workers associations were founded, they were concentrating on organization building, carrying out sharp ideological disputes, which were free from the national question. Social democrat workers organizations only grew in industrial agglomerations, that is, mainly in German and Czech speaking regions, and they maintained close contacts with the German Social Democrat Workers Party, which served as a model. In these years the leading German social democrats, in spite of their internationalist understanding, were conceiving the states of the German Confederation, that is, the Austrian and the Bohemian lands, as a natural part of a united German nation.[114] Biographies of most prominent Austrian social democratic leaders show their roots in the Austro-German movement, which was equally based on German-national and democratic principles.[115] The German orientation did not prevent non-German migrants from taking over leading positions in the Viennese working class associations, however. At the Austrian Workers' Day of 1868, a manifesto was presented in German, Magyar, Czech, and Polish—not without provoking critique from the side of German-national comrades.[116] A second center of labor organization was located in the Bohemian lands, where in the last quarter of the nineteenth century big industry as well as workers' organizations and trade unions grew faster than in the other Austrian provinces.

When the conflict between Germans and Czechs on the internal use of language in public administration in the Bohemian lands became the key issue of the Austrian parliament in 1897, the Social Democrat Workers Party, which had entered parliament in this year for the first time, took a neutral position. At the same time

---

[113] Berchtold, *Österreichische Parteiprogramme*, 165–78.

[114] Kořalka, *Tschechen im Habsburgerreich*, 222.

[115] Fuchs, *Geistige Strömungen*, 99–112.

[116] M. John, "Die österreichische Arbeiterbewegung und der soziale Protest der Unterschichten 1867–1914. Bemerkungen zu moralischer Ökonomie versus "moderner" Konfliktaustragung," in *Archiv 1990. Jahrbuch des Vereins für Geschichte der Arbeiterbewegung* 6 (Vienna, 1990), 7f.

they realized that the party could not keep the national question out of their program any longer. The Nationality Program, which was passed at the Party Congress in Brno in 1899, reflected the problem of including the national demands of the non-German nations into the program.[117] The program asked for a democratic federation of nations, which would replace the historical crown lands. However, it did not relate this radical demand with other proposals that were in debate: František Palacký's proposal of a federation of nations, which was submitted to the Austrian parliament in Kroměříž/Kremsier in 1848,[118] Aurel Popovici's idea of "United States of Great Austria," which was supported by the Christian democrats; and a transfer of northern and southern slavic crown lands to Hungarian rule, which was supported by All-Germans and German-Nationals. The program did not make any reference with regard to the relationship between Austria and Hungary, nor did it take a position vis-à-vis the Bohemian Constitutional Rights. The program rejected the idea of a single state language. This did not mean the equality of languages, however. Instead of a state language, it evocated a common language of administration ("to be determined by the parliament"), which was an acknowledgement of the priority of the German language. So the social democrats took the same position as the German National Party (*Deutsche Volkspartei*) in their Pentecostal Program of 1899. This was a clear rejection of accepting German and Czech as equal languages for internal as well as external administrative use, as proposed by Prime Minister Badeni in 1897.[119] The social democratic proposal did not question the unity of the Austrian Monarchy—it counted on administrative reform from above, and the national question was addressed in terms of cultural autonomy without questioning the existing dominance of German speaking Austrians and the gap in income and national self-determination between the different nationalities. The Austrian Social Democratic Workers Party was not able to integrate the national with social questions. As a consequence the existing dominance of the German nation was taken for granted.[120] Finally, the secession of the Czech organization was inevitable. It started with a separate trade union commission in 1897, and ended with the foundation of the Czech Social Democrat Workers Party in 1911, obtaining 23 out of 82 social democrat seats in the parliamentary elections of 1911.[121] The

---

[117] Berthold, *Österreichische Parteiprogramme*, 144f; also see R. Löw, *Der Zerfall der "Kleinen Internationale." Nationalitätenkonflikte in der Arbeiterbewegung des alten Österreich 1889–1914* (Vienna: Europaverlag, 1984); H. Mommsen, *Die Sozialdemokratie und die Nationalitätenfrage im habsburgischen Vielvölkerstaat* (Vienna: Europaverlag, 1963).

[118] In his proposal to the Kremsier parliament, which he withdrew within a short period of time, František Palacký conceived the monarchy as a federation of eight states, each based on the maximum of national homogeneity; implying the partition of the Bohemian lands between the German and the Czech entity. Svátek, "Tschechischer und deutscher Nationalismus," 236; J. Kořalka, *František Palacký (1798–1876)* (Vienna: Österreichische Akademie der Wissenschaften, 2007).

[119] Compare following pages.

[120] Löw, "Der Zerfall."

[121] Berchtold, *Österreichische Parteiprogramme*, 28.

Austrian social democrats were stuck in a dilemma: in spite of their official abstract commitments to internationalism and the propagation of equal rights for all Austrian nationalities, they neither put into question the dynastic unity of the monarchy nor the hegemony of the German nation and language, both in the state and in the party. The price was the secession of the Czech organization before the empire fell apart. This position rendered the SDAP a loyal partner to the Austro-German alliance in the First World War.

The women's movement faced a similar situation.[122] Contrary to non-German women, who had to combine the struggle against inequalities of gender and nationality, German Austrian women's organizations did not feel obliged to raise the national question. Without questioning their role as part of the privileged German nationality, they would claim to represent women of all nationalities. The German-Austrian organizations saw themselves as the top organization, while to the other national organizations only regional significance was attributed. The imbalances in the relationship became crucial when representation in international women's organizations came on the agenda in the late nineteenth century. German Austrian organizations had to realize that Hungarian women's organizations were accepted as independent national representatives in the international women's organizations. Their independent membership reflects the Hungarian status as a sub-empire of the Dual Monarchy. Czech women were denied a separate participation in the International Council of Women, founded in 1888 by Western women's movements. They had to accept subordination under the umbrella of Cisleithanian organizations led by German Austrians. The International Women's Suffrage Alliance, founded in 1904, was more open toward non-German speaking Austrian women, accepting suffrage committees from different nationalities (German, Czech, Polish), which led to the nationalization of Austrian representation. This situation fueled tensions between German Austrian and Czech women, leading to competition between all-Cisleithanian (German speaking) and national (non-German speaking) committees for women's suffrage. Similar to the Bohemian State Constitution, a compromise between the Austrian and the Czech women's organizations failed.

Transforming the imperial into a (German) national core need not be the result of active political Germaniziation. It often resulted from very practical considerations about the usefulness of a single language of communication for state

---

[122] S. Zimmermann, "The Challenge of Multinational Empire for the International Women's Movement: The Habsburg Monarchy and the Development of Feminist Inter/National Politics," *Journal of Women's History* 17, no. 2 (2005): 87–107; S. Zimmermann, "Reich, Nation und Internationalismus. Kooperationen und Konflikte der Frauenbewegungen der Habsburgermonarchie im Spannungsfeld internationaler Organisationen und Politik," in *Frauenbilder, feministische Praxis und nationales Bewusstsein in Österreich-Ungarn 1867–1918*, eds. W. Heindl, E. Király, and A. Millner (Tübingen–Basel: A. Francke Verlag, 2006), 119–68; F. De Hahn, K. Daskalova, and A. Loutfi, eds., *A Bibliographical Dictionary of Womens's Movements and Feminism: Central, Eastern, and South Eastern Europe, 19th and 20th Centuries* (Budapest–New York: Central European University Press, 2006).

integration. Joseph II's administrative reforms were inspired by improvements in administration, education, and communication across ethnic and linguistic boundaries. They lacked any feeling for ethnic and linguistic identity from the side of non-German nationalities, however, and therefore failed. The rise of national movements in the first half of the nineteenth century, the Revolutions of 1848, and the exclusion of Austria from the German imperial project in 1866 paved the way for a multi-ethnic constitution of the Habsburg Empire—and led to the paradox of including into the Dual Settlement with Hungary the right of the Hungarian government to transform imperial Hungary into a Magyar nation-state.

Austrian statehood and citizenship were not defined on an ethno-national principle, but on a political one, united by the common dynasty—conceiving Hungary (until the Compromise of 1867) as part of the multi-national imperial project. The Austrian Empire before 1867 and Cisleithanian Austria after 1867 can therefore be interpreted as projects for developing Austrianness as a political nation. Constitutional rights did not mean ethnic and linguistic equality, however. Unlike various demands raised and elaborated in 1848 and later,[123] inspired by the democratic nationalism of revolution, Cisleithania was not transformed into a union of equal nations united by a common sovereign and a common constitution. Although based on a different mission statement than Magyar in Transleithania, the leading role of German in Cisleithania cannot be denied.

The use of languages in the Austrian *Reichsrat* illustrates the difficulties in practicing the equality of languages.[124] In theory all customary languages were acknowledged. In practice, minutes were only taken in German—contributions in other languages only were protocolled if the speaker provided a translation into German. This regulation exercised pressure on non- German nationalities to use German in debate. Despite seeming equality of languages, parliament became a German speaking domain.[125]

In the Habsburg military, which was a common k. u. k. domain under dynastic insignia, German was the language of command. Despite ethnic and linguistic diversity, which was acknowledged in regional units, the military was based on a leading nation principle, evoking strong resentment in Hungary.[126] Attempts to introduce Magyar as a second language of command were not successful. In 1900, when Vienna attempted to raise the annual recruitment quota to compete with other great powers,

---

[123] Svátek, "Tschechischer und deutscher Nationalismus," 235.

[124] G. Stourzh, *Die Gleichberechtigung der Nationalitäten in der Verfassung und Verwaltung Österreichs 1848–1918* (Vienna: Verlag der Österreichischen Akademie der Wissenschaften, 1985), 91.

[125] This regulation was lifted in 1917, when—as a measure of last resort—minutes in all customary languages were introduced.

[126] Christoph Allmayer-Beck, "Die bewaffnete Macht in staat und Gesellschaft," in *Die Habsburgermonarchie, 1848–1918, Band V: Die bewaffnete Macht*, eds. A. Wandruszka and P. Urbanitsch (Vienna, 1987); I. Deák, *Der K. (u.) K. Offizier 1848–1918* (Vienna–Cologne–Weimar: Böhlau Verlag, 1995); Kontler, *Millennium in Central Europe*, 279, 295f.

Hungarian politicians in return demanded the introduction of Magyar and Hungarian insignia for units recruited in Hungary. Franz Joseph insisted on the unity of his army, however, provoking a parliamentary crisis in Budapest, which led to the overthrow of Prime Minister Tisza, who was loyal to the royal position, and a majority for the Independence Party. In 1905–06, Hungarian attempts to insist on Magyar as a second language of command caused serious conflicts, culminating in the occupation of the parliament by the military and its dissolution by a royal commission in February 1906, before a "new compromise" restored order.

In civil life German was also as a necessary tool to work one's way up in Austria, hence promoting Germanization. While Austrianness for German speaking Austrians was based on historical and cultural features—the German language being considered a natural, more or less neutral tool—it often had a Germanizing aspect for non-German Austrians. The concrete level of the implementation of Czech, Polish, Slovenian etc. in education, administration, and law courts depended on a political compromise which had to be achieved in each crown land. Success and failure depended on the specific interest groups and power relations, leading to different regional and even local solutions. The Badeni riots of 1897 demonstrate very well the difficulties in achieving full equality for Czech with German languages in Bohemia.[127] At that time both languages were admitted in offices and courts for external communication: in other words, each citizen had the right to come into office or court with his or her native language, which implied that there had to be both German and Czech speaking officials. The Czech demand to extend linguistic equality to the internal communication in all parts of the Bohemian Lands met insurmountable barriers. When Prime Minister Badeni, in order to gain Czech support for the compromise negotiations with Hungary, presented the bill, it led to tumultuous scenes in the *Reichsrat*. Internal equality all over the Bohemian Lands would have required that every civil servant, regardless of whether he was serving in a predominantly Czech or German speaking region, had to be bilingual in order to guarantee internal communication. The case was politicized and the rejection of the Badeni law became a symbol for defending the privileged position of the German language. Practically, internal communication among Bohemian officials relied on Czech colleagues' self-understood bilingualism, German representing a precondition for a career in the public service. To oblige German civil servants to learn Czech, in order to enter public service in a bilingual province, was not tolerated. German speakers from all political parties vetoed the bill. Prime Minister Badeni was dismissed over the issue.

The example shows, that the multi-national character of Austrian society was challenged and undermined by the de facto use of German as a privileged language and the German speaking Austrians as the de facto leading nation. In spite of the multi-ethnic commitment of the constitution, the German language was an effective means of unification, at the same time encouraging resistance from non-German

---

[127] Bosl, *Handbuch der Geschichte*, 174–76; Hoensch, *Geschichte Böhmens*, 393f; Kořalka, *Tschechen im Habsburgerreich*, 157f.

nationalities and hindering the realization of an all-embracing Austrian political nation. When the imperial framework collapsed in 1918, German speaking Austrians immediately switched from a supposedly non-national to a national definition of their nationality: they declared *Deutschösterreich* part of the German state, which had become a republic.

MULTI-ETHNIC ELEMENTS IN THE HUNGARIAN SUB-EMPIRE

Looking at censuses in the lands of the Hungarian Crown reveals the survival of non-Magyar nationalities.[128] Compared to 1850, Magyar speakers in 1910 rose from 44.5 to 54.5% of the total population, while German speakers dropped from 11.6 to 10.4, Romanian from 17.3 to 16.1, Slovak from 15 to 10.7, Serb and Croat from 8 to 6.6%—while the total population increased from 11.6 to 18.3 million. This shows that Magyarization policies were not as vigorous as one could have assumed, considering the aims of language policies and the threatening picture drawn by non-Magyar representatives. What are the reasons for the survival of multi-ethnicity in spite of severe attempts to transform the country into a homogenous political nation, united by the Magyar language? The reasons are manifold and they impact one another.

First to be mentioned is the persistence of the rural population in maintaining their mother tongues, in spite of language policies imposed on them by schooling and administration. It is evident that nation building was not an elite-question, but dependent on the rural population and their use of languages. Slovak, Romanian, and Serbo-Croat in Transleithania mainly survived in rural neighborhoods. Magyarization of education and administration was meant as a factor of national homogenization, enabling all citizens to communicate in the Magyar state language. It had assimilating effects, but it did not put a ban on other languages, like France did on Breton, German, or Occitan from the seventeenth century onwards. Magyarization politics did not gain momentum before the 1880s, taking their rigorous form only around 1900. Furthermore, non-Magyar languages were tolerated as second languages.

Bilingual practices were favorable for the survival of non-hegemonic languages. Speaking different languages according to different contexts and imposing an official state language did not extinguish vernacular languages. Magyar in many cases was adopted as an additional language without replacing first languages. Marriage laws facilitating mixed marriages aimed at overcoming religious and ethnic boundaries in the process of state building. At the same time, mixed couples encouraged bilingual skills, contributing to the persistence of language diversity instead of overcoming it.[129]

Official Hungarian language policies aiming at the spread of the Magyar language were countered by the support of non-Magyar languages by national societies in the respective regions or from abroad. National associations were often sponsored by

---

[128] The census asked for the mother tongue, which here is used as a proxi for the shares of nationalities. Data from Niederhauser, "The National Question," 258.

[129] Hanák, *Ungarn in der Donaumonarchie*, 307f.

co-national elites in Vienna, which attracted migrants from all nationalities. Linguistic research was carried out in Vienna, and Viennese publishing houses printed grammars, dictionaries, and literature. So the non-Magyar languages—Croat, Serb, Slovak, and Romanian—developed in spite of Magyar dominance, rendering Hungary less homogeneous than the official ideology proclaimed.

In case of the Serb language, support for the National Foundation, *Matica srpska*, founded in Pest in 1826, and later (1864) moving to Novi Sad/Újvidék/Neusatz, came from diaspora Serbs in Vienna.[130] Austria had become a shelter place for Serbian national culture as Serbs were partners against Ottoman influence at a time when a majority of Serbs still lived under Ottoman rule. Vuk Karadžić's linguistic studies in Vienna led to the codification of the Serbian language, where the first books in Serbian were printed. Viennese support for Serbian national culture continued when a Serbian nation-state was founded, with both Vienna and Belgrade competing for the loyalty of Serbs in Hungary. Supporting Serbian culture in Hungary served as a means of counter-balancing the effects of Magyarization.

Slovak nation building was centered in Upper Hungary, where the majority of the population was Slovak. Bratislava/Pozsony/Pressburg, which had served as the Hungarian capital during the Ottoman occupation, was a multi-lingual town, with German, Magyar, and Slovak coexisting and interacting. Slovak migration was directed to Budapest as well as Vienna, representing a link between the rather separated migration networks of Austria and Hungary. When *Matica slovenská*, the Slovak Foundation (founded in 1863) was prohibited in 1875, Slovak national activities concentrated in Budapest. In 1900 more than 60,000 Slovaks lived in Budapest, rendering the Hungarian capital the biggest Slovak town. They did not only gain support from Slovak diaspora communities in Vienna, but also from the Czech national movement, which considered the possibilities of merging the development of the Czech and the Slovak languages.[131]

The Serb and the Romanian languages profited from the establishment of Orthodox bishoprics within the boundaries of the Habsburg Monarchy. In case of the Serb Orthodox Church the Patriarchal seat in Sremski Karlovci dates back to 1690–91, when a large group of Serbs fled to southern Hungary in the course of Habsburg–Ottoman fighting, in which Serbs had supported the Habsburg side. Initially the Serbian Patriarchate was responsible for all Christian Orthodox believers in the Habsburg Monarchy. Later, in 1868, Romanian-Orthodox believers achieved a Romanian Metropolitan seat in Sibiu/Hermannstadt/Nagyszeben, responsible for Transleithania, and in Czernowitz/Cernăuț/Cernivci and Kotor/Cattaro in 1873–74, responsible for Bukovina and Dalmatia.[132] The admission of Christian Orthodox

---

[130] M. Brković, and J. Kartalović, *Das serbische Buch in Wien, 1741–1900* (Vienna: Katalog der Ausstellung, Österreichische Nationalbibliothek, 2002).

[131] Glettler, "Ethnizität als gesellschaftliches"; Nemes, *The Once and Future Budapest*, 17.

[132] H. Hofbauer, and V. Roman, *Bukowina, Bessarabien, Moldawien. Vergessenes Land zwischen Westeuropa, Rußland und der Türkei* (Vienna: Promedia Verlag, 1993), 39f; Silbernagel, *Verfassung*, 208–10.

Churches because of their ethno-religious self-understanding indirectly promoted the use of Serbian and the Romanian languages. The churches served as a means of protecting their believers against assimilation into a dominant Magyar or German surrounding.

The persistence of the German language in Hungary is another story. In Budapest it suffered a rapid decline from 34.4% mother-tongue speakers in 1880 to 9% in 1910.[133] Magyar education and media had developed in a way that the German *lingua franca* lost its vital function. It did not disappear, however, surviving as a second language in educated circles. In order to survive under the dominance of Magyar culture, German associations in Budapest acted in a strictly non-political way, concentrating on cultural or commercial purposes.[134] German maintained its strongholds in the towns of Slovak Upper Hungary, Transylvania, and the Banat, competing and coexisting with Magyar and regional languages.

Non-Magyar cultures and their languages were indirectly stimulated by official language policies. In particular this was the case in those regions where Magyars were a minority. In towns with a Slovak, Serbian, or Romanian majority, not to speak of Croatia-Slavonia—where the Croat Compromise guaranteed priority for the Croat language—assimilation to the Magyar language did not promote the same social advancement as it did in Magyar core regions or in Budapest, where Magyarization was effectively carried out. Hungary was therefore divided into two parts: the core regions, with Budapest as their center, where social advent relied on the adaption of Magyar language and culture, making assimilation an attractive vehicle for non-Magyars. Conversely, Magyarization only took place on the surface in regions with overwhelmingly non-Magyar population, like in Upper Hungary, Transylvania, the Banat, and Croatia-Slavonia, without replacing regional language skills and national identities.

Last but not least the idea of the Hungarian nation, with its aspired identity of state territory, people, and language, also faced differentiation within the Magyar population. In the transition period from the noble to the political nation, the idea of national unity seized all layers of society across social and ideological differences, promising new forms of participation. After a while it became evident that the nation was not able to solve social inequalities and economic problems. Interest and class conflicts intermingled with regional and ethnic identities, preserving them as important factors of political life.

When the collapse of the Dual Monarchy became inevitable, non-Magyar nationalities in Transleithania were as prepared as non-German nations in Cisleithania to merge with existing co-national neighbors or to build new nation-states on former Hungarian territory. The national transformation of the imperial state had not been as effective as planned—Transleithania had preserved its multi-national character.

---

[133] Tóth, "Was wird im Schmelztiegel," 210.
[134] Nemes, *The Once and Future Budapest*, 177.

Summary and Conclusion

Summing up the nation-building processes within the empire along the categories of economic core/economic periphery and national/imperial state identity, one may distinguish several regional constellations and patterns of identification.

The Archduchies Lower and Upper Austria and the hereditary alpine lands identified themselves and were identified with Austrian statehood. They were predominantly German speaking areas, therefore assigning German a privileged place in the variety of languages spoken in the Habsburg Monarchy. When in the process of industrial development and market integration the more competitive regions, with the help of state support, were transformed into economic cores, these economic cores were located in the Archduchies in the Alpine provinces. Not all regions were economic cores; nevertheless all ducal and alpine provinces felt part of the overall imperial core. On a smaller regional scale, internal peripheries faced economic and social problems, which gave rise to regionalist expressions.

The Bohemian lands with their Czech and German inhabitants were also part of the economic core. Germans saw themselves as the leading nation, an attitude that was supported by the introduction of German as the language of the Bohemian chancellery after the estates' defeat in the Battle of the White Mountain (1620). In the nineteenth century social advent of Czech citizens re-introduced Czech language into public life without being able to achieve full equality. As Bohemian elites were denied Bohemian constitutional rights, which would have reconciled their regional identities with the imperial, multi-national, Austrian one, they shifted towards national identification—the Czech opposed to the German one, and engaged in a battle for national possessions, while each of them split into a bigger group which accepted the imperial framework and a smaller group which strove for unification within an alternative pan-German or pan-Slavic project. Austrianness met the limits of national identities, which undermined imperial unity but could not be fully realized in the framework of empire.

The Carpathian and the southern provinces of Cisleithania were internal peripheries from an economic and a political point of view. All of them had a multi-ethnic population, ethnicity in each case corresponding with regional, class, professional, and religious attributes, from which specific elite groups concluded their claim for leadership. In Galicia, leadership was claimed by Poles, in Dalmatia and the Littoral by Italians, while the settlement of the German population, especially Jews, in Bukovina had contributed to a situation in which multi-ethnicity was proclaimed within the German linguistic community.[135] The different ethnic elites first of all had a national identity—complicated by the fact that all ethnic groups had co-nationals in neighboring states and that their provinces were cohabitated by other ethnic groups. As a

---

[135] Hofbauer and Roman, *Transsilvanien*; C. Cordon, and H. Kusdat, ed., *An der Zeiten Ränder. Czernowitz und die Bukowina. Geschichte/Literatur/Verfolgung/Exil* (Vienna: Verlag der Theodor Kramer Gesellschaft, 2002).

consequence national elites, whether dominating or in a minority position, cooperated with the imperial court hoping that it would support them against competing ethnic groups as well as territorial claims from neighboring empires. Certain national elites, e.g. Galician Poles, were coopted as regional partners by the central government. In general, the variety and interwoven multiplicity of ethnic groups in the Carpathian and southern provinces, which could not be separated from each other, were a strong argument for maintaining the trans-national understanding of the Habsburg Empire's cohesion: an Austrianness, defined from above by dynastic unity and supported from below as a means for the survival of each ethnic group in the framework of the empire.

In the case of Hungary, an inclusion of the Hungarian nation into the empire was not possible, neither in its aristocratic nor in its democratic understanding. The lands of the Hungarian Crown, although consisting of internal core and peripheral regions, can be classified as an overall economic periphery. However, after 1867 economic peripherality was superposed by a state autonomy, which allowed the Hungarian government to carry out industrial policy aiming building up a complete national economy. The success was limited and showed the difficulties of overcoming a peripheral economic role, which Hungary did not only fulfill in the Habsburg Monarchy, but within the world economy. Like in the Habsburg Empire in general, economic cores and peripheries in Hungary were not congruent with the ethnicity of the population. Ethnic Magyars rather had a national vision of the Hungarian Kingdom, including and coopting non-Magyar groups into their notion of Hungarianness as long as they were ready to assimilate. In this case the imperial framework created the nation. Ethnic non-Magyars who were not ready to share this vision opposed Magyarization—hoping for support from Vienna, or from Prague, Bucharest, or Belgrade, as soon as their co-nationals had achieved independent nation-states. In the Revolution of 1848 some of them experienced imperial support that was linked with the instrumentalization of their uprisings against the Hungarian Revolution. After the Compromise of 1867, support for non-Magyar nationalities in Hungary was exercised by diaspora associations.

Regional integration in the Habsburg Monarchy in the second half of the nineteenth century was strongly shaped by international relations, first of all with the other imperial great powers, which interacted by cooperation as well as competition. Developments in one empire had reciprocal effects on others. Balancing of power and geopolitical constraints and necessities in turn impacted internal developments in individual empires. In the case of the Habsburg Monarchy, the military defeats that led to the loss of Lombardy and Venetia, the defeat against Prussia that forced the Habsburgs to give up their claim for leadership in the German Confederation, and the consequent consolidation of the German Empire set the framework for balancing power within the Habsburg Empire, in particular the Dual Settlement with Hungary, and the strategies of regional integration within the Austrian and the Hungarian entities. Germanness was not an appropriate solution for the Austrian sub-empire—it would have fueled the wish for German unity and provoked non-German nationalities. On the other hand, meeting the Bohemian demands for constitutional rights and full equality for the Czech language would have marginalized the German nationality in Bohemia, eventually mobilizing all-German aspirations. Instead of Germanness, the Cisleithanian statehood adopted Austrianness as its characteristic, defined by multi-ethnicity under a common dynasty, with German Austrians and the German language as a *primus inter pares*. This Austrianness did not comply with Czech ideas for autonomy in the Bohemian Lands and equality among Germans and Czechs. Conversely, Austrianness was compatible with the Dual Settlement with Hungary, which was based on exclusiveness and singularity. Hungarian secessionist ambitions, which in 1849 were repelled with the help of Russian armed forces, endangered the monarchy's status as a great power, especially in a moment when it was weakened by military defeat from outside and demands for democratic participation inside. In order to stabilize power, Austria sought compromise with Hungary and an economic agreement that met the interests of the big economic lobbies, the Lower and Upper Austrian, Styrian, Bohemian, and Moravian industrialists and the Hungarian, Bohemian, and Galician landed aristocracy. Hungary was granted autonomy in all internal affairs, allowing for a different way of handling the multi-ethnicity of its population and the non-Magyar national claims for self-determination. Hungary was not confronted with a co-national Magyar neighbor. Therefore they were free to follow the Western European model of nation building, relying on the identity of state territory, people, and language, aimed at the assimilation of national minorities to the dominant state culture and language.

Austria and Hungary were characterized by a different handling of the national question, which was strongly related to balancing regional representation. Roughly speaking, Austria followed a federal model, based on regional parliaments (*Landtag*) and governments (*Landesregierung*) in the crown lands, which respected the regional languages (*Landessprachen*). With the exception of Croatia-Slavonia, which was not part of the Hungarian Crown, Hungary was a centralist state without intermediary provincial levels, subdivided into counties (*comitatus, megye*). The only language admitted in the national parliament, on the county level, in communities and municipalities was Magyar. Non-Magyar languages were condemned to a second, subordinate level, from where it was difficult to integrate them into modern social, scientific, and technological developments. On the other hand, a general command of Magyar by all educated citizens improved communication between different nationalities, encouraging political as well as professional participation of non-Magyar nationals. In Austria, the acknowledgement of regional languages in regional parliaments and education respected diversity and enabled the languages to be developed for the needs of high administration and education. It did not prevent them from learning German if they wanted to make a carrier outside their home region. While all Hungarian citizens received Magyar training from the elementary school level onwards, Austrian citizens faced a dual system of education: local or regional languages for regional requirements (education, administration, regiments), German for official communication (*Amtssprache, Dienstsprache*), higher education, and public careers on the trans-regional level. So in spite of the different conceptions of Cisleithanian multi-ethnicity versus Transleithanian single state language, we face the hegemony of German in Austria, and the persistence of language diversity in Hungary. Both tendencies were mutually enforcing each other. Austrian or Austrian-based institutions helped to develop non-Magyar languages in Hungary, and nationalities followed Cisleithanian models of nation building. Equally, Magyar self-consciousness impressed German speaking Austrians, who—along with the widening access to voting—were pressed to make concessions to non-German nationalities. The nationality conflict hardened, and the multi-ethnic conviviality gave way to blockades and standstills of the parliamentary and administrative process.

The Dual Settlement of 1867 was a balancing of power relations between Austrian and Hungarian sub-empires. The pre-existing unequal division of labor between an industrializing west and an agrarian east were part of the compromise settlement. They made sure that the power relations within the entities remained stable, guaranteeing a huge, protected internal market for Austrian-Bohemian manufactured goods and mostly Hungarian agricultural cash crops—at the expense of alpine and small peasant agriculture and Hungarian agricultural laborers. The development of Hungarian industry faced regional and sectoral limits. The different necessities of industrializing and agricultural areas in education, professional training, labor, mobility policies, and socio-political participation were met by separate legislation, keeping incomes, standards of living and social welfare on different levels.[136] The result was an enormous heterogeneity of social and economic conditions, benefiting the dominant economic interest groups, including the Bohemian and Moravian ones. Hence, regional imbalances in economic developments represented a cohesive force. In periods of peace the huge single market made up for a lack of competitiveness of Austrian and Hungarian goods on international markets. However, in times of war—as the last chapter in the Austro-Hungarian Empire would soon make apparent—such a large heterogenous market did not promote the pace and quality of economic development necessary to keep Austria-Hungary competitive in the arms race, let alone stave off threats to its very existence.

---

[136] Melinz and Zimmermann, "Die aktive Stadt"; Zimmermann. *Prächtige drnwut.*

Modernization, Imperial Nationalism, and the Ethnicization of Confessional Identity in the Late Ottoman Empire

HOWARD EISSENSTAT

This chapter traces shifts within the nature of Ottoman identity over the long period of imperial reform (roughly 1826–1918), emphasizing the fundamental continuity that bound a wide variety of very different formulations of Ottomanism: that of "saving the state." It will suggest that the development of a new language of Ottoman political legitimacy in the empire's last century was less one of moving from one discrete ideological basis to another than a messy process of experimentation aimed at holding together, and indeed nationalizing, a far-flung empire in an age of nationalism.

Yusuf Akçura and the Framing of Late Ottoman History

In 1904, *Türk*, an Ottoman-language newspaper printed in British-controlled Cairo, published a three-part essay by a young Tatar intellectual, Yusuf Akçura (Akçuraoğlu). While obscure at the time, Akçura's essay, *Üç Tarz-ı Siyaset*, or *Three Types of Policy*, eventually came to be seen as a foundational work of Turkish nationalism.[1] In his essay, Akçura argues that there were three possible—and more-or-less exclusive—models for the Ottoman Empire to take in reorganizing itself along Western (and national) lines:

> I believe that, benefiting from Western models [*garpten feyz alarak*] and wishing to gain in strength and development, three separate and distinct policies have been conceptualized and pursued in the Ottoman lands: The first is to represent and unite the various peoples of the Ottoman

---

[1] Yusuf Akçura, *Üç Tarz-ı Siyaset* (Ankara: Türk Tarih Kurumu Basımevi, 1991).

state, creating an Ottoman nation. The second, is to politically unite all Muslims under the leadership of the Ottoman government through the Sultan's rights as caliph (What Europeans would call "Pan-Islamism"). The third, is to create a Turkish nation-state based on the concept of a Turkish ethnicity [*Üçüncüsü, ırka dayanan siyasi bir Türk milleti teşkil etmek*].[2]

What I would like to emphasize here is his essay's *historiographical* significance, which can hardly be understated. Perhaps because Akçura's work has been so fundamental to the way Turkish nationalism was shaped, it is also foundational in the way historians have read the landscape of the late Ottoman Empire. In particular, his analysis highlights two issues that have channeled the historiography of the period to the present day. The first of these, central to almost any analysis of the late Ottoman Empire, is that the Ottoman state, in its last decades, was engaged in an on-going and desperate search for a reframing of political legitimacy that would allow it to hold its disparate peoples together.

The second element of Akçura's analysis, however, is also remarkably well-established within the historiography, but considerably more problematic: the hard categories he defines as shaping Ottoman choices. Fundamentally, Akçura saw the empire as facing a choice between three distinct and mutually exclusive ideologies, namely Ottomanism (*Osmanlılık*), by which he meant some sort of Ottoman constitutional nationalism, Islamism, which Akçura understood as a policy of actively promoting a Pan-Islamic state with the Ottoman sultan/caliph at its head, and Turkism, by which he meant an Ottoman Empire based on an ethnically-defined Turkish nationalism.[3] As an émigré intellectual attempting to pull together the political destinies of both his Russian Muslim and Ottoman Muslim identities, this reification of terms was a useful ploy, if not particularly sound analysis.

Nonetheless, Akçura's terminology—and the tendency to see these terms as mutually exclusive possibilities—has enjoyed a remarkably large role within the historiography of the late Ottoman period. Attempting to explain the roots of Turkish nationalism, this historiography has largely viewed the transition from *Tanzimat* to Abdülhamit II to the Young Turks as representing the transformation, respectively, from Ottomanism (understood as a civic nationalism based on a common Ottoman identity) to Islamism (often glossed as Pan-Islamism) to Turkism (sometimes framed as Pan-Turkism).

The seminal work of the preceding generation shows how Akçura's terminology has filtered into contemporary historical narratives. Bernard Lewis, in the standard work of the last generation, describes the ideological choices in terms that are almost identical to those employed by Akçura, arguing that "Ottomanism had proved

---

[2] Ibid., 19.

[3] For a discussion of Akçura's definition of Turkism, see François Georgeon, *Aux Origines du Nationalism Turc, Yusuf Akçura (1876–1935)* (Paris: Éditions ADPF, 1980), 26–27. See also, Bernard Lewis, *The Emergence of Modern Turkey*, 2nd ed. (Oxford: Oxford University Press, 1968), 326–27.

a failure. Islamic loyalty still dominated the sentiments of the great mass of Turks ... but its modern political avatar, pan-Islamism, had won only limited success ...It was only slowly ... that the Turks at last began to recover a sense of their separate national identity as Turks."[4] Like Akçura, Lewis and his generation viewed Ottomanism as an experiment that not only failed but was *bound* to fail. Like Akçura, they viewed Turkishness as the natural outcome of national rebirth.[5]

This framework, while still powerful in its narrative force, has been complicated over the past two decades by a wealth of new scholarship. Kemal Karpat, for example, has drawn our attention to the ways in which cultural and social shifts in the status of Ottoman Muslims, and particularly Ottoman Muslims in the Balkans, created the social basis for a sort of Muslim proto-nationalism.[6] The reign of Abdülhamit II, in particular, has been the center of significant revision. While his reign's modernizing qualities have long been established within the historiography (the Shaws, for example, describe his reign as "the culmination of the Tanzimat"), works by both Karpat and Deringil have emphasized the innovative ways in which Abdülhamit utilized traditional symbols of Islam to create a very modern political discourse.[7] Scholars such as Ussama Makdisi and Hasan Kayalı have done much to undermine the still powerful tendency to "backread" present day identity politics onto nineteenth century actors.[8]

Modernization and Ottomanism

Ottomanism, like any language of citizenship, was a language of reciprocity, of what Charles Tilly has described as "mutually enforceable claims" between government and society.[9] The challenge was to develop a language of Ottomanism that was ac-

---

[4] Lewis, *The Emergence of Modern Turkey*, 344–45. Lewis' book remains a wealth of ideas and information, but has been largely superseded by Feroz Ahmad, *The Making of Modern Turkey* (London and New York: Routledge, 1993), and Erik J. Zürcher, *Turkey: A Modern History* (London & New York: I.B. Tauris, 1993).

[5] Note in this context, the language that Lewis employs in the above quotation, in which Turks "began to recover a sense of their separate national identity as Turks."

[6] Kemal Karpat, *The Politicization of Islam: Reconstructing Identity, State, Faith, and Community in the Late Ottoman State* (Oxford: Oxford University Press, 2001).

[7] Stanford J. Shaw and Ezel Kural Shaw, *History of the Ottoman Empire and Modern Turkey: vol. 2 Reform Revolution and Republic: The Rise of Modern Turkey, 1808–1975* (Cambridge: Cambridge University Press, 1977); Karpat, *The Politicization of Islam*; Selim Deringil, *The Well-Protected Domains: Ideology and the Legitimation of Power in the Ottoman Empire, 1876–1909* (London and New York: I.B. Tauris, 1998).

[8] Hasan Kayalı, *Arabs and Young Turks: Ottomanism, Arabism, and Islamism in the Ottoman Empire, 1908–1918* (Berkeley: University of California Press, 1997); Ussama Makdisi, *The Culture of Sectarianism: Community, History, and Violence in Nineteenth-Century Ottoman Lebanon* (Berkeley: University of California Press, 2000); Ussama Makdisi, "Ottoman Orientalism," *The American Historical Review* 107, no. 3 (June 2002): 768–96.

[9] Charles Tilly, "A Primer on Citizenship," *Theory and Society* 26, no. 4 (August 1997): 599–600.

ceptable—and meaningful—to political actors with widely ranging needs and goals. While this question is one faced by all states, it was nevertheless a particularly difficult one to negotiate in the context of an empire which spanned physical and cultural geography, that held a weak position in the world economic and political system, and which faced a variety of potentially rebellious local actors at home.

The Ottoman Empire entered the nineteenth century as a pre-national state *par excellence*, with a startling diversity of religions, languages, and local cultures represented among its subject peoples. By the late eighteenth century, it had suffered some territorial losses, but still spanned over large swaths of the Balkans and Middle East. Nevertheless, it was clear to even the most myopic of observers within the Ottoman elite that the state was under increasing threat from both European competition and centrifugal forces within the empire itself. First reluctantly and then with greater determination, this elite came to accept that only dramatic restructuring of not only the military, but of basic political and economic institutions could save the empire.

The history of the empire's last hundred years, starting in the first half of the nineteenth century and continuing through the empire's defeat and dismemberment at the end of World War I, was defined by a long and bitter process of attempting to transform the state from a decentralized empire, based on negotiated arrangements and loose, local control (what Ariel Salzman has described as a system of "vernacular politics") to a modern state capable of competing economically and militarily with European incursion, while addressing the growing threat of nationalist separatist movements within its own boundaries.[10] To meet these twin threats, the empire modernized basic infrastructure, developed military efficiency through the adoption of European strategies and technology, and centralized control of the state through the development of a modern and efficient bureaucracy. At the same time, there was a concerted effort to change the nature of state legitimacy by developing a sense of citizenship and membership in a common "Ottoman" political identity, an Ottoman nationalism.

Traditionally, the beginnings of this transformation are dated to the second half of the reign of Mahmud II (r. 1808–39), who in 1826, destroyed the Janissary Corps and, with it, the main internal military threat to Ottoman modernization.[11] This "Auspicious Event," as it was described by Ottoman historians, opened the way for Mahmud to initiate a series of reforms that included almost every aspect of Ottoman life. In a move that would foreshadow integration of religious authorities into state

---

[10] Ariel Salzmann, "Citizens in Search of a State: The Limits of Political Participation in the Late Ottoman Empire," in *Extending Citizenship, Reconfiguring States*, eds. Michael Hanagan and Charles Tilly (Lanham, MD: Rowman & Littlefield, 1999), 38. Salzman provides in this essay perhaps the most succinct and useful overview of the recent literature on the changing sense of Ottoman legitimacy in the nineteenth century.

[11] Most scholars also note attempts at modernizing reform under Selim III (1761–1808). These reforms, more tentative than those which were to come later, were cut short by a Janissary revolt which overthrew Selim in 1807.

bureaucracies in the post-Ottoman period, the *Şeyhülislam*, or chief Muslim religious authority, was transformed from a quasi-state functionary, capable of acting as a potential check on the sultan's powers, to the head of a state religious bureaucracy (and thus directly responsible to the sultan), the *Bab-ı Meşihat* or *Fetvahane*.[12] Religious foundations, *evkaf* (singular, *vakıf*), were brought under direct governmental control as well.[13] Anew, a western-style army corps was instituted and old units were subject to reorganization. To help in the recruitment of men for new units, a census system was established.[14] Technical schools were developed to train officers and specialized troops and, eventually, to man the growing Ottoman bureaucracy.[15] New ministries were created and the central and provincial governments were formalized along European models. To help pay for these new reforms, taxation was rationalized and the central government began to work more insistently at coopting local notables.

Efforts at developing popular support and participation for this increasingly centralized and invasive bureaucracy were a natural corollary to these structural reforms. The Mahmud II's new military corp was named the *Muallem Asakir-i Mansure-i Muhammadiye* (The Trained Victorious Soldiers of Muhammad)—underlining that the unit's new technological proficiency did not detract from its "Muslim" character. Other units were created under the cover of "reforming" already extant units.[16] From 1831 on, the government published what is often described as the first Ottoman-language "newspaper," *Takvim-i Vekayi*, a weekly record of new laws and proclamations along with what Bernard Lewis describes as "pompous descriptions of the sultan's progress on state occasions."[17]

Pompous or not, however, the *Takvim-i Vekayi* served as an important means of disseminating information through the Ottoman bureaucracy and for reminding isolated bureaucrats of their role in the larger state program. Moreover, Mahmud pushed his officials to use plain language that would "say little but mean much," and

---

[12] Kemal Karpat, "The Transformation of the Ottoman State, 1789–1908," *International Journal of Middle East Studies* 3, no. 3 (July 1972): 255. For a discussion of the changing status of the Şeyhulislam, see Doğu Ergil, "Secularization of Islamic Law in Turkey: A Socio-Historic Analysis," *Studies in Islam* (April 1978): 73, 87–88.

[13] Zürcher, *Turkey: A Modern History*, 42.

[14] For details on the development of the Ottoman census under Mahmud II, see Stanford J. Shaw, "The Ottoman Census System and Population, 1831–1914," *International Journal of Middle East Studies* 9 (1978): 325–27.

[15] Shaw and Shaw, *History of the Ottoman Empire*, 20–32, 47–48. The Ottoman bureaucracy was not necessarily large in comparison with other empires of the day. Nevertheless, its growth during the course of the nineteenth century was remarkable, from an estimated 2000 men in the scribal service at the end of the eighteenth century, to about thirty-five thousand by the end of the nineteenth century. See Carter V. Findley, *Ottoman Civil Officialdom: A Social History* (Princeton: Princeton University Press, 1989), 22–25.

[16] For an analysis of this new military unit, see Avigdor Levy, "The Officer Corps in Sultan Mahmud II's New Ottoman Army, 1826–1939," *International Journal of Middle East Studies* 2, no. 1 (Jan. 1971): 21–39.

[17] Ibid., 35; Lewis, *The Emergence of Modern Turkey*, 94–95,

had official pamphlets published for popular consumption that used a simpler form of Ottoman Turkish.[18] The beginnings of an Ottoman-reading public—and state concern for enlisting its support—had begun.

Perhaps most famously, Mahmud instituted a program of sartorial reform, including the adoption of the fez as the headgear for Ottoman officialdom in 1829. The fez served to erase symbols of old elites, while, at the same time, regularizing the bureaucracy. As Donald Quataert has argued, "when he placed the identical fez on all officials... he laid claim to a new kind of sultanic control. Before him, all officials appeared equal."[19]

This uniformity within the bureaucratic corps also began the process of erasing the most important distinction between Ottoman subjects—that of religion. Distinguishing Muslims from non-Muslims (and, indeed, between Muslims of different status) had long been an element in policing intra-religious relations in Islamic societies.[20] At a time when the Ottoman state was being challenged by rebellion in Greece that was both religious and national in nature, Mahmud seemed to be offering non-Muslims a new place within the social order through an undifferentiated Ottoman identity, "stripped of its religious component."[21] Indeed, Mahmud is quoted as saying "I distinguish among my subjects: Muslims in the mosque, Christians in the church, Jews in the synagogue, but there is no difference among them in any other way."[22] As Quataert has shown, among the Ottoman middle strata, and particularly among non-Muslims who were anxious to escape from discrimination, many were anxious to imitate Ottoman bureaucracy in its new headgear.[23] The idea of an Ottoman public identity was born.

The Tanzimat and Ottoman Non-Muslims

After Mahmud's death in 1839 (reputedly of a broken heart at the news that his modernized army had been defeated by the forces of the equally reform-minded Muhammad Ali Pasha), restructuring continued apace. The most notable figures of the Tanzimat (generally translated as Reorganization or Reform) era which followed Mahmud's death were, however, not sultans but members of the expanding

[18] Şerif Mardin, "Some Notes on an Early Phase in the Modernization of Communications in Turkey," *Comparative Studies in Society and History* 3, no. 3 (April 1961): 260–61.
[19] Donald Quataert, "Clothing Laws, State, and Society in the Ottoman Empire, 1720–1829," *International Journal of Middle Eastern Studies* 29, no. 3 (August 1997): 413.
[20] See Lewis, *The Emergence of Modern Turkey*, 100–01.
[21] Ibid., 413.
[22] Quoted in Roderic H. Davison, *Reform in the Ottoman Empire, 1856–1876* (New York: Gordon Press, 1973), 31.
[23] Quataert, "Clothing Laws," 414.

bureaucracy which Mahmud had helped develop.[24] As Feroz Ahmad has noted, the era of the Tanzimat saw a change in the relation of the bureaucracy to the state, in which loyalty to the state could supersede loyalty to a particular sultan.[25] The development of a modern military and bureaucracy under Mahmud was extended after his death and combined with an elaboration of the concept of an Ottoman community (as opposed to a mere polity) under his successors. This occurred first within a bureaucracy that increasingly identified itself with the Ottoman state, but eventually extended into the reading public and amongst those in the middle strata that shared with the bureaucracy common tastes and educational background.

One of the earliest elaborations of this new conceptualization of Ottoman legitimacy, known in Western historiography as the Gülhane Rescript of 1839 (*Hatt-i Şerif-i Gülhane*), offered, in effect, a social contract:

> If there is an absence of security as to one's fortune, everyone remains insensible to the voice of the Prince and the country; no one interests himself in the progress of the public good ... If, on the contrary, the citizen keeps possession in all confidence of all his goods ... he feels daily growing and doubling in his heart not only his love for the Prince and country, but also his devotion to his native land.
>
> These feelings become in him the source of the most praiseworthy actions.[26]

Good governance was assumed to be the requirement for loyalty to the state. More importantly within the context of this discussion, the social contract was "extended to all our subjects, of whatever religion or sect they may be."[27]

Lip service was paid to Islamic norms, while secularizing reforms continued apace. Selim Deringil notes that the same Gülhane Rescript which formally initiated the Tanzimat era, "[stated] as its first principle that, 'it is evident that countries not governed by the şeriat [Islamic law] cannot prevail,' even though much of what it decreed was indeed in contravention of the Şeriat."[28] In a break from traditional practice, no one requested that Şeyhülislam issue a *fetva* in support of the new document.[29] It was not, as Davison has argued, that the religious language of the Gülhane Rescript

---

[24] Both grammatically and ideologically, the term *Tanzimat* holds much in common with the Gorbachev era term *Perestroika*. Both terms specifically refer to reorganization (the root of *Tanzimat* is order, *Perestroika* literally means "restructuring"). Both were meant to radically change the state and the state's relation to its citizens in order to save it. Both opened up ideological forces that they were ill-equipped to contain.

[25] Ahmad, *The Making of Modern Turkey*, 25–26.

[26] Text given in J. C. Hurewitz, *Diplomacy in the Near and Middle East, A Documentary Record: 1535–1914 vol. 1* (New York: Octagon Books, 1972), 114.

[27] Quoted in Davison, *Reform in the Ottoman Empire*, 40.

[28] Selim Deringil, *The Well-Protected Domains*, 9.

[29] Ergil, "Secularization of Islamic Law," 93.

was "mere window dressing"; rather the nature of public Islam was changing as elites worked to balance the state's Islamic identity with the goal of creating modern institutions that would be inclusive of all Ottomans.[30]

The Ottoman elite was painfully aware of both the difficulty and urgency of this project. A series of internal rebellions at the beginning of the nineteenth century was followed by the territorial loss of some of the empire's wealthiest provinces in the years up to 1839, including Greece (independent after 1830), Serbia (autonomous after 1835), and Egypt (increasingly a rival rather than a vassal province after 1805). Greater central control required greater efficiency, despite the misgivings of both local notables and peasants regarding increased central government meddling and more effective taxation. Moreover, one of the central pillars of Ottoman legitimacy, the claim that the Ottoman state represented Islamic orthodoxy and implemented God's law on earth had little saliency for either the wider "international community," (which meant, of course, the great powers of Europe), or for its non-Muslim population.

The non-Muslim population of the Ottoman Empire was of central importance. The Balkan provinces were amongst the empire's wealthiest and most developed territories. Nor were non-Muslims a marginal group. In the 1820s, Muslims made up just under 60% of the empire's total population and, in the vital European provinces, Ottoman Muslims represented a mere 32% of the population.[31] In an age of nationalism, a weak state, anxious to prevent uprisings, needed to take these demographic realities into consideration.

Nonetheless, the support from Ottoman Muslims, the traditional base of the empire, could not be assumed. Davison notes that the Gülhane Rescript was met by:

> public disturbances in some Anatolian cities, of hopes voiced in İstanbul that Mehmed Ali [the ruler of Egypt] would deliver the Ottoman government from European influence and the control of the gâvur [infidel] pasha Reşid [the main author of the Gülhane Rescript], and of expressions that equality was simply against the natural order of things. A Muslim, hauled to the police station by a Christian for having insulted the latter with the epithet gâvur, was told by the police captain: "Oh my son, didn't we explain? Now there is the Tanzimat; a gâvur is not to be called a gâvur."[32]

For Ottoman reformers, this created a conundrum: the same language of equality they hoped would tie the empire together in a common Ottoman identity was often seen as absurd or counter-intuitive at the street level.

The problem with the new language of Ottoman inclusion was that it ran counter to long established boundaries and hierarchies. It was not, as Davison would have it,

---

[30] Davison, *Reform in the Ottoman Empire*, 38–39.
[31] Kemal H. Karpat, *Ottoman Population, 1830–1914: Demographic and Social Characteristics* (Madison: University of Wisconsin Press, 1985), 72.
[32] Davison, *Reform in the Ottoman Empire*, 43.

simply that the new Tanzimat reforms "forbade calling a spade a spade."[33] Ottomans were confronting a world in which different categories, different value systems, were being used simultaneously and their meanings were in flux. Ussama Maksidi's study of Mount Lebanon, for example, shows how the Ottoman reformer, Şekib Efendi, argued for allegiance to a common Ottoman identity while simultaneously formalizing and, indeed, solidifying rival sectarian identities.[34] It was not that he believed the Ottomanist ideal was false, rather he believed that there were other realities that existed simultaneously.

As public institutions were secularized, the equality promised in the Gülhane Rescript slowly and imperfectly came into effect. One of the most awkward questions in the reform movement was whether, as full Ottoman citizens, non-Muslim men were to participate in the military. The rescript's language had suggested that military service was the obligation of every Ottoman, but no specific provisions for non-Muslims was made.[35] This question of military service was of fundamental importance. In traditional Islamic practice, one of the primary markers of Muslim superiority was that Muslims bore arms, while non-Muslims paid a tax, the *cizye* (Arabic: *jizya*), in lieu of military service.[36] While, in practice, many pre-modern Muslim armies, including the Ottoman army, used non-Muslim troops, this formula had Koranic basis and had, in more recent times, become both a key symbol of identity for Ottoman Muslims and a welcome protection against conscription for non-Muslims.

In 1837, Mahmud II had begun the process of integrating non-Muslim Ottomans into the military, by attempting to recruit Christians into the navy. The plan was to recruit 1,500 Orthodox men per annum from the coastal regions of the Aegean basin.[37] In theory, this was a fairly safe avenue of reform, in that use of non-Muslim naval troops (mostly captured seamen or Ottoman subjects from the Greek islands) had been a prominent part of the Ottoman navy right up until the 1820 Greek Revolt.[38] In practice, however, the recruitment process gave little cause for optimism. News of

---

[33] Roderic H. Davison, "Turkish Attitudes Concerning Christian–Muslim Equality in the Nineteenth Century," in *The Modern Middle East*, eds. Albert Hourani, Philip S. Khoury, and Mary C. Wilson (Berkeley: University of California Press, 1993), 73.

[34] Ussama Makdisi, *The Culture of Sectarianism*, 84–86.

[35] For a translation of the relevant section of the text, see Shaw and Shaw, *History of the Ottoman Empire*, 60–61.

[36] For a detailed discussion of the roots of the tax as well as the ways in which various states implemented it, see P. Hardy, "DJizya," in Bernard Lewis, et al., *The Encyclopedia of Islam New Edition* (Leiden: Brill, 1965), 559–67.

[37] The reliance on Orthodox Christians was probably based on their traditions of seamanship. Later, when discussion of the recruitment of Armenians was raised, it was in the context of service in the army, particularly on the Russo-Ottoman front. Recruitment of Jews, a relatively smaller population, was apparently not discussed until the beginning of the twentieth century. See Stanford J. Shaw, *The Jews of the Ottoman Empire and Turkish Republic* (New York: New York University Press, 1991), 156.

[38] Daniel Panzac, "The Manning of the Ottoman Navy in the Heyday of Sail (1660–1850)," in *Arming the State: Military Conscription in the Middle East and Central Asia, 1775–1925*, ed. Erik J. Zürcher (London: I.B. Tauris, 1999), 53–54.

the new policy was met with widespread dismay in places like Rhodes and Chios and many men fled to smaller islands where they believed they would be safe from conscription.[39] The youths of whole towns were suddenly declared to be infirm and, of those who were conscripted, many managed to escape on their way to training. While the recruitment quota for 1837 was nearly met, Ottoman officialdom ended the initiative the next year.[40] Nevertheless the issue of non-Muslims in the military, at once so sensitive and so singularly symbolic of a common Ottoman identity, remained prominent. Christians began to attend the Ottoman military medical school after 1839.[41] In the same year, there were high-level discussions in the Ottoman military establishment regarding the use of Armenians in the Ottoman army.[42] In 1847, a decade after Mahmud II's attempts to recruit non-Muslims into the Ottoman navy, Christians were again called to naval service. Indeed, enough Christians were now serving in the Ottoman navy that the admiralty began to discover the challenges of this diversity and was forced to develop new policies to allow Christian sailors to worship while in service.[43] Military conscription, however, remained deeply unpopular and was resisted both by potential draftees and community leaders.[44]

In these difficulties, the Ottomans were encountering many of the same problems that the Russian and Habsburg Empires were having in "nationalizing" their own diverse populations. The Habsburgs, for example, only began the serious recruitment of Muslims in 1881 and, although serious consideration was given to Muslim cultural and religious concerns, first news of the draft was met by uprisings in Krisvosije, Hercegovina and Southern Bosnia, which were only put down with considerable difficulty.[45] Even after

---

[39] Ufuk Gülsoy, *Osmanlı Gayrimüslimlerinin Askerlik Serüveni* (Istanbul: Simurg, 2000), 31–32.

[40] Ibid., 32–33.

[41] Davison, *Reform in the Ottoman Empire*, 44.

[42] Gülsoy, *Osmanlı Gayrimüslimlerinin*, 33–34.

[43] Ibid., 42–45.

[44] Ibid., 49–53. There is a strong element of opprobrium in Gülsoy's account. For Gülsoy, Christian rejection of military conscription is an indication that they wanted the advantages promised by the *Tanzimat* reforms, but not the accompanying responsibilities. While there is, no doubt, some truth to this, it should also be noted that the imposition of the draft on populations that had been exempt was seldom popular and often marked by resistance. Neither is it at all clear that conscription was any more popular among Muslim populations of the empire, for which examples of evasion and resistance are legion. Finally, Gülsoy overstates the extent to which the promises of *Tanzimat* equality in other fields of life were actually realized.

[45] Gunther E. Rothenberg, *The Army of Francis Joseph* (West Lafayette: Purdue University Press, 1998), 103–04. It is not clear how significant the religious component to this resistance was. Extension of forced conscription in other regions of the Habsburg Empire in 1868 also met wide-spread discontent and significant resistance. Long-term, the Habsburg army was probably more successful in integrating Muslims than the Ottomans were in integrating non-Muslims, and the *Bosniaken* became a particularly renowned regiment in the Habsburg Army. Taking the problem from another perspective, in the 1830's, when Bosnia was still under Ottoman control, the Ottomans attempted additional recruitment there which also resulted in a long-running sequence of revolts and resistance. See, Odile Moreau, "Bosnian Resistance to Conscription in the

the successful integration of Muslim troops, Muslims remained underrepresented in the Habsburg officers' corps.[46]

In many respects, sixteenth century Russian provisions for Muslims were parallel to those delineated by the Ottomans for non-Muslim subjects: the payment of an additional tax in lieu of military service and limits on their right to bear arms.[47] Nevertheless, Sergei Kudryashev is mistaken when he states that "under the Russian system of conscription at the beginning [of the twentieth century], the non-Slavs of the empire were never conscripted."[48] The case of the Russian Empire is longer and more complex. While there was often distrust of non-Christian troops, there was also a parallel but contradictory tradition of using particular Muslim populations as "native units."[49] Crimean Tatars, for example, had been used in the Russian military since 1784, only a year after their incorporation into the empire.[50] Nevertheless, the Russians were careful in how they introduced conscription and, despite a language of universal devotion to the state that paralleled those increasingly employed by the Habsburgs and Ottomans, were content to apply conscription on a case-by-case basis. The Russian general, Mikhail Skobelev, for example argued in the 1870s that only those *inorodtsy* (roughly, native foreigners) who were most devoted to the regime should be incorporated into the military.[51] The reaction to conscription also varied greatly in the Russian Empire. Russians had readily recruited Crimean Tatars and Bashkirs.[52] During World War I, Muslims in the Caucasus were conscripted without difficulty.[53] At other times and in other places, conscription was met by widespread and sometimes violent resistance. A report from the 1890s, for example, complains that Tatars (presumably Volga Tatars) and Jews were using self-mutilation to avoid military service.[54] The decision to

---

Nineteenth Century," in *Arming the State: Military Conscription in the Middle East and Central Asia, 1775–1925*, ed. Erik J. Zürcher (London & New York: I.B. Tauris, 1999), 130.

[46] István Deák, *Beyond Nationalism: A Social & Political History of the Habsburg Officer Corps 1848–1918* (Oxford: Oxford University Press, 1992), 170–71.

[47] Geoffrey Hosking, *Russia: People and Empire, 1552–1917* (Cambridge, Mass.: Harvard University Press, 1997), 10.

[48] Sergei Kudryashev, "The Revolts of 1916 in Russian Central Asia," in *Arming the State: Military Conscription in the Middle East and Central Asia, 1775–1925*, ed. Erik J. Zürcher (London & New York: I.B. Tauris, 1999), 139.

[49] Robert F. Bauman, "Subject Nationalities in the Military Service of Imperial Russia: The Case of the Bashkirs," *Slavic Review* 46, no. 3/4 (Autumn–Winter 1987): 489.

[50] Ibid., 499.

[51] Bauman, "Subject Nationalities," 499.

[52] Ibid., 498.

[53] Josh Sanborn, "More Than Imagined: A Few Notes on Modern Identities," *Slavic Review* 59, no. 2 (Summer 2000): 334.

[54] Austin Lee Jersild, "From Savagery to Citizenship: Caucasian Mountaineers and Muslims in the Russian Empire," in *Russia's Orient: Imperial Borderlands and Peoples, 1700–1917*, eds. Daniel R. Brower and Edward J. Lazzerini (Bloomington, IN: Indiana University Press, 1997), 107. Self-mutilation and other, less extreme, forms of draft evasion were, of course, not limited to non-Christian populations.

draft Central Asian Muslims into work battalions in 1916 resulted in a major rebellion that was only put down with great difficulty.

Evidence of popular resistance notwithstanding, when taken as a whole, the introduction of conscription of minority groups in these two neighboring empires was considerably more successful than similar attempts in the Ottoman Empire. The reason for this, however, lies less in the "cultural" arguments offered by scholars such as Davison, than in the political and economic strength of religious minorities in the Ottoman Empire. Non-Muslims in the Ottoman Empire were, on the whole, a relatively wealthy and well-educated population; unlike groups like the Bashkirs, they were unlikely to seek the military to improve their economic status. The Ottomans profited more from the exemption taxes non-Muslims paid than they would have from the additional supply of conscripts.[55] Moreover, non-Muslims in the Ottoman Empire often had access to sympathetic foreign powers which could—and often did—act as intermediaries and protectors against the state. In the Ottoman context, forcible conscription, such as that which the Habsburgs implemented, would have been politically unthinkable. This is not to say that no non-Muslims volunteered for service, nor that the goal of universal conscription was unreachable. But the path to broad non-Muslim conscription was long and its resolution, during World War I, tragic. In regulations from 1870, the first article states: "All Muslims of the Well-protected domains of His Majesty are personally obliged to fulfill the military service which is incumbent upon them."[56] The documents made no mention of the responsibilities of non-Muslim Ottomans.

Other aspects of Ottoman reform met with easier success. In 1840, a revised penal code was established and from 1843 on, Ottoman courts recognized the equality of Muslim and non-Muslims.[57] The evolving legal code simultaneously pushed *şeriat* principles to the periphery and asserted the primacy of the central state.[58] Secular secondary schools (*rüşdiye*) and a rudimentary university designed to develop young men for Ottoman service were also instituted (discussion of the emancipation of Ottoman women wouldn't begin in earnest for several decades). If few in number, these schools nevertheless pointed to the increasingly state-centered and secular direction of Ottoman society.[59] Beginning in the mid-forties, councils comprised of non-Muslim and Muslim notables were attached to some governors and the governors

---

[55] Erik Jan Zürcher, "The Ottoman Conscription System in Theory and Practice," in *Arming the State: Military Conscription in the Middle East and Central Asia, 1775–1925*, ed. Erik J. Zürcher (London & New York: I.B. Tauris, 1999), 88–89.

[56] Zürcher, "The Ottoman Conscription System."

[57] Davison, *Reform in the Ottoman Empire*, 44. Lewis, *The Emergence of Modern Turkey*, 109–10; 112–13.

[58] Ruth Austin Miller, *From Fikh to Fascism: The Turkish Republican Adoption of Mussolini's Criminal Code in the Context of Late Ottoman Legal Reform* (Ph.D. diss., Princeton University, 2003), 68–92.

[59] Lewis, *The Emergence of Modern Turkey*, 113–14.

were required to get council approval for many actions.[60] In 1847, the slave market in Istanbul was abolished (though slavery continued to thrive in the empire for decades).[61] By the late forties, there was evidence that non-Muslims who had emigrated to Greece and Russia were now returning to the Ottoman Empire.[62]

For most historians, the Crimean War (1854–56) was a turning point in the development of the Tanzimat reforms. There were several interrelated reasons for this. First, Ottoman troops were still not performing well enough to ensure the survival of the empire, creating an appetite for more radical reform.[63] Second, the Ottoman public had, through the empire's alliance with Britain and France, far greater direct contact with Western styles and modes of contact.[64] Third, Ottoman officers and officials were given firsthand contact with European administrative and technical organization. This contact facilitated not only the expanded use of new technologies, such as the telegraph, but the greater formalized technical training as well.[65] Fourth, and perhaps most significantly, as an ally of Britain and France, the Ottomans felt the renewed need to display their liberal intentions, particularly regarding non-Muslims.[66] The result of this desire to prove Ottoman good intentions can be found in the Imperial Rescript (*Hatt-ı Hümayun*) of 1856, in which the central tenets of the Gülhane Rescript were effectively restated, and the issue of equality was given even greater prominence.[67]

Even before the new rescript was issued, the Ottomans were taking further steps to address the question of the *cizye* and of non-Muslim military service. While for many scholars, the question was entirely of foreign manufacture, Gülsoy demonstrates

---

[60] Ibid., 48.

[61] Ehud R. Toledano, *The Ottoman Slave Trade and its Suppression* (Princeton: Princeton University Press, 1982), 107–08. Oddly, few Ottoman reformers—and few historians of Ottoman history—have reflected on the place of slaves within the context of Ottoman citizen reform. Presumably, Ottoman reformers were not overly concerned with a group that—by its very nature—could not press its demands. In any event, the slow abolition of slavery in the Ottoman Empire seems more closely tied to a grudging Ottoman acquiescence to British demands than any concern that it conflicted with Ottomanist ideals.

[62] Toledano, *The Ottoman Slave Trade*, 50–51. While this may provide evidence that conditions in the Ottoman Empire were improving for non-Muslims, Davison notes that it may simply indicate that Russian and Greek tax collection services were becoming more efficient at a better rate than Ottoman tax collection was.

[63] Lewis, *The Emergence of Modern Turkey*, 115.

[64] Shaw and Shaw, *History of the Ottoman Empire*, 141.

[65] Roderic H. Davison, "The Advent of the Electric Telegraph in the Ottoman Empire," in *Essays in Ottoman and Turkish History, 1774–1923: The Impact of the West*, ed. Roderic H. Davison (London: Saqi Books, 1990), 135–36.

[66] The Imperial Rescript was meant to curry favor with the Ottoman's wartime allies and ease its further incorporation into the European state system at the Treaty of Paris a week later. See, particularly, the brief discussion in Davison, *Reform in the Ottoman Empire*, 413–14.

[67] Ibid., 3.

that the domestic picture was more complex.[68] On October 5, 1853, the same day that the Ottoman Empire declared war on Russia, representatives of the Ottoman Armenian community delivered a letter to the Ottoman sultan, Abdülmecid I, indicating their willingness to enter into government service, including military service.[69] This was part of a general program on the part of Ottoman non-Muslims to demonstrate their participation in the war effort and was followed by a countrywide fundraising campaign.[70] On the eastern front, the governor of Trabzon, Hafız Paşa, authorized the conscription of men from both Muslim and non-Muslim communities in preparation for the defense of the city in 1855.[71] Finally, in May, 1855, the government officially announced in the *Takvim-i Vekayi* that the *cizye* burden was lifted and, in its place, non-Muslims, like other Ottomans, would be subject to obligatory military service.[72]

Despite early indications that the time might be ripe for such a policy shift, the attempt to integrate non-Muslims into the military was again met by widespread discontent among Ottoman Christian populations and a mixture of disinterest and disdain on the part of Muslims. When local officials attempted to draft Orthodox youths in the province of Niş, for example, most either escaped to the mountains or attempted to cross the border into Serbia.[73] Within a relatively short time, obligatory military service for non-Muslims effectively ended through the institution of a new tax, the *bedel-iaskerî*, or military tax, that simply replaced the old *cizye* with a new, more secular-sounding equivalent.[74]

Areas outside of military service saw greater change in the period after 1856, however. In the civilian bureaucracy, as in the military, a fundamental question was the integration of non-Muslims. The difference here was that many non-Muslims were anxious to enter into the Ottoman bureaucracy, which was both a major employer and an important source of business contacts. For this reason, the acceptance of non-Muslims into the bureaucracy became, in Carter Findley's words, "the acid test" of state

---

[68] Lewis, *The Emergence of Modern Turkey*, 116; Shaw and Shaw, *History of the Ottoman Empire*, 100; Gülsoy, 55–60.

[69] Gülsoy, *Osmanlı Gayrimüslimlerinin*, 55. Non-Muslim community leaders attempted to demonstrate loyalty to the state by offering their youths for military service on a number of occasions in late Ottoman history. On the whole, and perhaps unsurprisingly, they had considerably more difficulty convincing their young men of the wisdom of this than they did the Ottoman government.

[70] Ibid., 56.

[71] Ibid.

[72] For the text of this document, see ibid., 191–94.

[73] Ibid., 60.

[74] A small number of non-Muslims voluntarily entered the military. See Carter V. Findley, "The Acid Test of Ottomanism: The Acceptance of Non-Muslims in the Late Ottoman Bureaucracy," in *Christians and Jews in the Ottoman Empire: Vol. I The Central Lands*, eds. Benjamin Braude and Bernard Lewis (New York: Holmes and Meier, 1982), 342. Conversely, wealthy Muslims could also use the *bedel-i asker* to avoid military service.

commitment to Ottomanism.[75] Findley demonstrates that, while non-Muslims were able to find their way into the bureaucracy, they generally were less favored than what he terms "modernist Muslims."[76] Nevertheless, there were efforts on the part of the state to make sure that non-Muslims were represented. For example, imperial schools, such as *Mekteb-i Mülkiye-i Şâhâne*, or the Imperial School of Administration, that were meant to produce the leading professionals of the Ottoman state, had a quota in which thirty-three percent of the seats were allocated for non-Muslim students.[77] Moreover, non-Muslims did, overtime, take on increasingly important positions within the Ottoman bureaucracy.[78]

The legal code shows similar shifts. In 1859, the criminal code was revised through the translation and adoption of large sections of the Napoleonic Code. Commercial and maritime law were similarly reformed using French models in 1861 and 1863.[79] While most areas of private law remained under the purview of religious authorities, this aspect of legal reform too was progressively secularized, and through much of the nineteenth century, there was a reliance on both the new legal codes and *şeriat* in which each was "supported by and [supported] the central authority."

Despite this secularization, however, through the 1860s, Christians often found it necessary to petition the central government regarding the failure of local courts to accept their testimony.[80] This suggests two contradictory trends. Firstly,

---

[75] Ibid., 339–68. It might be argued that, from the perspective of the central government, non-Muslims in the civilian bureaucracy was less problematic than non-Muslims in the upper reaches of the military. The 1855 decree announcing the conscription of non-Muslims and the abolition of the *cizye*, stipulated that non-Muslims could hope to obtain the highest positions in the civilian bureaucracy, while they would be allowed to rise to the rank of colonel in the military. This distinction, while largely theoretical, might have been based on "security" concerns (though it is hard to argue that control of a major bureaucracy would be less strategically important than control of a brigade) and may have simply reflected the bias of the authors regarding what had heretofore been assumed to be a "Muslim" army. See Lewis, *The Emergence of Modern Turkey*, 337.

[76] Findley, "The Acid Test," 356–57. See also Findley, *Ottoman Civil Officialdom*, 264–72. In his study, Findley distinguishes those "modernist" Muslims who knew French (and thus had presumably come out of the new secular training facilities) and those who did not (whom he terms traditionalists). On the whole, non-Muslims (almost all of whom had at least one foreign language) fared worse than the first group and better than the second. For a comparison of Greek and Armenians in the nineteenth century Ottoman bureaucracy, see Charles Issawi, "Introduction," in *Ottoman Greeks in the Age of Nationalism: Politics, Economy, and Society in the Nineteenth Century*, eds. Dimitri Gondicas and Charles Issawi (Princeton: Darwin Press, 1999), 4–9.

[77] İlber Ortayli, "Greeks in the Ottoman Administration During the Tanzimat Period," in *Ottoman Greeks*, eds. Gondicas and Issawi, 163–64. This example can be understood in two contradictory ways: on the one hand, it demonstrates a seriousness on the part of the Ottoman state regarding the integration of non-Muslims into the state bureaucracy. At the same time, given the relative wealth and education level of non-Muslim communities, it might be that they would have actually gotten *more* positions if there had been no quota at all.

[78] Findley, "The Acid Test," 364–66.

[79] Lewis, *The Emergence of Modern Turkey*, 119.

[80] Davison, *Reform in the Ottoman Empire*, 105–06.

legal reforms formulated at the center were often resisted at the local level by officials, indicating that "the state" was working with multiple definitions simultaneously.[81] Secondly, non-Muslims were confident enough of their situation—and of the state's commitment to an inclusive Ottoman identity—that they were willing to lodge complaints to central authorities regarding failures of implementation at the local level.

Slowly, imperfectly, the institutionalization of an Ottoman identity shorn of religious connotations was taking form. An 1869 law defined Ottoman citizenship broadly, based on either residency or birth (through paternal descent).[82] This trend was further formalized in the Ottoman constitution of 1876. The new Ottoman constitution codified equal rights and responsibilities for all Ottomans, stating plainly that "Any individual who is a citizen of the Ottoman State, regardless of religion or sect, is without exception, [to be] called an Ottoman."[83] Nevertheless, article 11 of the constitution, while protecting freedom of conscience, declared Islam the state religion, while articles 2, 3, and 4 reinforced the sultan's dual role as caliph.[84]

More important than changes in the legal code was the extent to which the sultan's subjects came to see their Ottoman identity as intrinsic to themselves rather than merely an accident of the political regime. There are examples of non-Muslims who took the promises of Ottomanism seriously. The Maronite intellectual, Butrus al-Bustani, was quick to embrace the new language of Ottoman nationalism and, in 1874, wrote in his periodical, *al Jinan*:

> It is the duty of each easterner to say that I like to preserve the present [political] situation and avoid all causes of split (*inshiqāq*) in order to remain [a member] of a great national called the Ottoman nation (*'umma*), which even though composed of many racial groups (*ajnās*) is one in [common] interests.[85]

A few years after the Ottoman constitution was promulgated, an Ottoman Orthodox Christian, Alexander Istamatyadi would pen a play, *Gazi Osman*, extolling the virtues of Ottoman patriotism and commemorating the Ottoman defense of Plevna.[86]

---

[81] An attempted coup d'état by military officers and students resentful of the movement away from şeriat, the so-called Kuleli Incident of 1859, is further evidence that there was considerable mid and low level resentment of the reforms. See Davison, "Turkish Attitudes," 75.

[82] Ariel Salzmann, "Citizens in Search of a State," 45.

[83] http://www.belgenet.com/arsiv/anayasa/1876.html.

[84] http://www.belgenet.com/arsiv/anayasa/1876.html.

[85] *al-Jinān* 5 (1874), 110. Quoted in Butrus Abu-Manneh, "The Christians Between Ottomanism and Syrian Nationalism: The Ideas of Butrus al-Butani," *International Journal of Middle East Studies* 11, no. 3 (May 1980): 298. For a comparison of Bustani's Ottomanism with that promulgated by the state, see Ussama Makdisi, "After 1860: Debating Religion, Reform, and Nationalism in the Ottoman Empire," *International Journal of Middle East Studies* 34 (2002): 601–17.

[86] Issawi, "Introduction," 12.

Nevertheless, such examples appear to be exceptional. Davison has argued that, because much of the reforms directed at non-Muslims were run through millet institutions, the reforms served to reinforce rather than diminish loyalty to the millet over the greater Ottoman whole.[87] Non-Muslims preferred to develop their own schools or attend missionary schools rather than attend state schools (this was not necessarily an ideological decision, the millet-run, and particularly, the missionary schools were, on the whole better than the state schools).

The continued sense of separation did not, however, necessarily translate into separatism. While the Ladino-language newspaper, *El Tiempo*, argued in its very first editorial for the need to learn Ottoman, it did so "because we find ourselves under a Turkish government."[88] This is not, Sarah Stein dryly notes, a powerful expression of Ottoman patriotism.[89] Ottoman Jewry, having few options for a counter-nationalism to compete with their loyalty to the empire, was perhaps the most sympathetic non-Muslim group to the language of Ottoman nationalism.[90]

Of the Christian populations, the weak position of Ottoman Armenians precluded early development of Armenian nationalism within the Ottoman Empire. As Ronald Suny has suggested, "until the end of the 1870s the sense of the nation for Ottoman Armenians was still largely of an ethno-religious community that needed to work within the context of the empire to improve its difficult position."[91] When a revolutionary Armenian movement developed in the 1880s and 1890s, its main impetus would come from the Armenians of the Russian Empire, who had developed their political consciousness in the context of Russian radicalism, but who saw the Ottoman Empire as their most likely field of action.[92]

---

[87] Davison, *Reform in the Ottoman Empire*, 132.

[88] Quoted in Sarah Abrevaya Stein, "Ottomanism in Ladino" (San Domenico di Fiesole, Italy: EUI Working Papers, 2002), 5.

[89] Ibid. According to Stein, a more full-hearted embrace of Ottomanism by the paper began in the 1890's.

[90] Zionism, it should be remembered, only developed as a serious political movement after 1881. Even after this date, Ottoman Jews, relatively free of the sort of discrimination witnessed by their Russian counter-parts, tended to view Zionism with more distrust than hope, fearing that it would jeopardize the gains that they were making under Ottomanism. See ibid., 17–22; Shaw, *The Jews of the Ottoman Empire*, 222–28; Sarah Abrevaya Stein, "The Permeable Boundaries of Ottoman Jewry," in *Boundaries and Belonging: States and Societies in the Struggle to Shape Identities and Local Practices*, ed. Joel S. Migdal (Cambridge: Cambridge University Press, 2004), 49–70; Michelle U. Campos, "Between 'Beloved Ottomania' and 'The Land of Israel': The Struggle over Ottomanism Among Palestine's Sephardi Jews, 1908–1913," *International Journal of Middle Eastern Studies* 37, no. 4 (November 2005): 461–83.

[91] Ronald Grigor Suny, "Empire and Nation: Armenians, Turks, and the End of the Ottoman Empire," *Armenian Forum* 1, no. 2 (Summer 1998): 31.

[92] Ibid. and Ronald Grigor Suny, *Looking Toward Ararat: Armenia in Modern History* (Bloomington: Indiana University Press), 19; 102–03.

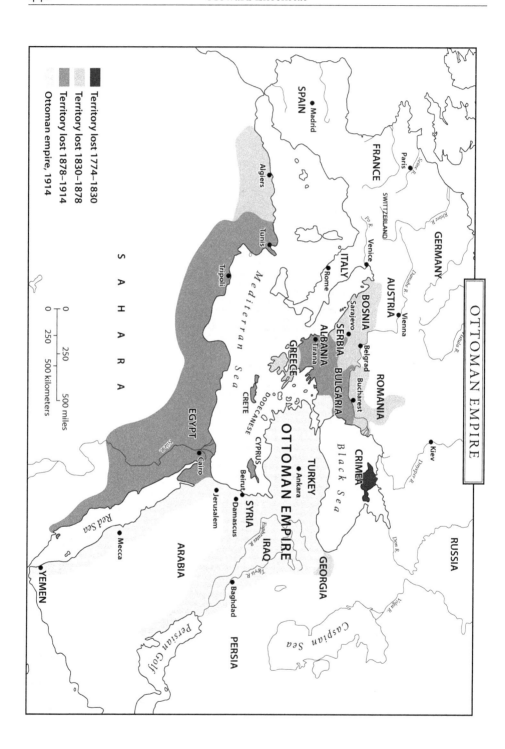

OTTOMAN EMPIRE

SPAIN
● Madrid

FRANCE
● Paris

GERMANY

SWITZERLAND

Algiers ●

Tunis ●

Tripoli ●

Venice ●
ITALY
● Rome

AUSTRIA
● Vienna

BOSNIA
● Sarajevo
SERBIA
● Belgrad
ALBANIA
● Tirana
GREECE

BULGARIA
● Bucharest
ROMANIA

Mediterranean Sea

CRETE

DODECANESE

CYPRUS

TURKEY
● Ankara

Black Sea

CRIMEA

● Kiev

RUSSIA

S A H A R A

EGYPT

Cairo ●

Beirut ●
● Jerusalem
● Damascus
SYRIA

IRAQ

● Baghdad

GEORGIA

Red Sea

● Mecca

ARABIA

● YEMEN

Persian Gulf

PERSIA

Caspian Sea

Territory lost 1774–1830
Territory lost 1830–1878
Territory lost 1878–1914
Ottoman empire, 1914

0   250   500 miles
0   250   500 kilometers

"Turks," Muslims, and the Late Ottoman Empire

Ottomanism in the strategically and economically vital Balkan provinces proved less successful. The Bulgarian Orthodox (the Bulgarians had, for decades, lobbied for a separate millet, which they finally won by sultanic order in 1870) and to a lesser degree, the Greek Orthodox had the economic strength and geographic coherence to envision their own state as a practical possibility in a way that neither Ottoman Armenians nor Ottoman Jews could have. With their economic relations largely facing westward, the model of independent, or Habsburg-controlled territories readily available to them, and the occasional support of outside powers, enticing Balkan non-Muslims into a sense of membership within the Ottoman nation proved next to impossible.

If Ottoman nationalism success among non-Muslim Ottomans was limited, however, it nevertheless succeeded in winning over an important group of western-oriented Muslim intellectuals, known collectively as the "Young Ottomans." Yet this group's strong identification with the state proved both a major success and a significant challenge for the central government. Fiercely connected to the idea of an Ottoman identity, these intellectuals were, simultaneously, highly critical of the very centralization of power that had been one of the keystones to Ottoman reform.

Very much affected by liberal currents in Europe, Young Ottoman intellectuals like Namık Kemal and İbrahim Şinasi believed that Tanzimat failures in development and in creating a broader sense of Ottoman nationalism were based on a lack of representative government. In this, they turned the statist reformism of Mahmud II and the men of the Tanzimat on its head, seeing the overwhelming centralizing tendencies of the previous generation as a barrier rather than a basis for successful reform.

Moreover, the argumentation that the Young Ottomans employed pointed to nagging contradictions within liberal Ottomanism. On the one hand, the Young Ottomans were clearly devoted to the ideal of an inclusive Ottomanism that would win the loyalty of non-Muslims and Muslims alike. Even the most "Islamist" of the Young Ottomans, Ali Suavi, would write "All the populations which today compose the Ottoman Empire constitute only one nationality: the Osmanli."[93] Namık Kemal's vision of *vatan*, or homeland, was one of territorial and constitutional nationalism, in which all citizens, non-Muslim and Muslim alike, would voice a common will through a democratically elected parliament.[94] Indeed, the Young Ottomans played key roles in the formulation of one of the key documents of Ottoman liberalism, the Ottoman constitution of 1876.

Nevertheless, a fundamental concern of the Young Ottomans was the relatively advantageous economic position of non-Muslims in the post-1856 period and

---

[93] Quoted in Davison, *Reform in the Ottoman Empire*, 222.
[94] Şerif Mardin, *The Genesis of Young Ottoman Thought* (Princeton: Princeton University Press, 1962), 328.

they nurtured a profound resentment of what they perceived as a lack of loyalty on the part of non-Muslims to the Ottomanist project.[95] There was also a powerful sense of Muslim self-identification in their program and a considerable element of what can be termed "Islamic modernism" in Young Ottoman thought that had little attraction for non-Muslims who might otherwise have been attracted to the Young Ottoman's agenda of parliamentary, representative government. The Young Ottomans were keen to demonstrate the Islamic basis of liberalism, arguing, for example, that there was Koranic basis for such concepts as "parliament" and "democracy."[96] They were also deeply critical of what they saw as a facile secularism and a lack of respect for Islamic law within the Tanzimat reforms.[97]

Blended into this already confused mixture of constitutionalist optimism and Islamic modernism was evidence of a growing sense of Turkishness as a salient feature of identity. The term, "Turk," of course, is ancient, but its meaning changed fundamentally over the course of the nineteenth century. For most of the Ottoman period "Turk" had a descriptive quality, merely referring to those populations or individuals who spoke Turkish. In some contexts, the term even had a pejorative quality, suggesting a backward rural peasantry, a bumpkin.[98] Like a number of mid-century Ottoman intellectuals, the Young Ottoman, under the influence of European historiography and philology, began to express an interest in Turkishness as a politically and culturally salient identity, one which they should embrace with pride. In exile in Paris, they came into contact with, and were influenced by, the works of Léon Cahun, whose romantic portrayal of Central Asian Turkic history seems to have helped spark their imagination.[99] In 1873, for example, Ali Suavi published his work on the Khanate of Khiva, in which he emphasized not only shared religion, but also ties of blood.[100] An Istanbul newspaper closely associated with the Young Ottoman movement, *Basiret*, argued that the Turkic Muslims of the Russian Empire were "united with us from the point of view of both faith (*diyanet*) and nationality (*milliyet*)."[101] In political terms, however, this newfound interest in Turkishness was folded into the general "Ottomanist" mix. Like Arab intellectuals who saw an Arab cultural renaissance developing—and helping to

---

[95] Ibid., 18–29; Karpat, *The Politicization of Islam*, 96.

[96] Niyazi Berkes has described Namık Kemal's patriotism as "pan-Ottomanism with Islamist 'nationalism' at its base." See his discussion in Niyazi Berkes, *The Development of Secularism in Turkey* (Montreal: McGill University Press, 1964), 221. For examples of their argumentation, see Ali Suavi, "Democracy: Government by the People, Equality," trans. M. Şükru Hanioğlu, and Namık Kemal, "And Seek Their Counsel in the Matter [Qur'an, Sura 3, Verse 159]," trans. M. Şükru Hanioğlu in *Modernist Islam: A Sourcebook*, ed. Charles Kurzman (Oxford: Oxford University Press, 2002), 138–48.

[97] Davison, *Reform in the Ottoman Empire*, 225–26.

[98] Lewis, *The Emergence of Modern Turkey*, 2.

[99] David Kushner, *The Rise of Turkish Nationalism*, 1876–1908 (London: Frank Cass, 1977), 10, 29.

[100] Ibid., 42.

[101] Quoted in ibid., 42.

guide—Ottoman political development, the Young Ottomans saw their Turkish identity as contributing to rather than at odds with their Ottoman patriotism.

Constitutionalism and patriotism were the two guiding lights of the Young Ottomans' program, but the elements which they relied on were varied and contradictory: Islamic pride was combined with desire to develop an Ottoman patriotism that would attract non-Muslims as well as Muslims. A newfound interest in Turkishness was woven into a patriotism that spoke equally of the contributions of Farabi and Avicenna to the "nation."[102] As Şerif Mardin, in his classic work on the Young Ottomans has argued, "Namık Kemal, enthusiastic as he was in eliciting an undivided allegiance to 'the fatherland,' was not entirely clear as to what the fatherland consisted of."[103] This interweaving of varied, often contradictory, narratives of the self was one that would continue until the end of the empire.

As a matter of imperial survival, the principal question regarding membership in the "Ottoman nation" in the period through to 1876 was whether or not non-Muslims could share membership in a community that also made claims of Islamic legitimacy. In the face of national movements developing among the Christian populations in the rich Balkan provinces, a new language of legitimacy that would tie non-Muslims to the state had been paramount. Political realities shifted in a fundamental way after defeat in the Russo-Turkish War of 1877–78—the peace treaty agreed to at the Berlin Congress meant the loss of approximately one third of Ottoman territory, with most of the losses occurring in the relatively rich Balkan territories. The sultan, Abdülhamit II (r. 1876–1909), prorogued the newly established constitution and quickly consolidated political power. For the first time since the beginning of the Tanzimat, the palace was the unquestioned center of power in the Ottoman Empire.

Traditionally, the historiography of the Ottoman Empire has followed Akçura in arguing that the Hamidian period was marked by a shift from "Ottomanism" to "Islamism." Abdülhamit's reign, in this view, marked the rejection of Ottoman nationalism or Ottomanism and a movement towards Islamic legitimacy. This framework, however, tends to reify these streams, suggesting that they represented mutually exclusive choices. Yet, as has been outlined above, even in the writings of those most associated with liberal Ottomanism, Islam was a prominent symbol of political legitimacy. The same constitution that called all citizens of the empire Ottomans, without regard to religion, emphasized the Islamic nature of the state and the dual role of the sultan as political leader and leader of the faithful.

Moreover, recent scholarship on the regime of Abdülhamit has noted an increasing attention to Turkish identity as part of the Hamidian Ottomanism. Kemal Karpat argued that Abdülhamit saw Turks as more than simply one of the myriad of ethnic and confessional groups within the empire—they were the empire's founders and its leading element.[104] A palace memorandum from around 1890 stated that:

---

[102] Lewis, *The Emergence of Modern Turkey*, 336.
[103] Mardin, *The Genesis of Young Ottoman Thought*, 327–28.
[104] Karpat, *The Politicization of Islam*, 336.

Turks constitute the real strength of the state. As long as the Turks survive, the rest will [follow] and sacrifice themselves for the dynasty as part of their absolute [religious] obligation. This is the reason for which the Sublime Sultanate should place on a higher level the national fate [kadr-i millet] but also respect the Arabs, with whom we share the language of faith ... instead of addressing them as "fellahs" as our ignorant officials insult them in Arabia ... [All this] naturally makes the Arabs hate the Turks.[105]

This quotation is suggestive in a number of ways. First, it demonstrates that policy makers saw ethnicity as a key component of managing the empire. Moreover, Turkishness was increasingly seen as constituting a core of the Ottoman polity. This did not represent a burgeoning Turkish nationalism, however. The state did not exist to represent Turks; Turks were simply a reliable bulwark of the state.

More important than a reliance on ethnic Turks was the increasing importance of Ottoman language and metropolitan culture on the empire's elite. The Ottoman path to modernity was based on widespread acceptance on the part of Ottoman reforms for European definitions and constructs in what Selim Deringil has described as an "Ottoman mission civilisatrice" and Ussama Makdisi has framed as "Ottoman Orientalism."[106] Ottoman Turkish, long the language of administration and of the ruling elite, was being promoted, through state-sponsored education and as a means of securing higher level postings, as one of the defining characteristics of the elite. Imposition of the language and culture of the metropole, served the double purpose of both "civilizing" an unruly periphery and integrating them into a modern Ottoman citizenry. Modernity in late Ottoman Empire, increasingly bore a Turkish stamp.

Nonetheless, cultural pride and nationalist project are two different things. Turkish nationalism would certainly emerge from this language, the emphasis on Turkishness seen in Abdülhamit's language was not in itself nationalist because it saw Turkishness as a useful rather than a necessary quality of the state. Abdülhamit may have seen Turks as a particularly reliable population, but he was determined to broaden and deepen support beyond this population. In this effort, the Arab provinces took on new importance. With the loss of the Balkans, these territories and their populations made up a significantly larger portion of the empire than they once had. Additionally, the Levant had witnessed a high degree of European economic and diplomatic encroachment and thus was a point of potential dangers for the Ottomans in a way that central Anatolia was not. The Hamidian reaction to this was greater integration, greater recruitment of Arabic speakers into the central government, and greater interest in the administration of the region.[107]

---

[105] Quoted in ibid. All parentheticals are from Karpat's translation.
[106] Deringil, *The Well Protected Domains*, 158; Ussama Makdisi, "Ottoman Orientalism," 768–96.
[107] Fatma Müge Göçek, "The Decline of the Ottoman Empire and the Emergence of Greek, Armenian, Turkish, and Arab Nationalisms," in *Social Constructions of Nationalism in the Middle East*, ed. Fatma Müge Göçek (Albany: State University of New York Press, 2002), 29.

Ariel Salzmann has convincingly argued that rather than abandoning Ottomanism, the Hamidian regime reinterpreted it to fit new demographic realities: with the loss of most of the Balkan territories, religious pluralism ceased to be a primary concern.[108] Instead, Ottoman citizenship was increasingly framed in ways that would maintain legitimacy among the remaining population. The Ottoman Empire, after 1878, had, for the first time in its six hundred year history, an overwhelming Muslim majority and Abdülhamit's revision of Ottomanism reflected this new demographic reality by emphasizing Islamic legitimacy. Indeed, Muslim demographic dominance increased as time passed. Muslim populations in the Balkans were expelled or encouraged to leave the newly constituted states, causing a rapid influx of Muslims into the Ottoman Empire. Thus, in addition to losing Christian populations, the regions which remained within the Ottoman Empire became more Muslim as well.[109] Massacres of Christian populations, such as those perpetrated against the Armenians in 1894, along with increasingly frequent sectarian tensions and violence, precipitated increased migration among some of the Christian populations who remained.

As the empire became more Muslim, the symbols of legitimacy became more Islamic. Yet, as Selim Deringil makes clear, the Islamic elements of Abdülhamit's regime were not simply a return to past practice. Rather, Islamic symbols of legitimacy were re-employed to defend the modernization program of the Ottoman state.[110] Karpat notes that "the rapid expansion of the modern school system after 1880 and the use of textbooks glorifying the Ottoman-Muslim past aimed at consolidating internal unity and the sense of a common past."[111] One might add, however, that, in developing this narrative of a common history, little room was left for the non-Muslim Ottomans who remained in the empire.

Nevertheless, even in this context of increasing emphasis on Islamic symbolism and despite sporadic state-sponsored violence against non-Muslims, inclusion of non-Muslims into the Ottomanist project was not wholly abandoned under Abdülhamit. On the whole, Ottoman Jews continued to see integration and support of the empire as their best political option.[112] Indeed, Stein has argued that the support of the Jewish press for inclusion in the Ottoman nation increased over the long reign of Abdülhamit. By the 1890s, for example,

[108] Salzmann, "Citizens in Search of a State," 50–51. Kemal Karpat refers to Abdülhamit's formula as one of an "Ottoman-Muslim" nation. See Kemal Karpat, "The *Hijra* from Russia and the Balkans," in *Muslim Travelers: Pilgrimage, Migration, and the Religious Imagination*, eds. Dale F. Eickelman and James Piscatori (Berkeley: University of California Press, 1990), 147.
[109] Ibid., 133.
[110] See, especially, Deringil, *The Well-Protected Domains*, 44–46.
[111] Karpat, *The Politicization of Islam*, 185.
[112] Eugene Abraham Cooperman, *Turco-Jewish Relations in the Ottoman City of Salonica, 1889–1912: Two Communities in Support of the Ottoman Empire* (PhD diss., New York University, 1991), 30–31 and *passim*.

... *El Tiempo* was evolving to accommodate a changed political climate. On the one hand, by this decade, the paper was intent on fashioning itself as a proponent of the imperial system. It began to oppose separatist nationalism of all forms and to support the Turkicization of all Ottomans ... [The] contributors to *El Tiempo* subdued their lionization of Western Europe and began to argue that Jews were guaranteed a secure homeland in the Ottoman Empire. By 1899, an article spoke of the importance of Jews' "Ottoman nationality," a notion that was unthinkable two decades earlier.[113]

The relationship of the Greek Orthodox and Armenians to Ottoman nationalism under Abdülhamit remained ambiguous. Wealthier and more numerous than the Jews, they had more potential options. Nonetheless, the emphasis on Islam by the Hamidian regime did not wholly end Christian participation in Ottomanism. For example, Vangelis Kechriotis has shown that "Greek" and "Ottoman" often coexisted as identity markers and many Greek Orthodox merged enthusiasm for the Greek national state with active participation in Ottoman institutions and public life.[114] Throughout the Hamidian period, Armenian nationalist agitation remained primarily generated from Russian Armenia, though the focus of its revolutionary energies was consistently on the Armenians of Anatolia and both the *Hnchak* (Bell) Party and *Dashnaksutiun* (Armenian Revolutionary Federation) were able to successfully recruit members in Ottoman territories.[115] At the same time, Mesob Krikorian notes similar participation (and state recruitment of) Armenians in all aspects of the Ottoman state, even in regions that suffered from attacks on Armenian communities.[116] Non-Muslim Ottomans, no less than the Ottoman ruling class, found themselves employing a variety of identities that seemed mutually contradictory, hoping to benefit from the ambiguity of identity.

Ottoman legitimacy under Abdülhamit was marked less by a wholesale rejection of earlier trends than by a shift in emphasis towards a new merging of national and religious symbols.[117] His efforts, however, broadened and in turn were nourished by an increasing self-awareness and political engagement on the part of Ottoman Muslims. Public intellectuals like the Young Ottomans were one example of this, but

---

[113] Stein, "Ottomanism in Ladino," 10.

[114] Vangelis Kechriotis, "Greek-Orthodox, Ottoman-Greeks or just Greeks? Theories of Coexistence in the Aftermath of the Young Turks Revolution," *Études Balkaniques* 41 (2005): 51–72. See also, Vangelis Kechriotis, "Hellenic Smyrna: Communities in the Pantheon of History," paper presented at conference Nationalism, Society and Culture in Post-Ottoman South East Europe, St. Peter's College, University of Oxford, May 29–30, 2004.

[115] Suny, *Looking Toward Ararat*, 85; Göçek, "The Decline of the Ottoman Empire," 52–53.

[116] Mesrob K. Krikorian, *Armenians in the Service of the Ottoman Empire, 1860–1908* (London: Routledge, 1977).

[117] As Selim Deringil, among others has noted, in this regard, Abdülhamit II's formulation of Ottoman legitimacy was following a similar trajectory to that of his Russian contemporary, Alexander III.

this new political awareness was by no means limited to an Istanbul elite. There were a wide range of factors which facilitated Muslims seeing themselves in a new way, to see their religious identity as not merely a matter of confession or even of community, but as a primordial category.

Perhaps the most significant basis for this increased self-awareness resulted from Muslim emigration from former Ottoman territories in the Balkans and, to a lesser extent, from the Russian Empire.[118] The demographic unraveling of much of the diversity of former Ottoman territories was accompanied by what can best be termed "ethnic cleansing," as victorious Christian populations used violence and terror to push the remaining Muslims out of the newly won territories. The economic and social strain of caring for these new refugees was overwhelming. In 1878, over one hundred thousand refugees were housed in Istanbul alone.[119] This in a city with a population of just under 700,000.[120] Kemal Karpat has estimated that some 250,000–300,000 Muslim civilians died and 1.5 million emigrated to the remaining territories of the Ottoman Empire in the aftermath of the Russo-Turkish War of 1877–78.[121] At the same time, there is some evidence that Abdülhamit actually was facilitating this immigration, not simply out of sense of moral obligation, but as a way of cementing his control of problematic Ottoman territories, particularly in East Anatolia, but also in parts of the Levant. When the Habsburgs enlisted the mufti of Tuzla to help limit the exodus of Bosnian Muslims from the region, the sultan demanded that steps be taken "to increase the size of the Muslim population [in the Ottoman state] by permitting the Muslims living under the authority of neighboring governments to come here."[122]

As noted above, these changes meant new demographic equations for the central state as it sought to maintain control of its remaining territories, now largely defined by Anatolia and the Arab Middle East. The effects of this continuing influx of refugees had, naturally, a powerful effect on public consciousness as well. In this upheaval, the primary marker of which side of the conflict and, eventually, which side of the border one found oneself on was religious. Confessional identity was taking on additional meaning as it became associated with membership in competing national programs—it was becoming "ethnicized" as the Western-educated Muslim of the city found him or herself sharing the same political fate as the illiterate Muslim of the countryside.[123] This sense of common destiny was intensified through an expanding popular press and shared in coffee shops. As one British consular report had it:

---

[118] These shifts are most graphically detailed in Justin McCarthy, *Death and Exile: The Ethnic Cleansing of Ottoman Muslims, 1821–1922* (Princeton: The Darwin Press, 1995). See also, Nedim İpek, *Rumeli'den Anadolu'ya Türk Göçleri, 1877–1890* (Ankara: Türk Tarih Kurumu Basımevi, 1994).

[119] Ibid., 78.

[120] Karpat, *Ottoman Population, 1830–1914*, 117. The population of Istanbul in 1872 was 685,000.

[121] Karpat, *The Politicization of Islam*, 75.

[122] Quoted in ibid., 185. Parenthetical in Karpat's translation.

[123] Ibid., 97–98 and *passim*.

They now take a keen interest in national and foreign political affairs, and follow up and ventilate events which affect their country and religion.

The usurping views of Austria on Bosnia and Macedonia, our occupation of Cyprus, the action of France in Tunis, and our proceedings in Egypt, are all burning questions now eagerly discussed among the higher as well as the more ignorant and fanatic classes ...[124]

The Boundaries of Ottoman Identity

In many respects, Abdülhamit, despite—or perhaps because of—his use of Islamic symbolism, had been remarkably successful in modernizing the Ottoman state. Basic infrastructure improved throughout the empire and, in fundamental ways, Ottoman urban life became increasingly defined by European norms. Elizabeth Frierson, in particular, has pointed to the ways that the Ottoman press developed a sense of Ottoman identity.[125] Railway and telegraph, the ties that bound states into nations, were expanded rapidly during his reign. Railway lines, minimal and local in nature before his reign, were greatly expanded and, by 1908, there were nearly 6,000 kilometers of track, including lines connecting Anatolia and Mesopotamia and the still unfinished Hijaz Railroad.[126] Telegraph lines expanded even more rapidly, with almost 50,000 kilometers of line by 1904.[127]

Despite these gains, the boundaries of the empire, both ideologically and geographically, were unclear. Despite the profound centralizing ambitions of the state, rural areas still largely were defined by local interest and local and confessional identities. The relationship of rural Muslims to the state was based on time honored tradition and a sense of Islamic identity and was mediated through local notables. At best, they had a sense of personal obligation to the sultan/caliph; they were not, however, Ottoman in a national sense. While it is true that some non-Muslims saw their political future within the Ottoman Empire, it is likely that, for most, identification with the empire represented hopes for the future more than anything else. While there were certainly exceptions, it was less that Ottomanist Jews and Christians felt that they were fully part of the body politic than hopes that one day they would be. Ottoman nationalism, by the end of the empire, was likely still a limited affair, centered primarily on educated Muslims in urban areas. Ethnicity and language seem to have played a relatively little role, though by the end of the Hamidian regime many secularly

---

[124] Quoted in ibid., 152.
[125] Elizabeth Brown Frierson, "Mirrors Out, Mirrors In: Domestication and Rejection of the Foreign in Late-Ottoman Women's Magazines (1875–1908)," in *Women, Patronage, and Self-Representation in Islamic Societies*, ed. D. Fairchild Ruggles (Albany: State University of New York Press, 2000), 177–204.
[126] Shaw and Shaw, *History of the Ottoman Empire*, 227.
[127] Shaw and Shaw, *History of the Ottoman Empire*, 228–29.

educated Ottomans were able to read and write passible Turkish whether they lived in Damascus or Smyrna.

The Young Turk Era: From Constitutionalism to Genocide and the End of Empire

The Hamidian regime was brought to a close in the Constitutional Revolution of 1908, though Abdülhamit remained on the throne as a figurehead until an attempted counter-coup in 1909. The CUP, or Committee for Union and Progress (*Ittihadve Terakki Cemiyeti*), the so-called Young Turks, were mostly military officers and bureaucrats, convinced that Hamidian repression was to blame for the empire's weakness. Their initial reaction was to attempt a return to the liberal path that Abdülhamit had ended in 1878. In the cities, Christians, Muslims, and Jews rejoiced together at the restoration of the constitution. The territorial and constitutional descriptors of Ottoman identity initially formulated in the Tanzimat era were brought to the fore once again.

Whereas Abdülhamit had cloaked his nation-building and modernization programs in the garments of traditional and royal paternalism, the CUP was forthright in its devotion to modernity as mood as well as method. Like the Tanzimat reformers, the Young Turks saw their hope in a liberal Ottomanism which would tie all citizens to a modernized and efficient state. The Young Turks had two important advantages over their Tanzimat predecessors, however: firstly, as relatively junior figures who had come to power through armed revolt, they were less tied to the status quo; secondly, they had the very significant advantage of being able to participate in the steady development of education and infrastructure under Abdülhamit. Despite their acceptance of democratic opposition, the CUP position was further supported by the relative disorganization of potential opposition groups.[128] They enjoyed both the legitimacy of reasonably fair elections (in 1908) and—at least initially—a lack of serious opposition.

The goal of creating a sense of common Ottoman identity was pressed forward on all fronts. Military service was now required of non-Muslim as well as Muslim Ottoman males.[129] At the educational level, the state instituted citizenship classes to develop a sense of patriotism among its youth.[130] More controversially, the CUP instituted what has been referred to as a "Turkification" of the bureaucracy, attempting to make Ottoman Turkish more fully the language of the state while increasing the level of Turkish-language education in the schools. Yet, the extent to which these policies marked a rejection of Ottomanism and the adoption of a self-consciously Turkish nationalist agenda within the CUP has been a point of considerable debate within recent

---

[128] Salzmann, "Citizens in Search of a State," 53.

[129] Zürcher, *Turkey: A Modern History*, 105.

[130] Füsun Üstel, "Les 'Foyers Turcs' et les 'Turcs de l'Exterieur,'" in *Cahiers d'études sur la Méditerranée orientale et le monde turco-iranien*, no. 16 (July–December 1993): 168–69.

scholarship. Some, like Şükrü Hanioğlu, see the Young Turks as convinced Turkish nationalists from the start and portray their apparent sympathy towards a liberal Ottomanism in the early years of their rule as a necessary "political opportunism."[131]

Yet what is most striking about the Young Turks is not their ideology, but their pragmatism. The CUP's "Turkification" was fundamentally an attempt of the Young Turks to rationalize the state and create a sense of shared Ottoman identity, an intensification rather than a break from long-term goals of the Ottoman state.[132] To take as an example, their emphasis on broadening the use of Turkish as a common administrative language was, after all, a long-term Ottoman goal. The constitution of 1876 stated in article 68 that, starting in 1880, knowledge of Turkish would be a requirement for members of parliament.[133] The goal throughout this period was the integration of local elites into a unified, "rational," and modern state.[134] At the same time, Abdülhamit's policy of "Islamic Ottomanism" did not die in the Young Turk period and the CUP made active efforts to increase the economic power of Muslims over their non-Muslim countrymen.[135]

There is no question, however, that the decrease in local privileges, coupled with foreign intervention, increased the inclination of local populations to contemplate a political future free of Ottoman rule and made political implementation of "national" imaginings more attractive. Among Muslim elites of the Ottoman Empire, the influence of national metaphors of identity, of an "awakening" to a linguistic and cultural past outside of political and religious identity were, despite their attractions, framed in the context of continued allegiance to the Ottoman political state. This was true even for Muslim regions that went into armed revolt. Albanians, who eventually gained full independence at the insistence of the Habsburgs in 1913, were initially resisting only taxation and military recruitment—the twin scourges of an increasingly efficient state—while the leadership in Yemen was satisfied with autonomy under an Ottoman umbrella.[136]

Among non-Muslims, the situation is largely defined by opportunity. In most parts of the empire, local Jewish populations seem to have placed their hopes in a liberal Ottomanism and remained deaf to the call of Zionism. In Palestine, the political landscape was more complex, but here too, the indigenous Jewish population seems

[131] M. Şükrü Hanioğlu, *Preparation for a Revolution: The Young Turks, 1902–1908* (Oxford: Oxford University Press, 2001), 295–302. A. Holly Shissler, in her work, *Between Two Empires: Ahmet Ağaoğlu and the New Turkey* (London and New York: I.B. Tauris, 2003) directly addresses this issue of opportunism through her analysis of a key figure in Turkist thought, Ahmet Ağaoğlu, arguing that Turkism developed out of a gradual process of formulating and reformulating what the "national community" would constitute.
[132] This argument is made particularly forcefully by Kayalı, *Arabs and Young Turks*, 79, 90–94.
[133] See Suna Kili, *Türk Anayasaları* (Istanbul: TekinYayınevi, 1982), 18.
[134] Kayalı, *Arabs and Young Turks*, 92.
[135] Salzmann, "Citizens in Search of a State," 54.
[136] Zürcher, *Turkey: A Modern History*, 109–12.

to have felt more secure in supporting liberal Ottomanism.[137] Greeks and Armenians were more divided, with some following the Jewish model, while others hoped for European intervention that would offer them the opportunity for independent rule. Nevertheless, as late as 1913, significant numbers of non-Muslims fought alongside their Muslim countrymen to defend Ottoman territory.[138]

The loss of many of the remaining Balkan territories at the end of the Balkan Wars (1912–13) and the corresponding influx of Muslim refugees increased the inclination to frame Ottoman identity in Muslim terms. While the "citizen-based" framework of Ottoman nationhood did not completely die out after this time, the demographic realities made appeals to Muslim unity all the more vital, particularly after the empire entered into World War I the following year (1914).[139] Zafer Toprak, in particular, has shown the extent to which the CUP actively worked to develop a Muslim bourgeoisie at the expense of both foreign capital and native Ottoman Christians.[140]

In 1913, the Ottomans concluded an agreement on population transfers with the Bulgarians aimed at ensuring that the region around the Ottoman–Bulgarian border would be demographically secured through the transfer of Muslims living close to the border on the Bulgarian side to Ottoman territory and Bulgarians living close to the border on the Ottoman side to Bulgarian territory.[141] On the eve of World War I, the Ottomans began a process of forcibly relocating parts of its Greek Orthodox population. Over the course of the war, nearly 300,000 Greek Orthodox Christians were driven from Western Anatolia and Thrace into Greece and another 85,000 were forcibly relocated to Central Anatolia. Negotiations between Greece and the Ottomans to regularize this process began in May of 1914 but the Ottoman entrance into the war rendered these discussions moot.[142]

---

[137] For a detailed analysis of this issue, see Michelle Campos, *"A Shared Homeland" and its Boundaries: Empire, Citizenship and the Origins of Sectarianism in Late Ottoman Palestine, 1908–1913* (Ph.D. dissertation, Stanford University, 2003).

[138] Salzmann, "Citizens in Search of a State," 54. The support of many non-Muslims for Ottoman rule when they saw it as offering them opportunities for security and advancement were matched in the (rare) cases when the new government in former Ottoman territories gave Muslim citizens similar opportunities. In British-administered Cyprus (an Ottoman territory until 1878), for example, Muslims supported British rule in World War I against the Ottoman Empire and played key roles in the administration of the island. See: Nergis Canefe, "Türklük Tarihive Kıbrıs: Kıbrıslı Türk Kimliğin Hikâyelenmesinde Bir Yolağzı," in *Hatırladıklarıylave Unuttuklarıyla Türkiye'nin Toplumsal Hafızası*, ed. Esra Özyürek (Istanbul: İletişim, 2001), 54.

[139] Kayalı, *Arabs and Young Turks*, 174–77.

[140] Zafer Toprak, *Türkiye'de Millîİktisat, 1908–1918* (Ankara: Yurt Yayınları, 1982).

[141] Stephen P. Ladas, *The Exchange of Minorities: Bulgaria, Greece, and Turkey* (New York: Macmillan Company, 1932), 18–20. For a wider perspective on these negotiations, see Fuat Dündar, *İttihatve Terakki'nin Müslümanları İskân Politikası, 1913–1918* (Istanbul: İletişim, 2001), 66–72.

[142] Ibid., 15–16; 20–23; Erol Ülker, "Contextualizing 'Turkification': Nation-building in the Late Ottoman Empire, 1908–18," *Nations and Nationalism* 11, no. 4 (2005); 626.

These transfers represented a long-standing Ottoman strategy of moving populations as a means of controlling territory. As noted above, this policy had been intensified under Abdülhamit, who had used the inflow of Muslim émigrés from the Balkans and Russia to increase his control in parts of Anatolia and the Levant. Under the Young Turks it rose to the level of what Fuat Dündar has referred to as "demographic engineering," as the central government attempted to preclude revolt through the massive transfer of populations.[143]

It also represented a hardening of the sometimes vague geographic boundaries of the Ottoman nation. Over a century of territorial loss, the Ottomans were surprisingly adaptive in reframing their sense of what represented "Ottoman lands." As territories were lost, Ottoman elites were remarkably quick to refocus on maintaining lands they still controlled. By 1913, however, many Ottoman Muslims, both inside and outside the government, felt profoundly besieged. The remaining territory of the empire had been Ottoman since at least 1517 and was overwhelmingly Muslim. Many Ottomans, including many in the ruling elite, were themselves refugees or the children of refugees. World War I and its immediate aftermath, for many Muslims, were understood as an existential war.

This "existential quality" to the Ottoman efforts in World War I help explain both the remarkable defenses they made of Iraq and Gallipoli, but also the shocking brutality of the World War I in the east. The most obvious example of this is the Armenian Genocide, which, in many respects represents a culmination of the ethnic cleansing that had occurred before the war. Beginning in 1915, Armenians, along with some smaller Christian populations in the east, were targeted for forced relocation, which was accompanied by a broad program of massacre and terror. The number of dead are hotly disputed, but were at least 800,000 and might well have been much more.

Many scholars have seen in CUP policies during the course of World War I the emergence of the "true face" of the Young Turk movement as a Turkish nationalist project. Certainly, Turkist themes were of greater utility to the Ottoman government after the outbreak of the First World War and the freedom of émigrés in the Ottoman Empire to argue for political union with Russian Muslims widened accordingly. The government made common cause with non-governmental, Turkist groups in maintaining ties between the Ottomans and Muslim independence movements in Russia and émigrés from the Russian Empire were particularly important in these efforts.[144] Nevertheless, while Turkist themes were utilized to gather support in the Russian Empire during World War I, the language of Muslim brotherhood was far more central to (and effective in) Ottoman propaganda efforts abroad. Moreover, Ottoman interest in Russian Muslims was primarily a reflection of the hopes of undermining

---

[143] Dündar, İttihat ve Terakki'nin.

[144] Jacob Landau, *Pan-Turkism: From Irredentism to Cooperation* (Bloomington: Indiana University Press, 1995), 53–55; Füsun Üstel, "Les 'Foyers Turcs' et les 'Turcs de l'Exterieur'," *Cahiers d'etudes sur la Mediterranée orientale et le monde turco-iranien*, no. 16 (July–December 1993): 86–87.

Russian control more than a decisive concern regarding the fate of Muslims under Russian rule.[145]

It is also fair to note that, while the Young Turks had come to view Anatolia as a secure "core" of the empire, they were still fully committed to maintaining as much control over the Arab provinces as they possibly could. Yet the importance of both Turkification and Arab nationalism, even in the context of World War I, can easily be overstated. What is perhaps most striking about the response of most of the Muslims of the Ottoman Empire, regardless of religion, social class, or language, is the extent to which they remained loyal to the institution of empire until its final defeat as well as the alacrity with which they sought new national projects after the Ottoman Empire finally collapsed.

The centrality of geopolitics in Ottoman thinking during World War I is underlined by the fact that the CUP, in their search for allies against the Russians, also supported Christian groups such as the Georgians and Ukrainians whom they saw as potential allies, while simultaneously engaging in the massacre and displacement of groups such as the Armenians, whom they saw as a threat.[146] As Michael Reynolds concludes, "Ottoman policy toward the Caucasus was dominated by considerations of *realpolitik*, not identity."[147]

Over the course of the nineteenth century, Ottoman elites attempted to address the questions of international competition and internal dissent through a program of radical, top-down, modernization. In the Ottoman Empire, a key element to this project was the development of "Ottomanism," a sense of national identity and purpose within its population. Three aspects of this attempt need to be underlined here. First, the central motivation for Ottomanism was based not on ideology, but on the practical need to integrate the population and bind them to the state. Second, because the state had to address different populations simultaneously, and because political realities shifted over time, Ottomanism was not a consistent ideology; rather, it was a shifting set of themes which were emphasized more or less depending on audience and circumstance. Third, the relative failure of this program among Balkan Christians ensured that Ottomanism would take on an increasingly Muslim aspect in the last years of the empire and helped to create a sense of "Muslimness" as an ethnic category that would, in large part, create the basis for the brutal ethnic cleansing that marked Ottoman collapse in the Balkans and Anatolia.

---

[145] Michael A. Reynolds, *The Ottoman-Russian Struggle for Eastern Anatolia and the Caucasus, 1908–1918: Identity, Ideology, and the Geopolitics of World Order* (Ph.D. dissertation, Princeton University, 2003), 157–58 and *passim*.

[146] Ibid., 234–46.

[147] Ibid., 595.

Nation-Building and Nationalism in the Oldenburg Empire

Uffe Østergård

In the nineteenth century, Denmark, or rather the Oldenburg Monarchy, changed from a middle sized composite state in northern Europe that had for centuries controlled most of the Baltic Sea and large parts of the North Atlantic Ocean, to a small homogeneous nation-state. The "Oldenburg Monarchy" or "Oldenburg Empire" is an unusual denomination for "Denmark" or the "Danish Monarchy." In the eighteenth and nineteenth century, the most used concept was "Helstaten" (in German *Gesamtstaat*). Yet it seems appropriate to name the state on a par with larger and better known empires such as the Habsburg and Romanov because of the composite and multilingual nature of the far-stretched state that dominated the entrance to the Baltic Sea but also controlled almost half of Europe's coastline towards the Atlantic Ocean. Despite some forerunners, it is generally agreed that Denmark as a state dates back to the tenth century, when it was recognized by the Papacy as a Christian monarchy on a par with Poland, Bohemia, Hungary, and Croatia, as a reaction to the Ottonian kings in Germany who aspired to unite all Christendom under their banner as emperors of the Holy Roman Empire. The kings were recruited from a series of indigenous families, first of all the Valdemars in the High Middle Ages. After the extinction of this line, the first king of the Oldenburg family from northern Germany was elected king of Denmark in 1448 under the name Christian I. Oldenburg (in *Plattdeutsch* or Low German Ollnborg) is situated in today's Federal Republic of Germany, divided between the present Bundesländer Rheinland-Westfalen and Niedersachsen. The first known count of Oldenburg was Elimar of Oldenburg (d. 1108). When the emperor Frederick I (Barbarossa) dismembered the duchy of Saxony in 1180, the counts were elevated to the rank of dukes and thus joined the ranks of potential royalty. In the thirteenth century, the duchy expanded at the cost of its Frisian neighbors to the north and west. In 1448 the young duke Christian was elected king of Denmark, based on his maternal descent from Danish kings. In 1450, Christian was elected king of Norway and in 1457 king of Sweden (due to the Kalmar Union of 1397 of all three Scandinavian kingdoms). In 1460 he was elected duke of Schleswig and count of Holstein, after having handed over Oldenburg to his brother Gerhard in 1454.[1]

From the nineteenth century onwards this composite state is normally referred to as "Denmark" but that does not correspond to historical truth, even though the whole of the state came to be governed from Copenhagen at the central waterway Øresund (the Sound) which was the maritime and economic center of the far-stretched state and thus expressed the geopolitical logic of this Northern European state that controlled the entry to the Baltic Sea. Through a series of military defeats over a period of four hundred years, this state was reduced to its present state as a small, nationally homogeneous country. But this state of affairs was anachronistically written back in history after the loss of Norway in the Napoleonic Wars in 1814 and the predominantly German speaking duchies of Schleswig and Holstein in 1864. So profound was the change "Denmark" underwent in the nineteenth century that Danes and even the majority of Danish historians forgot about the multinational past and began to depict all of Danish history from the end of the Viking Age in the eleventh century as the very epitome of a small state at the mercy of aggressive and treacherous neighbors, in particular a non-existing entity called "Germany" and neighboring Sweden.[2] In 1523, Sweden (with Finland) broke away from Danish domination. The Vasa dynasty subsequently succeeded in building a Swedish empire in northern Europe around the Baltic Sea between 1560 and 1720 at the expense of Denmark, Russia, and Poland—in Swedish called *Stormaktstiden* or the "Swedish Imperial Experience."[3] Although reduced in size after losses of a third of its territorial holdings to Sweden in 1658, the Oldenburg Monarchy in the eighteenth century still ranked as a middle sized power with a fleet that controlled the western parts of the Baltic Sea and the Atlantic Ocean north of the British Isles between Norway, Iceland, and Greenland, as well as a small colonial empire. Yet this history, together with Danish participation in the trans-Atlantic slave trade, has been forgotten in today's Denmark.

From a traditional point of view on Danish history, the title of this contribution thus seems a meaningless contradiction in terms. How can we talk of nation-building if the Danish nation-state already existed as a small homogenous nation in the Middle Ages? Nevertheless, the question is relevant as Danish historians

---

[1] Gerd Steinwascher, *Die Oldenburger. Die Geschichte einer europäischen Dynastie* (Stuttgart: Kohlhammer Verlag, 2011).

[2] Uffe Østergård, "Schleswig and Holstein in Danish and German Historiography," in *Disputed Territories and Shared Pasts: Overlapping National Histories in Modern Europe*, eds. Tibor Frank and Frank Hadler (Houndsmill: Palgrave Macmillan, 2011), 200–23; and Uffe Østergård, "Fortidens nutid—dansk nationalisme og national identitet," in *Her og nu! Fortidsforståelse i kunst, kultur og videnskab*, eds. Erik Bach, et al. (Copenhagen: Carlsbergfondet, 2012), 22–39.

[3] Michael Roberts, *The Swedish Imperial Experience 1560–1718* (Cambridge: Cambridge University Press, 1979).

recently have begun to admit. Two historians have used the title the "Rise and Decline of the Danish Empire" in a recent reinterpretation of Danish history from the Middle Ages until 1864.[4] In their understanding, Denmark was an empire from the end of the Viking Age until 1864. I share this understanding of Denmark as a multinational state, although technically speaking Denmark never was an empire but a composite or conglomerate state held together by the king of Denmark who ruled the various parts in different capacities. It is this fact which justifies the denomination of "empire" for the entity often referred to as "Denmark."

Until the loss of the Norwegian part of the realm in 1814, the name "Denmark" or *Kron zu Dennemarck* referred to a composite state, typical of the early modern European era of territorial states.[5] Today, to the extent this entity is remembered at all, it is called by such politically correct terms as "the Dual Monarchy of Denmark and Norway" or "the Twin Kingdoms." However, these polite terms are so imprecise as to be misleading since the king of Denmark ruled all his lands from Copenhagen, except for brief periods when a viceroy was appointed for Norway. As a consequence of the loss of the provinces of Skåne, Halland, Blekinge, Bohuslen, Herjedalen, and Gotland in 1658, the Danish king in 1660 became the absolute ruler of the kingdoms of Denmark and Norway and duke of parts of Schleswig and Holstein. Holstein belonged to the Holy Roman Empire (in Latin, *Sacrum Imperium*), which complicated the constitutional situation considerably. As duke of Holstein, the Danish king formally was subordinate to the emperor, while as duke in parts of Schleswig he owed loyalty to himself as king of Denmark. The situation was further complicated by the fact that the aristocracy (*Ritterschaft*) of the two duchies, when electing Christian I as duke in 1460, had forced him to recognize that the two duchies should "always be ruled together"—in Low German "dat se bliven ewig tosamende ungedelt."[6]

In addition to the four main realms, Denmark (which until 1658 included today's southern Sweden), Norway, Schleswig, and Holstein, the Oldenburg Empire comprised the North Atlantic territories of Iceland, the Faroe Islands, and Greenland. Originally affiliated with Norway, these three provinces in the course of

---

[4] Michael Bregnsbo and Kurt Villads Jensen, *Det danske imperium—storhed og fald* (Copenhagen: Aschehoug, 2004).

[5] The concepts "composite state" and "conglomerate state" have become accepted technical terms for the territorial states in early modern Europe. A definition is proposed by J. C. D. Clark, "Britain as a Composite State," in *Britain—Nation, State, Decline*, ed. Uffe Østergård, special issue of *Culture and History* 9, no. 10 (1991): 55–85. The Swedish historian Harald Gustafsson has coined the concept "conglomerate state," see Harald Gustafsson, "Conglomerate State: A Perspective on State Formation in Early Modern Europe," *Scandinavian Journal of History* 23, nos. 3–4 (1998): 189–213.

[6] In an interesting article a German historian, Carsten Jahnke, has challenged this interpretation of the treaty and convincingly proven that the treaty was misinterpreted by the Schleswig-Holstein movement in the 19th century for political reasons Carsten Jahnke, "dat se bliven ewig tosamende ungedelt," *Zeitschrift für die Geschichte Schleswig Holsteins* 128 (2003), 45 59.

the seventeenth and eighteenth centuries gradually came to be directly ruled from Copenhagen. Finally, the Danish monarchy acquired a number of colonies in the West Indies (St. Croix, St. John, and St. Thomas), in West Africa (Christiansborg fortress in today's Ghana), and in India (Frederiksnagore, today Serampore, north of Calcutta, and Tranquebar in the south). By virtue of this colonial empire Denmark played a role, however small, in the Atlantic triangular trade between a European center, the slave-producing West Africa and the sugar-growing West Indies, plus a considerable role in the East Asian trade. The Oldenburg Monarchy "only" ranked number seven in the ranks of those responsible for the Atlantic slave trade. According to the late historian Svend Erik Green Pedersen, at least 85,000 black slaves were exported on Danish (i.e., Danish, Norwegian, and Schleswig-Holsteinian) ships from the Danish fort Christiansborg to the Danish West Indies between 1700 and 1792, when the slave trade (but not slavery as such) was abolished.[7] The multinational character of the realm is demonstrated in the fact that by the end of the eighteenth century the biggest cities of the composite state were Copenhagen in Denmark proper, Altona and Kiel in Holstein, Flensburg in Schleswig and Bergen in Norway, while the seaports of Charlotte Amalie in St. Thomas and Frederiksnagore in India were second and sixth, respectively, as measured by trade volume.

Customs duties on maritime traffic to and from the Baltic through the Øresund contributed significantly to the relatively large revenue of the monarchy. In general, the Oldenburg Empire owed no small part of its strong position to its location at the entrance of the Baltic. In 1420, Erik of Pommern built the fortress Kronborg at Elsinore (Helsingør) and one in Hälsingborg (Kärnan) on the other shore of the sound in order to enforce his command over the traffic. King Frederik II converted the grim fortress into a spectacular Renaissance castle, a castle which was sufficiently well-known in Europe to allow Shakespeare to use it as setting for his famous play *Hamlet* in 1601. For a while, the Oldenburg kings ruled over a loosely organized empire in Northern Europe, formalized in the Kalmar Union which lasted from 1397 to 1523. But even after the dissolution of the Kalmar Union in 1523, the Oldenburg Empire comprised many different provinces, although gradually ruled directly from Copenhagen. The quest for maritime control over the Baltic Sea, in Latin *Dominium Maris Baltici,* in competition with the more centralized Swedish Empire, remained the principal theme in the history of Northern Europe.[8]

The multinational character of the state is further evidenced by the history of its universities. Normally, the university in Aarhus from 1928 is considered Denmark's second. True, Copenhagen University is the oldest Danish university, established by Christian I in 1479. But the second was Kiel University, established in 1665, though its language of instruction was German and founded by Count Christian Albrecht of the

---

[7] Svend Erik Green-Pedersen, "The Scope and Structure of the Danish Negro Slave Trade," *The Scandinavian Economic History Review* 19, no. 2 (1971): 149–97.

[8] Nils Ahnlund, "Dominium Maris Baltici," in *Tradition och historia*, ed. Nils Ahnlund (Stockholm: Almquist & Wicksell, 1956), 114–30.

House of Gottorp, who, although he was a vassal of the Danish king, simultaneously was his competitor and an ally of his Swedish enemy. In the eighteenth century the Gottorp parts of Schleswig and Holstein were incorporated into the Danish monarchy which meant that Kiel became a Danish university, although German speaking. The third university was inaugurated in Christiania (today's Oslo) in 1811 just before the separation of Norway from Denmark; but it did begin its existence as a Danish institution.[9] The fourth university was established in Frederiksnagore (Serampore) in 1821 under the name "College for the Instruction of Asiatic and Other Youth in Eastern Literature and European Science." Its aim was to educate Christian Indian youth in Sanskrit, other Asian languages and European science. Though the university was run in English by British Baptist missionaries, the charter (*oktroy*) was issued by King Frederik VI and kept in the Danish National Archives in Copenhagen.[10] Even after the dissolution of the composite state in 1864, universities using languages other than Danish were founded in different parts of the surviving state, such as the university in Reykjavik (Háskólí Íslands) in 1911, Frodskapasetur Føroya in Tórshavn, Faroe Islands in 1965 and the University of Greenland, Ilisimatusarfik, in Nuuk in 1983 after the establishment of home rule for Greenland in 1979.

A similar history could be written of the multinational Swedish (Vasa) Empire, beginning with the university in Uppsala 1477, a college in Tartu (Dorpat), established by Gustav Adolf in 1632, Åbo Academy in 1640 and Greifswald University, founded in 1456 and Swedish from 1648 to 1815. Thus, the university in Lund from 1668, which is usually considered Sweden's second, is actually the fifth in the line of Swedish universities. Incidentally, it was established with the explicit purpose of influencing the loyalty of the population by educating Swedish-oriented ministers to succeed the Danish priests after the conquest of the provinces that today constitute southern Sweden. In the Catholic Middle Ages, Lund in Skåne (Scania) was the seat of the Danish arch bishop and the ideological center of the Danish Kingdom. When in 1658 the Danish king was forced to cede Skåne, Halland, Blekinge, Bohuslen, Herjedalen, and Gotland to Sweden, the Swedish state immediately established a new university as an alternative to the University of Copenhagen, which previously had been the natural center for the provinces. Øresund, the narrow strait between Denmark and the newly acquired territories Scania, Halland, and Blekinge, became a divide to such an extent that only in the 1820s could Swedes and Danes legally cross the sound. The political logic behind Lund University was to Swedenize the rural population of the conquered provinces, or at least to direct its loyalty away from the Danish crown. This policy was

---

[9] Uffe Østergård, "For konge og fædreland. Universiteterne i den multinationale dansk-norsk-slesvigsk-holstenske Helstat," *Rubicon* 11, no. 2 (2003): 17–41; and Uffe Østergård, *Universiteterne i den dansk-norsk-slesvigsk-holstenske Helstat.* www.cbp.cbs.dk (2007).

[10] Uffe Østergård, "College for the Instruction of Asian and Other Youth in Eastern Literature and European Science in Serampore," in *It began in Copenhagen: Junctions in 300 years of Indian-Danish Relations in Christian Mission*, eds. George Oommen and Hans Raun Iversen (Delhi: Indian Society for Promoting Christian Knowledge, 2005) 204–20.

far more successful than in comparable European states such as Bohemia-Moravia or Alsace, even if today several modern historians rather think the policy ought to be understood as "Scania-nization"—that is, neither Danish nor Swedish but Scanian—than "Swedenization."[11]

The weakening of the Oldenburg Monarchy after the defeat in 1658 led to the introduction of absolutism in 1660, which implied an administrative reorganization or "modernization." At the same time began a geopolitical reorientation towards Schleswig and Holstein in the south, which were now gradually incorporated into the core of the kingdom. This realignment was almost of the same magnitude as the simultaneous transformation of Sweden from an east–west to a north–south axis. The Oldenburg Monarchy was unsuccessful in its attempts to regain the provinces lost to Sweden in the two wars of revenge from 1675–79 and 1709–20. To a degree this loss was compensated through the annexation of the Gottorp parts of Schleswig in 1720 and Holstein in 1773. This incorporation, on the other hand, changed the composition of the empires' population toward domination by German speakers, born within the state as well as outside its borders. In 1720 the Law of Succession of 1665 (*Lex Regia*) was extended to the whole of Schleswig. Administratively, however, Schleswig was to remain ruled together with the royal parts of Holstein, administered by the so-called *Deutsche Kanzlei* (German Chancellery), which in 1523 had moved from Gottorp in Schleswig to Copenhagen at the accession of Frederik I. In 1762, after a major military crisis with the Russian Empire, an agreement with the Gottorp heirs who had married into the Russian ruling dynasty was reached. According to this agreement the Danish king gained unchallenged possession of all of Holstein. The act of incorporation was put into effect in 1773. Thus, the foundations were laid for a great reform process in the various parts of the empire from 1784 to 1814. These reforms were initiated primarily by representatives of the German speaking aristocratic elite within the composite state. This aristocratic elite, however, saw no reason to make any adjustments to the administrative division of the realm, so the Danish speaking parts in Schleswig continued to be administered together with Holstein in German, as promised in 1460.

Even after the loss of the eastern third of the realm in 1658 the composite state was geographically large. The Danish king ruled over lands stretching from the North Cape to Hamburg, a distance equal to that between Hamburg and Sicily, plus the sparsely populated islands in the North Atlantic Ocean. The military, technological, and political backbone of the empire was the fleet, manned to a large extent by fishermen from Norway. This fleet had been big enough to fight the Swedish rival in the Baltic and to protect the extensive possessions for more than 150 years. Even after 1660 the Danish fleet proved capable of inflicting massive losses on Sweden in the Scanian war of 1675–79. Only the superiority of the Swedish land forces and the Swedish success in the battle at Lund on December 3, 1676 enabled Sweden to safeguard the newly conquered territories of what since has been considered southern Sweden.

---

[11] Hanne Sanders, *Efter Roskildefreden 1658. Skånelandskapen och Sverige i krig och fred* (Göteborg: Makadams förlag, 2008).

As mentioned, the Danish response to the defeats was the introduction of absolutism which resulted in a tightly organized state ready for war. The foundations were laid in the 1670s and 1680s, when the absolutist monarchy reformed itself on the pattern of absolutist France under Louis XIV.[12] The all-encompassing bodies of laws, *Danske Lov* of 1683 and *Norske Lov* of 1687, modernized, systematized and made uniform the many varying Medieval provincial laws, introducing government according to modern European standards.[13] A new survey of the productivity of arable land and other natural resources enabled the state to collect taxes on a more efficient basis than before. The central administration was rebuilt on the Swedish-European model of specialized colleges somewhat similar to today's ministries. The administration of the army and navy was the first to be modernized. The next step was a change of the administration of finances which was taken care of in a collegium made up of four nobles and four burghers. That the path to a government career in this way was opened to persons of non-noble birth was something quite new. The old regional administration of state territories in the Danish and German chancelleries, respectively, was incorporated into the college system as "domestic" and "external" administration, and by the end of the seventeenth century the territorial state had gradually been replaced by a tax-based *"Machtstaat."* The modernization implied a heavy influx of German speakers who came to dominate the court and the central administration in Copenhagen. The Oldenburg court in the eighteenth century on the one hand was heavily German in language and culture. On the other hand, as the largest state in Northern Europe until the rise of Prussia, it exercised a considerable cultural influence over Northern Europe, an influence that can be seen in the role of the Royal Academy of Arts from 1754. Many famous artists studied at this academy before they went on to pursue their careers at smaller German courts. The Oldenburg court also served as a channel for cultural impulses from France and Italy in Northern Europe.

The navy was still dominated by Norwegian and Danish speakers, with a core of officers and non-commissioned officers living in the main base of the fleet, Copenhagen. But the army was fundamentally changed as a result of the defeat of the traditional aristocratic army in the seventeenth century. It now mainly consisted of a standing, professional army, recruited among German speakers and stationed in Copenhagen and in the fortress of Rendsburg on the border between Schleswig and Holstein. The officers were primarily recruited among German speaking aristocrats from all over Europe and as a result the language of the army and the officers' academy

---

[12] According to the research by Gunner Lind and others, the structural foundations for these legal innovations actually date back to the wars between 1614 and 1660, the Danish version of the European wide military-political revolution of the 17th century, see Gunner Lind, *Hæren og magten i Danmark 1614–1662* (Odense: Odense University Press, 1994). Whether this is correct or not does not effect the degree of modern centralization which characterized the Oldenborg Empire from the 1680s onwards.

[13] Henrik Horstbøll and Uffe Østergård "Reform and Revolution—The French Revolution and the Case of Denmark," *Scandinavian Journal of History* 15 (1990): 155–79.

was German in most of the eighteenth century.[14] This resulted in a major change of the composition of the population in the capital Copenhagen which now was the by far largest city in the empire.

Language and National Identifications in Copenhagen before 1800

Copenhagen played a particular role in the nation building process in Denmark when the country changed character from a far-stretched, Danish-Norwegian-German-North Atlantic multinational composite state into a small, homogeneous national state. Copenhagen was the capital in the large multinational empire as well as in the subsequent mono-national state, but played different roles in the two. In the multinational empire before 1814, and even until its defeat by Prussia and Austria in 1864, Copenhagen was the administrative and military center of a centrally ruled absolutist state. Though it was by far the largest city in terms of population, other centers such as Bergen in Norway (until 1814), Altona, Kiel, and Flensburg in Schleswig and Holstein (until 1864) and Charlotte Amalie in the Danish West Indies (Danish until 1917) rivaled the capital in importance as harbors and commercial centers.

Copenhagen was founded around 1200 in the High Middle Ages as part of the eastward expansion of the Danish kingdom in the Baltic region. Because of its position in the geographical center of the monarchy the town gradually became the administrative capital of all of the Oldenburg Empire, even though the king and his court still traveled among the king's castles as an itinerant court until the end of the sixteenth century. Helsingør (Elsinore) and Copenhagen rose to economic centers of the Danish state with the introduction of customs on the international traffic through the sound (Øresund) from 1400 (Øresundstold). This became even more the case when the administration of the customs duties was transferred to Copenhagen around 1500. In 1660, as a result of the defeat in the wars with Sweden over the hegemony in Northern Europe, absolutism was introduced and the remaining parts of the state reorganized as a centralized and heavily militarized state with Copenhagen as the undisputed administrative and economic center of the manorialized agrarian economy.[15]

The Lutheran Reformation of 1536 marked the victory of the Schleswig-Holstein branch of the Oldenburg dynasty (Frederik I and his son Christian III) over a merchant backed, "Danish" branch of the Oldenburg dynasty (Christian II) and his supporters in Copenhagen and Malmö on the opposite side of the sound. This victory was symbolized in the move of the so-called German Chancellery (*Tyske Kancelli*)

---

[14] Karsten Skjold Petersen, *Geworbene krigskarle. Hvervede soldater i Danmark 1774–1803* (Copenhagen: Museum Tusculanums Forlag, 2002).

[15] Michael Bregnsbo, "Copenhagen—the Capital of an Empire," in *Danish Towns During Absolutism. Urbanization and Urban Life 1660–1814*, eds. Søren Bitsch Christensen and Jørgen Mikkelsen (Aarhus: Center for Urban History, 2008), 133–52.

from Gottorp in Schleswig to the castle of Copenhagen in 1523 (*Slotsholmen*). From then on, the administration consisted of the so-called Danish and German chancelleries that divided the administration of the monarchy between them. With the absolutist revolution of 1660, Copenhagen became the basis of a standing army of hired soldiers together with Rendsburg in Schleswig. Copenhagen was now situated on the easternmost rim of the state, apart from the island of Bornholm which had stayed Danish after a successful uprising against Swedish occupation in 1659. Because of geography Copenhagen became the base of the navy that was a precondition for holding the far-stretched lands of the multinational state together. The navy had to be based in Copenhagen in order to protect the exposed capital against the arch enemy Sweden and to control the main entrance to the Baltic Sea, *Øresund*. The primary sea route today, *Storebælt* (Great Belt), was only opened by the British fleet and mapped during the war of 1807–14. This peripheral position was slightly inconvenient for the navy's other role, to protect the sailing routes to and from Norway and the remote islands in the North Atlantic Ocean and help protect the merchant commerce that began to spread all over the Atlantic Ocean, the Mediterranean, and even to the Indian Ocean and China.

Thus, Copenhagen in the eighteenth century must be characterized as a military and naval fortress with an absolutist court of some standing—although of course provincial compared with Versailles and other major European courts—built on a small Medieval town. The Royal Academy of Arts from 1754 played an important role in the training of artists, not only from the Scandinavian countries, but also from most of Northern Germany.[16] German in two versions, Low German (*Plattdeutsch*) and High German (*Hochdeutsch*) was spoken at the court and in the army, whereas Danish and Norwegian dominated in the navy's quarters at *Nyholm* and *Nyboder*. For a period, Dutch (*Nederlands*) was spoken by immigrant farmers on the island of Amager in the immediate vicinity of the town who had been invited to grow vegetables for the supply of the expanding court. This was the situation until the nationalist break-up of the state in the nineteenth century with the rise of competing national programs and identifications. Until the 1850s Copenhagen remained a cosmopolitan and multi-lingual town. According to Ole Feldbæk, in 1700 a quarter of the 100,000 inhabitants in Copenhagen were German speakers and Germans could make

---

[16] An exhibition at Hamburger Kunsthalle and Thorvaldsen's Museum in Copenhagen in 2000 pointed to this rather overlooked aspect of German–Danish cultural exchange, cf. *Under samme himmel. Land og by i dansk og tysk kunst 1800–1850* (Copenhagen: Thorvaldsens Museum, 2000). One of the famous German artists who studied at the Royal Academy of Arts in Copenhagen was the Romanticist painter Caspar David Friedrich (1774–1840) from Geifswald, who studied in Copenhagen from 1794 to 1798 under the sculptor Johannes Wiedewelt and the painter Nicolai Abildgaard before he left for Dresden, see in particular: Kasper Monrad, "København—Dresden tur/retur. Friedrich set med danske øjne," *Under samme himmel* (2000): 37–62.

themselves understood even in the early nineteenth century as was enthusiastically reported by many German visitors.[17]

Furthermore, the city was home to many Norwegian speakers and a few
Icelanders and Faroese. These latter have left their imprint on today's city in the
form of the so-called Faroese Ware House (*Færøske Pakhus*) near the political center, *Slotsholmen* and *Nordatlantens Brygge* in Christianshavn on the other side of the
inner harbor. The latter was a warehouse for the products from the North Atlantic
dependencies built in 1766–67, now converted into a cultural center for Greenland,
Iceland, and the Faroe Islands and seat of their political representations in Denmark.
The Norwegians have left only few traces apart from their significant role in the common Danish–Norwegian literary heritage, as the written Norwegian language largely
had become Danish by 1700 (except in southwestern parts of Norway). The founder of modern Danish as a literary language in the first half of the eighteenth century
was a Norwegian from Bergen, Ludvig Holberg (1684–1754). He spoke with a heavy
Norwegian accent and was once arrested on the return from a long travel in Europe
accused of being a Swedish spy. Yet he never thought of changing his Norwegian pro-
nunciation of the common language. As professor at the university in Copenhagen
he was a prolific writer, primarily on history and law. Today Holberg is primarily remembered because of the comedies in the style of Molière and Goldoni he wrote in
the 1720s and 1740s and his essays in moral philosophy (*Moralske Tanker* and *Epistler*).
Through his influential writings he helped change the grammar in Danish (and
Norwegian) away from long sentences influenced by Latin and German into a style
closer to English and French.[18]

In 1800 Copenhagen thus was a peculiar combination of a small Medieval
trading town as revealed by its name, *Køpmanæhafn*[19] and an absolutist administrative
and military center. The court and the central administration long counted for the lion's part of the city's income whereas up to a third of the population was constituted
of professional soldiers mostly recruited in German states. This did not even change
fundamentally in the long period of explosive growth of the overseas trade in the last
half of the eighteenth century which left its imprint on the city in the form of a number of impressive palaces built by successful merchants. The period is remembered in
Danish as the "epoch of the flourishing trade" (den florisante handels epoke) and lasted until 1801, when Britain attacked Copenhagen.

---

[17] Ole Feldbæk, "Clash of Culture in a Conglomerate State: Danes and Germans in 18th Century
Denmark," in *Clashes of Culture*, eds. C. V. Johansen et al. (Odense: Odense University Press,
1992), 80–89; and Uffe Østergård, "Seien Sie herzlich Willkommen in Kopenhagen. Deutsche
Spuren in Kopenhagen," *www.goethe.de/ins/dk Gesellschaft* (2008).

[18] Jens Hougaard, *Ludvig Holberg. The Playwright and his Age up to 1730* (Odense: Odense
University Press) 1993.

[19] *Købmanahafn* or just *Hafn,* in Latin *Hafnia* or *Mercatorum portus* (Saxo Grammaticus, *Gesta
Danorum* around 1200) literally means the merchant's harbor. The name first appeared in a letter
from Pope Urban III in 1186, according to Gunnar Olsen and Kjeld Winding, *Københavns historie* (Copenhagen: J. H. Schultz Forlag, 1941).

National Identifications in the Eighteenth Century

German speaking elites had played an important role in the Oldenburg Empire ever since the civil war and the Reformation in the 1530s, when the Holstein nobility obtained dominant influence at the Danish court under Frederik I and his son Christian II. Their influence diminished somewhat in the first half of the seventeenth century under Christian IV's long rule from 1588 to 1648, but rose again after the losses of the eastern parts of Denmark, today's southern Sweden, and the introduction of absolutism in 1660. A new nobility was created to serve the absolutist king, replacing the traditional nobility whose holdings had been spread all over the Nordic countries. These aristocrats where recruited among rich merchants who had financed the unsuccessful wars, but in particular among lesser nobles and university graduates from northern Germany. When the Scanian War 1675–79 ended without restitution of the lost lands in the east, the monarchy began to incorporate the two duchies Schleswig and Holstein and thus reorient the state toward the south, even though Danes and Norwegians still constituted the overwhelming majority of the population.

The Oldenburg Empire was multilingual. According to Ole Feldbæk's account, the Norwegians spoke a language fairly close to Danish and the language of the church, the schools, the administration, and the courts of justice was Danish. The Same nomads in the far north spoke Lappish. On the Faroe Islands the small population had kept its Old Norse language, but Danish was preached in the church and used by the administration. The Icelanders used Old Icelandic, which was (and still is) close to Old Norse, in their daily life as well as in the church and in administration. In Greenland, missionaries since 1721 preached to the Eskimos in their own language and translated the gospel into what now came to be called Greenlandic. In the two duchies High and Low German dominated, especially in the towns and among Holstein's German speaking nobility, even though the majority of the peasant population in northern Schleswig spoke Danish, albeit a particular dialect, *sønderjysk* (Low Danish), while German was used by the church, in the schools, and by the administration. The population along the North Sea coast until today's border spoke Frisian, a language related to both German and English. As long as language was not considered a vital component of identity, this multilingual situation did not cause any problems. On his birthday the king would receive congratulatory poems not only in Latin and French, but also in Danish, German, Icelandic, and Lappish.[20]

As mentioned, the reorientation of the Oldenburg Empire met with success in 1720 with the incorporation of the Gottorp parts of Schleswig and in 1773 of the Gottorp parts of Holstein. As Holstein in particular was economically and culturally more advanced than the rest of the state and both duchies held a much larger urban population, the reorientation of the state toward the south meant a growing influence

---

[20] Feldbæk, "Clash of Culture," 81.

of German speakers in the rest of the state, Norway included. Furthermore, the crown encouraged the entry of German artists, administrators and skilled workers in order revive the country after the intellectual and economic devastations caused by the wars and occupation of foreign troops, allied as well as enemy, in the seventeenth century. Thus German speakers came to possess considerable influence in the Oldenburg Empire in the eighteenth and early nineteenth century. According to calculations by the British historian William Carr, there were some 3,500 civil servants and 9,000 teachers and church officers in the two duchies Schleswig and Holstein.[21] Most teachers and lower officials in the county districts in Schleswig spoke Danish. But the most important officials, the *Amtman* and his assistants, the pastors and officials, and the intermediate authorities for Schleswig and Holstein in Glückstadt and in Gottorp (the town of Schleswig), were invariably German speakers, even in such Danish speaking counties as Aabenraa and Sønderborg. In Copenhagen around 1800, about 60 Germans from the duchies occupied key positions in the administration, especially in the so-called *Deutsche Kanzlei*, which was responsible for the duchies and most of the foreign policy of the whole state. All in all, between 400 and 450 German officials were employed in Copenhagen.[22] Such was the situation in the empire when an aristocratic, primarily German speaking elite in the late seventeenth century decided to reform the country in order to avoid the problems that were to explode in the French Revolution a few years later.[23]

Enlightened Reforms from the Above and National Reactions

The relatively poor and sparsely populated Oldenburg Empire was characterized by a higher degree of militarization than the affluent and densely populated Central European states.[24] It is, then, rather remarkable that the geographically far-flung and economically overburdened Oldenburg Monarchy succeeded in modernizing itself through a kind of revolution from above at the end of the seventeenth century and once again in the late eighteenth century. The Oldenburg Monarchy underwent a revolution akin to the French through a timely self-reformation in the years 1784–1814. In many respects, this northern European monarchy personified the

---

[21] William Carr, *Schleswig-Holstein 1815–48: A Study in National Conflict* (Manchester: Manchester University Press, 1963), 27.

[22] J. Paulsen, "Tyske embedsmænd i København i Tiden 1800–1840. En oversigt over deres Indflydelse paa Udviklingen af den nationale Modsætning indenfor den danske Helstat," *Sønderjyske Aarbøger* (1936): 48.

[23] Uffe Østergård, "Republican Revolution or Absolutist Reform?" in *The French Revolution of 1789 and Its Impact*, eds. G. M. Schwab and J. R. Jeanneney (Westport, CT: Greenwood Press, 1995), 227–56.

[24] Erling Ladewig Petersen, ed., *Magtstaten i Norden i 1600-tallet og dens sociale konsekvenser* (Odense: Odense University Press, 1984).

ideals of enlightenment thinkers. Thus, from Venice to London the political system of the Danish state was eagerly debated among political observers—though not always in flattering terms, as we know from Montesquieu's criticism of absolutism in Denmark.[25]

Theoretically, the political system was the most autocratic in Europe, even formalized in a kind of absolute "constitution" (*Kongeloven* or *Lex Regia* from 1665). But the political reality was far from despotic, a state the Norwegian historian Jens Arup Seip somewhat paradoxically has termed "absolutism informed by public opinion."[26] This tradition of consulting public opinion is the main reason why the Danish monarchy succeeded in revolutionizing itself from above through a series of relatively continuous reforms of the agrarian system, civil rights, customs, trade, education, and emancipation of the Jews between 1784 and 1814.[27] In contrast, the French king lost legitimacy to the tax-granting assembly of the States General and thus unleashed an uncontrollable democratic revolution, subsequently hailed by much of French history writing as the only meaning of history, despite the enormous cost and the brutal terror it also involved.[28]

Between 1770 and 1772 Johann Friedrich Struensee (1743–81), a German-born physician of the absolutist King Christian VII, tried in vain to revolutionize the whole state of Denmark and Norway by introducing radical reforms from above of the types recommended by enlightened philosophers. Though having practiced in Altona (today a suburb to Hamburg), that is within the borders of the multinational Oldenburg Monarchy, most of his career had taken place outside Denmark and he was thus perceived a foreigner by the majority of the population. His reforms quickly ran into disrepute when he was exposed as the British-born queen's secret lover. When he was arrested and subsequently executed in February 1772, anti-German sentiments among the Danish-speaking middle classes who hoped to profit from the expulsion of the so-called Germans came to the fore. Struensee's sixteen months in power thus marked a turning point in the relations between Danes and Germans. Before Struensee, Germans had been criticized because they were foreigners who occupied positions that rightfully were seen as belonging to Danish. After his aborted revolution they were criticized simply because they were Germans, that is, not Danish.[29] The feelings of the time were summarized in the sentence: "All our troubles are German," which the poet Johannes Ewald (1737–72) let one of his protagonists

---

[25] Franco Venturi, *The End of the Old Regime in Europe, 1768–1776: The First Crisis* (Princeton: Princeton University Press, 1989); and Østergård, "Republican Revolution."

[26] J. A. Seip, "Teorien om det opinionstyrte enevelde," *Historisk Tidssktift* 38 (1958): 397–463; reprint in *Politisk ideologi. Tre lærestykker* (Oslo: Universitetsforlaget, 1988), 13–66.

[27] Østergård, "Republican Revolution."

[28] C. Løfting, H. Horstbøll, and U. Østergård, "Les effets de la révolution française au Danemark," in *L'image de la révolution française vol. I*, ed. M. Vovelle (Oxford: Pergamon Press, 1989), 621–42.

[29] Feldbæk, "Clash of Culture," 87.

utter in the play "Harlekin Patriot eller Den uægte patriotisme" (Harlequin Patriot or the False Patriotism) in 1772.[30]

When the new government led by a commoner—a professor of history from Sorø Academy, Ove Høegh Guldberg (1731–1808)—took over, it immediately made clear that it would tolerate no public debate which could lead to civil disturbances. Because of the informal restrictions of free speech it is difficult to analyze Danish attitudes towards Germans. Struensee had abolished censorship as part of his attempts to introduce enlightened reforms, but instead of producing positive ideas, the new freedom of the press had unleashed an avalanche of pamphlets that in the end contributed to the downfall of the well-intended despot. The new government had learned the lesson and although it did not reintroduce censorship it let it be understood that further debates would harm the careers of those involved. Furthermore, it launched a pronounced "national policy" in the interest of the Danish speaking middle class audience that contributed to the downfall of Struensee. In February, the government let the king ordain that in the future the government should be composed of men "who knew the laws and institutions of the country," that "the administration of Denmark and Norway should be conducted in Danish" and that "Danish should succeed German as the language of command in the army." For the first time since 1660, the council of the king was now composed of men born within the realm, four Danes and a Holsteinian born in the king's part of Holstein. An ordinance of 1775 decreed that "boys should be taught Danish in order to write it fluently and that they should be taught the history of their country and be imbued with love of the fatherland."[31] On top of this, the government in 1776 passed a law reserving government jobs for those born inside the realm, the so-called Indfødsret (Law of Indigenous Rights). Such a law was unique in *ancien régime* Europe. The law was backed by a whole series of well meant—but futile as it turned out—attempts to build a common patriotic feeling in the whole of the realm in general and for the king in particular.[32] Examples of this ideological enterprise were the publication in 1776 of Peter Suhm's *History of Denmark, Norway and Holstein* and Ove Malling's *Lives of Eminent Danes, Norwegians and Holsteinians*, the latter in the tradition of Plutarch from 1777 and meant for teaching in grammar schools (Latinskoler). Whether this program was an expression of Danish nationalism as claimed by Ole Feldbæk in a major investigation of Danish identity,[33] though, is highly debatable. At a closer look, the program involved a deliberate attempt to install a kind of "patriotism from above" intended to unify the three peoples of the realm as

[30] N. F. Christiansen, "Danmark og Tyskland i det 19. århundrede," in *Fjendebileder & fremmedhad*, eds. K. K. Kristiansen and J. R. Rasmussen (Copenhagen: FN-forbundet, 1988), 161–74.
[31] Feldbæk, "Clash of Culture," 88.
[32] Jens Rahbek Rasmussen, "The Danish Monarchy as a Composite State," in *European Identities, Cultural Diversity and Integration in Europe since 1700*, ed. N. A. Sørensen (Odense: Odense University Press, 1995), 28–29.
[33] Ole Feldbæk, ed., *Dansk identitetshistorie vol. I–IV* (Copenhagen: C. A. Reitzels Forlag, 1991–1992).

demonstrated by Tine Damsholt in a convincing analysis of "love of the Fatherland" in this period.[34]

This attempt to roll back the enlightened reforms and substitute them with a "patriotic," anti-German ideology for the whole composite state in its turn provoked a virtual revolution from above led by the young heir to throne, son of the insane King Christian VII, Crown Prince Frederik, who only in 1808, on the death of his father, was crowned King Frederik VI. On April 14, 1784 he carried out a peaceful *coup d'état* in alliance with a group of primarily German speaking aristocrats who had lost influence under the former "patriotic" regime from 1772 to 1784. At the very first meeting of the royal council he attended after having reached the age of sixteen, he persuaded his father Christian to dismiss the prior cabinet and grant himself the reins of government. The former ministers were caught completely off guard and put up no resistance. The young prince was not well prepared for this task, but had the good luck of an extremely gifted group of advisers. They were headed by the minister of foreign affairs (the German Chancellery), count Andreas Peter Bernstorff (1735–97) and the minister of finance and trade, Count Ernst Schimmelmann (1747–1831). Both men followed illustrious German born predecessors bearing the same family names, an uncle and a father respectively. They were joined by the influential aristocrat Count Christian Ditlev Reventlow (1748–1827) who had influential relatives in Holstein and the Norwegian lawyer Christian Colbiørnsen (1749–1814).

With the exception of Colbiørnsen these were all noble landowners, among the biggest in the country. Yet they immediately set off to follow up earlier endeavors of agricultural reform, which had been discussed in learned journals from 1757 onwards. Andreas Peter Bernstorff, together with Christian Ditlev Reventlow, from 1786 chaired the Great Land Commission, with Colbiørnsen as secretary. The commission worked with unprecedented speed and immediately effectuated a series of measures which eventually granted the Danish peasant as much personal freedom as his English counterpart, but better protection against economic exploitation and thus laying the foundation for the social rise of the peasant farmers in the nineteenth century.[35] First, in 1786 and 1787, landlords were deprived of their right to impose degrading punishments on their tenants such as riding the "wooden horse," and tenants were granted the right to economic compensation for improvements they had made if they were evicted from their plots. In 1788 the Danish equivalent of serfdom, the so-called Stavnsbånd, was abolished. Literally the "Stavnsbånd" means adscription. It was a peculiar form of servitude enforced by the state on tenant peasants that had come into existence as late as 1733 in order to secure soldiers for the army. Serfdom in the East-Elbian sense never made it further north than Holstein, but the "Stavnsbånd" came close. It was to be terminated in stages which would leave all peasants completely free

---

[34] Tine Damsholt, *Fædrelandskærlighed og borgerdyd* (Copenhagen: Museum Tusculanums Forlag, 2000).

[35] Claus Bjørn, "The Peasantry and Agrarian Reform in Denmark," *Scandinavian Economic History Review* 25 (1977): 117–37.

by 1800. But 1788 was from the beginning seen as the point of no return for agrarian reforms in particular and the whole complex of reforms in general. Lately, the degree of servitude under the "Stavnsbånd" has been questioned by Danish historians, and the intention of the legislation seems primarily to have been to secure peasant recruits for the army which again relied on adscription of peasants from the Danish core lands.[36] Yet, the abolition of the "Stavnsbånd" and the many other reforms then and later took on a symbolic importance which was to have an enormous political impact on the subsequent development of Danish society and the peculiar form of nation building based on the production and political culture of peasant farmers that characterized the rump state after 1870.

The Agrarian reforms of 1784–88 and 1793–96 were followed by a thorough overhaul of the legal system in the spirit of the Italian legal theorist Cesare di Beccaria (1738–94), bearing the unmistakable imprint of Christian Colbiørnsen. Legal processes were rationalized and prison conditions improved. A regular system of poor relief was instituted, financed by compulsory contributions from the peasants under the supervision of the priests in their capacity as local representatives of the state—the king was head of the church in this Lutheran country since the Reformation in 1536. The system worked relatively well until the middle of the nineteenth century when peasant farmers, as a result of the democratization, took over local government themselves and subsequently cut down on poor relief. A liberal tariff abolishing many import prohibitions was introduced in 1797 and the corn trade was liberalized. In 1792, Ernst Schimmelmann took steps to end the slave trade in the Danish West Indies—the first country in the world to do so. However, he failed to abolish slavery itself on these islands because of intransigent resistance among the planters and fear of lost revenue. He also presided over a commission which in 1789 proposed the introduction of universal free elementary schooling for all children between seven and fourteen, a measure to be enacted in the so-called Great School Law of 1814 in the midst of military defeat and economic catastrophe. Likewise, Jews were emancipated in 1798 with full rights to marry Christians and enter secondary schools.

The whole reform program was accomplished in an atmosphere of almost unlimited free debate, as censorship was banned in the period between 1770 and 1799. In the wake of the coup of 1784, freedom of the press was encouraged and the abolishment of censorship was put into law in 1790. The agents of these reforms were some of the most influential nobles in the double monarchy. They did not act on an impulse of pure idealism, although the noble landowner Reventlow, for one, like the American republican Thomas Jefferson, left office poorer than he entered. They were sufficiently far-sighted to give up untenable political prerogatives of their class and gamble on future economic gains. The majority of the owners of large estates were to profit from this policy in the nineteenth century as the initiators were sufficiently

---

[36] Jens Holmgaard, *Uden at landet besværes. Studier over Frederik IV's landmilits med henblik på spørgsmålet om bøndernes vilkår i øvrigt* (Viborg: Udgiverselskabet ved Landsarkivet for Nørrejylland, 1999).

well off to be able to risk the gamble. This was not the case for many of the smaller estate holders, especially in the peninsula of Jutland. In the summer of 1790, 103 of the greatest proprietors rebelled. Somewhat confusingly this rebellion took the form of a so-called Address of Confidence to the crown prince at the occasion of his betrothal to a German princess. The landowners protested against the newly proposed civil reforms and drew attention to the rising "insubordinance of the peasants encouraged by the French example." The latter was the real meat of the problem—noble anxiety over the rising expectations among the liberated peasants triggered off a reaction which has gone down in history under the name of the "Revolt of the Proprietors of Jutland."[37] The outcome, however, was to contrast completely with the noble protest in France two years earlier.

The reform ministry reacted swiftly and with determination to the challenge. Christian Colbiørnsen, besides serving as secretary of the Great Agrarian Commission in 1788, had also been appointed procurator general and legal porte-parole of the regime. In this capacity he published the address and a detailed refutation in October 1790. He stressed the privileges of the grand holders of estates and denounced the signatories and their motives publicly. This offence forced the main instigator of the protest, a German noble by the name of Lüttichau to sue Colbiørnsen privately in order to protect his honor. Thus, the ministry cleverly succeeded in maneuvering the revolt into the courtroom while mobilizing the predominantly non-noble "public opinion" of the capital to support its cause. Lüttichau was completely isolated as the signatories in the following months one by one withdrew their signatures or even denied that they ever signed. When the verdict in Colbiørnsen's favor was pronounced on April 7, 1791, Lüttichau was finished as was the Danish revolt of the nobles. He sold his manors and moved to Braunschweig in Germany while the reforms of the Oldenburg Empire continued as planned.

Even though the resistance against the reforms failed, the leading German speaking noble families, the Bernstorffs, the Schimmelmanns, the Reventlows, and the prince regent's brother-in-law, duke Friedrich Christian of Augustenborg (from the island Als in Schleswig), came under heavy attacks. In pamphlets they were accused of misleading the young prince regent, for conducting a policy harmful to "Danish" interests and for illicitly enriching themselves. The spiteful and even hateful anti-German tone which had characterized the opposition against Struensee now returned. And in 1789 the growing tension between Danes and Germans exploded into an open national confrontation, the so-called German Feud (*Tyskerfejden*) over the predominance of German speakers in public affairs. The origins of the public debate was rather insignificant, the premiere of an opera at the Royal Theatre in Copenhagen March 31, 1789. The opera, *Holger Danske,* was built over a figure from ancient Danish mythology dating back to the Medieval epic of Roland. The composer was German—F. L. Aemilius Kunzen—but the libretto was written by the Danish writer Jens Baggesen

---

[37] Claus Bjørn, "Den jyske Proprietærfejde," *Historie* XIII (1979): 1–70.

(1764–1824), a cosmopolitan European who wrote in both German and Danish (which is why only half of his writings are acknowledged as belonging to "Danish" literature today). Beginning as a debate over opera and literature, the polemic quickly spilled over to national antagonisms and differences between everything German and Danish. The debate touched upon many of the themes that came to characterize the confrontations between Danes and Germans over the next seventy years, reflecting a Danish inferiority complex against the larger culture to the south.[38] This was bad enough, but when the minister of trade and finance, count Ernst Schimmelmann, let himself be provoked into taking up the challenge, the affair became politically important.

In an anonymous pamphlet he accused Danes of cultural mediocrity and of placing narrow personal interests before common humanity. Through his intervention the debate spilled over from aesthetics to politics and became potentially dangerous for the multinational state. In the subsequent heated debate, resentment against the German speaking Holsteinians surfaced. Some Danish pamphleteers even went as far as suggesting that if Holsteinians should have any posts in the state it should be in Holstein, not in Denmark proper. And the national confrontation went both ways. The leading German participant, count Andreas Peter Bernstorff had already in 1776 been unwilling to see why his royal master should prefer lesser qualified servants simply because they were born in the state. Now in 1789–90 the German speaking elite saw the attacks on them as directed against both law and (enlightened) reason. It was unlawful because the criticism violated the Law of Indigenous Rights, and against reason because it was "neither expedient nor right that they should give up their superior language and culture in order to serve a king who was theirs as well as the Danes.'"[39] The debate eventually died out, overshadowed by the demonstrations of loyalty toward the young the crown prince at the occasion of his marriage. But the debate had revealed dangerous tensions and beginning national identifications that eventually broke through in the 1830s and split the Oldenburg Empire into two national groups who fought a civil war over the province of Schleswig.

Before that, however, the empire had already lost a third of its territory and population as a result of defeat in the Napoleonic Wars, where Frederik VI allied himself with the losers after the British attack on Copenhagen in 1807. In order to keep his empire together and be able to supply Norway with grain from Jutland—the geopolitical *raison d'être* of the empire—he entered a coalition with Napoleon and thus prevented him from occupying Jutland. Frederik remained loyal to the bitter end and lost Norway to Sweden under a new—French—king, Carl XIV Johan, formerly known as Jean-Baptiste Bernadotte, at the peace treaty in Kiel 1814. Before that, however, the Norwegians under the Danish viceroy—the later Christian VIII—had proclaimed their independence and produced one of the most liberal constitutions

---

[38] Ole Feldbæk and Vibeke Winge, "Tyskerfejden 1789–1790. Den første nationale konfrontation," in *Dansk identitetshistorie vol. II*, ed. Ole Feldbæk (Copenhagen: C. A. Reitzels Forlag, 1991), 9–109.

[39] Feldbæk, "Clash of Culture," 91.

since the American at Eidvoll in 1814. Only an armed intervention by the battle hard-ened Swedish army forced the Norwegians to relinquish independence and join into a union with Sweden. The union was of two separate kingdoms, who only shared the king, foreign policy, and a small common army while the Norwegians were able to keep their treasured free constitution.

Norway in the Oldenburg Empire

The deeper social, economic, and national reasons for the separation of Norway from Denmark in 1814, after the Danish defeat in the Napoleonic Wars, have only recently come into focus for Scandinavian historians. Norwegian historians have mainly con-centrated on the history of independent Norway in union with Sweden after 1814, whereas the majority of Danish historians have ignored the common history lead-ing up to the separation altogether, until the publication in 1997–98 of a history of Norway and Denmark from 1380 to 1814 in four volumes. In particular, the volume on the period 1720–1814 by Ole Feldbæk broke new territory in studying the Norwegian movement through a university in Christiania (Oslo).[40] Most recently a young Danish historian, Rasmus Glenthøj, has investigated the formulation of separate national pro-grams among the bourgeois elites in the two countries between 1807 and 1830 and the development of an independent Norwegian national identity before and after the separation from Denmark in 1814 and the writing of the constitution in Eidsvoll the same year.[41] Much more research will see the light in 2014 as a series of conferences and research projects are planned to celebrate the bi-centennial of the Norwegian constitution. Glenthøj's result is that some Norwegian merchants and civil servants had begun to cultivate a common Norse (Nordic) history as part of the Oldenburg patriotic supranational identity which they shared with their Danish—and to a degree Schleswig-Holsteinian—fellows since the introduction of the program of patriotism from above for the whole of the empire. Whether this program could be reconciled with the broader patriotic ideology for the whole state was never put to test because of the isolation of Norway from Denmark during the war with Great Britain and the sudden break in 1814 following the Swedish conquest of Norway. A small debate on differences between Danes and Norwegians and Danish so-called exploitation during the four hundred years of the Oldenburg Empire continued, but was soon overtaken by confrontations with the king of Sweden within the union of the two kingdoms.[42]

---

[40] Ole Feldbæk, *Nærhed og adskillelses 1720–1814. Danmark-Norge 1380–1814 vol. IV* (Oslo: Universitetsforlaget, 1998).

[41] Rasmus Glenthøj, *Skilsmissen. Dansk og norsk identitet før og efter 1814* (Odense: Syddansk Universitetsforlag, 2012).

[42] Uffe Østergård, "Union, Federation or 'merely' European Cooperation: Norden as a Result of 1814," *Baltic World* (March 2013): 46–51.

The war with Great Britain 1807–14 caused an economic and political up-heaval which opened up the formulation for new national ideas from urban elites in France, the German states, and across Europe. In Norway this development looked back to the proud history of the country in the High Middle Ages when the Norwegian monarchy before the Black Death and the agrarian crisis of the Late Middle Ages was one of the strongest and most centralized states in Medieval Europe. Language, culture, and history was studied in much detail in order to back up a national identification which could set Norway apart from Sweden and Denmark. Prior to 1814, the Danish elite tended to downplay differences between Danish and Norwegian nationality in favor of a common Danish-Nordic identity contrasted with a concept of German culture—with or without Holstein and Schleswig—as witnessed in the heated debates in 1789–90.

Some Norwegian patriots, however, had already before 1807 come to believe that the close cultural community between Denmark and Norway would threaten a separate and "authentic" Norwegian identity. According to Glenthøj, some members of the Norwegian elite who were trained at the university in Copenhagen developed a complex double concept of fatherland, distinguishing between the fatherland as their state, that is, the Oldenburg Monarchy, and their "natural" fatherland or homeland, Norway. This led to a split in Norwegian nationalism between the "Danish-minded" who constructed their reborn Norwegian culture in the image of the former Danish-Norwegian state, culture, and language, and the so-called Swedish-minded who tried to create a national culture in contrast to the former state, seeking their inspiration in a "true" and "independent" Norwegian past. The most striking example of this latter tendency was the writer Henrik Wergeland (1808–45) who fought against what he called "Danomania." Danish intellectuals actively fought against this attempt to separate Danish and Norwegian culture and history from each other, but often only succeeded in alienating Norwegians even more. This cultural war continued in the nineteenth century as a conflict over which language was the "real" Norwegian language. Norwegian nationalists attempted to create a "true" Norwegian language on the basis of dialects spoken in the isolated southwestern parts of the country while the rest kept to their Danish inspired language. This struggle has not yet been resolved and has resulted in the existence of two official Norwegian languages today, the so-called *bokmål*, which is close to Danish and spoken by more than 80% of the population, and the so-called *nynorsk* (new Norwegian), which is preferred by 17% as their written language.

Danes, on the other hand, did not seem to have the same need to distinguish between the concept of state and nation, at least not when confronted with Norwegians. Their fatherland (nation) and their state bore the same name, Denmark (which is why I have attempted to separate the two by introducing the denomination "Oldenburg Empire" in my analysis). In confrontations with German speakers in Denmark and Schleswig and Holstein, the situation was different. This Danish double speak was brought out in the open in 1845 in an interesting booklet by a young Danish linguist and ethnologist Svend Grundtvig (1824–83), son of the influential priest Nikolaj Severin Grundtvig, on the linguistic situation in the Faroe Islands. In the booklet—*Dansken paa Færøerne. Sidestykke til Tysken i Slesvig* ("Danish in the Faroe Islands—a parallel to German in Schleswig")—Svend Grundtvig compared the oppressive role of Danish against the Faroese language (which was close to Old Norse) to German versus Danish in North Schleswig. His argument was that it was untenable to deplore the oppression of Danish in Schleswig by the German language and at the same time ignore the oppressive role of Danish in the Faroe Islands. This book has been utterly ignored in Danish debates, but has played an important role in Faroese intellectual and political circles.[43]

The Treaty of Kiel of 1814 separated two peoples who had a shared history and state for more than 400 years. As a result, the notion of a Danish national identity as different from the common Nordic identity was propagated under the heading of "Scandinavianism" and strengthened at the expense of the former state sponsored *Helstats*-patriotism. Both elites began to look back to different versions of the culture and history of the High Middle Ages. The elite in the young Norwegian nation-state displayed a strong need for national recognition by other states and thus embarked on an extensive construction of national symbols. In Denmark, Frederik VI did his best to make Danes "forget" Norway. The reason was that the loss constituted a personal trauma for him, but also that a Norway with the most liberal constitution in Europe represented a fundamental challenge to his own absolutist rule. Among Danish intellectuals, the loss of Norway led to a growing interest in the duchy of Schleswig, becoming a battleground between Danish, German, and regional identifications.[44] As a result Holstein came to be seen by Danes as a foreign element in the state instead of "Danish Holstein" which had been the dominant denomination for the two duchies in the eighteenth century. Until the rise of national tensions in the 1830s, Holstein in

---

[43] Although largely ignored in Denmark this pamphlet and political actions by Faroese representatives led to the resurrection of the Faroese language in the 1880s. Under the slogan: "Nú er tann stundin komin til hand" (Now is the time to act), the Faroese newspaper *Dimmalætting* (December 22, 1888) informed its readers that on the afternoon of December 26, 1888 a public meeting would be held in the Parliament House (*Tinghuset*) in Tórshavn, the tiny capital of a far away North Atlantic periphery of the anyway very small Danish state. The topic of the meeting was to discuss ways "to defend Faroes' language and the Faroes' customs." Despite weather so wet and windy that people from outside Tórshavn could not participate, many came and thus originated the modern Faroese nation. Its program has proven successful in shaping an independent Faroese intellectual, political, and economic life. After a protracted and somewhat tumultuous political and cultural struggle, the Faroe Islands acquired home rule in 1948 within the loosely organized Danish realm. The extent of Faroese autonomy today is best demonstrated by the fact that the Faroese opted not to join the European Community together with the rest of Denmark in 1973 and still today does not belong to the European Union. See: Uffe Østergård, "Der Aufbau einer fäöischen Identität. Nordisch, norwegisch, dänisch—oder färöisch?" and "Der Staat Dänemark—Territorium und Nation," *Tjaldur. Mitteilungsblatt des Deutsch-Färöischen Freundeskreises e.v.—Týskt-Føroyskt Vinafelag*, nr. 33–34 (2005): 73–103 (English version: *www.cbs.dbp.dk*).

[44] Østergård, "Schleswig and Holstein," n. 1.

German literature was depicted as a "Nordic" country because of its centuries old affiliation with the Danish kingdom, albeit German speaking.[45]

Intellectual Preparations for the National Break-up of the Oldenburg Monarchy

Around 1800, the Danish king, despite losses in the seventeenth century, still ruled over a vast though thinly populated realm, stretching from Greenland, Iceland, and Norway to the suburbs of Hamburg, encompassing half of Europe's Atlantic coastline. According to a reliable census of 1801, the total population of the kingdom was 2.5 million. Denmark and Norway had 1.8 million inhabitants, 51% of which lived in Denmark proper; Schleswig and Holstein had 600,000 inhabitants, of which 54% lived in Holstein. Other German possessions counted for some 90,000 people and the North Atlantic islands some 50,000.[46] No reliable censuses for the colonies exist as their status was different. The loss of Norway in 1814 after the Danish defeat by the United Kingdom and Sweden in the Napoleonic Wars completely altered the balance between German and Nordic elements in the composite state. The number of German speakers rose from less than 20% to 35% and nationalist sentiments soon began to tear the state apart. In 1806, the Duchy of Holstein was annexed to Denmark as a consequence of the disintegration of the Holy Roman Empire. However, with the establishment of the German Confederation in 1815, Holstein was reestablished as an independent duchy, which implied that the Danish king participated in the German Federal Assembly in his capacity as Duke of Holstein. As was the case with the Habsburg Empire, the multinational state soon was to be torn apart by two antagonistic, national programs, a "Danish" (either a Danish-Danish or a Scandinavianist, that is Danish-Swedish, variant[47]) and a "German" (either a Schleswig-Holsteinian or a pan-German variant). The main proponents of these two programs were the academic elites in the two cities with a university, Copenhagen and Kiel.[48]

Until 1814 the three major linguistic and national groups in the multinational state had balanced each other. The influence of the economically more advanced German speaking parts was balanced by the much larger number of Danish and Norwegian speakers, roughly two thirds. Whether these three groups and the other

[45] Steen Bo Frandsen, *Holsten i Helstaten. Hertugdømmet inden for og uden for de danske monarki i første halvdel af 1800-tallet* (Copenhagen: Museum Tusculanum Press, 2008).
[46] Rasmussen, "The Danish Monarchy," 25.
[47] This relationship and the interpretation of the political implications of Scandinavianism is described in Uffe Østergård, "The Geopolitics of 'Norden'—From Composite States to Nation-states," in *The Cultural Construction of Norden*, eds. Øystein Sørensen and Bo Stråth (Oslo: Scandinavian University Press, 1997), 25–71; and Østergård, "Union, Federation."
[48] Frandsen, *Holsten i Helstaten*; and Hans Schultz Hansen, "Nationalitetskamp og modernisering 1815–1918," in *Sønderjyllands historie vol. 2, Efter 1815* (Aabenraa: Historisk samfund for Sønderjylland, 2009), 11–240.

small peoples such as the Icelanders and Faroese perceived of themselves as nations and not just people with different languages under the same ruler is debated among contemporary historians. As almost all intellectuals, primarily priests, had been trained at the University in Copenhagen they had a shared language and outlook on the world. It was only later in the nineteenth century that proper national identifications developed and national programs were drawn up by nationalized intellectuals. The only exception to this general lack of nationalist identifications was the antagonism between Danish and German speakers since 1814. The reason for that was primarily due to the influence of the rising German nationalism which was channeled into the Oldenburg Empire through Kiel University in Holstein.

One of the results of the final settlement between the Romanov rulers and the Oldenburg Monarchy was the survival of the university in Kiel.[49] The exchange of property with the Russian rulers meant that Christian VII obtained the Gottorp parts of Holstein in return for Lauenburg-Delmenhorst. At the same time, he pledged not only to respect the privileges of the university but also to uphold the so-called *biennium*, that is, the requirement that students from the Duchies had to study for two years in Kiel as a condition for jobs in Schleswig and Holstein.[50] This was a reversal of his grandfather's policy from 1743. Thus, the university in Kiel was saved from closing due to lack of students which otherwise had been an imminent threat. This decision was to have far-reaching consequences for the relationship between Denmark and the Duchies. Interestingly, simultaneously with this concession to the regionalists in Schleswig and Holstein, a request to establish a university in Norway was dismissed by the king.[51] The 1773 agreement calmed the atmosphere in the Oldenburg Monarchy—at least for a while. Now the state had two universities plus the aristocratic academy in Sorø which after a glorious opening soon fell behind. The universities in Copenhagen and Kiel witnessed very different developments even though both were given the task of training state officials after the introduction of the earlier mentioned Law of Indigenous Rights in 1776, whereby positions within the state administration were reserved for residents born within the borders of the realm. As a result of this law, the crown could no longer import its officials from abroad as had been the case in past centuries, but had to train their own. Copenhagen University was given a new charter in a great hurry, but nevertheless remained a rather mediocre institution,

---

[49] Christian-Albrechts-Universität zu Kiel was founded in 1665 by the duke of Gottorp as part of his attempts to establish the small duchy as an independent state in alliance with Sweden. As this attempt failed with the defeat of Sweden by Russia in 1720, the Danish king was 'returned to his rights' in Schleswig and Holstein. One result of this was that the small German university became an institution for training civil servants to the German speaking parts of the multinational Danish Oldenburg Monarchy, in other words a German language, "Danish" university between 1720 and 1848/64, cf. Feldbæk, "Clash of Cultures"; and Østergård, "For konge og fædreland," 2003.

[50] Feldbæk, "Clash of Cultures."

[51] Ibid.

concentrating on administrative and theological studies during the revolutionary years in the 1790s and the Napoleonic Wars.

Kiel University, on the other hand, thrived and gained a reputation for excellence within the German speaking parts of Europe. The number of students began to grow after 1768 as a result of the *biennium,* and in the 1770s the number of recently matriculated students stabilized between 50 and 60, compared to the eight in 1767 when the university hit its lowest point. In the 1780s, Kiel became a cultural center with the establishment of the monarchy's first college of education for teachers in 1781 and a "Patriotic Circle" in 1786. The hiring of a range of highly qualified younger professors within a short time turned Kiel University into one of the most modern in the German speaking area, a position it managed to keep until the late nineteenth century. The Chancellery for German Affairs in Copenhagen (*Deutsche Kanzlei*), which was responsible for German foreign policy plus Schleswig and Holstein, watched the young university closely. The same was the case among the politically and culturally conservative aristocracy in Holstein. After 1789, the nobles were wary of any signs of sympathy for the French Revolution. When a professor and fervent admirer of the revolution, C. F. Cramer, praised one of the Girondists, Jérome Pétion (who later voted for the execution of Louis XVI) in a public lecture, he was not only fired but exiled from Kiel. After the death of the moderate president of the chancellery, Andreas Peter Bernstorff, in 1797, controls were tightened further.[52] These attempts peaked in 1806 with the incorporation of Holstein into the Oldenburg Empire after the dissolution of the Holy Roman Empire.

The incorporation of Holstein and the attempt to centralize the Oldenburg Empire failed as a result of the political turmoil in Europe in the wake of the Napoleonic Wars. Historians in Denmark as well as Germany have pretty much agreed that this result was logical as well as beneficial. It became a dogma that multinational states were unviable and had to be divided into their respective national parts. And the dogma about "the right of a nation to self-determination," still today remains a fundamental doctrine in spite of all the logical inconsistencies and political misfortunes it has led to. Yet it is still an open question whether the result was a foregone conclusion. It is correct that a similar reform in the multinational Habsburg Empire under Joseph II between 1780 and 1790 failed because it was perceived as a Germanization among the non-German speaking peoples of the empire. Nevertheless the realm survived for a long time and even though many today regard the dissolution of the Habsburg Empire in 1918 as a necessity, the many shortcomings of the successor states have led to doubts.[53] Furthermore, for a while at least, a sense of "British" identity actually came into existence in Great Britain in the eighteenth and nineteenth century, an identification that still plays a role in the United Kingdom despite "devolution" and independence for Wales, Scotland and Northern Ireland.[54] In Spain, too, a common Spanish identity undeniably developed after 1714, even though it still competes fervently with

---

[52] Ibid.

[53] Uffe Østergård, *Europas ansigter* (Copenhagen: Rosinante, 1992), 213–68.

[54] Linda Colley, *Britons: Forging the Nation 1707–1837* (New Haven: Yale University Press, 1992).

especially Catalan and Basque identities.[55] In this light, the attempts between 1776 and the 1850s to reach a federal status for Schleswig and maybe even Holstein within a multilinguistic, multinational Oldenburg Empire were perhaps not as hopeless as they may seem through today's anachronistic hindsight.

The "Schleswig-Holstein question" played an important and instrumental role in Danish nation-building—not to speak of bringing a united Germany into existence.[56] Kiel University took a leading role in the process of nationalization. Even though it was under Danish sovereignty, Kiel University was able to attract a surprising number of talented German scholars, especially historians. Among the best known were Friedrich Christoph Dahlmann (1785–1860), who taught in Kiel from 1812 to 1829 and Johann Gustav Droysen (1808–84), who taught in Kiel from 1840 to 1851. Furthermore the historians of Ancient Rome, Barthold Georg Niebuhr (1776–1831) and Theodor Mommsen (1817–1903), grew up in Holstein and studied at Kiel University, even though its teaching apparently did not leave important impressions on either.

Niebuhr, one of the founders of modern critical historical research, was a typical child of the Enlightenment in the pre-national Oldenburg Empire. Son of Danish civil servant and explorer of the Near Middle East, Carsten Niebuhr (1733–1815), he was born in Copenhagen but grew up in Meldorf, Dithmarschen in Holstein.[57] After wide ranging studies in Kiel he got a Danish scholarship to study in England and Scotland where he concentrated on agriculture and mathematics. In 1800, he entered the Danish civil service in Copenhagen and eventually rose to director of the Danish National Bank. While working at the bank he published his first studies of Roman agriculture in 1803 and 1806. He continued his studies of Roman history in Berlin at the age of 35 after having joined the Prussian civil service allied with the reformers around Freiherr von Stein. Niebuhr represented the best of the pre-nationalist period, when

---

[55] *Er Spanien anderledes? Den Jyske Historiker* (2001), 91–92.

[56] Uffe Østergård, "Dänemark und Deutschland als europäische Nachbarn—Geschichte und Erinnerung," in *50 Jahre Goethe-Institut Dänemark*, eds. Susanne Fabrin and Matthias Müller-Wieferig (Copenhagen: Goethe-Institut, 2011), 219–24.

[57] In Medieval times the marshland villages of Dithmarschen in the western parts of Holstein enjoyed remarkable autonomy. In the 15th century they confederated in a peasants' republic. Several times the kings of Denmark and the dukes in Holstein without success tried to subdue the independent peasant state. In 1500, the greatest of these battles took place at Hemmingstedt, where the outnumbered peasants defeated the army of Holstein and the Danish king. Only in 1559 were the peasants forced to give up their autonomy after the successful invasion of Count Johan Rantzau from Steinburg, one of the best strategists of the time. Since then, the coat of arms of Dithmarschen has shown a warrior on horseback, representing Rantzau as a knight. This knight has been identified with St. Georg, the patron of Dithmarschen. The conquerors—King Frederik II, Duke Adolf, and Duke Johann II—divided Dithmarschen into two parts: the south became part of Holstein in personal union with Denmark, while the north came into the possession of the other Duke of Holstein. From 1773, all of Holstein was united in personal union with Denmark and remained so until 1864, when Schleswig and Holstein were annexed by the Kingdom of Prussia as the Province of Schleswig-Holstein. For more see: Ulrich Lange, ed., *Geschichte Schleswig-Holsteins* (Neumünster: Wachholtz Verlag, 1996).

the elites moved from one country to another, feeling at home wherever they felt use-ful. Contrary to other eminent historians from the same region, it is not possible to detect any anti-Danish feelings in his writings, nor was he engaged in the indepen-dence movement for Schleswig and Holstein.[58]

Mommsen and Droysen, on the contrary, were politically extremely active in the movement for an independent that is, German, Schleswig-Holstein state and wrote pamphlets against the Danish cause in favor of unification with a united and liberal Germany. Especially Theodor Mommsen—together with his contemporary Karl Marx and many other German republican liberals at the time—hated everything Danish. They saw Denmark as an autocratic and backward peasant state that imped-ed liberal progress and the unification of all German speakers. Mommsen, the ardent republican and anti-Dane, is reported to have answered the question of a Danish col-league—the Classical philologist and politician Johan Nicolai Madvig (1804–86)—when he would finish the fourth volume of his famous *Römische Geschichte* on the period of Caesars, with the biting sentence: "Dass kann Jedermann schreiben, dass können Sie schreiben" [that everybody can do, even you]. In 1847, having just returned from research in Italy, Mommsen as a writer with a sharp pen joined the political bat-tle with a series of articles in the *Schleswig-Holsteinische Zeitung* in order to further the case of a united Germany. This effort has earned him the characterization, *"journalis-tischer Schlachtenbummler"* [journalistic bully].[59]

Johann Gustav Droysen was born in 1808, two years after Napoleon's victory over Prussia at Jena and nine years before Mommsen was born. After being called to the chair of history in Kiel in 1840 from Berlin, where he had specialized in Greek history and literature, he changed his area of research and teaching to contemporary German history. In 1842–43 he lectured on the era of the German wars of liberation in the early nineteenth century which he revised and published as a book in 1846. In the preface, Droysen declared, "Our youth no longer believes in the deeds of prowess and the enthusiasm of that age. My object is to express and justify the love of and belief in the fatherland."[60] In 1843, on the occasion of the thousand year jubilee of the Treaty of Verdun in 843, Droysen gave a public lecture on the continuity of German histo-ry in general and Schleswig-Holstein's German character in particular. Its effects can be compared to those of Dahlmann's Waterloo lecture in 1814 (see later). When the Danish king tried to tighten the Danish hold on the duchies in the 1840s, Droysen is-sued a pamphlet urging the king not to sever the ties with Germany. In 1848, Droysen was elected member of the parliament in Paulskirche in Frankfurt by the provisional government in Kiel. Here he proclaimed "that all Germans should rally round Prussia as the vacant place of the House of Hohenstaufen now with history's right belonged to

[58] Karl Christ, "Barthold Georg Niebuhr," in *Deutsche Historiker vol. VI*, ed. H. U. Wehler (Göttingen: Vandenhoeck & Ruprecht, 1980), 23–36.

[59] Albert Wucher, "Theodor Mommsen," in *Deutsche Historiker vol. IV*, ed. H. U. Wehler (Göttingen: Vandenhoeck & Ruprecht, 1972), 18.

[60] G. P. Gooch, *History and Historians in the Nineteenth Century* (London: Longmans, 1952), 126.

the Prussian House of Hohenzollern."[61] As a determined supporter of Prussian ascendancy he was one of the first members to retire from the assembly after King Friedrich Wilhelm IV did not accept the imperial crown in 1849.

In the following two years of civil war over Schleswig, Droysen continued to support the cause of the duchies. In 1850, with his colleague at Kiel University, the lawyer and politician Karl Samwer (1819–82), he published a history of the relations between Denmark and Schleswig-Holstein[62] seen from the point of view of the pretender to the throne as duke of Schleswig and Holstein: *Die Herzogthümer Schleswig-Holstein und das Königreich Dänemark seit dem Jahre 1806*. An English translation was published in London in the same year under the title *The Policy of Denmark towards the Duchies of Schleswig-Holstein*. The work was of great political importance and heavily persuaded the German public opinion of the rights of the duchies in their struggle with Denmark. Because of that, the conservative Danish historian, Caspar Paludan-Müller (1805–82), later the same year published a refutation of Droysen and Samwer's pamphlet in another pamphlet, *Bidrag til en Kritik over Droysens og Samwers saakaldte aktmæssige Fremstilling af den danske Politik siden Aar 1806*. Paludan tried to discard their arguments in favor of the claims of the family of Augustenburg (in Danish Augustenborg)[63] to rule in both Holstein and Schleswig. In 1851, when Holstein

---

[61] Ibid., 126.

[62] In German literature, Schleswig-Holstein is traditionally spelled with a hyphen to indicate the unity of the two historic provinces since 1460, whereas the Danish usage is to treat the two entities as separate because of the different international legal status in relation to the Holy Roman Empire and the Danish affiliation of Schleswig.

[63] Duke Christian Carl Frederik August of Schleswig-Holstein-Sonderburg-Augustenburg (1798–1869) is usually simply known by just his first name, Christian, Duke of Augustenburg. He claimed the inheritance of the provinces Schleswig and Holstein and held the fiefs Augustenborg and Sonderborg (hence his title). He was a prince of the House of Oldenburg and a cadet-line descendant of the Danish royal house. He was the eldest son and heir of Louise Augusta of Denmark and Frederik Christian II, Duke of Augustenborg. As such, he was close to succeed in the Danish throne. He was the brother-in-law of King Christian VIII and nephew of Frederik VI. In 1848 a provisional government was established in Kiel under the Duke of Augustenborg, who secured help from the King of Prussia to assert his rights. However, European powers were united in opposing any dismemberment of Denmark. Emperor Nicholas I of Russia, who spoke with authority as head of the elder Holstein-Gottorp line, regarded the Duke of Augustenborg a rebel as Russia had guaranteed Schleswig to the Danish crown by the treaties of 1767 and 1773. A peace treaty between Prussia and Denmark was signed in Berlin on July 2, 1850. Here both parties reserved all their antecedent rights. Denmark was satisfied that the treaty enabled the King/Duke Frederik VII to restore his authority in Holstein with or without the consent of the German Confederation. Augustenborg was ousted from power when the victorious Danish troops marched into the duchies in 1851. The question of the Augustenburg succession made an agreement between the big powers impossible, and on March 31, 1852 the duke of Augustenburg resigned his claim in return for a money payment. Duke Christian sold his rights to the Duchy of Schleswig-Holstein to Denmark in aftermath of the Treaty of London, but later renounced his rights in favor of his son Frederik August. In 1864, his son Friedrich of Augustenborg proclaimed himself as Duke of Schleswig and Holstein, but to no avail.

passed to Denmark, Droysen rightly feared for his position and prudently left Kiel for a chair in Jena.

In the narrower field of scholarly studies of the history of the two duchies, the legal historian Friedrich Christoph Dahlmann (1785–1860) was the most influential on the German side. Dahlmann was born in the then Swedish Wismar in 1785 and was a nephew of the legal historian and secretary of the *Ritterschaft* (Corporation) in Schleswig-Holstein, Frederik Christian Jensen. In 1802 he began to study philology in Copenhagen under the protection of his uncle. Later Dahlmann moved on to Halle and Wittenberg and eventually defended his thesis (*Habilitation*) in Copenhagen. His family connections helped him become a Danish citizen even though he did not live up to the strict law of citizenship from 1776, which restricted citizenship to people born within the borders of the multinational Danish state. In 1812, he received a call to the chair in history at Kiel University where he stayed until 1829. His biography, thus, in many ways seems similar to that of Niebuhr, but in reality they represent two different eras, before and after the advent of nationalism.

As thrilled as Dahlmann was by the German successes in liberating the German states from Napoleon's yoke, as bitterly disappointed he was over the economic bankruptcy and demise of the Oldenburg Empire in 1813 and 1814. Together with many other German intellectuals he wanted Schleswig and Holstein to join a new unified German state. In this situation he laid the scholarly ground for the Schleswig-Holstein movement with his studies of the Ribe Accord of 1460. According to this document, Christian I, as a condition for his accession to the Danish throne, promised to rule the two duchies as one unit, "*ewich tosamende ungedelt*" as the document rendered the promise in Low German (*Plattdeutsch*). The document had already been published in 1797 by his predecessor as professor of history in Kiel, Dietrich Hermann Hegewisch (1746–1812, professor from 1780) and his uncle, the formerly mentioned F. C. Jensen. They were loyal supporters of the Danish monarchy and enemies of the rising German nationalism. They advocated the historical rights of the aristocracy in Schleswig and Holstein (in German *Ritterschaft*) and vehemently refused the incorporation of Schleswig and Holstein into the Danish state after the dissolution of the Holy Roman Empire in 1806. Instead they wanted to uphold the multinational state with separate rights for its historical components while still recognizing the Danish king as their legitimate master. Before 1806 the document hardly played any role. After the incorporation and in particular in the discussions on how to share the economic burdens after the bankruptcy of the National Bank of Denmark in 1813, however, the document was instrumentalized as the legal basis for the demands of the aristocracy and liberals in both duchies as a forerunner of the Schleswig-Holstein movement of the 1830s.

In contrast to Dahlmann, his colleague at Kiel University and competitor for the job as secretary of the corporation of the Ritterschaft, the legal historian Niels Nicolai Falck (1784–1850), was a German speaking patriotic regionalist and supporter of the Danish multinational monarchy, "Helstaten." Falck was born in Schleswig as a son of peasants in Emmerlev near Tønder (Tondern) north of the present border, and wanted to uphold the status quo of Schleswig and Holstein within the Danish realm.

For Dahlmann, on the contrary, defense of the traditional "Landesrechte" of Schleswig and Holstein primarily served as a means to an end, namely German national unification. This he demonstrated in a series of well attended public lectures in 1814 and 1815 on the eve of Napoleon's—and Denmark's—defeat, particularly a lecture he gave to mark the anniversary of Napoleon's defeat at Waterloo, "Rede zur Feier des Siegs vom 18ten Junius 1815; gehalten am 7ten Julius, im grossen academischen Hörsale, bei der durch die Kieler Universität angeordnete Feierlichkeit." Interestingly, Dahlmann's advocacy of German unification at first did not catch on at all among the students in Kiel. On the contrary, they were reported to have reacted rather coldly to his proclamation of a united Germany.[64] Dahlmann kept up his political activities for a time, publishing a journal called *Kieler Nachrichten* from 1815 to 1821 in collaboration with Falck. But he also succeeded in publishing solid historical research on Scandinavian and German history which has earned him a good name, even among Danish historians. Another result of Dahlmann's work was that he helped popularize the idea of a particular democratic tradition among the peasants in Dithmarschen in the western parts of Holstein, a democratic tradition which he rightly blaimed the Oldenburg kings for having crushed.

In Göttingen, Dahlmann met the two linguists, Jakob Ludwig and Wilhlem Karl Grimm, who along with their many scholarly results played an ominous role as spokesmen for a pan-German reduction of the languages of their neighbors to the north and the east to mere dialects. In 1848 Jakob Grimm (1785–1863) claimed that the original language of the inhabitants of Jutland was German, and Schleswig thus ought to be united with Germany for purely linguistic and cultural reasons.[65] The only problem with this reasoning was that the majority of the population in North Schleswig spoke Danish and thought this was a different language from German, be that *Hochdeutsch* or *Plattdeutsch*. These claims by the brothers Grimm and others provoked responses from Danish historians who wanted to demonstrate the Danish character of Schleswig and Denmark in language and culture. The most influential was *Haandbog i Fædrelandets Historie* from 1840 by the historian Carl Ferdinand Allen (1811–71). In 1857–58 Allen published *Det danske Sprogs Historie i Hertugdømmet Slesvig eller Sønderjylland* in two massive volumes with an in-depth treatment of the languages in Schleswig from the oldest time until the present. A Danish nationalist, Allen was also an ardent Scandinavianist, and at the end of his life he published *De tre nordiske Rigers Historie 1497–1536* of which he managed to finish the first five volumes covering the history of the Scandinavian kingdoms until 1527. When the civil war over the national affiliation of the two duchies erupted in the spring of 1848 the intellectual ground was thus well prepared by historians and propagandists on both sides.

---

[64] Ruth Hemstad, *Historie og nasjonal identitet. Kampem om fortiden i det dansk-tyske grenseland 1815–1840* (Oslo: Norges forskningsråd KULTs skriftserie nr. 57, 1996), 48–53.

[65] Inge Adriansen, *Fædrelandet, folkeminderne og modersmålet. Brug af folkeminder og folkesprog i nationale identitetsprocesser—især belyst ud fra striden mellem dansk og tysk i Sønderjylland* (Sønderborg: Skrifter fra Museumsrådet for Sønderjyllands Amt, 1990).

THE OLDENBURG MONARCHY, 1814–1864

Civil War over Schleswig 1848–51

The largest town in Schleswig was Flensburg which played an important economic role in the entire realm. Together with Bergen in Norway and Altona in Holstein, Flensburg was the largest commercial center outside Copenhagen and home to an important part of the Danish merchant fleet. Flensburg's position in the so-called triangular trade between Europe, the West Coast of Africa and the West Indies explains why the production of rum played such an important role in Flensburg until recently—*Hansen Rum* for instance. Sugar was grown in the Danish Virgin Islands by slaves imported from the Danish colony Christiansborg in nowadays Ghana and ended up as rum, which was drunk in the shipyards of Flensburg by the Danish craftsmen and workers who built the ships that served the trading routes.

Aside from its economic importance in the multinational Danish monarchy, Flensburg also played an important role in the economic and cultural life of the province of Schleswig. This may be difficult to understand today, where Flensburg has become just another sleepy German provincial town, albeit with a Danish flavor. But it is not long ago that the town was an active metropolis whose interests extended all over the globe. In the 1830s Flensburg was the economic center of a separate province within the Oldenburg Monarchy. In order to avoid the influence from the "unruly masses" of this large town, the Consultative Estates Assembly ("Stænderforsamling") for the province of Schleswig, which existed from 1834 to 1848, was convened in the much smaller and quieter town of Schleswig, south of Flensburg.[66] Aside from an upper class of merchants and officials, the majority of whom spoke German, Flensburg comprised a large Danish-speaking class of workers and craftsmen. Danish and German, or more accurately the South Jutland dialect (*sønderjysk*) and Low German (*Plattdeutsch*), co-existed, occasionally supplemented by Standard Danish and High German as the languages of the churches and the legal system.

In the western parts of Schleswig, furthermore, Frisian was spoken in the area between the Ejder and the present border just north of Niebüll and the North Sea islands. In the 1840s the Frisians sided with the German speakers, but in the wake of World War I the Frisians split into two groups, the larger one identifying itself as Germans with a regional culture (and coming dangerously close to Nazism), whereas the minority, the so-called National Frisians claimed to be a distinct national minority, although cooperating with the Danish minority. Since 1945 the National Frisians have allied themselves with the Danish minority and run on the same political ticket, the SSW. Altona in Holstein, which today is a rather sleepy suburb to Hamburg, was one of the busiest economic centers in the state. It, too, owed its independence and affluence to the Oldenburg Empire (*Helstaten*). In Holstein the town was seen as "foreign" and too Danish, a fact which is still witnessed today in a row of impressive villas on the road along the Elbe, the *Palmaille,* drawn by the Danish neo-classical architect Christian Frederik Hansen (1756–1845) who served as chief royal architect in Holstein 1784–1845 and set his imprint on the whole region. Apart from this effort, Hansen is primarily known as the chief architect of Copenhagen from 1800 to his death in 1845. The capital Kiel was rather small and together with Itzehoe only grew rapidly in the last half of the nineteenth century as a result of industrialization, militarization, and the building of the North Sea Channel from Kiel to the Elbe from 1887–95.[67]

The Schleswig-Holstein program of the 1830s advocated by German intellectuals and aristocrats did not build on the Schleswigian regional identity of old. The Schleswig-Holstein movement rather represented a modern national-political program

---

[66] Hans Jensen, *De danske Stænderforsamlingers Historie 1830–1848 vol. I–II* (Copenhagen: J. H. Schultz Forlag, 1931, 1934).

[67] The Kaiser-Wilhelm-Kanal which connected the Baltic Sea and the North Sea was primarily built for strategic reasons. From 1907–14 it was expanded in order to allow the passage of dreadnoughts from Kiel to Bremerhaven. In 1948 the name was changed to Nord-Ostsee-Kanal.

in competition with a Danish-national program that called for the incorporation of the whole of Schleswig as far as the river Ejder into a centralist Danish national state. As the Danish nationalist Orla Lehmann (1810–70) put it in the debates over a liberal constitution in 1838: "There are no regions in Denmark" ("I Danmark gives der ikke regioner").[68] But a region or province was exactly what Schleswig had become since the Early Middle Ages. The Danish call for an incorporation of all of the province of Schleswig provoked a separatist reaction in Holstein in the 1830s and 1840s out of fear that the Danish state would "Danisize" the province. Because of that the majority moved from loyalty to the Danish king to separatism for Schleswig-Holstein. This change is witnessed in *Itzehoer Wochenblatt* according to Steen Bo Frandsen's recent research.[69] In the long run, the old Schleswigian identity almost disappeared as a result of the civil war from 1848–51 and incorporation into Prussia in the united Germany after 1870.[70] The principal losers were the concept of a tolerant multi-nation Danish state, "*Helstaten*" and the idea of an independent Schleswig-Holstein. The two duchies of Schleswig and Holstein did remain "ungedeelt," as assured by the Ribe Accord in 1460, but only as a rather neglected and militarized periphery within the new German Empire.

On the Danish side, a program for an ethnically and historically defined nation was formulated by the National Liberals in the 1830s under the leadership of a Danish politician who had spoken German in his home in Copenhagen in the 1820s, the earlier mentioned Orla Lehmann. The years between 1830 and 1848 saw the rise of modern political ideas in Denmark. As a result, the peasant farmers began to organize for their own interests. According to the liberals, members of society ought to organize themselves on the basis of ideas and compete for political power in free elections—although the liberals meant that only those who "understood how to govern" should have the right to vote. Demands for a liberal constitution in the absolutist Danish monarchy were first formulated in minority circles of liberal academics in the first half of the nineteenth century, primarily among students and civil servants. In Denmark as well as Holstein, the move away from international or supranational liberalism to national liberalism occurred between 1836 and 1842. Until that point, the liberals in Copenhagen and Kiel had been allied in their resistance against the absolute monarchy, which continued to prevail even after the introduction of the consultative assemblies in 1830–34.[71] The bourgeoisie alone was so small in numbers that it was in no position to shake the absolutist regime. Had this not been apparent before, it certainly became so after the accession of Christian VIII to the throne in 1839. The

---

[68] Steen Bo Frandsen, "Men gives der da Provindser i Danmark?" *Historie* 19, no. 1 (1991).

[69] Steen Bo Frandsen, "Helstatens første opinionsavis: Theodor Olshausens Kieler Correspondenz-Blatt som forum for en liberal holstensk regionalisme (1830–1848)," *Historie* 2 (2006): 283–317; and Steen Bo Frandsen, *Holsten i Helstaten. Hertugdømmet inden for og uden for det danske monarki i første halvdel af 1800-tallet* (Copenhagen: Museum Tusculanum Press, 2008).

[70] Carsten Jahnke, "Die Borussifizierung des schleswig-holsteinischen Geschichtsbewusstseins, 1866–1889," *Zeitschrift für die Geschichte Schleswig Holsteins* 130 (2005): 161–90.

[71] Jensen, *De danske Stænderforsamlingers*.

liberals nurtured high hopes in Christian VIII who had presided over the writing of the free constitution in Norway in 1814 before the forced union with Sweden. Much to their disappointment, the liberals soon realized that the new king had absolutely no desire to limit his own powers and deliver himself into the hands of the increasingly nationalist liberals. His main intent was to preserve the composite *Helstat* and defend it against the rising nationalist antagonisms.

Under these circumstances, the two liberal reform groups in the capitals of Copenhagen and Kiel each established their own strategic alliances. In Denmark, the liberals allied themselves with the peasant farmers, an alliance which in 1846 led to the establishment of a political party, *Bondevennerne* (Friends of the Peasant). In Holstein and parts of Schleswig, a more informal alliance was established with the landed aristocracy that later developed into the Schleswig-Holsteinian movement. The confrontation of 1848 was not the only possible result of the national confrontations in Schleswig as it has been depicted in nationalist historiography from both sides. But neither of the two national liberal groups was able to gain power without a "national" polarization over an abstract ideology that allowed them to mobilize allies among the other strata of the population. Thus nationalism came to tear apart the relatively well-functioning composite state, *Helstaten*, or the Oldenburg Empire.

The nationalist radicalization of the language employed eventually led to rebellion and subsequent civil war in 1848. In Danish historiography the revolution is normally presented as a peaceful and consensual change from absolutism to democracy.[72] In fact, it was a bloody civil war over Schleswig, primarily fought in Jutland and at sea where the Danish fleet blockaded German harbors.[73] The proponents were two nationalist coalitions that both appealed to "the people." In the first years of the conflict, Prussia and other German states supported the Schleswig-Holstein rebels militarily and politically. Eventually, though, the European powers led by Russia, sided with the legitimate ruler, the king of Denmark, and restored status quo. After the Prussian forces were forced to withdraw, the Danish army won a narrow victory over the Schleswig-Holstein army led by German voluntaries at Isted near Schleswig on July 25, 1850. After the defeat of the rebels and the survival of the unstable bilingual *Helstat*, the Danish administration took revenge and tried to roll back German language and culture in the disputed territories.[74] Neither this episode, nor the Danish revenge over the Schleswig-Holstein liberals who were driven into exile in the US, and the demise of the castle of Gottorp in Schleswig which was stripped of its paintings and sculptures (they can now

---

[72] A criticism of this traditional understanding is formulated by Claus Bjørn, *1848. Borgerkrig og revolution* (Copenhagen: Gyldendal, 1998).

[73] Uffe Østergård, "1848 aus der Sicht von 1998. Der Bürgerkrieg im dänisch-deutschen Gesamtstaat 1848–50 unter der Perspektive des Bürgerkrieges in Ex-Jugoslawien," in *Die deutsche Revolution von 1848/49 und Norddeutschland*, eds. W. Beutin, W. Hoppe, and F. Kopitzsch (Frankfurt: Peter Lang, 1999), 251–62.

[74] Lorenz Rerup, "The Danes in Schleswig from the National Awakening to 1933," in *Formation of National Elites*, eds. A. Kappeler, A. Adanir, and A. O'Day (London: Hearst, 1992), 259–60.

be seen in the official Danish collections in the museums in Copenhagen) and turned into barracks for Danish troops, has been treated by Danish historians.

Neither the Danish nor the German side wanted to give in, and after long and fruitless deliberations an intransigent Danish government in 1863 proclaimed the annexation of the whole of Schleswig. The international political climate and international agreements notwithstanding, the ruling National Liberals demanded a Danish nation-state within the "historical" framework, that is all of Schleswig to the river Ejder, regardless of the opinion of the inhabitants. This move would have resulted in a large German-speaking minority within Denmark. After a crushing defeat of the Danish army at Dybbøl on April 18, 1864 and the subsequent occupation of all of Jutland, this unilateral act provided Bismarck's Prussia and Austria with an opportunity to take all of Schleswig and Holstein. A narrow Danish victory at sea against an Austrian fleet at Helgoland—which the Austrians too remember as a victory with a *Siegessäule* in the Prater in Vienna—did not change the military outcome. Denmark lost two fifths of her most developed territory and a large group of Danes came to live as a Danish minority in North Schleswig.[75]

Stubborn and intransigent quibbling on the part of the Danish national liberal politicians and their misunderstanding of the international situation enabled Bismarck to establish a united Germany, without Austria, under Prussian dominance.[76] Denmark had gambled and lost all. The state survived as a sovereign nation-state only by the skin of its teeth, primarily because its monarchy still was regarded as a legitimate part of European politics, combined with the interest of the great powers, first and foremost Russia and Britain, in maintaining a neutral power at the entrance to the Baltic. Had this not been the case, the country would have become either German or Swedish (the latter eventuality being termed Scandinavianism) or divided between the two powers. Today Danes have grown used to considering the small state of Denmark as both inevitable and positive. The reason for this was that new political movements exploited the exceptional situation with a sovereign state so weak that it opened the door for the political take over, first of the peasant farmers and later of the Social Democratic Party. Immediately after the defeat in 1864, the demand for national, social, and even physical integration of all people and districts was formulated in a popular slogan, "Outward losses must make up for by inward gains" ("Hvad udad tabes skal indad vindes").[77] This laid the foundations for a consensual and relatively egalitarian Danish political culture, which is often portrayed as the opposite of the more authoritarian outcome in victorious Germany, what self critical German historians referred to as the German *Sonderweg*. Such popular movements were not altogether uncommon in an international context, but it was quite unique for such movements to gain cultural, economic and eventually political hegemony over a sovereign state.[78]

---

[75] Troels Fink, *Geschichte des Schleswigschen Grenzlandes* (Copenhagen: Munksgaard, 1958).
[76] Johannes Nielsen, *1864—Da Europa gik af lave* (Odense: Odense Universitetsforlag, 1987).
[77] Uffe Østergård, "The Danish Path to Modernity," *Thesis Eleven* 77 (2004): 25–43.
[78] Uffe Østergård, "Dänemark und Deutschland," 219–24.

The Peasant-Farmer Roots of Danish National Identity

Contrary to the situation in most other nineteenth century nation-states, the small size of the amputated Danish state allowed economic and political take over by a numerous class of relatively well-to-do peasants turned independent farmers. Not without opposition, but gradually throughout the last part of the nineteenth century, the middle peasant farmers took over from ruling elites. These elites were recruited from the tiny urban bourgeoisie, officials of the state trained at German style universities inside the monarchy as well as outside, and the manorial class. They had lost faith in the survival of the state after the debacle of 1864, followed by the subsequent establishment of a strong united Germany next door. Some even played with the thought of joining this neighboring state which already dominated the culture of the upper classes.

In this situation, however, an outburst of so-called popular energy proclaimed a strategy of "winning inwards what had been lost to the outside." This *bon mot* was turned into a literal strategy of retrieving the lost agrarian lands of Western Jutland which had become deserted after the cutting of the forests in the sixteenth and seventeenth centuries. It also took the form of an opening up of the so-called Dark Jutland in an attempt to turn the economy of the peninsula of Jutland away from Hamburg and redirect it toward Copenhagen. This movement has provocatively been called "the Discovery of Jutland,"[79] meaning the exploitation of Jutland by its capital Copenhagen, which is situated on the far eastern rim of the country as a left over from the former empire, much like Vienna in present day Austria. This battle is not yet over, as demonstrated in the heated controversies of whether first build a bridge between the islands Fyn and Sjælland or between Sweden and Copenhagen in the 1980s. The attempt to keep the Danish nation-state together and Jutland away from Hamburg won out as the former bridge was built first. However, it was decided on a very narrow margin.

What is more important, though, is the cultural, economic, and political awakening of the middle peasants who became peasant farmers precisely during this period. The reason for their success lies in the relative weakness of the Danish bourgeoisie and late industrialization. The industrial take-off only happened in the 1890s, and the final breakthrough as late as in the 1950s according the economic historian Svend Åge Hansen.[80] Hansen's definition of industry, though, is debatable as he follows the tradition of counting dairies and slaughterhouses as agriculture and not industry. This may have been correct in the early nineteenth century but misses the point later on in the century and rather testifies to a particular Danish ideology than economic reality.

---

[79] Steen Bo Frandsen, "The Discovery of Jutland: The Existence of a Regional Dimension in Denmark," in *European Identities, Cultural Diversity and Integration in Europe since 1700*, ed. N. A. Sørensen (Odense: Odense University Press, 1995), 11–126; and Steen Bo Frandsen, *Opdagelsen af Jylland. Den regionale dimension i danmarkshistorien 1814–64* (Århus: Aarhus University Press, 1996).

[80] Svend Åge Hansen, *Early Industrialization in Denmark* (Copenhagen: Academic Press, 1970).

The peasant farmers developed a consciousness of themselves as a class and understood themselves to be the real backbone of society. Their ideology supported free trade which is of no surprise as they were beginning to rely heavily on export of bacon and butter to the rapidly developing British market. This was the case to such a degree that Denmark, economically speaking, became a de facto part of the British Empire from the mid-nineteenth to the mid-twentieth century. What is more surprising is the fact that their ideology also contained strong libertarian elements because of their struggle with the existing urban and academic elites. The peasant movement won out basically because it succeeded in establishing an independent culture with educational institutions of its own. This again was possible because of the unique organizational device applied in the organization of the agrarian industries—the cooperative.

The basic agrarian production was still pretty much a typical individualistic production on independent farms, albeit of an average size somewhat larger than usual in a European context. However, the processing of these products into exportable products took place in local farm industries run on a cooperative basis. The cooperatives were run democratically on the basis of equality regardless of the initial investment. The cooperative movement formulated this in a slogan of votes being cast "by heads instead of heads of cattle" (i.e., one man, one vote). This pun (in Danish *hoveder* and *høveder*) is less true when one starts investigating the realities of the cooperatives.[81] Yet the myth stuck and produced a sense of community which through means of various political traditions has been transformed into a hegemony that lasted long enough to lay the groundwork for a national consensus. The libertarian values, though, were not originally meant to include other segments of the population. The agrarian system was based on a crass exploitation of agricultural laborers by farmers. These were, together with the urban elites, often not even considered part of "the people" (*folket*) by the peasant-farmers. However, in an interesting and surprisingly original ideological maneuver, the rising Social Democratic Party adapted its ideology to the unique agrarian-industrial conditions in Denmark and developed a strategy very different from the Marxist orthodoxy of the German mother party. The Social Democratic Party even agreed to the establishment of a class of very small farmers called *husmænd* (cottagers). Thus they fulfilled the expectations of their landless members among the agricultural workers but at the same time undermined the possibility of ever obtaining an absolute majority in the parliament as did their sister parties in Sweden and Norway.[82]

Danish social democrats understood the importance of agriculture in the Danish rump state in their practical policies. They failed, however, to turn this understanding into coherent theory. At the level of doctrine, the party stuck to the orthodox Marxist formulations in the 1913 program. These formulations reflected the

[81] Claus Bjørn, "Dansk mejeribrug 1882–1914," in *Dansk mejeribrug 1882–2000*, ed. Claus Bjørn (Copenhagen: Landbohistorisk selskab, 1982).
[82] Uffe Østergård, "Peasants and Danes," *Comparative Studies in Society and History* 1 (1992): 5–31 (reprinted in G. Eley and G. Suny, eds., *Becoming National: A Reader* (Oxford: Oxford University Press) 1996: 179–222).

international debates in the Second International rather than Danish reality and the practical policy of the party. The very fact that the program of 1913 remained unchanged until 1961 testifies to the lack of importance attributed to theory in this the most pragmatic of all reformist socialist parties. The party was never strong on theory, but the labor movement, on the other hand, produced an impressive number of capable administrators and politicians, at least until recently. The lack of explicit strategy enabled remnants of the libertarian peasant ideology to take root early on. The social democrats embarked upon a policy for all the classes, and not just for the working class, after World War I. This new policy was provoked by the shock of the outbreak of a war which the socialist parties proved unable to prevent through international cooperation. This testifies to the importance of the liberal-popular ideological hegemony dating back to the last third of the nineteenth century. It is also proof that the leaders realized that they would never gain power on their own. The farmers proper only constituted a fragment of the population as a whole, but small scale production permeated the whole society.

Originally the Danish social democrats followed the internationalist paroles of the international socialist movement, but as a result of their electoral success they had to adapt to the general anti-German feelings of the population. Socialists in all European states faced the dilemma of operating as followers of an international movement and ideology in nation-states that underwent a rapid nationalization as a result of the new mass politics that followed successful industrialization. In theory the Danish social democrats subscribed to the anti-militarist and internationalist paroles of the Second International after 1889 but in practical politics they turned out as national as the other socialist parties, only with a different social profile. In economic policy Social Democracy, as mentioned, took a more liberal course than other socialist parties out of respect for the agrarian character of the country, even in its most modern sectors of which a substantial part was organized in cooperatives. The Danish social democrats only organized as a party in 1870 after the devastating defeat of 1864. From the beginning it tried to distance itself from conservative nationalism as well as the more populist nationalism of the liberal peasant farmers in the party, *Venstre*. This policy of distance turned out to be difficult as the social democrats entered an electoral alliance with *Venstre* from 1883 in order to oust the ruling conservative party from power. Furthermore, the conservatives had some success in appealing to the national sentiments of the urban workers and artisans.

In the 1870s, the Danish Social Democratic Party, though not seeing itself as anti-national, urged urban workers in Schleswig to vote for German socialist candidates instead of Danish candidates.[83] This recommendation was based on the principle

[83] N. F. Christiansen, "Socialismen og fædrelandet. Arbejderbevægelsen mellem internationalisme og national stolthed 1871–1940," in *Dansk identitetshistorie vol. 3 Folkets Danmark 1848–1940*, ed. Ole Feldbæk (Copenhagen: C. A. Reitzels Forlag, 1992), 512–86; Søren Federspiel, "Socialdemokratiet og de tyske partistridigheder. Det nordslesvigske spørgsmål og det danske socialdemokrati i 1970'ernes begyndelse, på baggrund af striden i den tyske arbejderbevægelse,"

of national self-determination which all socialist parties, at least in theory, subscribed to. The party, operating in a small country, was one of the most ardent followers of the principles of internationalism and anti-militarism whereas it was more difficult for parties in larger and stronger states to persuade their voters of the value of abstaining from the use of force in international relations. This internationalist policy, which implied acceptance of international borders, meant that the party abstained from organizing workers in Schleswig. One consequence was that the majority of workers in Flensburg in particular, which underwent a rapid industrialization before 1912, joined the German socialists, from 1890 officially recognized as *Sozialdemokratische Partei Deutschlands, SPD*. Flensburg gradually changed from a Danish speaking majority in 1864 to a German majority in 1920.[84] On the other hand, the German Social Democratic Party condemned the official policy of Germanization from 1897–1901 and cooperated with the Danish social democrats north of the border in the interest of internationalism and the policy of national self-determination. In the other towns in North Schleswig, the outcome was different even though the Danish social democrats abstained from organizing workers. Even though an influx of German civil servants and railway workers, a German military presence in Sønderborg (Sonderburg), and general Germanization of the urban middle classes resulted in German majorities at the referendum in 1920, most workers in North Schleswig preserved their Danish language and identification with Danish culture. And as the surrounding districts demonstrated an overwhelming Danish majority, they all fell to Denmark as part of the first zone where national affiliation was determined en bloc at the referendum in 1920.

The national affiliation of Flensburg remained an open wound in Danish politics in the years after 1920. The Social Democratic Party suffered a split over the national question in Schleswig in 1920, albeit of minor importance.[85] Basically it stuck to its acceptance of the outcome of the referendum and even threatened to call a general strike when the king exercised his powers and appointed a new government as the social liberal government that had steered the country through World War I lost

---

Årbog for arbejderbevægelsens historie 4 (1974): 147–63; and Søren Federspiel, "Die dänische Arbeiterbewegung und der Internationalismus 1870–1900," in *Arbeiterbewegung in Nord- und Mitteleuropa zwischen nationaler Orientierung und Nationalismus, Schriftenreihe der Akademie Sankelmark*, ed. E. Krüger, *Heft* 30/31 (1976): 28–35.

[84] Gerd Callesen, "Die Schleswig-Frage in den Beziehungen zwischen dänischer und deutscher Sozialdemokratie von 1912 bis 1924," *Aabenraa* (1970); Hans Schultz Hansen, *Danskheden i Sydslesvig 1840–1918 som folkelig og national bevægelse* (Flensborg: Studieafdelingen ved Dansk Centralbibliotek i Sydslesvig, 1990); and Hans Schultz Hansen, "Nationalitetskamp og modernisering 1815–1918," in *Sønderjyllands historie vol. 2, Efter 1815* (Aabenraa: Historisk samfund for Sønderjylland, 2009), 11–240, in particular 193–204; Dorrit Andersen, "Die dänische Arbeiterbewegung und die Schleswig-Frage in den Jahren 1900–1924," in *Arbeiterbewegung in Nord- und Mitteleuropa zwischen nationaler Orientierung und Nationalismus, Schriftenreihe der Akademie Sankelmark*, ed. E. Krüger, *Heft* 30/31 (1976): 52–60.

[85] Jens Topholm, *Emil Marott. Socialdemokrat med sociale og nationale særstandpunkter* (Aarhus: Universitetsforlaget i Aarhus, 1980).

its majority. This led to the so-called Easter Crisis in 1920, which helped secure the principle of parliamentarism, that is, that a government should command a majority in parliament.[86] Even though some workers signed a petition "to get Flensburg back" regardless of the convincing electoral result, the party succeeded in holding its line together with social liberal allies and a few conservatives. The so-called Flensburg question surfaced again in 1945–47 and helped bring down a liberal-conservative government. The question was only settled in 1955 with the signing of the Bonn-Copenhagen agreements which were based on a mutual recognition of the individual's right to national self-determination and protection of the national minorities on both sides of the border. In German, the principle behind the so-called Schleswig model is rendered as "Minderheit ist wer will," that is, only the individual has the right to declare his or her national affiliation and no authorities have any right to interfere with the decision of individuals.[87]

Grundtvigism: National and Social Consensus in the Left Overs of the Oldenburg Empire

The main reason why a libertarian nationalist ideology ended up dominating a whole nation-state was the small size of this particular state. Danish historians and sociologists have eagerly discussed whether the peasant ideological hegemony resulted from a particular class structure dating back to the 1780s or even further back to the early sixteenth century, when the number of farms was frozen by law, or whether it was the other way around—that ideology created the particular class-structure of Danish nineteenth century society. Put in such terms the discussion is almost impossible to solve as both of the protagonist's positions reveal some part of the truth. A better explanation of the outcome is to stress the particular ideology of populism or "popular" (*folke-lighed*) in Danish nationalism. This concept was first and most coherently formulated by the important but virtually untranslatable philosopher, historian, priest, and poet Nikolaj Frederik Grundtvig (1783–1872).

Depressed by the defeat of Denmark by Great Britain in the war of 1807–14, the young priest Grundtvig took it upon himself to reestablish what he took to be the original "Nordic" or "Danish" mind. He translated the *Icelandic Sagas*, the twelfth-century historian Saxo Grammaticus, the Anglo-Saxon poem *Beowulf*, and many other sources of what he considered the true, but lost, core of "Danishness." His sermons attracted large crowds of enthusiastic students. His address on *The Light of*

---

[86] Christiansen, "Socialismen og fædrelandet," 528–29.

[87] Jørgen Kühl and Marc Weller, eds., *Minority Policy in Action: The Bonn-Copenhagen Declarations in a European Context 1955–2005* (Flensburg and Aabenraa: European Center for Minority Issues and Department of Border Region Research, University of Southern Denmark, 2005); and Uffe Østergård, "Danmark og mindretallene i teori og praksis," in *Mindretalspolitik*, ed. Jørgen Kühl (Copenhagen: DUPI, 1996), 44–106.

the Holy Trinity, delivered in 1814 to a band of student volunteers willing to fight the English, inspired a whole generation of young followers, including the priest Jacob Christian Lindberg (1791–1857) who later organized the first Grundtvigian movement. When Grundtvig embarked upon a sharp polemic with his superiors in the church on matters of theology, he was banned from all public appearances and publishing. This drove him into what he called his "inner exile" in the 1830s. This inner exile, however, gave him time for reflection where he formulated a program for a revival of the stagnant official religion. When the ban was lifted in 1839 he burst out in a massive production of sermons, psalms, and songs, a literary legacy which at least until a generation ago constituted the core of the socialization of most Danes. Grundtvig formulated an all-embracing view of nature, language, and history. In 1848, after the outbreak of the civil war over Schleswig, he produced a refined definition of national identity which helped set the tone for a nationalist identification less chauvinistic than most in the nineteenth century. As is sometimes the case with prolific writers, his most precise theoretical expressions were to be found in the restricted form of the verse: "People! What is a people? What does popular mean? Is it the nose or the mouth that gives it away? Is there a people hidden from the average eye in burial hills and behind bushes, in every body, big and boney? They belong to a people who think they do, those who can hear the Mother tongue, those who love the Fatherland. The rest are separated from the people, expel themselves, do not belong."[88]

This definition, though produced in the heat of the battle with the German speaking rebels in the duchies of Schleswig and Holstein, resembles most of all the definition of national identity produced in 1882 by the French thinker Ernest Renan in what has since become one of the standard texts on nationalism, *Qu'est-ce qu'une nation?* Originally Renan's intention was to "scientifically" demonstrate the right of the French population in Alsace-Lorraine to its French nationality, even after the provinces had been signed over to Germany by the peace treaty in 1871. After their defeat, the French changed their minds as to whether nation should be defined in cultural or political terms. The same happened in Denmark after the defeat in 1864 which in 1867 was followed by the incorporation into Prussia of all of Schleswig. But Grundtvig anticipated this change of thinking—at least in some of his writings. Renan's statement has since become the standard formulation of an anti-essentialist definition of national identity. This could be labeled a voluntarist-subjective definition as it stresses the importance of the expressed will of people. The rival definition in modern European thinking could be called the objective-culturalist definition. It dates back to the German thinker J. G. H. Herder and has permeated all thinking in the nineteenth and twentieth centuries up until Fascism and Nazism.[89] It is surprising that the Danish thinker Grundtvig should present a democratic definition of nationality as early as

---

[88]   N.F.S. Grundtvig, *Folkelighed,* written in 1848 in the midst of the civil war over Schleswig, author's translation.

[89]   Uffe Østergård, "Definitions of Nation in European Political Thought," *North Atlantic Studies* 1, no. 2 (1991): 51–56.

1848. No immediate military defeat had preceded it as was the case in France. Until 1870 French thinkers had defined nationality in terms no less essentialist than any German would after that date. On top of that it must be remembered that Grundtvig wrote these lines in a highly explosive political situation when a majority in the two predominantly German-speaking provinces of Schleswig and Holstein had seceded. Admittedly Grundtvig left those who opted for the German language to their own choice as non-Danes, which in his opinion was a most deplorable fate. But he left them the choice and would never dream of interfering with it.

Through a long and complicated history this understanding of national identity gradually became official Danish policy and has successfully been applied in the border region between Denmark and Germany after 1920 and in particular after 1955. There is much more to say about the thinking of Grundtvig and his influence on Danish political culture. The core of his thinking was the assumption that culture and identity are embedded in the unity of life and language. Although this kind of thinking invites the labeling of chauvinism, Grundtvig himself, like his opposite number Herder, did not assume a hierarchy of nationalities. Cultural diversity yes, cultural dominance no. Whether these assumptions are really viable need not concern us here. What does concern us, though, is the fact that his thinking caught on among a class of people in the small state left over from the wars of the middle of the century. It began with students immediately after 1814. The breakthrough only happened around 1839 when different religious and political movements decided to transform his thinking into practice. First, it influenced the revivalist religious movements; later, more explicitly political movements; and eventually, his thinking came to serve as the foundation for independent economic and educational institutions. Grundtvig himself did not seek such popular support. He delivered his message either in writing or orally, and then stood aloof when others decided what to make out of it. This is why some of today's guardians of the thoughts of Grundtvig speak of him as having been "taken prisoner by the Grundtvigian movement" when his message was transformed into an ideology by the name of "Grundtvigism."

The revivalists came to Grundtvig of their own accord. The religious movements in Denmark of the first half of the nineteenth century resembled many other Pietist movements throughout Europe. Because of the negative attitude of the official Lutheran state church they chose to meet outside the churches, and were called *Forsamlingsbevægelsen* (the meeting movement). They were attracted by Grundtvig's independent interpretation of the Lutheran heritage because he succeeded in giving an optimistic tone to the normally somewhat gloomy Pietism of German origins. In their struggles with the officials of the absolutist state, these revivalists learned an organizational lesson which they would soon put to political use. The leaders of the peasant movement of the 1840s were recruited from their ranks. Initially, working under the tutelage of the liberal intellectuals, the peasant party gradually broke away from the national liberals, as they called themselves. Soon, though, the various political factions of the peasant party began to establish independent institutions. They began with the church. With the transformation of the monarchy from an absolutist to a constitutional regime in 1849, the organization of the church had to be changed accordingly.

The result of these endeavors differed in important ways from the otherwise comparable situation in the Lutheran monarchies of Sweden and Norway. A state church with a proper constitution never came into existence, though it had been envisaged in the constitution of 1849. This was a result of the influence of Grundtvig and the revivalist movement. They wanted guarantees of religious freedom, so the church should be the creature of the state, or its agent of socialization, as it had been under absolutism. These guarantees they found best preserved in an anarchic state of church affairs.[90] In this way, Denmark has acquired a most peculiar mixture of freedom and state control in religious matters. There is a minister of religious affairs called minister of the "People's Church"—a contradiction in terms that does not seem to bother Danes. He or she presides over church administration and the upkeep of church buildings. Most of this is financed by a separate tax. However, it is left to individual priests and their congregations to interpret the actual teachings of the church within a broad understanding of Christianity. Local councils elected every four years run these congregations. Still today the most influential groups in these councils are the vaguely fundamentalist Inner Mission in alliance with the social democrats. In spite of their differences they often collaborate in order to control the freedom of the academically educated priests. These latter are normally trained at the universities and represent an intellectually refined Lutheran theology which does not appeal to ordinary believers.

Yet almost 80% of the apparently non-religious and secular Danish citizens belong to this church in the sense that they pay the taxes even if relatively few attend service except for Christmas, baptisms, burials, and weddings. Still, I think, the Lutheranism of the People's Church plays an enormous and insufficiently recognized role in defining the political culture. In fact, we should probably talk of Lutheran or Protestant democracy rather than social democracy when analyzing the social and political model advocated by Denmark in particular and the Nordic countries in general.[91] In the 1870s the ideological battle was carried into the educational field. The national liberals who now sided whole-heartedly with the conservative owners of the manors in a party called *Højre* (the Right) wanted a comprehensive school system under the supervision of the state. This, the majority of the farmers' party *Venstre* (the Left) resisted vehemently. They believed in the absolute freedom of education

---

[90] Cf. Jes Fabricius Møller and Uffe Østergård, "Lutheran Orthodoxy and Anti-Catholicism in Denmark 1536–2011," in *European Anti-Catholicism in a Comparative and Transnational Perspective*, eds. Jonas Harvard and Yvonne Werner (Amsterdam: Rodopi Press, 2013), 132–51.

[91] Uffe Østergård, "Lutheranism, Nationalism and the Universal Welfare State—National Churches and National Identity after the Reformation and the Development of the Welfare State in the Nordic Nation-states," in *Europäisches und Globales Christentum: Herausforderungen und Transformationen im 20. Jahrhundert* [European and Global Christianity: Challenges and Transformations in the 20th Century] *Arbeiten zur Kirchlichen Zeitgeschichte*, Reihe B, Band 54, eds. Katharina Kunter and Jens Holger Schiørring (Göttingen: Vandenhoeck & Ruprecht, 2011), 78–101.

and attacked the "black" schools of learning where Latin was still taught. They could do this because the peasant movement from 1844 had established a network of "Folk High Schools" throughout the country. Over the years, Grundtvig had produced a series of programs for a new and more democratic educational system. Like most of his other thoughts they did not constitute a coherent system. Rather, they can be seen as an appeal for a practical schooling in democracy. However, what these schools lack in coherent programs they make up for in flexibility. Today most of them are institutions of adult education, supplementing the formal educational system.

On top of this, the anti-institutional thinking of Grundtvig in the end permeated the Danish educational system to such a degree that even today there is no compulsory schooling, only compulsory learning. Whether one is educated in a state school or a so-called free school is a personal choice. Again, this might not sound terribly surprising for an American audience, but taken in the context of the highly centralized European states with a Lutheran heritage, it is most surprising. What is more, these free schools helped produce what can best be termed an "alternative elite." Until very recently there were two or maybe three different ways of recruiting the political, cultural, and business elites. The university system was one, the workers movement another, at least until the democratization of the official educational system in the 1960s. Both are well-known in other countries. The third line of recruitment through the folk high schools, however, is (or rather was) a peculiarly Danish phenomenon. Grundtvig and his followers accomplished what amounts to a real cultural revolution. He hated the formal teachings of the official school system and favored free learning with an emphasis on story telling—"the living word"—and discussion among peers. This program gave rise to a system of free schools for the children, plus folk high schools and agrarian schools for the farmer sons and daughters in their late teens and early twenties.

It is difficult to estimate the importance of the Grundtvigian schools in precise quantitative terms, as their influence has been almost as great outside the schools as in them. There is no doubt, however, that the very fact of the existence of two competing elites has helped agrarian and libertarian values to make inroads into the mainstream of Danish political culture and thus has contributed heavily to defining "Danishness."[92] The informal and anti-systematic character of the teachings of Grundtvig was the reason why they suited the peasant movement so well. His writings in prose and poetry provided inspiration without restricting innovation. It also helps explain why Grundtvig has never been a favorite of academics—his thinking does not amount to a coherent theoretical system. His enmity toward all systems led him even to deny that he himself was a "Grundtvigian" (much as Marx denied that he was a "Marxist"). "Grundtvigians" never used this term themselves but talked of "Friends"

---

[92] Richard Jenkins, *Being Danish: Paradoxes of Identity in Everyday Life* (Copenhagen: Museum Tusculanum Press, 2011); and Uffe Østergård, "Danish National Identity: A Historical Account," in *Global Collaboration: Intercultural Experiences and Learning*, eds. Martine Cardel Gertsen, Anne-Marie Søderberg, and Mette Zølner (Houndsmill: Palgrave Macmillan, 2012), 37–55.

and organized "meetings of Friends." This organizational informality turned out to be a major advantage, at least in the early stages of the movement, while later on it led to long series of splits and fractional fighting. Furthermore, it is the reason why the influence of this farmers' ideology was able to cross the boundaries of the class it originally had served so well and was able to influence the worker's movement in the Danish rump, which became the quintessential "small state" because it survived its territorial losses and even succeeded in turning these defeats into a strength.[93]

Urbanization, Industrialization, and Nationalization in Danish Nation Building

As the class of peasant farmers gradually won political, cultural, and economic influence in the second half of the nineteenth century, their program prevailed as the backbone of a successful national democracy. In the twentieth century, this national democracy was transformed into a tightly knit social democracy as a result of the rise of the workers' movement, organized in the Social Democratic Party. This party had already become the largest party before World War I, primarily due to the industrialization of Copenhagen combined with a successful mobilization of the landless agrarian laborers. Because of the agrarian dominance, the level of urbanization was relatively low apart from the capital of Copenhagen.[94] Copenhagen played an un-proportionally large role in the otherwise agrarian country because of its former role as center in a much larger multinational composite state. Copenhagen was much larger than all other towns in the realm and seat of the major merchant houses and overseas trading companies, home to a rapid industrialization that attracted huge immigration from the rest of the country and southern Sweden. The importance of this unbalanced process of urbanization for the formation of national identity has not been addressed by Danish historians who have taken the imbalance between the capital and the rest of the country as "normal." The contradictory role of a city that at the same time was a cosmopolitan and Baltic city and a national capital in a small state where peasant farmers gradually established an economic, political and cultural hegemony, though, has left an important mark on the political culture.

Danish political mobilization in the 1830s and 1840s and the narrow defeat of the Holsteinian rebellion in the civil war of 1848–51 led to what modern observers might call an "ethnic cleansing" of German speaking population in Copenhagen. This process has never been investigated in any detail as it was seen as the "natural" outcome of the conflict by later Danish historians. That is why we do not know whether

---

[93] Uffe Østergård, "Danish National Identity: Between Multinational Heritage and Small State Nationalism," in *Denmark's Policy towards Europe after 1945: History, Theory and Options*, eds. Hans Branner and Morten Kelstrup (Odense: Odense University Press, 2000), 139–84.

[94] In 1860, urban dwellers accounted for 24% of the total population. By 1911, it was 40%, according to: Vagn Dybdahl, *De nye klasser 1870–1913* (Copenhagen: Politikens Forlag, 1965), 33.

this "ethnic cleansing" was the result of forced migration or a change of language and national affiliation. We only know that Copenhagen was nationally homogeneous at the onset of the war in 1863. As a result of the disastrous defeat in 1864 and the loss of almost two fifths of the population, Copenhagen, although relatively small compared with other European capitals, came to loom even larger in the tiny nation-state that was left. Despite the city's higher degree of linguistic homogeneity it must be remembered that Copenhagen still was the capital for the remnants of a North Atlantic empire, large in geography though small in inhabitants, composed of Iceland, the Faroe Islands, and Greenland. Furthermore, Copenhagen was still considered the cultural capital of Norway even though this nation politically was in union with Sweden. Thus, the city never was as nationally homogeneous as has been assumed by Danish historians. Even though the city in a European context must be considered a small city, even after the opening up of the Medieval walls in 1857 and subsequent expansion, politically and culturally Copenhagen was a large head on a small body, pretty much in the same situation as Vienna in the reduced Austria after 1918.

Copenhagen's political and cultural dominance over the rest of the country was reinforced with industrialization in the nineteenth and twentieth centuries. The industrial revolution in the second part of the nineteenth century in Denmark to a large degree took place in Copenhagen, combined with the small scale dairy industry in the agrarian sector outside the capital. The industrialization implied a huge in-migration of landless laborers from all over Denmark and from southern Sweden—the provinces which has been lost in 1658–60—the so-called forgotten immigration as it was called by the late economic historian Richard Willerslev.[95] At the same time, Copenhagen developed into a trading and commercial center of the Baltic area because of its informal alliance with the Russian Empire that allowed a company like *Store Nordiske Telegrafkompagni* (Great Northern Telegraph Company) to establish telegraph lines through the huge Russian Empire all the way to China.[96] This expansion, combined with Denmark's role as the prime exporter of agrarian products to Britain, allowed Copenhagen a much larger and more cosmopolitan status than the size of Denmark would provide. In 1891–94 a duty free harbor (*Frihavnen*) was established to serve as trading hub for international trade in the Baltic area. Thus the modernization of Denmark was the result of two different processes that at the time were as mutually antagonistic and exclusive. On the one hand, the

---

[95] Richard Willerslev, *Den glemte indvandring* (Copenhagen: Academic Press, 1983).

[96] The two dominating entrepreneurs of the second half of the 19th century who succeeded in transforming Copenhagen into a center of global business, C. F. Tietgen (1829–1901) and H. N. Andersen (1852–1937), are critically treated in formidable biographies by the business historian Ole Lange, in *Finansmænd, stråmænd og mandariner. C. F. Tietgen, Privatbanken og Store Nordiske. Etablering 1868–76* (Copenhagen: Gyldendal, 1978); Ole Lange, *Partnere og Rivaler. C. F. Tietgen, Eastern Extension og Store Nordiske. Ekspansion i Kina 1880–86* (Copenhagen: Gyldendal, 1980); Ole Lange, *Den hvide Elefant. H. N. Andersens eventyr og ØK 1852–1914* (Copenhagen: Gyldendal, 1986); and Ole Lange, *Stormogulen. C. F. Tietgen—en finansmand, hans imperium og hans tid 1829–1901* (Copenhagen: Gyldendal, 2006).

modernization of the agrarian sector was primarily initiated by the cooperative movement and Grundtvigism which came from the west in Jutland and stopped short
of Copenhagen. On the other hand, a more traditional modernization process was
spurred by industries set up mainly in Copenhagen, in combination with a number
of successful transnational companies such as *Østasiatisk Kompagni, ØK* (East India
Company), *Store Nordiske Telegrafkompagni* (Great Northern Telegraph Company),
and *Det Forenede Dampskibs-Selskab, DFDS* (United Steamship Company), not to
speak of the breweries Carlsberg and Tuborg (today merged into one large company, *De Forenede Bryggerier*, United Breweries). Unfortunately this double character of
economic modernization in Denmark has not been analyzed in depth by Ivan Berend
in his otherwise brilliant analysis of the industrialization of Europe in the nineteenth
century.[97]

Because of all these factors, Copenhagen came to play a contradictory role
in the development of Danish nationalism. On the one hand, the city was the undisputed political, cultural, and economic center after the victory of the anti-federalist
and centralizing national liberals in 1848–49 that led to the introduction of a free
constitution. On the other hand, the urban classes in Copenhagen joined hands with
the manorial class in the party of the Right (*Højre*) in the political struggles with the
representatives of the rising agrarian class of peasant farmers, the Left (*Venstre*) in the
second half of the nineteenth century. The outcome of this struggle came to determine
the political culture of the country. These urban classes primarily comprised civil servants and the many new craftsmen and independent businessmen in the upcoming
urban trades after the introduction of free trade in 1857.[98] The capital was thus both the
ultimate theater for political struggle, the main seat for the newspapers that formed
the national public sphere (in German *Öffentlichkeit*), and an active participant in
politics with its own economic interests towards Hamburg and the Danish provincial
towns. This is the background for the extreme centralization of the infrastructure, in
particular railroads and steamship routes, that began with the founding of the united
steamship company DFDS in 1866 by the most successful businessman of the period
Carl Frederik Tietgen (1829–1901).[99] The intellectuals in the city thought themselves
cosmopolitan and European as can be demonstrated by the example of the leading
Danish and European intellectual Georg Brandes (1842–1927), whose self-proclaimed

---

[97] Ivan Berend, *Nineteenth-Century Europe: Diversity and Industrialization* (Cambridge: Cambridge University Press, 2013).

[98] This alliance was investigated in 1969 by the business historian Vagn Dybdahl in an original analysis of the political organization and importance of the urban trades in Denmark in: *Partier og
erhverv. Studier i partiorganisation og byerhvervenes politiske aktiviteter ca. 1880–ca. 1913 vol. I–II*
(Århus: Universitetsforlaget, 1969). Before this he applied this perspective in a masterly overview
in his contribution to a multi-volume history of Denmark in 1965 with the revealing title "The
new classes," in Dybdahl, *De nye klasser*. Unfortunately, very little of his path-breaking research
into the urbanization processses is translated into English.

[99] Hans Helge Madsen, *Skæv og national. Dansk byplanlægning 1830 til 1938* (Copenhagen:
Bogværket, 2009).

"Europeanness" and cosmopolitanism in reality only amounted to an urban version of Danish small-state agrarian nationalism.[100]

Brandes was born in 1842 when the Danish-Schleswigian-Holsteinian-Icelandic multinational state approached its final demise in the civil war of 1848–51 and total defeat by the Prussian and Austrian armies in 1864. The latter event left an enormous impression on the young Brandes as it did on all his contemporaries. As earlier mentioned, the small, rather provincial capital of Copenhagen between 1800 and 1850 was home to a surprisingly large group of artists, writers, and philosophers, some of whom acquired world fame in their own time or later, foremost among them the philosopher Søren Kierkegaard (1813–55), the writer Hans Christian Andersen (1805–75), and the natural scientist Hans Christian Ørsted (1777–1851) not to speak of a range of painters who have given rise to the denomination of the period as the "Golden Age" of Danish culture. According to the authoritative multi-volume biography of Georg Brandes by Jørgen Knudsen, he saw himself as a Jew, a Dane, and a European.[101] In this order, though the sequence today seems slightly politically incorrect. Knudsen demonstrates convincingly that Brandes' Jewishness played an important though largely ignored role for him all his life. But in contrast to his two other identities, the national and the European, his Jewishness has not attracted much attention in scholarly literature, though it was very much noticed at the time. Anti-Semitism probably was an important factor in his difficulties in obtaining a professorship at Copenhagen University even though the official reason was his lack of national credentials, his so-called Europeanness.

Brandes himself did not see any problem with the two identities of Dane and European, neither in theory nor in practice. Through the influence and widespread reception of his writings in the dominant European languages, Brandes acquired the status of the most respected and best known European intellectual since Voltaire. In his later years, he alone constituted a European public sphere (*Öffentlichkeit*). Yet, this all-European intellectual, well versed in most European languages, cherished his national identification as a Dane, at times even a nationalist Dane. Most of his life he was in strong opposition to the extremely conservative regime under the county squire Estrup who dominated Danish politics between 1870 and 1894. Nevertheless he took a strong stance in favor of the suppressed Danish minority in Prussian-ruled Schleswig. In his farewell address when taking leave of Berlin in 1883 after a successful six years stay,[102] he openly criticized the German suppression of his countrymen in

---

[100] Cf. Uffe Østergård, "Georg Brandes e l'Europa di oggi," *Studi Nordici* 9, Pisa (2004): 35–41.

[101] Jørgen Knudsen, *Georg Brandes, vol. 4: Magt og afmagt 1896–1914* (Copenhagen: Gyldendal, 1998), 16, under the chapter heading "I am myself alone. Jøden, danskeren og europæeren" [the Jew, the Dane, and the European].

[102] This stay among other publications resulted in the intense description of the new united Germany: Georg Brandes, *Berlin som tysk Rigshovedstad* (Copenhagen: Gyldendal, 1885) [German translation, *Berlin als deutsche Reichshauptstad: Erinnerungen aus den Jahren 1877–1883* (Berlin: Colloquium Verlag) 1989]; cf. Jørgen Knudsen, *Georg Brandes, Vol. 2: I modsigelsernes tegn 1877–83* (Copenhagen: Gyldendal, 1988).

this northernmost part of the newly united German Empire. This intervention falls well in line with his later interventions on behalf of other suppressed nationalities such as the Poles in Russia, the Armenians in the Ottoman Empire, and the Alsacians in Germany where he advocated the principle of national self-determination. These interventions were courageous as they ran against the dominating mood in the country whose reading audience he depended on the most for his international fame, Germany. But his political interventions were not anti-German, which became obvious when he under World War I broke with his former ally, Georges Clemenceau (1841–1929), because he refused to place all blame for the war on Germany and upheld a neutral stance in a war which he right from the beginning saw as the catastrophe for Europe it was.[103]

That Georg Brandes was a European with a specific national background does not mark him out as anything particular. But we should go a step further in understanding the very "Danish" nature of this very epitome of a European intellectual who, regardless of all the languages he mastered, still only felt fully at home in Danish. As he put it in 1871 when his Italian friend Giuseppe Saredo tried to lure him to Italy with all the opportunities this step would open for a man of his abilities: "I love the Danish language much too much to ever leave it." And as he wrote to his editor Henri Nathansen (1868–1944) in 1903: "The Danish language is my fatherland."[104] The program for a romantically, ethnically, and historically motivated definition of the nation was originally formulated by the national liberals who predominantly were recruited among the administrative and commercial elites in Copenhagen. This concept, however, was out of tune with the political and social realities of the agrarian economy of the country, farmers as well as owners of manors. The clash between these forces came to dominate parliamentary politics from 1870 to 1901. This clash is best understood as a conflict between two variants of nationalism, an urban small-state nationalism primarily based in Copenhagen and an agrarian version expressing the rising self confidence among peasant farmers. As the intellectual and administrative center, Copenhagen was both victim and prime mover in the nationalization process from 1830 to 1914.

Because of the industrialization of the country in last half of the nineteenth century, almost a third of the Danish population lived in the greater Copenhagen area in the eastern part of the country around 1900. Even though the main economic development of agricultural products and processing took place in the countryside outside Copenhagen, this urban milieu was the main center of the political and intellectual modernization of Denmark. In the parliamentary struggles of the nineteenth century, the city was for a long time solidly in the hands of the conservative party, *Højre*.[105] The

---

[103] Jørgen Knudsen, *Georg Brandes, Vol. 5: Uovervindelig taber 1914–27* (Copenhagen: Gyldendal, 2004), 127–75.

[104] Knudsen, *Georg Brandes, vol. 4*, 34.

[105] The Right recruited its voters from the old urban middle classes but also from the urban craftsmen and even workers, as witnessed in the name of its political organization "Højres Arbejderog Vælgerforening" from 1881 [Worker's and Voter's Association of the Right]; between 10

political majority in Copenhagen eventually changed because of the immigration of thousands of rural workers from all over Denmark and southern Sweden in the wake of the industrial revolution.[106] But until the rise of social democracy in the 1880s and 1890s, many of the urban workers voted for *Højre*. Only when the social democrats after 1878 succeeded in organizing trade unions and later began to collaborate with *Venstre* in the elections, the political climate in the capital changed. This victory was possible because, contrary to the situation in many other capital cities, the percentage of workers who voted was almost the same as other classes.[107] In 1903, the rapid increase in social democratic votes gave a social democrat the post of mayor for finances. In 1917 the Social Democratic Party obtained the majority and the position of lord mayor of the city, a post the party has held until today.

Legacy of the Oldenburg Empire: Populist and Democratic Nationalism in a Rump State

The notion of "Denmark" is far from unequivocal. On one hand, the name refers to a typical multinational empire, the Oldenburg Empire, which has played a role in European politics for centuries. On the other hand, this very same name refers to an atypical homogeneous small nation-state. This duality is nicely reflected in the use of two national anthems. The first is *Kong Christian* ("King Christian") written by Johannes Ewald in 1779. This martial song praises the warrior king who defeats the enemies of the country—and politely forgets how he lost everything in the end. The other song is *Der er et yndigt land* ("There is a lovely land") written in 1819 by the romanticist poet Adam Oehlenschläger, praising the beauty of the friendly and peaceful country and its national inhabitants. This latter is the one sung at national football games, regardless of the result. Denmark, Danes and "Danish" national consensus are caught between competing and at times even antagonistic notions of Danishness. Both notions are legacies of the Oldenburg Empire, albeit at odds with each other. This duality also explains the all dominating role of the capital of Copenhagen in the economy as well in the political culture and why the country until recently understood itself as agrarian, albeit in a capitalist and industrialized way. All these contradictions stem from the complicated and misunderstood nation-building process in the remnants of the Oldenburg Empire in the nineteenth century.

---

and 40% of the party's voters were urban workers; cf. Dybdahl, *De nye klasser*, 151–55; and Dybdahl, *Partier og erhverv*, 1969.

[106] Richard Willerslev, *Den glemte indvandring. Den svenske indvandring til Danmark 1850–1914* (Copenhagen: Academic Press, 1983).

[107] Dybdahl, *De nye klasser*, 226.

Empire, City, Nation: Venice's Imperial Past and the "Making of Italians" from Unification to Fascism

DAVID LAVEN AND ELSA DAMIEN

In the aftermath of the 1848–49 revolutions, even amongst those political commentators most deeply sympathetic to the cause of Italian unification, it remained commonplace to decry not only the politically fragmented nature of the peninsula but also the deep internal divisions within the Italian people. Thus, for example, the French historian François-Tommy Perrens, writing in a work completed shortly after the New Year in 1857, reflected that, "Agreement is no more than a dream. Everywhere division rules, between subjects as much as between princes, between one province or city and another, even within the very heart of an individual city. Nothing can be done that requires collective effort. Much has been spoken of federations and leagues, without a single one ever having been formed. In vain has it been desired to unite Rome with Florence, Lombardy with Piedmont, Sicily with Naples; but no one can agree on anything, even on the battlefield ... These suspicions, these universal jealousies have made Italy fail in favorable circumstances that perhaps will not be seen again for many years."[1]

At first glance it might appear as though Perrens spoke too soon: four years after the publication of his book, the new Kingdom of Italy was constituted, albeit without Venetia and Rome, which would not be acquired until 1866 and 1870 respectively. Yet despite the formation of a united constitutional monarchy under the rule of the House of Savoy, Italy's new rulers, and indeed most of those who had played a pivotal role in the unlikely process of unification, were painfully aware that while a single Italian state had been created for the first time since the fall of the Western Roman Empire, the overwhelming bulk of the population was at best indifferent, and at worst actively resentful and hostile toward the new political structure. Despite the massive

---

[1] F. Perrens, *Deux ans de révolution en Italie (1848–1849)* (Paris: Hachette, 1857), 357–58.

endorsement offered by (heavily rigged) plebiscites, which were held in all the House of Savoy's newly annexed territories bar Lombardy, it was not possible to avoid the obvious conclusion that, for the majority of Italians, the process of unification was an alien or fundamentally negative experience. A process of centralization—in large part a panicked response to widespread public opposition to the new order—was greeted by popular unease. In the south especially resistance took the form of violent unrest and open insurrection, misleadingly labeled the *grande brigantaggio*, in an attempt to demonize a movement that was political and social in its aims as purely criminal. It was in such a climate that the great Piedmontese moderate, Massimo d'Azeglio, is commonly alleged to have uttered the phrase, "Fatta l'Italia, bisogna fare gli italiani" ("With Italy made, it is necessary to make Italians"). In fact, d'Azeglio seems never to have made this remark,[2] but awareness of the problem it so succinctly expresses was without doubt general within Italy's ruling elites; it would remain so until the fascist era. Despite recent attempts by Alberto Banti to argue that the Risorgimento was a "mass movement,"[3] contemporaries were well aware that those who had actively supported unification had never amounted to more than a tiny percentage of the population: Italians needed to be made. The systematic use of repression by the new state (characterized by a calculated brutality that far exceeded anything ever adopted by any of its restoration predecessors), the undemocratic nature of its political system until the eve of the Great War,[4] and the fiercely anticlerical nature of the regime in an essentially Catholic country combined to create a climate in which the creation of a strong sense of national identity was little more than a fantasy. To make matters worse, the bulk of the population continued to identify the new order with unprecedented rates of taxation, and burden of military service.

It was in part in response to these problems that, during the final decades of the nineteenth and the beginning of the twentieth century, Italian governments pursued an imperial mission. Although often justified in strategic, economic, and demographic terms, Italian attempts at empire-building had two principal goals: first, to raise Italy's international status, and, second, to try to construct a stronger sense of nation at home. Indeed, it is hard not to see the former of these ambitions as largely arising from the latter: international recognition of Italy as a major imperial power would help build public confidence in the new state. It is not, however, our intention in this essay to offer a comprehensive analysis of the way in which the idea of the

---

[2] For a discussion of this phrase see the introduction in: S. Soldani and G. Turi, eds., *Fare gli italiani. Scuola e cultura nell'Italia contemporanea. I. La nascita dello stato nazionale* (Bologna: Il Mulino, 1993), vol. I, 17. See also A. M. Banti, *La nazione del Risorgimento. Parentela, sanità e onore alle origini dell'Italia unita* (Turin: Einaudi, 2000), 203.

[3] A. M. Banti, "Per una nuova storia del Risorgimento," in *Storia d'Italia. Annali. Vol. 22, Il Risorgimento*, eds. A. M. Banti and P. Ginsborg (Turin: Einaudi, 2007), xxiii–xli, xxiii.

[4] The Zanardelli law of 1882 extended the suffrage to slightly under 7% of the population. It was only during Giolitti's fourth ministry of 1911 to 1914 that steps were taken towards the adoption of a system approaching universal male suffrage; this was to be finally introduced in the 1919 elections.

Italian nation was fashioned through the government's efforts to acquire an empire, through the inevitable conflicts that this generated with other powers (most notably the Ottoman Empire, France, and Austria-Hungary), or through the invention of "Italianness" outside the peninsula (a process, after all, that was as likely to take place amongst emigrants in Buenos Aires, New York, or New Orleans as in the outposts of the nascent Italian imperium). Rather we intend to take a different approach, namely to focus on how debates surrounding empire, the practical consequences of imperial policy, and a "colonial imaginary" played a part in shaping attitudes to the nation in a particular city—Venice—and eventually played a pivotal role in the "making of the Italian nation," or perhaps more accurately "the imagining of the Italian nation," in that urban center.

A case study of a single city is particularly fruitful as an approach to understanding spatial identities in post-unification Italy. On the one hand, such a case study recommends itself because, given the severe reservations entertained by many Italians with regard to the new order established by unification, it is perhaps unsurprising that much of the population continued to look to local rather than national allegiances. Indeed, it is something of a historical commonplace to emphasize the resilience of local and municipal particularisms as one of the great obstacles to effectively attaching Italians to the national idea in the liberal era. On the other hand, research on Germany and France has increasingly demonstrated not only that national and local loyalties were not necessarily at loggerheads, but also that they were often mutually-reinforcing.[5] This sense that local identity could actually be the basic building block for creating the nation has been recently applied to the Italian case, perhaps most persuasively by Axel Körner in his study of Bologna.[6] It is our intention in this essay to build on these approaches, but to address them from a slightly different perspective, asking how far Venetian responses to both unification and "the making of Italians" were shaped by imperialist ambitions and the experience of empire. In doing this we shall examine both the historical legacy of the *Serenissima's* imperial past, and the practical consequences of contemporary Italian imperialism, but most significantly the interplay of the two.

---

[5] A. Confino, *The Nation as Local Metaphor: Württemberg, Imperial Germany, and National Memory, 1871–1918* (Chapel Hill: University of North Carolina Press, 1997); C. Applegate, *A Nation of Provincials: The German Idea of Heimat* (Berkeley: University of California Press, 1990). Similar arguments have been put forward for nineteenth-century France. See especially the works: A. Thiesse, *Écrire la France: le mouvement littéraire régionaliste de langue française entre la Belle Époque et la Libération* (Paris: PUF, 1991); A. Thiesse, *Ils apprenaient la France. L'exaltation des régions dans le discours patriotique* (Paris: Maison des Sciences de l'Homme, 1997). See also: J. Chanet, "Maîtres d'école et régionalisme en France, sous la Troisième République," *Ethnologie française* 18 (1988): 244–56; J. Chanet, *L'école républicaine et les petites patries* (Paris: Aubier, 1996); J. Lalouette, "L'éducation populaire au canton: Edmond Groult et les musées cantonaux," *Jean Jaurès cahiers trimestriels* 152 (1999): 91–104.

[6] A. Körner, *Politics of Culture in Liberal Italy: From Unification to Fascism* (London: Routledge, 2009).

Venice, it must be remembered, was one of the last significant parts of Italy to be united under the rule of the House of Savoy. Although the war of 1859, which had pitched French forces—inadequately supported by the Piedmontese—against the Austrian army, had originally been intended to liberate the whole of Venetia from Habsburg rule, peace had been made at a point when only Lombardy had been secured. Despite the outrage of Cavour, who resigned in protest at the failure to pursue the originally-agreed war aims and to push on to the Adriatic, the lands to the east of the River Mincio were not secured for the House of Savoy for another seven years. The acquisition of Venice was a fairly ignominious process,[7] dependent on the victory of Italy's Prussian allies at the battle of Königgrätz-Sadowa and the good offices of Napoleon III rather than on the military glories dreamed of by Vittorio Emanuele and his generals; only when the Austrians withdrew the vast bulk of their men to defend Vienna did the Italians make any significant headway—more-or-less unopposed—into Venetian territory. Significantly, while inhabitants of both the *Terraferma* and Venice itself welcomed the advance of the Italian army, there was no spontaneous insurrection in support of unification. Moreover, while observers recorded the delighted celebrations of the local population,[8] disillusionment followed swiftly. Even the departure of the garrison from Venice seems to have been marked by a certain melancholic display of affection for the Habsburg "whitecoats." The overwhelming support for unification in the plebiscite held on October 21–22 saw 647,246 votes in favor of annexation, and only 69 against. The result reflected in part optimism about a new order, but the huge margin in favor of annexation had other explanations: the presence of heavily armed Italian troops at the polling stations, the use of easily distinguishable "Yes" and "No" voting slips in public view, the intimidation of clergy to guarantee that they preached in favor of unity, and the lack of any alternative proposal to the immediate establishment of Savoyard rule, left Venetians with little choice but to accept the outcome as a foregone conclusion. Disillusionment followed rapidly, as Venetians switched from patriotic excitement to confronting the reality of the situation in which they now found themselves.[9] Not only was it clear that rule from Vienna had permitted much greater levels of autonomy than was the case under Italian rule, but it was also the case that, perhaps paradoxically, the need to balance the competing interests of diverse peripheries within the structure of a multinational empire meant that the authorities in

---

[7] The poor showing of the Italian army and, most especially, navy in 1866 led to an outpouring of self-lacerating articles, pamphlets and books. The most famous of these was the short work of the Neapolitan historian and academic, Pasquale Villari, in the Milanese journal *Il Politecnico* of 1867, entitled "Di chi è la colpa? O sia la pace e la Guerra," later republished several times as a free-standing pamphlet, *Di chi è la colpa?* (Milan: Francesco Zanetti, 1866).

[8] See, for example, the descriptions offered by Dickens's friend and sometime collaborator, G. A. Sala, *Rome and Venice: with other wanderings in Italy, in 1866–67* (London: Tinsley Brothers, 1869), 217–21.

[9] R. Camurri, "Istituzioni, associazioni e classi dirigenti dall'Unità alla Grande guerra," in *Storia di Venezia. L'Ottocento e il Novecento I, L'Ottocento. 1797–1918*, eds. M. Isenghi and S. Woolf (Rome: Istituto della Enciclopedia Italiana, 2002), 225–303, 237.

Vienna were more responsive to local needs than was the new national government in Florence. As a consequence of unification, Venice also found itself relegated from the position of the Habsburgs' second port with a vast imperial hinterland containing a seventh of Europe's population, to a distinctly subsidiary status, facing competition from Genoa, Livorno, Ancona, Naples, and a host of smaller Italian maritime cities. Any chance of a commercial renaissance was distinctly limited. To aggravate matters, Venice was annexed at a moment of fiscal crisis: in the aftermath of the creation of the Kingdom of Italy in 1861, a major campaign of state investment had been undertaken, in part to improve the national infrastructure for its own sake, and in part to create vested interests in defending unity amongst the disparate parts of the peninsula. Much of this expenditure had taken the form of heavy investment in railways, but, in the years up to 1866, the young Italian state had also indulged in heavy expenditure on public health, welfare, and education. By the time of the acquisition of Venice such government largesse had come to an end. The cost of policing the unrest in the south between 1861 and 1865, and dealing with the uprising in Palermo in 1866, coupled with the massive expenditure on the ultimately disastrous war against Austria left Italian coffers empty. Matters were aggravated by inheriting Venetia's share of the Austrian national debt, and by peace terms under which the Italians undertook to pay compensation for Austrian fortifications and railways in the annexed territories. This all dictated that the Italian government could no longer consider sustaining an annual budget deficit of over 25%. Retrenchment was essential in order to address huge debts. This meant that Venice and its mainland were suddenly obliged to shoulder a share of Italy's huge state debt, when they would not benefit directly from the heavy expenditure that had generated it. To make matters worse, annexation aggravated Venice's economic situation in other ways. During the American Civil War, which had disrupted cotton production and exports to Europe, Venice—albeit far from flourishing economically— had become a key port of entry for Egyptian cotton destined for the Central European market. Venice now found itself marginalized as a place of entry for this Egyptian product. This was less because peace in America led to renewed competition from the former Confederate states anxious to regain lost markets, than because Venice was now deprived of access to consumers in the Habsburg lands. Similarly, Vicentine woolen manufactures—largely destined to clothe Austrian soldiery—collapsed as a consequence of annexation.[10] Venetians who had hoped for prosperity and liberty as a result

---

[10] On unification and its economic impact on Venice, see A. Schram, *Railways and the Formation of the Italian State in the Nineteenth Century* (Cambridge: Cambridge University Press, 1997), 82–86. On the already depressed state of the Venetian economy in the period 1859–66, see also A. Bernardello, "Iniziative economiche, accumulazione e investimenti di capitale (1830–1866)," in *Storia di Venezia*, eds. Isnenghi and Woolf, 567–617, 584–86. For more general reflections on the Venetian economy, see G. Luzzatto, "L'economia veneziana dal 1797 al 1866," in *La civiltà veneziana nell'età romantica* (Florence: Sansoni, 1961), 85–108; G. Zalin, *Aspetti e problemi dell'economia veneta dalla caduta della Repubblica all'annessione* (Vicenza: Comune di Vicenza, 1969).

of unification, found themselves impoverished, their autonomy snatched from them, and with little voice in government.

If the immediate consequences of unification were largely negative for Venice, then it was also far from easy to appeal to Venetian involvement in the Risorgimento, which rapidly became the foundation myth for unity. On the one hand, Venice and its surrounding territories had a longstanding reputation for political passivity. Although a fair number of Veneti had participated in Garibaldi's expedition to Sicily in 1860, the region was widely considered to lack patriotic fiber. During the restoration years, the likes of Pellico and Mazzini had despaired of its inhabitants' refusal to challenge Austrian rule, and the one famous Venetian conspiracy, that of the Bandiera brothers, had ended in a tragicomedy of errors that scarcely added lustre to Venice's association with the national struggle for independence.[11] In neither 1859 nor 1866 did Venetians rally in significant numbers to the Italian cause. The one episode in recent Venetian history to which patriotic appeal might legitimately be made was the Venetian rising of 1848–49. Indeed, by the early 1870s, its most famous protagonist, Daniele Manin, had been successfully repackaged as a national hero. This process was facilitated by Manin's open condemnation of Mazzinian republicanism, and his adoption of a pro-Piedmontese monarchist stance in the years between his flight from Venice in 1849 and his death in 1857, a transformation that was symbolized on the one hand by his broadside against the former Roman Triumvir in the pages of the *Times*,[12] and on the other hand by his pivotal role in the formation of the moderate *Società Italiana Nazionale*.[13] Already by September 1861, a monument had been erected to Manin in Turin; in March 1875 a huge bronze statue, with a reclining winged lion at its pedestal was inaugurated in Venice in Campo San Paternian, subsequently renamed Campo Manin. Nevertheless, the incorporation of Manin and the Venetian revolution of 1848–49 into the patriotic prehistory of Italian unification was deeply problematic.[14] As a member of Turin's *consiglio comunale* vociferously protested in 1861, Manin had

---

[11] On the politically passive, even supine, nature of Venetians in the Restoration era, see D. Laven, *Venice and Venetia under the Habsburgs, 1815–1835* (Oxford: Oxford University Press, 2002), 149–212.

[12] *The Times*, May 27, 1856.

[13] The definitive account of the SNI remains R. Grew, *A Sterner Plan for Italian Unification. The Italian National Society in the Risorgimento* (Princeton: Princeton University Press, 1963).

[14] The key values of the Venetian revolution found expression within the historiography of the *Serenissima* in the monumental work of Samuele Romanin, his vast *Storia documentata di Venezia*, 10 vols. (Venice: Naratovich, 1853–64). Romanin's work remained the fundamental reference point for historians of the city until the twentieth century, but his desire to extol ideas of democracy and republicanism, as well as the fundamental distinctiveness of Venice rested uneasily with a political climate that sought unity through the House of Savoy, and utterly rejected any federal solution to the Italian question. See E. Damien, "Narrating Venice in nineteenth-century Italy: the notions of municipal and national in Samuele Romanin's patriotic project, the *Storia documentata di Venezia* (1853–64)," *Journal of Modern Italian Studies* 16 (2011): 19–36.

been part of a fiercely republican tradition and a statue of him was, therefore, inappropriate in the Savoyard capital.[15] Indeed, attempts to incorporate Manin in the patriotic pantheon raised as many problems as they solved. For while there was no doubt that, as Vincenzo Gioberti observed in 1851, Manin's name was inseparable from that of the "eroica città,"[16] then the Venetian resistance to the Austrians was both widely perceived as essentially particularist, and hostile to the Piedmontese (who had failed to provide the besieged city with any tangible support).[17] In addition, 1848–49 had been characterized by squabbling between Venetians and non-Venetian patriots, by clashes of interest between genuine *veneziani* and *veneti* from the *Terraferma*, and by class and ideological fissures within the population of the city itself. These were all symptomatic of the historical divisions that had traditionally made the peninsula so vulnerable to outside domination: the mid-century revolutions did not automatically make for an edifying spectacle. Attempts to use the events of the *'quarantotto* to embed Venice firmly within a narrative of national liberation nonetheless continued. They came both from Venetians anxious to seek accommodation and influence within the new order, and from those nationalists who sought to foster a strong and uniform sense of Italian national identity.[18] Such conscious myth-making ran the risk of alienating the Venetian public still aware of the betrayal of 1848–49 and skeptical about the far from positive consequences of 1866.

---

[15] C. Lanfranco, "L'uso politico dei monumenti: il caso torinese fra 1849 e 1915," *Il Risorgimento* 48 (1996): 207–73. On the Venetian monument, see L. Alban, "Il monumento a Daniele Manin," *Venetica* 5 (1996): 11–44. We are grateful to our research student, Laura Parker, for bringing the existence of the Turin monument to our notice.

[16] Vincenzo Gioberti, *Del rinnovamento civile d'Italia* (Turin & Paris: Libraio S.S.R.M., 1851), 295.

[17] A famous *Times* headline on the heroism of the Venetians from September 1, 1849 referred significantly to the fact that Venice constituted a nation in its own right.

[18] See, for example, the two long articles in the *Archivio Veneto* dating from much the same period as the erection of the Manin monument. R. Fulin, "Venezia e Daniele Manin," *Archivio Veneto* 9/1 (1875): v–ccxxvi; and A. De Giorgi, "Venezia nel 1848 e 1849," *Archivio Veneto* 9/1 (1875): 1–50. Significantly, Fulin stressed that Manin's life was "so glorious a part of the modern history of the city," while simultaneously pointing to the wider service both the revolutionary leader and the city had rendered "to the common *patria.*" De Giorgi, a neo-Thomist expert on Roman Law, sometime editor of Romagnosi and friend of Manin, was, in contrast, at pains to emphasize that even Venice's fourteen centuries of glory "are in the final analysis Italian glories." Similarly, he underlined the ease with which Venetian republican traditions could be reconciled to "a national monarchy" (13). Was De Giorgi, who was purged by the Italian authorities in 1867 from his chair in Roman Law at Padua University, which he had held since 1849, perhaps trying to appease the new order? On De Giorgi's career, see A. Manfredi, *Vescovi, clero e cura pastorale. Studi sulla diocesi di Parma alla fine dell'Ottocento* (Rome: Editrice Pontifica Università Gregoriana, 1999), 150–51. See also A. De Giorgi, "Memorie della mia vita (1865)" with a preface by Roberto Treves in *I tempi e le opere di Gian Domenico Romagnosi*, eds. E. A. Albertoni and R. Ghiringhelli (Milano: A. Giuffrè, 1990).

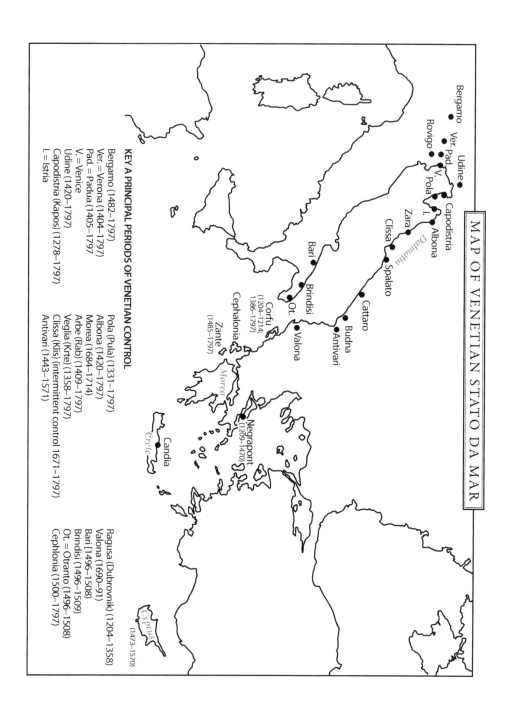

MAP OF VENETIAN STATO DA MAR

KEY A PRINCIPAL PERIODS OF VENETIAN CONTROL

Bergamo (1482–1797)
Ver. = Verona (1404–1797)
Pad. = Padua (1405–1797)
V. = Venice
Udine (1420–1797)
Capodistria (Kapos) (1278–1797)
I. = Istria

Pola (Pula) (1331–1797)
Albona (1420–1797)
Morea (1684–1714)
Arbe (Rab) (1409–1797)
Veglia (Krte) (1358–1797)
Clissa (Klis) (intermittent control 1671–1797)
Antivari (1443–1571)

Ragusa (Dubrovnik) (1204–1358)
Valona (1690–91)
Bari (1496–1508)
Brindisi (1496–1509)
Ot. = Otranto (1496–1508)
Cephlonia (1500–1797)

A far more successful means of stitching the Venetians into the Italian boot than any patriotic appeal to its part in the Risorgimento was to be found in the imperialist project—or, at least, in aspects thereof—that had its origins in pre-unification debates about overseas expansion and Italy's role as a Mediterranean power, but which blossomed in the liberal era. Central to this are two key elements. First, that the Republic of Saint Mark's experience as a major imperial power permitted Venetians not only to reinvent themselves as integral to a new state from which they had initially felt alienated; and second, that those who championed *irredentismo*, and the extension of Italian domination in the Balkans and Eastern Mediterranean, not only sought legitimacy through presenting their ambitions as harking back to Venice's *Stato da Mar*, but also sought to link them to the fostering of commercial, military, and cultural projects that brought genuine advantages to the city. Imperialism thus played an important role in making Venetians less inward-looking, less likely to seek refuge in *venezianità*. In short, through looking to Italian expansionism, Venetians were able to position themselves at the center rather than on the periphery of Italian nationalism. At the same time, the adoption of so-called Adriatic nationalism—to a great degree championed by Venetians—and pursuit of irredentist claims were pivotal to bringing Italy into the Italo-Turkish War of 1911–12, in its jettisoning of its partners in the Triple Alliance, and in its hesitant entrance into the Great War in 1915. The latter of these two conflicts turned Venice into a frontline city, threatened by Austrian bombardment, which in turn helped cement its place in nationalist rhetoric: during the Great War and in its immediate aftermath there was renewed emphasis on Venice's history of resisting the Habsburgs, which both encouraged its citizens to turn to the nation as their protector against "teutonic" aggression, and underpinned demands for imperial expansion into the lands of the former *Stato da Mar* for reasons of strategic defense. Under the Fascists, *venezianità* would be seen as a link with *romanità*, legitimating attempts to build a new Roman imperial edifice with the *Duce* at its head.

Venice and the Prehistory of Italian Imperialism

Just as Italy was a late comer as a European nation-state, so it was tardy in its acquisition of overseas imperial possessions. This does not mean that nineteenth-century Italians never thought about possible colonies long before unification was achieved. As Maurizio Isabella has recently demonstrated there was a long history of Italian imperialist thought prior to the establishment of the Kingdom of Italy. Perhaps surprisingly, even Giuseppe Mazzini (so quick to vilify the Habsburgs for stifling national independence) and the brilliant federalist Carlo Cattaneo could on occasion be found defending colonialism, although a marked ambivalence always informed their writings.[19] For

---

[19]   M. Isabella, "Liberalism and Empires in the Mediterranean: the view-point of the Risorgimento," in *The Risorgimento Revisited. Nationalism and Culture in Nineteenth-Century Italy*, eds. L. Riall and S. Patriarca (Basingstoke: Palgrave Macmillan, 2011), 232–54.

Vincenzo Gioberti, geographical determinism dictated that Italy should dominate the Mediterranean.[20] But the Piedmontese cleric also stressed in his enormously influential *Primato* of 1843—the work that triggered the neo-Guelf movement, so influential in the outbreak of revolution in 1848—that the strong historical precedent for Italian imperialism within the Mediterranean basin was to be found not only in the glories of the Roman Empire: the tradition lived on long after the collapse of the western empire; both Venice and Genoa (which we shall discuss briefly by way of comparison later in this essay) possessed extensive overseas territories.[21] Moreover, it was to Italian military and cultural prowess that all other Europeans owed their current glories. Indeed, Britain's maritime prowess, on which its own empire was built, would never have existed without the lessons taught by Italy's maritime republics. "You, brave Britons, would not be able to dominate the seas and be the Romans of the oceans ... if the Catholic fleets of Amalfi, Pisa, Genoa, Venice had not taught your forefathers the art of mastering the waves."[22]

Two key elements can be detected in the way that the imperial and Mediterranean role of the former Republic of Venice was located within pre-unification discussions of a potential imperial mission for Italy. On the one hand, authors stressed the importance of Venice's former Mediterranean presence, both as a bastion of *italianità* and as a bulwark in defense of a wider western and Christian culture. On the other hand, it was also widely presented as a model of maritime hegemony and imperial rule, and as a bridge between eastern and western economies and cultures. Such sentiments were already evident in the years immediately after the fall of the *Serenissima* in 1797: they are, for instance, neatly encapsulated in the opening lines of William Wordsworth's much-quoted "On the extinction of the Venetian Republic"

> Once did she hold the gorgeous East in fee,
> And was the safeguard of the West: the worth
> Of Venice did not fall below her birth,
> Venice, the eldest child of Liberty.[23]

There is not space to treat exhaustively here how this view of Venice's past imperial and hegemonic role developed in the course of the Risorgimento era, but it was clearly extremely widespread. Let us offer just a few examples. Take the position adopted by novelist and *garibaldino* Ippolito Nievo in his pamphlet "Venezia e la libertà d'Italia."[24]

[20] V. Gioberti, *Del Primato morale e civile degli Italiani* (Lausanne: Bonamici & co, 1846), vol. 2, 52. Gioberti bizarrely argued that the only other country destined for imperial grandeur by virtue of its geographical position was Guatemala. Ibid., 387–88.

[21] Ibid., 91–2.

[22] Ibid., 72.

[23] The piece was written in 1802, but not published until 1807. William Wordsworth, *The Poetical Works of William Wordsworth* (Boston: Cummings, Hilliard, & Co., 1824), vol. 2, 320.

[24] I. Nievo, "Venezia e la libertà d'Italia," in *Ippolito Nievo. Opere*, ed. S. Romagnoli (Milan & Naples: Riccardo Ricciardi Editore, 1952), 1033–52.

Elsewhere, Nievo had been critical of the late Republic, most notably in his posthumously published novel, written in 1857–58,[25] but in this propagandistic pamphlet Venice—"after Rome it is the most Italian city of our fatherland"[26]—embodied not only all the virtues of the "spirito antico italiano" but was presented as the unparalleled champion of Italian freedom and culture against a hostile other: "Liberty and civilization, behold the ancient characteristics of the Latin people lost in Medieval Italy, yet preserved always by Venice and defended through an innumerable series of wars, treaties and internal tumults ... the same shield that defended Venetian trade and commercial establishments against the Turks of Constantinople, against the Uskoks of the Don, and against the Barbary Corsairs of Tunis, while at the same time defending the literary, scientific and artistic rebirth of Italy and the whole world."[27] Venice was above all to be celebrated as the shield of Christendom, *italianità*, and western culture, betrayed by an ungrateful Europe both during its seventeenth-century defense of Crete and on the eve of Campoformido; it was to Venice that Europe owed centuries of freedom from the Ottomans.[28] But there was another side to Venice's existence, which Nievo identified clearly in the *Confessioni*: Venice's mercantile contact with the East had made it "la mediatrice dei due mondi" ("the bridge between two worlds").[29]

Cesare Balbo similarly pointed to the pivotal role of Medieval Venice, likening it to modern London as an imperial, military, commercial, and industrial center,[30] while Carlo Cattaneo extolled Venice as a model of maritime hegemony in the Mediterranean in 1846, advocating Venetian-style imperialism as a way forward for European influence in North Africa. Rather than occupying great swathes of territory, argued the Milanese, the French would be well-advised to copy the Venetian example and to limit their presence to urban centers on the littoral: "... a chain of maritime stations, similar to the colonies of the Phoenicians and the Greeks and to the Venetian cities in Dalmatia, in which latter the Italian and Slav races of such different levels of civilization, nonetheless lived together in the most stable peace."[31] Significantly in this passage, Cattaneo emphasized the ability of the Venetians to reconcile their non-Italian subjects to their rule. This notion of local acceptance of Venetian rule became a

---

[25] I. Nievo, "Le confessioni d'un Italiano," in *Ippolito Nievo. Opere*, ed. S. Romagnoli (Milan & Naples: Riccardo Ricciardi Editore, 1952), 3–883. See especially the opening pages of Chapter 6, 211–18.

[26] Nievo, "Venezia," 1033.

[27] Ibid., 1035.

[28] Ibid., 1034.

[29] Nievo, "Confessioni," 400.

[30] "Venice was like the London of today; its Arsenal was Woolwich and Plymouth; its piazzetta and its canal were the Docks [....] its mastery of one quarter of the eastern Roman Empire, held for some time, and then of Crete and Cyprus and Morea, were within the context of the times, equivalent to modern day European colonies." C. Balbo, *Pensieri sulla storia d'Italia* (Florence: Felice Le Monnier, 1858), 187.

[31] C. Cattaneo, "Di alcuni stati moderni," in *Alcuni Scritti* (Milan: Borroni e Scotti, 1846), vol. 2, 229–65, 257.

commonplace: Gioberti, for example, stressed the benign nature of the Republic's rule—"un paterno dominio"—of its colonies.[32] Much more critical had been the Swiss economist and historian, Simonde de Sismondi, who, while happy to portray the Venetian state as the most systematic defender of Europe from the ravages of the Turks, cruelly "abandoned by all Christendom,"[33] and a kindly overlord of its Italian *Terraferma*, nevertheless damned attitudes and conduct in their Greek, Albanian, and Illyrian possessions. According to Sismondi, Venetians were disdainful of their "sujets levantins" ("All the Greeks were deemed false and corrupt, all the Illyrians barbarian"), incapable of affection for their overseas empire, and prepared to spend time there purely with a view to amassing a fortune.

> Finally, the inhabitants of the overseas provinces formed a third class, de-
> spised, oppressed, and whose interests were always sacrificed to those of
> the two others [Venetians and inhabitants of the *Terraferma*]. Their ports
> were markets preserved purely for Venetians, where the latter exercised
> an odious and exclusive monopoly; their fortresses were designed to con-
> trol their subjects through fear, and to guarantee the domination of the
> Adriatic; but these fortifications did not defend the frontiers, nor protect
> agriculture or peace through an unbreachable barrier; their militias were
> frequently left unarmed; the troops levied in this land of warriors, were
> not incorporated with the rest of the Venetian army, but were relegated
> to the very lowest rank of the military establishment.[34]

Amongst Italian authors, however, Venetian rule of the *Stato da Mar* was generally portrayed in a positive light. This was particularly true of the Venetian presence on the eastern shores of the Adriatic. A powerful narrative both of affection for Venetian rule, and of the cultural as well as commercial benefits that Dalmatia and Istria derived from close connection with the Republic of Saint Mark became widespread.[35] This

---

[32] Gioberti, *Del Primato*, ii, 91.

[33] Jean-Charles-Léonard Simonde de Sismondi, *Histoire des Républiques Italiennes du moyen âge*, 16 vols. (Paris: H. Nicolle, and subsequently Treuttel & Würtz, 1807–1818). The quotation comes from the abridged English translation of Sismondi's work, *A History of the Italian Republics, being a View of the Origin, Progress and Fall of Italian Freedom* (London: Longman, Brown, Green & Longmans, 1832), 259.

[34] Sismondi, *Républiques italiennes*, vol. 10, 262–63. Elsewhere he argued that "In maintaining this system, the Republic of Venice manifested at least vigour and foresight; but in the overseas terri-tories, there was nothing to be seen except corruption, negligence and embezzlement. The Greek subjects of the Republic came to be so vexed by the injustice of Venetian governors, and by the monopolies of the Venetian merchants, that they were nostalgic for the Turkish yoke." Ibid., vol. 14, 340–41.

[35] To some degree this harked back to earlier writings on the intimate links between Venice and its Slav subjects. The eighteenth-century playwright Goldoni, for example, stressed the tight and mutually-beneficial links between Venice and Dalmatia. On the eighteenth-century attitudes

relationship was probably most powerfully stated in the work of Niccolò Tommaseo. Hero of the 1848 revolution, brilliant lexicographer and linguist, accomplished polemicist and author, Tommaseo was extremely proud of his Dalmatian origins, and certainly never an advocate of renewed Italian rule of the eastern Adriatic coast.[36] Nevertheless, he was passionate in his defense of both the Venetian legacy and of the wider Italian cultural influence in his homeland, albeit in part as a means of undermining Croat "Illyrianist" claims to the region. Repeatedly returning to this theme, he was perhaps at his most eloquent in his *La questione Dalmatica* of 1861. Tommaseo was dismissive of those who sought to vilify Venetian rule, whether Daru in an attempt to legitimate Napoleon—"his patron, great master of liberty, as everyone knows"— or Croat propagandists seeking to blacken the name of and marginalize the littoral's educated, Italianized community. The Venetians merited affection and esteem not merely because no other European power would have saved the region from Ottoman control ("If it were not for Venice, Dalmatia would have Pashas instead of Bans"), but also because they had been an actively positive influence.[37] Mocking those who echoed Sismondi in alleging the hatred felt for Venetian misrule, Tommaseo remarked: "But if the tyranny of these foreigners was so abominable, why was it that the Dalmatians did not shake it off during the League of Cambrai, or when other opportunities presented themselves? ... Subjugated Dalmatia loved Venice; Saint Mark was a sacred name, gave the sacred banner; until the very last Dalmatians fought for her, and over her [defeat] they wept."[38]

By the time Venice was annexed to Italy, there already existed a strong sense of its distinctive place within Italian history. On the one hand, it had for centuries retained its independence far more effectively than other states within the peninsula; on the other hand, it had wielded an influence across the eastern half of the Mediterranean, which had not only brought wealth, but had also played a pivotal part in the protection of Italy and the rest of western Christendom from Ottoman subjection. In the years immediately after 1866, historians appealed to these traditions in an attempt to find past glories that linked an unenthusiastic Venetian population to a

---

to Venice's relationship with Dalmatia, see L. Wolff, *Venice and the Slavs: the Discovery of Dalmatia in the Age of Enlightenment* (Palo Alto: Stanford University Press, 2003). See also L. Wolff, "Venice and the Slavs of Dalmatia: the Drama of the Adriatic Empire in the Venetian Enlightenment," *Slavic Review* 56 (1997), 428–55.

[36] Significantly, despite his position of prominence within the anti-Austrian revolution of 1848–49, Tommaseo sought to block attempts made by Venetian propagandists to appeal to Dalmatians to support the insurrection. See D. Reill, "A Mission of Mediation: Dalmatia's Multi-national Regionalism from the 1830s–60s," in *Different Paths to the Nation: Regional and National Identities in Central Europe and Italy, 1830–70,* ed. L. Cole (Basingstoke: Palgrave Macmillan, 2007), 16–36, 16–17.

[37] N. Tommaseo, *La questione dalmatica riguardata ne'suoi nuovi aspetti* (Zare: Fratelli Battara, 1861), 18.

[38] Ibid., 18–19.

national narrative, which also increased Venice's chance of attaining benefits from the new government.[39]

The Arsenale and Venezianità

One of the central hopes of Venetians in the years immediately after 1866 was that the *Arsenale*—for centuries the biggest industrial enterprise in Europe, and still a significant producer of warships even in the final years of the Republic—might be revivified. In the years after 1860, the Italian government had spent lavishly on constructing a modern, armored, steam-powered fleet, only for Persano's ironclads to be crushed by Tegetthoff's mostly wooden ships with crews drawn predominantly from formerly Venetian lands, who apparently celebrated victory with shouts of "Viva San Marco!" Despite the need for post-war retrenchment, there was widespread recognition after the humiliating defeat of Lissa that naval construction had to continue, both to defend Italy's shores and as a prerequisite for any future extension of Mediterranean influence. Days before the plebiscite of October 21–22, 1866, a decree had been passed promising regeneration of the Venetian *Arsenale*. Yet it was not long before a petition signed by over 1400 Venetians was sent to parliament demanding that action be taken for the purposes of "restoring it to its natural glory."[40] Of course, one of the problems with developing Venice as a naval center was that it was in competition with other ports with similar claims: La Spezia—preferred naval base of Cavour, and once the favored site

---

[39] Interesting in these terms is a review published in the *Archivio Veneto* of a three volume work in Italian published in Zara (today's Zadar) in the early 1870s under the auspices of the Habsburg regime. The reviewer acknowledged that geographically the eastern Adriatic "is nothing more than a westward extension of European Turkey," but was anxious to stress its historical and cultural links with the west. In medieval and early modern times Dalmatian valor had helped save Italy from the Ottomans, and in return the Italians had sowed the seeds of culture, which had flourished in Dalmatian soil. "This long strip of land, that alongside Rome and Venice will share one day the sorrows and the glories of the fatherland—that rulers of Italy have always seen as their natural extension—and it is pointless to keep quiet about the fact that Venice held it as an integral part of its territories, and as the best guarantee of the Adriatic Sea, and always showed herself extremely jealous of its possession, so that only when she was absolute master of it, did she proclaim herself Queen of the Adriatic—is Dalmatia." N. Battaglini, "Review of L. Maschek, *Manuale del Regno di Dalmazia*," 3 vols. (Zara: Fratelli Battara, 1872; G. Woditzka, 1873–74) in *Archivio Veneto* 8/i (1874), 157–79, 158–59.

[40] May 7, 1867, *Rendiconti del Parlamento Italiano. Sessione del 1867. Discussioni della Camera dei Deputati vol. I dal 22 marzo al 6 giugno 1867* (Florence: Eredi Botta, 1867), 559. The phrase is that of Galeazzo Giacomo Maldini, elected as deputy for Venice, naval captain and member of the Società italiana geografica. Maldini would later serve on a government committee to establish priorities for the development of a railway network around Venice. See G. Collotta, ed., *Intorno alle questioni ferroviarie nei riguardi della provincia, della città e del porto di Venezia: relazione della commissione nominata nella seduta del 26 settembre 1872, composta dei signori Maldini, Bertoli e Collotta relatore* (Venice: Stabilmento di G. Antonelli, 1873).

for an arsenal in the Napoleonic regime—had already become the premier naval base of the new kingdom despite the jealousy of the Genoese. Many in Naples also hoped for greater investment in military boat yards in the hope of economic benefits.[41] Just as rivalry between the Ligurians and Neapolitans had played a key part in the defeat of the Italian fleet at Lissa, so the competition for investment in developing shipyards generated antagonism between different Italian cities. Even by the mid-1870s imperial ambitions within the Adriatic had led to a preference for Taranto and Brindisi in Puglia—in large part because of their region's proximity to Albania, seen as a potential Italian acquisition.[42] Nevertheless, Venice's historical role in the Adriatic, coupled with the somewhat diffident attitude of the bulk of its inhabitants towards the newly united state, recommended that investment be ploughed into the *Arsenale* as a means of winning over Venetians and strengthening Italy's naval position. This was championed with especial determination by Nino Bixio, disciplinarian *garibaldino*, regular army general in 1866, and senator. Perhaps improbably for so dedicated a man of action, Bixio spent long periods in 1867 studying the history of the *Serenissima*'s navy as a means of legitimating its role once more as a key port for the pursuit of Italian naval power in the Adriatic and Mediterranean.[43] The eventual drive for the expansion of the *Arsenale* was triggered in large part by the opening of the Suez Canal in 1869. This project—once mooted by the Venetians in the early sixteenth century in response to Portuguese rounding of the Cape—shifted considerable focus toward the eastern Mediterranean, the traditional sphere of Venetian influence. The possibilities it opened played a pivotal part in the formation of the *Società Veneta*, established in Padua in January 1872.[44] Its president was the future senator Vincenzo Stefano Breda who would later also establish the *Cantieri Navali Breda*—the shipyards—at Marghera on the mainland facing Venice across the lagoon. The *Società Veneta*—which by 1881 had a technical and administrative staff of over 700—became one of the key contractors for public works in Italy, and was instrumental in the massive redevelopment of the *Arsenale* from the early 1870s onwards, dramatically adapting and expanding its structures to make it capable of producing modern warships.[45] One of the first major warships to be constructed in Venice was the *Francesco Morosini*, appropriately named after the seventeenth-century naval and land commander, and doge, who had been one the last great military heroes of the Republic in its wars against Ottoman

---

[41] G. Bellavitis, *L'Arsenale di Venezia. Storia di una grande struttura urbana* (Venice: Cicero, 2009), 221–23.

[42] M. Gabriele and G. Fritz, *La flotta come strumento di politica nei primi decenni dello stato unitario italiano* (Rome: Ufficio Storico Marina Miltare, 1973), 160.

[43] B. Cecchetti, *L'Archivio di Stato di Venezia. Nel decennio 1866–75* (Venice: Naratovich, 1876).

[44] On the formation of the Società Veneta, see A. M. Banti, *Storia della borghesia italiana. L'età liberale* (Rome: Donzelli, 1996), 147.

[45] Bellavitis, *L'Arsenale*, 231

expansion, famously portrayed by the artist Giacomo Favretto in 1879.[46] By the turn of the twentieth century, dreadnoughts were also in production in the *Arsenale*. This revivification of the historical military boat yards, brought about in large part to pursue an imperial mission, helped to breathe new life into Venice's moribund economy,[47] as well as creating a link between Venice's past and a more dynamic modernity. But while linked to the past there was also a sharp contrast, as the patriotic writer Gabriele d'Annunzio observed in his great novel of 1898, *Il fuoco*: "... the clamour of the Arsenal workers on their way to their warlike work, all the emanation of the water's edge where one could still smell the old rotten galleys of the *Serenissima* and where the iron-cladding of Italian ships reverberated under the blows of the hammer."[48]

Venetian hopes that rejuvenation of the *Arsenale* might bring material benefits to the city co-existed with a very different sense that the city's future lay not in modernization but in an emphasis on its distinctive past and picturesque present. While new wharves and workshops were erected and English-built industrial cranes began to compete with Venice's bell towers, the 1870s to 1890s saw a flowering of slightly kitsch Venetian art, best represented in the works of Giacomo Favretto and Ettore Tito, that celebrated both past glories and the *Venezia minore*—the everyday life of the city's ordinary, contemporary inhabitants. The emphasis on this distinctive *venezianità* could be seen in the works of both Venetian and non-Venetian scholars and commentators. Thus the Roman-born but Venetian-trained architect, critic, and novelist Camillo Boito, now best known for *Senso* (his novella set against the backdrop of the 1866 war), wrote an eloquent defense of the disappearing popular Venice in the influential *Nuova Antologia*.[49] A host of Anglophone artists from Sir Samuel Luke Fildes to John Singer Sargent and Maurice Brazil Prendergast sought to cap-

---

[46] Ibid., 222–23; M. Plant, *Venice: Fragile City 1797–1997* (New Haven: Yale University Press, 2002), 175. In both Fascist and post-war Italy, warships and submarines have been named after the warlike doge. In 1961, Morosini's name was also adopted by Venice's naval collegio, the "Scuola navale militare 'Francesco Morosini,'" which still seeks to emphasize the links between Venice's former maritime grandeur and the modern Italian navy—according to the Italian navy's official website, its pupils past and present are "[...] breathing the maritime nature, the history, the culture of this great city, the pride of the nation and of every seafaring man [....]" http://www.marina.difesa.it/morosini/cerimonia.asp.

[47] Some indication of the economic impact of enlargement of the *Arsenale* can be drawn simply from the numbers of those working there. The only other industrial enterprise to approach it in terms of providing work was the Manifattura Tabacchi, which employed, like the *Arsenale*, around 1500 workers in 1871; by 1911 the *Arsenale*'s workforce had risen to over 2,400. See L. Pes, "Le classi popolari" in *Storia di Venezia I*, eds. Isenghi and Woolf, 771–800, 779 & 782. It should, of course, be noted that, perhaps paradoxically, among the *arsenalotti* themselves support for imperialism or militarism was not especially strong as a consequence of their tendency to align with the political left.

[48] G. d'Annunzio, *Il fuoco* (Rome: L'Oleandro, 1933), 198. On d'Annunzio and *venezianità*, see M. Isenghi, "D'Annunzio e l'ideologia della venezianità," in *D'Annunzio e Venezia. Atti del Convegno*, ed. E. Mariano (Rome: Lucarini, 1991), 229–44.

[49] C. Boito, "Rassegna artistica: Venezia ne'suoi vecchi edifici," *Nuova Antologia* 20 (1872): 916–27.

ture scenes of everyday life with varying degrees of verisimilitude, while writers such as the American novelist and consul William Dean Howells and the British historian Horatio Brown produced what amounted to affectionate ethnographies based on long residence and familiarity.[50] Ruskin—who actually hated modern Venetians—championed all aspects of Venetian gothic.[51] Such emphasis on the distinctive nature of Venice helped, alongside the growing trend in sea bathing,[52] to transform the city into a highly seductive tourist destination by the final quarter of the nineteenth century.[53] This both encouraged a fierce emphasis on what was characteristically Venetian (and, therefore, appealing to the visitor), and often went hand-in-hand with resistance to modernization and an emphasis on continuity. Such views were perhaps most fervently articulated by the social historian, school teacher, parliamentary deputy for Brescia, and eventually senator and briefly undersecretary of the state for the fine arts, Pompeo Molmenti, both before and in the aftermath of the Great War. A fierce opponent of anything that might threaten the unique beauty of Venice, Molmenti was perhaps at his most outspoken in the essays, published four years before he died in 1928, in *I nemici di Venezia*,[54] in which his principal targets were the so-called *pontisti*, the supporters of a road bridge linking Venice to the mainland.[55] But well before the debate over linking Venice to the mainland with a second causeway, Molmenti had made clear his position regarding the need to conserve what was distinctive about the city:

> Certainly modern times have declared war on the old poetry, and whoever says that with poetry you die of hunger is quite right. It is a good thing, therefore, that work and industry come to Venice. But why not try to reconcile today's requirements with ancient beauty? Is there really such a rift between duties owed to the past and the needs of modern civilization? No one can oppose some partial widening of roads, and the demolition of miserable and filthy hovels, but whoever destroys something ought to feel the obligation to replace it with something better ... Venice certainly cannot remain unchanging, immutable, lifeless, while everywhere around it is movement and progress, but whoever might want to reduce the most distinctive city in the world to the same level as many tedious

---

[50] W. D. Howells, *Venetian Life* (Boston: Houghton Mifflin, 1881; originally published 1866); H. Brown, *Life on the Lagoons* (London: Kegan Paul, Trench & Co., 1884).

[51] See especially: R. Hewison, *Ruskin on Venice: 'The Paradise of Cities'* (New Haven: Yale University Press, 2009).

[52] See unpublished PhD thesis, L. Levantis, *Venise un spectacle d'eau et de pierre. Architecture et paysage dans les récits de voyageurs français (1756–1850)*, Université Pierre Mendès-France, Grenoble II, 2009.

[53] A. Zannini, "La costruzione della città turistica," in *Storia di Venezia*, eds. Isenghi and Woolf, 1123–49.

[54] P. Molmenti, *I nemici di Venezia*, ed. E. Zorzi (Bologna: N. Zanichelli, 1924).

[55] On the debates between *pontisti* and *anti pontisti*, see Plant, *Venice*, 282–84.

and monotonous modern cities ... would be committing a crime against art, against all those who still feel love for the cult of beauty.[56]

Yet in championing the preservation of a city he loved, Molmenti also stressed its specific mission and its connection with an imperial past.[57] Take for example his engagement with the memorialization of Sebastiano Venier, the Venetian commander at the victory of Lepanto and subsequent doge.[58] Molmenti wrote extensively on both the naval victory and Veniero himself, always prefering the Italianized version of the latter's name in his titles ("... why not simply say 'Venier' in proper Venetian fashion?" remarked one of his reviewers),[59] but he was also the driving force behind the transfer of Venier's bones from Santa Maria degli Angeli on Murano to the church of SS. Giovanni e Paolo in Venice itself. Having won the approval of the *consiglio comunale* in April 1896, the move took place in the presence of Queen Margherita, the duca di Genova, and Venice's *sindaco* on June 30, 1897, during a carefully orchestrated ceremony involving a considerable naval and military presence.[60] As Stouraiti has argued, Molmenti's emphasis on a Venetian who owed his fame to an attempted defense of Venetian dominance in the eastern Mediterranean made him an unlikely ally of some of the modernizers who sought radically to change his native city.[61] In this he

---

[56] P. Molmenti, *Venezia* (Bergamo: Istituto Italiano d'Arti Grafiche, 1905), 125–26.

[57] See, for example, his brief *Veneziani e Turchi in Dalmazia* (1915). On Molmenti's career, see M. Donaglio, *Un esponente dell'eélite liberale: Pompeo Molmenti politico e storico di Venezia* (Venice: Istituto veneto di scienze, lettere ed arti, 2004). Also useful is M. Donaglio, "Il difensore di Venezia. Pompeo Molmenti fra idolatria del passato e pragmatismo politico," *Venetica* 13 (1996): 45–72.

[58] On Molmenti and Lepanto, see A. Stouraiti, "Construendo un luogo di memoria," in *Meditando sull'evento di Lepanto. Odierne interpretazioni e memorie*, ed. M. Sbalchiero (Venice: Corbo e Fiore, 2004), 35–52. Also available electronically at: http://www.storiadivenezia.net/sito/saggi/stouraiti_lepanto.pdf, 1–17.

[59] P. Molmenti, *Sebastiano Veniero e la battaglia di Lepanto* (Florence: G. Barbèra, 1899); P. Molmenti, "Sebastiano Veniero dopo la battaglia di Lepanto," *Nuovo Archivio Veneto* 15, no. 30 (1915): 3–146.

[60] Stouraiti, "Costruendo un luogo," 13–14; P. Molmenti, "Sebastiano Veniero e la sua tombe," *Nuova Antologia* 66 (1896): 240–73. For pictures of the ceremony, see G. Secrétant, "Fra la grandezza e la decadenza di Venezia. (Lepanto, il suo eroe, i suoi monumenti)," *Il Secolo XX* 10 (1907): 793–813.

[61] "An initiative of Molmenti, a fierce defender of *venezianità* and one of the principal apologists for the old regime, appeared to fit perfectly with a specifically Venetian valuation of war, seen as the opportunity to conquer territories that had in the past belonged to the *Serenissima*, which in turn concurred entirely with the ambitions of figures such as ... Volpi to conquer the lands of the 'quarta sponda' as territories that would be of economic advantage to Italian capitalism." Stouraiti, "Costruendo un luogo," 14. Molmenti's interest in the Republic's imperial possessions was not limited to Venier or Lepanto. For example, he collaborated on a heavily illustrated work stressing the Italian artistic legacy in Dalmatia (produced almost simultaneously in French and Italian), contributing a chapter on the *Serenissima*'s role in the artistic and architectural patrimony of the eastern littoral of the Adriatic. A. Venturi, E. Pais, P. Molmenti, and T. Sillani, *La Dalmazia monumentale* (Milan: Alfieri & Lacroix, 1917); *La Dalmatie monumentale* (Milan: Alfieri & Lacroix,

had a surprising amount in common with the imperialist and naval vision of Gabriele d'Annunzio, and was not so different from key opponents in the campaign to modernize the city, notably the energetic businessman Giuseppe Volpi, the most dynamic of all Venetian industrialists and one of the most effective and energetic advocates of Adriatic expansionism.[62]

D'Annunzio, Volpi, and the Problems of a Roman Model of Imperialism

For all his desire to conserve the uniqueness of Venice, Molmenti saw the *Serenissima*'s past as a model to which other Italians might aspire. Repeatedly calumnied by the proponents of "the myth of terror and mystery," the Republic and its citizens had been restored to their rightful place in Italian historiography by modern archival history: "... the glorious life of this people presents itself as one which did not await the outcome of fortune, but knew how to conquer it with courage and wisdom, that expanded this task as an act of liberation and guaranteed the state by laws and by justice, that fought effectively against the religious infidels and against those who had no faith in liberty, seizing, by means of immense struggles, the sceptre of the seas, never bowing in the face of the most powerful enemies, passing the centuries resolute, united, in concord, amid the Italians who were divided, fractious, defenseless, deprived of practical political ideas, wanting in high civil goals."[63]

Molmenti's notion of Venice as historically superior to the rest of Italy was, therefore, premised in part both on its capacity to resist outside threats, most notably from the Turks, and on its dominance of the seas. Through the final decade of the nineteenth century and the first three lustra of the twentieth, these views would receive clearer and clearer articulation, yet a complete consensus was never achieved even amongst Venetian nationalists. Take, for example, the response to the imperialist and militaristic message that underpinned d'Annunzio's controversial play *La Nave*. First performed on January 11, 1908 in Rome before an audience that included Queen Margherita, the play told a tale of the origins of the Venetian Republic in the sixth century, with the Venetian population attempting to assert its independence against Byzantium. The text of *La Nave* is littered with phrases urging an aggressive maritime policy: "La patria è su la nave!" ("The fatherland is on the ship!"), "Patria ai Veneti tutto l'Adriatico!" ("Fatherland for Venetians is the whole Adriatic!"), "Arma la prora e salpa verso il mondo!" ("Arm the prow and weigh anchor for the world!"), "Il Mondo!

1918). This was one of a number of volumes officially accredited by the Italian delegation to the Paris Peace Conference at the end of the Great War. See: *A Catalogue of Paris Peace Conference Propaganda in the Hoover War Library* (Palo Alto: Stanford University Press, 1926), 51.

[62] Still the standard work on Volpi is S. Romano, *Giuseppe Volpi: Industria e finanza tra Giolitti e Mussolini* (Milan: Bompiani, 1970).

[63] Molmenti, *Venezia*, 122.

Il Mondo! arma la Nave grande!" ("The World! The World! Arm the great vessel!"). In an event stage-managed by Piero Foscari—a Venetian naval officer and capitalist from one of the most famous of all the city's patrician lines who, in 1910, would be a founding member of the *Associazione Nazionale Italiana*—d'Annunzio came to Venice in April 1908 to present the manuscript of his verse tragedy symbolically to the city.[64] The *sindaco* Filippo Grimani, initially hostile to the idea, was eventually pressured into accepting the gift, delivered by d'Annunzio himself, who carried it along the Grand Canal in Foscari's gondola. Lauded by the *Gazzetta di Venezia*, the newspaper[65] edited by Luciano Zuccoli, which sought to represent both the established *notabili* and the new financial-industrial elite of the city, both the play and those who fawned over its author drew the fire of the conservative and Catholic *La Difesa*: sexual immorality, and historical inaccuracies made "questa porcheria" repellant: "... Catholics and Venetians it is time to rebel! If conte Zuccoli, a foreigner, a guest of Venice, wants to burn incense in honor of D'Annunzio, he is welcome to do so, but could he please leave *venezianità* to us, because whatever happens, we shall defend it to the last man, and our word will sound a warning and rebuke all those who wish to impose this vileness, this shame on our dear, our very own Venice."[66]

This sense of a home-grown, Catholic, conservative, yet distinctively Venetian opposition, respectful of the history and myths of the Republic, is indicative of a widespread underlying resentment in Venice of outside attempts to appropriate *venezianità* to legitimate Italian overseas territorial expansion.[67] It was not just the Swiss Zuccoli—born in Ticino/Tessin and bearing the title Graf von Ingenheim—who was

---

[64] On the episode surrounding the production and dedication of *La Nave*, see: M. Isnenghi, *L'Italia del Fascio* (Florence: Giuntí, 1996), 50–53; J. Woodhouse, *Gabriele d'Annunzio: Defiant Angel* (Oxford: Oxford University Press, 1998), 240; M. A. Leeden, *D'Annunzio: The First Duce* (Baltimore: Johns Hopkins University Press, 2009); A. Bonadeo, *D'Annunzio and the Great War* (Madison, NJ: Farleigh Dickinson University Press, 1995), 29–34. Useful on the general place of Venice and the idea of the Mediterranean in d'Annunzio's work is F. Caburlotto, "D'Annunzio, la latinità del Mediterraneo e il mito della riconquista," *Californian Italian Studies Journal* 1 (2010): available on line at: http://escholarship.org/uc/item/7gx5g2n9;jsessionid=D37D5EE65B-D0042A2C84171D63C8EB57#page-1. For an example of Foscari's agitation based around his involvement with both irredentismo and the Lega Navale pressure group, see P. Foscari, *Il porto di Venezia nel problema adriatico, conferenza tenuta nella sala maggiore dell'Ateneo Veneto a beneficio della Dante Alighieri e della Lega Navale* (Venice: F. Garzia, 1904).

[65] On the emergence of *La Gazzetta di Venezia* as a nationalist mouthpiece, and its role in transforming nationalism from a minority movement of a largely literary nature into a powerful political force, see R. Drake, "The Theory and Practice of Italian Nationalism, 1900–1906," *Journal of Modern History* 53 (1981): 213–41, 215–17.

[66] April 18, 1908, *La Difesa*. Cited in Isnenghi, *L'Italia del Fascio*, 52.

[67] Despite the anger of some Venetians at d'Annunzio's liberties with the past, Gino Damerini recognized that, even with the liberties taken by the poet, the first five chapters of Romanin's *Storia documentata* and the first hundred odd pages of Molmenti's *Vita privata* clearly provided d'Annunzio with the historical material for his play. See G. Damerini, *D'Annunzio e Venezia* (Venice: Albrizzi editore, 1992; originally published 1943), 95–125.

considered an outsider by many Venetians; d'Annunzio himself was also seen as an alien imposter.[68] Yet at the same time *La Nave* succeeded, as Margaret Plant has remarked, in repositioning Venice "in the Adriatic as powerfully as in the days of the first Republic" and in offering "a vision of historic energy with contemporary relevance." This vision of Venice came to be deeply seductive to the city's elites, both to the *nobil homeni* or *patrisi* (because it spoke to the past grandeur of Venice), and to the new class of entrepreneurial industrialists and financiers (because it offered a historical/ mythical legitimacy to their plans for future grandeur).[69] *La Nave*'s potential to inspire nationalist and imperialist claims to the Adriatic was such that it was widely rumored that the Austrian naval minister kept a copy on his desk as a reminder of the Italian threat.[70] Certainly the work chimed with a new spirit amongst a new Venetian bourgeoisie increasingly determined to resolve the problems of the city through a fusion of radical patriotism and a more dynamic, aggressive emphasis on economic innovation.[71] Moreover, the gap between, on the one hand, the patricians and the older, liberal bourgeoisie, and, on the other hand, a more energetic and imperialistic *nuovo capitalismo veneziano* was bridged by the nationalist patrician Piero Foscari, whose business interests focused largely on electrical enterprises. However, it was Giuseppe Volpi, who, like Foscari, had based his fortune on an electrical company (the *Società Adriatica di Elettricità*) but who, unlike Foscari, did not come from ancient aristocratic stock,[72] who really embodied the new spirit of aggressive and opportunist expansionism, and

---

[68] On d'Annunzio's appropriation and uses of *venezianità*, see M. Isnenghi, "D'Annunzio e l'ideologia della venezianità," *Rivista di Storia Contemporanea* 19 (1990): 419–31.

[69] These assessments of the significance of *La Nave* are taken from Plant, *Venice*, 208, 251. It is striking that in 1912 a film version was made of *La Nave*. Originally d'Annunzio was paid an advance of 10,000 lire to produce a number of film scripts, but he actually provided almost nothing after banking his fee. The Turin-based Film Ambrosio subsequently employed the prolific scriptwriter Arrigo Frusta (whose real name was Augusto Sebastiano Ferraris) and Ricciotto Canudo to fill the gap left by the poet. This first cinematic version of the film was directed by Eduardo Bencivenga. In 1920 the film was remade with a script by d'Annunzio's son Gabriellino in collaboration with Mario Roncoroni. Despite d'Annunzio's outrage at the "vittoria mutilata," the remake was something of a financial flop. On the transformation of *La Nave* for screen, see M. Cardillo, *Tra le quinte del cinematografo. Cinema, cultura e società in Italia, 1900–1937* (Bari: Dedalo, 1987), 47, 59–60. See also C. Quarantotto, "Cinema di D'Annunzio e cinema dannunziano (1908–1928)," in *D'Annunzio e il suo tempo: atti del Convegno di studi. Genova 19, 20, 22, 23 settembre; Rapallo 21 settembre 1989*, ed. F. Perfetti (Genoa: SAGEP, 1992), vol. 2, 169–97. An interesting perspective from the fascist era is F. Soro, *Splendori e miserie del cinema. Cose viste e vissute* (Milan: Consalvo, 1935). On d'Annunzio's failure to deliver the promised scripts, see Woodhouse, *D'Annunzio*, 260.

[70] Ibid., 233.

[71] G. Riccamboni, "Cent'anni di elezioni a Venezia," in *Storia di Venezia II*, eds. Woolf and Stuart, 1183–1254, 1186; L. Pes, "Il fascismo urbano a Venezia. Origine e primi sviluppi 1895–1922," *Italia Contemporanea* 58 (1987): 63–84, 70.

[72] Volpi was ennobled as the conte di Misurata only in 1920.

proved the most dynamic advocate of Venice's economic growth (symbolized by the development of the port and industrial zone of Marghera)[73] and Adriatic nationalism.

Even before he had become the principal force behind the electrification of the Veneto, Volpi had developed commercial interests in the Balkans at the turn of the century, dealing in agricultural produce, selling insurance, and mining. Volpi's business interests would eventually become truly international—in the 1930s he owned the Altrincham and mid-Lincolnshire electrical supply companies, as well as controlling the Italian activities of Thomas Cook—but his real obsession was with the economic penetration of the Adriatic, Balkans, and Eastern Mediterranean.[74] Backed by the Milanese Banca Commerciale, he led Italian penetration of Montenegro, and was the pivotal figure, albeit often in an unofficial capacity, during negotiations with the Turks at the end of the Libyan War.[75] At the center of the so-called *gruppo veneziano* of nationalist economic modernizers, his vision of an imperial and industrial Venice, both forward and backward looking, helped him to place the city firmly within the framework of nationalist agendas both under the liberal and the Fascist regimes.[76] As both governor of Tripolitana from 1922–25 and as minister of finance from 1925, he pushed hard for a policy of Mediterranean expansionism, which echoed that of his Fascist masters. But while Mussolini turned to *romanità* to legitimate his pursuit of the Mediterranean as *mare nostrum*, Venetian nationalists continued to emphasize claims to Adriatic territories on the basis of the cultural, commercial, and historical links with the *Serenissima*. Of course, many historians sought to establish tight links between a Roman inheritance and the Venetian Republic, portraying Venice in some senses as the direct heir to the Roman imperial tradition. But there lay a number of distinct dangers in placing too much emphasis on *romanità*. During the Risorgimento, anxiety about the internal divisions, civil wars, and ultimate decadence of the Roman Empire caused concern even if it did not preclude entirely looking to Roman models for inspiration. Much more problematic was the manner in which other Europeans— and even Americans—had seen fit to stress their own close relationship and lines of continuity with ancient Rome. Just as the Catholic church was both too universal and

---

[73] On the growth of Marghera and Volpi's part in it, see: M. Reberschak, "Gli uomini capitali: il 'gruppo veneziano' (Volpi, Cini e gli altri)," in *Storia di Venezia II*, eds. Woolf and Stuart, 1262–66.

[74] Romano, *Giuseppe Volpi*; on Volpi's involvement with Thomas Cook, see R. J. B. Bosworth, "Tourist planning in Fascist Italy and the limits of a totalitarian culture," *Contemporary European History* 6 (1997): 1–25. Volpi's interest in developing the tourist trade in Venice—he owned both the Excelsior and the Grand Hotel—was fused with his prominent role in both the *biennale* and the associated film festival, which was launched in 1932. See M. Stone, *The Patron State: Culture and Politics in Fascist Italy* (Princeton: Princeton University Press, 1998), 38–39, 82–83.

[75] T. W. Childs, *Italo-Turkish Diplomacy and the War over Libya, 1911–12* (Leiden: Brill, 1990), 152–59.

[76] R. Sarti, "Giuseppe Volpi," *Uomini e volti del Fascismo*, ed. in F. Cordova (Rome: Bulzoni, 1980), 521–46; F. M. Paladini, "Velleità e capitolazione della propaganda talassocratica veneziana (1935–45)," *Venetica* 17, terza serie 6 (2002): 147–72, 148–49. Also available at: http://www. storiadivenezia.net/sito/saggi/paladini_propaganda.pdf

too reactionary for Papal Rome to become the focus of nationalist aspirations (despite the hopes of Giobertian neo-Guelfs before 1848), so classical Rome was simply insufficiently Italian, too obviously international. As the cosmopolitan scholar Arturo Graf—he was himself half-German, half-Italian, and Athenian-born—stressed, Rome was both a symbol of universal citizenship and a common *patria* with which everyone identified.[77] This in essence was why nineteenth-century Italians were more inclined to look to the middle ages and, indeed, to the unification itself for their foundation myths.[78] But if ancient Rome was problematic when seeking historical justification for Italian unity, it was perhaps even more awkward a model for imperialist ambitions. The Roman Empire was not only international in its extent, but included the lands of most of Italy's rivals as European powers—lands to which the new Italy could certainly not risk laying claim. Above all, comparison with the Roman Empire simply highlighted the inadequacies and insignificance of modern Italy. This is probably no more clearly demonstrated than in the panels erected by the Fascist regime in the Via dei Fori Imperiali in Rome, which illustrated the expansion of Rome from city state to its maximum extent under Trajan. A final panel, no longer displayed today, showed the modern Italian empire, and its ambitions in Africa and the Mediterranean. These panels were just one symbol of Mussolini's dream of rekindling the spirit and ambition of ancient Rome amongst modern Italians.[79] But while Mussolini's desire to turn the Mediterranean into a *mare nostrum* was not entirely fantastical, and his aspirations to break free from Anglo-French-Yugoslav encirclement certainly convinced many Italians,[80] any sense that Italy might one day become a new Rome with even a fraction of the territory of the caesars was absurdly unrealistic. In contrast with the ancient Roman model, the notion that Italy might aspire to the influence of the former maritime republics was more clearly consonant with nationalist ambitions and even possibly reconcilable with the policies of at least some of the major powers. Venice (and Genoa) made better models for expansion than Rome.

---

[77] A. Graf, *Roma nella memoria e nelle immaginazioni del medio evo* (Turin: Loescher, 1882), 13–14.

[78] A. Lyttelton, "Creating a National Past: History, Myth and Image in the Risorgimento," in *Making and Remaking Italy: The Cultivation of National Identity around the Risorgimento*, eds. A. R. Ascoli and K. von Henneberg (Oxford: Berg, 2001), 27–74; D. Laven, "Italy: The Idea of the Nation in the Risorgimento and Liberal Eras," in *What is a Nation? Europe 1789–1914*, eds. T. Baycroft and M. Hewitson (Oxford: Oxford University Press, 2006), 254–71, 265–68.

[79] H. Hyde Minor, "Mapping Mussolini: Ritual and Cartography in Public Art during the Second Roman Empire," *Imago Mundi* 51 (1999): 147–62.

[80] While heavily criticized by historians such as Richard Bosworth, MacGregor Knox, and Paul Preston, R. Quartararo, *Roma tra Londra e Berlino: la Politica estera fascista dal 1930 a 1940* (Rome: Bonacci, 1980) argued convincingly for the coherence of Mussolini's planning to seek Italian hegemony within the Mediterranean. For a very different version of Mussolini's Mediterranean imperialism, see D. Rodogno, *Il nuovo ordine mediterraneo. Le politiche d'occupazione dell'Italia fascista in Europa 1940–1943* (Turin: Bollati Boringhieri, 2003); the English version of this work is published as *Fascism's European Empire: Italian Occupation during the Second World War*, trans. Adrian Belton (Cambridge: Cambridge University Press, 2006).

Venice's Imperial Legacy and Adriatic Nationalism from an International Perspective

The story of *irredentismo* has been told many times and it is not our intention to re-peat it here.[81] What is significant for our argument is the way that irredentist goals helped place Venice at the center of arguments about the nation, and how this in turn enabled Venetians increasingly to consider themselves Italian. Italian nationalists in the late nineteenth century laid claim not only to lands where the majority or even a substantial minority of the population was Italophone (Trieste and Trento), as well as to regions that were in some sense within Italy's "natural frontiers" marked by the mountains and the sea (the German-speaking South Tyrol). But the desire to annex significant territories on the opposite side of the Adriatic (Dalmatia and Albania) was less easy to legitimate internationally, and even more likely to lead to clashes with neighboring states. In the aftermath of the Great War, such pursuit of "unredeemed" lands seemed at loggerheads with the alleged (although inconsistently respected and applied) adoption by Italy's allies of Mazzinian and Wilsonian principles of self-de-termination. Yet strikingly the notion that the former extent of the Venetian empire justified a modern Italian claim on these lands remained extremely vibrant both within the peninsula and beyond.

In both the Anglophone and French press the view that a widespread *itali-anità* persisted on the eastern shores of the Adriatic was frequently articulated from the 1890s. By contrast there was generally rather less sympathy for Italian claims to the so-called *quarta sponda* (the Libyan coastline), or, indeed, for Italian penetration in the Horn of Africa. For Venetians, imperialist aspirations were usually focused on these nearby lands that had once been part of the *Stato da Mar*. Admittedly some Venetians entertained wider ambitions. Indeed, the nationalist Foscari had seen ac-tion as a naval officer in East Africa in 1896, bombarding Mogadishu in revenge for a Somali attack on Italian sailors; he subsequently emerged as an eloquent spokesman for a wider-ranging imperialism. Similarly, Volpi had an obvious interest in Libya, of which, as we have noted, he was governor in the early years of fascist rule. However, most Venetians, in common with other northerners, were less expressly interested in African colonies and preferred to look eastward in pursuit of essentially European

---

[81] For a good recent introduction to questions of irredentism, see M. Cattaruzza, *L'Italia e il con-fine orientale* (Bologna: Il Mulino, 2007). See also, M. Cattaruzza, ed., *Nazionalismi di frontiera: identità contrapposte sull'adriatico nord-orientale: 1850–1950* (Cozenza: Rubbettino Editore, 2003). The classic contemporary text remains A. Vivante, *Irredentismo adriatico. Contributo alla discussione sui rapporti austro-italiani* (Florence: Libreria della Voce, 1912). With particular ref-erence to the Dalmatian question, see Luciano Monzali, *Italiani di Dalmazia: dal Risorgimento alla Grande Guerra* (Florence: Le Lettere, 2004); the English version of this volume is published as *The Italians of Dalmatia: From Italian Unification to the World War*, trans. S. Evans (Toronto: University of Toronto Press, 2009).

expansionist designs.[82] We shall return later to the underpinning that was offered to these Adriatic and Aegean claims by historians writing in Italian for mainly domestic consumption. First, however, it is worth reflecting on the degree to which they seem to have been supported by both foreign authors' and foreign editors' commissioning of Italians to write for foreign journals and papers. Thus in 1902, Luigi Villari—son of the astute political commentator, historian, and famous biographer of Savonarola and Machiavelli—wrote a piece on Dalmatia for a popular English periodical.[83] The younger Villari, an English-schooled diplomat, was at the time working on book about the Republic of Ragusa, which was far from complimentary about the devious and oppressive policies pursued by the Venetians against their fellow maritime republic.[84] As one reviewer remarked of the conflict of Ragusa (today's Dubrovnik) with "her hated rival," "the only yoke that galled her elastic neck was that of Venice."[85] Yet writing in his handsomely-illustrated article on Dalmatia, Villari stressed not only the coast's essential *italianità*, but also that this was the direct consequence of a powerful Venetian inheritance in the region. This is underlined from the very opening of his article: "Of the many thousands of travelers who annually spend a few weeks in Venice, who know the towns of the Venetian mainland as well as those of their own country, only a very small proportion push on a little further and visit the former territory of the Venetian Republic on that wonderful Eastern coast of the Adriatic. There a group of towns may be seen, thoroughly Italian in character, which once formed one of the chief bulwarks of Christendom against the advancing Turk."[86] Time and again Villari emphasized the fundamentally Venetian nature of the ports of the eastern littoral. The reader is reminded that the architectural and artistic highlights of each town are Venetian in style, design, and production; there is talk of "the handsome Venetian doorways," the use of "the best style of Venetian Gothic" for public buildings and palaces, the presence of the Lion of St. Mark.[87] Villari leaves no doubt that—in contrast to the rural hinterland, home to a picturesque and hardy Croatian peasantry—the true urban character of Dalmatia is Italian because it is Venetian. "The language spoken by

---

[82] It is something of a commonplace that whereas northern apologists for imperialism looked to the Balkans and eastern Mediterranean, southerners were more inclined to look to Africa. As one foreign correspondent remarked, "Broadly speaking, the advocates of the Abyssinian colony and the war to extremity are to be found in the southern provinces of Italy, the principal organs of the continuation of the war and the retrieval of the honour of Italy [after the humiliation of Adowa] are the Neapolitan journals; whereas the advocates of peace at any price and the abandonment of colonial honors are to be found in the north of Italy, in the plains of Lombardy and Venetia, where the newspapers are taking up a unanimous line on this point." T. J. Bent, "The Italians in Africa," *Fortnightly Review* 60 (1896): 363–73, 364.

[83] L. Villari, "Dalmatia," *English Illustrated Magazine* 225 (June 1902): 239–49.

[84] L. Villari, *The Republic of Ragusa: An Episode of the Turkish Conquest* (London: J. M. Dent & Co., 1904).

[85] M. Vaughan, "Ragusa," *The Speaker* (July 23, 1904), 390–91.

[86] Villari, "Dalmatia," 239.

[87] Ibid., 244–47.

the people is to a great extent Italian," wrote Villari, "especially at Zara, and it is pronounced with the soft lisping Venetian accent. Another thoroughly Venetian feature is
that in no Dalmatian town, save Ragusa, are carriages seen in the streets ... Outside in
the harbour flocks of gaily painted Venetian sails add another Venetian touch."[88]

Such views on the fundamental "Venetianness" of Dalmatia had perhaps
been articulated most forcefully in the work of the Oxford architect Jackson, who
traveled to the Adriatic three times with his wife in 1882, 1884, and 1885, both to help
with the construction of ecclesiastical architecture and to research his vast three volume work on the region's history and material patrimony.[89] For Jackson, Istria and
Dalmatia possessed an evident and unchallenged superiority over all other lands in the
Danube-Balkan region because of the enduring contact with Italy, which permitted
the local population to retain the language and political traditions of "civic liberties,"
"civil order" and "settled law," as well as "an ancient culture" in the face of "barbarian
colonization."[90] "To this day they cling to their *coltura Latina* with passionate affection; and though the Croats backed by the Austrian government, are fighting hard to
Slavonize the cities and reduce them to the same rule as the rural districts, the issue
of the struggle is still doubtful. The survival of these waifs and strays of the Roman
empire is unique; it is an historical phenomenon of almost unparalleled interest; and
one cannot contemplate without regret the possibility of its disappearance."[91] Jackson
saw the cultural and political superiority of Dalmatia as descending directly and with
unbroken continuity from Roman times. He was also both matter-of-fact and not entirely uncritical in his narrative of Venetian conquest and control. But his discussion
of the architecture of the region makes the case repeatedly for the *latinità* of Dalmatia
and Istria as being owed directly to the Venetian presence. Moreover, he stressed in uncompromising terms the enormous debt owed by Europe as a whole to "the resolution
of the Republic of St. Mark, and the stubborn valour of her Dalmatian subjects" for
saving Italy from Ottoman rapacity.[92] In adopting such a line, Jackson departed slightly from the position put forward by the John Wilkison Gardiner forty years earlier.
Writing at a time when British observers still tended to view Venetian history through
the distorting lens of Daru and Sismondi, and before the city's redemption in the eyes
of the British public through their resistance to the Austrians in 1849,[93] the eminent

---

[88] Ibid., 240.
[89] On Jackson's ambitions to emulate Ruskin, and his Dalmatian sojourns, see W. Whyte, *Oxford Jackson: Architecture, Education, Status and Style 1835–1924* (Oxford: Oxford University Press, 2006).
[90] T. G. Jackson, *Dalmatia, the Quarnero and Istria with Cettigne in Montenegro and the Island of Grado* (Oxford: Clarendon Press, 1887), vol. 3, ix.
[91] Ibid.
[92] Ibid., vol. 1, 143–44.
[93] See, for example, the *Times* headline of September 1, 1849, which wrote of "the heroic defence of the Venetians, the good use they made of their liberty" arguing that "never did a people vindicate their claim to be enrolled in the virile populations of Europe with more determined spirit, or in a more effective way."

Egyptologist gave a relatively even-handed assessment of Venice's role in the region. Yet at the same time he hinted at an over-all opinion of the *Serenissima's* dabbling in Dalmatian affairs that was not always favorable. For example, while he was at pains to stress the anguish felt by Venice's Slav troops at the fall of the Republic in 1797, pointing to their readiness "to resist the French to the last drop of their blood" and the "great honour that they coveted, that of fighting for the cause they had sworn to defend,"[94] he wrote of his own arrival in Ragusa thus: "Here for the first time, the winged lion of St. Mark ceases to appear; and the absence of this emblem of Venetian subjugation, the boast of the Ragusans, cannot fail to inspire every one with respect for a people, who preserved their country from the all-absorbing power of Venice."[95] Jackson by contrast, despite an awareness of occasional misdeeds perpetrated in the name of Saint Mark, saw the Venetian presence—even in reluctantly subdued Ragusa—as almost without exception a force for good. At the very end of his monumental work he wrote of how: "In every place we visited on mainland and island Venice had set her stamp; her architecture fills the streets, her silversmiths' work and broidery enriches the treasuries, her evangelistic lion guards every gate, presides over the judge's bench, frowns from every bastion, and the accents of her smooth softened dialect strike the ear at every turn ... no European state since the days of the Romans has more strongly stamped its individuality on its empire than Venice ... her influence may still be traced wherever the standard of St. Mark has been planted; and if the defects of her political system become apparent as one wanders over her ancient dominion, one learns to appreciate her greatness."[96]

So strong an endorsement of the Venetian legacy in the eastern Adriatic fed powerfully into later propaganda in favor of irredentist claims to the region. In August 1915 an article was published in the *Fortnightly Review* entitled "Italy and the Adriatic" by Antonio Cippico. Criticizing those who alleged Italy's tardy intervention in the conflict in May lay in "sheer imperialist motives," Cippico argued that Italy's actions were based principally on defending Italians within the Dual Monarchy: the Habsburg policy of favoring Croats and discriminating against the Italian community

---

[94] J. G. Wilkinson, *Dalmatia and Montenegro: with a journey to Mostar in Herzegovina and Remarks on the Slavonic Nations; the History of Dalmatia and Ragusa*, 2 vols. (London: John Murray, 1848), vol. 2, 294. It should be remarked that in general earlier nineteenth-century Anglophone commentators had a much lower opinion of Venetian imperialism than those writing after Romanin. For example, G. Finlay, *The History of Greece under Othoman* [sic] *and Venetian Domination* (Edinburgh & London: William Blackwood and Sons, 1856) portrayed the Venetians in Greece, Crete and Cyprus as inclined to brutality and cruelty. Similarly, an article of 1832 spoke of "the usual arbitrary exactions of arbitrary governors were the principal proofs of the maternal protection of Venice." "The Ionian Islands," *Chambers' Edinburgh Journal* 24 (July 14, 1832): 189–90.

[95] J. G. Wilkinson, *Dalmatia and Montenegro*, vol. 1, 273–74.

[96] Jackson, *Dalmatia*, vol. 3, 438–39. For another clear example of this late nineteenth-century British recognition of the venezianità of Dalmatia, see H. K. Scott, "A visit to Dalmatia and Montenegro," *Belgravia. A London Magazine* 96 (1898): 98–126.

in Dalmatia was the absolute justification for hostilities. While acknowledging the presence of Slavs on the eastern coast of the Adriatic since the seventh century, the author stressed that "the Latin and Italian element is the sole and autochthonous element of the country and of the country's history, civilization and art."[97] Such views were to be deployed again and again during the Great War and the Peace Conference, as the Italian government pursued its war aim, recognized by the allies in the Treaty of London of April 1915, of dominating the Adriatic. This became more significant as Clemenceau grew determined to foster a Yugoslav state as a counterbalance to Italy, with a view to reducing Italian potential to challenge France's position within the Mediterranean and in North Africa. While some Italian army officers warned of the danger of acquiring a province where the bulk of the Slav population might be permanently on the brink of insurrection, fomented by Yugoslav irredentists, there was widespread belief that Italy required possession of the Dalmatian coast for reasons of security. Thus in the summer of 1917 the *Review of Reviews* cited an Italian general who made "… a strong case for the possession by Italy of the Dalmatian coast as a measure of defence vital to her [Italy's] well-being … From Brindisi to Venice the Italian coast is so straight that there is no possibility of creating a decent naval port, whereas the deeply indented coast of Dalmatia, protected by many islands, forms the most admirable naval base that any sea power could desire."[98]

Increasingly, the French, British, and Americans became less tolerant of the deployment of arguments focusing on the *venezianità* or *latinità* of Dalmatia in favor of Italian imperialism. Take two examples of responses to the massive work produced by the Triestine irredentist and friend of James Joyce, Attilio Tamaro,[99] *La Vénétie Julienne et la Dalmatie: Histoire de la nation italienne sur les frontiers orientales*, with a view to legitimating annexation of the territory stretching from Trieste in the north to the most southerly tip of Dalmatia. In the *American Geographic Journal*, the skeptical reviewer, W. E. Lunt, pointed out that Tamaro "practically acknowledges" the work as little more than "an attempt to justify the Italian claims to territory on the northeastern shores of the Adriatic." Lunt's unnamed British colleague, while apparently more convinced by Tamaro's line that "Venice always looked upon Dalmatia as the bastion

---

[97] A. Cippico, "Italy and the Adriatic," *Fortnightly Review* 98:584 (Aug. 1915): 296–304, 299.

[98] *Review of Reviews* 55:330 (June 1917): 585. In an article by Virginio Gayda of 1919, the arguments of redemption, the legitimacy of the Treaty of London, the desirability of Italianization, and the strategic necessity of expansion were combined with the "continuity of historical possession throughout twenty centuries, first by Rome and then by Venice." "The Adriatic Problem and the Peace Conference," *Fortnightly Review* 105:627 (March 1919): 478–91.

[99] Tamaro, former archivist and future diplomat for the Fascist regime, was the author of a number of irredentist works. See, for example, Attilio Tamaro, *L'Adriatico—Golfo d'Italia, L'italianità di Trieste* (Milan: Fratelli Treves, 1915); *Italiani e Slavi nell'Adriatico* (Rome: Athenaeum, 1915); *Le condizioni degli italiani soggetti all'Austria nella Venezia Giulia e nella Dalmazia* (Rome: G. Bettero/Società italiana per il progresso delle scienze, 1915); *Il trattato di Londra e le rivendicazioni nazionali* (Rome: Reale Società geografica italiana, 1918); *Storia di Trieste* (Rome: Alberto Stock, 1924).

for defending her territories against the common enemy of Christendom," was equally alert to the fact that the book was "avowedly a work of propaganda, written in support of Italy's claims for presentation to the Peace Conference."[100] But, while outside observers had started to challenge the propagandizing invocation of Venice, in one sense this served to cement the city's place firmly within nationalist rhetoric. The denial of Dalmatia, a prize which had been promised to the Italians by the terms of the Treaty of London, came to be seen by Italian nationalists as central to the so-called *vittoria mutilata*. Given that Italian claims to the region were so tightly associated with its fundamentally Venetian character, the refusal of Clemenceau, Lloyd George, and Wilson to contemplate seizure of the littoral from the new Yugoslavia was a blow not only to Italian pride but to *venezianità*. The offence to Venice and nation helped to make Italian nationalists of Venetians.

Venetian Historians, Empire, and the Impact of the Great War: Battistella and Fradeletto

If Venice's historical role as Mediterranean power, protector of Christendom, and benign exporter of Italian culture to the Balkans was widely extolled abroad, it was even more significant in shaping opinion in the city itself. Rare were the occasions in home-grown historiography when even the smallest criticism of Venice's imperial mission was offered by Venetian authors. Nevertheless, there developed, during the final years of the nineteenth and the early years of the twentieth century, a far stronger emphasis on Venice's *Stato da Mar* than can be detected in the earlier historiography. Probably the most eloquent and persistent exponent of this position was the Udinese-born Antonio Battistella, who wrote two general histories of Venice, published in 1897 and 1921 respectively. These two works are worth looking at in some detail as they highlight the changing Venetian perspective on empire either side of the Great War.

Battistella's first volume came out of a series of eleven lectures delivered at the *Ateneo Veneto* in the spring of 1896 to mark the fall of the Venetian Republic a hundred years earlier.[101] The timing of these lectures was pivotal in that they coincided with a sense of national disaster following the humiliating defeat of the Italian army by an Ethiopian force at the battle of Adowa in March 1896. When fused with the growing threat posed to the political status quo in Italy by increasingly restless and well-organized socialists and anarchists, many conservatives and nationalists seemed to revert to the sense of collective woe that had greeted the military failings thirty years beforehand. The threat of the left (felt at a municipal as well as a national level), fused with Italy's failure in Abyssinia to trigger a backlash in Venetian politics. This

---

[100] W. E. Lunt, "Review of *La Vénétie Julienne et la Dalmatie: Histoire de la nation italienne sur les frontières orientales*," *The Geographical Journal* 54 (1919): 314–15.

[101] Antonio Battistella, *La Repubblica di Venezia dalle sue origini alla sua caduta, 11 conferenze tenute all'Ateneo Veneto nella primavera del 1896* (Bologna: Zanichelli, 1897)

saw the municipality fall to a coalition of Catholics and conservatives, and ultimately
led to the long tenure in office of Filippo Grimani. Battistella was principally known
as a historian of his native Friuli, but the series of lectures he delivered—destined to
be published by Zanichelli for an essentially popular audience—were delivered with
a clear political agenda that emphasized the Venetian Republic and nationalism. Put
at its crudest, Battistella's aim was to hold up republican Venice as a model for a failing modern Italy. In common with Molmenti, Battistella was eager to stress Venice's
distinctiveness and past grandeur, but unlike Molmenti this was not premised on any
whimsical nostalgia or myths of benign government.

  Battistella's Venice was an independent, aggressive, expansionist state. Its government firm, determined and unashamedly oligarchic, possessed of a constitution, the
justification of which lay principally in efficient administration and the ability of the
Serenissima to mobilize military resources: the implicit criticism of modern Italy as it
lurched towards democracy was none too hidden.[102] Jettisoning a growing wealth of evidence that showed the extent to which the early Venice had been subject to Byzantine
rule,[103] he argued that Venetians had tolerated the authority of the eastern emperors
principally to further their own commercial interests, and that any "sudditanza politica"
was far from total.[104] Later when Dandolo led the sack and seizure of Constantinople
during the Fourth Crusade in 1204, it was a simple issue of wanting "to settle old scores
with the Greek Empire."[105] Such unashamed celebration of aggression and *sagro egoisi-
mo* could not have been further from Molmenti. Battistella was not unusual in arguing
that Venice, having never known outside rule, had remained essentially Roman in character, in contrast with the rest of the peninsula, which had been subjected to barbarian
domination and foreign rule.[106] However, more than any previous historian of the city,
he sought to fuse this delight in a Roman heritage and Venetian grandeur with a near
mystical and messianic nationalism. This had the interesting consequence of his stressing Venice's superiority over the Piedmontese and the House of Savoy in terms both
of patriotism and the defense of Italian independence.[107] Rejecting the recent work of
Vincenzo Marchesi, who had disapproved of a policy he accused of wasting colossal financial and military efforts in a useless cause, Battistella was relatively conventional in

---

[102] For Battistella, the Venetian administration and constitution constituted "a masterpiece of practical good sense." Ibid., 373.

[103] The emphasis on the Byzantine origins of Venice were already a center of historiographical debate in earlier decades. Central to this was the posthumously published work of A. F. Gfrörer,
Geschichte Venedigs von seiner Gründung bis zum Jahre 1084, ed. G. B. Weiss (Graz: Vereins-
Buchdruckerei, 1872), which the *Archivio Veneto* reviewed and subsequently started publishing
in Italian translation. F. Brunetti, "Review of *Geschichte Venedigs*," *Archivio Veneto* 7/I (1874),
372–93; and F. Brunetti, "Storia di Venezia dall sua fondazione fino all'anno 1084," *Archivio
Veneto* 12–16 (1876–78).

[104] Battistella, *La Repubblica di Venezia*, 36.

[105] Ibid., 90.

[106] Ibid., 23.

[107] Ibid., 320–21.

his assessment of Venice's pivotal part in resisting the Ottoman threat:[108] fighting the Turks was "Venice's historical task and the most brilliant if not the principal reason for its glory."[109] But even here the nationalist historian added a novel twist: in Battistella's account, the power of Ottomans had been much exaggerated. In effect this was a call for contemporary Italy not to be intimidated by the Turks in its pursuit of colonial expansion, and to see in early-modern Venice a model for glory, expansion, and national pride. It was indeed in the Venetian empire and its defense that Italian greatness lay, and to which modern Italians should now look. "O what vast powers there were in these memories of past glories that made the name of Italy great even when Italy did not exist, that live on and will always live surrounded by eternal splendor, keeping alive the cult of beauty and scourging with their immortal wings the stagnant and laziness airlessness of a prosaic and matter-of-fact bourgeois era."[110]

Battistella's second general history, *La Repubblica di Venezia ne' suoi undici secoli di storia*,[111] was originally commissioned for the inauguration of the new bell tower in 1912. The *campanile* had collapsed July in 1902, and its reconstruction was both widely portrayed as a symbol of the rebirth of Venice—the tower now embodying the strength and prestige regained by the *nuova Venezia*—and was exploited to emphasize continuities with the Republic.[112] However, it was not until 1921 that Battistella's work was published: by this stage the Great War and the outcome of the Paris peace settlement had radically changed approaches to Venice's imperial past. In his 1897 volume, Battistella had tended to praise Venice and to blame any failures and shortcomings on Italy. In his second account of Venice's "eleven-hundred-year" history, Battistella's text offered a rather different perspective. Now, rather than sniping at the House of Savoy, Battistella sang the praises both of Venice and of a triumphant contemporary Italy, now presented as a fully-fledged nation-state, sanctified by the blood sacrifice of the Great War. In his new work Venice became a bridge linking ancient Rome directly with the nation; notions of *venezianità*, *romanità*, and Italian nationalism were increasingly conflated. And whereas Spain had been set up as the arch-enemy of the *Serenissima* in his 1897 text, Battistella now switched his target to Austria. The Habsburgs were presented both as the Republic's main rival within the Adriatic itself and for territories along its coast; even the disaster of 1797 was presented as principally the work of Vienna rather than the young Bonaparte.[113] In adopting this stance,

---

[108] V. Marchesi, *La Repubblica di Venezia (appunti critici)* (Udine: Tipografia cooperativa, 1894), 49.

[109] Battistella, *La Repubblica di Venezia*, 56.

[110] Ibid., 266.

[111] A. Battistella, *La Repubblica di Venezia ne' suoi undici secoli di storia* (Venice: Carlo Ferrari, 1921).

[112] Plant, *Venice*, 234–38.

[113] Battistella, *Venezia ne' suoi undici secoli*, 649–52, 700. Battistella had already developed his argument about the pernicious nature of the Austrians in a work published during the Great War. See A. Battistella, "Venezia e l'Austria durante la vita della Repubblica," *Nuovo Archivio Veneto*, nuova serie 62 (1916): 279–320.

Battistella not only linked the history of Venetian imperialism to the Risorgimento foundation myth (which identified the Austrians as the great enemy of the Italian nation),[114] but he also emphasized a powerful continuity with the recent bloody conflict.

Of course, one problem thrown up by the irredentist successes of Italy in 1918 was the acquisition of Trieste, which, while a traditional target of Italian nationalist expansion, was much better adapted as a modern port than Venice, even when the wartime expansion of Marghera was taken into consideration. Battistella's approach to Venice's Adriatic rival (and the favored maritime outlet of the Habsburgs) is informative, given that he showed scant sympathy for its inhabitants, and was perfectly content to narrate the attempts of Venice to stifle the ultimately more successful mercantile city. However, like so many Venetian historians before him, his main interest lay with Istria and Dalmatia, highlighting their longstanding cultural, commercial, and military links with the *Dominante*. Significantly, he felt more uncomfortable regarding faraway adventures involving the control of large territories. Even in the highly charged nationalist and colonial debates, Venetian historiographers tended to favor interventions around the Adriatic, and inclined towards skepticism over African enterprises: imperial ventures in the Adriatic offered the advantage of keeping Venice at the center of the stage, nationally and internationally. Battistella's 1921 account of the history of Venice was thus very much of its time: imperialist ambitions in the Adriatic had a new resonance as Italy was denied Dalmatia at the Peace Conference, and as d'Annunzio briefly occupied Fiume/Rijeka, but they also meant much more to a city that during the war had found itself on the frontline of attack by the Austrians, subjected to bombardment, with much of the population evacuated, especially in the aftermath of Caporetto, when the numbers living in Venice were reduced to little more than a quarter of those resident at the time of the 1911 census. The city also became increasingly militarized, subject to martial law, surrounded by barrage balloons, and with a significant presence from the armed forces.[115] While many Venetians undoubtedly resented the authorities'

---

[114] Battistella was by no means the sole historian of Venice to emphasize the Austrians as the key enemy of the Venetian state or to identify the interests of the extinct Republic so closely with the new nation. Thus, for example, even before the outbreak of the Great War, Antonio Santalena took aim at both the Habsburgs and the French. A. Santalena, "La resistenza veneta contro la Lega di Cambray," *Rivista dell'Ateneo Veneto* (July–August 1909): 220–36. The final paragraphs of the article were particularly inflammatory, as Santalena commented on the new lion of St. Mark inaugurated on the Santi Quaranta gate of Treviso. The winged lion, he proclaimed, "in Istria ... in Dalmatia, in Corfu, Crete, Cyprus, where our blessed language is heard, it indicates the shining memory of a naval and warrior Venice. It is the lion that roared in chains under the Austrian domination ... that rebels against the eternal enemy, and resists unbowed with the prophetic cry of the former Republic 'Italy and Liberty,' and which would still know how to use its claws in defence of the common fatherland. It is the lion that—with Venice reunited with the Great Mother—is a sacred bond to the past of the great state that felt itself truly Italian and worked over the centuries in a truly Italian manner, for an always more flourishing and powerful future for our Fatherland." Ibid., 235–36.

[115] B. Bianchi, "Venezia nella Grande guerra," in *Storia di Venezia I*, eds. Isnenghi and Woolf, 349–416.

handling of the way the war impacted on their lives, the transformation of Venice into a frontline city kindled memories of resistance both to the League of Cambrai and to the Austrians in 1848–49. This helped "nationalize" Venice; at the same time, the war aims—closely linked to the reacquisition of lands once held by the *Serenissima*—also emphasized the tight links between *venezianità* and *italianità*.

No other writer expressed these views so forcefully as Antonio Fradeletto, who at the end of the war would be made the Ministro delle Terre liberate dal Nemico in the Orlando government. Fradeletto—who had the interesting distinction of introducing the young Margherita Sarfatti, future lover of Mussolini and fascist journalist, to the work of John Ruskin[116]—is perhaps best remembered now as a driving force in the organization of the *Biennale*.[117] In 1916, however, he published a brief and extremely polemical history of Venice.[118] This work is remarkable in the way it almost completely ignores the Venetian constitution and structures of government, considered of such pivotal importance in almost every other historical narrative of the city. Instead, the book concentrates almost entirely on territorial aggrandizement and conflict. Beginning by pointing to the fact that the war that Italy had entered the previous year was "the first in which the entire population participated," he repeatedly derived lessons from Venetian history and drew parallels between the city's past glories and the patriotic struggle of Italy of the moment: "Modern Italy is today re-entering a furrow ploughed by little old Venice."[119] Geographical determinism underpins Fradeletto's arguments for Adriatic expansionism,[120] but at the same time he was clearly anxious to stress the longstanding and friendly relations with the people of Dalmatia and Istria. "Bit by bit the country was pacified; it rallied to the Republic with unbreakable sentiments of devotion; it furnished it with soldiers, sailors, and galley commanders; its maritime cities assumed in their buildings, in the streets, in their customs, in their language, such an intense degree of *venezianità* that it speaks not of subjection but of brotherhood."[121]

Thus while emphasizing the need to emulate the Venetian Republic in dominating the Adriatic as a prerequisite for further eastern expansion, Fradeletto also

---

[116] E. Braun, "From the Risorgimento to the Resistance: One Hundred Years of Jewish Artists in Italy," in *Gardens and Ghettos: The Art of Jewish Life in Italy*, ed. V. B. Mann (Berkeley: University of California Press, 1989), 137–190, 167.

[117] J. A. May, *La Biennale di Venezia: Kontinuität und Wandel in der venezianischen Ausstellungspolitik 1895–1948* (Berlin: Akademie Verlag, 2009); G. Donzello, *Arte e collezionismo: Fradeletto e Pica, primi segretari alle Biennali veneziane, 1895–1926* (Florence: Firenze libri, 1987); D. Ceschin, *La 'Voce' di Venezia: Antonio Fradeletto e l'organizzazione della cultura tra Otto e Novecento* (Padua: Il Poligrafo, 2001).

[118] A. Fradeletto, *La storia di Venezia e l'ora presente d'Italia* (Turin: STEN, 1916).

[119] Ibid., 14.

[120] "Above all, it was necessary to extend its own jurisdiction to the other side of the sea, because it was precisely this rugged and treacherous coastline, hemmed with islands, and studded with ports, that permitted a watch to be kept over the Adriatic, and the mastery of that sea." Ibid., 20.

[121] Ibid., 23.

insisted, in a fashion almost worthy of Tommaseo, on the benign and civilizing mission of the former imperial venture, as well as pointing to the exemplary heroism of Venetian commanders such as Francesco Morosini, even when "abandoned by Europe."[122] Only in neutrality—the ultimate sign of eighteenth-century decadence—was Venice to be condemned; yet even as the Republic fell, victim of its own "unwarlike submissiveness," both its *popolo* and its Slav subjects remained determinedly loyal.[123] Fradeletto's propaganda, therefore, combined a militaristic and expansionist rhetoric with a myth of benevolent imperialism. If this really was an accurate reflection of Venice's role in the Mediterranean, those values would not persist when the Fascist state began its concerted plans for hegemony in the Balkans. The conduct of the Fascists would too often echo that of the arbitrary and bloodthirsty Venetian troops and auxiliaries described by George Finlay in *The History of Greece under Othoman* [sic] *and Venetian Domination* of 1857, rather than the sympathetic rulers portrayed by Fradeletto and his ilk. The arguments of Fradeletto, however, would continue to be deployed in justification of territorial expansion.

A Comparative Perspective: Genoa, Historians, and Empire

Throughout the liberal era it was something of a commonplace amongst historians and political commentators to refer to Venice and Genoa as the eastern and western "lungs" of the peninsula. Yet it is striking that while historians of Venice constantly emphasized its imperialist role, ultimately using this as one of the key arguments for inserting *venezianità* within the national narrative, this seems not to have been of such paramount importance to the writing of Genoese history, or at least insofar as attempts were made to integrate Genoa into the national narrative. One reason for this was the much earlier integration of Genoa into the Savoyard monarchy. Although, as we shall show, the Ligurian population quite often regarded the Piedmontese ruling house with suspicion, and sometimes downright hostility, the advantages of rule from Turin (and later Florence and Rome) were significant and tended to distract from a nostalgic engagement with the past. Moreover, historical research was inclined to focus on the internal instabilities that led to the gradual erosion of Genoa's independence, rather than on its imperial grandeur, even if the latter remained an important subtext in general histories of the city.

After the collapse of the Napoleonic Empire, Genoa had been almost immediately annexed by the Kingdom of Sardinia-Piedmont. Although many Ligurians had been reluctant to accept reactionary Piedmontese rule, and had rebelled in May 1849 (the insurrection was brutally repressed by royal troops), the lands of the former

---

[122] Ibid., 52.
[123] Ibid., 56–57.

Republic of Genoa had in fact been among the first to be fully integrated into the administrative and constitutional structures imposed by Turin. And Genoa benefited hugely from Savoyard rule, its wealth expanding dramatically in consequence of the commercial and economic policies imposed by Cavour and his successors. Unification brought further benefits, as Genoa, always the favored port of the Lombards, found itself once again in a tight economic synergy with this most prosperous of Italian regions. Since the city had from the 1790s always been more fully part of the process of the Risorgimento, nationalists and municipalists alike felt happy to praise Genoa's imperialist past, but it was not so essential to deploy the quest for empire as a means of attaching the city to the national cause.[124] The frequent internal disorders that made Genoa so vulnerable to invasion and foreign control—in a sense a sort of Italy in miniature—also made its past less attractive as a field for the manufacture of historical myths of stability, resistance, and independence, which were so fundamental to the Venetian narrative.[125] Thus, when the marchese Girolamo Serra's history of the city was published in 1834, it emphasized that "In three centuries of memorable wars, Genoa acquired stupendous possessions, and a significant share of global trade,"[126] yet it was in "the loss of its eastern colonies and the awful period of civil discord" that there existed the "two principal causes, which reduced this almighty naval power to the status of a small state."[127] Much the same emphasis was to be found in Carlo Varese's history of the Republic, which came out the following year. For Varese, the key topic was "[t]he perpetual struggle between the nobility and the people, and the shifts between narrow oligarchy and democracy that was the consequence of these struggles," even if he was also anxious to underline the importance of Genoese history for all Italians, observing that it was impossible not to find fascinating "the fortunes of a people that is of such glory to the story of our peninsula."[128]

By the time the *Congresso degli Scienziati italiani* met at Genoa in 1846 it had become normal for the organizers of these annual meetings of scientists and scholars to produce an official or, at least semi-official, book on the host city. The work on Genoa contained a substantial historical sketch. Once again what is striking about this sketch is the relatively peripheral role played by Genoa's colonial past. Stressing from the outset the martial qualities of the Ligurians not least in their resistance to Roman domination in ancient times, the author, Michele Giuseppe Canale, above all else emphasized domestic instability, changes in regime, and how these

---

[124] S. Serra, *La storia della antica Liguria e di Genova* (Turin: Giuseppe Pomba, 1834).

[125] The greatest patriotic moment in Genoa's history was perhaps the famous rebellion sparked by a street urchin, "Balilla," who threw a stone at occupying Austrian soldiers in 1746. The Italian patriots were less eager to recall that at the time of the Genoese revolt, the Habsburgs were in alliance with the Piedmontese.

[126] Serra, *La storia della*, viii.

[127] Ibid., ix.

[128] Carlo Varese, *Storia della Repubblica di Genova dalla sua origine sino al 1814* (Genoa: Yves Gravier, 1835), A.

ultimately left the city open to foreign domination.[129] In Canale's historical sketch even Genoa's last remaining colonial possession, the island of Corsica, was presented as essentially problematic. This was not an equivalent to Venetian Dalmatia—a source of soldiers and solidarity in the face of the Turk—but rather as a rebellious and vulnerable territory, the rule of which that had the added disadvantage of bringing Genoa into conflict with both France and the House of Savoy. Indeed, Canale went further, justifying the cruel repression of Corsican insurgents by the Genoese authorities as the legitimate action of colonial masters over rebellious subjects.[130] The views expressed by historians after the dramatic events of 1848–49 and during the course of unification did not alter much. It was the domestic situation in Genoa's stormy history from which most lessons could be learned. Mariano Bargellini in his substantial *Storia popolare di Genova* of 1857 could not, of course, avoid engaging with Genoa's at times vast seaborne empire, commenting, for example, of the loss of much of it three hundred years beforehand that "With the loss of its colonies, Genoa had its arms hacked off,"[131] but his principal interest was with the internal organization, constitution, and power-struggles of Genoa itself.[132] Indeed, on the one hand, Bargellini presented successful imperial expansion largely as a product of domestic harmony and order; on the other hand, failure of empire, while contributing to domestic problems was also above all a symptom of these shortcomings.[133] As Bargellini's work was appearing, so too was a new, multi-volume, and never completed study by Canale. The basic themes remained much the same, although it is perhaps particularly striking with what virulence he lambasted the parasitic and oppressive nature of the Roman Empire. Indeed, while Venetians tended to present themselves as direct heirs to a Roman tradition, Genoese historians were more inclined to write of themselves as victims or resisters of a decadent and burdensome ancient imperial domination, even preferring barbarian rule to that of the caesars. "The vices and the infinite lusts of the emperors were a vast chasm into which excessive public monies were cast; the municipalities, the provinces the colonies, enjoying no rights of citizenship, seethed that the Roman sewer swallowed up their wealth. Often

---

[129] M. G. Canale, "Storia civile," in *Descrizione di Genova e del genovesato* (Genoa: Tipografia Ferrando, 1846).

[130] Ibid., 38–39.

[131] M. Bargellini, *Storia popolare di Genova: dalla sua origine fino ai nostri tempi* (Genoa: Enrico Monni, 1856–57), vol. 1, 566.

[132] As one German reviewer wrote "History cannot say much that is good about the aristocracy of the former Republic of Genoa, which, through the intrigues of the powerful, brought about its own downfall." The reviewer continued to remark that the study "is principally concerned with internal unrest and faction." No mention was made of Genoa here as a past imperial power at all. Neigebaur, "Literaturbericht aus Italien," *Heidelberger Jahrbücher der Literatur* 35 (Aug. 1857): 545–60, 557.

[133] As Bargellini remarked in his introduction, "Under the auspices of this brotherly harmony between the popular and aristocratic elements of society were begun the first conquests in the east that opened the road to the future power of the nation." Bargellini, *Storia popolare*, ix.

deeply galled, the subject peoples rose up en masse when greedy and unjust proconsuls and governors made a hated rule even worse and more intolerable through their cruel exactions."[134] Meanwhile, Canale continued to reiterate his earlier reservations about colonies, most especially Corsica, "a legitimately acquired possession, greedily coveted, and unjustly lost."[135] "The island of Corisca," he continues, "held by the Republic ... [constituted a] great and continual reason for wars and calamities from the moment it was conquered, brought worries and upheavals."[136] When the great historian of Genoa and the Genoese—biographer of both Columbus and Mazzini— Federico Donaver, wrote his two volume work on his home town, once again the focus was domestic rather than imperialistic. The aim of his work was to concentrate on: "... important occurrences, which had a fairly extensive influence on the political and commercial life of the Middle Ages ... acts of heroism and ... virtuous acts of unnamed self-sacrifice, interwoven with revolts, sometimes demagogic and sometimes sublimely patriotic ... the history of our republic is varied, rich in anecdote, educational, an admonition both to peoples and to individuals."[137]

Despite the obvious need for any history of Genoa to address the city's involvement in the Black Sea and Mediterranean, it is clear that the focus of historians of the Ligurian capital was almost invariably on foreign invasion or domestic affairs. Its colonial past could not be overlooked but its place within the Italian nation was never dependent upon it. It was only under the Fascist regime, with the development of an even more aggressively expansionist attitude toward the Mediterranean, that, on the eve of renewed European-wide conflict, Roberto Lopez wrote the first systematic study of Genoese expansion.[138]

---

[134] M. G. Canale, *Nuova istoria della repubblica di Genova, del suo commercio e della sua letteratura dalle origini all'anno 1797* (Florence: Le Monnier, 1858–64), vol. 1, 274–75. It should be noted that Canale's fourth volume only took the narrative to 1528.

[135] Ibid., vol. 2, 582.

[136] Ibid., vol. 1, 109.

[137] F. Donaver, *La Storia della Repubblica di Genova* (Genoa: Liberia Editrice Moderna, 1913), vol. 1, xiii.

[138] R. Lopez, *Storia delle colonie Genovese nel Mediterraneo* (Bologna: Zanichelli, 1938). However, it is noteworthy that when this work was commissioned for the *Collana di studi giuridici e storici* edited by Pier Silverio Leicht (academic historian and lawyer, president of the *Società alpine friulana*, and Fascist—serving as a deputy from 1924 and a senator from 1934), it was because apparently no other such survey existed on the subject. See A. Varsoni, *Roberto Lopez. L'impegno politico e civile (1938–45)* (Florence: Università di Firenze, 1990), 356. For earlier statements of the significance of Genoa's colonial status and relations with a wider Mediterranean world it is worth looking at the A. Oliviero, "Prefazione," in *Atti della Società ligure di storia patria, 1* (Genoa: Tommaso Ferrando, 1857), v–xi; V. Ricci, "Parole del Presidente provvisorio," ibid., xiii–xxxvi, and P. V. Marchese, "Per la inaugurazione della Società ligure di storia patria," ibid., xxxvii–lx. The *Atti* do not, however, seem to have overly concerned themselves with Genoa's relations with the eastern Mediterranean.

Venetians, Empire, and the Rhetoric of Fascism

The lines of continuity between the imperialism of the liberal Italian state, and that of the Fascist regime are extremely strong. Thus the final process of pacification of Tripolitania and Cirenaica under Volpi, Pietro Badoglio, and Italo Balbo can be seen as little more than a continuation and intensification of the policies initiated in Libya by San Giuliano and Giolitti.[139] Much the same can be said of the expansion of power, based on superior military strength and technology, in what came to be known as Africa Orientale Italiana. Nor did the writing of history radically alter. Claims on the Adriatic, at least until the increased Fascist emphasis on race in the late 1930s, also changed little after 1922. Of course, the emphasis on *romanità*, underscored by repeated appeals to "Roman" symbolism, grew stronger under the Fascist regime.[140] But when Mussolini, and his generals and admirals, ministers and advisors sought to pursue a policy of *spazio vitale* in the Mediterranean with a view to transforming it into a *mare nostrum*, it was still possible to legitimate imperial expansion through appeals to *venezianità*. As Stefano Cavazza has shown, the Fascist state was not above annexing the local as a means of attaching Italians to the nation-state.[141] Just as the festivals and traditions studied by Cavazza were appropriated for this end, so too was essentially municipal history. Consequently, Venice continued to be able to relate to the nation in large part through the history of its *Stato da Mar*. As Filippo Maria Paladini has remarked, the notion of the Adriatic as "Golfo di Venezia" was pivotal: "... one of the most obsessive themes in national-fascist propaganda was Italy's penetration of overseas' territories, the Balkan East, the Levant and the Mediterranean as Italian 'spazio vitale.'"[142]

In the aftermath of the Great War, such appeals to Venice's historical importance as the dominant power of the Mediterranean assumed a special significance. As we have noted above, the acquisition of Trieste by the Italians posed a major threat to Venice's position. To safeguard its significance and to encourage economic expansion, it was essential to push Venice's claim to a hegemonic status within the "Golfo." This led to a renewed emphasis on links between Venice and Dalmatia—widely perceived as the essential bridgehead for any Balkan expansion—which stood to benefit both broader Fascist plans for territorial expansion, and more focused Venetian defense of local interests. This would receive articulation through the foundation in the early

---

[139] There is a large literature on the Italo-Turkish war and the conquest of Libya. See, for example T. W. Childs, *Italo-Turkish Diplomacy*; F. Malgeri, *La guerra libica (1911–12)* (Rome: Edizioni di Storia e Letteratura, 1970); S. Romano, *La quarta sponda: la guerra di Libia 1911–12* (Milan: Bompiani, 1977).

[140] See, for example, R. Visser, "Fascist Doctrine and the Cult of Romanità," *Journal of Contemporary History* 27 (1992): 5–22; L. M. Bechelloni, "Le mythe de la romanité et la politique de l'image dans l'Italie fasciste," *Vingtième Siècle—Revue d'histoire* 78 (2003): 111–20.

[141] S. Cavazza, *Piccole patrie. Feste popolari tra regione e nazione durante il fascismo* (Bologna: Il Mulino, 2003).

[142] Paladini, "Propaganda talassocratica," 147.

1930s of the *Istituto di Studi Adriatici*, which went hand-in-hand with the fascistization of key cultural Venetian institutions, such as the *Deputazione di storia patria per le Venezie*, and the *Istituto Veneto di scienze, lettere ed arti*.[143] The ISA became a key propaganda tool for promoting Venice through an emphasis on the study of the Adriatic, and rapidly attracted the patronage and involvement of key figures. In its early stages, the Rovigo-born academic at the University of Padua, Roberto Cessi—a left-wing scholar with no nationalist credentials, who in 1908 at the age of 23 joined the *Partito Socialista Italiano*—played a key part in stressing the significance of Venice's maritime past as a thalassocracy. Cessi grew less happy with the brief of the ISA when Volpi took over its direction, replacing Mussolini's first minister for the navy, Admiral Paolo Thaon di Revel. Nevertheless, the fact that Cessi never distanced himself entirely from the project is symptomatic of the extent to which the Venetian intelligentsia was prepared both to collaborate with the regime, not least with a view to ensuring the centrality of their city within its expansionist projects.[144] Of course, many Venetians were utterly unconvinced by such propaganda. If Italians nationally celebrated the successful war in Abyssinia in 1935 with enormous and almost universal enthusiasm, they were less excited by the annexation of Albania in 1939. Nevertheless, the seizure of Albania did trigger, in some sections of society, a renewed Venetian interest in laying claim to historical rights in the Adriatic, Balkans, and Mediterranean, cementing Venice's place in the national-Fascist imperial scheme, with, for example, the proposal to produce *Le fonte veneziane per la storia albanese*.[145]

The increasingly aggressive Italian policy in the Adriatic and Balkans following the successful conquest of Abyssinia led some among the Fascist hierarchy to justify expansion on the grounds of the racist ideology that became *de rigueur* following the *Manifesto sulla purezza della razza* of July 1938. However, in general the Venetian perspective on imperial expansion continued to stress cultural and economic legacies as the basis for legitimate involvement in areas once ruled by the *Serenissima*. In 1927, Francesco Pullé, in his anthropological and linguistic study of the peninsula, had asserted the inherent unity of the Adriatic peoples; by extension this was the rationale for Venetian/Italian expansion on the eastern coastline.[146] Writing in September 1941, six months after the Italian annexation of the bulk of the Dalmatian coastline (a smaller area was left in the hands of a German-controlled Croatian satellite state), the Sicilian historian, folklorist, philologist and ethnographer, Giuseppe Cocchiara—himself an extremely prominent supporter of the Fascist regime's move toward racism—argued in *La Difesa della Razza* that "Dalmatia is fundamentally an extension of the Venezie, as Malta is of the Sicilies." Yet Cocchiara echoed Molmenti when he pointed to the way in

---

[143] Ibid., 152.
[144] Ibid., 153–66.
[145] Ibid., 150, 161.
[146] F. Pullé, *L'Italia, genti e favelle. Profilo antropologico-linguistico*, 4 vols. (Turin: Bocca, 1927) cited in Sandra Puccini, "Le immagini della razza balcaniche nell'antropologia italiana tra le due guerre," *La Ricerca Folklorica* 34 (1996): 59–70, 62.

which monuments demonstrated the fundamentally Venetian nature of Dalmatia, but more importantly "Venice was present in Dalmatia through its festivals, its customs, its popular literature. But with this literature it was not just Venice but Italy that was present in Dalmatia."[147] It was not just in the conquest and "re-Italianization" of Dalmatia that *venezianità* was exploited.[148] As both Davide Rodogno and Marco Cuzzi have observed, the history of Venetian economic penetration was also used to legitimate intervention in Slovenia.[149] In this climate perhaps the clearest statement of the link between Venice's historical imperialism and the implementation of plans to dominate a Mediterranean *spazio vitale* was to be found in a work written by the Dalmatian Italian, Bruno Dudan, published under the auspices of the *Istituto nazionale di cultura fascista* in 1938.[150] Dudan's was an extensive, reasonably comprehensive and *longue durée* survey, which ended rather abruptly with Campoformido and the collapse of the Republic in 1797. Dudan identified in the Republic's energy, determination, and "... its intransigent and inflexibly egoist determination to concentrate wealth and power at a single geographical point for centuries on end" confirmation of the lesson "... that it is to enduring action that are entrusted the destinies of peoples wishing to continue their course and to construct a path through the world."[151] But while he saw in Venetian expansion a certain degree of *sagro egoismo*, which chimed no doubt with both liberal and Fascist policy, he also stressed the notion that Venice was both bastion against the threat from the east and "erede della sovrantità dell'Impero romano d'Oriente." Despite the book's appearing in a series that was expressly Fascist, that bore the imprint of the *fascio littorio* on its cover and frontispiece, and that was edited by the die-hard PNF supporter Pier Silverio Leicht (who was one of relatively few academics actually purged by the allies after the collapse of Mussolini's regime), the message it carried was not so very different from that of authors writing in the years before the Great War.

Conclusion

In 1943 as Italy spiralled toward defeat, Gino Damerini, nationalist journalist and author of wide-ranging cultural and historical interests, who was often seen as the unofficial spokesman of Giuseppe Volpi, published a study of the Ionian Islands under Venetian domination. In this work, he argued that Campoformido and the fall of the Republic would never be avenged or forgotten until all Venice's imperial possessions

---

[147] G. Cocchiara in *La Difesa della Razza* 4 (Sep. 1941), 6–9, cited ibid., 60.

[148] Rodogno, *Fascism's European Empire*, 73–76.

[149] Ibid., 82; M. Cuzzi, *L'occupazione italiana della Slovenia (1941–43)* (Rome: Stato maggiore dell'esercito, 1998).

[150] B. Dudan, *Il dominio veneziano di Levante* (Bologna: Zanichelli, 1938). Dudan's other historical works included a study jointly authored with T. Teja, *L'italianità della Dalmazia negli ordinamenti e statuti cittadini* (Varese & Milan: ISPI, 1943).

[151] Dudan, *Il dominio*, 271.

were once again under Italian rule.[152] Not only did Venice have to be redeemed, so did the whole *Stato da Mar*. Given the precarious military position of the Italians when Damerini was writing, such a position was, at best, profoundly and ridiculously unrealistic. In defeat Italy was stripped of her imperial possessions (generating perhaps surprising protests from left as well as right). Italians fled in large numbers from Tito's Yugoslavia and returned from other outposts of empire. Yet there is little doubt that, by the end of the Fascist regime, empire had played a far from insignificant part in the formation of the Italian nation. Strikingly, however, this process of making the nation could be extremely localized. Pursuit of an Italian empire, of Italian *spazio vitale*, again and again emphasized the contribution of a particular city; and elites within that city saw the advantage of supporting such a project because it served their own very local interests. Paradoxically, while both the liberal state and the Fascist regime periodically expressed their frustrations at the *municipalismo* of the *cento città*, *venezianità* could be harnessed as a key tool in legitimating empire, which was in turn designed to strengthen the nation. In the Venetian case, the *piccola patria* helped make Italians by justifying a short-lived and fundamentally unsuccessful imperial experiment.

---

[152] G. Damerini, *Le isole Jonie e il sistema adriatico dal dominio veneziano a Buonoparte* (Varese & Milan: ISPI, 1943), 186

COMMENTS

The European Old Regime and the Imperial Question: A Modernist View of a Contemporary Question

Jean-Frédéric Schaub

Modern and Contemporary History: Imperfect Gaps and Real Revolutions

The texts collected by Stefan Berger and Alexey Miller in this volume all answer the same question. Effectively, they deal with the formation of national sovereignties in Europe in the age of liberalism and early industrial revolutions, when imperial structures, whether inherited from the old regimes or born as a result of colonial conquest, gave shape to the majority of European states. Consistency in questioning, carried out by the editors of the volume, is a necessary condition to make the comparative approach successful. However, the empirical framework is also important to make the study effective. If we accept the fiction of sovereign states being actors, we will recognize that every one of them develops in interaction and competition with multiple other actors. Thus, the comparison itself takes place in a space dominated by exchanges, conflicts, and possibilities of mutual influence. This is why studies collected here all fall within both comparative history and *histoire croisée*.[1]

The point of view of a historian specializing in the early modern period can help to reveal the historical strata that remained present after the cycle of revolutions that took place between the end of the eighteenth and the end of the nineteenth centuries. The framework of analysis could become an answer to a remark made by Jane Burbank and Frederick Cooper in their book dedicated to empires in world history. "There was and is no single path from empire to nation—or the other way around. Both ways of organizing state power present challenges and opportunities to the politically ambitious and both empires and nation-states could be transformed into something more like the

---

[1] Michael Werner and Bénédicte Zimmermann, "Penser l'histoire croisée: entre empirie et réflexivité," *Annales HSS* no. 1 (2003): 7–36

other."[2] European societies that had experienced the great cycle of continental revolutions between 1789 and 1848 had to undergo deep legal and institutional changes. They did it at very different paces. But there is hardly any doubt that they started the process of accepting new political and legal forms of the state. Normative systems, forms of decision-making, and available political ideologies present at the end of the nineteenth century are extremely different from what had been the legal order of the old regimes, expressions by political authorities, and princely images at the end of the seventeenth century.[3] This statement, a very banal one, is necessary insofar as the temptation to emphasize the continuity of the European old regimes, despite the political realities of the long nineteenth century, is reasonable and well-grounded.[4]

As far as the history of Europe is concerned, one understands that the question of telling empires from nation-states, if it is legitimate, cannot be formulated without, at the same time, questioning the analytical and didactical difference of early modern and modern. Also, regarding the history of European colonies, whether situated overseas or in geographical proximity to the metropolitan territory, the distinction between the colonial period and the national one seems, roughly speaking, to match the opposition between the early modern and the modern era. However, this correspondence is today under heavy criticism, especially in the United States and in Brazil. The hypothesis of the "Tropical Old Regime" of Portuguese America surviving the end of dependency between Brazil and Portugal is not just a cultivated field of research, it's a very fertile one.[5] Similarly, the illusion that the "Founding Fathers" of 1776 transformed North American society, turning it from colonial into national, needs to be thoroughly reexamined.[6]

Relations of opposition and inclusion between the imperial system and the nation-state nurture this temptation. Should we follow Alexis de Tocqueville, who thought that the French absolutist administration had done the bulk of the work that the Jacobins only finalized? Should we think that the prohibited craft guilds were just the last hurdle ahead of the already triumphant capitalism? Were vandalism and

---

[2] Frederick Cooper and Jane Burbank, *Empires in World History* (Princeton: Princeton University Press, 2009), 9.

[3] Denis Richet, *La France moderne, l'esprit des institutions* (1973) (Paris: Flammarion, 1991).

[4] Arno Mayer, *The Persistence of the Old Regime: Europe to the Great War* (New York: Pantheon Books, 1981).

[5] João Fragoso, Maria Fernanda Bicalho, and Maria de Fátima Gouvêa, eds., *O Antigo Regime nos Trópicos. A Dinâmica Imperial Portuguesa (séculos XVI–XVIII)* (Rio de Janeiro: Civilização Brasileira, 2001); Maria Fernanda Bicalho and Vera Lúcia Ferlini, eds., *Modos de governar. Ideias e práticas políticas no império português, séculos XVI a XIX* (São Paulo: Alameda, 2005); Rodrigo Bentes Monteiro, Daniela Buono Calainho, Bruno Feitler, and Jorge Flores, *Raízes do privilégio. Mobilidade social no mundo ibérico do Antigo Regime* (Rio de Janeiro: Civilização Brasileira, 2011).

[6] Jack P. Greene, "Colonial History and National History: Reflections on a Continuing Problem," *The William and Mary Quarterly* 64, no. 2 (2007): 235–50; Kariann Akemi Yokota, *Unbecoming British. How Revolutionary America Became a Postcolonial Nation* (Oxford: Oxford University Press, 2011).

de-Christianization just the culmination of a long process of secularization, which bore fruit in 1792? These questions are not conceived to impose a franco-centric vision of the European political arena, but the fact is that the French case appears to concentrate the entire capacity of European societies to overthrow their structures. Whether we speak about the appearance of a centralized administration, deregulation of labor, or the retreat of religion, European societies before 1789 were far from laying the foundations of the liberal systems. And if it was not the case, it would be self-evident that the cycle of revolutions was indeed revolutionary in its intentions and its legal outcome. Did European societies digest these changes and these promises in a hundred or in a hundred and fifty years? That is another question. Thus, the visible continuities between the periods on both sides of the revolutionary era invite scholars to identify in the anterior period's political forms, rules of law, methods of social and economic regulation, and representations of the "public thing" which had been profoundly different from those of the age of liberalism.

It is here that the work of historians should show its critical functions. On the one hand, national mythologies, born in the same age as romantic and liberal movements, tried to forge long continuities around the idea of a genius of every nation, across the political accidents and succession of regimes.[7] On the other hand, the historiography, also indifferent to political institutions and attentive to economic evolution, built its discourse on long-lasting social processes. In both cases, the gap between historical periods on both sides of the revolutions is minimized. However, the approach that confronts the depth—intellectual and chronological at the same time—of social and economic history with the superficiality of political and institutional history, seems nowadays quite outdated. On the contrary, history can evaluate normative systems, institutional models, and discourses of political justification of the old regimes and of the liberal era to find both similarities and differences.[8]

Universal Empire: General Political Horizon

Thus, a critical approach to historical research can permit, for example, the study of theories of universal empire, created and spread from the Middle Ages to the seventeenth century, taking them for what they really were: royal propaganda devices.[9] Historians should avoid two dangers. The first one is taking the discourses (and

---

[7] Patrick Geary, *The Myth of Nations: The Medieval Origins of Europe* (Princeton: Princeton University Press, 2002).

[8] António Manuel Hespanha, *Guiando a mão invisível. Direito, Estado e lei no liberalismo monárquico português* (Coimbra: Almedina, 2004).

[9] Alexandre Haran, *Le lys et le globe, messianisme dynastique et rêve impérial en France aux XVIe et XVIIe siècles* (Seyssel: Champ Vallon, 2000); Fernando Bouza, *Imagen y propaganda. Capítulos de historia cultural del reinado de Felipe II* (Madrid: Akal, 1998); James Muldoon, *Empire and Order: The Concept of Empire, 800–1800* (New York: St. Martin's, 1999).

images) of imperial majesty for the description of the authority really upheld by the monarchs who sponsored these works. The second one is confusing the *mise en scène* (dramatization) of the majesty with the theory of sovereignty, produced by the philosophers for the same monarchs. In reality, there are three types of objects in need of investigation (myth of the Universal Empire, *mise en scène* of the majesty, and legal and philosophical theory of sovereignty). These have some sort of connection with each other, but they were wrongly mixed up for a long time.[10]

So, the theories of national sovereignty, including the one of unity and indivisibility, French style, can be studied as ideological arguments serving government authorities. But there can be no doubt that the diffusion of such theories had specifically legal implications, insofar as they influenced the choices of assemblies that gave birth to modern constitutions and legal codes.[11] Even if the discourses were different before and after the revolutions, they had one thing in common: ancient ones as well as modern ones were based on fiction. Under the old regimes, the Universal Empire was never anything other than a utopian horizon in Europe, in the same way as national unity, which remains an idea or a theoretical framework.[12] Nowadays, historians who study politics, whether on a national or imperial level, do not see sovereignty anymore as a self-evident framework of analysis but as one of the regulatory discourses established by modern political systems to build their authority or to justify their actual power.

It is the relationship with imperial heritage which makes the modern period politically different from the earlier one. European monarchies liberate themselves from the symbolic tutelage of the Roman Imperial institution. They affirm their pre-imperial roots, located in the barbarian past, the very birthplace of the singularity of every kingdom.[13] But, at the same time, the monarchies, deploying this kind of argument, assume the symbols of imperial authority.[14] Many of the authors of the volume show that the imperial institution and the build-up of national identities strengthened each other during the early modern era. In the same way, the consolidation of the European powers and the renovation of the imperial image went hand in hand.

---

[10] Fanny Cosandey and Robert Descimon, *L'Absolutisme en France. Histoire et historiographie* (Paris: Seuil, 2002).

[11] Jacques Krynen, *L'Empire du roi. Idées et croyances politiques en France, XIIIe–XVe siècle* (Paris: Gallimard, 1993); Jacques Krynen, *L'état de justice. France, XIIIe–XXe siècle*, vol. I *L'idéologie de la magistrature ancienne* (Paris: Gallimard, 2009).

[12] Franz Bosbach, *Monarchia universalis: ein politischer Leitbegriff der fruhen Neuzeit* (Gottingen: Vandenhoeck & Ruprecht, 1988).

[13] Richard Helgerson, *Forms of Nationhood. The Elizabethan Writing of England* (Chicago: University of Chicago Press, 1992); Françoise Crémoux and Jean-Louis Fournel, *Idées d'Empire en Italie et en Espagne: XIV–XVIIe siècle* (Rouen: Publications des universités de Rouen et du Havre, 2010).

[14] Frances A. Yates, *Astraea: The Imperial Theme in the Sixteenth Century* (London: Routledge, 1975); Pablo Fernández Albaladejo, "'Imperio de por sí.' la reformulación del poder universal en la temprana edad moderna," in *Fragmentos de Monarquía* (Madrid: Alianza, 1990), 168–84.

Thus, in the Church domain, the evolution of the relationship between the throne and the altar had been marked by a phenomenon identified by German historians as "confessionalization." While Christendom was not fragmented into a number of autocephalous churches equal to that of countries, it seems that the universalist aspirations of Roman Catholicism were broken. Every kingdom established its own relationship with Roman authority, going from the most obedient ultramontanism to mutual anathemas. The Church of England detached from Rome and created a special bond with royal power. France, with its honorific title of the "eldest daughter of the Church" and its magic-working king, negotiated with the Holy See and its clerical assembly a special path. The Spanish monarchy built an identity of a Catholic sentinel defending the religion against its interior and exterior foes.[15] The Austrian monarchy established the same type of relation between the royal institution and the Roman church. Portugal, organized as a "pluricontinental monarchy," was a seat of a universal evangelizing mission.[16] Emerging powers of the north, Denmark, The United Provinces, and Sweden, based their legitimacy on choosing the Reform. The one great European institution that could not present itself anymore as a religious unity, that being a fundamental failure of Charles V, was precisely the Holy Roman Empire, which had elected him as its head. In a dialectic way, at the moment when Christian Roman unity was broken forever, it was broken in the very heart of the empire. On the contrary, most kingdoms of Western and Central Europe maintained a certain religious unity, consolidating at the same time the alliance of throne and altar.

The evolution which produced this result was not a rational one, let alone a peaceful one. In Europe, the religious question led to the civil wars of religion starting from the first third of the sixteenth century and lasting until the monstrous destructions of the Thirty Years' War, multiplying the diasporas and collective exiles.[17] The loss of unity and of the universality of Roman Christendom was more than a disaster of the ecclesiastical order; it was accompanied by an outbreak of political violence.[18]

During the long early modern period, the breakup of Roman and imperial unity was not the only reconfiguration in Western Europe. Indeed, in the field of diplomacy, the concert of nations, as it was understood in the nineteenth century, did not take the place of the empire. On the contrary, certain monarchies reached a level which permitted a pursuit of supremacy, if not of universality. All the European

---

[15] Pablo Fernández Albaladejo, *Materia de España. Cultura política e identidad en la España moderna* (Madrid: Marcial Pons, 2007).

[16] Pedro Cardim, "La aspiración imperial de la monarquía portuguesa (siglos XVII–XVIII)," in *Comprendere le monarchie iberiche: risorse materiali e rappresentazione del potere*, ed. Gaetano Sabatini (Rome: Viella, 2010), 37–72; Giuseppe Marcocci, *L'invenzione di un impero. Politica e cultura nel mondo portoghese (1450–1600)* (Rome: Carroci, 2011).

[17] Natalia Muchnik, "'S'attacher à des pierres comme à une religion locale….' La terre d'origine dans les diasporas des XVIe–XVIIIe siècles," *Annales. Histoire, Sciences sociales* (2011): 481–512.

[18] *Eadem Utraque Europa* vol 10/11, dir. José Emilio Burucúa, 2011.

discussion between the middle of the sixteenth and the middle of the seventeenth century was dedicated to the accusation of Spain for its excessive ambitions. Then Louis XIV, between the symbolic splendor of Versailles and quite real territorial conquests in the Netherlands, in Franche-Comté, in Alsace, in Roussillon, superseded Spain and was in his turn accused of aspiring to a Universal Monarchy.[19] Finally, the maritime, commercial, and financial triumph of Great Britain in the eighteenth century provoked mistrust and resentment on the continent, before and after the final clash with Napoleon. The Central European powers also faced the same change of fortunes, from the powerful Polish-Lithuanian Commonwealth fighting the Ottoman Empire, to the territorial successes of the Russian and Austrian Empires. Whether looked at in synchronic or diachronic fashion, systems of territoriality remained informed by aspirations for imperial hegemony. On the one hand, European powers learned to create a provisional balance, organizing congresses, of which the Westphalian was a mold. On the other hand, in a contradictory way, the aspiration for hegemony remained and, at least in the case of the France of Louis XIV, it was connected to a providential and imperial ideology.

Territorial Expansion: Triumphs and Weaknesses

European expansion, started by Iberian powers in the overseas, followed by French, English, Dutch, Danish, as well as the continental expansion of the Tsars' power eastwards and southwards, played a crucial role in the perpetuation of providential political horizons. Indeed, the survival of the imperial culture was largely due to the dynamics of conquest and colonization started by many European societies and political entities. Naturally, much more than just the survival of the old imperial ideals was at stake during this period. True, almost everywhere lawyers tended to describe the new political realities with the help of vocabulary borrowed from the compilations of Roman law, even when the institutional reality did not have anything in common with one of the Roman Empire. Charles V was Caesar only in disguise, Suleiman was no Islamic Constantine and Moscow was never recognized as the third Rome. Still, the great phenomena of conquests and annexations adopted a pace and reached a scope never realized before. This is why it would be an illusion to think that it is possible to study the supposed domestic development of government institutions in the early modern period without taking into account the imperial or colonial dynamics deployed at the same time. Whether we study competition for power in Europe or rivalry in overseas expansion, the very definition of the old regime political entities remains naturally mobile and fragile. At the same time, speaking about political entities whose territorial definition is permanent conquest, it is very difficult and doubtless artificial

---

[19] Jean-Frédéric Schaub, *La France espagnole. Les racines hispaniques de l'absolutisme français* (Paris: Seuil, 2003).

to distinguish between a state of peace and a state of war, and even between an exterior war and a civil one.

That is why historians took an interest in a phenomenon which deeply affected European societies in their mutual relations: the establishment of state borders according to the new procedures. The best-known examples are Spain in its relations with Portugal, and France in its relations with all the neighbors. The Spanish–Portuguese example is very instructive. On the one hand, jurisdictional boundaries dividing the Kingdom of Portugal and the Kingdom of Castile are almost unchanged since the thirteenth century, making one of the most ancient borders in Europe.[20] But in that legal framework, cross-border exchanges were very intensive both on a local level and between the two crowns in general, so the separation function of the border remained purely theoretical. On the other hand, after a period of dynastic union between two empires (1581–1640) the war known as the Portuguese Restoration War (1641–68) transformed the border into a ditch full of fire and blood.[21] Indeed, as both parties found themselves incapable of financing their armies, troops started living exclusively off the land imposing conditions of horrific violence and extortion on border societies. Until the nineteenth century, peasant traditions from both sides of the border remembered these atrocities. Consequently, two societies which had been deeply interlinked before 1640 turned their backs on each other in the middle of the seventeenth century and it lasted until the admission of Spain and Portugal to the European Community in 1986.

The second well-known example is the complex shaping of the "French border" in the seventeenth and eighteenth centuries. Works by Peter Sahlins and Daniel Nordman showed how closely these processes were linked with the political evolution of the entire society, from the localities in the border regions to the political definition of the kingdom and its global defense system.[22] France, at the moment of its expansion, was a growing power gaining territory at the expense of its neighbors. This is why the strategy of the Bourbon kings was perceived everywhere in Europe as an aspiration to a universal monarchy or else an establishment of a continental empire. The Napoleonic adventure was interpreted in its time at least as much through the prism of this ancient accusation as through the denial of the principles of the French Revolution.

---

[20] Rita Costa Gomes, *A Ring of Castles. Fortresses of the Portuguese Frontier 1—Beira* (Lisbon: Instituto do Património, 2002); *A Ring of Castles. Fortresses of the Portuguese Frontier 2—Trás-os-Montes* (Lisbon: Instituto do Património, 2006).

[21] Fernando Dores Costa, *A Guerra da Restauração, 1641–1668* (Lisbon: Livros Horizonte, 2004).

[22] Peter Sahlins, *Boundaries: the Making of France and Spain in the Pyrenees* (Berkeley: University of California Press, 1989); Daniel Nordman, *Frontières de France: de l'espace au territoire: XVIe–XIXe siècle* (Paris: Gallimard, 1998).

Politicization and Institutionalization

Starting from this point, historians can work in two opposing directions, both of them necessary. On the one hand, they must identify the phenomena distinguishing the early modern from the modern period. Three examples can be named among many others: extension of the citizenship at the level of the state and its territory beyond local roots; growing distinction between political exercise of authority and obedience, economic activity and, eventually, religious communion; and the establishment of language policy to reinforce the political cohesion of the population. On the other hand, to remember the warning of Jane Burbank and Frederick Cooper, historians should learn not to exaggerate the phenomena of rupture between the periods, especially when it is possible to reconstitute the experience of actors in the past really close to the processes in which they had participated. In this case, the framework of analysis dominating in this volume of studies, that is, articulation of imperial structure and national construction rather than opposition between them, makes perfect sense. In such a framework of analysis, historians of the old regimes find themselves in a position where dialogue with specialists of modern history is easy.

Classical historiographies construct a framework corresponding with the development of the government institutions and the extension of territories depending on the same authority. Successive stages of the establishment of the political institutions are the chronological references to which all the other phenomena are adjusted.[23] Happily, more than thirty years ago the teleological scenario of the ascent of the modern state came under criticism which changed our view on the evolution of political institutions in Europe between the thirteenth and the eighteenth centuries. It is well known that Joseph Strayer formulated the model of the "Medieval origins of the modern state." This proposition dominated the field of political studies for a long time.[24] Two series of volumes organized by Jean-Philippe Genet, *Genèse de l'Etat moderne* [Genesis of the Modern State] and *Origines de l'Etat moderne* [Origins of the Modern State] are based on the general framework summarized by Strayer.[25] Significantly, even the study of the diversity of old configurations of society was started from a central model of an emerging nation-state. This is how Hendrik Spruyt described his political analysis, a confrontation of the "Sovereign State and its Competitors." And why can

---

[23] Jean-Frédéric Schaub, "Le temps et l'Etat: vers un nouveau régime historiographique de l'Ancien Régime français," *Quaderni Fiorentini per la Storia del Pensiero Giuridico Moderno* 25 (1996): 127–82.

[24] Joseph R. Strayer, *On the Medieval Origins of the Modern State* (Princeton: Princeton University Press, 1970).

[25] Jean-Philippe Genet, ed., *L'Etat moderne. Genèse: bilans et perspectives* (Paris: Éditions du CNRS, 1990).

we not think that the state was at the same time a competitor and a challenger of an imperial form much more powerful than the state itself?[26]

If it is demonstrated that political institutions had been functioning continuously and coherently since the thirteenth century up to the Enlightenment, contradictory conclusions could be drawn. The hypothesis of continuity opens up to the historians the opportunity to choose the episodes or the processes which fit into their theoretical framework. Thus, it is possible to maintain that the thirteenth century was already modern or, quite the contrary, that the seventeenth century was still archaic. In the first case, one would refer to a number of indications of the coming modern state: the English *Magna Carta*, territorial concentration of France under Philip II Augustus, the criminal code fixed by Rome at the Fourth Council of the Lateran, or *Siete Partidas* of the King Alfonso X the Sage of Castile. To illustrate the second case, one would note the inheritance of public offices which existed until the end of the old regimes, magic powers of French and English Kings until the very century of Enlightenment, never-ending religious persecutions, legal plurality which was a rule in the countries of *Ius Commune* as well as in those of the Common Law, and the absence of linguistic policies.

The Law without the State

During the last twenty years of the twentieth century, certain historians from the Catholic countries in the south of Europe—Italy, Spain, and Portugal—maintained the hypothesis of political and legal archaism of the early modern period.[27] On the academic level, this disposition does not at all reflect a delay in development of these societies. On the contrary, it is linked with the persistence of an ancient legal culture which was never separated from its Medieval genealogy and its roots in Roman Christianity. Indeed, in these countries historians of law restored the thread of another continuity, the one of legal culture, since the rebirth of the commentary to the *Corpus Iuris Civilis* in the University of Bologna at the end of the twelfth century until the establishment of police administration in the second half of the eighteenth century.

---

[26] Hendrik Spruyt, *The Sovereign State and Its Competitors: An Analysis of Systems Change* (Princeton: Princeton University Press, 1994).

[27] The bibliography is very abundant. See among others: Paolo Grossi, *Dalla società di società alla insularità dello Stato fra Medioevo ed età moderna* (Naples: Instituto universitario suor Orsola Benincasa, 2003); Luca Mannori, "Genesi dello Stato e storia giuridica," *Quaderni Fiorentini per la Storia del Pensiero Giuridico Moderno* 24 (1995): 485–505; Bartolomé Clavero, "Institucion politica y derecho: acerca del concepto historiografico de 'Estado Moderno,'" *Revista de estudios politicos* 19 (1981): 43–57; Jesús Vallejo, "Paratonía de la historia jurídica," *Mélanges de la Casa de Velázquez* XXXI, no. 2, 109–41; António Manuel Hespanha, "Pré-compréhension et savoir historique. La crise du modèle étatiste et les nouveaux contours de l'histoire du pouvoir," *Rättshistoriska Studier*, serien II, Lund (1993). 49–68.

Doing this, they were less dependent intellectually on the heritage of the modern period, representing the state as the guarantor, the last resort, the initiator of a system of legal norms. Indeed, the modern state does not only have a monopoly on the legitimate power of coercion, but it also embodies sovereignty which is the primary source of all institutional legitimacy. The state guarantees the regular functioning of a system of legal norms founded on the primacy of law over all other instruments of regulation. However, under the old regimes the relationship between law and government institutions did not obey this scheme.

In order to show this difference, historians of law make use of two types of research. On the one hand, they analyze the system of norms which ensured the cohesion of the ancient society. During this operation, they deploy the legal science in a number of cases mobilizing very ancient normative reasoning and arguments.[28] On the other hand, they run socio-historical surveys on the networks of holders of authority in the old regime societies, especially the social power of lawyers. Indeed, already many decades ago, a number of surveys were made on professional bodies of magistrates and officers wielding judicial authority delegated by the princes. The majority of these works produced a historical sociology of the professional groups which were at the same time kinship systems and networks of friends. Indeed, an appointment to a post did depend on competence and performance, but not uniquely. Various processes of public offices becoming heritable, with or without their legal sale, enhanced the cohesion and the autonomy of lawyers, without undermining their intellectual prestige.

These different types of works lead to two converging conclusions. On the one hand, it seems that the legal order we are referring to was an architecture of norms much larger and deeper than just a collection of laws and orders emanating from kings and princes. Indeed, compilations of laws and orders voted by state assemblies were put together—and sometimes printed—in many kingdoms and principalities, from Lisbon (*Ordenações Filipinas*, 1603) to Moscow (*Sobornoe Ulozhenie*, 1649). But these instruments covered just a part, most often a minimal one, of the legal resources at the disposal of magistrates, litigants, and notaries wishing to take a decision or to find a motivation. In reality, legal order was an aggregate of textual authorities of theological and legal nature including, among others, the Holy Scriptures, Fathers of the Church, collections of *Corpus Iuris Civilis*, canon law, and layers of commentaries and glosses accumulated since the thirteenth century. This civil law, *Ius Commune,* formed a complex normative culture. But it was understood by lawyers in all the regions dominated by Roman Christianity and even beyond. It is remarkable, indeed, that after the political schism provoked by the Reformation, Protestant lawyers never stopped learning about the development of the *Ius Commune* as it was taught in the Catholic universities of the Southern Europe.

---

[28] Ernst Kantorowicz, "Kingship under the Impact of Scientific Jurisprudence," in *Twelfth-Century Europe and the Foundations of Modern Society*, eds. M. Clagett, G. Post, and R. Reynolds (Madison: University of Wisconsin Press, 1961), 89–111.

From the other side, after studying this aggregation of references, lawyers drew the conclusion that the model of decision-making is not an affirmation of a unilateral arbitrariness, but rather an arbitration between different interests in the name of a superior judicial authority. It was qualified as jurisdictional paradigm.[29] The dominant form of decision-making is through a judge weighing the arguments of the different parties soliciting him and not by an administrator determined, on his own initiative, to amend the rules of the social life. To be able to mobilize these resources, which were complex, encyclopedic, often conflicting with each other, a professional body of specialists was formed. Since the institution of universities and their chairs of civil law (that is Roman law, commentary of *Corpus Iuris Civilis*), canon law and theology, the lawyers of the old regimes were organized as a body endowed with authority in society. This professional body was stratified and the rules of its reproduction were made by the body itself. It enjoyed relative autonomy from the royal authority, let alone from the power games of the court. Continuities in the legal system found by historians of law are reflected in social relations. It is enough to think about the very long duration of the feudal system[30] or, in the cultural arena, about the Latin language, persistently used by learned people.[31]

In the High Middle Ages, lawyers created the theory of their own eminent position with regard both to society and royal or princely power. Let us take, for instance, three notions which seem to go beyond the law proper: custom as a social reality, equity as a moral imperative, and grace as a religious truth. Lawyers mobilize their culture to determine the border dividing the learned law from the customs; but those who only practice the customs cannot symmetrically define the territory of their competence, defending it from invasion of the written law. One might think that equity concerns only moral assessment, but in fact it is an object of legal and jurisprudential regulations from which the judges cannot digress, if they cannot in their turn produce technically solid legal argumentation. Finally, concerning the pardon, that is the supreme power of the prince to throw off the rules of social life, it is nonetheless the object of councils and consultations, of formulating and justification, mobilizing lawyers. This is why it is essential to recover the literal meaning of the notion of absolutism. The neologism was based on an adage *"Princeps est a legibus solutus"* which means that the prince is not bound by princely laws. But it does not mean at all that he is free to throw off general legal norms, "the order of things," the infinitely larger realm of rules governing divine creation as well as human society.

Speaking of professional experience of historians, an element should be added to this presentation concerning the intellectual and political power of lawyers in the old regime societies. They were the ones, indeed, who dictated the conceptual framework in which the vast majority of archival sources was produced, without which we

---

[29] Pietro Costa, *Jurisdictio: semantica del potere politico nella pubblicistica medievale, 1100–1433* (Milan: Giuffrè, 1969).
[30] Renata Ago, *La feudalità in età moderna* (Rome–Bari: Laterza, 1998).
[31] Françoise Waquet, *Le latin ou l'empire d'un signe, XVIe XXe siècle* (Paris: Albin Michel, 1998).

would not know anything about old societies. Minutes, notarial acts, contracts, corporative deliberations, surveys, registers: all these tools of social life obey legal models. This is why, moreover, it is illusory to think that the manuscript archives of the ancient institutions give us direct access to their society while literature and printed books only give access to heavily mediatized representations. It is better to realize that all these manuscript instruments keep in line with legal qualification of social facts and recount them in a shape acceptable for political and legal institutions. When one loses this *naïveté*, it seems essential to learn the culture and professional techniques of the producers of archives, from a modest notary to the highest magistrate, before embarking on a study of the old regime documents.

Growth and Accumulation of Authority

The researchers of early modern history often took a keen interest in the concentration of political, social, and cultural authority in a more and more restrained and more and more abstract circle of institutions.[32] But they could also emphasize the contractual character of the relations negotiated between political authorities and social bodies that they pretended to govern, and they could highlight the religious bases of their legitimacy which were partly lost because of the rise of contracts. Recently, an enlightening study dedicated to the construction of the fiscal state in the Spanish Empire showed the negotiated character of this process of political institutionalization.[33] Nowadays, the idea of absolutism being also a regime of negotiation does not seem very scandalous. Forty years ago, after the success of the great dogmatic or logical descriptions of intractable totalitarian regimes, a new period started. Whether the study reveals the chaotic character of the Third Reich or existence of discontinued spaces of negotiation in the heart of the Soviet institutional system, the specialists in modern history taught us to distinguish the self-declared ideal of state omnipotence from the discrete systems of arrangements at all levels of society. Is it possible not to take into account these historiographic achievements when approaching the old regime societies, in their local and imperial dimensions?

The thesis of continuity of the institutions is based on the persistence of social organization centered on the ecclesiastical model and religious imagination of society. If, according to Jérôme Baschet, the Church stays "the dominant institution of Feudalism" in the Middle Ages, the early modern period does not liberate itself from this structure, despite all the disruptions provoked by the wars of religion.[34] Indeed,

---

[32] Stefano Mannoni, *Une et indivisible. Storia dell'Acentramento Amministrativo in Francia, vol. 1, La formazione del sistema (1661–1815)* (Milan: Giufré Editore, 1994).

[33] Alejandra Irigoin and Regina Grafe, "Bargaining for Absolutism: A Spanish Path to Nation-State and Empire Building," *Hispanic American Historical Review* 88, no. 2 (2008): 173–209.

[34] Jérôme Baschet, *La civilisation féodale. De l'an Mil à la colonisation de l'Amérique* (Paris: Flammario, coll. Champs, 2006).

Alain Guerreau shows that the analytical distinction between "religion," "politics," and "economy" as three autonomous spheres of social experience, became conceivable only as a result of the work started by the men of the Enlightenment.[35] Consequently, there is no point in trying to trace secularizing dynamics in the sixteenth and seventeenth centuries, which would have had emancipating effects on politics at the end of the Middle Ages.[36]

The conclusion of religious peace to put an end to the disastrous conflicts did not mean a stable disengagement of a political sphere placed above religion.[37] The historiographic topic of confessionalization was born in Germany: Heinz Schilling and Wolfgang Reinhard used this grid of reading to give an account of political and territorial composition of the aggregate of Germanic societies divided by the issue of religion.[38] This historiographic framework shows that there is no point in trying to separate the study of political institutions from the study of religious structuring of societies in the early modern era. Various studies show the progress of the skeptical attitude even among the lower classes, especially the extraordinary survey of Stuart Schwartz dedicated to the "tolerance" of the common people in the Iberian Peninsula and Spanish and Portuguese America.[39] Others bring in evidence that religious peace, to use the term introduced by Olivier Christin, leads to a long-term regulation of social relations between the faithful of opposing confessions.[40] However, these studies do not deny the persistence of religious control of social and political life. Nor did the conflicts between throne and altar, which affected the Roman church as well as some Orthodox patriarchies, trigger the process of secularization. Philip II, the king of Spain, was in an open conflict with the Papacy over the question of ecclesiastical patronage: who would advance an idea to interpret these tensions as heralds of secularizing processes?[41] The France of Louis XIV persecuted the Protestants and the Russia

---

[35] Alain Guerreau, "Fief, féodalité, féodalisme. Enjeux sociaux et réflexion historienne," *Annales E.S.C.* 45 (1990): 137–66.

[36] Pedro Cardim, "Religião e ordem social. Em torno dos fundamentos católicos do sistema político do Antigo Regime," *Revista de História das Ideias* 22 (2001): 133–74; Bartolomé Clavero, *La grâce du don. Anthropologie catholique de l'économie moderne* (Paris: Albin Michel, 1996).

[37] Olivier Christin, *La paix de religion: l'autonomisation de la raison politique au XVIe siècle* (Paris: Seuil, 1997).

[38] Heinz Schilling, "Confessional Europe," in *Handbook of European History 1400–1600: Late Middle Ages, Renaissance and Reformation II: Visions, Programs and Outcomes*, eds. Thomas A. Brady Jr, Heiko A. Oberman, and James D. Tracy (Leiden: Brill, 1995), 612–81; Wolfgang Reinhard, *Papauté, confessions, modernité* (Paris: Editions de l'Ecole des hautes études en sciences sociales, 1998).

[39] Stuart B. Schwartz, *All Can Be Saved. Religious Tolerance and Salvation in the Iberian Atlantic World* (New Haven: Yale University Press, 2008).

[40] Christophe Duhamelle, *La frontière au village. Une identité catholique allemande au temps des Lumières* (Paris: Editions de l'Ecole des Hautes Etudes en Sciences Sociales, 2010).

[41] Ignasi Fernández Terricabras, *Felipe II y el clero secular. La aplicación del concilio de Trento* (Madrid: Sociedad Estatal para la Conmemoración de los centenarios de Felipe II y Carlos V, 2000),

of Alexis hunted for Old Believers: the policies of these monarchs did not lead to the separation of throne and altar, but they pointed exactly in another direction. Speaking about the imperial expansion of the early modern era, it was deeply marked by the religious dimension of authorities. Indeed, the exportation of European societies to the overseas territories was at the same time accompanied by missionary ambition and, in any event, was given a religious definition.[42]

In Central and Southeastern Europe, in the Mediterranean and in the Indian Ocean, politics of territorial and commercial expansion were seen as a chapter in the chronicle of the clash between Christendom and Islam. In the Americas and in Western Africa the presence of Europeans, merchants or representatives of princely powers, was doubled and sometimes preceded by a wide range of missionary ventures. During the seventeenth century, installation of settlers coming from the British Isles to the Caribbean and the continent of North America was fully connected with the question of religion, from the voluntary exile of Puritans to Cromwell's enterprises. If European historians cease to treat colonial processes as secondary ones, separating them from the histories of mother countries, they will be undoubtedly less tempted to reproduce the fiction of a precocious coming of secularized political culture.[43]

Power Techniques in an Unstable World

The French case may be useful to cast light on the historiographic opposition between empires and nation-states. France as expanding power is at least an ambivalent example. Since the nineteenth century, French national historiography (and equally the French studies of the Anglo-Saxon world) especially emphasized the phenomena of administrative centralization and rationalization. It was a kind of trademark: the cultural and political identity of France had to be situated at the junction of the *raison d'état* (reason of state) of Richelieu and the philosophical reason of Descartes.[44] These two reasons stood for uniformity and coming universality. But in fact, this political rationalism reflects much more the retrospective myth than a program imagined under the monarchy. The reason of state for the principal minister of Louis XIII referred to two intellectual traditions without any link with nascent rationalism. On the one hand, the art of government is rooted in the Medieval corpus, on the other hand, it

---

[42] Carla Pestana, *Protestant Empire: Religion and the Making of the British Atlantic World* (Philadelphia: University of Pennsylvania Press, 2009); Charlotte de Castelnau-L'Estoile, Marie-Lucie Copete, Aliocha Maldavsky and Inès Zupanov, eds., *Missions et circulation des savoirs (XVIe–XVIIIe siècles)* (Madrid: Casa de Velázquez, 2011).

[43] Jean-Frédéric Schaub, "La catégorie 'études coloniales' est-elle indispensable?" *Annales HSS* 63, no. 3 (2008): 625–46.

[44] Stéphane Van Damme, *Descartes. Essai d'histoire culturelle d'une grandeur philosophique (XVIIe–XXe siècle)* (Paris: Presses de Science Po, collection "Facettes," 2002).

is rooted in the Catholic answers to the challenge of Machiavelli.[45] The means of dissimulation, to take just one example, did not have much in common with the way of reasoning found on observation and logical deduction.[46] On the contrary, Bourbon France allowed for a linguistic plurality and did not try to reduce it by any political means.[47] The kings of France had to negotiate all the time with powerful aristocratic families, with urban oligarchies, and with the clergy which constituted the Church of France.[48] From this point of view France was never an exception: under the theatrical majesty of absolutism, legal pluralism remained the framework for politics. When the royal authority strengthened and its ability to command increased, it was a fruit of violent clashes, in other words, of civil wars. The capacity of kings taking action increased much more as a result of interior war than as a result of the help of absolutist ideology.

Other essential elements should also be taken into account. On the one hand, the effectiveness of the *mise en scène* of royal majesty.[49] Religious celebrations, urban festivals, erection of statues and festive gates, diffusion of medals, images, panegyrics: all this helped to spread the impression of the divine and at the same time the pastoral character of the king's person, incarnating the political order in the kingdom.[50] On the other hand, at all levels of society and everywhere in the country there were clients of the king and his court. There were also political, economic, and family bonds of dependency. Municipal magistrates, military governors, financiers, and shopkeepers: thousands of people everywhere were affected through their patron-client links by a fraction if not of royal authority, at least of a capacity to take part in the implementation of the king's will. It goes without saying that these agents did not place themselves at the service of this policy without receiving immediate profit in return, protection, or prestige.

Thus, the progress of the King's authority rested upon four modes of action: violence of internal war, seduction of the court propaganda, corruption through patron-client links penetrating the heart of the provinces, and formalization of conflicts

---

[45] Michel Senellart, *Les arts de gouverner. Du regimen médiéval au concept de gouvernement* (Paris: Seuil, 1995); Claude Lefort, *Le travail de l'œuvre Machiavel* (Paris: Gallimard, 1972).

[46] Rosario Villari, *Elogio della dissimulazione. La lotta politica nel Seicento* (Bari: Laterza, 2003).

[47] Michel de Certeau, Dominique Julia, and Jacques Revel, *Une politique de la langue: la Révolution française et les patois, l'enquête de Grégoire* (Paris: Gallimard, 1975); Hélène Merlin-Kajman, *La langue est-elle fasciste? Langue, pouvoir, enseignement* (Paris: Seuil, 2003).

[48] Katia Béguin, *Les Princes de Condé. Rebelles, courtisans et mécènes dans la France du Grand siècle* (Seyssel: Champ Vallon, 1999); William Beik, *Absolutism and Society in Seventeenth Century France: State, Power and Provincial Aristocracy in Languedoc* (Cambridge: Cambridge University Press, 1985); Claude Michaud, *L'Église et l'argent sous l'Ancien Régime. Les receveurs généraux du clergé de France au XVIe–XVIIe siècles* (Paris: Fayard, 1991).

[49] Gérard Sabatier, *Le prince et les arts: Stratégies figuratives de la monarchie française de la Renaissance à l'âge baroque* (Seyssel: France, Champ Vallon, 2010).

[50] Paul Kléber Monod, *The Power of Kings: Monarchy and Religion in Europe, 1589–1715* (New Haven: Yale University Press, 1999)

of interests through the development of institutions regulated by law. This is a complex system, associating from one side a regime of perpetual negotiation, discouraging any standardization attempt, and from the other side a use of force turning entire groups of population into interior enemies. Between these two extremes, the factual power mobilized law as a technical source of legitimacy, spirituality as an ideological base, and court arts as a means of seduction.

The negotiation could proceed upwards or downwards, depending on the chains of the hierarchical interests of clients linking the smallest towns with great lords, with kings' courtiers or even with the royal family itself. The powerful relied on their network of trusted persons to get their fidelity and economical resources; in exchange, they guaranteed security and distributed places and honors. Various regional versions of such systems were described in very different regions of Europe. This way of functioning can be found in all the great types of political societies: kingdoms centered symbolically around a royal or princely court (among others England, Castile, Austria, France, Denmark, and Russia); private dominions of a royal court (among others Naples, Aragon, Scotland after 1603, Norway, Bohemia after 1620); and overseas colonies in Asia, Africa, and America.

Speaking about violence, it is sufficient to set the terms of the problem without entering into a long discussion. In the most common teleological perspective one can analyze the couple revolt/repression on the model of crime/punishment. In this case, the historian marks the emergence of disorder and describes the coercive or negotiated mechanisms of the return to order. And that implies a preceding stability of balance of power and institutional framework, of which it matters to regain the serenity shaken for one instant. However, it is also possible to think in other terms. A return to order is not necessarily a return to the previous situation. On the contrary, it may be argued that the deployment of force in the social space against a part of the population is an essential mechanism to found a political regime and command obedience. In other words, the war the prince is compelled to wage against his own subjects is the very foundation of his political authority. The king can devastate his own country with impunity in the name of order, he can murder his rivals and great lords in the name of defending the dynasty, he can destroy the city walls to make townsfolk respect his supreme authority: acting in this way, the king accumulates the force available in society around himself and his circle of associates, and tends to acquire a monopoly on the use of force.

In such a perspective, Weber's formula on the legitimate use of force being a special attribute of state, takes a different sense from the one that historians of early modern states wished to illustrate during the decades. Indeed, if one argues that violence is not a failure of authority but a condition of its establishment, then Weber's formula could mean that the violence of social forces, which manage actually to monopolize the force, succeeds also in imposing the ideological framework affirming its own legitimacy. Procedures of magistrates and prayers of the priests do not contribute to creating a rational political order: they transform force in law and disorder in order. The object of these remarks is not to suggest a moral criticism of these old processes of politicization of which we are incessantly reminded that they form the genealogy of our own political experience. My remarks are aimed simply at suggesting that the monarchical state is not less dynamic and uncertain, expansive and violent, fragile and brutal, than the great imperial and colonial enterprises.

Thus, the institution of royal power was built with the help of unstable processes. Its cumulative abilities were often tested, for example in the realm of the capacity of European powers to mobilize more and more impressive armies. But it could be swept away, as it happened two times in England during the seventeenth century. Its crisis could be brought about by forms of a fiscal, financial, and political deadlock, as it was the case in France in the eighteenth century. It could also be led to accept a persistent autonomy of its components under the apparent unity of the façade, as it was the case in the Spanish monarchy during all of the early modern era. Negotiations between the titular holder of supreme authority and his subjects never stopped. This is why the fight for internal order and for external borders was never finished and doubtless never will; this is why the deployment of ideological instruments continues to be essential to fuel belief in the foundations of the legitimacy of existing order. In light of these assessments, historians of "early modern states" may question their colleagues studying the history of early modern and modern empires. And the question they can ask is: Are we sure we can analytically distinguish national kingdoms from multinational empires?

"Imperial Nationalism" as a Challenge for the Study of Nationalism

Philipp Ther

For a long time, empires and nationalism with its ultimate goal of nation-state forma-tion were viewed as antagonistic principles. According to Dominic Lieven, empires are multinational entities which are based not on a democratic but a dynastic and tran-scendental legitimization of power secured by military might.[1] Indeed, the continen-tal European empires tended to suppress national movements throughout the long nineteenth century, the period of modern nationalism. The exceptions to this rule, the attempts of some of the European empires to enhance nation building at their cores—one of the major topics of this volume—and the limited support for specific national movements according to the *divide et impera* device, need to be left aside for a moment here. In spite of the fact that most national movements came to flourish in an imperial framework, the standard reading of twentieth century historiography used to be that national movements have led a long and tough struggle against the empires, but even-tually achieved national independence and the creation of a nation-state. One could summarize this viewpoint as a "Völkerkerker" or "prison of nation" paradigm that has been prevalent especially among twentieth century successor states of the Habsburg, Romanov, Ottoman and German Empires.

In German historiography, there was yet another line of criticism against the imperial past. The Bielefeld school of historiography has put the Prusso-German

---

[1] See Dominic Lieven, *Empire: The Russian Empire and its Rivals* (New Haven: Yale University Press, 2001), xiv. Of course there are also more recent definitions of empire, see among many books in a burgeoning field: Jane Burbank and Frederick Cooper, *Empires in World History: Power and the Politics of Difference* (Princeton: Princeton University Press, 2010).

Empire into a line of continuation with Nazi Germany.[2] Kemalist historians in Turkey have viewed the Ottoman Empire as incurably backward and suppressive. Soviet historians argued in a similar vein and of course damned the policy of the Romanov dynasty. Marxist historians generally shared a view of empires as having been anti-national and anti-modern. By contrast, the formation of nation-states was seen as a telos of modernity. The antagonism between empire and nation-states was constructed on a political, social, and cultural level in dichotomies such as multi-national vs. national, autocratic vs. democratic and feudal vs. market oriented. To be sure, in the recent two decades, there has been a re-evaluation of empire, especially in post-soviet Russia and in Turkey, and of course on the international level. Yet, in view of the entire historiography on empire that is presented in the contributions to this volume, the antagonism between empire and nationalism still appears to be conventional wisdom. That might also explain why the term empire is so contested in the United States.[3] To be labeled as an empire goes against the grain of mainstream American politics and academia, because empire is still viewed in opposition to democracy and in context of imperialism and colonialism.

In view of this antagonism between empire and nationalism, the term "imperial nationalism" appears to be a paradox and untenable. Yet reflections upon the imperial setup of nationalism are pivotal for further advancing nationalism studies. So far, there is a surprising lack of attention for empires in canonized works of nationalism studies although it is clear that empires have served at least as a context for all cases of modern nation formation. Ernest Gellner's point of reference is an imagined "Ruritania," as if the empires all had been backward, feudal, and agrarian.[4] Benedict Anderson reduces empires to pre-modern, sacral "dynastic realms," the official nationalism of empires is characterized as a "reactionary, secondary modeling" of western European nationalism.[5] Miroslav Hroch considers empires in a more substantial way. According to him, the attempts of empires to modernize and homogenize themselves provoked resistance and eventually nation building efforts from population groups, who were not native speakers of the imperial language. Yet, following his more recent opus magnum it is the formation of a modern state, rather than imperial rule that

---

[2] This was the brunt of the "Sonderweg" argument, which is paradoxically more convincing in its dimension of cultural history, e.g. regarding mentalities, than it is in its socio-historical parts, e.g. the thesis about a weak German "Bürgertum." See about the Sonderweg debate: Jürgen Kocka, "Asymmetrical Historical Comparison: The Case of the German *Sonderweg*," *History and Theory* 38, no. 1 (1999): 40–51.

[3] See for more on the controversy: Charles Maier, *Among Empires: American Ascendancy and Its Predecessors* (Cambridge, Mass.: Harvard University Press, 2006); and more recently the masterly review article: Paul A. Kramer, "Power and Connection: Imperial Histories of the United States in the World," *American Historical Review* 116 (December 2011): 1348–91.

[4] See Ernest Gellner, *Nations and Nationalism* (Ithaka: Cornell University Press, 1983), 63–75.

[5] See Benedict Anderson, *Imagined Communities: Reflections on the Origin and Spread of Nationalism* (London: Verso, 1991), 19–22. For quote on the cultural artifact, 4; for quote on reactionary nationalism, 87.

triggers modern nationalism.[6] Eric Hobsbawm stresses the relevance of imperial rule for the nationalism in the late nineteenth century and blames empires for their futile attempts at suppressing various nationalities. According to him, suppression contributed to hardening nationalism and making it "ethnic" in the eastern half of Europe.[7] Hence, one can summarize that empires are either bedevilled as backward and suppressive or not dealt with substantially in mainstream theories of nationalism and nation building.

The common root of the, one is tempted to say, ignorance or at least lack of attention for empire in nationalism studies and mainstream western historiography in the postwar period is a mostly implicit, modernist take on history. According to the liberal and Marxist understanding of history as a process of progress, at least in terms of time, empires are a part of the past, forms of state organization that needed to fail and to be replaced by an order of nation-states. This is also the reason why there were so many books about the fall of empire while few addressed the question of why many empires lasted such a long time. Nationalism was seen as a linear process as well, hence it spread from the West to the East and changed its character along the way. Although Hans Kohn's model has been refuted many decades ago, traces of the old West–East division and other traditional assumptions can still be found among the "holy triangle" of nationalism studies—Ernest Gellner, Benedict Anderson, and Eric Hobsbawm. Because of his footing in modernization theory, Gellner stresses that nationalism was a result of industrialization and the modern bureaucratic state. Like many other Central European intellectuals of his generation, Gellner would not like the thought that something which is copied could be as good as the original. Therefore, he juxtaposed a civic, subjective Western and an ethnic and violent Eastern European nationalism, epitomized in his chapter on "diaspora nationalism." Ernest Renan usually serves as the key identification figure in the pantheon of benign Western nationalism, while "diaspora nationalism" embodies all possible evils, an inflexible ethnic identity built upon common descent, which was incompatible even with states built upon a civic identity such as Czechoslovakia, where Gellner spent most his childhood. Eric Hobsbawm is less explicit in his normative juxtaposition of good Western and bad Central or Eastern European nationalism than Gellner, but his narrative also moves in this direction. Hobsbawm locates the later, radical and violent variants of nationalism almost entirely in Central and Eastern Europe. One wonders how the Basque or the Irish movement and their history of terrorism fit into this picture.

---

[6] Miroslav Hroch, *Das Europa der Nationen. Die moderne Nationsbildung im europäischen Vergleich* (Göttingen: Vandenhoeck & Ruprecht, 2005). See also his earlier book: *Na prahu národní existence. Touha a skutečnost* (Prague: Mlada Fronta, 1999), which develops this argument based on the Czech case. Hroch contends convincingly that the Josefinian reforms and later attempts to build up a modern bureaucratic state created a new kind of inequality for non-German speakers in the Habsburg Empire.

[7] Eric J. Hobsbawm, *Nations and Nationalism since 1780: Programme, Myth, Reality* (Cambridge: Verso, 1992). It takes Hobsbawm more than 40 pages to use the word empire.

Benedict Anderson is less prone to follow this West–East dichotomy, because his model is also built upon extra-European cases of nationalism. His idea that print capitalism was the key factor for spreading identities and creating alterities is close to Gellner's industrial capitalism as the underlying concept of modernization. Yet his book on the invention of the nation could also be taken as the basis for a different interpretation of modernity. Following Anderson, modernity is not necessarily based upon the existence of heavy industry and railway tracks. Means of mass communication, especially the rotating press, are his key prerequisites and components of modern nationalism. According to Anderson's take on modernity, empires, and even their most rural parts like Austrian Galicia, Western Prussia, the Caucasus, Ireland, or Spanish Galicia, could be regarded as modern due to their vibrant print media and public sphere. One could radicalize Anderson by the idea of "modernization without industrialization." This model of modernity was characteristic for large parts of continental Eastern Europe as well as southern Europe that may have had a traditional economy but were modern in their mass communication. If nationalism is based upon communication, a point already made by Karl Deutsch, one can assume that nationalist or any other political propaganda has shaped rural societies as much (although differently) as the more urbanized societies of the "Blue Banana" in northwestern Europe.

Of course, more attention was dedicated to the connection between nation building and empire in the historiography about specific countries. A seminal work in this regard is Andreas Kappeler's multi-ethnic history of the Russian Empire.[8] The Habsburg policies vis a vis various nationalities and their reactions are also well researched.[9] Yet, these important works still need to be paralleled by studies on other European empires. There is not yet a similar multi-ethnic history of the German or British Empire.[10] But Irish nation building was a similar challenge for the British Empire like the Polish national movement for Prussia and the German Empire.[11] As

---

[8] See Andreas Kappeler, *The Russian Empire. A Multiethnic History* (Harlow: Longman, 2001). See also the various books by the co-editor of this volume on nationalization policies and nationalism in the Russian Empire. In English there is Alexei Miller, *The Romanov Empire and Nationalism: Essays in the Methodology of Historical Research* (Budapest–New York: Central European University Press, 2008).

[9] See Jan Křen, *Konfliktgemeinschaft. Tschechen und Deutsche 1780–1918* (Munich: Oldenbourg, 1996). Křen's book is one of the few publications which mastered the task of writing a history of relations between two polities which cannot be understood in isolation from each other.

[10] A collective volume by Sebastian Conrad and Jürgen Osterhammel about the transnational dimensions of the German Empire went in that direction. See Sebastian Conrad and Jürgen Osterhammel, *Das Kaiserreich transnational. Deutschland in der Welt 1871–1914* (Göttingen: Vandenhoeck & Ruprecht, 2004). Yet, there is still is no book that compiles the history of the non-Germans in the German Empire and the reverberations of their existence on the politics of the center. Moreover, there still is a widespread presumption of homogeneity concerning the German Empire.

[11] There is, however, a comparative book about Polish and Irish migrants. See John Belchem and Klaus Tenfelde, ed., *Irish and Polish Migration in Comparative Perspective* (Essen: Klartext, 2003).

is shown in this volume as well, Spain faced the national movements of Catalans and other ethnic minorities on its mainland territory. Like in the German Empire, the autonomist or even separatist ambitions of various nationalities got a push, when wars and overseas territories were lost, that is, when the country had forfeited part of its imperial prestige and power. Hence, there are clearly close connections between nation building and empire on various levels.

These examples and the imperial setup of most national movements in Europe put into question longstanding distinctions between Western vs. Eastern, subjective vs. objective, civic vs. ethnic nationalism. They also counter the conventional wisdoms that nationalism moved from West to East or might be regarded as an indicator for social and economic modernity. Reflecting upon the various dimensions of the term "imperial nationalism" can help to create a more dynamic picture of nationalism in modern European history, and a model of nationalism which is not built upon an internalist perspective on singular national movements but communication and interaction between them.

Dimensions of "Imperial Nationalism"

Within the term "imperial nationalism" one can distinguish three dimensions that changed dynamically over time: 1) There were imperial nations in a narrow sense which tended to be loyal to the respective empire, e.g. the Germans in the German Empire, the Russians in the Russian Empire etc.[12] It is quite characteristic for these imperial nations that their transformation into a modern nation occurred relatively late and on a rather small, elitist social basis, at least compared to the national movements who operated without the framework of an already existing state. Moreover, since these movements depended on the support of the state and/or the emperor, they tended to be politically conservative. 2) Since one should avoid analyzing the history of empires in the categories of nation-states, one also needs to take into account imperial nations in a wider sense. There were national movements who struck a coalition with the empire and its ruling dynasty, although they did not have any prospect to become an imperial nation in the narrow sense, and did not speak the main or administrative language of the empire. Examples for this are the Baltic Germans in the Russian Empire, the Jews in the Habsburg Empire and for a long time the Armenians in the Ottoman Empire. These nationalities were mostly in support of the empire and were rewarded for their loyalty. 3) There were clearly anti-imperial movements such as the prototypical Italian Risorgimento nationalism or Polish nationalism in the long nineteenth century. But most national movements striving for emancipation attempted to strike deals with the empire, at least temporarily. The reason was that based on historical experience and reasonable calculations about the future in the long nineteenth

---

[12] One could also use the term "empire nations" (probably derived from "Reichsnation") used by Stefan Berger in his contribution to this volume.

century, the great European empires were expected to last for the foreseeable future. Sometimes, there was also a compromise in order to avoid worse alternatives, such as the rapprochement of the Czech national movement, that did not want be located in a greater Germany, with the Habsburg Empire. The empires had various options for how to deal with their nationalities that ranged from the proverbial carrot to stick. For example, the Russian Empire pursued a cooptation strategy with the Polish nobility until the November uprising of 1830, and Austria accommodated the Hungarian elites in a much more comprehensive way in the *Ausgleich* of 1867.

All these constellations show that empires had a large array of possible strategies for how to integrate, slow down, or suppress upcoming national movements. The empires were also quite creative in changing their course over time. Inevitably, this had a tremendous impact on national movements. Hence, empire was also a big challenge for national movements, not only vice versa. Above all, empires served as a common point of reference. Even if a national movement stood in clear opposition to a specific kind of imperial rule and its actual national policy, the emperor and the dynasty, the military or the imperial high culture could still serve as objects of identification.[13] Again, one needs to remember that empires were the given order in large parts of Europe, an order that was shaken only relatively late by the nation-state formation in Italy, the foundation of the German Empire in 1871 (which was propagated mostly as a nation-state then, although today there are good arguments for historians to regard it as an empire) and in Southeastern Europe. Yet the failure of the uprisings in Poland, the various alliances between the continental empires (even Italy chose to form an alliance with the Habsburg Empire and the German Empire up to World War I) and the continuous expansion of all European empires (with the exception of the Ottoman Empire and partial exception of the Habsburg Empire) in the age of imperialism confirmed the imperial order. Only the defeat of Spain in the 1898, of Russia in 1905, and of the Ottoman Empire in 1912 clearly put into question the imperial order of Europe.

Military defeats are hard to swallow for democratic nation-states, but even harder for empires which by definition are built upon military power. Therefore, defeats often had a deep impact, especially in drawing empires nearer to the model of the nation-state. In the end of the nineteenth century, when at least in Europe there was a crisis of imperial rule, more and more empires chose a strategy of becoming more national. Those empires which partially or entirely took over the agency of national movements can be labeled as "nationalizing empires." Examples for this are the Russian Empire after the Polish uprising in 1863, the German Empire established in 1871, and the Ottoman Empire after the revolution of 1908. In fact, only the Habsburg Empire

---

[13] See about the term loyalty the introduction to a volume about interwar Czechoslovakia (after all, a multinational state): Martin Schulze Wessel, "'Loyalität' als geschichtlicher Grundbegriff und Forschungskonzept: Zur Einleitung," in *Loyalitäten in der Tschechoslowakischen Republik 1918–1938. Politische, nationale und kulturelle Zugehörigkeiten*, ed. Martin Schulze Wessel (Munich: Oldenbourg, 2004), 1–22.

followed a different strategy by clearly accepting its multinational character and attempting to find *Ausgleiche* with and between its nationalities.[14]

The term "nationalizing empires" obviously creates problems of distinction—what is the difference between empire and nation-state if both forms of modern states chose similar strategies in pivotal areas such as schooling and other arenas of identity formation, administration, and even the military? Defining this term is further complicated by the fact that the terms nation (and hence nationalization), state, and empire were often used interchangeably in various European languages. Alexei Miller has outlined this for Russia—according to his contribution to this volume, the state was so strong and the society so weak (in terms of self-organization and consciousness as a society) that the empire and the nation were seen as synonyms for a long time. Contemporary politicians and intellectuals also mixed up the terms nation and nationality (*Narodnost'*), hence the nation was regarded as a state of being and not as an active political and social entity.[15] In the United States and England one can again observe synonymous usages as well, but based on opposite premises. In these countries (and therefore in the English language) the society was so strong that "nation building" took on a meaning that the closest equivalent in continental European languages would be state formation. Hence, seemingly specific imperial or nation-state policies in supporting or fighting nationalism and developing an imperial or national identity might be more similar than one would assume if one still follows the liberal and Marxist tradition of setting apart empires and nation-states on a linear scale of modernity and the old West–East division in European history that overlooks how "eastern" many southern European countries were in terms of social structures and in the case of Spain even ethnic mixture.

Yet, one should not underestimate the differences between empires and nation-states regarding the legitimization of power, the maybe grudging, but still existing acceptance that the state is inhabited by various nationalities (e.g. in population counts) and deliberate or at least tolerated mixture of the personnel in the state administration and military. However, ethnic mixture is itself a problematic argument for distinguishing empires and nation-states, because the latter ones were more mixed than officially admitted. Moreover, terms such as "ethnic," "multi-ethnic," or "multi-national" are rooted in the categories of modern nationalism.

In fact, another line of distinction needs to be made here. While the continental empires in Central and Eastern Europe were never concerned about mixtures between various nationalities inhabiting their territory or even encouraged mixing, e.g. by integrating foreign elites, the maritime empires in Western Europe (and the German Empire after the acquisition of colonies) were preoccupied with keeping their cores homogenous, e.g. by prohibiting marriages with colonized people who were

---

[14] See Gerald Stourzh, *Die Gleichberechtigung der Nationalitäten in der Verfassung und Verwaltung Österreichs 1848–1918* (Vienna: ÖAW, 1985). See about the late Ottoman Empire: Donald Quataert, *The Ottoman Empire, 1700–1922* (Cambridge: Cambridge University Press, 2000).

[15] See Alexei Miller's article before footnotes 15 and 22.

defined with racial categories. Even more important than detailed measures like marriage politics was that fact that the maritime empires could define a historical core already at the given period of expansion, whereas in the case of the contiguous empires this is a highly difficult task. As the article on Austria in this volume demonstrates, the very identification or definition of a core is difficult if not impossible, therefore it must have been even more difficult for contemporaries who could not employ the wisdom of hindsight.

The last remark points to another possible reward of the category imperial nationalism: Discussing the various dimensions of empire can influence our vision of place and time in nationalism studies. Although national movements usually referred to and demanded a bounded territory, in empires they were de facto transterritorial. They acted in several centers, which also means that they had to overcome space with less or no national activities. In those centers, the national movements were often confronted with competing nationalisms and hence shaped by external communication. Nation building was rarely a linear process like Eugene Weber's "Turning Peasants into Frenchmen," but underwent phases of growth and decline like other political and ideological movements. It is important to stress these changing dynamics in view of the prevalent teloi of nationalism studies, the increasing mobilization and ultimate "success" of national movements. Finally, one can view this as an opportunity to reflect on concepts of time, and related to this on terms such as backwardness, progress, or modernity. If one accepts that national movements grew, declined, and maybe grew again, then obviously their state of development varies over time. A national movement acting in the late twentieth century can have many features of nineteenth-century national movements.

Following Alexei Miller's pluralization of the term nationalization for the Russian Empire, one can also question the singular of the terms "nation building" or "nationalism" pertaining to one ethnic group. The imperial setup created and implied a confusing choice of cultural, ethnic, and political orientations among its various nationalities including imperial nations. The fact that there were several nationalisms within one potential nation, however, is again characteristic of the imperial setup and should be further explored in a comparative dimension.

In spite of the initial critical remarks about the lack of reflection on empire in mainstream nationalism studies, one should take the best out of them for advancing a discussion and highlighting the potential of this volume for nationalism studies. Benedict Anderson and Karl Deutsch were already mentioned because of their emphasis on communication. Rogers Brubaker has offered an even more refined model in his book "Nationalism Reframed," where he stresses the conflictual interaction between nationalizing nation-states, external homelands, and national minorities.[16] This model is important because it breaks with the traditional internalist vision on nationalism. Brubaker stresses the transborder connections and orientation of national movements.

---

[16] Rogers Brubaker, *Nationalism Reframed: Nationhood and the National Question in the New Europe* (Cambridge, Mass.: Harvard University Press, 1996).

With regard to empires, one could add that the competition between various national movements at one single place, e.g. in cities like Prague, Budapest, Kiev, or Istanbul, was as important. Brubaker's book is also relevant for a second reason. His focus on the nationalizing agenda of states is useful for understanding the policies of the German, Russian, and eventually Ottoman Empires in the late nineteenth and early twentieth century. Based on his term "nationalizing nation-state" one can indeed categorize certain empires as "nationalizing."

Another author who deserves mentioning as a source of inspiration for this essay is Miroslav Hroch. In his synthesis on national movements in Europe published in 2005, Hroch distinguishes between state and non-state national movements. It allows him to consider cases such as the Catalan, the Irish, and Norwegian national movements, who in fact share many commonalities with Central and Eastern European cases. Hroch's new book, which will hopefully be translated into English sooner than his earlier work, demonstrates that a geographic division of nationalism in Europe does not make sense. One can find similar types in Western and Eastern Europe. The key factor shaping the ideology and social composition of a national movement is the state context in which it operates.[17]

Historical Patterns of Imperial Nationalism

The paradox contained in the term imperial nationalism is reduced if one takes a look at the map of Europe in the first half of the nineteenth century, the takeoff phase for most national movements on the continent. During this period, almost all of Europe east of the river Rhine was governed by multinational empires. Hence, acting within the framework of empires was rather a rule than an exception for national movements. It is the goal of the following subchapter to highlight the structures of this imperial constellation.

It was characteristic of nationalism in these empires that it was activated at first by what Hroch has called non-dominant groups.[18] Only in reaction to these nation building activities of various nationalities did core imperial nations develop and politicize their own modern national consciousness. Obviously this model invalidates the idea that nationalism moved from West to East or that it was connected with the degree of industrialization.

---

[17] The only doubt could be directed against the terminological distinction between "Staatsnationen" and "Nationalbewegungen," which indirectly implies that national movements operate without a state, i.e., that not having an own state is a deficit. Moreover, imperial nations could also activate something like a national movement.

[18] See the hardly cited eight volume book series: Christopher Harvie Thompson, ed., *Comparative Studies on Governments and Non-dominant Ethnic Groups*, 8 vols. (Aldershot and Dartmouth: Publishing for the ESF and New York University Press, 1991–93).

The case of German nationalism (again one might think about using national-isms in the plural) can provide empirical backup for the outlined pattern. The literature on nation building in the German Lands (Germany is in certain ways an anachronism for the periods prior to 1871 or at least 1866) has been dominated by empirical stud-ies on the history of the national movement in the relatively liberal and ethnically ho-mogenous southwest.[19] There are less studies about German nationalism in Prussia and Austria, and the impact of the Polish and the Czech national movement on the local German speaking population and eventually the various strands of German nationalism.

In 1830–31, the Polish national movement was relatively advanced compared to the German national movement that was still eagerly suppressed by the Prussian and Austrian Empires. The Polish national activists had already universally agreed upon symbols such as a flag and an unquestioned capital city, and they had a tradition of heroes and martyrs commemorated already in quite modern ways. In short, all the ideology, myths, and symbols that are a prerequisite for a modern national movement are present in the Polish case. During the same period, German national activists had yet to decide about the future size of the Germany nation-state, needed a consensus about its capital and future core, and were equally undecided over symbolic items such as the national flag and anthem. As is well known, the enthusiasm for the Polish move-ment soon changed into rivalry. During the 1848 revolution the German conservatives and liberals denied the Prussian Poles their own national ambitions and confirmed im-perial rule over the Polish partition.[20]

The imperial context also shaped the relationship between German and Czech nationalism. Although the Czech national movement was delayed compared to its Polish equivalent, it influenced the mobilization and nationalization of German speakers in Bohemia. This became especially visible during the revolution of 1848. Palacký's refusal to send Czech delegates to the national assembly in Frankfurt pro-voked the German speaking areas of Bohemia to set up election committees for their delegates. In other words, first came the agitation for the Czech national movement and then the reaction of German speakers.[21] In 1848 a similar situation evolved on the regional level in the Prussian partition of Poland. The Polish movement mobi-lized supporters, and only then did the German speakers in Poznań/Posen organize themselves. The revolution was not exported to the Russian Empire, but one can draw parallels to 1863, when the Polish uprising with its Ukrainian components pro-voked a response of the state, which then decided to implement various strategies of Russification.[22]

---

[19] See as an example Dieter Langewiesche, *Nation, Nationalismus, Nationalstaat in Deutschland und Europa* (Munich: Beck, 2000).

[20] The debate is summarized in Michael G. Müller and Bernd Schönemann, *Die 'Polen-Debatte' in der Frankfurter Paulskirche* (Frankfurt: Diesterweg Verlag, 1991).

[21] See Gary Cohen, *The Politics of Ethnic Survival: Germans in Prague 1861–1914* (Princeton: Princeton University Press, 1981, 26.

[22] Miller, *The Romanov Empire and Nationalism*, 45–65.

Between 1848 and the 1860s, a structural interdependence came about between mobilization from below by national movements and dependence on the state by the imperial nations. This anticipated a conservative twist of the German national movement after 1848 and its coalition with the state in Prussia and Austria, which can again be compared with the Russian case. Russian nationalism developed on similar tracks like its German counterpart, also because the Polish national movement played an important role for activating Russian, and eventually Ukrainian nationalism. The Prusso-German, Russian, and Polish triangle has been well analyzed on the level of diplomatic history,[23] but there also was a common link in nation building.

The continuous suppression of the Polish national movement by the Holy Alliance (until Austria followed a completely different course after 1867) provoked even more organizational efforts on the Polish side. The Polish national movement reacted to the imperial rule by Prussia, Austria, and Russia with the *praca organiczna*, the organization of a modern and autonomous society.[24] The response was even more organizational efforts of the Prusso-German state to assimilate its Slavic speaking minorities. But the activation of Germans in the mixed areas always met a major obstacle: The political and social hegemony of the imperial nation was already in place (on the state, regional, and local level), hence a strong national commitment did not serve any immediate political or social goals. Being a prominent member of the Polish or Czech national movement in Prague or Poznan could add a lot of social prestige among their respective peer groups; loudly propagating a Russian identity in Kiev or Germanness in the Prussian East or in Bohemia did not promise the same social rewards.

A similar pattern can be observed in the areas of the Habsburg Empire, where the German speakers were in a minority position, but had been part of the social and political elite for a long time. As Gary Cohen has shown for the Prague Germans, their nationality was in a sense perceived to be given. Being German had for a long time a cultural, not a political, meaning. This was advantageous for establishing an imperial high culture, but not for building up a modern national movement that mobilized all classes of society. The cultural orientation only changed in the second half of the nineteenth century, at first during the 1848 revolution, in the 1860s, when the anti-imperial nationalisms reached the phase of mass mobilization and again in the late nineteenth century, when the hegemony of the German elites and culture was threatened. The preservation of Germanness then required organizational efforts, and the construction of a common identity.

Due to its imperial status, the Prussian state wavered for a long time on how to deal with the anti-imperial nationalisms and how to counter it with the construction of its national identity. Interestingly, a Prussian identity, which would have been a parallel creation to the Austrian one after 1806, never caught on, probably because

---

[23] Klaus Zernack, *Polen und Russland. Zwei Wege in der europäischen Geschichte* (Berlin: Propyläen, 1994), 337–46.

[24] These efforts are well compiled in Norman Davies, *God's Playground: A History of Poland. Vol. 2: 1795 to the Present* (Oxford: Oxford University Press, 1981).

of a lack of cultural resources. There was another problem that deserves attention in a comparative perspective. The long lasting incongruence of language and state, the very fact that the spoken language was German, not Prussian or Austrian, also means that the Russian Empire was in a relatively advantageous situation for its nation building efforts (like Italy or France), while the Ottoman Empire clearly was not. It deserves further attention how the British Empire moulded Englishness in its imperial identity, and how it succeeded in exporting its language far beyond the originally English speaking domains on the British Islands.

Evidently, the Prussian and then the German Empire were less successful in implementing German, even in areas that were ruled by Berlin for quite a long time. Instead, the government launched several waves of suppression against the Poles, but there was no clear concept whether and how to activate the German speaking population. Eventually Bismarck decided to rely on a triple backup for Germanness—language, religious denomination, and eventually descent. Russian *narodnost'* was defined in a comparable way, but since orthodoxy covered large areas of Eastern Europe, it was potentially much more expansive or, one might argue, inclusive.

Paradoxically, the triple definition of German imperial nationalism was the basis for its peculiar weakness in the eastern territories. The social base of Germanization was too small, and the national code too narrowly defined to attract large numbers of the slavophone population. Moreover, the dependence of the national movement on the existence and support of the empire reinforced a conservative turn that went back to the 1848 revolution. The political constellation was somewhat similar in Bohemia, where the Czech national movement demanded democratic reforms in order to be represented according to their share of the population, whereas the German minority in Bohemia (it was already remarkable that it perceived itself as such) defended their power position with open or indirect support of the imperial government.[25] This mixture of conservative and anti-democratic attitudes and defending old power structures became a common feature of the German national movement in the Prusso-German and the Austrian Empire.

The anti-imperial mobilization of the Polish, Czech, and comparable national movements occurred mostly based on ethnic criteria of in- and exclusion. The nationalisms operating in the framework of empires were not directed against the Hohenzollern, the Habsburg, or the Romanov dynasty, but against *the* Germans and *the* Russians. This pattern can be observed in other anti-imperial national movements as well. This had repercussions for imperial nationalism. Imperial Germans and Russians also came to define themselves increasingly on ethnic grounds. This marks a difference to the maritime empires in Western Europe, where the imperial nations were able to keep up relatively open versions of nationalism that facilitated the assimilation of various nationalities (although not that of other "races" inhabiting the colonies). But in the case of Spain the defeat in the war of 1898 and the subsequent loss

---

[25] Jan Křen, *Konfliktgemeinschaft. Tschechen und Deutsche 1780–1918* (Munich: Oldenbourg Verlag, 1996).

of most of the remaining empire weakened the efforts of imperial nation building at the core and indirectly strengthened the competing national movements in Catalonia and other regions.[26] Since various options of national identification were available in empires, nationalism remained a matter of competition and to some degree of choice. In nation-states the hegemony of the titular nation is usually not contested, hence even a severe economic or political crisis did not usually have effects on national identification. In empires and especially late empires, national identities were less stable.

The imperial setup also shaped the social composition of the German national movement. In the Prussian East and in Bohemia a cultural consciousness of being German was widespread. But this idea of belonging to a wider area of German culture was restricted to the educated classes and should not be equated with a modern national identity. The German speakers only slowly developed an identity as a *national* minority. This was also true for the German speaking population in Poznań and other cities in the Polish partition. Only when these groups were ever more confronted with Polish and Czech organizations and the very fact that they could become minorities, did they organize themselves.

However, especially pertaining to rural areas and the suburbs of industrial cities, nationally conscious Germans still remained a minority among German speakers for a long time.[27] In the eastern parts of Prussia and the German Empire, the state and its national ideology were mostly represented by state servants, factory owners, and the military. Workers and peasants, especially if they were Catholics, remained distant to national ideology. The *Kulturkampf*, when the protestant state got into conflict with the Catholic clergy and Catholics at large, was also counterproductive for nation building efforts. Bismarck's policy may have helped to further enhance the national consciousness of the protestant bourgeoisie, but it alienated Catholics, and in particular Slavophone Catholics. The restrictions against minority languages and the Germanizing settlement policy provoked even more resistance. One can conclude that an active policy of nationalization was usually counterproductive, in the German Empire and elsewhere.

But did the *Polenpolitik* indeed fail, as William H. Hagen contended in his important book thirty years ago?[28] He is right regarding the expectations and the results of the attempted Germanization of the Prussian East. Viewed from a comparative perspective, nationalization efforts there were relatively successful. Alexei Miller has shown how the Russian Empire failed to Russify most of its Ukrainian population, in spite of the given religious and linguistic proximity. Based on common religion, the

---

[26] See the article by Xosé-Manoel Núñez in this volume.

[27] See Philipp Ther, "Die Grenzen des Nationalismus: Der Wandel von Identitäten in Oberschlesien von der Mitte des 19. Jahrhunderts bis 1939," in *Nationalismen in Europa: West und Osteuropa im Vergleich*, eds. Ulrike v. Hirschhausen and Jörn Leonhard (Göttingen: Vandenhoeck & Ruprecht, 2001), 322–46.

[28] William W. Hagen, *Germans, Poles and Jews: The Nationality Conflict in the Prussian East, 1772–1914* (Chicago: Chicago University Press, 1980).

Ottoman Empire succeeded in assimilating various brands of Turkish speakers, but did not integrate Albanians or Bosniaks into an Ottoman or Turkish nation, although their Christian neighbors used to call them Turks.

The Prusso-German, the Russian, and the Ottoman Empire are interesting comparative cases also for other purposes. One can ask with a comparative vein, whether the nationalization policy mobilized the imperial nation and fortified national identities. The Polish uprising in 1863 boosted the development of an official, imperial policy of strengthening nationality (*narodnost'*). Like in Prussia, there was a top-down, but also a bottom up dimension in developing imperial nationalism. When Ivan Glinka's *Žyzn za Tsaria* was staged in Moscow in 1866 in the Bolshoi Theatre, the audience reacted to the staged Polish–Russian confrontation with riots. At certain points the spectators stormed the stage and shouted "down with the Poles, down with the Poles."[29] This might seem like a singular incident, but the nationalism of the imperial nations came to be a factor in mass politics. This was demonstrated by the 1907 elections in the German Empire, when the social democrats and left liberals were defeated by a coalition of nationalist parties.[30] The earlier victory of the Christian socialists in Vienna was also due to their negative stance regarding Jews, Czechs, and other non-German nationalities.[31]

The Germanization of the Prussian East had a popular dimension on the regional level as well. There are little studies about the attitudes of the colonists who moved to West Prussia or the Grand Duchy of Poznań. Probably only few of them did act as national missionaries. But among the small bourgeoisie in medium and small size cities in the Prussian East, ethnic German nationalism was rampant. The increasingly racist nationalism closed the ranks of those who were already committed, but abhorred parts of the mixed population. When the German Empire lost World War I, especially in Upper Silesia the autonomy movement and separatism were strong. One could explain this with a genuine weakness of German nationalism, but one should not forget that 1918 brought the end of the monarchy. The dynasty, the emperor, and all other points of identification offered by the empire were gone. The deeply Catholic Silesians revolted against "red Berlin," which was more alien to them than the Protestant dynasty.

One should discuss in a comparative perspective what the Bolshevik Revolution meant for the peasants in the Russian Empire, who still formed a vast majority of the population. What bound the peasants to Russia when the czar was gone, especially in Ukraine? Again, the breakdown of an empire lead to a rise of nationalism at its fringes. In the previous lands of the Ottoman Empire, the end of the Califate and the final demise of transcendental objects of identifications had strong effects as well,

[29] See a letter of Piotr Tchaikovsky's brother to the composer, quoted from Sigrid Neef, *Handbuch der russischen und sowjetischen Oper* (Berlin: Henschel Verlag, 1985), 193.
[30] See the article by Stefan Berger, before footnote 54.
[31] See John W. Boyer, *Culture and Political Crisis in Vienna: Christian Socialism in Power, 1897–1918* (Chicago: University of Chicago Press, 1995).

especially in Albania. Only after 1922 did the Osmanlı and the Turkomans lose their previous influence and secular Albanianism prevail. But one can also add the question of whether the successful or less successful attempts of establishing nation-states in the post-imperial space was a result of successful mobilization by national movements or rather a result of alienation from a center that ceased to be an empire and attempted to build a state on completely different premises. Independently of this question it is clear that even when the empires ceased to exist, they had a tremendous impact on various nationalisms, that of the titular nation and that of competing movements.

It is difficult to analyze a void—the attitudes or level of identification with an object that ceased to exist. But one can get closer to the issue by reflecting on loyalties shown to the empires in public and in private space and paying attention to the multiple objects of identification offered by empires. The most important was the ruler itself. As much as the Poles, Silesians, Sorbs, or Kashubs might have detested the Germanizing petty bureaucrats or school teachers in their neighborhood, they did not necessarily dislike the king and the emperor. Włodzimierz Mędrecki has shown in his historical-anthropological studies the important and often idealized place of the czar among peasants of all nationalities.[32] The myth of the just ruler, that was especially strong in the late Habsburg Empire, surpassed linguistic and denominational divisions.

Last, but not least, the official languages and cultures of the empire were attractive, even for writers, composers or artists who later were elevated as "founding fathers" of national culture. Figures like Palacký or Hruševskij were fluent in the imperial language or even preferred it over the language of their nationality for a long time—they rose to prominence in the educational system of the empires, and showed loyalty at various occasions. There were many cases of academics or professionals who were born into Czech families like the founder of the Institute for East European History at the University of Vienna, Konstantin Jireček, and easily could have become ardent nationalists in view of their family history, but instead made careers in the imperial bureaucracy and usually took on a loyalist stance.[33]

Like the universities, the imperial high culture and its institutions, opera theatres, museums, galleries and associated educational institutions such as conservatories and academies of art enjoyed a superior prestige until the very end of empire.[34] These institutions were the basis of genres that can be described as imperial in many ways. Composers from the Russian and the Habsburg Empires were very successful in

---

[32] See Włodzimierz Mędrecki, *Młodzież wiejska na terenie Polski centralnej 1864–1939. Procesy socjalizacji* (Warsaw: DiG, 2002).

[33] Benjamin Schenk (Basel) and Martin Aust (Heidelberg) have started a joint research project about imperial biographies which certainly will reveal further results. See http://dg.philhist. unibas.ch/departement/personen/person-details/forschungsprojekte/projekt-detailseite/person/schenk/?tx_x4euniprojectsgeneral_pi1[showUid]=6531&cHash=328b5aef499e108f-75c418f8ef9940af (accessed on March 5, 2013).

[34] See Philipp Ther, ed., *Kulturpolitik und Theater: Die kontinentalen Imperien in Europa im Vergleich* (Vienna: Böhlau/Oldenbourg, 2012).

adapting the model of the French Grand opera and filling it with an imperial content that eventually could be interpreted in a national way. Glinka's *Zhyzn za Tsaria* could serve as a classic example; in the Habsburg Empire, Grillparzer's drama about King Ottokar's rise and fall was an expression of imperial loyalty; later on, Karl Goldmark's opera *The Empress of Saba* could be considered a "Habsburg-opera."[35] In Prussia, by contrast, the attempts to create an imperial opera did not have lasting results. Meyerbeer's opera *Agnes von Hohenstaufen* was a failure; soon after Richard Wagner's star was rising, but his operas conveyed a clearly anti-imperial and anti-aristocratic stance. Wagner's political ideal was an ethnically homogenous nation-state with his home region Saxony serving as the German Piedmont. In the Ottoman Empire there was less artistic creativity in composing opera or developing other representative imperial genres of art. The reason was that the court limited its high culture mostly to the palace and did not have a strategy for reaching the public. Nevertheless, the operatic life in centers such as Istanbul and Cairo was rich and built upon a mix of Armenian entrepreneurs, multi-ethnic audiences, and a laissez faire policy of the state regarding cultural institution building for most periods.[36] French opera of the late nineteenth century also bore the imprint of empire, one just needs to think about *Lakmé* by Léo Delibes, which is, however, set in British India. It is quite obvious that even composers, who were later revered and instrumentalized as having been "national," followed universal models of composition, worked with plots that were interesting not just for their own national, but also imperial audiences and tried to make careers in imperial institutions of music.

The key question is, when and why did this integration through social advancement cease to function. It is stunning how many Polish activists had received an excellent education at German universities or even in the state administration, but who at a later stage of their life acted against the German state. This change occurred in the last two decades of the nineteenth century, when German students replaced the imperial elements of identification with a *völkisch* nationalism, when Prussia indeed became Germanized.[37] Polish and Ukrainian students at Russian universities changed in a comparable way. One can conclude that the empires lost parts of their attraction when they were transformed into "nationalizing empires" instead of "empires of nationality" like in the Austrian case.[38]

---

[35] See Peter Stachel, "Eine 'vaterländische' Oper für die Habsburgermonarchie oder eine 'jüdische' Nationaloper'? Carl Goldmarks, 'Königin von Saba' in Wien," in *Die Gesellschaft der Oper: Kulturtransfers und Netzwerke des Musiktheaters in Europa*, eds. Oliver Müller, et al. (Vienna: Böhlau/Oldenbourg 2010), 197–218.

[36] See Adam Mestyan, *"A garden with mellow fruits of refinement." Music Theatres and Cultural Politics in Cairo and Istanbul, 1867–1892* (PhD dissertation, Central European University, 2011).

[37] See Konrad Jarausch, *Students, Society and Politics in Imperial Germany: The Rise of Academic Illiberalism* (Princeton: Princeton University Press, 1982).

[38] See for these two and other terms the very useful categorization in Kramer, "Power and Connection," 1366.

But even the nationalizing empires could offer a larger array of points of identification than nation-states. This had a strong impact on national movements acting in the framework of empires. There are only few cases in which every element of imperial identification was rejected. Especially religious ties created cohesion. In the Austrian partition, the Polish national movement could reconcile itself with Habsburg rule because of the common Catholicism. Even in much more agnostic Bohemia religion attracted the conservative wing of the Old Czechs. Among the Kashubs and the Masurians, Prussian language policy was not popular, but Protestantism created loyalties to the Prussian state. Moreover, religious ties surpassed linguistic and sometimes state borders. The Russian czar had an almost mythical status among Russian and Ukrainian speaking peasants. The Russophiles in Galicia were attracted by Orthodoxy even beyond the borders of the empire. The Albanian Osmanlı stressed ties to the sultan and the Turks, viewed as a non-secular nation.

These various offers of identification resulted in different and competing currents among national movements operating within empires. In the German lands, the split between adherents of a greater Germany and what one can label—in a comparative vein—as Prussophiles in the 1850s and 60s was notorious and even outlived the establishment of the Wilhelmine Empire. The Ukrainian national movement was split into three currents—Russophiles, Ukrainophiles, Ruthenians.[39] Despite the much smaller size of the potential nation, Albanians were divided into Grekomans, Osmanlı, Turkophiles, and Albanianists.[40] In Bohemia there were the Bohemists, the loyalist Old Czechs, and the more radical Young Czechs, loyal Bohemian or Habsburg Germans, and pan-German Germans. Can one speak at all about one Czech, Albanian, Ukrainian, or German national movement or were there several movements? Studying nationalism in the framework of empires implies that one cannot privilege the one fraction of the national movement that eventually turned out to be the strongest and formed a nation-state.

Empires were also a breaking ground for ephemeral national movements. Examples for this are the Ślązacy/Schlonsaken in Upper Silesia, the Moravians in the Czech lands, or the Ruthenians in Galicia, who all became active in empires, but did not form nation-states and lost their steam in the course of the twentieth century.[41] Hence, empires compel nationalism studies to look not only at successful, but also at failed cases of nation building.

---

[39] See Veronika Wendland, *Die Russophilen in Galizien: Ukrainische Konservative zwischen Österreich und Rußland, 1848–1915* (Vienna: ÖAW, 2001).

[40] See Nathalie Clayer, *Aux origines du nationalisme albanais: La naissance d'une nation majoritairement musulmane en Europe* (Paris: Karthala, 2007), 611–706.

[41] See about Silesia and Moravia the articles in Philipp Ther, and Holm Sundhaussen, eds., *Regionale Bewegungen und Regionalismen in europäischen Zwischenräumen seit der Mitte des 19. Jahrhunderts* (Marburg: Verlag Herder Institut, 2003). See about the Ruthenians (with a nation building purpose): I. I. Pop and Paul Robert Magocsi, *Encyclopedia of Rusyn History and Culture* (Toronto: University of Toronto Press, 2002).

The key factor for understanding the multiplication of national movements is communication. Every modern national movement in Europe had one or more models of nation building it could refer to. The exchange between nationalisms has been studied quite a lot with a trans-border dimension, but usually under the premise of spatially distant nations.[42] It is characteristic for empires that several nationalisms were acting within one political space, and that two or more national movements were active at the very same place. Hence, the national activists could learn from each other, take on certain elements of ideology while repudiating other ones, and beat competitors with his own or new weapons.[43]

Conclusion

There is no question that nationalism was shaped by empires in large parts of Europe. The continental empires created a specific context for nation building. Often the non-dominant nationalities were pioneers of nationalization. Their activities provoked or fostered the mobilization of imperial nations such as the German and Russian. One can also speak about a mutual mobilization, which was so strong because the empires were a space of communication between various national movements. Communication and competition greatly contributed to the fast rise of nation building in Europe, also in areas where modernity had only arrived without industrialization. It is remarkable how quickly the level of nation building in Eastern Europe caught up or surpassed that of Western European cases in spite of bad structural preconditions such as high rates of analphabetism. This defies traditional modernist ideas that nationalism was dispersed in an West-East direction or that it depends on a traditionally defined modernity.

Although nation building progressed quickly in all parts of Europe since the second half of the nineteenth century, one should not underestimate the cohesion created by empires. The imperial dynasty, above all the monarch, his religious position, and imperial culture still attracted agents from all layers of society. Empires continued to serve as an object of identification, in competition or in accordance with national movements. But the universal appeal of empires was weakened when they were transformed into "nationalizing empires." Policies of nationalization turned out to be counterproductive even among populations which were close to the imperial nation in terms of culture, language, and religion, such as the "Little Russians," who eventually turned into Ukrainians. The lack of integration, however, was also due to the fact that the Polish national movement and culture in the "Kresy" could serve as an example of

---

[42] Especially the German–French case is rather well studied. See e.g. Jakob Vogel, *Nationen im Gleichschritt. Der Kult der "Nation in Waffen" in Deutschland und Frankreich, 1871–1914* (Göttingen: Vandenhoeck & Ruprecht, 1997).

[43] See as an excellent example Kai Struve, *Bauern und Nation in Galizien: Über Zugehörigkeit und soziale Emanzipation im 19. Jahrhundert* (Göttingen: Vandenhoeck & Ruprecht 2005).

how to build up a national movement. All these cases demonstrate the modernity of the empires as spaces of communication and hence as a hotbed of nationalism.

This leads us to the conceptualization of "imperial nationalism." Taking sincerely into account the imperial context beyond a modernist view of empires as backward, feudal, and anti-nationalistic is obviously relevant for studying nineteenth century nationalism and nation building. There also might be an indirect gain. A stronger awareness of the structural impact of empires on nation building in the long nineteenth century may help to recognize what was specific about nationalism in a post-imperial context. Although the "nationalizing empires" can be seen as precursors of the later "nationalizing nation-states," the main difference is that in the twentieth-century nationalism became steered by states rather than by national movements. Nation-states had different and much more far reaching possibilities and tools than empires to spread ideologies, homogenize their populations, and mobilize them. Like empires, they deserve special attention and terms. Rogers Brubaker has developed a set of terms for the interwar period, but similar books are needed for the postwar period that was already perceived prematurely as a time beyond the peak of nationalism. It remains to be studied in more detail why and how nationalist movements and ideologies were rising in the Soviet Empire (especially after World War II). If indeed the EU can be regarded as a neo-Medieval empire,[44] it might also provoke more nationalist counter-reactions in the near future, especially if a common economic policy is regarded as yet another expression of hegemonic if not imperial ambitions.

---

[44] See Jan Zielonka, *Europe as Empire: The Nature of the Enlarged European Union* (Oxford: Oxford University Press, 2006).

Nationalizing Imperial Armies: A Comparative and Transnational Study of Three Empires

Alfred J. Rieber[1]

A rmies played a crucial role in imperial state-building in the three great Habsburg, Romanov, and Ottoman continental empires, and their competition with one another raised questions of the most effective means of mobilizing their elites and the mass of their populations. Was it to be by appealing to dynastic loyalty, or to a common religious faith, or to ethno-linguistic commonalities that gradually evolved into nationalizing projects? Could these three elements, especially the imperial and national be reconciled within a single state system? Or would the potential tension between them precipitate a crisis in imperial rule? This essay is an attempt to address these questions from a transnational as well as a comparative approach. This double valence stems from the fact that they were long-term rivals for territorial and cultural hegemony along their common frontiers, and their policies, especially with regard to military affairs, were deeply influenced by the actions and performance of their rivals. As rivals, they measured their position and status as great powers by their successes or failures in warfare. Their internal stability and external security depended upon the loyalty and effectiveness of the army. Thus, their ruling elites were, consciously or not, constantly comparing their military power with one another. The task here is to follow them in this comparative pursuit. Because they were multi-cultural conquest states which had acquired culturally distinctive borderlands, there was always the danger that a serious defeat in warfare could lead to dismemberment and dissolution. Their fates as state systems were closely intertwined. As other essays in this volume demonstrate, the process of nationalizing reveals a surprising flexibility in responding to changing circumstances over long periods of time, a flexibility that helps to explain their longevity. Of the

---

[1] I should like to thank Virginia Aksan, Charles Ingrao, and Alexei Miller for their careful reading and critical comments.

multiple factors of this entanglement outlined by the editors in their introduction, the one which receives less attention than its due, in my view, is the institution of the army. The aim of this essay is to place the army along with bureaucracy and ideology as one of the three main pillars of imperial rule and to demonstrate how it evolved through an interaction between imperial and nationalizing processes from the seventeenth century to 1914.

To be sure, the military interaction among the three empires took place within a changing international environment. The multiple frontiers of the three empires exposed them to conflicts outside the triangular space of their common frontiers. The expansion of the imperial Russian frontiers into the Caucasus, Trans-Caspia and Inner Asia embroiled them with the Iranian empires of the Safavids and Qajars and the Qing dynasty in China. The Ottoman Empire also actively competed with the Russians and Iranians in the Caucasus, while defending its turbulent southern and North African periphery against Arab and Berber tribesmen. The Habsburgs faced challenges to its hegemony in the Italian and German states until it was excluded from playing an active role in their unification in the middle decades of the nineteenth century. Finally, the complex relationship between the three powers was further entangled by the imperial expansion of Great Britain, in particular its support of the Habsburg Monarchy and defense of the Ottoman Empire against what it regarded as the Russian menace. But the main parameters of interaction among the three continental states were determined by the territorial contiguity of their land frontiers, and hence the importance of the army.

This essay proposes a double thesis. First, the reform of the military establishment through improvements in the organization, recruitment, training, and financing of the army was the main if not the only aim of the periodic reforming impulses that gripped imperial rulers and elites, especially when the regime was faced by internal and external threats to its authority. These reforms encountered opposition from entrenched elites and were not fully implemented in any of the competing empires. But they were instrumental in holding the empires together in times of crisis until the cataclysm of World War I brought about the almost simultaneous collapse of all three. Second, by the end of the nineteenth century these reforms acquired more of a nationalizing character. By this time the long course of creating modern, professional, mass armies provided increasing evidence that an army imbued with loyalty not only or perhaps not even primarily to the dynasty, but to the hegemonic nation within the imperial system would perform more effectively on the field of battle. This awareness stemmed in part from comparisons with the armies of nation-states, but was also a reaction to the rising tide of national sentiment within the imperial borderlands. At the same time, the military reforms transformed the army into one of the most highly modernized institutions of the imperial state and society, threatening to diminish the power of the older elites or subvert the absolutist ethos of imperial rule.

Although the nationalizing process in the three empires revealed strong similarities, the effects on the combat effectiveness of the army and perceptions of the ruling elites were different. In Russia, by the end of the nineteenth century the professionalization and democratization of the officer corps opened up a gap between the reformers on the one hand and defenders of the traditional order including Nicholas II, on the other. In the Habsburg Monarchy, the nationalizing process proceeded much more rapidly among the Hungarians than the Austrians, leading to the growth of ethnic tensions that affected the cohesion of the army and threatened its very existence after defeat in World War I. In the Ottoman Empire, the most progressive elements among intellectuals and in the army regarded autocratic imperial rule as increasingly ineffective. Acting often as an autonomous force, especially during a *crise de régime,* army officers among the Young Turks contributed to the dissolution of the state they had been created to preserve. This dialectic of the modern produced a new role for the army officers in the struggle for control over the successor states. They emerged from the wreckage of imperial rule to become one of the main contenders for the reconstruction of the old and domination over the new political order. This essay is organized around the different trajectories of nationalizing imperial armies, a process which was still incomplete before the three armies were plunged into a total war, from which their subsequent defeat led to dissolution into national components and then, inevitably, to the collapse of the imperial project.

The Russian Empire

Peter the Great may not have had an imperial plan in mind, but arguably he did have a vision. It emerges from his military reforms, his three military expeditions, and his design of inland waterways. His predecessors had tried unsuccessfully to break out of the inland position and tame the wild frontiers of the Muscovite state. With the encouragement of France, the three barrier states on Muscovy's western frontier—Sweden, the Polish-Lithuanian Commonwealth, and the Ottoman Empire (all it should be noted parenthetically, also multi-cultural states if not empires in *sensus strictus*)—blocked the entryway into a European state system with its commercial and cultural advantages. The Ottoman and Safavid (Iranian) states blocked access to the northern shores of the Black Sea and western shores of the Caspian, both of which could secure passage to the trade of the East and anchor the southern frontiers. To accomplish a breakthrough required an armed force which could compete with Peter's rivals for domination over the Baltic, Black, and Caspian seacoasts. In the course of these initiatives he laid the foundations for nationalizing the army.

Like many of Peter's other reforms, the creation of a professional, European style army had its origins in the Muscovite period.[2] His innovations aimed first,

---

[2] R. Hellie, "The Petrine Army: Continuity, Change and Impact," *Canadian American Slavic Studies* 8, no. 2 (Summer 1974): 237–52; R. Hellie, "Warfare, Changing Military Technology and the Evolution of Muscovite Society," in *Tools of War: Instruments, Ideas and Institutions of Warfare,* ed. J. A Lynn (Urbana: University of Illinois Press, 1990), 74–99 and especially M. Poe, "The Consequences of the Military Revolution in Muscovy: A Comparative Perspective," *Comparative Studies in Society and History* 38, no. 4 (October 1996): 603–18.

however, at replacing the archaic chain of command and outmoded battlefield tactics of the old Moscow army and to destroy its most inefficient, conservative, and rebellious military formation—the musketeers (*strel'tsy*). In their place, he pushed hard to adopt the advances of the Western military revolution and build Russia's first naval arm. The Russian army he created was in some ways unique. Unlike the armies of Western Europe and the Habsburg armies, it was not composed mainly of mercenaries. Although Peter hired foreign officers to command his regiments in the early days of the Great Northern War, he soon replaced most of them with Russians. Unlike the armies of the Ottoman Empire, the elite formations of the Russian army were not composed of slaves. The army was made up primarily of Russian peasants, although all social strata were required to serve, commanded by Russian nobles and a few foreigners. Most of the rank and file had been serfs but they lost that status when they were enrolled. To be sure they were obliged to serve for life, a term reduced to twenty-five years at the end of the eighteenth century. Over the following decades the amenities changed but the essentials remained. Soldiers were provided with uniforms and paid, if miserably and not always on time. They could be promoted and decorated if they performed courageously under fire. Under the husk of harsh discipline they were able to organize themselves into small working collectives, *artels*, in order to provide many of their daily necessities. Homogeneity and social bonds must have contributed to the high level of unit cohesion and discipline that were noticed even by their opponents.[3] Was this what drove Frederick the Great to exclaim: "It is easier to kill these Russians than to defeat them"?[4]

With the aim of mobilizing the human and material resources for his armies, Peter the Great undertook a massive reorganization of the economy and society. Did he create a "garrison state?" The term is provocative and has been challenged.[5]

[3] J. L. H. Keep, *Soldiers of the Tsar: Army and Society in Russia, 1462–1874* (Oxford: Oxford University Press, 1985), part 2; E. K. Wirtshafter, *From Serf to Russian Soldier* (Princeton: Princeton University Press, 1990), chapter 5; J. Bushnell, "Peasants in Uniform: The Tsarist Army as a Peasant Society," *Journal of Social History* 13 (1979–80): 565–76.
[4] W. M. Pintner, "Russia's Military Style, Russian Society, and Russian Power in the Eighteenth Century," in *Russia and the West in the Eighteenth Century*, ed. A. G. Cross (Newtonville, Mass.: Oriental Research Partners, 1983), 265. Pintner also questions, however, whether ethnic homogeneity made much of a difference in the army's combat effectiveness.
[5] J. L. H. Keep, "The Origins of Russian Militarism," *Cahiers du monde russe et soviétique* 26 (1985): 5–20. Keep, *Soldiers of the Tsar*, 116, 142, seems to have been the first to use this term. See also R. Hellie, *The Economy and Material Culture of Russia, 1600–1725* (Chicago: University of Chicago Press, 1999), 536; and E. Lohr and M. Poe, "Introduction: The Role of War in Russian History," in *The Military and Society in Russia 1450–1917*, eds. E. Lohr and M. Poe (Leiden/ Boston: E.J. Brill, 2002), 1–15, who make the term central for the entire period of Russian history. The challenge has come from W. C. Fuller, Jr., *Civil Military Conflict in Imperial Russia, 1881– 1914* (Princeton: Princeton University Press, 1985). See especially the discussion on xix–xxii for the later period. For the earlier period see: J. M. Hartley, *Russia, 1762–1825. Military Power, the State, and the People* (Westport, CT: Praeger, 2008), 4–5, who also rejects the idea that the army was an instrument of modernization.

Whatever terms are used, there can be no doubt that Peter's reorganization of finances and the tax system and the administrative subdivision of the country into *guber-
niia*, provinces, and districts were initially designed to provide the necessary revenue
and recruits to fight the Great Northern War. His mercantilist industrial policies established state monopolies and encouraged private entrepreneurs in key sectors by attaching state peasants to private factories and mines producing uniforms, equipment,
and firearms. By the end of his reign, the Russian armaments industry was largely
self-sufficient and was producing a sufficient surplus of iron to become a net exporter. By mid-century the army could boast of an artillery train second to none.[6] Thus, a
Russian army and military tradition had come into existence before the great expansion that created a multi-national empire.

Peter's administrative organization of the country into eight gigantic *guberni-
ia* in 1708 was a direct consequence of his requirements in fighting the Great Northern
War against Sweden. The entire structure was highly militarized following the earlier
practice of creating "unified frontier districts in large military regions." By ruthlessly
subordinating the administrative, economic, and social life of the country to the needs
of the armed forces, Peter established the precedents for future reforms, enabling the
Russian army repeatedly to defeat its rivals throughout the eighteenth and much of the
nineteenth century in the struggle over the borderlands.

For Peter and his successors, the state was always represented as the Russian,
not the Romanov Empire, in contrast to the dynastic terms used to characterize the
Habsburg (not German) and Ottoman (not Turkish) Empires. Substituting for the
Byzantine-Muscovite images of the ruler, Peter represented himself as the founder of
Russia by virtue of his heroic deeds and military victories. His subjects embellished
the themes of a Russian emperor as an amalgam of classic and contemporary personas.
He was the "new Philip of Macedon" and "the all-Russian Hercules."[7] From Peter on,
the imperial state-building project was also a Russian state-building project and the
Russian army was its primary instrument.

The institutional and symbolic foundations he had laid down proved resilient enough to survive forty years of dynastic turmoil over the succession to the
throne, during the so-called era of palace revolutions, 1724–62. The Preobrazhenskii
and Semenovskii Guards Regiments comprised the embryo of a national army, recruited from the Russian nobility with a highly developed corporate spirit. At such

---

[6] A. Kahan, *The Plow, the Hammer and the Knout: An Economic History of Eighteenth Century
Russia* (Chicago: University of Chicago Press, 1985), 96–99, 111–12; W. M. Pintner, "The
Burden of Defense in Imperial Russia, 1725–1914," *The Russian Review* 43 (1984): 231–35.

[7] R. Wortman, *Scenarios of Power, Myth and Ceremony in Russian Monarchy* Vol. 1: *From Peter the
Great to the Death of Nicholas I* (Princeton: Princeton University Press, 1995), 48–49. This emphasis on the "Russianness" of the ruler countered the foreign (or "Western") models of dress and
deportment adopted by Peter and his successors to which after Catherine was added their predominantly German blood lines

crucial moments as the Decembrist Revolt in 1825 and the revolution of 1905, the Preobrazhenskii Guards provided crucial support for the dynasty.[8]

Throughout the eighteenth century the Russian army acquired a European reputation through participation in wars against the Swedes, Prussians, and French. The steadfast behavior of the infantry under fire and the power of its artillery were generally recognized as the equal if not the superior of the other European armies.[9] However, this was an army conscripted from serfs for life who were often selected as the least valuable to their communes. There could be no question of patriotic to say nothing of national sentiments inspiring them.[10] For ambitious and talented nobles, on the other hand, military service became the preferred profession. It offered the best opportunity for social advancement and political influence at court and in the higher offices of the bureaucracy, predominantly staffed by military officers until the mid-nineteenth century. The creation of the first Cadet Corps in 1732 and the expansion under the direction of a palace favorite, Count Peter Shuvalov, laid the foundations for a military and general education that greatly enhanced the prestige of its noble graduates and even its drop outs.[11] By the end of the eighteenth century a military intelligentsia began to emerge. The penetration of Western ideas into the cultural life of the upper classes promoted ethical ideals tinged with Stoicism. Virtue, bravery, and the attainment of rank were identified with personal merit rather than birth, although the nobility monopolized all avenues leading to that goal. The attitudes and values of what Marc Raeff has called the "military ethos" left a strong imprint on the institutions of imperial rule.[12]

---

[8] On the Preobrazhenskii Guards under Peter see: E. Boltunova, *Gvardiia Petra velikogo kak voennaia korporatsiia* (Moscow: RGGU, 2011). In general, see Keep, *The Soldiers of the Tsar*, 96, 98, 121–22 and D. Beyrau, *Militär und Gesellschaft im vorrevoliutsionären Russland* (Cologne: Böhlau, 1984), 190–93.

[9] C. Duffy, *Russia's Military Way to the West: Origins and Nature of Russian Military Power 1700–1800* (London: Routledge and Keegan Paul, 1981) demonstrates the gradual acquisition of professional competence through experience on the battlefields of Europe. But he also attributes the peculiar strength of the army to its ethnic and religious homogeneity and its offensive philosophy gained from open warfare on the steppe against the Turks.

[10] Hartley, *Russia 1762–1825*, especially 45–47.

[11] L. G. Beskrovnyi, "Voennye shkoly v pervoi polovine XVIII v." *Istoricheskie zapiski* 42 (1953): 285–300; M. J. Okenfuss, "Education and Empire: School Reform in Enlightened Russia," *Jahrbücher für Geschichte Osteuropas* 27 (1979): 59. Okenfuss is critical of the quality of instruction given in the cadet corps.

[12] M. Raeff, "L'état, le gouvernement et la tradition politique en Russie impériale avant 1861," *Revue d'histoire moderne et contemporaine* 9 (October–December 1962): 302; M. Raeff, *The Origins of the Russian Intelligentsia: The Eighteenth Century Nobility* (New York: Harcourt Brace, 1966), 48–50. The term military intelligentsia was coined by Soviet historians and adopted by Keep, *The Soldiers of the Tsar*, 239–45. The same "military ethos" could erupt into a revolt against the autocratic mode of government as in December 1825. Cf. I. Lotman, "Dekabristy v poslevoennoi zhizni: bytovoe povedenie kak istoriko-psikhologicheskaia kategoriia," in *Literaturnye nasledye dekabristov* in eds. V. G. Bazonov and V. E. Vatsuro (Leningrad: Nauka, 1975), 25–74.

Successive rulers continued to devote close attention to the maintenance and improvement of the armed forces. Catherine II lavished attention and rewards on the Guards who had brought her to power. She employed her favorites, especially Count Grigory Potemkin, to consolidate her power in the army. Potemkin made the clearest commitment to transforming the Russian army into a national force. While accused of currying favor with the rank and file, he sought to free the ordinary soldier from the grip of foreign officers by redesigning their uniforms and humanizing their treatment in the Russian manner. Catherine also made certain that scions of the great Russian noble families occupied leading positions in the military, thus assuring her of support on that side as well.[13] The enormous expansion of the Russian Empire under her reign, mainly at the expense of the Polish-Lithuanian Commonwealth and the Ottoman Empire, was due mainly to the brilliance of her military commanders—A. V. Suvorov, P. A. Rumiantsev, Z. G. Chernyshev, along with Potemkin—and her ability to control their rivalries.[14] But the army was also critical in repressing internal rebellions, such as the great Pugachev rising in the early 1770s, the last of the great Cossack-led peasant revolts to threaten the throne until 1905.

Catherine's son Paul attempted to introduce uniform standards, diminish the political role of the Guards, and improve the lot of the common soldier. But his reforms were tainted in the eyes of the army elite by what they regarded as his worshipful attitude toward Frederick the Great, his slavish adherence to Prussian methods of training, the adoption of Prussian style uniforms, and his bizarre attempt to impose the ethos of the Knights of Malta on his bewildered officers. This was, after all, a Russian army. Paul was overthrown and murdered by a cabal of high ranking officers.[15] After his death his superficial innovations were eliminated. But he left an important legacy. His three sons, two of whom became emperors, Alexander, Konstantin and Nicholas, were raised in a strict military environment. This tradition continued in the training of the last three emperors, Alexander II, Alexander III and Nicholas II, all of whom cherished their formal role as officers in the Guards; they delighted in reviewing elaborate parades and reviews, wearing uniforms and displaying decorations. Alexander II and Nicholas even believed their symbolic presence on the battlefield was vital to maintain the image of the Russian emperor as supreme war lord.

The nationalizing effect of the Napoleonic Wars on the Russian army officers has often been noted, particularly on those who served in the Army of Occupation in France. Napoleon's campaign of 1812 marked the first time in a hundred years that

---

[13] J. P. LeDonne, *Ruling Russia: Politics and Administration in the Age of Absolutism, 1762–1796* (Princeton: Princeton University Press, 1984), 5, 26, 60.

[14] *Zapiski L'va N. Engel'gardta, 1766–1835*, quoted in I. de Madariaga, *Russia in the Age of Catherine the Great* (New Haven: Yale University Press, 1981), 353.

[15] B. W. Menning, "Paul I and Catherine II's Military Legacy, 1762–1801," in *The Military History of Tsarist Russia*, eds. F. W. Kagan and R. Higham (Basingstoke: Palgrave Macmillan, 2002), 77–86. For a vivid description of Paul's use of military display as a symbol and model of imperial rule, see Wortman, *Scenarios of Power*, I, 181 86, quotation on 186.

a large enemy force had invaded Russian soil. The patriotic surge was felt through throughout the upper reaches of Russian society. Dominic Lieven has expressed doubt that it penetrated very deeply into the peasantry or the rank and file of the army despite Tolstoy's display of emotional patriotism in *War and Peace*.[16] On the other hand, there was a veritable flood of popular woodcuts (lubki) celebrating the Russian resistance to Napoleon, especially the partisan movement.[17] More lasting was the transfer of nationalist-democratic ideas into the junior ranks of the officer corps. Dismissed by the Russian historian Vasili Kliuchevskii as "Frenchmen yearning to be Russians," they were, nonetheless, patriots who sought to adopt the ideas of the French Revolution to Russian conditions. They returned from the battlefields of Europe determined to bring about change at home. Disillusioned by the failure of Alexander I to implement the reforms they expected from him, they formed a number of secret societies, several of which participated in the revolt of December 1825. The officers involved in the conspiracy were mostly highly educated scions of the aristocracy.[18] They constituted a new generation of a military intelligentsia, one imbued with nationalist ideals. The Decembrists proposed different political programs which had in common opposition to all forms of autocratic rule and demands for reforms of basic institutions, above all the creation of a truly national army which required the abolition of serfdom.[19] This desire to close the yawning social gap between the nobility and the peasantry in the name of forging a new nation permeated their diaries, memoirs and correspondence with one another.[20]

The Decembrists, in particular the leader of the Southern Society, P. I. Pestel', sought to infuse the idea of empire with a strongly nationalist spirit and to retain the multi-cultural character of the state under highly centralized if republican institutions. He titled the draft of the program which he and other Decembrists produced *Russkaia Pravda*, consciously invoking the ancient Russian legal charter as a sign of the continuity of the national historical tradition.[21] Pestel's national-imperial vision

---

[16] The significant number of foreigners or non-Russian subjects of the tsar among the senior officer ranks were loyal but hardly motivated by nationalist sentiments. See D. Lieven, *Russia Against Napoleon: The True Story of the Campaign of War and Peace* (New York: Viking, 2010), 23–24.

[17] D. Rovinskii, *Russkie narodnye kartiny,* 2 vols. (St. Petersburg: R. Golike, 1900), II, 448–58. The woodcuts had a tradition of celebrating Russian military heroes going back to eighteenth century commanders, field marshalls Suvorov and Rumiantsev. Ibid., I, 148, 151–56.

[18] Of the 570 men brought to trial, 456 were from the military including 17 generals and 115 staff officers. Of the total, 125 had completed the course in military academies, 30 in the naval schools, 28 in the Page Corps with many of the rest having military tutors in their home education. See: E. A. Prokof'ev, *Bor'ba dekabristov za peredovoe russkoe voennoe iskusstvo* (Moscow: Akademiia Nauk, 1953), 98–99, 101.

[19] N. M. Lebedev, *Pestel'. Ideolog i rukovoditel' dekabristov* (Moscow: Mysl', 1972), 202–25, based on the documentary collection *Vosstanie dekabristov. Materialy i dokumenty*, seven volumes (Moscow–Leningrad, 1927), VII, 158–203.

[20] The older two volume work of M. V. Nechkina, *Dvizhenie dekabristov* (Moscow: Akademiia Nauk, 1955) is still valuable but needs updating.

[21] Lebedev, *Pestel'*, 130–31.

was encapsulated in his phrase, "Russia (*Rossiia*) is a unified and indivisible state." Although opposed to federalism, he recognized the multi-cultural character of the state in a section called "On the various tribes (*plemia*) united with Russia." He separated the peoples of the empire into two groups. First he designated the "minute variations (*ottenki*) of the indigenous Russian people" by which, apparently, he meant the Great Russians, Little Russians, and Belorussians. Then he lumped together all the others as Finnish, Latvian, Moldavian, and Tatar "tribes," the Caucasian, Siberian, nomadic and Jewish "peoples" (*narod*) followed by Cossacks and colonists settled in Russia, and foreigners. The conclusion of the *Russkaia Pravda* exuded a spirit of what later generations of Bolsheviks would call Great Russian chauvinism: "All the tribes inhabiting Russia should be fused into one people." The one exception were the Poles, who had created a strong and independent state in the past and deserved national independence, but only if they accepted the mandates of *Russkaia Pravda,* eliminated their aristocracy and maintained a "close alliance" in times of peace and war.[22] The vision of the army as the instrument for uniting national with imperial ambitions was widely shared but failed to win over the bulk of the army which remained loyal to the dynasty. The revolt was crushed by loyal army units, its leaders tried and harshly sentenced, but the idea of a national army based on the abolition of serfdom remained just below the surface of debates on improving the military under Nicholas I.[23]

By the mid-nineteenth century the Russian army had fulfilled the imperial dreams of Peter the Great. It had advanced the Russian frontiers deep into Europe, securing a position of the ultimate mediator in the Prussian–Habsburg rivalry. It had cleared the Ottoman Turks from the northern shores of the Black Sea and established a Russian presence on the Danube. From this strategic position it could dominate the Principalities and invade the Balkans at will. It had expelled both Ottoman and Iranian power from the South Caucasus. As a participant for over a century in the major European Wars, it had followed up its victory over Charles XI by defeating Frederick the Great and Napoleon, the three outstanding military geniuses of their time. It had raised its standards over Berlin and Paris. Paul I, Alexander I, Nicholas I and his heir, the future Alexander II, had increasingly identified imperial rule with the success of their armies. As Richard Wortman has written, "Nicholas merely reformulated the myth of conquest in contemporary terms. He, like his predecessors, was the Russian monarch who ruled because he appeared foreign, but now this tradition was defined as peculiarly Russian."[24] From the perspective of the soldiers themselves,

[22] Ibid., 145–46, 154–55. These views corresponded very closely to the war aims of the tsarist government during World War I and the Soviet government during and after World War II.

[23] F. W. Kagan, *The Military Reforms of Nicholas I: The Origins of the Modern Russian Army* (New York: St. Martin's, 1999). The major reform under Nicholas was the creation of the General Staff Academy that bore his name.

[24] Wortman, *Scenarios of Power*, I, 298. This perception of the tsar was reflected in popular tradition through the portrayal of Nicholas in wood cuts (*lubki*) in the pose of a frontier warrior of old Russia, the *bogatyr*. Ibid., 313.

the unity of tsar and fatherland, of dynasty and nation was closely intertwined, as John Keep has written. The evidence for this derives in part from the ordinary soldier's' "indifferent if not actively hostile [attitude] to ethnic groups whose ways so differed from his own."[25] No wonder then that defeat in the Crimean War on Russian soil and the humiliating Treaty of Paris in 1856, imposing demilitarization of the Black Sea littoral, administered a terrible psychological blow to the new emperor, Alexander II, and the ruling elite.

In the wake of defeat, the tsar and his closest advisers recognized that Russia's great power standing could only be restored by reforming an outmoded army and restoring the empire's financial stability.[26] Serfdom stood in the path of creating a more efficient army with a large ready reserve and the construction of a modern fiscal system with a European style budget. A fundamental reform of the army could not be carried out without the abolition of serfdom. The first steps were taken in 1855, serfdom abolished in 1861, but the long process of carrying out a full scale reform took another thirteen years.[27]

In the meantime, the cohesion and loyalty of the imperial army was put to the test by the Polish insurrection of 1863. After the independent Polish army had been disbanded following the Polish revolt of 1830–33, thirty-five thousand Polish officers and soldiers had been incorporated into Russian formations. When the insurrection broke out in Warsaw in January 1863, several hundred Polish officers deserted and took command of the insurgent forces.[28] Russian officials and the educated public were shocked. The country was rallied mainly by the nationalistic propaganda of M. N. Katkov, a formerly liberal journalist and editor of *Moskovskie vedomosti*, which became the leading voice of Russian nationalism over the following two and a half decades. Foreign observers were struck by the spontaneous surge of nationalist sentiment that swept Russia: "Recruits hurried to enlist with unprecedented enthusiasm firmly convinced of the inevitability of war for their faith," wrote the British ambassador. The loyalty of the Russian units remained unshaken.[29] Unlike the Decembrists, the Russian officer corps exhibited very little sentiment for Polish independence.[30] There was

---

[25] Keep, *Soldiers of the Tsar*, 221, distinguishes this "chauvinism" from the "nationalism that was now [in 1812] gaining currency in educated circles."

[26] "Ob opastnosti v 1856 g. voennykh deistvii," *Istoricheskii arkhiv* 1 (January–February 1959): 206–08; and discussion in A. J. Rieber, ed., *The Politics of Autocracy: Letters of Alexander II to Prince A.I. Bariatinskii, 1857–1864* (Paris/The Hague: Mouton, 1966), 23–40, 59–60.

[27] A. Rieber, "Alexander II: A Revisionist View," *Journal of Modern History* 43, no. 1 (March 1971): 42–58; and discussion in Rieber, *The Politics*, 18–19.

[28] Keep, *Soldiers of the Tsar*, 327, 359–64.

[29] D. M. Miliutin, *Vospominaniia general-fel'dmarshala grafa Dmitriia Alekseevicha Miliutina, 1963–1864*, ed. L. G. Zakharova (Moscow: Rosspen, 2003), 246–54, quotation on 249.

[30] There appears to be no firm evidence for the accusation, attributed to Grand Duke Nikolai Nikolaevich (the Elder), that the chief of staff of the Second Guards Division, N. N. Obruchev, later known as the Russian Moltke for his brilliant strategic planning, had requested transfer to the General Staff rather than participate in a "fratricidal war." But the story haunted Obruchev

hardly a better example of an increasingly nationalized army in defending the empire against its internal enemies.

For all its powerful effect in arousing and broadening Russian nationalism, the financial strain and organizational problems imposed by the massive repressive effort delayed the plans to create a truly national army by introducing conscription. In the meantime, under the leadership of the war minister, Dmitri Miliutin, veteran of the Caucasus wars and a key figure in crushing the Polish insurrection, the army, virtually stripped of its Polish elements, had become more than ever an ethnically Russian force.[31] Yet its role in state-building remained unclear and disputed. Strategic factors aside, different characteristics of the far flung frontiers gave rise to different concepts of the army's imperial mission. In the Caucasus and Central Asia, the Russian army assumed the role of promoting a civilizing mission, nourishing its own form of "Orientalism." In Poland it was to prevent the restoration of a large Polish state which would reverse Peter's and Catherine's policy of bringing Russia into Europe. On the Danube it was to support and advance the cause of the Slavs. In all cases, Russia and the Russians occupied a central place without being conceived as a nation-state.

In the second half of the nineteenth century the idea that the soldiers and officers of the Russian army represented national heroes began to take hold among the educated public. It was nourished by articles in the popular press and the works of major writers of *belles lettres*. Leo Tolstoy's *Sevastopol Tales* may be seen as the beginning of this trend. Later, in *War and Peace*, Tolstoy represented General Kutuzov as the epitome of the most admirable Russian characteristics of a soldier, eclipsing Tsar Alexander I in native wisdom. In the eighteen seventies and eighties, the press romanticized and celebrated the exploits of such famous paladins of Russian imperialism in the post-Emancipation generation as M. G. Chernaiev, M. D. Skobelev, K. P. von Kaufman "of Turkestan," creating a new pantheon of Russian national heroes.[32] In his

---

all his life, and despite an impressive career probably blocked him from becoming minister of war. Cf. O. R. Airapetov, *Zabytaia kar'era 'russkogo Mol'ke.' Nikolai Nikolaevich Obruchev (1830–1904)* (St. Petersburg: Alateiia, 1998), 83–84, passim.

[31] M. I. Dragomirov, a leading strategic thinker and head of the Nikolaev Military Academy from 1878 to 1889 was frequently rumored not be a "pure Russian" because he was of Little Russian origin. His dismissive reply was "You can't satisfy everyone, I was born in the heart of Little Russia—the town of Konotop in Chernigov province—I cannot emerge suddenly as a man of Tambov, Mogilev, or Kaluga, still less of Berdichev—each to his own." M. I. Dragomirov vo vremiia Avstro-Prusskoi voiny," *Russkaia starina* (May 1910): 621.

[32] D. MacKenzie, *The Lion of Tashkent: The Career of General M. G. Cherniaev* (Athens: University of Georgia Press, 1975) and N. S. Kiniapina, M. M. Bliev, and V. V. Degoev, *Kavkaz i Sredniaia Asiia vo vneshnei politike Rossii. Vtoraia polovina XVIII-80e gody XIX v.* (Moscow: Izd. Moskovskogo universiteta, 1984), 273–78. A contemporary sympathetic editor later recalled that "the Slav movement arising in 1875 was for him [Cherniaev] an affair not just of foreign but also of domestic politics ... He believed in Russian national enthusiasm and expected from it the most favorable effects upon the country." These favorable effects would be to block further reform and sweep men like himself into power. MacKenzie, *The Lion*, 118.

journalism, Dostoevsky broadcast their vision of the army as the instrument of Russia's messianic, pan-Slav mission and expansion in Central Asia.[33]

When Miliutin's military reform was finally instituted in 1874, universal military service was supplemented by plans to equip the army with modern rifled weapons and organize it into military districts, led by officers professionally trained in military academies with the elite being selected for the General Staff. An activist in bureaucratic politics, Miliutin was an ardent advocate of rational and centralized imperial rule, knitting together strategic railroad building, expansion into the borderlands of the Caucasus and Trans Caspia and, in support of his brother Nikolai, the reorganization of rebellious Poland after 1863.[34] But nationalizing the army to serve imperial interests in the Russian as in the Habsburg and Ottoman Empires ran into opposition and encountered cross currents. Miliutin's vision of a truly representative citizens' army was clouded by the intervention of the minister of interior who introduced a number of exceptions to conscription, weakening its universal design.[35] Nevertheless, the dominant position of Russians in the army at all levels was assured by the rule practiced to the end of the empire of setting their number (including Great Russians, Belorussians, and Ukrainians) in a unit at 75% and non-Russians at 25%.[36]

After Miliutin left office in 1881, according to William C. Fuller, military professionalism in the Russian army steadily declined to a low level in comparison with the great European armies. Conflict with civil authorities over financing and the role of the army further eroded Miliutin's program.[37] On the other hand, the post-Miliutin years witnessed the growth of a new generation of the Russian military intelligentsia. Under the leadership of such reformers as Miliutin's protégé, General N. N. Obruchev, chief of staff in the 1880s and 90s, and his protégé General A. N. Kuropatkin, appointed minister of war in 1898 , the attempt was made to modernize the army and broaden the social base of its officer corps by stressing talent over birth. They ran into opposition from the court, conservative ministers, and Nicholas II, all imbued with the parade ground ethos and aristocratic mentality that had long pervaded Russian military life.[38] Nevertheless,

---

[33] See especially his panegyric to Skobelev in his article "Geok-Tepe. What is Asia to Us?" in *The Diary of a Writer*, trans. and ed. by B. Brasol (New York: Charles Scribner, 1949), II, 1043–52. For the close relations between Cherniaev and the Pan Slav Ivan Aksakov, see: D. MacKenzie, *The Serbs and Russian Pan-Slavism, 1875–1878* (Ithaca: Cornell University Press, 1974), 74–75, 117–25, and 136–43.

[34] The standard work on the military reform remains: P. A. Zaionchkovskii, *Voennye reformy 1860–1870 gg. v Rossii* (Moscow: Izd. Moskovskogo universiteta, 1952). See also F. Miller, *Dimitri Miliutin and the Reform Era in Russia* (Nashville: Vanderbilt University Press, 1968).

[35] See the debate in the highest echelons of government over the issue in: Zaionchkovskii, *Voennye reformy*, 308–19.

[36] W. Beneke, "Die Allgemeine Wehrpflicht in Russland. Zwischen militärischen Anspruchen und zivilen Interessen," *Journal of Modern European History* 5, no. 2 (September, 2007): 258.

[37] W. C. Fuller, *Civil-Military Conflict in Imperial Russia, 1881–1914* (Princeton: Princeton University Press, 1985), 32.

[38] J. W. Steinberg, *All the Tsar's Men: Russia's General Staff and the Fate of the Empire, 1898–1914* (Baltimore: Johns Hopkins University Press, 2010), especially chapters 2 and 5.

the democratization of the officer corps proceeded steadily as nobles found more lucrative and socially rewarding occupations outside the military and plebian officers rose rapidly in the ranks.[39] It was only during World War I that the last obstacles to a citizen-soldier were swept away under the pressure of replacing large losses. By this time, too, a new spirit of comradeship and enhanced feelings of masculine pride developing out of the reforms of 1908 was building toward a full "nationalization of the army."[40]

A more favorable overall picture of Russia's military achievement emerges if the traditional comparison is shifted from Western European armies to those of Russia's main rivals in the struggle over the borderlands. As recent revisionist interpretations have pointed out, the army fought better during World War I than had previously been portrayed in Western and Soviet literature. It held its own against three enemies on a front extending from the Baltic to Eastern Anatolia. It repeatedly defeated the Habsburg forces in Galicia and the Turks in the Caucasus. By the end of the war it had surrendered less territory than the Red Army in 1941–42. In the final analysis, it was only outmatched by the best army in Europe. But once again as in 1905 it lost the war on the home front.[41] During the critical days of February 1917, the army command played a key role in orchestrating attempts to limit the power of the tsar and then to force his abdication.[42] Their overriding concern was to win the war and preserve the social order. If this meant cooperating with the republican provisional government then General M. V. Alekseev, the chief of staff, like his fellow commanders was "willing to accept the revolution in order to contain it."[43] Within less than two years the high command of the German army also demanded the abdication of Wilhelm II in order to preserve the army and the old social order.

Habsburg Monarchy

Habsburg foreign policy from the acquisition by the dynasty of Bohemia and Hungary in 1526 to the end of the monarchy may be seen as "largely dictated by the monarchy's attempts to enhance its security by the maintenance of buffer zones in each of four distinctive geographical areas: Germany to the northwest, Italy to the southwest, Turkey and the Balkans to the southeast, and, to a somewhat lesser degree, Poland

---

[39] Steinberg demonstrates in his prosopographical study that "these statistics reveal the democratization of the officer corps had penetrated the ranks of the Russian General Staff." Ibid., 287.

[40] J. A. Sanborn, *Drafting the Russian Nation: Military Conscription, Total War and Mass Politics* (DeKalb: Northern Illinois University Press, 2003).

[41] D. R. Jones, "The Imperial Army in World War I, 1914–1917," in *The Military History*, eds. Kagan and Higham, 228–48 with a review of the literature.

[42] G. Katkov, *Russia, 1917: The February Revolution* (New York: Harper and Row, 1967), 306–58; and T. Hasegawa, *The February Revolution: Petrograd, 1917* (Seattle: University of Washington Press, 1981), 487–507. Both of these volumes deal in great detail with the abdication and agree on the main points summarized below.

[43] Hasegawa, *The February Revolution*, 501.

and later Russia to the northeast."[44] Although priorities among these regions shifted during this period, the task of the army in holding together the disparate parts of
the monarchy against multiple external attacks was as fundamental to the existence
of the state as in any other continental empire but also fraught with greater internal
problems. The absence for most of its existence of a centralized rational administration of finances and the poly-ethnic character of the army had by the mid-nineteenth
century led to military defeats that terminated its policies to keep Germany and Italy
divided, stripping its buffers in the northwest and southwest and forcing it to shift the
prime object of its mission to the southeast. There it sought to maintain the buffers
by dividing the Balkans into spheres of influence with the expanding Russian Empire.
From the Great Northern War to the Napoleonic Wars the Habsburg and Russian
Empires were frequent allies, sharing the spoils of the partitioned Polish-Lithuanian
Commonwealth and a common enemy in the Ottoman Empire. After the Habsburgs
acquired Venice and the Dalmatian Coast in 1815, it generally favored status quo in the
Balkans. Throughout the nineteenth century the main stumbling block to a continu-
ation of their quondam alliance was the question of which power would replace the
Ottoman Empire as the dominant force in the Balkans. The problem for the Habsburg
Monarchy was that the military establishment had not kept pace with its putative
rival; it was in no condition to fight a major war alone.

A regular Habsburg army began to emerge from the destructive military excesses of the Thirty Years War. The first real standing army was created by Ferdinand
III in 1649 when he refused to disband the imperial forces. In this way he sought to
circumvent the resistance of the traditional estates represented in the provincial
Landtag to furnish recruits. His initiatives broke the authority of mercenary colonels whose private armies were the scourge of Central Europe. Thereafter, the emperors were also able at times of crisis to raise contingents from other states in the
Holy Roman Empire.[45] But Ferdinand's successors were not able to centralize financing, supply, and recruitment which remained mainly in the hands of the hereditary
lands (*Erblande*) until the mid-eighteenth century.[46] Still, the ability to raise a powerful army was in striking contrast to what was happening in the Polish-Lithuanian
Commonwealth. Ironically, the Polish army was a national force. But the *szlachta* refused to support the creation of a mass army for fear of granting their elective king too
much power which might be used to establish a hereditary monarchy. The key to the
greater success of the Habsburgs in forging a mass army was not by nationalizing it,

---

[44] C. W. Ingrao, *In Quest and Crisis: Emperor Joseph I and the Habsburg Monarchy* (West Lafayette:
    Purdue University Press, 1979), 4–5.
[45] K. A. Roider, *The Reluctant Ally: Austria's Policy in the Austro-Turkish War, 1737–1739* (Baton
    Rouge: Louisiana State University Press, 1972); J. A. Mears, "The Thirty Years War and the
    Origins of a Standing Army in the Habsburg Monarchy," *Central European History* 21 (1988):
    125–39.
[46] Michael Hochedlinger, *Austria's Wars of Emergence: War, State, and Society in the Habsburg
    Monarchy, 1683–1797* (London: Pearson Education, 2003), 98–111.

but by gradually and often painfully creating the central governing bodies necessary to administer and finance its operations. This meant that, unlike the more centralized and militarized Russian Empire, the Habsburg Monarchy had to rely for several centuries on contributions for the upkeep of the army from a complex process of bargaining with the provincial *Landtag*. As a result, the Habsburg army was a more heterogeneous, not to say cosmopolitan force, than the Russian. This was a source of strength until the nineteenth century when nationalizing trends within the monarchy turned this advantage into its opposite.

The army had long been composed of loosely organized congeries of regiments under mercenary colonels who raised their own forces and hired the commanders of smaller units irrespective of origin or status. This so-called military entrepreneur system had a strong effect on the social structure of the Habsburg officer corps. Unlike the Prussian and Russian armies, where nobleman and officer were virtually synonymous in the eighteenth century, the Habsburg army was largely staffed by commoners except for the highest ranks and the elite guard and cavalry regiments.[47] Neither the funding of the army nor the membership of its officer corps provided the basis for nationalizing the army.

Under the reign of Leopold I (1657–1705) the Habsburg Empire appeared to have stabilized its strategic frontiers in all four directions. The emperor had recognized that the army was the sole institution together with the court that was subject to his personal authority without the need to rely on the local elites and their elective institutions. His policy of recruiting foreigners independent of local diets or orders to positions of command and then ennobling them was another method of assuring loyalty of the army. Throughout the seventeenth century, the army absorbed approximately eighty percent of the budget. By the late seventeenth century, the Habsburg army had become a match for the Ottomans, their main rival in the struggle over the Balkan borderlands. In the early eighteenth century it was able to fight on both ends of the double frontier during the Hungarian rebellion in the east (Kuruc War, 1703–11) and in the west (War of the Spanish Succession, 1700–13).

A large part of the credit belongs to a trio of brilliant foreign military organizers and commanders, Raimondo Montecuccoli, Duke Charles of Lorraine, and Prince Eugene of Savoy. In the pre-nationalist age, the monarchy benefitted from its freedom to employ the most talented commanders in Europe. As president of the *Hofkriegsrat* from 1668–81 and commander in chief, Montecuccoli unified civil and military control of the army. A man of the Renaissance and a Renaissance man, he was one of the first commanders to develop a general theory of war.[48] That the commanders were also military planners who organized finances, constructed arsenals, and improved

---

[47] F. Redlich, "The German Military Enterprise and Work Force," *Vierteljahrsschrift für Sozial-und Weltgeschichte* 47 (1964).

[48] A. Gat, *The Origins of Military Thought from the Enlightenment to Clausewitz* (Oxford: Oxford University Press, 1989), 13–24. For Prince Eugene, a brilliant field commander with little interest in theory, see D. McKay, *Prince Eugene of Savoy* (London: Thames and Hudson, 1977).

logistical support contributed to the establishment of a standing army of 100,000 that ranked with the best in Europe.[49]

The main shortcoming of the army continued to be its recurrent dependence for recruits and finances on local diets, a problem that was never entirely overcome especially with respect to Hungary. Under Maria Theresa alternative proposals to solve the problem reflected the different challenges on the double frontiers. The advocates of a Prussian-style conscription supported by Joseph II and leading military figures were responding to the challenge of Frederick the Great on the northern frontier. Count Kaunitz advocated a strict separation of the army and society by proposing the highly militarized Military Border facing the Ottoman as a viable model. The "military party" won over Maria Theresa and her advisers. Conscription was introduced first into the Austrian-Bohemian provinces and then to Hungary. Recruitment of foreign mercenaries was extended, regular regiments were formed, and a furlough system eased lifelong service which was only abolished in 1802. German became the language of command and a whole set of improvements were introduced in the training and education of officers. The overall effect was to increase vastly the control of the sovereign over her subjects. By the end of her reign the army, now called "imperial-royal" (kaiserlich-und-königliche or k-u-k.), numbered 200,000 men.[50] The revitalized army had not been able to prevent Frederick II from seizing and holding Silesia, but it did help preserve the monarchy during one of its many moments of crisis.

These reforms were supplemented by equally far-reaching changes on the military border. It was turned into a reservoir of manpower for the regular armed forces. Joseph II sought to reduce expenditures by encouraging troops stationed more or less permanently on the military frontier to undertake some kind of gainful employment in peacetime.[51] There was even an "enlightened" aspect to these measures, for Joseph believed these activities would contribute to the welfare and happiness of the soldiers.[52]

Of all the European armies, the Habsburg Army was ethnically the most highly diversified. Recruited from all corners of the empire and beyond, its soldiers spoke German, French, Czech, Flemish, Serbo-Croatian, Italian, Hungarian, Romanian, and Polish, although the language of drill and commands remained German. During the Napoleonic Wars, reforms were introduced by Archduke Charles, the brother of the king and the ablest general in the army. But there was no attempt to emulate the French or the Prussians in creating a truly national army. Charles strongly opposed a

---

[49] Berenger, *Leopold I*, chap. 10, gives full details on the organization and finances of the army.

[50] C. Duffy, *The Army of Maria Theresa: The Armed Forces of Imperial Austria, 1740–1780* (New York: Hippocrene Books, 1977), 218, 43, 46, 208–09; and Hochedlinger, *Austria's Wars*, 303–16.

[51] H. Freudenberger, "Introduction" to part three, "Government and Economy," in *State and Society in Early Modern Austria*, ed. C. Ingrao (West Lafayette: Purdue University Press, 1994), 141–45; Dickson, *Finance*, II, 117.

[52] J. C. Allmayer-Beck, "Das Heerwesen unter Joseph II," in *Österreich zur Zeit Kaiser Josephs II* (Vienna: Niederösterreichische Landesausstellung, 1980), 42–43.

mass army on the French model arguing that "such a mobilization would ruin industry and national prosperity, and disrupt the established order, including the system of government." He even distrusted the citizen militia (*Landwehr*) which was inspired by local patriotic motives.[53]

The performance of the Habsburg army in the Napoleonic Wars was mixed. Its mere staying power, however, greatly assisted Metternich in gaining for the monarchy a leading role in European politics down to the revolutions of 1848. The main problem confronting the makers of military policy in Vienna was the dissatisfaction of the Hungarian elites with their role in the army. Although the Hungarians persistently opposed Vienna's control over the military border, they continued to supply light cavalry units for the army. When the chips were down, the Magyar nobility rallied around the dynasty to resist Napoleon, unlike their Polish counterparts who supported him. Up to 1848, the Hungarians constituted 68% of the infantry stationed in Hungary and 43% of the army as a whole.[54] But ever since 1790 the Hungarian diet had repeatedly demanded the establishment of national units composed of Magyar speaking officers and soldiers. Growing nationalist sentiments produced similar if less sharply defined frictions between the German command and Czech, Italian, and even Polish troops. Vienna's response was two-fold. The predominantly aristocratic officer corps and long term recruitment for soldiers (up to the 1840s) was complemented by the well-known policy of stationing troops of one nationality in the territory of another, which paid off in the revolutions of 1848–49.[55]

The supreme test for the army came in 1848–49. Rebellions throughout the entire monarchy appeared to presage the disintegration of the state. But the army did not disintegrate into its national components. Regional commands in Bohemia, Lombardy-Venetia, and Croatia rallied to the dynasty. In Lombardy-Venetia one half to two thirds of the troops remained loyal.[56] Although the fighting in Hungary took on some aspects of a national uprising, it also resembled a civil war. In fact, the loyal units of the "imperial and royal" army were a mix of all the nationalities including Hungarians. Germans and South Slavs counted one third of the officers in the

---

[53] G. E. Rothenberg, "Archduke Charles and the 'New' Army," in *East Central War Leaders: Civilian and Military*, eds. B. Király and A. Nofi (Boulder: Atlantic Research and Publishing, 1988), 187–95, quotation from Charles's memorandum of 1804 on 191.

[54] A. Sked, *The Survival of the Habsburg Monarchy: Radetzky, the Imperial Army and the Class War, 1848* (London: Longman, 1979), 49. The main problem for the army was insufficient funding. Ibid., part one.

[55] G. E. Rothenberg, "The Habsburg Army and the Nationality Problem in the Nineteenth Century, 1815–1914," *Austrian History Yearbook* III, pt. 1 (1967): 71–73.

[56] L. Sondhaus, *In the Service of the Emperor: Italians in the Austrian Armed Forces, 1814–1918* (Boulder: East European Monographs, 1990), 42. Emperor Franz Joseph pardoned those Italians who had deserted in the early phase of the uprisings. The navy, almost exclusively manned by Italians, remained wholly loyal.

rebellious Hungarian army.[57] Individual soldiers were often confused, switching sides or deserting according to circumstances. To be sure, under the leadership of Louis Kossuth the Hungarian diet declared independence. But the greater Hungarian state he envisaged was like the monarchy—multi-national with its own borderlands in Slovakia, Transylvania, the Banat, and Croatia, a sure fire recipe for generating opposition in these regions. When Nicholas I intervened at the request of Franz Joseph, the Russian army was used not only to put down a Hungarian national uprising but to forestall its spread to the Kingdom of Poland.

The unsteady loyalty of the poly-ethnic army contributed to the defeats in the wars of Italian and German national unification against France and Piedmont in 1859 and against Prussia in 1866. Desertions of Hungarian regiments at the battle of Solferino led to the withdrawal of the Hungarian corps from military operations. In 1866, two Italian regiments defected to the Prussians, and Hungarian prisoners of war formed an anti-Habsburg legion. These defeats persuaded the ruling elites of the necessity for reforms in the army and a political settlement with Hungary in 1867 that effectively divided the monarchy into two separate parts, linked by common foreign, financial, and military institutions. The terms of the economic compromise had to be re-negotiated every ten years which gave rise to periodic conflicts over the size and apportionment of the military budget. The military provisions of the compromise provided for the common imperial-royal army, with dynastic insignia and German remaining as the language of command, two sources of resentment among Hungarians. In addition, two militias were created, the *honvéd* for Hungary and the *landwehr* for Austria. The *honvéd* (defenders of the fatherland) had first been raised in 1848 as the core of the Hungarian national revolutionary army and its re-creation was clearly a concession to Hungarian national sentiment.[58]

The re-organization of the armed forces entrusted to the head of the Austrian military chancellery, Friedrich Beck, offered something to everyone, but satisfied no one.[59] In contrast to Miliutin, he followed the Prussian model by erecting a general staff to replace the system of ministerial domination and required completion of courses at the *Kriegsschule* for entrance into its membership. This preserved German domination of the officer corps. The two militias were intended for home defense, but

[57] G. Bona, "Revolutionary Army, Professional Officers: Active Imperial and Royal Officers in the Hungarian Army in 1848–49," in *The East Central European Officer Corps 1740–1920s: Social Origins, Selection, Education and Training*, eds. B. K. Király and W. S. Dillard (Boulder: East European Monographs, 1988), 55–60, provides a summary of the monograph *Tábornokok és törzstisztek a szabadságharcban 1848–1849* (Budapest, 1983).

[58] L. Kontler, *Millennium in Central Europe: A History of Hungary* (Budapest: Atlantisz, 1999), 251, 279, 290, 295, 300. According to Deák, "because these laws also [along with the political provisions] dissatisfied nearly everybody, they likewise survived essentially unchanged until 1918." István Deák, *Beyond Nationalism: A Social and Political History of the Habsburg Officer Corps, 1848–1918* (Oxford: Oxford University Press, 1990), 55.

[59] S. W. Lackey, *The Rebirth of the Habsburg Army: Friedrich Beck and the Rise of the General Staff* (Westport: Greenwood Press, 1995).

the Hungarians aspired to transform the *honvéd* into something resembling a national army with Hungarian the language of command.[60] There was no comparable movement by the Germans with respect to the *landwehr*, and it never evolved in the direction of an Austro-German national army. But Beck sought to integrate the *landwehr* and *honvéd* into the regular army and substitute new levies called *landsturm* for home defense. The imperial and royal army was never turned into a national force, although it was dominated by Germans through the language of command and the preponderance of Germans on the General Staff (60% to 18% Slavs and only 4.5% Hungarians at the end of the nineteenth century) and the officer corps in general.[61] The monarch Franz Joseph retained his role as supreme commander and was perfectly confident in using the *honvéd* to support Hungarian landowners in repressing agrarian disorders of their discontented peasants.[62]

Efforts to instill a supra-national, dynastic loyalty in the army reached a peace time climax during the celebrations of the imperial jubilee in 1898. Franz Joseph had adopted a military way of life as if to signal that the army (along with the church) was the highest form of state unity; in this he was like the Russian tsars. The symbolic fusion of the military and the Church, the two supra national pillars of the empire infused the ceremonies throughout the jubilee year. The massive awarding of medals to the troops was accompanied by the distribution of a thirteen page, *Commemorative Pamphlet for the Soldiers on the Occasion of the Fiftieth Jubilee of His Majesty Franz Joseph I*. It was "in effect, an attempt to immunize the joint Army against the threat of radical nationalism."[63]

By this time the implementation of conscription had produced an army whose ethnic composition closely corresponded to that of the empire as a whole. Correspondingly, a regimental language was introduced, chosen on the basis of the unit's ethnic composition: if at least twenty percent of the regiment's soldiers spoke a native non-German language, then the officers had to learn and speak it well. But attempts to achieve integration through a manipulation of imperial symbols and concessions to local nationalist sentiments fell short of creating a truly integrated army representing society as a whole. Only around twenty percent of those youths liable for military service were actually called to the colors, and the number who failed to show up for mustering kept increasing up to 1910, when it reached a figure of twenty-two percent.[64]

---

[60] Rothenberg, "The Habsburg Army," 77–78.

[61] Between 1895 and 1910 the percentage of German officers in the joint army was between 77% and 80%, according to the calculations of T. Hajdu, *Tisztikar és középosztály 1850–1914: Ferenc József magyar tisztjei* (Budapest, 1999) quoted in G. Romsics, *Myth and Remembrance. The Dissolution of the Habsburg Empire in the Memoir Literature of the Austro-Hungarian Political Elite* (Boulder: East European Monographs, 2006), 216, n. 3.

[62] P. Hanák, "Hungary in the Austro-Hungarian monarchy: Preponderancy or Dependency?" *Austrian History Yearbook* III, pt. 1 (1967): 296–98.

[63] D. L. Unkowsky, *The Pomp and Politics of Patriotism: Imperial Celebrations in Habsburg Austria, 1848–1916* (West Lafayette: Purdue University Press, 2005), 97–104, quotation on 99.

[64] C. Hämmerle, "Die Allgemeine Wehrpflicht in der multiethnischen Armee der Habsburgermonarchie," *Journal of Modern European History* 5, no. 2 (September 2007): 227–35.

The Austro-Hungarian armed forces were designed not to fight a major war but to maintain a delicate balance between the major ethnic constituencies of the empire. Measured by the size of the defense budget and the percentage of the population annually conscripted, the Austro-Hungarian forces lagged behind the major European powers. In 1914 the army fielded fewer infantry battalions than in 1866.[65] Piecemeal reforms did not aim at the creation of a national army. There was no unified command or concentration of authority in the War Ministry as was the case in the reformed Russian army. Franz Joseph played arbiter among the factions and rival departments with disastrous results in World War I. By this time the high command was in the hands of Conrad von Hötzendorf, the talented, modernizing chief of staff who was committed to the idea of a preventative war but pessimistic about the chances of the monarchy surviving it. The officer corps was socially isolated from the rank and file as well as the civilian population—first, by its oath to the emperor and direct subordination to him and second, paradoxically, by its cultivation of a form of prestige based on an artificial, caste-like, social distinction between non-noble officers and the rest of society and not on the hereditary privilege that bred a natural *noblesse oblige*. The result was a "bureaucratic army" ill-suited to fight wars in the nationalist era.[66]

The performance of the army in World War I may seem to have refuted such a pessimistic conclusion. Aside from a few exaggerated incidents of unit mutiny or desertion, the army maintained its cohesion in the face of severe battlefield losses to the Russians, for example, in 1915. However, by the spring of 1918 the warning issued by Count Kasimir Badeni in 1895, was turning out to be correct: "a state of nationalities can make no war without danger to itself."[67] It might have been more correct to have said: "a state of nationalities can suffer *no general defeat* without *mortal* danger to itself." Once the compromise with Hungary had been sealed, the monarchy had two options in re-organizing the army in Cisleithenia. It could have permitted the formation of national units comparable to the Hungarian. This is what the Czechs advocated in their petitions to create a Czech national guard. Or it could have embarked on a program of Germanization of the army. Both options were fraught with political dangers. The monarchy reacted, as it often did, by pursuing neither course. The fragile compromise ensured only a modicum of loyalty to the dynasty.

The memoirs of former high ranking officers, both German and Hungarian, reveal their belief that during World War I the army, even including the Czech front

[65] H. H. Herwig, *The First World War: Germany and Austria-Hungary, 1914–1918* (London: Arnold, 1996), 12–13, 238–39. Herwig is much more critical of the officer corps than Deák.
[66] R. Kann, "The Social Prestige of the Officer Corps in the Habsburg Empire from the Eighteenth Century to 1918," in *War and Society in East Central Europe* I. *Special Topics and Generalizations on the 18th and 19th Centuries*, eds. B. Király and G. E. Rothenberg (New York: Brooklyn College Press, 1979), 113–37.
[67] Cited in Rothenberg, "The Habsburg Army," 79.

line units, were loyal to the end.[68] However, even before 1914 two different attitudes toward the primacy of imperial or national tendencies had already begun to show up among German-speaking officers. Those who called themselves Old Austrians identified themselves with the dynasty and imperial rule. Another group, who perceived the process of nationalizing the empire as having advanced much farther, considered themselves to be primarily Germans or Austro-Germans. A similar line dividing Hungarian officers is more difficult to draw because of their more highly developed identification with Hungarian nationalism and their ambivalence toward the imperial idea both as a protective cover for their national aspirations and a brake on the further development of those aspirations.[69] Underneath the surface, the rank and file were vulnerable to nationalist propaganda. In a time of a long and hard war this loyalty would become increasingly frayed.

In the first half of 1918 the Austro-Hungarian army was sorely tried by internal disturbances. In January a mass strike movement with radical social and economic demands began in Vienna, spread to the *Erbland* provinces, then to Brno and Budapest, where soviets were formed for the first time. With the Bolsheviks negotiating for peace, the government was able to move seven full strength divisions from the Russian front to check the disorders. But fresh outbreaks occurred in the mining districts of Moravia. Again the army was forced to intervene. In early spring mutinies broke out among Slovene, Ruthene, and Serb regiments, followed by the Czechs. Loyal units of the army suppressed them. But this was not 1848. In the view of Z. A. B. Zeman the army had become "a blunt instrument; it eventually failed the Habsburg dynasty in its hour of need." By repressing the mass strikes it enabled the nationalist leaders inside and outside the country to rally support without splitting the revolutionary movements into their potentially antagonistic national and social currents.[70] By August 1918 the Habsburg army was disintegrating into its component ethnic parts, beginning with the mass defection of the Croatian regiments. The new emperor, Charles, refused to use the army to check the national councils in the imperial borderlands that organized the dissolution of the empire.[71]

As the imperial army disintegrated, its officers and men attempted to reach their homelands, which were in the process of forming new states under national banners. But the tasks of defining and defending new boundaries along ethno-linguistic lines were formidable given the highly mixed populations in the imperial borderlands. While the great powers in Paris sought from afar to trace new boundaries for successor

---

[68] Romsics, *Myth and Remembrance*, 14–15, 24, 27–29. The Austrian memoirists nourished their own *Dolchstoss* ("stab in the back") theory, blaming everyone from Emperor Charles to the nationalists on the home front, with the Hungarians taking most of the blame. Ibid., 36–39

[69] Ibid., 51–58, 101–10.

[70] Z. A. B. Zeman, *The Breakup of the Habsburg Empire, 1914–1918: A Study in National and Social Revolution* (Oxford: Oxford University Press, 1962), 134–35, 139, 140, 143, 146, and for quotation, 219.

[71] Herwig, *The First World War*, 436–37.

states by balancing the principle of national self-determination with economic and strategic requirements, local nationalist forces fought one another over disputed ground. For example, the Polish forces, made up of former soldiers of the Russian and Habsburg armies and General Haller's regiments from France were engaged at one time or another on three fronts—against the Germans, the Bolsheviks, and the Hungarians. Czech units battled at home against the Hungarians and abroad against the Bolsheviks in Siberia as a way of winning Allied support for an economic and strategically viable but multi-national Czechoslovak state that they would dominate. The Hungarians, though a defeated power, still fought under both a liberal and Soviet government against the Romanians, Serbs, and Czechs. The k-u-k army had finally given birth to a set of quarreling national offspring.

Ottoman Empire

The Ottoman armed forces evolved from frontier raiders in the *gazi* tradition on the frontiers of Byzantium in the fourteenth century to one of the most formidable regular armies in Europe in the sixteenth century. As early as the late fourteenth century, they completed the reorganization of their military forces on the basis of a unique combination of two social components unified by the Islamic faith. The cavalry was largely recruited from Turkic tribesmen (*sipahi*) who were granted land for service (*timars*). The elite units of the infantry (Janissaries) were composed of young Christian boys from the Balkans converted to Islam and serving as slaves to the sultan (*devşirme* system). It was far from being a national army, but it possessed a cohesiveness that was just as effective. At the height of Ottoman military power in the fifteenth and sixteenth century, the *sipahi* and Janissaries were the foundations of Ottoman military success. The origins of both exemplified the adaptation of the nomadic society to state building under a hereditary dynasty. The result was the creation of a permanent mass army in a pre-capitalist economy, which developed earlier than the Russian variation but shared many of the same characteristics.

The *timar* was not unlike the Russian *pomestie*. These were not hereditary fiefs but held only so long as the *sipahi* fulfilled his military obligations. He was authorized to collect taxes from the peasant cultivators on his land, who were not serfs but enjoyed a kind of permanent tenure, in order to support himself and his retainers. By virtue of conquest and confiscation of Christian secular estates and monastic lands, the state disposed of almost all arable lands outside those granted to religious communities. As long as new territories were conquered, the *timar* system and the cavalry arm it supported could be constantly expanded. As long as the state exercised its authority, the *sipahi* was bound to the center and not to personal or local interests. When those two conditions changed, the foundation of state power was seriously weakened.[72]

---

[72] H. Inalcik, *The Ottoman State, Economy and Society, 1300–1600* (Cambridge: Cambridge University Press, 1994), 305–07.

The Janissary Corps derived from a Central Asian Turkic tradition of recruiting slaves for military service adopted by the Ottomans for their own needs. They were formed by selecting outstanding physical types from annual levies of Christian boys in Balkan villages who were then obliged to convert to Islam. Trained as an elite military unit they developed a legendary *esprit de corps*. The dual aim, originally introduced by the founder of the Ottoman dynasty, Orkhan, was to create an absolutely loyal body of servitors who would have no other ties except to the person of the sultan, thus avoiding the need to create a nobility of birth. The Janissaries were supplied with the most modern weapons as a sign of their elite status. The system worked well until the Janissaries began to lose their exclusive military character and to act as an interest group in defense of their own privileges against the introduction of military reforms that challenged their elite status.[73] In this, they were similar to the Russian *strel'tsy*, who were not to be sure slaves or converts.

Despite the Islamic basis of the army, the early sultans were not opposed to technology transfer from Christian Europe. However, Mehmet the Conqueror rapidly freed himself from dependence on foreign experts, enlisted a growing number of Muslims in a corps of gunners and introduced a process of forging cannon from gun metal and scrap during sieges, as well as establishing permanent gun foundries.[74] During their final siege of Constantinople in 1453 they employed the largest cannon ever seen up to that time to breach the walls of "the strongest fortification of the Middle Ages."[75] Even more astonishing, these steppe warriors adapted to naval warfare and were able to challenge the great maritime power of Venice in the Mediterranean.

Over the long run, the internal cohesion of the army suffered from a combination of changes in the nature of Ottoman rulership and financial problems. The shift in the Turkic nomadic style of rulership, essentially from the saddle and tent, to the luxurious court atmosphere, signaled a shift from the warrior sultan to the sedentary or symbolic sultan and the breakup of the imperial household into family factions.[76] Palace favorites began to dispose of *timar* lands, reducing the land fund available for *sipahis*. As a measure of compensation, the number of Janissaries increased, supported by public taxation as they were not permitted to hold land. The *sipahis* themselves were increasingly attracted to the pleasures of life in the towns and became absentee landlords who irregularly performed their service obligations. After the 1580s the influx of silver and the price revolution began a long spiral of economic

---

[73] Ibid.; C. Fleischer, *Bureaucrat and Intellectual in the Ottoman Empire* (Princeton: Princeton University Press, 1986); A. Hourani, *A History of the Arab Peoples* (Cambridge, Mass.: Harvard University Press, 1991), 214–22.

[74] C. Imber, *The Ottoman Empire, 1300–1650* (Basingstoke: Palgrave Macmillan, 2002), 252–86.

[75] H. Inalcik, *The Ottoman Empire: The Classic Age, 1300–1600* (Oxford: Oxford University Press, 1973), 7–8, 21, 23.

[76] C. V. Findley, "Political Culture and the Great Households," in *The Cambridge History of Turkey*, ed. Suraiya Faroqhi (Cambridge: Cambridge University Press, 2006), 66–68.

crises.[77] Inflation and the circulation of counterfeit money particularly affected fixed income groups like the Janissaries who responded by rioting and the *timar* holders who resorted to squeezing more out of the peasants. The state steadily lost the ability to protect the tax-paying population of peasants, artisans, and merchants (*reaya*), whether Christian or Muslim, from the depredations of local officials and wandering bands of demobilized soldiers. Various kinds of adventurers, rural bandits, and deserters, who were themselves a product of the economic crisis, took advantage of the gradual disappearance of *timar* holders in the countryside to seize land and then offer protection to the peasants from the depredations of others. The weakening of the link between service and land-holding gradually gave rise to the conversion of the *timar* into tax farms or large holdings for court officials and the harem (*çiftlik*) managed by a powerful overseer who imposed a second level of economic exploitation on the peasantry.[78]

The weakening of central authority and growth of insecurity in the countryside throughout the seventeenth century gave rise to various forms of peasant resistance ranging from falsification of feudal documents and refusal to pay taxes to mass flight and brigandage. The traditional division between the *askeri* and *reaya* began to break down. The separation had never been rigid, but by the early seventeenth century the government increasingly turned a blind eye to the flow of non-*timar* holders into the army and the Janissaries. Volunteers were drawn from a variety of social categories, constituting as many as twenty percent of the armed forces by the end of the sixteenth century. Their use created other problems. The failure to meet promises of rewards in the form of prebends (*timars*) in the fierce competition for limited resources and demobilization after military campaigns created bitterness and frequently led to the formation of armed bands of demobilized soldiers that roamed the countryside.

An early account in 1636 records the flight of peasants from the district of Bitolja into the mountains to join the bandit gangs (*hajduks*) who supported their

[77] H. Inalcik, "Bursa and the Commerce of the Levant," *Journal of Economic and Social History of the Orient* III, no. 2 (1960): 131–47; R. Mantran, "L'empire Ottoman et le commerce asiatique au XVIe et au XVIIe siècle," in *Islam and the Trade of Asia*, ed. D. S. Richards (Philadelphia: University of Pennsylvania Press, 1970), 169–80. In the long run this may have been less serious than the inability of the Ottoman economic system rooted in Islamic law to secure new economic resources or accumulating capital for major infrastructural improvements in the industrialization of the eighteenth century; see: H. Inalcik, "Capital Formation in the Ottoman Empire," *Journal of Economic History* 29, no. 1 (March 1969): 97–140.

[78] I. M. Kunt, *The Sultan's Servants: the Transformation of Ottoman Provincial Government, 1550–1650* (New York: Columbia University Press, 1983), 80–85; B. Lewis, "Some Reflections on the Decline of the Ottoman Empire," *Studia Islamica* 9 (1958): 111–27; and S. Faroqui, "Crisis and Change, 1590–1699," in *An Economic and Social History of the Ottoman Empire*, 2 vols., eds. H. İnalcik with D. Quataert (Cambridge: Cambridge University Press, 1994), 447–51.

refusal to furnish provisions for the Ottoman army in Hungary.[79] The *hajduks* existed at all stages of Ottoman rule. But by the seventeenth century the bands were spread wide throughout the Balkans although they clustered in regions like Macedonia where the terrain and the prevalence of large *çiftliks* provided suitable conditions. *Hajduks* often collaborated with foreign armies, especially during the Habsburg–Ottoman wars (1586–1606 and 1683–99) when their harassment of supply lines and attacks on isolated Turkish posts took on all the character of a full scale guerilla war.[80]

After their re-conquest of Belgrade in 1739, the Ottoman armies failed to win any major wars against their Habsburg or Russian rivals although they fought well, especially on defense. But it was hardly a national army. During the Crimean War, it was made up of many nationalities, fighting under the command of British officers.[81] The reasons for this military decline and the subsequent steady loss of territory have been hotly debated. The more recent literature based on Ottoman sources has replaced the older interpretation that attributed defeats to Islamic conservatism as an obstacle to technological innovation. Instead a more complex picture has emerged.

In the late sixteenth century the evolution of the Janissary Corps from an elite unit of the sultan's army to an unreliable, often disorderly force opposing military reforms was already noticeable. One of the important functions of the Janissaries had been to garrison frontier fortresses. From thirty to sixty percent of the Janissaries served on frontier duties. The rest were stationed in Istanbul. Although their number increased throughout the seventeenth century, their proportion of the combat troops declined.[82] By the end of the eighteenth century the Janissaries numbered about half a million men, but only one in ten were engaged in military activities.[83] Once they were allowed to marry, the opportunities opened up for their sons to inherit their functions. Inflationary pressures cause by the influx of silver brought additional pressure on the Janissaries to seek supplementary employment in artisanal or commercial enterprises. They often resisted paying taxes, considering themselves by virtue of their previ-

---

[79] B. Cvetkova, "Mouvements antiféodaux dans les terres bulgares sous domination ottomane du XVIe au XVIIIe siècle," *Études historiques à l'occasion du XIIe congrès internationale des sciences historiques, Vienne, août-septembre, 1965* (Sofia, 1965): II, 153.

[80] The argument has been made by K. Barkey that the state once again responded flexibly to the crisis by employing a combination of tactics ranging from bargaining and cooptation to fierce repression: K. Barkey, *Bandits and Bureaucrats: The Ottoman Route to State Centralization* (Ithaca: Cornell University Press, 1994). See also: K. Barkey "In Different Times: Scheduling and Control in the Ottoman Empire, 1550–1659," *Comparative Studies in Society and History* 38 (1996): 460–83.

[81] O. Figes, *Crimea: The Last Crusade* (London: Penguin, 2010), 120–21, 172–73, 398–99. The British commanded at the defense of Silistria, and at Kars. The most famous if not the best Ottoman general, Omer Pasha, was a converted Croatian Serb.

[82] Gábor Ágoston, "Military Transformation in the Ottoman Empire and Russia, 1500–1800," *Kritika* 12, no. 2 (Spring 2011): 303–08.

[83] V. H. Aksan, "Whatever Happened to the Janissaries? Mobilization for the 1768–74 War," *War in History* 15 (1998): 22–36.

ous military service members of the ruling, non-taxpaying population. They used their military training in order to coerce and intimidate local tradesmen. The de-militarization of the Janissaries contributed to social discontent and increased their resistance to any form of innovation in the army.[84] Even their loyalty to the sultan eroded over time. They became a law unto themselves and their conduct in battle was often unpredictable and disorderly.[85]

There was no lack of attempt to overcome the weaknesses in the Ottoman armed forces identified by its most perceptive critics. In their view, two major problems that continued to preoccupy reformers to the end of the empire were first, keeping apace with innovations in military technology in Western Europe and Russia; and second, obtaining sufficient financial resources and manpower to defend the increasingly imperiled frontiers. There were crucial differences between the Ottoman, Habsburg, and Russian responses to the same problem. The Ottoman solution was to borrow and bargain. Up to the eighteenth century, the Ottoman army had kept pace with advances in military technology. A major source was the transfer of weapons technology among the Muslim gunpowder empires.[86] Attempts to create a domestic armaments industry were sporadic and largely unsuccessful. Under Selim III the government undertook to construct factories to arm or equip the military by transferring European technology. Usually tax farmers supervised the strategic industries like gunpowder, ships, cloth for uniforms, and strategic metals. But this meant that production remained "locked into older patterns, shutting out the possibility of new efficiencies based on the division of labor or new technique."[87] The Ottoman Empire managed briefly to achieve self-sufficiency in arms production at the beginning of the nineteenth century. Thereafter, it relied increasingly on imports, becoming totally dependent on them by 1914. In this way they were able to obtain high quality military equipment quickly through the international arms market without creating a national armaments industry.[88]

---

[84] H. Inalcik, "Military and Fiscal Transformation in the Ottoman Empire, 1600–1700," *Archivum Ottomanicum* 6 (1980); V. J. Parry, "La manière de combattre," in *War, Technology and Society in the Middle East*, eds. V. J. Parry and M. E. Yapp (Oxford: Oxford University Press, 1975), 218–56; I. E. Petrosian, "Ianicharskie garnizony v provintsiiakh osmanskoi imperii v XVI–XVII vv," in *Osmanskaia imperiia i strany tsentral'noi, vostochnoi i iugo-vostochnoi Evropy v XVII v*. pt 1 (Moscow: Akademiia Nauk SSSR, 1998).

[85] V. H. Aksan, *Ottoman Wars, 1700–1870: An Empire Besieged* (Edinburgh: Edinburgh University Press, 2007), 38–40, 53, 117.

[86] Murphey, *Ottoman Warfare*, 50 and passim; Aksan, "Military Reform," 264–65; J. Grant, "Rethinking Ottoman 'Decline': Military Technology Diffusion in the Ottoman Empire, Fifteenth to Eighteenth Centuries," *Journal of World History* 10, no. 1 (Spring 1999): 179–201.

[87] B. McGowan, "The Age of the Ayans," in *An Economic and Social History*, eds. İnalcik and Quataert, 717; and E. C. Clark, "The Ottoman Industrial Revolution," *International Journal of Middle East Studies* 5, no. 1 (January 1974): 65–76.

[88] J. Grant, "The Sword of the Sultan: Ottoman Arms Imports, 1854–1914," *Journal of Military History* 66, no. 1 (January 2002); and more generally J. A. Grant, *Rulers, Guns and Money: The Global Arms Trade in the Age of Imperialism* (Cambridge, Mass.: Harvard University Press, 2007) is more positive about Ottoman industrial policy than Clark.

A corollary of the "civilianization" of the Janissaries was a militarization of the borderlands. The growth of local militias formed on ethnic-regional bases increasingly shouldered the burden of defending the frontier. At the same time, the devolution of many governmental functions from the central bureaucracy to the local level allowed a variety of social types to gain access to the *askeri*.[89]

Up to the end of the seventeenth century, proponents of Ottoman military reforms had mainly resorted to what Avigdor Levy has called "restorative measures." That is, they argued for the return to the Ottoman institutions that had fallen into decay. This strategy gave them protective cover to introduce technological innovations in weaponry borrowed from the infidels but it also imposed limitations on the extent of the borrowing.[90] Two big defeats at the hands of the Habsburgs forced a reconsideration of the type and pace of reform. At the Treaty of Karlowitz in 1699, the Sultan was obliged for the first time to enter the European state system and to accept a new legal concept of state boundaries, one based on negotiations rather than conquest. The peace negotiations also illustrated the need to train diplomats who could deal with their European counterparts as equals, thus opening a path for the penetration of European ideas of statecraft.[91] Reacting to a second defeat in 1716–17 and the surrender of Belgrade, the Ottoman ruling elite felt the need to broaden their interest in European culture from pursuing fads like growing tulips to instituting far-reaching military reforms. The more serious aspect of the so-called Tulip Era was the dispatch by Grand Vizier Damad Ibrahim Pasha of five missions to Vienna, Moscow, Poland, and Paris with instructions to report in particular on military and technological matters. This foreshadowed the first of three spurts of military reform in the eighteenth century.[92]

Sultan Mahmud I (1730–54) and his advisers took the first tentative steps to introduce the latest Western techniques by engaging a converted French officer, the Comte de Bonneval, to reorganize the entire military. The Janissaries once again blocked all the major changes. At the same time, another convert, a Hungarian known only as Ibrahim Müteferrika, was one of the first to advocate publicly the virtue of absorbing the lessons of defeat by the Christians. In 1731 he founded the first Muslim printing press in the empire. All of the first sixteen books printed by his press dealt with political-military matters. Citing the reforms of Peter the Great, he declared that

---

[89] H. Canbakal, *Society and Politics in an Ottoman Town: Ayntāb in the 17th Century* (Leiden: E.J. Brill, 2007); and C. L. Wilkins, *Forging Urban Solidarities: Ottoman Aleppo 1640–1700* (Leiden: E.J. Brill, 2010). I owe these references to Virginia H. Aksan.

[90] A. Levy, "Military Reform and the Problem of Centralization in the Eighteenth Century," *Middle Eastern Studies* 18, no. 3 (July 1982): 229–30.

[91] R. A. Abou-El-Haj, "Ottoman Attitudes towards Peace Making: The Karlowitz Case," *Der Islam* 51 (1974): 131–37; S. Akgun, "European Influence on the Development of Social and Cultural Life of the Ottoman Empire in the Eighteenth Century," *Revue des études sud-est européenes* 21 (1983): 92.

[92] Levy, "Military Reform," 231–32. Damad Pasha had no time to implement any new ideas before he was overthrown in 1730 by a Janissary-led revolt sparked by economic causes and the defeat in a war against Iran but cloaked in anti-European terms.

adopting the new military techniques of the enemy could restore Ottoman greatness because the Ottomans possessed the moral superiority of the *sharia* and the *jihad*.[93] But the pressure for military reform lifted, ironically, as a result of their last successful campaign against the Habsburgs in the war of 1738–39 when they won back Bosnia and Serbia, including Belgrade. Thirty years of peace followed, apparently lulling them into a false sense of security. The outbreak of a new war with Russia in 1768 jogged Sultan Mustafa III (1757–74) out of complacency.

Responding positively to the crushing defeat at the hands of the Russians in the war of 1768–74, Mustafa's successor, Abdülhamid I (1768–89), recruited his top advisers from the professionally trained and salaried bureaucracy which had gradually been evolving along European lines.[94] They purchased military equipment from Europe, purged the Janissary Corps of the most disorderly elements, and introduced improvements in the navy. They sought to curb the power of the provincial notables and introduce more efficient methods into the central administration. Their efforts fell short of a radical transformation of the army and bureaucracy under the burden of growing financial constraints due to the cost of the war and mounting opposition to imperial rule. The latter arose not so much from religious conservatism, as from cultural differences and opposition by the entrenched interests in the army and *ulema* to what they perceived as threats to their preeminent position as the ruling elite.[95]

The third reforming spurt came under the reign of Selim III (1789–1807), once again under the pressure of an unsuccessful war against an alliance of the Habsburg and Russian Empires.[96] One of the most ambitious reformers among the Ottoman sultans, he was strongly influenced by events in France during the first years of the revolution. But the urgency came once again from the 1787–92 war with Russia ending with the Treaty of Iaşi. Even before the defeat was registered, he solicited reforming proposals from his closest advisors. Most of these dealt with the need for military reform, taking Russia as the example of what could be done and France as the model of how to do it. In the vanguard of reforming bureaucrats, Ahmed Resmi provided the intellectual inspiration. A seasoned diplomat, he was second in command to the grand vizier for much of the Russo-Turkish War of 1768–74. His comprehensive report on the reasons for defeat outlined ten major shortcomings of the Ottoman army, its organization, tactics, and provisioning. He was also one of the earliest and most profound Ottoman analysts of the struggle over the borderlands. He warned

---

[93] Aksan, *An Ottoman Statesman*, 186–88.

[94] V. Aksan, "Breaking the Spell of the Baron de Tott: Reframing the Question of Military Reform in the Ottoman Empire, 1760–1830," *The International History Review* 24, no. 2 (June 2002): 258–63, has shown that the influence of a few French advisers has been exaggerated.

[95] Levy, "Military Reform," 235–38; Aksan, *Ottoman Wars*, 198–202.

[96] The older account of the reign: S. J. Shaw, *Between Old and New: the Ottoman Empire under Sultan Selim III (1789–1807)* (Cambridge, Mass.: Harvard University Press, 1973), has been superseded in many ways by Aksan, *Ottoman Warfare*, which is the main source for the following account of military reform.

against the dangers of imperial overextension into [border]lands that could not be easily defended, citing the examples of Genghis Khan and Suleiman I and prophesying the same fate for the Russian Empire. An advocate of settling disputes by negotiation, he rejected the concept of limitless frontiers of the *Dar-al-Islam* in favor of Ottoman integration into a European state system as the best guarantee of stable borders.[97]

As Virginia Aksan has argued, Selim's military reforms must be placed within the context of "the climate and articulation of reform within Ottoman society." The new triad of imperial power linked those reforms to bureaucratization, the incorporation of new elites into the center of power, and reformulating dynastic and religious ideology.[98] Faced with the lack of order and discipline among the *sipahis* and Janissaries under combat conditions, Selim created an entirely new force known as the "New Order Army." Trained in the European manner with an independent financial base and recruited from Turkish boys from Anatolia, it was to be officered by graduates of the new technical schools he established. Special attention continued to focus on the development of the artillery arm. But Selim lacked the ruthlessness of a Peter the Great. He failed to crush his opponents in the old army: the provincial notables (*ayans*) in the Balkans who opposed conscription into the New Order Army and the *ulema* who condemned his consorting with the infidel. His only allies were drawn from the non-Muslim population. There were other problems as well: the lack of a technical vocabulary to facilitate technology transfer, and the unfamiliarity of the ruling elite, except for non-Muslim minorities, with Western ideas.[99]

Under the reign of Selim, internal reforms became entangled in a dense web of international relations formed by shifting alliances in the era of Napoleonic imperialism. The sultan maneuvered among the great powers, aligning himself alternately with the British and French in order to ward off the Russians and to obtain military advisers and transfers of technology. Finally, he fell victim to an internal revolt against his policy of conscription and his support of the French. Deposed in 1807, his reforms were aborted.

The revolt that brought Mahmud II (1808–39) to the throne was sealed by a Deed of Agreement between him and the provincial notables. Sometimes called the Ottoman Magna Carta, it established the foundation of public law in the empire. It also committed the provincial notables to providing troops for the defense of the

---

[97] Aksan, *An Ottoman Statesman*, 196–98, who notes that his advocacy of negotiation was "a bit equivocal" given the fact that the Ottomans started the war, but his deeper convictions were reinforced by his own humiliating role in signing the Treaty of Kuchuk-Kainardji. Ibid., 204.

[98] Aksan, *Ottoman Warfare*, 180–81. The author points out the similarity with the pattern of military reform in Muscovy as suggested by M. Poe, "The Consequences of Military Revolution in Muscovy." See above note 1.

[99] Shaw, *History of the Ottoman Empire*, I, 261–66; Aksan, *Ottoman Wars*, 202–06 and chapter six; Levy, "Military Reform," 239–41. Aksan, *An Ottoman Statesman*, 200–03, also notes that many of Ahmed Resmi's ideas had become part of the reforming discourse by this time. For an analysis of the expanded role of the ulema in government and diplomacy in the eighteenth century, see M. C. Zilfi, "The Ottoman Ulema," in *The Cambridge History of Turkey*, III, ed. Faroqui, 223–25.

empire and provided the financial guarantees by reaffirming the tax farming system. The agreement freed the hands of the sultan and his advisers to revive the reforming process and, of the greatest importance, to break with the traditional mold of reform in 1826 by destroying for the first time an established institution—the Janissary Corps—rather than as in the past tinkering with its leadership and organization. To suppress them he relied on remnants of the disbanded New Order Army, the soldiers forced out of the ceded territories and the flotsam and jetsam of the "masterless men" in the provinces. Mahmud skillfully used the *ulema* to accuse the Janissaries of being polluted by infidels under the influence of the heterodox *Bektaşi* sect.[100]

The parallel has often been drawn between the destruction of the Janissaries and Peter the Great's repression of the Musketeers (*strel'tsy*) supported by the schismatic Old Believers. But there were important differences. Ottoman society was more complex than Muscovy's. Peter was able to create a new army by reorganizing and westernizing the noble elite, separating church and state, and abolishing the Patriarchate as an alternative source of authority. There were no powerful urban elites or independent local notables to challenge him. In Peter's empire the population was still overwhelmingly Russian and Orthodox; the Muslim Tatars were concentrated in the interior provinces far from the porous frontiers. These conditions favorable to greater centralization were absent in the Ottoman state where the non-Muslims, who constituted about half the population, were located on the vulnerable frontiers.

Nonetheless, Mahmud's reforms, particularly the Deed of Agreement and the replacement of the Janissaries with an army increasingly recruited from Turkish peasants in rural Anatolia, may be seen as the first major step in the direction of nationalizing the empire and the army by creating "an Ottoman absolutism based on a more rigorously defined (Turkish and Muslim) citizenship."[101] The term "Turk" gradually assumed an ideological content for the Ottoman rulers, particularly in the army where it first began to replace the traditional meaning of "hick" or "rube" which long survived outside the military sphere. In part this was a result of the difficulty encountered by army recruiters in enrolling recruits from the borderlands where the local notables controlled their own militias. Instead, they had to rely increasingly on the "Turkic" peasantry of Anatolia, from the districts near the capital in the Balkans and on the Caucasus frontier. In part, too, it was a response to the growing nationalist agitation among the non-Muslim population and the demands for reform by the European powers in support of their rights guaranteed by the Ottoman reforms. The value of the "Turkic" soldiers was recognized by the governor of Egypt, Mehmed Ali, who was carrying out a major economic and military transformation of his province, and his

---

[100] Aksan, *Ottoman Warfare*, 261–65. U. Heyd, "The Ottoman Ulema and Westernization at the Time of Selim III and Mahmud II," reprinted from *Studies in Islamic History and Civilization* in *Scripta Hierusoly Mitana* IX (Jerusalem, 1961).

[101] Aksan, "Military Reform," 258 for quotation and 274.

son, Ibrahim Pasha, who commanded his army, as well as Ottoman commanders in the fortresses on the Danubian frontier fighting the Greek rebels.[102]

The two major obstacles to a comprehensive and effective reconstruction of the army and administration reflected the deep structural faults within Ottoman imperial rule. First, there was a recurrence of a financial crisis, but this time in the form of runaway inflation unprecedented in scope.[103] Second, the prevalence of the patriarchal system beginning with the sultan and distributed through favoritism and factional rivalry throughout the ruling elite hampered the professionalization of the army and the rationalization of the bureaucracy. To be sure, fresh talent continued to filter into the bureaucracy; new regiments were created to replace the Janissaries.[104] But Christians, though not allowed to join, were surely alienated by the name of the new formations, the "Victorious Army of Muhammed," and by the new taxes imposed to support them. The frontiers continued to be defended by militias under the command of provincial notables. Mahmud did not create an officer's training school until 1834, more than a century after the Russian Cadet Corps. The greatest weakness of the new army was the junior officer ranks.[105] It proved difficult to break ingrained cultural practices of favoritism, corruption, and intrigue. Mahmud's decision to go to war with Russia in 1827 under the banner of jihad revealed improvements in the fighting capacity of the army but once again exposed the failure to mobilize adequate numbers of able bodied males in the Turkic population. The Sultan's insistence on fighting the war as a jihad and his suspicion of disloyal ethnic elements in the population, including converts, heterodox Muslims, Greeks, Albanians, Kurds, and Arabs, further cut into the potential reservoir of recruits. The new army fielded only forty thousand men (as opposed to 120,000 in the Russian army), only half of what the Ottoman commanders has deemed necessary.[106]

The renewal of the reforming impulse under the name of Tanzimat or "Auspicious Reorderings" (1839–76) by Mahmud II's successors was largely the work of a small number of Europeanized officials. The military reforms aimed at correcting the major shortcomings in the chain of command and financial support that had led to defeat in the Greek Revolution and the Russo-Turkish War of 1828–29. Its defining

---

[102] V. H. Aksan, "The Ottoman Military and State Transformation in a Globalizing World," in *Comparative Studies of South Asia, Africa and the Middle East* 27, no. 2 (2007); H. Erdem, "Recruitment of the 'Victorious Soldiers of Muhammad' in the Arab Provinces, 1826–1828," in *Histories of the Modern Middle East: New Directions*, eds. I. Gershoni, H. Erdem, and U. Wokök (Boulder: Lynne Riener, 2002), 198–200.

[103] M. Genç, "L'economie ottoman et la guerre au XVIIIe siècle," *Turcica* 27 (1995): 177–96; and especially Ş. Pamuk, "Prices in the Ottoman Empire, 1469–1914," *International Journal of Middle East Studies* 36 (2004): 463.

[104] The weaknesses of the reforms are clearly set out in Aksan, *Ottoman Warfare*, 328–36.

[105] A. Levy, "The Officer Corps in Sultan Mahmud's New Ottoman Army, 1826–39," *International Journal of Middle East Studies* 2 (1971): 21–39.

[106] Aksan, "The Ottoman Military," 266–67.

dual feature during reigns of Abdülmecid (1839–61) and Abdülaziz (1861–76) was to create an Ottoman citizenship with equal rights and responsibilities for all subjects and to create a new army based upon this new foundation. One of the three basic principles of the Gülhane Rescript of 1839 that inaugurated the new wave of reform was "an equally regular system for the conscription of requisite troops and the duration of service, it being "the inescapable duty of all the people to provide soldiers for the defense of the fatherland."[107]

Under Abdülaziz who was particularly interested in the army, Minister of War Hüseyin Avni undertook the first major military reform since the 1830s. In the wake of the Crimean War in 1856 the empire extended conscription to all Ottomans, but in practice most non-Muslims purchased exceptions or were excluded.[108] The difference between the theory and practice illustrates the dilemma persistently facing Ottoman reformers: how to reconcile the imperial, inclusive Ottoman idea of a common citizenship with the Turkic and Sunni Islamic cultural ideal of a nation-state. Gradual and cautious though it was, the reforming process ran into the familiar structural obstacles and political opposition that ultimately doomed its architects and brought it to a crashing end. First of all there was the growing resentment within the army against working with "infidel" advisers and protests by the *ulema* against the idea of civic equality for non-Muslims. By the early seventies, a new wave of Muslim revivalism broke over the reformers. It was generated in part by preachers like al-Afghani in Istanbul and Cairo. Their popularity was nourished by stories of Russian atrocities against the Turks in their conquest of Trans Caspia and news of the great Muslim uprising of Ya'qub Beg in the Chinese province of Xinjiang followed by the arrival in the Ottoman lands of refugees from these embattled areas.[109]

Despite these reactions, the army officers graduating from the reformed military schools developed a corporate spirit, becoming increasingly professional and politicized under the reign of Abdülhamit II (1876–1909). They were outraged by the rapidly declining international position of the empire, its loss of control in Tunisia to the French (1881), in Egypt to the British (1882), and the intervention of the great powers in 1876–78 and again after the army had defeated the Greeks in the war of 1896–97. Still devoted to the imperial idea, they were increasingly disillusioned with the ability of the civilian administration to defend it. Toward the end of the century, however, a growing nationalist outlook penetrated the officer corps. Revolutionary cells within the army began to appear which bore such names as the Motherland Society, Motherland and Liberty Society, and Ottoman Liberty Society. In 1902 they

---

[107] J. C. Hurewitz, *The Middle East and North Africa in World Politics*, second edition, 2 vols. (New Haven: Yale University Press, 1975), I, 270.

[108] E-J. Zürcher, "The Ottoman Conscription System in Theory and Practice," *Arming the State: Military Conscription in the Middle East and Central Asia, 1775–1925*, ed. Zürcher (London: I.B. Tauris, 1999), 21–39.

[109] Shaw, *History of the Ottoman Empire,* II, 157.

formed a coalition of intellectuals and military men, constituting what is known as the Young Turk movement.[110]

From 1908 to 1918 the Young Turks dominated the Ottoman government except for short intervals. But already in 1907 the German inspector general of the Ottoman military schools, General Colmar Freiherr von der Golz, observed that "during my recent visits and contacts I have seen that, in the military, feelings of Turkish nationalism have grown astonishingly, and found supporters. If this sentiment develops and becomes widespread, it will be necessary to add the reaction against incidents which are corrosive of Turkish nationalism among the military's reasons for an effective intervention in the politics of the state."[111]

The Young Turks were, in the apt phrase of Erik-Jan Zürcher, "children of the borderlands." They came from a wide range of social origins, and were drawn from many ethnic backgrounds, Turks, Arabs, Kurds, Albanians, and Circassians. They were all educated in the modern schools founded along European lines. Before 1906 the civilians dominated; from 1906 to the revolution of 1908 the officers were in control. The majority came from the provinces, mainly the Balkans (48% after 1908) where they had been exposed to the small scale warfare against Serbs, Bulgarians, and Greek guerillas and the widening gap between Muslims and Christians in schools and economic activity.[112] But the army was not united behind the Young Turks. Shortly after they came to power a counter-revolution broke out spearheaded by elements of the First Army in Istanbul allied to an Islamic Party, demanding the restoration of Islamic law (*shari'ia*). They were repressed by troops from Saloniki.[113] It would appear that Turkish nationalism remained a minority ideology until the collapse of the Ottoman Empire in 1923.

Was Turkification a conscious policy of the Young Turks? Was it the irritant that aroused Arab nationalism? These remain hotly debated issues and they cannot be easily resolved by examining the national component of the army because here too the evidence is mixed. The problem does not arise merely from the sources, although contemporary perceptions on both sides are important. Rather it reflects the absence of clear cut criteria for identifying the relevant categories and separating them from

---

[110] The most important of these was the Committee of Progress and Union, later the Committee of Union and Progress. For the varieties of organizations, coalitions and factions see M. Ş. Hanioğlu, *Preparation for a Revolution: The Young Turks, 1902–1908* (Oxford: Oxford University Press, 2001).

[111] M. N. Turfan, *Rise of the Young Turks: Politics, the Military and Ottoman Collapse* (London: I.B. Tauris, 2002), 65–66.

[112] E-J. Zürcher, "The Young Turks: Children of the Borderlands," in *Ottoman Borderlands*, ed. K. Karpat, 275–85. In addition to a mixture of Turkism, Ottomanism and Islam within the CPU, strong anti-European (mainly anti-Austrian) and anti-Russian feelings were omnipresent. When expedient, the Young Turks flirted with the possibility of cooperation with the Armenian Dashnaks and the Macedonian revolutionaries (IMRO) before the revolution of 1908. Hanioğlu, *Preparation for a Revolution*, 175–81, 191–97, 243–49, 296–99.

[113] F. Ahmad, *The Young Turks: The Committee of Union and Progress in Turkish Politics, 1908–1914* (Oxford: Oxford University Press, 1969), 40–43.

one another. Aside from ethno-linguistic categories, which may be anachronistic, over-lapping ideological affinities were in play—Ottomanism, Turkism, Islam. According to the press organ of the Young Turks the top nine army commanders counted two Arabs, two Albanians, two Circassians, a Georgian, a Tatar, and a Bosnian, although the language of command was Turkish.[114]

Whatever the balance of forces among the Young Turks, military men played an increasingly prominent role in the movement, especially after the Ottoman defeats in the Balkan Wars of 1912–13. Two of the so-called ruling triumvirate, Enver Pasha and Djemal Pasha, had been graduates of the War College.[115] The outbreak of the war intensified the Turkification of the army. As minister of war in the cabinet of 1914, Enver Pasha instituted a purge of Arab officers, retiring 300 of them. As military governor of Syria, the third member of the triumvirate, Cemal Pasha, instituted a reign of terror against the Arabs in the belief that they constituted a nationalist movement that threatened the security of the empire. Their policies aroused the Arab leaders to launch a rebellion. Cemal's reprisals radicalized elements among the Arab army officers who emerged as the main adherents of national independence.[116] The common ties of Ottomanism and Islam broke asunder as the long gestating national rivalries rose to the surface. But even after the Ottoman defeat and loss of the Arab provinces, a full-blown nationalist movement was slow to develop. It came mainly as a response to European plans to partition the Empire.[117] When it did come, not surprisingly, it was led by Kemal Pasha (Atatürk) another Young Turk member of the War College and a man of the borderlands (Saloniki). Although his relations with Enver and Djemal was not cordial, he came out of the same professional, increasingly nationalist milieu within the army that characterized the most secular and modern institution of Ottoman life.[118] His assumption of power completed the process of forging a nation

---

[114] H. Kayali, *Arabs and Young Turks: Ottomanism, Arabism and Islamism in the Ottoman Empire, 1908–1918* (Berkeley: University of California Press, 1997), 88. A Young Turk spokesman attempting to refute the accusation of Turkification wrote: "[The Young Turks] too are attached to their nationality [*milliyet*]. If they had the choice and if this were possible they would lose no time to make Turks out of all nations [*akvam*] within the Ottoman Empire." Ibid., 87. The author's tendency to downplay Turkism has been questioned. Cf. the review by C. Herzog in *Die Welt Islam* 39, no. 2 (July 1999): 249–51.

[115] B. Lewis, *The Emergence of Modern Turkey* (Oxford: Oxford University Press, 1965), 221.

[116] Kayali, *Arabs*, 178, 195,197.

[117] See M. A. Reynolds, *Shattering Empires: The Clash and Collapse of the Ottoman and Russian Empires, 1908–1918* (Cambridge: Cambridge University Press, 2011), 256, who concludes that the national forces supporting the creation of a Turkish Republic were not bound together by ethnic identity but rather by "the corporate ties of the military officers and state officials who formed the movement's cadres and the common Muslim identity that linked those cadres to the population of Anatolia" including the Kurds and Circassians.

[118] A. Mango, *Atatürk* (London: John Murray, 1999), 49–54, 71–75, 301, 316 and 319–23. By contrast to Kemal's Anatolian Turkism, Enver Pasha was fascinated by the prospect of unifying all Turks. His fanciful and fatal adventure in Central Asia merely demonstrated that Pan Turkism was as unrealistic a political ideology as Pan Slavism.

out of empire. The Ottoman army, for so long the sword and then the shield of empire, produced the Young Turk officers who launched the constitutional revolution of 1908 and then in the person of Kemal Pasha overthrew the dynasty. Kemal's new *nationalist* army defeated and expelled the Greeks, created a secular Turkish republic and dominated its politics for the next eighty years.

Conclusion

The role of the army in strengthening the national component of the imperial state building in the three empires evolved in tandem with professionalization, following different and irregular rhythms of reform. In all three empires, both processes were responses to external competition with one another and to movements of domestic resistance and rebellion. From 1700 to 1918, the Russians and Ottoman fought nine wars; the Habsburgs were at war with the Ottomans throughout much of the sixteenth and seventeenth century and fought two more wars with them in the eighteenth century, incorporating the Banat, Hungary, Bukovina and finally in 1907 annexing Bosnia. Russian–Habsburg rivalry was mainly political in the nineteenth century, focusing on their competition to control the Principalities and their influence south of the Danube. But by the end of the nineteenth century the military leadership of both countries were convinced that they would have to fight one another, and then to the death.

In the sixteenth, seventeenth and eighteenth centuries the identification of the army with the dynasty was reinforced by powerful attachments of the officers and men to Orthodoxy, Catholicism, and Islam in the Russian, Habsburg, and Ottoman Empires respectively. In the nineteenth century the conscious manipulations of religious symbols within the three empires to increase army morale became part of the nationalizing process.[119] But it was not until the twentieth century and the ordeal of total war that nationalist movements in the empires became wholly secular. In the eighteenth century a pronounced shift took place in the relative strength of the competing states. The tendency in the Habsburg and Russian armies was toward greater centralization of command and tactical innovations based on stricter discipline.[120] The wars of the French Revolution created the first mass citizen armies, but this model was abandoned throughout Europe in the post-1815 period by conservative governments who preferred long term professional armies to the nation in arms. The empires undertook their first real efforts to institute universal conscription within two decades of one another—the Ottomans in 1856, the Austro-Hungarians in 1867, and the Russians 1874. Reflecting different degrees of relative economic backwardness, the three empires were slow to develop indigenous armaments industries, which remained small compared

---

[119] See the stimulating insights in Aksan, "Military Reform," 277.
[120] See, for example, the excellent comparison in G. Ágoston, "Military Transformation in the Ottoman Empire and Russia, 1500–1800," *Kritika* 12, no. 2 (Spring 2011): 281–320.

to other European powers.[121] The military reforms aimed primarily at centralization and professionalization tended to promote nationalizing tendencies if only through the uniform training of officers and the standardization of the language of command.

The armies were the glue that held the multi-cultural empires together. They were employed both to maintain domestic order, especially in the culturally distinctive borderlands, and to defend or even expand the military frontiers. Imperial ideologies and bureaucracies could not by themselves guarantee the territorial integrity of the empire. Recognition of this fact explains the periodic burst of institutional reform, seeking to mobilize new resources for the army. The vital need to compete required an increase in technical, tactical, and technological improvements to provide an increasingly professional force. By the second half of the nineteenth century the Imperial German army had given dramatic proof that only a nation in arms could forge the psychological bonds and supply the manpower necessary to perfect a well-trained, disciplined, and dedicated force. Following their lead, the imperial armies' officer corps emerged as corporate interest groups for whom the preservation of the army assume primary importance even when the dynasty was at stake, as the Russian, Turkish, and German armies demonstrated. The army had become the most modern institution of imperial rule. With their disastrous defeat, the empires collapsed.

With the dissolution of empire, the remnants of the imperial armies broke into their component national parts and the former officers and men of the imperial armies became the standard bearers in the process of nationalist state building in the successor states. The Turkish army battled the Greeks, Arabs, and Armenians. The White or Volunteer Army made up exclusively of Russians and the Red Army which was predominantly Russian fought one another and at various times against most of the nationalities from Finland to the Caucasus. The new armies produced many of the founders of the successor states. They included such leading political figures as Piłsudski in Poland, Skoropads'kyi in Ukraine, Horthy in Hungary, Mannerheim in Finland, and Kemal Pasha in Turkey. In addition, army officers played a key role in the creation of Czechoslovakia. If the Bolsheviks had not won the civil war in Russia, General Denikin or Admiral Kolchak would have come to power.[122] What this suggests is that the officer corps as a corporate group served both to defend imperial rule but also to nurture the growth of a different national loyalty which emerged full blown when the empires passed from the scene.

---

[121] M. Reinschedl, *Die Aufrüstung der Habsburgermonachie von 1880-bis 1914 in internationalen Vergleich. Der Anteil Österreich-Ungarns am Wettrüsten vor dem Ersten Weltkrieg* (Frankfurt: Peter Lang, 2001), 143–81.

[122] See the suggestive views in J. Sanborn, "The Genesis of Russian Warlordism: Violence and Government during the First World War and the Civil War," *Contemporary European History* 19, no. 3 (August 2010): 195–214.

Multi-Ethnic Empires and Nation-Building: Comparative Perspectives on the late Nineteenth Century and the First World War

Jörn Leonhard

Introduction

When President Woodrow Wilson developed his vision of a new world order in 1917, his focus on the right of national self-determination, particularly that of small nations, played an almost fundamental role: "No nation should seek to extend its polity over any other nation or people, but ... every people should be left free to determine its own polity, its own way of development, unhindered, unthreatened, unafraid, the little along the great and powerful." Against the background of the First World War and the hitherto unknown number of victims, contemporaries sought to uncover the causes of this catastrophe. Wilson's answer pointed to the suppression of nationalities in continental Europe: "This war had its roots in the disregard of rights of small nations and of nationalities which lacked the union and the force to make good their claim to determine their own allegiances and their own forms of political life."[1] The American president's own premise of democratic and national self-determination represented a counter-model to what he and others came to regard as autocratic and anachronistic empires with their complex ethnic compositions.

When, as a result of the First World War, all continental European empires—the German and Russian Empires as well as the Habsburg Monarchy and the

---

[1] Woodrow Wilson, "'A Peace Worth Preserving,' Address to the Senate on Essential Terms of Peace in Europe, 22nd January 1917," in *Americanism: Woodrow Wilson's Speeches on the War, Why He Made Them and What They Have Done. The President's Principal Utterances in the First Year of War; with Notes, Comments and War Dates, Giving Them Their Historical Setting, Significance and Consequences, and with Brief Quotations from Earlier Speeches and Papers*, ed. O. M. Gale (Chicago: Baldwin Syndicate, 1918), 22–28, 27; second quotation: "'Only One Peace Possible,' Address to Congress Analyzing German and Austrian Peace Offerings, 11th February 1918, containing the 'Four Points'" in ibid., 103–109, 106.

Ottoman Empire—collapsed and new nation-states emerged in Central, Eastern, and Southeastern Europe, these events seemed to justify Wilson's interpretation. Hence, the outcome of the war in 1918 led to a particular narrative in historiography regarding the somehow inevitable end of traditional and autocratic empires on the European continent. According to this interpretation, the First World War only completed a process which had been obvious already prior to 1914: Multi-ethnic empires seemed to be anachronistic political entities, old prisons of young nations, which could have survived only by the violent suppression of national movements and ethnic groups. This paradigm of interpretation had a lasting impact on the historiography of empires in the twentieth century. For many years, the model of the nation-state seemed to be much more attractive for historians: The complex structures of Europe's multi-ethnic empires were seen as inferior compared with the apparently homogeneous and efficient nation-state with its promise of external strength and internal unity through participation of all citizens. Furthermore, this model corresponded more convincingly with the premises of modernization theories which assumed that traditional—religious, local, or dynastic—loyalties would gradually be replaced by an identity of territory and nation.[2] In this view, multi-ethnic, religious, and legal diversity pointed to the backwardness of empires in contrast to the apparently unstoppable progress of ethnically homogeneous nation-states. The dissolution of the continental empires seemed to strengthen notions of unavoidable decline, which manifested itself in the paradigmatic formulae of "rise and fall," thereby applying Edward Gibbon's influential eighteenth-century metaphor to the complexities of imperial structures in the nineteenth and early twentieth centuries.[3]

     However in recent years empires have come back on the historiographic agenda, and different reasons stand behind this change and the new interest in empires. First, the dissolution of the Soviet Union resulted in a number of new nation-states in Central, Eastern, and Southeastern Europe, highlighting the character of the Soviet Union as a multi-ethnic empire that had long been overshadowed by Cold War antagonism. Second, through an ongoing process of institutional Europeanization and a general focus on transnational and supranational processes as well as economic and

---

[2] J. Leonhard and U. von Hirschhausen, "Europäische Nationalismen im West-Ost-Vergleich: Von der Typologie zur Differenzbestimmung," in *Nationalismen in Europa: West- und Osteuropa im Vergleich*, eds. J. Leonhard and U. von Hirschhausen (Göttingen: Wallstein Verlag, 2001), 11–45.

[3] E. Gibbon, *The History of the Decline and Fall of the Roman Empire*, 6 vols. (London: Strahan & Cadell, 1776–1789); O. Jaszi, *The Dissolution of the Habsburg Monarchy* (Chicago: University of Chicago Press, 1929); S. Eisenstadt, ed., *The Decline of Empires* (Englewood Cliffs, NJ: Prentice Hall, 1967); A. Sked, *The Decline and Fall of the Habsburg Empire 1815–1918* (London: Longman, 1989); P. Kennedy, *The Rise and Fall of Great Powers: Economic Change and Military Conflict from 1500 to 2000* (New York: Random House, 1987); R. Lorenz, ed., *Das Verdämmern der Macht: Vom Untergang großer Reiche* (Frankfurt: Fischer Taschenbuch Verlag, 2000); E. Brix et al., eds., *The Decline of Empires* (Munich: Oldenbourg Verlag, 2001); A. J. Motyl, *Imperial Ends: The Decay, Collapse, and Revival of Empires* (New York: Columbia University Press, 2001).

cultural globalization, the notion of the nation-state seems to have lost much of its credibility. Third, the outburst of extreme ethnic violence in former parts of the Soviet Union and Yugoslavia underlined the problem of how states accommodate ethnic plurality or fail in doing so.[4] Finally, after the end of the Cold War the United States developed a new international strategy to maintain and partly expand its international engagement. The particular role of the United States as the last remaining empire has provoked controversial discussions on chances and limits of empires in past and present.[5] For all these political debates, the re-discovery and re-interpretation of past empires has become an important point of reference.[6] These developments have led to a new interest in historical alternatives beyond the nation-state, not only among academic historians but also to a wider public, which may explain the focus on European empires of the early modern period and later as well as a particular interest in comparative studies of empires.[7]

In contrast to the long held premise of unavoidable disintegration and decay, the present focus is rather on the questions of why empires were able to last for so long, in which ways they contributed to the stability of the international order between 1815 and 1914, and where the limits of their potential for integration lay. A shift from the paradigm of "rise and fall" toward the question of chances and crises is obvious in many recent studies on the topic.[8] For example historians of Austria-Hungary

---

[4] H. A. Winkler and H. Kaelble, eds., *Nationalismus, Nationalitäten, Supranationalität* (Stuttgart: Klett-Cotta, 1993); B. Jones and M. Keating, eds., *The European Union and the Region* (Oxford: Oxford University Press, 1995); Aleksandar Pavcovic and Ivan Misic, eds., *New States and Old Conflicts: Nationalism and State Formation in the Former Yugoslavia* (Canberra: National Europe Centre, 2002).

[5] For a critical assessment see H. Münkler, *Imperien: Die Logik der Weltherrschaft—vom Alten Rom bis zu den Vereinigten Staaten* (Berlin: Rowohlt Berlin, 2005); M. Hardt and A. Negri, *Empire* (Cambridge, Mass.: Harvard University Press, 2000).

[6] Niall Ferguson, *Empire: How Britain made the Modern World* (London: Penguin Books, 2003); Niall Ferguson, *Colossus: The Rise and Fall of the American Empire* (London: Penguin Books, 2004); for a critical review see J. Leonhard and U. von Hirschhausen, "'New Imperialism' oder 'Liberal Empire'? Niall Fergusons Empire-Apologetik im Zeichen der 'Anglobalization,'" *Zeithistorische Forschungen. Studies in Contemporary History* 3 (2006), 121–28.

[7] See A. L. Stoler, C. McGranahan, P. C. Perdue, eds., *Imperial Formations* (Santa Fe: School for Advanced Research Press, 2007); J. Burbank and F. Cooper, *Empires in World History: Power and the Politics of Difference* (Princeton: Princeton University Press, 2010); J. Leonhard and U. von Hirschhausen, *Empires und Nationalstaaten im 19. Jahrhundert* (Göttingen: Vandenhoeck & Ruprecht, 2011); J. Leonhard and U. von Hirschhausen, "Historisierung und Globalisierung: Titel, Themen und Trends der neueren Empire-Forschung," *Neue Politische Literatur* 56 (2011), 389–404; J. Leonhard and U. von Hirschhausen, eds., *Comparing Empires: Encounters and Transfers in the Nineteenth and Early Twentieth Century* (Göttingen: Vandenhoeck & Ruprecht, 2012).

[8] J. Osterhammel, *Die Entzauberung Asiens. Europa und die asiatischen Reiche im 18. Jahrhundert* (Munich: C.H. Beck, 1998); J. Osterhammel, *Kolonialismus: Geschichte, Formen, Folgen* (Munich: C.H. Beck, 2010).

have pointed to the failure of many nationalist movements to gain widespread support for secessionism before and even during the first years of the First World War.[9]

Against this background, this article looks at the complex relation between multi-ethnic empires and nation-building from a comparative point of view, concentrating on moments of imperial crisis: the first and shorter part of the article focuses on some exemplary constellations of inner-imperial conflicts regarding national movements and processes of nation-building on the one hand and what may be called imperial conflict management before 1914 on the other: Which motives for resistance against imperial rule can be differentiated, and which forms did conflicts actually take? How successfully did imperial conflict-management develop in different crises? What does the analysis of such conflict situations reveal about the nature and structural character of the empires' integrative potentials and their limits? The second part of the article concentrates in more detail on the particular situation of the First World War: What did the ideal of a "nation in arms" mean in the concrete situation of multi-ethnic empires? How did the crisis of integration and loyalty affect the empires' stability during the First World War? By integrating four empires—the Habsburg Monarchy, Tsarist Russia, the Ottoman Empire, and the British Empire—this comparison includes West, East, and Southeast European examples with very different political and imperial traditions, and it moves beyond the classical separation between maritime and continental empires. The article operates from a bird's eye perspective and concentrates on a symptomatic, not a systematic comparison.

The Experience of Inner-Imperial Conflicts Before 1914

The experience of increasing international competition as well as rising nationalisms in the second half of the nineteenth century posed a particular challenge to all multi-ethnic empires under review. Yet the responses to particular conflict situations varied from case to case, and the following examples illustrate why it is difficult to speak of one uniform crisis of empires prior to and after 1900.

In the case of the Habsburg Monarchy the two conflicts over Hungary in 1848–49 and 1867 are particularly illustrative: The revolution of 1848 underlined the fact that Hungarian nationalism never succeeded in reconciling its aspirations for its own Magyar nation with other competing nationalities. Instead the Hungarian revolution turned into a series of aggressive ethnic exclusions against ethnic minorities which tried to tear themselves away. The imperial monarchy's military defeat of 1859–61 against Piedmont and France replaced the older connection between nationalism and revolution with that between nationalism and war, and Hungarians began to re-define

---

[9] P. Judson, *Guardians of the Nation: Activists on the Language Frontiers of Imperial Austria* (Cambridge, Mass.: Harvard University Press, 2006); L. Cole and D. Unowsky, eds., *The Limits of Loyalty: Imperial Symbolism, Popular Allegiances, and State Patriotism in the Late Habsburg Monarchy* (New York: Berghahn Books, 2007).

their revolutionary experience of 1848–49 as a war of independence. In contrast to 1848, the *Ausgleich* of 1867, which established the dual monarchy following yet another military defeat against Prussia in 1866, resulted in a new legal construction and constitutional framework. But it was connected to the revolution of 1848 in that it was based upon the fiction that the Habsburg monarch Franz Joseph in 1867 agreed to the Hungarian reform agenda of April 1848, thereby fusing two levels of historical time. On the other side and in contrast to their former efforts to demystify the imperial monarchy, Hungarian nationalists now used the coronation rites of 1867 as a symbol of the sovereign, recognizing the position of king of the Hungarians rather than that of a conquering emperor. However, the Hungarian nation in 1867 was not only represented in the Buda cathedral. It was also found among the urban crowds in Pest, thereby connecting and temporarily reconciling the crowd with the new imperial order—the same crowd which had been regarded as a revolutionary threat in 1848. In contrast to the military repression in 1848, the solution of 1867 was based on a combination of constitutional autonomy for the Hungarians and symbolic union through the very person of the emperor and king. However, the concessions made to the Magyar elites allowed them to assume a colonizing role with regard to the many ethnic minorities in Hungary. In consequence, these elites provoked resistance from other nationalities in Cisleithania, where for instance the Czechs criticized that there had been no equivalent to the *Ausgleich* for them. Although this fuelled anxieties of a pan-German dominance in the other part of the dual monarchy, these were still far from developing secessionist nation-building before 1914, but rather pointed to the necessity of enlarged autonomy.[10]

What Hungary had been to the Habsburg Monarchy, Poland was to the Tsarist Empire throughout the nineteenth century—a focal point of ever renewed conflicts within the empire. The two Polish uprisings of 1830–31 and 1863–64 became watersheds in imperial responses to secessionist nation-building, but there were also important differences: In 1831 when the Tsarist Empire was in a powerful position, the original policy of careful limitation of autonomy after 1815 could be replaced by the abolition of the constitution and by a drastic reduction of autonomous rights—although the revolt caused anxieties about the empire's military security under the conditions of serfdom. In stark contrast, the Polish uprising of 1863 took place after the Russian defeat in the Crimean War and against the background of the Great Reforms in the Tsarist Empire. This constellation made impossible any idea of a restoration of the autonomy of the Kingdom of Poland. Fuelled by Russian nationalist public opinion

---

[10] A. Freifeld, "Conflict and De-escalation—The Hungarian People and Imperial Politics from 1848–1849 to the '*Ausgleich*' of 1867," in *Empires*, eds. Leonhard and von Hirschhausen, 409–24; A. Freifeld, *Nationalism and the Crowd in Liberal Hungary, 1848–1914* (Baltimore: Johns Hopkins University Press, 2000); A. Freifeld, "Empress Elisabeth as Hungarian Queen: The Uses of Celebrity Monarchy," in *Limits*, eds. Cole and Unowsky, 138–61; L. Deme, *The Radical Left in the Hungarian Revolution of 1848* (Boulder, CO.: East European Monographs, 1976), 14–23; István Deák, *The Lawful Revolution, Louis Kossuth and the Hungarians, 1848–1849* (New York: Columbia University Press, 1979).

and the press, the 1860s witnessed the competition between two concepts of nation and nationality: Different from 1830–31, the Poles of 1863 wanted to foster a nation which would unite the nobility and the unprivileged classes, especially the peasants, whereas the Russian government now tried to impose a Polish identity from above by including concepts of loyalty to the dynasty and to a "Slavic unity." Furthermore, the Russian strategy focused on the Polish peasants and tried to alienate them from the Polish national movement by promising social and land reforms. After 1863, the struggle over Russification—especially regarding school policies—between the Polish movement and the Russian Empire provoked many local nationalisms, for instance in the Ukraine, Lithuania, and Belorussia, which further complicated the implementation of an all-encompassing Russian nation building. While the 1830 uprising reflected a conflict between a traditional empire with a traditional regional and noble elite, the conflict of the 1860s involved more and different groups of Polish society now confronted with a modernizing empire that referred to nationalism as an instrument of popular legitimization and mobilization. The new formula for imperial ideology "Orthodoxy—Autocracy—Nationality," coined by Count Sergei Semenovich Uvarov as the new minister of education, reflected this attempt to turn to a nationalist policy in order to legitimize tsarist rule and provide the means for the acculturation of borderland elites.[11]

Conflicts in the Ottoman Empire in the second half of the nineteenth century reflected a particular constellation characterized by reform policies initiated by state elites and secessionist nationalisms in many Southeast European parts of the empire. This constellation was made even more complicated by the international situation, the continuous threat of foreign intervention, and the competing powers of Habsburg and Russia which followed their own strategy to gain control over Ottoman territories as in the case of the Habsburg annexation of Bosnia in 1908 or Russian support for secessionist nation-building as in the case of Serbia—both contributing to the crisis in the Balkans prior to the summer of 1914. Traditionally, the Ottoman state had not interfered in its peripheries as long as a minimum of stability and loyalty was secured, so that ethnic conflicts could be contained. In the course of the so-called Tanzimat reforms of the nineteenth century—aiming at a combination of effective state control and a development of the state's infrastructural power—this policy came under increasing pressure, because Ottoman authorities were determined to install direct

---

[11] A. Miller and M. Dolbilov, "'The Damned Polish Question'—The Romanov Empire and the Polish Uprisings of 1830–1831 and 1863–1864," in *Empires*, eds. Leonhard and von Hirschhausen, 425–52; C. A. Whittaker, *The Origins of Modern Russian Education: An Intellectual Biography of Count Sergei Uvarov, 1786–1855* (DeKalb: Northern Illinois University Press, 1984); P. Wandycz, *The Lands of Partitioned Poland: 1795–1918* (Seattle: University of Washington Press, 1984), 155–79; F. Kagan, *The Military Reforms of Nicholas I: The Origins of the Modern Russian Army* (New York: Palgrave Macmillan, 1999), 209–41; A. Renner, *Russischer Nationalismus und Öffentlichkeit im Zarenreich* (Cologne: Böhlau, 2000); M. Dolbilov, "Russification and the Bureaucratic Mind in the Russian Empire's Northwestern Region in the 1860s," *Kritika: Explorations in Russian and Eurasian History* 2 (2004): 245–71.

control, for instance in the virtually autonomous mountain regions of Northern Albania.[12] But in order to integrate the Catholic tribes of the Albanian highlands into the Ottoman administrative and fiscal regime and to prevent a further destabilization of the region which could have provoked foreign intervention, the Ottoman authorities had to recur to their proven policy of cooptation of and bargaining with the local population. Refraining from enforced taxation and conscription reflected the constricted freedom of imperial action, but at the same time it contradicted the very idea of the Tanzimat ideology of civilization and rigid order. This clash between theory and practice, between wide ranging reform expectations and limited freedom of political action, called the whole fabric of the reform agenda into question. The combination of a reform-ideology that could not be implemented and at times even resulted in more ethnic conflicts proved to be much more fragile than the traditional praxis of flexible ethnic containment: The Tanzimat idea of a final order propagated by the Ottoman elite challenged the experience of imperial routine and led to new ethnic tensions, with which the authorities proved unable to deal. In the Ottoman case, reforms had thus provoked expectations of stronger imperial rule among the progressive parts of the imperial elite that could not be fulfilled in practice, as the secessionist movements in Southeastern Europe proved. In turn, this experience called into question the imperial elite's capability to deal with ethnic and religious diversity and thereby to guarantee the empire's existence in the face of mounting international pressure. The revolutionary upheaval of the Young Turkish military in 1908, the turn from inclusive Ottomanism to an exclusive notion of a Turkish nation, was a direct reaction to this constellation.[13]

In the nineteenth-century history of the British Empire, both the Indian Mutiny of 1857—a revolt of sepoys of the East India Company escalating into civilian rebellions in central India—and the South African War of the 1890s marked fundamental watersheds of Britain's imperial history.[14] Although, in contrast to 1848 or 1867 in the Habsburg Monarchy or the conflicts in the Ottoman Empire since the 1870s, they never questioned the empire's very existence, these were nevertheless critical moments leading to different responses of conflict management. These conflicts highlighted the structural differences between a conquered colony without a settler tradition and a former white settler colony: Whereas in the case of India the upheaval

---

[12] E. Rogan, *Frontiers of the State in the Late Ottoman Empire: Transjordan, 1850–1921* (Cambridge: Cambridge University Press, 1999), 3–5.

[13] M. Reinkowski, "The *Imperial Idea* and *Realpolitik*—Reform Policy and Nationalism in the Ottoman Empire," in *Empires*, eds. Leonhard and von Hirschhausen, 453–71; R. H. Davison, "Nationalism as an Ottoman Problem and the Ottoman Response," in *Nationalism in a Non-National State*, eds. W. Haddad and W. Ochsenwald (Columbus: Ohio University Press, 1977), 25–56; G. Heer, *Territorialentwicklung und Grenzfragen von Montenegro in der Zeit seiner Staatswerdung, 1830–1887* (Bern: Peter Lang, 1981).

[14] J. Leonhard, "Pax Britannica and Imperial Conflict Strategies—The Indian Uprising 1857/58 and the South African War in Comparison," in *Empires*, eds. Leonhard and von Hirschhausen, 393–400.

was no consequence of secessionist nation-building, the Boers in South Africa aimed at an independent republic. In India the crisis led to a shift from an older ideal of inclusive Europeanization, applied by the proponents of the East India Company before 1857–58, to a mixture of economic modernization, a return to the fiscal military state and an invented imperial monarchy, which highlighted the notions of positive imperial civilization and negative oriental barbarism. This constellation postponed rather than solved conflicts, and it undermined Indian elites' trust in Britain's willingness to apply substantial reforms to India. The world of the invented monarchical *durbars*— royal gatherings with Indian princes—reflected a British image of India that could no longer be reconciled with the reality of politically and socially self-conscious Indian middle classes. In time this fostered a new kind of Indian nationalism.[15]

In contrast, the South African War of 1899 was a conflict over secessionist nation-building. As such, it attracted global attention and was intensely monitored not only by Irish advocates of home rule and independence, but also by contemporaries in Poland and Finland. The war took place in front of a new international audience of imperial crisis, challenging the notion of geographically distant "small wars" which had characterized Britain's imperial conflict management so far.[16] The conflict in South Africa ended with a transfer of power to the dominant white elite with the Dominion-model as a firm basis to secure British rule in the area, but at the cost of excluding native Africans from any participation. Thus, the Dominion-model also revealed the empire's structural weakness: the increasing independence of Dominions from London would sooner or later become a model for all parts of the British Empire. In consequence, Britain came under pressure to expand into new territories or to control others in order to keep them as safe bases. In both cases, however, military success was not accompanied by decisive and carefully planned integration strategies. Instead, military violence was followed by piecemeal solutions which tended to postpone major issues in order to solve others. This became ever more obvious in the course of the First World War, when many of these problems resurfaced.[17]

---

[15] T. R. Metcalf, *The Aftermath of Revolt: India, 1857–1870* (Princeton: Princeton University Press, 1964); V. Nünning, "'Das jeder seine Pflicht thue.' Die Bedeutung der Indian Mutiny für das nationale britische Selbstverständnis," *Archiv für Kulturgeschichte* 78 (1996): 363–91; P. Burroughs, "Defence and Imperial Disunity," in *The Oxford History of the British Empire, vol. 3: The Nineteenth Century*, ed. A. Porter (Oxford: Oxford University Press, 1999), 320–45; D. A. Washbrook, "India 1818–1860: The Two Faces of Colonialism," in *History*, vol. 3, ed. Porter, 395–421; G. Chakravaty, *The Indian Mutiny and the British Imagination* (Cambridge: Cambridge University Press, 2005), 1–18; Leonhard and von Hirschhausen, *Empires und Nationalstaaten*, 23–30.

[16] C. E. Callwell, *Small Wars. A Tactical Textbook for Imperial Soldiers*, 2nd ed. (London: HMSO, 1899).

[17] A. Porter, "The South African War (1899–1902): Context and Motive Reconsidered," *Journal of African History* 31, no. 1 (1990): 43–57; A. Porter, "The South African War and Imperial Britain: A Question of Significance?," in *Writing a Wider War: Rethinking Gender, Race, and Identity in the South African War, 1899–1902*, eds. G. Cuthbertson, A. M. Grundlingh, and M. L. Suttie

The empires' crises before 1914 were as complex as the empires' structures. On the one hand, new measures of integration were necessary in order to balance the centrifugal forces of national movements in imperial contexts, and different strategies to reconcile imperial sovereignty with demands for autonomy were conceived. On the other hand, many responses and attempts to manage inner-imperial crises led to new problems that reduced the empires' freedom of political action. What becomes obvious from the comparison is that these were, in varying degrees, "empires in transition."[18] More traditional instruments of integration—such as monarchy and dynasties and religion—were re-invented and re-formulated, as the Habsburg and the British cases illustrated. In the Ottoman Empire, Ottomanism as an inclusive, reform-oriented imperial ideology developed. Contrary to many contemporary expectations, new constitutional institutions such as parliaments—after 1905 in Russia and after 1908 in the Ottoman Empire—did not have an integrative effect but could turn into a forum of competing visions of the empire and competing nationalisms, as would be the case with the Vienna parliament, the Reichsrat, in 1917. By increasingly applying nationalizing methods and turning, as in the Russian and Ottoman case, to core nationalisms as a means of stabilization, the traditional *realpolitik* toward ethnic plurality changed significantly.[19]

The Experience of the First World War and the Limits of Imperial Loyalty

The suggestive image of continental empires as prisons of nationalities that had such prominence in twentieth-century historiography never reflected the complex reality before 1914. Rather, this image was itself in many ways the result of war experiences and war propaganda after August 1914. As the examples of new constitutions and forms of state citizenship, of general conscription, national banks, and invented monarchies

---

(Athens, OH: Ohio University Press, 2002), 287–302; D. J. Denon, "Participation in the 'Boer War': People's War, People's Non-War, or Non-People's War," in *War and Society in Africa: Ten Studies*, ed. A. B. Ogot (London: Frank Cass, 1992), 109–22; M. Legassick, "British Hegemony and the Origins of Segregation in South Africa, 1901–14," in *Segregation and Apartheid in Twentieth-Century South Africa*, eds. W. Beinart and S. Dubow (London: Routledge, 1995), 43–60; K. Wilson, "The Boer War in the Context of Britain's Imperial Problems," in *The International Impact of the Boer War*, ed. Keith Wilson (Chesham: Acumen Publishing, 2001), 158–77; D. Omissi and A. Thompson, eds., *The Impact of the South African War* (Basingstoke: Palgrave Macmillan, 2002).

[18] Alexei Miller, *The Romanov Empire and Nationalism: Essays in the Methodology of Historical Research* (Budapest: Central European University Press, 2008), 27–28.

[19] J. Leonhard, "Wie legitimieren sich multiethnische Empires im langen 19. Jahrhundert?" in *Die Legitimation von Imperien. Strategien und Motive im 19. und 20. Jahrhundert*, eds. H. Münkler and E. M. Hausteiner (Frankfurt: Campus Verlag, 2012), 70–93; J. Leonhard, "Imperial Projections and Piecemeal Realities: Multiethnic Empires and the Experience of Failure in the Nineteenth Century," in *Helpless Imperialists: Imperial Failure, Fear and Radicalization*, eds. M. Reinkowski and G. Thum (Göttingen: Vandenhoeck & Ruprecht, 2012), 21–46.

show, elites in many empires had started to copy and import, at least selectively, the model of the homogenizing nation-state in the course of the second half of the nineteenth century. Similarly, infrastructure projects and new means of categorization and visualization such as the census and maps as well as new concepts of Russification, Magyarization, pan-Germanization, and Turkification shaped the perception of the progressive "nationalization" of these empires. Yet in contrast to these nationalizing features, a relative flexibility in dealing with multiethnic diversity remained a prime characteristic and highlighted the continuous meaning of composite state structures. Although under mounting pressure, imperial routines, based on broad experiences in responding to spatial, legal, ethnic, and religious diversity, were never completely replaced before 1914. Without idealizing the ethnic, religious, and social multiplicities in cities such as Czernowitz, Riga, or Thessaloniki, it was never inevitable that such multilayered structures were doomed to violent disintegration. In Riga, the later tensions and conflicts between German, Russians, Latvians, and Jews had been successfully defused over a long period of the later half of the nineteenth century.[20] With the rise of the national paradigm and its transformation into a collective phenomenon, which called for an identity of state and nation in order to survive future wars, however, they came under increasing pressure. The ideal of a whole nation in arms and the concept of coherent conscript armies were direct consequences of this new constellation, which proved particularly challenging in the ethnically mixed regions of Central, Eastern, and Southeastern Europe, since it questioned the traditional dynastic and religious-confessional bases of imperial sovereignty and legitimacy. It was no accident that the critical war experiences of all empires—1899 for the British, 1905 for the Tsarist Empire, and the period after 1908 for the Ottoman Empire—were widely discussed and that questions about the empires' preparedness for a future war were often used to challenge their legitimacy in a world of apparently successful nation-states.

On the other hand, however, we must not overstate the antagonism between empires and nation-states prior to 1914. In practice, a number of obvious overlaps between the two developed: Besides nationalizing empires which copied elements of the nation-states there were also imperializing nation-states, which focused on colonial expansion in order to strengthen their legitimacy as political actors in Europe and beyond, such as in the cases of France, Germany, Italy, Belgium, or the Netherlands. In some respects, all European states and certainly the United States and Japan before 1914 operated on an imperial agenda.[21]

---

[20] U. von Hirschhausen, *Die Grenzen der Gemeinsamkeit: Deutsche, Letten, Russen und Juden in Riga 1860–1914* (Göttingen: Vandenhoeck & Ruprecht, 2006).

[21] S. Conrad and J. Osterhammel, eds., *Das Kaiserreich transnational: Deutschland in der Welt 1871–1914* (Göttingen: Vandenhoeck & Ruprecht, 2004); J. Osterhammel, "Europamodelle und imperiale Kontexte," *Journal of Modern European History* 2, no. 2 (2004): 157–81; J. Osterhammel, *Die Verwandlung der Welt: Eine Geschichte des 19. Jahrhunderts* (Munich: C.H. Beck, 2009), 565–672; C. A. Bayly, *Die Geburt der modernen Welt: Eine Globalgeschichte 1780–1914* (Frankfurt: Campus Verlag, 2006), 248–300.

Against this background, alternatives to historical empires were widely discussed before 1914, from the idea of an imperial federation as a basis for the British Empire and the numerous plans to reform the Habsburg Monarchy with its two states and ten historic peoples to the concept of a Turkish nation as the Ottoman Empire's core. The fact that many of these concepts were not put into practice often had little to do with secessionist nationalisms. For example only a small minority of Czechs and Slavs really thought of national independence in 1914, and still in 1918 the Austrian Socialist Karl Renner favored a Habsburg "state of nationalities, in order to provide an example for mankind's future national order."[22] In many cases, secessionist nation building only resulted from the dynamism of the First World War itself—although it determined regional conflicts in the Balkans, it was less a cause of the Great War than a consequence of it: In all societies, political and military leaders used national arguments in order to win allies or to stabilize the home front, including the promise of establishing independent nation-states after the war. Besides provoking expectations of social and political participation, the war catalyzed competing national expectations, thus creating the context for an escalation of rising expectations with revolutionary consequences after 1916–17. This basic factor was behind British and American support for Tomás Masaryk's campaigns in exile, German help for Ukrainian and Finnish nationalists, the German and Austrian promise of a Polish nation-state, as well as the British and French promises for Arab and Palestinian independence movements, fuelled by British fear of an Ottoman-led "jihad" as an anti-colonial war against the British in India.[23]

According to the war theories developed since the 1860s and 1870s and widely read in all European capitals prior to 1914, a war fought in the name of the whole nation and fought by a whole nation in arms, provoking new expectations of political and social participation, would directly challenge the traditional empires with their multi-ethnic populations. The close relation between war and nation-building was a legacy of all European wars since 1792, and the ideal of a nation in arms was much discussed in the imperial capitals of London, Vienna, St. Petersburg, and Istanbul before 1914.[24] It was based on the new ideal of the politically participating citizen as the natural defender of the fatherland, combining with connotations of citizenship and political participation. The connection between franchise and conscription was the most obvious example. The First World War with its hitherto unknown numbers of victims challenged these concepts of loyal nations in arms, and for the empires this challenge was even more radical: Would the multi-ethnic empires, with their traditional or newly invented bonds and languages of loyalty, be strong enough to survive a totalized war? What did the ideal of a

---

[22] Quoted in: M. Mazower, *Dark Continent: Europe's Twentieth Century* (New York: Vintage Books, 1999), 46.

[23] Mazower, *Continent*, passim.

[24] J. Leonhard and U. von Hirschhausen, eds., *Multi-Ethnic Empires and the Military: Conscription in Europe between Integration and Desintegration, 1860–1918*, Journal of Modern European History 5, no. 2 (Munich, 2007).

"nation in arms" mean for multiethnic empires, and how did the crisis of integration and loyalty affect the empires' stability during the First World War?

Mass mobilization, militarization of societies, and heightened expectations of political participation transformed traditional notions of national wars into the distinct war nationalisms that became characteristic of all societies between 1914 and 1918. Given the enormous number of casualties, the war turned into a test of loyalty on all levels, and state wars could turn into ethnic warfare, as the multi-ethnic zones of war and occupation in Eastern and Southeastern Europe would soon demonstrate. With the crisis of traditional languages of monarchical, dynastic, or religious loyalty, the war became a plebiscite over imperial legitimacy, further complicated by external pressures from the counter-models of Wilson's Fourteen Points and Lenin's program after 1917. Against this general background, the comparison between the four empires at war helps us to better understand the crisis of the various empires' legitimacy not just by pointing to the conventional combination of war, revolution, and imperial collapse between 1917 and 1918 but by differentiating a spectrum of experiences of nation-building in imperial contexts.[25]

Prior to 1914, many contemporaries had feared an imminent military collapse of the Habsburg Monarchy in a major European war. Its multiethnic army seemed particularly badly prepared for the challenges of large-scale warfare on multiple military fronts.[26] Yet despite these predictions, the Habsburg Monarchy survived the first tests of the war, and although nationalist propaganda and ethnically motivated distrust contributed to a latent destabilization and erosion, for instance among the Germans vis à vis the Czechs and vice versa, traditional bonds of loyalty focusing on the person of the monarch and the army as integrative institutions functioned for quite a long time. Recent research has underlined that the monarchy's military, despite its multi-ethnic character, military defeats, and imminent supply crises, was not more affected by mutinies and desertions than other armies before 1916–17. The image of unreliable Czech deserters had much to do with narratives arguing from the point of view of the war's outcome when trying to identify early signs of secessionist nation-building during the war.[27]

---

[25] A. Roshwald, *Ethnic Nationalism and the Fall of Empires: Central Europe, Russia and the Middle East, 1914–1923* (London: Routledge, 2001).

[26] L. E. Miller, *Politics, the Nationality Problem, and the Habsburg Army 1848–1914* (Ann Arbor: University of Michigan Press, 1992), 305–07; C. Hämmerle, "Ein gescheitertes Experiment? Die Allgemeine Wehrpflicht in der multiethnischen Armee der Habsburgermonarchie," *Journal of Modern European History* 5, no. 2 (2007): 222–43.

[27] M. Zückert, "Imperial War in the Age of Nationalism—The Habsburg Monarchy and the First World War," in *Empires*, eds. Leonhard and von Hirschhausen, 500–17; M. Zückert, *Zwischen Nationsidee und staatlicher Realität. Die tschechoslowakische Armee und ihre Nationalitätenpolitik 1918–1938* (Munich: Oldenbourg, 2006); D. Strigl, "Schneidige Husaren, brave Bosniaken, feige Tschechen: Nationale Mythen und Stereotypen in der k.u.k. Armee," in *Zentren, Peripherien und kollektive Identitäten in Österreich-Ungarn*, eds. E. Hárs et al. (Tübingen: Francke, 2006), 129–43; R. Lein, *Pflichterfüllung oder Hochverrat?: Die tschechischen Soldaten Österreich-Ungarns im Ersten Weltkrieg* (Vienna: Lit Verlag, 2011).

National belonging as an isolated factor did not explain the Habsburg Monarchy's ultimate disintegration, neither at the beginning nor in the last phase of the war. However, in the context of intensifying supply crises and military defeats after the summer of 1916, a conversion of conflicts took place: Social, economic, and political conflicts became increasingly ethnicized. An erosion of trust resulted when these conflicts made visible the monarchy's inability to protect the population and highlighted the empire's fragile structure and the fundamental faultlines within the monarchy, especially between the two parts of the dual monarchy: Whereas in Cisleithania symbolic acts of national belonging by Slavic soldiers or civilians were violently suppressed by the authorities, and the Germans' collective obsession with an apparent inner enemy led to a climate of increasing mistrust, identification with the nationally defined state in Hungary was openly supported. Yet at the same time, the war radicalized the suppression of national minorities in Hungary. The imperial test of war only began to question the empire's existence when a particular combination of a supply crisis, military defeats, and general war-weariness questioned the monarchy's ability to fulfill its traditional functions. Only then did social and economic conflicts become ethnicized.[28] On another level, the collapse of economic, social, and administrative structures after 1916–17 was also the result of eroding languages of loyalty, as the example of the imperial monarchy demonstrated: The Habsburg Emperor Franz Joseph had been regarded as an authentic symbol of imperial unity before the war, but neither he nor his successor Karl were monarchs fit for war and able to defend their position vis-à-vis the army high command and the German military. Traditional imperial loyalty could be secured in peacetime, but not in a war with radically new experiences of loss and conflicts over the equal distribution of the unexpected costs of war.[29]

In the Tsarist Empire, the army was less affected by the problems of multi-ethnic structure than by the high number of desertions as a response to serious mismanagement of supply and catastrophic military decisions resulting in exceptionally high numbers of soldiers killed or taken prisoner. Together with the experience of military defeats and a widening gulf between peasant soldiers and the officer elite,

---

[28] M. Healy, *Vienna and the Fall of the Habsburg Empire: Total War and Everyday Life in World War I* (Cambridge: Cambridge University Press, 2004).

[29] M. Cornwall, "Morale and Patriotism in the Austro-Hungarian Army, 1914–1918," in *State, Society and Mobilization in Europe during the First World War*, ed. J. Horne (Cambridge: Cambridge University Press, 1997), 173–91; M. Cornwall, *The Undermining of Austria-Hungary: The Battle for Hearts and Minds* (Basingstoke: Palgrave Macmillan, 2000); M. Cornwall, "Auflösung und Niederlage—Die österreichisch-ungarische Revolution," in *Die letzten Jahre der Donaumonarchie. Der erste Vielvölkerstaat im Europa des frühen 20. Jahrhunderts*, ed. M. Cornwall (Essen: Magnus Verlag, 2004), 174–201; Z. Kárník, "Die Idee der Donaumonarchie und das Verhältnis der tschechischen Parteien zum Deutschen Reich," in *Der Erste Weltkrieg und die Beziehungen zwischen Tschechen, Slowaken und Deutschen*, eds. H. Mommsen et al. (Essen: Klartext Verlag, 2001), 15–46.

this had a devastating effect on the army's morale.[30] Furthermore, the outbreak of war in August 1914 and the course of the war in Russia were accompanied not only by the development of the national movements in the periphery, but also by a particular kind of Russian core nationalism. Aggressive war nationalism directed against national and religious minorities such as Germans, Jews, and Poles became closely connected to the changing war economy and conflicts revolving around the distribution of the costs of war. Russian core nationalism relied on a broad social base and soon began questioning the domestic and international status quo. Contrary to the cosmopolitan model of imperial modernization, with which the tsarist regime had entered the war in 1914, state authorities and elites soon embraced and encouraged Russian core nationalism. This strategy resulted in the isolation of "enemy" populations in Russian society, their deportation, and confiscation of their private properties. This practice of radical war nationalism, including purges and pogroms against those regarded as internal enemies, stood in clear contrast to the mainly cultural notions of Russification that had been developed and employed before 1914. The war thus generated a new understanding of the imperial state, no longer comprising a single entity but representing a conglomerate of antagonistic and competing nationalities that in the eyes of Russian contemporaries necessitated and justified radical means of exclusion. In this context, more traditional means of imperial assimilation were replaced by mobilization, segregation, and punishment of distinct national groups. An obvious line of continuity between the practice of Russian war nationalism and future policies of the Soviet regime became visible.[31]

The Ottoman Empire's experience of the First World War was characterized by a particular combination of demographic engineering, military violence, and imperial disintegration.[32] Against the background of earlier experiences of foreign inter-

---

[30] J. Sanborn, "The Mobilization of 1914 and the Question of the Russian Nation: A Reexamination," *Slavic Review* 59, no. 2 (2000): 267–89; D. Beyrau and P. P. Shcherbinin, "Alles für die Front: Russland im Krieg 1914–1922," in *Durchhalten! Krieg und Gesellschaft im Vergleich 1914–1918*, eds. A. Bauerkämper and Elise Julien (Göttingen: Vandenhoeck & Ruprecht, 2011), 151–77.

[31] E. Lohr, "Politics, Economics and Minorities—Core Nationalism in the Russian Empire at War," in *Empires*, eds. Leonhard and von Hirschhausen, 518–29; E. Lohr, *Nationalizing the Russian Empire: The Campaign against Enemy Aliens during World War I* (Cambridge, Mass.: Harvard University Press, 2003); E. Lohr, "Russian Economic Nationalism during the First World War: Moscow Merchants and Commercial Diasporas," *Nationalities Papers* 31, no. 4 (2003): 471–84; E. Lohr, "Patriotic Violence and the State: The Moscow Riots of 1915," *Kritika. Explorations in Russian and Eurasian History* 4, no. 3 (2003): 607–26; L. Siegelbaum, *The Politics of Industrial Mobilization in Russia, 1914–1917* (New York: St. Martin's Press, 1983); H. Rogger, "Conclusion and Overview," in *Pogroms: Anti-Jewish Violence in Modern Russian History*, eds. J. D. Klier and S. Lambroza (Cambridge: Cambridge University Press, 1992), 314–71.

[32] E.-J. Zürcher, "Demographic Engineering, State-Building and the Army—The Ottoman Empire and the First World War," in *Empires*, eds. Leonhard and von Hirschhausen, 530–44; E.-J. Zürcher, "The Ottoman Conscription System in Theory and Practice, 1844–1918," *International Review of Social History* 43, no. 3 (1998): 437–49; E.-J. Zürcher, "Young Turks, Ottoman

ventions, the Young Turk military leadership feared that neutrality could provoke yet another intervention, ultimately leading to the empire being carved up by the victors. From the perspective of the Young Turkish military elite, the war brought about more freedom of action, especially once supported by the German military. The war radicalized processes of forced migration and expulsion of minorities which had been under way since the later nineteenth century. It served as a means to replace provinces that had been lost before 1914, as well as to replace the non-Muslim bourgeoisie, especially Christian and Jewish merchants which had hitherto dominated many sectors of the economy. The practice of segregation, deportation, and ultimately genocidal violence that ensued was also derived from the ideal of a national economy dominated by Muslims. Some of these mechanisms were very similar to the Russian war nationalism. Under the pressure of military defeats on the Russian front, traditional experiences with forced migrations transformed into aggressive demographic engineering, ethnic cleansing, and extermination—not just as a result of neglect, but by the systematic and intended combination of deportation and massacres. The suspicion of national disloyalty, coupled with connotations of religious otherness, was directed against particular minorities: from questioning the loyalty of Armenians and other Christian communities, to disarming Armenian soldiers in the Ottoman army and putting them into labor battalions, to pogroms against Christian villages and piecemeal deportations of Armenians in the rear of the front. This process intensified when Armenians were accused of joining forces with the advancing Russian army, leading the Young Turk government to decide in favor of large-scale deportations of the Armenian population of Anatolia to Syria and northern Mesopotamia.[33]

Although such forced migrations through deportations had been part of a traditional Ottoman policy to generate loyalty and stability, the deportations of 1915 were without precedent, not least because they were accompanied with systematic massacres. In contrast to the situation in Russia, these violent measures were not primarily justified by linguistic or ethnic categories, but by religious criteria which in the Ottoman context had become the primary marker in the previous decades. The experience of the war not only radicalized this concept of exclusion but it led to something new: The Armenian genocide showed a transformation from state war to systematic ethnic warfare. Although the Young Turkish elite did not succeed in making the army

Muslims and Turkish Nationalists: Identity Politics 1908–1938," in *Ottoman Past and Today's Turkey*, ed. K. H. Karpat (Leiden: Brill, 2000), 150–79; A. G. Altinay, *The Myth of the Military Nation: Militarism, Gender, and Education in Turkey* (London: Palgrave Macmillan, 2004); H. N. Akmese, *The Birth of Modern Turkey. The Ottoman Military and the March to World War I* (London: I.B. Taurus, 2005); M. Aksakal, *The Ottoman Road to War in 1914. The Ottoman Empire and the First World War* (Cambridge: Cambridge University Press, 2008).
[33] J. McCarthy, *Death and Exile: The Ethnic Cleansing of Ottoman Muslims 1821–1922* (Princeton: Princeton University Press, 1995); E.-J. Zürcher, "Ottoman Labor Battalions in World War I," in *Der Völkermord an den Armeniern und die Shoah. The Armenian genocide and the Shoah*, eds. H.-L. Kieser and D. J. Schaller (Zürich: Chronos, 2002), 187–96; T. Akçam, *A Shameful Act: The Armenian Genocide and the Question of Turkish Responsibility* (New York: Metropolitan Books, 2006).

a truly Ottoman nation in arms copying the example of other European nation-states, the army did become the institutional and symbolic nucleus of the Turkish Republic as a nation-state, especially after the successful revision of the immediate post-war order by the Lausanne Treaty of 1923.

In the case of the British Empire, the war did not lead to any disintegration, although the Irish Uprising of Easter 1916 was a moment of serious crisis. More important, however, was the peacemeal transformation of the empire's structure and of hierarchies in the relation between Britain and her empire. In India, which contributed more than a million soldiers and laborers to the war theatres of France, Mesopotamia, East Africa, and the Mediterranean, many contemporary observers expected a different status as the result of these war contributions, which were at least comparable with those of white dominions such as Canada or Australia. Yet the situation in India was even more complicated: Despite opposition against British colonial rule, the outbreak of war at first provoked a wave of inter-imperial solidarity, not only in the empire's white dominions, but also in India where the annual Indian Congress was poorly attended. Indian war contributions became vital for Britain's European and global position.[34] In the course of the war, however, the difference between Indian soldiers fighting for the empire and the Indian national movement turning against British imperial rule became ever more obvious. The result was a dual marginalization of Indian soldiers: first by the Indian national movement, and second by British war narratives. For India, the experience of the First World War became ever more closely connected with anti-colonial resistance, so that mass conscription and middle-class support for the war went hand in hand with nationwide home rule agitation and increasingly aggressive demands for self-government. A process which had already become obvious during the South African War of 1899 was intensified: In order to defend her European and global position, Britain depended more than ever on the empire's war contributions. Yet this constellation would also lead to a changing balance between London and the different parts of the British Empire. Imperial war contributions underlined the need for representation or autonomy according to the Dominion-model or even independence. In that respect, the Irish Easter Uprising of 1916 and the Indian Amritsar massacre of 1919 both reflected the limits of imperial loyalty.[35]

---

[34] J. Greenhut, "The Imperial Reserve: The Indian Corps on the Western Front, 1914–15," *The Journal of Imperial and Commonwealth History* 12, no. 1 (1983): 54–73; R. Visram, "The First World War and the Indian Soldiers," *Indo-British Review. A Journal of History* 16, no. 2 (1989): 17–26; G. M. Jack, "The Indian Army on the Western Front, 1914–15: A Portrait of Collaboration," *War in History* 13 (2006): 329–62.

[35] Santanu Das, "Heart and Soul with Britain? India, Empire and the Great War," in *Empires*, eds. Leonhard and von Hirschhausen, 479–99; D. Omissi, ed., *Indian Voices of the Great War: Soldiers' Letters, 1914–1918* (Basingstoke: Palgrave Macmillan, 1999). U. N. Chakravorty, *Indian Nationalism and the First World War (1914–1918)* (Calcutta: Progressive Publishers, 1997); K. Jeffery, *Ireland and the Great War* (Cambridge: Cambridge University Press, 2000).

Conclusion: Some General Observations and Hypotheses

(1) This article has analyzed the problem of multi-ethnic empires and nation-building in a period of rising nationalisms and increased international competition since the second half of the nineteenth century. Its main goal has been to overcome the antagonistic narrative, still dominant in historiography, which explains the apparently inevitable decline and fall of empires and their disintegration in the course of the First World War in terms of rising nationalisms and nation-building processes. In contrast to this premise, this article argues in favor of focusing on different traditions and transformations of imperial conflict management prior to 1914 and on different war dynamics and their consequences between 1914 and 1918.

(2) The short and symptomatic overview of inner-imperial conflicts underlines how all four empires experienced changes in the character of their inner conflicts and in the means of responding to them. Against this background the conflicts of the later nineteenth century—the *Ausgleich* of 1867, the second Polish uprising of 1863, the conflicts in the Ottoman Empire since the 1870s, and the South African War as a watershed in the history of the British Empire—stood under a dual influence: the dominant model of a homogenous nation-state, indigenous national movements and international competition on the one hand, and the relative loss of conventional and traditional imperial routines in dealing with ethnic, legal, and religious diversity on the other. New actors and media—from national movements and the urban masses to the penny press—reduced the flexibility of imperial elites' responses. A widening gap between projections of imperial rule—often developed with reference to the order of a well-regulated nation-state which made traditional empires "nationalizing empires" towards the end of the nineteenth century—and the practical need for piecemeal bargaining or violent forms of repression was the consequence. Yet despite many contemporaries' critical view of the empires, the almost complete dissolution of the continental empires as a result of a great war was far from inevitable. Without idealizing the realities of multi-ethnic empires before 1914, secessionist nation-building was not a general trend leaving no other alternative.

(3) Against this background, the First World War as an experience of total warfare on the military and home fronts put the empires' military efficiency, mass loyalty, political mobilization, and social coherence to the test. The comparison highlights the particular dynamism and distinct logic of war constellations. These went far beyond any pre-war anticipations, which again helps to challenge the historiographical premises of inevitability. From that perspective, what is surprising is rather how long the empires survived under war conditions. The continental empires were faced with particular challenges that could, under specific, but not inevitable constellations, threaten their existence. Three factors proved to be important in this respect: First, in order to destabilize and ultimately destroy enemy empires, the use of secessionist nation-building

as a means of totalized warfare and the competing promises of new nation-states became common. Second, a conversion of conflicts took place: Against the background of mounting supply crises, hunger, and the transformation of war societies through the realities of war economies, many social, economic, and political conflicts became increasingly ethnicized, and military defeats were explained in terms of disloyal behavior of particular ethnic groups. This in turn fuelled the experience of imperial failure and the expectation that only solution to the inner crisis was the creation of separate nation-states. Third, strong war nationalisms developed, which transformed notions of cultural Turkification, Russification, pan-Germanization, and Magyarization, as they had characterized the "empires in transition" before 1914, into a practice of political and social exclusion, in turn provoking counter movements. The British position in the European war was, in contrast, rather strengthened by imperial war contributions. Still, it led to a changing balance between Britain and the different parts of her empire. From that perspective, the First World War continued a process which had already been obvious during the South African War: Confronted with the reality of a global war, Britain depended more and more on the empire, thus reversing the imagined relation between the colonizing center and colonized peripheries.

(4) Contrary to contemporary expectations, the Habsburg multi-ethnic conscript army did not disintegrate, whereas core nationalisms in both Russia and in the Ottoman Empire turned to aggressive practices of exclusion and demographic engineering. Sometimes the war served as a catalyst, and not a primary cause, for nationalistic exclusions which had started earlier, as the radicalization of forced migration in the Ottoman Empire demonstrated. In the context of war—and this seems to be elementary to understand nation-building in imperial contexts during the war—ethnicity was not an isolated factor, causing imperial disintegration, especially not if one looks at the soldiers' and the home fronts' experiences. Dynamic and radicalized core nationalisms, as in the Ottoman and Russian Empires, could have a strongly disintegrative effect when they clashed with national movements in the peripheries. The examples prove that the various combinations of military successes and failures, supply crises, war-weariness, and the erosion of traditional languages of loyalty allowed the ethnicization of political, social, and economic conflicts within imperial societies. This constellation, which was far from obvious in the summer of 1914, but became an everyday reality from 1916–17 onwards, challenged the empires' ability to deal with diversity and balance multiple loyalties in a totalized war.

Empires and Their Core Territories on the Eve of 1914: A Comment

DOMINIC LIEVEN

Polities calling themselves empires are many and various. That remains true even if one confines oneself to European empires of the nineteenth and early twentieth centuries. There was, for example, in this period an obvious difference between the dynastic land empires of Eastern Europe and the West European mostly transoceanic empires in which sovereignty belonged in principle to a distinct metropolitan nation and its parliamentary representatives. Nations and national identities also exist in many shapes and sizes. It is therefore difficult to come up with clear and useful generalizations about the relationship between the European empires of that day and nationalism in their core territories.

Amidst the confusion, it is perhaps useful to remember some fundamental points about empires, politics, and power. Great power is the core and essence of empire but not all Great Powers are empires. Some of them are nations. So empire and nation can share key similarities, can even indeed overlap. In some key respects, however, "empire" and "nation" are based on different and even often contradictory principles, the most fundamental of which is that the nation embodies the principle of popular sovereignty which most historical empires denied. Empires, however, are very often diverse and hybrid polities, some parts of which may be much closer to being nations than others. To flourish, any polity needs to reflect the dominant interests, capabilities, and values of the society it governs. But it also needs to be able to surmount the external challenges which confront it in the international arena. By the early twentieth century, in most of Europe the nation appeared most readily to "fit" domestic socio-economic and cultural realities but the realm of international relations was dominated by empires. This was a key dilemma of statesmen at the turn of the twentieth century and helps to explain why some major polities of that era appear to be hybrid imperial nations or national empires.

Today we live in the second era of Anglophone, liberal globalization. Just as American power buttresses our era, so British power was the main political framework for the first era of liberal globalization, which lasted from the second quarter of the nineteenth century until 1914, or in certain respects until 1929. Globalization and British global power encompassed more than the British Empire but the empire was crucial to their survival. As the world's largest and richest empire, it was a source of emulation and envy. Both the empire and British global power depended on the peculiar nature of European geopolitics. Unlike in East Asia or the western hemisphere, where a single hegemon often dominated an entire region, in Europe since the mid eighteenth century a rough balance of power existed between a number of polities. After 1815, Britain was by some margin the most powerful of the European states but it never attempted to achieve hegemony in Europe. Instead it threw its weight against any continental country which appeared most powerful, and in particular seemed to be a potential hegemon. By so doing it ensured the security of the British islands without itself usually having to make a major military or financial commitment in Europe. That was a key reason not just why Victorian-era Britain was able to maintain worldwide predominance but also why it could do so, by the standards of most empires in history, at a very small price in blood and treasure. The continental powers often resented this British grand strategy but each of them feared a European hegemon more than they disliked British domination of the maritime and colonial world.[1]

As Neil Evans notes, contemporary British observers were at pains to stress that their empire was very different to most empires of the past. If they nevertheless used the term "empire" it was because they could find no other more appropriate word to sum up the totality of British power and territory. Over the centuries there were really two overseas cores of the British Empire: one was the white and mostly Anglophone self-governing colonies, the other was India. The former mattered most in the eighteenth century and the latter in the nineteenth but by 1900 many British politicians and intellectuals believed that in the coming century the so-called white Dominions would once again regain their pre-eminence. That was partly because of the rapid growth in their economies and populations. But it was above all because, as John Seeley put it, the Dominions were potentially part of a broader worldwide British nation and only empires which were rooted in a single over-arching national identity could be secure in the long run.[2]

Of the many territories possessed by the British crown, only India was formally speaking an empire ruled over by an emperor. The adoption of the imperial title in 1876 both reflected and established international fashion. In this era, empire conferred status on the people who ruled and possessed it. In the last quarter of the nineteenth century it appeared to be the wave of the future. One-fifth of the world's land surface

---

[1] John Darwin provides an excellent analysis of the geopolitical basis of British imperial power: John Darwin, *The Empire Project: The Rise and Fall of the British World-System 1830–1970* (Cambridge: Cambridge University Press, 2009).
[2] J.R. Seeley, *The Expansion of England* (London: Macmillan, 1885).

changed hands between 1870 and 1913. For many British people, empire had traditionally conveyed the whiff of despotism but they swallowed whatever doubts they possessed by stressing their own empire's unique civilizing mission. Once again, this is a
very common imperial theme and one noted for their specific empire by many of the
contributors to this book. To a certain extent British rule in India could be equated
with older patterns and models of imperial rule. This was a territorial empire inhabited
overwhelmingly by peasants, based on a land tax but tapping mercantile wealth, and
ruled over by an imperial bureaucracy but in alliance with native elites. It was harder
to find historical antecedents for the autonomous white Dominions though at a high
level of generalization one might perhaps find parallels with an imperial confederation
such as the Holy Roman Empire.

Quite rightly, Neil Evans lays heavy stress on the United Kingdom which was
always the empire's power-political core. It is when the Scots and Irish come into the
picture that it is easiest to make comparisons between the British and continental
empires. Traditionally Ireland under the Union was not much discussed by imperial
scholars since it was seen as a domestic British issue. It is certainly true that the integration of Ireland into the metropolitan polity had extremely important consequences
both for it and for the United Kingdom as a whole. But in reality, Ireland never entirely shed its heritage as a colony and remained to some extent an imperial issue. This was
particularly the case in the years immediately before 1914. In these years, the survival
of a number of empires seemed to be in question because of the nationalist challenge
and this was a source of acute international tension and instability. In Europe, the most
obvious case was the Ottoman Empire but the First World War's immediate cause was
a pre-emptive strike by Austria's rulers against what they perceived to be a dangerous
south Slav nationalist threat to their empire's security and status. Ever since 1914 historians have puzzled over why a conservative European regime adopted so radical a
remedy. Comparisons with Britain are perhaps useful. In 1911–14 the Conservative
Party and most of the British elite were prepared to condone mutiny in the army and
armed rebellion in Ulster to block Irish home rule. For this unprecedented radicalism
of British conservative elites there were a number of reasons but the most important
one was fear that giving way to Irish nationalism would be the first step in the disintegration of the British Empire and of Britain's entire global position.

The greatest overt challenger to British pre-eminence before 1914 was
the German Empire. Unlike the communist and fascist powers between the wars,
Germany did not seek to destroy the existing international order but to assert its
power within it. Sharing rather than replacing British hegemony was the hope of most
intelligent Germans. To the extent that Wilhelmine *Weltpolitik* was designed to legitimize the imperial polity by a successful foreign policy, to defend global economic expansion and assert German prestige, it had some parallels with the strategy of British
elites in the eighteenth century when landowning, financial, and commercial interests
came together in pursuit of a brilliantly successful policy of global commercial and territorial expansion. But Germany's rulers never clearly defined the goals of *Weltpolitik*
nor were the institutions of the Wilhelmine Kaiserreich adept at coordinating grand

strategy. In addition, unlike eighteenth-century Britain, Germany's rulers were operating in an era of mass politics. Placed in the center of Europe with great powers on
either flank and Britain standing astride all Germany's maritime communications with
the non-European world, the Kaiserreich also faced inherently greater obstacles to the
pursuit of a successful British-style *Weltpolitik*.

Unlike in the British case, the German polity did call itself an empire, though
the word Reich has connotations lacking in the British and French usage of the word
"Empire." In his discussion of some of these connotations Stefan Berger does not
mention one that mattered significantly at the empire's foundation in 1871. Since this
new Reich was a federation of princes and included three royal dynasties as well as the
Hohenzollerns, its ruler more or less had to be called an emperor to emerge above the
ruck.[3] Berger does discuss the link in the German imagination with the old Reich. The
new Hohenzollern polity was conceived from the start as a national empire, in contrast to the German Confederation which preceded it and the Holy Roman Empire
in its later centuries. It was the heir of the Reich of the Hohenstaufens, which German
nationalists (most of them Protestant) were inclined to see as a national empire in embryo, destroyed by Rome before it could establish deep roots.

If these connotations of empire existed from the start in the Kaiserreich, others
came in time. These included the overseas colonial empire which got underway in the
1880s. In power-political and economic terms the basic point about this empire was
that it was pathetic. In no way could it assuage German thirst for first-class status in the
world or make any significant addition to German power. It is possible and interesting
to compare German and British ideas about empire and globalization in this era but to
the extent that Neil Evans's chapter on Britain is partly concerned with the governance
of Britain's empire it can have no parallels in Stefan Berger's account of Germany.

As Berger points out, a much more credible basis for empire were the 24 million Germans who lived in Europe but beyond the Kaiserreich's borders when the state
was formed. A greater German Empire in Eastern and Southeastern Europe had not
just numbers but also history and culture to recommend it, for in many of these areas
Germans formed a social, economic, or cultural elite. It was in these regions that an attempt to create a German Empire was attempted in incoherent fashion in 1914–18 and
then with far greater and murderous coherence in 1933–45. One does, however, have to
be very careful about tracing the later history of German Empire building in Eastern
Europe back to the pre-1914 Kaiserreich. Advocates of German territorial expansion
eastwards were marginal before 1914. German capitalism saw its field as worldwide,
not regional. German schoolchildren were taught about a fatherland bounded by the
borders of the current Reich. Bismarck had created this *Kleindeutsch* Reich precisely
in order to square the requirements of German nationalism with the interests of the
Prussian kingdom and those who dominated it. To some extent—but only to some
extent—Wilhelmine Germany had burst the confines of Bismarck's Reich even before

---

[3] An insight I owe to a conversation with Professor John Rohl.

1914 but it was the war itself which completed most of this process. It opened up possibilities in the east and it persuaded many members of the German elite that the era of liberal globalization had gone for good.[4]

In one key respect, however, Bismarck was responsible for laying the foundations for German Empire in the east. In 1879 he engineered an alliance between those ancient enemies, Hohenzollern Prussia and Habsburg Austria. Initially this was a narrow diplomatic and military alliance rooted in *Realpolitik*. But in time it came to be more than that: ethno-cultural solidarity came to play a role, particularly but not exclusively at an elite level. Both Austrian-Germans and Hungarians came in time to see the alliance as a German guarantee of the Habsburg Monarchy from the external and internal threat presented by Russia and Slavdom. To an extent, the Dual Alliance allowed supporters of *Grossdeutschland* a consolation prize for their defeat in 1866–71.

In mixing *Realpolitik* with cultural, linguistic and ideological solidarity, the Germans were in fact typical in this era. The fate of twentieth-century Europe was to be contested between three blocs, all of them rooted in *Realpolitik* but much influenced by broader cultural, ethno-linguistic, and ideological sympathies. Of the other two blocs, one was Russo-Slavic and the other Anglo-American. In the end it was the enormous resources of the Anglophone global community which were to triumph. Already in the 1890s, Britain was intent on removing all sources of possible conflict between itself and the USA, appeasing American claims where necessary and accepting American hegemony in the western hemisphere with good grace. Faced with the need to sustain a global empire in the face of rising challenges, the hard-headed rulers of Britain made cool calculations of *Realpolitik*. But the success of British grand strategy was made easier by growing cultural ties between the two countries' elites and by increasing ideological solidarity as the traditional British "mixed constitution" made way for democracy. If France was always number three in the triumvirate of Western democracies that was owed above all to her geopolitical weakness. But particularly after 1918, it did not help that she was the odd one out in a democratic community dominated by Anglophones. The French overseas empire, ably discussed by Robert Aldrich in this volume, was too weak to alter this basic equation.[5]

Like its German ally, the Austrian monarchy called itself an empire. The Habsburgs were the direct heirs of the old Reich. When they abandoned this title in the early nineteenth century they called themselves emperors of Austria. Flanked by the Russian Empire and by Napoleon's new empire in the west, they could hardly allow

---

[4] On what German schoolchildren were taught (specifically about Germany and Russia) see: Troy Paddock, *Creating the Russian Peril: Education, the Public Sphere, and National Identity in Imperial Germany, 1890–1914* (Rochester: Camden House, 2010). As my comment suggests, I believe that Fritz Fischer's works underestimated the radical impact of the war on not just German but all other European imperialist strategies and projects.
[5] An interesting insight into this is provided by Robert Boyce's work on the breakdown of liberal globalization after 1929: Robert Boyce, *The Great Interwar Crisis and the Collapse of Globalization* (Houndmills: Palgrave, 2009).

themselves to decline to the rank of mere kings of Bohemia and Hungary. The Habsburg Empire is usually presented as above all a composite polity, made up of disparate lands which were acquired through marriage and by lawful inheritance, thereby never losing their separate identities and constitutional rights. There is real truth in this idea though it does gloss over the fact that both the Czech and Hungarian lands were subsequently re-conquered after rebellions and for a time subjected to various degrees of absolutist rule from Vienna. Comparing Andrea Komlosy's analysis of the Habsburg polity with earlier chapters on Britain and Germany is a reminder that the United Kingdom and Imperial Germany were themselves composite polities, uniting but by no means eliminating a range of ancient and not-so-ancient states. The key differences included the fact that England and Prussia dominated the United Kingdom and Germany in a way that no single territorial unit could dominate the Habsburg Empire. In the eighteenth century, the creation of common Austro-Bohemian institutions to some extent filled this gap. But the Austrian and Bohemian crownlands were retained and in the nineteenth century their separate identities were reinvigorated. Moreover, the Habsburg Monarchy in 1900 had no potential over-arching identity equivalent to British loyalties in the United Kingdom or German solidarity in the Kaiserreich.

The Habsburgs could never appeal with any confidence to ethno-linguistic nationalism in the empire's core population. To the extent that the monarchy traditionally had a core population it was German, but they were a heterogeneous group with an often limited sense of solidarity with fellow German-speakers beyond their own province. Moreover they made up less than a quarter of the total population. In any case, the logic of German ethno-linguistic nationalism led to the dissolution of the Habsburg Empire and to the unification of all Germans under Berlin. In many ways the situation with the Hungarians was even worse. An empire's concessions to nationalism could easily lead to policies that alienated other peoples and thereby weakened legitimacy. This happened after the monarchy allied itself with Hungarian nationalism after 1867 and the situation deteriorated, as Komlosy illustrates, as the Hungarian government increased its pressure on ethnic minorities in the early twentieth century. But because the alliance was never unequivocal and Hungarians never saw the dynasty or empire as truly their own, they actually continued to suspect Vienna's intentions and to weaken the military and fiscal bases of Austrian external power. In a sense, therefore, the Habsburgs got the worst of every world in their bargain with Hungarian nationalism, which is not necessarily to say that there were better alternatives available to this bargain or that it did not at least buy the monarchy time.[6]

Most of the empires covered in this book are more or less the polities which one would expect to find. The biggest exception is Uffe Østergård's chapter on nation-building and nationalism in the Oldenburg Empire, which uses the imperial perspective to say a number of surprising things about Danish history and the national

---

[6] The emperor's own comment at the time of the 1867 Compromise to his daughter sums up the narrowness of the available options: J. P. Bled, *Franz Joseph* (Oxford: Blackwell, 1994), 39.

historiographical tradition. Some common themes do, however, link this and other chapters. One is the advance of "peasant" nationalisms at the expense of Germanic elites across a broad swathe of the continent. Another is the role of "metropolitan" nationalism in undermining multi-national, composite empires. Østergård explains how Danish nationalism's rise and its attempts to impose a unitary national model on Schleswig-Holstein ended by inviting intervention by the Germanic great powers and destroying the "Oldenburg Empire."

In very different political contexts the same story is often told about Hungarian, Russian, and Turkish nationalism's role in the decline of the Habsburg, Romanov, and Ottoman Empires, respectively. Nineteenth-century Ottomanism was in one sense a watered-down version of civic nationalism. All subjects were equal, religious disabilities were removed, careers were open to talent, and security of property was promised to all. But the people were not sovereign and Ottomanism was a very top-down experiment with little support outside the upper reaches of the imperial bureaucracy. Not surprisingly, this version of Ottomanism did not get very far though large sections of the non-Turkish and non-Muslim population were happy in traditional fashion to enjoy the peace, security, and tolerance of Ottoman rule so long as the empire did not make too many demands on them. The Young Turks were now, however, taking Ottomanism one step further. The peoples of the empire were to be not Ottoman subjects but Ottoman citizens. This sovereign people was to be represented in a parliament. In good Jacobin style, the Young Turks expected that the members of the sovereign people would now be ready to die for the state. When this proved not to be true, the CUP fell back on Turkish ethnic nationalism as the only basis for a polity which needed to fight if it was to survive.[7]

As these examples show, the relationship between empire and its core ethnic community is complicated and equivocal. For example, empire could matter a great deal to the people of its core territory in economic terms but as the chapters in this book show, this varied greatly from one empire and one era to another. The chapters on the British and Spanish Empires argue that empire had a much bigger impact on the metropolitan British and Spanish economies than is commonly perceived by historians. In the French case, empire's economic impact on the metropole was concentrated on certain industries and regions. With regard to Germany, the colonial empire was of minimal importance in the context of the enormous dynamism of Germany's world trade. Empire mattered more to a country if it could not compete in open global markets or if, as in the 1930s, the latter had ceased to exist. The British Empire was more important to the British economy in the 1930s-1950s than it had been for a century. The enormous benefits of the integrated Habsburg imperial market only became fully evident after it had disappeared in 1918.

---

[7] On Ottoman options in the immediate pre-war years see in particular two recent works: Kemal Karpat, *The Politicization of Islam* (Oxford: Oxford University Press, 2001); Francois Georgeon, *Abdul Hamid II. Le Sultan Caliph* (Paris: Fayard, 2003).

As to the cultural impact of empire on the metropolitan people and territory, opinions differ. So undoubtedly too do realities from one empire to another. In culture as in economics, specific cities or regions in the metropole could exploit their link to empire to push their individual interests and agendas. David Laven and Elsa Damien make this point in very interesting fashion when discussing Venice's use of its imperial past within the new Italian kingdom. The overseas colonial empires no doubt did often enhance the consciousness of race, the prestige of militarism, and the arrogance of easy conquest in wide circles of the metropolitan populations. But empire was not the only source of militarism or race, let alone of metropolitan national identity. To take two examples: anti-Semitism had a long history independent of empire and British identity was defined more against a French, Catholic, and despotic European others than against non-whites. Nor was the growing influence of ideas rooted in science and specifically in biology just the product of empire.

In the century before 1914 what strikes me is the enormous difference between the deep cultural impact of many European empires on their colonies and the far weaker non-European impact on the metropolitan population. This is also true if one compares the European empires of the Victorian era with many past empires, most notably in China and the Middle East, where (often nomadic) military conquerors were themselves conquered and transformed by the high cultures of the peoples they subjected to their rule. These comparisons bring home rather starkly the meaning of cultural hegemony. The really great impact of colonial peoples on the European imperial metropoles came after the end of empire and resulted largely from mass immigration. Metropolitan populations who had rejected the idea of sharing a common imperial citizenship with non-whites now found themselves forced to forge a common color-blind national citizenship in their own home countries.[8]

Did empire strengthen "metropolitan" nationalism? In many cases it did. Disraeli, for example, used pride in Britain's empire to consolidate mass support for the Conservative Party and the British state. The empire symbolized the fact that Britain was a world leader, powerful and respected by other peoples. Bülow attempted a similar use of empire in German domestic politics. In both cases pride, power, and security were linked. An imperial polity could stand up for its interests against foreign aggression. Failure at the game of empire could on the contrary de-legitimize a polity. The Portuguese monarchy never recovered from the humiliation of 1890. The Italian liberal monarchy suffered a deep crisis after defeat in Abyssinia in 1896 and the Spanish liberal monarchy did not survive defeat in Morocco in 1921. Defeat in the war against Japan led to the Russian revolution of 1905. Failure, defeat, and humiliation of

---

[8] As this passage suggests, as regards the British case I tend to support Bernard Porter's line. See: Bernard Porter, *The Absent-Minded Imperialists: Empire, Society and Culture in Britain* (Oxford: Oxford University Press, 2004). Above all, when one compares Britain to a wide range of empires what strikes me is the extent of metropolitan cultural hegemony in the British Empire and the relative weakness of contrary influences.

course often bring down many governments and regimes, and empire is far from their only source. But in this era to have an empire was seen as a mark of success, virility, and the ability to survive in a world of Darwinian struggle. Not for nothing was the agonized debate in Spain after defeat against the United States in 1898 linked to concepts of degeneracy and regeneration.

But there is another side to the picture. As already noted, metropolitan nationalism could force rulers into policies which alienated minorities and de-legitimized empire. Moreover, enthusiasm for empire in the metropolitan population was also often shallow and ephemeral. Salisbury's Khaki Election of 1900 and Bülow's Hottentot Election of 1907 successfully exploited empire to win votes for the right but the result in the next elections were dramatic victories for the left-wing parties. Very few electorates accepted that their sons should be conscripted to die for empire in colonial wars. In general, domestic issues prevailed over imperial ones. Imperial glory was fine so long as it came quickly and cheap.

Most important, empire does not seem to have been of decisive importance in determining the success or failure of metropolitan nation-building. The existence of a British Empire was undoubtedly important for Scotland's allegiance to the Union and the creation of a British identity. But Protestantism, victory over France, and the impact of the world's first Industrial Revolution were at least as important.[9] Nor was empire the reason why France succeeded in integrating Brittany into a unitary nation-state or why Spain failed to do the same with regards to the Basques or Catalans. In this era, it was crucially important that the Russian government failed to stop the emergence of a Ukrainian national identity or to forge a common all-Russian political identity out of the three Orthodox east Slav peoples. But empire was not the basic cause of failure. The resources of the metropolitan state, the commitment of its educated elites, and the socio-economic and geographical context mattered much more than empire in the French, Spanish, and Russian cases. In the Russian case, Alexei Miller points out that it was by no means a forgone conclusion in 1914 that the still relatively weak sense of national identity among the Ukrainian masses would form a basis for independent statehood. But, unlike the French and Spanish, the Russians faced the challenge of a Ukrainian irredentist base in Galicia on the other side of an international border.

At least in principle, nation and empire are rooted in opposing principles. Most great empires in history were ruled by monarchs who claimed religious legitimation for their power and took pride in ruling by conquest over a wide range of peoples. On the contrary, both civic and ethnically-based concepts of nationalism root sovereignty in the people. They stress the ordinary citizen's active engagement in the polity. Although in principle the ethnically blind concept of civic nationalism may seem less incompatible with empire than is the ethnic nation, this is to a great extent an illusion. In reality, few ethnically blind civic nations have existed in history, not least because

---

[9] This is of course Linda Colley's argument in: Linda Colley, *Britons: Forging the Nation. 1707–1837* (New Haven: Yale University Press, 1992). The book deservedly remains a classic.

they find it hard to engage their citizens' loyalty. Who in the end is willing to die for the purely civic nation? Revolutionary France provided the model for the nation of citizens but in reality it was anything but ethnically blind. For the French, the revolution seemed to be confirmation that *La Grande Nation* was indeed where they always knew it was, in the vanguard of civilization and progress. As Michael Broers makes clear, it was precisely this blend of civic and ethnic nationalism which informed Napoleonic officials' imperial ideology of a French civilizing mission.

In the decades before the First World War, the key dilemma for statesmen was that whereas the national model seemed best to "fit" the domestic requirements of most European polities, the world of international relations and power politics seemed to belong to empire. The power of the nation lay partly in the ideas that sustained it. Above all, this meant popular sovereignty, democracy and citizenship on the one hand and the almost sacred uniqueness and value of communities rooted in specific languages, cultures, and histories on the other. Only within the nation—so it was asserted—could the individual achieve meaning and a sort of immortality. Intellectual and socio-economic factors combined to encourage nationalism's spread. Urbanization, mass literacy and the extended national market disrupted traditional communities and identities: the nation was seen as filling the void. Politics was also vital. Modernity meant the ever greater size and intrusiveness of the bureaucratic state, whose operations became somewhat more tolerable when clothed in the metaphor of nation-family. For many European elites, nationalism became the right's most popular battle cry against socialists and radicals. It was seen as a way to consolidate societies whose unity was threatened by industrialization, naked inequality, and at least in most urban areas by declining religious allegiance.

Nationalism also had specific attractions regarding military power. In 1792–93, the European powers had believed that the invasion of France would be little more than a police action to suppress disorganized mobs. Instead they were faced by the *levée en masse*, a people's war, and twenty years of devastating subsequent conflict. Clausewitz became the philosopher of the nation at war. In some ways he perceived more the potential than the reality of the wars he had experienced in his era. Napoleon's armies were some way removed from the volunteers of 1793 or the nation in arms. Moreover he was defeated precisely by the European Old Regime, modified in certain respects (especially in Clausewitz's Prussia) but essentially a somewhat more efficient but above all much more united version of the coalition of Great Powers which had sought to crush the revolutionary nation in 1792–23. But if Clausewitz's vision did not entirely fit the realities of 1814, it came much closer to reflecting the world of 1914. By this time one did approach the reality of total people's war. Millions of civilian reservists recalled to the colors after relatively short immersion in military life had to be persuaded to die for the state. The loyalties and habits that motivated the old long-service professional armies were no longer appropriate, or at least sufficient. Moreover the old armies had fought in close order with a NCO standing behind every fifth soldier's back. In the new warfare, men would have to be motivated to fight in dispersed groups and to advance across the killing ground which modern firearms had

created. For many generals and politicians, the only solution appeared to be the inculcation of fervent love for the nation.[10]

The main problem was that the future appeared to belong to polities of continental scale and resources. Few nations, however defined, could encompass whole continents. Only empires seemingly could do so. Part of the turn towards empire in the
second half of the nineteenth century was rooted in awareness of growing American
and Russian power. If some successful modern polities were of continental scale then
all countries wishing to remain great powers would need to match them. Hence the
need of the nations of Western Europe for overseas empires. Technological development was also important. Railways in particular allowed the penetration, settlement,
and exploitation of continental heartlands. The trend towards protectionism that set
in from the 1870s increased the attractions of direct political control over territory. So
too did growing competition between rival empires as Britain's economic dominance
was undermined by the spread of the Industrial Revolution. With all "free" areas of
the globe being eyed by one empire or another, it made good sense, in Lord Rosebery's
words, to peg out claims for the future in good time.

This was all the more true because one never knew what hidden riches might
lie under the soil of some seemingly barren territory. In earlier times, for example, the
British had tolerated the de facto independence of Boer farmers in the Transvaal and
Orange Free State. Once it became clear that these lands contained the world's richest
treasure of gold and diamonds, which modern mining technology could now exploit,
the situation changed dramatically. The Boer republics would clearly become the economic heartland of southern Africa, drawing into their orbit the British Cape Colony,
most of whose population was Boer. Moreover, unlike thirty years before, by the 1890s
other European empires were becoming very interested in Africa. The British therefore fought a very expensive war in 1899–1902 to control territories which they had
light-heartedly abandoned a generation before. The logic of pegging out claims in
good time was thereby underlined. So too, however, was the logic of European—and
above all German—resentment at British imperialism. The British already controlled
the lion's share of Africa in particular and overseas colonies in general. Their naval hegemony combined with the workings of the European balance of power now enabled
them to correct their earlier error and make off with the most valuable territory in
southern Africa. It was such resentments but also realities that provided part of the
impetus for German *Weltpolitik* and naval construction.[11]

---

[10] For fuller discussion of the Napoleonic era and Clausewitz see Dominic Lieven, *Russia against
Napoleon: The Struggle for Europe. 1807–1814* (London: Penguin, 2009).

[11] On the origins of the Boer War see A. N. Porter, *The Origins of the South African War: Joseph
Chamberlain and the Diplomacy of Imperialism* (Manchester: Manchester University Press,
1990). Iain R. Smith, *The Origins of the South African War 1899–1902* (London: Longman,
1996). For new insights into German navalism and Weltpolitik see: Patrick J. Kelly, *Tirpitz and
the Imperial German Navy* (Bloomington: Indiana University Press, 2011).

Of the European powers, it was clearly the British who had the best chance of consolidating an overseas empire on such a scale as to match American or Russian power. In the long run there had to be doubts about whether Britain could retain a dependent non-white empire far larger and more populous than the United Kingdom. But as many British observers at the time reckoned, the creation of a broader Greater British imperial identity and federation among the white colonies was more feasible. Neil Evans discusses this issue with great insight. One undoubted obstacle was the development of colonial nationalism. Any attempt to keep the white colonies as agrarian dependencies of industrial Britain in a neo-mercantilist relationship would merely invite a repeat of the American revolution of the 1770s. British conceptions of parliamentary sovereignty were also an issue. So too, however, were considerations of power and security. In the mid-nineteenth century when the white Dominions established their autonomy, they were very weak and Britain's global supremacy was unchallenged. Had autonomy come in 1900 when the Dominions were much more formidable and Britain's global position was slipping, then it seems likely that internal autonomy for the Dominions would have been combined with more serious efforts at an imperial federation. Whether in the long run this would have made a difference is a moot point. Except in the short run, there was no chance that Britain could preserve the enormous economic lead it had achieved over its rivals by 1850. In geopolitical terms, the United Kingdom was a very small base on which to build and defend an empire stretching to every corner of the globe. That remained the case even if a tacit global condominium was conceded to the Americans and accepted by them on terms that preserved Britain's imperial power.

To write in these terms offends contemporary sensibilities. The study of geopolitics suggests a logic to German imperialism's eastward expansion and to the merging of empire and nation which was the essence of Hitler's Reich. The sheer evil of Hitler's regime and the appalling suffering it caused the world (and also the Germans) makes this a very unpalatable message. But there is also the basic point that German imperialism failed, as did all the other empires covered in this book. At which point the discussion of geopolitics, international power, and the various projects of European imperialists seems not just unpleasant but also futile.

A key point to remember, however, is that European geopolitical realities put great obstacles in the way of empire. If that was the case with Britain's global empire, it was if anything even more true of empire on the continent of Europe. Even facing the European balance of power, it was possible—albeit difficult—for a would-be European emperor to conquer the Carolingian core of Europe—France, Germany, the Low Countries, and northern Italy. Napoleon achieved this and so did Hitler. Europe's potential master then, however, faced two formidable concentrations of power on the continent's periphery in Russia and Britain. Even if he satisfied himself with a limited Carolingian empire the emperor could not feel secure since the very existence of such an empire posed a major threat to British and Russian security. The two peripheral empires were therefore always likely to gang up on him. To mobilize sufficient resources from a Carolingian base to defeat these two peripheral powers was extremely difficult.

To make matters worse, one required different types of power: a maritime power to get the emperor across the English Channel and a military-logistical power sufficient to sustain his dominance of the heartlands of Russian power east and south of Moscow. Meanwhile, however, both the British and the Russians would mobilize the immense resources of their non-European territories against the would-be heir to Charlemagne.

The task facing a would-be conqueror of Europe was not completely impossible, merely very difficult. The Russians and British might fail to gang up against him in effective and timely fashion, thereby giving him a window of opportunity. One or other of the peripheral empires might disintegrate under the strain of war, as happened to Russia in 1917. It is arguable that much of twentieth-century Europe's fate turned around the winter of 1916–17. Had Germany not brought the United States into the First World War on the very eve of a revolution that destroyed Russian power then it is certainly possible that some version of lasting German imperial dominance in Europe could have been achieved. But conquering empires is often easier than establishing the institutions and the legitimacy which will allow them to survive. Quite apart from raw considerations of power and geopolitics, successful German empire-building would have required leadership of a subtlety and coherence which the Kaiserreich had not achieved since Bismarck's retirement.

The great questions of empire and nation, of power and legitimacy, have not gone away, however. They have merely been displaced to regions of the world better suited to empire than is the case with Europe. The United States has been the undisputed hegemon in the western hemisphere since the end of the Civil War. China has achieved something close to hegemony—in terms of both hard and soft power—in East Asia intermittently for much longer. American and Chinese power is rooted in their continental scale and resources, as potentially is that of India. Effective mobilization and channelling of these resources depends to a great degree on the existence of coherent policies, coordinated institutions of government, and a polity which is legitimate in the eyes of the dominant elements in the society over which it rules. That polity must to a certain degree guide its people's efforts without stifling the individual initiative which is the essential basis for any country's wealth and power. Meeting these criteria is a necessary but not a sufficient guarantee that a polity will be able to surmount the external challenges which traditionally have been the major cause of the rise and fall of empires. The imperial nation—in its varying American and Chinese forms—seemingly remains the best way of reconciling the requirements of external power and internal legitimacy and unity.

During the last decade we have been inundated with works debating the existence or otherwise of an American empire. The literature on growing Chinese power is also increasing exponentially. At one level, China is more easily compared with historical empires than is the case with the United States. Beijing holds or claims all the territory ruled by the empire of the Qing. If 94% of the population are Han Chinese, 40% of the territory (including vast assets of energy, minerals, and water) are in non-Han areas. Moreover, unlike the USA but like almost all empires, China is not a democracy. Contemporary China is not an empire, however, if comparisons with its imperial predecessor are anything to go by. The Qing took explicit pride in conquering and ruling over many peoples. Not merely did they preserve their separate identity as Manchu warrior-conquerors but they used multi-nationality as a system of rule, balancing Manchu, Han, and other nationalities under the overall sovereignty of a supra or rather multi-national monarch who stood between all his peoples and the heavens. Unlike in contemporary China, the Qing had no intention (or means) to use modern state institutions to create a united and dominant Chinese nation.[12]

Faced by the challenges to empire a century ago, many imperial elites dreamed of forging as much as possible of the empire's population into a core national community, united in language and ethnicity and loyal to the polity. The Chinese have come closest to achieving this feat. China is in most respects more truly a nation than an empire. But the elements that go into specific national identities not just vary enormously but also go far to explaining both how a community sees itself and how it relates to outsiders. China's history and its power make it inevitable that it will be an imperial nation. It is true that, unlike the USA, China lacks a universalist ideology. At most it will seek regional, not global hegemony. This can be a source of both strength and weakness, on the one hand limiting the appeal of its "soft power" but on the other reducing the dangers of imperial overstretch. Like the Kaiserreich and unlike Hitler or Stalin's regimes, China seeks to share and modify the existing international system, not to overthrow it. Since most of Europe's woes in the twentieth century sprang from the failure to integrate Germany peacefully into the first era of Anglophone liberal globalization we can only pray that history does not repeat itself.

---

[12] Given the scale and quality of recent scholarship on the Qing (even works in the English language read by a Russianist amateur like myself) it is extremely hard to know where to start when providing support for these comments: see, for example: Pamela Crossley, *A Translucent Mirror: History and Identity in Qing Imperial Ideology* (Berkeley: University of California Press, 1999); L. Hostetler, *Qing Colonial Enterprise: Ethnography and Cartography in Early Modern China* (Chicago: University of Chicago Press, 2001); Evelyn Rawski, *The Last Emperors* (Berkeley: University of California Press, 1998). Lynn Struve, *The Qing Formation in World Historical Time* (Cambridge, Mass.: Harvard University Press, 2004).

Contributors

ROBERT ALDRICH is Professor of European History at the University of Sydney. He has written widely on French and British colonialism, colonial sites of memory, and colonialism and sexuality. Recent publications include *Vestiges of the Colonial Empire in France: Monuments, Museums and Colonial Memories* (Palgrave Macmillan, 2005), published in an updated French translation as *Les Traces Coloniales dans le Paysage Français. Monuments et Mémoires* (Société Française d'Histoire d'Outre-Mer, 2011), and *Cultural Encounters and Homoeroticism in Sri Lanka. Sex and Serendipity* (Routledge, 2014). With Kirsten McKenzie, he has edited *The Routlege History of Western Empires* (Routledge, 2014). He is a Fellow of the Australian Academy of the Humanities and of the Academy of the Social Sciences in Australia.

STEFAN BERGER is Professor of Social History at Ruhr-Universität Bochum, where he is also director of the Institute for Social Movements and executive chair of the Foundation Library of the Ruhr. Previously he held chairs for comparative European history at the University of Manchester and for contemporary history at the University of Glamorgan. He has published widely on comparative labour history, social movement studies, the history of historiography, historical theory, nationalism and national identity studies as well as the history of memory. Among his most recent publications are: *The Past as History: National Identity and Historical Consciousness in Modern Europe*, with Christoph Conrad, (Palgrave MacMillan, 2015); *Writing the History of Memory*, ed. with Bill Niven (Bloomsbury, 2014); *Erinnerungsorte. Leistungen und Grenzen eines Erfolgskonzepts in den Kulturwissenschaften*, ed. with Joana Seiffert (Klartext, 2014); *Writing Popular National Histories, 1750 to the Present*, ed. with Billie Melman and Chris Lorenz (Routledge, 2012), and *Friendly Enemies. Britain and the GDR, 1949–1990*, with Norman LaPorte (Berghahn Books, 2010).

MICHAEL BROERS is Professor of 18th and 19th century Western European History at Oxford University and he was Leverhulme Research Fellow for the academic years 2011–2013. He has published widely on theories of cultural imperialism and the Revolutionary-Napoleonic period as well as on regionalism, popular Catholicism and modern state-building. Amongst his most recent publications are *Napoleon. Soldier of Destiny* (Faber&Faber 2014).

ELSA DAMIEN is an independent scholar, language teacher, and translator. She was a research associate and co-investigator on the AHRC-sponsored Venice Remembered project, and is the French translator of novels by Davide Ferrario, Elena Ferrante, and Valerio Manfredi. She is the author of *La notion de guide à l'épreuve du tourisme naissant: Les voyageurs anglo-saxons en Italie à l'ère industrielle* (2004), and of articles on the historiography and identity of Venice after its loss of independence. She is co-authoring a monograph on Venetian identity and historiography with David Laven.

HOWARD EISSENSTAT is Assistant Professor of Middle East History at St. Lawrence University New York (since 2009) and serving also as Country Specialist on Turkey for Amnesty International USA (since 2006). He has published widely on the Late Ottoman Empire and the Turkish Republic focussing on critical race theory, nationalism and state building processes. Amongst others, he published "The Gezi Park Protests: Time for a New U.S. Approach to Turkey" (*Project on Middle East Democracy (POMED)*, 2013), "Turkey's Season of Struggle: Unrest in Istanbul" (*The Christian Century*, 2013).

NEIL EVANS is an honorary research fellow in the School of History, Archaeology and Religion at Cardiff University. He was joint editor of *Llafur: The Journal of Welsh People's History*, 1994–2010 and has published on a wide variety of topics in Welsh and British history. Recent publications include: *Writing a Small Nation's Past. Wales in Comparative Perspective, 1850–1950*, ed. with Huw Pryce (Ashgate, 2013) and *A Tolerant Nation. Revisiting Ethnic Diversity in a Devolved* Wales, ed. with Charlotte Williams and Paul O'Leary (University of Wales Press, 2015).

ANDREA KOMLOSY is professor of Social and Economic History at the University of Vienna, where she is coordinator of the Global History programs. She is also faculty member of the Doctoral Program "Austrian Galicia and its multi-cultural heritage". In 2014/15 she is Schumpeter fellow at the Wheaterhead Center for International Affairs at Harvard University. Komlosy has published widely on economic and social history of the Habsburg Monarchy with a focus on uneven development, regional disparities, borders and mobility. See *Grenze und ungleiche regionale Entwicklung. Binnenmarkt und Migration in der Habsburgermonarchie* (Promedia, 2003). She approaches global history by linking the local with the global. Recent books *Theorien und Methoden der Globalgeschichte* (Boehlau, 2011); *Arbeit: Eine globalhistorische Perspektive. 13. bis 21. Jahrhundert* (Promedia, 2014).

DAVID LAVEN is Associate Professor in the Department of History at the University of Nottingham. He is the author of Venice and Venetia under the Habsburgs 1815–1835 (Oxford University Press, 2002), and is currently completing Venice Remembered a monograph on Venetian identity and historiography. He has published numerous articles and essays on nineteenth-century Venice, the British and Italy, and Italian identity.

JÖRN LEONHARD is Full Professor in Modern European History at the History Seminar of Freiburg University. He received his Doctorate (1998) and his Habilitation (2004) at the University of Heidelberg. From 1998–2003 he taught as Fellow and Tutor in Modern History at Oxford University, from 2004-1006 as Reader in West European History at Jena University before coming to Freiburg. From 2007 to 2012 he was one of the Directors of the School of History of the Freiburg Institute for Advanced Studies (FRIAS). In 2012/13 he was Visiting Fellow at the Minda de Gunzburg Center for European Studies at Harvard University, where he completed a general history of the First World War.

His main publications include *Liberalismus. Zur historischen Semantik eines europäischen Deutungsmusters* (Munich, 2001); ed. [together with Ulrike von Hirschhausen], *Nationalismen in Europa: West- und Osteuropa im Vergleich* (Göttingen, 2001); *Bellizismus und Nation. Kriegsdeutung und Nationalbestimmung in Europa und den Vereinigten Staaten 1750–1914* (Munich, 2008); *Empires und Nationalstaaten im 19. Jahrhundert* (together with Ulrike von Hirschhausen), (2nd ed. Göttingen, 2010); ed. (together with Ulrike von Hirtschhausen), *Comparing Empires. Encounters and Transfers in the Nineteenth an Early Twentieth Century* (Göttingen, 2nd ed. 2012); and ed. (together with Christian Wieland), *What Makes the Nobility Noble? Comparative Perspectives from the Sixteenth to the Twentieth Century* (Göttingen, 2011); *Die Büchse der Pandora. Geschichte des Ersten Weltkriegs* (Munich, 5th ed. 2014).

DOMINIC LIEVEN is a Senior Research Fellow at Trinity College, Cambridge (since 2011) and a Fellow of the British Academy (since 2001). From 1978 until 20111 he was lecturer and then professor at the London School of Economics. He has written widely on imperial Russia, on European aristocracy and on empires. His book, *Russia against Napoleon. The Struggle for Europe*, was published in 2009 and won the Wolfson Prize and the annual prize of the Fondation Napoleon. His latest book, *Towards the Flame. Revolution, War and the End of Tsarist Russia*, was published by Penguin in May 2015.

ALEXEI MILLER is Professor at the European University in Saint-Petersburg and recurrent visiting professor at Central European University in Budapest. He has published on comparative history of empires, on history of the Romanov Empire and nationalism, on history of concepts in Russia, and on memory politics in Eastern Europe. Among his books are: *The Ukrainian Question. The Russian Empire and Nationalism in the Nineteenth Century* (CEU Press, 2003); *Imperial Rule*, ed. with Alfred J. Rieber (CEU Press, 2004); *The Romanov Empire and Nationalism. Essays in Methodology of Historical Research* (CEU Press, 2008); *The Convolutions of Historical Politics*, ed. with Maria Lipman (CEU Press, 2012).

XOSÉ M. NÚÑEZ SEIXAS is Full Professor of Modern History at the University of Santiago de Compostela, and since October 2012 also Full Professor of Modern European History at the Ludwig-Maximilian University, Munich. His work focuses on comparative history of nationalist movements and national and regional identities, as well as on the analysis of overseas migration from Spain and Galicia to Latin America, and the study of modern war and war experiences in the twentieth century. Among his most recent books are *¡Fuera el Invasor! Nacionalismo y Movilización Bélica en la Guerra Civil Española 1936–1939* (Madrid, 2006); *Patriotas y Demócratas. El Discurso Nacionalista Español Después de Franco* (Madrid, 2010); *Ser Españoles. Imaginarios Nacionalistas en el siglo XX*, ed. with J. Moreno (Barcelona, 2013); *Icônes Littéraires et Stéréotypes Sociaux: L'image des Immigrants Galiciens en Argentine (1800–1960)* (Besançon, 2013); *Las Patrias Ausentes. Estudios Sobre Historia y Memoria de las Migraciones Ibéricas* (Oviedo, 2014), and *Banderas de Nieve. Experiencia y Memoria de la División Azul (1941–1945)* (Barcelona, 2015, forthcoming).

UFFE ØSTERGÅRD is Professor in European and Danish History, Department of Business and Politics, Copenhagen Business School, formerly director of the Danish Center for Holocaust and Genocide Studies and Jean Monnet professor in European Civilization and Integration, University of Aarhus. He published widely on political cultures in various European states, among others *Europas Ansigter* (1992 and 2001); *Dansk Identitet* (1993); *Den Globala Nationalismen*, ed. with Björn Hettne, Sverker Sörlin (Pocket, 2006); *Europa. Identitet og Identitetspolitik* (Munksgaar/Rosinante, 1998 and 2000). He also published many articles in Danish, Italian, German, French, Spanish, English and other languages.

ALFRED J. RIEBER is University Professor Emeritus at the Central European University and Professor Emeritus at the University of Pennsylvania. He has been chair of the History Department at both universities. Previously he taught at Northwestern University and Columbia University. He has published widely in the history of Imperial Russia and the Soviet Union. His articles have appeared in *Slavic Review, Kritika, Cahiers du Monde Russe et Sovietique, Jahrbücher fur Geschichte Osteuropas* and *Istoricheskie Zapiski*. Among his major works are *Stalin and the French Communist Party, 1941–1947* (Columbia University Press, 1962), *The Politics of Autocracy* (Mouton, 1966), *Merchants and Entrepreneurs in Imperial Russia* (North Carolina Press, 1982), and *Struggle for the Eurasian Borderlands. From the Rise of Early Modern Empires to the End of World War One* (Cambridge University Press, 2014). A sequel, *Stalin and the Struggle for Eurasia*, is in press with Cambridge.

JEAN-FRÉDÉRIC SCHAUB teaches at the École des Hautes Études en Sciences Sociales (Paris). He is researcher at the *Mondes Américains* EHESS' center. Together with Silvia Sebastian, he recently prepares a new book on the creation of racial categories in Western societies from the Late Middle Ages to the Enlightenment. He has published as single author: *L'île Aux Mariés. Les Açores entre Deux Empires. 1583–1642* (Madrid, Casa de Velázquez, 2014), *L'Europe a-t-elle une Histoire?* (Paris, 2008; trad. Spanish, Akal, 2013), *Oroonoko, Prince et Esclave. Roman Colonial de l'Incertitude* (Seuil, 2008); *La France Espagnole. Les Racines Hispaniques de l'Absolutisme Français* (Editions du Seuil, 2003; trad. Spanish, Marcial Pons, 2004), *Portugal na Monarquia Hispânica. 1580–1640* (Livros Horizonte, 2001), *Le Portugal au Temps du Comte-Duc d'Olivares 1621–1640. Le Conflit de Juridiction Comme Exercice de la Politique* (Casa de Velázquez, 2001), *Les Juifs du Roi d'Espagne. Oran, 1507–1669* (Hachette Littérature, 1999; trad. Hebrew, Taupress, 2012).

PHILIPP THER is Professor of Central European History at the University of Vienna. Previously he was a Professor of comparative European history at the EUI in Florence. He has published several books dealing with nationalism, among them *The Dark Side of Nation States. Ethnic Cleansing in Modern Europe* (Berghahn Press, 2014), *Center Stage. Operatic Culture and Nation Building in 19th Century Central Europe* (Purdue University Press, 2014). His most recent publication is *Die neue Ordnung auf dem alten Kontinent. Eine Geschichte des neoliberalen Europa* (Suhrkamp Verlag, 2014).

Index

COMPILED BY STEFAN BRAUN

CPSIA information can be obtained
at www.ICGtesting.com
Printed in the USA
LVHW081604040123
736433LV00004B/127